It's All News to Me

To my distinguished Roomie

Kermit McFarland

With admiration

Bob Considine

N.Y.C. May 25 '69

Books by BOB CONSIDINE

MacARTHUR THE MAGNIFICENT

THIRTY SECONDS OVER TOKYO (with Capt. Ted W. Lawson)

WHERE'S SAMMY? (with Sammy Schulman)

INNOCENTS AT HOME

GENERAL WAINWRIGHT'S STORY (with Jonathan M. Wainwright)

THE BABE RUTH STORY (with Babe Ruth)

DEMPSEY (with Bill Slocum)

RAPE OF POLAND (with Stanislaw Mikolajczyk)

RED PLOT AGAINST AMERICA (with Robert E. Stripling)

THE MARYKNOLL STORY

KHRUSHCHEV (with W. R. Hearst, Jr., and Frank Conniff)

THE MEN WHO ROBBED BRINK'S (with Specs O'Keefe)

IT'S THE IRISH

PANAMA CANAL

IT'S ALL NEWS TO ME

It's All News to Me

A Reporter's Deposition

by

BOB CONSIDINE

A Duell, Sloan and Pearce Book

MEREDITH PRESS

New York

Third Printing, October 1967

Library of Congress Catalog Card Number: 67-12635

MANUFACTURED IN THE UNITED STATES OF AMERICA FOR MEREDITH PRESS

VAN REES PRESS • NEW YORK

For Mil

who wouldn't marry a Government clerk

Pride Goeth Before . . .

It takes a roaring amount of conceit to practice daily journalism, particularly if it assumes the form of a column. The deep-domed cosmic thinker who either rattles or soothes the President of the United States is of the same species as the gassy advice columnist who counsels "Puzzled" to stop sprinkling her corn flakes with powdered LSD. Each plays God.

The straight newswriters, who operate more often than not without the dazzling shield of a by-line, are not immune to the contagion of earthbound divinity. They dream of a day when their names, too, will be "on the trucks"—breathtaking lithographs plastered to the sides of delivery vans careening through the streets of great cities: "READ JOE DOAKES, EXCLUSIVELY IN THE. . . ."

The Almighty, apparently concerned, has arranged that certain little setbacks, comeuppances, shake the pretenders to the throne firmly enough to remind them they must remain mortal—for a time, at least.

I speak with the accent of experience. Somebody always pulls a rug.

My column, features, and news stories were appearing in perhaps three hundred papers here and abroad at the precise period when a child of ours named Dennis chose to jump out a window of an abandoned inn in Allenhurst, New Jersey, where we were summering. He was intent not upon suicide, but was a dutiful participant in a game of follow the leader. The leader, an Irish-Catholic kamikaze, jumped first, as befits authority, and better, too. Dennis plunged into a large bush which seemed to offer a good landing place.

Alas. The bush was in fact a new burgeoning of an old tree, flourishing from the original stump. Dennis' right leg, ill-protected by a very short pair of shorts, hit the spear of the broken stump. It turned out to be as bad a wound as if it had been inflicted by a bazooka.

The boy was on the operating table at Fitkin Memorial Hospital in Neptune, New Jersey, an excruciatingly long time. Then a woman who seemed to have emerged from Surgery walked down the long hall toward the waiting room where Millie and I sat, silently reciting the Rosary. The woman advanced resolutely toward where we sat; the closer she came, the more ominous she loomed. At last she was in the waiting room.

"I understand there's a newspaperman here," she said. Our hearts stopped. She, clearly, was the bearer of terrible news.

"I am," I said huskily.

"Oh, fine," she said brightly. "I'll buy one."

Then there was the exclusive interview with Frank Hague, perennial mayor of Jersey City. Hague held the key to whether racing would return to Jersey after years in hibernation. A mutual friend approached me one day at Belmont and said that Hague was in his box on the mezzanine and was in the mood to give me the scoop of the ages: Racing would indeed resume in Jersey.

"He wants to break the news in a big syndicated column like yours," the bloke said. [I was either flattered or fulfilled.]

So we trooped to Hague's box. He had apparently just blown a big bet and was glaring straight ahead, black derby rammed down close to his nose. Ten feet short of the box, the pal who had professed to be closer to Hague than his wallet took off his own hat, held it on his chest as if he had picked up the distant strains of the national anthem, coughed, and whimpered, "Mr. Mayor, sir, I want you should meet Bob Considine, one of the greatest sportswriters in New York."

It must have taken Hague's head a full minute to turn to the point where he could survey me with his glacial eyes.

"No," Hague said.

I was doing nicely in the papers with my column on the night Millie showed up forty minutes late for a sit-down dinner at the apartment of our friends, the Walter Shirleys. The host was not amused.

"Millie, dear," Walter said gently but firmly, "Bob's column isn't that good."

I was indeed "on the trucks" but not on the wagon one night, late, when I asked a cabdriver to take me for a spin through the old Swamppoodle section of Washington, near the Union Station. It was undilutedly Freudian, of course.

The driver remembered he had picked me up in front of the Washington *Herald*. I was then its sports editor.

"Know anybody on that paper where I picked you up?" he asked as we tooled down Second Street, N.E., where I had lived as a child.

"Sure."

"Know that fellow Considine?"

"Yeah," I said uneasily.

The driver chuckled.

"I knew that bum when he didn't have shoes," he said.

I once had the privilege of introducing Harry S. Truman to a dinner gathering at the Overseas Press Club. In searching for something meatier than "Ladies and gentlemen, the former President of the United States," I hit upon and delivered the following:

"President Truman will be remembered by the future historian as the Chief Executive who had more difficult decisions to make than most of the others combined. He faced and overcame with courageous decisions more crises than confronted Washington or Lincoln, Wilson or FDR. Six come readily to mind.

"He had to make the agonizing decision to drop the atomic bombs on Hiroshima and Nagasaki, which killed tens of thousands and opened the Atomic Age.

"He set in motion, with a firm decision, the wheels of the greatest humanitarian effort in history, the Marshall Plan.

"He proposed and implemented the Point IV program that revitalized the industrial complexes and economic security of friend and foe.

"He drew the line in Greece and Turkey and told the Communists on that side of the world that they must not cross it.

"He stopped Communist aggression on the other side of the world by making a stand in Korea.

"And he re-established civilian control over the military by firing the most popular military figure in modern history, Douglas MacArthur."

Throughout the introduction I could hear Truman clucking agreement and whispering to Margaret Truman Daniel, who sat next to him, "By golly, that fellow's right." Or "Yessirree." Or "He can say that again!"

Then with a great hambone gesture I said, "And now, ladies and gentlemen, here he is—President Harry S. Truman!"

He jumped up, plainly pleased, and said, "Thank you, Eric Sevareid!"

It was, I believe, the loudest laugh ever recorded at the club. Mr. Truman looked baffled. Margaret tugged at his coat tail, and he bent over to hear what she was trying to tell him.

"His name is Considine, not Sevareid," she whispered.

Mr. Truman straightened up and shrugged.

"I made a natural mistake," he said. "I got two fat reporters mixed up."

Playing God can be a taxing role.

Contents

Illustrations

(following page 114)

A Newspaperman's Prayer

by Bob Considine

(Distributed by King Features Syndicate)

Dear God, may I be fair. Circumstances and dumb luck have placed in my thumby paws a degree of authority which I may not fully comprehend. Let me not profane it.

Give me the drive that will make me check and countercheck the facts. Guide me when, lost for want of a rudder or a lead, I stumble through the jungle of speculation. Grant me, as the poet sang:

> The courage to change
> The things I can change;
> The serenity to accept
> Those I cannot change, and
> The wisdom to know the difference.

The twenty-six sharp-edged tools we call our alphabet can do what other tools do; build or destroy. Let me build. But let me know clearly, also, what should be destroyed, what darkness, what bigotry, what evil, what curse, what ignorance.

Never let me slip into writing *down,* in fatuous fear that readers will not understand. Let me write from the shoulder, and always with the assumption that those who read know more than I.

Such news as I find or comes my way, let me tell it quickly and accurately and simply, with an eye to my responsibilities. For news is precious. Few could live without it. When it is stopped or thwarted or twisted, something goes out of the hearts of men it might have nourished. Confront a starving man with his choice of a succulent meal or the promise to reveal instantly news of great importance, and he will first take the news. *Think* pieces, as we say in the trade to identify articles and columns contrived out of airy nothingness, or from a prone position, can never replace the meat and potatoes of news.

Let me champion just causes, avoid expediency, never lose the stimulation engendered by printer's ink. Remind me to be kind to copyboys, for I'll meet them on the way back down—when they are editors. Protect the innocent from me when, with deadlines pressing, my aim grows fuzzy.

Make me use my legs and eyes, the better to track down and see the truth. Deafen me to the Lorelei song of rootless hearsay, rumor, and the gossip of town loafers. If word that could cause great harm comes to me, even from sources far above reproach, let me have the dexterity and decency to pick up a phone and ask the subject about it.

When the customers write in to accuse me of being a bum, let me consider carefully the possibility or probability that I am . . . and try to do better. Let me work harder, try harder, and recall with proper humility that history produced some notably abler reporters, including four journeymen named Matthew, Mark, Luke, and John.

Let my stomach rebel at plucking meat from publicity handouts and let me not be miffed when someone says, "You had a pretty good piece last week but I can't remember what it was."

As long as our men fight, sweat, freeze, and die in actual or cold war, sacrifices which at times should make our food stick in our throats and our luxuries a torment, let me never cheaply use the words "courage" or "guts" to describe the means by which a pitcher wins a ball game, a gridman bucks a line, a golfer sinks a putt, or a fellow makes a speech.

And above all, let me recall repeatedly what the great teachers of the past . . . Moses and Socrates and Christ . . . would have done if by some alchemy they had been given the breathtaking break of swift and farflung communications.

It's All News to Me

1. *Caveat Emptor*

FOR ME, this blessed peonage of newspaper work began under the warped scepter of Edward R. McLean during his last and not always lucid years as owner of the Washington *Post.* That was September, 1930, and it would seem to me neat and proper to clean one's desk of his memories at least every third of a century.

I had been poking gingerly at sportswriting since discovering shortly after the middle of the 1920's that Considine was a hard name for the sports department of the Washington *Herald* to spell. By that time I had begun to reach the third and sometimes even the fourth round of local tennis tournaments and was consequently injured one morning, while still suffused in the blush of a previous day's victory, to read in the *Herald* that the match had been won by Robert Constantine. I repaired to the desk of the paper's sports editor, William Henry Coyle, who silently accepted the correct spelling of a name he had seen only in the agate type beneath "Other results."

Then Coyle said that there was little interest in tennis in Washington and none whatsoever among members of his staff. "If you want to see any tennis news in this paper, you'll have to write it yourself," he said resignedly.

Not long after that I was approached by Orrel Mitchell, a crack young athlete and scholar who lived two doors from our house in the Swamppoodle section of the city, hard by the railroad tracks leading into Union Station. Orrel was working part-time on the Washington *Post.* He explained unhappily that he had been stuck with the task of writing a review of the tennis season just past. Would I write it for him? There was two dollars in it for me if I did.

It was in all probability the fastest-concluded business transaction in the entire Hoover administration. The following Sunday my affront on basic English appeared in one of the obscurer reaches of the *Post*'s sports section. I was pink with pride, a color which matched that of the page on which this delible piece was printed. (When the *Post*'s ebbing fortunes prompted replacement of the pink stock by regular white newsprint, a reader complained bitterly that this compromised his habit of reaching thumb and forefinger into the edge of his *Post,* pinching off the edges of the sports section, "and shaking the rest of the paper on the floor.")

The *Post*'s résumé of that long-interred tennis season was by-lined "By Orrel Mitchell," of course. But I treasured it as if it were a page from the Book of Kells. "By Bill Henry" was another by-line that raised goosebumps all over me and nurtured the blooming-ham factor without which no writer, however unsung, can exist. I became Bill Henry the hard way. I was at that time playing in and had reached one of the late rounds of the Maryland indoor singles championship at the Fifth Regiment Armory in Baltimore. William Henry Coyle called me in with an odd proposition. Was I going to *win* the tournament? I nodded as if I knew what I was nodding about. He then said that such a win would enable him to give the story an unusual (for tennis) amount of space, "because," he added, "you're a Washington boy and it figures to be a dull Monday paper anyway."

He ordered me to go home, fetch my tennis clothes and a racquet, and report back to the paper's photo studio.

The three-column cut was made hours before the final round of the tournament began. Dutifully, I won the tournament, wrote a glowing story about the conquest—comparing it roughly to the triumph of Judas Maccabeus over the Hellenized Assyrians—and wired it to the *Herald.* It appeared Monday morning, wrapped around my picture, under the "By Bill Henry" credit. It was the greatest notice I've had so far.

Coyle said, as he handed me a voucher for ten dollars the next day, that he used his first two names as the by-line to spare me possible prosecution by the U.S. Lawn Tennis Association, whose rules forbade an amateur's writing about a tournament in which he was a participant. Coyle was as ignorant as I about the existence of an authentic and thriving Bill Henry on the other side of the country—Bill Henry of the Los Angeles *Times.*

The evening of that Monday the story appeared I just happened to have the clipping in my pocket when I slid into my seat in Prof.

Douglas Bement's Creative Writing course at George Washington University. Several members of the class read it, after slight prodding, and muttered congratulations. But a middle-aged lady who, like myself, was a Government clerk taking night classes at the University, had a question unrelated to the triumph. She said, "The fellow who wrote this story, this Bill Henry, says here that you lost the first set because you were 'too caustic.' What do you suppose he meant by that?"

"I meant . . . I mean *he* meant, or I guess he meant, that I should have taken more chances in the first set," I stammered, blushing.

She eyed me steadily, a gaze that was depressingly omniscient.

"I think you meant to write 'too *cautious*,'" she said, and left the impostor for dead.

The experience should have made me grateful for and content with my job as a clerk in the State Department's Division of Communications and Records. The job paid a good steady $1,680 a year. If I worked at it long enough I would be eligible for consular work without having to take the consular corps examination. All that Secretary of State Frank Billings Kellogg appeared to demand of me, aside from facelessness, was that I appear each morning no later than 9 A.M. and keep in alphabetical, numerical, and geographical order certain department files. These included the Kellogg-Briand Pact which condemned "recourse to war for the solution of international controversies." It was signed by fifteen peace-loving nations, including Germany, Japan, and Italy.

The dream of a permanent by-line of my own remained a troubling burr on the backside of this otherwise secure existence. And so one fine day in 1929 the obstructing curtains parted and there, ahead, stretched the way. I would write a weekly column of tennis news, gossip, playing hints, history, fact, fancy, call it "Speaking of Tennis," sign it with my own name, properly spelled, and see it emblazoned on the sports pages of the Washington *Star!* After all, the *Star* was the only paper our house subscribed to. It thumped against our paint-peeling door each evening and every Sunday morning and was thoroughly devoured by my mother, beginning with the obituary page. The *Star* was the fattest and most respected paper in Washington and thus, I felt, best fixed financially to sustain the additional burden of paying me for "Speaking of Tennis."

I wrote and rewrote that first column until I could have recited it backwards in Urdu. Then I walked it down Pennsylvania Avenue from the State Department to the *Star*. The *Star*'s meticulous sports editor, Denman Thompson, read the long piece in unnerving silence, instinctively correcting it with a blunt pencil as he proceeded. When he finished, he handed it back to me with the suggestion of a shudder.

"Sorry," Denman said. "We take Tilden's weekly column."

The totally uphill path back to the State Department led past the *Post*. I climbed to its rickety sports department and by extraordinary coincidence its young sports editor, Shirley Povich, was at his desk. I believe he had slept on it the night before. Anyway, Shirley was the only person around the premises at that time of day. He read the piece, and said he'd let me know. I went back to clerking in the State Department, properly deflated.

"Speaking of Tennis" appeared, every inconsequential word of it, by God, the following Sunday in the *Post*. Shirley paid me five dollars and ordered one for each Sunday thereafter. I took my best girl, Millie Anderson, to dinner. It seemed like found money.

It still does . . . most of the time.

In the late summer of 1930 Bill Dismer, the regular reporter of high-school sports for the *Post,* told Povich that he intended to retire to, or advance to, his family's hardware business. There were several applications for his job, mine among them. I was hesitant to ask Shirley outright to hire me. Instead, I communed with Walter Haight, Shirley's rotund assistant. Walter said he thought he could fix it.

Shirley was notoriously argumentative at that period in his life. If someone pressed a point of view upon him, Shirley would move to the other side, take up a position, and argue the opposite side. He had not gone to Georgetown Law for naught. Haight bided his time, and one day the trap was sprung.

"I'm thinking of hiring Considine to take Dismer's place," Shirley told him.

"Don't do it," Walter said. "He's a tennis player."

Shirley was immediately offended. "What's wrong with tennis players?" he demanded.

Walter shrugged. "They're either Filipinos or finks," he said, airily.

That did it, as Walter guessed it would.

"Well, I'll show you!" Shirley said heatedly, in what may have been a defense of both categories.

He offered me the job, and after a decent interval of soul-searching and compulsion, I took it. The soul-searching had to do with security.

The Government offered it; the staggering *Post* did not. The compulsion was provided by Millie.

"Take it," she said. "If you flop, well, I'm working. Whatever, I have no intention of ever marrying a Government clerk."

Have been winning bread for kith and kin through newspaper work since that dire ultimatum.

Thanks to (1) Millie and (2) God, who surely won't mind the billing.

It was a wonderful change of pace for me. Suddenly, it was not necessary that I report to work at 9 A.M. On the *Post,* even if one showed up at 3 P.M., he might find the dilapidated sports department totally deserted. I therefore was able to sleep the sleep of a laborer who dreams tormentedly of being late for work, awakens in a dismal sweat, and then discovers to his utter bliss that it is Sunday. Beyond that homely creature comfort there was an additional joy to this new work. Meager and obscure as the job and I were, I had a feeling of massive fulfillment. I had acquired a "local habitation and a name." I was no longer a State Department clerk subject to slights (unquestionably deserved but nonetheless painful) imposed by superiors I considered outrageously rude. For example, I had experienced difficulty forming a State Department tennis team to play in the Government League, though I was the singles champion of the city's public courts and the Department had some reasonably good players among its younger career diplomats. John Farr Simmons, later of ambassadorial rank and still later President Truman's Protocol Officer, finally made that State Department team possible. He explained to others in the Department that it was not a bad idea even though the suggestion had come from a noncareerist. At the *Post,* too, there would be no chance that I would ever again be upbraided by John Carter, a State Department career man who dabbled in journalism under the by-line of "Jay Franklin." He once ordered me to wrap some article of his clothing and send it to an address in Chevy Chase, presumably his home. It seemed hardly a task to impose on one busily engaged at the time in misfiling the documents of the London Naval Conference. By happy inadvertency, I dispatched the laundry to a wrong address. Mr. Carter was not amused.

Now, thanks to Shirley Povich, I ventured forth each day with credentials that proclaimed I represented the majesty of the Washington *Post.*

We were a shabby outfit, soon after plunged into receivership when McLean's physical, mental, and financial troubles transported him to a sanitarium at Towson, Maryland. Like certain beach crabs which continue to observe the rise and fall of tides, even though transported in tanks far from the beach, our salaries submerged with McLean's decline. My substantial $25 a week, plus $10 additional for "Speaking of Tennis," was reduced to a total of $31.50.

I had dreamed for years of moving to New York and finding fame and fortune there. Now, in January, 1931, with better newsmen than I selling apples on freezing street corners, I had the ignorance and the nerve to ask Shirley to help me conquer New York. Patiently, he sat down and wrote letters of recommendation to eight New York sportswriters he knew. I gambled an entire week's salary on the expedition.

And blew it. It was a disaster. The then plentiful New York papers were firing, not hiring. I could not even get inside the sports departments of five of the eight names on my list. The three men who sent word out to the guard at the door that it was safe to pass me were Joe Williams of the *Telegram,* Richards Vidmer of the *Herald Tribune,* and Bill Hennigan of the *Mirror*. I had lied at each of their reception desks when asked to fill out a form stating why I wanted in. I swore that my purpose was not to seek work but to offer startling news: Emmett Pare, an amateur tennis player of some skill, was about to turn *pro!*

Williams, one of the most trenchant sportswriters of my time, explained wearily that I was a fool to look for a job in New York when I had one in Washington. But as I left his office, he stopped me at the door.

"I'll read the clippings you brought with you," he said.

For some inscrutable reason, I was offended.

"I don't carry clippings with me," I said, and plunged out into the Labradorian weather in a steamy huff.

It was a long ride back to Washington.

The debacle made me more grateful than ever for the job on the *Post.* The pure joy and privilege of working in that sports department transcended the need for more money to pay the rent and buy the groceries. None of those exploited around our shop, in the pre-Newspaper Guild days, gave a damn how many hours we worked. The paramount ambition was to get the paper on the street more or less on time and write something for it worth reading.

Even at its nadir, the *Post* rewarded industry above and beyond the call of duty. Aubrey Taylor and Don Reed, who were running the paper in those early thirties under the beady eye of some fiscal wraith we knew only as "The Receiver," agreed to pay me an additional five dollars a week for a Sunday piece by-lined "The Drifter." (Walter Haight suggested that we liven it up a bit and call it "The Grifter.") It was a different sort of Washington column and an extraordinarily dull one to boot. Each week's effort was expended on exploring a Washington thoroughfare from its source to its mouth, or delta. I'd walk its length, note its features (equestrian figures, flophouses, etc.), study its origin—which in some cases reached back to the majestic genius of Pierre Charles L'Enfant, the French-born American soldier, engineer, and architect who was assigned by President Washington to draw plans for a capital city, driven to distraction by Thomas Jefferson, and dismissed after rejecting five hundred guineas and a patch of muddy Washington real estate for his timeless designs.

Slowly, surely, Shirley rounded out my lopsided sports knowledge. Once, in preparing for the composing room a routine AP story about a ball game played by the Brooklyn team, I wrote a head that read: "EAGLES WIN, 7-5."

Shirley looked at it and sighed.

"They are better known as the Dodgers," he said witheringly, plainly wondering what he had bought in the way of boobs.

Another time I complained in my "Speaking of Tennis" column: "Didn't see a line in the newspapers about the recent meeting of the Middle-Atlantic Tennis Association." Shirley read copy on the piece. When I glanced at it the following Sunday I was struck by a small but ever-so-crisp prefix. The edited sentence read: "Due to my reportorial shortcomings, I didn't see a line in the newspapers about the recent meeting of the Middle-Atlantic Tennis Association."

In 1932, when Jack Espey left the *Post* to handle publicity for George Washington University, Shirley upgraded me from high school sports to college games. And because the *Post* was always shorthanded in those days, the city side let me work a bit on the story of the Bonus Marchers and their humane, but still terrible, rout from Washington by troops commanded by Gen. Douglas MacArthur, Army Chief of Staff. On the ultimate day of the exodus, the splendid World War I hero, then a stylish fifty-two, rode down Pennsylvania Avenue on his white horse, followed by a handful of men, machines, and horses from

Fort Myer, Virginia. With him that day was his public relations aide, a forty-two-year-old major called Ike, whose quick, radiant grin and easy manner with reporters helped cushion the shock of seeing U.S. troops with bayonets bared, and a primitive tank or two, push ragged and bemedaled World War I veterans and their families out of their nation's capital. Tear gas was used to stir the more determined squatters.

My chief memory of that dismal day was experiencing the heat from a blazing encampment in Anacostia which had been set afire by the troops after the siege and defeat of the bonus-seekers. My sadness and muddled indignation were tempered by a feeling of relief that my main beat, my niche in the news business, was sports . . . wherein all was clean and noble and inspiring. I never expected to see General MacArthur or Major Eisenhower, his aide, again.

In January, 1933, halfway through the hiatus between the election and inauguration of Franklin D. Roosevelt, a considerably less historic event occurred. One bleak day during that period Shirley decided to replace a fine older man named Frank Young as the *Post*'s baseball writer. It broke Frank's heart and loosened his tears, for he loved the game in general and the Senators (or Nats, as they were then more frequently called) in particular. What was even more depressing for Frank, understandably, was that Povich—with the consent of managing editor Don Reed—chose me for the job. I couldn't carry Frank's typewriter, so far as knowledge of the game was concerned.

Once again, Shirley took me by the hand. This time the path led first to the office of Clark Griffith, the remarkable old fellow who meant as much to baseball, the so-called national pastime, as did Connie Mack, John McGraw, Ban Johnson, Charles Comiskey, or any other founding father. Griff originated the slick gimmick of having the President of the United States toss out the first ball of the season. For years, the Washington club's opener was scheduled a day ahead of any other, the better to frame this bold exploitation of the Chief Executive.

As time and administrations passed, a President would no more think of missing the opportunity to lend his presence on opening day than he would think of denouncing the sound dollar and motherhood. Many years after President William Howard Taft became the first patsy of this dodge, President Eisenhower said to hell with it: he had a golf date in Augusta, Georgia, that particular day. His decision struck consternation on all sides, not one side of which would have blamed him for neglecting to throw out the first football of the Washington Redskins season or the first two-year-old at Laurel race track, to name two other profit-making sports promotions in the area.

Griff sized me up that day, through the filter of his shaggy gray eyebrows, and didn't much like what he saw. Frank Young had never caused him any trouble, but how could he be sure of a tennis player?

Turned out that his misgivings were fairly well-founded. As suzerain of his tight little organization, surrounded by his doting wife, "Aunt Addie," five adoring nephews and nieces, and reverent retainers, Griff was distressed or angered by a number of pieces I later wrote. He had been a radical in his days as a player and later as a manager. He had helped raid the established National League for a cadre of stars around which the American League had been formed. But by the time I darkened his doorstep, or so he believed, he was somewhat more conservative than Louis XIV and just as sensitive to criticism.

What burned Griff especially was to be reminded in print that he was a delightfully inconsistent cuss.

One night at his ballpark while we watched a feebly lighted local charity game involving local celebrities who were expected to ride out their base hits mounted on donkeys, I asked Griff if he thought big league baseball would ever be played under the lights. His answer was an explosive *"Never!"* and I duly recorded it. A few years later he was night baseball's most wanton entrepreneur—so much so that Shirley wrote that Griff had applied to the baseball commissioner's office to play seven *day* games during the upcoming season. I bugged him along the same lines, suggesting that his keen sense of commerce had overcome righteous principle.

He threatened to denounce me to the other Washington papers as a fraud when I arranged a meeting between him and George Preston Marshall, who was eager to move his Boston Redskins to Washington, and then wrote that they had discussed the possible shift. This was technically true, but barely so. Griff had been an outspoken enemy of pro football ever since two local semi-pro teams of some years before, the Mohawks and the Apaches, had failed to pay him for the use of his park. He and Marshall had talked mostly about baseball, but I featured the fleeting mention of the Redskins move.

I watched the other papers for a day or two, fearing the worst. Nothing appeared. Then, not too many weeks later, a grand announcement appeared. The Boston Redskins would become the Washington Redskins and present, at Griffith Stadium, a star-studded team that had a fair little backfield manned by Ernie Pinckert, Riley Smith, Cliff Battles, and Sammy Baugh. It won the National Football League championship, and Griff made enough from the rent he charged and the food and program concessions he demanded to pay his entire baseball-team roster—and then some.

From the first day I met him, Griff assured me, as he did all others within earshot, that he was the sworn enemy of "those rich fellows" who threw their bankrolls around and were arrogant enough to think they could "buy" a pennant. Real baseball men, like himself, won their pennants by shrewd horsetrading and the purchase of promising youngsters. He proved his point dramatically that season of 1933 when he assembled, via trade, a team that had Goose Goslin, Earl Whitehill, Luke Sewell, Heinie Manush, Joe Kuhel, Al Crowder, Monte Weaver, and other solid senders, and appointed young Joe Cronin their manager.

The club won the American League pennant, but fell apart the following year. Griff sold Cronin, by then married to Griff's fine niece and adopted daughter, to Tom Yawkey of the Boston Red Sox, the richest of "those rich fellows." The price, $250,000 plus an able-bodied shortstop replacement named Lynn Lary.

I don't want to imply that Griff was generally sore about what I wrote about this ball club, such as "Buddy Myer's eighth-inning home run upped the team's output for the season to 32, only 14 behind Lou Gehrig." Or, just before Christmas, 1934, a year of disaster which saw the team finish deep in the second division, "Old Griff, mellowed by the approaching Yuletide, made a magnanimous gesture of good will today. He conceded the 1934 pennant to the Detroit Tigers."

I liked Griff and his family very much. In a fit of admiration, as one of his seemingly endless birthdays approached, I took up a collection from Jack Keller and Francis Stann of the *Star,* Buck O'Neill and Kirk Miller of the *Times,* Dick McCann of the *News,* and Shirley, of course, to buy him a present. Keller made discreet inquiry of Aunt Addie as to what Griff might need.

"Get Clark a suitcase with his named spelled out all the way in great big letters," the formidable matriarch of the clan decreed. "Some dirty rat stole the one that only had his initials on it."

Keller and I brought the bag to Griff's office in the midst of his birthday party, which was limited to the family, the staff, and Arch McDonald, the team's marvelous radio broadcaster.

Griff was touched and asked us to thank "my boys." So was Aunt Addie. As Keller and I prepared to leave the family affair, after a swift gulp of red wine out of a Dixie cup, Aunt Addie touched my sleeve.

"You know something, Mr. Constantine," she said warmly, "I've never believed all those terrible things they say about you."

Shirley sent me to Biloxi, Mississippi, with the ball club in the Spring of 1933. It was a hardship trek. There was not enough money available at the *Post* to buy me a train ticket. Millie and I, who had been married in the summer of 1931, rode down in the car of Louie Jordan, then a *Post* photographer. He had a Ford coupe, and it was one hell of a long, cramped trip.

But it changed my life. Some pieces I wrote during the days and weeks at Biloxi appealed to Mike Flynn, managing editor of the rival Washington *Herald*. He delegated his sports editor, Bryan Morse, to offer me a job at the end of the Biloxi stay and just before the season opened. It was a heady offer: $38.50 a week, seven dollars more than I was making on the *Post*. It was tempting. Millie was making $35 a week in the State Department, to my $31.50, and there was already talk that I had married her for her money. I wanted to shoot past her like a rocket, so I told Bryan I wanted at least $45. He was understandably shaken and said he would have to check with Mike Flynn.

When I told Shirley what had happened, he tried to get me $45 from the *Post*'s "receiver." The man said no.

By a curious coincidence, I knew another receiver, or representative of a receiver. He was George Allen, at that time administering mouth-to-mouth resuscitation to stately old (and half-filled) Wardman Park Hotel. George, an "I'm Just a Country Boy from Booneville, Mississippi" type from way back, had a strong streak of Mississippi in him, true. Mississippi riverboat. He was to move from his hotel baby-sitting job to Commissioner of the District of Columbia, confidant of Presidents Roosevelt, Truman, and Eisenhower (he wrote the best-selling *Presidents Who Have Known Me*), head of the Reconstruction Finance Corporation, treasurer of the Democratic National Congressional Committee, and a place on the boards of more

U.S. corporations than Nicholas Murray Butler had degrees. But when I approached him, the money involved was insignificant—to all but myself.

"Ask the *Herald* for sixty bucks a week and a year's contract," George advised fearlessly.

I did, all set to join in the laughter that followed.

But I got it, just in time to cover the opening game. Millie—no fool, she—promptly quit working.

A few weeks after I joined the *Herald,* Bryan Morse took drunk. This offended Mike Flynn, who had won a stirring battle with the jug not too long before. Mike fired Bryan and to the astonishment of all, in that obscure pocket of American letters, named me sports editor. I knew nothing about makeup, handling a staff, giving assignments, getting proper (free, if possible) seats for advertisers, and a host of other details alien to a person content merely to write.

My first act of office as sports editor was vainglorious. I assigned myself the task of writing a daily column, indented with a 6-pica cut of my bar mitzvah picture. What to name the column was a problem. (It was a big thing in those days, a catchy name.) All the good stock heads seemed taken. Arthur Brisbane, who appeared daily in the *Herald,* wrote under a simple and arresting roof: "Today." Damon Runyon, long a fixture on the *Herald*'s sports pages, had chosen "Both Barrels." Shirley, with an envious sense of immediacy, had copyrighted "This Morning." Grantland Rice had a lock on "Sportlight," Bill McGeehan owned "Down the Field," Westbrook Pegler "Fair or Foul."

There wasn't much time to make up my mind. I had gotten the assignment from myself about four o'clock in the afternoon and the paper was going to press at six. After dining lightly on my fingernails, I rolled a sheet of copy paper in the typewriter and wrote: "ON THE LINE."

Then, under it, I typed: "By Bob Considine."

Something was wrong. I x'd it out and made it read:

"ON THE LINE
With Considine"

It moved no earth, not even under its creator, but it was a handy enough stock head in that it covered considerable latitude. It would apply to all sports that need boundary markings on their playing fields, including dice. It suggested that I might be calling a reader personally to impart some toothsome morsel of news. It hinted of straightforwardness, as in "I'm laying it on the line, see?"

Moreover, it might help readers learn to pronounce Considine properly, for it rhymes with line. But that turned out to be a forlorn hope. I've been called Consideen more often than Considine ever since.

Having firmed up a stock head, there was the little matter of what to write under it. But that, too, came. Ring Lardner had died that day, and if that could not bring forth words there was scant chance they'd ever come. During four slipshod years of night classes at George Washington I had figuratively and sometimes literally sat at the feet of Douglas Bement, who conducted a class in creative writing. He was married to an exciting-looking woman, for a professor's wife, either French or Spanish or both. He sometimes sauntered into class in plus-fours, puffing a slender pipe. He was Ronald Colman, playing a quietly gay dean. He introduced me to Lardner, not the man, alas, but his product . . . Champion . . . Haircut . . . The Golden Honeymoon . . . Liberty Hall . . . and the sports coverage.

I wrote my first "On the Line" column about Lardner as if I had lost a dear friend—and in a sense I had.

"Pretty good piece," Mike Flynn said the next day. "Runyon's the big shot today, but Lardner's the one they'll be reading twenty-five or fifty years from now. His stuff will live."

It is a grand feeling to have a column in a metropolitan daily, replete with a carefully selected (and somewhat retouched) photo betokening manliness, courage, strength—but also hinting of good nature, kindliness to dogs and cats, and other rare qualities. But from the start there was a cloud over me. I was a fifth-rate sports editor. Simple as that.

I had neither the stomach nor will to fire anybody, even when ordered, as I was in the case of a great old cartoonist, Bud Counihan. When one of the staff got drunk for a few days it seemed best to phone his wife and ask her to keep him away from the office and I'd write his pieces until the fogs dispersed.

But this was not my trouble. My failing, mainly, was that I considered the symmetrical makeup of the *New York Times* sports page, the first page, that is, and Shirley's first page at the *Post* constituted the ideal way to present the news. I became symmetry-happy, balancing heads, boxes, and story lengths to such a fine degree that the first page of *my* sports section could have walked a tightrope across Niagara Falls without recourse to a parasol. Also, I kept all cuts to discreet sizes and considered it unwarranted to splash a headline across the top of the page each day, willy-nilly. Worse, I stubbornly resisted the pleas of our circulation manager, Happy Robinson, to pour on a lot of early Fall football stories and features about Georgetown, George Washington, Catholic University, Maryland, Navy, and other resident or adjacent teams. Instead, I gave by far the biggest play to Griff's baseball club, which was hammering toward its first pennant since 1925 (and the last it was to cop for decades, by the way).

I was out of my depth. Without the sure touch of George Garner on the copy desk, the *Herald* would have hit the streets now and then without a sports section. George and I had attended St. Aloysius grammar school together, and Gonzaga High until I became a dropout after two years. He had gone on to Georgetown and preceded me to the *Herald*.

Now, as if we were back in the sixth grade again, under the watchful eye of Sister Bernard, George helped me with my lessons. He kept our holey craft afloat, particularly when I was on the road with the ball club, competing against the man who had brought me into the business and directing my first faltering steps. Shirley and I were now equals, in grade at least: each was a sports editor, sports columnist, and baseball writer covering the Senators. Rivals!

"Anything I can do to help you, let me know," he said the day Mike Flynn had made the announcement.

Without thinking how ridiculous it must have sounded to him, I made the same offer. The difference in the twin offers, of course, was that I had nothing in the bank.

Just before the World Series of 1933, in which the New York Giants beat Washington four games to one, I began feeling hot breaths on my neck. Bryan Morse had been editing our sports pages by remote control. Whenever he spotted an error, though it be ostensibly a typographical fluff, he would circle it with a red pencil and mail the page to Mike Flynn. To boot, Ray Helgeson, our mercurial City Editor who had worked on the New York *Mirror* and the Chicago *Examiner*, burst into the sports department one night and said to me, "Get me twenty more tickets to the Series." I told him that the *Herald* had been given its full quota, the same as Griff allotted to the other Washington papers.

Ray looked at me with surprised disgust.

"What the hell kind of sports editor are you?" he asked. He didn't wait for an answer. It was just as well, for I didn't really know.

I was soon told.

The *Herald* was on lease from the Hearst chain, but many pipe lines were kept open between New York and Washington. Through one of them one day came Ed Frayne, sports editor of the New York *American*. He was a quiet-spoken man with heavy lenses, impersonally friendly and, to me, vaguely ominous. His sports pages were colorfully explosive compared to mine. And that's why he was in Washington, I began to comprehend.

Shortly after he returned to New York, I was leaving the *Herald* building late one night, so punchy from work that I was trying to remember where I had parked my car. I stopped by the lobby counter to pick up a fresh copy of the paper. The old fellow who manned the counter looked at me.

"You know you're out as sports editor, don't you?" he asked.

It was my introduction to one of the peculiarities of my craft: Everybody knows the verdict before the condemned man is told.

Bernie Harter, a decent, industrious man who had been Frayne's work-horse assistant on the *American* replaced me and granted me a last request. He hired Vincent X. Flaherty, who had been doing some piecework for me, as a regular member of the staff. Vinny and I grew up in generally the same area of Washington. He became a rolling-stone college football player, an end, in a day when it was comparatively easy to touch down at several campuses in quick succession without awakening sleeping eligibility dogs. Somewhere along the athletic scholarship road—not known for the finer things of life—Vinny picked up not only a voracious appetite to write but also the gift of fulfilling the desire.

He had something else that made him a natural for a sports section. He was an instinctive promoter.

In the years that stretched from there, Flaherty, overriding a speech impediment that would blast most men's careers, was responsible for some pretty profound sports developments. He wangled a berth on the College All Stars for a comparatively obscure George Washington University halfback named Tuffy Leemans, Tuffy's steppingstone to the New York Football Giants and a place in the pro-game's history. After World War II, in which he served as a correspondent, Vinny arranged two fund-raising TV telethons, featuring Bob Hope and Bing Crosby, that raised several million dollars for U.S. Olympic teams. After he moved his typewriter to the Los Angeles *Examiner* as its sports columnist, he began a campaign—mainly at his own expense—to bring big league baseball to California. More than any other individual, he must be given credit for inducing the Dodgers to move from Brooklyn to L.A. and the Giants to find their way to San Francisco. Vincent Xavier Flaherty, who was once paid fifteen dollars a week by a grateful Washington *Herald,* made the national pastime national, brought millions to Walter O'Malley and Horace Stoneham . . . and had difficulty persuading the Dodgers' management to sell him two good seats to the 1966 World Series at Chavez Ravine.

The reason for that is he no longer writes a column.

A similar fate faced me when I went to spring training camp with the Washington ball club in 1934. I had flopped as sports editor and seemed to be more or less on probation as sports columnist and baseball writer. My precious sixty-dollar-a-week, one-year contract, only one of its kind in Washington, was a guttering flame. There was no word from the office about its renewal. So I called George Allen, by that time District of Columbia Commissioner (in charge of making F.D.R. chuckle).

"What's your problem?" George asked cheerfully.

It took twenty minutes to tell him, even in the *Reader's Digest* version. My lament ended with, "What do you think I should do?"

"Demand one hundred twenty a week and a two-year contract," George snapped and hung up. He was busy.

Taking a firm stand on the quicksand of my predicament, I did just that. A week passed, an inch at a time. Then a telegram from Mike Flynn. I had to read it twice to believe it. It read, "OKAY FOR $120 A WEEK. TWO-YEAR CONTRACT MAILED YOU TODAY FOR SIGNING."

I learned later that when my demand first arrived at the office it evoked derisive laughter. Several days after its arrival, someone at the *Herald* called Ed Frayne in New York to tell him about the preposterous attitude.

"If you don't want to give him what he wants, we'll take him on the *American,*" Ed said.

This remarkable bid was brought to the attention of Mrs. Eleanor Patterson, absolute ruler of our domain in her roles as publisher, editor, and executive in charge of paying for the paper's million-dollar-a-year deficit. She had never shown the remotest interest in me or the sports department in general. But now that someone else was interested . . . well, by God, nobody was going to steal "one of my boys," Mrs. Patterson cried out.

That's why my terms (George Allen's terms, really) were met.

Moreover, that's how I was transported into the cast of characters who supported her, the star in a daily newspaper soap opera which could have been called "Life With Cissy."

Cissy. That's what everybody called her, except to her face.

2. *Cissy*

THIS was Cissy. . . .

There could never have been anyone quite like her before and little likelihood of a duplication in the future. She spun through the thick atmosphere of American journalism like a maverick meteor, then flamed out. No person who witnessed that incandescent passage can forget her, any more than the elderly astronomers forget Halley's Comet. No reporter she touched was precisely the same thereafter.

Eleanor Medill Patterson Gizycka Schlesinger was a female buccaneer, her transient son-in-law, Drew Pearson, decided. She could weep over a sick kitten and call the crippled President of the United States, Franklin D. Roosevelt, a slacker. She was the most extraordinarily generous publisher in newspaper history, and she was also a niggardly bitch.

I loved her.

Cissy was an arresting-looking woman, tall, with good movement, equally at home in rough-riding togs as in something by Dior. She was no chick when she came around to the newspaper business. But more than one of the younger bucks who worked for her mused over what it might be like to work with her on a different plane. She had the kind of hair that used to be portrayed in the shampoo ads, a cascade of darker Titian that fell to her hips, and strange dark eyes that could be as merry as Mrs. Santa Claus's and malevolent as Mrs. Medici's. No man really *knew* Cissy, but God knows a lot of them tried.

Some tried too hard; that could be fatal.

Cissy stood on the edge of the business for years, watching her mercurial brother Joseph Medill Patterson and her difficult cousin Robert Rutherford McCormick carve and sometimes hack their niches. She beheld and benefited from the harvest when Joe and

Bertie together converted their grandfather's Chicago *Tribune,* always a substantial winner, into the most successful newspaper in the publishing world. She watched with interest, and perhaps envy, when Joe moved along to New York to found the tabloid *Daily News,* which swiftly won and held the nation's circulation peak.

Cissy bided her time, but hardly in purdah.

She had two debuts, the additional one in Washington, which did not happen to every gangly rich girl from Chicago. When at nineteen she married Josef Gizycka, a high-octane Polish count with a low-calorie bank rating, the feature writers of those early 1900's hinted as bluntly as the libel laws permitted that this was yet another sorry example of a fine young American girl having her pretty head turned by a fortune-hunting cad with a waxed mustache. Whatever the justification for this sort of scandal-mongering, Cissy and her swain gave them something *really* to relish. After three years of generally jarring life with Gizycka, Cissy fled his mortgaged castle, baby Felicia in her arms, and made good her escape to London. Gizycka countered by kidnapping the child and taking her back to Poland. The *Tribune* and just about every other U.S. newspaper thundered. The State Department fumed; President William Howard Taft wrote pointed letters to Czar Nicholas; Pope (later Saint) Pius X expressed concern. Cissy got Felicia back in 1908 and came back to America. Including what amounted to ransom, the adventure of getting back her child cost Cissy about half a million dollars.

It would have been worth it, if they had ever become warm friends.

But Cissy and her vibrant daughter fissioned as the daughter grew, and in the end Felicia, hardly felicitously, charged that her mother must have been lunatic when she signed the will that left her only certain real estate, household effects, and $25,000 a year for life.

How much of that split could be traced to Cissy's busy but generally unproductive life during Felicia's maturing years is not measurable. But it was the life of a gadabout. She traveled restlessly at times, secreted herself on a ranch near Jackson Hole, Wyoming, at other times, knew the rollicking social life of Washington during Warren Harding's earlier days in the White House, and wrote two novels. One of them, *Glass Houses,* filled with thinly veiled or completely exposed well-known habitués—and sons of habitués—of Washington's top-drawer social set, was a kind of blueprint of the intemperance and intolerance she would later show as an editor and publisher. The other, *Fall Flight,* concerned a betrayed American heiress.

Washington was evolving as her home. Felicia fell in love and married up-and-coming Drew Pearson whose activities in those precolumn days in the early 1920's included such posts as director of the American Friends Service Committee in Serbia, Montenegro, and Albania; instructor in industrial geography at the University of Pennsylvania; lecturer; and occasional contributor to newspaper syndicates: "Europe's 12 Greatest Men," etc. Cissy gave her blessing, packed them off in style, and the following month in 1925 married her old friend Elmer Schlesinger, a New York attorney who had served as a dollar-a-year man in Washington with the Shipping Board.

Schlesinger's death in 1929 is a date totally unnoticed in the story of American journalism. But it is a significant milestone. Cissy was deeply attached to him; had great respect for him, she once told me. There is some good chance, therefore, that had he lived, she would have been content to share his life in the law and high finance.

But now she was alone, more alone than she had ever been before or would ever be again. The dynamos began to spin faster. She needed something to sink her teeth into, to occupy her restless mind. She tried writing again, factually this time. And she decided that she must have a writing name: thereafter, she was Eleanor Patterson. Period.

She needed something to write *on,* and that was provided, too. When she approached her friend William Randolph Hearst, Sr., and asked him to sell her his feeble Washington *Herald,* a pale competitor of the Washington *Post* in the capital's morning field, the laird of San Simeon laughed and asked her why she would want to add to her troubles.

The *Herald* had been a money-burning furnace for years. It had reached one of its drearier depressions while controlled, oddly enough, by one of its most well-heeled patrons: Herbert Hoover. Little is known of the late President's dip into daily journalism. But he had the *Herald* for a period after World War I and used it to promote the political fortunes of good friends in government and espouse the blessings of Prohibition. In those pre-Guild days, several members of the City Room staff worked for nothing, including future Pulitzer Prize winner Eddie Folliard. Desks were so scarce that Folliard and other lesser staffers sometimes were forced to use two huge rolls of newsprint as office equipment, one roll to plant a typewriter on, the other to sit on while working. Work was interrupted or demolished when either roll had to be trundled to the press room and fed into the hungry maw of the roaring machinery. It is not known why Mr. Hoover lost interest in the publishing business, but a possible clue lingered in the folklore of Washington journalism for years after he moved on to more rewarding fields, including the Presidency. Seems that Barney Hughes, a distinguished old copyboy, lost his balance one day while taking a refreshing drink of Ed Pinaud's Hair Tonic, tumbled down a flight of steps, and crashed through a dozen clouded glass doors stacked at the foot of the steps, awaiting installation.

Whatever was the case, or loss, Mr. Hoover surrendered, and it was from the National Savings and Trust Co. of Washington that Mr. Hearst bought the dubious "good will, etc." of the *Herald* on November 16, 1922, for $100,000. He made it a corporate part of his Washington *Times* Company, which had cost him more dearly. Hearst editor-columnist Arthur Brisbane (ostensibly acting on his own) bought the *Times* from Frank Munsey in 1917 for $500,000. In 1919, Mr. Hearst assumed the purchase contract from his employee for $325,000 and picked up unpaid notes to the amount of another $250,000.

Now, in 1930, with Cissy breathing heavily on his neck, Mr. Hearst had two, not one, losing properties in Washington. The feebler was the *Herald* whose circulation was 60,000. Cissy asked her friend to sell it to her. Mr. Hearst was not selling anything in those days, whatever the drain. But he shrewdly reckoned that she might be just the right transfusion the paper needed. He appointed her its editor at $15,000 a year. She accepted instantly, despite the protests of her brother and cousin, Joe and Bertie, that there was something nutty about working for $300 a week for a rival publisher while deriving a million-dollar-a-year income from her share of the Chicago *Tribune* and New York *Daily News*.

Cissy could not have cared less about the improbability of her position. She had a new baby in her lap, a new toy, a pulpit, a power, all rolled into one. It was enough to make her sensitive nostrils flare. And it did, on the front page of her *Herald* on July 26, 1930, just four days after she took over. The cause of the flaring was a report that Alice Longworth, still an impressive figure in the political and social life of Washington, would campaign for Ruth Hanna McCormick, then a candidate for the U.S. Senate from Illinois.

"INTERESTING, BUT NOT TRUE" read the startling box on Page 1 of the normally dull *Herald*. "The news is that Mrs. Alice Longworth will not only be a confidential adviser to Mrs. Ruth Hanna McCormick, but that she will campaign publicly for her lifelong friend.

"Interesting, but not true. Mrs. McCormick takes no advice, political or otherwise, from Mrs. Longworth. Mrs. Longworth gives no interviews to the press. Mrs. Longworth cannot utter in public. Her assistance will, therefore, resolve itself, as usual, into posing for photographs.—ELEANOR PATTERSON"

The *Herald* was never the same after that. Nor was Washington.

Cissy gave every outward appearance of being a dilettante stray in the newspaper game. The first person she hired after becoming editor was an interior decorator to fortify her Spartan office with chintz. The lengthening bread lines and increasing number of apple vendors in Washington made a sorry background for her arrival at the office each day in her chauffeured sixteen-cylinder Cadillac or the Duesenberg landaulet. She was often accompanied by her flock of big playful French poodles, all of them apparently descended from a dour dog she called affectionately the Old Bitch. Sometimes at night she would sweep into the office in an evening gown—in sharp contrast to her frequent daytime appearances in riding habit—en route to the theater or perhaps a White House party.

But as a matter of fact, Cissy worked exceedingly hard at her job. She was in many regards as keen as any cub reporter, and as eager to learn the trade.

"What can I do to get closer to our readers?" she asked managing editor Mike Flynn.

Mike was a real pro—a good, tough Irishman who had won an exhausting marathon against the bottle and now found himself burdened not only by a weak paper but a Hearst-blessed appendage who dressed and talked a bit like Rosalind Russell. His Humphrey Bogart brow furrowed in thought.

"Get out and meet them," he answered. "All you know is Society people and they don't buy the *Herald*."

Out of this exchange emerged "Maude Martin, jobless maid." In this disguise, Cissy haunted Washington's relief agencies collecting material for the series that was to launch her as a woman-of-the-people. It was a genuine hardship for her, but she was game right up to the incident that turned out to be her breaking point. It occurred during her brief stay at the Gospel Mission, a grubby haven for derelicts in Washington's Skid Row, not far from the glittering Capitol.

The adventure was notable in several ways. Cissy was the first person ever to arrive at the Mission in a Duesenberg, and the first claimant of a cot there ever to have journeyed from No. 15 Dupont Circle, her superb town house designed years before by Stanford White. She was certainly not the first waif ever granted asylum in the Mission who arrived with alcohol in the veins, but probably the first who ever brought aboard a load induced by vintage Mumm's. Cissy liked good champagne, and this seemed as good a night as any to fortify herself with it. It also seemed a good idea to take along some proper sheets and pillow cases, night gown, dressing robe, slippers, toiletry case, and that paragon of able-bodied chauffeurs, LaForte.

"Wait," she commanded LaForte as she sailed into the Mission. She was escorted to her freshly deloused room, ordered in advance by the *Herald,* and prepared herself for sleep. In the morning, there would be some sample bums to talk to, for her story.

Cissy never got to meet them, as it turned out. Dressed like a silken model for Harper's Bazaar caught anachronistically in a Barbary Coast bawdy house, Cissy reclined on her pillow, tucked her familiar sheets around her chin, and tried to forget the unshielded light overhead. She had coldly resisted the suggestion that most Mission residents, when able, turn out their lights at night.

Cissy's eyes were not very strong. She suffered from occasional attacks of conjunctivitis, or "pinkeye" as she called it, which occasionally caused associates to believe she was less than cold sober. "Mother, you're drunk!" Felicia accused her once at an otherwise pleasant party at Dupont Circle. It was a case of pinkeye, not pink champagne, Cissy tried vainly to explain.

But now as she lay in the Gospel Mission there was no question in Cissy's mind about her eyesight. The creature walking across the garish ceiling was a cockroach. She found the sight completely demoralizing. She let loose a cry that must have startled her fellow inmates, threw her mink over her nightgown, put on her slippers, and quit the premises.

LaForte had the motor running.

The series was bound to be an attention-grabber. The *Herald*'s promotion department, eager to bask in her good graces, composed full-page panegyrics heralding the coming series.

There was reason to believe that Cissy herself believed her notices. At least, there must have been considerable pride of authorship involved because of her violent reaction to a sorry snafu that struck the first article of the series. By a freak of fate and bad composition, the first edition of that fated night's run came off the presses with her story wildly garbled.

The by-line was there all right, bigger than life, but the story started out with some bewildering paragraph that belonged far down in the pillars of type. Somewhere else in the typographical Babel reposed the misplaced lead.

Even in those early stages of her editorial career there were *Herald* employees bucking to be mentioned in her will, apparently. One of these seized the first few papers off the press that sorry night and sped off for Dupont Circle, where Cissy paced impatiently. He never read below her impressive by-line.

But Cissy did, and her yell of rage shook the mansion. LaForte was summoned and the primed Duesenberg shot to the *Herald,* bearing in its back seat an author whose emotions ranged from helpless tears to mule-skinning profanity.

All was quiet in the *Herald*'s City Room when Cissy swept in like an unannounced cyclone. The early edition had been swiftly replated when the error was caught and was by now running smoothly; most of the staff were out for "lunch," as dinner time was always called on morning papers.

Her stentorian *"Who is responsible for this!"* would have scared a dog out of a boneyard. Heads swung in shock, and the City Room went into what might be called Condition B—for buck-passing. The instinct for survival, highly developed in newspaper people, impelled those present at the time to point toward the Copy Desk.

Cissy closed in on it. What followed might have been the most magnificent firing act of her life. But, as noted before, it was "lunch" time. The disorderly half-moon table which had been pointed out to her as guilty was manned at the moment only by a graying lush who had dropped in to bum a quarter and was awaiting the return of a copyreading benefactor.

"You are fired!" Cissy thundered, pointing like Brünnhilde ordering a war.

The bum laughed at her, which did not help matters. It was the first time he had ever been fired from the *Herald* while not employed.

When Cissy arrived at the office the next day, she looked into the City Room and noticed a graying man busy at a desk not far from the Copy Desk. She sailed resolutely into Mike Flynn's nearby office.

"I fired that man last night; get him out of here," she said, livid.

Mike looked in the direction she was pointing, took off his glasses, and shook his head.

"That's Bob McClellan, our Day City Editor, Mrs. Patterson."

"I don't care who he is," Cissy said. "Get him out of here."

It was useless, Flynn discovered, to explain that (1) she was wrong, (2) Bob had only recently battled his way up to the position after being canned for drinking too enthusiastically at the wrong times; and (3) a cruel blow like this would knock him off the wagon again. But Cissy was running the paper now, as any phone call to San Simeon would confirm. Mike fired McClellan, whose first act of outrage was to prove Mike's third point.

The remarkable aspect of Cissy's inhuman conduct in McClellan's case was that she did not almost immediately rehire him and appoint him Pope. Cissy could blow hotter and colder than the surface of the moon. She made a special point of saving sway-backed old work-horses ticketed for the LePage's plant. Her disparagers swore this dated from an impetuous chapter in her life as a horsewoman. They assured all who would listen that Cissy extracted a dramatic price from a favorite hunter who threw her and trotted back to the barn at Dower House, Cissy's place in the Maryland hunt country which had once belonged to Lord Baltimore. Cissy is suppose to have walked home in her fashionable jodhpurs, fetched a pistol, and killed the animal.

Whether true or false, Cissy was a big woman. She always had room for remorse. McClellan in time went back to work for her and married one of her prettier reporters.

The desire to catch her eye, join her shifting court, became one of the major preoccupations of the *Herald* staff. Reporters got hair-cuts more frequently than in the past and admired her dogs. Composi-tors began wearing neckties. Pressmen replaced their ink-stained paper birettas with fresh ones. Bill Shelton and his business office people became, if possible, ever more unctuous. Eddie Bratburg, who might have carried a spear in *The Front Page,* devised a signal system with the front counter to alert him whenever Cissy entered the build-ing. He was an assistant city editor and had every intention of bettering his position. Whenever Cissy would enter the City Room en route to her office, the phones on Eddie's desk and those adjoining it would be ringing urgently and he would be reaching for them and barking hosts of orders. Cissy was pleased by such industry until she learned about the hoax, probably from a rival for her uncertain smile.

Then one day there was a new man at Eddie's desk: handsome, rakish, pencil-thin Ray Helgeson, fresh from Hearst's Chicago *Examiner* and the hard school of knocks whose dean was Walter Howey. He was but one of a stream of men and women Mr. Hearst was happy to send to her aid in Washington from his enormous pool of executives, editors, specialists, and ordinary working stiffs.

"He sincerely admired her journalistic enterprise," W. A. Swanberg was to write years later in *Citizen Hearst.* And he added, "When Mrs. Patterson, who rode in her own private railroad car, arrived at San Simeon for a visit, he invariably had the other guests out on the terrace to meet her with armfuls of flowers, and hired a band to furnish a musical welcome."

Cissy was making her mark in the Hearst complex. "Publisher" was added to her title. The *Herald* was beginning to be talked about and bought. Local and national advertisers who had been avoiding the paper like a plague for years began showing an interest. The *Herald* was still operating in the red, but a deal was made whereby Cissy was given a percentage of all new advertising revenue. Cissy responded magnanimously by giving up her $15,000-a-year pin money. She remained a director of the Chicago *Tribune,* which was in bitter competition with Hearst's *Examiner,* and of the New York *Daily News,* then engaged in lethal conflict with Hearst's two New York morning papers, the *American* and the *Mirror.*

Cissy revered the man who had entrusted his sick *Herald* to her doting care. She saw eye to eye with him on every subject from politics to vivisection. They shared a lively interest in the former and deplored the latter in fulminating editorials. Mr. Hearst played an important role in gaining the Democratic nomination for Franklin D. Roosevelt in 1932. Cissy echoed the confidence. "He is a real American," she wrote of the candidate. "There is surely a special radiance about this man." She and Washington's other renowned Eleanor—Mrs. Roosevelt—became close friends.

Hearst talent wore a path to Cissy's *Herald* in the early days of the New Deal. Courtly, competent Tom White, Hearst's general manager, began dividing his valuable time between Hearst's over-all problems, which involved tens of millions of dollars, and Cissy's infinitely smaller-scaled fiscal aches and growing pains. She got her share of Hearst's efficiency experts, too, but more often than not ignored their recommendations—another trait she shared with W.R.

A particularly aggressive one named Bart Guild, who struck dismay wherever he roamed in search of heads to lop off the payrolls, struck no terror in Cissy. One night during his Washington stay, in the heady after-dinner dialogues at Dupont Circle, Guild held forth at some length about the number of Hearst people he had fired over the years. He concluded the grisly tale by announcing, ". . . but if I had my choice in this business I wouldn't be in this end of it all. I'd like nothing more than to be a simple newsboy selling papers on the corner."

He must have noted my look of disbelief, for he wheeled and roughly demanded, "And what would *you* like to be?"

I would mainly have liked to be someplace else at the moment, but the silence of the room—particularly of the hostess—required an answer.

"I'd like to be a newsboy, too," I said, "and have the corner opposite your corner."

"I'd run you off it," the hatchet man said angrily.

"Like hell you would," I said, bravely defending my nonexistent territory.

"Good for you," Cissy cut in, giving Guild a look that indicated he was not to stay very long in Washington.

Others came to help her make good.

Down from Boston, to be followed next day by the wife and children, came a lean redhead billed as just the picture-page editor Cissy needed. His arrival on the job coincided with a banquet given that night at the Willard Hotel for *Herald* newsboys. The paper had sandbagged local dignitaries into attending, and for these Cissy gave a special reception in a private dining room before the group joined the apple-cheeked youngsters for the dinner. Drinks were served. Among the many pictures taken was one which caught Cissy gesturing with her highball glass as if she was proposing a toast to the camera's lens.

With that infallible skill which picture-page editors have for selecting the worst of a choice of available shots, the eager-beaver from Boston chose the shot of Cissy confronting the camera with her drink.

She was again suffering from pinkeye at the time and thus looked plastered. The relative positions of her well-groomed body and the outstretched glass gave the drink the distorted size of a Jeroboam. To compound the felony of drinking at a newsboys' dinner, as his caption indicated, the benighted Bostonian ordered the picture set four columns and featured it in the center of a layout of potential advertisers, Y.M.C.A. types, and selected cherubs among the newsboys.

After the first edition came up, the man from Boston had misgivings. He ordered the drink air-brushed—erased—from the picture and a new cut made. In the next edition, which Cissy saw, she appeared with extended claw, apparently bent on garroting any newsboy who came within reach. The man from Boston was fired by phone. There was later a legend around the *Herald* that in his resultant state of shock he forgot to tell his wife he was returning to Boston and that the poor woman and the children caught a glimpse of him—a ghostly face in a window—as their trains shot past each other the next day.

Cissy inherited Hearst star Adela Rogers St. John for a spell, too, and they hit it off as only two women of the world could. An incurable matchmaker, Cissy tried to marry Adela off to Helgeson, but there were complications. Like other mates. Adela gave the girl reporters of the City Room and the chaste ladies of the Women's Page and Society a vicarious taste of what it was like to be in combat on big national stories. She had covered them all.

Adela astounded one and all by her facility. One day she spent a couple of hours with a Government stenographer and in short order produced a series of articles about Government Girls which, if produced today as a TV series for afternoon consumption, would clobber all competition. *Herald* people stood in awe of the prolific whirlwind from the big time. One day she tripped and dropped her purse as she entered the City Room. The purse opened and its disemboweled contents littered the floor.

"What a novel that'll make!" one of the *Herald* rewrite men gasped.

Pat Frank, who was to write the best-selling *Mr. Adam,* and a lot of other winners before he died, was brought in by Helgeson to nail down the kind of tough stories Ray wanted to break—and did. Pat hid in the broom closet of a grand jury room on one occasion, and the *Herald* broke the story of its deliberations. He nearly went to jail for his scoop. Cissy, exercised over the case, would willingly have gone to jail with him.

Nobody awed Cissy. The stimulation of battle over real or imagined wrongs to herself brought a flush to her cheeks and a glint to her swimming eyes. She was properly outraged when Eugene Meyer, who had bought the rundown Washington *Post* in 1933 and began to pump impressive sums into its rebirth, made Hearst an attractive offer for the *Herald* without so much as consulting Cissy. Hearst ignored the offer, but from then on Cissy regarded Meyer and his *Post* as her worst enemies. She delighted in luring *Post* people into her pasture. When the papers became embroiled in a court fight over "Dick Tracy," the adventure strip which was in effect owned by her brother Joe and cousin Bertie, and Meyer won the case, Cissy sent him a pound of raw meat with her card, on which she scrawled, "Have your pound of flesh!"

Another who chose to square off against Cissy was George Preston Marshall, then owner of the highly profitable Palace Laundry chain in Washington, bon vivant, sportsman, friend of Broadway and Hollywood folk and, on orders from San Simeon, publisher of Hearst's Washington *Times*. That afternoon paper used the building, presses, and some of the clichés left over from the morning *Herald*. George and Cissy, both headstrong and colorfully independent, had been friends for years. But in 1934, after Marshall was deputized as publisher of the *Times,* in the hope that he might inject as much zing into it as Cissy had into the *Herald,* there was a noticeable cooling off on Cissy's part. She came to regard him, quite correctly, as a rival for the major share of the dollar which advertisers earmarked for space in Hearst papers in Washington.

Their ultimate collision was characteristic of Cissy's sensitized explosion point, unlike anything known in nature until the isolation, some years later, of Uranium-235. One day Marshall ordered *his* side of the third floor hall painted a bluish-purple, the hereditary hue of the family laundry. Worse, he chose to have the work done during one of Cissy's trips out of the city. When she returned, she took one look at the *Times* side of the hall wall and ordered *her* side painted a clashing green. Both claimed victory to their now separate coteries of friends, but neither could arouse much enthusiasm among those, particularly those with hangovers, who had to walk through the hall each day.

Cissy won that one. Her impact at San Simeon was understandably greater than that of Marshall. He was thanked and returned to his mangles.

It was Cissy's building after that, and she shaped it and its inmates into the image and likeness of her steel-clad whims.

One of her surest innovations was pure Cissy. All the creature comforts she had known since birth—good food, proper wines, gracious service, travel, and chi-chi rampant—found expression on her expanded pages for women. Martha Blair, who was to marry Arthur Krock, introduced *Herald* readers to life behind the closed doors of the 1925 F Street Club. Igor Cassini, dashing son of an old friend, in time became her provocative society editor-columnist, and on one occasion provoked a group of blue-blooded ruffians from the Virginia horse country into tarring and feathering him.

Cissy was a stickler for good style. One night she dropped by the office on the way to a party dressed in a stunning gold lamé gown, with train held delicately across her left wrist as she moved to her office, dusting ashes from a cigarette held in a quill-tipped holder. She approved the first-edition pages spread before her, then floated regally back to the elevator. It held a motley group: respectful or ogling reporters, printers, publicity people, a souse or two, and up front and ready-get-set, a Western Union boy. When the door slammed open, the boy shot out across the lobby, bent on his errand. Cissy picked up her tight dress and sprinted after him, a frightening sight to the lad when he looked over his shoulder. She seized the terrified youngster by the collar, marched him back through the crowd that was still leaving the elevator, waited until it was empty, pushed him inside, stepped in after him, adjusted her train over her wrist again, and walked out ahead of him.

"Ladies first, young man," Cissy cooed.

Reporters found they could take advantage of Cissy up to a point. The trouble was the task of locating the point. Like the night of Betty Hynes's farewell party for Ray Helgeson. Ray had taken two major steps. He had fallen in love with a beautiful young girl reporter, and he had decided to return to Chicago. Cissy was certain to be offended on both points.

So Betty, who worshiped Cissy but never became a part of her innermost court (as did among a few others Evie Robert, personality-flashing wife of Roosevelt's Under Secretary of the Treasury), did not invite Cissy to the Helgeson bash. But if Cissy was out of sight that night, as we sat around the little apartment's chairs and floor drinking the fresh squeezings of Repeal, she was not out of mind. About 2:30 A.M. the *Herald*'s top crime reporter, Laz Sommers, who had come to George Washington University as a gifted athlete and had moved on to greater things as a speakeasy impresario, put in a call to Dupont Circle. It roused a butler and, in time, Cissy.

"Hello, you old bag," Laz said. "Get on your feet and come over to Betty Hynes's joint. We're having a hell of a party for Helgeson."

Then Laz, my friend, handed the phone to me. Cissy was asking a question. It was an ominous-sounding question.

"Who *is* this?" she was asking.

I told her it was me . . . I. Surprisingly, she was not the least bit angry.

"It sounds very gay," she said sleepily. "I'm sorry I can't come over, but I'll tell you what: Why don't you bring your little party over here to the house, and we'll have a nightcap and a bite to eat?"

There were thirty of us. Thirty-one, actually. Maybelle Jennings, the dear movie critic, was missing for a time after the alarming rabble arrived in the driveway of the splendid mansion. A search party quickly discovered her. Upon alighting from one of the cars and taxis that transported the well-oiled mob from Betty's to Cissy's, Maybelle had collapsed and fallen through a high hedge and was flat on her back in the formal garden on the other side of it, feet in the air. We were all accounted for now and filed into the stately foyer, chastened suddenly by the outrageous intrusion of our leader's domain. At least, we felt chastened until Sommers relieved the tension.

He goosed Cissy's butler, who was bowing us in with understandable disdain. The man must have leaped a yard in the air in the course of surely the most extraordinary experience of his life.

Cissy was a radiant hostess. She appeared in a lovely dressing gown, again with a train, and ordered out the kind of good whiskey and champagne we would have been drinking earlier if we had been able to afford it. She danced with some of us, and very well, too, laughed when one exuberant drunken employee tried to hitch a ride across the slick ballroom floor on her train, and found it not unamusing when the husband of one of her embarrassed girl reporters passed out. Cissy had seen lots of friends pass out before, but never one as dramatically as this. The man was seated in the middle of a divan facing a coffee table. He was stoned but upright. Then a butler came in and put down in front of him a silver tray filled with a huge mound of scrambled eggs, garnished with bacon and decorated with parsley twigs. It proved too much for the man to bear. He keeled over face first into the mountain of eggs and with such force that his head was almost completely submerged. Fast work prevented his becoming the first known American to die in scrambled eggs.

There was a touch of dawn when the party dissolved. George Waters, one of the *Herald*'s best police reporters, sought out Cissy and found her in the spacious kitchen, still serene.

"Thanks very much, Mrs. Patterson," George said. "You're a great sport to put up with a thing like this. Can I help with the dishes?"

Cissy looked at him glacially.

"I have sufficient help to do my dishes," she said. "You're fired."

Cissy was the utter mistress of the bold gesture. There was that pilgrimage to Edgar Allan Poe's room. . . .

One day she appeared in the doorway looking into our scabrous sports department, searched the room uncertainly, recognized me, and beckoned.

"We're going to the University of Virginia at Charlottesville," she said. "I've never seen Poe's room there. Be at Union Station at five."

"I've got to cover the doubleheader today," I said. "Washington's playing the Yankees. Its the biggest. . . ."

"Who's interested in baseball?" Cissy said impatiently. "Be at the station at five. Just ask the station master where the Ranger is."

The Ranger was her private car, a handsome gift from the late Schlesinger. It had a shiny brass-railed observation deck, a paneled drawing room fit for the queen who owned it, four bedrooms equipped with comfortable poster beds, not berths (and showers and hand basins whose spigots were marked 18 k.), a handsome dining room with a fine oval table and glittering ware, and beyond that a spotless galley and quarters for the two-man crew. No. 1 boy's Ranger insignia on the cap that topped his special uniform was spelled out in gold; No. 2 boy's in silver.

"They're fags, but cute," Cissy would say when conducting a tour of the fabled Pullman. It cost $5,000 a year just to park the Ranger in the station yard at Washington, and twenty-eight round-trip first-class fares every time she ordered it hitched to a train headed some place she wished to visit—even if she rode alone, as she sometimes did.

We had a nice ride south that night, just Cissy, Maybelle Jennings, and the fellow who was supposed to have covered a doubleheader that day at Griffith Stadium. Our drinks were elegantly served on the observation deck as the sun set. There was a leisurely dinner whose main course was the tender hearts of lamb chops, after-dinner coffee and liqueurs in the car's living room, and a good night's sleep. We awakened in the morning to find the Ranger parked on a siding at the foot of the hill leading up to the University campus.

LaForte was parked in the mud-splattered Duesenberg a few feet from the steps of the Ranger. He had driven through the night over Virginia roads, just to be there. We breakfasted, stepped into the car, purred up the hill, were led to Poe's room, and looked in. A stuffed raven peered down glassily from a beam.

"Nice," Cissy said. She turned and we followed her back to the car and rode down the hill in the early morning sunshine. That's right, she told the university's man, that's all she wanted to see.

At the little station at the foot of the hill Cissy said, pleased as a child with a ginger of an idea, "Let's go to Williamsburg now and see the Rockefeller restorations." Maybelle said she could not dream of anything nicer to do. I could not think. It was the earliest I had been up since I was an altar boy.

The overwhelmed station manager was delighted with the new plan.

"A wonderful coincidence, Mrs. Patterson," he beamed, bowing and tipping his little hat. "There's only one train down there and back each day and it'll be along in, let me see"—he flipped the lid of his big watch—"just two hours, by cracky. We'll hitch your Ranger on, and down you'll go." He seemed about to go into a joyful jig.

"I don't want to wait two hours," Cissie said, evenly. "Bring around an engine."

I waited for the man to fall over dead. But he survived.

"I don't think you understood me, Mrs. Patterson," he said. "I said the regular train—the only train today—is coming through soon and—"

"And I said bring around an engine," Cissie interrupted firmly. "You're in that business, aren't you?"

"But the *cost* to you, Mrs. Patterson. . . ." the poor man mewed. He looked at her and swallowed noisily. "There *is* a spare freight engine here, but. . . ."

It took an hour to fire up the steamy monster and attach the Ranger to it. Cissy and Maybelle retired to their staterooms for a morning nap as we moved down the tracks in solitary grandeur, pulled by an engine that could have dragged two hundred freight cars. I fixed one of those much-too-early-in-the-morning Scotches and repaired to a chair on the observation deck to contemplate (1) my navel, and (2) the occasional sight of the smoke of the regular train following not too far behind.

Cissy wrote a piece for *Editor and Publisher* once upon a time which began:

> Arthur Brisbane once said that the only two men in the world he knew who never do anything they don't want to do are W. R. Hearst and Joe Patterson. It would be truer to say that neither of these men pays the slightest attention to nonessentials.

Like Cissy . . .

Exhausted from her assorted labors, feuds, fads, and crusades, Cissy took off for Miami Beach in the Ranger with her dogs, trunks, and trappings one bleak Washington morning, bound for a full month's vacation in the sun at the Flamingo Hotel. She had reserved the better part of an entire floor in its tower at stiff seasonal prices and looked forward eagerly to the respite from work and worry. Happy Robinson would join her there in a couple of days.

Happy, straight from the Hearst stable and a crackerjack, was her circulation director. He bowed to no man in the shop when it came to expressing and displaying undying loyalty to Cissy. Happy was a survivor of the mob-ridden circulation wars between Cousin Bertie's *Tribune* and Hearst's *Examiner*. He wore his scars with pride, as he did a .38 slug which had been shot into him and which he had never gotten around to having mined.

Happy's trip to Miami was to be a little reward, a bonus. The *Herald* was by now streaming into front doors in Washington, too. Circulation was mounting toward the 100,000 mark, and it was noised about that Eugene Meyer had made another futile effort to buy the property from Hearst, this time for a million dollars.

Happy breezed into the lobby of the Flamingo like a song and dance man coming on stage at the old Palace. "It's Happy, Chief, I'll be right up," he sang into the house phone. He did a kind of clog over to the elevator, beckoning to the bellhop to bring along his bags.

Then a man with striped trousers and a white carnation in his lapel tapped him on the shoulder.

"Sorry, sir," the man said. "You're not permitted above the ground floor."

Happy could be tough.

"Listen, buddy, I'm the guest of Mrs. Eleanor Patterson."

The man sighed.

"This," he said, "is a restricted hotel, sir."

Happy had eaten tougher men for less. But now he walked quietly back to the house phone, called Cissy and said, "Chief, they won't let me come upstairs because I'm a Jew."

There was an imperceptible pause on the other end of the line, then Cissy said airily, "Well, Happy, if that's the case I'll come down and see you."

"I'm gettin' out of this goddam joint, Chief."

"Now you stop," Cissy chided. "I'll be down."

Happy clumped to the nearest chair and glared at the imperturbable manager. After ten minutes he could no longer bear it. He snatched the house phone again, got Cissy, and shouted that he was leaving immediately.

"Happy," she said, "I *told* you I'll be right down."

And in a few minutes there appeared an explosive scene at the elevators. The doors flung open and out spilled Cissy, her boisterous French poodles, trunks, bags, gowns streaming from hangers—and a stricken manager trying to kiss her hand and implore her to change her mind.

Cissy had had enough of Meyer's overtures to Hearst. On April 18, 1937, she leased the *Herald* for five years. It was a complicated deal: $350,000 a year for the first year and thereafter for each year the paper lost money, minus 50 per cent of the amount the losses in the previous year were reduced below $700,000. If there should be a profit, the rental would be 50 per cent of the net. Three months later Cissy wrote out a check for a million dollars, which in effect gave her both the *Herald* and the *Times*. On January 1, 1939, the purchase of the papers was formalized. In the end they cost Cissy $1,557,500.

They were losing $1,750,000 a year.

Now came the full flowering of her colorful, courageous, even reckless skills. She combined the two failures into the whopping success that became the Washington *Times-Herald,* an around-the-clock no-holds-barred daily bombshell. No target was too big to tackle, including That Man in the White House, and in time two of the columnists who had helped so greatly in bolstering circulation, Walter Winchell and Drew Pearson.

Cissy told me once that the whole thing between Roosevelt and herself was smashed forever when the President, having consented to see her brother Joe, who wished to offer his services to the Army immediately after Pearl Harbor, "let Joe stand there like an office boy and then turned him down."

Actually, there had been a cooling off over a period of years. Cissy accompanied Hearst, Brisbane, and publisher Paul Block when the titans trained to Topeka in the summer of 1936 to look over (and enthusiastically approve of) Gov. Alf M. Landon as Presidential timber. But she remained friendly with Mrs. Roosevelt through the late thirties and with the more personable men around Roosevelt—notably Joseph P. Kennedy, Harold Ickes, and Harry Hopkins.

In time, she was to belt them all, sometimes in a manner that shocked even the most case-hardened of her editors. Ash DeWitt, probably the most capable executive who ever worked for her, walked out when—over his bitter protests—Cissy insisted on running a full page of dead U.S. Marines, killed on the beach of Tarawa. At a slant across the whole page she had ordered written Roosevelt's prewar pledge: "AGAIN AND AGAIN AND AGAIN I SAY, AMERICAN BOYS WILL NOT FIGHT ON FOREIGN BATTLEFIELDS. . . ."

In July, 1944, FDR rejected an appeal to allow draft deferments for premedical students under twenty-six. Cissy filled another picture page, this time with twenty State Department career men—ages twenty-four to thirty-seven—"who do not choose to fight."

Her accompanying editorial "hissed"—as *Time* magazine put it—"If the Army really needs *all* the able-bodied young men it can get, it can find in Secretary Hull's fold an assortment of rich, able-bodied and unmarried boys of no particular use to anyone. . . . There are plenty of intelligent girls available to more than adequately fill the jobs of these young men." *Time*'s account continued:

> "It would really be good for 'the panty-waist brigade' (and isn't *that* vulgar?)," snapped Cissie, to have a taste of war. Even Bill Bullitt "might have lost his insatiable appetite for intrigue before the present disaster" if he had "risked *his* young blood and guts and tears in the last World War instead of cutting dramatic capers at the Versailles Peace Conference."

> And just while she was on the subject, "the President himself has no firsthand knowledge of war either, we might add. Like his little boy friends, Pearson and Winchell, he stayed far away from the battlefield of the first World War. Although at that time a young man, and in perfect physical condition, he did 'his bit' as Assistant Secretary of the Navy—right here in Washington."

Cordell Hull raged at his next press conference. He produced the deferment record, age, and marital status of every career man whose picture Cissie had printed. All but four were overseas, he said, many in jobs directly related to the military. Nobody in his department under twenty-six was draft deferred, he said. Cissy's attack, he said, was "violent and unfair, grossly unfair."

Cissy died one night; there probably was nothing more interesting to do at the time. She was in bed at Dower House reading a book when her time came. A maid named Eva Barowik tapped on her door and came in—that morning of July 24, 1948—with a message that the office was on the phone; she found Cissy. Her eyeglasses were on the pillow beside her head; her book was on her chest. The reading light was on. She was sixty-three.

Her sealed coffin was centered in the ballroom of the Dupont Circle home she had known so long. Dr. Dudley E. Stark of St. Chrysostom's Episcopal Church, Chicago, who did not know her very well, said some kind words. Daughter Felicia and granddaughter Ellen were there. Happy Robinson shed honest tears. The body was taken to Chicago by train and buried there.

Drew Pearson wrote the best obit. He and Felicia had managed to stay married three years. Ellen was a year old when they broke up in 1928. For a long time he and Cissy remained firm friends, but when they broke up her vilification was total. Still, on her death, Pearson wrote with grace and affection:

> A great lady died the other day—a lady who had caused me much happiness, and much pain. She was my ex-mother-in-law, Eleanor Patterson, who used to write about me in such scathing terms that even the very frank *Time* magazine had to interpret them with dots and dashes. And, though I never answered her, I want to write about her now because she represented a great newspaper cycle which may be coming to an end.
>
> Cissy Patterson's one ambition was to be as great a newspaperman as her brother Joe, and though she may not have realized

it, she was. She and Joe had grown up together, and she worshiped him. That was how Cissy got her nickname; for Joe, as a little boy, could not pronounce "Eleanor."

Both inherited part of the Chicago *Tribune*—wealthiest newspaper property in the world. But neither was satisfied merely to be a cog in the *Tribune* machine, and their genius built up two great newspapers in other cities, the New York *Daily News* and the Washington *Times-Herald.*

Cissy Patterson always reminded me of the house on Dupont Circle in which she lived. Her mother, bored with Chicago, had moved there. The house was designed by Stanford White. Cissy's home was the scene of luxurious parties, hatched conspiracies to kill the League of Nations, official residence of frugal Calvin Coolidge, who moved in with 30 pairs of shoes, half a dozen pairs of hip boots, an array of flannel nightgowns and 100 woolen socks. It still stands, a monument to the past.

Her method of running a newspaper was brilliant, sometimes vitriolic, always personal. It was her paper, and she ran it as such. There was not a night she did not pass on its banner headlines and Page 1 makeup. Even when in Florida, she checked by phone.

Sometimes Page 1 featured headlines about "The Headache Boy"—Cissy's description of her ex-son-in-law. Not only did she play up every speech attacking me on the Senate floor, but she kept a file and I know helped Senators write those speeches.

Today, Senator Brewster of Maine has his offices stacked high with 75,000 reprints of a speech largely taken from Cissy's diatribes against me, which he is mailing to constituents at the taxpayers' expense.

People used to ask me why I didn't answer Cissy or sue her for libel. Well, she and I had been through a lot together and I concluded the public is the best judge of such things and will eventually decide that.

But I shall miss the personal journalism of my ex-mother-in-law, though I do not agree with it. I shall even miss her excoriating me. . . . And so the house on Dupont Circle now goes to the Red Cross and a great lady, representing a great age of journalism, will be troubled by such headaches as me no more.

Cissy's will, filed the day after her Chicago funeral, made instant millionaires of seven "loyal employees," to whom she bequeathed the *Times-Herald* and all that went with it. They were William C. Shelton, general manager; Frank C. Waldrop, editor-in-chief; Edmund P.

Jewell, advertising director; Mike Flynn, supervising managing editor; Happy Robinson, circulation; Irving Belt, mechanical superintendent, and Mason Peters, night managing editor. Federal taxes on their windfall were paid out of an estate which was valued tentatively at $16,-586,571, a conservative estimate.

Nothing approximating such a gesture had ever been made before in the newspaper business.

It was Cissy's hope, forlorn as it turned out, that the men to whom she willed her newspaper would cherish it until death did them part. But, ever the realist, she inserted a clause in her testament calculated to dampen defection. Heirs to the paper were expressly forbidden to sell "without the consent of all the beneficiaries."

They cashed in their chips at the first good invitation to become ex-newspapermen. Rejectıng an offer from the Hearst organization that would have continued to utilize all their skills, they sold out to Bertie McCormick for good safe *Tribune* stock and cash, indifferent to the memory of Cissy's repeated differences with him. McCormick made a botch of the paper in attempting to make it an eastern Chicago *Tribune*. He, in turn, despite last-minute efforts by favorite niece Bazie Tankersley to salvage the paper, abruptly sold it to Eugene Meyer of the Washington *Post,* the man and institution Cissy abhorred. The *Post* soon devoured all of its flavor.

Cissy would have come to hate her newspaper heirs. Indeed, she was in the process of changing her will, as if she sensed what they would do, when her light went out. Several weeks before her death, Cissy decided that the person best fitted to carry on with the *Times-Herald* was her niece, Alicia Patterson Guggenheim, Joe's daughter and the wife of Harry F. Guggenheim, multimillionaire head of the foundation bearing his father's name, patron of many of the pioneers of the aerospace age, Navy captain in World War II and co-founder, with Alicia, of the nation's most successful post-war daily, *Newsday,* of Nassau County, New York. All of Cissy's love of her brother had been transferred to Alicia upon Joe's death.

So minded, Cissy wrote out a new will that dumped the loyal editors and company officials and named Alicia her sole heir to that thriving property, which by that time was grossing well over a million dollars a year profit. She knew Joe would have approved, but Joe was gone. She turned to Cousin Bertie, mailed him the draft of the proposed new will, and in due time received a reply from him.

Cousin Bertie, difficult as ever, wrote her a note criticizing the *syntax* of the new will. Cissy was furious. She shot back a singeing reply (in the course of some other differences of opinion they were having over how the New York *Daily News* should be operated).

The two were in the midst of this exchange when death put an end to it. Cissy had never gotten around to having the new will legalized. The oversight cost Mrs. Guggenheim, who died in 1963, a ten-million-dollar property which today—had it maintained the kind of drive Cissy had gaited it to—would be worth several times that sum. Less enchanted newspapers in New Orleans and Omaha have sold for about forty million dollars in recent years.

Cissy's will left Felicia the estates in Sands Point, Long Island, and the shooting lodge in North Dakota, the bulk of her jewelry, paintings, and furniture, and $25,000 a year for life. The granddaughter was provided for before Cissy died. Josephine Patterson Reeve Albright, another niece, was given the ranch at Jackson Hole, Wyoming. A Maryland neighbor, Ann Bowie Smith, was willed the magnificent Dower House with all its lands and accoutrements, including a huge hothouse wherein Cissy had raised prize orchids. Evie Robert, who had given Cissy so many laughs in life, became owner of her fabled black pearls, a sable scarf, and a half-a-million-dollar slice of Connecticut Avenue. Rhoda Christmas, who wrote about horses and dogs for the *Times-Herald,* wound up with Cissy's horses and dogs and was admonished in the will not to sell any of them and to "put them to death painlessly" when she felt their times had come. Margaret Barney, the diminutive personal secretary who had been at Cissy's side for years, was awarded a diminutive $10,000.

On successive days in September of the same year, Felicia contested the will on the grounds that her mother was demented when she drew it, Betty Hynes died beside a row of emptied sleeping pill bottles, and Charles B. Porter, Cissy's former treasurer at the paper, dived to his death through a screened window of his room in a cheap Clarksburg, West Virginia, hotel. (Later, big and handsome Joe Brooks, a trustee of Cissy's estate and one-time husband of Alicia Patterson, committed suicide.)

Felicia's petition charged that her mother was "not of sound mind" when the will was drawn two years before her death, and that "undue influence, duress, and coercion" had been brought to bear, by persons unnamed, to cause Cissy to sign the document. She asked for a jury trial of the unnamed Svengalis. After some weeks of dreary charges and countercharges the heirs to the *Times-Herald* silenced her with a lump sum of $400,000.

Friends of Betty Hynes had found her ill and distressed after publication of the will showed that she—who had worked so hard for Cissy—had been forgotten. She believed, and had reason to believe, that Cissy planned to help her pay the mortgage on a home she had purchased in Georgetown, in which she died.

Porter's death was harder to fathom. It remains something of a mystery. Drew Pearson, among others, contested the suicide conclusion reached by the Clarksburg police.

"Apparently some people believed Porter knew too much," he wrote darkly. "The circumstances surrounding Porter's death are strange indeed, including the fact that he jumped or was pushed through a window screen. This is not an ordinary act of suicide."

Like so many others, Porter had been in and out of Cissy's favor since their association began. Precisely where he stood with her at the time of her death has never been clarified. On the day the will was printed in the *Times-Herald,* Porter dispatched a long letter to a young friend named Roland De Corneille, a divinity student. It read, in part:

> E.P. was out to destroy me. That is certain. Dr. [deleted] predicted that I would be called back to the *Times-Herald* for more slaughter. Always there were indications that it would be so.
>
> Her death stopped it. [The doctor] said: "You had better discuss with me here and now what you will do in such an eventuality." I told him I would never go back. He said, "Wise indeed, because the next time you would be destroyed."
>
> Today's *Times-Herald* prints the will *in extenso.* The name "C. B. Porter" is shown all along the line being eliminated. That would give E.P. strange delight. Perhaps there are others too who will enjoy it. A last attempt to carry over after death one's hates.
>
> I am relieved because E.P. would have hounded me through her life as long as I remained here in Washington. She was forever asking why I did not get out of the country. . . . Please keep this letter. I might want to end it some day in the future.

Actually, Porter saw Cissy just before her death, and it was agreed that he would return to the fold—but not in his former role as one of her trustees—after he took a short trip back to Scotland. He was a product of Edinburgh University, held a degree in criminology and in law. He joined the business office of the *Herald* in 1933, interested Cissy, and rapidly rose to the posts of treasurer, trustee, and loosely defined overseer of her personal fortune. He was a bachelor and—though he worked for a 110 per cent patriot—never yielded his British passport.

According to De Corneille, an Amherst Phi Beta Kappa whose college training had been underwritten by Porter, Porter came under heavy pressure from "a person highly connected with the *Times-Herald*" after Cissy's death when it became known he had in his possession many documents related to Cissy's fiscal affairs. He was also believed to be writing a book about her.

Porter's last movements and last testament appeared to contradict the image of a man at baleful odds with the Patterson Establishment.

According to Washington cabdriver Henry Shepherd, who drove Porter 140 miles from Washington to Keyser, West Virginia, a week before he died, the cab had been hired for the trip by Mrs. Sibilla Campbell, Cissy's housekeeper.

Porter's will, penned but not validated four days before his plunge, named Mrs. Campbell as his executrix. When informed of this, Mrs. Campbell at first expressed surprise. She told County Coroner Dr. Kenna Jackson that she and the dead man had never been close friends. When Dr. Jackson described over the phone the three packed bags found in Porter's room, Mrs. Campbell told him that the small black one belonged to her. She would send someone to Clarksburg to claim the broken corpse and the man's property, she promised. This was attended to the following day by Stanley Epstein and John T. Barger, *Times-Herald* men bearing a notarized note, on plain stationery, signed "Sibilla Campbell, executrix in the will of Charles Bell Porter." Still later, Mrs. Campbell's lawyer, Charles F. R. Ogilby of Washington, was court-appointed to administer Porter's estate, the will having been ruled invalid for lack of witness.

Wholly forgotten because of these dire aftermaths were Cissy's large bequests to "needy children, especially homeless and orphaned children, in order that they may have some measure of advantages enjoyed by children more fortunately situated."

Somewhat to the chagrin of *Times-Herald* newsmen and women and faithful executives who were given the back of Cissy's perfumed hand, in the will, the favored heirs fared well despite the burden of millionaire status. There were lurid reports at one point that Mason Peters, youngest and gayest of the lot, had been lost at sea while sailing the yacht he had acquired with his bonanza. Untrue. Mason came up dry and solvent. Then it was whispered, with many a "Didn't I tell you?" nod, that the bookies had picked Happy Robinson clean. Untrue. They dented him, but not deep enough to draw blood. Mike Flynn, everybody's favorite millionaire, lived out his remaining years in happy retirement, moving between Washington and Florida whenever the sun did.

All but inevitably, Frank Waldrop and Bill Shelton used their windfalls to build more substantial fortunes.

It was only natural that all who passed through Cissy's hands wondered whether at any time she ever toyed with the thought of including them in her unprecedented will. Terrible legends took shape after her death, as to why this or that one was ignored. The worst of these folk stories concerned Charles Duffy, Cissy's colorful and competent city editor during the paper's best days. Duffy was commissioned in the Navy at the time of Pearl Harbor and Cissy gave him a loving farewell. He emerged a full commander, was given a hero's reception when he returned to the city room, took an independent Irishman's discerning look at the obsequiousness of his troops whenever Cissy hove into view, said to hell with that, and went back into the Navy. He became a four-striper.

Then (the legend went) came the day he and his loving Irish wife were instructed by Cissy's executors to appear for the reading of the will. "You're mentioned in it," he is said to have been told. Then the reading: Cissy had left the paper to *eight* loyal employees, including Charles Duffy! The Duffys sat there immersed in tears of gratitude, their years of labor finally miraculously rewarded.

But the lawyer was still reading. And in time he is said to have come to a codicil which read, in effect, that this was the way Cissy wanted all things done with one exception: "Wherever the name Charles Duffy appears it shall be stricken."

There were less substantial legends. Cissy at one time had been attracted to Eugene Warner, the handsomest of her reportorial staff. One day she invited my wife and me to bring him along on a date we had with her at her Sands Point place. When we arrived, Cissy was seated next to her pool, brushing her magnificent hair. Her poodles were galloping about.

She waved us a pleasant welcome as we approached and called out to my wife, "Guess what the Old Bitch did today?"

Before my wife could inquire about Cissy's favorite poodle, Gene spoke up.

"That's easy, I see you've been swimming," he volunteered.

Turned out to be a somewhat chilly day. But if Warner ever wondered why he did not make the will, despite his understandable mixup on which bitch was which, it did not crush him. He later became vice president of McGraw-Hill.

Other and closer associates of Cissy who were excluded—men who meant as much to her success as DeWitt, Helgeson, sports columnist Vincent X. Flaherty, editorial assistant Dick Hollander, etc.—had one serious flaw in Cissy's curious mind: They left her for better jobs.

I speak with a measure of authority.

One day early in December, 1936, I received a wire from W. R. Hearst, Sr., asking me to come to New York the following day and meet with him at his suite in the Ritz-Tower. ". . . with a view to working with the New York *American*." The reaction around the *Herald* was a warmhearted one. "A wire like that is like money in the bank," Mike Flynn said when he read it. "Ask him for at least three-fifty a week, to start. Salary doesn't mean anything to Hearst, if he wants you." I was making $140 at the *Herald*.

Cissy seemed delighted. "Another one of my boys has made the big time," she said. I must come by Dupont Circle that evening when she called Hearst in New York.

I did. The champagne was nicely iced in a bucket near her favorite divan. We sipped as she put in the call to New York, and after a bit I could hear Mr. Hearst's surprisingly little voice spilling out of the receiver. Cissy said some very flattering things about me, urging "Pay him well, W.R., he's a poor boy," and concluded with an astonishing statement.

"One more thing about him, W.R.," Cissy said into the phone, "he's my illegitimate son by Calvin Coolidge."

I went to New York the next morning, met and was deeply impressed by Mr. Hearst (who flustered me by repeatedly calling me *Mr.* Considine), and was directed to go to the office of one of the empire's top nabobs, J. D. Gortatowsky, where the contract was awaiting signature.

It called for $140 a week.

I thanked Mr. Gortatowsky, asked him to thank Mr. Hearst for me, and told him I was returning home to my job in Washington. On the train en route I wrote a sports column from some notes I had taken during an interview with a stern-looking little Japanese diplomat a few days before. The gist of the column was that the Japanese game of judo is not so much a sport as it is a demonstration that a fast and determined man, striking without telegraphing his attack, can defeat a much bigger and less alert man.

I took a cab from the station to the *Herald* and tossed my column on the desk of Bernie Harter, the sports editor, and told him I had turned down the New York *American* offer. Bernie was getting red in the face by now, and making voice-clearing sounds.

"Bob, I can't print this," he said, nodding at the column. "Mrs. Patterson sent me a memo today saying that you are off the payroll and nothing more of yours can ever be printed in the *Herald*."

I was out of work. All efforts made to reach her, even by phone, were fruitless. But finally Miss Barney, the secretary, gave me the Word.

"She's mad at you because you *wanted* to leave the Herald," she said.

And that's how I happened to go to work in New York. For $140 a week.

I never expected or especially wanted to see Cissy again. But some months later she called me from Washington as if she were still my illegitimate mother.

"Did you see what that [censored] brother of mine, Joe, wrote in his editorial in the *News* today?" she asked indignantly. I had. It was a piece which called the elder Mr. Hearst a faker.

"Well!" Cissy said, in her best "they can't do that to me" manner. "That [deleted] Joe Patterson forgets that I've got a newspaper, too, and that I'm not going to stand by and see anybody—including my brother—say anything bad about that dear W.R. I'm going to devote an entire page to him. I've written the eight-column streamer already: 'A Tribute to a Great American—W. R. Hearst.' I've sent Jackie Martin out to San Simeon for a new picture. It's going to be wonderful. I'll show that [unprintable] brother of mine!"

I asked her what this had to do with me.

"Silly, I want you to write all the nice words on the page," Cissy said, as if I should have known all along.

I worked for a month on the assignment, in addition to my regular work in New York as a sports columnist and feature writer. The research involved a lot of reading and talks with a number of Mr. Hearst's old associates, including the legendary S. S. Carvalho, about the first associate he had when he stormed New York late in the nineteenth century. My article ran twenty typewritten pages, and it was with a feeling of mingled relief and pride that I sent it off to Cissy in Washington, airmail, special delivery, registered.

Three silent weeks passed. Then I called her. Had she received it? Yes. Well, what did she think? There was a pained pause.

"Bob, I'm so sorry," Cissy said. "I lost it before I could read it. Would you possibly have made a carbon copy of it?"

I had, and rushed it to Washington.

Three even more silent weeks went by. Again I called. Had she received it? Yes! Had she read it? Yes!

"Not only read it, Bob," she said, making my head swim, "but it's simply great! I've never read anything about W.R. quite like it. You looked into that great man's soul."

There was time for a sigh of happiness before I asked her when she was going to run the big tribute.

It seemed a lifetime before she answered.

"Bob," she said, "I'm not going to run it."

I couldn't believe her. But why? *Why?*

Cissy cleared her throat.

"I made up with Joe," she said.

She was saying something else and I was not listening attentively.

"What was that?" I asked, a trifle numbly.

"I was saying that I know how hard you worked on this and that I want to pay you for all your pains," she said. "How much do you want?"

I answered somewhat haughtily that I did not want anything. I would charge it off to experience.

"Well, I know how we can do it," Cissy said. "Let's think of it as you'd think of a magazine piece. What did you make from your last article in *Cosmopolitan?*"

I said, "Mrs. Patterson, I made seven hundred and fifty for my last article in *Cosmopolitan,* but that has nothing to do with a piece about Hearst that you don't need. Please skip it. Forget it. Good-bye."

Several days later I received a letter from her. Enclosed was a check for $500. There was a note attached. It read:

"Dear Bob:
I *called* Cosmo.
Affectionately,
Cissy."

3. *New York*

I HAD LONGED for New York for years, had dreamed of riding into it triumphantly, wanted, heralded, able to dictate the terms of its surrender. But Cissy's petulant rug-pulling deprived me of leverage, upended me. Reversing a classic humiliation, I was ridden *into* town on a rail.

New York, the newcomer soon learns, never adjusts itself to him; he adjusts himself to it.

Some are driven mad by its breathtaking bigness. On my first assignment to cover a fight at Madison Square Garden, I found myself seated in the press section next to a shabby-looking little guy. I introduced myself.

"Yeah, I heard about you," he said. "New, huh? Well, boy, you've got a lot to learn about New York. But it's a great feeling when you finally learn the ropes. I get over here from Staten Island, that's where my paper is, at least four or five times a year. Coming across, I always stand up in the front of the ferry. I look at the skyline, all lighted up. Then I shake my fist at it and I say to myself, 'I licked that!' "

I never saw him again, and that was 1937.

The adjustment process can take ludicrous turns. It is quite hard to learn to walk faster than the gait you have chosen as the speed at which you prefer to march through life. Until I picked up the pace, I had the uneasy feeling that New Yorkers walking behind me, and always gaining, were of a mind to walk right up my back, jump off my shoulders, and continue on their way without breaking stride. I was a slowly tumbling stone gathering moss in a churning millrace.

The speedy New Yorker is not necessarily going any place. He has simply been wound up to maintain a velocity in consonance with that of his fellow New Yorkers and maintains it to the death.

There were adjustments to be made in the matter of dress. I didn't know until I met Mark Hanna, the pin-neat agent for Quentin Reynolds and other well-known figures like Leo Durocher, that it was gauche to wear a blue shirt after sundown. Some years later, after Mark's funeral services at Campbell's, several of the members of the funeral party walked briskly to the nearest bar. It is in the Stanhope Hotel on Fifth Avenue, and the only time it loses its built-in decorum, as sterile as that of the neighboring funeral parlor, is when it is visited by mourners.

"How about that creep who did the eulogy, calling Hanna 'Mr. New York'?" Toots Shor grumbled, stirring his brandy and soda with a stout forefinger.

"Yeah," said Jack O'Connell, then editor of *Cosmopolitan,* "and all the business about the great things he did for his clients." He looked at me. "What did he ever do for you?" Jack asked.

What I said made them laugh, but I meant it from the heart.

"Mark taught me not to wear white shoes in New York," I said.

The atmosphere of working in New York was so different. On the *Herald* one thought of himself as an inhabitant of an atoll at the extreme end of the Hearst archipelago. We were under a benevolent trusteeship, seldom involved with central authority. The *American* was at the heart of the Establishment.

That courtly disciplinarian, Ed Frayne, placed strange store on his staff's reporting to work each day at 3 P.M., if the staff member was not on specific assignment in or out of the city. He frowned through his heavy lenses if the lesser members of his stable called him and said, for example, "I'm uptown, Ed. Is it okay if I drop by Jimmy Johnston's office at the Garden and see what I can pick up?"

No, I soon learned, that was not the way to do it. One came down to the *American* by three o'clock. It was a chore at any time of day or night, if the price of a cab ride was prohibitive. Arthur Brisbane had urged the selection of a site on South Street, downwind from the Fulton Fish Market, and we accepted as Gospel the malicious whisper that he also had an interest in the construction firm that won the bid from the incredibly patient Mr. Hearst. We believed, too, the story that Mr. Hearst had paid only one visit to his multimillion dollar eyesore. That solitary visit ended, it was said, several feet inside the cramped little lobby. At that point, the legend went, Mr. Hearst made an abrupt 180 degree turn, walked to his limousine, and was never seen again around the premises.

Whatever, Ed Frayne must have liked it, because he was so determined that we share it with him by no later than 3 P.M. each day. There would be a short round of pleasantries and story suggestions. Then, and only then, would Ed approve any "Is it okay if I drop by Jimmy Johnston's . . . ?" proposals. And you'd head uptown again via the rattly *American* shuttle bus to City Hall, a walk over to Chambers Street for the Eighth Avenue subway, express to Forty-second, and local to Fiftieth. Sometimes Jimmy would have had his traditional afternoon tea and departed. But, at least, the three o'clock crisis had been faced and resolved.

My first good assignment was the fight between Joe Louis and Bob Pastor at Madison Square Garden. Pastor put up a surprising resistance to the great young Negro who was soon—the following June—to win the heavyweight title from Jim Braddock (under circumstances that imperiled my job, by the way).

Pastor set out to last the full ten rounds of the Garden fight and succeeded. He was in reverse gear through much of the fight, but switched and charged now and then and bloodied Louis' nose. The packed house bellowed, scenting an extraordinary upset. Louis was given the decision after ten rounds, which was proper, but there was no question that Pastor had infuriated and embarrassed him. Only a strong finish had sufficed.

Typewriters on all sides of me began to be belabored by more experienced sportswriters the moment the decision was announced by Harry Balogh. But my fingers became becalmed after typing my byline. Here was my big chance, and I had come up empty. I stared at the barren page through distressed exhalations of cigarette smoke. The sound of the surehanded industry around me grew alarming. My Western Union operator sat there vamping with his key and trying not to look at me.

Miserably, I plagiarized myself. I fell back on a lead I had written a year or two before to describe an obscure fight in a dismal former brewery named Portner's Arena, in Alexandria, Virginia. In its original form, the tired little lead read: "Brushing away the crimson cloud that steamed from his battered nose, Joe Blow made Herman Bananas pay dearly for his indiscretions last night at Portner's Arena."

The story did not attract so much as a postcard, nor any verbal comment.

But that was not the case with the lead I wrote that night at the Garden: "Brushing away the crimson cloud that steamed from his battered nose, Joe Louis made Bob Pastor pay dearly for his indiscretions last night at Madison Square Garden."

Frayne was delighted. Damon Runyon, who had moved over to writing a general column, but kept his hand in the sports department, so long his preserve, wrote a report or letter to the great old Hearst editor, Edmond D. "Cobbie" Coblentz, Hearst's liaison with his publishers and other editors, about the new crop of Hearst sportswriters. Excerpt: "One of them, a chap we've already got—Considine. I think he will be a corker when he gets his sights adjusted. He is terrifically ambitious and a hard worker."

I got some mail, too, about the Louis-Pastor story. But as heady as it was, for a newcomer, it was clear that genius had not spurred this response. What had spurred it was New York . . . Madison Square Garden . . . instantly recognizable gladiators.

The experience came back to me when, shortly after that, Frayne handed me the annual Westminster Kennel Club dog show at the Garden. In Washington I had covered a much lesser mutt meet and had caused something of a ripple, at least in church circles, by getting away with a story that began: "Ch. Beauregard van Updyke of Terwilliger, a son of a bitch named Ch. Imogene Brockstine Agincourt, took Best-of-Breed in the Yorkshire class last night at the Auditorium."

With names and locale stepped up to the big leagues, my name would soon be on every New Yorker's lips. I thanked Ed for the assignment and prepared to depart from South Street to the yip-laced Garden.

"One last thing," Ed said, stopping me at the door. "Don't knock Kerry Blues."

To my astonishment, he was serious.

"I don't think I ever knocked a Kerry Blue in my life," I swore.

"Well, don't start tonight," Ed said.

It was not too much to ask.

"Why?"

Ed gazed at me solemnly.

"Mrs. Hearst, senior, has a Kerry Blue," he said.

Doomed, so far as a replay on the son-of-a-bitch theme was concerned, I went to work.

It was a vaguely troubled time, those cold winter months in early 1937. Millie and I missed Washington. We had acquaintances now, and though they were better known than our friends in Washington and nice to us when we occasionally met, we missed the older and truer ties. There wasn't enough money to take care of living costs in New York. We now had our infant son, Michael Riley (named, respectively, for Monsignor—later Bishop—Michael Ready and the baby's godfather, George Riley). We also had a wonderful nurse-cook named Veronica, and an apartment off Central Park West, after a cramped sojourn at the Hotel New Yorker.

It was that same winter that I managed to offend the undisputed star of our organization, Runyon. That was not particularly difficult. The creator of all those tough-tender Broadway characters was as thin-skinned as an aging Met soprano. He had everything his less distinguished colleagues might have wished for: prestige in the newspaper business, in magazines, and in Hollywood. He dressed expensively and well. (Hype Igoe, the New York *Journal*'s pixie boxing writer, broke in Runyon's custom-made shoes for him.) He was fussed over by owners and headwaiters at Lindy's, to which he gave great if passing fame as the Mindy's of his Broadway stories, the Stork Club, and wherever else he chose to patronize. He knew and was respected by a huge cross section of the citizenry, ranging from President Roosevelt to Al Capone, with whom he had a closer affinity. He was married to a still-beautiful ex-showgirl, his second wife, maintained a fine apartment at the Parc Vendome in Manhattan, and owned a white plaster jewel box of a home on one of the better islands in Biscayne Bay.

My troubles with him emerged, preposterously enough, from a small get-together Millie and I had at our apartment for a few equally impoverished yet hopeful friends in sportswriting, among them our friends from Washington, Dick and Mary McCann. Mary was Damon's daughter by his first wife. My wife and I had reason to believe that he treated his daughter, son-in-law, and Damon, Jr., with something considerably less than paternal affection. He just didn't give a damn, but we stood steadfastly in awe of the summits he had scaled by his drive and talent.

"I'd sure like to be able to cover a range like that," I said in the course of many tributes to him uttered during our party. There were fervent amens from all sides. A few weeks later, Mary, who hadn't been feeling too well, was at our apartment again.

"I told Daddy about what you said about him," Mary said.

"Oh? Was he pleased?"

"No, he didn't like it one little bit," Mary said.

I was suddenly alarmed.

"What did you tell him?" I asked.

"What you said," Mary said. "That you're out after his job."

There was nothing to say to her or to her father. So we had another Manhattan. We drank them, even after dinner, in those days.

Next, there was a piece I felt compelled to write for the "Home Magazine," a supplement in each Saturday edition of the New York *Journal* and the Chicago *Herald-American*. There was civil war in the boxing business at the time. The Garden, with Johnston as its current matchmaker, had ruled the game at its highest level since Tex Rickard's day as promoter of Jack Dempsey's early fights and his two memorable ten-rounders against Gene Tunney. After Tunney's retirement, the game began to disintegrate under the combined assaults of the Depression and less entrancing champions and contenders. Max Schmeling won the title in the finals of a loose elimination tournament when Jack Sharkey may or may not have fouled him in the fourth round of their fight. Brisbane's shouts of "Foul!" from ringside may have had as much to do with the referee's and the commission doctor's decision as Max's dented aluminum "cup" that protected his privates from blows below the belt line. Sharkey later won from Schmeling in fifteen rounds and lost to Primo Carnera under suspicious circumstances. Carnera was toppled by Max Baer in a kind of rehash of a movie they both played in called *The Prize Fighter and the Lady,* and Baer then lost to a solid underdog, Jim Braddock.

In the latter portion of that sequence, Joe Louis appeared, a product of a Golden Gloves tournament in Detroit. For reasons best known to the two suave Negroes who controlled him—John Roxborough of Detroit and Julian Black of Chicago—Louis cast his lot with the Twentieth Century Sporting Club. The ostensible head of the club was Mike Jacobs, who had been Rickard's trusted ticket scalper. His silent partners, it was eventually revealed in an explosive revelation by Harry Grayson, of the Scripps-Howard chain, were Runyon, Frayne, and the rollicking, hard-living Bill Farnsworth of the New

York *Journal*. Each owned 25 per cent of Twentieth Century's stock. Louis was the company's goldmine, but the Garden controlled the heavyweight title's succession. The title belonged to Braddock, a poor drawing card. His obvious challenger was former champion Schmeling, who had catapulted back into prominence (to the joy of the Nazi Party) by giving Louis the worst beating of his life and knocking him out in the twelfth round of their 1936 fight.

Now, a year later, the Garden matched Braddock and Schmeling. From the start it was a forlorn gesture. I wrote a piece for the "Home Magazine" predicting that Schmeling would somehow be gypped out of his chance to become the first man ever to regain the heavyweight title. It turned out that way. Braddock obtained a Philadelphia court decision—the ruling was handed down by a Judge Fake—to fight Louis instead of Schmeling. Either would beat Jim for the title, but Louis was the more desirable conqueror. In the first place, "it would keep the title in America" instead of seeing it packed off to Hitler's Germany. In the second place, Louis was willing to give Braddock 10 percent of his ring earnings for the next ten years in payment for being granted the opportunity to flatten Jim.

The New York State Athletic Commission would not permit the Braddock-Louis fight to be held in the state, but Chicago gladly accepted it. The Garden went through with the pathetic pretense of a Braddock-Schmeling fight, even to the point of printing tickets for it. It was somehow fitting that the printer also gaffed. He spelled it "Schmelling."

As expected, Louis beat Braddock. There were moments of concern, however. Jim courageously decked the younger, stronger man for a two or three count in the first round. For the next six rounds Louis chopped him like a lumberjack would strip a great old oak of its limbs, one by one. In the eighth Joe hit him with a right hand that would have broken a moose's jaw. Jim crashed with a thud that shook the ring. It was a great night for all concerned: the new champion, his managers who cut him 50 percent, Mike Jacobs and his partners, and the loser—shorn of his title but now heir to 10 percent of Louis' purses for what looked like ten years of boom.

Runyon was angered and Frayne upset by the "Home Magazine" piece. They considered it "unloyal," and both stopped speaking to me. Farnsworth didn't give a damn. He liked to shock young sportswriters (and distress his associates) by boasting about a Cadillac he had bought in the immediate wake of a fight he had helped to promote for the benefit of Mrs. Hearst's Free Milk for Babies charity. Jacobs, too, remained friendly to me. He was as proud of the publicity my piece had given his iniquity as he was when he told me later, in the course of an interview for a magazine piece, that he had soaked Boo Boo Hoff, the Philadelphia mobster, $25,000 for twenty-five last-minute ringside seats for the first Dempsey-Tunney fight. (Boo Boo paid in thousand-dollar bills and was walking away with the tickets when Mike said to him, "Just a minute. The twenty-five grand was for getting the tickets for you. They're fifty bucks apiece." Boo Boo paid.)

Between the time the offending "Home Magazine" article appeared and the Braddock-Louis fight there were several reports that my days on the *American* were numbered; that Damon was going to have me fired. The charges were always vague, but depressing. As it turned out, it was the *American*'s days which were numbered. It succumbed to assorted ailments, man-made and banker-dictated, in June, 1937, a day or two after the Chicago title fight. As far as its sports section was concerned, the *American* went down with its flags flapping valiantly. It covered the Louis-Braddock fight with its varsity team: Runyon, Frayne, Sid Mercer, Jimmy Cannon, Bugs Baer, Bill Slocum, Sr., and me. In the tense minutes after the knockout, with all our typewriters going full tilt, Mercer's Western Union wire to New York broke down. Precious minutes passed while the operator worked fruitlessly to bring it back to life.

"Dammit, get that wire fixed or I'll miss an edition," Mercer snapped, writing against our deadline.

Cannon had a wry extension of that remark. Jimmy said, "Get that wire fixed or he'll miss a newspaper."

The afternoon *Journal,* which immediately became the *Journal-American,* got custody of most of the *American*'s best. I was shifted over to Hearst's morning *Mirror,* a hell-raising slapdash tabloid packed to its perpetually leaking seams with some of the worst and best journalism in New York. Its payroll was studded with the likes of Walter Winchell, Mark Hellinger, Jack Lait, Lee Mortimer, John McNulty, Jim Bishop, Jim Whittaker, Tex McCrary, who had been Brisbane's son-in-law, and good editors: Glenn Neville, George McDonald, Charlie Barth, Selig Adler, Mort Ehrman, Eddie Markell, and Hinson Styles.

The *Mirror*'s sports department was one of the most-admired and best-read (except by the proofreaders) of any in the land. It had the city's best horse handicapper, Fred Keats, an astral seer who had not set foot in the building for years, Murray Lewin, who had done some fighting and knew everybody in that bitter-sweet business, and talented baseball writers Ben Epstein (Yankees), Ken Smith (Giants), and Gus Steiger (Dodgers). Our rod and gun man, Jim Hurley, was considered the best of the lot. There was a covey of bright young men struggling up from copyboy status, Harold Weissman, John Hennigan, Leonard Lewin, Frank Blauschild, and Arthur Richman, a remarkable lad who chose to spend his vacations traveling with the acknowledged worst team in the majors, if not the world, the St. Louis Browns.

Holding the immediate reins on the staff were veteran toy department men, Bill Hennigan, Frank Kearns and Bill Carver, and over them sat the *Mirror*'s crowning anachronism, Clarence Cassin, head of the desk. He was a saintly soul put down by Providence into the profane bustle of tabloid journalism. No one in our department said even "Damn" more than once in his presence, for it upset him so much. It is questionable whether he ever even looked at some of the leg art which Manny Elkins and other fanciers among the picture editors assembled for each edition. Clarence set an example of diligence for all of us which few could or would emulate. Not for him the soothing dram after a long night's work; not for him the word that purged.

Not long after Braddock retired, after winning a surprising ten-rounder against Tommy Farr at the Garden, there was a report that he would try a comeback and even aim at a second fight against silent-partner Joe Louis. I asked Jim if it were true.

"Hell's bells, I'm not going to let them make a football outta my head," Jim said.

I used that quote as the lead on my story, turned it in to Clarence, and went my way. Clarence made only one change. He made it read: " 'Heck's bells, I'm not going to let them make a football outta my head,' Jim Braddock said yesterday."

Thus did piety persevere in one small corner of a babbling blat whose front page that very day may have proclaimed: "SEX FIEND SLAYS TOT."

Our proofreaders were sometimes less than abstemious. When Don McNeill, a handsome young man with flaxen hair, won the National

Indoor tennis championship, my lead sent from the Armory began: "Tow-headed Don McNeill blazed his way to victory yesterday . . ."

It ran through all editions as: "Two-headed Don McNeill . . ."

The most astonishing coincidence of my life in newspaper work happened while on the *Mirror*. I wrote a lead about the victory the greatest U.S. polo team (led by Tommy Hitchcock and all ten-goalers) scored over a crack British team at Westbury, Long Island. It went: "Yankee Doodle went to town here today, a-ridin' on a polo pony."

At the other end of the press box, perhaps sixty yards away, the New York *Herald Tribune*'s Harry Cross simultaneously was writing: "Yankee Doodle went to town here today, a-ridin' on a polo pony."

It may have been the first reporting by ESP. Walter Winchell, no mean phrase maker himself, liked the lead. A few days later in his column in the *Mirror,* under a paragraph he called "Literary Lace," he warmly congratulated Harry Cross of the rival *Tribune* on his unique lead. It was never compulsory for *Mirror* writers to read other *Mirror* writers.

An air of the risqué and the rogue hung over the City Room. Jack Lait had engaged in countless larks and rumbles on Hearst's Chicago papers and never ran out of stories late at night, as long as the Cutty Sark, which he took neat, held out. Then there was Lee Mortimer, with whom Jack collaborated in several "Confidential"-type books that sold furiously and attracted some equally furious libel suits and threats of mayhem on sight. Indeed, Frank Sinatra did slug Mortimer. The *Mirror* wreaked a stern revenge. Frank's name was dropped from the agate-type "Birthday Greetings" which always concluded the daily prose and poetry turned out by the paper's poet laureate and radio columnist, Nick Kenny.

Both Hinson Styles and a good, hard-working, hard-drinking general assignments man named Walter Marshall were members of the Henry the Eighth club, a loosely knit, if not loosely living organization made up of men-about-town who had been married at least five times.

The *Mirror*'s most loyal readers were followers of Keats's race tips, and those dispensed by Ken Kling in his "Joe and Asbestos" strip. Through some unspelled-out alliance, beyond the control of the sports department, we also were the official record for the day's "number," at a time when countless millions of dollars were being wagered in dribs and drabs in the city's policy racket. We even carried tips on numbers concealed, more or less, in a delightful little single-column cartoon drawn by dapper Fred Weatherly, who kept his mustache waxed as if momentarily awaiting inspection by the colonel of the Coldstream Guards.

It is hard to believe, looking back, that the *Mirror* had a Society Editor. He was Howard Shelley. He came from quality folks and wrote under the name of Barclay Beekman. Almost every event he attended appeared to call for white tie and tails and decorations. The Horse Show at the Garden was hardly held to be constitutional unless Barclay was in his box, silk hat in place, Tiffany pencil and pad on his chubby little lap. He was a magnificent snob and possibly the most near-sighted of them all. At the opening of the Metropolitan's season he always took along a *Mirror* photographer, usually the handsome and well-groomed Tony Sarno, and was more selective about the pictures he ordered than, say, his contemporary from the *New York Times*. As this or that superbly gowned lady emerged from her limousine, followed by a chivalrous escort, Barclay would bustle forward, search their faces from a range of a foot or two, then wheel and tell Sarno whether or not to waste a flashbulb.

"They're nobody!" Barclay would shout more often than not, thus saving money for Mr. Hearst, who was somewhat strapped financially at that stage of the Depression and that stage of his relationship with the Roosevelt Administration.

(We could never understand FDR's antipathy toward WRH. After all, Mr. Hearst had been largely instrumental in winning the 1932 nomination for him, by swinging California, and just about wholly instrumental in having him opposed four years later by Alf M. Landon. Very late on Election Night, 1936, Bill Hearst, Jr., and his brother John came into Jack White's Club 18 on Fifty-second Street while the floor show was blasting away. White rapped his cane on the floor, stopped the music and dancing, and announced, "Quiet, please! Here comes Maine and Vermont.")

For all his boorishness, Barclay Beekman was a sensitive soul. Late one night as I toiled, soiled, over some forgotten story, he loomed over my desk like the fairy godfather he was—resplendent in his working clothes. He didn't know my name, or maybe he thought I was the sterling young righthander for the Cleveland Indians.

"Feller," he said, crisply, and a bit lispingly, "did you ever know the Dowager Mrs. Cornelius Vanderbilt?"

Silently cursing my forebears for never having stolen a railroad, I muttered an apologetic No.

"Of course, you wouldn't," Barclay said, starting back to his desk. I tried to make amends.

"But I've met the Dowager Mrs. Chick Wergeles," I said to him, referring, of course, to the dear wife of one of the best fight-publicity men on Jacobs Beach.

Barclay Beekman, who looked a great deal like Queen Victoria, was not amused. He was hurt. Nor did he join in the hearty laughter when a 10 by 12 glossy print of him in his best white tie and tails was tacked on the City Room's bulletin board. Elkins' retouch artist had inked an ambassadorial ribbon across Barclay's starched chest. It read: "EAT AT JAKE'S."

He wouldn't return to work until he received an apology.

Our drama critic, Robert Coleman, came from a fine old Southern family, wrote pithy and nondrawling reviews, had the longest haircut in the world of the theater, and between his dandruff and the ashes that cascaded from the cigarette he always kept in his mouth, he sometimes resembled a snow-topped Alp on tour.

For all we knew, Coleman may have inspired one of Nick Kenny's most enduring bursts of blank verse:

> Snow fell from Heaven
> Like dandruff from God's shoulders.

George Clark, our Night Club Editor, was a sophisticated cynic who went in for king-sized cigarettes, an oddity at that time, and for light-hearted contempt. One day a Broadway impresario offered him a job as a press agent, at more money than the *Mirror* was paying him. George turned it down. It would mean leaving the *Mirror*.

"I've lived in a ho'house half my life, why should I now become a streetwalker?" George asked.

Every newspaper draws odd visitors, but the *Mirror* magnetized more than its just quota. One evening a disheveled man with a glazed look walked into the City Room. That in itself was not extraordinary. He might have been a rewrite man. But this one was different. He had a big ugly revolver in his paw and his finger was on the trigger. The only man in the room whose eyes were not riveted on the nut was

Charlie Barth. Charlie's head was bent over his makeup pad. He spent a lot of time each day deciding where each gem would be placed in the paper.

The man with the gun stood over Charlie, and in back of him. The gun seemed aimed directly at the back of Charlie's skull, like the crowning phase of a coup de grace.

"Which one is Jim Hurley?" the man with the gun asked.

Charlie never looked up. He waved idly in the direction of the sports department at the other end of the large room.

The man started across the room. All hands hit the deck and tried to squeeze under desks and tables.

Finally, in the hush of the ordinarily noisy room he bent down and poked his gun under a desk. It was Jim's desk and Jim was under it.

"Jim Hurley?"

"Don't shoot me," Jim said. "I have quite a family."

"Shoot *you,* Jim?" the man said, hurt. "You're my favorite writer. I just shot my wife and I come right here to give you the story."

Larry MacPhail, the mercurial man who was running the Brooklyn Dodgers at that stage in his life, dropped by the *Mirror* one night to see me. He wanted to shoot me for a story I had written about a bum deal he gave his first baseman, Dolph Camilli. I wasn't there.

"Sorry, he isn't in," Larry was told, very politely.

"Oh," he said, and went back to Brooklyn, consoled in all probability by the philosophy on which baseball is built: "Well, you can't win 'em all."

Along with countless thousands of others, I read the *Mirror* because of one man, Dan Parker.

He was the last and in my estimation the greatest of a breed of sports columnists who was prepared to back up anything he wrote, not with a lawyer but with his bulk, heart, and, on occasion, fists. He was in the tradition of Bat Masterson, Sheriff Bill McGeehan, Boze Bulger, Dave Egan (who editorially asked for contributions to a fund for a Boston cabdriver who ran over Casey Stengel), and Tommy Laird (who didn't like something a San Francisco Seals player shouted at him, tore out of the press box, picked up a bat, and chased the terrified player the length of the field and out the center field gate).

Incorruptible Dan Parker wore no man's collar. Let the business office clutter his sports pages with the ads of the horse-touting services and Dan would continue blasting them in his column. Let Jimmy

Johnston threaten him with multimillion dollar suits or physical harm (which was ludicrous in view of Dan's 6-feet-5 altitude and 230-pound tonnage) and Dan would continue to refer to the bantam-sized promoter as the Boy Bandit.

Everybody wrote that Primo Carnera was controlled by The Mob, but Dan named the mobsters. One of them who came under Dan's withering scorn sent a platoon of goons to Times Square one night to buy up and tear up all copies of the *Mirror* delivered to the area's newsstands. Dan called Carnera a tottering tower of Gorgonzola whose opponents were bribed or terrorized into taking dives. Then one tense night the two men met on stage at a New York Boxing Writers banquet. Dan was the only sportswriter in the land big enough to look Primo straight in the eye. For a moment the two stood facing one another in the suddenly quiet place. Primo then assumed a fighting stance. Dan promptly extended his hands, like a kid about to plunge into a swimming pool, and dived onto the stage, which all but brought down the house, literally. It was the perfect pantomime of any of Primo's fixed fights.

Dan could use his hands in earnest, too. Somewhere in the course of his hammer-and-tongs writings he sideswiped the New York *Enquirer's* Marcus Griffin, a biographer of Jimmy Johnston. After a period of wrangle in print and over the phone, Dan sent him a note saying that the next time their paths crossed, he, Dan, would take great pleasure in flattening him. Their paths crossed in the crowded press rows at Mike Jacobs' Tournament of Champions, a unique boxing show featuring four title fights. Dan and I were seated side by side. The action in the ring was fast and furious, the noise was great, but Dan heard his name being mentioned roughly.

He turned his head. Marcus Griffin was the one using his name. Dan stood up, knocked Marcus down with a single right-hand punch to the jaw, sat back down, and continued writing. He had hardly missed a sentence of the action in the ring. He continued working subsequently when the loser of the short-lived fight returned with a cop and demanded Dan's arrest on the spot. The cop was delighted to meet Dan in person. He was such a fan that for a moment it appeared that he might arrest Marcus for momentarily disturbing Dan's train of thought.

But virility was only one of Parker's gifts. He had the most delightful sense of humor of anybody in his field and possibly the truest ear for the language—the many languages of sports people, for that matter—since Lardner. Dan framed classic, imaginary dialogues between announcer Harry Balogh (who once introduced thirty-three-year-old Gus Lesnevich: "And now—a man who, like old wine, goes on forever. . . .") and fight publicist Mushky Jackson ("George Washington slept right here in Pompton Lakes. . . . You know Washington, dontcha? He freed the slaves.") He interviewed at hilarious length a hypothetical Greek dialectician whose hero was Jimmy (Dan spelled it Dzimmy) Londos.

Dan heard, and presented to the American language, fight manager Joe Jacobs' shuddering remark during a terribly cold World Series game in Detroit: "I shoulda stood in bed!" He heard the guy yell from the top gallery at the Garden at two fighters who had failed to throw a single punch halfway through the first round: "Hit him now, y'bum, y'got the wind witcha!" He duly noted for posterity Charley Dressen's elegy, "The Giants is dead."

Dan knocked out many a critic with a single written punch, too. A particularly obnoxious radio sportscaster named Bert somebody wired him, "Listen to my program tonight. I'm going to knock your brains out." Dan printed the telegram and commented, "Why should I double his Hooper rating?" He printed other abusive letters, if they were signed, and would add, "I returned the gentleman's letter with a suggestion as to where on his person he might best deposit it."

The *Mirror,* in which many a fish was wrapped and many a subway car littered, became a collector's item whenever Dan's muse moved him to verse. The presence of a Jewish bronco buster from the Bronx at the Garden's Rodeo caused Dan to pen a rhymed saga that began:

I'm an old cow hand
From the Concourse Grand.

It ended, many marvelous lines later, with:

Yipee, ei ei—oy oy!

*Mirror*s were hard to find every March 17 because, as any fool knew, that would be the day Dan's St. Patrick's Day Parade poem would be printed. The scholarship of his effort that day was worthy of Padraic Colum and was as saucy as G. B. Shaw. Dan knew the prides, prejudices, failings, and foibles of every county whose colors were marched past the Cardinal.

But he reserved his best for boxing. As if in gratitude for his genius, boxing gave Dan the one, the only, Tony Galento. Dan wrote volumes about that incredible fat, hairy gladiator-bartender from Orange, New Jersey. The one sample picked by W. C. Heinz in his masterful *Fireside Book of Boxing* concerned Tony's fight against a harmless setup named Charley Massera. Dan sang:

Oh, Tony Galento, he trains on pimento
And gargles the ale when it's cool.
My pronunciamento concerning Galento
Is: "Switch to that pasta fazoole!"
They say a left hook
To the chops closed the book
Of the prize fighter Charley Massera.
Though it may not have landed
It left Charley stranded.
(And how is your dear old Aunt Sarah?)

It was Dan's kind of fight, and Tony's, for that matter:

Outside the Orange Armony thousands lingered, hoping to hear the thud. Everyone knew Massera was going out like an empty beer barrel, the only element of doubt being "when?"

Tony's belly rolled like jelly
And Massera's fist
Bounced into it—almost through it—
Right up to the wrist.

As a boxer, Tony uses the Ely Culbertson, or approach system. He approaches an opponent wide open, as if inviting a liver massage. After getting what he wants, he switches to the Irish attack, better known as "The back of me fisht to you!" Next, he tries "The Shoemaker's Revenge," or "Giving It the Heel." Two rounds of this and Tony decided the customers had had enough. Did I say Tony? I meant Charley. One of Tony's left hooks landed somewhere—no one is quite sure—and Charley landed on his haunches. He's up. He's down. He's out. It all happened in 45 seconds. Yussel Jacobs, in Tony's corner, summed it up succinctly when he warbled: "He certainly stood down the second time when you left him have that left."

Some of the boys said Charley almost choked on his mouthpiece after he had been counted out. If he did, it was from laughing.

> Tony was back behind the bar in his white apron, with most of the grease wiped off him, in about ten minutes, and from then until dawn his cash register burned out six bearings handling the biggest night's trade in the history of the jernt.

I was immensely proud of being on the same sports section with Dan Parker. He was great to work for, kind, considerate, and helpful when his advice was sought. Then one day, about a year after I went to work for the *Mirror,* Dan stopped speaking to me. For a day or two I supposed his ulcer was acting up again and that he was sore at the world in general. When it became abundantly clear that he was angry with only one guy in that world, me, I went into his office.

"What's up?"

"I'd rather not talk about it," Dan said, concentrating on a column he was writing.

"I've got to know, Dan," I said.

He paused for a long time, then turned in his chair and looked at me.

"I don't like what you've been saying around town," he said.

I asked him what I had been saying around town.

"That you're going to get my job," Dan said evenly.

The emotion that immersed me was not anger. It was disappointment.

When I could speak, I said, "Do you believe that, Dan? If you do, I don't want to work for you. You know damned well that I couldn't carry your jock strap."

Dan sighed. "I don't know what to believe . . ." He turned back to his typewriter.

"I can't leave it hanging like that, Dan. I've got to know who gave you that story. I have a right to know."

Dan must have thought so, too.

"Damon Runyon," he said.

I just didn't know what to say to him, so I walked out and went back to work. The frost stayed on the pumpkin as the date of the second Louis-Schmeling fight approached. I wanted to be there at ringside when it happened, having covered most of Joe's fights either for the Washington *Herald* or the New York *American.* But such was the spell that Runyon could exert, even over an honest sports editor like Dan Parker, that it was questionable up to a late hour whether there would be any need for me at the fight. Dan, of course, would do the lead story. That was proper and the best thing that could happen for the paper. Murray Lewin would do the expert story, and the dressing rooms would be adequately covered.

Dan did me a favor, unexpectedly. I could cover the fight for the *Mirror* with a feature. I sat behind him at what turned out to be Louis' finest hour or, rather, his finest two minutes and four seconds. When it was finished, and the ecstasy of the stadium had swept over and inoculated the reporters at ringside, Dan turned to me and shook my hand warmly. It was like a reprieve from the Governor. I sat back down and wrote a feature. It went like this:

> Listen to this, buddy, for it comes from a guy whose palms are still wet, whose throat is still dry, and whose jaw is still agape from the utter shock of watching Joe Louis knock out Max Schmeling.
>
> It was, indeed, a shocking thing, that knockout—short, sharp, merciless, complete. Louis was like this:
>
> He was a big lean copper spring, tightened and retightened through weeks of training until he was one pregnant package of coiled venom.
>
> Schmeling hit that spring. He hit it with a whistling right-hand punch in the first minute of the fight—and the spring, tormented with tension, suddenly burst with one brazen spang of activity. Hard brown arms, propelling two unerring fists, blurred beneath the hot white candelabra of the ring lights. And Schmeling was in the path of them, a man caught and mangled in the whirring claws of a mad and feverish machine.
>
> The mob, biggest and most prosperous ever to see a fight in a ball yard, knew that here was the end before the thing had really started. It knew, so it stood up and howled one long shriek. People who had paid as much as $100 for their chairs didn't use them—except perhaps to stand on, the better to let the sight burn forever in their memories.
>
> There were four steps to Schmeling's knockout. A few seconds after he landed his only real punch of the fight, Louis caught him with a lethal little left hook that drove him into the ropes so hard that his right arm hooked over the top strand, like a drunk hanging on to a fence. Louis swarmed over him and hit Max with everything he had—until Referee Donovan pushed him away and counted one.

Schmeling staggered away from the ropes at that, dazed and sick. He looked drunkenly toward his corner, and before he had turned his head back Louis was on him again, first with a left and then with an awe-provoking right that made a crunching sound when it hit the German's jaw. Max fell down, hurt and giddy, for a count of three.

He clawed his way up as if the night air were as thick as black water, and Louis—his nostrils like the mouth of a double-barreled shotgun—took a quiet bead and let him have both barrels.

Max fell almost lightly, bereft of his senses, his fingers touching the canvas like a comical stewbum doing his morning exercises, knees bent and tongue lolling in his head.

He got up long enough to be knocked down again, this time with his dark unshaven face pushed in the sharp gravel of the resin.

Louis jumped away lightly, a bright and pleased look in his eyes, and as he did the white towel of surrender which Louis' handlers had refused to use two years ago tonight [when Max beat Joe so badly] came sailing into the ring in a soggy mess. It was thrown by Max Machon, oblivious to the fact that fights can no longer end this way in New York.

The referee snatched it off the floor and flung it backwards. It hit the ropes and hung there, limp as Schmeling. Donovan counted up to five over Max, sensed the futility of it all, and stopped the fight.

The big crowd began to rustle restlessly toward the exits, many only now accepting Louis as champion of the world. There were no eyes for Schmeling, sprawled on his stool in his corner.

He got up eventually, his dirty gray and black robe over his shoulders, and wormed through the happy little crowd that hovered around Louis. And he put his arm around the Negro and smiled. They both smiled and could afford to—for Louis had made around $200,000 for two minutes and four seconds and Schmeling $100,000.

But once he crawled down in the belly of the big stadium, Schmeling realized the implications of his defeat. He, who won the title on a partly phony foul, and beat Louis two years ago with the aid of a crushing punch after the bell had sounded ending a critical round, now said Louis had fouled him. That would read better in Germany, whence earlier in the day had come a cable from Hitler, calling on him to win.

It made a couple of anthologies, including *A Treasury of Great Reporting,* assembled for Simon and Schuster by Columbia's Prof. Richard B. Morris and CCNY's Louis L. Snyder, and another by Frank Luther Mott, dean of Missouri's School of Journalism. But it never would have been written if Parker had not given me the opportunity.

The sports beat was an entrancing one in the last days of peace leading up to World War II. Paul Gallico's thesis in his memorable *Farewell to Sports,* to the effect that the Golden Age of Sports had turned to dross, found itself under attack in every field. We had no Ruth, Gehrig, or Grove, but we had DiMaggio, Williams, and Feller. We had no Dempsey, Tunney, or Greb, but we had Louis, Henry Armstrong, and Ray Robinson. Bobby Jones and Walter Hagen were gone, but in their stead stood Sam Snead, Byron Nelson, and a struggling young pro named Ben Hogan. Red Grange, Jim Thorpe, and Bronco Nagurski had vanished, but Sammy Baugh, Sid Luckman, and Don Hutson somehow sufficed. Big Bill Tilden and Little Bill Johnston had left the center court, replaced by pulverizing Ellsworth Vines, Don Budge and Jack Kramer. Helen Wills, Suzanne Lenglen, and Joyce Wethered had called it a day, and now we turned handsprings over Alice Marble, Pauline Betz, and Babe Didrikson. We had no Earl Sande, but there was a boy around who showed great promise named Eddie Arcaro. Man o' War was down on the farm in Lexington, but the youngest of his countless sons, War Admiral, was doing him proud—and then a beast named Whirlaway came along who could run faster (and wider) than both of them.

We had carry-over and developing sportswriters to tell the world about this transition from what Paul Gallico called the Golden Age and Westbrook Pegler, "The Era of Wonderful Nonsense."

All Gaul may have been divided into three parts, but Pegler's Law ruled that sportswriting could be divided into but two: the Gee Whiz group and the Aw Nuts clan. Unchallenged head of the former classification was Grantland Rice. He was the dearest, most gentle, and most successful man in the craft. He was extraordinarily kind and helpful to young and uncertain newcomers. He would spot a yearning younker on the edge of the crowd that always assembled around him during bull-session time and with an easy sweep of his arm bring him into the conversation, somehow remember his name. "What do *you* think about what we've been talking about, Bob (Joe, Bill, Ralph, Homer . . .)?

Bill Corum was much the same kind of openhearted, good-talking, good-drinking man, ready to pick up his battered portable and go anywhere in the land where the action was fast. And where the horses were fast. Bill could write warmly about every sport and all the people in each sport. But his heart belonged to racing. In his final year of covering the Kentucky Derby he picked the first four to finish in perfect order: Ponder, Capot, Palestinian, and Rockport. Ponder paid $34 to win, $11.60 to place, and $6.20 to show; Capot, $9.60 and $5.80; and Palestinian, $4.80. The favorite of the crowd of 100,000, Olympia, with Eddie Arcaro up, went off at 4 to 5 and finished far up the track. The mathematics department of Bill's alma mater, Columbia, asked by *Journal-American* sports editor Max Kase to calculate the odds against such an astonishing feat, threw up its hands in defeat. Bill never covered another Derby. He couldn't, because Churchill Downs made him president of the track.

John Kieran, whose authorship of the *New York Times*'s sports column spanned the transitional years, was the intellectual the fraternity always pointed to when we needed evidence to prove that mentally we were a cut above the status of arrested development. The New Yorkese flavor of his speech contrasted his immense scholarship. Patronizingly introduced by the stuffy headmaster of a fashionable prep school, John unconcernedly addressed the boys in Latin. He was as sweet-tempered and unassuming as Rice. One day, seated next to him at a noisy World Series game in Yankee Stadium, I noticed that between innings he'd put his nose into an antique book whose leather flaked on touch. I asked him what he was reading. "It's *Curiosities of Literature,*" John said. Hearing no response, he added helpfully, "By Isaac D'Israeli." John still wanted to help. "You know," he said, as if I were feigning ignorance, "Disraeli's father."

There were so many of these good men still around in those days, each with a helping hand outstretched, each more interested in boosting than knocking.

I think now of Frank Graham, who never wished to offend a player he was interviewing by pulling a pad and pencil, but who could later write everything the man had said and without a flaw. Frank, too, was one with Rice. So were other old-timers around the town and country: Harry Salsinger and Sam Greene in Detroit, George Cairns and

Austen Lake in Boston, Ed Danforth and O. B. Keeler in Atlanta, Fred Russell in Nashville, Sec Taylor in Des Moines, George Barton in Minneapolis, Curley Grieve in San Francisco, Jimmy Burns in Miami, Jimmy Isiminger and Red Smith in Philadelphia, John Carmichael and T-Bone Otto in Chicago, Gordon Cobbledick in Cleveland, Havey Boyle and Chet Smith in Pittsburgh, Red McQueen in Hawaii, Buck O'Neill in Washington, Roy Stockton and Jim Gould in St. Louis, Royal Brougham in Seattle, and in New York men of the caliber of Tommy Holmes, Stanley Woodward, the Bill Slocums, Sr. and Jr., Arthur Daley, Al Laney, Allison Danzig, Burris Jenkins, Willard Mullin, Tom Meany, Clem McCarthy, Al Buck, and Walter Stewart, Jack Singer, Richards Vidmer, Alan Gould, Ted Husing, Scotty Reston, Drew Middleton, Caswell Adams, Jack Mahon, Stu Cameron, and the best-rounded sportswriter of them all, Sid Mercer.

We had great cudgelers during that period, too, willing and able to pick up where Pegler left off when he took his look-of-eagles and his blackjack into the sphere he liked to call "cosmic thinking." Peg considered calling his new column "Sweetness and Light."

We had Dave Egan in a perpetual tantrum in Boston, Joe Williams and Davis J. Walsh jabbing superbly in New York, Prescott Sullivan and Tom Laird fulminating in San Francisco, Jack Miley and Jimmy Cannon ready to tackle anything or anybody around the big town, and Bill Cunningham trumpeting defiance from his Boston redoubt.

We had pixies galore. Let us consider just three of them.

Hype Igoe had been as close to Jim Corbett as he was to Jim Braddock, as much of a confidant of Joe Gans as of Barney Ross, as trusted by Stanley Ketchell as by Billy Conn. He was a ruddy, jolly little man who worked hard and lived harder. He was immune to the erosion of time.

Hype was drinking beer very late one night in Mickey Walker's saloon across the street from the Garden. Hype was worried. His companion Jack Miley, another impressive consumer of the suds, was assigned by the *Daily News* to cover the Army-Navy football game in Philadelphia some hours later that day. Hype implored his friend to leave the saloon and get to Philadelphia.

He said later that he must have dozed a bit. He remembered opening his eyes, seeing Miley sitting opposite him, as usual, and he ordered two more beers.

"For the last time, Jack, get to Philadelphia and cover that game," Hype said crossly. "Do you want to blow your job?"

Jack seemed surprised.

"I've been to Philadelphia, Hype," he said. "I covered the game. I took a slow train back, just dropped in here for a beer, and found you sitting in the same spot where I left you last night."

Hype got "rolled" in a strange town once, and showed up at the press gate of the fight arena minus his ticket and any sort of identification, and was turned away. He was feeling very bad anyway and this frustration made him sicker. He found his way to a public rest room nearby, for he was too fastidious a man to be sick in front of fans crowding into the arena.

As he was leaving his place of woe, Hype noticed with interest the enamel button which, when pushed, flushed the water closet he had been using. It bore a neat legend: "PRESS."

Hype unscrewed the button, attached it to his lapel, and sailed through the press gate unimpeded.

Hype was a devoted father for a man whose job and nature militated against his getting home much more often than Halley's Comet squirts past Earth. Whenever he did drop by, Hype liked to bring presents for the children. Detained late one night at the *Journal,* he despaired of finding anything suitable to take home with him. Then he was struck with a fine idea. He went up to the roof of the building, picked up a wire-mesh box of homing pigeons, and took them home to the kids. The *Journal* used pigeons for swift transit of undeveloped film and captions and notes from the baseball and football fields, remote disaster stories, shipboard interviews, and others events.

The Igoe children loved the birds, made pets of them, fattened them up, and happiness abounded until the search for the culprit who had made off with them, under cloak of night, narrowed down to Hype. He confessed after considerable grilling. The *Journal* sent its aviary keeper to Hype's house and he repossessed the birds, to the wails and laments of the children.

Hype was forgiven, but not for long. The same birds were pressed into service shortly thereafter. Some great dignitary was arriving from Europe and would submit to pictures and interviews on the ship as it reached Quarantine. Film and the story of the arrival, plus the interview, scribbled in "takes" on oiled paper, were stuffed in the little capsules the pigeons carried, and off they shot—straight to Hype's house instead of to the *Journal.* It was badly scooped by the *World-Telegram,* the *Sun,* and the *Post,* none of whose pigeons suffered from split personalities, or divided loyalties.

The pixie in Henry McLemore was so pronounced it tended to overshadow the fact that he was the nimblest sportswriter of that happy period. His impish manner and unpredictability combined to make him unique. He was to serve in the Army through all of World War II, but in the period leading up to the bombing of Pearl Harbor, he could not have cared less about its meaning: At a party given at Grossinger's resort in the Catskills, where Barney Ross was training for a fight, Henry seized the microphone during a floor show and suggested that the audience—predominantly Jewish—join him in singing the "Horst Wessel" song. He lived.

Introducing saintly Granny Rice at a distinguished dinner given in Rice's honor by members of the Detroit Athletic Club, Henry said fondly, "Over the years, Granny has taken more punishment than the mothballs in a public urinal." The first time Henry saw our daughter Debbie, who was then two, she was happily tubbing herself at our apartment, her hair pinned up prettily out of the way of the large bar of bath soap she was wielding.

"You're the most beautiful girl I've ever seen," Henry said, standing at the side of the tub. Then he joined her in the tub, fully dressed and they had a fine sloshing time together.

Henry was a rarity in other respects. Although he worked for the United Press, he could write well. He could write funny, write sad, and as must all wire-service slaves, write fast. There was no end to his imagination, in a pinch.

En route to a World Series in St. Louis, Henry got snarled in a card game and blew the entire $250 his office had pressed upon him to cover his expenses during the long trip. Later that day, burdened by not only the financial disaster but a ringing hangover, Henry stared unhappily at the sheet of paper he had rolled into his typewriter in the cramped confines of the press box at Sportsman's Park. I had drawn the seat directly behind him and slightly higher and thus commanded an unintended but uninterrupted view of Henry's typewriter and the tempests that afflicted him. He was on his deadline, suffering the unanaesthetized birthpangs of a lead. He looked up, as a hurt fighter does, and his eye riveted on a fat Goodyear blimp floating idly over the ballpark. Henry's typing fingers instantly sprang to action. I couldn't resist looking over his shoulder as he wrote: "By Henry McLemore. Aboard Goodyear Blimp over Sportsman's Park, St. Louis, Oct. 6.—The Cardinals, spilling out of their dugout, resemble a swiftly blooming and burgeoning flower, as I look down on the field far below me."

It went on and on, a virtuoso performance. But there was more to his mad flight of fancy. At the end of the story, Henry attached a memo to UP's New York office. It read: "P.S. Blimp hire cost $250. Rush."

Got it, too.

Harry Grayson, sports editor of Newspaper Enterprise Association, the mail-sheet department of the Scripps-Howard chain, trod the sports world of that era with the confidence of a man who was to the manner born and a law unto himself. He liked Runyon, Farnsworth, and Frayne personally, but saw that as no reason to prevent his documented report on their financial involvement in Mike Jacobs' Twentieth Century Sporting Club. Harry liked Mike, too, and Mike showered him with kindnesses. But one day as Harry looked down on Forty-ninth Street from the window of his room high in the Forrest Hotel and saw Mike sunning himself in a chair outside the Jacobs Ticket Office, he found no good reason to resist the temptation to lob a filled water pitcher out the window. It hit the pavement with a splintering crash just a few feet from where Mike dozed. If it had hit him on the head it would have driven him into the sidewalk like a croquet pole.

Harry smoked cigars that always appeared to be sputtering down the last half inch to the explosion. In fact, Harry himself always seemed on the point of detonation. Almost everything he said was delivered with gusto and finger-jabbing. He preferred to stand very close to the person he was addressing or arguing with. Harry had many fine traits, including love of his son and worship of his nephew, the Stanford All America Bobby Grayson. But attentiveness was not one of his strengths.

One night in the crowded confines of the Theatrical Grill in Cleveland, where Cleveland's night life began and ended, he stood up to illustrate how a fighter he liked had cranked up a right-hand punch. In the course of the backswing, Harry's fist hit a souse at the next table. The guy tipped over backwards in his chair and his drink went flying through the smoky air. Harry looked down briefly on the chaotic scene, said "Oh," turned back to us, and resumed his story.

Harry hated Cleveland with all his heart, but that's where Scripps-Howard headquartered its NEA in a dismal building not far from the Stadium and the lake front. One ghastly winter morning before dawn Harry, unable to find a cab, leaned miserably against the sleet and snowstorm sweeping off the lake as he trudged to work. A car pulled over to the curb near him, and the motorist rolled down a window and shouted above the horrid storm, "Hey, Mac, how do you get out of Cleveland?"

Harry lunged at him and would have probably choked him to death if the window had been lowered sufficiently. Instead, all he could do was roar at the startled man, "You dumb son of a bitch, do you think I'd be in Cleveland if I knew how to get out?"

Harry was a real swinger and often had to prove it. His idea of a lively night, perhaps dating back to his days as a Marine in World War I, was to go into the toughest bar in town for a few beers. There was always an excellent chance that he would overhear a patron—usually the big tough guy down at the other end of the bar—say something Harry didn't agree with. He would drop everything to try to set the guy straight. Sometimes the guy didn't want to be set straight, didn't want to be interrupted by the gray-haired, blue-eyed stranger who stood inches from his face and blew cigar sparks and smoke. It was interesting to make the rounds with Harry when the moon was full, but not especially healthy.

I flew around the world with Harry near the end of the war, courtesy of the Air Transport Command. It may have been the junket that killed all junkets. A montage of that voyage remains vividly clear, each vignette in living color:

Harry, taking the occasion of a spit-and-polish dinner at the Officers' Club at Gander to deliver a stinging denunciation of their commander-in-chief, F.D.R.

Harry, in Casablanca's Old Medina, beset by two screaming Arab prostitutes when all he wanted was to see the sights.

Harry, shaking his head and muttering "This goddam Egypt!" as we looked down from the balcony of our room in a *Calcutta* hotel while buzzards wheeled over a cholera victim.

Harry, viewing with distaste a dirt-covered holy man lying in a prayer trance near a burning ghat in New Delhi, "Hey, get up, you filthy old faker!"

Harry, shaking hands with Chiang Kai-shek in Chungking (Chiang had a nervous habit of smiling and repeating "Hao . . . hao . . . hao") and saying to me, too loud, "This bum's in a rut!"

Harry, being threatened with eviction from the China Burma India theater for poking Gen. Albert C. Wedemeyer in his beribboned chest to stress a point.

Harry, still on probation while we were being entertained at Lord Louis Mountbatten's digs in Colombo, being hit a resounding whack on the back by Supremo—who was jolly pleased with some ribald story Harry had told him.

Harry, looking around Jerusalem and mulling over what I had just told him: that here in 70 A.D. more than fifty thousand Jews had been killed by Titus. "Thank Christ we got inoculated against *that,*" Harry said fervently.

But the prime feature of our global trip was Harry's meeting with Pope Pius XII and their wholly improbable togetherness.

The episode began on a low note. I woke up Harry at the crack of noon that warm Sunday in Rome. We had had a rough Saturday night in a wine cellar owned, if memory serves, by a family named Borgia. We suffered from the wrath of grapes.

"Get up, Harry, we're going to see the Pope."

Harry, sleeping in his shorts in the curtainless room in the war-stained Excelsior, stirred just enough to say, "To hell with the Pope."

The only course left to me as a defender of the faith was to get him up, see that he shaved and put his war correspondent's uniform on frontward. We reported to the bus on time and joined the other correspondents who had been granted an audience with the Pontiff.

"I'm only doing this for you because you're Catholic or something," Harry said unhappily as we marched into the papal palace. "But get this straight: I'm not going to kiss that guy's ring."

Feeling a bit faint, and fingering the rosary in my pocket, I led Harry along the glorious hallways, wondering if, after their having weathered the sin of purchased indulgences, they might now collapse on a former altar boy at St. Aloysius' in Washington, D. C., and on his militantly agnostic pal.

"Nobody wants you to kiss His Holiness' ring," I hissed at him.

But Harry wasn't listening. He had spotted the first Swiss guard he had ever seen. Naturally, he stopped.

"Are you kidding?" he said to the stiff and proper man, bedecked in the uniform that Michelangelo designed as a gag, only to have the Pope who gave him the demeaning assignment applaud his sketches and order the uniforms. "What are you, some kind of a nut?" The Swiss Guard never blinked, never got around to piercing Harry with his halberd.

And so it went until we reached the vicinity of the magenta silk-covered door that led into Pius XII's office. There at its threshold more bad news awaited. Franklin Gowen, a State Department career officer who served as the strong right arm of the White House's representative at the Vatican, Myron Taylor, took me aside. He said he had selected me as the member of the party who would introduce the others to the Pope. I can hardly remember my wife's name, much less casual acquaintances.

"No."

"Oh, yes, you will," Mr. Gowen said. "What's more, you must put His Holiness at his ease at the start with some compliment or discreet pleasantry, then explain the mission of your group and get along with the introductions."

"I've had very little experience putting Popes at their ease," I said lamely. Just then, to make things less bearable, two things happened. A papal household monsignor prematurely opened the door to the Holy Father's office and we beheld the spectacle of the Vicar of Christ busily engaged in the task of personally arranging the chairs we were to sit on during his proposed talk to us. The other happening concerned Harry.

"Remember, I'm not kissing that guy's ring, see?" he said.

It was just too much, with a hangover. But one manages to survive, somehow. Upon signal, we all trooped in and found His Holiness, a vision in white silk, standing serenely near his desk, on which there rested, among other objects, a white portable typewriter. As if in a dream I heard Mr. Gowen introduce me. I genuflected and kissed the ring on Pius XII's delicate, long-fingered, almost translucent right hand. (I was to kiss both those hands—described as "fluttering white doves"—under different conditions years later.)

"Your Holiness," I said on this occasion, voice cracking. "We are a group of American news correspondents on tour of the various theaters of war. We have only one thing in common with you as a group. We're all touch-typists together."

It was a demented opening. But Eugenio Pacelli smiled, as if he had been put at ease. Gowen nodded to me to begin the introductions. I don't remember the first ten in line. I kept worrying about No. 11, Harry. He was getting ever closer. And then at last there they stood, face to face, the spiritual leader of 400,000,000 Catholics and, well, let's face it, Harry.

"Hi'ya," Harry said, taking the Pope's hand and pumping it. "Harry Grayson of NEA."

Taking a long chance that the Pope had never heard of NEA, I said "Your Holiness, Mr. Grayson writes for a well-known news service named Newspaper Enterprise Association in our country. Its main office is in a state we call Ohio. The city where it is located is called Cleveland."

"Cleveland?" the Pope repeated. He looked at Harry with fresh interest. "I know Cleveland. I spent a most enjoyable time in Cleveland when I visited your country in 1935. Would you by any chance know my friend Bishop Ready in Cleveland?"

It was just too much. Grayson knew him. Now the two of them, perhaps the least likely acquaintances in Christendom, talked animatedly about their mutual friend. It was with some difficulty that I got the line moving again.

When we were all introduced and seated, the Pope sat down at his desk and gave us a little talk on our obligations as newsmen. Then he distributed rosaries and papal medals and it was time to bid him farewell. As we filed out, the Pope stopped only one of us. Harry.

"Our blessing on you and your family, Mr. Grayson," Pius XII said to Harry, the only one whose name he could recall. He made a gentle little Sign of the Cross over Harry's gray mane.

Suddenly, incredibly, Harry dropped to one knee, seized the Pope's hand, and kissed his ring. I turned away, not wishing to be a witness to what had to be a trying time for my friend. To have stared in wonderment would have been a rude and perhaps sacrilegious invasion of privacy.

Harry and I walked out together in silence unbroken except for Harry's occasional obscene references to Swiss Guards stationed here and there along the route. Once outside, Harry bit the end off a cigar and squirted the bitten part at the base of a Bernini column. He puffed on the cigar as he applied the match, got it going to his satisfaction, and cocked his head in the direction of the Pope's palace.

"That guy's okay," Harry said.

I felt that the papacy had seldom had a finer or less expected tribute paid it.

I sometimes miss sportswriting. There is within its narrow confines a blithe togetherness seldom apparent in other reaches of the news business. There will always be jealousies among men who write as competitors. But at day's end, it is easier for sportswriters to get together for a meal or a drink than for, let us say, editorial writers, financial editors, publishers, and even police reporters. The friendships I formed in sportswriting are more lasting and rewarding than any formed in the other fields I bumbled into. I don't subscribe for a minute to the old wives' tale that most of the best writing in today's newspapers appears on their sports pages. It is popular to repeat that a lot of prominent columnists, correspondents, and literary figures started out in sports: Brisbane (who covered the John L. Sullivan-Charley Mitchell fight at Chantilly in 1888 as part of an audience of forty spectators), Heywood Broun, Westbrook Pegler, Paul Gallico, Quentin Reynolds, James Reston, Frank Conniff, Stanley Frank, Drew Middleton, etc. But as many or more beat a path to fame without the stimuli of the crack of a bat, thump of a punch, thunder of hooves, and the encouragingly loose reins of the sports department's Copy Desk.

Still, there is always something special about a good sportswriter that the best in the other departments seldom attain. He attracts more and tenacious readers and holds them longer than the other featured stars. Nobody proved this more in life or death than Runyon. He had been out of daily sports journalism for ten years when he died of cancer in December, 1946. But it was as a sportswriter (rather than as a short-story writer, trial reporter, Hollywood scenarist, and man-about-town chronicler) that he was remembered. He was mourned by millions, this lonely and often irascible man. It is inconceivable that any outstanding pundit of Walter Lippmann's stature, or even an Ernie Pyle or Ernest Hemingway, could have served after death as the rallying point of the remarkable cancer research fund that bears Runyon's name. With Walter Winchell quietly footing the administrative costs for fourteen years, and Dan Parker, John Daly, Arthur Godfrey, Leonard Lyons, Ray Robinson, and others pitching in, some

$30,000,000 had been raised twenty years after Winchell started the ball rolling with a $5,000 check and a pitch on the air.

It was rewarding, being a part of the world of sports. It was a nice feeling to have a seat in the press row at every big event that came along. But the War pulled back a vast curtain and gave me my first view of the world, its wonders, and its peoples. Luckily, there was a handy steppingstone into that broader life.

It was called International News Service.

4 *INS—(R.I.P.)*

AT NOON, EDT, May 24, 1958, the teletypes of the United Press and International News Service paused briefly all over the nation and beyond some of the seas. The machines sounded their separate and intensely competitive bells to indicate that news of "bulletin" importance was about to move on their wires. And then the two old foes gave forth with the following: "The United Press Associations and International News Service joined forces today around the world in the creation of a single news agency named United Press International."

There were curses, consternation, and tears in the INS newsroom. Guildsmen had been assured a day or two before by general manager Joe Kingsbury Smith that all rumors that INS would be sold to UP were completely without foundation. He was correct in his notice to employees, Joe said subsequently. The Guild's inquiry had asked if it were true that INS was about to be *sold* to UP. Actually, Joe explained, it was *merged*.

A better verb would have been *swallowed*. The new organization, UPI, kept most of the old UP personnel. It picked up only a handful of INS men, several of whom soon quit. They could not endure the transition from their wild and wonderful news service to an atmosphere which, by comparison, was about as challenging as a Western Union branch.

Even as the keys of the teletypes clacked the doom of INS, two strangers entered the shocked newsroom. They strolled over to Milton Kaplan, then manning the news desk. One of the men introduced himself as a UP. Milt, who doesn't look unlike Michelangelo's Christ in the Pietà, graciously shook hands.

"I'll be working around here the rest of the day," UP said. "I guess you read the wire."

"Yes, I did," said one of the hardest-working and most dedicated INS men of all. "May I get you a desk . . . typewriter . . . phone?"

"Yes, thank you," UP said.

Milt turned to the other man, who looked as if he intended to buy a derby at the earliest opportunity.

"And may I do the same for you?" Milt assumed he, too, was UP.

"Naw," the mugg said. "I'm from Pinkerton. I'm here to see you guys don't steal nothing, see?"

We died with vinegar in our wounds.

A lot of us kidded INS. Unlike Avis Rent A Car, we could not claim to be only second best. We were, at most, third best among the wire services. Today, with the rise of the *New York Times* wire, and Los Angeles *Times*-Washington *Post,* Chicago *Daily News,* and other wires, we might have pushed down to sixth or seventh place among the most respected dispensers of spot news and features.

But for a long time, as we trailed behind UP and the Associated Press, scorned and often bad-mouthed by both, we were some of the proudest people in the news business. Proud and often deeply moved by events which the reading public never noticed, or considered trite: the big "play" an INS story might get in a paper that subscribed also to AP and UP. If the paper ignored us when we felt we had covered a big story better than the AP and UP and printed their accounts rather than our INS copy, we would be inclined to dismiss the paper's telegraph editor as a drunk or some old doddering teetotaler who had worked for either of our sworn enemies for years and had been hopelessly brainwashed against all things Hearst-owned.

There was astonishing opposition to us. When Clark Lee, the great AP correspondent resigned after Bataan and Corregidor to accept a much more remunerative job with INS, he dropped by AP's New York office to say good-bye to associates he had been close to for years. Kent Cooper, the top AP man at the time, would not see him; he was "busy." A day or two before actually starting writing for INS, Clark visited AP again. There was a bustle and hustle as he entered. Kent Cooper wanted to see him immediately.

Cooper greeted him with the deceptive smile of winter sunshine and congratulated him on risking his life so many times for AP—for a stipend, by the way, that would have caused the New York Yankees batboy to hold out. As a fruit of this noble service to the cause, Cooper went on, he was going to send Clark to South America to head up one of AP's bureaus.

"I didn't know what to say to him," Clark told me one night, as we leaned on the rail of the *Appalachian* on the way to the A-bomb tests at Bikini in 1946. "I knew he knew I had resigned. It had been in the papers and some of the AP guys had given me farewell parties. But I had to say it all over again for him. And I did. He said, and he acted very mad, 'INS! You can't do that, Clark. You *can't* resign. Your *father* worked all his life for AP. INS is *Hearst!*'

"I told him what he already knew, that I had signed a contract and was ready to go to work for INS," Clark said quietly, as we looked into the phosphorescent water. "Then I started for the door. I said good-bye and thanks for all the wonderful things that had happened to me at AP. But he wouldn't let me go. He said, 'Lee,'—he had called me Clark all those years—'a funny thing happened to me today at the meeting of the Pulitzer Prize selection group. I forgot to bring up your name.' "

We at INS were never sore at Mr. Hearst, senior, or his son and namesake, who took the folding of the wire service quite hard. They and their corporation underwrote our adventures, our fun, and our games to the extent of several million dollars a year during the last down-grade. That lost fortune provided a unique stage in the theater of news-gathering, filled to its proscenium with an arresting cast of characters.

I caught the last fifteen years of the act which had been opened in 1909 when the elder Hearst magnificently ordered the creation of a special news service to supply his own newspapers exclusively. He wished it to be as impartial as AP and UP, and maintained a most commendable hands-off policy toward it through the next forty-two years until his death in 1951. His editorials, policy direction, and often subtly couched "suggestions" moved to his papers along a separate wire service, Universal. INS went its own way as a separate entity, either impervious to, or ignorant of, what was known as "Hearst policy." It began to attract clients from the outside world, which threw it into direct competition with the much larger AP and UP.

So far as manpower was concerned, the odds against INS men were prohibitive in most of their jousts with the other two. We had one man—Jim Brown—covering India during most of World War II. He'd get an occasionally tart "bullet" from our foreign editor Jack

Oestreicher if he found himself in Lahore when the action was taking place in Trivandrum, 1,700 impassable miles to the south. No computer could calculate the number of times Jimmy Kilgallen, Dave Walsh, Inez Robb, Charlie Einstein, Lawton Carver, and other willing round-the-clock reporters were thrown into the fray alone, and expected to outproduce the rivals or, that failing, outwrite them.

I lost track of the number of times I was the loner from INS, but I remember that when Eisenhower went to Abilene, Kansas, in 1952 to announce his candidacy, INS convered that event with one man (me), UP with seven, and AP with twelve.

There were other times when we overcovered a story, surrounded it, permeated every cell of it. It would be like a four-alarm fire that had brought every piece of a town's equipment to the scene of the blaze. In the confusion, we'd sometimes squirt our hoses on each other, when we weren't squirting them on the opposition.

There was that sunny Sunday in Monaco when Father Francis Tucker, the ecclesiastic Cupid in the story-book romance of dashing Rainier III and beautiful Grace Kelly, mounted the pulpit to make a few final observations about the impending wedding. Monagasques found the news largely filled with newsmen and photographers. There were 1,700 of us assigned to that story from all parts of the world, as opposed to only 2,200 actual Monagasques.

Halfway through his sermon in which he showered blessings down on the betrothed the priest paused and branched off into spot news.

"It will never break up," the priest said as if tearfully denying some unprinted report. "I believe Rainier will keep his oath. As for Grace Kelly, she will keep her oath, or she won't be a Catholic. I can bear witness that this man [Rainier] is being faithful to his pledge to his country. Two years ago he broke off a sentimental friendship for your sake. . . ." It was another way of stating that the groom was finished for keeps with French actress Gisèle Pascal.

There was a scuffling in the front of the church. UP's Bob Musel was bolting out a side door. AP, in the person of Eddy Gilmore, was making a more discreet but still determined march up the middle aisle toward the main doors. I felt trapped, ground between Church and that portion of State called INS. This was the last Mass of the day, and my religion requires that I attend Mass each Sunday. On the other hand, there went UP and AP, headed for telephones, each bearing the story of Tucker's bad taste.

A fast decision had to be made, and it was. I decided that it would be easier to face my confessor than Barry Faris, my leader at INS headquarters in New York. So I rushed out, found a phone, called the INS agency which had been set up in a water closet and bidet shop in Monte Carlo, and dictated the story. Later that day I ran into a young colleague, Olga Curtis, a beautiful and talented girl who felt eclipsed by the presence on our team of our strikingly efficient and confident Dorothy Kilgallen. Olga had been crying, her eyes said. I asked her to have a drink. She shook her head.

"Why did you write the story about Father Tucker?" she wailed. "I was assigned to cover the Mass . . . the first good assignment I've had since I've been here in this damned place. I worked hard on my story, took it to the office, and that man on the desk said that your story had moved on the wire a long time before." I thought she would cry again, and I don't think she was listening when I told her that nobody had told me that she was assigned.

So now I had accumulated two sins for the day: leaving Mass early for commercial reasons (thus emulating the originator of that practice, Judas Iscariot), and inadvertently hurting a fellow INS'er. (Olga recovered to become women's editor of the *Denver Post.*)

But on big stories of that nature, we had an incomparable *esprit de corps* and sometimes even teamwork. It was a heady experience to field as many or more troops than either AP or UP chose to commit. But the rare occasions of our numerical superiority had its penalties. We must be perfect in order to justify the terrible expense. Perfect was subject to different interpretations.

The trial of Dr. Hermann Sander in Manchester, New Hampshire, was a case in point.

The day the waspish doctor took the stand to deny the prosecution's charge that he had practiced euthanasia on an elderly woman patient with a terminal case of cancer, INS had the finest day's file I'd ever seen. It started before that wintry daybreak with Fanny Hurst's vivid feature about the women queued up in the snowy streets, waiting and hoping to be admitted to the ugly courthouse where a man that most of them seemed to know would face his worst moment of truth. The popular novelist had been retained for the duration of the trial, a familiar and generally rewarding INS ploy. Her feature drew a brilliant parallel between those waiting women and the crones of Place Concorde, knitting and waiting for the arrival of wailing tumbrels.

It was followed on the wire by an extraordinarily sensitive piece done by John O'Hara, another INS special. It was a reminiscence of his father's hard times as a small-town doctor. Dr. Patrick Henry O'Hara of Pottsville, Pa., led the same overworked life that had brought Dr. Sander to this spent and drained hour. It was pure *New Yorker,* but only INS had it.

Our *Q* and *A* during the doctor's long stay on the stand was handled by, in my opinion, the finest virtuosos of that black art of recording precisely what was asked and answered no matter how swift the give-and-take: Inez Robb and Jimmy Kilgallen. Their notebook pages hit me like a heavy snowfall as I sat at the end of our press table in the courtroom. With each highlight, I'd scoop up their work and run down to an evil little cubbyhole in the cellar, colder than a Deepfreeze, where sat Phil Reed, our editor in charge. I'd bang out a new lead, Phil would grab it from the typewriter in short takes, read it like lightning, and our teletype operators thrust it into the trunkline that reached newspaper, radio, and TV clients across the U.S.

It was one of those glorious days when all thought of food and drink is driven from one's system; when nothing mattered except to show those dull bastards from AP and UP that—given the manpower—we could leave 'em for dead every time we met. We actually shouted like schoolchildren when wires of congratulation came in from such clients as the Yankee Network ("... INS averaging six to eight minutes ahead of opposition.")

By 9 P.M. we had run out of story and steam. Inez had found strength enough to do her regular column in addition to her long hours of exacting additional reporting. Kilgallen had written an overnight. INS'ers from the Boston bureau had come up with half a dozen fine local stories. I had done my "On the Line" column; Phil had finished editing it, and pretty soon the teletypes choked to a stop. We all just sat there in our own chosen attitudes of collapse, wondering how we'd make it to the hotel in the storm.

Phil picked up the phone and called Barry Faris in New York. It was a good connection, and the acoustics in our refrigerator were excellent, alas.

"Now, about tomorrow," we could hear Barry say, and even thought we heard the rustle of his assignment sheets.

"Tomorrow!" Phil cried out in anguish. "What have you got to say about *today!*"

There was a dreadful pause, and we all hung on breathlessly.

"Long," Barry said. "Now, about tomorrow . . ."

Barry was our beadle. He kept order in the house—at least when he was physically present or watching things by telephone and cable—from the time he joined INS in 1915 until he went down with the sinking ship nearly half a century later.

He was a seasoned newsman for a decade before he joined INS: priceless experience lapped up hungrily while working for the St. Joseph (Missouri) *Gazette,* St. Louis *Globe-Democrat,* Fort Worth *Record,* Kansas City *Post,* San Francisco *Call,* Los Angeles *Tribune,* Denver *Post,* Indianapolis *Sun* and UP, an organization on which he was to declare a total war that lasted longer than the War of the Roses.

For years he ran a one-man show in a way that won grudging admiration from the competition. He was head of news and of personnel and handled both with a gruff exterior that camouflaged his infatuation with the former and his sentimental regard for the latter.

In his best years his faith in the integrity and efficiency of his troops could not be shaken in any emergency. He ignored Roy Howard's false Armistice exclusive that ended World War I—on the UP wire, at least—a week early. On the night the AP sent out its wrong verdict in the Hauptmann case and frantic and angry phone calls from INS clients demanded to know why INS had not confirmed the verdict, Faris stood in the New York newsroom next to the silent Western Union key manned by the veteran operator Tom Walsh. Jimmy Kilgallen was in the courtroom at Flemington, New Jersey. That was enough for Faris. He just stood there, quietly smoking. To hell with panicky clients.

After five taut minutes Jimmy sent a short lead: "A premature verdict of life imprisonment for Bruno Richard Hauptmann for the kidnap-murder of Charles A. Lindbergh, Jr., emanated from the courtroom at 10:21 P.M. The jury had not as yet entered the courtroom. . . ."

Someone shouted to Barry that more INS clients were on the wire, angry.

"Tell 'em to use the goddam AP!" he shouted back.

Many editors needed no such invitation. Their presses were rolling with extra papers. The New York *American* in a most unbrotherly disregard for not only Kilgallen but its own treasured Damon Runyon, who was posted in the half-empty courtroom, ran off 55,000 copies carrying the AP story. The Washington *Post* and countless other papers placed their trust in AP, caring not a whit that INS was saying "premature" and UP was saying nothing.

AP and INS shared a room just outside the courtroom, after much earlier wrangling for separate bureaus.

"Naturally, we weren't speaking," Kilgallen recalled a long time later. "Well, that night of the verdict we're hanging around, waiting for the jury to make up its mind. You know how it is. You wander in and out of the courtroom, in and out of the bureau. It came up 10:30, and no action. The judge was still at his home, four blocks down the street.

"Then 10:31 and suddenly the red light comes up on the AP teletype, and it starts chugging. It's a bad feeling. I felt so helpless. I couldn't just walk over there and see what the opposition was saying. I couldn't have gotten near the machine, with those AP guys. But I got a break. A few days before, by mutual consent, we had agreed to let Bill Chaplin share our room. Bill worked for one of the radio networks which subscribed to *both* our wires. He was my friend from a long way back. He took a look at AP's wire, sent a bulletin to his network, then told me. That's when I sent my short lead."

For the next sixteen terrible minutes, Faris stood his ground, refusing to query Kilgallen. During all that time, at the rate of sixty words a minute, the AP ground out its story—one of several alternates providing for as many types and gradations of verdict.

Then a sudden and horrible silence.

Kilgallen's flash had hit the world: "HAUPTMANN GETS ELECTRIC CHAIR."

"Barry had great gobs of common sense," Jim said of his old boss, in comparing him with some of the more famous editors of his time. "All the others were merely geniuses."

Faris' common sense filtered down to some of the hands he employed.

Quentin Reynolds used to say that if he never worked for Faris he probably never would have sent a cable from Paris in 1940 during his early days as a *Collier's* war correspondent. He handed the cable to a stubborn French official and demanded that it be sent to the White House. It read: "DEAR UNCLE FRANKLIN: I AM HAVING DIFFICULTY GETTING ACCREDITED TO THE FRENCH ARMY. TIME IS IMPORTANT. WOULD YOU PHONE OR CABLE PREMIER REYNAUD AND ASK HIM TO

HURRY THINGS UP? IT WAS GRAND OF YOU TO PHONE ME LAST NIGHT. PLEASE GIVE MY LOVE TO AUNT ELEANOR. QUENT."

It worked.

There was a Faris flair in Kilgallen's scoop on the release of Tokyo Rose from a remote West Virginia prison, long after she had been tracked down in Japan by Clark Lee. The only phone in the vicinity of the prison was in the kitchen of a neighboring farmhouse. UP had resourcefully tied it up by renting the only available bedroom in the house. Nothing daunted, Kilgallen rented the kitchen. Naturally, he refused to let UP use his phone when the story broke.

Faris had an uncanny rapport with his men bordering on ESP. Pierre Huss, INS's Berlin bureau chief in the early days of World War II, before the bombing of Pearl Harbor, was covering Hitler's panzers in Silesia in June, 1941, when he dispatched three expense accounts to INS-New York, care of the business office.

A harried accountant brought them into Faris' office.

"Your man Huss has lost his mind," he said. "Look at these."

Faris looked. All three slips had been dated ahead to June 21. One was a voucher for expenses incurred in Russian-held Poland. The second was from Minsk. The third was from Kiev.

"My God!" Faris cried out. "The Germans are going to invade Russia!"

The arrival of Seymour Berkson on the INS scene had an unsettling influence on Faris. Bit by bit, Berkson diminished Faris' authority. It was obvious from the day he was transferred from the Rome bureau to New York that Seymour had taken dead aim on Barry's title and chair. Moreover, he had the skills and everlasting drive needed—over and above the fact that the Hearst hierarchy admired him—to unseat the unseatable. Seymour was one of the most dynamic creatures I've ever met in the news business, an exasperating lint-picker, demanding, deflating, and the hardest-working man in the shop.

When I proposed after the war that my "On the Line" column be resumed as a general news and feature column, instead of sports, Seymour asked for six samples. I wrote them and, after a week or two, was sorry the matter had come up. He went over them word by word and had a question for every sentence. He was University of Chicago, linguist, author of a comprehensive study on the erosion of royal families, handsome, and stylish and—after hours—a most congenial host. But at INS he was frequently a terror and often impossible to communicate with. There were astonishing gaps in his fund of knowledge. Questioning a story of mine to the effect that the New York Yankees had signed the Georgia football star Frank Sinkwich to play both baseball and pro football, Seymour demanded to know how this could be possible.

"Why not?" I asked him.

"How can he be both a pro and an amateur?" Seymour demanded.

I told him I didn't understand him.

"If he's going to be a professional football player, how could he also play for the Yankees?"

"Why not?"

"The Yankees are amateurs, aren't they?"

In the course of his constant fine-tooth combing of my sample "On the Line" columns he came across a reference to St. Joseph. He wanted to know the saint's exact relationship with the Blessed Virgin and with Jesus, and demanded supporting evidence of his foster fatherhood.

I spent several hours with him in his office on Thanksgiving Day, 1946, going over the now thoroughly odious sample columns. Finally, I told him I had to get home. Millie had invited half a dozen of what she calls her "homeless" friends—childless couples and stray bachelors and spinsters. I was to mix the drinks and carve the turkey. Halfway through the carving job, the phone rang. It was Seymour. He had more questions to ask, and they were the least consequential or erratic that he had yet asked. After a few minutes on the phone, I began to hear peals of rage and shouts of hunger from the dining room. Two of our children, unfed, began to weep. It was too much.

"Goddam you, Seymour, you're ruining our Thanksgiving dinner," I said to him.

There was a pause.

"And goddam you, you're ruining mine," Seymour said.

He was still at the office.

When Seymour had reached a point where he began to exert at least as much authority as Barry, Faris went to Joseph V. Connolly, the debonair Hearst executive who had overall charge of both INS and profit-making King Features Syndicate and laid his predicament before that old friend.

"Stop worrying, Barry," Connolly told him. "You'll be managing editor of INS as long as I'm alive."

Whereupon, Joe went home—which was something of a novelty—and died.

Seymour's ascendancy produced a general edginess around INS. It introduced an era of "Who's responsible for this?" Sub-editors who once could clear up matters with an exchange of a few words now found themselves sending memos back and forth. Faris' iron-clad faith in his forces seemed now to waver on occasion, and peevishness sometimes replaced his lordliness. At one of the A-bomb tests at Yucca Flat, Nevada, the communications truck the Army had assigned to INS went on the blink. Instead of transmitting my story back to Las Vegas as I had written it, it sent only a long string of Z's. Jack Hanley, our San Francisco bureau chief, had moved over to Las Vegas to handle my story and was, of course, appalled when I seemed to have gone stark raving mad in the desert and forgotten the other twenty-five letters of the alphabet. With the aid of radio broadcasts of the big event, he patched together a story, put my by-line on it, and sent it out on the INS wire. It was about fifteen minutes behind AP's and UP's stories. Their communication trucks had worked perfectly.

Faris was soon on the phone to Jack. Jack explained.

"Don't give me that crap," Barry said angrily. "You know as well as I do that we were booby-trapped."

"But how?" Jack asked wonderingly.

"How!" Barry shouted across the country. "They cut our wires!"

"Who cut our wires?"

"The AP and the UP. Who the hell else would cut them!"

"But Barry," Jack said helplessly, "there weren't any wires to cut. Considine's story came down from Yucca Flat by wireless."

Faris was not a man to accept any such lunatic alibi.

"Wireless or not, they found some way to cut the wires—so watch it," he said and hung up.

Faris worshiped General MacArthur. He dispatched the whole varsity team of INS to San Francisco for MacArthur's Second Coming, his return after President Truman had fired him so unceremoniously. We soon ran out of things to write about. There are just so many ways of phrasing "Gen. Douglas MacArthur will come home next Thursday." But the words had to be turned out willy-nilly. Hanley vetoed my suggestion that he deploy one of our staff at the water's edge, to be on hand in case MacArthur walked in atop the Pacific. But a similarly ridiculous column of mine, scraping the bottom of the subject matter, easily passed muster and was sent out on the wire. In it I wrote that MacArthur was about to have one of the biggest letdowns of his life. I said that when he left Haneda Airport, Tokyo, Emperor Hirohito himself would be there to shake his hand. When he arrived at Honolulu he would find the outstretched hand of that renowned old salt, Adm. Arthur W. Radford. When he landed in San Francisco, there at the bottom of the steps, hand outstretched, would be his old comrade, Gen. Albert C. Wedemeyer.

"And when he reaches his destination, Washington, D. C., there to greet him—as President Truman's representative—will be none other save Gen. Harry Vaughan," I wrote meanly.

I was awakened the following morning before eight o'clock by a call from Faris.

"You've gotten us in one hell of a jam," he began. "That column of yours is absolutely libelous. The lawyers say that Vaughan can sue us right down to the bone. I want the name of the deskman who passed that column."

I told him I couldn't remember the name.

"Well, you haven't heard the last of this one," he said. "I'll be calling you back."

Jack Hanley called me a few minutes later.

"I'm quitting," he said. "I've taken a lot of abuse in my day, but what Faris just said to me is too much. He blames *me* for what you wrote, and I never even saw it before it went out. I'm quitting."

I asked him not to quit . . . at least not until Faris called back.

Barry never called back, and it was not until I reached New York a week later that I learned why he had not. As reconstructed by staffers, it went like this:

As was his custom, the first thing Faris did after reporting for work that frantic morning was to read the flimsies, the stack of yellow tissue carbon copies of all the golden words that had been expressed along our wire the night before. In time he came to and, with unconcealed delight, read my column. He came out of his fishbowl office into the newsroom, bearing the flimsies of my piece, slapped the pages on the news desk, and said to its editor, "By God, that's the way a piece should be written. This is the greatest column Considine ever wrote. By God, he really told 'em!"

Then he went back into his office, and all was quiet for about an hour. Then a roar of indignation sounded out of Berkson's office.

Presently, Seymour was seen rounding a corner at high speed, his fist clutching *his* flimsies of my column. He burst into Faris' office, and the startled desk men saw him thumping his fist (and my column) against the edge of Barry's desk. Then he slammed out of Barry's office, his face dark with rage, and slammed into his own.

All eyes were on Faris. After a bit he got up from his desk, picked up the crumpled remains of my column, strode out to the desk, and roared, "Who's responsible for letting this villainous attack on General Vaughan get on our wire!"

The phone calls to San Francisco followed, after our libel lawyer, Carl Helm, had been roused and alerted to the infamous attack.

"But why didn't he call back?" I asked those who were giving me the fill-in.

"The first edition of the *Journal-American* reached Berkson's office during the height of the storm," one of them said. "Your column was spread eight columns across the top of Page One. That's the kind of play Berkson has been hoping we'd get for a long time."

So it was a nutty shop at times, too.

"It was wild and wonderful," Einstein wrote when I asked him for his memory of the place he graced. Charles memoed:

> Bugs Baer called it the Unintentional News Service and changed our slogan from "Get it first—but first get it right" to "Get it first—correct it later." Seymour was not amused.
>
> A copyboy in the Chicago bureau thought he was working for the SIN and thus caroled the initials when he answered the phone; and it may not be wholly without symbolism that when the Mickey Mouse Club wanted to show a newsroom on television, it unerringly chose INS headquarters in New York.
>
> What remained clear, on the day of our doom, was that the magic and money-losing world of INS would be no more. The unpainted, plaster-cracked newsroom in New York, on the eleventh floor of the *Daily Mirror* building—where once an elevator slipped its cable and fell, only to find INS scooped on the story because an unresponsible elevator in their building did not strike staffers as being news—was gone to gather dust. So was the Chicago bureau, where the overnight shift staged cockroach races for enormous stakes; Philadelphia, where the bureau was behind a barber shop; the basement quarters in Columbus, the cubbyholes in St. Louis, Los Angeles, Detroit, and Boston. In Phoenix, the termination of the INS consisted of unplugging a teletype

machine, which was the entire bureau, occupying as it did four square feet of space in the newsroom of a local radio station.

No one can be so sentimentally nostalgic as a newspaperman, nor more instantly so, but surely the INS merits a niche apart even in a business where reminiscence sets in at the age of nineteen. In the newspaper trade, the phrase has it, you meet such interesting people, and all of them at one time or another worked for INS, including a Latin American cables man believed to be the only person in history with a medical discharge from the French Foreign Legion and a one-armed copyboy who inevitably, when harassed, would cry out, "For Christ's sake, I've only got two hands." In New York at one time there was another copyboy who planned a career as a prizefighter and who trained late at night in the newsroom, skipping rope while clad solely in a jock strap. On the staff also was Les Conklin, who used to report to work with a paper carton of martinis and who claimed to be one of the few persons ever to get thrown out of Bickford's—the beanery down the street.

Conklin, who was writing the INS baseball roundup at the time, gained revenge against the restaurant chain in time. Vern Bickford, then with the Boston Braves, pitched a one-hitter. "Bickford," Conklin's roundup began, "is still serving up the smallest portions."

On a less esoteric level, the INS personnel included Ferdinand Goodfellow, who once vomited into the lap of a teletype operator for the purpose of exploring, he said, the iron-clad rule that no operator can leave his machine while on duty. One unforgettable scene occurred in the New York headquarters the night the Germans overran Holland in the initial stages of World War II. The U.S. still was at peace in those days, and the staff of the bureau clearly indicated it. It included a German, a Briton, and a Japanese, whose tasks comprised the preparation of news reports for client papers in their respective homelands. An argument arose between the Englishman and the German as one inflammatory bulletin after another hit the news desk, and finally they came to blows in the middle of the newsroom.

Meanwhile, a mechanical worker in the traffic department, a little the worse for whiskey, stepped up to the Japanese. "You'll be next, you little son of a bitch," he declared with uncanny foreboding, and laid his fingers to the Oriental's throat, forcing him back toward a window. It was at this juncture that sports editor Lawton Carver, who had a cousin by marriage who was a singer, decided to call up the minstrel-in-law and hum a few bars of a song he recently had heard. Back at the foreign desk, the incoming war news was such that the cable department had sent out a hurry call for reinforcement. One newsman was located, off duty and experiencing no pain, in the Ink Well, a tavern on Third Avenue. He returned to the office but maneuvered only so far as the financial desk, where he fell to the floor, comatose. Another editor was reached at a formal-dress function at the Waldorf. He rushed back to the office dressed—spectacularly—as he was.

It was at this instant that Ed Kiely, who later reconstructed the tableau for a succession of awe-struck listeners, came to work. Kiely, who understandingly left INS to become an official of the Pittsburgh Steelers of the National Football League, then was a night rewrite man in sports. "I opened the door," he recollected, "and here were two guys beating the hell out of each other in the middle of the room. Over here somebody was trying to push a Jap out a window. Another guy was singing at the top of his lungs into a telephone. There was a man lying on his face on the floor. And the guy tearing off the carbon paper was wearing a tuxedo and a top hat. It was the damndest sight I ever saw."

But we also had Joe Smith's exclusive cable interview with Stalin, a forty-minute beat on the arrest of Hauptmann, Washington bureau manager Bill Hutchinson's remarkable scoops on the death sentences imposed on the six Nazi saboteurs who landed here by submarine, and his prediction that Hirohito would be retained as Emperor. Possibly the most important beat the news service ever chalked up, however, was one not of hours or even minutes, but of approximately fifty seconds. The ringing of four bells on the INS teletypes signaled the shortest flash in history: "F.D.R. DEAD."

My most valued keepsake is an autographed picture from Faris to me. I was in New York after INS folded and bumped into Barry at the restaurant Carver had opened. He began regaling witnesses as to how he discovered me in the bullrushes and transformed me into the Jewish George R. Holmes. Nothing would do but that we wind up at his apartment, which was then only a block away. We wound up crying over INS. He selected his all-time favorite photo of himself and inscribed it for me.

Just before I went to bed in my hotel, I looked at it closely, fondly. He had misspelled my name. In the morning I looked at it again and found out something else. He had misspelled his own name, too.

INS was a make-do wire service. We happened to have nobody in New Delhi on January 30, 1948, to cover the big prayer and pacification meeting led by Mahatma Gandhi. A Hindu who blamed the saint for the partition of India shot and killed him. Reuter's, of course, was well-staffed for this stupendous news event. In a matter of a minute or two its printers in papers all over the world were flashing the news of the assassination. One of those clients, happily, was INS-London. It quickly broke the news to INS-New York, which appropriated some additional material from AP and UP—by way of the *Mirror,* which subscribed to both. Hearst blood was thicker than water. With the vital statistics and purloined facts now in hand, all we needed was a by-line to prove that the sun never set on INS.

John Martin, who had successfully made the difficult leap from the AP's foreign desk to ours, reached for our slim deck of index cards containing the names and addresses of our overseas correspondents and stringers—a stringer being a locally employed reporter, expatriate, or beachcomber, sometimes reachable for special assignments. At AP the index was so voluminous, it was said, that among its Palestinian stringers was one listed as Christ, J. But now Martin's eye latched on to the yellowing card of an Indian stringer named J. B. Sahne. Nothing had been heard from him nor had his services been sought for many years. But in short order and shorter "takes," INS's wires across the country began rolling with a fine story of the death of the great leader, "by J. B. Sahne—International News Service Staff Correspondent." Martin never wrote a better story faster.

Not long after that Martin ran into an old AP friend, Charlie Grumich, who complimented him for the fine play INS had received in U.S. papers the day of the murder.

"Who's your man in India?" Charlie asked.

"J. B. Sahne," John said steadily.

"Of course . . . Sahne. I knew him well! First class."

John swallowed.

"I thought he was dead," he said.

Karl Von Wiegand was the last of his breed. He was a contemporary of and had been hired by W. R. Hearst, Sr., at some improbable time in the remote past. He broke one of the biggest stories of World War I: the German decision in 1916 to wage unrestricted U-boat warfare on all shipping. The decision, coming as it did a year after the sinking of the *Lusitania* (which claimed 1,195 lives, of which 128 were Americans) did much to end America's neutrality and send her into the war.

He had astonishing contacts in the Germany of that period. Many years later, Hal Boyle of the AP and I called on him at his estate, in the shadow of the pyramids, when the sun was low enough on the horizon. He was in his eighties, and almost totally blind, but still dapper, dauntless, aggressively goatee'd, and eager to relive his moments as an intimate of greats. It was not always easy to follow his train of thought because he assumed that his listeners had been on the same first-name basis that he had enjoyed with long-gone world figures. A treasured sample:

"I'll not forget the day Willie said to me, 'My dear Wiegand, tell Papa we've lost this war. Everytime I try to tell him, he gets furious at me.' "

I looked at Boyle and Boyle looked at me. One of us had to ask the crazy question.

"Willie who?" I said, weakly.

"Crown Prince Wilhelm, of course!" the old gentleman snapped impatiently.

Von Wiegand and his close friend Lady Drummond Hay made a spectacular trip around the world in 1929 in the Graf Zeppelin, commanded by Hugo Eckener and financed by the elder Hearst. The rise of Hitler in Germany gave von Wiegand so few qualms that INS clients began asking embarrassing questions about where his sympathies really lay. After World War II von Wiegand found Generalissimo Franco a figure deserving of weekly ovations in print, which offended liberal clients along the INS wire. Still later, when he moved to Cairo because he believed the sun and the dry heat would preserve his life indefinitely, von Wiegand commenced a lengthy infatuation with Nasser—which offended Jewish readers. And, worse, advertisers. After Seymour Berkson gained sufficient power in INS, he quietly dropped von Wiegand from the wire. His output during the last period of his life was airmailed, not cabled, and appeared in obscure sections of the Hearst Sunday papers.

Another star, spaced several million light years away from the run of us at INS, was Gobind Behari Lal, born in Delhi, one-time science professor at Hindu College, University of Punjab, hired by the elder Hearst in 1925 for the San Francisco *Examiner,* and co-winner of a Pulitzer Prize for science writing. His comings and goings as science editor of INS were scurries, not visitations. He would pop in, drop his copy on the news desk, smile timidly, and off he'd go. No one seemed to know where he went, or lived, but the legend grew that when he was not in the office, he affected a turban. And burned incense.

Then there was Les Conklin, much better known to one element of INS's readership than either von Wiegand or Gobind Behari Lal. He made our racing selections, even wrote a book or two on how to beat the races. Les lived somewhat less splendidly than the stereotype of a successful horseplayer. One night, after some formal function, Berkson dropped into the office to see how things were running. Les was sound asleep on a thin mattress he had spread on a table containing stories and flimsies either already filed or awaiting dispatch on the wire. Berkson's roar of indignation at this flophouse aura awakened Conklin, who had something about him faintly reminiscent of the wispy shabbiness of Charlie Chaplin. Les tried to explain, but Seymour thundered him into silence, then loudly berated the ever-patient Ferd Goodfellow for permitting such conduct.

Several nights after that, Carver spotted Berkson having a brandy at the Pen and Pencil, alone. That was always the best time to get through to Seymour, who was at most other times one of the most accomplished nonlisteners in history. Seizing upon this rare moment of mellowness, Lawton explained about Conklin: Les had worked out an arrangement for beating the high cost of drinking and low INS pay by making a deal with the Snug Bar and Grill down Forty-fifth Street from the office. He could drink all he wanted and eat periodically for a stipulated weekly amount. Certain, but insufficient, sleeping privileges were also thrown into the flat rate. Les bought a bedroll and would tote it each night from the Snug Bar and Grill to INS. When he had finished his racing selections and whatever else he had to do, he'd turn in for a few hours sleep at INS.

"Thereby making himself available for duty at all times," Lawton finished. Seymour ordered another brandy, and before the evening was finished, the whole arrangement seemed to make sense to him.

There was only one mishap in INS's career as a rooming house. One night Les rolled over in his sleep and squashed the spare pint of martinis resting in a paper container at his side. The cascade immersed a pile of flimsies ready to be moved on the wire. They had to be peeled apart and spread around various desk tops and even on the floor, to dry, before they could be discernible again. Held things up a bit, and when Faris heard about it, he shot off a memo to the desk stating that if things of this nature happened any more around there, well, there'd be some changes made.

In many respects our most remarkable man was Lou Allwell. He held half a dozen titles, including office manager, the vaguest of his portfolios. Lou's activities sometimes overlapped. He strolled into his friend Carver's sports department one night, shortly before it was converted into the ladies' room, and while the man on duty with the overnight work had his back turned, Lou put a match to the newspapers strewn all over the place. Then he walked out. So did the man on duty.

Lou was one of the first to return to the scene of the fire, and played a gallant role in putting it out. Inevitably, the next day brought a memo to Allwell—not as the arsonist but as office manager—asking for an estimate on the loss in flimsy "books" and carbon paper in the sports department fire. Allwell assessed the loss at less than a dollar and ordered posted still another memo about carelessness with matches.

Lou made the most interesting barroom bets in my experience: odd little wagers such as betting he could eat a dozen saltine crackers without taking a sip of liquid before Carver could run around the block and return to the bar. This turned out more spectacularly than planned. It was dead of night and Carver, lumbering up the deserted grade of pavement from Forty-sixth and Third to Forty-sixth and Second encountered a cop. The cop said "Halt!" Carver kept running. The cop gave chase. Carver couldn't explain. He'd need all his breath to win the bet. He was close to a heart attack, and perhaps a cop's bullet through the back, as he stumbled into the Pen and Pencil followed by the Law. Allwell was close to apoplexy. His eyes bulged. His mouth and chin were splattered with half-chewed cracker crumbs. He still had two crackers in his hand. When he tried to speak he made a sound like a man gargling ashes.

The Cop settled for a beer. We heard later that he had resigned.

After a long lunch at the Pen and Pencil, one day when the rain was coming down by the buckets, the question of getting back to work was reluctantly brought up. That, naturally, suggested a bet to Allwell. He bet the magnificent proprietor, John C. Bruno, he could run all the way up Forty-fifth Street to INS, backwards.

"And on one foot," he added.

John swore excitedly that he would buy everyone in sight a drink if Lou achieved such a miracle.

Lou opened a borrowed umbrella with the flair of a circus tightrope walker, gave a mighty leap backward on one leg, somehow retained his balance, and sloshed and slopped away on his mad race.

"He was doing great until he got a bad break," Carver later reported. "A cab splashed up to the curb beside him. Louie made the mistake of looking up. He found himself staring into Berkson's stupefied glare. This proved unnerving. Louie slipped and sprawled into a puddle, all snarled up with his broken umbrella. In a state of shock, Berkson ordered the cab to proceed, and Allwell came back to the Pen and Pencil to argue with Bruno over the bet. Allwell took the stand that he hadn't lost, really, because an outsider had interfered with his performance in a contest of skill and daring."

Allwell played an incomparable role at INS on national election nights. He set up a series of tables half as long as the deck of an aircraft carrier and divided the table space into sections reserved for returns from each of the states. Then he drew and tacked up an impressive chart which only he seemed able to decipher. He hired extra copyboys, laid in a supply of sandwiches, and kept the coffee-runners running. Our election headquarters lacked only one requisite: complete election returns. There wasn't enough of INS spread around the country to amass comprehensive tallies, identify trends, and obtain significant prognostications from the king-makers. We borrowed what we could from the *Mirror,* which had its own staff and a much more comprehensive coverage of AP and UP.

But somehow we held our own against these impossible odds—and sometimes we would breeze out in front. I wrote our night leads (for A.M. papers) for the 1952 and 1956 elections. Long before the polls closed in the West I'd yell across the room to Allwell, "Give me a projection, Lou." Lou would take his feet off a table, finish a soggy cup of coffee, riffle through the spiked flimsies of depressingly early returns from a few key states, look at his Rosetta stone chart, take a hot drag on his cigarette and say something like, "Ike by six million popular votes, and let's say four hundred fifty electoral votes." And I'd pound out a new lead. Lou was better than a Univac, and could run backwards on one leg to boot. Today's TV networks spend millions on what Lou gave INS for nothing.

I inherited that task of writing the election leads, something of an honor around our shop. The role had been played for some years previous by Bill Hutchinson, head of our Washington bureau, close friend of many national political figures, and one of the most sublimely pigheaded newspapermen I've ever met. His shouts and dark rages terrorized the Washington bureau. The only man there who was able to present even a slightly alternative point of view without being devoured was Art Herman. Most of the others, and they were good men, longed for friendlier fields in which to browse. But they stood in awe of Hutch's zeal and accomplishments as a lone wolf reporter and friend of the mighty on Capitol Hill, the White House, the FBI—and the Washington Redskins. The Iron Chancellor of INS-Washington was a slavering fan of that professional football team. He regarded owner George Preston Marshall's invitation to sit on the Redskin bench during a game as highly as he did his great newsbeats.

Hutch never worried too much about his troops' feelings.

He arrived in San Francisco in the heady spring of 1945 several days in advance of the opening of the assembly of fifty nations which cemented the United Nations, a not ill-considered verb. Jack Hanley whisked him to the hall, hard by the scene of the delegate meetings, where all the major news services of the world as well as all the great dailies and the news weeklies had leased space and set up on-the-spot bureaus. Hanley had wangled what all conceded to be the best space in the building. He had rented desks, typewriters, file cases, and had installed two teletype machines all geared and wired into the INS lines that reached across the land.

"Tear it out," Hutch said, in the sternly thin-lipped manner of a man who has just been grievously affronted.

"But Hutch, it's the best spot. . . ."

"Rip it up," Hutch thunderously ordered. "We'll work out of the regular bureau."

The regular bureau, housed in a forgotten wing of an almost as forgotten Hearst afternoon paper, the *Call-Bulletin,* was located on Howard Street. It did not matter that Howard Street lay in darkest Skid Row. Its bums had been netted by the police and placed elsewhere in escrow, so that delicate UN delegates from, say, Belorussia would not be offended by the sight of them. What mattered to Jack and the rest of us was that Hutch arbitrarily was screwing up our operation, making it even more difficult to compete with the better-manned, or at least more-manned, AP and UP.

Just as arbitrarily, Hutch changed his mind. There was a small marshmallow deep inside him, like the liquid core of a tough golf ball. It exerted itself in odd ways. He was very tough at the meeting he called on the first day he was in San Francisco. He laid down the law, and the assignments, to the Washington staffers who had come out for the story, and in the same tones that had given some of them ulcers and most of them shakes. Finally, he came to me, an outlander from INS-New York. He had given out all the possible assignments, including the job of writing the night lead, to his Washington staffers.

"What are *you* out here for?" Hutch asked.

It was a logical enough question, but I just didn't like the way he said it.

"To write the night lead," I said.

"The night lead, on a story like this?" he asked. "You're a sportswriter." He made it sound like a dirty word. So I went to the San Francisco Press Club, then unquestionably the world's best, to commune with its dollar steaks and twenty-five-cent Scotch.

The next morning at nine my phone at the Palace Hotel awakened me. It was Hutch. He was angry.

"Where the hell are you?" he demanded.

"In bed." After all, I had nothing to do but write a column, hours later.

"In bed! Don't you realize it's noon in New York and Washington and the A.M. wire is opening? Get the hell over here and start your night lead."

There was another day when Hutch made a greater mistake. He buzzed into the temporary bureau, leaned over the superbly groomed shoulder of Inez Robb as she was writing her column, and after a brief kibitzing job said, "What's *that* crap?"

Inez sprang to her feet, livid.

"How *dare* you!" she shrieked at what was probably the rudest man she had met in her newspaper life. Hutch flinched, genuinely startled by her reaction. Later he asked one of his Washington staff, "Why would she blow her top like that? What did I say that hurt her feelings?" He was flabbergasted.

Hutch was an incorrigible Republican, and that's how I wound up with his traditional job of writing the election leads. In November of 1948 he moved on New York with selected members of his Washington staff to handle the outcome of the contest between the overwhelming favorite, Gov. Tom Dewey, and the poor White House incumbent President Harry S. Truman. Hutch had no need for or confidence in the clairvoyance of Lou Allwell. Dewey would win—big. Hutch's leads reflected that conviction from the start, though INS prided itself in being as impartial as Charles Evans Hughes, once described by Bugs Baer as being so impartial that he even parted his beard down the middle.

I was assigned to cover Dewey's headquarters at the Roosevelt Hotel on the night of the election. I arrived at 8 P.M. and found things quite festive. Dewey workers were beginning to assemble in the ballroom for the victory celebration. There could be nothing less. The Democratic forces were hopelessly split among the President, former Vice President Henry Wallace, heading the Progressive ticket splinter, and Sen. Strom Thurmond, leader of the States Rights ticket.

Through much of the long night that followed, and as the orchids began to wilt on the fine committeewomen, some of whom surely had posed for Helen Hokinson, campaign manager Herbert Brownell made periodic descents from the candidate's suite aloft in the hotel to assure party-worker and press that things looked good. It seemed that every time he re-entered the elevator to be borne aloft, an AP printer that had been installed at the headquarters crackled out another bulletin indicating that Harry Truman, the 15 to 1 shot, was (1) not being swamped as the pollsters had predicted, and (2) was taking a pretty commanding lead.

No such heresy, of course, was getting on the INS wire. Hutch was in command. His leads had Dewey on the brink, verge, edge of a colossal triumph which would restore constitutional government, rout rascals, revitalize free enterprise, clean up the mess. And so it went through the night in a few selected circles, notably on the INS wire, at the Chicago *Tribune,* which went to press with a "Dewey Wins" edition that became a collector's item, and in the running radio commentary of H. V. Kaltenborn. At the Roosevelt, we knew differently. For one thing, Brownell had been commanded to make no more appearances. But more importantly, the photographers had ruled that it was all over. They staged pictures showing the night-charwoman shift tearing posters of the determined-looking candidate from the walls of Dewey headquarters, and other shots of brooms sweeping torn pictures and brave campaign quotes and pledges into trash bins. I kept the office alerted to these goings on.

Shortly before noon of the next day, Jim Hagerty, Dewey's press secretary, emerged from the elevator and headed for the crowded newsroom. He had a folded sheet of paper, like hotel stationery, in his hand. I picked up the phone that connected me immediately with the INS news desk. A voice said, "INS."

"Dewey concedes!" I said. "Flash it . . . bulletin it . . . something. Let's get going." I was conjuring a lead. After a moment I realized that there had been no rattle of activity on the other end.

"Did you get that?" I shouted. "Dewey concedes. Get cracking."

"Who's this?" the voice asked. I had been on duty and on and off the phone for sixteen hours. Alone.

"It's me—Considine," I said angrily. "Who the hell do you think it is? Now get going, goddam it. Dewey concedes." I could see Hagerty from where I was phoning. He was advancing into the mass of reporters and was obviously about to read whatever was written on the paper he held.

"This is Paul Allerup, Bob," the voice of INS said. "I just came on. I didn't know you. . . ."

"Paul, for Christ's sake get it on the wire: 'Dewey concedes.' "

There was an interminable delay, then Paul said, "How can we say Dewey concedes? Hutch's last lead has him out in front and. . . ."

I don't remember what I said, but it must have been a substantial enough oath to get Dewey's concession on the wire—three or four minutes after it might have been. The next week, *Editor & Publisher* carried a shameless INS advertisement, written by Berkson. It was one of those "First Again" blurbs which spread their bright pinfeathers through that pious blat. Glumly reading the ad, threaded with praise more fitted to describe a turn in the affairs of the Battle of the Bulge, I learned that INS had scored a "notable one-minute beat" over AP and UP on Dewey's concession. Berkson wrote something else about that time: a memo, as confidential as the recipe for the A-bomb, stating that thereafter the election leads would no longer be the automatic assignment of Bill Hutchinson. That's how I fell into, or rose to, the slot.

Hutch and Berkson had one strong trait in common: Either could inspire great wrath in a reporter, then turn it away. At five o'clock one afternoon at INS I decided that I had taken all I could tolerate from Seymour. I stood up, ready to do vulgar battle with him in the newsroom. At eight o'clock I was at his apartment at a black tie affair for some real or imagined client, and we were happily chatting over one of his most civilized martinis.

The day General MacArthur flew from San Francisco to Washington, where he was to make his "Old Soldiers Never Die" speech to the joint session of Congress the following day, I was one of twenty reporters invited by Rex Smith of American Airlines to "race" the General's Constellation across the country in American's first DC-6B. We covered MacArthur's speech and reception at San Francisco, then were rushed to the airport behind him, witnessed his takeoff for Washington, wrote our stories, filed them with Western Union, and boarded the DC-6B. It took off a half hour behind MacArthur, made what was then an extraordinary nonstop flight across the country, and reached Washington a half an hour before Col. Tony Story brought in the General's plane. It was still short of midnight in Washington. I realized with a slight shock that this was probably the first time on record that a reporter had covered two stories on opposite coasts within the same calendar day. I got to a phone and called INS-Washington. Hutch, of all people, answered. He was alone in the office, except for the teletype operator, for some unfathomable reason.

"Hutch, this is Considine. I've got a story I'd like to dictate about . . ."

"Get off the goddam phone!" Hutch bellowed. He seemed to be typing while he cursed me.

I tried again: a brief summary about what a unique gimmick it would be to have San Francisco *and* Washington datelines and by-lines by the same fellow, same day. . . .

"Will you get off the goddam phone?" Hutch shouted. It had been a long hard day for me. So I shouted, too. It was one of those senseless outbursts born of the twin devils of wounded pride and frustration. When I had finished, I could still hear typing for a time. Then Hutch spoke, and his voice was as tired as mine, but softer.

"Will you get off the goddam phone and let me finish the piece I'm doing under your by-line?" he asked. "We've been rolling with it since your goddam plane landed ten minutes ago."

Those two died like flashbulbs: one moment blazing, the next moment forever spent. Hutch, who was told little or nothing about the plan to shut down INS, read the abrupt announcement, went home, and died of a heart attack later that day. Berkson's heart gave off a warning skip not too long after that, but not particularly from any pang resulting from the death of INS. Seymour by that time had wired all of his built-in dynamos to the *Journal American,* as its publisher, and the paper was reflecting his tremendous drive and energy. Reluctantly, he consented to enter a San Francisco hospital for a check-up before returning to New York. On January 4, 1959, he called his assistant publisher, Charles Gould, with a long list of things he wanted done in the next day's paper.

"Seymour, for Pete's sake, I've taken care of all that," Gould said with a patient laugh. "Relax."

To ask Seymour Berkson to relax, really relax, was tantamount to telling him to get out of the news business, or roll over and die. Which is precisely what he did moments after talking to Gould.

"INS was a last frontier of the news business . . . free and easy, adventurous, awkward, short-handed, and constantly caught in money downholds," Carver elegized. Then he added:

> It was replete with all manner of harassments, including trends in office politics, and composed of an assortment of solid performers and misfits unsurpassed for talent and lack of it. Nothing made the slightest sense until you became accustomed to the contradictions. INS would spend thousands of dollars on a major story—"hit the big ones hard"—and then slash expenses in a panic so sweeping that Alwell would be confronted with a box of pencils only three-fourths used and berated for the office's extravagant waste.
>
> Berkson deplored office drinking, but learned to live with it as an epidemic he could not escape. Occasionally, he had reason to take a firm stand, such as the time our Western Union chief, Tom Walsh, enraged because Seymour had ordered some long story sent in by Postal Telegraph, deposited a large and very dead fish on Berkson's desk, with a thud. Another time he was vexed when, upon pulling out a paper towel in the men's room the rack flew open and a bottle of whisky fell out and hit him on the foot. He limped back into the newsroom letting it be known on all sides that if that ever happened again, well, disciplinary action would be taken.
>
> Drinking never seemed to interfere greatly with the flow of our wire. There was that Saturday afternoon when George Lait,

sitting in our Sunday desk with a monumental hangover, survived a shock that would have unsprung a lesser man: Gobind Behari Lal tiptoed out of his hiding place behind a file case and put down under George's nose at least a dozen books of copy. It was our science editor's pleasure to announce exclusively in this Sunday feature that science had solved one of mankind's most baffling puzzles: how to make practical use of urine.

George held his head in his hands for a time and prayed. He was also handling a bulletin story out of Washington, requiring New York follow-ups, and some big local story had burst in his face. George's staff, consisting of a cable-writer, wire-filer, and an officeboy to make up flimsy books, was two-thirds missing. Only the officeboy was visible. George ordered him to search the neighborhood bars for the cable-writer and wire-filer. The boy found them but he got drunk with them and didn't come back for a long time. Finally, people began drifting in, and George not only had his sparse Sunday staff but volunteers from the dayside, all pitching in. He borrowed two dollars from the sports department for dinner, drank it, returned to the office, and made a very touching talk. He said that this staff was undoubtedly the finest ever in any news-gathering organization. He vowed to call The Chief himself at San Simeon, first thing Monday morning, and get raises for everybody. Then he went to sleep peacefully, lulled by the fine sound of stories moving out on our teletypes.

The resourcefulness of INS men was seldom rewarded, but we rolled with the punches.

On his own initiative, and with his own money, Carver went to Boston once to play a horse he liked and to see his beautiful wife's relatives. While there, he wrote a superb feature about Don Meade, once a top jockey, then barred from the track "for life," but by this time attempting a comeback by the lowly route of exercise boy. Later that same day Carver attended a civic reception for Billy Southworth, who had been named manager of the Boston Braves, and persuaded him to write a signed story at no expense to INS. Lawton also wrote a couple of columns with a New England flavor, filed the whole batch, and an important client—the Yankee Network—sent a grateful wire to Berkson. When Carver returned to his New York desk the next day there was a memo from Berkson, congratulating him heartily on his string of exclusives. The memo had been sent via Faris' office, and Barry had added a P.S. It read: "Good job—*with some prodding.*"

The expense account Carver rendered after covering the America's Cup races off Newport was, of course, exorbitant. One item that repeatedly appeared was "Launch—$50." The account bounced Allwell.

"Louie, we've still got a horse on our books, bought by Damon Runyon when he was chasing Pancho Villa," Faris said. "We own an armed mule train Red Knickerbocker bought in Ethiopia. We're still carrying that Chinese junk Floyd Gibbons picked up in Hong Kong. Now Carver has added a fleet of launches. Looks like we're in the transportation business, mostly. Find out what it's all about."

Allwell found occasion to bring it up to Carver at the Pen and Pencil.

"The launch bit doesn't make any sense," he said. "Faris knows that you worked on the cutter the Coast Guard gave to the press. Remember me? I got your credentials for you."

"I still needed a launch every day," Carter said.

"But why?"

Lawton looked at his friend steadily.

"For shallow water," he said.

Allwell nodded sagely. And okayed the account.

INS covered several big and expensive stories in 1938, including Chamberlain at Munich, but one it skimped on turned out to be a triumph. Carver, about to cover the Poughkeepsie Regatta, was told that he must somehow get along without a wire at the finish line. Seems it would cost $150 to string it from a Western Union shack located on the Hudson shore about midway between the start and finish of the four-mile stretch. Resignedly, Carver chose the shack as the place he would work. He would not be able to see either start or finish of the eight-oared shell classic, but he could file into New York from there. And the AP and UP stories, sent from down at the finish line, had to come through there. With a little bit of luck . . .

Rain and choppy water delayed the race until near dark. Carver couldn't even see the crews as they swept past the Western Union shack. He went back to his blind spot and struck up an easy friendship with the shack's other occupants, venerable Western Union operators.

In time, two operators' old fashioned keys, using empty Prince Albert tobacco tins as amplifiers, came to life. AP and UP were flashing from the finish line: "Navy wins."

Carver looked over a cooperative operator's shoulder, sent the flash to INS on his own wire and began beating out a story about the big upset. Navy had not been given a chance by the experts. Either California or Washington would surely win.

Carver's story was rolling into INS-New York at a good clip when AP and UP had a violent change of heart at the finish line: "Kill Navy flash. California wins." A dismal silence then fell upon their wires. Carver sighed. Too much was too much. He continued with his story about Navy's dramatic victory over a storm-tossed Hudson in the face of stunning odds. Etc. What he was writing, in effect, was "To hell with INS" and its blind economies.

Then still another flash from AP and UP: "Kill California flash. Navy wins." Carver's story was so far along by that time and winning so many friends on the news desks of scores of client papers which also took AP and UP, that he had gotten down into the "color" of the victory: ". . . while the lights of battlecraft along the murky course blinked their salute. . . ."

Drenched, pooped, Carver returned to the office late that night, chiefly to type out a note of resignation. There was a memo in his typewriter. It was a flattering note from one of INS's most gifted writers, Walter Kiernan, who did not know Carver had been denied the advantage of a wire at the finish line. Kiernan's note congratulated Lawton for his "fast and excellent story written under pressure."

The *"under pressure,"* he figured later, was what prompted Carver to change his mind about quitting. He went to the Pen and Pencil instead.

INS lost some close ones, too.

On Monday, May 7, 1945, AP-London flashed the end of the war in Europe, followed by a two-hundred-word bulletin, and then a long and stirring account by correspondent Ed Kennedy of the surrender scene at the "little red schoolhouse" at Reims. It swept the world, sent millions spilling into the streets to celebrate. At San Francisco, the word was brought into the delivery room of the infant UN by a roly-poly Latin American delegate who disrupted a meeting by waddling up and down the aisles waving an Extra which had just spun off the presses of the *Call-Bulletin.* He kept shouting in incoherent and apoplectic Spanish. Joy reigned in the hopeful "parliament of man," and through the world. But not at INS. Or UP. Or any other news service. We had suffered a colossal beating. Only AP had the top story of the age.

At INS-New York, Jack Oestreicher, our foreign director, was in need of being tied down. He knew we had been double-crossed, but for an interminable two or three hours could not pin down the circumstances. The best we could do in the face of the masterful story by Kennedy was to speak of it on our own wire as an unconfirmed report and guardedly question its authenticity. That was not very convincing. Kennedy's story was complete, down to the names of the American, British, Soviet, and French officers who had presided over the surrender of the abject remnants of Hitler's general staff.

The most careful precautions had been taken and the most solemn assurances given on all sides before that to guard against a recurrence of Roy Howard's solo flight ending of World War I. U.S. editors had been told by Byron Price, the chief censor, that no announcement about Germany's surrender could be considered official unless it came either from General Eisenhower's SHAEF or a simultaneous broadcast by President Truman, Prime Minister Churchill and Premier Stalin.

Oestreicher had received a tantalizing message from Joe Smith, who was at SHAEF, several hours before the AP's bombshell. Smith messaged that Jimmy Kilgallen had left Paris. Period. Then Joe began a story that smacked of something much more significant than its subject matter, which, of course, had had to pass through the SHAEF censor's office. Joe wrote that Monday had dawned "almost like the birth of peace in Europe, with brilliant Spring sunshine flooding Paris." Shortly before Kennedy's story broke, Smith sent Oestreicher another pregnant message. It said simply that Jack could eliminate the word "almost" from his earlier story.

At San Francisco we gathered miserably around our INS printer, hours after AP's great beat. The word from Washington was that President Truman was about to make a statement. It could only be confirmation that the AP was right.

The bells rang inside the chattering machine. Then: "FLASH—WAR NOT OVER—HST."

We gave vent to a savage yell of joy. It was Inez Robb who brought us to our senses.

"What the hell are we cheering for?" she asked. Her husband, Ad Robb, was serving overseas.

When the official word came through from SHAEF the next day, it was a fat letdown. AP's promotion department crowed loudly over the scoop. But other sounds, shouts of betrayal, began to filter through from Ed Kennedy's colleagues. The full story pieced itself together as SHAEF censorship relaxed:

Seventeen correspondents, including our man Kilgallen, were flown from Paris to Reims May 6. They were permitted to watch Hitler's dream of a Thousand Year Reich end with the quavering signature of Adm. Karl Doenitz and the nervous silence of Adm. Gen. Hans Georg von Friedeberg, who was soon to commit suicide. The actual signing was at 2:41 A.M., May 7, Reims time. Brig. Gen. Frank Allen, in charge of the correspondents, briefed them pointedly on their responsibility. They could write their flashes, two-hundred-word bulletins, and as much of a story as they wanted to write. These could be deposited with Press Wireless at the Hôtel Scribe in Paris, to be held for release until SHAEF's consent or the aforementioned Big Three broadcast. All present gave their pledges.

Kilgallen and Kennedy, with their stories written and neatly enveloped, were in the first of the correspondents' cars that pulled up to the hotel late that morning of May 7, Paris time. The worthy competitors hit the curb before the car stopped rolling, burst through the door and headed across the lobby for the steps leading up to Press Wireless. Each wanted to get his flash, bulletin, and lead into the "Hold for Release" basket first—believing that the news would be moved on a first-come-first-served basis, when the time came to move it.

"Ed was gaining on me," Kil recalled a long time later. "He had longer legs than I did, which didn't seem fair. So I did a bad thing. I lobbed my typewriter at him, like a discus thrower. It was Faris' portable, come to think of it, but I knew he wouldn't mind. It caught Ed on the back of his legs and down he went. I shot past him, up the steps, and plunked down my story first: flash, bulletin of two hundred words, and thirty-one typewritten pages. Ed came in second, limping. I felt sorry about what I had done. They wouldn't allow that kind of thing at Aqueduct," the inveterate horseplayer was to muse in distant retrospect.

Kennedy exacted a terrible revenge. Learning (he said later) that the Flensburg radio had announced the Reims signing, Ed called AP-London through an Army switchboard, whose people had not been alerted to the lid that had been placed on the story, and dictated his flash, bulletin, and story from carbon copies he had made of his escrowed original. AP-London put a Reims dateline on everything and spread it through the world.

AP's pride of achievement was short-lived. Robert McLean, president and publisher of the Philadelphia *Bulletin,* and serving as president of the AP at the time, frigidly rebuked those in AP who permitted Kennedy's story to be released. AP-New York quickly cancelled its credit-taking promotion campaign. It pulled the red rug from under its conquering hero and cast him into exterior darkness. Years later, after serving out his time in a remote AP bureau and a quiet period on California papers, Kennedy met death most prosaically. He stepped off a curb and was hit by a car. The obits raked over his "shame." None of the dour last hurrahs that I saw got around to mentioning that if the AP had not chickened out on him, had stood by him as staunchly as, say, Faris stood by Kilgallen on the Hauptmann verdict, Ed would have been remembered as an intrepid reporter who saw his duty to his organization and answered the call.

If I could have afforded it, I would have paid INS to let me work for it. It was such a joy, over and above the frustrations. At INS, everything happened in Technicolor, and wide screen. . . .

We all trembled over Louella Parsons' bold announcement on the INS wire from Hollywood that Ingrid Bergman had an excellent reason for leaving hearth and home to marry her Italian director, Roberto Rossellini: she was pregnant by him. We trembled even more when there were indignant denials from the principals, the studios, and Louella's rivals. At the height of the tension, Louella returned home late one night to find her husband, Dr. Harry Martin, one of the most delightfully irreverent men in the nation, kneeling at his bedside reciting the Rosary. She dropped to his side, petrified that he was dying.

"Docky . . . Docky, what are you doing saying the Rosary?" she cried. "What's wrong?"

"Nothing," Docky said. "I was just saying a prayer that Ingrid *is* knocked up." *

INS had some homely reporters working for it, but not its girls. We had Inez, a good-looking woman who could type with her long

* She was.

white gloves in place, if the occasion warranted. And, whenever we could spring her from the *Journal American,* we had the services of Dorothy Kilgallen, whose face and style and keen mind were to be known to television's millions, too. We had Lee Carson, Phyllis Battelle, Dixie Tighe, and Peggy Diggins, all made to make men's heads wheel. And pert, pretty Rita Hume whose high school cheer leader looks and demeanor were misleading. She battled her way to Dongo, on Lake Como, on April 28, 1945, to see Mussolini, the life riddled out of him, strung up by his heels, and sent out the first story.

We had Doris Duke working for us briefly, too, for twenty-five dollars a week. The irrepressible Michael Chinigo, the Yale-trained Albanian who was the dominant figure in Roman journalism during his years with INS, put the richest girl in the world on the payroll and arranged with Col. Tex McCrary of the Eighth Air Force to get her to Berlin. There, at a dinner celebrating the short but sweet accord between the Soviet and American conquerors, Tex proposed a toast to a Russian woman tank-commander who was present. In response, the ranking Russian officer rose and proposed a toast to Doris.

"To a typical American girl," he said, probably the rarest compliment she was ever paid.

When our man at the Aly Khan-Rita Hayworth wedding, Irving R. Levine, filed the final words of stories of the nuptials by himself, Louella Parsons, Jack Lee, Elie Maissi, and whoever else we had buzzing around Cannes, he received a fond salute from Larry Klingman and Gerald Green, who handled the story at INS-New York.

"Mazeltov," they cabled him—a word breathed upon newly wedded couples by their Jewish relatives and friends which means "Good life." Faris appeared at their desk the next day, waving his "Mazeltov" flimsy and wanting to know what was going on around there. The boys explained that they were congratulating Levine and the others in simple, word-saving, money-saving Hebrew. Faris was pleased.

INS was sometimes accused by its jealous competitors of being edited by remote control, or osmosis. Actually, our stories were combed quite thoroughly, but never as completely as when the desk was manned by Paul Allerup. Hardly any lead ever really pleased Paul. Once, when an angry writer viewed a story Paul had dissected remorselessly, he cried, "You'd edit Shakespeare!"

Paul considered that for a searching moment. Then nodded.

"His stuff could have been tightened," he muttered.

But Paul did like at least one lead. It had been written for him without his knowledge by Klingman and Green as a gag, after they had wrapped up a story of a big plane crash in India. Before Paul came to work the next morning they slipped it into the pile of flimsies which had moved out during the night, sure that his eye would fall upon it. The eye did. It purported to be an eyewitness account of the crash:

By Ali Ben Ghouli

World Copyright, International News Service

The ways of Allah are mysterious indeed. . . .

"My God, what a great lead on this eyewitnesser," Paul exclaimed. "How did we ever get it from a guy in a rice paddy?"

We lost good men for bad reasons. Saul Pett left INS because Berkson insisted that the real lead of Saul's vivid account of the crash of a B-25 into the uppermost reaches of the Empire State Building was not the uniqueness of the collision but the number of persons killed: seven. Saul's fine work thereafter graced the AP wire.

Sid Eiges, a first-class man with responsible duties on the overnight desk, was being paid only seventy dollars a week. He asked Joe Connolly for a five-dollar raise. Joe mentioned it to Faris. Barry didn't like the chain of command Sid had used in his forlorn quest, and said so sharply to Sid. Sid quit, and eventually had to settle for a fifty-thousand-dollar-a-year job as a vice president of NBC.

One night Les Conklin failed to show up on time. Klingman called the Snug and learned that Les was asleep in his room over the bar, a room furnished mainly with a cot and his racing charts, past performance sheets, and losing parimutuel tickets. Larry called the police and reported that a man named Les Conklin was operating a bookie joint in bold defiance of the law in a little room over the Snug.

Les reported for work an hour later, carrying his bedroll, a carton of martinis, and his racing notes.

"Damnedest thing just happened to me," he said to Larry. "The cops busted in on me and accused me of running a bookie joint. They were going to lock me up until I managed to convince them that I worked for INS."

"How did you prove that?" Larry asked.

ABOVE: Bob Considine interviewing Henry Ford II
BELOW: With Gen. Douglas MacArthur

ABOVE: Considine and Gen. Jonathan M. Wainwright working on *General Wainwright's Story*. LEFT: Flying over the hump—India to China—June, 1945

RIGHT: Westbrook Pegler and Mrs. Franklin D. Roosevelt (*seated*); Deems Taylor and George Bye (*standing*). BELOW: Pat Morin, Jack Woliston, and Considine at Sing Sing prison to witness the execution of the Rosenbergs, June 19, 1953

ABOVE: Considine with Frank Conniff and William Randolph Hearst, Jr., interviewing Nikita Khrushchev, Moscow, 1957. BOTTOM LEFT: Considine and Babe Ruth celebrating the publication of *The Babe Ruth Story*. BOTTOM RIGHT: Boarding a plane with Toots Shor

ABOVE: President Dwight D. Eisenhower greeting Considine. BELOW: Frank Conniff and Considine discussing the latter's book, *It's the Irish,* with President John F. Kennedy, August, 1961

ABOVE: Considine and William R. Hearst, Jr., in a helicopter over the Mekong Delta, 1963
BELOW: Considine chatting with the Duke of Windsor

TOP LEFT: Watching an atomic bomb test at Yucca Flat, Nevada
TOP RIGHT: Considine with his wife, Millie. BELOW: And with his daughter, Deborah

LEFT: Bob Considine at work. BELOW: Just before taking off at Bien Hoa, Vietnam, September, 1966

Les fumbled through his Chaplinesque suit and pulled out a small savings account book.

"I showed them this," he said, pointing to his balance. His balance was $1.40.

To stay abreast or even ahead of AP and UP frequently called for resourcefulness above and beyond the INS-ers' already considerable dedication. Good imagination also contributed. We were not above employing a jeep and a boxer dog named Butch von Hohenzollern to turn the tides of news-gathering battles with the opposition.

The jeep had been scrounged in some mysterious manner by Lee Ferrero, the only man INS had in Korea at one of the more critical phases of that war—the tug and pull of the late winter of 1950–51. Lee graciously shared his transportation with the AP and UP correspondents while covering the battling Third Division's activities in mountainous country that permitted little other means of transportation. Without warning or replacement, Lee was ordered to leave the Third Division and report thereafter from Eighth Army Headquarters in Taegu. There was no way he could take his jeep with him.

The thought of leaving all those good stories behind him was intolerable to Lee. So he made a hard but—in view of the circumstances—fair bargain with Sam Summerlin of AP. Sam could have the jeep if he kept Lee (and thus INS) informed about everything that happened to the Third Division. Sam rejected this shocking propositon. Lee shrugged. He said he was sorry, but he would be forced therefore to immobilize the jeep by taking its key and distributor head with him when he left for Taegu. That clinched it. Sam got his jeep, Lee got his news, and the word soon spread that INS was getting fine coverage out of that theater of war by means of a "talking jeep."

Butch von Hohenzollern and God helped INS score a fine beat when Robert A. Vogeler, the I.T. & T. official, was released by the Hungarian government after imprisonment on charges of spying for the United States. Barry Faris had become convinced that Marvin Stone, of INS's London bureau, had the inside track on all news about Vogeler because he was friendly with Mrs. Vogeler, a good-looking blonde who had made several dramatic pleas to the Communist government in Budapest to release her husband. Marvin made repeated efforts to assure Faris that he had no better "in" with Mrs.

Vogeler than AP or UP types assigned to the story. But when word came that Vogeler was about to be released and would be reunited with his wife and family at a villa she had rented in Vienna, Faris cabled Stone that he expected a clear beat.

As ever, AP and UP had much superior communications. Vienna was plugged into their European wire networks, with immediate transmission to London offices on tap. INS would be forced to use the overhead cable—RCA—to New York. That would take, conservatively, twenty minutes longer than the direct Vienna–London–New York wires of the competition.

Stone dispatched his one-man staff, John Fiehn, to the Austro-Hungarian border at Nickelsdorff. Fiehn got through to Stone in Vienna by phone and dictated a good story about Vogeler's release.

"How about AP and UP?" Marvin asked him.

"It's a dead heat at this end," Fiehn said. "They've got everything I got."

Resignedly Stone dashed off the story, filed it with RCA, and waited for the "rocket" from Faris—a rocket being a damning notice that the opposition had come through first. Most rockets end with a morale-shattering demand, usually, "How, please?"

One hour later, Stone received a cable from Faris. Expecting the worst, he was flabbergasted to read a message of congratulations. INS had had a clear beat of five minutes on the AP and ten minutes on the UP.

In the case of UP, a singularly precise bolt of lightning had hit and destroyed its telex antenna on the roof of the Wiener Kurier building. It had been erected to flash the news with the speed of light. Instead, the harried UP staffers had to raise Frankfurt by phone, which was time-consuming, and holler the story and details over a faulty line. It took UP thirty minutes to get the story to New York.

Butch von Hohenzollern delivered the coup de grace to the AP. Seems that on this momentous day the AP's Viennese secretary, one Effie, brought to work a particularly aromatic luncheon featuring bratwurst. She deposited the paper bag that contained the lunch at the side of her desk, resting on the telephone-connection box. A change in the wind communicated the presence of the tempting lunch to Butch, who had been asleep in INS's quarters several doors away from AP's room in the Kurier building. The boxer roused himself and went sniffing down the hall, entered AP, and made a voracious lunge for Effie's lunch just as the call came through from Nickelsdorff. In seizing the bag, Butch tore the phone box from its place, cutting off communication from the border for twenty-five minutes. AP was very angry at Butch von Hohenzollern.

"Ordinarily, that kind of stunning and undeserved luck on a story is enough to hold a man for a long time," Stone, now one of the editors of *U.S. News and World Report,* recently noted. "But in this case, we also came through with a tremendous photo beat, reflected in the full page the New York Sunday *Mirror* gave it while the Sunday *News* was dragging with some inferior shots. Ours was a memorable picture: the Vogelers reunited at the gate of their home with their two handsome boys, and the tears spilling from Vogeler's eyes.

"We had waited overly long for that picture and the oppositions had sped off to the airport with earlier stuff to make a BEA flight to Paris, whence they could radiophoto to New York. In those days there were no radiophoto facilities in Vienna. Well, we missed the BEA flight to Paris and had to put our undeveloped film on a later flight, direct to London. When New York was told that we probably would take a shellacking on photos, Sid Mautner, in charge of International News Photos, sent me a real tough rocket advising me that I was directly responsible for ruining INS's reputation around the world.

"A few hours later, however, up turned a cable of ecstatic congratulations from Mautner. Seems that the BEA flight had been grounded in some remote European airfield while our later flight sailed right on into London.

"So ended one of those rare days when, instead of putting your luck to work for INS and peanut pay, you should have been standing at the tables at Monte Carlo."

INS men *looked* right, when they had to, when nothing else would suffice.

No reporters were permitted on the clubhouse grounds one day in the early 1930's when Bobby Jones was invited to play a round with the Prince of Wales. But Tom Watson of INS-London easily made it. No one at the gate dared challenge him as he swept through in his rented chauffeur-driven limousine, smoothing his British Colonel's brush mustache, bowler cocked just so, spats, umbrella tightly sheathed, and face set in bored disdain. Phoned a fine account of the match to INS in Fleet Street.

INS was represented at the Lying In of George VI in 1952 at Sandringham, though the British and world press was specifically barred. John Carlova, whose principal claim to fame before he covered the Lying In was that his father had played piano for Helen Morgan, had the countenance of an honest choirboy. Scotland Yard's men at the Palace gate were touched when John showed up and shyly told them his story: He was an American GI who had hitchhiked for hundreds of miles to pay a simple soldier's tribute to the gentle king he had admired so greatly.

He filed his scoop to INS-London, including mention of the ruse he had used. Then with rare intuition he remained in the area. The next day Ed Korry of the UP appeared at the guarded gates and appeared to be well on his way toward being admitted, after telling a story strikingly similar to John's moist-eyed lie. Then the rug was pulled from under him. John appeared, beaming. And in good voice.

"Hi, Ed," he said, as his rival made his pitch with Scotland Yard, "how are things at the United Press?"

Rivals were always expendable, in the opinion of good INS men. But sometimes colleagues were, too. If the conditions were right, of course.

Marvin Stone was running INS's Far East operation from Tokyo when Operation Big Switch started in August, 1953, shortly after the armistice was signed wrapping up the Korean War. The one returning American POW everybody wanted to know about was Gen. William F. Dean, captured early in the war.

All communications from the press center at the prisoner-reception area were routed through the press center at Seoul and thence to the Tokyo offices of the wire services and other media maintaining offices there. There were, in addition, two or three so-called "official lines," presumably reserved for VIP's and UN personages. Stone instructed Rowland Gould, a displaced Englishman INS had picked up in Tokyo and dispatched to Korea, to try by hook or crook to get access to one of the "official" phones. It was the forlornest of hopes. But Gould apparently looked *right* to the guardians of the phones, strolled by them casually, picked one up, and called INS-Tokyo, immediately after the long press conference in which General Dean denied authorship of statements the enemy had attributed to him during his captivity and related the full account of his grueling experience. Sid White, on the Tokyo end of the wire, took ninety minutes of notes which were transformed, as they arrived, into a fine running story in money-saving cablese put together by Stone and Bob Schakne, shot to San Francisco to the waiting typewriter of bureau chief Howard Handleman, and on to the INS wire. Because all regular press lines out of Korea were hopelessly loaded down that day, INS had Dean's entire story on the desks of its clients about twelve hours ahead of the others.

When AP and UP complained about INS's unauthorized use of an official phone from Korea, Stone was called to Gen. Mark Clark's headquarters, Pershing Heights, Tokyo, on command of Lt. Col. Rodger Bankson, Clark's deputy public information officer. The following dialogue ensued:

Bankson: "OK, Marv, what'll we do about this?"

Stone: "I don't think you ought to do anything. We were just paying AP and UP back for some of their tricks in the past. And retribution is sweet."

Bankson: "I know, I know. But something has got to be done; they're asking for blood."

Stone: "Why don't you throw Gould out of Korea? After all, he hates being there. Secondly, I need him back in Tokyo. Thirdly, his wife threatens to divorce him if he doesn't get the hell out of there and get back home."

Bankson (sighing): "Officially, I didn't hear the last three parts of that statement. Okay, as of this moment, Gould has lost his Korea war accreditation until further notice. No, make that permanently. That ought to satisfy everybody."

INS had magnificent young men in the Korean War, after a bad start. And one of them had a flying machine.

In the early days there was a period of more than a week when Lee Ferrero's schedule went as follows: In the morning he covered the Eighth Army briefing at Taegu, filed his story, raced to the airfield where he had talked himself into the use of a light liaison plane, and flew to I Corps Headquarters on the Western Front. From there, after picking up the news, the plane flew Lee across the peninsula to Eastern Front Headquarters, where he mopped up more news, then the flight back to Taegu in time for the early evening Eighth Army briefing. Lee finally cried out for help, and got it. Rival newsmen wrote a song about him, set to the tune of "Mañana." A fragment of the lyrics went:

My name is Lee Ferrero
And I work for INS,
I always like to write the truth,
But the lies come out the best,
I asked for correspondents and they sent me Irwin Tress,
My name is Lee Ferrero and I work for INS.

"Neither of the slurs was justified," memos Handleman, from his *U.S. News & World Report* desk. "Lee's reporting more than stood up. And Tress, a photographer, did a fine job doubling as a reporter. In fact, Tress scored one of the greatest beats of the war—and couldn't get it on the INS wire. He sent word to the Tokyo office late in October or early November, 1950, that a handful of Chinese 'volunteers' had just been captured. The fear of China's entry into the war had come true. But the young fellow who happened to be on the desk in Tokyo that night spiked the story and told nobody about it because, as he confessed after the oppositions had beaten our brains out on the story, Tress was 'only a photographer.' "

By the spring of 1951 INS was able to field one of the finest teams of young correspondents in wire service history: Frank Conniff, later National Editor of the Hearst papers and now editor of the *World Journal Tribune;* Don Schanche, who now edits *Holiday;* Bob Schakne, with CBS-Latin America; Cecil Brownlow, with *Aviation Week;* Rafael Steinberg, a leading writer on Far East affairs; Don Dixon, production chief of National Educational Television; Irving R. Levine, with NBC-Rome; John Rich, a Japanese language officer in the Marines at Kwajalein and Iwo Jima, now with NBC-Tokyo; Frank Emery, a wonderful kid with a world of promise, who was killed; and subsequently John Casserly, now with ABC-Washington; Ed Hymoff, space expert and biographer of Lyndon Baines Johnson; Robert Elegant, later with the *New York Times;* plus Bob Horiguchi, now IBM's public relations chief for the Far East, and an astonishing group of affluent and distinguished correspondents who became known as "INS's guerrillas."

The guerrillas were of particular usefulness. They were loners, men who commanded one-man Tokyo bureaus for their estimable newspapers. When a man would pop over to Korea to cover the fighting, he needed someone back in Tokyo to handle his material and move it along to his editors. INS's Tokyo bureau was manned twenty-four hours a day by a magnificent staff of Handleman and Horiguchi. They worked twelve hours a day and perhaps another six hours of overlap. Gordon Walker of the *Christian Science Monitor* proposed to Handleman, out of the blue, that if INS would take his dictation from Korea and file his copy we could extract anything we wanted from his superb reportage. He was so pleased with the arrangement—INS was not only pleased, it was stupefied—that he urged other fellow loners to do the same, and under the same terms. As a result of his endorsement, INS soon had working for it, at not a penny's cost, such renowned correspondents as Lachie MacDonald and, later, Ward Price of the London *Daily Mail,* Bill Stevenson of the Toronto *Star,* and Denis Warner, then with a group of Australian papers. Without the gratis services of Warner and MacDonald, INS could never have competed with AP and UP on the fall of Taejon and the capture of General Dean.

Horiguchi was a marvel composed of equal parts of Japanese culture, Domei, the respected Japanese wire service that became a propaganda tool after he left it, and the University of Missouri's School of Journalism. Handleman recalls:

> Bob worked out a filing system that gave us an edge over the oppositions.
>
> All wire-service offices were on the second floor of Radio Tokyo. The cable head was a block away at the old Domei building—by 1950 called the Kyodo News Service building. By pure chance, INS was located closest to the Kyodo building. The other bureaus were strung out down a long hall in this order: Agence France-Presse, AP, and, around the corner, Reuters and UP.
>
> All copy had to be hand-carried to Kyodo—where it would be moved on a first-come-first-served basis. Official war communiqués were handed out at the door of the PIO office which was also on the second floor of Radio Tokyo.
>
> Copyboys fought like tigers to get their copies of the communiqués. It was a matter of pride—face—to grab the first copies. Our copyboy raced down the hall like a track man and relayed his two copies—like a baton—to our second copyboy crouched at the door of our office. That boy then ran through the office, dropping one copy to me at my desk in the middle of the office and the other copy on Horiguchi's desk next to the window. Then

he'd jump back to my desk, where I would be finishing the first short bulletin written on a cablegram blank previously addressed and signed. He'd snatch this, run it to Bob, and Bob would pencil-edit it, stuff it in a box and toss it out the window. We had a third copyboy waiting below. He had a bicycle, and off he'd go to the Kyodo cable head like an Olympic cyclist.

Our senior copyboys, Yoshikazu Ohmachi and Sadamu Hoseya, were remarkable kids. They spoke little English, but they taught themselves how to use our typewriters and later learned to operate the teletype machines we installed. They became so expert as teletype punchers that when the Communications Ministry finally installed teletypes at Kyodo our two boys were called on to teach the Ministry's people how to handle them.

The first time anyone in the office knew that the copyboys had learned how to type was when Ohmachi, without a word, handed me an envelope perfectly addressed to Barry Faris. He had looked over my shoulder to see who I was writing a letter to, and addressed the envelope for me. We learned a lot from our copyboys, too. There was the time I was doing a story about the Emperor, and how Japanese regarded him. Ohmachi, who could not have been more than fifteen at the time, answered several questions through an interpreter. Unwittingly, I asked a question he resented. The boy, who earned more at INS than his father earned as a laborer, squared his shoulders, stood at attention, and put his high-paying job on the line.

"You stupid foreigners never will be able to understand our love and reverence for our Emperor," he said. To Ohmachi, such a statement to the boss meant that he would be fired out of hand. But he was willing to accept that rather than remain silent after hearing what he considered to be a slight to his Emperor.

World War II's ending—or the announcement of it by AP's Ed Kennedy—shook INS. The ending of the Korean War produced an INS achievement which compressed within it all of the drive, ingenuity, and sheer delight that made it unique among the wire services. Handleman, Who Was There, remembers it best:

It was July, 1953. Our INS suite in the Nadja Apartments in Seoul was crowded with competitors, shooting the breeze. Jack Casserly walked in, looking a little odd. After a bit he told me there was a fellow down at the bar who wanted to see me. When we got out of the room he told me what he had. He had the best beat of the war, a locked-up exclusive that armistice terms had been agreed to.

Then began some play acting. The story had to be written in the room with all the competitors. My typewriter and cable blanks, carbons and so forth were there. Jack and I strolled back in and I sat down and started to write what I said was a little feature. I called Bob Elegant over to read the lead and asked him if he would word it the way I had. He suppressed his excitement, grunted something, walked slowly out of the room, then took off like a sprinter to find the Korean foreign minister. Ed Hymoff came in just then from Eighth Army Headquarters. He read what was in my typewriter, shrugged, and started a poker game as a diversion.

After the story was wrapped up—including confirmation to Elegant from the foreign minister—we got a gratifying payoff. Relaxed and happy and drinking beer, we saw four AP men race past our door toward the press office, single file, to pick up their rockets.

Time was rotten to us when we died.

It hurt us all so much that I tried to retort in my column. It went like this:

> This is an open-faced letter to the young man—anonymous as a shady story—who wrote the obituary of International News Service in the Press section of *Time* magazine.
>
> You poor guy:
>
> You write, "On a Coronation story, editors could rely on the AP for the dimensions of the cathedral, the UP for the mood of the ceremony, and the INS (sometimes) for an interview with the barmaid across the way." There is also a reference to "splash-and-dash journalism." That's about all.
>
> The men and women who sat in our silenced newsrooms and read that farewell nose-thumbing felt more than anger. Many of them were seasoned at their trade when you, in all probability, were making your first little jabs at a typewriter. Their anger was tempered by a pity for you; a pity born of the sadness that one feels in the face of flippant ignorance.
>
> For one, I thought of Floyd Gibbons going down on one of the first ships torpedoed in World War I and surviving to write a brilliant story for INS. And of Jimmy Kilgallen tracking down Samuel Insull in Greece and practically bringing him back to trial, after turning him into a kind of legman for INS. And Inez

Robb in North Africa, and some years later in Texas City, being knocked flat by an explosion, and getting off the ground to get her story in to INS. And Davis J. Walsh who helped make sportswriting a profession.

I thought of Bill Hutchinson driving the opposition nuts at the Scopes trial and getting the great wartime beats on the capture and execution of the Nazi submarine-landed saboteurs, and the decision to retain Hirohito on his throne.

I also thought of Richard Tregaskis, Jack Mahon, and Bob Brumby, on Guadalcanal; of Pat Robinson in the New Guinea jungles; of Lee Van Atta, flying on so many bombing and strafing missions that MacArthur ordered him grounded. And of the incomparable H. R. Knickerbocker and irrepressible Sammy Schulman.

The memory of Pete Huss, Frank Conniff, Larry Newman, Graham Hovey, Joe Smith, Bill Hearst, Lee Carson, Joe Willicombe, and the others who went with the troops from the beaches to Berlin filled the cranial room where proud thoughts are stored. And of Mike Chinigo, crawling to a dead German sentry's phone on the beach in Sicily, making contact with the German commander whose artillery was shelling our landing troops, and (in perfect German) ordering him to cease—". . . We have driven the enemy back into the sea." (General Truscott put Mike in for the DSC.) And of Jimmy Young rotting in a Japanese prison, and Alfred Tyrnauer dumped into one of Hitler's death cells in Vienna for courageously writing the truth.

And of Clark Lee, who started the war with the AP on Bataan and ended it with INS in Tokyo. He and Harry Brundidge of *Cosmopolitan* magazine were the only reporters present when Tojo tried to kill himself. I thought, of course, of Runyon on a murder trial, or covering an execution, or describing the burning of the Morro Castle.

I thought of brave lads like Howard Handleman and Lowell Bennett, who was shot down over Berlin and not only escaped three times, but got the only stories out of Germany—INS stories, my poor friend. And of Tregaskis, who hungered to get close enough, walking down a mountain in Italy, his busted helmet in his hand, the top of his head left somewhere up on the hill. And of Larry Meier, wounded while covering the Dieppe raid. He never recovered.

I still don't think a wonderful friend I had named Jack Singer was getting an interview with the barmaid the day the Japanese killed him. Death came to him in the wardroom of the carrier Wasp, torpedoed into a funeral pyre. A young Navy pilot who survived brought along the unfinished INS story Jack was writing and finished it for him.

There weren't any barmaids on Okinawa the day John Cashman of INS was killed in action. John had lost an arm as a serviceman, hooked on with our sports department, went back to the wars as a correspondent, and died. The first reporter killed in Korea was Ray Richards, INS, who might have been home with his grandchildren. Four other INS men were killed there, too.

Someday, son, venture out of doors and ask a couple of good men like Frank Bartholomew and Alan Gould [Editor's note: editors of UP and AP, respectively] what kind of a time they used to have when they had even an undermanned team of INS reporters competing against them on a big, fast-moving story. Someday, son, if you improve, you'll be good enough to change the ribbons on their beat-up mills.

It made some of us feel a little better.

But not much. Something dear and exciting had died in our business, never to resurrect itself.

5. *Moonlighting*

THE TOUCH of arrogance that is a part of every reporter's makeup frequently drives him into thinly related fields in which he has no marked competence. He seldom reads a book or magazine article or short story without feeling he could have written it better. He makes a note, sometimes on the back of an unpaid bill, to get cracking on some "outside work," as he likes to call it. If he carries through with his intention, he finds the going a little rougher than anticipated.

He knows in his heart (and for good reason) that he knows more about news than a vast majority of the golden-voiced, beautiful news-givers on radio and TV. But the sight of a mike or the relentless glare of a klieg light fills his soul with doubt or dread. During the 114-day newspaper strike in New York, stretching through the winter of 1962–63, the local TV and radio stations made considerable use of the city's better-known newspapermen. We were, by and large, simply awful—especially those who held the lowest opinion of electronic journalism.

I don't think I ever met a reporter who agreed that Hollywood was capable of turning out a bona fide screen reporter, or a true picture about a reporter's life and times—or anything else.

The above is presented merely as prelude to experiences I've had in all three of those fields. I've grossed a million dollars moonlighting, but only have been able to save the memories.

The person who practices daily journalism and tries writing magazine articles on the side tends to wind up doing one or the other. Doing both becomes a bloody chore, even for the prolific. Paul Gallico's success in "outside work" caused, or forced, him to close his successful sports column in the New York *Daily News*. Others who left the daily grind and did well in magazine work—men like Stanley Frank,

Charles Einstein, Quentin Reynolds, and Stewart Alsop—never hankered to return. They had conquered greener pastures. But for every successful foray there have been countless failures and blizzards of rejection slips.

Runyon rode the two horses well, turning out his daily sports column by day and his fiction about even more fictional Broadway characters by night. Bob Ruark scored very well simultaneously with his columns, slick magazine pieces, and with books as flaky as *Grenadine Etchings* to such impressive and challenging undertakings as *Something of Value* and *Uhuru*. His posthumously printed *The Honey Badger* should have been interred with his bones. His newspapering had long since withered and died.

Most reporters who just know for certain that they've got a book in them, lurking somewhere between the pituitary gland and the liver, find it appallingly difficult to "give to airy nothingness a local habitation and a name." The endlessness of a book presents the spot-news reporter or 750-word columnist with the predicament of an Olympic one-hundred-meter sprinter suddenly called upon to run the marathon. There are just so many words stoked in a writer's gut each day. If he uses them all on a PTA meeting, or the death of God, he cannot then come home and find any more words for his book. If he has taken an advance against royalties from the publisher, a transaction which he was still celebrating when the money ran out and the publisher began writing and calling for action, he will feel sad about the whole deal, particularly after a third martini.

I returned the advances on two books, both of them complete in typescript form. The editors of Dodd Mead & Company considered my book on St. Patrick's Cathedral lacking in merit, substance, and general interest. I agreed, not heartily. It is very trying on a writer's frayed nerves to give back spent money, especially to a publisher. A book I did about the Christian Brothers of Ireland, for P. J. Kenedy & Sons cath pubs, as the firm is listed in the Manhattan phone book, might be called a remorse of a different color—a play on words fit to sicken even Bennett Cerf, who has been kind enough or unguarded enough to publish four of my books. I worked hard on the Christian Brothers book, made two trips to Ireland researching it, spent a great deal more money than the Kenedy people dared advance, and then gave back the advance. Moreover, I've never tried another publisher with the book.

What caused the cath pubs to gulp and wish out was a substantial section of the book which dealt with the efforts of jealous and entrenched Catholic Orders in early nineteenth-century Ireland to crush the congregation of teachers being fashioned by a well-to-do sports-minded merchant of Waterford, Edmund Ignatius Rice. Rice was a widower with a daughter. He and the first fellow monks he gathered, for an assault on the ignorance and delinquency of maverick boys of the city, were accused of homosexuality. How they erased the smear, and not only survived but expanded in a climate of British persecution and the hostility of fellow religious, seemed to me the heart of the book.

But it was a bit too much for conservative elements among the Brothers' leadership, though all of the material was selected from Vatican archives where it has been filed in the continuing effort to secure beatification for Rice. An unexpurgated Life of Rice must not be sold to the students of Irish Christian Brothers schools on five continents! The Order withdrew its support of the project; when Kenedy asked that its advance be returned, I borrowed the dough and swore a mighty oath never to write another book related to my faith.

As was once the case with the price of refrigerators west of the Rockies, the above oath is subject to change without notice.

Radio can be an easy and substantial buck, if you get a break, as I did.

I got into it by default. At the pit of its misery in the early 1930's the Washington *Post* arranged with radio station WMAL to provide a five-night-a-week news show—fifteen minutes. Volunteers were called but few answered. There were two reasons for their reluctance: (1) there would be no pay for this extra duty, and (2) what self-respecting newspaperman wanted to be caught red-handed in a radio studio? Radio was for "Amos 'n' Andy," not news.

When the final head count was taken of the volunteers, it showed only Harris Hull, our aviation writer (who much later became an Air Force general) and the paper's high school sports reporter and tennis columnist.

Harris and I divided the agony. There was never any thought of "taping" in advance; indeed, there was no tape as yet. Everything was "live" and, in my case, ill-prepared because of my time-consuming work in the sports department. One night, reading the hurriedly pasted-together script, I found myself recounting the AP's story of the arrival in Britain from Australia of the heroic over-ocean flier, Amy Mollison. Never given to believe the AP could possibly have a typographical error on its wire, I found myself saying, "As she stepped from her plane, the crowd shouted: 'Hurrah for our British Army!' "

I came to a ghastly stop, and so did WMAL.

"I don't understand why they were cheering for the British Army," I said after what must have seemed to management an eternity. Then, obviously crazed by the experience, I heard myself saying into the microphone, "Oh, I see. It's a typo. They must have yelled, 'Hurrah for our British *Amy!*' " Somehow, I escaped alive.

Then there was the night of February 15, 1933. I was fumbling my way through the pablum of a bland script when to my astonishment the station's announcer, Warren Sweeney, slid a hastily scrawled note to me. The *Post*'s telegraph desk had phoned an urgent bulletin to WMAL. An attempt on the life of President-elect Roosevelt had just been made in Miami. There were no further details. Should I promptly blurt the flash? Could it have been the fiercely competitive Washington *Herald* that had phoned a phony to me? Torn, I kept reading the immensely lesser news and then, as a final item, heavily qualified ("there is an unconfirmed report, etc. . . ."), the richest morsel of all.

WMAL was a good, safe last in the race to get that vital information to all those teeming hordes out there in radioland.

I still get a little ill every time I hear John Philip Sousa's "The Washington Post March." It was our theme song.

The first remuneration I ever received from radio was a quart of Chickadee Rye. Too many bottles of too many rare and rotten whiskies have clinked and clanked into me over the years. But that quart of Chickadee is unforgettable. Prohibition was still in effect, so far as the hard stuff was concerned. This was "prescription" whiskey from the private reserves of People's Drug Stores, Inc., which sponsored a fifteen-minute sports show featuring Arch McDonald, the classy country boy from Chattanooga who came to Washington in 1933 to broadcast the Senators' games and set a pennant-happy city singing his theme song, "They Cut Down the Old Pine Tree." A death in Arch's family sent him back to Chattanooga for a week during the winter of 1933–34, and he asked the several Washington baseball writers to substitute for him. Wholly inadvertently, we gave Arch's listeners a fuller appreciation of just how good he was. I was a terrible substitute, when it came my turn to step up there and make radio history. Shirley Povich advanced Arch's reputation, too. Six or seven minutes into the fifteen-minute show, Shirley said, "Well, that's it, sports fans. Good night." A tall, thin, black-browed announcer at WJSV (which we used to say stood for Will Jesus Save Virginia?) vaulted to the microphone Shirley had abandoned and talked smoothly about this and that for the remaining minutes. His name was Robert Trout.

But there was nothing much that Trout, the glibbest of them all, or anybody else could do when Dick McCann of the Washington *Daily News* stepped up to bat for Arch. Dick had prepared a witty script and had timed it down to the proper length. The "on the air" light blinked on, Trout introduced him, and Dick opened his mouth to speak the first word.

Nothing came out.

Nothing. The lips moved, the face contorted, the spasm of the born orator seized Dick. But for the first two minutes of The Arch McDonald Show the only sound that went out from WJSV was the rattle and rustle of the script in Dick's palsied hands.

Notwithstanding Arch presented us with our bottles of Chickadee. Each bottle came enclosed in an oval tin can featuring a garish painting of, what else?—a chickadee. How could one conceivably forget a drink that had to be challenged first by a kitchen can opener?

Radio paid better, once a fellow got to New York. But to the menace of a critical audience was added another factor not calculated to give a performer added confidence: the sponsor. He, or it, had to be pleased enough with the person's ability to sell his product on the air that he was willing to stand for the costs. Moreover, he or it had to remain pleased—or else.

My first brush with a sponsor was unnerving. Bill Corum, Caswell Adams, and I were invited to a Brooklyn brewery to lunch with its principal directors. They obviously wanted to see what they had been urged to buy in the way of a three-man radio sportscasting team. During the luncheon, glass after glass of beer was poured into glasses bearing the brewery's name and emblem. Bill, Cas, and I were loud in our praise of the beer. None of us noticed a subtle stiffening on the part of the beer barons.

"So," said the director who looked more like a pig than the others, "you like our beer, hey?"

We swore it was a beer fit for higher echelon gods.

"Well, chentlemen, we have been serving you the beer of our worst competitor—Rheingold!" he said contemptuously. "And you, chentlemen, didn't know the difference."

We lasted thirteen weeks.

There were random radio jobs during the war, including a stint on BBC, a two-season stretch giving General Electric's "institutional" pronouncements during lulls in Fred Waring's Show, and then one of those breaks for which there is no accounting. William L. Brooks, a first-class newsman and bureau chief for AP, had become vice president of NBC in charge of news and special events. He left repeated messages for me at my office and apartment before I overcame my lunatic reluctance to return phone calls. Bill's patience somehow weathered the apparent insult.

"Forgive me for bothering you," Bill said, "but I have a fifteen-minute spot for you on NBC radio each Sunday at 6:15."

In 1951, shortly after Bill provided me with this showcase, I was called by Morris Jacobs, former Omaha newsman and by then head of the Bozell and Jacobs advertising agency. His principal client, Mutual of Omaha, had instructed him to look about for a network radio and TV show. Jacobs said he had several types of show in mind and that he'd like to look me over. I invited him to lunch at Shor's.

If Toots likes you, he's a great asset when you're trying to impress a guest. He will see that you get one of the best tables, a lot of attention from the captains and waiters, the bowl of celery and radishes, and, from time to time, his own overwhelming presence for a brandy-and-soda "and set up a fresh one for these fellows."

All preliminaries were attended to. Morris was impressed by the position of the table, my somewhat studied ease with the captains and waiters, the friendly waves of patrons he recognized, and the service.

"Where's your friend Tooooots?" Morris asked.

I said I guess he had been detained somewhere and would be in a bit later. Just then, Toots appeared. There was no question that he had been detained—in a brandy vat. He fell into the seat opposite Morris and before I could get to the introduction, Toots said, "Who's this creep?"

I explained that my guest was one of the most distinguished citizens of Omaha, a great fund raiser for worthy charities, a prime mover in the city's inter-faith circles, the King of Ak-Sar-Ben, and a first-class gent.

"Nice to know you, Tooooots," Morris said. "I have an important client who is looking for a radio and TV personality, and I'm thinking seriously of recommending your friend here for the job."

"Why you four-eyed so and so from no place, who the hell you think you are, coming in here and insulting my friend Considine by saying you're going to do him some big favor. You're nothing but a piece of raisin cake."

It wasn't one of Toots's better days.

Morris was not going to take that sitting down. He began to talk just as tough as Toots, and at one point picked up a knife. I've always meant to ask him which he intended to stab: Toots for giving him such a hard time or me, for introducing him to Toots.

Subsequently, they became fast friends. Also, shortly thereafter, Morris offered me to Mutual of Omaha, and the world's largest health and accident insurance company accepted the package: fifteen minutes of prime network time on NBC-TV with the format left up to me, and fifteen minutes of radio time. The salary, embarrassingly enough, was almost commensurate with that of the president of Mutual of Omaha, V. J. Skutt, whose genius had built a parochial institution into international importance.

It was much too much for a fellow whose main job was to turn out six columns a week for INS, plus coverage of major stories at home and overseas, and the creation of a certain difficult series of special articles. The latter included about that time the first in-depth interview with Frank Costello (arranged by Toots Shor), a long, hard look at Las Vegas and what and who made it tick (which won a Sigma Delta Chi Award), and a progress report on cancer research (which won a Lasker Award).

But I managed, somehow, to serve both masters, W.R. and V.J. Mostly responsible for this trick was Ann Gillis Slocum, a frail but incredibly durable NBC producer. Ann had had much to do with the development of John Daly during his early days in Washington and made many important contributions to the success of Bob Trout, Morgan Beatty, Edward R. Murrow, and John Cameron Swayze. Now she took me in hand, taught me how to keep my hands out of my pockets on camera, personally edited out of my radio tapes every last "er" and "ah" until I sounded as if I spoke that way in real life. Few figures in public life, particularly during the 1952 political campaigns, resisted Ann's invitation to appear on my shows. They were uniformly better than I, having had much more experience, and I learned a lot from them. Particularly from a Senator from Texas named Lyndon B. Johnson.

The instant I finished asking L.B.J. the first question of the interview, his eyes darted here and there to the three cameras, latched on to the one whose red light was on, and gave his answer to it, not me. Thereafter, whichever camera director Martin Hoade chose to carry the action, L.B.J. faced it instantly and gave it the full impact of his answers. I interrupted him once, by nodding. It seemed dishonest to take the money for that particular show.

Averell Harriman was a memorable guest. He proposed to run for the Democratic nomination at Chicago and thus oppose his longtime friend, Gen. Dwight D. Eisenhower.

"I could beat Ike," he said on the air.

"What makes you think so?" I asked him.

He seemed surprised by the question.

"Because I'm a Democrat," Harriman said.

That was a chancy sort of interview. The Harrimans had me in for dinner at their mansion in Washington on the night of the show. It was a fine dinner and the after-dinner talk was so interesting that we lost track of the time. A slightly horrified glance at my watch showed that we had scarcely half an hour left before air time. I hurried the distinguished public servant toward his front door, explaining that it would take at least fifteen minutes to reach the NBC studios in the Sheraton Park Hotel, after which we would have to be made up, the lighting would have to be arranged for, etc.

Honest Ave sometimes didn't hear too well. He pulled on a brocaded butler's cord and sent the man off to a pantry as we stood near the front door. The butler returned presently, bearing a fifth of Johnnie Walker Black, ice, and two large old-fashioned glasses.

"I usually like a little drink before I go on the air," Ave said, pouring me a triple and himself a tipple. We drank, straight and fast. Then to my dismay, he poured another for himself and for me. We drank and fled.

We reached our chairs on the TV set about one minute before NBC would have had to announce, coast-to-coast, "Sorry, neither fellow showed up." Ann whipped out a powder puff, hit us each in the face, smeared it around a bit and jumped out of the picture just as our announcer, Bob Denton, began his introduction.

Harriman was excellent throughout the fifteen minutes, clear, concise, coherent. Then, as was her practice, Ann changed microphones, seated us in more comfortable chairs, and gave me the signal to go ahead with the radio version of the interview—to be played two days hence. The strong TV lights, the closeness of the studio, and the relaxation of tension built up before and during the TV show combined to give full sway to the whiskey in our systems. We wandered and meandered through twenty-eight minutes of tape, at the end of which time Ann sighed and said, "I guess that'll be enough for a fifteen-minute show."

It took her many hours of painstaking editing and re-editing, and the floor of the editing room was littered with probably the greatest number of *"Well*'s . . . *Er*'s . . . *Ah*'s . . . *I Dunno*'s . . . *Maybe*'s" plus grunts and reflective pauses ever discarded. But when the patched tape went on the air, we sounded briskly letter-perfect. Ave called me after he heard it.

"Bob," he said, and he was serious, "you're the only fellow knows how to interview me."

I don't have a strong enough personality for TV. In a day when there was only black and white TV I perfected another color—gray. My guests found no difficulty whatever in forgetting me, sometimes when we were on the air. I had what I thought was a most interesting interview with Sen. Robert Kerr one night. He called me Bob, and was real down-to-earthy in a best-pal manner throughout the show. Two mornings later, Shor and I, en route to the Kentucky Derby, got off the plane at Cincinnati to pick up a fast beer during the short stopover. There, in front of the terminal, stood my dear friend Senator Kerr, surrounded by a group of admirers.

"Hi, Senator," I called out to him.

He turned and looked right through me. He had never seen me before.

Toots laughed all the way to Louisville.

It was this certain grayness, I feel in retrospect, that made it almost impossible for me to shut off a TV interview on time. I marveled at my superiors who could slice into a guest's prattling like a guillotine and end things in time for the last commercial and the credits. I was always afraid of hurting the person's feelings or causing him to take a punch at me.

Ann got me out of an interview with Baseball Commissioner Happy Chandler on time by arranging for her brother-in-law Frank Slocum of the commissioner's office to toss a baseball to me from the corner of the set. The startling act rendered Happy speechless, a condition which he had never experienced before or since. He was mute just long enough for me to say, "Thanks, Hap. Good night, folks."

"The best way to get off on time is to frame a question and answer in advance," Ann told me. "Then tell the guest that when you ask that question he'll know that this is the end of the show; that he gives the rehearsed answer and that's that."

It worked pretty well, but then came the night when my guest was Gwen Cafritz, the Washington Hostess With Almost the Mostest. Before air time we agreed on the climactic question and answer:

Q: In the old days, Dolly Gann had a lot of trouble seating people properly at Washington dinners given by her brother, the Vice President. Do you have such protocol headaches?

A: Of course not! This is a democracy.

All went beautifully. As the second-sweep hand on the studio clock hit the predestined moment, and the No. 1 camera came inching toward us, I casually asked Mrs. Cafritz a question I had apparently plucked from the wild blue yonder.

"In the old days, Dolly Gann had a lot of trouble seating people properly at Washington dinners given by her brother, the Vice President," I said. "Do you have such protocol headaches?"

"I've been thinking about that since we talked it over before the show," I heard Gwen say, as if in a nightmare. "I don't have troubles because I stick to the rules. Now, let's say I have the Chief Justice. I put myself on his left. On his right, I put the wife of—"

"Thank you, Mrs. Gwen Cafritz, famous Washington hostess, for coming all the way up here to New York to—"

"On *my* left I usually have the dean of the Washington diplomatic corps while on *her* right I—"

"Sure grand of you to come all the way up here to New York—"

"Next to the dean on my left, and to his left, I put. . . ."

The floor director had, in deadly succession, held up his right index finger, meaning that we had one minute in which to wrap up the show; then had crossed that finger with his left index, meaning thirty seconds, then had clenched his fist, meaning time's up, than had slashed his right index finger across his throat, meaning get the hell off. The camera was in quite close on us now. Bob Denton, at his desk on the other side of the set, bore the puzzled look of a man wondering how best to explain to Mutual of Omaha why he had been unable to sell any insurance due to a last-minute reseating of The Last Supper.

"On *her* left, I put. . . ."

I reached for Mrs. Cafritz's leg, figuring I might be able to break it. Surely, the camera was by now so close to us that it was televising us only from the chest up. Alas, the red light blinked out just then, and I swiftly learned that the cameraman was using his wide-angle lens. The Mutual of Omaha show had gone off the air, for lack of time, showing its commentator lewdly grappling for the shapely leg of a fine woman who had come all the way up from Washington to do him a favor.

Mutual moved me to radio not long after that. V. J. Skutt is a very patient man. The *J* in his name must stand for Job.

I have come on from a lot of odd places, mostly via radio, over the years: London, Paris, Rome, Madrid, Moscow, Berlin, Brussels, Cairo, Monaco, Tel Aviv, Mexico City, Buenos Aires, Rio, Brasilia, Anchorage, Honolulu, Hong Kong, Tokyo, Seoul, Melbourne, Dublin, from Pope Paul's Alitalia jet between Rome and New York . . . and from Topeka, Kansas.

The last named was on opening night of one of the most ambitious and disastrous TV news shows ever concocted, NBC's "America After Dark." It was a noble effort to bring live TV to the arid reruns and old movies that clog America's screens late at night. It replaced the "Steve Allen Show" and preceded the "Jack Paar Show." It lasted six hazard-strewn months.

The sterling cast of commentators included Earl Wilson, Hy Gardner, and myself in New York, Irv Kupcinet in Chicago, Paul Coates and Vernon Scott in Los Angeles—and anybody who happened to be awake and around other NBC stations that late at night. If everything worked, we could cover anything from a prison break in Fargo to a midnight funeral in New Orleans, and live, man, live.

There were grumblings at NBC when I said I could not appear on the opening show because INS had assigned me to talk to a Rotary in Topeka that very day, at the request of one of our badly needed client papers. Then someone connected with the show slapped his knee and declared—and I use his very words—"This could be a plus!" My presence there would show the skeptics, provided they were still awake, that "America After Dark" could indeed fulfill its pledge to cover the darkness, live, from coast to coast. Pray, what better proof was needed than to switch to Topeka in the dead of night?

We lined up a dandy Topeka sequence, starring a prize-winning drum majorette, Alf M. Landon, sheepishly wearing a huge sunflower button like the ones that stampeded Maine and Vermont to his cause in his 1936 race against F.D.R., and Dr. William Claire Menninger, all live. My role before introducing them was to stand on the roof of the hotel that housed us, point out into one of the deadest nights Topeka ever had, and talk for thirty seconds about Topeka, the Chisholm Trail, the Atchison, Topeka, and the Santa Fe (which was picking up the line charges), and whatever other goodies came to mind.

On signal, I went into my bit like St. Vitus imitating a semaphore. After thirty seconds the red light blinked out on the camera and the local director ripped off his headphones with a gesture of disgust.

"No audio," he said. "Somebody forgot to throw a switch when Scott, in Los Angeles, turned it over to you. Made you look like a damned fool, standing there yapping and gesturing and not a sound coming out of you."

When the ghastly night ended, I called my mother-in-law in Kansas City, who had been sternly alerted by her daughter to watch the show.

"How did you like it, Mom?" I asked her.

"You were pretty good," she said. "But I couldn't hear a word you said at the start. Speak up, son, when you're on the air. Don't be bashful. You're as good as any of them."

"Something called the audio went wrong and. . . ."

"Never mind that," Mom Anderson said. "You just speak up and you'll be all right."

I spoke up repeatedly over the next six months, but it didn't stay the slow but sure death of the show. The unions began to get personal about the appearance on the show of such stars as Jimmy Durante, who did a number or two from the Chez Paree in Chicago, gratis, because his old friend Kup asked him to. In a valiant effort to stem the inevitable, Earl Wilson had his hair dyed bright red, live, at an all-night beauty salon patronized largely by chorus girls and insomniac prostitutes. Somehow, the fact that the show was in black and white detracted from this self-sacrificing show of *esprit de corps*. Hy Gardner and management stopped speaking because of a demented system of time allotments which turned his in-depth interviews into surface scratchings. The news department of NBC became upset with me for opening my five-minute spot news slot with, "Sorry, but there isn't any news tonight." (Jack Gould of the *Times* liked it.)

Our most steadfast critic was Jack O'Brian in the *Journal American*. He called the show "America *in the* Dark," hammered away at it like Gutzon Borglum chopping a new head on Mount Rushmore.

America After (or in the) Dark lived six months. The next to last item on its final show was a remarkable shot of a fire raging in Boston, live, which I described on the air as a dramatic, if belated, confirmation of the program's original premise. The final shot was humiliating. It showed a big moving van filled with the show's cast and some of its accouterments slowly pulling away from the curb in front of NBC. Jack Lescoulie, our M.C., smiling as bravely as he had on opening night, announced that he and the others were headed for Cain's warehouse, traditional boneyard of Broadway flops.

I wouldn't lend myself to the finale. Too stuffy for that sort of self-ridicule, I guess. Ann and I walked around the corner to Toots's. He was waiting.

We had a few.

I was a bit player in what I feel was Hollywood's last Golden Age, the period that reached from a point near the end of World War II until 1947 or 48. Television had not drugged the nation. The studios made great sums of money with pictures that had nothing to do with perversion, dope addiction, seduction, incest, sodomy, murder-for-kicks, and miscegenation. All was right and decent in the picture world, and L. B. Mayer was in his heaven. So were Sam Goldwyn, who chartered Robert Sherwood to write *The Best Years of Our Lives,* Jack Warner, Darryl Zanuck, David O. Selznick, Cecil B. DeMille . . . and other giants, authentic geniuses, court jesters, knaves, and fools. The knaves and fools had more intrinsic class than most of today's screen tycoons, who are little more than glorified smut peddlers bent—as are their bankers—on filming any tawdry tale that might lure the televiewers from their nightly spells. Our newspapers compound the felony by printing lewd advertisements of such pictures and all the paid-for, lascivious words, while at the same time editorially deploring the decline in juvenile moral standards.

When I was in Hollywood, the intent of most film makers was to turn out pictures that had some meaning, some social significance, some hope of enduring. Whatever their backgrounds and penchant for emulating Julius Caesar, these men possessed all but indestructible taste. And a passion for detail that expressed itself in ways as varied as DeMille commanding the dusty charge of an army of extras to Goldwyn crankily supervising the proper mixture of developer in the darkroom where that day's film was being processed.

There were "hawks" and "doves" in the paradise of Hollywood in those days, but of a different nature. The screenwriters, by and large, were intensely liberal: Russia could do no wrong. They had a few cohorts among the directors, most of them foreign-born. The executives, on the other hand, were preponderantly Republican. L. B. Mayer could expound for an hour on the nation's need for Douglas MacArthur in the White House.

But there was laughter, too, and remnants of the hell-raising that had marked previous Golden Ages, and splendid pride in achievement. One night in Mike Romanoff's a conversation I was having with John Lee Mahin, one of the finest writers extant, was rudely interrupted by a complete stranger. He had recognized Mahin.

"The trouble with you goddam Hollywood writers is that you're all alike," the man said, poking Mahin in the chest with a punctuating forefinger. "Whenever one of you writes a religious story it's about one of two things. It's about a goddam Catholic priest who can sing like a bird, play baseball, and knock out the town bully, or it's about a goddam Jewish rabbi who is always so sweet and gentle and gets up the mortgage money to save the Catholic school.

"This is a Protestant country, goddam you," he continued loudly. "This is the greatest goddam Protestant country in the world. Now for Chrisakes why don't you make a movie about a Protestant minister?"

John put down his drink and looked at the fellow.

"One of the greatest pictures ever made in this town was about a Protestant minister," he said quietly.

"That's a goddam lie," the boor brayed. "Name it!"

"Rain," John said.

On most of my half-dozen raids on Hollywood I hitched my modest wagon to a wobbly star, MGM's mercurial old producer, John W. Considine, Jr.

On occasion, usually while drinking, we claimed a state of cousinship whose genealogy became mired in a peat bog in County Clare, whence sprang (or were driven) both our paternal grandfathers. But if there was a relationship, it was a tenuous one. John grew up in Seattle under the stern domination of a father who was tough as nails (killed a foe in a close-range duel), shrewd enough to amass a fortune out of the Sullivan-Considine vaudeville circuit, humanitarian enough to found the Loyal Order of Eagles, and foolish enough to think he could shape his son into his exact image and likeness. John, Jr., was the kid who lived in the big house, had a cart and pony, was packed off to the best prep school, then Stanford, Yale, and a year at Oxford after World War I.

He had a story to fit every stop he made in life: "An embarrassing thing happened to me just after I was mustered out of the Navy," he'd say. Then, self-cued, he'd continue:

> I decided that since I was overseas at the time I might as well go up to Norway. I had never seen the fjords. Well, there I am, a handsome young and virile bachelor, alone on a cruise. Then I saw her at dinner. I've known a lot of beauties around this town, and in a few other places, you might say. But I never saw anything like this before or since. When I learned she was traveling alone, it was almost too much to bear. I worked on her as quietly and unhurriedly as I could, but she was an iceberg until the last night aboard ship. Then all the woman in her surfaced and she said Yes, Yes, indeed, she would meet me on the top deck that night.
>
> You should have seen me in those days, hard as a rock from head to foot, no belly, just beautiful. And this was my night. To make sure she knew from the start that I was all man I decided to wear my lieutenant's uniform. I had had it made in London, of course.
>
> Well, there I am in my cabin, smelling like a rose after my bath, putting on my uniform, whistling away. But then a strange thing happened. When I buttoned my collar it was uncomfortable. I wondered if I was putting on a little weight without knowing it. But that was impossible. I loosened it for a moment and felt better. Then I buttoned it again, and I felt worse than I did the

first time. I began to sweat and it was only then that I realized that I was becoming seasick—me! a representative of the great navy of the United States.

It just couldn't be; it couldn't be happening to me on a night when I was going to score with the most beautiful girl in the world.

I straightened my shoulders, finished dressing, and started for the big tryst. She would be waiting, I knew. There would be a few preliminaries, then back to her place, or mine. It was a two-deck climb to the top. Inboard. When I cleared the last of the first set of steps, one deck below, I knew the awful truth: I was going to be very sick very soon. I stumbled down the passageway, looking for a men's room. There was not one in sight. Then I saw a cabin whose door was open. I lunged into it—its lights were out. There was a fine-looking Gladstone bag on a bag-rack. It was open and partly filled, I could see from the light in the passageway, with beautifully laundered shirts.

I put my head in the opened bag and, well, I've never been sicker. When there was nothing left in me I staggered weakly out of the cabin and leaned against a wall. Then I heard footsteps approaching. I fled back to the landing of the staircase, stood behind something, and looked down the passageway. My dining room tablemate, a retired British colonel who wore a Sherlock Holmes deer-stalker, was coming down the way. I knew, sure as hell, that it had to be *his* cabin I had been in.

Sure enough, he turned into it. I leaned against a wall, too weak to move. And then it came, a roar that must have sounded over half of Norway: "GOOD GAWD!"

I was too weak to make it to the top deck. She looked right through me at breakfast the next morning. But my tablemate didn't. "Glad to see you, old chap," he said as I sat down. "Been wanting to talk to someone. The most extraordinary thing happened last night when I was taking my constitutional. Some bounder fouled my luggage!"

John Considine was one of the finest producers the film industry ever knew. His taste was impeccable, when sober. His imagination was boundless, drunk or sober. Traveling east on the Union Pacific one day, he stepped off the train at Omaha, picked up a copy of the *World Herald,* returned to his drawing room, and read it cover to cover. Somewhere buried in its depths he noticed a tiny story about a talk given the previous night by a local priest named Flanagan who operated a haven for homeless and rudderless boys. The talk was titled "There Is No Such Thing as a Bad Boy."

That single atom fissioned into MGM's *Boys Town,* starring Spencer Tracy and Mickey Rooney. John assigned Dore Schary to do the script. It was a tremendous success, propelled the priest to an international reputation, and expanded the school to its present dimensions with students from all parts of the nation.

John was the producer of many MGM moneymakers, including a very good tough-guy picture named *Johnny Eager* with Robert Taylor, an early *Born Free* named *Sequoia,* and *A Yank at Oxford.* I shared only in his defeats, and they were as monumental in their way as his triumphs.

MGM had him either on probation or off the payroll during my times with him. He waged through that period as desperate a battle against the bottle as I've ever observed. On days (or parts of days) when he was good, he was very very good. On days when he was bad, he could be a totally different person. There were in-between periods when his wasting system struggled to clear itself of the vapors. These were the saddest times of all to share with him. They were spent for the most part in endlessly recounting stories of his father. It was a complex any psychiatrist worth his salt would have paid to listen to.

"My father used to say. . . ." and off he would go, a trace of sweat on his forehead, hands fluttery. I lost track of the number of times he said "My father used to say that the worst drink a man can take is his first."

The first was John's worst. He grew up in a hell-raising period in Hollywood, long since departed, but would never touch a drink. But one night at a dinner party at the home of Joan Bennett another actress, somewhat the worse for wear, commandeered the table conversation with a shrill interrogation of John on the question of his sobriety—which offended her.

"If you've got any guts, take a drink," she said to him.

He gave her his handsome, virile smile and said, for the dozenth time, "I'm sorry, but I don't drink."

"You're yellow," the woman said, and a depressing silence fell on the room.

John looked at her for a time, then turned to Joan's butler.

"I'll have a drink," he said.

"What shall I serve you?" the man asked, his composure ruffled.

"Doesn't matter," John said.

The butler returned with a Scotch, and John drank it, looking over the glass at the woman.

I worked as a writer on three of John's best nonproductions: a sequel to *Boys Town* and a brace of projects titled *The Church of the Good Thief* and *Gripsholm.* The pay ranged from minuscule to nothing because during the course of the three separate labors John was under suspension by MGM and his handsome salary of $3,250 a week cut off. He alternately proposed to produce them independently, interest other studios, or sail back to MGM basking in the radiance of their potential. I wrote reams of script, but not one foot of film ever emerged.

There were novel extenuating circumstances.

The *Boys Town* sequel was pursued by John in the face of odds which only he seemed unable to see. There was no chance that he could ride back to MGM on it; Metro had worked that claim dry. No other studio seemed interested. We took a trip to Omaha where I was to soak up enough Boys Town lore to etch a story line, while John was to hold a series of summit meetings with Flanagan and his advisers, notably Ted Miller, the wizard who headed Boys Town's mail solicitation, sale of stamps, booklets, and souvenirs. It was a distressing visit. Miller, who had grown quite well-to-do on the percentage he took of each contribution to Boys Town, made no effort to camouflage his contempt for John's proposition which, I learned to my embarrassment, was to have Boys Town provide the capital for the film. Father (by then Monsignor) Flanagan was impervious to John's plans and pleadings in an amused way. John and I attended his Vespers one bitter, ice-clad evening, and that turned out to be the saddest part of the trip for me. The honors that had come to him firmed up his image as the gentle shepherd of an unruly and pathetic flock of boys. He was the good man welcoming the kid standing in the snow carrying a kid almost his size. ("He ain't heavy, Father, he's my brother.")

During Vespers, conducted by a curate, Monsignor rose from the first pew on the left of fine Boys Town church where he had sat in solitary splendor. Then he walked slowly toward the rear of the church, pausing first on this and then on the other side of the center aisle, to gaze benignly at the boys and lay a hand on a scruffy head.

"Beautiful, wasn't it?" John said later at the Blackstone over his alarmingly receding case of Haig and Haig Pinch.

"No."

He was surprised. "No?"

"No. Didn't you notice that as he passed down the aisle every kid's head turned and looked at him in wonder?"

"So what?"

"So he hadn't done it before. He was putting on an act for us."

John plunged into his next nonproduction, *The Church of the Good Thief* with sporadic vigor. I arranged to take a short leave from International News Service, trained to California, caught him on a good day, and soon shared his vision. John had found (or vice versa) a priest named Ambrose Hyland, chaplain of Clinton State Prison at Dannemora. The upstate New York jug was as tough as Alcatraz and bleak as Siberia. But its inmates of all creeds, or none at all, had built a house of God within the prison's high walls. The priest had had to remove many barricades erected by state and church, and raise much money, before the erection and consecration of *The Church of the Good Thief*. The good thief so honored was not the prison's most distinguished inmate, Lucky Luciano. It was Dismas, the repentant hood who was crucified with Christ. On the day of dedication the warden learned for the first time why somebody had stolen the glass from the stop lights of his official car. They had been incorporated into the church's stained glass windows.

John dispatched me to Dannemora to soak up the atmosphere, after a few vaguely troubling meetings with Father Hyland on the Coast. Father was a swinger who didn't seem to care a great deal if we ever left Chasen's. I spent a couple of days around the prison and came to know some of the willing craftsmen who had built and decorated the church. Two, at least, had rechanneled their criminal trades in interesting ways. A convicted counterfeiter and forger produced some very good copies of the better-known sacred art. A burglar famous for his work with a jimmy and other tools turned out to be a fair sculptor. Prison and inmates took such redemptions in stride. Once, when a Dannemora warden's office safe went out of kilter and resisted efforts to open it by twiddling the combination the warden just called in a prominent safecracker he had in custody—and presto!

The day I left Dannemora the incumbent warden took me for a little ride around the reservation. In time we hove into a rare sight in those days of steel-rationing. The framework of a very large structure was being erected with all the clatter which attends such creations. I asked him what was going up.

"New cell blocks," he said, proudly. "Plenty of 'em."

I was puzzled.

"But you told me just a minute ago that Dannemora is only half full," I said.

"That's right," he said cheerfully. "But we've got to be ready for the boys coming home from the war, don't we?"

When I felt well enough to think, I thought it might be a good idea to expose the State of New York for the infamous precautions it was taking at the patriotic taxpayers' expense. But cooler thought prevailed. If I wrote it for INS, it would be picked up immediately by the Japanese, and good men fighting a terrible war in the Pacific would be further taunted by Tokyo Rose.

I swallowed it. Almost simultaneously, John swallowed *The Church of the Good Thief*. He had had a falling out with Father Hyland, he explained weakly over a transcontinental telephone line.

"What happened?"

"I'm afraid the good padre drinks," John said, passing irrevocable judgment on the damned.

Gripsholm, which was to have been the story of that great white ship's merciful services to refugees and POW's, ran into an early snag. John made the long train trip from California to join me. The ship was in dock, steady as a rock. John was something less. He was ruefully unable to sign his name to the form which the security guard insisted we fill out before permitting us to board. He was unmoved by a long story John told which commenced, "My father used to say. . . ."

Things were better the next day and for a number of days after that. We mapped out a misty story line: Japanese diplomats and merchants we picked up after Pearl Harbor was bombed and sent to the Greenbrier, White Sulphur Springs, West Virginia, are seen enjoying their golf, tennis and good food; Americans rounded up in Jap-held lands are seen living in great want and bravely enduring vile justice; Lap Dissolve. Mournful sound of *Gripsholm*'s great horn: "Ooooooooooooooo . . ." Jap diplomats bow politely as they and others leave U.S. to be exchanged for Americans, then turn despotic and dictatorial as neutral ship leaves U.S. territorial waters. Ragged Americans come aboard at Goa. Pathetic. "Ooooooooooooooo . . ."

Big buffet table on sunny deck. Starvelings attack it as if playing giant xylophone. Charley Ruggles type keeps trying to say, "May I have a drink first?" and/or "Where is the bar?" but is drowned out each time by "Oooooooooooooo." Intrepid correspondent files story to his paper about U.S.-educated Jap prison official who had kicked him in groin; story saying U.S.-educated Jap had privately castigated Hirohito, Tojo, etc. and was secretly rooting for U.S. victory. Sort of steal from *Address Unknown.*

John returned to his headquarters-redoubt, set up on the second floor of his fine home on Canon Drive, Beverly Hills, and informed me by wire that things were moving along fine: He had retained the directorial services of his old friend and mine, Norman Taurog. I should rush out and, with his guidance, shape up the script.

I checked into the Beverly Hills Hotel and called John. He was not available, so I called Norman. He said he had just heard from John.

"What did he say?" I asked.

"Oooooooooooooooooo," Norman said.

"Anything else?"

"No, that seemed to be it."

John and I had some productive sessions on *Gripsholm,* particularly early morning meetings. But things had a way of becoming derailed before the sun was high enough to cut the smog. One morning I was busily typing away on the script, copying down some fine dialogue his wonderful mind was concocting, when without prelude he said, "Look at your shoes!"

I thought I had stepped into something on the walk from the hotel to his home. But they looked about the same.

"What's wrong?"

"What's wrong? When did you last have them shined? Or repaired?"

I apologized and said maybe it would be better to wear the pair of size thirteen tennis shoes John had borrowed for me from his good friend Walter Pidgeon. But the dialogue had chased his muse from the house, and we both had to wait for a better morning.

It came, of course. No one with John's talents could stay unproductive for very long. One morning we worked together so well, so productively, that I—a good touch-typist—could scarcely keep up with the flow of words and ideas. It was a joyful creativity I had seldom before experienced, and I marveled once more at the skills of this battered but still brave genius. For a precious period that morning I would have bet my arms that John stood on the brink of a comeback that would shake the industry to its gizzard.

"Excuse me a moment," he said, interrupting the torrent of his talent. He left the room. I continued to type, trying to catch up with what he had dreamed. He was back in a minute.

"Answer the phone," John said in a voice that was oddly unlike the one I had been listening to during the morning.

I assumed I had not heard him correctly.

"Okay, let's go, John," I said, putting a fresh sheet in the typewriter.

"I said answer the phone, goddam it," John said with terrible intensity.

I suddenly felt drained.

"It's not ringing, John," I said, looking at him as if we were utter strangers.

He got up impatiently and snatched the phone off its cradle. I could hear the dial tone.

"Yes, Admiral," John said into the phone.

It was too much. I went down to his bar. There was a little shot glass sitting next to the bottle of Scotch. I poured myself one or two, as John had moments before, and went back to his office. He had finished his nonexistent dialogue and was relaxing in his favorite chair.

"It was Admiral Ernest King again," he said. "He keeps calling, asking me to be Secretary of Navy."

It seemed as good a time as any to go back to work with INS. Millie and I had dinner with Norman and Sue Taurog the night before we left. Norman mixed a drink for us. He touched glasses with me. "Oooooooooooooo," he said, affectionately.

It was much more profitable—$2,500 a week, actually—writing scripts that were produced, but not nearly as entrancing as working with John.

Shortly after the A-bombs fell on Hiroshima and Nagasaki, and I had finished a stint for INS that involved interviews in Washington with Lt. Gen. Leslie R. Groves, Col. (now Judge) William Consodine, top security officer of the incredible organization that created the Bomb, Dr. Robert Oppenheimer, and others involved, I received a call from MGM producer Sam Marx. Sam was enormously engrossed with the subject of the Bomb's creation, application, and the morality of the act. He assigned me to write the script of MGM's *The Beginning or the End.* Jim McGuinness was the executive producer, Taurog the director. Comdr. Spig Wead, the paraplegic former Navy test pilot who did the screen play for *They Were Expendable,* was assigned to help me write a filmable script.

It was my first brush with the "story conference." We'd all meet in Jim's big office, and after an exchange of pleasantries I'd read aloud what I had written that day or the day before. As the lowest man on that particular totem pole my words were expected to move up through channels. I recall one sequence where our young nuclear physicist, who had been virtually torn from the brink of his connubial couch by an order to proceed immediately to Oak Ridge (then Los Alamos, then Tinian) says to his forlornly unfulfilled bride, "Well, with us I guess it's a case of touch and go."

Spig, the next man up on the totem pole, chuckled appreciatively. "Good line," he said.

"That'll play," Norman said.

"I'll buy that," Sam said.

All eyes turned to Jim, the executive producer. After a bit he shook his head.

"It has a dirty connotation," he said.

"Let's hear it once more," Sam said.

"Well, with us I guess it's a case of touch and go."

"I think Jim's right, we shouldn't risk it," Sam said.

"On second thought, I'm not sure it *would* play," Norman said.

"Here's a better line," Spig said.

Some months later I went through L.A. with Frank Conniff on the way to Bikini to cover the A-bomb tests against captured Japanese and obsolete U.S. ships. Sam Marx was kind enough to ask us out to MGM to see some of the rushes of *The Beginning or the End.* One particularly alarmed me. I had patiently researched and worked into the script an important, at least to me, step in the development of the Bomb. Included in the research was a trip to Stockholm to talk with Dr. Lise Meitner, who had been an important part of the little research team that had proved at the Kaiser Wilhelm Institute in Berlin in 1939 that uranium-238 when bombarded by radium emissions showed, under chemical analysis, that portions were transmuted into barium and krypton, whose combined weight on the nuclear scale was just short of the weight of the uranium atom involved. Therefore, atoms had been split, and every book on physics had to be rewritten. Something had escaped in the form of energy.

Dr. Meitner had been expelled from Germany shortly after the staggering discovery on the ground that she was part Jewish. She made her way to Denmark and divulged the news to her friend Niels Bohr, who had won the Nobel Prize in Physics for related studies and theories having to do with the enormous potential of atoms historically considered unsplittable. Providentially, Dr. Bohr was about to depart for the United States on a lecture tour. He alerted his friends in the nuclear physics community and a small group that included Enrico Fermi greeted him at the pier upon his arrival in New York. The men proceeded immediately to Columbia University and there proved, as Albert Einstein had proposed years before, that Energy really does equal MC square.

Now there were half a dozen or so in the Free World who knew that man was on the verge of unleashing stupendous power. But they were mostly men who had little knowledge of the workings of the American system of give and take. There was, for example, Fermi, the genius who had refused to take his brilliant Jewish wife Laura and their children back to Fascist Italy after he won the 1938 Nobel Prize for his experiments with radioactivity. And the Hungarians Leo Szilard and Eugene Wigner. Suffice it to report that in time one suggested that the terrible secret they shared should be presented to President Roosevelt. But how?

Then a thought: Why not call upon Professor Einstein, inform him that he had been right all along about matter being converted into energy beyond the dreams of avarice, and urge him to present the findings to the President? After all, was he not the world's foremost scientist?

A group visited Einstein in July, 1939 at a cottage he had rented near Spring Lake, N. J. He listened to the presentation but said, when he had heard it out, that he could not possibly ask for an appointment with President Roosevelt. The President would not know him, the Father of Relativity protested. As a compromise, he would write a letter. He did that, explaining the research that had been done, alerting the President to the fact that Dr. Meitner's associates,

Otto Hahn and F. Strassman, were still around in Germany, that Hitler was showing a deep interest in the uranium-bountiful pitchblende mines of Czechoslovakia. He, the ultimate pacifist, proposed that it was theoretically possible to manufacture what he, of all persons, called an atomic bomb. He envisioned it as something so huge that it would have to be transported by ship into an enemy harbor, whereupon the crew would light some form of fuse, abandon ship, and the whole thing would blow up—either knocking down or contaminating the adjacent port or town.

Anyway, as I brought out painfully in my script, Einstein and the other scientists decided that it was not safe to trust such a letter to the United States Post Office. It must be delivered by hand. A friend of the group, Alexander Sachs, Russian-born economist and science buff, volunteered to hand-deliver the crucial letter to the President. It took him some time to arrange an audience, whereas Einstein would have been granted an immediate hearing if he had asked for one.

The rushes of *The Beginning or the End* followed this entire sequence superbly—to a point. The scientists did not call on Einstein at his summer cottage. They trooped into his Princeton home in dead of winter, as attested by the swirls of ersatz snow that greeted their arrival at the great man's digs.

"It was summertime, Sam," I said to my leader in the darkness of the projection room.

"Shhh," Sam explained.

Then the actor who played Einstein, portrayed shivering near a blazing fireplace and bundled to the gills, gave an interesting reason why he would not make the short journey to Washington and tell President Roosevelt, who was actually very much impressed by him, that we had knowledge of a potential superweapon that must be fabricated before Hitler built his own.

"Why won't you go?" I heard an actor playing the role of a nuclear physicist ask on the sound track.

"I have a bad cold," the actor portraying Einstein said.

The lights came on in the projection room.

"Sam," I said after a time, "I worked pretty hard running down the story of how the men got through to Roosevelt. Now, the only reason I did the business of Einstein was to show how modest this great man was. Roosevelt was delighted to save his letter for the autograph alone. Why did you change the season, and the reason that he didn't go to Washington. The picture makes him sound like a nutty hypochondriac."

Sam shrugged.

"The actor looked better in a muffler," he said.

Then there was *The Babe Ruth Story,* produced by Allied Artists, directed by Roy Del Ruth, no relation, and starring William Bendix as the Babe. I tried to get Paul Douglas for the Ruth role. Paul was an athlete, knew Babe, looked like Babe. But Paul was not yet a star and naturally could not induce the casting department of the Allied Artists bank to vote for him. The department was happy to underwrite the film so long as Bendix played Babe.

I met Bill in the office of a decent Hollywood fellow named Steve Broidy, a very uncomplaining sort. I had the film's technical adviser, Pat Flaherty, with me. Pat, who had played big league ball for McGraw's Giants, was a man no studio could do without if it ventured into baseball. He could not only teach actors how to handle themselves in a baseball uniform and in position, but could appear in bit parts with them and tolerate their utter ignorance. The day he first went out to work as adviser/actor for Sam Goldwyn's *Pride of the Yankees* he said to Gary Cooper, cast as Lou Gehrig, "Let's loosen up a bit, Gary." He tossed a baseball at Cooper, and it hit the actor in his chest. Pat thought he was clowning. But Cooper failed to catch the next few easy tosses.

"I'm sorry," Cooper said in the end. "I never played baseball. You see, I fell off this horse when I was a kid and did something to my pelvis and, well, I never got around to playing baseball. Then I came out here and. . . ."

"And what?" Pat asked after a long pause.

"Well, don't tell anybody," the actor said, "but I've never even *seen* a ballgame." As it turned out, Coop *became* Gehrig under Pat's tutelage.

Now, in Broidy's office, Pat and this time myself were appraising the Ruth book I had ghosted with the help of Fred Lieb, and whose script I had written. In came our hero, Bendix. He looked about as much like Babe as I looked like Elizabeth Taylor, a virginal kid who had just made *National Velvet.* The talk turned naturally to hitting styles, and Pat and I commented on Babe's magnificent posture, right-leg-tuck-in, weight-on-left-leg, body-turned, ready-and-waiting stance.

"That's wrong," Bendix said. "I know all about the way the Babe used to hit. I was a batboy at the Polo Grounds when he played there with the Yankees before the opening of Yankee Stadium. Here, I'll show you."

He picked up the *Herald-Examiner,* rolled it into a makeshift bat, took his position at the side of an imaginary home plate, studied a mythical pitcher, then ran several steps forward in the direction of that pitcher, and swung the newspaper.

"Babe always ran a few steps toward the pitcher before he swung at the ball," Bendix said.

Pat looked thoughtfully at the ceiling, I at a passing Good Humor truck. There wasn't anything to say.

Everybody concerned seemed satisfied with my shooting script. It was an easy one to write, of course. Just about everything Babe did in life was dramatic: early hardships around his father's saloon, the rough and tumble days at St. Mary's Industrial School (where the monks decided he might make a good shirtmaker), the discovery by Brother Matthias that the kid was a ballplayer in a million, the move to the old Baltimore Orioles, the trade to the Boston Red Sox, the pitching heights he reached there, the great sale to the New York Yankees, dazzling home runs, living it up, shooting his money out of a cannon, the slow decline, frustration over not being named a manager, the cancer he refused to believe he had, the croak-voiced farewell in Yankee Stadium. . . .

I went back to work at INS. Perhaps a month later I received a note from Joe Kaufmann, Allied Artists executive. A staff writer had "made a few changes," Joe wrote. He was sending me the new script for quick approval before the filming began.

The new script had everything but dancing girls in the Yankee locker room. I sent it back with a note:

"Very interesting, but who is it about?"

Joe called. Would I come out to Hollywood again, at $2,500 per and all expenses, including car, and make the script "right" again? I did and restored it to its original form.

They filmed the other one.

I took our son Mike, then twelve, to see the preview. He had hung more or less breathlessly on the fashioning of each word of the book, and the prospect that the book would become a moving picture was of great importance to him. "Pop," he said, when I turned in the script, "please arrange for a screening at our school. It'll make me the biggest kid in the whole place."

He was silent for some time after we left the preview. Then he said, "Pop, don't bother about showing it at the school. I'd hate to see you lugging all those heavy cans up there."

I went through Hollywood once more, this time in my more natural role as a reporter. There was good news about John. He had shaped up and through the intercession of his good friend Neil McCarthy, who was close to L. B. Mayer, was back at work in MGM's Thalberg Building—known less respectfully as the Whited Sepulcher. John invited me to lunch with him the next day in his office suite. He sounded just fine.

He was late for the appointment, but that meant nothing. What mattered was that he was stoned, and drenched with self-pity. The handsome suite, he said, was an insult to him.

I said I thought it was swell.

"Come here," he commanded. "You call that swell?" He pointed out the window to a nearby mortuary. "They put me on the side of the building nearest the undertaker, that's what they did!"

Just then, several waiters from MGM's excellent commissary arrived bearing luncheon, kept warm by great silvery covers. I was hungry, particularly for the rich chicken soup which L.B. insisted be on each day's menu—as a reminder that in his youth he had dreamed of such soup but could not afford it.

The waiters were setting the spotless table under John's critical eye when suddenly he roared, "Get out, and take that junk with you! Out! Out!"

As they fled, dropping things, John said to me, "Why should I eat here when all those incompetent horses' asses are eating in the Executive Dining Room? Come on, I'm taking you up there with me."

It didn't matter, all of a sudden.

It was a slightly terrifying, but oddly magnificent, scene. John, his fine gray hair askew, flung open the heavy doors of the lordly dining room. MGM's brass was all there: L.B., Sam Katz, Eddie Mannix, Marvin Schenck. . . .

They froze.

"We're having lunch here, hear me?" he said. "My cousin *Bob* Considine and I, see? You can insult me, John Considine, all you want to, but nobody's going to insult *Bob* Considine. Nobody in this room!"

Several of the executives got up and left quietly. Marvin Schenck said cordially, "Come in, Bob and John. Have lunch with us."

All gone now, John . . . L.B. . . . the beauty and the flaky chivalry . . . crushed under the hooves of TV.

I miss John the most. I often wish I could remember some of the things *my* father said. He died when I was ten, and the only thing I can remember hearing him say is, "Boy, remember this: Never shake hands with an undertaker."

6. *Intrusions*

SOMETIMES you wish you had chosen Diesel engineering, say. Sometimes you feel like a vulture, hovering.

"Stop looking at me, you dirty sons of bitches," the accused murderess hissed at several of us who had been permitted to go into the cell area of the dismal jail at Snow Hill, Maryland. She was sitting on the side of her cot behind the formidable bars of her cage. Her great dark eyes blazed with indignation. She had been a beautiful and spirited woman, surely. But now she was a trapped animal, charged by corn-pone Eastern Shore police with the shotgun slaying of her husband. They had made a national case out of the ugly business by making her submit to a then novel test. They had dipped her hands in paraffin and deduced that the impurities the wax had sucked from her pores were caused by the acridly smoking gun used in the killing.

"Who the hell gave you the right to stand there, looking at me?" she said. Every word was a knife.

Who, indeed, gave us the right?

I have no memory of a more poignant scene than that at the graveside of a girl named Beverly Burda, one of ninety-five children burned to death in the tragic fire that leveled Chicago's Lady of the Angels parochial school in December, 1958.

"The services for the girl will be held in advance of the mass burial ceremony," a windblown and shivering young priest said to us as the pathetic white casket was placed on its lowering apparatus. "It would be too much of a strain on the family to wait until the others arrive."

And so, while one after another funeral procession snaked into the bleakly frozen and terribly misnamed Queen of Heaven Cemetery, the last rites of the Catholic Church were given to this little girl alone. The Burda family and friends came forth, trodding the imitation grass and sorely stricken. The mother, a short woman whose rough woolen scarf was a frame for a searing portrait of grief, was supported by two larger women who wept loudly. The mother was silent. Behind her spellbound eyes was the question that had lain heavily on all the bereaved: "Why?"

But it was not Mrs. Burda with her inexpressible grief who commanded the thunderstruck attention of those nearby.

It was the father of the dead child. He had no visible face of human skin. Instead, he wore a startling leather mask that extended from his hairline to his sensitive mouth. Out of the right side of the mask, at eye level, protruded what seemed to be a jeweler's eyepiece with a pinpoint opening instead of a full lens. He stood there, erect and silent, on the arm of a male member of the mourning party, oddly aloof to the wails of the women supporting his wife and the even louder cries of other women farther back in the group immobilized at the graveside.

The priest from Our Lady Help of Christians droned into the familiar ritual. I could not take my eyes off the shocking leather mask. Another priest saw my rude consternation, and above the weeping, the Word, and the marrow-freezing wind he whispered:

"He just came from the hospital against the doctors' wishes. Had an operation for detached retinas a few days ago. He's been told that if he cries the salt of his tears will enter the open incisions and destroy his sight for good."

There this man stood, surrounded by tears, alone in his midnight at noon, and I, too, wept to see him fight for control of his exposed chin, wept to watch him try not to weep. The service went on and on, mixing as of old the melancholy fact of death with the promise of life hereafter. The mortal remains and the soul of the schoolgirl were urged to rest in peace. But what of the benumbed mother? What of the father who must not cry? I found myself praying other prayers than those for the repose of the little girl, prayers that Burda somehow would not do the most natural thing in the world—and let free his scalding blinding tears. I watched the telltale jaw, for there was no way to know what agony lay expressed behind the harsh leather mask. It was not the jaw of a fighter or a male model. It was just the ordinary jaw of a poor man who worked hard and had been visited by more woe than human spirit could endure. Once the jaw trembled, then firmed up, fluttered again, and recovered.

It was time to go now. The weeping women led the stumbling mother away. The man at Burda's arm pointed him down a narrow line between open graves. His head was high, as if he were reaching for his breath. His jaw was like a rock.

The Secret Service, Boston Police, and guards at the hospital ordered the lobby cleared of all reporters and cameramen. President Kennedy was momentarily due to come down from the room where he had spent half an hour with doctors who had been given the impossible task of saving the life of Patrick Bouvier Kennedy. The infant had been brought to the hospital earlier that day by police-escorted ambulance from Otis Air Force Base, where he had been born the day before and where his mother was recovering. A last-resort decision had been reached. The baby would be given emergency treatment inside the hospital's monstrously large "iron lung," as big and as ugly as a section of a submarine. There was little or no hope that the first son born to an incumbent American President in 68 years would live to know he had moved millions of hearts great and small. I had flown from New York to cover.

In the confusion of clearing the hospital lobby, I was either overlooked or forgotten. Whatever, I was there alone when the President came out of the elevator with Jim Rowley and another Secret Service man. Jim directed the President's attention to me. He crossed the lobby with a smile and shook hands.

"Hi, Bob," he said, "what are you doing here?"

It knocked the wind and all composure out of me. I could not answer.

"Are you on vacation?" he asked.

I clutched gladly at that. "Yes, oh yes," I said, eager to lie. "Vacation."

"Have a good time," the President said, shook hands again, and moved through the door to the waiting press, the bulb-popping cameramen, and the sympathetic crowd.

The baby died at four-thirty the next morning, August 9, 1963. The President, summoned from a room he had returned to in the hospital, was outside the great pressure boiler when the end came. He asked to be alone. For ten minutes he rested his forehead on a small porthole that commanded a view of the infant's bed inside the brightly lighted apparatus. Then he walked out, silent, and a much older man than he had been.

In the press room at the hospital a doctor gave me a signal to join him outside the room. I followed him by a circuitous route to the building that held the pressure chamber. The baby's body had just been removed. A doctor, dejected and exhausted, slumped in a chair near the chamber, smoking a cigarette under a large NO SMOKING sign. Inside the boiler, another doctor and two interne assistants were lying on the deck, undergoing decompression.

"Didn't work, this time," my doctor-guide said, looking at the evil thing that filled the room.

About a hundred of us gathered later outside the plain, barracks-like base hospital at Otis, watched the President enter to join his wife, and settled down to wait for him to reappear.

But after a bit, it seemed so obscene, so indecent for us to be standing there like grave-robbers.

"It *is* obscene," our White House correspondent Marianne Means agreed. We were walking toward her Hertz rental to drive to Hyannis Port, where there would be a briefing still later in the day. "Terribly, terribly obscene. But most of them will stay on, in fear of being beaten on the story."

There was a period when the death sentences imposed on the Rosenbergs seemed patently proper. Just. Had to be done. They asked for it, see?

But then there came a night at Sing Sing. . . .

At the beginning of any scrutiny of the Rosenbergs, their lives, crimes, legalistic gyrations, propaganda roles, electrocution, and red-labeled "martyrdom," it should be stated that theirs was essentially a clear-cut spy case.

They violated the provisions of Title 50, Section 32, the United States Code, by funneling atomic, fire-control, submarine-detection, and other guarded U.S. military secrets to Soviet Russia. They were caught, indicted, tried, and given the maximum sentence: death.

The Rosenbergs, parents of sons then nine and five, might have died in comparative obscurity during the originally assigned week of May 21, 1951, and been remembered chiefly as the first persons ever sentenced to death for espionage by a U.S. Civil Court and the first to die in Sing Sing by federal decree.

But shortly after the couple stoically heard the death sentence handed down by Federal Judge Irving R. Kaufman, the Communist Party made a discovery which must have impressed even the most avid Red.

The Rosenbergs were "safe." They were not only willing but determined to go to their deaths without revealing the names of others who worked with them in the Communist apparatus set up to steal American military information for the Soviet Union. They would not "talk" as did other atomic spies such as Dr. Klaus Fuchs, Harry Gold, and Sgt. David Greenglass, Mrs. Rosenberg's brother, whose remorseless testimony helped send her and Rosenberg to the chair.

Their fellow Communists had kept their hands strictly off the Rosenbergs during the trial of the New York couple. For example, the *Daily Worker* did not cover the trial or display any interest in their arrest and indictment.

But, once convinced of the Rosenbergs' complete loyalty to the Soviet Union and their eagerness to die for it, the Kremlin itself filtered word down to party functionaries to launch a sweeping propaganda campaign against the United States, its judicial system, etc.

In the end, the campaign exceeded even the Kremlin's virulent "germ-warfare" line in its open animosity and violent rupture of known truths.

The once-mute *Daily Worker* seethed with grotesque panegyrics about the Rosenbergs, letters the unrepentant couple sent from the death house, sobbing features about the sons, and protests from Communist fronts, left-wingers, and fuzzy humanitarians from all over the world.

The purpose was to invest two not overly bright espionage agents with the dignity of martyrdom, an estate which the Reds hoped to trade upon in the future. The Rosenbergs entered wholeheartedly into the macabre plan.

According to prison sources, they were "happy to die for the cause," though they obviously had enough Communist training to realize they were being used as few condemned persons in history have been exploited.

The Russians used them in a variety of ways. Gullible areas of the world and captives of Communist-dominated countries and organizations were repeatedly told, for example, that the Rosenbergs were condemned to death because they were Jewish. This was an effort to fan hatred of the U.S. and to help take the curse off the newly ordered wave of anti-Semitism in the U.S.S.R. It blithely overlooked the fact that Julius Rosenberg forsook rabbinical training to become a Communist. It ignored such facts as that Judge Kaufman was also Jewish, as were U.S. Attorney (now N.Y. State Supreme Court Judge) Irving Saypol, Chief Prosecutor, and Judge Jerome Frank of the Court of Appeals, who upheld the verdict.

The Russians used the Rosenbergs also to tell countless millions that the U.S. judicial system was corrupt. Half-clothed primitives in parts of darkest Africa may still mull over reports, received from Red infiltrators, that American witnesses and such agencies as the FBI indulge in mass perjury.

The Rosenbergs were not tried as Jews, nor because "they spoke for peace," nor because they were members of the Communist Party. They were tried under a statute which Congress laid down in 1917.

This statute, boiled down, states that any person who in any way delivers or conspires to deliver to a foreign country any information of any kind relating to U.S. national defense shall, in time of peace, be sentenced to prison for not more than twenty years. If espionage was committed, as in the case of the Rosenbergs, at a time when the nation was at war, the maximum penalty becomes death.

Julius Rosenberg and his wife, three years older than he and even more immersed in Communism and its requirements for regimentation, inhaled secrets as avidly as a vacuum cleaner gulps dust. Julius stole a complete proximity fuse from the Emerson Electric Company. This fuse—a device that exploded a shell or bomb with deadly effect near a target and without contact—was one of America's most jealously guarded World War II secrets. He and she gathered information about the latest U.S. Navy sub-detection devices, processed bizarre data on a man-made satellite to be rocketed beyond the gravitational pull of the earth, acted as paymasters and patrons of lesser wartime spies, and continued their activities after it became abundantly apparent that Russia was no longer an ally.

As Judge Kaufman put it, Ethel Rosenberg was a "full-fledged partner."

It was their work in the field of the atomic bomb, however, that was the principal cause of the death sentence imposed by Judge Kaufman, a gravely concerned man who spent many hours of contemplation and prayer in his synagogue before rendering the hard verdict.

In gathering and submitting to their Russian superior, Soviet Vice Consul Anatoli Yakovlev, a treasury of atomic information via their willing dupe, Sergeant Greenglass, the condemned Rosenbergs committed a crime which Judge Kaufman denounced as "worse than murder." In passing sentence, the federal jurist, shaken physically by the experience, said:

"It is not in my power, Julius and Ethel Rosenberg, to forgive you. Only the Lord can find mercy for what you have done."

Judge Kaufman was subjected to enormous pressure after imposing sentence. The full scope of that pressure probably will never be known. But he never wavered, never failed to give the Rosenbergs' defense counsel, Emanuel H. Bloch, recourse to every available avenue of appeal.

When every legal facet was explored and exhausted, from the setting aside of the judgment to a reduction of the sentence, the case was sent to the White House.

It was to no avail. Execution inexorably awaited this couple who, until a few years before, were hardly distinguishable from other New York couples of moderate means, eager to improve their lot in life. Yet veteran court attendants agreed they were the "coldest fish" they had ever seen.

Julius and Ethel sang "Good Night, Irene" and "Battle Hymn of the Republic," and smiled fondly at each other as they were taken away from Federal Court in New York City after hearing themselves condemned to death.

At forbidding Sing Sing, while she waited to be the eighth woman to die in the prison's electric chair and the first ever to die as a spy convicted by a U.S. Civil Court, soft, little Ethel Rosenberg was no trouble to matrons assigned to her.

While pickets paraded before the White House and before U.S. embassies and consulates throughout the world, demanding that she and her husband be spared, the placid woman continued her reading and wrote an occasional letter to her sons Michael and Robert or to her doomed husband in another wing of the death house.

Sometimes she played handball for exercise. She ate regularly, slept well, and took pains with the soft brown curls that framed her round face.

Julius kept up a heavy correspondence, much of which found its way into the *Daily Worker*. He was quite indignant when the prison librarian, either by accident or design sent him several books about the growth, glories, and humanitarianism of the United States.

"I will not crawl," he assured the *Worker* in his next message. He regarded the selection of the books as another effort by U.S. authorities to persuade him to gain clemency by naming co-conspirators in the wartime espionage apparatus and by giving details of its workings.

Rosenberg, a neat bespectacled man whose engineering training was received at the College of the City of New York, evidenced no outward emotion when he described the electric chair and its operation to his two curious sons, come to visit him in prison. He, too, played handball within what amounted to first-bounce distance of the room in which he was due to die.

"Their lips have remained sealed and they prefer the glory which they believe will be theirs by the martyrdom which will be bestowed upon them by those who enlisted them in this diabolical conspiracy (and who, indeed, desire them to remain silent)," wrote Federal Judge Irving Kaufman in denying their application for a reduction of sentence.

The Rosenbergs sprang from desperately poor Lower East Side, New York, families. Intelligent, ambitious, and seemingly devoid of harmful complexes, they went their separate ways through the public school system, grade school and junior high, and met at Seward Park High School.

Julius went on through CCNY and graduated in 1939 as an electrical engineer. Ethel became an accomplished stenographer who dreamed of being a singer. They were married in the summer of 1939 and for a time she supported him, while he looked for work, by clerking in the Census Bureau in Washington, D.C.

The record is vague on why they became Communists, though Julius probably was recruited by friends at CCNY. But each embraced Marxism with zeal and in time prepared to die in its name. They labored mightily to spread Communism among their friends and relatives. Most of their prospects shied away; but one who did not was Ethel's younger brother, David Greenglass.

He stood in dumbfounded awe of the learning of his sister and brother-in-law. And he was grateful for the gifts Julius would bring to him—occasional tools, elementary machinist manuals, and always some Communist literature. He was delighted to join the Communist Youth League when the Rosenbergs assured him it was the "right" thing to do, just as he later considered it "right," as a sergeant at Los Alamos, to give them the atomic secrets they passed on to Russia.

By 1942, Julius Rosenberg had ingratiated himself enough with his superiors to become a semi-official leader of Communistic or left-wing government employees connected with the Federation of Architects, Engineers, Chemists, and Technicians. He was by then a civilian expert assigned to the Army Signal Corps.

By November, 1944, Julius had reached his goal. He had moved on beyond his cell and his recruiting activities to the status of spy. He was no longer reporting to fellow American Communists. He was reporting directly to Russians who obviously had satisfied themselves as to his loyalty to the U.S.S.R. To them, among other things, he had delivered the proximity fuse, audaciously carried out of the Emerson plant in his briefcase after an inspection tour in his Signal Corps capacity. The fuse was subsequently used against U.S. and UN aircraft in Korea.

Julius and Ethel were now ready for the biggest job of their lives, and they laughed at how easy it was going to be.

Poor, naïve David Greenglass—on a million-to-one shot—had been sent by the Army to Los Alamos, New Mexico, to work on the very weapon Russia wanted most of all—the atomic bomb! Rosenberg was delighted with the information Greenglass sent back, and still more pleased when Greenglass arrived in New York City, January 1, 1945, on furlough.

Rosenberg easily persuaded Greenglass to write down everything he knew about the project. The notes were retyped neatly by Ethel, who was accustomed to her brother's bad writing. Among the information revealed was a description of the "lens" device which is the heart of the A-bomb, the mechanism through which explosive fission is achieved.

During the furlough Greenglass was introduced to a Russian and, during a twenty-minute automobile ride through deserted New York slums, told him all he knew about the bomb. Greenglass borrowed the car for the occasion and was its driver.

Before the furlough ended Rosenberg introduced Greenglass to a

Russian courier named Ann Sidorovich at the Rosenberg apartment and told him to be on the lookout for her when and if she came to Albuquerque—where, it had been decided, Mrs. Greenglass would set up an apartment to be paid for by Rosenberg's Russian friends.

To make sure of the proper identification, Rosenberg took an empty raspberry Jello box, tore off one side of it, cut it in half in irregular style, and gave one part to Mrs. Greenglass for safekeeping. The other part, he explained, and the salutation, "I came from Julius," would properly identify any agent who called on the Greenglasses.

On the first Sunday in June, 1945, about six weeks before the A-bomb was tested, Harry Gold arrived at the Greenglass apartment in Albuquerque with the Jello tear-out. It had been given to him by Rosenberg's superior, vice consul Anatoli Yakovlev. So had an envelope containing five hundred dollars, which Gold—who drew thirty years for his part in the conspiracy—gave to Greenglass after the latter had turned over sketches of the "lens mold" and other data. Yakovlev eventually told Gold that the Greenglass material was "extremely excellent and very valuable."

In September, 1945, shortly after V-J Day, Greenglass was given another furlough. With him this time he brought sketches of the improved "trigger" used in the Nagasaki bomb and the makeup of the bomb itself. Ethel typed an eleven-page report from his revelations.

Julius, who had by that time been secretly awarded the Soviet Order of the Red Star and had been given a special console table designed to facilitate the microfilming of other secret documents and plans he was receiving, gratefully pressed two hundred dollars on his brother-in-law.

Rosenberg strongly urged Greenglass to apply for civilian work at Los Alamos when it came time to be mustered out, so that he could continue his spying. But Greenglass took his honorable discharge as a sergeant and returned to New York to enter the machine-shop business with Rosenberg.

Rosenberg had by then been fired from his Army Signal Corps job. The FBI discovered a record of his membership in the Communist Party and the Army promptly dismissed him. Rosenberg entered a fuming protest but told intimates he was secretly relieved. The FBI report made no mention of espionage, just party membership.

Julius and Ethel were happy people as 1950 dawned. In addition to other favors from their Soviet masters they could now point to handsome watches, and they could bask happily in the shock of horror that had swept the United States when President Truman announced that Russia had successfully completed and tested an atomic bomb.

But one day in February, 1950, the Rosenbergs were struck across their faces with a shattering headline. Their world was beginning to collapse. Klaus Fuchs had been arrested in London. Worse, he was talking. Rosenberg raced to the miserable cold-water flat of the Greenglasses on New York's Lower East Side to tell him the significance of the news.

David Greenglass did not know Fuchs. But he had met and had passed atomic information to Gold.

What Rosenberg did not know was that Fuchs never knew Harry Gold's name, his profession, or his place of business. Fuchs knew Gold only as "Raymond." From a casual description Fuchs gave of the meek-looking Gold, an obscure Philadelphia chemist, the FBI tracked him down by May, 1950, one of the more masterful manhunts in the history of crime detection.

The three-month period between the arrest of Fuchs and that of Gold was a frantic time for Julius and Ethel. They had had personal troubles with Greenglass. The machine shop in which he had become a partner with Rosenberg was doing badly; Julius appeared to be the only one prospering, and Greenglass had repeatedly asked for just recompense for his work therein.

Now, as he urged Greenglass to leave for Mexico immediately, in the wake of Fuchs's arrest, Rosenberg promised to pay the ex-sergeant's debts. He made inquiry of a doctor about the "shots" the Greenglasses would need, ascertained the least conspicuous place to pick up travel cards, and outlined the path they would travel to safety behind the Iron Curtain.

Greenglass would not budge. When the newspapers announced Gold's arrest, Rosenberg took more positive action. He gave Greenglass one thousand dollars and promised that an additional six thousand dollars would be forthcoming. The Greenglasses were to go first to Mexico, thence to Sweden, Czechoslovakia, and from there to Moscow, where a job would await David. There were bizarre instructions as to how he could recognize Soviet agents while passing through the escape route.

On May 30, 1950, Greenglass finally stirred. He had six sets of passport pictures taken of his little family and early in June accepted four thousand dollars from Rosenberg. He wavered again, to the horror of the Rosenbergs, and delayed his departure. He turned the money over to another brother-in-law, one Louis Abel, for safekeeping.

Harry Gold was by then "singing" one of the longest confessions in U.S. crime annals. In time he came to Greenglass' role. Greenglass was taken into custody and appeared to be relieved to tell what he knew.

He quickly agreed to become a Government witness, and because of his complete cooperation—which brought his sister and brother-in-law to the death chair—he drew only a fifteen-year prison sentence. Mrs. Greenglass, chiefly responsible for persuading her husband not to attempt to flee, at a time when the family might have made a clear getaway, was given no sentence.

The arrest of Greenglass caused Ethel to call immediately on Mrs. Greenglass and promise to shower her with gifts if she could prevail upon her husband not to implicate the Rosenbergs.

For reasons never properly explained, the Rosenbergs tarried in this country for weeks after sounding their first alarms to the Greenglasses. It was not until late May or early June, 1950, that the Rosenbergs appeared at the photo shop of a Ben Schneider, at 99 Park Row, and had passport photos taken of themselves and the children.

Schneider, a stunning surprise witness produced by the government at the end of the Rosenberg trial, who was permitted to testify over the protests of defense attorney Bloch, said that he recalled the Rosenbergs because they came in on a Saturday—usually a bad day for him—spent nine dollars, their children acted up, and Mrs. Rosenberg volunteered that they were traveling to France to pick up a bequest left to her.

The government used Schneider's testimony to prove to the satisfaction of the jury that the Rosenbergs contemplated flight. And the jury ruled that this act was, indeed, "an indication of the consciousness of guilt."

The historic three-week trial of Julius and Ethel Rosenberg suffered a partial eclipse of an improbable nature. It conflicted in dates with the less significant but more sensational Kefauver Committee hearings involving Frank Costello, Joe Adonis, Virginia Hill, and former Mayor and Ambassador William O'Dwyer. I covered that ham-ridden farce, as well as the Rosenberg drama, and marveled that the meaning and nuances of the spy trial were consequently lost on millions of Americans captivated solely by the sight of Costello's knuckle-kneading on their television screens. Overseas, the Rosenberg trial took clear precedence. So vast and effective was the spread of Communist propaganda about the trial that the U.S. State Department felt forced to send a lengthy review of the case, outlining the charges and the evidence presented, to forty U.S. diplomatic missions throughout the world.

There followed also one of the most vigorously appealed cases in U.S. criminal history. First the case was sent up to the Court of Appeals—composed of Chief Judge Thomas Swan and Judges Harrie Chase and Jerome Frank—and the verdict was unanimously upheld in February 1952.

Petitions for a rehearing in the Court of Appeals were denied in April, 1952. The Supreme Court then declined to review it because the high court seldom, of course, reviews any case that has no bearing on the Constitution. There were appeals and upholdings through the fall of 1952 and the early part of the winter, and finally one which sought to set aside Judge Kaufman's judgment.

Kaufman himself was assigned to judge this but withdrew and Chief Judge John C. Knox referred it to Judge Sylvester Ryan. On December 10, Judge Ryan denied the application. Judge Ryan's decision was argued before the same Appeals judges. Then defense counsel Emanuel Bloch went back to Judge Kaufman for a reduction of sentence. It was an emotional scene.

"Tell me where I erred," Judge Kaufman said to Bloch at one point. "I'm anxious to know." He had been the target of thousands of wires and letters from all over the world, many of them parroting phrases and distortions which followed the known Communist line on the case.

"When the day comes when we are swayed by pressures, we might as well close the doors of justice," the deeply concerned jurist said in this respect.

"You have in your hands the fate of two human beings," Bloch told him with muted passion. "... Your Honor should have witnessed the scenes with the children.

"The Rosenbergs are soft, sweet, tender people whose hearts are no different than yours or mine—what is it that causes them to say 'we are innocent'? Why don't they take the easy way out and confess if they are guilty? What stops them?"

Judge Kaufman broke in soberly. "I have pondered that over and over," he mused.

"Is it fair to forfeit these lives when you have some doubt?" Bloch appealed. "Any doubt—one little iota of doubt? It's such a terrible thing to take the lives of people who stand up in the shadow of death and still say, 'We are innocent!' knowing that if they came to this court now and said, 'Guilty!—have mercy!' you'd commute their sentences. Millions cry, 'Don't kill these people!' All humanity cries out against it.

"Once the current passes through the bodies of the Rosenbergs nobody can ever right the wrongs done to them, their children, and American justice.

"God, your Honor, you have a heart! These are parents! They love their children as you love yours. Please think. Please consult with your conscience. You'll never be able to look in a mirror again, or at your children. . . ."

"If I felt that way for an instant," Judge Kaufman said evenly, "I'd change."

In denying the clemency appeal and opening the door to the Rosenbergs' appeal to the White House, Judge Kaufman wearily explained that the espionage act of 1917 gave him no opportunity to hand down a verdict of life imprisonment. It had to be a prison sentence up to thirty years, or death. He found death in any form heart-rending, he said, and he was "deeply moved by considerations of parenthood." But, he added, "My personal feelings or preferences must be pushed aside, for my prime obligation is to society and to American institutions.

"This court," he observed near the end of a remarkable document, "has no doubt but that if the Rosenbergs were ever to attain their freedom they would continue in their deep-seated devotion and allegiance to Soviet Russia, a devotion which has caused them to choose martyrdom and keep their lips sealed."

Then the little man who had resisted perhaps incomprehensible pressures in an effort to make him change his mind looked around his courtroom—packed with Rosenberg cohorts who had hissed U.S. attorneys in the corridors—and quoted from the English novelist Mary Ann Evans, who called herself George Eliot:

"There is a mercy which is weakness, and even treason against the common good."

Julius and Ethel, particularly Ethel, died bravely. I was one of three wire-service reporters permitted to see them go. Guards frisked us for hidden cameras, and even took away our fountain pens. I never again wore the expensive wrist watch I used that night at Sing Sing to measure the last seconds of their lives. I threw away some of the clothes I wore, for they stank of death.

As in life, Ethel was stronger than Julius when death came toward them.

He went first, but not from choice. He had spent the last afternoon, Saturday, June 20, 1953, in Ethel's wing of the death house. The cell that had been given to him there was closer to the chair room's door than that of his wife. This meant that if Ethel were designated to be the first to go she would have to pass his cell en route to the chair. Sing Sing recoils from that sort of salting of wounds. So it was Julius who led.

His familiar black mustache had been shaved away. He was the picture of a soberly stricken but silent man as he walked behind Rabbi Irving Koslowe, of Mamaroneck, New York. He seemed to be trying to keep step with the Rabbi's sonorous Biblical quotations.

Rosenberg had been told that two "open" telephone lines, one to Attorney General Herbert Brownell and the other to the governor's mansion at Albany, were at his disposal—if he wished to name fellow conspirators. The big ugly switch on a nearby wall would not be activated if he spoke out.

Julius did not utter a sound. He was strapped to the chair, rather roughly gagged with a black cloth, and the current was applied. He quivered under his bonds, and his neck seemed to grow several sizes. Three charges killed him. Dr. George McCracken, a jaunty-looking old political appointee in a sports jacket, applied his stethoscope to Julius' chest and confirmed his death. The body was unstrapped and wheeled off.

Then Ethel. Her little procession into the shockingly silent and bright room was led by Rabbi Koslowe, who had retired after leading in Julius. The Rabbi's resonant voice had sounded the coming of the macabre parade before a coatless guard opened the huge oak door that leads to the chamber.

Now, somber in his vestments, the Rabbi walked in quoting from the 15th and 31st Psalms. His voice replaced the eerie silence of the room. . . .

"Who shalt sojourn in Thy tabernacle . . ."

Ethel wore a Mona Lisa smile. Her little minnow of a mouth was curled at the edges in the faintest possible way. She was dressed in a dark green print of cheap material, a prison dress that revealed her plump legs below the knee.

Her dark brown hair, apparently freshly washed, was set in an almost boyish manner. Her head had not been shaved, only clipped short on the top. Like Julius, she wore brown cloth slippers.

Just before she reached the chair, for which she showed no revulsion, she turned and looked at the two dumpy, gray-haired matrons who had followed her into the room.

With an impulsive gesture she reached out her right hand to them. It was taken by the elder of the two, Mrs. Helen Evans, who had guarded her for two years. Ethel's iron composure melted briefly as she took Mrs. Evans' hand and pulled the woman into a quick and affectionate embrace.

She kissed Mrs. Evans on the left cheek, but even as she turned away to retrace her steps toward the chair, the tight little smile came back to her lips.

Ethel was cooperative with the little swarm of death-house attendants now collected around her. She stretched out her hands along the arms of her ghastly throne to facilitate their buckling on the black electrode straps. She cocked her head in such a way as to help those who were fitting the monstrous crown. She tucked in one fat leg to help a guard adjust its strap.

Only once did she change her expression before the mask came down over her eyes. That was when an attendant roughly adjusted the electrode that reaches down through the center of the hood and makes contact with the scalp.

But her face quickly regained its composure. As the hood was lowered over her eyes and the black strap placed across her mouth, she was looking straight ahead, almost triumphantly, her gaze directed at the wall over the heads of the ashen reporters sitting on hard benches before the chair.

Executioner Joseph Francel, a wasp-waisted little man as innocuous-looking as his regular pursuit might indicate—he was an electrician in Cairo, New York—walked quickly into the little alcove which contained his switches and meters, stared pensively across the room at the grimly enthroned woman, and without a change of expression went about the grisly work for which he was paid three hundred dollars.

As the torrent of electricity swept through her body, Ethel braced herself. Slowly, surely, the index finger of her right hand rose as if in silent rebuke. From every pore of her body there seemed to emanate a strange, unearthly sound made up almost exclusively of the letter *Z*. Now she seemed about to stand. Her hands contracted into fists. Thus she sat, lifted off her seat as far as the straps would permit, and I had the startled feeling that she would break those bonds and come charging across the floor, wielding those tight little fists.

Out of the left side of the gear that covered her head rose a heavy cloud of blue-gray smoke that ascended straight up in the deathly room until it flattened out in an ugly cake against the skylight overhead.

Slowly and majestically she began to descend again in the chair, as if the executioner could no longer conquer the law of gravity with his switches. The smoke continued to rise from her head. From the chair there continued the sound of the skillet.

It was a three-second jolt. Francel left his instrument board and, hand on hip, speculatively studied the smoking figure in the chair. He shook his head, went back to his panel, and shot the second jolt into her—a fifty-seven-second surge. The woman's index finger rose again, then slowly subsided.

There was a stir in the room now. The executioner had signaled that the woman had received a sufficient charge to cause death. Dr. McCracken and a younger assistant, Dr. H. W. Kipp, moved over to Ethel and pulled at the front of her round-collared dress.

The collar was not large enough for them to introduce their stethoscopes. They ripped it. An attendant unleashed the black strap that had been tied tightly across her breasts. Other attendants unbound her arms and a leg.

The doctors hovered over Ethel, stethoscopes attached to the white skin beneath the sleazy dress. Then they stared at each other dumbfounded, held a whispered consultation, and beckoned to the executioner.

Francel seemed surprised. He came over to them, lips pursed.

"Another?" he asked, vexed.

"Yeah," one of the doctors muttered.

Now the business of restrapping her had to be attended to. Two more fifty-seven-second jolts went through her. The plume of smoke reappeared, and the room was heavy with the smell of electrocuted death.

She could relax now. What had been a woman who once dreamed of the operatic stage and settled for espionage, sat there loosely composed. The doctors advanced again, listened and agreed.

"I pronounce this woman dead," said Dr. Kipp.

They took the mask off Ethel Rosenberg now and her face possessed the same quizzical half-smile that had been painted upon it minutes before. She was freed of her straps. Two guards picked her up and placed her on the wheel-table and pushed her out of sight. Ethel's right leg was flexed in an easy and almost nonchalant posture.

Relman Morin of AP, Jack Woliston of UP, and I were bundled into a paddy wagon and taken back to the Visitors Room of Sing Sing, where thirty-eight reporters from half a dozen countries waited for details. All three of us were supposed to brief them, but neither AP nor UP cared to do so. It was left up to me. I was put behind the elevated desk that commands a view of the screen-separated tables where inmates normally converse with their visitors from the outer world.

It was a trying experience for a reporter, particularly when the first question asked—after blunt details had been given—was a shrill one from a lady reporter.

"What did Mrs. Rosenberg wear tonight?" she called up to me.

It just seemed so damned callous.

There are other sins of intrusion. . . . Killing is so damned impersonal, in the electric chair or a war like Vietnam.

That's the second reaction you're likely to experience after flying in the back seat of an F-100F on a combat strike.

The first reaction, of course, is a swarming surge of relief that they didn't shoot you down. Now you can unpeel about sixty pounds of flying gear: suit, gut-corset, parachute, life jacket, survival-vest kit, pistol, knife, head-shrinking helmet, and suffocating oxygen mask. And you can stand up, rub your aching butt, and slip into a cold beer.

The second reaction hits you as soon as there is an evaporation of the bubbly elation of still being alive, still having a chance to make something of yourself in life's miserably short span. It is a sobering reaction. You realize that you were a kibitzer to a killing.

At least, you suppose it was a killing. You don't see anybody spin and fall. But Viet Cong were known to be lurking in the patch of woods Capt. Carl Young of Towson, Maryland, hit with two 750-pound canisters of napalm, two 500-pound bombs, and only God and the VC know how many slugs of 20-mm. shells during what seemed like endless low-level passes over the target at 450 miles an hour.

In the course of a seat-grinding zoom-out after Captain Young dropped his bombs, I heard his airborne spotter come on the pipe with his molasses drawl and say, "Would you believe it? A secondary explosion." There were two such detonations in the wake of the strike. Apparently, something the VC had dragged into their cover had blown up, perhaps killing some of those who planned to use it to blow up others.

For Captain Young, father of two sons, Pat and Mike, and veteran of twelve years of Air Force service, it was just another day's work. This was his 220th sortie since he went into action at this base nine months ago. With a little bit of luck he'd fly dozens more during the remaining three months of his tour.

For me, well, it wasn't quite routine. I walk around ants to keep from stepping on them. The epitaph my stone will bear is "Here lies a bum who never swatted a fly."

So come along and share the experience of an uneasy greenhorn.

There was an infernally prolonged prelude. The Bien Hoa air base is less than twenty miles from Saigon along the best road in Viet Nam, but it took well over an hour to reach it. The maze of traffic around Saigon is all but impenetrable and ranges in nature from growling fifty-ton tanks to lovely bicycling Vietnamese girls in gossamer garments that float like butterflies.

Lt. Jim Farley, an Air Force flack who drew the gloomy task of delivering me intact to the Third Tactical Fighter Wing of the 308th Tactical Squadron, made interesting small talk as we inched toward the field.

"I've been over here eight months, but the war never hit me until last night," he chatted. "I dropped by a mortuary in Saigon, and there were thirteen soldiers stretched out on slabs. Dead," he explained. (There were seventeen other mortuaries operating around the clock.)

Now even the turtle's pace decelerated. On the right-hand side of the road, a mop-up crew was doing something about what was left of the Sealand Motor Pool. It had been hit several hours before by VC mortars, grenades, and rifle fire. There were still some bodies among the sixty battered vehicles.

Suiting up for a ride in an F-100F takes another hour if you're my size and girth. This is a slim, flat-bellied war. But they found a stylish stout in the fly-suit inventory, and an airman named Jones went to work on me.

First you strip down to your shorts and climb into a long-zippered jumper that looks like Churchill's "blitz suit." Then you are ornamented like a macabre Christmas tree. The gut-corset, designed to hold your insides during dives and pull-outs, is strapped around you tight enough to shape you like a dumbbell.

Then everything else is piled on. In time, you can hardly move. You're bent over like an old man, the crotch-straps of the chute having been tautly pulled.

With all this goes a running commentary about what each bit of equipment means—how to unzip, unbuckle, unsnap, and uncrank in case you must bail out. After a bit you stop listening. You know in your heart that you'll either not remember or be too petrified to unanything.

Now, everything is taken off you except the jumper suit. This was just a fitting, so to speak. Besides, a monsoon weather has settled over the target, and there will be a delay. A briefing fills part of the void.

"We've lost five birds in the past twenty-four hours," the young briefing officer said briskly. "I guess you've heard about Jerry. His F-One-hundred ran into a wall of fire, and he never pulled out of his first dive. Watch it. Your MIG alert call today is 'Phillies,' and you are Sabre Two. Any questions?" When there were none, he compressed his pointer like a retractable radio antenna, put his map under his arm, and went off on some other mission of good cheer.

Captain Young was doodling a problem on his pad. Now he looked at his two wing men, Capts. Gerald D. Cannon, of Tremonton, Utah, and Charles W. Bradley, of Goff, Kansas.

"You should have a hundred twenty-nine knots after three thousand feet of roll, and go off at a hundred eighty knots and sixty-one hundred feet," he murmured. Then he turned to me and said, "We've got ten thousand feet here at Bien Hoa. With the help of the braking chute, we can still stop in time if something goes wrong at a hundred sixty knots with four thousand feet to go."

Then a bewildering account of the various switchings that would have to be made from one radio band to another. One band would tell him more about the weather, another would give him general details about the target, and still another—the band reserved for the daring young man in a tiny plane who would find the target and lead us to it by dropping a phosphorescent marker-bomb squarely on it.

"FAC [Forward Air Controller] will give us additional information," Captain Young said casually. "Oh, such as the best places to bail out if we get shot up—places where there are more friendlies than VC, let's say." He turned back to the pilots.

"I want each of you guys to come in at different angles than the one I'll use," he said, drawing a sketch. "If you come in on my tail, they are ready for you, and they shoot you down. Make them guess where you're coming from. Make as many dry runs as you need. You've got to do that sometimes to make it good when you finally drop. One-second bursts with the guns. No more. Save thirty rounds, enough to cover one of us if he goes down. That should hold them off until we can get a chopper in for a rescue."

Another hour dragged by. The pilots dropped off to sleep on their chairs, as effortlessly and peacefully as children. Lt. Col. Ed Derryberry, Information Officer, had something for me to do.

He led me to the next hut, that of the 510th Tactical Flight Squadron, to see its mascot. The mascot was asleep on top of a partition that formed a briefing room. It was a python, nine feet two inches long. A pilot reached up and rubbed what I assumed was its belly. It stretched contentedly.

We rode through the sullen rain to the Officers' Mess and were having a cup of coffee when in from the downpour, shaking himself like a wet terrier, came one of the bravest hands in aviation history—Col. Chuck Yeager, first man to fly through the sound barrier. After years of test-piloting at Edwards AFB, California, and training Air Force astronauts (among them Jim McDivitt, Frank Dorman, Mike Collins, and Dave Scott), Chuck was working as Wing Commander of the 405th Fighter Wing based at Clark AFB, Philippines.

"Are you going to fly while you're here?" Colonel Derryberry asked him.

"Me?" Chuck snorted. "No sirreee! They don't pay me enough."

A phone rang in the Ready Room. Captain Young said something into it very quietly and hung up. "Let's go," he said.

You're redressed at the side of the F-100F, and you weigh a ton as you climb the ladder and wriggle into the little seat. An airman attaches all the straps and plugs you in to the oxygen and communications system. The Pratt and Whitney J-57 you're squatting on bursts to life with a convulsive shriek, the canopy comes down and locks in place, and pretty soon you're rolling down the runway faster than you've ever moved before on the ground.

Then up through the dirty overcast like a rocket and into the blue. And suddenly, as intimately as if he were sitting on your lap, the easy voice of FAC.

"Good afternoon," FAC said with disarming cordiality. "I have some news about your target. I'm over it now. I'm over to your left at nine o'clock. I have red wingtips. There was a big operation around here couple days ago, and the only place Charlie could have gone is back into these woods. Target elevation sixty feet. The houses in the woods are considered friendly. They are unoccupied. We don't want to hit them. If you're ready, I'll go in with the smoke."

"That's fine," Captain Young said. "I'll make a dry run just to be sure."

We sluiced down four thousand feet through a small hole in the cloud cover. It was like jumping off a cliff. Just about the time and altitude where it seemed likely that I had become a silent partner in a suicide pact, Captain Young flattened us out, and I was pushed down into my seat as if a thousand pounds had been dropped on my shoulders.

A mile or so ahead of us a creamy cloud rose from the woods and hung there. We raced at it at about two hundred feet altitude, shot past on the right, and knifed sharply up and away. I wondered what it would be like, going right through the bottom of the F-100F.

The next time was for keeps. The fighter-bomber shuddered as explosive charges punched the big streamlined napalm bombs from the underside of our wing. As we went through the hamburger grinder of the pull-out and getaway, FAC spoke—as if he were in the jet with us.

"Right on it!" he applauded. "Beautiful. Now for snake eyes [the two 500-pound bombs]. I'd like you to come in a hundred meters to the left of the napalm."

"Thank you," Captain Young said. "But I'll try a dry pass first." He switched from FAC to me. "A dry pass at this stage tends to change their minds about popping up and shooting at us," he said.

We did the dry pass. It tends to make the throat dry, too. Then FAC was back.

"I'm over the target now," FAC remarked laconically. "The friendlies have moved out of the way."

"That demonstrates the importance of tactical airpower," Captain Young commented. "There's been criticism back home, I understand, but we can work very close with people on the ground, clear out enemy positions maybe fifty meters in front of friendlies."

And so it went—airpower and comparatively small talk—for the next half hour. There were belching thrusts of 20-mm. fire from the four guns. And FAC was on and off.

FAC was full of gossip about the target. In addition to the two secondary explosions there was some kind of fire raging that interested FAC. "I can't tell what it is," he said, "but it's burning real good. White smoke."

We sprang up and away from the business at hand, our wings free of the awesome and ugly bombs, the arsenal of 20-mm. shells down to the minimum thirty rounds. The F-100F was about a ton and a half lighter. It was a jaunty fighter again; not a lumbering fighter-bomber. With Captains Cannon and Bradley alarmingly close to his wing tips, Captain Young reached for the deep blue overhead, as if hungering for its cold, antiseptic absolution.

We went over the top at thirty thousand feet, and then down. Captain Young switched on his afterburner, and five thousand more pounds of thrust surged through the engine.

"You won't notice much when you go through sound," he said. "Maybe a little nudge."

Sure enough, there was a nudge as the needle touched Mach 1 and moved on to Mach 1.1. Captain Young switched off the burner, and though we were in a steep dive, it seemed as if we had run into a thick layer of transparent gelatine. We were flung against our shoulder straps but leveled off in time, and were talked back to the field through the gray potage that lay just over the trees and paddies.

Colonel Derryberry was there at the bottom of the ladder. He had a can of beer ready.

"Thing like that can vitiate a fellow," he said.

The judgment in the debriefing session, back in the rickety office, was that it had been a successful mission. Eventually, somebody among the friendlies would venture into the woods and count the dead, if any.

Somebody else, Lt. Jim Farley, let's say, would write a little piece about it, which none of the newspapers would use. It would be, at most, a footnote in the endless annals of war, memorable only to those who were hurt, and to a kibitzer to a killing.

7. *It Broadens One . . .*

. . . sometimes in the wrong places.

The first long trip I remember was to Chesapeake Beach, Maryland, a resort a few miles out of Washington. Tension ran considerably higher than, let's say, a subsequent Sabena jet flight which involved breakfast in Moscow, luncheon in Brussels, and dinner in New York. Minutes before the train for Chesapeake Beach huffed into action (it looked like the one that carried Lincoln to Gettysburg) my brother-custodian Charles got off to buy a bag of peanuts. When the train began to move and he had still not returned, I panicked. I went to the platform of our car and sat down on the steps that led to the ground, now slipping by faster and faster. I was abandoned, penniless, in the alien corn. I thought of trying to jump off, but the dizzy acceleration of the train warned of disaster. So I just sat there and wept.

Charles and a conductor found me in that position and condition. My keeper had gotten back on the train by way of another car and was somewhat concerned to find our seat empty. The meeting between Stanley and Livingstone could not have been more emotion-filled. I was led back to our seat somewhat the worse for wear. Between tears and cinders (whatever happened to railroad cinders?) my face was a surrealist painting in black and white. One cinder stuck in my eye the rest of the day, eluding what was the open-heart operation of that day, pulling the eyelid down as far as human tissue permitted and groping for the snug little obstruction with the saliva-moistened and twisted corner of a handkerchief.

It was a day to remember.

There were other great voyages in my youth but none to compare with the annual outing at Marshall Hall, Maryland, engaged in by the families of St. Aloysius parish.

That one took a lot of preparation. There was money to raise by means of selling old papers and scrounged scrap to the neighborhood junk yard, by delivering repaired shoes for an old Irish cobbler who lived down the street from us in the Swamppoodle section of Washington, and running errands for Laddon's drug store at the corner of Third and H Street, Northeast. A fellow needed a pretty good pile to do Marshall Hall correctly. The roller coaster cost a nickel a ride and though breathtaking beyond description, wasn't a very long ride.

The voyage was made by ship. The *Charles McAllister* was a noble white sidewheeler with a fine black rocker-arm on its top deck and a steam-horn that made us clap hands to our ears and dance with joy. My father had been one of the organizers of these yearly adventures, usually staged on August 1. After he died, my mother carried on the tradition of attending and provisioning us. She would make the fried chicken and the baloney sandwiches the night before, and the hard-boiled eggs, and see to it that there were tomatoes and pickles and even potato chips. I'd help squeeze the lemons into a Ball-Mason jar, to be made into lemonade with iron water pumped out of the earth of Marshall Hall's picnic grounds the next day.

We'd eat and play ourselves into exhaustion, then back to the *Charles McAllister* for the long, sleep-filled twenty-mile voyage back to the pier at the foot of Seventh Street. If the night had turned chilly as we stretched out across the ship's canvas chairs, our mother would cover us with newspapers.

I've sometimes wondered since if osmosis was involved.

The first time I journeyed all the way to New York was to play in the National Indoor championship. At that time the Pennsylvania Railroad maintained a station-platform in adjacent Jersey called Manhattan Transfer. When the conductor stuck his head into the coach and bellowed its name, I hurriedly put on hat and coat, grabbed bag and tennis racquets, and labored down the aisle, convinced that the train would start again before I could get off and I'd be carried to some hostile place farther to the north, say, Albany. The conductor's contempt was withering as he told me that Manhattan Transfer was not Manhattan even though many transfers were made there. Equally flabbergasting was an examination of the Manhattan phone directory which I opened immediately after reaching my room in the then brand-new New Yorker Hotel. I turned to the McIntyres. There was a small forest of them listed in the book. But no O.O. I wondered how in the name of God the writer whose every word about New York was gospel to me couldn't afford a telephone.

The big war gave wings to a lot of us who had never dreamed we'd see far-off places. Americans spread around the earth like a blessing or a plague, depending on the viewpoint of the hosts. For this reporter, sometimes, and wrongly, regarded as the "travelingest," there is no substitute for travel, no comparable adrenalin. And one is not likely ever to forget his first important break with immobility. . . .

"Step outside, sergeant," the portly lieutenant colonel at 90 Church Street in New York crisply ordered. The enlisted man retired and added to the mystery by closing the door as if it were mined. Then and only then did the light colonel lean across the desk he had commanded so faithfully.

"Pier 90," he whispered. "Be there no later than 1800. Destroy that note you just made! Dress in civilian clothes, not your correspondent's uniform. Don't take a cab all the way to the pier. Get off two or three blocks away and walk the rest of the way."

It was the early summer of 1943.

I kissed Millie and Mike and Barry good-bye and patted the one in the oven—who turned out to be Dennis six months later. Mike, who was seven, gave me the first and only salute I ever rated as a correspondent.

I did as my leader had commanded, though it made no sense. All those German spies who followed me in black limousines with drawn blinds must have suspected that something was up when they saw me get out of the taxi and begin lugging my gear—including helmet and gas mask—in the direction of the *Queen Mary*. I clanked like a pots-and-pans peddler. It was a blazingly bright 6 P.M. The ship's proud bow and nameplate hovered over a busy West Side Highway. The spies' lingering doubts may have vanished completely during the night. An entire division marched aboard to the accompaniment of a brass band. The next noon the *Mary*'s horn rattled windows as far away as New Rochelle while tugs nuzzled her on her way. As we edged down the river toward the sea, thousands waved handkerchiefs from skyscraper windows. Tugs honked a farewell. Thus did we surreptitiously slip out of town.

"Attention! All men on deck!" the brass-lunged public address system boomed. Thousands cluttered to the decks.

"Face inboard!" we were ordered. The *Mary* was passing through the antisubmarine nets strung across the Narrows. They must not be looked upon by us who were about to die.

Later that first day out I was startled to hear myself being paged and asked to appear immediately at the purser's office. A young British officer in immaculate whites, with shorts, was looking vexedly at an immigration declaration I had filled out earlier.

"I'm sure you've made a mistake here, old boy, under 'Nationality,' " he said. "You've put down 'American.' "

"I *am* an American," I said, vibrating with an inner orchestration of "Yankee Doodle," "Dixie," and "The Battle Hymn of the Republic."

He looked at me as only the British Navy can.

"Are you a Red Indgeon? They are the only Americans."

I said, "That would come as a big fat surprise to the fourteen thousand guys on this ship who are going over to fight for you."

He ignored that, handed me a pen, and said, "Under 'Nationality' please write 'U.S.A.' "

At sea we zigged and zagged with metronomic monotony. Even an incurably cockeyed U-boat commander could not have failed to send us to the bottom. But nothing violent happened, except the day a big Negro kid blew his stack and began throwing his equipment overboard, yelling incoherently as he did so. A Negro sergeant as old and wise as Jersey Joe Walcott walked up slowly and said, almost soothingly, "Boy, don't do that." The kid wheeled and reached for his knife pocket, but he never got it out. The old sarge, who had been sucking on a bottle of Coke, hit the boy across the face with it and it cut him like the swipe of a machete. There wasn't any trouble after that.

A couple of the blacked-out nights we sat wherever possible, including the side of the bathtub, in the cabin I shared with Lt. Col. John Staige Davis, Air Force doctor, while Willie Shore and his USO troupe sang a song soft and low and, somehow, poignantly. A handful of Red Cross girls dropped by for these sessions, including Taty Spaatz, daughter of the Army Air Force general, and Kit Kennedy, cheerfully freckled daughter of the former ambassador to the Court of St. James's.

We debarked at Greenock while a Spitfire, a breathtakingly beautiful fighter when first (and last) seen, rolled over us beneath the low, gray overcast. The train to London took all day and well into the dark. A truck awaited us at the terminal and carried a full load of us—

standing and reeling—through the shrouded streets to the faintly lighted doorway of the Savoy. Dr. Davis and I had confirmed reservations there for the night, as did our fellow shipmate and truckmate, Walter Rothschild, the Brooklyn merchant prince and philanthropist who was a dollar-a-year man in Government service.

"As bedraggled a group as ever entered this lobby," observed a gaunt, gray, black-caped, black-suited old man whose cigarette ashes flowed like dry lava down his clothing. Turned out to be the beloved eccentric of Fleet Street's critics, Hannen Swaffer. We were to become good friends in the ensuing months, but that first meeting left something to be desired. So did the first meeting with the desk clerk the Savoy must have ordered from Madame Tussaud's. He introduced us to the most implacable expression of that period of austerity in Britain.

"You've had it," he clicked when I asked if we could have supper. The train had been foodless, and, foolishly, I mentioned that. He shook his head. "You've had it," he repeated, meaning an assortment of things: We were too late to be served, we had had such luxuries in the long ago past, we should be nourished by memories of better days. . . .

The only lodging available at the Savoy was a magnificent suite. John Staige Davis had three small cans of rations. I drew the beef stew. We held our repasts under the hot-water tap, and Walter somehow opened the cans with his penknife. We ate with our fingers, perhaps the first time that lack of couth had been seen in a Savoy suite since Henry VIII week-ended.

John Staige went off to his airfield in the Midlands the next day, and Rothschild disappeared on one of those unspelled-out dollar-a-year missions. The man from Tussaud's, or one just like him, moved me into more sensible quarters in the hotel. I was just settling in for the night in my pitch black room when the air-raid sirens went off. I was frightened, experiencing an alert for the first time, particularly after the anti-aircraft guns in Hyde Park began to cough and mutter and vaguely shake the deeply hooded windows. The rules of the hotel were that all guests must retreat to the air-raid shelter in its venerable bowels, but there was scant hope of finding it in the dark. At least, I must dress. No sense being blown out of one's room in pajamas. It was surprisingly difficult to find the necessary bits of clothing in that strange inky room. Halfway into them, with doom now swiftly approaching, I remembered more sobersided counsel given to me by the desk-flying lieutenant colonel back at 90 Church. He had put me through a crash course in how to don, secure, and operate my gas mask.

"Those Krauts will be using poison gas before very long," he said as he helped me through the incomprehensible.

Now, trapped in my posh cell, pants at half-mast and a left shoe on my right foot, I somehow found the mask. But it had been folded and packaged so ingeniously that I could not have opened it within a week. I was still struggling with it, using Braille, when the "All clear" sounded.

Thereafter, it seemed simpler during raids on London late at night to put a pillow over your head, pull the covers up around your shoulders, and go back to sleep.

This was hardly sheer bravado. This was the period between the Battle of Britain and the coming of the V-1's and V-2's. "Look at it this way," a correspondent with more experience put it. "Suppose the Germans dropped a half dozen fifty-dollar bills on this city of seven or eight million. What do you think your chances would be of catching one?"

Reactions to air raids were manifold, I soon found. Elderly ladies in London tended to have upset stomachs on mornings after emphatic raids. The Ministry of Health professed to have diagnosed the reason for this. If the bombing and cannonading grew menacing enough, the dear old girls would get out of bed, repair to the pantry, and eat some carefully harbored luxury item, long since disappeared from London's better grocery shelves: tinned deviled lobster, say. These were riches one *could* take with him to the grave.

One of the older cocks at INS, which ran a tight little bureau at 78 Fleet, found his long-dormant sexual prowess rejuvenated whenever the sirens sounded at night. Conveniently, he shacked up with another type of siren: a big blonde Scandinavian suspected of wishing that the Luftwaffe would bomb more often.

From Italy came still another report on the antics of the reflexes when bombs are dropping. Former heavyweight champion Jack Sharkey and the fabled Yankee pitcher Lefty Gomez were caught one night in a raid while doing a USO job. All hands were ordered to hit the slit trenches on the double. Sharkey dived into one head first, a belly flopper, and Gomez landed on top of him. The racket of the raid grew intolerable.

"We're going to die in this rotten place," Sharkey mourned into the dirt that pressed against his face. "We're going to die."

"You think so?" Gomez asked, his lips close to the former champion's ear.

"I know so," Sharkey muttered.

"If that's so," Lefty said, "may I ask you a question?"

"Heluva time to ask questions," Sharkey growled. "What is it?"

"Did you go in the tank for Carnera?"

The most senseless bomb that fell on England while I was there in 1943 was not meant for the target it hit. It was the one-bomb blitz against East Grinstead on July 1. A German bomber pilot fleeing home after an ineffectual daylight raid on London apparently shook loose a five-hundred pounder that had jammed in its release mechanism and was slowing down his escape. It fell into the thick overcast and plunged through the roof of an East Grinstead movie house that was showing a Western. Most of those killed or wounded were children. Nearly every family in the town was affected by that one bomb. But there was no time for mourning. The people of East Grinstead had to be cheerful.

On the edge of town sat the Queen Victoria Cottage Hospital where a wizard plastic surgeon from New Zealand, Archibald McIndoe, remade the faces and arms and hands of badly burned RAF men. There had been trouble at the hospital before the catastrophe of the movie house. A patient had committed suicide in the room later assigned to me. The bullet had passed through him and torn an unrepaired chunk out of a wall. He had looked at himself in a mirror for the first time since extensive surgery and grafting and found his noseless, earless, scorched face, hung with wattles of flesh from other parts of his body, too much to bear. Mr. McIndoe forthwith ordered all mirrors removed from the hospital. But then he gave a second and stunning order which must be obeyed: All patients able to walk must stroll through the streets of East Grinstead each day as part of their psychological therapy. No man, however ghastly, was excused—if he could walk.

Mr. McIndoe had prepared the people for their ordeal. They must not stare at the macabre strollers. They must not turn away. By all means, they must not become ill. They must make these horribly disfigured young men welcome. They must show them that normal people wanted them to come back to a normal life. They must invite them in for a spot of tea, or something stronger. On Saturday nights the pretty girls of the town and magnificent young nurses from the hospital would dance with these effigies of young men.

"Nursey, you'd never know it but I was a good-looker and the girlies couldn't get enough of me," a faceless and all but fingerless Spitfire pilot croaked with a jaunty laugh one day as I passed through his ward.

The girl came over to him and put her hand on what was left of his. "Don't I know!' she said. "That's what the whole lot of them tell me." And here and there in the ward sounded ghostly chuckles.

Then the bomb. Heartbreaking, but the town must rise above it. There was work to do.

I spent some time with Bob Hope on that trip, writing a Sunday feature on how he managed to keep going with his entertaining all day and most of the night. I never found out, and still haven't. But trying was interesting. At the end of a backbreaker of a day Bob and his writer-friend, Hal Block, who was to mean so much to the early success of television's "What's My Line?" would kick fresh gags around, weighing them, making notes to put the good ones into the next day's inventory. Sometimes they'd finish at four in the morning and have to start for the car or the airfield at six, headed for another round of camps and hospitals.

In the course of that trip Bob asked me to accompany him to the funeral of his British grandfather who had died one month short of his one hundredth year. I wondered if his presence in the little village might not eclipse the day's main event.

"Not a chance," he laughed. "I went back to the old place just after making it big on Broadway. My grandfather MC'd a show they put on in my honor. Nearly everybody in town turned out. He had them in stitches all the way. When I went on I gave them the full routine, everything that had made me big in New York. Laugh?—I thought they'd never start. In fact, they didn't. Then my grandfather introduced a couple of bell-ringers in bloomers—locals—and they broke up the joint."

At the old homestead a cousin led Bob into the little living room where the body lay in an open coffin.

"He looks better than I do," Hope said, and may have had something there.

One day Bob took over the controls of a small twin-engined plane provided for us by the RAF, and for the next few miles I felt I was on an invisible roller coaster. Holding on with one hand I scribbled a note to him with the other. It read, "Stop ad-libbing!" It led later to a revealing side of his labors overseas. The subject of insurance came up from nowhere. It reminded me of a bleak fact I tried to forget throughout the war: that if I were killed my insurance was worthless and Millie would be penniless. I asked Bob about his infinitely larger insurance.

"I'd blow it," he said with a shrug.

With other members of his troupe—Frances Langford, Tony Manero, and Jack Pepper—Bob showed up the next dawn at a field near Londonderry. The plane that was to take us to Belfast was the saddest-looking B-17 imaginable. It was patched like a clown's coat and gave every appearance of running on tired blood rather than gas. A sleepy airman in a shack of a terminal looked at Hope, unshaven, and pooped, did not recognize him, and handed him the usual chilling form the Air Force reserves for civilian passengers. Under "Person to be notified in case of death" Bob wrote:

"Louella Parsons."

We brought a precious cargo back to London from Belfast: two dozen real eggs. My quota was four. The eggs were the first I had seen in weeks. The Atheneum Court, where I lived by that time, was no different from any other war-rationed hotel in London. Its eggs were powdered, its sausages had only the barest acquaintance with meat, and its Spam was endless. It was imperative that the real eggs arrive in London unscathed. However, upon landing at tiny Hendon, there was a bad minute or two when we as well as the eggs seemed about to be cracked. The bucket-seat Lockheed Lodestar hit the short runway with a wallop, bounced crazily a time or two, and then the pilot gave his engines full throttle. We staggered off the end of the runway and somehow cleared the chimney pots of a residential area just beyond. We were all alarmed and terribly silent as the plane swung around for another landing attempt. I was sure the first one had mortally ruptured our landing gear. I looked across the tin aisle at Hope, sitting bolt upright among his shillelaghs, his blackthorn walking sticks, his bottle of Irish whisky, and his eggs. He was looking at me intently.

"What sort of billing do you think you'll get in the story of our crack-up?" he asked.

We landed safely, smuggled our loot into the egg-beleaguered city, and in gratitude for having survived the rough landing, I gave away three of my four. The fourth and last egg spent a peaceful, chilled night on my windowsill.

Next morning the floor waiter came in aglow with news.

"No Spam for you this morning, sir," he said. "We're serving real by-con. It's the first we've had in a long time."

I told him that the gods clearly had chosen this day to stand out like a star in the annals of wartime Britain's cookery. I fetched my egg off the ledge (the Luftwaffe had been thoughtful enough not to bomb the night before) and handed it to the waiter like the Kohinoor.

"Sunny side up with my bacon," I said.

He looked stricken.

"Sorry, sir, it's against regulations to have by-con and aig on the same dish," he said.

"But it's my egg. . . ."

He sighed. "There's not a thing I can do about it, sir. Regulations. I can fry your aig for you, but no by-con if I do. Or I can serve the by-con alone."

It was a somewhat less majestic compromise than the Missouri. In came the bacon and when the man was gone I locked the door, put my treasure in a glass and let the not-quite-hot-enough bathroom water run on it. After half an hour I had the first one-minute egg I ever sucked. Ghastly.

The greatest hero I interviewed while in England was Sgt. Maynard Smith, a B-17 waist-gunner inevitably called Snuffy, after Billy De Beck's testy little comic strip hillbilly. Col. Tex McCrary, the intrepid mission-flying Eighth Air Force public relations officer, arranged transportation so that I could be present and write something about Snuffy's sublimest hour. Turned out to be an unnerving hour, too, for Snuffy wasn't precisely the type the Air Force was featuring on its enlistment posters. He didn't fit the public's image of a Congressional Medal of Honor winner, which he was about to become in a glittering ceremony at Bassingbourn Airdrome, Cambridgeshire. Indeed, he'd be the only one in the whole ETO.

There was no question that he rated the highest decoration a grateful nation can offer. On his first mission over Germany, the previous May 1, his B-17 was jumped and set afire amidships by German fighters. It turned for home without fighter escort and was harder hit. Snuffy's fellow waist-gunner, the bombardier, the navigator, and the belly-turret gunner bailed out. Snuffy manned first one and then the other waist-gun position and shot down two of the enemy. Between times, he beat on the flames with his gloved hands or rolled his body against them. The tail-gunner crawled up to Snuffy's fiery section, shot through a lung. Snuffy gave him first aid and positioned him so that the lung would drain. He went back to firing his .50 calibers at the fighters again, but the fire grew hotter. He picked up the portable latrine and flung its contents on the fire.

Miraculously, the B-17's pilot and co-pilot coaxed the scorched wreck across the Channel and landed on an RAF grass strip at the water's edge. As the fire engines and ambulances arrived at the ravaged bomber's side, Snuffy was observed dousing the remaining flicker of flame by urinating on it.

Throughout the century and more of its existence there has never been a bestowal of the Medal of Honor quite like the day the hallowed ribbon and medal was hung around Snuffy's neck. Twelve generals including Ira Eaker, commander of the Eighth Air Force, and Jacob Devers, commander of ETO ground forces, lined up beside Secretary of War Henry L. Stimson, old in the service of his country but proud to be present on such a momentous occasion. Old Glory never fluttered better, airmen never marched in review with as much cadence, and a dozen B-17's drummed low over the noble scene.

The only one who seemed to be out of uniform was Snuffy. He had been roughed up in a happy free-for-all in a public house in Oxford the week before, made the constables very mad at him, was turned back to the Air Force, and drew a most unusual punishment for a man on combat: KP duty, peeling potatoes. A larger sergeant loaned him his coat for the great occasion, Snuffy's having been ripped beyond fast repair in the Oxford caper.

When it was all over, I met Snuffy. He had been given the short pin-on ribbon of the award and the rosette. But he was still wearing the round-the-neck ribbon and its dangling medal. After a few routine questions and answers, I asked him if he would like a drink.

"Are you some kind of a nut? Of course I would."

It was a good half-mile walk to the Nissen hut where I had a cot. Halfway there I noticed an Air Force captain striding in the opposite direction. He obviously had missed the ceremony, didn't know Snuffy, and was excessively salute-conscious. As the gap closed, his right arm stiffened, ready to return Snuffy's salute. Snuffy ignored him, continuing to talk to me. They were abreast now. The captain stopped and glared at Snuffy, his right arm now half-up.

"Buzz off," Snuffy said to him. We kept walking, with Snuffy chatting as if he did not share my expectation of our both being shot in the back by the flushed and angry officer.

"There's a bum who don't know history," Snuffy remarked. "I guess he never heard that no Congressional Medal of Honor winner ever has to initiate a salute. The other guy salutes the Medal, first."

We had a drink out of the bottle and then Snuffy said he must be getting back to his Nissen to see his fellow noncoms and go to chow. I walked back with him, taking more notes. He lay down on his bed and lighted a cigarette.

" 'Ten-shun!" an airman barked near the door of the hut. A bird colonel entered. Every man leaped to his feet and stood at attention. Except Snuffy. The colonel walked to the foot of Snuffy's cot and reddened as Snuffy lay there and regarded him indifferently through an exhalation of cigarette smoke.

The colonel braced and saluted the reclining figure of Sgt. Maynard Smith.

"General Eaker's compliments, Sergeant Smith," the colonel said. "The General would be pleased to have you at the officers' mess for lunch."

Snuffy looked at the proud and distinguished officer for what seemed an eternity. Then he spoke, ever so casually.

"Tell him I'm busy," Snuffy said.

The colonel turned and marched out faster than he had entered.

"You shouldn't have done that, buddy," I volunteered after the hut had relaxed with a wheeze of admiration.

"Why not?" Snuffy asked with great honesty. "I didn't make the rules. Everybody's got to salute the Medal, salute me first. Eisenhower's got to salute me."

That was hard to top, but I tried.

"MacArthur doesn't," I pointed out.

"Yeah? How come?"

"He's got the Congressional Medal of Honor."

Something died in Snuffy.

"Oh, rats!" he said.

Unbeknown to the poor slob, the American taxpayer (circa 1944–45) underwrote some of the most senseless expeditions in the history of transportation. I should know. I was both a taxpayer and a beneficiary.

I had felt until the junkets of 1944–45 that the war's high point in useless expenditure would remain an exercise in England in the early fall of '43. Mr. Churchill called it Harlequin. Thousands, maybe tens of thousands, of troops were trucked, trained, bussed, flown, and marched to embarkation points, along with all their gear. Some never-revealed number boarded ships and troop carriers, headed for what was then never called Festung Europa, but made U-turns about a mile out in the Channel and came back to port. That whole section of England seemed to shake under the roar of planes just before daybreak. They, too, returned to their bases. Coastal anti-aircraft batteries blazed away, shooting blanks.

Harlequin, indeed.

The realization that it was just a show, a sham, somehow increased the chill in the air as I stood with a group of British war correspondents on a windy promontory at Newhaven, Sussex East. A great slash of pink began to show its lovely face in the east. We watched the rebirth of day in silence and wonderment. That is, all but one of us.

"Bugger the rosy-fingered dawn!" a British correspondent muttered.

It remains one of the worst obscenities I've ever heard.

Harlequin (which was said to have greatly annoyed Stalin, who was pressing the Allies hard for the opening of the Second Front) at least could be condoned as a dress rehearsal for D-Day. I was never able to discover the true purpose, if any, of an Air Transport Command visitation to the North country in November, 1944. ATC billed it as a trip which would prove for all time that no degree of Arctic violence could stay those winged messengers from the swift completion of their appointed rounds, occasionally rounds of drinks. Arctic Safety Trip; that was the way our orders were cut.

The Safety Trip got off to an interesting start. Our bucket-seat C-46's port engine burst into flames shortly after takeoff. The pilot put the flying gas tank (there was a big one inside the cabin, too) into a sharp 180-degree turn. We limped back into the landing pattern on one engine, with the other one smoking like a chimney on its gas-heavy wing. We hit hard about one third down the runway. I caught a blurred view of several pieces of fire-fighting apparatus and an ambulance giving chase. The pilot gave his craft all the brakes it had, and when they proved insufficient he managed to bring us to a stop by making a 180-degree turn at the end of the runway.

"Out!" someone ordered, as if the whole business was about to erupt in one vast fiery belch.

We moved as fast as we could to the now-open door in the rear. The last wisp of smoke fluttered from the engine, which the pilot had immersed in the fire-throttling chemical foam with which planes are equipped. Just then the first fire truck drew up with a screech of brakes. A boy dressed in what looked like a deep-sea diver's outfit made of asbestos, head encased in a weird cylindrical helmet with a glass peephole, leaped off the still-moving truck, pulling a hose behind him. He pointed the nozzle of his fire-fighting weapon at the burned and foam-flaked engine. His gloved fingers twitched on the nozzle's trigger. But there was no fire left to put out. He took off his helmet and looked at the former fire in disgust.

"Shit," he said.

It seemed like such an unusual reaction that I sought him later—while someone in charge was ordering another plane—and asked him to explain.

"I been chasing planes ever since I got in the service two years ago," he said. "Something always happens at the last minute, and I don't get to squirt my hose. Today looked like the day more than any other time. Then just as I got there the goddam fire goes out. It's driving me nuts."

There wasn't much to do except apologize and go to the new plane, a C-47. The Safety Trip began all over again. All went well until we arrived at LaGuardia, where our group was transferred into another C-47 bound for Presque Isle, Maine. ATC's handling of the group's typewriters left something to be desired. They were put on a plane going somewhere else. There was another jarring note. Just before the pilot buttoned up the C-47 and prepared to taxi away for the takeoff, a general arrived with his staff and all their gear. The pilot remonstrated as vigorously as he dared that the plane was already overloaded and not another pound could be carried without endangering all hands. The general outvoted the other forty of us by a healthy majority of 1 to 40.

ATC could fly in the teeth of the Arctic's iciest gale, perhaps, but it couldn't get off the ground at Presque Isle for forty-eight hours because of a slight drizzle. During the wait, somebody back at headquarters concluded that perhaps it might be better to spring a better airplane for that increasingly restless platoon of reporters. We drew a four-engined C-54. It took us to the U.S. airbase at Stevenville, Gander, where another chapter was added to the saga of the Safety Trip.

"Anything happening around here?" Carl Levin of the New York *Herald Tribune* asked an airman as we deplaned.

"Nothing much," the kid said, "except the crash."

"Crash! What crash?"

"Oh, a '54 like the one you're on. It pranged a mountain out there last night, trying to find the field."

Unluckily, the Air Transport Command had deposited a whole plane load of reporters at a point near a crash which, under normal wartime conditions, would have attracted, at most, an obscure paragraph. It was not the kind of story ATC wanted spread at any time; now countless thousands of words began pouring from our reclaimed typewriters. The tour's ATC public relations officer, Maj. Lynn Mahan, a decent man, made the lot of us what a few of us considered a fair proposition: ATC would supply all the details of the crash, names of the dead and names of the survivors. In exchange, he asked us to spare the feelings of the next-of-kin of the dead by limiting the more grisly details of the crack-up and concentrate on the good job done by rescue forces who climbed the wild peak and saved lives. It was depressing to hear several of our number accuse him bitterly of trying to throttle the free press.

I never wondered again why so many good public relations people hate our guts.

The by now numb Safety Trip reached Bluie West 8, Greenland, just in time to be present when an Army Air Force officer who had been stationed there a bit too long blew his stack in front of some of us and launched into the worst condemnation of ATC we had ever heard. Printable portions made some of the papers represented in our group.

There seemed to be no statute of limitations on the trip's bad luck. One of the officers assigned as our keepers got himself pleasantly involved with a six-foot version of Ingrid Bergman within ten minutes after our arrival in Reykjavik. He was deeper involved three days later as we prepared to leave. The massive rosy-jawed beauty came to the airport to see him off. One hazarded a guess, judging from appearances, that they had not spent all of their time together discussing U.S.-Icelandic cod-fishing treaties. Our roué stood several inches shorter and fifty degrees colder than his girl. She enveloped him in a great hug and cried on the top of his head in the course of the most one-sided farewell since Rhett Butler took leave of Scarlet O'Hara.

It was time to go. Our man, who couldn't wait for the propellers to start turning, broke away from a last kiss, with the noise of a rubber suction cup pulled off a glass pane, patted her paternally on her buttocks, and spoke the line that was used more often and less sincerely than any other sentence uttered overseas in World War II:

"Good-bye, honey," he said. "If you ever come to the United States, be sure to look me up."

On Christmas Eve the following year, our hero was assembling the toys after tucking in the three kids for the night. His ever-loving wife, about to have their fourth, was knitting contentedly in her chair. There was Peace on Earth in cozy little Peaceful Glade, Virginia, for men of such good will.

There was, at least, until the phone rang. Our man picked it up and—as was his wont—officiously announced his name. Then he froze.

"Dolling!" a deliriously happy Icelandic voice crackled in the phone. "It's your Poopsie. I'm here!"

The China-Burma-India theater was a bypassed arena of World War II by mid-summer of 1945. Japanese forces still held most of the China coast, but there was little fighting. Chiang Kai-shek's armies and those of Mao Tse-tung, ostensibly allied in the common cause of casting the Nippon devils out of China, were busily engaged instead in caching arms against the inevitable postwar day when they would fight for possession of the world's most populous country. In Burma and India there was hardly a memory of the war. Each was more concerned with the kind of postwar world it would inherit or be forced to accept.

China was America's problem child, exasperating but tolerated, expensive but endured. If any American in or out of public office at that time suspected that one day China would be considered a major menace to the welfare of the United States, he held his tongue. Its excesses were conversation pieces, but hardly alarming. There were dozens of reports that Chinese recruits being transported like cattle in C-47's across the Hump to India, for training, occasionally would throw one of their number out of the plane's open door for laughs. Tons of Chinese paper currency, printed in the United States, were jettisoned by cargo planes experiencing engine trouble, it was said. Everybody seemed to accept the story that Chinese co-pilots on Hump-flying runs made fortunes trafficking in penicillin, Parker 51's, and Scotch. It was unquestionably true that Chinese farmers along the fuel pipeline we built from the Persian Gulf to Kunming regarded it as their own. They'd occasionally crack it open just to fill a primitive lamp with a few ounces, and let the precious stuff gush for hours, sometimes days, until U.S. repair crews could find the precise breach and patch it. Other Chinese would break open the pipe at night, light the spilling gas, and gather around to enjoy the impressive flames. The fuel was estimated to cost twenty-five dollars a gallon by the time it attempted to slip past the Chinese farmers.

Chinese military and civil officials sometimes unnerved and shut up indignant Americans who protested against Chinese robbers by seizing the robber, or a reasonable facsimile, and chopping off one of his hands. Exhausted Hump fliers learned to sleep fully clothed in their Kunming bunks after their more trusting buddies had been virtually robbed naked by Chinese while sleeping off the rigors of flying aid to the same Chinese. In July, 1945, the United States presented the Generalissimo with a C-47 whose interior had been fitted to serve as his combination airborne headquarters and executive suite. The plane was named the Mayling, for Madame Chiang. It reached Kunming too late in the afternoon to risk continuation of its ultimate deliverance on Chungking's unlighted side-of-the-mountain airstrip. So the U.S. ferry crew parked it at Kunming for the night. Chiang, pleased over the present from the grateful democracy on the other side of the world, flew in his honor guard to police the plane through the night. The next morning, when the American crewmen reported to fly the plane to Chungking, they found it stripped of most of its furnishings. Even the springs in the seats had been carried away. Obviously, the honor guard had rifled it.

Still, China was preferred to India, almost equally poor but much more forlorn about its status. There was always something antic about China. The fierce regimentation eventually imposed on it by the Communists was nowhere in evidence. In India the poor shrank from an American's efforts to be friendly. In China the people met you half way, with a smile and often a prepared plan to relieve you of your shirt at the earliest opportunity. They laughed. The Indians and Burmese preferred heavy sighs. The consensus was that the Chinese would be first-class allies forever if they patched up their petty political differences. Toward that end, the United States insisted in time that Chiang integrate Mao people into his Kuomintang government —with historically disastrous results.

Chiang's younger son by his first wife tried to be helpful during our stay there. He had trained in Arizona as a flier and had picked up many American ways and expressions which he tried, with lamentable results, to implant in his father. I was witness to one setback in his attempted Americanization of the Gimo. In the course of a luncheon Chiang gave us at the graduation ceremonies of China's "West Point," near Sian, I related to young Major Chiang a story Pat Hurley had told me not long before. I asked Hurley how he, an old soldier and politician, sank into diplomacy. He answered with a typically thundering anecdote. Seems (he said) he was caught in a Japanese bombing raid on Port Moresby, New Guinea, early in the war. While running for a slit trench he was hit in the back of the head by a bomb fragment.

"I was unconscious for two or three days, and when I woke up I was a diplomat," he told me. Young Chiang enjoyed the story much more than it warranted.

"You must tell that to my father just the way you told it to me," he insisted, and would brook no protest. "Don't worry about the language problem," he said. "You just tell it to him, and I'll interpret as you go along. He'll love it."

It laid an egg. A five-hundred-year-old Chinese egg. As I reached the pallid punchline, young Chiang was laughing so robustly he had trouble sputtering his words. He slapped his knee with joy and searched his father's face for a reaction. So did I.

Chiang's face remained an inscrutable mask throughout. His luminous black eyes never left mine as I spoke. An infernal ten seconds or so after his son's laughter and the translation had died away, Chiang muttered a few words in Chinese, still with no change in expression. His son sighed and led me away.

"You know what he said?" young Chiang asked me. "He said, 'I trust General Hurley was not injured badly.' "

I often think of Sian and wonder if its pleasant people still water down its wide and dusty streets each evening to keep the dust at bay. It was the thriving capital of the Ch'in dynasty, which gave China its name, 250 years before Christ. For me, it provided two enduring memories. I lay ill and homesick in a rickety hotel there one afternoon when the door was flung open by Bob Rodenberg, an old friend I had worked with on the Washington *Herald* ten years before. Bob was stationed nearby at an OSS camp, had wandered into Sian, spotted one of the correspondents with our group, and, making small talk, remarked that he had a friend who was a reporter—name of Considine.

"He's at that fleabag down the street, dying of the crud or something," Rodenberg was told. He took me to the OSS camp and nursed me back to health with repeated applications of Four Roses and apple pie.

Harry Grayson supplied my other indelible memory of Sian. One day the neighborhood shook with the approach of a brassy band playing the "Wedding Hymn" from *Lohengrin.* Behind the musicians followed four Chinese carrying a sedan chair whose curtains were drawn. We followed it to the site of the wedding, a public room in our hotel. The bespectacled and extraordinarily homely groom was waiting. The bearers put down their burden near him and out stepped one of the loveliest creatures I've ever seen, a shy but radiant young Chinese in her wedding robes.

It was a beautiful wedding, somewhat marred by my friend Grayson. "Poor son of a bitch," he'd say from time to time, chewing his cigar. Harry felt sorry for the groom for getting married. Hooked, Harry said.

It is difficult to equate the Chinese I came to know in 1945 with, let us say, the Chinese who have nuclear weapons, the Chinese who underwent without audible protest the "cultural revolution" of 1966 which was hazily delineated in Peking's *People's Daily* as follows:

> China's masses of workers, peasants, and soldiers and revolutionary cadres and intellectuals have started to criticize the old world, old things, and old thinking on an unprecedented scale, using as their weapon the thought of Mao Tse-tung.
>
> We criticize the system of exploitation, the exploiting classes, imperialism, modern revisionism, all reactionaries, landlords, rich peasants, counter-revolutionaries, bad elements, and rightists.
>
> We criticize the representatives of the bourgeoisie and bourgeois "scholars and authorities." We criticize the bourgeois conception of history, bourgeois academic theories, pedagogy, journalism, and theories of art and literature, and all bad plays, films, and works of literature and art.
>
> In sum, we criticize the old world, the old ideology and culture, and old customs and habits which imperialism and all exploiting classes use to poison the minds of the working people; we criticize all nonproletarian ideology, all reactionary ideology which is antagonistic to Marxism-Leninism, to Mao Tse-tung's thought.

. . . Poor son of a bitch.

In the summer of 1946 the United States produced a nuclear spectacular which, if presented today, would bring down on its head the frowns and fulminations of much of the civilized world—excepting France and Communist China, which would wish for such an entrepreneur's role. We tested two twenty-kiloton A-bombs at Bikini Atoll in the Ralik chain of the Marshall Islands. Their targets, securely anchored, were rusty relics of World War II's naval engagements: obsolete American, Japanese, and German warships, plus complements of laboratory animals, mostly rats but also goats and pigs. The project was named "Operation Crossroads," into which some of us on hand tried to read a certain significance. It engaged 42,000 men from the Army, Army Air Force, Navy, and Marine Corps, some of them against their wills. It was a time when most servicemen wanted out of uniform. It was also a time when the national conscience was first being pricked by the massive horror we had rained on Hiroshima and Nagasaki (and would have flung down on Tokyo, which was to have been the target of Bomb No. 3). On the "Big Apple" (as our ship was called) and elsewhere there was mirthless jesting about the possible effect of the Bikini bombs on visiting genitals.

We had a monopoly on the Bomb but were hardly adverse to demonstrating what it could do. Eleven nations accepted our far-flung invitations to send observers, as did the United Nations Atomic Energy Commission, members of Congress, representatives of the scientific community which had produced the weapon, and a motley army of newsmen. The latter journeyed from Oakland to Bikini aboard the *Appalachian,* a communications ship noted for its abominable communications. The Navy insisted on the ship as the very least it could contribute to an experiment designed primarily to show the uselessness of having a surface Navy in Year One of the Atomic Age. We ploughed westward for many days at eight knots, followed by an eight knot wind which thus lay on us like an oven's continuous breath. Some were driven to drink and, surprisingly, did not find it hard to get. Sensing the probable need for such relief, the Navy had been unusually clement in the language in which it couched our orders. Our papers read that alcoholic beverages were strictly forbidden aboard all U.S. Navy ships, but for Operation Crossroads there would be no baggage inspection. Thus, many reporters brought two bags aboard at Oakland: one for clothing, one for comfort.

Still, it was an infernally long voyage. The "Big Apple" had never before been asked to carry as undisciplined a party. The executive officer, a ludicrous martinet, was soon reduced to a perpetual rage at the sight of our lolling about the decks for days on end, dropping cigarette butts on his spotless craft, and ordering ice brought to our stuffed cabins as if we were aboard a bloody *Queen.* Powerless to do anything about us, he spent his venom on the crew. They chipped a vast fortune in paint during that trip, and several times each day they were forced to line up in front of us for a spit and polish review in which the exec set new U.S. Navy records for lint-picking. We urged the crew to mutiny against him and set him adrift in an open boat with a pint of water and two breadfruit, but they never took this excellent advice.

A Russian reporter, whose bunk was on the lowest level of a four-tier job in the largest and most crowded cabin, pinned the picture of a hula girl on the bottom of the mattress of the bunk just above him and would lie for hours looking up at it, two or three inches above his nose. Now and then on the long first leg of the trip he was heard to mumble "Havaii . . . vimmen!" But the pleasure of expectation must have been diminished by his need to throw up again. He was our only seasick newsman, but generously made up for the rest of us. In the same gamy cell a fine-looking young reporter who had been shot up during the war haunted the evenings with his nightmares. In his torment he would call for his mother like a frightened child in the dark.

Honolulu was a happy respite, save for the man from Tass. He remained too ill to accomplish the dreams that had sustained him for 2,200 miles at eight knots. My friend Red McQueen, sports editor of the Honolulu *Advertiser,* and his dear wife Glenn adopted a good half of us and made their pleasant waterside home in the Kahala area ring with hospitality. It was interesting and enlightening, too, to meet Clark Lee's wife—incongruously called Baby—a robust and fullback-sized granddaughter and heiress of the last Queen of the Hawaiian Islands, Liliuokalani. I arrived at their palatial home bearing a lei and commenced the pleasant ritual of draping it about her shoulders. "Please," Baby said, waving it aside, "I'm allergic to leis."

Sometimes one must go a great distance to learn a small thing. The long second leg of the trip to the bomb-test area was a case in point. One learned, for example, that the U.S. Navy will not stop one of its ships—specifically, the "Big Apple"—to retrieve a medicine ball erratically heaved overboard during a game. When we lost the third and last of the ship's supply, we exercised our talents instead of our tired blood. We wrote a theme song, to be sung to the easiest-remembered melody of Gilbert and Sullivan's *H.M.S. Pinafore.* We dedicated it to the patrician officer in charge of us, Capt. Fitzhugh Lee, U.S.N., named for his illustrious grandfather, the Confederate cavalry general who so well served his own uncle, Robert E. It was a poor verse, but there was little else to do at eight knots:

We are the boys of Fitzhugh Lee
We hate the Navy and we hate the sea
We hate the Army and we hate this ship
But we're all signed up for the atomic trip.
(We're all signed up for the atomic trip.)
We're all signed up and ready to go
To offer up our testicles for UNO.

There was a verse near the end that poked fun at the two most distinguished science writers aboard, Howard Blakeslee of the Associated Press and William L. Laurence of the *New York Times,* who had written about the explosive properties of uranium as far back as 1940, was the only journalistic witness of the Nagasaki bombing, and the sole pool man for the entire development of the Bomb. The verse had something feckless to say about the impressive scholarship of the two men, made so bold as to doubt if they knew what they were talking about, and ended with what we all felt was a superior rhyme, composed by two of our better wits, Steve White and Tom Priestly. It went (still to the rhythm of Messrs. Gilbert and Sullivan):

Oh, the goddam thing will hang in midair
And Energy will never equal MC square!

Once at the scene, which had overtones of a grisly Gauguin depicting natives being moved away to avoid contamination with radioactive fallout, all newsmen aboard the "Big Apple" became painfully aware they were the helpless victims of Navy communications. Most of our early stories elicited starts of surprise from stateside offices. They arrived in badly garbled condition or out of sequence. Clark Lee and I, along with our counterparts with AP and UP, offered our services to the Navy as impartial wire-filers who could keep the stories in order and pass them along in proper sequence to the ship's teletype operators. Navy was hurt. Navy said the ship's communications center was off-limits to civilians. Navy said it had been handling messages since long before Admiral Farragut's "Damn the torpedoes! Captain Drayton, go ahead! Jouett, full speed!" How that ever emerged without its syntax scrambled, though it passed through Navy hands, remains a mystery.

But Fitzhugh Lee presented a comforting compromise. He issued an order to the ship's communications center to turn the story-basket upside down, when the transmission period began, and thus the story that was first in the basket would be the first to be sent.

The day before the first test, a freelance type nobody seemed to have much respect for—probably because he wore a black homburg with shorts and aloha shirt—handed me ten typewritten pages and asked me to read them. It was a lurid, eyewitness account, or vision, of the next day's event. It had borrowed heavily from Bill Laurence's Pulitzer Prize-winning descriptions of the first A-bomb test at Alamogordo, New Mexico, and the Nagasaki detonation—without credit. Our hero portrayed himself as having been knocked to the deck by the concussion, following which (I read on) he shook off the terrible blow of twenty-thousand tons of TNT, fought his way back to his post at the rail of the *Appalachian,* and beheld an enormous conflagration "brighter, more dazzling, than 100 suns." I laughed when I finished it, but he was serious.

"Laugh all you want," he said, "but I just filed it. My newspapers will have it in hand, in type, and ready to go as soon as the flash comes in that the bomb has been dropped."

He must have read my face.

"Okay, it ain't ethical," he said. "But it'll get through."

The bomb was dropped on schedule, July 1, 1946, from a B-29 passing over the chained flotilla at thirty thousand feet. Its aim left something to be desired, but it sank five of the ninety target ships, ignited an escort carrier's deck, further scorched an already crisp and ugly Japanese battleship, gutted the superstructure of a sub, and ruptured the boilers of the handsomest of the doomed ships, the German pocket battleship *Prinz Eugen.* From where we tried to watch it wasn't nearly as exciting as Black Homburg's story, by now snugly arrived at its several destinations. We were positioned fourteen miles from the blast and our vision was almost completely blacked out by welders' glasses. As for the sound of the bomb, it was like the sound of a discreet belch at the other end of a bar. But there was a torrent of activity on our typewriters. A blizzard of stories hit the communications center almost simultaneously.

Captain Lee's orders were scrupulously obeyed. The first story placed in the basket that day ran six pages. The seaman in charge of impartiality turned the filled basket upside down and handed the six pages to the seaman assigned to send it. That seaman, obeying the order as he understood it, sent the story in just that order, beginning with Page 6 and persevering backwards to Page 1. I wrote fifteen pages. I learned later that Page 15 was the first to arrive at INS-San Francisco. My "lead" came in the next day. A patient man named Harry Bergman, at INS-San Francisco, put together the scrambled stories he received from me and from Clark Lee, updating mine for the morning papers along our circuit, Clark's for the afternoons, as we used to say, dropping the apostrophe. "My" stories, liberally laced with Lee's words, won INS's George R. Holmes Award, named for the late great head of our Washington bureau. That's show business.

Forty-eight hours after the shot Bikini lagoon was judged safe enough for correspondents, and vice versa. Our tour of the damage was made memorable by our leader, Captain Lee. For reasons comprehensible only to Annapolis graduates, he was cheered by what short-sighted newsmen considered a pretty beat-up array of targets.

"Good as ever!" the captain boomed as we tooled slowly past a submarine that looked, in retrospect, like the fish in Hemingway's *The Old Man and the Sea* just before it docked at Havana. "Any good crew could have her under way in short order," he pronounced as we passed the wavy-decked and flaky escort carrier. Maj. John Moynihan, the Army Air Force public relations man who had been all the way with the Bomb, from the tinkering stage to Tinian to Hiroshima and Nagasaki to Bikini, had a hard time getting in *his* word. His word was that an unlucky thing happened to the bomb as it slid out of the B-29's bomb bay. It scraped, or something, and one of its several chubby tail wings was knocked off, which compromised its true aerodynamism, or some such. Instead of detonating smack over the ugly old Japanese battleship, which deserved nothing more, it blazed immediately over a light Japanese destroyer and crushed it like a sardine can, which may have been the inspiration of its designer.

The second test put the Bomb in a more properly somber perspective. It was our first underwater experiment with a weapon whose proliferation would haunt all mankind. It regurgitated a monstrous fountain whose falling waters contaminated everything they touched. It ripped the guts out of nine ships. The *Prinz Eugen,* which seemed to have been spared, later plunged to the bottom of the sea while being towed to the United States.

I haven't the foggiest notion of how many plane trips I've taken in search of news or to cover a story. But I have a clear memory of a flight I did not take. In 1949 I received an invitation from Lynn Mahan, by that time doing public relations for The Netherlands, to join a press junket he was leading to Batavia (Djakarta) for a last look at Dutch colonialism before it succumbed to Sukarno. I was the first to accept the invitation. But Barry Faris came up with other plans for me. He assigned me to Germany for the last runs of the Berlin Air Lift and the birth of the Federal Republic of Germany. The KLM Constellation carrying Mahan and his press group, including the legendary H. R. Knickerbocker, crashed at Bombay and killed all aboard.

My borrowed time has been spent gratefully.

There was that touch of Korea, circa 1950, in the stunned early weeks of the war.

("What's on the other side of that hill?" I asked a dog-tired, sick-of-retreating GI. "Another hill," he said.)

And getting to know MacArthur at one of the most tempestuous periods of his life as a folk hero. He had just shaken Washington, and London, and the UN by flying to Taipei without President Truman's permission to engage in what appeared to be war talks with Chiang Kai-shek. There might have been fewer jitters back home if the full text of the Supreme Commander's remarks had been printed.

("Tony, look at the leg on Madame Chiang," he whispered to his aide and pilot, Colonel Story, as he stood ramrod stiff at the top of the plane steps while the band played and the Chiangs waited to welcome him. The wind was doing little tricks with Madame's beautifully tailored split-gown. "The leg of a girl of twenty . . .")

And a productive swing through Europe in 1951, with a stopover at Villa Taverna for a TV interview with Ambassador Clare Boothe Luce.

("Where shall we set up the camera?" I asked. "Let's case the joint," Her Excellency said in her grandest manner.)

Then back to Korea in '52, this time with President-elect Eisenhower. Our departure was spooky. Ike was spirited out of his Columbia University president's mansion in the dead of a cold November night, after the Secret Service had tricked the mansion's sentry, a New York cop, into going around the corner to an all-night beanery for a cup of coffee. As soon as the cop was out of sight, Eisenhower, who had been waiting behind the door, stepped outside and trotted to the limousine parked down the street. The car's headlights had been killed. The little bulbs inside the car that light up when a door is opened had been unscrewed, so no mortal eye could recognize the figure who stepped into the shrouded car and was swiftly driven away. For days thereafter, John Foster Dulles, Secretary of State-designate, appeared at the mansion with an impressively stuffed briefcase and, upon leaving hours later, calmly told reporters he had had another stimulating meeting with the President-elect. The getaway of the press pool was equally clandestine. The Secret Service would not let us alert our offices as to takeoff time.

But nobody was pulling the wool over the eyes of Bob Rodenberg. Trust an old OSS man to find a weak link in what appeared to be the strongest security chain since the gestation of the A-bomb. By accident, Bob called our apartment at some unconscionable hour the morning of the takeoff. Deborah, then three, was the only one awake. She had only recently discovered the telephone.

"Hello, baby," Rodenberg said patiently. "Let me speak to your daddy."

"He's not here," the cunning little spy lisped. "He's flying to Korea with General Eisenhower."

There was an odd little scene at Iwo Jima, where we took a two-day breather after pausing only long enough at Hawaii, Midway, and Wake to refuel. The commanding officer of Iwo's air base laid on a string of jeeps to carry Ike and his party to the Marine memorial atop Mt. Suribachi. It was a hot day filled with the island's stench of sulfur and swarming with tiny, indigenous black bugs that hit like pebbles. Ike, in fresh khaki, collar spread open, strolled from his Nissen-hut quarters toward his jeep. Gen. Jerry Persons stepped up close to him and whispered something that caused Ike's face to become a sternly upset mask. He turned on his heel, reentered the hut without a word, and reappeared minutes later wearing a necktie —and a sorely put-upon look.

"Dammit," he muttered as he climbed aboard his jeep, "one of these times I'm going to do something the way *I* want to do it."

If I had gone with Lynn Mahan, as I had wanted to, I would never have seen the gloriously girlish smile of Elizabeth II at the end of her incredibly taxing coronation in '53. Or Khrushchev's childish pushing and shoving of Bulganin, in order to enter the Soviet limousine ahead of the premier at the Geneva Summit Conference of '55. And I would have missed the vintage year of '56.

In the spring of that year the Defense Department let the world in on the test of an H-bomb, for the first and presumably the last time. Repeated delays kept us in the Bikini-Eniwetok area for most of the month of May. This time, the entrepreneurs wanted to be sure. Two years earlier an unexpected shift in the wind carrying a giant radioactive mushroom across the Pacific from its point of birth at Bikini had changed the hot cloud's course and its fallout pattern. It seriously contaminated a stretch 240 miles long and 40 miles wide, struck and sickened 236 Marshall Islanders and 31 U.S. test personnel on Rongelap and Utirik islands, and dripped its "ghastly dew" on the 23-man crew of the *Fukuryu Maru* ("Fortunate Dragon") which was tuna-fishing 85 miles from Bikini. The Japanese were hospitalized for a year, and when one died the relations between the two countries reached their lowest ebb since the War. The miscalculation cost the United States millions in reparations and incalculable face.

Now in May of '56 a bigger and hotter bomb was to be tried, the first hydrogen bomb to be dropped from a bomber. One of the postponements, made necessary by a last-minute weather reading, occurred while the B-52 bearing the H-bomb was airborne and all hands on the observation ships had been told to prepare to put on their protective glasses. The bomber returned its megaton monster safely to Eniwetok, but from somewhere out of the night a two-man B-60, one of the jets scheduled to flirt around the edges of the radioactive cloud and scoop in samples of its poison, plunged into that forlorn area of the Pacific. Our press ship, the *Mt. McKinley,* joined in the fruitless twenty-four-hour search that followed. On what amounted to the second night of the hopeless hunt our restless searchlight spotted something glowing in the water. The bullhorns gave a breathtaking command for a boat to be lowered. I strained my eyes against the night, praying that the tantalizing glow would become a flashlight held by a man, two men, on a raft. Nightmarishly, throughout this throat-catching scene, a claptrap movie blared on deck and commanded the absolute attention of perhaps a hundred officers and seamen.

The glow in the water was a reflection from a tin can.

The test was a deeply moving experience. Just to sense that the ship's loudspeaker system said, "Bomb away," not "Bombs away," was to dwell moodily on how science had miniaturized and neatly packaged the art of overkill. Each with his own thoughts, we sweated out the long seconds of the bomb's fall. We were forty miles from the islet intended for extinction, but one could toy with the possibility that the bombardier had lost his bearings. . . .

And then our whole world became a hell that erupted on the predawn horizon and engulfed us in its fiery spell. Instinctively, our heads dropped and our shoulders hunched, as if bracing against and warding off a blow we could not comprehend. Instant and alarming heat swept over us. But the light, the indescribable light, was worse. It was a scalding thing, condition, presence. It permeated, pierced, and nothing could stop it. It plunged through welders' glasses, through our clothing, our skulls, our marrow.

I raised my head and beheld through the black glasses a conflagration I knew I could never reduce to words, a huge and tormented and boiling and seething and flaming Thing that now was reshaping itself as it rose against its gray-black backdrop. For a moment it became a flaming red arm bloodily holding aloft a white-hot sword, the bottom of the arm encased in a huge lace cuff tailored of the boiling and steaming sea. And then the thing was a huge brazen ball ascending and sucking behind it that part of creation where it had been born. It seemed safe enough by now to look upon it without protective lenses. Something warned me as I raised the left side of my black glasses to direct my gaze downward at my typewriter rather than at the Thing. It was just as well. The light from the bomb was still blinding to the naked eye.

There was still no sound. It was still en route. And in that eerie silence, like a film that has lost its soundtrack, a seaman said in a voice that went boyishly off key, "Christ. Suppose that had been my home town. . . ."

In time the white mushroom cloud grew and spread until it measured one hundred miles across its crown. Jets flying so high that only their vapor trails were visible, slender as slim white woolen threads, stitched at the edges of the great cloud as if trying to sew it to the blueing sky.

"I'd say it was two or three megatons," remarked a scientist at the ship's rail.

Bill Laurence, our doughty dean, held up a separated thumb and forefinger, peered at the departing cloud through the aperture, and ruled, "I make it at least five megatons."

This learned dialogue was too much for Ed Lahey of the Knight papers.

"Megatons schmegatons, it was one hell of a bomb!" he snorted.

It would have been hard to find a greater change of pace than the following month's assignment to cover the wedding of Grace Kelly to

Prince Rainier. It was the difference between malevolent muscle and merry meringue, the difference between the scalding light of the H-bomb and the cool chic of having tea with Dorothy Kilgallen at a table off the bar at Hotel de Paris. Dorothy and the Kelly clan were not on speaking terms for the nonce because of a misunderstanding over something Dorothy had written in her column. Coupled with the fact that Rainier was not speaking to anybody, including his own family, this made news scarce.

"I've never known such a dearth of news," Dorothy said, staring moodily into my teacup, which had been drained down to its tea leaves. I put my hand over the cup.

"Stop reading my notes," I said.

It was an antic time, hardly likely to happen again. The original cast could never be reassembled: eccentric Lady Docker, playing Ping Pong on her yacht and denouncing both the Kellys and the Grimaldis for slighting her . . . the hefty Matt McCloskeys of Philadelphia being robbed of their jewels . . . French cops beating photographers with their fungo-sized billies . . . Irwin Tress, our International News Photos photographer, who ran his car over a French cop's toe for revenge, and was promptly jailed . . . Conrad Hilton, representing President Eisenhower . . . the breezy conjecture around the town's bars over whether Rainier could forget Gisèle Pascal . . . the story mischievous George Schlee spread at the Hotel de Paris bar that it would be a double wedding with Rainier's estranged father, Count Pierre de Polignac, marrying Gloria Swanson . . . Art Buchwald's pieces about the ancient feud between the Grimaldis and the Buchwalds, culminating in his not being invited to the wedding and their not being invited to one Becky Buchwald's wedding in Brooklyn . . . Rainier, handsome as John Gilbert in an old Garbo movie, chain-smoking as he swept out of the picture postcard harbor of Monte Carlo to fetch his bride-to-be from the S.S. *Constitution,* and his return with her at his side on the white honeymoon yacht, while church bells rang, ships' horns sounded, and Aristotle Onassis' yellow seaplane from his huge *Christina* bombed the Rainier yacht with pink carnations.

"I think I'm going to cry," announced a stout lady from New Jersey I happened to be standing near. And she did. On me.

Only five of us were permitted to cover the civil wedding performed at the palace by Chief Justice Marcel Portanier. It was limited to INS, UP, AP, Reuter's, and Agence France Presse. It was a most uncivil

civil wedding. Rainier was angry, for reasons unknown. He stared straight ahead at the judge throughout the barren ceremony, ignoring an occasional and ever-so-entreating look from the beautiful Philadelphia girl who sat at his side in an identical ceremonial chair-throne. The ceremony finished, Rainier marched his bride out of the room, gave Conrad Hilton and other dignitaries in an anteroom a curt brusque-off, and started down a long second-story gallery toward his apartment. Grace walked shyly at his side, chastened by his moody silence. There was nothing in my invitation that urged me to join the newlyweds after the ceremony. But the father of the bride, Jack Kelly, was a good friend. I found myself walking with him and chatting as he and all the Kellys and a sprinkling of Grimaldis strolled along twenty paces behind the forbiddingly silent couple whose great romance was being heralded around the world. AP and UP eyed me warily, torn between the clear call to duty—writing the story of the wedding—and the nagging fear that I, or INS, was moving toward some bigger story under the protection of Jack Kelly. After a bit of agonizing soul-searching, they decided to tag along, too.

Just short of the entrance to his lost-bachelorhood lair, Rainier stopped and shook off whatever it was that was bugging him. He turned to Grace, gave her his most dashing smile, and they embraced happily. An audible wheeze of relief was exhaled by the Kellys. Jack lost the somewhat preoccupied look in his eyes, stopped rambling about sports, as he had been, and said something direct, hearty, and nice about his new son-in-law. The Dom Perignon soon popped like vintage corn.

The religious ceremony in the nineteenth century cathedral the following day was part God, part Schubert. Rainier was in full military dress, down to an ancestor's sword; Grace was a vision. Every available crowned head was on hand, and at least one uncrowned one. Farouk filled part of a front pew like a sad, beached whale. Halfway back in the cathedral, some guest, if that he was, read a newspaper through the early part of the wedding Mass, turning its pages from time to time with a loud rustle. At one point Rainier appeared on the verge of going back into his saturnine slump, but snapped out of it. On the whole, it came off much better than the civil wedding. It, too, had its interesting aftermath: the unforgettable sight of Dorothy Kilgallen, bless her, busily beating out her story in the strange headquarters INS had established near the cathedral. She was surrounded, in all her bouffant glory and magnificent raiment, by the regular product of the place: sample water closets and bidets.

Later that same entrancing year I saw peace break out. That had happened seldom before in my life as a reporter, and never since. Peace broke out on the final day of the Olympics in Melbourne. The Games had opened in the traditional manner: the parade of the chauvinistically segregated teams, each behind its flag and banner, each aloof of the others. Much the same ceremony was planned for the final day, but sheer inspiration intervened. On signal, at the parade-assembly area beneath the crowded reaches of Olympic stadium, the teams happily scrambled. Flags and banners and identification cards were put aside, and when the athletes of most of the nations of the world marched on to the stadium's running track they marched arm in arm, short, tall, fat, lean, white, black, brown, yellow, Communist, Socialist, Democrat, Republican, Jew, Christian, Moslem, Buddhist, agnostic, atheist—all their competitive fires doused, furies spent; no cares, no Big Brother watching. The crowd of 100,000 began singing the bitter-sweet "Waltzing Matilda," which can be as enspiriting as "Dixie" and as hauntingly sad as "Greensleeves." The athletes picked up the chant and sang, or hummed, or whistled it. And the whole place was one.

Peace lasted a good ten minutes. It was glorious.

I was covering the 1958 World Series between the Yankees and the Milwaukee Braves when Frank Conniff sent me winging on a more somber mission. Pope Pius XII, eighty-two years old, lay dying at Castel Gandolfo. Several years before that, he had survived another serious claim on his life, a prolonged and nearly fatal siege of hiccups. Upon recovery he informed members of his hierarchy that during his periods of unconsciousness he had been visited by and had been spoken to by Jesus. Now, once more unconscious, there was no thought of divine intercession. The time had come for aristocratic Eugenio Maria Giuseppe Giovanni Pacelli.

His mission had ended. He had lived through one of the most trying reigns since Peter's.

If the Roman Catholic Church maintained a Central Casting Office, it would have selected Pacelli as its future Pope from the time he began his studies for the priesthood at age fourteen. He was born of a mother who was a marchioness and a father who was a prominent Vatican attorney. He was the favorite grandchild of Marcantonio Pacelli, founder of *L'Osservatore Romano*. He was top man in his class at Gregorian University, the State University of Rome, and the Papal Atheneum of the Apollinare. With his doctorates showing, he brought his priestly scholarship and zeal into the Vatican's Secretariat of State, which soon expanded his horizons by sending him to London to present to Edward VII the sympathy of Pope Leo XIII upon the death of Queen Victoria. In time Pacelli was being depended upon as the Church's chief pact-maker, but it was a time when pacts were not easily arranged. He failed badly when he tried to convince Kaiser Wilhelm to end World War I in 1917 before America's entrance—a failure which cost the United States 126,000 dead, 250,000 wounded, and direct and boldly indirect veterans' benefits which have amounted to billions of dollars. A comparatively young man of fifty-three, Pacelli, as papal nuncio, was dean of the diplomatic corps in Berlin in 1929, when he was called back to the Vatican to be consecrated a cardinal by tough-minded Pius XI. In February, 1930, three months after being given his red hat, Pacelli was named papal secretary of state, then archpriest of St. Peter's Basilica. He was author/architect of the daring ploy which saw Monsignor Francis J. Spellman spirit out of Vatican City Pius XI's statement accusing Mussolini of violating the Lateran Treaty. The future cardinal archbishop of New York called in key correspondents, once he reached Paris, and distributed the bombshell.

Pacelli was voted Pope by the sixty-two cardinals of the conclave that followed the death of Pius XI. The election came on March 2, 1939, his sixty-third birthday. It was reached on the third ballot, and the legend firmed up that the margin of victory was 61 to 1; he voted against himself. Nevertheless, he was the first cardinal secretary of state elected to the papacy since 1667, and he had taken over an awesome job at the brink of the biggest war in history. His conduct during that war was accepted by the antagonists as that of a humane neutral. But after his death he was the target of a play, *The Deputy,* and a book, both of which condemned his silence in the face of Germany's treatment of Jews. Vatican denials were timid and tentative.

Actually, Pius XII was a good friend of oppressed Jews. When the Nazis took over Rome from their halfhearted Italian allies in 1943, Pius opened Castel Gandolfo to fifteen thousand Jews living in Italy and gave shelter, food, and clothing to thousands more inside the Vatican walls. In September, 1943, the German commandant of Rome demanded a million lire from Dr. Israel Zolli, chief rabbi of Rome. If it were not paid by noon of the following day, along with one hundred pounds of gold, the Jews who had not put themselves under the Church's wing would be "dispersed." Dr. Zolli, unable to raise but a fraction of the money and gold, appealed to Pius. The ransom was paid on time. Melted sacred vessels helped provide the demanded gold. A month later the Nazis broke the pact, smashed and looted Jewish homes and shops, broke up families, and dispatched hundreds to concentration camps. Pius protested and, astonishingly, many Jews were returned to Rome. A month after the Allied liberation of Rome, Dr. Zolli praised Pius' good works and not long after that was received into the Catholic Church.

I ended Pius' noble life forty-eight hours earlier than God chose, which may have seemed presumptuous to both. My scoop will not be remembered with Roy Howard's unilateral shutdown of World War I some days before the November 11, 1918, Armistice. But I'd wager I suffered greater pangs of remorse because of my false report, which was never printed, than Howard suffered during the chaotic week that followed his great gaffe, for Roy had a tremendous amount of "Aw, to hell with it!" compressed in his hide.

What happened in my case was a combination of unpardonable gullibility and bad reporting. I was working on a piece at the Hearst service's office in downtown Rome after being assured at Castel Gandolfo that the Pope was still battling, when John Casserly came in to report that the Pope was dead. Jack, head of our diminished operation in Rome, now that INS had folded, still retained an Italian wire service. It was the Italian wire which flashed the Pope was dead. With Jack translating, I wrote a long piece about Pius' death and not a little about his life, and we sent it off to New York, via Radio Stampa, at urgent rates. Then I suggested that we go to Stampa Estera, probably the worst press club in Christendom, to salute the late-lamented pontiff with a drink.

There was nobody at the bar and very few correspondents in the workroom upstairs. Moreover, there was a stunning reason for this: The Pope was still alive. I rushed back to Radio Stampa and sent through a kill on my story, despairing of its ever getting to New York in time to repair the damage, then back to Stampa Estera, which has a phone service, and put through a call to New York.

The circuits were busy.

"Three . . . four hours," the lady who booked calls at the club said. She couldn't have cared less. Romans, most of them professedly Catholic, have about as much interest in Popes as do delegates to a Baptist convention in Philadelphia, Mississippi.

It was one of the worst sweats of my life as a reporter. I could see the presses at the *Journal American* crunching out hundreds of thousands of copies with my florid blunder spread across the front page. But with the phones clogged, and the wireless completely irresponsible, so far as back-and-forth communication was concerned, there was no way to stop this nightmare, this Niagara of wrongness emblazoned with my by-line.

At long, long, long last my call to New York came through. It was late enough in New York by that time for the *Journal American* to have completed most of its run. But I felt I could salvage some of the final thousands of papers with a correction. I had it, all of it, on the tip of my tongue, ready to dictate.

"Kill the story I filed hours ago," I shouted into the phone, one of Marconi's first. "I have a new lead . . . the Pope's still alive. Ready?"

"Relax," a voice from the *Journal American* said, across the ocean. "When AP and UPI didn't confirm, we decided not to use your death story." It was the only insult I ever welcomed.

I did not go directly to the bar on the floor below. I paused on a marble step at the head of the staircase, knelt down, and breathed a "Hail Mary." *Then* I went to the bar.

First things first.

As soon as the word came officially that the Pope had died, Casserly and I drove to Castel Gandolfo. The pleasant little square in front of the papal summer place was filled with newsmen. The limousines of cardinals and other dignitaries were drawing up solemnly, disgorging distinguished mourners. I settled down with the others for the long wait, until that distant hour when the Church's public relations division, which has not been noticeably altered since the Inquisition, awakened to the fact that perhaps the entire world might be interested in Pius' postmortems.

Then, a chance in a million. A bustling, black-haired monsignor emerged from the main gate of Castel Gandolfo, which faces the square. He seemed bent on facilitating the entrance of some distinguished mourner.

"That's your friend Paganuzzi," Casserly said. "He celebrated that Mass for the Hearsts and you when you came through Rome last year on the way to. . . ."

We were at his side in a moment. To our complete consternation and troubled delight, he led us past the guards and through the great gates. I could feel the glares of dozens, hundreds, of restrained colleagues on the back of my neck. I also became acutely aware that I was wearing a light, excessively noisy blue-checked sports jacket—donned earlier with little thought of attending a Pope's wake.

All that remained of Pope Pius XII, the most graceful world figure I ever met, lay on the simple brass-barred bed in which he had died. The ghastly black tubes which his reprehensible doctor, Galleazzi-Lisi, had inserted in his nose and mouth before death, and then photographed for profit, had been removed. The dead Pope looked as sparse as a sparrow in robes that seemed to have been summoned by the papal household as an afterthought. His head was covered by the kind of tam o'shanter in which pontiffs of the Middle Ages posed for papal court artists. His hands, which *Time* likened in life to two fluttering white doves, had become the alabaster holders of Crucifix and Rosary. At each corner of his bed stood a young priest. Several grief-stricken nuns knelt on the sparse-rugged floor of the bedroom, hammering their beads. A beautiful Italian woman in her sixties, swathed in black, knelt on a prie-dieu in the center of the room and did not take her great, sad eyes from him while we were there. The room was heavy with candle fumes. I felt like an outrageous intruder, in my obscene sports jacket.

"Kiss his hands," a voice whispered, interrupting my silent recitation of my Rosary. It was Paganuzzi. He was looking at Casserly and at me. We hesitated.

"Kiss his hands!" he repeated in a louder tone.

I got up from my knees, went to the bed, and bent over it. It was a three-quarter bed. The body of the Pope was directly in the middle of it, necessitating something of a stretch or reach. One couldn't very well cock a leg up on the mattress, for balance. To compensate, I leaned on the side of the bed with my hands, momentarily expecting to tip it and wind up on the floor with the late Vicar of Christ on Earth on my lap.

His hands were as cool and white and graceful and sad as the hands in Michelangelo's Pietà. I can never forget what they felt like on my lips.

On the way out, Paganuzzi told us touching stories about the Pope's final hours. We took the Great Circle route around the waiting correspondents in the square, slipped into a Radio Stampa mobile transmitter, and I riffled the keys of the van's typewriter. Alas! It had the European keyboard, not a suitable arrangement for any typist ever turned out of Business High School Night School, Washington, D.C. So in quiet desperation I fell back on the hunt and peck system, which to a touch typist is as tedious as pushing a peanut up Pike's Peak with one's nose. I tapped out: "Castel Gandolfo, Oct. 9."

Jack was watching over my shoulder. He had not served INS in vain. Or vice versa.

"Don't you think the dateline should be 'At the Pope's Bedside'?" he asked in a way that would reach any INS man. And so that was the way it went out. It won the Overseas Press Club of America's award that year for the Best Foreign Correspondence from Abroad. It also won a sobering comment from Red Smith, the thinking man's sports columnist.

"It was a pretty good story but I kept worrying as I read it," Red said at Shor's one night not long after.

"Why?"

"Well," Red said, "I had a vision of you typing away on a typewriter you had put on the side of his bed."

I promised him it would never happen again.

Pius XII's successor, John XXIII, came as a big surprise to about 300,000 gathered in St. Peter's Square—300,001, actually. I had kept a vigil atop the roofing of the Bernini Colonnade for hours during the third day of the balloting, watching more black smoke emerging from the Sistine Chapel's chimney than the old engine that took me to Chesapeake Beach. So as the dusk of another day gathered over Rome, I sought the counsel of an adjacent bishop who assured me that nothing more could happen that day; the old cardinals were probably hungry, crotchety, obviously divided, and feeling for their pasta and bed. That was enough of a horse's mouth for me, so I started down the endless flights of steps toward the square, cunningly bent on getting a taxi before the exodus started. Surprisingly, I saw Bill Hearst and Frank Conniff coming up the same staircase I was descending. They had heard that the election was imminent. Patiently, I told them what I had heard from a bishop, no less, and went my way, feeling a little let down by their stupidity.

I threaded through the dense crowds in the square to the head of Via Conciliazione, where sat a Radio Stampa trailer, fully staffed with technicians but empty of correspondents save for an American priest who said he hoped to write an article, eventually, for his diocesan newspaper. He could speak Italian.

"Why do you suppose the crowd is still sticking around?" I asked him.

"They must know something," he said. "Vatican Radio just broadcast that there won't be anything more tonight. But they stay."

I was about to go on in search of a cab when an enormous shout went up from the crowded square. A light had appeared in the vast ceremonial salon that stretches the width of incredible St. Peter's and opens on to the familiar loggia that soars over the main entrance to the basilica. Now more lights shone and the roar swelled.

"They've got a Pope," the American priest said.

"But the smoke has been black. . . ."

"They've got a Pope."

I asked him to ask the Radio Stampa man to get me a circuit to New York.

It came through like magic. I requisitioned the only typewriter in the trailer. Incredibly, it had the style of keyboard that fitted my touch-typing. Now the great doors leading to the loggia were lighted and opened. Members of the household appeared and draped a huge papal banner over the stone railing of the loggia. Immediately, the balcony was filled with what appeared to be doddering old men groaning under the weight of their vestments. They had a Pope all right, and said so.

"What's his name?" I asked the American priest.

"Roncalli. Angelo Giuseppe Roncalli," he said, then held up a hand for silence, when the papal chamberlain droned on toward the name the strange new occupant of the Throne of Peter had chosen.

"He'll be John XXIII," the priest said. "I have some dope on him. . . ."

I beat out the story as fast as my fingers could fly over the keys, but there was time to wonder, too. Why did they select an old fellow like that—seventy-seven!—so different in size and shape and looks from the image—Pius XII's image? He couldn't speak English and had spent much of his career in places like Turkey and Bulgaria. And why did he choose the same name as one of the worst scoundrels who ever laid claim to the papacy?

(Baldassare Cossa, the original John XXIII, was an on-again off-again pope from 1410 to 1415. He apparently had done well as a pirate, though he came from a good Neapolitan family. He led a dissident group of Romans in and out of the Church who withdrew their support of Pope Gregory XII *and* the current anti-Pope Benedict XIII. He was largely instrumental in convening the Council of Pisa which elected a third reigning pope, Alexander V. But Alexander died in 1410 and his followers elected Cossa pope. Thereafter, he was largely in flight, protected first by one king and then another. He was incapable of inspiring confidence or obtaining succor for any great length of consecutive months. The Council of Constance, which he called in 1414, excommunicated him as one who was *scandalizator ecclesiae.* He was jailed in Germany for three years, came back to Rome as a layman, threw himself at the feet of the now legitimate and uncontested Pope Martin V, and asked for mercy. In 1419, Martin V made him cardinal bishop of Tusculum, just southeast of Rome where the rich had had their summer places since Nero's time. Cossa lived only a few months thereafter. He is remembered chiefly today for the magnificent tomb in Florence which Cosimo de' Medici ordered to cloak his last remains.)

The new John XXIII answered the question of his choice of papal designations and many other questions in the swift four and a half years of his astonishing reign. He took the name John XXIII, he said in effect, to cleanse the numerical succession and perhaps inspire some pope of the future to carry it onward without misgivings. He set out on the first Sunday of his stewardship to visit the least of his flock in his secondary role of Bishop of Rome: the raucously pious jailbirds in Rome's main jail. "I, too, am a prisoner now," he told them. For all his age and avoirdupois he proved himself an industrious pedestrian, and, having been something of a fancier of wines at an earlier age, was said to be delighted when he learned that Romans—who usually don't like popes too much—were beginning to refer to him as "Johnnie Walker." Unlike his predecessor, a man of infinite dignity and sceptered mien, he liked to laugh, joked about his homeliness, occasionally would look about—as if searching for someone else—when he was addressed as "Your Holiness." Pius XII was by El Greco; John XXIII by Rubens.

In 1901, when Roncalli was a country boy from Bergamo studying in a Roman seminary and faceless as any other seminarian, Pacelli was a patrician young priest with the Congregation of Extraordinary Ecclesiastical Affairs, an important division of the Papal Secretariat of State. Pacelli went up; Roncalli went into the Italian army for three years, emerged as a sergeant, returned to the seminary, and was ordained a priest in 1904. Almost simultaneously, Pacelli was becoming a monsignor, a leading authority on canon law and a professor of law at the Academy of Ecclesiastical Nobles. He was the regal papal ambassador to Germany in World War I while Fr. Roncalli, once more in uniform, was medico-chaplain in trench warfare.

In short, John XXIII came to the Throne of Peter as much more a man of the people than was his predecessor, and people in general were quick to recognize that this man was no mere seat-warmer until a true successor of Pius XII could be found. On January 25, 1959, he removed all remaining doubt. He announced that he would convoke an ecumenical council to "open the windows of the Church to fresh air." It was to draw to Rome the Fathers of the Church and observers from most other religions, and to promulgate changes, reforms, concessions, and guidelines without precedent in the centuries-old Church. The last of John XXIII's encyclicals, *Pacem in Terris,* issued two months before his death on June 3, 1963, was the first papal social document addressed to the world in general. It was much more encompassing than his surprising first encyclical, *Ad Petri Cathedram* ("Unto the See of Peter") which invited the "separated brethren" to return to the Church of Rome. "Peace on Earth" rang bells not only in the capitals of Christendom but in Moscow, Peking, Mecca, and Jerusalem. The encyclical called for a nuclear-test ban, disarmament, rights of minorities, support of the UN, freedom of conscience, and cooperation between the Communist and free countries to alleviate poverty, disease, and ignorance; and it preached the brotherhood of man more ardently than any previous pronouncement from the Vatican. As it was being prepared for release, "Good Pope John," as he had come to be known, received in audience Aleksei Adzhubei, Khrushchev's son-in-law who edited *Izvestia,* a journal not known for its deference to popes. Roman conservatives complained bitterly that this single act of brotherhood resulted in a million increase in the Italian Communist Party's vote in the next election. But the effect it had on lessening world tensions and its appeal to basic reason far outweighed parochial setbacks.

John's agonizingly prolonged death touched hearts and minds never before moved by any event of the papacy. When at last it was official, there was relief as well as fond sadness. He had suffered enough. His last prayer, "May they be one," has not been answered. But they are more "one" than they were when he came out of nowhere, so far as the world knew, and pried open stained-glass windows that had been locked for centuries.

Count Enrico Galeazzi, the elegant "Mayor" of Vatican City, provided me with a credential that permitted me to view the body of John along with the diplomatic corps attached to the Vatican. Embalmment, Italian style, had rendered the jolly red-faced man a dismal green. The flat catafalque was tipped to a daring 10 or 20 percent grade, suggesting that strong ropes attached to it beneath his excessive layers of unduly (for him) crusted sacerdotal robes prevented a downhill slide. It was an unreal scene, until a woman in deep mourning a few people ahead of me in line genuflected and kissed the sandal of the good man that death had turned into an effigy. All who followed her did the same, and for the first time there was meaning to this ritual.

The chief surprise about the election of Giovanni Battista Cardinal Montini was that it took all of three ballots. The irreverent betting around the pizzerias had made him an overwhelming favorite. This was made painfully apparent to him at the solemn Mass of the Holy Ghost, always celebrated in St. Peter's just before the cardinals retired into the purdah of the conclave. The number of pictures taken of him by photographers of the world press approximated the margin of the edge he held over the others. He was visibly perturbed by the attention.

My own luck held. With INS gone, there was no longer any way for me to get through to New York in a hurry. Radio Stampa was perpetually swamped with the endless words of hundreds of newsmen on hand. There were hours-long delays on trans-Atlantic phone calls. Just for the Heaven of it, so to speak, I booked a call to the *Journal American* early on the morning of June 20. The operator at the Cavalieri Hilton said she could not even guess as to when there would be a circuit available. I went back to bed. At 11 A.M. an old St.

Peter's bell sounded quietly. Just once, it seemed, but I jumped up and switched on the television. White smoke was coming from the Sistine Chapel's skinny chimney.

I was trapped. If I went to St. Peter's square and the Radio Stampa van was engaged, as it would most certainly be, there would be no way to get my story in. If I found a cab and we were lucky with the impossible Roman traffic, I might be able to get from the hotel to downtown Radio Stampa in forty-five minutes or an hour, during which time I'd be out of contact with what was happening at the Vatican. I picked up the phone and inquired about the status of my earlier call to New York. Sorry . . . it might be several more hours. I felt as frustrated as an old firehorse tethered in a firehouse while a four-alarm blaze roared on the other side of town. The smoke from that blaze continued white.

I called my friend Luca Salvatore, public relations director of the Cavalieri, and asked him if he would come up to the room and act as my interpreter of the event that would soon be taking place on the loggia. There wasn't much I could do about sending a story, but at least I wanted to *know*.

Three things happened simultaneously. Just as Luca walked in the TV camera switched to the loggia and its great doors began to open. And my telephone rang! The *Journal American* was on the line, clear as crystal. Al Robbins, the fastest and best man we had, was ready. I spread my reference books on a bed, pulled up a chair facing the TV set, and said, "Let's go, Al. It's coming now. . . ."

I dictated for an hour and a half, the news, the background, the significance. Everything fell into its exact place. Every fact, date, reference I needed literally sprang from the books spread on the bed. It was just one of those times, one of those impossible successions of breaks, that warm a reporter's memory the rest of his days.

"How did you do it? You were from five to eight minutes ahead of the wire services," *Journal* Editor Paul Schoenstein asked me later, plainly expecting some whispered admission of a popish plot.

"The phone happened to ring," I said. It didn't sound very heroic. Richard Harding Davis would have been made uncomfortable.

Paul VI turned out to be a remarkable combination of the two opposites who immediately preceded him. He looked like and spoke like his mentor, Pius XII, but his words and viewpoint were those of

John XXIII. Vatican II would continue. The fresh winds would continue to air out the Church.

He was to make his revered mentor and predecessor appear sedentary and timidly sequestered by comparison. He flew to the Holy Land, India, and New York. On the Mount of Olives he embraced the towering and holy Patriarch Athenagoras I, and, as the Patriarch told me with simple eloquence the next day at a meeting arranged, extraordinarily enough, by Spyros Skouras of Twentieth Century-Fox, "We wept over divided Jerusalem." It was the first such meeting between a pope and a patriarch of the Orthodox Eastern Church in eight hundred years. In Bombay Paul was mobbed by countless poor peoples of other faiths among whom the word had spread that he was a saint of sorts from a remote part of the world, come to Bombay to distribute food and favors. In New York, he drew several millions to the sidewalks, spoke before the UN, had warm exchanges with celebrities as varied as Jacqueline Kennedy, Soviet Foreign Minister Andrei Gromyko (who later called on him at the Vatican), and President Johnson, celebrated a Mass for eighty thousand at Yankee Stadium, took in a portion of the World's Fair, and flew back to Rome the same day he had left it.

I carried a spear in the small armies of reporters who followed him to Jordan and Israel early in 1964 and to New York in the fall of 1965.

As mad an hour as I ever expect to experience was that at Damascus Gate the evening of the Pope's arrival. Perhaps a montage approach would best describe what it was like:

Dusk, and a chill the TV and newsreel kliegs could not diminish. . . . A torrent of unruly Jordanians surging through police and military barriers, screaming like dervishes. . . . Land Rovers and troop carriers prodding into the packed and shoving thousands in front of the gate, with troops beating the people with canes and sticks. The helpless inability to breast the human tide, the fight to keep from being knocked underfoot. . . . The holy men of several faiths, so bearded and serene only ten minutes before, being tossed around in the chaos like everyone else. . . . A nun no bigger than your arm being crushed against a wall as old as time (I muscled my way to her, braced my hands against the wall over her head, and pushed back as hard as I could against the insensate mob. It was like trying to hold back a ten-ton truck in low gear). . . . Then, more sensed than seen, Paul VI was convoyed through the center of the jam, a frail white bark led and flanked and followed by burly black-suited ice-breakers in the form of his Italian security guard and a few Jordanian officers and police who had kept their heads . . . and all the while, overhead, the deep-voiced young ruler of the Hashimite Kingdom of Jordan, Hussein, swept back and forth in his chattering helicopter.

Inside the Old City, just as one enters or is propelled through the Damascus Gate, it is necessary to take a sharp left to the street that leads to the Via Doloroso—along which the Pope proposed to retrace the steps of Jesus carrying His cross to Calvary. The human avalanche that burst in through the closing gates just behind the Pope managed to make the left turn, but could not then make the right turn into the narrow street that winds into the center of the city. Tons of flesh and bone spilled through the primitive windows of a fruit store, disentangled itself somehow, picked the glass splinters out of its composite hide, and plunged on. Oranges spilled from the showcases and were trampled and squeezed under successive feet. In the crush, as I was pressed along like a log in a millrace, I felt an empty shoe beneath my foot and momentarily expected to find myself involuntarily walking over the ankle, shin, thigh, torso, and head of some poor soul invisible underfoot. But it was just a shoe. Somewhere up ahead of me its owner was hobbling along the cold cobbled street with no chance of reversing his course. The shoe owner, like me, was going where the crowd took him.

Paul VI strove like a saint to meditate and pray at the Stations of the Cross. But it was not feasible by any stretch of piety. At one point a photographer's flashbulb exploded near his face and peppered him with glass needles. At another he had to seek the shelter of a doorway to avoid going down under a new tidal wave of humanity that swept the mob in his wake. And in the midst of the solemn ceremony that followed at the Church of the Holy Sepulchre, a badly wired TV light short-circuited and threatened to set fire to the holiest place in Christendom, as if it did not already have its share of troubles, having been quarreled over for centuries by Franciscans, Copts, Syrian Jacobites, and Gregorian Armenians.

Paul's trip to India later that year for the Eucharistic Congress saw his life endangered by Turkish air-force fighter pilots who playfully buzzed the Alitalia DC-8 bearing the Pope and his suite as it flew over

Turkey en route back to Rome. By comparison, his flight from Rome to New York was as uneventful as it was historic. The fifty-five of us who were aboard to report it were snugged into the tourist section of the Alitalia charter. The Pope's party, cardinals, aids, and Alitalia officials, occupied the center section of the plane, as aloof from us as the Pope was from them. Paul VI had a compartment to himself in the forward area behind the flight deck. In tourist, through the night and into the dawn of the New World, we saw quite a bit of the flying Princes of the Church in a new and highly informal light. The only gentlemen's room they could attend was at the rear of our ghetto. It was interesting to see them thread their way down the narrow aisle in their rustling silk, bent on the commonest of man's poor but rewarding endeavors.

We had no hopes that Paul VI would come our way. But as the jet swung near Newfoundland on its long parabola reaching for New York, the plastic gate that segregated us from the rest of the passengers was pulled back a foot or two and an Italian head poked itself through the opening. It was one of the Alitalia types.

"Il Papa!" the head said. The eyes of the head seemed to be saying, "What the hell does he want to see *you* people for?"

The accordion barrier was retracted, and there stood the Pope looking quite relaxed about the ordeal of invading our lair, a lair cluttered with typewriters, cameras, clusters of lights, tripods, half-eaten meals, and half-finished drinks. Lights blazed, microphones were extended toward him, and cameras whirred as he moved down the aisle. He added a few words in English to a tape Walter Cronkite, Irving R. Levine, Serge Fliegers, and I had made for CBS, NBC, Mutual, and ABC, respectively. Then he was gone as suddenly as he appeared, only to return to us about an hour later to give each of us a silver medallion commemorating the flight.

I thought once more of Harry Grayson's ultimate accolade to another pope: "That guy's okay."

President Eisenhower's trips at the end of his White House stay probably were the costliest goodwill voyages ever undertaken. But anyone who was lucky enough to go along would have been a fool to complain. What man, what economist, what computer can put a price on goodwill . . . or would be daft enough to try?

The first trip, December 3 to December 22, 1959, covered 18,520 miles. It remains a magnificent blur, in Technicolor.

Rome: Rain. Scrawled insults on wet walls suggesting that our leader go home. The colors of welcome banners, running. The meaningless communiqué after the meeting with John XXIII. Seems they discussed peace, and both were believed to be in favor of it.

Ankara: Ataturk's stark mausoleum, and a swarthy trumpeter's single, piercing, frightening note as Ike laid a wreath on the grave. Ike (reading): "If I couldn't be an American, I'd be proud to be Turkish. . . ." The Turkish official beamed. He was executed in 1965.

Karachi: Gorgeous, maybe a million in the streets, brassy cymbaled bands, splendid Sikhs in superb turbans, red-coated horsemen right out of Kipling roaring through the superb exercise of "tent-pegging," and, always at Ike's shoulder, President Ayub Khan, impeccably Sandhurst—and slightly annoyed when Ike looked at his watch and said he guessed he'd have to leave the bloody boring cricket game before the tea break.

Khyber Pass: U.S. helicopters fluttering over the invasion routes of Alexander the Great, Tamerlane, Baber, Mahmud of Ghazni, and Nadir Shah, prospecting the weather for the jet of the President of the United States of America, his $6,000,000 reserve jet, the C-130 and C-54 supply planes, and the crowded Pan Am Boeing 707 press plane wherein beautiful stewardesses, for whose favors Alexander and the others would have given minor kingdoms, moved up and down the aisles ladling prebreakfast Bloody Marys.

Kabul: Crazy, awesome Afghanistan. Marrow-freezing cold. Russian-built jet strip of great octagonal cinder-blocks. MIG's, always sinister to regard, roaring off boisterously to escort the President's jet. Roughest-looking honor guard on record. Mad ride in busses and trucks over inconceivable roads into the dung-colored capital, with veiled women peering from roofs and windows like caged animals. Crowds that allowed only inches of freeway for the open car—a Mercedes convertible—bearing the President, wearing his anachronistic black homburg . . . crowds that hit him repeatedly in the face with wads of confetti at point-blank range. He was up to his ankles in the stuff by the time his car pulled up to the modest palace of King Mohammed Zahir Shah for lunch. When he tipped his homburg to a reception group, a small and varicolored Niagara spilled from its brim. He was spitting confetti and finding the patented Eisenhower grin a bit hard to summon as he entered. A wild ride back to the airport in the press busses. The driver of our bus kept dozing at the wheel, waking up just in time to avoid plunging bus and us down some nameless rocky gorge. "Give him a cigarette," somebody suggested. The driver accepted it gratefully. Then he ate it.

New Delhi: Nehru, fussing like a hen over the exact placement of this and that official he had appointed to the reception committee at the airport. He moved them like obedient chessmen, scolded them shrilly if they did not move fast enough. Ike's jet swept in silhouetted against an incomparable Indian sunset, but it was pitch dark as the procession began the long crawl into the capital. Nehru, determined to have India outwelcome Pakistan, had emptied every village along the parade route. Their people came to the side of the route by foot, bicycle, bullock, cart, and car. Placed at regular intervals were human lamp posts, holding garish butane lights aloft. Barefooted men and boys ran crazily through the narrow and dangerous gaps between the cars and busses of the entourage. Dozens climbed the walls of the bus I rode in. You could hear their bare feet and sandals scraping on the roof. Now and then the driver would apply his brakes savagely, for no other reason than to catapult a few rooftop passengers off their perch to the roadway. A twenty-mile blanket of dust hung over the parade route in time. As the car bearing the President and Nehru neared the outskirts of the city, the crowds spread across the road in impenetrable bulk and would give way and make room only when Nehru would leap agilely from the car and angrily demand that they do so. The first thing Ike ordered when he reached the haven of his quarters was an oxygen tent.

Agra: Blinding sun. Perfect blue sky. Nehru, proud, arranged it so that he and his distinguished visitor would not behold the Taj Mahal until the last possible second—for the sake of exquisite impact. Ike, unaware of this presentation, was engrossed in a monologue about U.S. wheat surpluses and the problem of reducing them. "There she is!" Nehru interrupted, gesturing gracefully to the most beautiful edifice on earth. Ike squinted at it. "Pretty," he said, and went back to wheat.

Tehran: Our ugly press bus, so far behind the President's car that a brace of camels and a wine truck were ahead of us, crunched over a million dollars worth of superb Persian rugs spread in the dirty street leading to Shah Mohammad Reza Pahlavi's digs. It seemed a regrettable waste, if not a sacrilege against artistic craftsmanship.

Athens, Tunis, Paris, Madrid, Casablanca . . . peace to you, King Paul, and you, your Excellency President Habib Bourguiba, and you, dear General, and you, Generalissimo, and you, too, Your Majesty Mohammed V—and if it doesn't offend you I don't think I'll have another serving of chocolate-covered goat.

Things didn't go as well on the next trip, in February, 1960: Brasilia, Rio, Sao Paulo, Santiago, Montevideo, Buenos Aires, Mar del Plata, San Carlos de Bariloche, and Laurance Rockefeller's Dorado golf club near San Juan, Puerto Rico.

At Brasilia, as spectacularly lonely as Lhasa, President Juscelino Kubitschek was late arriving at the muddy airport to greet Ike. Then with Ike still aboard, tapping his foot, a brilliant red carpet was unrolled from the temporary air terminal of that day to the steps of the plane. Alas, either the plane was too close to the terminal or the terminal had been built too close to the plane. The roll of carpet was still a yard thick when it reached the bottom step, presenting the leader of the Free World with the problem of needing to vault to the receiving line. A disgusted-looking airman from the President's plane leaped over it, pulled his knife, and chopped it to the right length.

At Rio, U.S. Ambassador and Mrs. John Cabot asked the U.S. Marine Band, which was making a concert tour of South America at the time, to fly a contingent to Rio for the scheduled Eisenhower reception. Its plane collided with a Brazilian airliner over Sugar Loaf and all were killed.

At a housing project outside Santiago, a haggard young Chilean woman carrying a pathetic baby broke through police and Secret Service lines during a politician's speech about how well things were going, held out the baby to Ike, and cried, "Cure my baby!"

At Montevideo, police with armored water-squirting trucks and tear gas were needed to break up a violent pro-Castro demonstration as the President's car passed the university.

Trout the size of fireplace logs and golf on a course as lush as the Masters were prospects dangled temptingly before the President by what amounted to the Chamber of Commerce of San Carlos de Bariloche, Argentina's spectacularly colorful Swiss-like mountain and lakes resort. It was a long flight for what turned out to be a few fingerlings and a rocky, alpine course.

At least, we all said, the exhausting trip would end pleasantly for Ike. He'd get to play Dorado, justly rated one of the world's finest courses. Our jets made a record, nearly four-thousand-mile flight up through the wild heart of South America from Buenos Aires to Ramey Air Force Base in Puerto Rico. And bright and early the next day the nearly one hundred newsmen on the trip piled into buses for the long ride from the air base to the Rockefeller pleasure dome.

Everything was laid on for him, the President learned to his disgust. Several hundred guests of the resort were gathered around the first tee when he arrived, all armed with movie and still cameras.

He had always loathed playing golf in front of a crowd, and this day was no exception. His tee shot, which he hurried in order to separate himself from the crowd, was a humiliating pop fly into the palmettos on the right.

"Take a Mulligan, Mr. President," said his friend and golf mentor Ed Dudley, the pro who had flown there from Colorado Springs to be his partner for what had now become a most involved little round. Ike, very angry, accepted the invitation. This time he tried to kill the ball. It followed the same dismal trajectory as the first shot and may be remembered with it as among the most-photographed bad shots in the game's annals. Ike stalked to his golf cart and sat down. Dudley drove a long one down the fairway, followed by the adequate drives of Maj. John Eisenhower and his partner.

Dudley slid into the cart seat next to the President, and what since has always seemed to me a slightly poignant procession began: Ike still brooding over his bad beginning in front of all those damned newspapermen and tourists, with three carts bringing up the rear. In the first of these sat John and his partner. In the next cart, riding alone, came Gen. Howard McC. Snyder (ret.), long-time personal physician, carrying a few simple first-aid items: oxygen, glycerin, and, inevitably, his number-one remedy for every Presidential ill from coronary to ileitis, milk of magnesia. In the fourth cart rode two strapping fellows who did not look like golfers, though the cart carried two golf bags on its rear deck. They were Secret Service men. The bags contained a few token clubs, but the main contents were (1) a machine gun, for use in case of ambush, and (2) a walkie-talkie tuned to call in the reserves. An Air Force Sikorsky hovered noisily over the Presidential party. At each spot along the course where trees and/or heavy vegetation grew close to the edge of fairways, uniformed members of the Puerto Rican constabulary faced the suspect foliage, guns at ready.

Ike's game was off kilter that day. . . .

The President's last grand tour was a shade short of grand. A pall was cast over it before it could get underway. White House press secretary Jim Hagerty, advance man for what was to have been a triumphant Presidential visit to Tokyo, ran into trouble at Haneda airport two weeks before the President's expected arrival in mid-June, 1960. Wilder members of the Zengakuren (All Students League) massed against Jim's Embassy limousine and threatened to turn it over. It took the downwash of the blades of a helicopter to disperse the rock throwers. The protest was against the signing of a treaty the previous January under the terms of which the United States would guarantee Japan's security and maintain military bases on her soil. The pacifist students demonstrated their objections in a most warlike manner.

For safety's sake, the government of Premier Nobusuke Kishi endured great loss of face and asked the President not to come to Japan. It then resigned under heavy attack from Leftists and neutralists.

It was a great disappointment to the President. But there was balm for his hurt in the fine welcomes he received at other points of the farewell flight: Anchorage, Manila, Taipei, Seoul, and Honolulu.

Okinawa was difficult. The U.S. military and their wives on hand as Ike's jet whistled up to the Terminal at our great air base at Naha were as loyal and loving as could be expected. But just outside the field's guarded gates the President's entourage encountered unexpected hostility. Little knots of grim-faced Okinawans, liberated from Japan at the cost of much American blood and treasure, held banners reading: "GIVE US BACK TO MOTHER JAPAN," and, worse: "GO HOME IKE."

Four of the nine Ryukyuan councilmen elected under our patiently taught system of government refused to appear at the official welcome ceremony in the council hall. The chants of the crowd that assembled outside made it difficult to hear the exchange of cordial remarks. The Secret Service and Air Force Security took the President out a rear door to a waiting jeep for a fast and bumpy ride to a waiting helicopter and thence to his plane.

It was distressing. Hot, dirty, and not a little indignant, the reporters and cameramen climbed aboard the Pan Am charter. My seatmate, Rene MacColl of London's formidable *Express,* a great foreign correspondent in the old tradition, was fathoms deep in brooding silence until the girl brought the martinis. Rene downed one in a swallow, turned to me, cocked a thumb back in the direction of Okinawa, and said something so right I'll never forget it. "If that's a sample of your outpost of Empah," he said, "I'll take Poona!"

President Kennedy's trips, a saga as slim as Blake's verse and as eloquent, presented an entirely new cast of characters and mostly new backdrops: Vienna (where Khrushchev misjudged him badly enough to presume Cuba could become a strong Soviet base), Paris (where he introduced himself as the fellow who was touring Europe with Jacqueline Kennedy. And where a cartoonist depicted General and Mrs. De Gaulle asleep in their double bed, with de Gaulle dreaming of Jackie), Berlin (*"Ich bin ein Berliner!"*), Rome (and Paul VI), Naples (for a much warmer reception than blasé Rome wished him), and, of course, Ireland.

Ireland was a green loving cup, overflowing wherever he ventured there. He was Prince Charming and Brian Boru combined, home to reclaim his lands in freedom.

Everybody on the press plane wished to find the proper words to pin down the scene, and then gave up. The *Irish Press* of Dublin had said it all:

> Ireland welcomes you, Mr. Kennedy, President of the greatest Republic in the world's history. You have come to the home of your forefathers and history fulfills itself in your journey and your arrival, and in the welcome from the heart that the Irish people offer you.
>
> It is a mere forty-four years since President De Valera crossed the Atlantic to appeal to the United States as the President of the Irish Republic at a time when the chosen government of the people had been declared a dangerous association and prohibited and suppressed.
>
> Your great free land then welcomed and aided our country's cause. They expressed by their welcome the longings and aspirations, even the just anger of generations, driven out by hunger and injustice, who had sought freedom and opportunity under

> the star-spangled banner of a new world. In the person of the President, those who came to support him saw the hope that the dreams of dead generations would become real, that the Irish Flag might fly in freedom east of the Atlantic as the Stars and Stripes did in the West—and because of their support it is possible today for an Irish President to welcome to Ireland a President of the United States who is the great-grandson of an Irish exile.
>
> Today, visiting the homeland of your people, you stand for almost two centuries of turbulent and always valiant endeavour. You join together as no man has ever done before the stories of this country and of that vast nation to which Ireland has made so many contributions, including that important one in the name of Kennedy.
>
> Ireland—North, South, East, and West—joyfully welcomes you; from the rocks of Connemara and the Western ocean to the streets of Dublin, from the Glens of Antrim to the Reeks of Kerry, from Donegal to Cork and to your own Wexford, where the statue of the great sailor—Barry—looks forever out at the sea he was to sail in the name of freedom.

It was not a long way from Tipperary . . . but, by God, it was some distance and some years from a train ride to Chesapeake Beach.

It is hard to top traveling with a President. But if you will bear with me, it is even harder to top traveling with a man named Hearst.

8. *Task Force*

THE HEARST TASK FORCE, which has won journalism prizes from the Pulitzer down, was built on the thoroughly improbable proposition that someone named William Randolph Hearst, Jr., could get through to the men in the Kremlin. The risk would have given Lloyd's of London pause. Hearst, senior, waged total editorial war against Bolshevism/Communism from the day of its birth in the Great October of 1917. He numbered Stalin among the infamous mass murderers of history, never tired of writing (or ordering written) uncompromising frontal attacks on the ideology and its disciples abroad and at home. He did not consider the U.S.S.R. a true ally in World War II, said so repeatedly, and was pilloried as a hopeless—if not seditious—reactionary.

His namesake son made an effort to get into Russia in 1945 through the Army Air Force's shuttle-bombing missions: takeoff from England or Italy, bomb deep in Germany, and fly on to Russian-held fields. Bill also sought the good offices of U.S. Ambassador Harriman. All seemed in order. Bill then informed his father and ran into a veto. The elder Hearst cabled his war correspondent son that Stalin had only recently ruthlessly liquidated the survivors of the Warsaw uprising against the Germans to clear the way for the scheduled takeover of Poland by the Lublin Government, yet had received no real censure from Washington and London. Therefore, why would he not just as callously liquidate someone named William Randolph Hearst, Jr.?

That ended that. But in December, 1954 (Hearst, senior, had been dead three years) the chief of the Hearst bureau in Washington, Dave Sentner, urged Hearst to think again about a Russian trip. Stalin had been dead a year, his heirs were generally unknown and just might be willing to talk—preferably to a popular American newspaper chain totally aloof from ideological involvement. Hearst was willing to try, and go if permitted. His wife, mother, and members of the company's hierarchy were not amused. One member of the Establishment, J. D. Gortatowsky, most trusted of the trustees, predicted that if Hearst ever got to Russia he'd wind up burning the Communist flag in Red Square. Everyone joined in the laughter over that absurdity.

On December 23, 1954, Sentner sent a special-delivery letter to Konstantin G. Fedoseev, counselor of the Soviet Embassy in Washington. It read: "W. R. Hearst, Jr., chairman of the editorial board of the Hearst Newspapers, has requested me to take up an important matter with His Excellency, Soviet Ambassador Zaroubin. I would like to have a preliminary discussion of the matter at your convenience."

Fedoseev called Sentner on Christmas Eve and suggested that the next day at noon would be a good time to get together. They met in the otherwise empty National Press Club bar. The only witness to the conception of the Hearst Task Force, which was to set a wholly fresh pattern in reporting, was a bartender.

Fedoseev said after a drink or two that things had changed in Russia since Stalin's death. Dave asked if they had changed enough to allow a person named Hearst to obtain a visa.

"I don't see why not," the Russian said. "Permit me to say that I think it could be arranged."

Dave permitted him. It was arranged, miraculously enough. But before accepting a prized visa that many newsmen had been seeking for years (the application of the *New York Times*'s C. L. Sulzberger had been on the waiting list for seven years), Hearst asked for two additional visas for Kingsbury Smith and Frank Conniff. After much grumbling and presumably a great deal of coded cabling, the additional visas were produced. Shortly thereafter, Hearst, accompanied by Conniff, was received in audience by Ambassador Zaroubin at the Embassy on Sixteenth Street. While they were waiting to be admitted through the locked iron outer door, Conniff waved at the National Geographic Magazine office building across the street.

"What's that for?" Hearst asked.

"I wanted the FBI to get a better picture of us than one just showing the backs of our necks," Frank said.

Zaroubin's butlers spread the good caviar and vodka before the Ambassador's guests, and the Ambassador, apparently expecting to be thanked, informed them that in addition to all other courtesies being extended the Embassy had plotted their itinerary. They would fly toward Moscow first by Air France as far as Prague, then transfer to Aeroflot for the rest of the voyage.

Hearst said no. He and his associates would fly to Moscow via Paris and Berlin. What he did not tell the Ambassador was that he wanted a final briefing from U.S. intelligence and diplomatic and military people before taking the next big step.

The trip turned out spectacularly. Doors that had been shut for decades creaked open at the precise hour of dramatic change in Soviet policies, portfolios, and personnel. A single question aimed at Molotov, artfully composed by Smith and blandly asked by Hearst, elicited an answer that led to the withdrawal of the Red Army and Allied forces from Austria. A brusque command by Khrushchev—to the effect that he would accept no telephone calls while being interviewed by the Hearst team—was the world's first inkling that this relatively unknown First Secretary of the Party had no superiors among Stalin's heirs.

Marshal Zhukov, bristling with eight rows of medals, three Hero-of-the-Soviet-Union stars, and gusts of good humor, was happy to see the Americans whose interviews with Molotov and Khrushchev had filled the entire front page of Pravda. He recalled affably, over tea in his office, his last meeting with General Eisenhower in 1945 during which each man pledged with a handshake that his country would never attack the other. Conniff, who teethed on a hard-cover edition of Clausewitz, asked him two questions that drew forth in masterful brevity explanations which subsequent historians felt required a million words.

"What was Hitler's greatest strategical mistake in the invasion of Russia?" Frank asked.

"The decision to invade Russia. He launched an operation for which he never had the necessary means. The conquest of Russia was simply beyond the means at his disposal."

"What was Hitler's greatest tactical mistake?"

"His dependence on aircraft at the expense of artillery. The Luftwaffe was a very formidable instrument, certainly, but there would be days at a time here in Russia, even weeks, especially during the winter months, when airplanes couldn't fly at all. Then he missed the artillery, which could function in any weather, and which we had in abundance."

The Task Force was present in the Supreme Soviet when Malenkov abruptly stepped down as premier and Bulganin—at Khrushchev's suggestion—was unanimously elected in his place. The team saw the new premier, heard him express the hope of a rapprochement with the United States. Before the remarkable trip was concluded—it covered less than three weeks—the trio entertained and were entertained by Galina Ulanova, Maya Plisetskaya, Yuri Zhdanov, Nicolai Fadeyechen, and Georgi Orvid, hitherto unapproachable Bolshoi greats, were permitted to see and talk to Stalin's daughter Svetlana (who wept when Hearst asked her whatever became of her brother Vassily, once a top-ranking commander in the Red Air Force), and spent some time with Patriarch Alexei and the sequestered monks at Zagorsk. Dmitri Shostakovich recanted all over Conniff.

It was a trip that could never be topped, but Hearst set forth again late in 1957, this time with Conniff and myself as his spear carriers (Joe Smith had moved upward and onward to general manager of INS). The timing of the trip was again exquisite.

Khrushchev, having denounced Stalin, had narrowly survived a power play aimed at ousting him and had emerged stronger than ever and banished Molotov, Malenkov, Kaganovich, and Shepilov, the prime conspirators. On top of this, he then made an unperson out of his friend Zhukov, whose skillful employment of Red Air Force transport planes had rounded up enough members of the far-flung Central Committee to give Khrushchev the vote of confidence he needed. This was a perfectly sensible move on Khrushchev's part, I was told later, because when Zhukov had demonstrated his ability to save Khrushchev he had thus demonstrated his capability to destroy him!

Sputnik I had startled and alarmed the world in early October of '57. Sputnik II, weighing a then awesome half a ton and carrying Laika, the immortal dog, went up on November 3 of that year while we paused in Rome on our way to Moscow. The word reached us as we were being given a tour of St. Peter's by Monsignor Paganuzzi, a good friend of the Hearst family who had just celebrated Mass for us at the tiny altar near the Tomb of Peter in the depths of the basilica. I have been judged (falsely) a pious person, but it was a genuine relief to be done with the good monsignor and be on our way to atheistic Prague later that sunny Sunday.

Prague was a study in gray depression. Hungering as I was to dig my typing fingers as deep into Russia as they'd be permitted to plunge, I found every Czech hour a burden. It wasn't so much the grayness of the old city as it was the grayness of its people. The people who had known the wand of Woodrow Wilson and been stirred by the Masaryks and Benes seemed to have surrendered abysmally without even token struggle—a crude generalization, I'm sure, but one which subsequent visits tended only to strengthen. Our three days there would have been farcical if pity had not enveloped the laughter. Whenever we ventured from the Alcron Hotel for a walk, day or night, we were followed by two ludicrous security agents, burlesques right down to their greasy raincoats, slouch hats, and squeaky shoes. When we whipped off one night in a car to file a story with the couple who represented Press Wireless, a security car followed us and remained parked at a distance while the saddened couple took our copy and served us coffee and slivovitz. At the Alcron bar, better attended by the three imperialists in town than by Playboys of the Eastern World, the bartender George liked to regale us with accounts of his adventurous travels. He had been all the way to Paris. But Paris had nothing on Prague, he would conclude strongly if there were other Czechs at the bar. Late one night there was just us and George. It was my birthday, as good a time as any to ask him to have a drink. He poured it carefully, marked it down on our check, drank it, looked around, then leaned over toward us.

"Myself, I am a Catholic," he confided in the voice of the confessional. We felt like promising not to turn him in.

Katherine Clark of INS took us to the airport through the early morning smog the first day, followed by the two clowns assigned to tail us. There sat the rakish TU-104, a jet transport we could not match at that time. It had been built as a Bison, the Red Air Force's medium-range bomber, and only modestly altered to enter commercial servitude. The plexiglass nose compartment had exchanged its bombsight for navigational equipment. But being a plane buff I found it enchanting and couldn't wait to get aboard.

The seventy Moscow-bound passengers moved restlessly toward the terminal's proper gate as the scheduled time of departure neared. But the gate remained closed. There was no announcement when the departure hour came and went, nor could the Czechs behind the counter give us any reason for the delay. Hearst, the Compleat Traveler, is not a man to tolerate such indignities. He flushed a Scandinavian Airways man who surmised, sotto voce, that one or two factors probably were involved: (1) The weather in Moscow was bad and the Russians didn't want to admit it. (2) Aeroflot might be sweating out the arrival from other places of Communist VIP's ticketed for that particular flight.

The passengers remained in that bleak, cushionless, foodless terminal until nearly dusk without information. Then a Czech behind a counter rapped for attention.

"Tomorrow," he announced helplessly.

The next morning, dull and early, we thought it best to inquire before making the long trip to the airport.

"Certainly the plane is leaving this morning," the Alcron's travel desk man said flatly. "It is scheduled to go, so it will go." He gave the appearance of a man talking for the benefit of a concealed "bug."

We vegetated at the airport all day. When dismissed again, Hearst braced the Czech behind the counter and asked him why he hadn't made his announcement hours earlier.

The poor man said, "The Russians won't tell us *anything.*"

The next morning, November 6, the fortieth anniversary of the Great October and a day of tumult and shouting and marching and missile-brandishing in Red Square, dawned with a deluge in Prague. We seemed doomed to spend another unbearable day far from the action and the news. We went to the airport more from habit than lively anticipation and to our astonishment were told we must hurry—the TU-104, cascading rain, was primed and raring to go. First, however, we must obtain exit permits. We found our way to the right bureaucrat's desk and restlessly watched as he made out the endless forms without which the whole Communist world would collapse. When he had finished, the man behind the desk held onto the permits and said that the cost would be seventy-five korunas—about ten dollars at the official rate. Our leader dug in his pocket, a familiar movement for him, and produced the seventy-five korunas. The man shook his head and held on to the permits.

"We are not permitted to accept Czechoslovakian money from persons leaving Czechoslovakia," he said by rote. "It must be in American dollars." Hearst said something defamatory about korunas in general and Czechoslovakia in particular and paid in dollars.

Now we were outside under a leaking shelter of sorts; a Czech girl in uniform was calling out the names of those permitted to proceed to the TU-104. We discovered that all passengers were members of official delegations en route to the meeting of the clan in Moscow. France's Duclos and Italy's Togliatti swept past us with their suites when called. After fifteen minutes the girl obviously had begun to scrape the bottom of the barrel.

"Deligazie Sudanese!" she shouted. That group of towering Africans stiffened to attention and filed past us into the rain. Each seemed seven feet tall. They had protected themselves against the raw day by wrapping scarves around their heads from chin to crown. On top of the scarves they had balanced their cheap little fedoras. They resembled the Harlem Globetrotters in a comedy routine.

"Regards to Abe Saperstein," Conniff said to them as they went by us.

"Deligazie Hearst!"

Our friend from SAS appeared out of nowhere and hurried us through the rain to the steps that led to what turned out to be the rather plush first-class section of the jet. We had just settled down happily in the three remaining empty seats when a heavy-set hostess loomed over us and gave us the brusque signal used by umpires to indicate that a runner is out. We retreated in disarray to the narrow-aisled tourist class of the classless society's jet and squeezed into seats designed especially for passengers with one-cheek bottoms and six-inch legs. And after an alarmingly long run down the semi-inundated runway the jet's two huge engines flung us aloft. We were still climbing when a hostess plopped lunch in front of us—a small portion of cold veal, vegetables too sodden to offer ready recognition, and a small glass of red wine. The wine made it a happy ship. One by one the heads of delegations aboard would rise in his place, make his voice heard above the considerable roar of the engines, and shout a toast to the U.S.S.R. and Comrade Khrushchev. I had the empty feeling of being a long way from home. I touched my glass to Bill's and Frank's and said "The President of the United States," and we had our separate (but equal) sip. Then Conniff rattled a spoon against his glass and a silence fell on nearby comrades as they readied their glasses for his toast.

"To the president of the National Association of Manufacturers!"

Frank sang out. It must have sounded like a newly formed Soviet industrial front to most of the comrades around us, for they drank to it.

The early night had fallen on Moscow, the parade had gone off to wherever Russian parades disappear. But a carnival air prevailed in Manezhnaya Square when we pulled up in front of the National Hotel, where Hearst and his troops had stayed on their first trip. The chambermaids on our floor were delighted to see Hearst again. *"Gospodin Gearst!"* cried the biggest of them and threw her arms around him. She was saying "Comrade Hearst," or, stretching the point a bit, "Citizen Hearst." The Russians have as much trouble with *H* as the Cockneys, but in a different way. *H* becomes *G*. Before our trip ended we were to hear many strong denunciations of Adolf *G*itler, but none of *G*erbert *G*oover.

Bundled in his wraparound camel's hair coat and muffler, Hearst led us into the living room of the four-room suite from the balcony of which Lenin once harangued throngs as dense as those which now populated gay Manezhnaya and, just beyond, Red Square. It was one of the most entrancing moments of my life: the gaudy Czarist suite with its ceiling painting of peacocks pulling a cushiony nude's troika, "people's" music thundering in from flung-open French doors, the invigorating rush of wintry air that accompanied the music, the huge illuminated pictures of Party leaders hung from the walls of neighboring buildings and spotlighted on captive balloons, the formless symphony of sound of the mobs just below, and the clucking and shoulder-dusting of the elephantine maids. The delirious, delicious cacophony was pierced suddenly by the urgent ringing of the living room's antique telephone. Hearst snatched it off its cradle and a torrent of cackling Russian bombarded his ear.

"Speak American, we've taken over!" he shouted into the phone, and hung up. Beautiful.

He and Conniff showered, shaved, dressed, and went off to the formal reception given that night to the visiting Communist delegations in the great George Hall inside the Kremlin walls. For want of a ticket, I remained in the suite with Serge Fliegers, INS's Man in Moscow, a remarkable young correspondent with a gifted command of a half dozen languages coupled with a driving curiosity and an ability to write well whatever he witnessed or heard. He had taken extensive notes on the day's parade, particularly on the missiles displayed and the first appearance in the forefront of Marshal Rodion Malinovsky, who had replaced Marshal Zhukov.

As I began to stitch the story together on my typewriter later that night, Hearst and Conniff piled in with more news: The two stars of the big reception had been Khrushchev and Mao Tse-tung. Bulganin, still premier, looked gray and tentative—had laughed nervously when Hearst asked for an audience and said, "No, it is Khrushchev you should see." Khrushchev had danced up a storm, had bussed a giggling matron or two, and had joined the Red Army chorus during one of its virile numbers.

It was an easy and colorful story to write: Red Summit, clank of military might, dancing in the streets, bygone saints exhumed, corks popping under glittering George Hall chandeliers. . . .

Serge's phone call to INS-London went through just as I finished the first page. I handed it to him and he began to dictate, as his predecessor, Charles Klensch, had during Hearst's earlier trip. But he had hardly begun before a loud click sounded through the system. London had disappeared. The voice on the phone now spoke Russian. Fliegers listened for a bit, then broke into an angry torrent of Russian himself. We couldn't understand a word, but it was clear he was losing the argument. Finally, he hung up.

"We're not permitted to file out of here by phone," he said. "Everything must go through the censor's office at the Telegraph Building."

Suddenly, I realized it was very late. The streets and squares had emptied their multitudes. The loudspeakers had fallen mute. The lights were going out, accentuating the bloody Red Stars that protruded into the night from the parapets and towers of the Kremlin across Manezhnaya Square. A night that had started as a glorious lark had descended into ominous silence, and doubt had taken the place of doughtiness.

Obtaining interviews with top Soviet officials can be a humbling pursuit. You just don't call up one of them and put in the request, any more than a Russian reporter visiting Washington could ring the White House or the State Department and ask for the man in charge. But at least that hypothetical Russian reporter would have the satisfaction of knowing that the phone on the other end of the line rang. Russia has not discovered phone books as yet. Phone numbers of even some of the office buildings which house newsworthy Russians are difficult to obtain.

But we did get through to the commissar of the foreign press, Leonid Ilychev, on the morning of our first full day in Moscow. Interviews? Why, that was out of the question; everyone was too busy with the meetings and celebrations of the Fortieth Anniversary. Premier Bulganin said you should see First Secretary Khrushchev? Well, he'd look into that. In the meantime, write a letter explaining why we had come to Moscow.

The hotel produced a Cyrillic alphabet typewriter, Intourist provided a typist, Bill composed the letter, and Serge dictated it to the girl. Bill signed it, sealed it, and Serge deposited it where Ilychev had dictated—in a mailbox hung on a Kremlin wall.

If that was utterly baffling, the next ten days were equally as deflating. True, there were pleasant distractions. Intourist chose as our official keeper a relentlessly cheerful and efficient little woman named Zoya Novikovo. As do all Intourist guides, she made us feel like Cossacks as she shepherded us past long and frozen queues of true aficionados. She steered us unerringly into *Swan Lake* at the Bolshoi, where Khrushchev and Mao Tse-tung sat together in ordinary orchestra seats while Anastas Mikoyan occupied alone the huge royal box on the mezzanine. She had the password and the last-minute tickets for such perennial sellouts as Moscow's unforgettable one-ring circus with Popov and a monstrous hippopotamus which mingled with front-row patrons like a lap dog. She knew the best way into the puppet show, the museums, into any place except the places we wanted to go: to the offices of newsmakers.

We spent a depressing number of hours shamelessly waiting for Ilychev to call. I began to wonder about the incidence of stir-craziness. But this was averted largely by two diversions: (1) Hearst's daily breakthrough against the impenetrable language barrier, and (2) an eerie fulfillment of the prophecy of J. D. Gortatowsky.

One of the hardest things to obtain from the room-service waiter at the ice-bound National was ice. We couldn't get through to him even with such overwhelming documentation as our English-Russian Dictionary:

> **ice** *sb* лёд *m* (1d)[1) thick тóлстый, thin тóнкий, hard крéпкий, clear чи́стый, transparent прозрáчный, artificial искýсственный, slippery скóльзкий, dry сухóй; 2) breaks ломáется, melts тáет, cracks трещи́т; 3) cut рубить, crush кроши́ть, break разби́ть, melt растопи́ть]; the river is covered with ~ рекá покры́та льдом; she slipped / fell on the ~ онá поскользнýлась / упáла на льдý; they fished through holes in the ~ они́ уди́ли ры́бу подо льдóм; the water under the ~ was cold водá подо льдóм былá холóдной; put some more ~ in your glass! положи́те себé в стакáн ещё льду!; your fingers are as cold as ~ у тебя́ пáльцы как лёд.

Our leader cracked the code. He faced the puzzled waiter and called for his careful attention. Then Bill flung his arms around himself, did a jig, shook his head, rattled his teeth and said:

"Br-r-r-r-r-r-r-r!"

The man marched out immediately and returned with a pitcher of ice.

"Eggs" were as bewildering to the waiter as "ice" had been until Bill squatted on the fine Persian rug of the living room, made a series of faces indicating pain, then beamed beatifically and began to cluck. Thanks to Hearst, Conniff and I could have our eggs boiled as we wished. For example, he would stand in front of the waiter and point to the glass or pitcher he was holding. Then he'd do "egg" again (the deep knee-bends kept him in excellent condition), tenderly deposit the "egg" into the receptacle and wiggle his fingers under its bottom. That, of course, was "fire" or "flames." Then he'd hold up, say, three fingers and point to Conniff. And Frank would get his three-minute eggs.

We ate better when Serge was present. All waiters moved on the double when Serge—who looks as if he posed for Van Gogh's pork-pied *Young Man*—snapped orders in Russian. He was generally at our sides at the endless rounds of diplomatic receptions whenever a story might be afoot. I always marveled at his command of one of the world's most difficult tongues, but never more keenly than the night he lost his way while driving to a party at the Liberian Legation—an indication of the condition of our desperation. Serge spotted a Moscow policeman standing his lonely vigil on a remote side street, pulled over to the curb, reached past me in the front seat to open the window, and engaged the fur-hatted man in what turned out to be five minutes of animated dialogue. There was much gesticulating on the part of the officer as he apparently told Serge when to turn left, right, and do an outside loop. Gravely impressed, I sat between them in the eye of a hurricane of lively exchanges, using neck muscles that had lain dormant since my days as a tennis reporter. Finally, Serge rolled up the window and we were again on our way. He started to laugh.

"Did you ever hear such an atrocious accent as that?" he asked *me*.

As for Gortatowsky's curse:

"Hey, we're on fire!" Hearst announced one night in the suite. Conniff was in his neighboring room taking a bath. I was engrossed in my typewriter attending the birth of a column by Caesarian section.

Hearst pushed open the doors that led to the main balcony and the suite was instantly filled with the music and crowd noises of the continuing Great October celebration . . . and smoke.

We *were* on fire. The big Hammer and Sickle flag that adorned the balcony of a man named William Randolph Hearst had drooped its tail end low enough to become enmeshed in a neon sign that hung just below our balcony. The sign, one of the most familiar in Moscow, read "PECTAPAH," meaning (and more or less pronounced) "RESTAURANT." The flag's tail, wet from the day's rain and snow, short-circuited the sign. The sign sent out a small fireworks display of sparks and the flag burst into sullen smoke and flames.

Hearst dashed across the living room, picked up a pitcher of drinking water, sped back to the balcony and heaved the contents upward and outward at the unnerving blaze. I found a bucket in one of the bathrooms, filled it, and let fly. Hearst was right behind with another pitcher full. We weren't quelling the blaze but we were certainly risking a bad electric shock, for the tail of the flag was still enmeshed in the sputtering wiring. Moreover, we discovered with a jolt, we were making a lot of Muscovites mad at us. We had forgotten the milling crowds in the street below. Every time we missed with the water, they got it on their heads. There seemed to me to be shouts of rage mixed somewhere in the ear-splitting street music that swept the mad scene. A few shook their fists up at us, blaming us for either setting fire to the Hammer and Sickle during a most hallowed anniversary period, or giving them an unrequested bath.

Bill and I were still playing energetic firemen when Frank Conniff entered the smoky living room with naught but a towel wrapped around his middle. He was delicately fanning the smoke away with his hand.

"Fire? What fire?" he asked, addressing his remarks to what we felt was the "bug" in the ceiling nude's navel. "I don't know anything about a fire. When the secret police arrive, I'll be given a clean bill of health."

Help arrived. It wasn't very friendly help. A swarm of chambermaids, porters, and probably electricians stormed into the living room like a pandemonium scene from the Winter Palace, circa 1917. The fire was doused, the desecrated flag lowered and bundled, and then for good measure they took the other flags off our proud balcony and trundled them off, with many a dark look. Serge wasn't around to explain the whole thing, and Bill couldn't come up with a quick pantomime depicting a sodden and drooping flag, short circuit, smoke, flames, valiant effort, so sorry. . . .

More deadly days of waiting, and then the logjam stirred.

We were permitted to see Andrei Gromyko, the first interview he gave after being named Foreign Minister. He was much more relaxed and affable than during his years at the UN in New York. He asked with mock alarm if Bill Hearst's compact tape recorder was a bomb, listened to it for a moment, and then said, "It doesn't tick. It keeps saying 'bleep . . . bleep . . . bleep.' " That was the sound of Sputnik I, and we still had nothing to match it at that time. Gromyko laughed at his joke and was chatting agreeably about New York in his flawless English until one of us asked him the first question of the interview.

Immediately, he switched into Russian. Presumably, he was "bugged" too and wanted to make certain that whatever answers he gave to us thereafter were clearly understood by superiors who presumably would add the tape to his dossier. He didn't say enough to fill three sticks of type. The next bone we were tossed was Yuri Zhukov, a crude oaf who had previously edited *Pravda* and was now staggering under the title of Chairman of the Soviet Union's Committee on Cultural Relations with Foreign Countries. He explained why the U.S.S.R. was jamming Voice of America broadcasts: "There is an old Russian proverb which goes 'When a man is trying to throw a stone into your window you try to protect your window. You close your blind.' "

That was the last day we had Serge Fliegers' services as our official interpreter. At one point in the interview, Zhukov's interpreter translated into English a Zhukov reference to Anthony Eden: ". . . but then, after certain events that took place in Hungary, the Conservative Eden . . ."

"Mr. Zhukov didn't call Eden a Conservative, he called him a Fascist," Serge spoke up. Filled with surprise, confusion, and anger, Zhukov acknowledged that he had. Thereafter, we were minus our miraculous linguist during formal interviews. And by coincidence or design, Serge was ordered out of Russia some months later.

Khrushchev bounced into the reception room of his modest suite in the Central Party headquarters building. He shook hands all around, giving each of us penetrating looks not quite in keeping with his feckless gold-toothed smile. The little glacial eyes paused a bit longer on me. He clearly remembered Hearst and Conniff. Bill explained that I had replaced Kingsbury Smith on this trip. Khrushchev muttered in Russian and laughed. Victor Sukhodrev, the testiest of Khrushchev's interpreters, also laughed as he translated:

"He's bigger than Smith, but is he as good?"

At last we were gathered around the big table of his inner sanctum. The hour I had actually prayed for, but doubted would ever come, was at hand. We arranged our scores of questions in front of us, carefully selected during hours of work back at the hotel. All the major INS bureaus in the world had contributed to our treasury of pertinent and impertinent inquires. But first the ice must be broken. Our icebreaker moved into the barrier.

"It *is* the same office as the last time, isn't it?" Hearst asked, scanning the inevitable picture of Lenin and Khrushchev's memento-laden desk.

"Of course," Khrushchev said, through Sukhodrev. "We don't change in this country as you do in yours."

Hearst started all over:

"Frank Conniff and I have noticed a lot of changes in Moscow since our visit of two years ago. For instance, there are many more cars on the streets. . . ."

"We're not interested in automobile production," Khrushchev cut in when he got the gist. "It has no important role in our country."

We weren't getting out of the batter's box, and this predicament obviously pleased Ilychev. The mean little man was silently laughing at us.

"Now, about these questions . . ." Khrushchev said, picking up the bundle we had sent him on Ilychev's telephoned demand. He looked at them with impatience showing, pushed them aside, and said, "Ask me whatever you wish."

He gave us three hours and thirty-five minutes.

It was one of those once-in-a-lifetime exclusives. The man's grasp of the spectrum of human events and crises was phenomenal. Only once during the crammed session did he refer to his notes, in order to quote accurately a portion of a speech President Eisenhower had delivered several days earlier in Oklahoma. The rest was off the top of his head, or lower. It ranged through war and peace, mutual suspicions, integral differences in the two ideologies, the arms race, Russia's ability to kill tens of millions in the United States with its ICBM's ("Your cities and bases could be stricken from the earth"); NATO, West German rearmament, Hungary ("It could have been different"); creature comforts, consumer goods, the need of East-West trade, hybrid corn, Soviet pre-eminence in space, aspirations of the workers of the world, disarmament, inspection. He left no base untouched. His words were weighed around the world by government leaders and policy makers. Popularly, however, the chief impact of the interview emerged from an area in which apparently he had never been questioned. I asked the question that loosed the little avalanche:

"You have made several references to God, the human soul, and spiritual freedom under Communism. How is it that any man who might believe in all those things is denied advancement in the Communist Party?"

Surprisingly, Khrushchev rose from his place at the conference table and started toward the rear door of his office. I feared the question had guillotined the interview before we had exhausted all the darts in our quivers. But he stopped at the door, poured himself a glass of his country's noxious seltzer water, and strode back to the table. He was angry but in full control.

"Because the situation is incompatible," he said, "We are atheists! Certainly we use the name of God, as in 'God's truth,' but it's only a habit, an expression. We could just as easily say, 'I give you my word.' We are atheists, but we have a tolerant attitude toward all religion. There is no contradiction in this attitude."

Then he hit the table with his fist. Pencils bounced.

"But if the acceptance of religion is intermingled with political activity that works against the Communist Party, that's different. If they intrude on political activity, that is against our constitution. It is not permitted. We are not going to fight for God's body. We don't fight for an empty coffin so that other coffins, filled, will cover the world. That's what the Crusades were fought for."

The mood interested Hearst, who is hardly gulp-prone in the presence of any world leader, however menacing. He told Khrushchev that no great country or civilization had ever risen without deference to or dependence upon some form of divine guidance and dared him to deny it.

"Let them believe what they want," Khrushchev said, sweeping the previous affairs of man to one side.

"That's the basic difference between us," Hearst said. "When we give our word, we consider it is a pledge to God. In your case, the pledge remains on paper only." It was a slap Khrushchev obviously never expected in his own office or anybody else's. In the tense silence that followed I wondered idly if we'd get out alive.

"We set high value on our pledges and on our word," Khrushchev said, picking up a blue-handled letter opener and wagging it at Bill. "We Communists, we atheists, are fighting actively to prevent another war. We mean it when say we are doing everything possible in order that there will be no new war. That is where the discrepancy lies. Such people (religious) seek to present things as if their activities really proceed from divine commands. In actual fact, they contradict the very principles of humanity and, consequently, of the whole of human society." He was getting louder.

"Your John Foster Dulles wears the mask of God, but behind the mask is the Devil. I've seen pictures of priests throwing holy water on tanks, guns, blessing these weapons that murder innocents and enslave the colonial peoples. Your priests brought the Cross and the Bible to strange lands and peoples and took their riches, leaving only the Cross and Bible." He hit the table again with his chubby fist, then calmed.

"I recall a story I once heard," he said, "about robbers who killed a man. Among the loot they took from the victim was a chunk of fresh ham. After a time, the robbers stopped to rest and eat the ham. They had distributed it among themselves when one asked what day of the week it was. He was told it was Wednesday or Friday—I can't remember the exact day named in the story. He declared he couldn't eat the ham, for his Church prohibited meat on Wednesdays and Fridays.

"You see how it is! The robber killed a man, took his life and everything he had, but didn't eat the ham taken in the loot for fear of committing a sin! Don't the deeds of certain Western statesman remind one of the sacrilegious people mentioned in the story? For they, shielding themselves with the name of God, quite often do things which bring death to thousands and millions of people."

When it was over and we were back in the hotel we compared our books of notes and I sat down at the typewriter. I wrote for nearly seven hours, never wanting food or drink. When the two long main pieces, the feature on his religious tirade, and a column on what it was like were finished, Serge read proof on the thick stack of material and took it to the censor's office in the Telegraph Building. A woman behind the counter stamped the original and carbon, to note the time of arrival, and carried both through a door beyond which no newsman ever was permitted to pass. Hearst got through to New York by phone that night—a Friday—and sketched the scope of the interview for the promotion department. He ordered the first of the two main articles to be released in Sunday papers. Consequently, the Hearst Papers and a great many INS clients the following day, Saturday, carried the following blurb:

> KHRUSHCHEV SPEAKS
>
> For three hours and 35 minutes—in one of the most significant interviews of our times—the dominant figure of Soviet Russia has answered the questions of three famous newsmen.
>
> No subject was out of bounds, no holds barred as William Randolph Hearst, Jr., Frank Conniff, and Bob Considine explored Khrushchev's views on war, peace, coexistence, science, satellites, missiles, nuclear power, and the probable directions of Soviet policy. Don't miss it. Sunday!

There was one fly in the ointment, we discovered when we woke up Saturday morning after celebrating the completion of the big coup. Every word, comma, period, dash, and exclamation point was still being held by the censor's office. Nothing had moved, nine hours after Serge had delivered it for approval and transmission. At 10 A.M. we made an aborted effort to reach INS-London and dictate it. The call never got beyond the nearest Russian switchboard. At 11 A.M. we craftily put in a call for Communist Prague, where we knew the two courageous Press Wireless people would take it. We were cut off before we could start. Just before noon it appeared that Hearst would be forced to tell our papers and clients in the United States and elsewhere in the world that the stories would not be forthcoming until, let's say, the publishing of our memoirs.

But at the stroke of noon, with Serge pacing back and forth near the counter in the censor's outer office, a woman emerged from the mysterious door with the stamped and approved carbon copy of everything. Not a word had been changed. The entire works was on its way to New York. We were given to understand later that Khrushchev had asked to see a translation of the material that Saturday morning and had personally passed it.

The Hearst team saw more of that remarkable rogue between this time and his downfall. The meetings were never nearly so productive, but they were lively. Hearst and Khrushchev were as separated as the earth's poles, but instinctively enjoyed a rapport. Each time the Russian spotted Hearst, sometimes as just another face in the crowd, he greeted him cheerfully, if sardonically, with such as "Ah!—my old monopolistic friend." Hearst once said to him, a bit ruefully, that he wished the Hearst papers *were* monopolies here and there because they were taking a financial pounding from the determined opposition in those markets. Khrushchev obviously didn't believe him, judging from his laughter. At the end of their first meeting, which had been heated at times, Khrushchev patted Hearst on the shoulder and said, "When you return to America and are called before the McCarthy committee investigating subversion—and you are sure to be after sitting down for hours with a Communist leader in Communist headquarters—I am prepared to testify for you that you defended your country's position well and ably." In the course of their long second meeting, after Khrushchev had expounded at length on what he called the plight of the American working class, Hearst said, "I've heard everything you've said and don't believe a word of it." Khrushchev was more amused than offended by being called a liar. Tapping his letter opener's blade on the conference table, he beamed and said, "When the time comes when the United States worker will say, 'I am the boss. I create all the values, and I will vote in the interest of myself and other members of the working class,' don't be afraid. We who will be in overall charge then will tell the leaders of the working class in the United States, Mr. Hearst, that you were not a bad capitalist at all."

"Gee, thanks," Hearst wheezed.

There were shrouded chapters in Khrushchev's life that suggested strong evidence he might be among the most ruthless hatchet men of the twentieth century. He was in at least partial command of putting down lawlessness in his native Ukraine after World War I. He was again there on orders in 1924 with his boss, Lazar Kaganovich, to wipe out Trotskyism. He was part of the prosecution in the forgotten but bloody purge of 1932 which led to the suicide of Nadyezhda Aliluyeva, Stalin's wife, which facilitated the dictator's marriage to his mistress Rosa Kaganovich, sister of Khrushchev's patron. Khrushchev was moving fast within the Party. Stalin was amused by his rough-hewn manner, barnyard humor, unquestioned loyalty, and the aggressive manner in which he danced the native *gopok*. He made him political overseer of the engineering endeavor that is still one of the man-made wonders of the world, the Moscow subway system. Of that phase, Edward Crankshaw, one of the foremost Western authorities on the Soviet Union, wrote searchingly: *

> With his cloth cap, his sloppy clothes, his brash, overbearing manner, and his ability to coax disgruntled workers and jolly them along as well as to bully them and lash them with his tongue, he was the practical man who knew how to get things done. High office and a host of sycophantic subordinates at his command had not changed him. As in his early days . . . he still liked to get out into the field and face his problems on the ground instead of keeping his boots clean and operating from behind a barricade of paper. At the same time the talent for intrigue, for smelling out heresy, for paying out rope in the most calculated manner until his enemies stumbled and a short, sharp twitch of the halter broke their necks, put him in the front rank of Party hatchet-men.

Eugene Lyons, longtime student of the U.S.S.R., testified before a Congressional committee just before Khrushchev's visit to President Eisenhower in 1959: "He was sent in 1937 as Stalin's trusted killer (to the Ukraine). . . . His first move was to summon a conference of the entire Ukrainian government, staged as a social occasion. The gathering was surrounded by the secret police, arrested en masse, and most of his 'guests' died in the cellars of the Kiev and Moscow secret police. When his two-year Ukrainian purge was over, an estimated 400,000 had been killed and terror gripped the whole population."

During World War II Khrushchev held a number of important jobs that were never mentioned in dispatches: military commissar for the Kiev area, commander of a partisan force in the Ukraine, and he was at Kharkov and Stalingrad with the rank of lieutenant general. In the postwar years he nimbly kept his balance in the face of Stalin's senile rages and outfoxed and outmuscled his fellow heirs when Stalin died.

Still, there was no noticeable demonstration of joy when his luck and his gall ran out and he became an unperson, another faceless member of his society's living dead. Indeed, he seemed to have sympathizers in the West, persons who had grown accustomed to his wacky ways and preferred him to his solemn-faced and unplumbed

* *Khrushchev: A Career.* The Viking Press. Copyright © 1966 by Edward Crankshaw.

successors, Leonid I. Brezhnev, Aleksei Kosygin, and the always mysteriously well-placed "theoretician" Mikhail Suslov. In the United States many felt they knew Khrushchev, could guess his future moves quite accurately from such risky and ridiculous past performances as planting missiles in Cuba and then chickening out and removing them, pounding his shoe in the UN, giving the Allies "notice" in West Berlin and then conveniently doing nothing about his ultimatums, expressing shock over the scantily dressed chorus line on the *Can-Can* set at Twentieth Century-Fox, complaining shrilly about not being permitted to go to Disneyland.

A lot of Americans remember him with mixed emotions . . . notably Richard Nixon.

Before he flew to Russia on a trip which for a time at least seemed a solid stepping stone to the White House, the Vice President invited the Hearst team to fly to Washington and brief him on the temper of the man he was to face.

We assured Nixon that Nikita Sergeyevitch (or Sergeivich) was tough as nails, rough as a cob, sharp as a tack, smart as a fox, mean as a razorback . . . and exciting to be around. I suggested to him that he collect a series of good waterproof American proverbs before he set foot on Soviet soil, for he'd surely be assailed by sentences beginning "There is an old Russian proverb which goes. . . ." Khrushchev used proverbs not only to sum up his arguments but conclude them triumphantly.

Actually, there was little that anyone could do to steer Nixon through his Russian trip without turmoil. In the first place, his credentials lacked distinction. As President Eisenhower assessed them, they called on Nixon to pay a visit to the U.S.S.R. and officially open the American Exhibition in Moscow's Sokolniki Park. This would repay the visit to New York the year before (1958) of Khrushchev's First Deputy Frol Koslov, who had opened the Russian fair at the New York Coliseum.

"It is a goodwill gesture, and we wanted to have a prominent American to officiate at the opening of our exhibit," the President told a news conference. The feeble fiat offered Nixon precious little armor for his inevitable brushes with Khrushchev and other assailants. The Hearst group and seventy other United States correspondents found themselves fending for Nixon as best they could, cheering him on his uncharted path, giving him a "press" back home that removed much doubt that he would be the GOP nominee in the following year's presidential campaign.

He needed every friend he found. Early on July 24, 1959, his first full day in Moscow, Nixon decided that he'd jump right into the life of the city. With a Secret Service man at his side, he left U.S. Ambassador Llewellyn Thompson's residence, Spaso House, and set out on a brisk constitutional. In time, the pair came upon a market-grocery, Danilovsky's by name. The inveterate politician compulsively entered, waved to customers and clerks, and sought out the manager. The manager and others recognized him, to Nixon's keen pleasure, and there was enough English afoot to pursue a dialogue. He signed a few autographs and smiled for the Secret Service man, who had brought along his 8 mm. home-movie camera.

All would have gone well if the manager of the store had not remarked that he and many others were unable to buy tickets to the eagerly awaited American Exhibition. Nixon, not knowing that Soviet officials had limited ticket sales to thirty thousand a day to suppress excesses of public endorsement of the fair, assumed the manager meant that he and others could not afford the price of admission tickets.

"I'll see to it personally that there are tickets for everyone here in the market," he announced generously. He had not picked up any Russian currency as yet, so he borrowed a hundred ruble note from the Secret Service man and offered it to the Russians to buy tickets. They laughingly protested that it wasn't a question of being unable to afford to go, and some applauded him as he left the place. But the next day's *Moscow News,* an English language tabloid, berated him pitilessly for his "insult" to well-paid Russian workers and accused him of bringing along a photographer to make a propaganda film.

Later that first morning he met Khrushchev in the latter's office in the Kremlin. Echoes of the introductions had barely died away when Khrushchev began to question Nixon sharply on a resolution passed in the U.S. Senate a day or two before expressing sympathy for the "captive nations" behind the Iron Curtain. In the course of its passage, several Senators from states where large numbers of refugees and others tracing their roots back into Eastern Europe lived and voted, attacked Khrushchev as an arch despot.

Khrushchev demanded to know whether this resolution marked an official change in American foreign policy. Nixon attempted to explain that there is a difference between a resolution and a fact of policy. Then why, Khrushchev wanted to know, was it passed just at this time when Nixon was embarking on a good-will tour? Nixon said that something of this nature was voted on at the tail end of just about every Senate session. But what does it *mean?*

Distressed, on his own, hoping to get his tour off on the best foot, Nixon said in a roundabout way that the Senate resolution didn't mean anything, despite the fervor of its language and the publicity it got.

Khrushchev was genuinely puzzled for a time.

"You mean it is just horse shit?" he asked incredulously.

Nixon nodded and the tension disappeared. Khrushchev skipped over to his desk, scooped up a miniature of Sputnik I, and brandished it before Nixon like an old child braying proudly over a new toy. His gamesmanship was showing badly, but Nixon saw nothing to do about it, then. They rode to the fair together in Khrushchev's limousine.

John Daly, then chief of news and special events at ABC, and I were luckily positioned at the entrance of the Exposition grounds as Khrushchev and Nixon arrived, followed by Mikoyan, Klimenti Voroshilov, the powerless president Khrushchev pointedly ignored, Kozlov, and bumbling Yuri Zhukov. Khrushchev, wearing a cheap little white hat with a brim that was in contrast to his breadth, beckoned Mikoyan to his side and gruffly introduced Nixon.

Determinedly polite, Nixon shook hands warmly and enthused, "Oh, yes, I met Mr. Mikoyan when he was in Washington. In the United States we have great respect for Mr. Mikoyan's ability as a trader. Everybody in our country recognizes Armenians as the greatest of traders." Through his interpreter, Khrushchev barked, "Then your country has forgotten how to trade. Mikoyan couldn't make a single deal while he was there." With that, Khrushchev led the way to heavy wire gates behind which at least a hundred cameramen fired away. Nixon turned to Daly and me as the procession began.

"Maybe I shouldn't have gotten into that," he said of the abruptly demolished talk about U.S.-Soviet trade.

There wasn't a kitchen in sight when the famous "kitchen debate" began. The wrangle between the temporal tsar of all the Russias and the man from Whittier, California, began in RCA's color TV pavilion. The schedule called for Nixon to show it off as an American scientific marvel, make a brief video tape with him, and move on. But Khrushchev noticed that the glassed-in gallery that looked down into the studio where they paused was crowded with attentive and admiring constituents. The prospect of appearing on a tape that would be seen on American TV a day or two later also struck Khrushchev as a lively challenge. The camera's red light glowed. A floor director nodded to Nixon. He was on. He had just plunged into a description of color TV for Khrushchev's benefit when Khrushchev grumpily said that Russian scientists had developed the same thing years before. And from that curious springboard he launched into a sputtering attack on U.S. overseas bases. Before Nixon could speak (Khrushchev's words were already being applauded by Russians in the gallery), the dictator also charged that the United States was deliberately fomenting a war over Berlin.

It was embarrassing. Nixon's smile became a grimace. Once he tried, "Now back to color TV . . ." but that's as far as the bullying monologist in the crazy white hat would let him go. Nixon was being held personally responsible for the lag in U.S.-Soviet trade, continuity of cultural exchanges, and what Khrushchev decreed was the average American's contempt for all Russian achievements. The camera was still on.

Clearly, it was then or never for Nixon. Suddenly he jabbed his right forefinger at his truculent guest.

"Just a moment," he said, louder than Khrushchev had been talking. "You're trying to dominate this talk. You would've made a good lawyer. Don't give *me* your ultimatums."

"Who is giving ultimatums?" Khrushchev spouted through his interpreter.

"This is hardly the time and place to hold a debate," Nixon beefed, looking around the studio at the litter of the scheduled plans.

"Why not now?" Khrushchev dared. He looked up at his fans and when they got the translation from the monitors placed strategically in the gallery, they cheered. Khrushchev tried a new tack.

"You will forgive me for raising my voice?"

Nixon turned to his own interpreter, Alexander Akalovsky, supplied by the State Department.

"Tell him not to worry. Tell him I've been insulted by experts."

"Will this exchange be broadcast in the United States?"

"Yes, it will."

"It will be so edited," Khrushchev declared, "that it will hardly be recognizable."

"It will be played just as it has been done here. I give you my word on that. But will it be shown to the Russian people?"

"Of course," Khrushchev said expansively. "If you show it, we'll show it. But I have reason to worry about how much of it you will show. You suppress."

"*We* suppress! Listen, for every word you print in your papers from a speech by our President, we print a hundred words of your speeches."

I found myself suddenly shouting, "That's telling him, Dick!" a most lamentable lapse in reportorial impartiality. I was not alone.

"So you will show it all?" Khrushchev repeated.

"Of course we will."

Khrushchev suddenly reached his right arm straight up, brought it down like a semaphor, seized Nixon's hand, and pumped it like a handle.

"Shake," he said, somewhat redundantly.

Khrushchev acted just as rudely later in front of the kitchen exhibit in the model American home. There was a preposterous exchange that grew out of a misinterpretation of the word "dictate." Nixon took advantage of a semicolon in one of Khrushchev's nonstop sentences to observe piously that no country, however strong, should attempt to dictate to a lesser nation. Khrushchev replied heatedly that he resented being called a dictator.

"We will answer your threats with threats," he shouted while reporters and cameramen jostled in the dense crowd around the antagonists. "We have means at our disposal which can have very bad consequences for you."

"We have, too!" Nixon answered toughly, poking him in the chest.

Subsequently, the GOP distributed tons of copies of that stirring picture of the nominee "standing up to Khrushchev." But not enough tons, apparently.

It was not much of a fair we spread before the visitors to Sokolniki Park, but they loved it. The eyes of stolid housewives were moist but enormously proud as they accepted their free shampoos, sets and hairdrys. A large head of Abraham Lincoln commanded the same bovine attention one observed at the mausoleum in Red Square. Shoes, pots and pans, vacuum cleaners, toasters, refrigerators, stocked deep-freezers, textiles, and carpentry sets created a constant chatter of admiration and bashful (or fearful) inquiries as to how such wonders might be purchased. The library, although pruned of 150 volumes the Russians considered offensive, was a top attraction. Several Russians were arrested by covertly deployed Soviet police for attempting to spirit books out of the exhibit. The weight of the law also fell on a group of Russians employed by the Pepsi Cola exhibit. One night when no one was looking they drank the thick, gagging Pepsi syrup-concentrate.

A carefree lull before subsequent and most ominous storms—the U-2 debacle, collapse of the Eisenhower-Khrushchev-de Gaulle-Macmillan Summit, and the Cuban missile crisis—permeated Moscow with Nixon and the Exposition on view. Moscow was "in" that summer for the more adventurous American tourists. Newsmen were everywhere, among them that noteworthy anachronism on the fabled scene, Westbrook Pegler. That's how far the bars had been lowered in the U.S.S.R. of that vintage year of '59. I wrote a column about him that started: "Moscow—Westbrook Pegler and I picked up our copies of the London Daily Worker today and hurried off to 10:30 Mass."

We did, too. Peg's prime cause of choler, Franklin Delano Roosevelt, had wrung a modest concession from Stalin in exchange for U.S. diplomatic recognition of the Soviet Union in 1933: One American priest would be allowed to maintain residence and chapel in Moscow. The Assumptionist Fathers were selected to staff this outpost. Peg grumbled a bit about going to Mass. He hadn't been since shortly after the Council of Nicaea, or thereabouts. But once we were on the way his interest quickened. I alerted him to be on the lookout for the Russian cop stationed in the phone booth/pill box near the entrance of the eight-story apartment house and office building on whose top floor was hidden the tiny chapel and living quarters of Fr. Louis F. Dion. Peg gave the cop a comprehensive sneer.

Father Dion, a large man who is now president of Assumption College in Worcester, Massachusetts, was delighted to meet Peg. He showed him his tiny domain: a tight-fitting sanctuary just big enough to hold the small altar, a good-sized wall ikon of the Virgin and Child, and himself; an adjoining room which could seat a congregation of perhaps eighteen or twenty on two divans and folding chairs, and a small bedroom and kitchen in the rear. The heady scent of a coffee pot percolating on the stove was Father Dion's favorite incense. He weaved and bobbed into his vestments and was off about his holy business. Peg and I took the two remaining chairs and tried to lose ourselves in certain old truths by now wholly alien to the land around us.

Pegler's somewhat surprisingly reverent reverie was dissolved by the arrival, late, of an attractive young woman—probably from one of the Latin embassies—and her son of three or four. Peg rose in his courtliest manner and offered his seat to her. She gave him a brief but dazzling smile, but put the child on the seat—whereon he squirmed and fretted and made a general nuisance of himself for the remainder of the service. On the way back to the huge, homely Hotel Ukraina Peg was still warmed by the morning's experience and uncommonly mellow.

"Isn't that something, persevering like that priest does?" he asked, not expecting an answer. "And how about that beautiful girl? Imagine a beautiful thing like that stuck over here in Russia." I began to worry a bit about my friend, and wondered if he was feeling well. But the worry was soon erased.

"How about that kid?"

What about the kid?

"The goddam kid the mother plunked down in my seat instead of sitting on it herself," Peg said, letting winter back into his eagle eyes. "The Catholic Church is wronger than Hell on its stand against birth control."

Now Nixon and his camp followers were given unprecedented permission to advance en masse on Novosibirsk, the largest industrial center of Siberia, and Sverdlovsk, chief heavy machinery complex in the foothills of the Urals and (when it bore its original name, Ekaterinburg) scene of the mass execution of Czar Nicholas II and his family by the Bolsheviks in 1918. It was a journey that could be called tensely hilarious.

Mir i druzhba! ("Peace and friendship") was our slogan and just about exhausted our knowledge of the language. At times the motto lacked meaning. Yuri Zhukov was our shepherd and set out each day to wring the neck of any peace dove which might flutter into view. His people had been sent out in advance to choose and brief the "typical workers" Nixon would be steered to. During his tour of a Novosibirsk plant Nixon found himself blocked by a "worker" who asked him a question which must have constituted Topic A at night around the samovars of every worker's hovel in the city: "When will the United States cease atomic tests, which imperil the peoples of the world with fallouts of strontium 90?"

There was seldom any effort made to answer the planted questions because the interrogators had been trained only to ask, not to engage in subsequent dialogue. Usually when Nixon tried to answer he'd be interrupted by another question on a wholly new subject, and that, too, called for no reply. The *Tass* and *Izvestia* reporters who accompanied us dutifully filed stories about the American vice president's inability to find honest answers to the searching questions of peace-loving workers. One day at Sverdlovsk a man who identified himself as a foreman stopped the Nixon party and proclaimed in a loud voice, "Look at the lovely sky! Do you see any Iron Curtain keeping you from getting through?"

Browned off, Nixon blazed, "Yes, I can. Let's take radio, for instance. We can listen to your broadcasts. But you can't listen to ours because your government jams them."

This was not the way his script was written, so the man started a different question. Nixon wouldn't let him finish. Tough and audible he now said, "Mr. Khrushchev says many things we don't like, see? Such as his statement that our grandchildren will live under Communism. But those things are printed in our country and are heard on our radio. We expect our people to listen, to read, and make up their own minds as to whether this is a fair prediction. We believe sincerely that you've made great progress in the Soviet Union. But we also believe that you would make greater progress if you had, or were permitted to have, a full exchange of ideas."

When he had his interpretation the foreman came up with an answer indicative of the futility of *mir i druzhba*. His reply was, "What you say about our progress is correct. But how you say it is a dirty slander."

Occasionally, a member of Nixon's official party would come to his aid.

"What about your rocket bases?" someone in a crowd of workers taunted as Nixon passed.

"What about *your* rockets?" a sharp and commanding voice retorted. It was Vice Admiral Hyman Rickover, who had been doing a slow burn since his arrival with the Nixon group. He strode up to Nixon's heckler, armed with an interpreter, looked him over with contempt and said, "You're not a worker, you're a politician." The admiral made it sound like a bad word. "I don't want to talk to politicians." As he turned and started to walk away, the man protested that he was not a politician. Rickover turned again.

"Then you're a Communist," he said, sizing him up.

"No," the man said, "I'm just a candidate for party membership."

"All the same thing," Rickover said, breaking it like a stick. "I don't want to talk to party members either. I want to talk to the people, if we can ever find them."

But there was laughter, too, and a fresh look at life in the Soviet hinterland.

The press hostel at Novosibirsk was a bit Spartan for the tastes of the American newsmen. The lone rusty toilet and cold-water sink at the end of the corridor of tiny rooms produced an unhappy queue in the mornings. One morning James Reston of the *Times,* having braved the primitive plumbing, strolled back to his crib past a line of his waiting confreres. He spotted George Healy, New Orleans *Times Picayune* editor who had recently conducted a campaign that resulted in the confinement in a mental institution of Louisiana Governor Earl Long.

Reston stopped and regarded his friend Healy, standing there in Siberia in his pajama bottoms, holding a ragged little towel, and waiting his turn to use a water closet that wouldn't flush.

"And you called Earl Long crazy," Reston said, shaking his head.

One night in Sverdlovsk the big band at the hotel's dining room and cabaret drew an unexpected guest drummer, William Randolph Hearst, Jr. The band's repertoire offered no problems to him. All the arrangements were from Glenn Miller, Tommy Dorsey, and other American maestros whose works had been pirated by means of shortwave radio and laborious counterarrangements. Another night Conniff and I discovered that we could drink a massive amount of vodka if we sat all evening with the mayor of the oblast. Conniff would pour a drink, neat, all around, we'd click our little glasses, say *"Mir i druzhba!"* and down the hatch. Then I'd pour one around and we'd do the same. Then the Mayor. It was the only thing we had to say until closing time, but Hearst had something to say after closing time. He said, "Watch it, you two. You were hitting it awful heavy tonight." He was unaccountably serious.

We wished him a cordial *mir i druzhba,* and were immensely relieved the following night to find him back in the drum section, flailing away at "Tiger Rag."

The homestretch of the Nixon visit was a trial to him and a time for sober assessment of Soviet ways on the part of those with him. John Daly worked long and hard to provide Nixon with proper technical aids for his appearance on Soviet TV. But just before air time two of the three studio cameras suffered suspicious power failures. Daly was somehow able to browbeat the remaining camera's crew into changing the angle from time to time to give variety to Nixon's discourse.

It remains the bluntest talk the Kremlin ever permitted its peoples to hear from a foreigner's lips. Simultaneously interpreted by Akalovsky, Nixon said in part:

"Both of our peoples want peace, but both of us also possess great strength, and much as we want peace, neither of us can or will tolerate being pushed around. . . . If you doubt that the American government and the American people are as dedicated to peace as you are, look at our record and you can reach only one conclusion, that only aggressor nations have anything to fear from the United States of America. . . .

"Why do we maintain military bases around the world? Well, let's look at the record. We disarmed rapidly after World War II. Then came a series of events which threatened our friends abroad as well as ourselves. The Berlin blockade and the war in Korea are typical of the actions which led the United States and our allies to rearm . . . Whenever the fear and suspicion that caused us and our allies to take measures for collective self-defense are removed, the reason for our maintaining bases will be removed. The only possible solution of this problem lies in mutual rather than unilateral action leading to disarmament. . . .

"Let us expand the concept of open skies. What the world also needs are open cities, open minds, and open hearts. Let us have peaceful competition not only in producing the best factories but in producing better lives for our people. Let us cooperate in our exploration of outer space. As a worker told me in Novosibirsk, 'Let's go to the moon together.' Let our aim be not victory over other people, but the victory of all mankind over hunger, want, misery, and disease."

There was no way to calculate the number of TV and radio stations that carried the broadcast. But one indication that it may have had widespread impact was the last-minute decision to have Frol Kozlov make a twenty-minute speech at the airport when Nixon departed a day or two later. Kozlov's speech rehashed everything Khrushchev had been saying, with a little of Stalin thrown in for good measure. It was an insulting farewell. The newsmen were given something of a grilling, too, before they were permitted to board the TWA Boeing 707 they had chartered to take them out into the free world. The closer they came to leaving, the cooler the Intourist guides became. In Novosibirsk the four rather prim young ladies from Intourist who had been assigned to us blossomed in much more feminine suits and dresses, took a drink and even danced with us. Alexander Rogow, manager of the big Intourist bureau in the National Hotel, became the soul of conviviality once we had put some distance between ourselves and Moscow. But at the airport Rogow had become stiff and stern, and it was "Mister" here and "Mister" there instead of "Bill" or "Frank." Three of the four girls disappeared into the rotting woodwork at the terminal and the survivor seemed petrified by some nameless dread.

Our passports were held up for an unnervingly long time. Then a dozen or so were returned to their owners, who promptly proceeded to board the waiting jet while the rest of us sweated matters out in Customs and Passport. But after a time those who had boarded the plane were ordered to return to the terminal. They had to yield their passports once more for further mysterious scrutiny. We concluded that somebody was attempting to make a break for freedom in the general hurly-burly of our noisy leave-taking, and the Russians were out to thwart his/her/their plans.

At long last, passports repossessed and clutched in our hands, we walked to the steps of the jet. But there was still another barrier. At the top of the steps, blocking the door, stood three Russian police who would have had to be cast as turnkeys in the darkest dungeons of Lubyanka prison. The goon in the middle demanded my passport. He opened it to the identifying picture, and then he and the other two glared at it, then at me, then at it, then at me, grunted, shoved it back to me, and opened up enough room for me to enter. In all my travels, it was the only time I ever felt happy about looking like my passport picture.

The pattern of the Hearst Task Force remains unique. At the start of its operations, Kingsbury Smith and Conniff presented Hearst with a format that made our subsequent newsgathering unlike any method that had preceded. Hearst would be presented to the celebrity who was to be interviewed as an equal rather than as one of several story-seeking reporters. He scoffed at the notion at first but came to realize that his name was a most effective door-opener, and in just about any chancellory in the civilized world. From that posture of equality ensued a writing style which sets a Hearst Task Force interview apart from all others. I have lost track of the number of stories, written under my by-line, which began: "Prime Minister so and so told William Randolph Hearst, Jr., today that . . ."

This tacit rapport between Hearst and the personality being interviewed has additional advantages. It enables Hearst to ask tougher and meatier questions—questions which if asked by one who is known simply as a reporter might antagonize the person being interviewed. During some of our interviews I've detected that the figure being interviewed—no matter how unapproachable and clam-mouthed under ordinary circumstances—went out of his way to reveal or explain first-rate stories to Hearst. Intuitively, Hearst is at home with any world figure. Moreover, he comes endowed with a low boring point. That can be a prodding force. In our 1957 Khrushchev interview, his most illuminating information was given to us after the first hour, at which precise point Bill had looked at his wristwatch and said to Conniff and me, "Isn't that about enough?"

Hearst's status in our reportorial apparatus was perhaps best recognized by Sukarno, who gave us one of his rare interviews at his palace in Jakarta in the fall of 1963. He welcomed Hearst with open arms as we entered, then piercingly inspected the editor-in-chief's companions.

"What was your name again?" he asked me. I repeated it.

"Considine . . . Considine . . . what kind of a name is that?"

I said it was an Irish name springing chiefly from County Clare. Astonishingly, the man knew Clare and its foremost product, Eamon de Valera, and excitedly recalled how he had emulated de Valera's revolutionary tactics.

He turned to Frank and repeated the question he had asked me. "Conniff . . . Conniff . . . and what kind of a name is that?" Conniff told him Irish. He beckoned us into comfortable chairs around his desk, pried the top off a round tin of Gold Flakes, and lighted one. He exhaled happily, looked at the cigarette, and said, "The only good thing about the British—their cigarettes."

For the next half hour the jaunty popinjay sprayed a stream of invective over just about every subject from Malaysia to motherhood. He let us know when he had finished by snapping his fingers to a waiting guard and saying, "Tell my Cabinet to come in."

It entered, an odd mix of civilian and military, intellectual and thug. Some were executed in the purge of 1966. Hearst, Conniff, and I stood up. Sukarno remained sprawled comfortably in his chair. He held out a languid hand for each Cabinet officer to touch or shake. When they were all present and accounted for, Sukarno put the identity of the visitors in focus for his ministers.

"Gentlemen," he said, "I want you to meet the very distinguished American journalist, William Randolph Hearst, Jr. And two Irishmen."

Task Force memories do not lend themselves to orderly sequence, nor is it invariably the headlines that linger.

I think of Henry Cabot Lodge, starchy in his air-conditioned embassy in ovenlike Saigon, assuring Hearst, Conniff, Warren Rogers, and me that when we called on Ngo Dinh Diem the next evening, as scheduled, we'd find a broken man who had lost his hold. Diem turned out to be enormously vigorous and positive in his plans ("We won't need your American troops after the end of 1965"). He defended his sister-in-law's right to act like a female. He said he had no intention of acceding to demands from Washington that he fire his brother and political adviser Ngo Dinh Nhu. ("What would be President Kennedy's reaction if Vietnam asked him to fire Robert Kennedy?") Diem further demanded that Lodge turn over to Vietnamese authorities a Buddhist rabble rouser then being given asylum in the Embassy—one Thich Tri Quang. The Embassy refused. On a subsequent trip to Vietnam to cover the Constitutional Assembly elections, the Ambassador told me that he felt Tri Quang would have been killed if he had been turned away the night he burst into the Embassy, hotly pursued by police. The following day Lodge was instructed by the State Department to keep the monk indefinitely. Lodge, informed of the impending CIA-supported coup to unseat Diem, made two attempts to persuade the doomed President to accept asylum at the Embassy. Diem refused, insisting that he would be able to cope with any threat to his position. Lodge then wrung from Maj. Gen. Duong Van Minh, soon to take over, a pledge that he would guarantee Diem and his brother safe-conduct out of the country. They were murdered while in the custody of Minh's men.

I think of Jawaharlal Nehru elegantly descending the great staircase of his residence in New Delhi, delicate rosebud peeping from an opening in his impeccable tunic, snow-white Congress Party cap cocked just right, great dark sultry eyes set in his ascetic's head. He was approaching seventy-four, yet had spent most of that day inspecting Indian Army positions, on foot and without added oxygen, along the 11,000 to 13,000 foot Ladakh front facing the Red Chinese Army. He led us to an elegantly decorated sitting room, clapped softly for tea, and tried patiently to explain to his highly skeptical friend, Hearst, that (1) he felt there was an opportunity for the generally hated Krishna Menon to make a comeback in government; (2) that the aggression by the Chinese had not altered India's determination to remain a neutral and unaligned power; and (3) if Red China's name came up for membership in the UN, India would vote affirmatively.

I think of Walter Ulbricht, goateed chairman of East Germany's Council of State, giving us the full treatment in East Berlin: conference room, lights, cameras, beaming fellow puppets, hearty handshakes for the East German TV newsreels, and the booming voice with which he began reading his statement. Hearst stopped him. "We didn't come here for a statement," he said. "We came to ask questions." The lights began to go out, one by one. Ulbricht grew unhappier with each question. It ended on a ludicrous note. He declared at length that West German forces were secretly armed with atomic weapons whereas East German troops and their Red Army colleagues had only conventional weapons. I remembered Khrushchev had bragged to us that his troops in East Germany packed every known modern weapon. So I stopped Ulbricht in mid-flight and with mock shock asked, "Are you calling Comrade Khrushchev a liar?" That put out the last light.

I think of *Der Alte,* Konrad Adenauer. As we marched into his office in Bonn we were Hearst, Conniff, Fliegers, our UN chief Pierre Huss (who had known Hitler before the war), and four West German press officers. Adenauer looked at the group, eyes smiling through the wrinkled iron mask that was his face. "Who's to be shot?" he asked. I remember his mild condescension toward Khrushchev: "He's not a Communist, he's trying to be either Ivan the Terrible or Peter the Great. He doesn't have nearly the naked power Stalin had." And I can still hear the old man say, "Someday, and I will not be alive, China will attack Russia with millions and millions of troops, and whoever rules the Kremlin at that time will turn his face to the West and cry out, 'Save us. We are white. Save us from this Yellow horde.' " The old man was quiet for a moment. Then he added with a weary chuckle, "And you will."

I think of the pomp and circumstance of our interview with Franco. It had more of the trappings of an audience than a press conference. We were led through a series of ornate salons and galleries all but as impressive as those that lead to the throne room of the Pope. The generalissimo wore his sunburst of medals, insignia, lower chest medallions and sword. He said that some of his best friends were Americans. He told of resisting great pressures brought to bear on him by Hitler to persuade him to permit the panzers to sweep through Spain and attack Gibraltar. Ideologically, he had become disillusioned with Hitler. The fact that Hitler had deigned to do business with Stalin, even for a brief period, stuck in Franco's craw and he told him off at great risk. Would he mind letting us see the correspondence with Hitler? Yes, indeed, he would mind. He'd mind very much.

I think of the following day in Lisbon. The tin gate to the modest residence of Antonio de Oliveira Salazar, premier since 1932, was guarded by two drowsy policemen, whereas the long driveway leading to the doors of Franco's palace had been double-lined with gorgeously uniformed mounted guards. The drowsy Portuguese cops swung back the door and our car crunched across a pebbled drive to the little flight of stone steps leading to a green front door straight from Main Street. We rang and a painfully shy rosy-jawed maid showed us into a dim, drab sitting room. Everything was as gray as a funeral parlor. After five minutes alone we were joined by a gray-faced, gray-haired, gray-suited, and slightly harried man, obviously some sort of clerk in the dictator's office. He stuck out his hand toward Hearst. "Salazar," he said.

I think of Generalissimo Chiang Kai-shek, and brittlely brilliant Madame. They couldn't wait to see us, that late afternoon at their pleasant summer place in the hills up from Taipei. They had moved the interview up twenty-four hours because two days before in Tokyo Premier Hayato Ikeda had told us (and we had reported) that nobody any longer took seriously Chiang's wordy pledges to liberate mainland China. Madame hardly waited for Hearst to blow on his tea. She quietly blazed, "This Ikeda person you give so much attention to is a nobody, a nothing. Why, he was a *clark* in Manchuria when my husband was a general. Why did you publish such an interview?" Hearst said he published it because it was news, but that made Madame angrier. "And I say you should not have," she said indignantly. Chiang sat through the exchange with the set, uncomprehending smile of a polite old man. Bill looked at him, and then at Madame. "Looky," he said to her, "I'll run my newspapers; you run your country."

There are so many other memories, born of the wondrous fact that Hearst cared enough to be a reporter as well as an editor, publisher, and rich man's son.

An ominous roadblock across a hazardous Tunisian highway, at night. Premier/President Habib Bourguiba had sent out word to stop Hearst's car! And invite him back to Tunis for a late dinner. . . . A strange omelet served to the Task Force and their wives at a luncheon given by Venezuela's President Romulo Betancourt. "What's in it?" Mrs. Hearst asked sweetly as we all chewed tentatively. "Many flowers," Betancourt said proudly. We all stopped chewing, our mouths filled. "He means many *flavors,*" the President's interpreter laughed. Chewing resumed. . . . An open window in the Elysée Palace, commanding a view of the magnificent gardens. Charles de Gaulle, having peremptorily ended a general press conference, had marched out of the conference room. Now he appeared in radiant profile, moving past the window like a newsreel. Fliegers cried out to him to pause and meet *le journalist plus grand,* William Randolph Hearst. De Gaulle reached his hamlike hand right past Bill and shook hands with me. Aghast, Serge tried again. Once again de Gaulle's big mitt came through the open window. This time he seized and shook *Serge's* hand, and moved off like a huge wound-up doll.

With Winston Churchill, who had once worked for W. R. Hearst, Sr., Bill always had it made. The old man tended to hate reporters in his later years. But he always made a point of seeing Bill in the wake of a Task Force venture. He'd be damned, however, if he'd see any of the rest of us.

Just Bill.

Just Our Bill, a kind of one-man Navy whom you can join and see the whole blinking world.

AUTOGRAPH
HIS NOVEL
"1 2 3
ALARY"
2 TO 3 AM
CORKA
for Bob Considine - Corka

9. *The Fraudulent Art of Spooking*

ONE OF THE more lugubrious callings within the literary stockade is ghostwriting. As in other reaches of the supernatural, there are good ghost-writers and bad ghost-writers. The bad ghost-writer inflicts his own words, thought patterns, philosophy and morality on the facade of another man's story. The good ghost-writer emulates a sheep dog who merely keeps the flock cohesive and headed in the proper direction, and he never yearns to join it.

The *Concise Oxford Dictionary* makes no such distinction. Its fourth definition of *ghost* (*gō-*), *n.*, & *v.t.* & *i* glacially states: "Artistic or literary hack doing the work for which his employer takes credit."

That's not quite true, or adequate. The employer, whose by-line dominates the book or article or speech prepared for him by the spook, does not automatically take credit in the wake of publication. It all depends on how the offering was received by the audience. If it is praised, all's well and good. He wonders why he needed a ghost in the first place; he could just as easily have done it all on his own. But if the effort with the bogus by-line is condemned or, worse, ignored, then there is no vestige of credit-taking. The ghost is to blame. He didn't capture the *real* me, the employer will swear all the way to his distant grave.

There are other complications that tend to militate against the integration of ghosts and their masters. When Zsa Zsa Gabor failed to marry her ghost, Gerold Frank,* at the climax of their rapt literary rapport, I, as a paid-up member of the ghostly guild, was willing to wager that never would the twain, between hack and employer, meet.

Gerold Frank is a self-effacing wraith, perhaps the best in the strange business. Others are not so selfless. Insensitive hacks who produce win-

* Gerold was happily married, it seems.

ners for their inarticulate employers can sometimes make themselves quite obnoxious. I've known spooks who thought they were worth as much as a three-fourths financial interest in a successful book they wrote under a nonwriter's name. One such boor is said to have had the bad manners to show up at a New York Herald Tribune Book Luncheon honoring the author-of-record. Another put in an appearance at NBC one bleak dawn to offer to help his straw man answer Hugh Downs's distressingly searching questions about a book. Worst of all, certain ghosts have been known to get stoned late at night in public houses and loudly reverse the pattern of the Concise Oxford's No. 4 definition by taking all the credit themselves.

One would think that the relationship between spook and master would smack of the cozy togetherness of the confessional. Not so. There is always a certain reserve, particularly at the beginning. In the days before I was exorcised of my spook quotient, I'd generally try to evade the assignment altogether.

"Try writing it yourself," I'd say as earnestly as I could. "You're the only person in the world who really knows what happened to you, or what you want to say. So do it."

"But I can't *write,"* was the standard complaint.

"Then speak it into a tape machine, hire somebody to transcribe it, and, presto!—you'll have your book in your own inimitable style, your kind of words."

They never believed me. Looking back, I'm glad some of them didn't, for they enriched my life.

I felt throughout my ghosting days that the doer of the deeds to be chronicled deserved to feel that he was a cut above the scrivener he had fetched to put the glorious saga into high-school English at least. Douglas MacArthur would have agreed with my outlook. In his forgotten but gorgeous report to a probably confounded Calvin Coolidge, after commanding the victorious 1928 U.S. Olympic team, MacArthur dipped his pen deep into his purple inkpot and wrote:

> In undertaking this difficult task, I recall a passage in Plutarch wherein Themistocles, being asked whether he would rather be Achilles or Homer, replied: "Which would you rather be, a conqueror in the Olympic Games or the crier who proclaims who are conquerors?" . . . I can but record the bare, blunt facts, trusting that imagination will supply the magic touch to that which can never be forgotten by those who were actually present. . . ."

MacArthur was writing about a reporter's plight in this case, of course. But a ghost is a reporter of sorts. He is an interviewer who is expected to give the employer—ugly word!—his head, see what he can do to make the story sing like a high-tension wire, and provide protective covering for all exposed feet of clay.

Ghosting is a major industry in this country. A vast majority of all statements, proclamations and communiqués which shower down on the public from high places is written or polished by obscure professionals. The nation has been blessed with a large number of responsible Presidents, particularly in times of national and international stress. But only a handful were able to write their way out of a wet paper bag: Jefferson . . . Lincoln . . . Teddy Roosevelt . . . Wilson . . . Kennedy. I would think the list ended there.

The more stirring phrases of Franklin Delano Roosevelt, trumpets that heralded a new social order and a call to arms to protect it in a great war, were his thoughts filtered through the golden vocabularies of pros like Robert Sherwood. The poetry that laced John Fitzgerald Kennedy's public utterances was a reflection of the man himself, but also adorned with the clean glitter imparted by Arthur Schlesinger, Jr., or Ted Sorensen.

The two worst deliverers of good ghosted material in my time as a member of the White House Correspondents were Harry S. Truman and Dwight D. Eisenhower. Each gave the impression that he had never seen the document at hand before plunging into the cold water of its first sentence. Neither had the foggiest notion about when to pause for audience reaction; each always looked up impatiently from the text when their audiences exercised their constitutional right to applaud. By that time, each would have charged well into the next sentence.

Emmett John Hughes, who can write like a sexy Walter Lippmann when the moon is full, composed many memorable speeches for President Eisenhower. But if Emmett had written another Gettysburg Address, Ike could still have made it sound like a 4-H Club's silage report. Like Truman and some of the others, Ike read speches for his own amazement. In the thick of the 1952 campaign, he appeared to start with surprise when he announced that, if elected, "I will go to Korea."

President Johnson wants no traffic with what he clearly feels were the dude words put in his predecessor's mouth by the Harvard hacks, and thus has gathered to his court spooks closer to his style and gait. His style is John Wayne waiting, steely-eyed, for Geronimo to start playing dirty again. His orbit, one would estimate without ready recourse to a tracking station, is Dr. Billy Graham. In slow motion.

I once ghosted a speech for Herbert Hoover which, I like to think, contributed something to his latter-day image as one of the mellow fellows. The occasion was a sports rally at Madison Square Garden to raise funds for Finland, at that time giving the Red Army an inspiring pasting in the ice-caked forests of the Karelian Isthmus. Sports columnist Joe Williams of the New York *World Telegram* and other Scripps-Howard papers was chairman of the affair and thus in a position to order me, a simple spear carrier on the lengthy committee, to compose something to put on Mr. Hoover's tongue.

Thousands at the Garden marveled at the former President's keen knowledge of Paavo Nurmi, and the David-like Stanley Ketchel's courage the day he flattened Goliath-sized Jack Johnson. No ghost is ever completely satisfied with the way a person reads his words, but the thirty-first President's delivery was better than average. We once had a New York mayor who, in the course of reading a ghosted speech to a distinguished audience at the Waldorf, lunged into a passage which began:

"All of which reminds me of the story of Pat and Mike. One fine day while walking past St. Patrick's Cathedral, Pat said to Mike. . . ."

The mayor's voice trailed off absently and died away, and the surprised audience beheld him silently scanning his script.

Suddenly, he burst into loud laughter. He had never read the joke before. Looking up, he seemed startled to find he had company. Then he plowed onward with his speech.

Herbert Hoover never knew who wrote his brave-little-Finland speech. Other famed Americans exercised much closer control over my ghosting services.

One was Gen. Jonathan M. Wainwright, author of *General Wainwright's Story* (. . . edited by Robert Considine, the dust jacket stated).

The fine old soldier had suffered through nearly four harrowing years as a prisoner of the Japanese. He was beaten, starved, humiliated. But his most constant worry during all that time was that he had let his country down by surrendering. He kept a sketchy diary during his years as a POW, a thin three-by-four-inch notebook in which he inscribed, in a script more suited to the head of a pin, certain events and disasters of his confinement.

Long periods, sometimes months, might be encompassed in a single terrible word, such as "hungry." Other abysmal trials went unrecorded, such as the quarrel among the distinguished senior officers in his POW billet. One of them was accused of not sharing the worm he had discovered in his bowl of dirty rice. Such was the craving for protein.

The longest passages in the general's notebook dealt with his soul-searching explanation of why he considered it better to surrender than fight to the last man. He had said it all in his last two messages from Corregidor, one to President Roosevelt, the other to General MacArthur in Australia.

The message to the President on May 6, 1942, read:

> With broken heart and head bowed in sadness but not in shame I report to Your Excellency that today I must arrange terms for the surrender of the fortified islands of Manila Bay.
>
> With many guns and anti-aircraft fire control equipment destroyed we are no longer able to prevent accurate bombardment from the air. With numerous batteries of heavy caliber emplaced on the shores of Bataan and Cavite the enemy now brings devastating crossfire to bear on us, outranging our remaining guns. . . . There is a limit of human endurance and that limit has long since been passed. Without prospect of relief I feel it is my duty to my country and to my gallant troops to end this useless effusion of blood and human sacrifice. . . . With profound regret and with continued pride in my gallant troops I go to meet the Japanese commander.
>
> Good-bye, Mr. President.

The message to MacArthur was more personal, for MacArthur had repeatedly urged him to hold on. It read, in part:

> American and Filipino troops have engaged and held the enemy for nearly five months. . . . We have done our full duty for you and for our country. We are sad but unashamed. I have fought for you to the best of my ability from Lingayen Gulf to Bataan to Corregidor, always hoping relief was on the way. . . .
>
> Good-bye, General, my regards to you and our comrades in Australia. May God strengthen your arm to insure ultimate success of the cause for which we have fought side by side.

Wainwright was haunted throughout his captivity by the thought that the messages may not have gotten to their destinations, or been given short shrift if they did. By an unnerving coincidence he was interviewed one day in the worst of his several prison camps by a Domei correspondent whose first question was, "Do you think you will be court-martialed if you ever returned to the United States?"

Instead, Wainwright was promoted to four-star rank, given a hero's welcome when he reached home—gaunt as a skeleton but straight as a sword. President Truman pinned the Congressional Medal of Honor on his chest at the White House, King Features Syndicate paid him $155,000 for newspaper rights to his story (plus $5,000 to me for writing the forty-two part series), and Doubleday gave him a $25,000 advance for the book rights.

It was a memorable experience.

Each morning for a month, that saffron autumn of '45, I'd climb the hill to his cottage overlooking famous old Greenbrier, White Sulphur Springs, West Virginia, then known as Ashford General Hospital. He would be seated on the porch if the weather was fine, lean and spent in his fresh khaki, coatless, shirt open at the collar, Adam's apple bobbing with a courtly "Good morning." A few yards away, in a quiet corner of the porch, Sgt. Archimedes Giacamantonio, the sculptor, shaped a blob of greenish clay into an increasingly taut likeness.

I would bring with me a first draft of what he had related the day before and which I had put through the typewriter the previous night. He'd put on his glasses, take a stubby pencil out of his breast pocket, and carefully read the material. He used the pencil more as a scanning tool than an editorial implement, I was always relieved to notice.

Indeed, during the entire time I spent with him, he made only two changes, each time wetting the little pencil's point in his mouth before applying it to the script.

The first of these changes had to do with the vanity that is in all who have a story to tell. MacArthur had willed Wainwright two jars of shaving cream and a box of cigars before leaving Corregidor for Australia. On April 28, 1942, having enjoyed a shave with the cream, Wainwright breakfasted in the convalescent mess inside Malinta Tunnel and then headed for an exit to breathe some fresh air and inspect a nearby battery.

About forty feet short of the barrier that protected the mouth of the tunnel, Wainwright stopped to light up one of the precious MacArthur cigars. The decision saved his life. If he had continued walking he would reached the barrier just as it was struck by a 240 mm. Japanese shell.

Wainwright's left eardrum burst and the right ear lost much of its hearing. Armed with those facts, I had written, ". . . as a result I have been quite hard of hearing ever since." Actually, questions to him often had to be half-shouted.

The general drew a line through that phrasing and in his neat hand replaced it with ". . . and the right ear since then has never been up to its old standard."

The other change he made was an addition, a touching assessment of a scene that can have had no parallel in American military history, his departure from Corregidor in defeat. This is how he told it to me:

> Under guard, Colonel Haba led me and five of my staff officers out of the Tunnel's west end. And again we passed through my captured men. They were standing there in the blazing sun in the area where I had seen them the night before. Obviously, they had not been fed or given any water during that terrible time.
>
> They were in very bad shape. But as I walked through them they all got to their feet. Some stood at attention and saluted as I passed, and I raised my hand to my old sun helmet. Others just stood, took off their hats, and held them across their chests.
>
> Again I felt the tears welling up in my eyes and could do nothing to stop the emotion.

The general read the section without comment. Then, after priming his pencil, he slowly wrote:

> I am a student of the Civil War, but not until then did I know how General R. E. Lee felt after Appomattox.

Wainwright was among the less formal World War II generals. "Call me Skinny," he said cheerfully, the day we met. "Everybody else does except Douglas [MacArthur]. Douglas calls me Jonathan. Only man in the world who calls me Jonathan. So call me Skinny, Bob."

It was "Skinny" and "Bob" until the chronological narration reached that point where the general told of the first of several beatings he suffered. Under prodding, he described the scene: the grim prison compound at Karenko, on Formosa; the attack of beriberi which had stripped him to the bones, the drudgery on the prisoners' truck farm, the starvation . . . and a trip one night to the vile latrine. As he was returning to the barracks, a young Japanese sentry shouted at him. Wainwright related that he dutifully stopped, bowed, and waited for whatever it was the sentry had in store for him. Other prisoners "froze" nearby, silently watching the confrontation.

"The Jap swung very quickly and slapped me across the face," the general said calmly as we sat on the hushed porch. Mrs. Wainwright came out, sat near him, and composed herself.

"It was a stinging blow," he continued, "and in my throat I felt a rising gorge of hate and despair."

Suddenly, tears rolled down the old soldier's lined and weather-crusted cheeks.

"I stood there," he went on. "Encouraged by what he had done, the Jap slapped me again, then again, and then a fourth time. Each time he hit me he shouted, 'For Japanese in America!'

"The blows made my legs weaker, but I was determined not to fall at the feet of a rat like that. He saw that I was not going down, so he took a lunge at me and hit me on the left jaw with his fist. And then I fell. I was only half-conscious from the blow, but the part of my consciousness that was alive told me that this was the very pit of my life."

The general stopped talking. Mrs. Wainwright cupped her sad face in her right hand. I felt tears in my eyes.

"That dirty son of a bitch," I sympathized. But the reporter in me recognized that this was a moment when I must extract every last drop of the doleful episode.

"What else went through your mind as you lay there, Skinny?" I asked tenderly.

Wainwright slowly stiffened in his chair. His shoulders, which had dropped as he told his story, squared off. He fetched a newly laundered handkerchief from his pocket, dusted the tears from his cheeks and eyes, blew a thunderous blast from his nose, and regarded me coolly.

"I'll tell you what else went through my mind as I lay there, Mr. Considine," he said curtly. "And this is it: a private should never strike a lieutenant-general!"

I never dared call him Skinny again.

There were other exchanges which, like this one, did not get in the book. It soon was apparent to me that Mrs. Wainwright did not share her husband's dogged, if sometimes humor-tinged, loyalty to MacArthur. At dinner on two occasions, Mrs. Wainwright left the table at the first glowing reference to the Supreme Commander. It was abundantly clear that she felt MacArthur easily could have selected her husband among the fifteen top aides he took with him to Australia, along with Mrs. MacArthur, young Arthur, and the boy's amah.

"She always does that," the general explained the first time his wife departed. The second time he shouted, "Dammit, cut that out and come back to dinner!"

For all his admiration, Wainwright could poke fun at MacArthur, too.

"One day Douglas came over to Bataan to see me," the general recalled with the trace of a smile.

" 'Jonathan, where are your 155 mm. guns?' he asked. I told him where the six of them were, and since two of them were fairly close, I suggested that he walk over with me and take a look at them.

" 'Jonathan,' he said, 'I don't want to *see* them. I want to *hear* them!' "

He chuckled and remembered another one, which he did not want in his book:

"After the surrender ceremony on the Missouri, Douglas invited me to return to Yokohama with him on the destroyer that had brought us to the battleship. On the way he said, 'Well, Jonathan, I hear that you've been offered a lot of money for your memoirs.' I said that was true. 'Bully!' he said. 'You write them, then send them to me and I'll check them and send them on to the War Department.' "

Wainwright glanced sideways at me, smiled tightly and whispered, "I didn't do any such thing."

Only once during our long days together did Wainwright show even the faintest tinge of bitterness toward the man whose orders had caused him so much grief.

In the last days of the Battle of Corregidor, President Roosevelt sent a message to MacArthur in Australia, which was to be relayed to Wainwright "if you concur." Wainwright's radio people intercepted the message, said to have been written by Robert Sherwood. It read:

> During recent weeks we have been following with growing admiration the day-by-day accounts of your [Wainwright's] heroic stand against the mounting intensity of bombardment by enemy planes and heavy siege guns.

> In spite of all the handicaps of complete isolation, lack of food, and ammunition you have given the world a shining example of patriotic fortitude and self-sacrifice.
>
> The American people ask no finer example of tenacity, resourcefulness, and steadfast courage. The calm determination of your personal leadership in a desperate situation sets a standard of duty for our soldiers throughout the world.
>
> In every camp and on every naval vessel soldiers, sailors, and Marines are inspired by the gallant struggle of their comrades in the Philippines. The workmen in our shipyards and munitions plants redouble their efforts because of your example.
>
> You and your devoted followers have become the living symbols of our war aims and the guarantee of victory.
>
> FRANKLIN D. ROOSEVELT.

Wainwright waited several days. MacArthur did not forward the tribute.

"Naturally, I was burned up," the general told me in retrospect. "So I repeated the entire Roosevelt message in a wireless to Douglas, and at the end of it I added one sentence: 'Apparently you did not concur.' "

MacArthur apologized briefly in a message to Wainwright in the final hours of the bloody defense of Corregidor, pleaded that the pressure of work had caused the oversight, and urged Wainwright to do his best to hold out.

Publication day, as always, was a happy one. The general had regained some of his weight and looked fine. The teeth that the sentry had knocked out had been replaced. He was at peace with the world. I hovered on the fringe of the admiring crowd which came forward at the party to ask him to autograph their copies of the book. When the crowd thinned out, I handed him my copy and asked him to sign it.

He did, in his firm hand. I treasure what he wrote:

"To 'The Gost'..."

The Pentagon presented no problem in the case of the Wainwright book, in contrast to the roadblocks it erected earlier in the path of *Thirty Seconds Over Tokyo,* by Capt. Ted W. Lawson, and "edited by Bob Considine."

I met with Ted the first time at the Mayflower Hotel in Washington in the Fall of 1942. He had participated in the Doolittle Raid the previous April as pilot of one of the sixteen B-25's used and lost on the mission. He had crashed just off the China coast after bombing Tokyo and been spirited out of the clutches of the occupying Japanese forces by friendly Chinese. His gangrenous left leg, gashed when he burst through the windshield of his plane—the bomber was prophetically named *The Ruptured Duck*—was amputated by the mission's flight surgeon, Capt. Thomas R. White, in a primitive Chinese hospital. But he lived and made it home in time to be near his wife Ellen when their first child was born.

Ted told the whole enthralling story in a couple of hours, without embellishment, painstakingly careful not to make himself sound heroic. But, bare as he outlined it, it had (as *Time*'s review stated much later) all the ingredients of an epic.

When he finished, I called Charles Colebaugh, editor of *Collier's,* and asked him to wait in his office until I could get to New York. I couldn't tell him over the phone. The Doolittle Raid's details were still top secret, months after the fact.

I had to return to New York by train, airplane seat priorities being what they were at the time. During the four-hour ride, I wrote thirteen single-spaced typewritten pages from the several pages of notes I had typed while Lawson relived his adventure. Colebaugh was alone in the big editorial room when I arrived at 250 Park Avenue that night. I read him my notes in the otherwise stilled and blacked-out place.

"Forget about doing it as an article," he said when I finished. He was quite touched. "It'll be at least six articles, I'd say, and of course it'll be a book." I hadn't thought of that.

I wrote it in less than a month, dictating parts of it and continuing on my typewriter when the stenographer took off to transcribe her shorthand. There was also the necessity of writing my daily sports column for International News Service, and feature assignments.

As the story took shape, my association with it weakened. Bennett Cerf of Random House had been tuned in and wanted rights to the book so keenly that when I suggested he give Ted a five-thousand-dollar advance he said, "Nonsense! I'll give him seventy-five hundred." But other publishing houses got wind of it. One approached Ted with two suggestions: (1) unload Random House, and (2) dump me. In respect to the second suggestion, the publisher said (and I was inclined to agree) that this was the kind of saga that needed the sure touch of Antoine de Saint-Exupéry.

I had a friend at court, however, in the person of Teddy Hayes.

The former trainer of Jack Dempsey, and U.S. Commissioner at the New York World's Fair of 1939–40, had met Lawson during the time Ted was undergoing painful additional surgery on what was left of his left leg. They became fast friends. Teddy kept me in the picture.

When I had written everything Lawson had told me I asked him to search his memory for some last little fact about his story. He furrowed his brow.

"I forgot to tell you about a funny thing happened to me at Walter Reed," he said with a laugh. "You see, I hadn't told Ellen I was back in this country, hadn't told her I had lost the leg. What I wanted was to get my face fixed up, get a good artificial leg, learn how to use it, and then just walk in on her some fine day like I was good as ever.

"Well, Doolittle called her in California and told her all about what had happened to me, without telling me. He also arranged for her to fly to Washington so we could be together, without telling me.

"So one day I'm sitting in my wheelchair in the room at the hospital and, all of a sudden, there she is at the door. I jumped up from the chair and started for her, forgetting about the leg. I skidded flat on my face right at her feet."

Ted laughed again. I couldn't join in.

I incorporated the scene in the book. When Dalton Trumbo wrote the script for Metro-Goldwyn-Mayer he chose this afterthought of Ted's as the ending of the motion picture. To this day, the sight of Van Johnson (Lawson) taking his header in front of Phyllis Thaxter (Ellen) jolts sleepy viewers of the Late Late Show wide awake with its naked impact.

Eleanor Roosevelt, who often visited Ted and Ellen during and after Ted's siege at Walter Reed, did not like that ending of the motion picture, she firmly informed me after the picture had been run for the President at the White House projection room.

"You should never have had the actress stoop down and try to pick him up off the floor," she scolded in her unusual voice.

"But that's what actually happened," I said, surprised.

"That doesn't matter," Mrs. Roosevelt continued, firmly. "A lot of our boys are going to come home without legs and arms. Their families must be taught that they prefer to do things by themselves, no matter how difficult. They won't want to be pampered. It would have been much better if you had ended the picture with the actress just standing there while he tried to get himself off the floor."

I couldn't think of anything to say except, "Mrs. Roosevelt, they'd throw rocks at the screen."

The six *Collier's* articles and the longer book manuscript were held in the deep freeze of censorship for months after they were completed. One entire episode, about the low-level flight of *The Ruptured Duck* across the country from Eglin Field, Florida, to Alameda, California, to be put aboard the carrier *Hornet* (Ted flew the bomber *under* the Golden Gate Bridge as he came in for a landing) was deleted because, as the censor explained, "We must not reveal to the Japanese that we have a landing field at Alameda."

"How about changing 'Alameda' to 'a West Coast field,' " I proposed.

"Oh, that's different," the nut said, and restored the whole exciting scene to the script.

The Pentagon was less amenable in the debate over the original title of the book. My wife had suggested, and all hands had accepted, *For Thirty Seconds Over Tokyo.* It was a title that explicitly expressed and delineated the high cost of waging war against a far-off enemy. The months of preparation and training, the daring investment of a full task force deep in Asian waters, the loss of all the planes, the capture of two crews, the execution of three of the fliers, and Ted's amputation, were the price paid for a thirty-second bomb run.

But a title like that smacked of defeatist thinking, the censor ruled. He struck the *For* and would never relent.

Publication was held up for a year after the mission because F.D.R. had said, in his arch manner, that the B-25's had flown to their several Japanese targets "from Shangri-la." Also, the first Pentagon communiqué insisted that no planes had been lost on the mission. The Shangri-la ploy persisted even after the Japanese torpedoed and sank the *Hornet* many months after the raid and announced to the world that this was the carrier from which the Doolittle fliers had taken off.

Weeks after the Japanese announcement, I was called to the Pentagon and sternly reprimanded. It had learned that someone at Random House had made copies of the script which was supposed to be under lock and key and had distributed them to selected friends of the publishing house. A Colonel Fitzgerald spoke darkly of the prospect of a year in prison and a ten-thousand-dollar fine if this sort of proliferation ever occurred again.

But at long last, *Thirty Seconds* was liberated. It was the longest series *Collier's* ever ran. The Book-of-the-Month chose it. It appeared in British, Spanish, Swedish, Norwegian and other editions, including two rival Chinese editions. The latter was puzzling until one afternoon at a cocktail party I attended in Chungking in 1945. An attractive Chinese girl said to me proudly, above the standard din, "I was the first to publish your Lawson book. I beat my competitor by several months."

I congratulated her warmly and asked her how she managed it.

"Easy," she said. "I stole it from the *Collier's* articles as they came out. He waited to steal it from the Random House book."

The Chinese publishers gave their looted properties the same title, *I Bombed and Destroyed by Fire the Great Eastern Capital.* Through 1945 it was topped on the Chinese Best Seller list only by *Within Four Seas All Are Neighbors,* by Wendell Willkie, a tome known elsewhere in the world by the much more prosaic title *One World.*

Babe Ruth's story, "as told to Bob Considine," presented no such foreign and domestic complications. Babe cut out only one scene. Speaking of his wastrel years, before Christy Walsh put a damper on his reckless spending, Babe recalled that on an excursion to a Havana race track he was approached by a pack of Cuban operators who assured him that they'd be happy to fix the next race for him as a gesture of inter-American amity.

Babe was delighted to join the conspiracy. The sharpies had a heart-to-heart talk with the jockeys, then returned and gave Babe the name of the next winner. Babe said fine, he'd bet thirty thousand dollars. To win. The startling size of the bet so impressed the hoods that they re-fixed the race, and all got away with parts of Babe's money.

"No good for the kids," Babe said, scratching the item out of the script.

Ruth was dying of cancer during the time we put his book together. I was assured by his attorney, Melvyn Gordon Lowenstein, and his good friend J. Paul Carey, that he did not know. I was instructed not to bring it up in any way during the interviews. If I did, I was assured, Babe might "go out the window." The disease had eaten his once basso voice into a rasping whisper. His stomach hung like a deflated basketball from what had been the chest of a grizzly.

"Goddamned teeth," he'd say, shaking his head. Babe had made his own eccentric diagnosis of his massive trouble, ". . . a couple of infected teeth." To humor him, his doctors (at one time he had eight) ordered the teeth extracted. It had no more or less effect on his condition than the major surgery which revealed the depressingly malignant tumor at the back base of his brain.

The surgery was performed by Dr. Hippolyte Wertheim, an internationally known specialist, and watched with fixed fascination by several doctors who shared a secret that Dr. Wertheim was not privy to. They knew that Dr. Wertheim's "ulcer," about which he had been complaining, was cancer of the stomach. Thus a doomed man worked fruitlessly to save another doomed man. The doctor died shortly after Babe's death on August 14, 1948.

Babe's book should have written itself, but it became so difficult I had to call on Fred Lieb, the veteran baseball historian who had covered Babe's capers on and off the field since 1914, to fill in the salient facts of his colorful life. Even in his prime there were two things Babe couldn't remember about people: their names and faces. The cancer compounded that failing. Babe was always too busy making history to bother with remembering it.

Working with what was left of Babe Ruth stirred dusty memories within me. I remembered particularly a hot day in 1918 in the Swamppoodle section of Washington, D.C. A tipsy sailor rolled into our street, noticed a bunch of us sitting on the curb in front of our plumbingless house, and said, "How would you kids like to go to the ball game with me?" We yelled happily and soon were on a streetcar with our benefactor, headed for Seventh and Georgia Avenue, home of the Washington Senators. The sailor bought tickets for the twenty-five-cent benches in right field. We were properly awed. It was the first big league game any of us had seen.

We rooted shrilly for the Senators but they lost to the Boston Red Sox 1 to 0. Jim Shaw, who grunted on nearly every pitch, was our pitcher. Young Babe Ruth pitched for Boston. Everybody knew that pitchers were not supposed to know how to hit, but late in the game Ruth hit a home run over the right-field wall and won his own game.

Now here we sat in the trophy room of his Riverside Drive apartment thirty years—or was it centuries?—later. The withered titan found it difficult not to immerse himself now and then in waves of self-pity. All the real or imagined slights he had suffered during his last years with the Yankees and his brief and aborted stretch with the Boston Braves bugged him as he neared his death.

"How do you like this dumb bastard!" he husked angrily one day, jabbing a bony finger at a sports page feature about him. I had read the article and found it highly flattering.

"What's wrong with it?"

"What's wrong with it? I'll tell you what's wrong with it. It calls me 'the former home run king,' that's what's wrong with it. Where's he get that 'former'? Answer me, who ever beat sixty?"

The apartment fairly bristled with mementos of the fifty-four records Babe broke or equalled during his twenty playing years. But his favorite was not a trophy. It was the framed original of a cartoon by Burris Jenkins, Jr., which appeared in the New York *Journal* in 1933, Babe's last year with the Yankees. It showed Babe as a mighty giant striding majestically past Yankee Stadium, "The House that Ruth Built," while at his heels snapped vicious-looking animals representing fans who had been booing him and owners who hesitated to appoint him manager.

"The best thing ever done on me," Babe would say, gazing at the picture.

There was never anyone quite like Babe. Nobody ever looked like Babe or was shaped like Babe, except his saloon-keeping father. Certainly nobody could ever play more positions more superbly than Babe. A new generation forgets that he was one of the greatest defensive outfielders the game ever knew, could relay a ball to the infield or home plate like a rifle shot, and was never known to throw to the wrong base. He was the finest left-handed pitcher in baseball when Ed Barrow began easing him into the Red Sox outfield on days when he was not scheduled to pitch and the club was opposed by a right-handed pitcher. His World Series pitching record of 29⅔ scoreless innings survived all assaults from 1918 until Whitey Ford surpassed it in 1963. His fifteen World Series home-run mark endured from 1932, his last series, until Mickey Mantle edged past him in 1964. His record of sixty home runs, set in 1927, stood up until 1961 when Roger Maris of the Yankees hit sixty-one in the course of a season that had been expanded from 154 to 162 games. Babe's 714 lifetime home-runs record appears inviolable. Willie Mays would have to live as long as Methuselah to top it.

It was difficult to relate these Ruthian feats with the shell I worked with near his end. He would not give up, however. Occasionally he'd get bored with the labor of remembering something that had happened to him years before, get up from his comfortable chair and say, "Let's get the hell out of here and hit a few." We'd go down to his Lincoln Continental and head for the golf course.

The first stop would be at an Italian butcher shop on crowded Ninth Avenue, where his appearance always evoked shouts of delight. Babe had a bizarre routine at this place. He'd pick up a meat cleaver and give mock chase to the proprietor, calling out, "Hey, you crazy dago bastard, give me some decent meat for a change." It made everybody happy, including the Babe. Then we'd drive to Bayside, a flat and busy little public course in Brooklyn, and change into golf gear while the club's cook prepared the meat, always a hamburger.

More often than not, Babe could not swallow the meat. He would settle for a couple of eggs boiled so briefly that he could drink them. His friend Toots Shor sometimes supplemented that egg diet by having his chef prepare Babe a puree of mashed lobster meat.

The frustration of an egg meal at Bayside was generally alleviated by the arrival of several cold bottles of National Premium beer, a Baltimore brew Babe preferred. He'd down them, belch sonorously, and approach the first tee—always the cynosure.

Babe had taken up golf comparatively late in his baseball career, but his inherent sense of timing, magnificent wrists, and coordination had quickly shrunken his scores down into the high seventies. He could, of course, hit a wood shot a country mile. But now you did not want to watch him. He'd breeze the clubhead through a few easy practice swings to loosen up, settle down, plant his feet, regard the ball intently, and swing away at it with all his might.

There wasn't enough might. The ball would lob lazily down the fairway and stop about 150 yards away. Or less, sometimes. Babe could never believe his eyes. He would stand there for a terrible moment at the end of his follow through. One day he simply dropped his club and blubbered helpless curses through the ashes of his throat.

It was stifling, even inside the deep shade of St. Patrick's Cathedral. Babe's flower-draped coffin was borne in slow cadence toward the great doors and the hearse that waited at the curb. Handkerchiefs showed everywhere in the crowded pews, some used for perspiration, some for tears.

Old teammates Joe Dugan and Waite Hoyt, who had shared a thousand and one days and even more nights with Ruth in the Golden Days, walked side by side in the line of honorary pallbearers.

"I could use a cold beer right about now," Dugan whispered to Hoyt.

They walked a few more measured steps before Hoyt replied.

"So could the Babe," he said with simple reverence.

Stanislaw Mikolajczyk, the last free premier of Poland, wanted his story written for him twice: a series for King Features Syndicate's newspaper clients here and abroad, and a book. He felt there was a difference between journalese and literature. He had just escaped from what would have been certain imprisonment and probable death at the hands of a government which had been taken over by his Communist countrymen, Wladyslaw Gomulka, Jakob Berman, and Boleslaw Bierut. He wished to sound an alarm that would ring from every front page, shake the complacent West, warn it that it could expect only trouble from the Soviet Union and her new Eastern European satellites.

As for the book, Mikolajczyk wanted it to be his enduring report on his life and times, his interpretation of the events which transformed the largest Catholic nation in Europe into a Marxist state.

He had a peasant's patience, this former leader of the Peasant Party. He'd spend an hour explaining to me some tricky nuance of, say, the Polish Referendum of June 30, 1946, which might then take up hardly a full sentence in his story. All our work was done in the dim parlor-office of his suite in a seedy West Side hotel in the Eighties. The door to the suite was kept bolted, guarded by a young Pole prominently armed with a .38 poked tentatively in his chest holster. Now and then arrived callers: Poles in stiff black suits reminiscent of old newsreels of international conferences, or of some lesser Hitchcockian charade. I'd be asked to leave the room. Polish tongues would be flying back and forth like shrapnel as I departed.

Mikolajczyk's grasp of English was tenuous, but he preferred to work in that language rather than filter his revelations through an interpreter. Problems arose. There were times when he would lead me down a path of increasingly flabbergasting contradiction, and I would have to call for a halt and retrace our steps back to the fork in the narrative road where we embarked on that particular tack. There I'd find that the trouble was a simple semantic breakdown. He'd smile in his engaging way, shrug, and say, for example, "I meant to say that Stalin was *not* a good man. So I forgot the not. I must be more careful, yes?"

But at long last my job ended. The articles had gotten much attention around the world, and the matter of the book had been cleared up. There had been a political disagreement with the editors of Viking, the first choice of Gertrude Algase, who had become Mikolajczyk's agent at the request of another of her clients, Francis Cardinal Spellman. Viking recoiled at Mikolajczyk's strong anti-Communism. The ideological climate was much more comfortable for Mikolajczyk at Whittlesey House, a wing of McGraw-Hill.

On the night my long chore ended I asked the premier if he would kindly step to the desk and look over my shoulder.

"I want you to read the two most beautiful words in the English language," I said. The rubicund little exile peered down solemnly as I put my fingers on the typewriter keys and wrote at the bottom of the final paragraph, "THE END."

He was confused for a bit. Then, wreathed in smiles, he exclaimed, "Ah! Now we go drunk!"

And that we did.

One of the more lethal banes of a ghost's life is the hero's lawyer, that is, if he tends to search through a completed manuscript and throw out everything that may conceivably harm his man's image. A chilling example of this kind of renovation came after Bill Slocum and I put the finishing touches on *Dempsey—By the Man Himself* (Simon and Schuster). Slocum is a second-generation ghost; his father spooked for Ruth.

Working with Dempsey was akin to being given box seats at the unfolding of one of the greatest, rawest, wildest stories in the history of sports. Jack spared nothing: the grinding poverty of his early days, his saloon fights to stay alive, the brutish beatings he took as a boy (one so savage that he was carted away from the fight unconscious in a wheelbarrow), his slacker trial after World War I, his wives, wrangles with Jack Kearns . . . the works. He told his story in the only way it could be told, in basic English that was always closer to the Anglo-Saxon than to Mayfair. And so we faithfully recorded it.

Jack's lawyer blanched when he read the manuscript. He shredded it of most of its vitality, to the distress of the publishers and of *Look*, which had the magazine rights. Dan Mich, *Look*'s editor, sent an urgent plea to Dempsey to permit *Look* to print the story as it was first written.

But the lawyer was adamant. Not only that, he had swung Dempsey to his prim point of view.

"Hell," Jack said to *Look*'s man, "those two bastards Considine and Slocum had me cussing on every ——— page!"

It was engrossing working with Specs O'Keefe, too. Specs is one of the poorest insurance risks in the nation. His testimony after he turned state's evidence sent eight of his fellow Brink's robbers to prison with life sentences, plus eighty years "beyond life." One of his associates in the $1,218,211.29 cash heist, Joseph F. McInniss, was given *nine* life sentences, plus three additional stretches of eight to ten years, two and a half to three years, and, to crown the anticlimax, a two-year bit "to take effect from and after the (other) sentences imposed upon you," intoned Judge Felix Forte.

O'Keefe had been criminally bent long enough to share the underworld's contempt for a man who would "sing" on his friends. But he had been provoked beyond endurance. The Brink's robber with whom he trusted his $100,000 share of the booty, to hold while he served a term in a Pennsylvania brig for a relatively minor robbery that backfired, lost Specs's nest egg on the races. Free at last, Specs demanded of the mob that it live up to a quasi gentlemen's agreement it had voted for several years before: a share-the-loot plan designed to take care of just such emergencies. The mob gave him a quick answer. It hired Trigger Burke, one of the nation's foremost assassins, to get rid of him.

Trigger missed Specs twice at close range. On the first try, made with a machine gun that sped past Specs's car on a dark Boston street, Specs instinctively threw himself sideways across the front seat a split second before the burst of shells streaked past the point where his head had been and blew out the windshield. Burke nearly got him the second time, when he caught Specs fleeing into a parking lot. Specs made strategic use of several parked cars as shields. But his wristwatch was shot away by one bullet that left a bloody crease where the timepiece had been. Another bullet struck a breast-pocket notebook that deflected it oddly. It entered Specs's chest and emerged a few inches away, and all he lost was blood. He picked himself off the ground and blazed away at the departing car with his .45.

"They flew," Specs remembered in his meticulous way.

His neatness, his impeccable manners, quiet voice, and keen humor were somewhat unnerving to encounter. But that was Specs. He thoroughly captivated Bennett Cerf when (having been made a sort of present of him by the FBI) I took him to meet the publisher. Bennett, a master of the concise, gave the resultant book the longest title in the history of Random House: *The Men Who Robbed Brink's —The Inside Story of One of the Most Famous Holdups in the History of Crime as told by Specs O'Keefe one of the Ringleaders to Bob Considine in cooperation with the FBI.*

Gazing admiringly at Specs as if he had just identified the Mystery Guest on "What's My Line?" Bennett asked, "If you fellows had gotten away with the Brink's robbery, what would you have done for an encore?"

Specs shrugged. "Fort Knox, I suppose," he said.

Cerf was delighted to press a five-thousand-dollar advance on Specs. It represented, Specs told me, the first legitimate money he had ever made in his life. He liked being legit, liked the hotel where I had stashed him (the stately Plaza), liked the long sessions over a recording machine in my cluttered office, like being able to step up to the men's bar at the Bull and Bear in the Waldorf at day's end and buy a drink in the open. He no longer felt "hot," and soon I, too, lost that vaguely uneasy feeling that it was risky to consort with him.

He charmed everyone I introduced him to, including Louella Parsons and the dowager Mrs. William Randolph Hearst, whom he met at a gay party at Luchow's. They hadn't the remotest idea who he was. As the wine flowed, a suggestion was made that Joe, as we were calling him, elope with Mrs. Hearst ". . . and unite your two great fortunes." The beautiful lady laughed happily. The man who led the tip-toe parade of hooded hoods into the Brink's counting house on a clammy night in Boston, bowed gallantly.

The book was finished now, and it was time for Specs to leave New York and return to the less secure preserves of Boston. I called from the lobby of the Plaza on get-away-day and Specs said he was all packed and would be right down. I told him I would meet him at the cashier's cage. I had paid his modest bill by the time he arrived bearing his suitcase and somewhat out of breath.

"I'm sorry I'm a bit late," he said in his gentlemanly way. "I had to spend a little time . . . unpacking."

"Unpacking?"

Specs shook his head bemusedly. "I packed my clothes, shoes, toilet articles, and so forth," he explained, "and then their towels, soap, light bulbs, ashtrays . . . you know. I was closing the suitcase when I guess a wonderful thought hit me. I said to myself, 'What the hell am I doing this for? I don't *have* to do it any more.' It took me a little time to put the stuff back."

He was distressed that I paid the bill. He looked thoughtfully through the cashier's grille at the matronly employees and beyond them to an old safe.

"You probably won't understand this," he said quietly. "But all of my life I, and most of the people I ran with, would have found it impossible to do what you just did—pay a bill—without figuring, inside, 'Now, how do I take it back from them so I won't be a sucker?' " Specs took another wistful look through the grille.

"It would be so easy," he sighed.

At least one review of *The Men Who Robbed Brink's* etc., the one printed by the Boston *Record American,* set a record as book reviews go. It did not appear in the book-review section. It covered almost the entire front page of the newspaper through all editions and spilled over to two more pages. It wasn't that the book was worthy; it was just that it was newsworthy. In an offhand way it solved three Boston stick-ups which had stumped the police for ten years past, and which had deprived Boston organizations of $182,000.

A special puzzler for the police had been the $43,000 holdup of the accounting office of Boston's big busy Hotel Statler on the day before the titanic Brink's robbery. The statute had long since run its limit in the Statler case, but not the humiliation of the police who could never locate a clue until Specs's book came along with his casual solution:

> Gus and I had watched this one for a long time, and we probably would have waited still longer if we hadn't been so edgy over all those delays on the Brink's thing.
>
> It was a big day for the Statler. Lots of people in the lobby, lots of activity. We went up the steps to the office on the mezzanine, steps that aren't used much. Near the top we took off our hats and put them on a step. Then we pulled a couple of

brown paper bags—with eye-slits in them—over our heads, took out our guns and walked in.

Well, they froze. We must have looked pretty terrible at that. There were some poor people at their desks, on one side of the room. They sat there like statues. There was a poor old fellow in uniform there, too, a guard of some kind. Gus stuck his gun at him, made him lie down, and tied him up. A nice-looking kid, a messenger, I guess, suddenly made a break for the door we had come through. I got in front of him and showed him what I had.

"Don't do that, son," I said to him, quiet. "You wouldn't want to get hurt now, would you? You just go over there and lie down next to the guard and nothing will happen to you."

We scooped up the cash, told them all to stay put, backed out, took off the bags, put our hats on and quickly joined the crowds in the lobby.

People were all excited. Some were clapping. Former Secretary of State General George C. Marshall was coming in a door. The manager was there, bowing and showing him in.

We went out another door with the forty-three. . . .

There were others I helped: war photographer Sammy Schulman, FDR's favorite lensman, Harold Stassen, Robert E. Stripling, chief investigator of the House Un-American Activities Committee, and a forgotten number of inarticulate ballplayers, fighters, and war heroes for whom I did magazine pieces. The least-rewarding were the ballplayers. They have a genuine horror of controversy. Years ago a Philadelphia baseball writer assigned to spook a daily article signed: "By Jimmy Foxx," during the World Series conscientiously called on the slugger and asked him if he had thoughts about the tone of the upcoming articles.

"Yeah," Jimmy said, "don't hurt nobody's feelings."

It's a philosophy that runs as steadfastly as the Amazon through this realm of legitimate fraud.

10 *You Meet Such Interesting People*

I MET Toots Shor the day I went to work for the New York *American.* He had come a considerable distance since his own arrival in New York in the late twenties, a big, cheerful, apple-cheeked fellow out of Philadelphia. He had been a doorman and a bouncer at rough-and-tumble places like the Napoleon and Leon and Eddie's and had worked for a spell for Sherman Billingsley at a time when Billingsley owned a fleet of drugstores. Billingsley's interests were hardly pharmaceutical. Owning a drugstore during Prohibition was tantamount to being a legalized bootlegger.

From a lowly and sometimes bruising beginning, Bernard Shor had risen in stature to the post of manager of Billy LaHiff's Tavern, one of the classic restaurant-hangouts in the annals of pre-war New York. He was soon to split with LaHiff's son over who had first dibs on the cash register.

Now in 1937 he was on the verge of hustling a bankroll with which to build a place of his own. He spoke of it as his "store."

"Follow him and you'll learn about New York," Bill Corum promised, turning me over to him.

The first place he showed me on the day we began making the rounds was Jimmy Johnston's office in Madison Square Garden. That testy little terrier of a man, a master raconteur, was nearing the end of his reign as boxing's leading matchmaker. He was slowly but surely being muscled out of the picture by Mike Jacobs, the veteran ticket speculator, and Jacobs' slightly undercover partners, Damon Runyon, Bill Farnsworth, and Ed Frayne. Their Twentieth Century Sporting Club had Joe Louis. The Garden monopoly, and thus Johnston, was stuck with heavyweight champion Jim Braddock, a much less glamorous soul than Louis.

But if the clouds were gathering around Johnston, neither he nor Toots gave any indication. Toots's respect for the man over whom he towered was infectious. I swiftly felt the same reverence and maintained it through a subsequent period when Johnston sued me for two million dollars for writing in a *Saturday Evening Post* article about the coups and double crosses that led to Johnston's downfall and resulted in his becoming financially dependent on his conqueror, Jacobs.

On that first day we spent together Toots took me directly from Johnston's office to Tony Canzoneri's bar.

Looking back, the wonder is that we didn't go there first.

We had many things in common from the start of our friendship: sports, growing families, our separate religions, financial problems, politics. But primarily I think he was attracted to me because I shared his enormous and wholesome respect for booze.

Toots is the greatest drinker I ever saw. When he holds up one of his short drinks of Hennessy and soda and says, "Booze . . . beautiful booze," it is not unlike Harry Winston's admiringly candling an egg-sized emerald. People who do not know Shor well are inclined to think his main occupation is drinking. They see him drinking with his customers at lunch, with friends who drop into the store after lunching elsewhere, with the early evening diners, the middle evening crowd, the late diners, and the after-theater people. Sometimes after the last customer has stumbled into the night and the chairs have been stacked on the tables to prepare for the clean-up, Toots goes to the bar and drinks with his bartenders.

If the above appalls, let it hastily be added that Toots never lets his drinking interfere with his business. As for those who presume that drinking *is* Shor's business, have a care. He is sternly pragmatic about this. He may have lived through a night that would have killed a Guardsman (and his horse), but Toots will be at work at 9 A.M. No matter what the morning and afternoon bring in the way of fueling and refueling, Toots always makes the family dining table promptly at six, to have dinner with the children and the smallest member of the household—Mrs. Shor.

Toots has strong feelings about friends who complain of hangovers or who miss a day's work after trying to keep up with him. He tells them they shouldn't drink, that they give drinking a bad name. He is easily offended also by the inevitable challenges he receives. Most of these confrontations subside before the first bottle is opened. Toots has a disarming trick that tends to deflate a challenger at what amounts to the weigh-in. He will regard the would-be champion with a look of withering pity and say, "You're amachoor night. Tell you what: I'll drink a bottle of brandy for a warm-up, and then we'll start." Even the dumbest of Toots's challengers somehow comprehend that he means what he is saying.

Jackie Gleason, a good minor-league drinker with commendable staying powers, fine bladder, and a liver which many feel is up there in the class of Toots's, insulted the champion with a loud challenge one midafternoon after Toots had polished off a few Madison Avenue friends and sent them dazedly back to work. He ordered two fifths of cognac brought to the table, and the "bottle of the century," as it came to be known, was on. Like the Dempsey-Firpo fight, it didn't go the distance. Or, more specifically, Gleason didn't go the distance. He had hardly finished his bottle (Toots had already lapped him by ordering his own second bottle) when he faltered in a most humiliating way. He had to go to the bathroom. He got as far as the archway that divided the restaurant from the bar and collapsed. Joe Harrison, the captain, and several waiters rushed to him.

"Leave him there!" Toots bellowed.

And there Gleason lay, stretched out stiff, while Toots enjoyed a few more drinks at the nearby table. Pretty soon, the first of the early diners began arriving. These are almost always out-of-towners who read about the place or hear references to it—or Toots—on the air. The early diners of that particular evening found themselves forced to detour around one of the most familiar stomachs on the American scene as they were led to their tables by an impassive captain.

Toots almost always drinks cognac, but discourages such steadfastness in others. He is particularly wary of martinis; calls them "bombs." Corum once spent a day in Toots's, which is not an unusual incident in the life of the pub. Bill had a few martinis before lunch, a couple during lunch, and a few more during the afternoon and evening. Naturally, as dinner time approached, he ordered a martini or two. After dinner Toots asked him what he'd like to drink.

"I'll have a martini," Bill said to the hovering waiter.

"Jiminy crickets, Bill, you shouldn't drink the same drink all the time." Toots said, supping his brandy and soda. "You should mix 'em up, change over to something else after you've eaten."

"Okay," Bill said. "Bring me a Gibson."

Toots feels it is his duty to drink.

"I owe it to my friends," he told me early in the great game of knowing him. "Suppose you're stuck in some joint like Hollywood, let's say, and you haven't been to New York for a long time, and you keep thinking about having a drink with me when you get here—what kind of bum would I be if I said, 'Sorry, Sam, I'm not drinking today.' I've got to fade guys like that."

Toots is a firm believer in the proposition that once a person steps outside the confines of Manhattan, he's in Bridgeport. One night in the store he listened to his friend Tom Coleman, the Wisconsin Republican national committeeman, extolling the wonders of Wisconsin steaks.

"I'll grant that this is a pretty good steak you serve here," Tom said as he knifed one of Toots's sirloins. "But the kind of steaks I get in Madison, Wisconsin, are something else again. Toots, you can cut them with a butter knife, and when you go to bed that night you go to sleep with the satisfaction of knowing that you've had the best steak in the world."

Toots looked at him.

"And when you wake up in the morning you're still in Madison, Wisconsin," he muttered.

Toots is a concise commentator on any passing scene.

He attended a War Bond sales luncheon at the Waldorf on a day when ballplayers from the New York Giants were "auctioned" off to various corporations which had taken tables for the patriotic affair. In a burst of chauvinism beyond the call of duty, a corporation head "bid" three million dollars for Lou Chiozza, a .200 hitter.

"That's an insult to money," Toots said grimly.

On another occasion while drinking with a table of sportswriters Toots began a sentence, "That was a good piece Jimmy Cannon had. . . ."

"Who read it to you?" one of the writers brayed.

Toots dropped his head and appeared to blush.

"You hurt his feelings," another writer said to Toots's heckler.

"No, he didn't," Toots said, looking up. "I was just trying to think who *did*."

When Corum became President of Churchill Downs and entrepreneur of the Kentucky Derby, Toots accepted the appointment as a call to arms. He ordered a full turnout of all available friends of Bill, from Bob Hope down to busted sportswriters whose fare and keep Toots quietly paid.

"Friendship," Toots said piously. Many feel that Toots is best known for saying "Crumb-bum," or "Creepy crumb-bum." His word is "friendship." On the rather frequent occasions when he is called upon to make a talk he implores all friends who have the faintest command of the language to "write a little something for me." At times by actual count he has had a dozen ghosts banging out bon mots and lyrical panegyrics. But when the time comes for him to get to his feet and give forth with the amalgam of all their skills, he dismisses the script, kicks an imaginary pebble or two, and in the manner of a whale, beached, he wheezes into his "Friendship" speech. It's all about friendship; what friendship has meant to him.

One had better not tamper with friendship, if he wishes to remain in Toots's somewhat harried and shaky circle. He is the only Puritan Jew I know, a man of almost tyrannical morality. With one or two exceptions, he will not permit any married man to bring a woman other than his wife into his restaurant. His long-term friendship with Ted Husing was terminated abruptly one night when Ted said a bad word at a table within earshot of a family at another table. That violated friendship, Toots decided. If Ted wanted to curse, let him curse at the Stork—owned by Toots's eternal foe, Billingsley.

Flying to the first Derby which Corum ran, Toots surprised me by ordering a bourbon when the stewardess asked what we'd like to drink.

"Bourbon?" I said, hoisting an eyebrow.

"I'm only going to drink bourbon on this trip," Toots said solemnly. "I owe that much to Bill, now that he's operating in Kentucky."

It made him sick, but he stuck with the stuff.

What made him sickest at that Derby, however, was to have a friend foully double-cross him. It had been a long day and a costly one. But now the ninth and final race was under way, and Toots's box rang with the exhortations and shouts of his guests: Baby, his wife, Frank and Liz Conniff, and John Daly. They all had the same horse and had bet all they had (and some they borrowed) on it.

The field swept into the backstretch with their horse running a steady sixth. But he looked good to everybody, and everybody was saying so at the top of his lungs. Everybody except the only guest who knew the first thing about racehorses, Don Ameche. Ameche had his glasses trained on the horse.

"We're dead," he quietly announced.

As the cheering subsided in sighs, Toots's party became aware that great excitement began to boil in the next box which held Horatio Luro, the famous Argentine trainer, and a group of friends.

Their screams reached a shrill ecstasy when a rank outsider, trained by Luro, passed under the wire a winner. It paid forty-four dollars.

"How about Luro, that filthy, slimy bum?" Toots grumbled as he led his depleted troops back to the hotel. "Friendship! He don't know the meaning of friendship. Imagine having a good thing like that running and not even telling us. Some friendship!"

Conniff was surprised.

"I didn't know you two were friends, Toots," he said, "When did you meet?"

"Last night," Toots said, stricken by the treachery.

Toots is very religious, in a somewhat informal and often unnerving way. When his good friend Joe Noonan was faced with a palpably political prison sentence (some said Joe took the term to escape drinking with Toots), Toots each day prayed at Temple Emanu-El, St. Thomas' (Episcopal), and St. Patrick's (Roman Catholic). I asked him why.

"I'm touching all bases," Toots said piously.

One hot day in Jersey, where he takes a place for the summer, Toots took his Catholic children to Mass at St. Mary's in Deal. They were gone for more than an hour. When the car drove up to the house the children bounded out buoyantly and went their separate ways. Toots got out wearily, sweating profusely and looking spent.

"We caught a double-header by mistake," he explained. He meant he had stumbled into a high Mass.

When Baby's mother died, and a wonderful old Irish lady she was, relatives Toots had never heard about swarmed to Campbell's funeral home on upper Madison Avenue. Some of them were marvelous stereotypes of the professional keeners best described in O'Connor's *The Last Hurrah*. More than one of them appeared to keep one eye on the late lamented and the other on Toots—to be sure to accompany him whenever he returned to his bar. The dear people didn't want him to be alone at a time like that, particularly drinking alone. All of them, with all their laments and endearing reminiscences, kept the fragile Baby Shor in a constant state of tears.

One night during the wake I looked in on the room where the bier rested. The place was empty, except for torrents of floral pieces. A fresh batch of relatives had come in from Jersey, had found Baby in an adjoining room, and had started her crying again.

Toots spotted me as I advanced toward the bier, Rosary in hand. "Thank Christ you're here," he said, stepping through a Gates Ajar arrangement. "These goddam Catholics are driving me nuts."

Toots has positive opinions on just about every person he ever met, and many he never will. He reserves for his large and enthusiastic list of enemies a singular phrase of damnation. "He's a piece of raisin cake," he'll say of some foe. It somehow makes him feel better, as if he had stuck a pin in a small effigy of the person involved.

When Toots heard a rumor that a New York mob planned to kidnap Billy Rose, he scoffed derisively. He and Rose were not friendly.

"What's wrong with it?" his informant said. "Billy is rich and small enough to pick up and run with if the cops try to break up the snatch."

Toots shook his head.

"It won't happen," Toots said. "Who could they contact?"

Toots took a remote dislike to Rev. Billy Graham during the preacher's first New York crusade.

"How about that Billy Graham?" he demanded one night at a table where he was having a drink with Baby and a few friends. Toots always introduces vituperation by asking a "how about" question. Those of us at the table had known him long enough to know that the question didn't require an answer; he was simply cueing himself.

"Two hundred and fifty dollars for a suit, that's what he pays," Toots said, scandalized. "I read it right in the paper: two hundred and fifty bucks for a suit!"

Baby cupped her pretty chin in her hand, sighed, and silently heard him out. It was quite a monologue, a ringing call for the return of the simple ecclesiastical life, a condemnation of the frills and showmanship of the Graham crusade, a dour suggestion that New York's resident Men of God needed no outside psalming.

Baby is a patient woman, but when she reaches the limit of that patience, she has an amazing knack of silencing her outsized mate with one rapier thrust. She waited until Toots had made a particularly righteous point. Then she garroted him with one line.

"Get a load of Bishop Sheeny," she said to the rest of the table.

Toots takes a lot of abuse from his friends; not as much as he dishes out, to be sure, but a lot.

"You've got the head of a pig," he remarked one day to Gleason as they exchanged thoughts.

"And you've got the body of one," Jackie responded.

Before great fame came to Gleason he had a spell of hard luck, and Toots gave him signing privileges. It was a secret only the two shared. Few out-of-work comedians had ever eaten better. As the weeks lengthened, Jackie put on weight and, alas, importance. He began signing ten-dollar tips onto the bill, which the waiters immediately collected from the till.

It hurt Toots to say it to his friend, but it had to be said.

"Jackie, please don't sign such tips on those checks of yours I'm picking up," Toots said.

Jackie was thunderstruck.

"And have your waiters call you a cheap bastard?" he demanded.

Gleason more than evened matters when he struck it rich. He stayed with Toots's place.

"Every creep I help moves right over to Twenty One soon as he makes good," Toots likes to moan. He is sensitive about lost customers, though he is first to admit that he has driven more people away from his place perhaps than any other publican in history.

"I'll never come in this place again," a tough guy who felt he and his girl had been kept waiting too long for a table shouted at Toots one night. He pushed the girl into the revolving door, then paused for one last shot at Toots, who was regarding him blandly.

"What's more, I'm going to tell all my friends to stay out of here," he blazed, stepping into the door.

"Tell him," Toots said, yawning.

Movie mogul Louis B. Mayer never came back to Toots's after the night he complained about bad service.

"I've seen some of your pictures," Toots said in answer to the complaint.

Toots gets a lot of mail, some of it distressing. He was very proud of being invited with Baby to dine with the Trumans at the White House until Bob Hope, who read about it in Hollywood, wrote:

"They put a hog in Tiffany's window."

A complete stranger wrote:

> Dear Mr. Shor: My wife and I dined at your restaurant during our recent trip to New York. We found the food delicious, the drinks very nice, the atmosphere and service fine. But if you expect to make a success in your business, you'd better get rid of that fat slob of a headwaiter who spent most of his time insulting patrons who seemed to be old friends.

Toots thinks anybody who orders wine with his dinner is a show-off. The legend has spread that his wine cellar consists of a five-gallon jug of Gallo. That's not true. He has been seen drinking Dom Perignon on the premises, but only because Don Ameche or Frank Conniff, two professional winos, ordered it. It was once believed that Shor's restaurant did not possess a wine bucket. But that was a lie spread by some piece of raisin cake. It did own one.

Toots won't have anything on his menu that he can't pronounce. This imposes certain hardships—and risk of scurvy—on his regulars. But it is all elementary to Toots. His friend Mel Ott invited him to New Orleans years ago to feast on the delicacies of Antoine's, La Louisianne, and Galatoire's. Toots returned unimpressed.

"Sauces," he said, dismissing the whole area with a word. "If you got good meat who needs sauces?"

Toots's is a meat and potatoes joint. He's intensely proud of his cuisine and demands respect for it, to which his waistline and those of many of his more persistent and loyal customers attest. Strangers in the place sometimes marvel at the enthusiasm of Toots's eaters; even tend to grow huffy about it. They don't understand that it is difficult to order anything in small portions in Toots's.

"No wonder you're getting fat," former baseball commissioner Ford Frick said to me one day as the waiter brought my simple late breakfast which the menu swore was Roast Beef Hash with Egg. There was a blob of roast beef bigger than home plate, and some sort of chain reaction had taken place with respect to that egg. It had become an imposing mound of scrambled eggs.

Frick, commendably trim, was having his customary lunch: a sweet Manhattan and a peanut butter sandwich. Toots has a built-in reverence for rank and prestige, particularly if those holding it prefer his place. If anybody named Gus Fink ever ordered a sweet Manhattan and a peanut butter sandwich within Toots's hearing range, the proprietor would order him thrown out and barred for life.

Frick's comment was not the first, or last, of its kind heard in Shor's. One afternoon a good regular eater named John Begley ordered and easily consumed four of Toots's Bloody Marys, a bowl of oxtail vegetable soup, a large slab of roast beef, baked potato, salad, several bottles of beer, a wedge of graham cracker pie, coffee, and a couple of post-luncheon stingers.

A guy at the next table tapped him on the shoulder.

"What time are you being electrocuted?" he asked John.

Toots maintains a box at Yankee Stadium, at Shea also, always has a block of tickets in the second ringside row at Madison Square Garden on fight nights, and serves as a philanthropic dispenser of tickets to Broadway shows that are complete sellouts for months to come. He pays silently through his impressive nose for such seats, but nothing is too good where real palship is involved.

Sports are his forte, but Toots doesn't exclude the other arts, even though uncomfortable things happen to him when he strays afield. Mike Todd, when the two were speaking, once persuaded Toots and Baby to attend the opening of Maurice Evans' *Hamlet.* Toots joined in the small talk during the first intermission; when the bell summoned the Shakespearean buffs back into the theater, Toots boomed, "I bet I'm the only bum in the joint that's going back just to see how it turns out." He liked *Faust* well enough, he told a friend after he had been liberated from the Met and was safely back at his store, "But there's too much music in it." The movie version of one of the master works of Feodor Mikhailovich Dostoyevsky left him unmoved. "I just took in a movie about a bunch of crazy Russian actors running around and yelling," he told me one night as he came into the store. "It's called 'The Brothers Kalamazoo.' "

Leopold Stokowski hurt Toots's feelings the night a friend managed to get him to Carnegie Hall. Toots looked on with astonishment and rising gorge as Stokowski took a dozen bows after the first number. "Look at that creep," Toots said to his friend. "I saw Hubbell pitch a no-hitter and he didn't take no bows. Let's leave at the half."

It was his second and last ordeal at Carnegie. Previously, he had gone there to see his friend Paul Draper dance. When he weathered that exposure to elfin grace, Toots lumbered to the curb and dissolved into a taxi. "Toots Shor's," he commanded. The driver's head wheeled in wonder.

"Mister, I've been working this stand for ten years," the hacker said, "and this is the first time I ever took anybody from here to there."

Toots has an overriding contempt for thrift. He can't understand, during those times when he is raising money to expand his store, move into a new one, or double-deck the martinis, why the banks do not readily come forth and offer him unlimited credit. When William Zeckendorf paid him $1,500,000 for his Fifty-first Street place to make way for what is now a routine Sixth Avenue skyscraper with much less character, Toots took a terrible revenge on his bank. It had previously given him a hard time. So he carried the check in his pocket for an unnervingly long time, thus depriving the bank of making money on it by lending it out at fancier rates to other stiffs in need. It cost Toots a lot of money in the interest he would have received in a regular savings account, but he feels it was worth it.

A real estate dealer in Deal, New Jersey, who had been renting Toots and his family a furnished summer place for several seasons at four thousand dollars, said to him in a burst of conscience, "Toots, I can get you this place, for keeps, for twenty thousand dollars, lock, stock, and barrel." Toots didn't like to be hustled in that manner.

"Lissen," he said, "why should I buy it for twenty grand when I can rent it for the next twenty years at four grand a summer?" The man went away, somewhat confused. So did Shor's auditor who some years ago suggested to him that if he closed his place on Sunday during the summer time—when business was slack—he could save five hundred dollars a week. Toots made a fast count on his fingers.

"Jiminy Crickets," Toots swore mightily, "at that rate I could close seven days a week and save $3,500."

Though no fool, Shor and his money were soon parted. He was out of action for two years because his original benefactor, Zeckendorf, could not help him to return—as promised. Toots had to make the same weary rounds that he had made nearly a quarter of a century before, when a few grand here and a few grand there built his original place. This time, because of rising costs and a dream of bigger and better things, a lot more money was involved. Several millions . . . a lot of money for a fellow who, with Baby and sportswriter Jimmy

Cannon, had approached the door of his first place on opening night with forty cents in his pocket. He paused on that occasion and threw the quarter and the dime and the nickel in the gutter and said, "I might as well walk in flat-pocket."

But he made it. He had a Friend at Chase Manhattan. The friend was the Teamsters Union Pension Fund, which invests in other profit-making organizations. Toots got his money and built his dream place. Everything was new, including new needlers. . . .

"Why don't you call the new joint 'Toots Shor's Hoffabrau'?"

"Oh, you're so funny, y'creep."

"By the way, Toots, I just came from Twenty One and one of the Kriendler boys said they're very grateful that you built your place next door to them; it's a place for their chauffeurs to eat."

"Oh, you're killing me, y'piece of raisin cake."

One midafternoon in the new place the lights suddenly dimmed ominously.

"Thank God they've electrocuted the chef!" Cannon said to Toots.

Toots had nothing to say.

That doesn't happen very often. . . .

Toots broke the only good leg he had, on the lamentable evening of March 13, 1966. He had attended the Gridiron Dinner the night before as a guest of Warren Rogers, then the chief Washington correspondent of the Hearst Headline Service and now in that same position with *Look*. Warren had just previously been admitted to the Gridiron, one of the choicest clans in the land, and been given the privilege of inviting two guests to the princely dinner whereat the only guest who did not appear in white tie and tails turned out—unpredictably—to be the President of the United States. Warren sent the first invitation to Toots, who was massively touched.

Warren had met Toots through Paul Garvey, former White House correspondent for the Voice of America and U.S. Information Service, and that was the best kind of credential to present to Shor. To Toots, Garvey's stamp of approval had no peer save perhaps the purple splendor of the Choice U.S. Prime Beef stamp. Garvey had become, in Toots's mind, a much more authentic wit than most of the big name stars that frequent his place. It was Garvey who observed, while serving in Seoul during the war, "There's nothing wrong with Korea that couldn't be helped by a seventy-five-story Airwick." And while on duty in Southeast Asia, Paul wrote two enduring song titles: "The

Rain in Laos Falls Mainly in the Ha-ouse," and "Every Little Breeze Seems to Whisper Disease."

But, as of 5:30 P.M., March 13, 1966, Toots wished that Garvey had never met Rogers, or had kept him a secret. He lay on the floor of his bedroom in the Statler Hilton, where he had been packing to fly back to New York. His right leg was twisted under his bulk, broken at the femur. Frank Conniff and I rushed in from neighboring rooms. Our friend was in intense pain. Frank and I pondered the difficult matter of whether to try to lift him onto the bed or obey the dictum of First Aid and leave him be—for fear of adding to his trouble by moving him. Toots made up our minds.

"Lift me up on the bed," he commanded through gritted teeth.

We did, and still plan to lay joint claim to the A.A.U. weightlifting record.

I went with Toots in the ambulance to Georgetown University Hospital, where during ensuing and highly expensive weeks he held a court that made Perle Mesta wince with envy. But on the night of the Great Fall, my friend was a pitiable sight as he lay racked with pain on an ambulance bed about as wide as a ruler. His moans were heartrending.

"Toots, it's Sunday, and this town's dry, but I'll get you a drink somehow," I said. "What do you want?"

My friend's face twisted with agony.

"A Coke," he said.

A thing like that could be remembered with "What hath God wrought?"

Arthur Baer was born in Philadelphia, the seventh of fourteen children, and was packed off to work at fourteen as a lace designer. He made twelve dollars a week drawing scrolls and flowers and was considered one of the most promising young southpaws in the lace dodge. At twenty, still promising and still at twelve dollars, he took a ten-dollar-a-week paycut to work as a copyboy on the Philadelphia *Ledger*. The paper was owned by Adolph Ochs. After that, Baer worked only for Pulitzer, Munsey, and Hearst, a parlay of titans deserving of his talent.

The *Ledger* gave him his chance to cartoon—sports cartoons which he signed with a whimsical-looking little bug in the corner. The bug got off some comment on the larger figure, usually derisive. Hence, Arthur Baer became Bugs Baer. One day in 1912, taken by too many tankards, he joined his friend Wally Wallgreen, later a fixture on World War I's *Stars and Stripes,* and roamed to Washington.

It was an eventful first day and night in town. Bugs coaxed a bartender at the old Ebbet House into drawing beer for him in exchange for a sketch. The sketch took longer than usual. When it was finished Bugs showed it to him. The bartender took a punch at him. Before the end of that momentous day, Bugs voted illegally for a Democratic candidate for the District of Columbia delegation to the Convention that in time nominated Woodrow Wilson, spent some time with the belles at Mahogany Hall (a bordello which Mrs. Wilson eventually caused to be shut down, to the dismay of many members of Congress), and slept in the White House on a couch in the press room.

Bugs became a writer by something akin to osmosis. He was sent by the Washington *Times* to the Charlottesville, Virginia, spring-training camp of the Washington Senators to draw cartoons of the ball club —then consisting mainly of Walter Johnson. It was a difficult assignment at the beginning, but it got considerably worse. The *Times*'s baseball writer took drunk for a week. Bugs protected him, writing reams of copy about the ball club and wiring it back to Washington under the writer's name. The man was unable even to open telegraphic assignments and suggestions he received. Bugs would open his wires and take care of the sports editor's requests, and somehow find time to do his own work. On the seventh day of double duty, Bugs opened a message addressed to the souse which read: "YOUR STUFF HAS BEEN GREAT LATELY. TELL BAER THAT IF HIS CARTOONS DON'T IMPROVE WE'LL HAVE TO LET HIM GO."

That is how the world lost a so-so sports cartoonist and gained one of the most remarkably trenchant craftsmen ever to hone the language.

"I don't care who runs the country as long as someone runs Bugs Baer twice a day," Ring Lardner once wrote. Matter of fact, somebody *did* run Bugs twice a day. In 1931, by which time Bugs was writing out of New York for the Hearst Newspapers, W. R. Hearst became attracted to the work of another humorist in the rival *Evening World.* The byline was "Graham Wire," the stock head was "Wiregrams by Graham Wire." The *World* thought so much of its man that it sometimes ran him on the front page. He wrote a great deal like Bugs, but frequently was even more hilarious.

Hearst ordered Bradford Merrill, his general manager, to hire Wire. Merrill assigned Damon Runyon to attend to the preliminary negotiations, Runyon being at heart a fixer and proselytizer. It was a difficult assignment for Runyon because he was only one of three men who knew that "Wire" was Bugs . . . Bugs in search of broader fields for his torrents of thoughts . . . Bugs in quest of a moonlit buck. The third man was Jack Wheeler, general manager of the North American Newspaper Alliance, who had talked Bugs into the ruse in the first place.

Runyon had become privy to the secret by his innate habit of prying. He could not approach any person's desk or typewriter without reading the man's correspondence or peering over a shoulder to see what was coming out of a typewriter. Because of his early years in the composing rooms of the papers to which his father had wandered, Runyon could read from any angle. Thus it was no great problem for him to discover one day at the New York *American* that Bugs was composing under the Graham Wire signature.

Runyon could not have been more pleased with the discovery. Now he "had" something on Baer.

Bugs looked at him steadily.

"You give me away and I'll break your arm," he said. Which he could have done without great effort, for Bugs was always in good shape.

That threat must have remained in the back of Runyon's mind during the days that followed the assignment from Merrill. He reached an interesting solution. He showed up at Merrill's office one day to report solemnly that he had talked at great length with Mr. Wire and Mr. Wire said he would not think of ever working for William Randolph Hearst.

Bugs's split personality as a writer soon after melded into the one that has since been uniquely identifiable. Henceforth he operated with only one spigot. Out of it gushed, in lively spurts, refreshment for his cult—and I am one of his true believers.

Bugs wrote the history of Europe in one sentence: "Europe's a place where they name a street for you one day and chase you down it the next."

That's what Toynbee was trying to say in five million words.

Nothing escaped the flash floods of his concise and explosive wit and wisdom.

He asked the same question that had perplexed world diplomacy as Khrushchev, possessor of appalling thermonuclear might, alarmingly thumped away at his desk in the UN Assembly. But a bit differently.

"Diplomats are wondering what kind of international omeleting is going on in Nikita's egghead when he sets the tempo with a half-soled Moscow metronome?" Bugs asked. "Will he use the same technique on the President, or will he pour it out of a boot?"

Bugs wrote sketches for Lillian Russell and Lew Dockstader, but was still fresh half a century after those two were wisps lost in space and time. Nothing he regarded, as he peered down from his tower of genuine walrus ivory near Stamford, Connecticut, failed to kindle his eye:

> Paying alimony is like buying oats for a dead horse. . . .
>
> There's no such thing as a little garlic. . . .
>
> He's so dumb they had to tear down the schoolhouse to get him out of the second grade. . . .
>
> What would you charge to haunt a house? (Bugs wrote that line for a comedian who wanted a devastating boffo with which to silence any heckler. The first time he used it, against a lady souse, the rest of the audience cheered. But when the cheer died down, the lady asked "Hic, how many rooms?")
>
> Chiang Kai-shek's troops have been on that island so long their stomachs have high and low tides. . . .
>
> Getting Toots Shor to Campbell's funeral parlor the night of Jimmy Walker's wake was like towing a sick whale without any hope of ambergris. . . .
>
> In 1918 I heard my Country's call. It had been calling since 1917. . . .
>
> Ping Bodie was out, trying to steal second. His head was full of larceny, but his feet were honest. . . .
>
> Pratt slid home on his surname. . . .
>
> DiMaggio [who popped to the catcher his first four times at bat in the 1950 World Series] could have done all of his hitting in a chimney. . . .
>
> [Of the Versailles Treaty] All it will do is fatten the wolf again. . . .
>
> Trying to get those Yankees out was like trying to throw a porkchop past a hungry dog. . . .
>
> [To the UN] Do something soon, or put back the brewery. . . .

[Of the UN] The world's first veto was a growl from the back of a cave. . . .

Success hasn't changed Toots a bit. He's still a bum. . . .

Shor gave Bugs a big black-tie dinner on his seventieth birthday. Bugs wasn't for the idea at all. He laid down harsh reservations: no politicians (except Jim Farley), and drinks at the bar would be served only to gentlemen wearing caps. Even after Toots agreed, Bugs was difficult. Bugs wired him:

TOOTS SHOR'S ROACH RANCH
51 WEST 51
NEW YORK CITY

YOURS OF THE 13TH INSTANT RECEIVED AND DULLY NOTED. HOLD EVERYTHING FOR 30 YEARS AND MAKE IT A CENTENNIAL.

It was as close to an Elizabethan revelry as the twentieth century has produced. Shor made the mistake of seating Bugs next to the lectern at the head table. At the most solemn moment of every eulogy to him, Bugs goosed the speaker. He had written during Prohibition that "the fellow who named it Near Beer is just a bad judge of distance." He demonstrated something along those lines at his banquet. After a while he could no longer lift his Burgundy glass as high as his waiting lips, but he retained the ability to tip the glass at the top of its rise, or perigee. The wine would cascade down what began as a spotless dress shirt. By the time the evening ended—if it did—Bugs looked like the sole survivor of the St. Valentine's Day slaughter.

It reminded him of a line he had written about an artful check-dodger: "He suffers from an impediment in his reach."

Just before Christmas 1963, Bugs faced a serious operation. It would be touch-and-go, and he knew it. As somberly as he was capable of putting it, he wrote:

"What kind of Christmas story do you write when you are not sure how much string is left in your ball of twine? What do you write just before they clap the cone over your schnozzola and you are in one of those rare rooms where Emily Post says it's okay to put your feet on the table?"

Bugs pulled through neatly and dropped a note to a friend at the Lambs Club: "I've got so many tubes in me I don't need a doctor. I need a switchboard operator."

But it took something out of him, as he felt he should explain when invited by Bob McCorkindale of King Features Syndicate to participate in the fun and games scheduled for the syndicate's next outing. He wrote:

> Owing to my advanced seniority, I no longer take part in capering on the greensward. The last time I competed in the father-and-son Olympics was in 1930 at the Friars outing. The contestants in the hundred-yard dash were Jim Corbett, Joe McGurk, Saturday Night O'Brien, Willie Collier, Steve Riordan, Rube Goldberg, and George M. Cohan. I was winning footily, but at seventy-five yards I had to go behind a bush and adjust my truss.
>
> But will come. Will be driven out there by my nurse, Thelma Orner, who permits me to eat very little. I rarely wrap up any food to take home, as you have nothing that matches my pet chameleon. Pardon my delay in answering your invitation but I soak all letters in a tub for two weeks.
>
> Yours until you hear different. . . .

Bugs sent Miss Orner to his dentist not long after that bearing two items, (1) a letter, and (2) his upper plate.

"Dear Docster," the letter read:

> It will surprise you to learn I am sending in my upper appetite by carrier pigeon, parcel post, and registered nurse. While taking my usual two cautious bites of a cherry, I stubbed my porcelain cuspidor on the second bite. Thereby losing one of the little whites of my artificial smile. Miss Orner has volunteered to carry the message to Garcia and has the ghastly dentifacts in her purse.
>
> A man is really rich when he has a spare upper maxillary in his vanity case. I looked up my spare and it fitted exactly, except for being a little on the Mortimer Snerd side. However, I will be glad to get the original back and popped into place. There's no use of your holding my bridgework for ransom as it is not worth 500 tractors, and also because I have that second set.
>
> I never take my plates out except to brush them. Some people keep theirs in a glass of water overnight. I tried it once and in the morning they looked much happier than I felt.
>
> Now, dickery old doc, you go ahead and vulcanize that old vacuum and give the finished gems to the nurse. I enclose the tooth that jumped the reservation. If it hasn't got a trade-in value you can donate it to the American Museum of Natural Curiosity.
>
> Yours till the last notch in your Adler Elevator Chair.

Once at a benefit where many Broadway people did quick turns, vaudevillian Al Trahan, caught without his writer, pleaded to Bugs, "Give me a couple of lines, I'm next on." Bugs said, "Just go out there, shoot a gun, and fall on your ass." Trahan did that, and only that, and broke up the audience.

"Humor is tragedy, standing on its head and with a rip in its pants," Bugs once said. His rule has been to make it sting, but never draw blood. He has been sued for libel only once over the long and saucy span. "I won the case," Bugs recalls. "The dame claimed I called her ugly, and I didn't at all. All I wrote was that she could safely cook naked in a lumber camp."

Irving S. Cobb said it best: "The Bugs Baers do not come in bunches like grapes. They appear but once in a millennium." Or longer, I've always felt. . . .

Bob Ripley, like many of his cartoons, was a bit hard to believe. After all, how many people have you known who owned a Chinese junk powered with a diesel robust enough to outrun most of the powered boats on Long Island Sound? He was the only American I ever knew who had a harem and made no bones about it. The talk of the neighborhood around Mamaroneck was that he took a daily steam bath with his beauties and often ran across them barefooted. To male neighbors stuck with monogamous natures, this seemed like the very last word in happy motoring.

It wasn't Nirvana, apparently. There was one party at his weird estate that did not come off too well. There were only four guests at B I O N that night. Rip had invited Bugs Baer, who wisely declined on the ground that Christmas was a day which should be celebrated in the bosom of one's family. Rip didn't agree. After all, he felt quite festive in the traditional Yuletide array of bright mandarin kimono, hat, and brocaded slippers.

Just before the chef brought the turkey, alas, the phone rang and one of Bob's oldest flames—long since relegated to limbo—was calling from the evil Mamaroneck station. With his Old World courtliness, he invited her over instantly to share the feast which even nonbelievers insist was built around the birth of Christ. She brought along her son, a child of fourteen who stood well over six feet and had dressed that day, dementedly enough, in a tight-fitting Boy Scout suit.

Regrettably, Rip's real guests were not getting along too well. One was a French actress, the other a Russian actress. Both were plastered. One was being moved out of a treasured bedroom at the spooky place and didn't like it one little bit. It was hardly the proper Dickensian setting. Matters were not helped when the Boy Scout announced that he had had so many milkshakes during the afternoon he no longer looked with joy on the traditional delights of a Christmas dinner. Worse, his mother, who had taken a seat of honor near Ripley, suddenly reached into a voluminous purse, brought out a picture of her late husband, and propped it up against an array of wine glasses. Every now and then she would look at the picture and burst into loud tears.

The Boy Scout, who was seated in the darkness of a corner in the wild dining room, would occasionally bray, "But Mama, where *is* Dad-dy?"

Meanwhile, the two whores who were Rip's prime guests were regarding each other with increasingly malevolent glares. Ultimately, one reached into the carefully stitched rear end of the turkey and seized, therein, a ball of dressing. She extracted it, at some expense to her wrist, cranked up, and hurled it across the table—smack-dab into the kisser of her foe for Rip's attentions.

"But Mama, where *is* Dad-dy?" the boy wailed.

"It wasn't a happy Christmas," Rip later told Mrs. Baer. It may have been that year's record understatement.

Things had to be right around Rip's place. My wife and I took a place just across Lake B I O N from him in 1942, shortly after the birth of our son Barry. An almost daily visitor, particularly at times when Millie was nursing the baby, was one of the more entrancing flowers in Rip's harem. She was an exquisite creature of Chinese-Japanese mixture, given to the more colorful gowns of both cultures. She invariably paddled across the little body of water in a small boat, and she made a delightful picture in a setting of quiet waters and great weeping willows. Just as invariably, she always brought the baby a little flower, and would tuck it daintily behind his ear as he nursed. Then she would sit through the procedure, her lovely face sometimes fathoms deep in thought. We often wondered about the dear girl's story.

One Sunday Rip invited us to one of his great parties. The girl was in the process of being chastised by being sent to her room. She had offended the laird and master, who was in full ceremonial robe, by playing gin rummy with Nick Kenny, who was to the Hearst organization at that time what John Masefield was to the British Crown and Edgar Guest to Henry Ford I. Nick had contributed some enduring gems to poesy. One piece about the death of his dog had sent countless readers of the *Mirror* into paroxysms of woe, particularly that line which said: "And don't forget what *d-o-g* spells backward!"

Another flight of fancy that involved the Almighty with certain unnervingly mundane matters ran:

"Snow fell from Heaven
Like dandruff from God's shoulders. . . ."

Then there was a touching refrain from what Nick called a Patty Poem, struck in honor of his daughter of the same name. She was a sentimental child, Patty, as the poems in her honor so winningly evidenced. Take, for example, Nick's threatened sale of "My Old One-Tube Set." Patty, naturally, objected to any such transaction. Nick asked why, in a kind of rollicking verse where even the rhyming of "orange" seemed faintly possible:

"She pointed to its dusty face,
Two baby lips were there.
'I kissed it last night, Daddy Dear,
When you were on the air.' "

There was every reason why a dear girl who had little claim to fame chauvinistically save the attack on Pearl Harbor would have been pleased and proud to be playing gin rummy with the poet laureate of the Burma Shave Company, but then Ripley hove into ominous view.

"How many times must I tell you not to mingle socially with my guests," Rip stormed. "Get off to your room!"

The girl ran, whimpering. It seemed an excessive punishment to Millie. My wife went off to search for her and found her in a darkened little bedroom which featured cohabiting Buddhas. The light fixture was made from a Japanese parasol. The girl lay on the bed, sobbing.

In an effort to make her forget the ugliness of the scene, Millie picked up a beautiful lacquered box from the dresser. "What exquisite work this is!" she said. She is one of the rare persons who pronounce "exquisite" properly.

The girl lifted her face from her pillow and looked around. "Oh," she said, and then, after a bit: "I keep my baby's ashes in there."

Millie put the box down swiftly, but sympathetically.

"Don't feel badly," the girl said. "The ashes are not there now. When Bob gets mad at me he hides them."

Years later, there was another brush with the rule of an American maharajah.

That would be my friend Bob Ruark, dead at forty-nine and stretched out inside a yellow pine box in the study of his hauntingly unfinished home in Palamos on the Costa Brava. He had died of his bad plumbing a week before in London after chartering a flight from Barcelona with a view to refueling his lost blood. It was a calculated risk, and Bob lost. There wasn't enough blood in all Middlesex to keep this robust soul going, so now what was left of him was back in the place he had on the water at Palamos, and all around him were people who knew nothing about him except his books and his bragging. Bob was a good writer, a marvelous illustrator, an excellent broadcaster, a pretty good speaker, a tireless companion, and a magnificent braggart. I don't speak of braggadocio meanly. It takes a certain amount of courage to be a braggart, for one must always be prepared to defend his position, substantiate his claims.

Bob Ruark could, more often than most.

His celebrated grandfather, endless source of wisdom for articles and, in time, for a book he and many fancied, was more a figment of yearning than one of fact. The Old Man was a concoction of personal need, born in great age and wisdom from his need for a forbear. Bob had no relatives he felt deserved him, and maybe he was right. He was prouder of knowing Bernard Baruch and shooting birds on Hobcaw Barony with that older braggart than he was of his own father and mother. It is doubtful if he ever introduced them to the self-confessed adviser to Presidents.

Bob would have liked some of the touches at his funeral, just as Winston Churchill would have reveled in seeing Queen Elizabeth II *and* Charles de Gaulle *and* Clement Attlee singing "The Battle Hymn of the Republic" in St. Paul's on the day he was consigned to peace eternal in ceremonies he personally had arranged. Bob would have liked for example, the thoughtfulness of the girl who stopped the Spanish newsreel cameraman from taking a shot of a great tiger Bob had killed in India years before. The tiger's skin and hideously fanged head were hung from a wall in such a manner that the beast seemed to be springing into the room.

"Stop!" the girl ordered, and the cameraman's light man snapped off the bulb in wonder. Then the girl raced about the place in search of a missing ingredient, as if under tacit orders from the dead man stretched out in his yellow box. Shortly she returned with the keys to Ruark's Rolls Royce, which dangled from a little case made of a leopard he had killed. The exposed key ring fitted neatly over one of the ominous teeth of the tiger on the wall.

"Bob used to sit where you're sitting now and look at his Rolls's keys in the leopard case hanging from the tiger's tooth and say, 'How rich can you get?' " the girl said.

I took another drink of Ruark's White Label Scotch.

The spoils of his safaris pressed around the coffin like creatures tremulously met at a water hole. The bier stretched across a rug made of hides of zebras his guns had felled. Like rigid acolytes, two enormous elephant tusks showed at the head of the casket. From the white walls of the library the glazed eyes and heads and flaring horns of an impala, a crant, a Robert's Eye, a great koodoo, lesser koodoo, sable, nyala, and two fierce black buffalo regarded the somber scene.

Not one relative had come to say farewell. But this man was not unmourned. Christian, the noble cook, sat in soundless grief in the dimly lighted room with Pascual, the gardener, Pascual's wife, and Pascualito, whose education my friend was underwriting when all his hot blood left him. There were, in addition, Gafarot the grocer, Reixac the butcher, and Samso the baker, all in stiff black and genuinely touched.

"Fourth head I've lost in a fortnight," the Polish sculptor Nicky Tregor said, as he drank the dead man's Scotch. "Nina Dyer commits suicide. George Litman just dies. Rubirosa hits a tree. Now Bob."

Four sad Spaniards in black carried Ruark out of the house and set his bright yellow box down in the emerald garden. The sun was intolerable. Father José Fonosas, a young priest given to gestures, stepped forward when the mourners stopped moving about. He fished notes out of his cassock, settled his glasses on his nose, and launched into a religious ceremony unlike any he had ever celebrated or witnessed in Catholic Spain. His bishop had not gone into any great detail about this assignment. He had simply said go ahead, it would be all right: Ruark's rich friend, Ricardo Sicré, had made a nice contribution to an orphanage.

The priest droned on in Spanish, pointing now and then to the box that embraced this spent skyrocket of a man. He had never known Bob. Bob was not one to take formal religion seriously and tended to laugh aloud at its emissaries. Once at our place in New Jersey he watched me lead my brood home from Sunday Mass at St. Mary's, Deal, all of us feeling outrageously pious. Looking me over as he lolled on our porch in his shorts, he said, "Okay, now take off your deacon's suit and mix us up a mess of martinis."

The beach life at the edge of Bob's garden went on uninterrupted for the most part. But some bathers who had noticed the little Spanish hearse and two cars into which erupting volcanoes of vivid flowers were being arranged came to the hedge and peered into the garden, straining to hear what the priest was saying.

What he was saying, and he summed it up at the end in painful English, was "Let God be mindful of his servant, Roberto Ruark, and grant him peace."

U.S. Consul General to Barcelona John Ford did not know Bob either, but he had done his homework.

"In twelve years the roots of a tree reach ever deeper," he said in Spanish. "They cling to the earth. It is difficult for them to be pulled out without leaving a deep scar. The people who have known Bob Ruark for the past twelve years in this region will remember how much affection and recognition he showered on Palamos. He will leave an empty space in this corner of Spain and a heaviness in the hearts of them who shared this part of his life.

"I recall a passage from his book *The Old Man and the Boy,* where the old man who was his grandfather is dying and he says to the boy who was Ruark, 'I gave you the best things I could give, and now you are the Old Man because I am tired and I am going to leave.'

"Ruark wrote that his eyes filled with tears, but the Old Man said to him, 'Let it alone. Like I've always told you, if there existed a way to mock death I would have already learned how. Your time will come, too, although it now looks impossible.'

"Ruark wrote, 'But How, When and Why?' because he couldn't find anything better to say.

"We have here the answer to his questions, really. Here in Palamos will sleep forever one who came to this land and planted here his roots."

My friend's casket looked too small for a fellow who had once flattened Bobo Newsom in a player-versus-writer fight, and during the war had decked a big union goon aboard a Merchant Marine war transport on which he commanded a Navy gun crew. When the four sad Spaniards slid it into the hearse a good foot of it protruded out the rear.

The funeral party emerged from the bottom of the garden and walked into town behind the hearse, behind the flower cars and Bob's Rolls Royce, which followed in empty elegance save for the chauffeur, like the riderless horse of a dead leader. I wondered if his boots were in the car, turned backwards.

And so we marched slowly between ranks of people who had come up from the beach, some in Bikinis, to look upon a cortege moving through a travel-poster town. One could hear my friend in the box saying, with his fierce black and white smile, "What a way to go!"

Ruark wanted to be Hemingway. But *Hemingway* wanted to be Hemingway, too. He would never move over, never give a tumble to the younger man who reflected so many of his facets. Bob never gave up the chase while Hemingway lived—hunting, guzzling, wenching, boasting, mimicking, trying on his mantle for size after his suicide.

Hemingway had too much of a lead.

I had only the flimsiest relationship with Hemingway and don't believe I could have called him Papa if I had known him well. The first knowledge I had that my hero was aware of my existence came in a letter from him which the *Mirror* forwarded to me one spring while I was covering the baseball training camps in Florida. I was deeply impressed and thrilled to turn the Havana-mailed letter over and read on its rear flap:

Ernest Hemingway
Finca la Vigia
San Francisco de Paula
Cuba

I assumed it was a response to a column I had written a week before, an interview with Quentin Reynolds in which Quent described the thrill and rigors of spending a weekend as Hemingway's guest. There was a particularly glowing reference to Hemingway's knockdown of Tom Heeney, the former heavyweight contender best remembered as the man Gene Tunney defended his title against before abdicating it. Reynolds told me Heeney was working for Hemingway as a sparring mate.

I assumed correctly. It was a response to the column. A retort.

"If I ever meet you I'm going to flatten you on sight," Hemingway's letter began. He denied that he had ever decked Heeney. Heeney, Hemingway wrote, was his friend, not his employee.

He seemed to have forgotten the whole thing by the time we met. He was in New York to see his publishers and do a little drinking at Shor's. We talked sports for hours and I dropped him off at his hotel. I asked him what his plans were for the next day, and he said he was going to work the whiskey out of himself at George Brown's gym in the morning—would I like to come along?

Puffed and puffing from the night before, Hemingway came out of his corner of the gym ring weaving and bobbing and glaring at his friend Brown, an accomplished and gentlemanly muscleman who catered physical fitness to select New York tycoons and blades. He got in close to Brown and tried to knee him in the groin. Brown stepped back and jabbed him sharply in the nose. Hemingway lunged at him like a bear, tried to stomp on his feet, and rubbed the lacings of a glove roughly up and down Brown's ear. Brown broke away, feinted him, and busted him a good right in the face. And so it went for three two-minute rounds. When it was over, Hemingway came over to where I stood and leaned his heavy hairy arms on the top rope. The blood from his nose had saturated his mustache. He smiled triumphantly and gasped, "Wasn't that a wonderful workout!"

A licensed referee would have stopped the fight and disqualified him at any point during the three rounds.

I saw him a few times after that at Shor's place where he liked to sit around and drink and talk sports. He had a good sports background in boxing lore and was fair on baseball. There's something about those dudes. Thomas Wolfe dreamed more about going home to Ebbets Field than to North Carolina. It becomes a big thing for them to be known as rooters for this or that team, or fighter, and the worse the team or fighter, the greater the reverence paid.

When Castro took over, Hemingway had a good word to say for him. When Simon Bolivar's skin peeled off of Castro and he was himself again, I tried and failed to reach Hemingway by cable, phone, and his agent to ask his comment.

When I next saw him at Shor's, he was bearded, subdued, and much thinner. He was standing alone at the bar; he beckoned to me and asked me to have a drink. We had several.

"You've blown some weight. How did you do it?"

He took a sip and thought.

"I stopped drinking with creeps," he said seriously. "As long as I can remember, I drank with creeps. I'd go into a bar anywhere in the world, somebody would spot me, make a big thing about buying me a drink, and finally I'd say sure, thanks, and now have one on me. So I'd wind up drinking with this creep I had never seen before and didn't want to be with and never wanted to see again. I took on a lot of booze that way over the years. One day I decided to stop drinking with creeps. I decided to drink only with friends. I've lost thirty pounds as a result."

Everybody at places like Shor's was sorry when the word came that Ernie was dead. To us, who didn't know him as well as the biographers lurking in the wings, there didn't seem to be any reason for putting the gun in his mouth and pressing the trigger. We held out some hope that, as had happened before, there would be a later bulletin canceling the obituaries. He had survived a couple of world wars, brushes with beasts, and a splintering plane crash on safari. On that occasion, after all the requiems, he emerged from the bush brandishing a bunch of bananas and a bottle of gin. His friend Shor, relieved to the extent of tears, sent him an insulting one-word cablegram. It read: "SHOWBOAT."

There was a lot of showboat in Ernie and some of its residue is still perpetuated at the place in Cuba where he spent, off and on, twenty-five of his best and most productive years. Castro has made it a museum of sorts which can be visited by appointment only. He has observed his promise to Mary Hemingway not to propagandize the place as the shrine of a renowned American who applauded his revolution.

I made the pilgrimage in 1964 when Castro invited a couple of dozen reporters to Havana and Santiago de Cuba to take a well-programmed look at how he was making out. Hemingway's place, twelve miles out of Havana, is as he left it on July 24, 1960, to go to Pamplona to see the bulls run and to explain *Bloody Summer,* his disappointing account of the *mano-a-manos* tour of Antonio Ordoñez and Luis Miguel Dominguin.

There are fresh flowers everywhere in the house, and the airy place is spotless. His favorite chair is still there in what must be called the living room. It is done in a chintzy pink print that is at odds with the heads of menacing beasts glaring down from the walls. The bar table still nudges at an arm of the deep chair, offering a variety of lived-with half-empties: White Horse, Gordon's, Noilly Prat, Martell. A large metal ice bucket snuggles at the foot of the bar. I had an uneasy feeling that it might be filled. There is a footstool near the chair on which Hemingway left a number of items he was reading or planned to read. On top of the pile is Allan Villers' *Give Me a Ship to Sail.* Luncheon for three is always about to be served at Finca la Vigia, but never is. The table is set each noon by Rene Villaralo, a now middle-aged Cuban brought into the ménage as a child to be a companion to Hemingway's sons. The china, silver, and glassware glitter from careful attention. The table flowers are sparkling fresh. There will be two wines. Papa will sit in the big chair facing Miss Mary and the guest beside her. . . .

It was something of a relief to get the hell out of the dining room.

Villaralo led us into Hemingway's combination bedroom-workroom. Directing our attention to the freshly made double bed on which there were a number of books and magazines and a Helen Wills white sun visor, he said that the master often fell asleep late at night amid such debris. This was what he had rolled in during his last night in that bed, the good and faithful servant said with his emotions gathering like a storm.

Ruark's *Poor No More* lay near one of the pillows of the uncommonly short bed. How much that would have meant to Bob!

Hemingway wrote standing up, his man recalled. He showed us the plain white bookcase that rose about as high as the author's once-barreled chest. He used its top layer as a desk. Hemingway would confront it every morning, write down his thoughts in longhand with a pencil, and then transcribe them on a beat-up portable he had carried through at least one war. That was atop another bookcase, where he also breakfasted: juice, tea, Rye-Krisp. He always wrote in his bare feet, Villaralo told us, because he said he could not think with his shoes on. In the wintertime he would protect his feet from the cold tiles with a thin rug made from the skin of some small animal he had shot. He kept a bookkeeper's account of how many words he wrote each day and marked the total on a writing board which would not be out of place in a drugstore inventory. Sometimes he wrote as many as seventeen hundred words a day ("if he was going fishing the next day," Villaralo explained). Sometimes he wrote only three hundred. Sometimes he just stared. He never used his regular desk except as a kind of display table. The day I was there it held a collection of bullets of different caliber, lined up like smart troops, his war correspondent brassard, a snapshot of Mary, and one of Marlene Dietrich singing to gaping GI's. Under the glass top of the desk was an illuminated religious card, a prayer of Ignatius Loyola: "Soul of Christ, sanctify me. . . . Soul of Christ, save me."

The Duchess of Windsor's 1957 Cadillac nuzzled to the curb on the Vendôme side of the Ritz in Paris. The chauffeur put my bag and beat-up portable in its yawning trunk as the Duchess reached a fashionably gloved hand out from the rear door of the car. She was brittlely hospitable under her thick car blanket. And off we went through a cold and clammy Paris to share a weekend that meant much to them, for it would be the twenty-fifth anniversary of the Duke's abdication because of her.

"He's actually playing golf in this weather," she said when I inquired about him. "He's playing with a couple of boys who are hardly thirty or thirty-five. It seems so foolhardy to me. But, then, I don't play golf." The Duke was sixty-four, she sixty. It had not been a good year for them, she said. He had lost the young British accountant who was so adept at helping them keep their financial affairs straight, and the Duchess' long-time secretary had abruptly quit.

It was something less than Bourse-shaking news, but I was glad she was talking at all. I had come to hear them talk, not to confront them with tedious questions.

"He had a wife and four small children in London," she was explaining, wielding her fine diction. "The wife couldn't see his spending three weeks out of every month with us. As for my secretary, she simply quit."

I tried to murmur sympathetically, but nothing came out. It would be a very long weekend. We watched the gray-green countryside slide by for a time.

"I am so sorry you won't see our place with the flowers out," the Duchess said in time. "We call it The Mill. It was built in the sixteen hundreds and remodeled in seventeen thirty. The agent did not want to show it to me. Got me halfway out here and tried to turn around and drive me back to town. I would not hear of it.

"Well it was almost as grim as he made it sound—no bathrooms and otherwise in terrible state. But the Duke loved it on first sight. He liked the space—it's twenty acres—and the water running through it. He works better, thinks clearer, out here, and we can make it in twenty minutes from the place we bought from the government in the Bois de Boulogne.

"We fixed it up nicely, I think you'll agree. You'll be sleeping in what was the cow barn."

It seemed appropriate, I said, and the Duchess nodded agreeably. We turned off the main road and into a twisting little lane that led past a well-stocked French farm.

"Sells all his milk to Maxim's," the Duchess noted.

The car slowed to a stop in time in front of a rustic and somewhat battered wooden gate.

"Well, this is it," she said. "The Duke lived in palaces all his life, but he loves this best of all. I lived in something less than palaces, a lot less, come to think of it. But, never mind, here we are. If the Duke likes it here, I like it here."

The gate was opened by a raw-jawed farmer's wife, and the widened view revealed a pleasant cobbled court surrounded by low-slung buildings constructed to mill grain in Elizabeth's age. A Mercury station wagon was being unloaded before the main lodge.

"The Duke's back from his golf," she exclaimed as we drove up to the door. She led me inside past a polished bell from the racing cutter *Britannia,* sailed by Edward VII and George V.

"Darling, where are you?" she trilled as she ascended a staircase with a balustrade made of the thick red plush roping one associates with the prize ring. There was no response.

"He must be walking the dogs," the Duchess said as we came into the large living room. She dropped her coat absently and began thumbing through her mail with the avidity of a school girl. It gave me time to look around: a room where grain once was stored now was miraculously transformed. The centuries-old beams, scrupulously whitewashed, looked down on a handsome decor: a huge red-and-white patterned rug, comfortable divans and chairs, fireplace, beautiful late fall flower-and-leaves arrangements, a large painting of the Duchess in blue taffeta by Étienne Drian and a larger one of the Duke, as Prince of Wales, astride his favorite chestnut hunter and wearing his nattiest pink coat.

The mail held no great attraction for the Duchess. She dropped it back on the table, crossed the room, and opened the French doors that led to a flat-stoned terrace marked by a sundial placed there in 1730. As we walked toward the mill race that once had turned the long-gone mill wheel, the Duke came up the lower path with the four pugs. He was hatless and wearing a red woolen shirt and red-and-white polka-dotted silk muffler.

He was kind enough to remember a meeting of twenty years before when, as Governor of the Bahamas, he invited a group of New York sportswriters to Nassau to cover a British Red Cross charity golf match involving Bobby Jones, Walter Hagen, Gene Sarazen, and Tommy Armour. He had served as scorekeeper and pin-holder.

We strolled inside. Tea was ready: intricately arranged shrimp in their shells, hot little squares of melted cheese and bacon on toast, cornbread, petits fours, jam, marmalade.

"It's China," the Duchess said of the tea, pouring her husband a second large cup, with milk.

"We much prefer it to India's," the Duke said, seriously. "We get it in New York. It's the same tea your J. Pierpont Morgan used to bring over for his grouse shooting. I carry it on all my trips, even to golf. Had a spot of it after today's round. The other chaps did a most unusual thing. They brought out splits of champagne and actually drank them. Imagine anyone having a *split* of champagne. . . ."

When tea was done, the Duchess retired across the room to a partly completed jigsaw which apparently had stumped but bemused her for some time past, and the Duke and I began a meandering dialogue that was to last the remainder of the weekend. First off, he produced an advance copy of the London *TV Times* in which, surprisingly, he had a signed article of a most intimate nature. He suggested I read it, and in the silence of the room I read:

> This I can say: in these past 25 years I have never, for one moment, regretted the decision I took then.
>
> That weekend party at Melton Mowbray in 1931, when I first met Wallis Warfield, changed the course of English history. It certainly changed the course of my life—but how empty my life would have been if I had never gone to that weekend house party.
>
> A man can come to a point in his life when there are two clearly defined paths ahead. He has to take one or the other and it is then when he is most alone. Only he can decide—no one can do it for him.
>
> As Shakespeare put it:
>
> "There is a tide in the affairs of men,
> Which, taken at the flood leads on to fortune;
> Omitted, all the voyage of their life
> Is bound in shallows and in miseries."
>
> My path led on to great good fortune, the fortune which comes from the knowledge that time has long since sanctified a true and faithful union.

The Duchess had read the article. Still puzzling over her jigsaw, she spoke up as I handed the magazine back to the Duke. She spoke without emotion.

"I was against the abdication," she said of the event that rocked Britain and the world. "Mrs. Simpson was more against the abdication than anybody. I'm not at all sure it would be different if it happened today. It is out of the question, I think, for anyone with the title of Defender of the Faith to marry a divorced woman. Perhaps if I had been a British girl it might have been more acceptable. The British didn't like Americans very much twenty-five years ago."

The Duke stuffed a small prepared barrel of tobacco in the bowl of his slender pipe and lighted it as he listened to the Duchess.

"If I had it to do over again the same thing would have happened," he said seriously. "There would be nothing different. We've had a fascinating life together. I had a great life before the abdication, certainly. But this life of ours for the past twenty-five years together has been simply flawless."

From the other side of the room the Duchess, still engrossed in her puzzle, asked, "Who said, 'Old men forget, young men don't know'?"

They had both been in London not long before, for business and Christmas shopping. I asked him if he had seen his niece, the Queen. He seemed surprised.

"Oh, no," he said. "I don't see my family any more, really, except of course at coronations and tragedies. I don't see them because they won't see the Duchess. Simple as that."

He cocked his ruddy, sandy-haired head quizzically. "Would you see your family if they wouldn't see your wife?" he asked.

I asked him if he would comment on an article, printed in France just previously, stating that he still enjoyed a handsome income from the British Crown.

"I never got a nickel," he said. "I've heard for years that great story that I inherited my grandmother Queen Alexandra's jewelry. I inherited absolutely nothing. I put in seventeen hard years of work for my country and the Commonwealth. I went straight from Oxford into four years of war, then came out in 1919 and worked until 1936. I'm not even assigned a secretary."

His show of polite indignation waned when I wondered aloud how things would be this day, had he taken the Duchess' advice and given her up.

"If I were king?" he asked, raising an eyebrow. "I don't think I could have done anything differently, really. I would have been bound, as my brother was bound, by the limitations of a constitutional monarchy. A king has no influence in government. My government was all against anything belligerent in its outlook toward Germany and Italy, though I must say that Anthony Eden quarreled with Hitler and Mussolini personally.

"It takes a king a long time even to partly influence his government. As you get older, you can point out to the politicians where they are wrong, wrong from your point of view, that is. But you have no power to disapprove of their acts. My father exerted a certain amount of influence at times near the end of his life, but surely not the power to disapprove."

Would there always be a British royal family?

The Duke of Windsor thought about that for some time.

"Always is a very big word," he said with a smile. "But the way things are going in the world, ours may be the last, one of these years.

I remember before the first World War that my family was constantly receiving and returning visits of what we called the foreign relations —Queen Victoria's host of descendants.

"I saw Kaiser Wilhelm II, my father's first cousin, at a shooting party at Sandringham. He could make himself very pleasant when he wanted to, though a real Prussian. I remember him mostly because that was the day I had my first automobile ride.

"Czar Nicholas, another first cousin, visited us eight years before he and his family were murdered. Alphonso XIII of Spain married one of my father's first cousins and used to come to us for shooting and polo. I was called to Windsor Castle from Oxford when my father entertained Archduke Franz Ferdinand, soon enough killed at Sarajevo. Very elegant sort of fellow. I remember Carlos of Portugal, too, fat and jolly little fellow. Assassinated, you know. And so on.

"Anyway, there were twenty monarchies in Europe when I was young. Now there are seven: Great Britain, Norway, Sweden, Denmark, Belgium, Holland, and Greece. Wars play hell with monarchies."

How had the years altered the Crown he wore?

"The colonies, chiefly," he said. "We had the lot when I was King."

"You were actually King-Emperor, weren't you?" the Duchess asked idly from her jigsaw.

"Yes, I was," the Duke said as if speaking of some remote relative. "But I wasn't the last. My brother was until 1947. That's when India went."

"This puzzle is just too much," the Duchess said. "The worst part of it is they say on the box how many hours it should be done in. It takes us days! It's disgraceful."

The Duke nodded, then continued, "Actually, there was always pressure about India from the Socialists. I never met Gandhi or Nehru. When I went out there as Prince of Wales they were both in jail. Later, I watched Gandhi when he came to London to see my father. Wore that extreme outfit.

"Now they've given Kenya independence. Mark my words, there'll be Mau Mau troubles there. But I suppose things will settle in time, even though some of those African nations aren't as yet fitted for self-rule. I'll say this for the British—they've always let their colonial peoples into the civil-service class. Would you have a drink?"

As we walked toward a small bar in the next room, I asked him about his golf.

"Oh, that," he shrugged. "I remember the old one about the golfer who was asked what his handicap was and he replied, 'me.' That's pretty much my own story. I must be an eighteen handicap right now. But I remember that once I had a seventy-five, holing all putts."

We were not out of range of the Duchess.

"You have pleasant memories," she observed cheerfully.

He poured me a Scotch and himself a bourbon. I asked for ice.

"Did you specify ice because of your experience with British hospitality?" he asked with a twinkle. "We always have ice here. This is an Anglo-American home."

"It's better for you without ice," the Duchess remarked, from fathoms deep in her puzzle.

Did they anticipate being interviewed on TV on the occasion of this anniversary?

"Not a chance," said the Duke, who once appeared with the Duchess on "Person to Person," on which program the Duchess had plainly startled Edward R. Murrow with how she could play jacks and balls.

"Everybody who gets off a plane after an eight-hour trip seems to get interviewed on television now," the Duchess said, giving up on her puzzle. "They're either motion picture people who want to advertise themselves or politicians."

"We're too old-fashioned for that sort of thing, really," the Duke said. "And handicapped, too. We cannot discuss politics, or express much of an opinion on anything."

"We don't have anything to say on TV," the Duchess agreed. "The Duke is right, we're old-fashioned. Why, I don't even fly. I flew from Miami to Nassau in 1940 and haven't been in the air since."

I asked her why she didn't fly.

"It's very simple," said the beautiful woman who rocked an empire. "I'm afraid.

"Now, shall we freshen up for dinner?"

The Duchess, in something black, with green shoes, emerald bracelet, and five strands of pearls, was standing before a dancing fire in the cozy reception room of the "big house" when I arrived from my plush cow shed for dinner. The fire was flattering, but hardly needed. She was stunning.

The Duke clumped down the sharp-turning staircase, with two pugs plopping behind him. The Duchess had said offhandedly earlier in the day that the Duke usually dressed for dinner, guests or not. It was an understatement. His dinner jacket was in one of his family's plaids. His shirt was fluffy and lacy. His "black tie" was as thick and broad as the mustache of a red-headed RAF ace. His socks were Argyle. We had a drink and, rather wildly, the talk turned to television again.

"I got interested in your television because I like baseball very much," the Duke said, looking into his little bowl of iced Polish vodka. "I was having a manicure at our place in the Waldorf, actually, and on came the Series. Fascinating! In time, I became so interested in your television that I began watching the late shows. That's shameful, of course. Worse, I even picked up some of your commercials."

I was about to ask a question when it became apparent he was not finished with the thought. He cleared his throat and then in the most jovial manner recited:

"Double your pleasure, double your fun, Doublemint, Doublemint, Doublemint gum!"

The Duchess smiled wanly.

"I learned another one during the TV golf matches," the Duke continued, and forthwith sang the Miller's High Life theme.

"French television is so sad," the Duchess said. "The news is excellent, but before you get it, and sometimes after you get it, there's a play or a sad song. French television women stars usually throw themselves into the Seine at the end of each show. Shall we dine?"

The candle-lit dining room nearby was in fine taste, a taste which included the food.

"The French oysters are much better," the Duchess, a renowned authority on haute cuisine, said during that course. "They have a coppery taste. I can't bear American oysters. They're so mushy. Now, Dungeness crab, that's different. There's nothing better than the Dungeness at Twenty One in New York."

The Duke interrupted to say that the main course would be grouse sent to him by the Duke of Buccleuch.

"It's spelled almost like Bookloosh and pronounced Baklush," he said. "Very odd, and I might say a very rich family."

The Duchess placed an immaculately manicured index finger on the button of a metal turtle near her plate and a bell-buzzer rang inside the iron reptile with startling clarity. I jumped.

"Whenever the Duke remembers a name at dinner I always ring the buzzer," the Duchess said merrily. "That's his reward. Women are so much better at names than men, haven't you noticed? Time and time again a husband fumbles around at a party and finally, in desperation, whispers to his wife, 'What's his name?' The wife always remembers. Women also make very good executives." She seemed to be daring one or both of us to challenge that. I waited for the Duke, but his concentration was on his grouse.

"Name ten," I said, after a bit. She plunged immediately into a list that included Mrs. Michael Paul, who headed the brokerage firm of A. M. Kidder; Mary Roebling, president of a bank in Trenton, New Jersey; Mary Lasker, Peggy Joyce, Marion Davies, Mrs. Mortimer Davis, Margaret Biddle, Dorothy Shaver, ". . . and I don't even know the people in the Middle West and the Coast, but I'm sure there are dozens of fine business women there.

"Oh, and what about Marjorie Post?" she continued, quietly triumphant. "Marjorie keeps tabs on everybody who eats a Post Toastie. She tests new products at General Foods. She's terrific at meetings. If I had a fortune like Marjorie's, I'd taste the products, too."

The phone had been ringing through the last half of the Duchess' tribute to the she-wolves of Wall Street, and now Robert, their all-around man, came in to whisper to the Duke, "Lord Dudley is calling from London, sir."

The Duke put down his utensils with a sigh. He had skipped lunch to play golf and had recently described himself as famished.

"Why do they always call at this time?" he asked. He got up and trooped off to a neighboring room and its uncertain French phone. "Hello, Dudley?" we heard him shout. Then, "Yes? . . . No! . . . Yes? . . . oh, no!"

"Something's wrong with Dudley," the Duchess divined. "He's the Duke's most faithful friend. A wonderful friend to us."

As the Duke continued his thunderous affirmative-negative responses over the thin, trembling line to London, the Duchess discoursed on grouse.

"There are three kinds of grouse," she said, "white, gray and black —or is it pink? Anyway, one type never leaves England. . . ."

The Duke returned to his place at that point, passing, as he did, a fine framed sketch of himself as he looked in his buoyant twenties.

"Poor old Bruce Ogleby," he said.

"Why, he was your aide-de-camp," the Duchess said, concerned.

"It's Primrose," the Duke said with simple eloquence. There was a decent period of silence, broken finally by the Duchess.

"What's the grouse that never flies away from England?" she asked.

The Duke looked up from his grouse, interested.

"I don't know," he said, ready to be told.

"But you did know when I asked you the other night," the Duchess pursued.

"Well, I don't know now," said England's foremost expatriate.

We moved on from the late lamented Primrose and home-based grouse to travel. Inevitably, I mentioned Switzerland.

"A terrifically well-ordered hospital, Switzerland," the Duchess said. "The Swiss have no show of wealth. They have developed the art of being inconspicuous. We know a couple of Swiss bankers who must be among the richest men in the world, but they always stay at small, cheap places."

The Duchess rose and moved serenely alone into the bar-TV room, and soon she called out that the news was on. The Duke and I went through the low-slung door, stooping. Chancellor Adenauer was on screen, arriving in Paris for his talks with President de Gaulle.

"Adenauer's a fine man," the Duke said, settling into his chair. He started into an anecdote about the Chancellor.

"Shhh!" the Duchess said without taking her eyes off the TV set. "I want to hear the news." Then she half-turned to me and said, "He always talks during the news."

The Duke chuckled amiably, lighting his pipe. "I do at that," he said.

As de Gaulle and Adenauer went through their paces and the commentator babbled in French, I looked about the pleasant room and was struck by an embroidered cushion in one of the chairs. On it was sewn, "Don't look now, somebody may be gaining on you." In my room in the cow shed there was a cushion emblazoned with, "Smile at the poorest tramp as you would at the highest king."

Scenes from the action in the Congo were on when I looked back at the TV set. The Duke had picked up Disraeli, one of the pugs, and was thoughtfully stroking him.

"We're living in terrible times," he said. He was about to go on but the scene changed to a discussion of French labor-management problems. The Duke, whose French was uncertain, shook his head. "Terrible," he said. "Now if they had social security in The States. . . ."

"They certainly do have social security in The States," the Duchess said, without turning away from the set. Then, "Wait a minute. This is marvelous!" The on-screen discussion enraptured her.

"The Duchess knows French so much better than I," the Duke said regretfully. But his mood soon brightened.

"That's football!" he said delightedly, as the picture turned to a Rugby match. "The French have become very sportsminded since the German occupation. I think our football is much more interesting than your brand in America. Your football, I must say, is quite boring. I don't speak ill of your baseball, however. That's enchanting. Who's playing, dear?"

"I think it's two French teams," the Duchess said, scanning the action.

"That's too French for me," the Duke boomed, and we all laughed heartily, and called it a night—another night—at Moulin de la Tuilerie.

The next morning, Sunday, the Duke gingerly picked his way across the cobbled courtyard from the main house to my cowshed guest quarters. A dismal rain, gray as slate, fell on the tableau: The Duke was hatless but his trim body was encased in a long woolen bathrobe of bright red. The four pugs were underfoot. White doves fanned about him.

"Halloooo!" he called through the opened upper half of the split door. "Anybody home?"

"Only us cows," I said.

"You must see my barn," he said. The dogs, doves and I followed him across the yard to a low-slung stone building, ancient before my country was born. The Duke, dogs, and I entered. The birds had other plans.

"I call it my museum," he said of the large room. It was at least that. There was enough memorabilia to stock a wing of the British

Museum, and only then did I understand the concern the Duchess had expressed the night before about the security of the estate. "A lot of what might have been is here," she had put it.

"This table might interest you," the Duke said, falling easily into the role of guide. The beautifully carved piece held a small forest of silver-framed photographs of certain illustrious forebears, a great green tongue of jade combed from some forgotten voyage, and a neat little gold plaque on which was engraved:

On this table King Edward VIII
signed the Instrument of Abdication at 10:30 A.M. December 11, 1936.

If the Duke attached any emotional importance to the object, his cheerful face masked it. He touched a long match to the kindling and crushed paper beneath the fireplace logs, and after a gay shower of sparks the chilled place was aglow with light and warmth. The Duke peeled off his robe and sat down in a deep chair near his hooded breakfast tray. He wore a turtleneck baby-blue sweater, fawn slacks with thin blue stripes forming large squares, and buff and green woolen socks.

I asked him about the abdication speech of a quarter of a century before, that superbly phrased and so touchingly delivered declaration of the heart. Was it true, as often hinted at in America, that Sir Winston Churchill had had a hand in its styling?

"I wrote it myself," the Duke said quickly, as if denying a Baconite claim. He uncovered his toast, buttered a bit, and relaxed.

"I did call him that day and told him I planned to go on the radio that night with a statement I had prepared," he said, his blue eyes re-weighing those crowded hours. "Old Winston said, 'I'd like to see what you have to say.' Naturally, I invited him to come to Fort Belvedere and I showed it to him. Wouldn't you? I think that if anybody was about to make a speech of that moment, that importance, and had Old Winston in his house, and didn't ask him to look it over, well, that person should have his head examined. Certainly, he made a few suggestions."

He shook his head, affectionately.

"He was always dramatic, Old Winston."

I asked the Duke which member of his family he felt he would most miss that early morning of December 12, 1936, when he sailed away from Portsmouth in H.M.S. *Fury*.

"I don't think anyone's ever asked me that," he said, cocking his head as if to recollect better.

"I really don't think I missed anybody, longed for anybody in my family," he said after a while. "I would miss Fort Belvedere. I made Fort Belvedere. As for persons, the only one in my mind was in France, getting her divorce. I hoped she would marry me."

I had read that the parting from his mother, Queen Mary, was a tearful one.

"Really?" the Duke asked with surprise. "The only nice thing, human thing, my mother said to me during that time when I was fighting a very lonely battle was, 'Isn't it a pity it'll be so long before you see her again?' "

The reference was to the then-prevalent six-month period of cloister during divorce proceedings.

"It was a strange age," he mused, lighting up his first pipe for the day. "My lawyer told me that if I even stayed in the same country with Wallis during that period, he would retire as my counsel."

We browsed the room after breakfast. There, under glass, rested the coronet he wore at the coronation of his father half a century before. About the place were arranged four yellow-skinned drums, one of which had shared his World War I service with the Grenadier Guards. Up and down the beams that framed the door were tacked the slender racing plates of hunters and jumpers he had ridden in a day when his hair-raising croppers were regarded as royal slapstick.

He took me for a climb through the large rock garden that rose from the boarded and winterized swimming pool. "Charlie Cushing—you knew him around New York—used to call this Cardiac Hill," the Duke called back as he negotiated the slippery stepping stones without drawing a deep breath. "Fine man, Charlie was. As friendly to caddie as to the president of the club." At the summit of the garden he turned and viewed the little walled complex of the old mill, and he could not have been more pleased by what he saw than if he were beholding Buckingham as Edward VIII.

It was time to join the Duchess and a newly arrived luncheon guest, their good friend Margery Wilson, an attractive American widow who lived in New York and Paris. As we walked toward the main house along the rushing mill race, the Duke chatted about a variety of things.

Christmas cards: "I wish I could stop sending them, as my cousin Mountbatten did, but the Duchess thinks it might offend old friends. . . ."

The Hoovers, Herbert and J. Edgar: "Great fellows!"

New York traffic: "Abominable! It's your Fifth Avenue busses, bumper to bumper for miles."

The then-delicate Berlin situation: "Your Roosevelt had a lot to do with that, I must say."

Suicidist Robert R. Young: "A great friend . . . poor Bob."

Clothing: "I'm not a full-fledged client of your man H. Harris, in New York. He does your President, you know. I met Kennedy when he was a boy living with his parents at the American Embassy in London. But that's neither here nor there. I just get my pants from H. Harris. They don't make good pants in England, for some reason, just as they don't make good coats in America. So I have the coats done on this side and the trousers in New York. The Duchess calls it 'pants-across-the-sea.' "

We rubbed mossy shoes on the mat outside the living-room French doors and came in out of the damp gray day, followed by four damp gray pugs who marched immediately to the fireplace and faced it like pleased figurines. Mrs. Wilson curtsied ever so briefly and affectionately as she accepted the Duke's outstretched hand.

"Here's the news," the Duchess called from among her treasury of British Sunday newspapers. She gave the Duke an astonishingly complete rundown of current happenings. It would have done justice to their favorite American newscaster, Bob Trout of CBS. Drinks came along as she finished, while the Duke leafed through the pages of the *Express*.

"Ah," he exclaimed, as he spotted a picture of the Duchess, taken the previous week at the opening of the new show at the Lido in Paris. She and the Duke had simply been part of a large party held there. But only the Duchess' picture appeared. The caption cruelly noted that the photograph of her was taken at a "strip" place.

"It's a jolly good picture of you, dear," the Duke said warmly.

A pleasant luncheon followed, with talk as varied as those opposite poles of subject matter, psychiatry and the Peppermint Lounge, then New York's busiest Twist parlor. The Duchess announced that she was determined to avoid the former like a scourge but look in on the latter when she and the Duke were next in New York.

"You have to be rich to go in for psychiatry," she observed, studying the neatly written menu near her plate, the better to describe the oncoming dish.

"Or lonely," Mrs. Wilson suggested.

"A good friend to talk to is the best thing," the Duchess said quietly. "There is nothing better than that."

The Duke nodded, and the little room was suddenly hushed, and I a witless intruder.

The sober mood was still about as the Duke walked me to the car that would take me back to Paris. I had one more question. The Duchess had said the night before, "He should've given me up. It would have been so much easier on him." I asked him if he wanted to say anything about that.

"She lost out in that argument," the Duke of Windsor said with steady pride. "I won."

Westbrook Pegler was the writer most of us chose to ape when I was coming along. Any young sportswriter who tried to write in Damon Runyon's patented present tense ("I am sitting in Mindy's . . .") was laughed at and thereafter suspect. But to write a good hard sentence like Peg was to be admired; not many could. Peg could keep a forty-word sentence under iron control, like Clyde Beatty in a cage of wild beasts, once he took command. Taking command was something else. At a fight, ballgame, or trial he would rip more unfinished leads out of his typewriter than the rest of us combined, crush them into balls, and drop them at his feet. It was sometimes difficult to resist stooping to appropriate something he had discarded as unworthy of his by-line, because it was probably better than the product on which I was about to settle.

Peg was a considerate man with his peers and inferiors. He would make a point of dropping a note to a newcomer in the business, if something the newcomer had written attracted him, compliment him, and wish him well. He gave me one of my first national notices. In an Esquire piece about New York sportswriters, he wrote that there were four others who worked on out-of-town papers who could hold their own if they ever chose to come to New York. He mentioned Bill Cunningham, then writing the sports column for the Boston *Post,* Ed Danforth of the Atlanta *Journal,* Warren Brown of the

Chicago *Examiner,* and me. It was a breathtaking experience to see my name in the body of an absorbing article about men ostensibly beyond me in prestige and skills.

After I reached New York, Peg and his wife, Julie Harpman, a former reporter who was as gentle in her estimate of mankind as Peg was barbed, were fine to Millie and to me. We discovered what so many before us had: that Pegler, the shatterer of images and piercer of stuffed shirts, was not the same Pegler one might run into at dinner or later. The latter Peg was filled with laughter, good stories, unswerving devotion to Julie—who had a heart condition—and his gallantry charmed all within sight and sound. It was another Pegler who pulled up a chair to a typewriter each day, lighted a cigarette as if it were a fuse, and exploded.

"Something snaps in his brain just before he hits the first key," became an awed cliché among his envious contemporaries.

One day at the *American* our sports department was filled with the noise of heavy hammering on the floor above, where construction work of some sort was under way.

"What's that?" Ed Frayne asked, as sledgehammer blows shook the place.

"That's Pegler, writing his column," Sid Mercer said without looking up from his typewriter.

Peg wrote several tender columns, as if to confound those who swore he was constitutionally incapable of sentiment. He enjoyed Walt Disney's *Snow White* and said so with considerable warmth. When Bill Corum was pinked by a bullet fired by the brother of an attractive lady Bill was, alas, in the very act of romancing, the cover-up story given to the newspapers was that Bill was struck by a stray shot while strolling along Park Avenue. Like everybody else, Peg liked Bill, even though Corum had once raked him sharply for predicting that the chief result of the Joe Louis-Max Baer fight at the Yankee Stadium would be a race riot in Harlem. Now, Peg sprang to his wounded friend's defense. He wrote a column soundly denouncing Park Avenue and all its people for hurting Bill.

He once wrote a kind piece about President Truman, too, but a closer scanning suggested that the tribute was not as inspired by Truman as by Peg's demoniacal hatred of Roosevelt. Two other Pegler columns that were honestly intended to be filled with sweetness and light (he once considered naming his column "Sweetness and Light") backfired. He had been rapping Knute Rockne for several years when Arch Ward, sports editor of the Chicago *Tribune,* arranged the first meeting between the two. They hit it off famously. Peg sat down to write what he considered an apologetic column. It was the only one Rockne sued on. In the other instance, Peg's good friend E. Phocion Howard, who ran a racing paper named the New York *Press* and often made a point of inviting prominent sportswriters to spend some time with him at his big rented house during the Saratoga meeting, died while Peg and Julie were his house guests. Peg's obituary-column was a moving tribute to his old friend "Phoce." For several paragraphs, that is. Then Peg launched into an attack on touting, on papers like the *Press,* and finally got around to the late-lamented.

"I guess he was just a bum," Peg's obit ended.

Peg and Julie, Runyon and his wife Patrice, and Millie and I spent a night at Tom Taggart's landmark spa at French Lick, Indiana, before moving on to Louisville for the running of a Kentucky Derby. It was a pleasant evening. Taggart sent a bottle of champagne to our table during dinner. The next day, Peg and I went to the cashier's cage to check out. He was the first in line. The girl in the cage smiled sweetly at him and said Mr. Taggart had instructed her that there would be no check for the Peglers. Peg protested at some length, stopping only when the girl said plaintively that she would lose her job if she disobeyed Mr. Taggart. I got the same treatment when I asked for our bill.

"Wasn't that nice of Tom?" Peg asked as we moved toward his car, following our baggage. He was going to drive us to Louisville.

"Sure was."

He was silent for a time, and I supposed he was reflecting on how nice Taggart had been. I was wrong.

"I can't wait to knock his brains out," Peg mused.

After Peg parted company with Scripps-Howard and joined Hearst's King Features Syndicate at more money, KFS attempted to capture his turbulent talents in a short biographical blurb to be distributed to prospective clients. It was a losing effort, of course. Finally, KFS's able public-relations man, Joe Willicombe, Jr., asked him to write the sketch himself. Peg snorted. But one day a sketch, unsigned, arrived.

It remains a treasured item in the syndicate's files:

Westbrook James Pegler was born in Minneapolis August 2, 1894, the son of Arthur James Pegler, an Englishman who had been a farm hand in Le Mars and other towns in an area of Iowa where there were a colony of English second sons whose fathers paid the Iowa farmers to teach them farming. For the most part they rode broad farm plugs over hill and dale yelling "Yoicks!" an Elizabethan term meaning, "I say, what ho!" and "tantivy," whose meaning is obvious to all right-thinking Americans. His mother was Frances Nicholson Pegler. The Nicholsons came from Conemara, Ireland, and are descendants of the Irish kings.

Arthur James was a third son, however, and had to work as a plow-jockey until he could escape to Council Bluffs where he painted front porches with a technique which was the basis of the school which employs the fried egg and a violin to depict the death of Aristotle.

After a while he went to Minneapolis where he became a reporter, sometimes working for three papers at once and earning up to $45 a week. There was no income tax in those days so thus, like E. H. Harriman, he was able to found a fortune. He later worked in Chicago where he became a tradition and in New York where he became a septuagenarian. Then he retired to live on a ranch near Tucson, Arizona, where now at 90 he writes letters of great vigor and beauty about his feet, which hurt from arthritis. He does this on a double-deck Smith-Premier, model of 1894 which burns soft coal.

Westbrook Pegler went to Horace Greeley grammar school and Lane Technical High School in Chicago and quit in disgust because he could not learn long division. He went to work for the United Press as cub in 1910 and, being a thoughtful little fellow, used to hang around police stations musing on the mysteries of long division, a series of reveries which gave the world the Westbrook Pegler Method, which is worked with salted peanuts. In 1912 he went to Loyola Academy, a Jesuit high school and, in the Spring of 1913 he went back to the U.P., his education completed. That Fall he got a job as cub on the Des Moines *News*. In 1914 he became bureau manager for the U.P. in St. Louis and in the Spring of 1916 he was sent to London. He was assigned to Queenstown with the destroyer *Flotilla* in the Spring of 1917, and after a spat with Admiral Sims he was sent to France with the AEF where, in due course, he had a spat with Pershing and was relieved and sent back to London, where he had a spat with Maj. Gen. Sir Frederick F. B. Maurice, the British chief of staff, because the boss told Pegler to ask Maurice who had supremacy in the air in France and Maurice gave him an oblique answer to which Pegler retorted, "Why don't you answer the question?"

After the war Pegler became markets editor of the United News in New York. He also held down the positions of sports editor, cable editor, fashion editor, society editor, and editor until he was hired by the Chicago Tribune Syndicate in 1925 to do sports. This phase ended in 1933 when he went cosmic for Roy Howard, spending a good deal of this time in Washington.

In 1944 he went to King Features and a lot of people wanted to know what he and Howard had scrapped about. Nobody would believe there had been no scrap and finally Pegler said "go to hell" and refused to discuss it any more. For God's sake has a man no privacy?

In 1942 Pegler received the Pulitzer Prize for distinguished reporting. He has an honorary degree as Doctor of Laws from Knox College and has twice won the National Headliners Club annual award, which don't mean a thing. He has also received the American Legion Award for Americanism.

In 1954 he received the "Silver Lady" Award for being "the outstanding reporter and columnist of the year" from the Banshees, a New York luncheon club composed of editors, writers, artists, and others in the creative trades. But it was awarded by King Features because King Features Syndicate wanted to make him feel good at the age of 60. It made him feel real good, too. At the same luncheon a remarkable and unique tribute was paid him by 25 winners of the Congressional Medal of Honor, who presented him with a special citation for Americanism.

He quit smoking in the year 1947, but not drinking. He likes to drink. Don't you? His hobbies are golf and thinking. Not very good at either but always in there swinging.

Peg's epic clash with Quentin Reynolds, which resulted in Reynolds' successful libel action, and his running wars with Walter Winchell and Drew Pearson, organized labor in general, and Eleanor Roosevelt in particular, the New York *Post,* Henry Luce, and the detractors of Sen. Joe McCarthy left him little time for laughter in his later years with King Features. Julie's untimely death in 1954, after she had enjoyed herself so much being with him in Geneva at the Eisenhower-Bulganin-Khrushchev-Eden-Faure summit meeting, knocked the remaining levity out of him. Fearless to the end of his stay with Hearst, he took on Hearst. Bill's Task Force, Peg wrote, reminded him of the Rover Boys.

I saw him at the office in New York just before he was about to leave, or be asked to leave, King Features. Peg said he hoped to take things easy for a bit, then start writing magazine pieces.

"Maybe even some fiction," he said.

"You'll be great, Peg," I said, and meant it. "You'll murder that kind of pitching."

It was a shock to learn later that he had decided to write for the John Birch Society's magazine. He left there soon enough, and the story spread that he had quit because he found the John Birchers too liberal for his blood. Whatever his reason for leaving, Peg dropped a notch in the profession he had graced so long and often so superbly. He found ventilation in *The Councilor,* a four-page sheet published twice monthly in Shreveport, Louisiana, as the official journal of the Citizens' Council of Louisiana. In its issue of February 20, 1966, the man who once was moved deeply by *Snow White* wrote:

> I have known Mike Quill for a hundred years as a cheap, flannel-mouthed shanty-Irish bum. The people of New York should have killed him cold stone dead on the sidewalk during his insurrection against the biggest and worst city in the world. This louse never was any good and should have been dumped for the benefit of our country 'way back in Roosevelt's time. And that big melodious pansy should have been run out of our capital because he was crazy from the effects of that disease which started in the marrows of his legs. The decay went to the brain about the time that he began to meddle with the world in an obsession that he was ordained by God or Fate or his own lantern-jawed, money-loving old lady to slaughter millions of human beings and deliver his own trusting country into ghastly carnage. Now Lyndon Johnson inherits tumult and is afraid to bring it to a halt.
>
> If Johnson had the trace of honor and the courage which his office calls for he should have moved right in and taken the initiative away from that long limpid faker named Lindsay who won the election to the City Hall in a clowning match with Bill Buckley. Johnson then should have clamped down some kind of material law to bring the idiot citizens out of their daze. This

> Quill donkey is a mush-mouth faker who has been getting by on his Irish brogue for God knows how long. There is an old fable that Quill walks with a limp in his r-r-rump, assisted by a blackthorn shillaleh because the Black and Tans or the Irish Republican Army kicked him out of some stinking cobbeen around Cork back in the days of the Thrubble over the Republic. Well, he does put on the limp but again, let us not forget that Roosevelt used that act, too.
>
> . . . When the State and the City of New York and Lyndon Johnson with his stinking Democratic Party can't run the buses in spite of such filthy apes as mush-mouth Quill, this country is shot to hell for sure.
>
> They still laugh at Calvin Coolidge, but you remember what he did when the Boston cops abandoned the people in a Police strike when he was mayor. He fired the whole rotten Irish mob and made them take it and like it. And not one of them ever got his job back. Not one. And every last one of those apes was a flannel-mouth mick from Dublin or Cork like mush-mouth Mike Quill.

An editorial note preceded Pegler's piece in *The Councilor*. It noted, "The late Mike Quill had fifty-five Communist and Communist-front citations in a 1944 Congressional report, now hidden from the public by Rep. Edwin Willis. Most of those listed were of Russian Khazar ancestry, but Quill said he was an Irishman. This Pegler column was written prior to his strange death, but it contains so many important references of historical value that it is being printed as written."

I miss Peg . . . the Peg one might run into at dinner, or later.

11. *Bigger Game*

THANKS chiefly to the Hearsts, father and son, my past thirty years have been crowded with the kind of opportunities and breaks all reporters dream about. They bought me a box seat near a world stage whose boards resound to the trod of a cast of characters unmatched in this century.

The dramatis personae include the glorious, inglorious, thrilling, boring, noble, despicable, kind, wicked, just, sadistic, immortal, transient. It holds every President since Hoover, every responsible hoodlum since Capone, three Popes, every renowned ballplayer since Walter Johnson, every football Hall of Famer since Jim Thorpe, every top fighter since Dempsey ruled, yes, and Churchill, Khrushchev, Nehru, Diem, Sukarno, de Gaulle, Franco, Castro, Ulbricht, kings and ex-kings, astronauts, atomic scientists, assassins, actors, actresses.

I have long since lost track of how many miles I've traveled in search of stories. It would be an impressive figure, for I've traveled in Afghanistan and Australia, Brazil and Burma, Chile and China, Denmark and the Dominican Republic, Eire and Eniwetok, France and Finland, Communism's Germany, Greece, Hungary and Helvetia, Iceland and India, Japan and Jordan, Korea and Kuwait, Libya and Liechtenstein, Malta and Monaco, Netherlands and Norway, the Philippines and Poland, Rumania and Rhodesia, Spain and Sweden, Thailand and Turkey, United Arab Republic and the Union of Soviet Socialist Republics, Vatican City State and Vietnam, West Germany and Westminster Abbey, Xochimilco and Xenia, have at least flown over Yap and Ypsilanti, but never once have set foot on Zambia.

Still, it's not too bad for a bloke who never ventured the 230 miles from his native Washington, D.C. to New York until he was twenty-three.

It is not easy or perhaps even sensible to attempt to choose one figure out of that fabled cast, or one scene or act that transcended all others. But near the top of those who played their historic roles would be Douglas MacArthur.

MacArthur would have risen to eminence—a comet trailing a tail of idolizers and critics—at any period in American history. His bearing (some thought it overbearing), his looks, voice, military skills, and sure sense of being one with history moved him with natural buoyancy to the top.

He was born with a silver sword in his mouth. His father, Arthur MacArthur, joined the Union forces in 1862 at the age of seventeen. He won the Congressional Medal of Honor at eighteen, at Missionary Ridge. He and his men were raiding a strong Confederate earthworks when the soldier who carried the regimental flag pitched forward with a bullet in his head. With a bravery that was later to be rendered hackneyed by a generation of lurid lithographers, MacArthur seized the flag and led the charge through a withering fire. He was the first man to mount the works, and there he planted the flag, changing the tide of battle.

His son Douglas won just about every honor West Point could bestow: highest scholastic marks since a cadet of twenty-five years before, John J. Pershing. He was First Captain of Cadets, first West Point ball-player to score a run against Navy . . . and first to have his mother, a militant matriarch who adored him, live on the campus.

After graduation, MacArthur was attached to his father's group of officers assigned by President Theodore Roosevelt to serve as observers of the Russo-Japanese War. The group was the guest of the Japanese, whose young officers young MacArthur came to know and admire. In fact, he participated in the Battle of Mukden with them, a classic carnage in which the Russians lost 97,000 dead and the Japanese between 40,000 and 50,000. At the height of the battle the elder MacArthur received an urgent message asking him to order his son back to the safety of General Nogi's headquarters. General MacArthur assumed that his son had left the safety of headquarters to find a position that gave him a better view of the gigantic battle. As a matter of fact, Douglas had done just that. But the sight of a Japanese company striving unsuccessfully five times to win a Russian position near his vantage place had been too much for his soldierly instincts. Whereupon, 1st Lt. Douglas MacArthur, U.S. Army Engineers, raced to the ranks of the deflated Japanese company, roused its spirit, and led it up the hill by a new route to capture the Russian battery.

In the Mexican border troubles he infiltrated the insurgent General Huerta's territory disguised, he liked to say later, as a "Mexican bum." (It was a description which later drew a snort of derision from his West Point classmate Gen. Hugh Johnson: "I'll say this much, Doug must have been the damned tallest Mexican bum that ever lived.") His most extravagant act in that disorder was the capture, single-handedly, of the crews of three locomotives. The entourage of flat-wheeled junk clanked into American-held territory in shabby grandeur —under the muzzle of Capt. MacArthur's revolver.

In World War I he was gassed, twice wounded, decorated thirteen times for bravery under fire, cited seven additional times for valor, led trench raids, became the youngest (thirty-eight) general in the AEF, returned home to become the youngest (thirty-nine) superintendent of West Point, married wealthy Louise Cromwell Brooks, who took her brother Jimmy (who was to marry Doris Duke, among others) along on the honeymoon.

The morning after the wedding night, the bride (who was later to marry actor Lionel Atwill) swept into the room where Jimmy was having his coffee and said blissfully, "He may be a general in the Army, but he's a buck private in the boudoir." Jimmy always classed it as one of the greatest tributes ever paid to the man, any man.

World War II seemed almost to be a staggering manuscript written especially for Douglas MacArthur: Bataan, Corregidor, The Escape, "I Shall Return," the island-hopping, Leyte, Manila . . . the stern but just terms of the surrender on the deck of the U.S.S. *Missouri.*

But there were frustrations that were never fully ventilated. He deeply resented the continued autonomy of the U.S. Navy though it gave lip service to his position as Supreme Commander of Allied Forces in the Pacific. He told me years later that he considered it the height of folly that FDR and his advisers in Washington had seen fit to favor Eisenhower and the Russians, ". . . while I was forced to operate against a far-flung enemy with scarcely 11 percent of the total output of the American war production."

Most of all, MacArthur was offended by being bypassed in the evolution of what turned out to be the deciding move of the war. In the latter part of July, 1945, he received a request from the Pentagon.

A Brig. Gen. Thomas Farrell was en route with a special message. Would MacArthur please see him?

It was a bother. The Pentagon had a distressing habit of inflicting its couriers on him. MacArthur had bigger things to contend with. He was drawing up plans for the invasion of Japan, scheduled for October. It would be the most mammoth military thrust of all time, and the accepted U.S. estimate was that 600,000 men would be killed or wounded before the expected fanatical defense of the islands was crushed.

Tom Farrell, a fine engineer and great gentleman, cooled his heels in MacArthur's outer office for some time—upon his arrival at the Supreme Commander's Philippine headquarters—before being told that MacArthur would see him. For fifteen minutes.

"For thirteen minutes he walked up and down his office telling me about his invasion plans," Farrell told me later. "He was a magnificent figure to behold, and the plans were wonderful, but I was worried about delivering my message. Then, with two minutes left, he looked at his wristwatch and asked me what I had come to see him about.

"I took a breath and told him that we had developed the atomic bomb; that we had tested it at Alamogordo, New Mexico, the previous July sixteenth; that the experts figured the bomb was the equivalent of twenty thousand tons of TNT; that we had two of them ready to be dropped and crews ready to carry out the mission from Tinian."

MacArthur was asked then to issue a directive which would keep the skies clear of routine U.S. air raids over certain Japanese cities during the first clear daytime weather that might accrue around the first week of August.

He agreed, dismissed Farrell, and went back to his invasion plans. Only after Hiroshima and Nagasaki did he learn, to his quiet indignation, that he had been cut out of the tiny top group who knew about The Bomb. It particularly irritated him that his one-time aide on the other side of the world, General Eisenhower, had been kept abreast of the years-long development and proving of the weapon that abruptly ended the costliest war in history.

I wrote the first MacArthur biography, *MacArthur the Magnificent,* published in 1942 by David McKay in this country and Hutchinson in England. It did not have his imprimatur nor his disapproval. It was not until 1950 that I met him, and then under somewhat strained circumstances.

Several days before my scheduled luncheon with the general I wangled a seat aboard his C-54 *Bataan,* bound from Tokyo's Haneda airport to the tin strip at Taegu, Korea. The passenger list was impressive: W. Averell Harriman, on orders from President Truman to review the continuing American retreat and discourage MacArthur from doing anything desperate to reverse the trend, Lt. Gen. Matt Ridgway, destined to replace MacArthur as Supreme Commander of UN forces, Lt. Gen. Lauris Norstad, who became head of NATO's forces, Maj. Gen. Roger Ramey USAF, and perhaps a dozen more generals.

The plane was commanded and piloted by MacArthur's aide and personal pilot, the intrepid Col. Tony Story. As it approached its destination, two events occurred: (1) U.S. fighter planes took up positions on all sides to protect the *Bataan* and its prized passenger list from enemy air attack, and (2) Story strolled down the aisle handing out .45's. He explained placidly that in order to land on the short emergency strip at Taegu it would be necessary for the *Bataan* to pass over positions occupied by North Korean troops and batteries spread along the Naktong River. We could be forced down and, if so, would need the guns.

Tony offered guns to Harriman and to me, in the order named, of course. Harriman waved his aside and I, the only other civilian on the plane, said "Thanks but no thanks," too. Curiously, General Norstad also disdained the offer. Tony went back to the cockpit and landed without further incident on the cramped runway. In a zillion miles of air travel, Story is the finest pilot I've known.

The visiting brass was warmly welcomed by Gen. Walton Walker, soon to meet his death in a jeep accident, and by other field officers. Immediately after a skimpy lunch, which he hardly touched, Harriman asked to see the war. Jeeps rolled up, and our party was taken first to division headquarters for a briefing that seemed to some of the group quite thorough.

"Now let's go to regimental headquarters," Harriman said. And off we went, in the direction of the enemy. There we had a splendid briefing that satisfied almost everyone in the group. But not Harriman. "I'd like to see a battalion headquarters," he said. To reach it we had to ride through ghost villages bereft of even the dogs. At one point the driver of the lead jeep lost his way and for a half hour the string of jeeps followed him down a wrong road.

"I'll take that gun now," General Norstad said quietly. "I'd look pretty silly if we were jumped and I didn't have one."

At battalion headquarters I noticed a single file line of Koreans approaching the group.

"Ours or theirs?" I asked General Gay, commander of the First Cavalry. The lean old pro who had fought under George Patton in World War II shrugged. "We'll know when they reach us. If they shoot, they're theirs."

The sun was getting low, but Harriman had not seen enough.

"Shall we go to a company headquarters?" he asked. Nobody answered. So the string of jeeps moved to the shoreline of the parched and pebbly Naktong. Our artillery was hitting their tree-shrouded encampments across the river with phosphorescent shells. The only adjacent company headquarters lay a half mile down a narrow dirt road that ran along the Naktong's edge and was exposed to the enemy throughout its length. Our group huddled like a football team awaiting the next play.

"Just as well we're not fighting Germans," General Gay said to me. "They'd have hit us with a round of their eighty-eights while we stood here trying to make up our minds."

It was eventually decided that the jeeps would make a dash for it, one at a time, at one minute intervals. Harriman's jeep would go first, carrying Walker and Ridgway with him. The driver gave it the gas, and it pounded down the dirt road, kicking up a plume of dust. We watched it with keen interest.

"Golly, I hope I don't get Averell Harriman killed here today," Gay sighed. Then he turned to me and said, "We're next, let's go."

The company HQ was a dismal hole filled with soiled and exhausted men. The lieutenant's voice was flat and tired. He had been retreating since the war began and now, in what was called the Pusan Perimeter, there wasn't much more room in which to retreat. A sergeant put it more bluntly to Harriman.

"They'll overrun us tonight," he said.

It turned out to be an accurate appraisal, but when it happened we were en route back to Tokyo after a hair-raising take-off by Colonel Story. In order to get up sufficient speed on the inadequate stretch of tin strip, Tony did not put his flaps down until within a few yards of the deep mud at the end of the runway. We leaped into the air in a manner most unbecoming to a matronly C-54.

It was a depressing ride back to Toyko. Harriman became air sick while trying to eat a bite of the cold dinner. The generals were morose or lost in their own appraisals of what they had that day witnessed: proud Americans being pushed toward the sea by Asiatic rabble.

I couldn't wait for the meeting with MacArthur and the golden chance to shower him with all the questions and misgivings that welled in me. But wait I did, and until the scheduled moment, the precise moment. The lieutenant colonel in charge of me appeared in the lobby of the Imperial exactly when he phoned that he would. As the driver of the car with the VIP license plate prepared to drive into the roadway that led to the handsome U.S. Embassy Residence, where MacArthur reigned, the lieutenant colonel let loose a nervous command.

"Take a turn around the block!" he half shouted at the driver. He rechecked his watch and explained. "We're not due until two," he said, "and it's only two minutes till two now."

I must have looked bewildered as the car sped around the block, sending chickens, old women, and children scampering.

"It's hard to explain," the lieutenant colonel said. "But when you're invited to lunch with the General and he says two o'clock, he means two o'clock. It's as bad to be two minutes early as two minutes late."

I began to shake, wondering what calamity would befall all of us if the car had a blowout. But we made it to the doorway so punctiliously that just as it was opened by a Japanese servant the grandfather's clock in the foyer chimed twice.

The chimes seemed to turn everything on. Gracious, vivacious Mrs. MacArthur, standing by herself on the far side of the living room, daintily skipped toward me, extending her hand. Simultaneously, there was a gruffly masculine command of " 'ten-shun!" just outside. The general had arrived and was passing through his towering guard of honor and entering his palace.

Eyes alight with excitement, Mrs. MacArthur dropped my hand and rushed to the general as if they were being reunited after a twenty-five-year separation, instead of a four-hour cleavage. MacArthur lifted her off the floor with his left arm around her slender waist and kept her airborne while her feet made little fluttering motions several inches above rug level, while he acknowledged her introduction of me with his right hand.

It was a frustrating luncheon. He never gave me the slightest opening to blurt the first of all the questions I had in mind. Nor would

Mrs. MacArthur or Col. Sid Huff, one of his aides, who completed the group at the table. MacArthur preferred to talk sports. His range of knowledge was flabbergasting. Though he had not been in the United States for fifteen years, he rattled off facts and figures about then-current athletes as if he were a daily companion. He knew the roster and even the physical condition of the West Point football players Coach Red Blaik would have on hand for the 1950 season (indeed, Blaik had sought and gained his approval before installing the two-platoon system).

Luncheon courses came and went, generally ignored by MacArthur despite Jean's pretty-please pleas that he eat more. My senses reeled. To be so close to a big story and yet so far was intolerable. Now he had embarked on a dissertation—I had missed the beginning of the story—having to do with the troubles he had had with West Point authorities when he, exercising his rights as manager of the football team, had scheduled a game against Bucknell.

"They didn't want to accept Christy as an amateur," MacArthur said, his eyes reliving a crisis of his youth. "Small wonder, Christy was the most superlative punter in the sport."

"Christy who?" I asked numbly. The general dropped his dessert spoon in pained surprise.

"Christy Mathewson, who else?" he boomed.

It was akin to hearing George Washington praised for his surveying or Lincoln for his rail-splitting.

To my dismay, the general dabbed his lips with his napkin, rose from the table, and steered a slow but steady course toward the front door, I at his side. Mrs. MacArthur bade me good-bye. Huff shook hands and disappeared with her into another room. The Japanese servant had opened the door by now, and I could see my car sitting at the end of a double line of spit-and-polish honor guards, all looking eleven feet tall.

It was too much.

"For God's sake, General," I said. "We're getting our brains knocked out in Korea. What are you going to do about it?"

He paused for a bit, turned and put his hand on my shoulder.

"Considine," he said very quietly, "I'll have my headquarters in North Korea in a month's time. Good day."

I left, troubled and empty-handed. I had reached for a momentous story affecting millions and finished with a forgotten footnote to the sports career of Christy Mathewson of John McGraw's New York Giants. I decided that MacArthur was becoming senile.

One month later he effected the Inchon landing, an astounding achievement in a bay the enemy had left poorly defended because next to the Bay of Fundy it has the greatest variance of tides. In another month MacArthur's forces took Pyongyang, capital of North Korea, and still another month later his Seventh Division reached the Yalu, the Manchurian border.

Military historians and buffs for generations to come will weigh and debate the debacle that ensued after some 200,000 Chinese "volunteers" streamed out of Manchuria. They used roads, a slender rail line, marshaling yards and depots, airfields, and maintenance sites which MacArthur had been forbidden to bomb. MacArthur, who had scoffed at fears in Washington and London that the Chinese would intervene, now effected a Dunkirk. About 105,000 UN troops and 91,000 Korean civilians were evacuated from Hungnam by Christmas, 1950, and regrouped below the thirty-eighth parallel. The Chinese and reheartened North Korean forces spread down the peninsula like spilled ink, recaptured Pyongyang, then Seoul, capital of South Korea. MacArthur's multilingual forces stiffened and stopped the counterattack along a jagged line that averaged seventy miles into South Korea.

On February 1, 1951, the UN General Assembly, aloof from Russia's Security Council veto, named China the aggressor in Korea. Seven weeks later, as he prepared to go back on the offense against Chinese forces now numbered at 600,000, MacArthur threatened the Peking government with air and naval attack.

He neglected to clear his threat with President Truman or the United Nations.

On April 11, 1951, with Seoul recaptured and UN forces headed northward again, the MacArthurs had luncheon guests at the Embassy Residence in Tokyo, among them Sen. Warren Magnuson. In the course of the meal, Jean looked over the general's shoulder and saw Colonel Huff beckoning to her. He looked stricken. She excused herself quietly, without disturbing the story the general was telling. The story was still unwinding, in the familiar purple, pear-shaped tones, when she returned and took her seat. She waited until the punch line, gave the laughter time to subside, then touched him gently on the shoulder, leaned close to his ear, and whispered the news that he had been fired.

His guests directed their attention elsewhere, fiddled nervously with their food, unaware that the world knew what their host had just been told. They did not hear what Mrs. MacArthur had whispered. Their first knowledge came when MacArthur's face relaxed. He looked fondly at his wife and said, "Jeannie, we're going home at last."

Huff then entered, tears running down his cheeks. He handed the general a Signal Corps envelope marked "Action for MacArthur." It might just as well have been stamped "Inaction for MacArthur." It was the message from President Truman:

> I deeply regret that it becomes my duty as President and Commander-in-Chief of the United States military forces to replace you as Supreme Commander, Allied powers; commander-in-chief, United Nations command; commander-in-chief, Far East; commanding general, U.S. Army Far East.
>
> You will turn over your command, effective at once, to Lt. Gen. Matthew B. Ridgway. You are authorized to issue such orders as are necessary to complete desired travel to such place as you select.

The rest of his life was bathed in lights and shadows.

The emotions he stirred by his homecoming and superb speech to the Congress were followed by the puzzle of his quasi-political tour. It began with a speech to the shirt-sleeved Mississippi Legislature at Jackson. He could have sprayed them with a Gatling Gun and never hit a Republican. The flight from New York to Jackson, made in a DC-4 chartered by H. L. Hunt, the shy, horse-playing Texas multimillionaire whose politics were well to the right of Louis XIV, was pure shambles. Tremendous headwinds at proper altitude caused the pilot to drop as low as five hundred feet in order to arrive in Jackson at the scheduled hour. For four hours and more the plane bounced and bucked in heavy turbulence. MacArthur, who was never much for flying, became airsick. So did Mrs. MacArthur, son Arthur, all four aides the general had with him, Hunt, and all but three or four of the remaining forty-odd passengers. Young Arthur was the first to make it to the toilet in the rear of the aircraft. He was in there a long time.

Thinking I'd cheer the general up a bit, I scribbled a note and had it passed up to MacArthur, who was in the aisle seat, first row, starboard. It read:

> Dear General: I am very happy to observe that in keeping with his distinguished military background Arthur got to the can fustest with the mostest.

It didn't do much for him. He tilted his seat back as far as it would go, interrupting the retching of one of his aides behind him, and leaned against the headrest. Mrs. MacArthur, feeling better now, got him a cold towel and put it over the face of the sick man who only a short time before had won acclaim that ranged from a courtly bow from Emperor Hirohito to an ear-splitting welcome to New York by a crowd of five million.

At last the plane put down at Jackson and taxied to the area where the band was playing, the honor guard was braced, and the cornpone officialdom awaited. MacArthur muttered something from beneath his towel. Mrs. MacArthur translated for the others. The general wished to be the last to deplane and would all others please get off now.

I stayed behind to see how he'd make it. He straightened the seat and wiped his face with the towel. His face was the color of liverwurst, or, commensurate with the man himself, pâté de foi gras. He put on his tailored trenchcoat and pulled his belt sharply around his waist. Then he moistened the palm of his right hand, spread his thinning hair sidewise over his bald spot and reached up to the hat rack. His unique, slightly crumpled campaign hat, crowned with seasoned gold braid, had made the trip on a small white airline pillow. He snapped it on at the rakish angle which only he could achieve and headed down the aisle for the door. I was sitting next to the door.

"Now may I have the Air Medal?" I asked him.

His eyes glinted a smile.

"No," he said, "but you rate the Purple Heart."

He stepped through the door and paused on the top step while the band thumped and flags fluttered. He put his slightly shaking right hand to the peak of his cap, as only he saluted.

He was a poster, as challenging as James Montgomery Flagg's Uncle Sam, pointing and saying, "I Want *You.*"

MacArthur was pitilessly exploited by the Old Guard of the GOP at the 1952 Convention. He made a rasping and not well-informed

Keynote Address in which some political reporters detected a subtle command to the Convention to choose Sen. Robert A. Taft over Dwight D. Eisenhower. At one of the Address' several nadirs, the old soldier who looked a foot shorter in civilian clothes complained querulously about the rising cost of a dozen eggs. He never bought an egg in his life. His generations of quartermasters had bought billions of them.

The general's keen disappointment over Taft's loss on the first ballot was comparatively mild compared to his reaction to his meeting, in mid-December of 1952, with the aide who once sat outside his office —President-elect Eisenhower.

I may have forced that rare confrontation.

While the President-elect was making his promised tour of the Korean battlefront, hopeful of finding an honorable way out of the frozen and costly stalemate, MacArthur told a National Association of Manufacturers convention at the Waldorf Astoria that he had an easy and efficient plan for just that. In Washington President Truman told reporters that if MacArthur had a plan he should send it to the Pentagon because he was "still on the payroll." MacArthur ignored that.

En route from Guam to Pearl Harbor aboard the cruiser *Helena,* which Ike and his party had taken somewhat against his will, I said to one of his designated Cabinet officers that I thought it would be a good idea if Eisenhower and MacArthur got together and exchanged thoughts on the best ways and means of bringing the war to a close.

He said he thought so too.

I probably would never have filed a story about the possibility of their meeting if I had not still been steaming over one of those communications foul-ups which only the Navy can contrive. Minutes after boarding the *Helena* at Guam, an Eisenhower aide took me aside and confided that the cruiser would slow down as it passed Wake Island and bring aboard by helicopter several Cabinet officers-designate, including John Foster Dulles. I whipped below to my quarters, knocked out the story, marked it "Urgent," and gave it to the ship's communications officer.

It was a nice feeling to return to the deck of the still docked ship and see my competitors, Don Whitehead of the Associated Press and Merriman Smith of the United Press, chatting idly at the rail—blissfully unaware that I had clobbered them.

Three days later I received a garbled message from INS-New

York. It was not too difficult to decipher. Barry Faris wished to know how in hell I was scooped by AP and UP on the big story each had about Dulles and others to be flown to the deck of Ike's cruiser. I had beaten Don and Smitty by forty-eight hours with the story. My scoop had been sent from the ship to the main communications center on Guam, and someone there simply forgot to relay it.

I deliberated a long time over whether to try a comeback with as flimsy a story as "Ike-Mac Meeting Favored." The more I thought about it the more I was convinced that it was the only course left to the two men if they were remotely interested in (1) ending a war that had already cost the United States nearly 30,000 dead, and (2) repairing the GOP's yawning gap between the Taft Republicans and the Eisenhower Republicans.

So I wrote it as if they had every intention of meeting. Papers on the INS circuit played it big. Don and Smitty received "rockets," churlish messages from their home offices suggesting they had gone off fishing while INS worked and won the day. Automatically, it became their duty to confirm the story or, better still, knock it down. The Eisenhower people were not talking; nor were they speaking to me. Two rather terrible days passed, and then Jim Hagerty called the three of us in the wardroom and handed us mimeographed handouts. The message was short and, to me, sweet. It said that President-elect Eisenhower and General MacArthur would meet in New York, shortly after Eisenhower's arrival back in the United States, to discuss the war.

They did, at the town house of John Foster Dulles. They had not seen or spoken to each other since shortly after World War II when Ike passed through Tokyo as Army Chief of Staff. After the meeting, they went their separate ways—Eisenhower back to Columbia University's presidential home, MacArthur to his huge and memento-laden suite in the Waldorf Towers. Neither would speak to waiting reporters. Instead, aides issued a barren handout which said simply that the two had met and discussed possible measures to end the war. MacArthur was not invited to the Inauguration of his one-time aide.

In the months that followed, the aging general sought and found the anonymity which had escaped him for half a century. Public appearances were rare. As chairman of the board of Remington Rand, an ornamental rank bestowed upon him by tycoon Jim Rand, the general journeyed in his chauffeured car to Rowayton, Connecticut, each weekday to attend luncheon at Rockledge, the posh lair where Rand's executives would gather each noon. It was somehow fitting and proper that MacArthur's workdays' travel was unique. Headed north out of the city each day his car traveled a practically empty highway, on the other side of which the cars of inbound workers nuzzled bumper to bumper. Returning home to his redoubt in the Waldorf the general's car also had clear sailing while Westchester-bound traffic on the other side of the road inched toward eventide's martini.

Obtaining an interview with him became roughly akin to scaling Everest. All calls to the Waldorf were answered with a firm request that the caller contact the office at 90 Church Street which the Army had provided for him for life as a five-star general. Those who found a shortcut and got through the Waldorf switchboard struck an even more imposing buffer: Maj. Gen. Courtney Whitney. General Whitney's devotion to MacArthur knew no horizon. It ran over into utter possessiveness. MacArthur became his prisoner as well as his idol. He had full veto power, or at least exercised it, over MacArthur's appointments list. He was willing to accept the bitterest protests from old friends of MacArthur he turned away.

As a protector, Whitney passed his severest test in a pitched telephone confrontation with MacArthur's landlord, Conrad Hilton. Hilton told me the story.

"It's my duty to my stockholders to return them as much as I can on their investment," he complained. "Well, as you know, I gave General MacArthur a ridiculously low rate when I knocked down walls and made that apartment for him, when he came back from Japan.

"I could get five hundred dollars a day for that suite today. But I can't get MacArthur on the phone . . . and I own the phone! I can't get through to him to tell him I want the suite. All I get is that goddam Whitney."

Connie could have gone through Mrs. MacArthur but he was too much of a gentleman. Jean was the one unblocked path to her man, the only member of the retinue Whitney could not dominate. It was through her good offices that I was permitted to see the general on January 27, 1954, the day after his seventy-fourth birthday. When the first opportunity offered itself, I asked him if he would tell me what had happened when he had met with Eisenhower at Dulles' place. Not a word beyond the skimpy communiqué had ever been forthcoming.

"I'd be happy to," he said surprisingly. "There were just the three of us in the study. I opened the meeting. I spoke for an hour and fifteen minutes. At the end of that time Eisenhower jumped up from his chair and paced the floor. His face was flushed. 'It's magnificent!' he said. 'It's . . .' What I had urged was that he become the world's peacemaker, in short, put an end to the Cold War.

"But Dulles interrupted.

" 'General,' Dulles said, meaning Ike, 'You will recall that on the ship returning from Korea we agreed we would undertake nothing of this nature for one full year. We agreed that we'd devote the first year to consolidating our position.' He spoke for perhaps fifteen minutes.

"I watched Ike. I could see his enthusiasm dying bit by bit. When Dulles finished, we were back where I had started. I stood up and almost took Ike into my embrace. I put my hands on his shoulders and I said to him, 'Ike, this is the last time I'll ever address you that way. You are about to assume a position that is the loftiest in this world. I'm proud that a man who has been as close to me as you have been has achieved this tremendous prominence.

" 'Your victory in Europe, your honesty, your integrity, your radiant and wonderful personality have combined to make you unique. You are loved and respected by every nation in the world. Even in Soviet Russia you are deeply respected. You have the greatest opportunity for good since the birth of Jesus Christ. You have in your hands today the power to make the greatest impression made on civilization since the crucifixion of Christ. If, when you go in the White House, you act instantly and dynamically on this program you cannot fail to be remembered in history as a Messiah.

" 'But you don't have much time. Through our blunders in Asia we have given the enemy a hold—ever strengthening—on half of the population of the earth and 60 percent of its natural resources when properly exploited. We have presented to him on a platter the warm ports which will increase his strength. We are letting him come toward Africa. By rejecting our ancient tradition that victory is the only reason to enter into battle, we have encouraged him everywhere.

" 'There is still time to turn the tide!' I said to my old comrade in arms. 'That tide can be turned only by you, the most beloved and respected man on earth today. You and I have soldiered together for a long, long time. We've had our ups and downs. I've made my share of mistakes, and you've made yours. [MacArthur smiled and nodded at this point.] I have from the start felt toward you the affection of an older brother for his junior. Don't hesitate to take command! Yours is a Messianic mission. Believe me, your name will be called Blessed!

" 'But if you wait a year, I predict, on my life, that for every day of your first three months in the White House your popularity will diminish. For every day of the next three months your influence will wane. And for every day of the following six months you will lose standing geographically. At the end of a year you will no longer be what you are today—a transcendent figure. You will be, by that time, chiefly titular head of the Republican Party and busy with the mean little tasks of holding your Congressional majority in the next year's elections.' "

MacArthur sighed.

"I could not have seen more clearly if I had been staring into a crystal ball," he said and then added, not without emotion in his voice. "There were tears in Eisenhower's eyes and in mine as we looked silently at each other. Then the silence of the room was broken by the cool, calculating voice of the lawyer. Dulles had taken the floor again. His mood was a bit patronizing, if good-natured.

" 'Very interesting, very interesting,' Dulles said. And turning to Eisenhower he added, 'You know, General MacArthur could be just as wrong in this as he was when he backed Bob Taft against you.'

"I could feel Eisenhower freeze. After a bit, I took my hands off his shoulders and said, 'I guess that's all there is to say.' We prepared to leave. But before we parted I said to him, 'You won't have to worry about me, once you're in the White House. I want nothing. I don't propose to take any part in public debates or attempt to push legislation or politics. Good-bye. God bless you.' "

It was too much for one interview, but nevertheless I asked him if he would spell out the never-before detailed "easy and effective" way in which he would have ended the war in Korea (where the uneasy armistice had been signed the previous July 27, 1953).

His hands shook.

"Of all the campaigns of my life—twenty major ones to be exact—the one I felt most sure of was the one I was deprived of waging," he said with an underlay of bitterness. "I could have won the war in Korea in a maximum of ten days, with considerably fewer casualties than were suffered during the so-called truce-period, and it could have altered the course of history.

"The enemy's air would first have been taken out. I would have dropped between thirty and fifty tactical atomic bombs on his air bases and other depots in that neck of Manchuria from just across the Yalu from Antung [northwestern tip of Korea] to the neighborhood of Hunchun [just north of the northeastern tip of Korea near the border of the U.S.S.R.]

"Between thirty and fifty bombs would have more than done the job. Dropped under cover of darkness, they would have destroyed the enemy's air force on the ground, wiped out his maintenance and his airmen. His only means of rebuilding would have been over the single-tracked trans-Siberian railroad. It is an excellently run railroad, but it could never have handled the matériel needed to rebuild the enemy's air force in a sufficient space of time.

"With the destruction of the enemy's air power I would then have called upon five hundred thousand of Chiang Kai-shek's troops, sweetened by two U.S. Marine divisions. These would have been formed into two amphibious forces. One, totaling four fifths of my strength and led by one of the Marine divisions, would have landed at Antung and proceeded eastward along the road that parallels the Yalu. The other force, led by the other Marine division, would have landed simultaneously at Unggi or Najin, hit the same river road, and charged very quickly westward. Forces could have joined in two days, forming a wall of manpower and firepower across the northern border of Korea. I had nearly all the shipping I needed, in Japan, and could have procured the rest from Pearl Harbor. That was no problem.

"Now, the Eighth Army, spread along the thirty-eighth parallel, would then have put pressure on the enemy from the south. The joined amphibious forces would press down from the north. Nothing in the way of supplies or reinforcements could have moved across the Yalu. North Korea, holding not less than one million to one million and a half of the enemy, could not have sustained him. It had been picked clean.

"The enemy commander would have been starved out within ten days after the landings. I suggest now he would have sued for peace immediately after learning not only that his air had been taken out, but that we had spread across his supply routes.

"You may ask what would have prevented the enemy's reinforcements massing and crossing the Yalu in great strength. It was my plan as our amphibious forces moved south to spread behind us—from the

Sea of Japan to the Yellow Sea—a belt of radioactive cobalt. It could have been spread from wagons, carts, trucks, and planes. It is not an expensive material. It has an active life of between sixty and one hundred and twenty years. For at least sixty years there could have been no land invasion of Korea from the north. The enemy could not have marched across that radiated belt.

"Russia? It makes me laugh when I recall the fears of the Truman-Acheson-Marshall-Bradley-General Staff group that Russia would commit its armies to a war in China's behalf at the end of an endless one-track railroad to a peninsular battleground that led only to the sea. Russia could not have engaged us. She would not have fought for China. She is already unhappy and uncertain over the colossus she has encouraged.

"The truce we entered into—that stupendous blunder of refusing to win when we could have won—has given China the breathing time she needed. Primitive airfields in Manchuria have been transformed into modern installations with ten-thousand-foot runways. China had only one concentrated arms-producing area before Truman relieved me. Now she has built or is in the process of building four more. In fifty years, if she can develop her plane-building facilities, China will be one of the world's top military powers.

"It was in our power to destroy the Red Chinese army and Chinese military power. And probably for all time. My plan was a cinch. I was refused the right to carry it out by a group of isolationists and the politically-minded Joint Chiefs. You may be surprised to hear Truman, Acheson, Marshall, and the others called isolationists. They were the true isolationists! They made only one revision in what we came to know as isolationism in this country. They expanded their walls to include Western Europe. They never comprehended the world as a whole. They never understood the enormous forces of Asia.

"Under Eisenhower—a naive and honest man who does not want to offend anyone—we have maintained that isolationism. In time, we will scuttle our holdings and interests in the Pacific."

And so it came time to put his house in order. If there was any doubt about the wisdom of taking inventory, it was removed by a somber—but traditional—inquiry from the Army. It asked him what kind of a funeral he preferred. It asked the same question of the two other retired five-star generals, Eisenhower and Omar Bradley.

Bradley, youngest of the three at seventy, said he preferred something simple. Eisenhower's answer was not revealed. MacArthur replied that he wanted a state funeral.

However grim the inquiry, which came to MacArthur after a grueling prostate operation, it is necessary. A state funeral involves planning in advance. The accouterments of ceremonial burials are not easily whistled up, even in Washington—which is itself a kind of national memorial ground, what with its monuments, sarcophagi, and statuary recalling Washington, Jefferson, Lincoln, Lee, the Unknown Soldiers, and John F. Kennedy.

The Army's purpose in questioning its rarest old soldiers was also to learn where in Arlington National Cemetery they wished to lie. MacArthur surprised the Army by stating that after his state funeral he had completed plans to be buried in Norfolk, Virginia. His mother was born there, and the city had discreetly offered him one of its architectural antiquities as his final resting place.

MacArthur chose to lie in state first in New York, then Washington under the Capitol Rotunda. He listed the type and number of military units he would prefer and accepted suggestions as to the routes of the funeral parade. The television networks were kept informed, so as to draw up plans for camera positions, lighting, direction, production.

That much out of the way, MacArthur began dedicating much of his days and nights to writing what he called his reminiscences rather than autobiography. He kept the early portion of this labor so secret than not even his almost constant shadow, General Whitney, knew about it.

"What are you doing, General?" Whitney asked him one day as MacArthur handwrote page after page on a yellow foolscap pad, discarding one dulled pencil point for a sharp one.

"After he told me, I had a new job," Whitney said later. "My job was to keep his pencils sharpened. It kept me busy, believe me."

When he had completed nine hundred pages of manuscript (some of it written on both sides), he handed the mound to Whitney and told him to find a purchaser. He said he thought of it as his legacy to Jean and Arthur.

Whitney called Henry Luce. It is problematical whether Whitney knew that in 1945 Bill Hearst, then a war correspondent, flew to Tokyo with a certified check for $500,000, signed by W. R. Hearst, Sr., to offer it to MacArthur for his memoirs. To Hearst's astonishment, MacArthur said he had no intention of ever writing a book about his life and his wars. As the years rolled on, and an assortment of approved and frowned-upon biographies appeared, it seemed he was carrying out his intention not to tell his own story.

Then this deluge. Whitney delivered it in a Japanese lacquer chest which exactly fit the manuscript. After the contracts were signed—amounting to about one million dollars divided between Time, Inc. and McGraw-Hill—Luce held a party for MacArthur in the Time-Life Building and professed to reporters that when Whitney first dumped the manuscript on his desk he nearly fainted, because it was the only copy in existence.

MacArthur was photographed holding the boxed pads, surrounded by Time, Inc. brass.

"How about letting me have a pad or two of it for the night?" I asked him. Time-Lifemen blanched, but recovered when MacArthur shook his head and smiled.

"Can't do that, I guess," he said. "But I'd like you to know one thing: not one word of this was written by a ghost."

Memories of West Point grew clearer and dearer to him near the end. One day he rang for Whitney and suggested they take a ride up to the Point, just to look around. It turned out to be something short of the Prodigal's Return. He was browsing through one of its hallowed halls, explaining things to Whitney—who was also in mufti—when a young duty officer stopped him.

"Sorry," the stiff young man said, "this is a restricted area. No visitors are permitted."

MacArthur's reply could have set a new A.A.U. record for understatement.

"I used to go to school here," he said quietly. "My name's MacArthur."

But that was not what it was like the lovely May day in 1962 when he was presented with the highest honor West Point bestows, the Sylvanus Thayer Award. He was eighty-two.

The military is traditionally unimaginative, blunt, hard, concise. But when it comes around to saying farewell to one of its beloved, it can do things that brings tears and make the tenderest of Broadway's plays seem like a peep show.

MacArthur seemed submerged in his funereal black suit and unfashionably wide-brimmed black homburg when he stepped to the side of the sun-washed parade ground. The Cadet Corps in all its starchy gray glory was lined up on the far ground. A jeep with a handrail behind the driver's seat pulled up and MacArthur climbed aboard, along with Academy Superintendent Maj. Gen. William C. Westmoreland, and they stood in the rear of the jeep, holding onto the rail, as it pulled across the field for the review.

Softly, so movingly, the band began playing the haunting songs he knew when he was the handsomest knight in all the AEF . . . "Tipperary" . . . "There's A Long, Long Trail Awinding" . . . "K-K-K-Katie" . . . "My Buddy."

It was hard to bear.

So was the valedictory later in the V-shaped dining hall which he had built as Superintendent.

"Duty-Honor-Country. Those three hallowed words reverently dictate what you ought to be, what you can be, what you will be," he said to the Corps. "They are your rallying points: to build courage when courage seems to fail; to regain faith when there seems to be little cause for faith; to create hope when hope becomes forlorn. Unhappily, I possess neither that eloquence of diction, that poetry of imagination, nor that brilliance of metaphor to tell you all that they mean."

For the next forty-five minutes he disproved that assertion in a way that cast the most melancholy spell over the assemblage. There were tears in the eyes of big strapping Cadets who wouldn't have shed one before a firing squad as MacArthur concluded:

"You are the leaven which binds together the entire fabric of our national system of defense. From your ranks come the great captains who hold the nation's destiny in their hands the moment the war tocsin sounds. The Long Gray Line has never failed us. Were you to do so, a million ghosts in olive drab, in brown khaki, in blue and gray, would rise from their white crosses thundering those magic words: Duty—Honor—Country.

"This does not mean that you are warmongers. On the contrary, the soldier, above all other people, prays for peace, for he must suffer and bear the deepest wounds and scars of war. But always in our ears ring the ominous words of Plato, the wisest of all philosophers, 'Only the dead have seen the end of war.' "

He took a step away from the microphone and rested a hand on the side of the lectern. Even those closest to him had difficulty hearing his finish, delivered without recourse to his notes:

"The shadows are lengthening for me. The twilight is here. My days of old have vanished, tone and tint; they have gone glimmering through the dream of things that were. Their memory is one of wondrous beauty, watered by tears, and coaxed and caressed by the smiles of yesterday. I listen vainly for the witching melody of faint bugles blowing reveille, of far drums beating the long roll. In my dreams I hear again the crash of guns, the rattle of musketry, the strange, mournful mutter of the battlefield.

"But in the evening of my memory, always I come back to West Point. Always there echoes and re-echoes: Duty—Honor—Country.

"Today marks my final roll call with you, but I want you to know that when I cross the river my last conscious thoughts will be of The Corps, and The Corps, and The Corps . . . I bid you farewell."

Dwight D. Eisenhower considered the Presidency a kind of sixth star to wear. He accepted it as a natural and inevitable promotion, as he had accepted all previous jumps in rank and extensions of duties. It was not something he campaigned for, or even secretly yearned for. It was simply a case of his number coming up at the right time and place. He had turned it down, earlier, when President Truman made his extraordinary offer to step aside in 1948 and present him with the Democratic nomination. The timing, the rhythm, wasn't right or perhaps seniority—sacredest of sacreds—was subtly involved. So he grinned and said no—to the utter consternation of the consummate politician who made the offer.

He was a bit more approachable four years later, but only a bit. Various emissaries to his court at SHAPE, notably Sen. Henry Cabot Lodge, perennial hopeful Harold Stassen, and old friend and President-fancier George E. Allen, returned to the United States without the vestige of his promissory note. All they seemed sure of was that if he ran, which was still questionable in view of his known antagonism toward politicking military men—MacArthur, let's say—he'd run as a Republican. That was considered a substantial straw. Like most career officers of his generation, Ike had never cast a vote in a national election.

But the wave continued to build, and it crashed loudly one night at Madison Square Garden, early in '52.

In subsequent months and years, many rose to take a bow for overcoming the inertia of Dwight David Eisenhower (who, incidentally, was originally named David Dwight Eisenhower). The woods were filled with kingmakers. But an authentic one was never mentioned, nor did she want to be. She was Jacqueline Cochran, intrepid wife of financier Floyd Odlum.

John Hay Whitney, destined to become Eisenhower's Ambassador to the Court of St. James's, and a foremost contributor to his campaign in word and deed, was chairman of the ear-splitting "We Like Ike" rally at the Garden. He asked Jacqueline to co-chair. She declined but offered to serve its best interests. She flew her plane to various places in Texas and Oklahoma and stimulated various groups to move en masse on New York for the big occasion at the Garden. Several chartered trains, even brought along their own horses.

It was a night to remember, even for the Garden. The place was jammed beyond the fire department limits and shook with "We Want Ike" chants led by radio-TV personality and former Eighth Air Force colonel Tex McCrary. There were about fifteen thousand outside the place, including a fine I'm-for-Ike worker who nearly got clubbed by a cop, Mrs. Jimmy Doolittle.

Jacqueline stayed with the film taken of the event while it was developed. Then, still sleepless, she carried the can to Idlewild, caught a TWA plane to Paris, and headed for Eisenhower's headquarters in the Astoria Hotel. She was told by a functionary in the outer office that the general would give her thirty minutes.

Eisenhower talked for twenty minutes before he gave her an opening. She has quick reflexes.

"General, you've been talking exactly twenty minutes and you haven't heard a word of my message," she snapped. "I think it's only fair that you let me talk the rest of the allotted time."

Eisenhower burst out laughing, and gave her the floor.

She talked (she recalled later) for eight minutes and thirty seconds. It was a report on the enthusiasm that had exploded at the rally. She turned over the can of film to him and, her work done, prepared to leave. But Eisenhower, the reluctant dragon, held her with a gesture. He punched a button and instructed an officer to take care of the luncheon date he had scheduled with an oil man. The general and the lady aviator lunched.

At five o'clock that afternoon the uncut film was shown to Eisenhower, Gen. Alfred Gruenther, his chief of staff, and other intimates. As it ended, and before the lights in the room were turned on, Eisenhower and his party got up and left the room. Jacqueline Cochran found herself the only patron for a time. When Ike and his group came back she launched into another pitch. Was not the film a symbol of his country's call? Could he any longer avoid the inevitable?

Suddenly, tears came into Eisenhower's eyes. "I wish my mother could've seen this," he said.

Then he dictated the letter—to be carried back to New York by Jacqueline, and to be seen by only a few. The letter said Yes.

Miss Cochran raised some of the basic rent money for the New Hampshire primary, where Eisenhower's victory illuminated "the clear-cut call." Gov. Sherman Adams called her just before the primary and told her he needed $25,000.

"When?" she asked.

"Yesterday," Adams said.

"You've got five from me and five from Floyd right now," she said, "and I'll get you the rest." She called John Hertz in Chicago. Hertz promised $10,000 but asked that his name not be mentioned. Jacqueline was indignant, though she was fonder of the Hertzes than of any other persons she knew.

"Then keep your ten thousand," she said over the phone. "I'm looking for people who are willing to stand up and be counted, people who believe in something and have the courage to let everybody know it." Hertz came through swiftly. Another $5,000 was found somewhere else—and Ike was on his way.

The preliminary scratchings of the historians have not been overly kind in their assessment of Dwight Eisenhower, the President. The decades may temper their judgment, swing them more to Herbert Hoover's conviction: "Ike is the most intellectually honest man we've ever had in the White House."

There was a human side to him that wasn't always too evident. In Korea in December, 1952, on his trip to "do something about the war in Korea" and in response to his declaration that if elected he would go to Korea, he visited, near the end of that trip, the area along the front where his son, Maj. John Eisenhower, was serving, I believe, as executive officer of a front-line group. There was an obvious warmth between the two, though John to outsiders was as cool and correct as the weather itself, and the weather was abominably cold.

As we were prepared to leave that section, having had lunch with the selected troops, and witnessed an embarrassingly planned napalm attack by Navy fighters on Chinese and North Korean positions scarcely two or three miles away from where we camped in the snow, the President-elect took his son John aside. None of us in the party could hear what transpired between them, but I'll never forget the sight. Eisenhower stood quite close to his son, facing him, and I could see his words, inaudible to me. I could see them because they were condensed into steam by the extreme cold. They came in short decisive puffs, faintly reminiscent of the Camel cigarette sign on Broadway, and broke against the son's receptive face. Occasionally John would say something and his smaller and less intense puff of breath would come back at his father. At the end of the ectoplasmic dialogue, the President-elected tapped his son on the arm, turned, and went back to his little plane.

Many days later we arrived at Kaneohe Marine Base in Hawaii on the island of Oahu. We were there several days, during which time we saw little or nothing of General Eisenhower. Merriman Smith, Don Whitehead, and I had filed a great deal of copy from the Cruiser *Helena* enroute from Guam to Pearl Harbor, much of it having to do with a major staff meeting that Eisenhower would hold once he reached Hawaii with Chief-of-Staff General Omar Bradley and other Pentagon figures. We were surprised, however, to find that Eisenhower's chief interest after arriving in Hawaii was golf. Scarcely half an hour after arrival at his cottage at Kaneohe, he emerged, not to confer with Bradley and the others, but in golfing gear. He moved quickly and decisively to the first tee where the other members of his foursome awaited him. They apparently had been alerted hours in advance because they were dressed ready to go. One was a Marine colonel who was champion of the base. I asked him, while waiting for Eisenhower to appear, what sort of game he shot. The colonel looked steadily at me and without cracking a smile said, "One shot worse than the General's game." I daresay he's a much higher ranking Marine officer today.

General Bradley made himself available on the first tee but, like the rest of us, was discouraged from following Eisenhower around the nine-hole course. So Bradley, some of the handful of reporters, and our photographer wandered in time to the ninth green to await the conclusion of the round. Bradley was very eager to get back to Washington. Indeed, his plane, he told us, was gassed and ready to leave. But as Eisenhower putted out, a deep frown furrowing his brow, it became apparent that the long-awaited conference was not going to take place then and there. The President-elect walked off the green immersed in a deep study and strolled within ten feet of where his five-star colleague and old friend, Bradley, stood.

"That old eight-iron sure let me down," Ike muttered. He continued walking to the practice tee, followed by his caddy, scattered a handful of golf balls about the tee, and proceeded to practice his eight-iron shots. Bradley left for Washington.

The next morning Merriman Smith decided to accompany John Foster Dulles on a tour of the islands by light plane. When Smitty leaves a story, that story can be diagnosed as dead, or nearly as close to death as news can become. Whitehead and I remained behind in our barracks not far from Eisenhower's cottage. We had breakfast together and in the course of discussing how remote we were from Eisenhower, although we had accompanied him thousands of miles and were sitting there within fifty yards of the man, I said to Don, "This is ridiculous. Let's go over and talk to him."

Don did not appear to think much of the idea, but being an alert reporter he thought less of letting me go alone. There was always an outside chance that I would get in, and if INS got in, AP would look pretty stupid not being there. A Marine guard blocked our way before we could put foot on the concrete pathway leading up to the step of the cottage. We explained that we had accompanied the President-elect from the time he left New York, but that of course meant nothing to the guard. He had his orders not to admit anyone.

I said to him, "At least send this message in to General Eisenhower. Tell him that Bob Considine is outside with Don Whitehead and that I would like to have a cup of coffee."

With great misgivings the guard turned, went to the door, and delivered the message. Out came an Army lieutenant who was serving as Eisenhower's secretary on the trip. If anything, he was as hostile as the Marine guard. But I insisted, more sternly than I can usually insist, that the message be delivered. I probably said that if it were not, I would see that the General heard about this lieutenant's refusal to do so. Well, that must have conjured up in his tormented mind the whole rigmarole of promotion and reprimand, because he went inside and after about ten minutes emerged again in the bright sunlight and said, "The General will see you with the understanding that it is only for coffee and that no questions will be asked."

That was better than nothing, barely better once we tasted the coffee. Ike seemed in a relaxed mood despite the restrictions that we were working under. He talked in general terms about the trip and then, unable to resist a question that I had wanted to ask him since I had seen him that day at the front with his son, I said to him, "General, it's none of my business, but what were you telling Major John that day we went up to his front?"

Eisenhower seemed almost pleased that someone had finally asked him.

"I'll tell you what I said to John," he said. "I said to John, 'John, if you get killed in this war, it'll be a terrible thing for your mother and for me, but that's a soldier's life. We take that risk when we put on the uniform. Somehow your mother and I could live through a thing like that. But for Godsake don't get captured. Don't let them capture you. If you should be captured and they held you over my head, I would not be able to serve as President of the United States!"

The silence that followed was broken by the hurried arrival of Jim Hagerty, somewhat the worse for wear from the night before, as was I. We had been at the same place together. He had been tipped off that we had gained admission to the sacrosanct confines of the cottage, probably by the nervous young lieutenant. Jim was red-eyed and unshaved, indicating he had hurriedly thrown on his clothes to perform his customary duty of buffer between Eisenhower and the press, which was his job, of course. Jim sat in on the rest of the small talk, and the longer it went, the smaller it got.

I don't recall what was said after Eisenhower's extraordinarily blunt revelation of what he had told his son. My mind was filled with an earlier scene, one that suddenly dovetailed with the present and made grim sense. I recalled a smoky autumn night at the home of a mutual friend, Howard Young, at Ridgefield, Connecticut. Eisenhower, then President of Columbia University, was a weekend guest and Mr. Young was kind enough to invite Frank Farrell of the New York *World-Telegram* and me to share the weekend with him.

Late on Saturday night of that weekend as we sat around over a drink of Scotch, I asked the General if he had ever known of any attempt to take him as a prisoner of war during World War II. He said with some show of heat that there was never any chance that he could ever be taken prisoner. But I reminded him that the Germans had been very adept at plucking high-ranking officers and even Mussolini out from under protective or hostile surroundings. They had captured several British generals, I recalled, in the desert warfare and had snatched Il Duce off what amounted to a mountainous crag as Italy went down the drain. *Reader's Digest* had carried a story that the Germans had made an elaborate plot to ambush and seize Eisenhower after D-Day and had failed chiefly because Eisenhower's driver had taken a wrong turn on a routine trip near the front.

Eisenhower repeated, "No, there was never any chance that I could be captured. It's completely out of the question."

And I further insisted, "But why?"

The future President of the United States looked at me steadily and then said very quietly, "I always had a gun."

What he had been telling his son, obviously, there in the snow in Korea, was to use his gun on himself rather than be captured.

An almost childish spark of jealousy sputtered back and forth between Eisenhower and MacArthur. They made no particular effort to conceal it. It must have baffled and even annoyed MacArthur to watch Eisenhower's swift rise from the rank of lieutenant colonel to Supreme Commander of Allied Forces in Europe.

Their differences began in the Philippines, or perhaps earlier. During and after the time when the Bonus Marchers were run out of Washington, the genial Maj. Eisenhower proved to be an ideal buffer between four-starred Douglas MacArthur and a sometimes critical press. But he resented other aspects of the job, as he sat outside MacArthur's splendid office. Years later, in the White House, he told an old friend, Maj. Gen. Melvin Maas (USMC, retired), a former Congressman from Minnesota:

"Mel, now you stop worrying about taking up too much of my time. I enjoy seeing you. You know, when I had a desk outside the office of the old general [MacArthur] quite a few of you Congressmen treated me like I was his batman. They'd toss me their coats and hats on the way in to see him and expect me to hang them up.

"I never forgot them. And I'll never forget how you used to hang your own hat and coat up, and say a friendly word."

Eisenhower's transfer from Washington to the Philippines was made at the request of MacArthur after he left his post as Chief of Staff and became military adviser to the Commonwealth in 1935. There is evidence that MacArthur received and accepted credit for much that Eisenhower did to beef up the lackluster Filipino military. Eisenhower did not approve when MacArthur took the baton and rank of field marshal of the Commonwealth's military forces in 1936. When Germany and the Soviet Union invaded Poland in 1939, Eisenhower requested transfer back to the United States.

"People think we're not friendly," Eisenhower volunteered in an interview he granted me in the summer of 1951 at Supreme Headquarters at NATO. "Why, when Mamie and I left the Philippines in 1939 he and Mrs. MacArthur came down to the ship to see us off."

On the occasion of the 1951 interview, Eisenhower was curious about details of the speaking- and personal-appearance tour MacArthur had engaged in during the weeks that followed his emotional pledge to the Congress and the nation to "fade away."

"I understand you've been on the road with the old general," Ike said, settling in his office chair. "What sort of reception did he get?"

I said he had received great welcomes everywhere.

"That's odd," Ike said. "I understood he had a bad turnout in Houston."

"No, sir. The police estimated about a million showed up for that one."

Ike frowned slightly. "They told me he had a bad turnout," he said. The room was silent, save for the sound of my swallowing. I was stoking a question that every reporter in the business wanted to ask him. Ike had successfully avoided involvement in the still raging debate over MacArthur's dismissal by President Truman and the conduct of the war in Korea. The President (who had appointed Eisenhower to head up NATO's military arm, and who had once virtually offered him the Presidency in 1948) stood firmly opposed to any escalation of the Korean War. He was particularly determined—as were most other UN allies—that the war did not spread beyond the Yalu.

"General," I asked, "what would you have done if you had been in the old general's shoes when the Red Chinese came over the mountain?"

He sat up quickly in his chair and his eyes turned a brittle blue.

"I'll tell you what I would have done," he said. "I would have put every plane I had in the air and bombed the hell out of their supply depots in Manchuria. What's more, I would not have asked Washington's permission, nor the UN's permission. And if either raised hell I would have simply told them that I had done what was necessary to save the lives of thousands of men from a dozen allied nations."

I changed the subject immediately and let his words sink deeply into my memory while we talked of lighter things—including a spur on Joe DiMaggio's heel. Twenty minutes later, we walked toward the door, the interview completed. I pondered over whether to speed to INS headquarters in Rue Caumartin by cab or phone my glorious scoop from the nearest booth. I had a story that would hit every front page in the world.

"Come back and see us soon," Ike said at the doorway. Then he reached out his hand, smiled his million-dollar smile, and said, "Of course, Bob, everything I've said today is in the room."

A scoop gives off a muted scream when it dies.

Ike made a show resisting the appeals of those who wanted him to run for the GOP nomination until the following May. Then the combined exhortations of Lucius Clay, George Allen, Henry Cabot Lodge, Harold Stassen, Sherman Adams, Tom Dewey, Herbert Brownell, and the others became too flattering to resist. He returned to America and early in June flew to his boyhood town of Abilene, Kansas, to make the formal announcement. It was an informal formal announcement, as things turned out. Wind and rain and bad acoustics ruined his painfully worded address, which he read as if for the first time. The next day at his first press conference—held in a movie house—he met some of the people he would have to put up with for most of the next decade.

For a good many years the general had found himself surrounded by a servile press. It wished to ask him nothing much more difficult to answer than, "How are you feeling, sir?" and "How are the Allies working together, sir?" But now he was in politics. The questions were no longer obsequious. Right off the bat, there in the little movie theater, some fellow he had never seen before threw him a curve. "Give us your feeling about socialized medicine," the fellow asked from the floor. As an Army man since 1911, when he entered West Point (after the bitter disappointment of being turned down by Annapolis) Ike had been the beneficiary of the service's type of socialized medicine. He paused a moment and delivered the first of what turned out to be a treasury of circumlocutionary answers.

"I don't like the sound of socialized medicine," Ike said. "Socialism leads down the path to anarchism. Anarchism leads down the path to communism." Pencils flew across notebook pages. But Ike had not finished. He continued, "On the other hand, every man, woman, and child in this country who needs it should have free medical care."

Pencils stopped flitting.

Then there was the distressing business about Edward R. Murrow. Murrow had made an almost preposterous request of James C. Hagerty, the excellent public relations man who had joined the Eisenhower camp as a kind of campaign gift from Tom Dewey. Murrow wanted to bring CBS's television cameras into the movie house and televise the press conference live.

Impossible, Jim ruled. Ike felt the same way. And so did a majority of the assembled "written word" reporters, a number of whom have long since left their newspapers and wire service jobs for greater fame and fortune in TV.

The protests failed to impress Murrow. Just after the press conference began, he personally led his crew and their cameras into the theater and turned on the tubes. The other networks followed suit. There were distressed mutterings from the candidate and from Hagerty. But Murrow knew he was on safe ground. It was hardly likely that a man who had just announced that he wanted to be President of the United States would then (on camera) deny to television what he was readily giving to the assembled paper and pencil reporters.

After becoming President, Eisenhower permitted his off-the-cuff news conferences to be filmed and selected excerpts used on TV later the same day. Live telecasts of these sometimes informative, ofttimes exasperating, affairs did not begin until John Fitzgerald Kennedy took over.

Ike's introduction to the rough and tumble political arena did not jar his basic simplicity or homely speech. Visiting the plain little house where he and his brothers grew up under the eye and counsel of his pietistic River Brethren parents, Ike looked around and said, nostalgia in his voice, "By golly, I didn't know until years later that we were poor."

He maintained that uncomplicated wonderment throughout his White House tenure. After one of the last of his long string of stag dinners, the President led his guests into the Red Room for the traditional demitasse, after-dinner drink, and talk. What turned out to be the last question we asked was that of Pat Weaver, then with NBC.

"Sir, you've had more in life than any other man who comes to mind," Weaver said. "Fine parents, happy boyhood, West Point, marriage to a wonderful girl, fine son, Supreme Commander of the greatest armed force in history, liberator of Western Europe, president of Columbia University, leader of a defense force reaching from Norway to Turkey, and President of the United States. Is there anything else you'd like to be?"

Ike gazed thoughtfully into his Chivas Regal.

"Yes," he said, looking up. "I'd like to be my grandson David."

Even if the Presidency should come eventually to Richard Milhous Nixon it is doubtful if that supreme achievement would bring him completely out from the state of shock into which he was plunged by the events of 1960. He lost to John Fitzgerald Kennedy by 118,550 votes out of 68,335,642 cast. The 34,108,546 votes he attracted, losing, was 172,294 more than Eisenhower drew, winning, in 1952. As long as he lives, Nixon and many of his followers will contend he was gypped by a fast count in Illinois's Cook County (Kennedy 1,378,343, Nixon 1,059,607) and elsewhere in tightly knit Democrat-bossed strongholds.

Commonly accepted reasons for the defeat were Nixon's agreement in the first place to debate J.F.K. on television, his poor showing and poorer appearance in the first of those confrontations, and "slanted" newswriting and reporting.

Any person assigned to cover that unique and arresting period in American politics knows that other reasons contributed heavily to Nixon's loss. His chosen running mate, Henry Cabot Lodge, was a colossal deadweight who confined himself to one speech a day during the campaign and seldom missed his long afternoon nap. Lyndon Johnson, working chiefly through old and powerful cronies in the Senate (who knew he would return to the Senate to help or haunt them if the Democratic ticket lost) was of enormous help to the Kennedy cause in those parts of the South steeped in misgivings about the candidate's Catholic background.

A clear majority of U.S. publishers supported Nixon. Their editorial pages reflected their choice. This, of course, did not inhibit contributing columnists. A notable example was the New York *Herald Tribune.* Its publisher, John Hay Whitney, President Eisenhower's Ambassador to the Court of St. James's and as determined a patron of the Republican Party in New York as, say, Tom Yawkey was of American League baseball in Boston, regularly featured the columns of Walter Lippmann and Joseph Alsop, who went all out for Kennedy.

The straight reporting on the campaign—the who, when, where, what, why—was down the middle, as it should be and almost always is. Editors alternated newsmen assigned to the candidates, a guard against either nominee's influencing or alienating. I made whistle-stop swings with both men. Traveling with Kennedy was more pleasant than with Nixon, and more rewarding from a news sense. Between stops, Kennedy would stroll down the aisle of the plane to pass the time of day or comment on what he considered the state of the union. Nixon, particularly near the crucial end of the campaign, retreated into his shell—his green-curtained enclosure in the forward section of his plane—leaving his man Herb Klein and his dear, brave Pat, smiling with everything except her eyes, to fend for him.

There were extenuating circumstances beyond these: Nixon's campaign was filled with the expected, the most likely to happen. There seemed to be some unwritten code that ruled laughter out of trips with him. Kennedy's voyages were marked by the antic, the unexpected: a kid in West Virginia who had obtained his autograph and now was turning the slip of paper this way and that in a bewildered effort to decipher his appalling handwriting; a feverish Negro in a car equipped with an ear-splitting loudspeaker system driving recklessly in the candidate's parade while he shouted into his mobile microphone, "Jack Kennedy is the greatest man ever walked the streets of Jersey City since Jesus Christ."

Nixon settled into a lucrative law practice after his defeat and appeared to have resigned himself, as Tom Dewey had before him, to the bitter realization he would never sleep in Lincoln's bed. On the morning after his stunning defeat by President Truman, Dewey announced he would never again run for public office. He kept his word. Nixon made no such promise. He yielded to pressures, some of them applied by General Eisenhower, to run for governor of California against Pat Brown, the incumbent. Most signs indicated that it was a good move. It would give him a platform from which he might launch a subsequent and perhaps even successful Presidential drive. He had beaten Kennedy in California (3,259,722 to 3,224,099) in face of a 3 to 2 Democratic registration in that politically eccentric state. But he lost badly to Brown, who had only a pale fraction of Kennedy's appeal. The day following that debacle Nixon made an embarrassing and poignant spectacle of himself at a news conference he attended against the best available advice. He didn't seem himself.

I had experienced a preview of that aberration. On July 4, 1962, I took my daughter Deborah to Rebild Park near Aalborg, Denmark, to make a film short and write a piece about that remarkable annual salute to the United States. It was the fiftieth anniversary of what long has been the best-attended Independence Day celebration anywhere in the world, including America. Eisenhower had been the scheduled speaker, but he canceled his laid-on trip to Scandinavia that summer after the Swedish press criticized him for a reference he had made about Sweden's suicide rate. He asked Nixon to substitute. Several Danish newspapers and politicians carped on the ground that Nixon was prepared to run for governor of California and the occasion traditionally called for a fully nonpartisan American speaker.

But all was serene as the crowd of about fifty thousand gathered on the benches and grassy slopes of the natural amphitheater. Luncheon was served to several hundred guests of honor under a big, cool tent. I was leading Deborah to a table reserved for reporters when Nixon spotted us and called us over to the table where he sat with the top officials of the event. I demurred but he insisted most generously. We sat down, and for the next few courses of the pleasant smorgasbord he could not have been a kinder host. We agreed that this entire affair gave a fellow patriotic goose bumps.

"And how about that amazing coincidence about the man who started this whole thing—what's-his-name Henius?" I asked, making minuscule talk.

Dick seemed to stiffen a bit.

"What about him?" he asked.

I pointed to a package of publicity handouts we had all been given. "He came back here from Wisconsin or some place on the thirty-fifth anniversary—fifteen years ago—and was killed right here on the grounds," I said. "Car hit him. Eerie, isn't it?"

Nixon turned to the chairman of the festival seated next to him.

"That's a typical American newspaperman for you," he said. "Notice that? He knows something about this occasion that I don't, and I'm the speaker." I thought for a moment he was joking and then realized with a start that he was terribly serious. "They always know more about everything than *you* do. And if they don't know, they make it up."

He turned back, looked at me blankly for a second or two, and then the anger dropped from him like a cloak. He grinned engagingly.

"Present company excepted, of course," he said, and the luncheon resumed.

He made a good hands-across-the-sea speech which was roundly applauded by King Frederik IX, Queen Ingrid, and their attentive subjects. I saw Nixon later at the hotel in Aalborg. All of us had been shaken by an even more unnerving coincidence than the one of fifteen years before which had so annoyed him when I brought it up. Nixon had been followed to the speaker's platform by Henry Henius, gray-haired son of the founder of the celebration. He had flown from Los Angeles for the occasion. He spoke warmly of his father's dreams for staunch U.S.-Danish relations, got a nice hand from the crowd, returned to his seat next to Nixon, sat down, pitched forward, and died of a heart attack.

It was a long time after the 1960 election before I had an opportunity to talk shop with Nixon. We met in his office in the Wall Street district. He sent out for sandwiches and coffee rather than take time out for a more formal meal, because he was quite busy. He was due to fly to San Francisco soon after for the Convention that nominated Barry Goldwater on the first ballot. Four years earlier, every mention of Nixon's name caused ovations through the Republican Party. Now, on this hot day in 1964, he had only two delegates who had announced they would vote for him—and even they dissolved in the strong solvent of Goldwater's gospel.

I asked him how he accounted for the Arizonan's enormous appeal.

"Barry makes a good appearance," Nixon said. "I like him very much, personally. He's intelligent, talks well, and he believes what he says. But the thing that draws people to him most is that just about everybody who is against something, who dislikes somebody or some group, or hates this or that, feels he has a friend in Barry. People like that feel he's on their side."

It seemed as good a time as any to ask him how he now assessed the 1960 election.

"What would you say was the one thing that beat you, the one incident or bad break that made the difference?"

He did not hesitate.

"When President Eisenhower was asked at one of his last news conferences at the White House to name a case or two where I had contributed to the shaping of his Administration's policy he said, in effect, 'Give me a week to think about that,' " Nixon answered, as if he had reflected on it many times. "He could have said something like, 'Well, we sent that fellow on a lot of trips around the world in the past eight years and he always came back with reports on what he had seen and people he had talked to. Naturally, some of his thinking filtered down into our policies.' But he didn't say that. He just said 'Give me a week to think about that. . . .' That beat me, more than the debates or anything else."

Nixon stood up, strode part of the way across his office, turned to me and added something.

"He's a great American," he said with ringing warmth.

Joseph P. Kennedy, Sr., approved of the series I proposed to write for INS entitled "The Amazing Kennedys." Millie and I were invited to lunch at his handsome home on the water at Palm Beach. It was early 1957. There were five of us: the Ambassador, as he liked to be called, in tan shorts and sunglasses; Mrs. Kennedy, dressed as if for a garden party and as fresh and young as any of her children; old family friend Bill Cunningham, the former sportswriter who often reflected in his writings and broadcasts Kennedy's ironclad conservatism; and Millie and I.

The sun on the patio was dazzling, the lunch delicious, the Ambassador's monologue relaxed. At seventy, the keen-eyed veteran of many a political and business war had the air of a man calling it a day. It had been quite a "day." His competitive fires had raged for more than half a century, reaching back to the decision to fight his way into Harvard instead of going submissively to the Jesuits at Boston College. He vowed that he'd show the Brahmins that the son of a saloonkeeper and parochial Catholic Democrat politician could be just as rich and just as intellectual and just as social as they. He did just that, made a mint, and turned to public service under Roosevelt. He was chairman of the Securities Exchange Commission and chief architect of most of the rules that regulate it today; Ambassador to the court of St. James's during the critical 1937–40 period. He brought his family home, campaigned so bitterly against the entrance of the United States in World War II that he was called pro-Hitler and anti-Semitic, and fell silent as three sons and a daughter went proudly off to war. But he was not a man to stay clammed for long.

"Preservation of our way of life is not assured by winning the war," he said in a speech at Colby College, Maine, a month after V-E Day. "We must defend it against cynics who would destroy our ideals and paralyze our aspirations, utopians who advocate plans to wreck our economic system; those who promote racial discrimination, industrial strife, corruption in public office, and those who would have us shun our responsibilities in a world order." With a glittering eye on the Truman Administration, then barely three months old, fellow Democrat Kennedy cried, "Men without training in economics, education in political science, perspective or balance, direct the future of this country because they are the only kind who take the trouble to participate in public affairs. Don't criticize these. Oppose them and all they stand for, by voice and by vote."

He was nominating John Fitzgerald Kennedy for Congress, but only he and his son knew that. And both knew he was nominating a substitute.

The elder Kennedy sounded off so vehemently on high taxes after the war that JFK was later to say of him, with the faintly amused reverence he held for him, "My father is a Democrat, a Taft Democrat."

The Korean War enraged Old Joe. World War II had claimed his oldest son and pride and joy, Joe, Jr., and his first son-in-law, Capt. John Robert Cavendish, Marquess of Hartington, eldest son and heir of the Duke of Devonshire. That death widowed Kathleen, eldest daughter of the Kennedys, and she in turn was killed in a plane crash in Europe several years later. The big war had so nearly taken Jack, too; indeed, a memorial mass had been said for him and other members of his PT-boat crew during the period when they were missing in action.

"Suicidal," Old Joe said of President Truman's Korean War policy in a speech at the University of Virginia Law School, as General MacArthur's forces retreated from the Yalu in the face of multitudes of Red Chinese. He urged that the United States withdraw from Korea "and any other place in Asia where we cannot hope to hold our defenses." He further urged that the United States get out of Berlin and thereafter devote a considerable portion of the defense budget to fortifying Canada and Latin America.

"We have no reason to believe that cooperation on their part will not be forthcoming," he told an audience that included his law student son Robert. "We can, and should, insist on it."

It was against a background as controversial as the above that we lunched and the master of the household sketched his new role in life.

"I'm just a has-been," he said, comfortably. " 'The doctor of sick empires,' as somebody once called me, is sidelined. The only one left to mind the store. I've cut all strings with public service. When I learned that Jack had support for the vice-presidential nomination at Chicago, and his name might be brought up, I resigned from President Eisenhower's commission studying our foreign intelligence. My day is done. Now it is my sons' day."

When the ripple of polite deprecations died down, I asked him for his capsule assessment of each of the Kennedys.

"Good idea," the Ambassador said in his steely and decisive way, but with a note of pride and affection in his voice. "Now you take Jack. Nobody's more courageous than Jack. He's a real intellectual, that boy, and a first-class historian, too. Don't let anybody tell you he had help when he was writing *Profiles in Courage*. I can see him now, lying on that couch out there on the lawn, working on that book by the hour. His back was killing him, but never a word out of him."

He ticked off the others, male heirs first:

"Now you take Bobby. Bobby's a tough one; he'll keep the Kennedys together, you can bet. He's a lot like me; he never forgets an enemy. And keep your eye on Teddy, too. That boy shows a lot of promise. He's just a kid now, but his class shows right through."

The Kennedy girls were dealt with swiftly, concisely. His voice saddened twice, once when he spoke of Kathleen, who served overseas with the Red Cross during the war, and when he mentioned Rosemary. "She's what we call our quiet one," the Ambassador said. The retarded eldest daughter was then at St. Coletta's, a Jefferson, Wisconsin, school for the handicapped—one of several beneficiaries of the Joseph P. Kennedy, Jr., Foundation.

He had left one out. Young Joe. I asked discreetly if he would say something about him.

The man who was one of the top financiers of the age, cool beyond calculation under fire, suddenly and terribly burst into tears at the luncheon table and for five aching minutes was racked with grief that cannot be described. Tears did not run, they literally cascaded down his bronzed, freckled face. He tried to speak, but nothing coherent issued. Mrs. Kennedy sat silent and composed. Cunningham stared at the ocean. Millie kicked me under the table.

"No," the Ambassador finally said, wiping his now reddened face. "No. I can't talk about Joe." He pointed at his wife. "*She* can. But I'll never be able to."

"Joe was a wonderful boy," Mrs. Kennedy said calmly. "A good boy. He had so much to live for. . . ."

My question had ruined the pleasant afternoon.

Young Joe's death seemed to have set a pattern for dramatic disasters that lay ahead for this vibrant, vital clan. He had completed his twenty-five bombing missions and his required number of dangerous reconnaissance trips as a Navy pilot by early August, 1944. He was scheduled to be returned to the States and spend the remainder of the war as a trainer of younger pilots. With the coming of peace, he would take up his life's work: politics. He had fully inherited his father's devouring curiosity about all things political, and the father's appetite to get in the thick of a fight and there take a stand. He had studied for a year under Harold Laski at the London School of Economics "the better to see both sides of the street." At Harvard Law he had raised his strong voice to support his father's stand against any weakening of U.S. neutrality toward the burgeoning war in Europe. He was a staunch isolationist, went to the isolationist-minded 1940 Democratic Convention as a delegate from Massachusetts, voted for James A. Farley (who, ironically, loathed Kennedy, Senior), and refused to make F.D.R.'s nomination for a third time unanimous.

But on August 13, 1944, when he could have come home, Young Joe volunteered for one of the more secret and dangerous missions of the war. The Nazis were hitting London and the invasion ports with the V-2 rocket, which flew so high and descended so swiftly that none was ever intercepted and few were even picked up on radar. The only defense Allied strategists could conceive was the destruction of the launching sites.

There were no bombs powerful enough to demolish these heavily built positions. Winston Churchill was later credited with the plan that proved to be the answer: cram as much TNT into a surplus bomber as it would hold, have a two-man crew take off with it, bail out over some Allied-held portion of France, and permit a "mother" plane to guide the unmanned bomber to the V-2 site and cause it to dive upon it.

Kennedy's co-pilot on the perilous mission was Sgt. Wilford Willy, USN, Fort Worth, Texas. Their four-engined B-24 lumbered into the sky with 24,000 pounds of high explosives, made its contact with the shepherding planes, and Kennedy and Willy prepared to parachute. The B-24 suddenly blew up so violently that nothing was ever found of either man.

A year later Jack Kennedy put together a tender little book, privately printed, which he called *As We Remember Joe.* Joe's brothers and sisters, his grandparents, war buddies, and friends each contributed. It was illustrated by a reproduction of the Navy Cross, awarded posthumously, and by a handwritten and poignant letter Secretary of the Navy James Forrestal wrote to the father. The touching book's tributes ranged warmly from the material to the spiritual.

Ensign James Simpson wrote, "I was in the plane testing and double checking three minutes before takeoff. I shook hands with Joe and said, 'So long and good luck, Joe. I only wish I were going with you.' He answered. "Thanks, Jim. Don't forget, you're going to make the next one with me. And, say, by the way, if I don't come back, you fellows can have the rest of my eggs.' We never saw him again."

Jack wrote, concluding his own chapter, "Through it all, he had a deep and abiding faith—he was never far from God—and so, I cannot help but feel that on that August day, high in the summer skies, 'death to him was less a setting forth than a returning.' "

A few days after the incident at Palm Beach I had a drink with the junior senator from Massachusetts at the Park Lane in New York and mentioned the Ambassador's emotional outburst.

"He always does that when Joe's name comes up," JFK said fondly. Then, after a pause, he said, "I'll tell you something about Joe. Joe was our star. He was the oldest, the smartest, and the strongest of the whole bunch. He was taller, could run faster, jump higher, hit harder. He got the best marks in school. And the prettiest girl. Joe would have been the Congressman from our district. Joe would have beaten Cabot Lodge for his Senate seat in fifty-two by a bigger majority than I did. Joe would have gotten the bid last Summer to run on the ticket with Adlai Stevenson, whereas I lost out by about twenty votes."

J.F.K. suddenly smiled.

"And Eisenhower would have run over him like a truck," he said of his brother, "and right now he'd still be picking up the tattered threads of his political career and trying to put it back together again."

He chuckled a bit.

"You know what I wanted to do," he said. "I wanted to be in *your* business, to write, to travel. But the moment I heard that Joe was dead, I knew I didn't have a chance. I was next in line. My father raised all of us to find our place or take an active interest in public affairs. When Joe died, I became *it*. If I had been killed, Bobby would have had to pick it up, because he was next in line. And if anything had happened to Bobby, it would be Teddy's duty."

The Ambassador sent me a flattering wire from Palm Beach when "The Amazing Kennedys" appeared in print. He expressed astonishment that on such short acquaintance I had caught "the true flavor of how things really are" with the family. A mutual friend later told me the elder Kennedy had liked the start of the first article especially. It read:

> In Sen. John Fitzgerald Kennedy, Roman Catholic Massachusetts Democrat, one of America's best-known families may have produced the man who will bring the dreams of three active generations of politicians to full flower.
>
> Possessed of a passion for public service, bright, handsome, decorated, young (39) Jack Kennedy has become a major spokesman for his party, a trusted figure on Capitol Hill in bipartisan work, and a man most prominently mentioned for a Democratic Presidential nomination—perhaps as early as 1960.

I saw the Ambassador at the Park Avenue offices of his empire shortly after his son was elected. He had taken the cliff-hanger in stride. He was most affable. Yes, Jack would make a fine President. Nobody ever had better training for the job. Sure, he would have troubles: Eisenhower had dumped a lot of difficult, unfinished problems in his lap. No (he laughed), there would be no fatherly advice given on how best to run the White House.

"I doubt if I'll ever go there," the Ambassador said with a laugh.

The *Journal American* photographer who had been taking shots as the Ambassador talked attracted his attention. He touched the knot of his own necktie.

"Mr. Kennedy, would you mind straightening your tie?" he asked.

The Ambassador raised his hand to the knot of his tie and wiggled it back and forth. As he did so, the photographer let go with another flash.

The father of the President of the United States sprang from his chair like an old but agile tiger, and for a split second it appeared, startlingly, that he would lunge for the cameraman's throat. Then he caught himself and, livid, said in the quietest but most menacing voice, "Goddam you, you tricked me into that picture. If you want a picture of me adjusting my tie, say to me 'I want a picture of you adjusting your tie,' and you'll get it. But goddam you, if you ever try to trick me again. . . ."

The thoroughly frightened photographer started to apologize, but was cut off by a glare that packed the glint of a scimitar. Then the Ambassador sat down again and continued talking to me about his son in the most matter-of-fact tones.

"How many states would Jack have taken if he had not been a Catholic?" I asked him, a trustee of Notre Dame, Knight of Malta, Knight of the Equestrian Order of the Holy Sepulchre, and Grand Knight of the Order of Pius IX.

"All of them!" he said instantly and emphatically.

At the Inauguration, the Ambassador was the picture of the restrained, quietly proud father who was watching the culmination of a mighty dream, the climax of a struggling saga that reached back to the Potato Famine of the 1840's and the awesome decision of young Patrick Kennedy to leave his thatch-roofed home in New Ross and join the ragged, starveling migration to a strange New World.

He seemed to listen more attentively and respectfully than many others to the long invocation offered by Richard Cardinal Cushing, a trying twenty minutes for the young President and countless more present in the subfreezing cold. Midway in the Cardinal's pious but unnervingly nasal peroration, a short circuit in the platform's heating apparatus sent whiffs of smoke ascending past his face.

"Fumes from Purgatory," someone whispered in the deep-frozen press rows.

The Cardinal persevered through the smoke, on and on and then on some more. Near the limit of endurance in the press section, whose flooring had not been cleared of the previous night's blizzard, another voice was heard. It was that of Bob Hartman, Washington correspondent of the Los Angeles *Times*.

"Well," Bob muttered grimly, "we *warned* you Protestant sons of bitches."

Herbert Hoover was an even eighty. He had had a busy day in West Branch, Iowa, at the little whitewashed house where he was born, also at the dedication of still another school bearing his name, and at a picnic in a public park arranged by the adoring committee so that young and old could mingle with the thirty-first President of the United States. Now he was en route back to New York and his more familiar digs at the Waldorf Towers. The conveyance was a United Air Lines Convair, Mainliner O'Connor, the executive plane set aside for him that day by UAL's president, Pat Patterson. Miss O'Connor, duenna of the company's stewardesses, was in charge of things aloft. She tucked a blue blanket around Mr. Hoover's shoulders and, at his request, brought him a martini.

His devoted little secretary, Miss Miller, had fetched the telegrams, cablegrams, and letters sent to West Branch for the occasion. All were affectionate. He listened attentively, with the help of his hearing aid, as she read a sampling, signed by the great and the humble of the world.

When the time seemed right, I asked him a rather personal question. I asked him if, at eighty, he harbored any bitterness toward old political foes who pilloried him in the past as chief architect of the Depression and who had coined or countenanced the use of Hooverville as a synonym for Shanty-town; indeed, had accused him of personally running the hungry Bonus Marchers out of Washington and Anacostia Flats.

"No, I bear no hard feelings," Mr. Hoover said, after taking a reflective puff on his pipe and a sip of his drink. Then a look of merriment in his clear blue eyes. "But what you ask reminds me of the story of the prayer meeting. The preacher's sermon was on brotherly love. When he finished, he addressed a question to the congregation. He asked if there was anybody in the house who could say in all honesty that he didn't have an enemy in the world.

"Well, there was a big silence, and then an old fellow about my time in life got up and said he personally didn't have an enemy. So the preacher praised him and urged the others in the house to lead the same kind of exemplary life. Then he asked the old fellow to tell the folks just how he happened to have no enemies.

"The old fellow said, 'I outlived the bastards!' "

The popularity polls listed Lyndon Baines Johnson as a casualty of the war in Vietnam. It hurt him deeply, aged him faster than a Chief Executive with the greatest string of legislative successes on record should have aged. As with Woodrow Wilson, and one supposes all the others, aging went forth without the comforting arm of mellowness.

He would see us—Frank Conniff, Marianne Means, who had been our girl at the White House and was now writing a national column, and me.

We entered the White House like burglars through the inconspicuous staff door. Mustn't be seen by the regular White House correspondents. They would be understandably angry and their relations with the President, already edgy, would worsen. And vice versa, in spades.

The guard at the desk gave us a friendly frisk with his eyes, breathed something into a phone, and pointed to a little elevator. There was a pause in what once was called the Fish Room, then a little march across one of the outer offices, and there in the doorway of the last redoubt of the Free World stood its loneliest man.

He looked deep into us as he offered his big, tough hand, a probing steel-blue look that was some kind of final assessment of the course he would take with us. Almost without words he motioned us to our places on the two facing divans, separated by a coffee table, that reach out from the fireplace in the wall opposite his desk. He lowered his well-tailored bulk into the rocking chair that faced us . . . just as John F. Kennedy used to marshal his guests. It was not the same rocker. Kennedy's was slender, darkly wooded, and with trim, squared beige cushions. L.B.J.'s was a rocker built for a man like L.B.J. He swung it heavily until he faced Conniff more squarely, leaned forward with a look as challenging as a sequence from *High Noon,* and said in a voice that was low-pitched but oddly menacing, "All right, now. Are you going to bomb Hanoi and Haiphong, bomb 'em off the map, or are you going to pull out? Let's have the answer right now."

Conniff said he never considered those extremes as the only alternatives.

The President hunched back comfortably in his rocker and some of the lines in his face seemed to ease. It was the answer he wanted to hear, and that had not been happening enough of late. He took off his glasses and rubbed his eyes and then his whole face. It was 6:30 in the evening and dark as pitch beyond the French doors that led into the garden. He would keep us pinned there—sometimes riveted there—until 9:30.

"I didn't start this," he said of the war in a voice that grew stronger and a shade angrier as the night wore on. "I inherited it. It was getting more difficult not long before the full responsibility fell on me. Right in this room, when Kennedy called on Ike after the election [1960] Ike told him that the big problem he was going to have as the new President would be in Southeast Asia.

"Just before Dallas, Kennedy told me that we were going to have to fight in South Vietnam, not just *advise.*" He swung his eyes at us and there was again challenge in them. "Now, is it going to be said of me that I let Kennedy down? Am I going to be remembered as the fellow who pulled out, who became as scared as a rabbit in the field?"

He did not need an answer.

"I sent ambassadors to thirty countries, tried everything," he said, frustration as well as anger welling in him. "They just don't want peace, don't want to negotiate—now." He lingered on *now* before going on.

"We keep the pressure on them all the time," he said. "Not too much, not too little. I read here and there that they still think they're winning, but every day we show them that they aren't winning, and eventually even they will realize it. We're killing them on the ground, day in and day out. The figures we released aren't estimates. We count every body we find. That isn't hard: they leave most of their dead and wounded. We're killing or wounding them at something like the rate of seventeen to one. How long can they last at that rate?"

He ordered a drink for us and a Dr. Pepper for himself when one of us suggested that it must be time for him to go on to dinner. And for the next hour he spoke almost without the prompting of questions, covering a score of troublesome national, international, and personal problems. It was plain he deeply resented what he felt were the more unjust accusations against and interpretations of his policy in Vietnam. Twice he picked up a phone and asked the girl in the outer office to bring in charts, graphs, and polls. His foes among the Washington columnists had that week abundantly noticed that his popularity quotient had subsided to fifty-four. That happened to be the same figure President Eisenhower ascended to in the heady wake of his first victory over Adlai Stevenson, one of the polls deduced.

"Yet they say I'm in a hell of a fix because I used to have a sixty," he said, genuinely perplexed.

He was more disturbed by several then-current stories that implied he had rebuffed certain overtures from the enemy to negotiate a peace. The most discussed of these stories was Eric Sevareid's article in *Look* detailing Ambassador Stevenson's last days, made sadder, it was charged, because his transmission of peace feelers had been short circuited at the White House.

"Do you think Adlai or anybody else could get a peace offer and I, the President, wouldn't hear about it?" he asked incredulously. "They try to give the public the idea that I'm purposely wrong in my handling of Vietnam. No President does what he thinks is wrong." He looked around the room, solemnly, and said, "Only thirty-five men have reached this office in history. I don't think any of them ever willfully set out to do something wrong." His eyes fastened on the soundproofed AP and UPI teletypes faintly chattering near his desk.

"But go over there to those tickers and you can find at least six mean statements about me on the wires," he invited.

We thanked him for giving us all this time. It was 8:30 and each of us had visions of his dinner being kept warm upstairs, and of Lady Bird trying to keep a soufflé inflated against catastrophe. L.B.J. ignored the murmurs of gratitude, ordered another drink for us and another Dr. Pepper for himself, and turned to a subject that had bugged every one of his predecessors: the failure of the press and/or public to get the real essence, the thrust, of a speech. He phoned the girl to fetch him his still-echoing Chicago speech of May 17, 1966. He marked several passages with one of the green-ink "seventeen-cent-souvenir pens" he had bestowed on us earlier.

"All that seems to have been stressed in my Chicago speech was the line about 'some Nervous Nellies and some who will become frustrated and bothered and break ranks under the strain and turn on their leaders, their own country, and their own fighting men.' But I don't see much about *these* passages," he said, pointing them out and handing me the marked text. These were his neglected words:

> As Commander in Chief, I am neither a Democrat nor a Republican. The men fighting in Vietnam are simply Americans. Our policy in Vietnam is a national policy. It springs from every lesson we have learned in this century. We fought in the First World War and then failed to build the system of collective security which could have prevented the Second World War.
>
> Standing in Chicago, October 5, 1937, Franklin Roosevelt said: "When an epidemic of physical disease starts to spread, the community approves and joins in a quarantine of the patients in order to protect the health of the community against the spread of disease."
>
> The country failed to back him. And then we saw what happened when aggressors felt confident that they could win all the way. That was what President Truman remembered in 1947 in Greece and Turkey. That is what he remembered during the blockade of Berlin and when the attack came in Korea.
>
> This is what President Eisenhower remembered in 1954 when he laid before the Senate the SEATO Treaty, and during the crisis over Quemoy and Matsu. That is what President Kennedy remembered when, in the face of Communist aggression in Laos and Vietnam, he began to send our forces there in 1962.
>
> We have learned over the past half century that failure to meet aggression means war, not peace. In carrying out that policy we have taken casualties in Berlin, in Korea, and now in Vietnam. Every morning I look at those casualty figures. I measure them not as statistics, but man by man.
>
> But I tell you that if we fail in frustrating this aggression the war that would surely come to Asia would produce casualties in the hundreds of thousands—perhaps in the millions. Your government is determined to resist this aggression at the minimum cost to our own people, to our allies, and to the world.

At 9:15, after another fruitless effort to thank him and go our way, I asked him what kind of a work day he put in. The details of it were more than fresh in his mind, he said, because he had spent some time earlier in the day with Jim Bishop, who was doing an in-depth book on him.

"I wake up at six, six-thirty as a rule," he said, relieved to be talking about something beyond Vietnam. "I get up, go to the bathroom, wash my teeth, and shave. I use an electric razor. Then I get back into bed and start working. The tea comes in. Might have four, five cups. Then the boys start coming with the overnight reports. I give them their instructions. At seven-thirty, McNamara calls. Then Rusk. Then I might talk on the phone about the budget. I might talk three, four times to McNamara before I get out of bed. He's not a fellow who talks very long.

"Then, of course, I read the casualty list.

"I get here to this office at ten-thirty or eleven and from then on it's one thing after another: a prime minister, a delegation from someplace, who knows?

"I'm not much for lunch. I never have any of those formal luncheons. Today I had a bowl of soup, a sandwich of some kind, and some tapioca. Then I keep going until maybe three-thirty, four. After that I used to take a swim with friends, friends I'd invite. But I've had to give that up. It's a terrible thing, but if a President starts out with, say, a hundred friends, well, he's lucky if he winds up with one.

"So now, mostly, I go from here back to my room and go back to bed. I mean really to bed: into pajamas, like you're going to bed at night. There aren't any telephone calls, unless it's important, of course. The room is as dark as night. I go sound to sleep. The rule is that I sleep until I wake up. That's usually about five o'clock or so. I take a cold shower, brush my teeth . . . like starting a new day.

"Matter of fact, I do have two days every day—one that lasts from the early morning until, say, four and the other day that lasts from six to ten or so. I always come back here about six and work. I go over and eat dinner about ten, not much, have a massage and watch the eleven o'clock news on TV. Frank Stanton put in three sets, side by side, just as I've got here in this office. I can put the picture on all three by this remote control gadget," he said, demonstrating. "Then I push this button and the sound comes on inside whichever set is showing a picture that interests me.

"I'm back in bed about midnight, reading the bulldog edition of the Washington *Post*. From then on, usually till two-thirty, sometimes three-thirty, I go over the memos and papers I've taken to bed . . . the ideas, speech outlines, things like that. I mark them 'Approved,' 'Disapproved,' or 'See me.' Then sleep."

Now he accepted our thanks, took a look at the AP and UPI, and showed us out. Marianne, two hours late for dinner at the Bill Whites, whistled up a cab. Conniff and I walked over to Duke Ziebert's place near the Mayflower, mostly in silence—not an ordinary condition for either of us.

All I could think to say was, "What a hell of a lousy job that poor man's got."

Endit

The Future of Journalism is a hardy topic that has begun to mesmerize discussion groups and pundits in increasing numbers. Endlessly soaring production costs, sometimes senseless strikes, and inroads made on the public mind and the advertiser's dollar by electronic news make some wonder if the Great American Newspaper is long for this world. Depression symptoms of decline are easily available. There are now only three cities in the nation—New York, Washington, and Boston—where the reading public has a choice of more than two shades of editorial opinion. New York once had a dozen thriving papers. Mergers blended many hallowed (and money-losing) mastheads into one, and united the shades of ruggedly individualistic titans who fought memorable newspaper wars in the long ago. New York City's *World Journal Tribune* alone stitched together the graves of Hearst, Greeley, Pulitzer, Scripps, Howard, and Bennett when its ten unions permitted it to publish. It lasted eight months, and lost millions.

The Cassandras are perpetually puzzled to learn that the newspaper business as a whole continues not only to survive but prosper in this land where it found its finest freedoms. As of September 30, 1965, there were 1,751 U.S. dailies and 9,392 weeklies. There has been little variation from the figures of ten years before, except in circulation. The 1955 total circulation reached 56,147,359; in 1965 it was 60,357,563, and in 1966 climbed to 61,400,000 plus.

Newspapers follow population movements as swiftly as do gas stations, shopping centers, and the PTA. Consequently, the suburban press is booming all around the great population centers. The off-beat and scruffy Bohemian press, springing up impudently in the land's Greenwich Villages, is growing like weeds. Some purists believe that portions of it should be weeded and burned, after a thorough examination of the First Article of the Constitution, of course. But who knows what splendid truffle this grubbing press might uproot?

There will always be room for and need of newspapers. The technology is bound to change. It has been relatively static for the better part of the century. Soon, the superb teamwork of tree chopper, newsprint maker, reporter, editor, compositor, and pressman will not be prey at the moment of fruition to a flat tire on a delivery truck. Or frustrated by a newspaperboy's toothache, or his bad aim. The family's morning newspaper may well emerge from the household's TV set or facsimile machine, which will silently "print" it while the family sleeps at night and drop it on the living room floor at dawn. The afternoon paper will be ready for the breadwinner as he returns at dusk to home and hearth, created in this same manner.

But however exotic the technology, reporters always will have to gather in the wheat and the chaff of every blessed day's news, editors will have the eternal task of separating that harvest, and those who live the charmed life of commentators will rise and fall on their interpretation of what the news means. There is perhaps only one achievement the computers will never be capable of, and that is the simple job of witnessing a happening and describing it swiftly, clearly, and honestly. How difficult that triple play can sometimes be! How warmly rewarding when it is realized!

I'll croak in this business, given the opportunity. Where else can a man hope to build a bridge between himself and others every day, whether it be as rickety as the one that snapped in half at Tacoma or as durable as the Golden Gate? On what other field of endeavor is a competitor called upon to come up each day with words and thoughts not used the day before? Every time a reporter picks up a phone to call in a story or spins a fresh sheet of copy paper into his typewriter, he shoots his roll—like a craps player going for broke.

Call it vanity, call it arrogant presumption, call it what you wish, but I would grope for the nearest open grave if I had no newspaper to work for, no need to search for and sometimes find the winged word that just fits, no keen wonder over what each unfolding day may bring.

Besides, it's better than working for a living.

Index

CONTEMPORARY AMERICA

CONTEMPORARY AMERICA

The National Scene Since 1900

HARVEY WISH

Western Reserve University

Harper & Brothers Publishers

New York and London

CONTEMPORARY AMERICA

I-X

To

Arthur M. Schlesinger

pioneer in the urban approach

to American culture

Contents

Preface

In recent years the professional writing of contemporary history, despite obvious pitfalls, has greatly increased, reflecting the general desire that history serve more directly as an instrument of social action. Since many of the movements and personalities are still alive, these studies of "only yesterday," to use Frederick L. Allen's phrase, have an unusual utility. Following in part such cultural historians as James Harvey Robinson, Charles Beard, and Arthur M. Schlesinger, I have sought to present patterns of historical behavior rather than a mere catalogue of the "past everything." This has meant, in terms of Robinson's New History, the use of the tools of analysis employed by the sociologist and the cultural anthropologist in order to reduce the chaos of overwhelming details to a meaningful scientific pattern. By a detailed picture of the impact of the metropolis and mature capitalism on American behavior this book seeks to integrate (where the facts justify it) the social, economic, and political phases of our times. Integration from the point of view of political affairs has been expressed in such terms as the recurrent rise and decline of the businessman's leadership in politics. Diplomatic history has also been related to this broad cultural setting as well as the myriad of special factors governing the conduct of the State Department.

Because of the diversity of the historical material, I have asked experts in almost every social science to read selected chapters. However, none can share the responsibility for any misinterpretation or error that may have crept in, since the suggestions made were not always accepted. I am particularly indebted to Isaac J. Cox of Northwestern, Thomas A. Bailey of Stanford, and Payson S. Wild, Jr., of Harvard, for reading the chapters on foreign affairs. The social and cultural chapters were read by Arthur M. Schlesinger, Talcott Parsons, Howard Mumford Jones, and Ralph Barton Perry—all of Harvard—and by Merle Curti of the University of Wisconsin. Those on government, business, and politics were read by William L. Crum,

William Y. Elliott, Merle Fainsod (all three of Harvard), and by Tracy Strevey of Northwestern. Professor Louis M. Hacker of Columbia read the entire manuscript and made certain fundamental as well as detailed suggestions. I have also profited from discussions with Roscoe Pound and from special training in American intellectual history afforded by a Post-Doctoral Fellowship at Harvard and Columbia granted by the Social Science Research Council.

Although the critical bibliography indicates the major sources to which I am indebted, special recognition for original interpretations, statistical analyses, and certain vital facts is due the authors of the various sections and monographs associated with *Recent Social Trends,* and the cited works of Philip Jessup, H. F. Pringle, H. U. Faulkner, Charles and Mary Beard, Mark Sullivan, J. T. Howard, P. W. Slosson, F. L. Allen, H. E. Luccock, J. C. Malin, and J. J. Garrison. The book owes much to Miss Dorothy Thompson, College Editor of Harper & Brothers, for her thorough, intelligent editing of the manuscript. Finally, I have profited greatly from the valuable suggestions and assistance of my wife.

Harvey Wish

January, 1945

CONTEMPORARY AMERICA

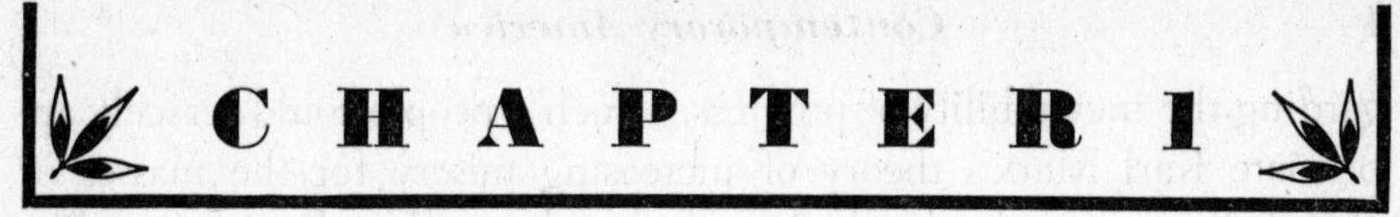

The Promise of American Life: 1900-1917

THE FAITH IN PROGRESS

The two colorful decades before the First World War, beginning with the economic recovery of 1897, were years of striking social and material achievement. This era of scientific planning in business enterprise has been regarded as the flowering of the middle-class individualist spirit. Although current literature and politics were dominated by the theme of social protest as in the preceding decade, the historic American faith in progress remained. A purposeful and expansive mood succeeded the pessimism of the early nineties. During the depression of 1893, Frederick Jackson Turner, the historian, had furnished a text for pessimists by calling attention to the fact that the era of the frontier, with its free lands, its self-reliant individualism, and easy opportunity, had passed. But the prewar generation refused to believe that the abundant life in America was a frail plant dependent on the now-disappearing resources of virgin lands. There would always be new frontiers of opportunity, they believed, as long as the road to advancement was kept free of corrupt men and monopolistic schemes. The rising industrial metropolis overshadowed the decline of free lands.

Herbert Croly, himself destined to establish in 1914 that journalistic champion of social planning, the *New Republic*, deplored the "irresponsible optimism" of the average American in his influential volume, *The Promise of American Life* (1909). He pointed out that this peculiarity of his fellow citizens lay in their expectation that "the familiar benefits will continue to accumulate automatically." A strong believer in social reform, he tended to attribute this simple faith in the American dream of unlimited opportunity to a Calvinist fatalism regarding the inevitability of progress. Such a people could scarcely appreciate Karl Marx's theory of increasing misery for the masses or cheerfully accept the hardening of class lines. The British novelist, H. G. Wells, who visited the United States in 1906, observed, "Most western Europeans have this delusion of automatic progress in things badly enough, but with Americans it seems almost fundamental." While Mr. Wells grudgingly admitted the strength and wealth of America, he assailed the prevailing indifference of the cities and of industry to the welfare of the masses as "pure nineteenth century."

He was addressing a generation happily past the great depression of the nineties and reared on the idealized success stories of the late Horatio Alger, a Harvard-trained Unitarian minister who was himself a frustrated individual. Alger's books for boys—most of the 119 volumes were of this variety—usually retailed the much-worn plot of the ambitious village lad who rose through hard work to wealth and distinction in the city. Besides, there were the living examples of the great business leaders—Carnegie, George F. Baker (president of the First National Bank of New York; he endowed the Harvard Business School), Ford, and Rockefeller—who had risen from small beginnings and now were able to offer the most extraordinary philanthropies in history, endowing libraries, universities, Negro training, charitable and religious foundations, medical research and health facilities, and movements to abolish war, as well as numerous other projects.

Side by side with the success story grew the middle-class fear that the mammoth enterprises of the Carnegies and the Rockefellers might forever block the rise of the aspiring small businessman by choking off competition. Working-class families complained of the high cost of living and showed resentment at the current disclosures of adulterated foods and drugs. Revelations of corruption in business and politics shook the popular faith in business leadership among large segments of the people. The ensuing Progressive movement added the powerful note of urban protest to the surviving Populism of the 1890's which embraced the farmers' revolt against the eastern creditor and the industrial interests. Confident in the efficacy of political and social experimentation, the Progressive elements sought to revive the competitive system and to remove the obstacles to that equality of opportunity which seemed a needed preliminary for individual success.

TAYLORIZATION

Despite the various irrational aspects of the Age of Trusts which had developed shortly after the Civil War, a strong underlying rationality of business organization was apparent. This period after 1900 marked the debut of the public accountant, whose scientific analysis afforded an indispensable tool for business planning. Commercial technicians, consulting engineers, and business economists began to appear in force, stimulated by the efficiency ideas of Frederick W. Taylor. Advertising expanded to include a national market for such products as packaged foods and factory-made clothes for women. Marketing as a specialty developed from its infant stages. The public relations counsel entered industry as the businessman became increasingly sensitive to adverse public opinion and its influence upon sales. These beginnings were to reach maturity during the 1920's. Planning, or "rationalization," as a later generation termed it, began to alter nineteenth-century individualism into an increasingly impersonal pattern of business behavior. Industrial capitalism was reaching maturity through the individualistic enterprise of the American middle class.

Foremost in the efficiency movement was Frederick W. Taylor, father of scientific management, who was trained as an engineer in a day when the profession was narrowly limited in scope. While employed as a gang boss for the Midvale Steel Company during the eighties, he found that the foreman's pressure on the worker for increased output resulted merely in conflict. "Throughout American industry," observed Taylor in later years, "management's concept of a proper day's work was what the foreman could drive workers to do and the workers' conception was how little they could do and hold their jobs."

From his determination to measure scientifically the manual operations constituting a fair day's work came his famous recommendations to engineers, "A Piece Rate System" (1895), involving a time-study and rate-fixing department in which the stop watch played a major role. In 1903 he read his significant paper, "Shop Management," before a group of engineers; in it he outlined the pioneer ideas of scientific management, which provided for shop organization according to function rather than adopting the usual over-all management of the factory as a simple unit. Novel specialized departments such as "routing," a "cost-and-time" division, and "disciplinarians" were set up according to their relationship to the planning process. The disciplinarian was the prototype of the personnel manager. A clearly defined task of reasonable difficulty, involving standardized conditions and high wages for its successful performance, was Taylor's ideal.

Adoption of "Taylorization," as this system was called, did not come spontaneously, largely because of the natural temptations afforded the less idealistic to introduce a ruthless speed-up system, thus antagonizing organized labor. The unions also feared the possibility that scientific management might increase unemployment. Taylor, who hoped that the higher wages resulting from lowered operating costs would bring labor and management together, did not reckon, according to some critics, with the unrestrained profit motive. Nevertheless, the Harvard Graduate School of Business Administration began its career in 1908 with complete acceptance of Taylorization. Even more significant was the publicity given scientific management in the Eastern Rate case heard before the Interstate Commerce Commission during 1910–1911. On this occasion the government's brilliant counsel, Louis D. Brandeis, took direct issue with the shippers, who demanded higher rates partly on the ground that the possibilities for further economies were exhausted. Brandeis attracted national attention by pointing out in some detail the high wages and managerial returns possible in competitive enterprises under the Taylor system. Although the Commission won its case on other grounds, this publicity for Taylorization led to its adoption by many industrialists.

URBANIZATION

Expanding industry and a maturing industrial capitalism required a larger and more mobile population. Between 1900 and 1920 the nation's inhabitants increased from nearly 76 million to over 105 million, a population equal to the combined total of the leading industrial nations, England and Germany. Despite considerable evidence of birth control among the business and professional classes—Theodore Roosevelt really meant this by his phrase "race suicide"—and a tendency toward deferred marriages, the birth rate decline was offset by an increased expectancy of life, which rose from a 48.2-year average in 1900 to over 51 in 1919, and by heavy recruitments from European immigration. Labor was assured to urban centers by the movement of native rural folk as well as new immigrants to the city. By 1920, the Census Office was to record the momentous fact that the population of the urban areas was practically equal to that of rural America. A new epoch in the nation's life had begun.

Reflecting the increased trend toward urbanization was the decline in the number of farmers, hitherto predominant among occupation groups, largely in favor of the manufacturing and technical trades. The concurrent rise of finance capitalism was revealed in the sharp increase of bankers and stock and loan brokers, who had numbered only 11,000 in 1870; this rose to 73,000 by 1900, and to the exceptionally high figure of 162,000 a decade later. Not all sections of the country were equally fortunate in growth, although the urban trend was general. In the South, Birmingham continued its sensational rise of a generation before as a leading iron center; and Atlanta, Georgia, strategically located as a commercial and industrial center, earned its reputation as "the New York of the South." The proud days of New England's industrial leadership seemed to be declining in favor of western and southern competitors. In southern California, Florida, and northern New Jersey, the suburban expansion of the 1920's was partly anticipated during the prewar era.

New York City, retaining much of the immigration that poured through Ellis Island, increased its supremacy as the nation's commercial and financial center; it gained at the rate of over one million people each decade beginning in 1900, the population totaling 5,620,000 by 1920. The second city of America, Chicago, with 1,700,000 people at the turn of the century, dominated the commerce of the Mississippi Valley through its pivotal railroad position, its meat-packing monopoly, and its central grain exchanges. By 1920 this medley of Poles, Bohemians, Germans, and Scandinavians, besides natives, had grown by another one million people. In the West, least Europeanized section of the country, Los Angeles, which was scarcely more than a sleepy village of a few thousand in 1870, became a city of 102,000 in 1900 and a metropolis of 576,673 by 1920, thus displacing San Francisco's supremacy on the Pacific coast. With the sensational growth of the automobile industry, Detroit and Akron made equally spectacular gains in population until an intricate web of neighboring cities had risen that were dependent upon the fortunes of that single industry.

THE COMING OF THE AUTOMOBILE

In the field of mechanical invention American genius found its peculiar realm, although it built upon foundations laid across the ocean. This was notably the case with the automobile. Frenchmen like Le Bon in 1799 and the Germans, Carl Benz and Gottlieb Daimler, during the 1870's and 1880's did much to create the essential elements of the gasoline automobile. Strongly contesting the field with Benz and Daimler was George B. Selden, a patent lawyer of New York and a graduate of the Sheffield Scientific School of Yale University, who apparently completed a gasoline "horseless carriage" in 1877. His unfortunate strategy of delaying the patent application until 1895, adopted for business reasons, involved him and his successors in an unsuccessful patent suit during 1902–1911 against Henry Ford and others for alleged infringement. By that time others like Charles E. Duryea and Elwood Haynes had already been able to market their own gasoline-driven carriages. Although steam and electric cars dominated the automobile field in 1900, the gasoline motor car soon outstripped them in popularity.

Selden managed to earn a modest fortune through a licensing arrangement with manufacturers desiring to use his patent, but the leadership in automobile promotion was reserved for another man, Henry Ford of Detroit. In common with Duryea, Haynes, R. E. Olds, and J. D. Maxwell, Ford was a practical mechanic who had been fascinated for many years by the prospect of building a successful automobile. Breaking with the farming career selected for him by his father, he built his first auto model in 1892. Despite an unsuccessful venture in automobile manufacture during the late nineties, he entered business again at the turn of the century with the Ford Motor Company; he owned one-fourth—and soon practically all—of the original $50,000 capital stock. With him were associated James Couzens, the Dodge brothers (Horace and John), and J. D. Maxwell, all names of great future importance. Long before the First World War, Ford had completed the "rags to riches" cycle so dear to American romanticism.

Ford's greatest contribution, which was to set him apart from the European forerunners in motor car invention, lay not in the ingenuity of his original model but in the adoption of the most far-reaching process of mass production known to industry anywhere. It is indeed indicative of the typically American character of mass production, a development based in part on the low ratio of population to effective resources, that the genealogy of Ford's process goes back to another American, the Connecticut Yankee, Eli Whitney. The latter had applied the principle of interchangeable parts to firearms over a century before. Nor were the names of Colt, Singer, and McCormick insignificant in the historical transition to mass-production methods. Ford chose to standardize a single inexpensive model in order to produce a car within the reach of the lower middle classes. When the historic but strictly utilitarian—even ugly—Model T emerged triumphantly in 1909 from a selective process in his plant, the great decision regarding a single model had been made. Not until the middle twenties did Ford bring out a new model. By that time over 5.5 million cars had been scattered over the nation's landscape.

The assembly line, propelled by a conveyor system, achieved the acme of standardized operations and equipment. Ford supplemented his technical successes by proceeding to confound his competitors with a five-dollar minimum daily wage for employees, a profit-sharing plan, and an eight-hour day; but true to his extreme individualist bias he turned a granite face to labor unions. His psychology had not a little of the paternalistic attitude of the eighteenth-century benevolent despots with all their vagaries.

The popularity of the automobile was destined to create a social revolution. Whereas in 1899 less than six million dollars was invested in automobiles, by 1914 over 407 millions were so allocated. Colonial American life had followed predominantly the contours of the seaboard, the inland seas, and the rivers. Our early national expansion had crept along the canals, then the railroads; now this pattern of urban penetration was to be radically altered by the diffusiveness of the great automobile highways. The islands of isolated rural cultures gave way to the sophisticated outlook of the city. This new integrative process wrought a revolution in recreation and transportation. The backward little red schoolhouse yielded to the central, well-equipped, consolidated school served by the bus. The metropolis expanded as middle-class car owners escaped to the suburbs. Congested factory areas were dispersed as a result of the automobile, as well as of electrical motive power (replacing steam) and the telephone.

PIONEER AVIATION AND WIRELESS TELEGRAPHY

Scarcely inferior in importance were the epoch-making airplane experiments of the Wright brothers, Orville and Wilbur, at Kitty Hawk, North Carolina, on December 17, 1903. Here again, invention of the first power-driven heavier-than-air machine capable of carrying its occupant in sustained flight was preceded by an impressive line of English and French experiments. The honor accorded the Wright brothers might have gone to Dr. Samuel P. Langley of the Smithsonian Institution, for he produced a successful man-carrying machine months before the Wrights did; but mistakes in launching this model obscured its merits. Only a subsequent demonstration flight by Glenn H. Curtiss revealed the truth. Langley's fiasco did much to discourage any general belief in the future of aviation.

The Wrights, like so many American inventors, were practical mechanics; they had experimented with gliders in 1900. Their special contributions included a light sixteen-horsepower gasoline engine and a working arrangement of the wings to solve the problem of balance from side to side. After reports in 1906–1908 of successful flights in France, particularly the performance of the Brazilian, Santos-Dumont, they abandoned their secrecy and in 1908 demonstrated the operation of their improved flying model. The United States Army eagerly adopted the Wright machine as a solid addition to the nation's armed strength.

By 1911 another such invention was made in Glenn Curtiss' "Hydro Airplane," the prototype of modern seaplanes. Curtiss, who liked to perform feats on motorcycles, had developed his interest in aeronautics while associated with Alexander Graham Bell, for whom he had constructed light gasoline engines. This was but another of a striking series of inventions in transportation and communication, which included a revolution in municipal transportation, with the subway, elevated, and electric street car assuming a dominant role in the great cities. Bell lived to inaugurate a long-distance telephone system connecting New York and San Francisco in 1915.

Wireless telegraphy, developed primarily through Marconi's genius, received one of its greatest applications in 1906 in the American invention by Lee De Forest of the vacuum tube amplifier, which controls and magnifies electric current; this not only was invaluable for the long-distance telephone but did much to create radio communication. By 1916, Secretary of the Navy Daniels was able to utilize the improvements in wireless by conversing at will with every naval station from the Atlantic to the Pacific.

SOUTHEASTERN EUROPE LEAVES HOME

This generation of Americans included the amazingly large proportion of ten million foreign-born whites in 1900, a figure which rose beyond thirteen million in 1910, although it increased at a much slower rate thereafter. The greatest period of immigration in our history was 1905–1914; the million mark was exceeded in at least six separate years. While the existing foreign-born population in 1900, reflecting an earlier trend, was predominantly German, Irish, and Scandinavian, the newcomers after that year came overwhelmingly from southeastern Europe, particularly southern Italy, Russia, and Austria-Hungary.

Southern Italians, living in the overpopulated, malaria-infested villages of the peninsula and hemmed in by a reactionary and absentee landlord system which embraced huge entailed estates, faced the choice of starvation or emigration. In the early years of the century the Italian emigrants were largely transients (80 per cent of them were male) who evidently hoped to send their earnings to distressed kinsfolk in Sicily and Naples. Soon, however, this migration became one of permanent, sturdy home builders, handicapped, it is true, by illiteracy and the popular myth of violence attributed to them. Elsewhere from southeastern Europe—from Austria-Hungary, Turkey, and the Balkans—came recruits for the factories, mines, and foundries. These people were accustomed to an average day's wage of fifty cents, and frequently less for farm labor; hence it was difficult at first to avert the consequent depressing influence on wages and labor conditions here.

The "Russian" migration belied its name, for it was essentially Jewish and Polish. Although the Jews of Austria-Hungary, like the Poles, were compelled to emigrate for economic reasons, the Russian Jews were driven forth by the lash of the worst era of persecution in their long sad history. Faced by rising popular discontent, in large part economic and in part a reflection of European liberal ideas, the Romanov dynasty sought the time-honored political safety valve of savage anti-

Semitism. Faithful servants of the Czar forged the infamous Protocols of the Elders of Zion to prove the intent of organized Jewry to dominate the world. High-ranking ministers like Plehve assured the neutrality of the Russian police amid unprecedented bloody pogroms which brought protests from almost every civilized nation, including the United States. The officially inspired massacre of Kishinev in 1903, the riots of the Black Hundreds in 1906—this was the Russian government's version of Ku Klux Klanism, but motivated by a desire to stem the tide of reform sentiment—and a host of lesser incidents of daily life conspired to destroy the final shreds of personal dignity for the Russian Jew. Unlike other emigrants, his numbers grew regardless of depression or prosperity and became the wholesale migration of a people.

In an alien and often hostile atmosphere which was aggravated by the persistence of Old World feuds, the immigrant sought social adjustment in segregated urban areas—"Little Italy," the "Ghetto," "Little Bohemia," and their equivalents among the other nationalities. Within these cultural fragments of the homeland flourished the powerful integrating force of the foreign-language press, which acted as a mediator with the strange outside world. In 1914 there were almost 2,600,000 subscribers to the various foreign-language publications; the German, Yiddish, Bohemian, and Polish were the largest. Newspapers like the polished *Illinois Staats Zeitung* and Abraham Cahan's socially-minded *Jewish Daily Forward* made a direct contribution to civic improvement. Inevitably assimilation, aided by the Americanization movement, weakened the distinctiveness of group lines. Israel Zangwill's play, *The Melting Pot,* in 1908 coined an apt term for the voluntary fusion of peoples in the New World.

This immigration tide, which brought in a heavy Catholic as well as Jewish element, awakened in some minds the hatreds of the old Know-Nothing movement of the 1850's and inspired a campaign, frequently by indirection, to maintain the domination of a native-white Protestant America. The notorious American Protective Association fought "Romanism" and parochial schools, demanded stricter enforcement of immigration laws, and urged new bars against the "foreigner." These forces were aided by a shortsighted sentiment within organized labor against immigration. While many employers favored unrestrained immigration as a source of cheap labor, others feared that "isms" were being imported from European shores and might precipitate another Haymarket Riot.

There were other evidences that the earlier spirit of hospitality toward the immigrant had waned. Prior to 1875, immigration laws had been largely designed to protect the newcomer from exploitation by steamship and industrial interests. After that year the idea of selection took root, and by 1900 various laws barred the Chinese, the alien convict, the prostitute, the insane, the contract laborer, the polygamist, the pauper, and the diseased. The assassination of McKinley in 1901 by the alleged anarchist Czolgosz inspired Roosevelt's successful demand for the addition of a political test to detect anarchist principles. Head taxes for immigrants were steadily increased. Organized labor's control over immigration was strengthened by the Act of 1913 which created a separate Department of Labor and subordinated the various federal immigration bureaus to the departmental secretary.

Republican platforms inspired by Senator Henry Cabot Lodge, scion of an old Massachusetts family, fulminated against "undesirable immigration." Lodge fought strenuously in Congress for almost three decades to convert the selection policy to one of restriction by demanding a literacy test. On four occasions during 1897–1917 a President's veto blocked the Lodge movement, on the principle that literacy is a test of opportunity rather than fitness. Despite Wilson's eloquent plea in a second veto message for the retention of America's tradition of hospitality, Congress secured the necessary two-thirds vote in 1917 to override the President. The melting-pot ideal of American society had cooled perceptibly.

NEGRO LEADERSHIP BECOMES MORE MILITANT

If the road for the immigrant was hard, the peculiar lot of nine million colored Americans, largely in the South, appeared far worse. The century opened with the most incredible wave of lynchings in post-Civil War history; there were 214 victims of mobs during 1900–1901. Even when these savage race riots ended, each year for some time thereafter saw about fifty extra-legal hangings of Negroes. Hitherto informal patterns of segregation in street conveyances and public places assumed a legal status. Housing conditions for the

Negro remained deplorable, especially in the South. "The nucleus of Negro population in southern cities is the alley," observed a scholar at the Southern Sociological Congress of 1914. Crowded hovels, lack of proper diet and sanitation, and disorganized family life fostered a heavy rate of illegitimacy and mortality. The civil rights of the race, which an earlier generation had attempted to protect in the Thirteenth, Fourteenth, and Fifteenth Amendments, had been whittled down by local custom, congressional prudence, and a Supreme Court which had become overconscious of the fact that the Fourteenth Amendment protected such minority "persons" as business corporations rather than the Negro from discrimination by hostile local legislatures and courts.

A modified form of slavery existed in the debt peonage of the Negro sharecropper to the landlord, a paternalistic situation which not infrequently included an element of fraud. During the nineties the softer hand of the aristocrat-planter and the ex-Confederate brigadiers who espoused mercantile and industrial power—the Bourbons—yielded to a revolutionary upsurge of the debt-ridden farmers and tenants who frequently regarded the Negro as a tool of Bourbon ascendancy. As a result, the Progressive movement in the South, for all its salutary economic reforms, bore heavily on the Negro and carried into power at the turn of the century the "demagogues"—Cole Blease in South Carolina, Hoke Smith in Georgia, James K. Vardaman in Mississippi, and Jeff Davis in Arkansas. These men, forerunners of Huey Long and "Gene" Talmadge, convinced their rural constituents that salvation lay not only in a campaign against corporate privilege but also in white supremacy. Negro expression was almost eliminated through grandfather clauses which restricted suffrage to descendants of voters, by literacy tests (color-blind to white illiteracy), and, most important, by white primaries (a peculiar use of a Progressive device) which were tantamount to election in the one-party system of the South. President Theodore Roosevelt committed a major political blunder in 1901, according to the southern press, when he invited the Negro leader, Booker T. Washington, to the White House for lunch.

Nevertheless, the Negro made important strides forward, aided by governmental and private agencies. From the bounty of the federal government arose some seventeen Negro land-grant colleges, provided by an amendment to the famous Morrill Land Grant Act of 1862. In the crucial battle against illiteracy the Rosenwald Fund, the Peabody Foundation, and the Rockefeller-endowed General Education Board played an important role. Negro youth between five and twenty years of age came to school in steadily increasing numbers; the proportion rose from less than one-third in 1900 to over one-half by 1920. More Negroes came to own land; a sharp increase in the number of skilled Negro workmen took place; and the war years brought them unprecedented economic opportunities.

Many thoughtful Negroes began to forsake the conservative leadership of Booker T. Washington, founder of Tuskegee Institute, who insisted that the race could save itself only by becoming indispensable to the white community through expertness in skilled trades. Since organized labor was cool to the prospect of increased Negro competition, Booker T. Washington found himself allied almost exclusively with the "best people"—to use his naïve phrase—the wealthy white employers. Among the more effective younger Negro leaders were men like Dr. W. E. B. DuBois, editor of *The Crisis,* who urged a program of agitation on behalf of Negro rights. As a result, the National Association for the Advancement of Colored People was organized in 1910; this heralded a new era of at least favorable publicity for the plight of the Negro. Inevitably the Negro population came to share a portion, however incommensurate, of the increasing well-being of American society.

TRIUMPH OF "PURE AND SIMPLE" UNIONISM

The opening of the century saw labor and capital closer to the oft-desired "honeymoon" than at any period since the Civil War, a situation promoted by the sensational increase of almost 100 billions in the national wealth during 1900–1920. Although the cost of living rose steadily, wage increases managed by a small margin to outstrip these advances. More important still, since American families frequently had more than one breadwinner prior to World War I, was the unique record of relatively full employment during 1897–1907. The building trades particularly made phenomenal gains in wages and employment.

This picture, however, is seriously marred by stationary or even declining conditions for hundreds of thousands of workers in various manufacturing fields, meat-packing plants, and mines. Thirty per cent of the steel workers in 1910 still worked seven days a week, largely because of the concerted strength of their employers. While it fared much better than it had in the preceding three decades, labor knew the bitter pinch of suffering during the short but acute depressions of 1907 and 1914. But in spite of this, recorded unemployment dropped by almost half in this period. Although the tendency still was to treat unemployment as the fault of the individual and to leave the distressed to the meager resources of private charities and church benefits, by 1913 there were evidences of another point of view. The Chicago *Tribune,* then in its militantly progressive period, asserted that unemployment was not a reflection upon the individual but a reproach to the nation. In an effort to aid the jobless, New York State led the way after 1911 in setting up employment offices, labor market bulletins, and a system of vocational guidance in the schools. Significant proposals made at this time for the alleviation of unemployment through well-planned state and national projects had to wait another generation for their fulfillment.

Faced with nationally organized employers such as the General Managers' Association of railroad companies and the National Manufacturers' Association, labor was not slow to organize effectively on a similar national scale. By 1900 unionized labor had accumulated a number of valuable lessons in organization and tactics from the failures of militant leaders. The decline of the Knights of Labor in the eighties convinced the skilled trades that to carry a large membership of unskilled laborers, easily replaceable in industry, meant a serious handicap in the struggle for better wages and conditions. Further extension of the principle of industrial unionism, i.e., unions organized according to shop rather than craft, had thus been discredited in favor of old-line craft unionism as advocated by the American Federation of Labor.

Under Samuel Gompers, its leader who espoused "pure and simple" unionism, the Federation rejected the notion of a labor party and the oft-mentioned cooperative commonwealth of Lawrence Gronlund and Eugene V. Debs. The Gompers slogan, "Reward your friends and punish your enemies," signified the opportunist ideal of the worker who denied class consciousness and emphasized the methods of economic pressure and negotiation. From a total of half a million paid-up members in 1900, the A. F. of L. membership nearly tripled by 1905; on the eve of our entrance into the First World War it had almost two million adherents.

The federal principle of this organization, by allowing for considerable local control, permitted—under protest of the central body—Jim Crowism among anti-Negro locals and unfortunate local differences in wages and conditions which were not conducive to the best interests of labor. The weapon of a labor boycott against the products of unfair employers turned out to be a boomerang in 1902 in the Danbury Hatters' case, when certain hat manufacturers successfully brought suit against 197 members of the United Hatters of North America on the ground that their national boycott was a violation of the anti-conspiracy provision of the Sherman Anti-Trust Act. Damages of $240,000 were granted the manufacturers and orders were given attaching the homes and savings accounts of the union members.

Four years later came another spectacular incident in the Buck Stove and Range Company case, when the employers secured an unusually sweeping injunction against a boycott by the A. F. of L. which resulted in a prison sentence for Gompers and other labor officials. Although the sentence was never served, this case, together with the Danbury decision, convinced many that the judiciary was hostile to organized labor. Once more the old cry of 1896, "No government by injunction," was raised and anti-labor forces gathered courage. Henry Ford refused to deal with the unions, justifying his stand by introducing a minimum daily wage of five dollars. Labor replied by charging that his assembly line process meant a heavy toll in human health. After its 1910 strike had collapsed, the United States Steel Corporation likewise succeeded in wiping out unionism, thus promoting a situation which culminated in bloodshed less than a decade later.

Leftist groups led by Eugene V. Debs, impatient with Gompers' labor statesmanship and anxious for the restoration of industrial unionism, hastened to join the militant Industrial Workers of the World (the I.W.W.), which had been formed in 1905 as the successor of the American Labor Union and the Western Federation of Miners. Its leader, the colorful William ("Big Bill") D. Haywood, was a Marxist revolutionary who advocated such syndicalist methods as the general strike and sabotage to achieve a socialist victory in "one big union." Despite a small official membership, the I.W.W. came dangerously close to winning the leadership of the labor movement when it gained a major victory in the Lawrence (Massachusetts) strike in 1912 for better wages and conditions for some twenty thousand textile workers. The popular assumption promoted by anti-labor forces, that the I.W.W. regularly practiced the violence implied in its creed, led to its ultimate destruction. However, even the cautious A. F. of L., with its "pure and simple" unionism, had to face the charge of alleged complicity in the dynamiting of the Los Angeles *Times* building in October, 1910, motivated supposedly by resentment of that newspaper's anti-union policies.

THE ADVANCE OF SCIENTIFIC FARMING

With the passing of the era of free land and the wasteful cultivation methods characteristic of it, the American farmer was compelled to meet the same problems of scientific agriculture and conservation that older European communities had faced long before. The successful commercial farm took on the aspect of a factory organization, with expensive farm buildings and equipment and a modern system of roads and communications. The annual factory value of farm machinery advanced by two-thirds during the prewar years. In 1916 almost 30,000 tractors were produced, bringing about a sharp reduction in the land hitherto used for forage crops. Thus the farmer as well as the automobile was bringing Old Dobbin's period of usefulness to an end. This stage of capitalist farming meant a sharp increase in the proportion of tenants throughout the nation, especially in the great single-crop areas of the South and the states of the Great Plains. As yet, however, much of this tenantry could be explained optimistically as the transitional stage to ownership rather than the permanent state of blighted opportunity that was too often the case during the postwar years.

On the whole the prewar farm picture seemed to justify optimism, despite the persistence of an ominous rural migration to the city in the New England and North Central States. The farm owner in most instances possessed a larger share of material goods than his forebears had had. His comfortable, well-furnished farmhouse with its telephone, piano, rural free delivery, and improved transportation facilities was a distinct advance over the more isolated nineteenth-century farm. This was the heyday of farmers' institutes, with their social as well as scientific aspects, that enriched the various rural communities with the knowledge of university agricultural specialists and practical farmers.

With Wilson's victory the farmers gained heavily in federal largess. The Smith-Lever Act of 1914 created a generous grant-in-aid system in behalf of agricultural education through university and governmental extension work in farm villages, and the Federal Farm Loan Act of 1916 attempted to ease the serious problem of oppressive interest rates by means of cooperative financing organizations and indirect federal assistance. The influx of Europeans and the progress of urbanization gave the farmer the largest domestic market he had ever enjoyed. The increase in land values that had been continuous since the nineties meant a substantial addition to the country's capitalized farm property. Examining the cheerful report of the Country Life Commission for the period, President Theodore Roosevelt in 1909 concluded that "the general level of country life is high compared with any previous time or with any other land."

"EMANCIPATED WOMAN"

The American home of this urban era showed some of the trends characteristic of the twenties and thirties and directly reflected the changed status of women. However insistently the arbiters of morals and etiquette might insist on the Victorian middle-class ideal of the carefully sheltered female, the necessities of industrialism conspired to create the "emancipated woman." Although work was still a temporary expedient until matrimony afforded an escape, increasing numbers of women poured into clerical, selling, and teaching positions. Woman's monopoly of elementary school teaching grew steadily and overflowed into the high schools, where men constituted a declining minority. Only in the universities and professional schools did women fail to make much headway. Compensation, however, was another matter, for in skilled types of work women averaged only one-third as much as union men. By 1903, the National Woman's Trade Union

League, a labor organization for women, had been formed to combat such conditions.

The urbanized woman meant inevitably a more individualist one, an attitude that was reflected in a steady increase in the divorce rate and a marked decline of births. Most militant in behalf of birth control was Mrs. Margaret Sanger, formerly a visiting nurse on New York's poverty-stricken East Side. In 1914 she issued the first number of *The Woman Rebel* and began to organize various birth control societies which ultimately became the National Birth Control League. There was also a marked growth in women's clubs; these tended to replace the old-fashioned literary societies by active reform groups.

One of the chief agitations was for woman suffrage, although American women fell far below their English sisters in militancy. By 1900 equal suffrage had been granted in four western states: Wyoming, Idaho, Colorado, and Utah; by 1914 the number had risen to eleven. Illinois' "presidential suffrage" provided an indirect way in which women could vote for President. The feminist leaders in the tradition of Susan B. Anthony were Carrie Chapman Catt and Anna Howard Shaw.

Serving the new feminism was the significant transformation of the middle-class home. In the city, with its sharply rising population, the expansive single-residence home of an earlier day yielded to the compact apartment dwelling. Smaller families, fewer rooms—the traditional guest room became a rarity—miniature kitchenettes, numerous "gadgets" to simplify housework, and commercial laundries meant more leisure for women and reflected their increased interests outside the home. The atmosphere of emancipation even affected women's styles, which slowly discarded long trailing dresses with voluminous sleeves in favor of a shorter and narrower skirt with a separate waist.

THE CITY-PLANNING MOVEMENT

Although urban middle-class people could boast of homes with such newly acquired "necessities" as telephones and incandescent lighting, the laborer's family, especially among recent immigrants, was too often squeezed into rickety, firetrap tenements that lacked all but the most elementary plumbing. Unregulated city expansion, poverty, and the huge influx of immigrants undoubtedly contributed to the growth of these slums. Housing laws remained unenforced, largely because of a corrupt alliance between politicians and absentee landlords. Press agitation in 1901, inspired by the new reform spirit, led to important changes such as the tenement house codes in New York and Chicago and removed the most glaring abuses. The effective inspection service that accompanied these salutary reforms incidentally brought fresh revelations regarding prostitution and other types of commercialized vice, and heralded the end of the old "red light" district.

To combat the disorderly growth of urban centers, a city-planning movement was initiated at the turn of the century and soon swept the nation. In 1901, Daniel H. Burnham, who had won a nationwide reputation as an architect while planning the significant Columbian Exposition of 1893 at Chicago, was invited by a Senate committee to head a commission of three experts to decide upon a building program for the city of Washington. Burnham sought to recover the spirit of the original L'Enfant plan, which provided for streets radiating from an axial center—a harmonious system which President George Washington had adopted for the national capital. The commission visited many European cities and studied the designs of the famous Versailles architects who had served Louis XIV and influenced L'Enfant. The eighteenth-century French ideal of symmetry and civic beauty marked by long tree-lined avenues tended not only to reanimate the decayed survivals of L'Enfant's plan but to stimulate national interest in the long-forgotten art of city-planning.

Sponsored by the leading merchants of Chicago, a city whose growth since the Great Fire of 1871 had been haphazard, Burnham in 1906 offered the outline of a comprehensive plan that stressed the efficient, orderly design of streets and buildings and, to a lesser extent, desirable living conditions as well. Details were elaborated three years later by a committee of several hundred citizens, headed by Charles Wacker, who presented the Chicago Plan that would require decades of work for its fulfillment. Henceforth, as the Wacker Plan, it was taught to Chicago's school children; they were to witness the transformation of rubbish-filled railroad yards along the lake front into an attractive series of parks, boulevards, and smooth automobile roadways. Building lines were eventually revised to form a more harmonious pattern.

The "Plan of New York and Environs," conceived by men who had participated in the Chicago Plan, reflected Burnham's influence. When San Francisco was partly destroyed by earthquake in 1906, Burnham sought vainly to persuade the city that here was an ideal opportunity for planning. Four years later President Taft chose him to be chairman of the National Commission of Fine Arts that was to plan the construction of federal projects. By this time Burnham's "city beautiful" idea had been expanded to include more desirable building and social arrangements. In 1916 New York City forged ahead in leadership by enacting the first zoning ordinance—the regulation of business, industrial, and residential areas to protect home surroundings and prevent incongruous building development. By the twenties, zoning had become a commonplace of city administration.

VOCATIONALISM AND ADULT EDUCATION

Education reflected the material progress and urban interests of the period. Although the prevailing labor scarcity brought about a slight increase in child labor up to 1910, there was a simultaneous rise in school attendance. By 1914 every state in the Union except six in the South had compulsory attendance laws and the laws were more effectively enforced than they had been in the past. Most spectacular was the sudden increase in vocational subjects, indicating the growing needs of industry and business for trained and specialized personnel. Although this was a world-wide trend, the added American emphasis on the practical made learning by doing almost a cult and resulted in a serious overburdening of the curriculum in the secondary schools, especially after 1910. The nine subjects offered by high schools in 1890 were increased to 23 in 1910 and to 43 in 1922. Classical subjects like Greek disappeared; Latin, however, held on with the tenacity of a century plant.

When Massachusetts established a State Board on Industrial Education in 1906, various states and municipalities quickly followed in making vocational subjects part of the curriculum. Congress, too, became convinced of the necessity of government assistance for the vocational movement. The Smith-Lever Act of 1914 subsidized adult training in agricultural and home economics. Much more significant in this field was the Smith-Hughes Act of 1917, supported by Wilson, which created a Federal Board for Vocational Education to administer a grant-in-aid system and generously subsidized state efforts in the teaching of commercial and industrial subjects.

College catalogues offered applied subjects like economics, education, journalism, and chemistry more frequently, and fewer courses in history, political science, French, Latin, Greek, and philosophy. At the opening of the century only the University of Pennsylvania had in its Wharton School a professional college for business subjects. In 1908 the Harvard Graduate School of Business Administration was established with the blessing of the industrialist Owen D. Young, who hailed it as a belated move in the right direction. That same year the first professional school of journalism was established at the University of Missouri; it was sponsored by the Missouri Press Association. A former Missourian, Joseph Pulitzer of the New York *World,* had agreed in 1903 to establish such a school at Columbia University, but its doors were not opened until 1912. By 1917 there were 172 teachers of journalism in 84 educational institutions. Huge endowment gifts to colleges by businessmen, such as those of Rockefeller to the University of Chicago (exceeding $32,000,000) and of George F. Baker to Harvard, guaranteed the sensational growth of these insitutions but without seriously impeding academic freedom. The junior college movement arose at this time to provide higher education for students nearer home and to serve the needs of those who did not intend to complete a four-year liberal arts program.

During these years schools and colleges tended to popularize their offerings, in keeping with the current Progressive trend toward mass education, especially for adults. The University of Wisconsin set up a model of effective extension work throughout the state that provided study centers, lectures, "package" libraries, and correspondence work; in 1913–1915 it reached some 525 communities and a total of 370,750 people.

Most sensational in the field of adult education was the mounting importance of the Chautauqua Institution, founded in 1874 at Fair Point (now Chautauqua), in western New York. Theodore Roosevelt (and others as well) was reported to have said during a visit in 1905 that Chautauqua was "the most American thing in America." It offered popular literary, religious, and scientific lectures by eminent authorities. William R. Harper, before becoming president of the University of Chicago, directed advanced Bible studies at Chautauqua; his Chicago associate, Shailer Mathews, organized in 1912 a Department of Religious Work which stressed the humanitarian spirit of the social gospel. In 1901 Melvil Dewey, originator of the famous Dewey decimal system of library classification, opened a pioneer library school affiliated with Chautauqua. A significant arts and crafts department carried over from England the romantic handicraft enthusiasm of William Morris, stressing the goal of good workmanship as a means of creative self-expression and better living conditions. Labor, feminism, settlement problems—all had their day or week among the discussion circles. A well-planned home study department attracted 8000 to 25,000 members annually and brought the benefits of Chautauqua to the villages and towns of the nation. Under the energetic and scholarly Dr. George E. Vincent, its president during 1907–1915, the Chautauqua Institution reached the peak of its influence, a worthy successor of the early nineteenth-century lyceum with its intellectual and reformist spirit.

THE CHURCH: DECLINE OF SECTARIANISM

The church and its organizations were faced with the need for a profound adjustment to the rising urban spirit. Just as business had revolutionized its organization in the direction of efficiency and centralized responsibility, so the churches, with property valued at $1,677,000,000 in 1916, turned the cares of administration over to expert laymen and specialized boards. New costly churches in the Gothic style, with elaborate organs and trained musicians, reflected the current well-being but invited repeated attacks from journalists who sought their standard of value in the simple origins of Christianity. Moreover, popular interest in religious subjects was ebbing. Although Protestant publications increased their circulation during 1900–1915 from 261,000 to 347,000, this advance was trivial compared to the rapid increase enjoyed by journals devoted to popular science, women's interests, and business. City life bred secular attitudes.

The higher-criticism movement of the late nineteenth century, which denied the miraculous in religion and treated the Bible as an ordinary historical chronicle not altogether free from error, dealt a sharp blow to the doctrinal distinctions of Protestantism and encouraged the tendency to interdenominationalism. This new quest for Protestant unity expressed itself in the expansion of Y.M.C.A. activities, the creation of the Home Missions Council in 1908 to direct a non-competitive missionary movement, and the substitution of interdenominational control over religious schools and colleges in place of the older, exclusively sectarian leadership. The crowning achievement of cooperation among sects was the organization in 1908 of the Federal Council of the Churches of Christ in America to give united expression to the moral and religious teachings of Protestantism.

Complete conciliation, however, was not achieved. The religious rift, North and South, of slavery days which separated Presbyterian, Methodist, and Baptist churches on the basis of the Mason and Dixon line remained unrepaired. Even more serious at the moment was the militant resistance of fundamentalism after 1910 to the teachings of modernism, a program favored in liberal Protestant congregations. Modernism stressed science as an instrument with which to discover the values in religion that could meet the needs of the modern world. Against this, the authoritarian defenders of historic Protestantism issued some 2,500,000 copies of a twelve-pamphlet series entitled "The Fundamentals," which urged the literal truth of the divine birth, resurrection, and imminent second coming of Christ, and the inerrancy of the Bible. The president of the Fundamentalist Association asserted that nothing held the liberals and fundamentalists together except the billions of dollars invested in church property. Most colorful of the opponents to modernism were traveling evangelists like the successful William A. (Billy) Sunday of Philadelphia, a former baseball player who carried over into the pulpit the vocabulary and gestures of that game.

Although Protestant sectarianism was declining, a relatively new organization, the Christian Science Church, founded in Boston by Mary Baker Eddy and based on faith healing, gained numerous adherents; it totaled 86,000 members by 1913, largely among the well-to-do classes. More significant was the fact that sectarianism gave way to a new secular emphasis on the social gospel; this inspired widespread welfare work in the slums by the Salvation Army and the Y.M.C.A., promoted the prohibition movement through the American Anti-Saloon League and the Women's Christian Temperance Union, and organized successive crusades against commercialized vice. All these efforts were eventually rewarded by sweeping local and national legislation. That the Protestant church was not insulated from the labor struggle received public confirmation in December, 1908, when the Federal Council of Churches adopted its famous "Social Creed," which insisted on the "most equitable division of the products of industry that can ultimately be devised."

The striking growth of the Catholic Church in the United States and its strong internal cohesion contrasted with developments among other religious groups. Immigration in this period brought in at least five million additional members from Italy, Austria-Hungary, southern Germany, Polish Russia, and elsewhere. The disruptive force of modernism was crushed as an error by the papal encyclical *Pascendi* in 1907; and Cahenlyism, which attempted to foster national church groups within Catholicism, was opposed by the hierarchy. In recognition of the flourishing state of the church in America, the Vatican removed it from the supervision of the Congregation of Propaganda in 1908 and gave it full ecclesiastical status by creating three American cardinals soon afterward. Protestant susceptibilities were spared through the leadership of such men as Cardinal Gibbons and Archbishop Ireland, whose understanding of American institutions was invaluable during a period of rapid Catholic expansion.

The Roman church in this era of secular interests put increasing emphasis on the teaching of social Christianity, basing its program on the famous encyclical *Rerum Novarum,* issued in 1891 by Leo XIII, "the workingman's pope." The most effective American apostle of this encyclical was the Reverend John A. Ryan, who in 1910 published *A Living Wage,* in which he condemned any wage system that could not provide workers with comfort, recreation, and security.

RISE OF THE SYNDICATED PRESS

Journalism rose to be a mighty industry during this period as the newspaper became thoroughly mechanized and integrated in organization. Two huge cooperative news-gathering agencies, the Associated Press and the Scripps-McRae Press Association, dated from the nineties; and a powerful newcomer, Hearst's International News Service, entered the field in 1906. E. W. Scripps, an outstanding journalist, developed the syndicated feature service in the Newspaper Enterprise Association, which furnished features, cartoons, pictures, and fashion articles to a lengthening list of newspaper clients. Since these "handouts" were sent to editors of every political persuasion, the Scripps editorial policy as reflected in these items became increasingly impersonal in tone after 1909.

Syndicated materials enabled many papers to reduce their staff, particularly on the large Sunday edition. Competition between the new journalistic giants put a premium on sensational features, a practice ornamented by scare headlines in which William Randolph Hearst's New York *Journal* and its satellites excelled. Only an unusually intelligent man like Adolph S. Ochs of the New York *Times* could depend solely on news and news features of the more orthodox variety. Inevitably the smaller newspapers faced the alternative of merger or disaster, and between 1909 and 1919 the number of papers actually declined despite mounting circulation. The "chain" had come to stay in journalism.

The American newspaper now took on the characteristic features of its later appearance during the twenties and thirties. H. C. (Bud) Fisher's "Mutt and Jeff" comic strip found such favor with Mr. Hearst's public that it earned a small fortune for its originator. Hearst himself managed to retain the highest-salaried editor in American journalism, Arthur Brisbane, who had been on the staff of Joseph Pulitzer's New York *World*. Beatrice Fairfax's column, "Advice to the Lovelorn," another syndicated feature, was destined to add its trite wisdom to our national life for three decades. Most creative of all talented humorists was Finley Peter Dunne of the Chicago *Journal*, whose witty column on "Mr. Dooley," an Irish saloonkeeper, and his unfailing client, "Mr. Hennessy," shrewdly analyzed the changing political scene.

The new syndicated press carried with it various social implications, some not altogether favorable. Journalism became an orthodox profession like law or medicine. The newspaperman, declared James

Keeley of the Chicago *Tribune* in 1903, "has moved from Bohemia into a steam-heated flat or a cozy suburban home." From the standpoint of public service, Pulitzer's New York *World* scored in 1905 by its sensational but accurate exposé of insurance corruption, which incidentally started the prosecutor, Charles Evans Hughes, off on a brilliant career that ultimately made him Chief Justice of the Supreme Court. The New York *Evening World* fought a telephone monopoly in 1915 and as a result compelled it to reduce its rates by five million dollars annually.

On the other hand, trial by newspaper became an increasing threat to judicial processes; the invasion of private rights was often without redress for the injured. Most scandalous was the revelation in 1907, inspired by the efforts of the Parkhurst Society, that the New York *Herald* was guilty of publishing "red light" personal columns regularly in its pages. Certain abuses in the press such as the publication of quack medicine advertisements, which came to popular attention through exposés by Samuel H. Adams in *Collier's Weekly,* were remedied by the self-regulation imposed by the Associated Advertising Clubs. There seems little question, however, that the sweeping charges of gross newspaper subservience to advertisers discussed by Upton Sinclair in the *Brass Check* (1920) were too extreme in their implications of a thoroughly corrupt press.

Magazine journalism, stimulated by Frank Munsey's drastic cut in the price of his magazine from twenty-five to ten cents, experienced a real renaissance. While the quality group of journals like *Harper's, Scribner's, Century,* and *The Atlantic Monthly* succeeded in striking a more popular note, other more venturesome magazines—particularly *Munsey's, Cosmopolitan, McClure's,* and *Collier's*—discovered a bonanza in the muckraking movement. Exposé-type material not only was of value to the public in many instances, but it *paid.* Samuel S. McClure wrote in 1904 concerning the generous rewards for exposé material, "None of the contributions of these staff writers has cost *McClure's Magazine* much less than one thousand dollars, and fully half of them have cost as high as two thousand five hundred dollars each." Even George H. Lorimer's mid-Victorian *Saturday Evening Post* and Edward W. Bok's *Ladies' Home Journal* found it useful to intersperse muckraking articles among otherwise conventional material—a policy which brought the *Post* a weekly circulation of one million and similar rewards to the *Journal*. (The social implications of muckraking will be examined again in a political setting.) Other magazines, less fastidious than these, found that there were unexploited frontiers for a scandalmongering journalism which might appeal to the semi-literate and to those seeking escapist fiction. Wild West weeklies, facing a jaded public, yielded to the lure of crime and adventure stories.

DECLINE OF THE GILD TRADITION IN THE THEATER

The theater of this era, while enjoying unusual prosperity, underwent a steady decline from an esthetic point of view. This tale of commercialization has a startling resemblance to the combination movement in business and finance. In 1896 six of the most successful theatrical managers met in Philadelphia to consider the prevailing competitive "chaos" in their field. The stock company, rooted in the creative traditions of the gild spirit, had been an independent group of actors who selected and managed their plays, arranged their own routes, and relied directly upon box-office receipts for their compensation. The Philadelphia conference led to the powerful theatrical syndicate of Klaw and Erlanger, and the organization of a chain of theaters that agreed to "sell time" only through the syndicate.

Stock companies faced extinction. When rebels like the renowned Sarah Bernhardt and David Belasco refused to submit to Klaw and Erlanger, they were barred from all first-class houses; Madame Bernhardt was compelled to perform in a circus tent. An independent movement sponsored by the Shubert brothers led to open warfare but failed to restore the nineteenth-century dramatic tradition. Actors feared the deterioration of talent beneath the grinding effects of profitable long runs which might confine an artist to a single role for years, thus preventing diversification of experience. An ambitious movement in 1909 for an endowed theater along the lines of the Metropolitan Opera Company failed after a brief existence, because of the lack of actors. Stars were attracted by the fabulous salaries which the Midases of the theatrical business could offer.

The more sensitive artist looked upon the Little Theatre movement that sprang up after 1912 as a possible avenue of salvation for the theater. Maurice Browne, an idealistic English actor, organized the pioneer Little Theatre of Chicago to experiment with an independent stage for the training of amateurs in the more creative types of drama. A leading critic, Walter Prichard Eaton, remarked in 1917 of the rising vogue of "little theatres," "They are a protest against the easy, safe professionalism which has divorced our drama from all serious contact with the problems of actual life, which has reopened the gap between the American stage and literature."

The results of the new commercialism, with its spectacular stage and over-lavish effects, were not altogether apparent in the early prewar era and were still far from wholly deadening either the public taste or the individual's talent. Arnold Daly's masterly performance in *Candida* during 1904 initiated a nation-wide vogue for George Bernard Shaw's plays. But Shaw's *Mrs. Warren's Profession,* a study of a prostitute, proved too much for the American Puritan tradition and the police were applauded for stopping the first performance. The blithe Maude Adams charmed audiences by her impish title role in Barrie's *Peter Pan* and brought tears to their eyes by her touching performance in *The Little Minister.* Richard Mansfield, then at the height of his peerless reputation, awed appreciative crowds who came to see *Beau Brummel* and *Ivan the Terrible,* as well as his famous Shakespearean roles.

The first decade of the century brought fame to other celebrities as well. David Belasco, greatest of play producers, won acclaim for his development of Mrs. Leslie Carter's dramatic talents and later those of David Warfield, outstanding character actor. Belasco's colorful dramas, *Madame Butterfly* (1900) and *The Girl of the Golden West* (1905), were the basis of two of Puccini's tuneful operas. Those hardy perennials the Barrymores—Ethel, John, and Lionel—won a faithful host of drama-goers during these years. Audiences crowded the performances of William Gillette, whose rendition of Barrie's *The Admirable Crichton* created a sensation in 1904.

More suited to the popular taste of the advancing decade was George M. Cohan, actor, playwright, composer, and manager, who formed his highly successful partnership with Sam Harris in 1910. Cohan, whom critics called "the Yankee Doodle comedian," attempted to portray the restless American spirit—"the cheeky go-aheadness of the hustling Yankee," as one dramatist put it. For the masses, melodrama reached its acme in Owen Davis' *Nellie, the Beautiful Cloak Model* and its many imitators.

BIRTH OF THE MOVIES

Rivals to the stage soon arrived. From Thomas Edison's kinetoscope of the late nineties, which was a peep show of figures in motion that lasted less than a minute, evolved the Age of the Cinema. In 1903 the Edison studio released Edwin S. Porter's *The Great Train Robbery,* a film 800 feet long which was one of the first complete stories in the history of movies; Porter scored so remarkable a success as to bring a strong flow of capital to the infant industry. Soon after, the nickelodeon era of one- or two-reelers took the country by storm, filling vacant stores and houses with such melodramatic themes as *Trapped by Bloodhounds* and *Raffles, the Amateur Cracksman.* Feature-length films emerged within a few years and the movies ceased to be "chasers" following vaudeville acts, becoming instead an independent form of entertainment and instruction.

By 1908, the inevitable signs of the consolidation spirit appeared. A Motion Picture Patents Company was formed to pool the patent rights of the industry and to "bring discipline" into the field by a system of licenses for trust members; exhibitors were restricted to films produced by the licensed inner circle. Aided by the rising Progressive sentiment against the trusts, independents like Carl Laemmle and William Fox fought back in the press and in the courts as well, and succeeded by 1914 in breaking down the film octopus. Meanwhile the independents, in their efforts to escape injunctions and subpoenas from the monopolists, fled from New York to Los Angeles, conveniently located near the refuge of the Mexican border. As a result, Hollywood, which was relatively free of the conservative restraints of New York finance and was endowed with varied scenic and climatic advantages, became the film capital.

Stars of the stage, attracted by princely salaries, deserted to the screen. Vaudeville and burlesque felt the competition of Mack Sennett's slapstick comedy, with its fantastic "Keystone Cops," custard pie battles, and bathing beauties. One of Sennett's famous protégés was the young English-born comedian Charlie Chaplin, whose getup of baggy trousers, enormous shoes, twirling cane, derby, and slight mustache became familiar to countless people by 1915; Chaplin's gift of pantomime, especially in expressing the pathetic humor of the underdog, gave him a universal appeal. Audiences also idolized Mack Sennett's Mabel Normand, who usually portrayed the simple maid caught in complicated love situations, and Fatty Arbuckle, whose comedy successes proved that everyone loves to laugh at a fat man. In both comedy and serious plots, however exaggerated, sympathy was frequently shown for labor and poverty in the current Progressive mode.

Setting the model for other directors was David W. Griffith, who possessed exceptional technical skill destined to raise the photographic realism of the movies to a high level. Griffith's Kentucky birth undoubtedly enhanced his sentimental love for the ante-bellum South and its chivalric traditions, especially its idealized notions of womanhood. To typify this ultra-romantic innocence, he helped to popularize such stars as Mary Pickford, "America's Sweetheart," Blanche Sweet, and Lillian Gish. *The Birth of a Nation,* his greatest film from the standpoint of direction and photographic art, appeared in 1915, and many individuals paid as much as $2.00 each for admission. So successful was it that President Wilson had it shown at the White House; he marveled at its effectiveness in teaching history. Unfortunately for the sake of race relations the film was based on Thomas Dixon's novel, *The Clansman,* which dealt with the Civil War and Reconstruction in the most exaggerated fashion, portraying the Negro as an inferior being for whom segregation was inevitable, and showing the old Ku Klux Klan as the shield of southern civilization. Race tensions were undoubtedly heightened by this emotional story, and protests came from liberal leaders of both races.

In expiation—so Lewis Jacobs, the historian of the movies, believes —Griffith produced *Intolerance,* a spectacle costing $1,900,000, a new record for expense in motion picture production. As Jacobs observes, this film story of persecution lost much of its point by the over-lavish scenes and intrinsic adventure value. For Griffith and his associates million-dollar pictures could be justified by the fact that in 1917 alone, motion picture audiences paid over $175,000,000 for admission. Middle-class patrons had ceased to regard movies as "lowbrow."

URBAN TRENDS IN MUSIC: TRADITION VERSUS RAGTIME

American taste in music underwent considerable transformation. Repeated efforts to establish a permanent opera in cities outside of New York failed despite heavy subsidies, but many thousands came to hear the musical art of Caruso and Galli-Curci. More successful was the extension of the symphony orchestra companies from the metropolis to the smaller cities. Theodore Thomas, America's leading conductor, who had come to this country from Germany as a boy in 1845, saw in the dedication of Orchestra Hall in Chicago in 1904 the triumph of his dream of a permanent home for his orchestra. His lifelong attempt to teach Americans appreciation of the best symphonic music through a well-planned series of programs was handed down to his talented young assistant conductor, Frederick Stock.

Men like Theodore Thomas and Anton Dvořák, the noted Bohemian composer, encouraged Americans to believe in the possibilities of native music, with its Indian, Negro, and cowboy traditions. Arthur Farwell of Cornell University, a rising young composer, established the Wa-Wan Press in 1901 to enable compositions on native themes to obtain an outlet hitherto denied by commercially-minded publishers. A vogue for Indian melodies soon developed, actively promoted by the foremost American composer, Edward MacDowell of Columbia University, whose "Indian Suite," written in 1896, offered a model to younger artists. MacDowell charged that the universities were materialistic in neglecting to provide adequate fine arts programs. His insistence upon a drastic revision of Columbia's fine arts curriculum in the direction of greater idealism brought about his resignation under fire and his tragic death soon afterward.

"American" music arrived in curiously devious ways and in keeping with the predominant tempo of the dawning machine age. Irving Berlin, a young Russian-Jewish immigrant who lived on New York's Europeanized East Side, found expression of the toiling urban masses in a fresh rhythmic version of the sentimental popular music of the nineties. His "Alexander's Rag-Time Band," written in 1912, emerged from the atmosphere of the Bowery saloons to captivate millions and herald the new urbanized spirit. That same year the "father of the blues," William C. Handy, an Alabaman Negro who managed a minstrel show, created a pioneer conception of modern jazz in the plaintive notes of "Memphis Blues." His subsequent "St. Louis Blues" achieved a fame that few composers could surpass. A well-integrated musical industry arose to sell these wares in "Tin Pan Alley," as West 28th Street in New York City came to be known.

While the infant stages of jazz were developing, crowded theaters found the acme of perfection in the operetta, listening to the romantic Viennese themes of Franz Lehar's *The Merry Widow* (1907) and Oscar Strauss' *Chocolate Soldier* (1909). Especially popular was the gifted and prolific Irish-American composer of light operas, Victor Herbert, who won a huge following with *Babes in Toyland* (1903) and *Naughty Marietta* (1910). Americans loved the sentimental notes of "Kiss Me Again" from his *Mlle. Modiste* and "Because You're You" from *The Red Mill.* But his attempt at more serious operas, as in *Natoma* (1911), which was based on an Indian theme, was only moderately successful; a second opera, *Madeleine,* was much less so.

The rising tempo of an urbanized culture was reflected in the swift popularity of the lively one-step, the fox trot, and the tango, which pressed hard upon the dominion of the more dignified waltz and two-step. These dances appeared in large part against the commercialized background of the newly imported cabaret and the dance hall. It is noteworthy that the creative American genius of Isadora Duncan, who rebelled against the artificiality of the ballet and sought her inspiration in the simple flowing expressions of classical dancing, required a European introduction to her native land.

URBANIZED RECREATION

Sport bore the undeniable imprint of this urban age of commercial organization, for crowded cities scarcely permitted the simple recreations of a rural society. In baseball at the opening of the century, two well-financed major leagues, the American and the National, faced each other in a bitter rivalry for city franchises, territories, and highly skilled players. By 1903 this was sublimated into the more entertaining rivalry which the public enjoyed. Detailed rules were drawn up for playing professional baseball and a national commission was appointed to enforce them. Then there revived the exciting annual World Series which became a colorful feature of our national life. Fans came to worship Frank L. Chance and John J. McGraw of the National League and Frank Baker and Ty Cobb of the American. The World Series of 1917 attracted 185,000 spectators to its six games and reaped $425,000 at the box office.

Football remained an amateur college sport in theory, but it too became an expensive regime of high-salaried coaches, an elaborate method of recruiting players, and a scientific study of strategy. The early years of the century seemed inauspicious for the sport when, as in 1903, 44 players were killed; many others suffered serious injuries each year. The climax was reached in 1905 when Columbia University abolished the game. To save a sport he greatly admired, President Roosevelt invited football leaders to the White House for a conference. This and subsequent sessions resulted in salutary regulations for the game which quickly restored its popularity. By 1914 football had become the breadwinner for the lesser college sports.

Boxing still retained its stigma as the sport par excellence of the underworld, despite considerable interest in the exploits of the mighty James J. Jeffries. Promoters found the race issue useful in stimulating attendance when they emphasized the search for a "white hope" able to defeat the Negro champion, Jack Johnson. Basketball advanced considerably under the pioneer sponsorship of Dr. James A. Naismith of the Y.M.C.A. School in Springfield, Massachusetts; it is famed as the only major sport to originate in the United States. Horse racing, hounded by reformers, led an irregular existence. When Governor Charles Evans Hughes of New York outlawed race-track betting in 1908, he delivered the sport a heavy blow that drove it to Havana, Tia Juana, and Montreal. Despite these handicaps, the year 1912 alone saw over six million dollars distributed in purses and stakes.

Golf and tennis became the middle-class sports of the "dude era" and inspired the expenditure of huge sums in suburban areas for golf links and courts. In his retirement, Roosevelt thought it necessary to warn his good friend William Howard Taft against indiscreetly publicizing his golf game and thus flouting the popular prejudice against dudes. Official sanction was lent to the world of sport in 1910 when President Taft recommended that Congress spend $50,000 to enable the United States to participate in the First International Field Sports Exposition at Vienna.

The middle classes enjoyed their flourishing fraternal societies; these practically doubled in membership during 1900–1917. In 1910 the luncheon club movement began among businessmen with the organization of the Rotary International. Among this class too, the automobile gained tremendous popularity during the first decade of the century; by 1916 there were at least four million cars in the nation. Henry Ford's mass production of low-priced cars enabled the lower middle classes, particularly the farm owner, to bask in the sun of the socially elite. The Ford car, despite the epidemic of good-natured jokes regarding its alleged flimsy construction, came to represent one-sixth of the automobiles in use.

The masses, however, patronized overwhelmingly the commercial amusement parks, a leading feature of urban recreation. One resort in New York's Coney Island collected no less than five million paid admissions in a single season. Nor was this tendency limited to the East. The five amusement parks in Kansas City reported a seasonal attendance of almost two million people in the summer of 1911, and receipts close to $670,000. The bicycle craze which had captivated both sexes in the nineties still held its appeal, supported by the practical consideration that this modest vehicle provided the workman with cheap transportation to his job. All classes of people were attracted to the various world's fairs which blossomed after the famous Columbian Exposition of 1893, and hundreds of thousands swarmed to San Francisco, St. Louis, and other cities where these elaborate pageants were held. So strong in fact was the urge for recreational outlets that the Sabbath-day observance of traditional Protestantism broke down as workmen demanded that amusement centers, including saloons, be kept open on Sundays.

Prewar America on the whole presents an attractive picture of energy and unbounded faith in the future. Although the essential pattern of a machine age culture, destined to reach fruition in the twenties, had begun to appear, there remained much of the color of late nineteenth-century society. The deadly uniformity of a thoroughly mechanized society which Emerson so much abhorred was yet to come. A later generation, disillusioned by the crash of fervid hopes, was to idealize this period as the golden age of American innocence. Both extremes of romanticism and cynicism seem unwarranted. There was indeed a sordid side of blighted hopes for many of that generation of 1900–1917, and the sober realist finds far more than social wreckage in the decade after 1929.

CHAPTER 2

The Pragmatic Spirit in American Thought: 1900-1917

EVOLUTION AND PRAGMATISM

The generation that reached maturity in 1900, like its parents, was largely under the spell of evolutionary thought. Charles Darwin's *Origin of Species* (1859) had explained the biological evolution of man from a simple life form upward by means of progressive adaptations to the environment through a process of natural selection which determined the organisms able to survive. There had ensued a bitter controversy both here and abroad over the conflicting claims of science and religion, compelling theologians in many quarters to yield their emphasis on the supernatural and on rigid sectarianism in favor of social Christianity and interdenominationalism. Following in the successful path of the biologists (and in many instances preceding them) were the social evolutionists, who tried to explain the origin and growth of social institutions like the family, the state, property, and law in Darwin's terms of gradual stages by adaptation toward a higher and more satisfying form.

For social Darwinists like Herbert Spencer and his American disciple William Graham Sumner, social evolution meant largely a struggle for existence leading to the survival of the fittest and presumably to a better world. Hence economic conservatives who defended *laissez faire* in business could criticize social reform as unscientific interference with the natural laws of business competition. Professor Sumner, ridiculing the socialist panaceas of Upton Sinclair, said bluntly, "This is a world in which the rule is 'Root, hog, or die,' and it is also a world in which 'The longest pole knocks down the most persimmons.' It is the popular experience which has formulated these sayings. How can we make them untrue?" Here was the anarchic individualism of the jungle in which the stronger survived. Despite the idealistic Declaration of Independence, only the inequality of men was self-evident.

But the intellectual leaders of Progressivism who combated extreme individualism during the prewar era also found comfort in the evolutionary philosophy. Instead of relying upon the blind forces of nature to select those qualities best fitted to survive, they believed that human intelligence, strengthened by a practical ethics, could direct the evolutionary process of society. So thought William James, John Dewey, Lester F. Ward, and many of their contemporaries. "I devoutly believe in the reign of peace and in the gradual advent of some sort of socialistic equilibrium," affirmed James in *The Moral Equivalent of War*. Ward attacked the notion that social control and reform constituted artificial interference with nature. Civilization itself, he observed, is an artificial product. "Every adjustment made at the behest of inventive genius is an interference with the course of natural law. Every object of art is such as nature would never have created." It is interesting to note that Woodrow Wilson spoke the individualist language of Spencer and Sumner on business and labor questions until his conversion a few years prior to his administration. To the Progressives, social evolution meant intelligent and persistent experimentation to attain the goal of progress.

The Spencerian individualists as well as their "collectivistic" opponents not only shared the evolutionary philosophy which they applied to the social sciences, but also tended to accept the related belief in pragmatism. This American development was a practical outgrowth of the evolutionary controversy and must be defined in its historical setting. The social evolutionists, by stressing the idea of constant change, helped to destroy the traditional world of absolute moral values. Their comparative studies of religion, society, and morals during the nineteenth century shattered much of the faith in revelation, the Bible, and the natural foundations of morality. What was right or wrong in a given society now appeared relative to place, time, and circumstance. In the United States, the frontier tradition and the practical problems arising from subduing a continent were unfavorable for purely abstract speculation. Life was too pressing for the fullest exercise of the logician's art. Tiring of the prolonged controversy over science versus religion, with its metaphysical subtleties, several American philosophers developed what was in effect a formula of compromise known as pragmatism. It was not precisely new, for practical Americans like Benjamin Franklin had long before been guided by its point of view.

Pragmatism became popular through William James, then professor of philosophy at Harvard University. Although born in New York City in 1842, he spent most of his life in New England, imbibing Emerson's optimistic ideal of individualism and self-reliance but also influenced by the reformist enthusiasms of his noted father, Henry James. After considerable travel and a stimulating education abroad, he turned to a career of teaching, first in anatomy and physiology, then after 1875 in psychology and philosophy. James was decisively influenced intellectually by the Leipzig psychology laboratory of Wilhelm Wundt, with its emphasis on experimentation and its sharp break with the philosophical tradition. In 1890 appeared his revolutionary two-volume work, *Principles of Psychology,* which embodied a new biological interpretation of the mind and was destined to convert John Dewey, among many others, to teaching psychology as an experimental science apart from mental and moral philosophy.

During 1906–1907 William James achieved wide fame by his lectures on pragmatism at the Lowell Institute in Boston and at Columbia University. Attributing this term to the philosopher Charles S. Peirce, James elaborated the concept until it became intimately identified with himself. He took issue with the professional philosophers, whose results he characterized as pure abstractions, verbal solutions, bad a priori reasons, fixed principles, closed systems, and "pretended absolutes and origins." "The whole function of philosophy," he explained in defining pragmatism, "ought to be to find out what definite difference it will make to you and me, at definite instances of our life, if this world-formula or that world-formula be the true one." The pragmatic method was but an instrument, not an answer to problems; only by examining the *consequences* of an act, rather than first principles, did one solve the problem of its goodness or badness, truth or falsehood. This was more than mere relativism, for, as he added, "If theological ideas prove to have a value for concrete life, they will be true for pragmatism, in the sense of being good for so much." James's realism rejected "inherent" or "objective truth" insofar as these concepts failed the pragmatic test of experience and everyday life. With Yankee instinct he stressed the "cash value" of ideas in terms of how they acted in a concrete situation.

Pragmatism was therefore a call to action and achievement, a fit product of an age which produced Taylor's efficiency system in industry and Progressivism in politics. In Europe after the First World War, it is true, pragmatists like Mussolini rejected democracy and intellectualism to teach a crude national expediency which suited the Fascist mentality. Whatever served the fatherland was necessarily good to these pragmatists of the Fascist variety, regardless of the injury done to other nations. Later critics were to point out that if thought without action was sterile, as the pragmatists claimed, action based on doctrines of the will or racial instinct produced moral chaos. In the prewar era of Rudyard Kipling's shining imperialism, not a few American writers, from Professor John W. Burgess to Jack London, believed in the mission of the Anglo-Saxon peoples to make over civilization in their own image. American pragmatism, however, was tempered by favorable economic conditions and by the frontier tradition of democracy. As it happened, at least for this era James's pragmatism had an undeniable creative value at home.

The majority of American philosophers did not accept pragmatism in the technical sense, but there were numerous rebels against the absolutism of the hitherto dominant school of idealistic philosophy represented by Professor Josiah Royce, a friend of William James. In 1910 a small academic group of "new realists" led by Ralph Barton Perry of Harvard, a student (and later biographer) of James, not only tore down the ivory tower of the idealists by their criticism, but also assailed the extreme relativist conception of truth implied in James's pragmatism. American philosophy, according to Professor William P. Montague, who was one of these insurgents, recovered its health after being out of touch with science and was thus rescued from the "paradoxical and the unimportant."

JOHN DEWEY: "LEARNING BY DOING"

James took occasion to commend the brilliance of the Chicago School, led by John Dewey, whose instrumentalism was the fulfillment of the Harvard professor's own pragmatic method. Born in Burlington, Vermont, on October 20, 1859, Dewey was trained under the pioneer psychologist G. Stanley Hall, who himself had worked (as did William James) to overthrow the older rational psychology in favor of an experimental science. James's *Principles,* containing an early statement of pragmatism, proved to be a revelation to Dewey and opened the road to those observations in educational psychology upon which the latter's reputation rests.

In 1894 Dewey came to the new University of Chicago, which had blossomed overnight through the millions of John D. Rockefeller as a formidable rival to Harvard and Johns Hopkins. The zealous president, William R. Harper, had won him from the University of Michigan by offering him a philosophy and psychology professorship which included a branch of pedagogy. Interested parents and associates aided Dewey in establishing a pioneer experimental elementary school, popularly known as the Dewey School and the predecessor of a later crop of progressive education schools. His able colleagues in philosophy helped to complete his conversion to experimentalism along democratic lines. An academic difference with the university administration over control of the laboratory school led to his resignation in 1904 and his subsequent transfer to Columbia University, the scene of his later contributions in philosophy and education.

During the prewar period Dewey's writings in logical theory and ethics attracted considerable comment because of their pragmatic temper. In discussing educational theory at Teachers College, Columbia, he declared that the primary task of the school was to train children in cooperative living rather than in artificial assignments, and that the root of all educational activity must be sought in the "instinctive, impulsive attitudes and activities of the child." He stressed industrial subjects and the cultivation of individual interests by participation in meaningful tasks. Dewey's instrumentalism, which rejected thought divorced from action, reflected the practical yet idealistic American attitude at the turn of the century. His "learning by doing" became the theoretical ideal of an ensuing generation of teachers to whom his *Democracy and Education,* published in 1913, represented indisputable authority.

The intensive application of philosophy, pedagogy, and psychology to everyday life brought forth as one of its chief fruits educational psychology, which was simultaneously developing as an independent discipline in Germany. To Edward L. Thorndike of Columbia University, psychology was not a study of mind in the abstract, but rather a mechanistic science of behavior in which mind appeared as an evolving organism adapting itself to its environment through a physiological habit system. In an attempt to achieve objectivity, Thorndike applied the methods of exact science to educational problems and stressed experiments with animal learning. His significant three-volume work, *Educational Psychology* (1913), helped to make this study an applied science and won for him a large academic following.

TRENDS IN ECONOMICS

In economics, the pragmatic temper left a definite pattern of dynamic thought that moved toward a closer alliance with the concepts of business and industry. Large numbers of economists were called into governmental and private service, the study of business economics became popular, and a sharp increase in commercial subjects offered by schools and colleges occurred. Economic theory tended to forsake purely abstract speculation regarding immutable classical laws; instead it embarked upon experimental formulas which carried more immediate applications for the everyday world of the market place and the ethical distribution of wealth. As a result, this period witnessed major advances in price theory, welfare economics, and economic history.

In the closing years of the nineteenth century there arose a group of economists who charged that the orthodox school, with its neat axioms of supply and demand, failed to deal adequately with the economic behavior of real human beings and a changing society. Like other pragmatists, these men—they were known as institutionalists—saw life as a continued flux and hence sought explanations in terms of actual observation rather than in static rules. To them, economic institutions evolved by constant adaptation not only to new inventions and technical methods but also to the ever-changing attitudes of society. Instead of using the formal logic of orthodox economics, they studied causation through sociological analyses and heavily factual studies covering such institutions as trade unionism, business cycles, the wage system, the business corporation, and the class structure of society. As a result, their findings sometimes enriched all the social sciences simultaneously. Reformers often found grist to their mill in these challenging interpretations of economic motives.

Thorstein Veblen, who had come as an economist to the new University of Chicago with J. Laurence Laughlin, was the arch-proponent of the institutionalist school. His famous book, *The Theory of the Leisure Class* (1899), appeared to have nothing in common with the conventional idea of economics, for it was a psychological and historical analysis of class relationships, written with a wealth of ethnological details. Economic institutions, like other human arrangements, he pointed out, grew out of human instincts which conditioned man's survival and development. Property institutions were associated with acquisitive or predatory instincts, whereas creative technological methods were an outgrowth of the service ideal. Veblen's *Instinct of Workmanship* (1914) and similar books which followed stressed the clash in society of the predatory element of self-interest (to which he attributed the origin of various exploitative institutions) with the creative instinct of true achievement. There is not a little suggestion of Marxism in this twofold struggle in which the dominant group fashions all institutions in its own interest.

Another institutionalist, Wesley C. Mitchell, offered a more practical economics than did Veblen. Mitchell's *Business Cycles* (1913) was a historical and statistical study of economic trends in the United States, England, and France from 1890 to 1911. In common with certain contemporaries both at home and abroad, Mitchell refused to deal with recurrent economic crises as purely accidental. His analysis of the periodicity of these crises, together with the contributions made by Henry L. Moore's *Economic Cycles* (1914) and the work of Warren M. Persons in 1915, opened the way toward the refined statistical technique of forecasting general business conditions. Economics thus moved a step further into the intimate counsels of American captains of industry.

APPLIED SOCIOLOGY

Sociology too, like economics, was remolded under the challenging spirit of pragmatism. It tended to ignore metaphysical systems altogether in its concern for the pressing problems of the immediate future and the forging of scientific tools to deal with these problems. The year 1900 saw the preeminence of Lester Frank Ward of Brown University, one of the founders of sociology, whose *Dynamic Sociology* (1883) was to be supplemented by his *Pure Sociology* (1903) and *Applied Sociology* (1906). Ward stressed the psychological basis of sociology, teaching that the feelings, ambitions, and desires of men drive them on to action; that group restraints and approvals are "social forces" and are organized into social institutions; thus feelings are the dynamic aspect of mind, and in sociology this dynamic aspect is fundamental. These social forces were to be channelized into desirable ends. Rejecting the paternalism of Comte and the *laissez-faire* ideas of Spencer, Ward taught that sociology's mission was to provide the scientific direction of society toward a democratic goal of achievement. Science, rather than charity, would achieve social melioration.

Among the first generation of academic sociologists whose work extended to the twentieth century was Albion W. Small, who had studied at the universities of Berlin and Leipzig as well as at Johns Hopkins. He was one of "that distinguished band of scholars," attracted by unrivaled facilities for research and by the unprecedented salary of $7000 paid to each department head, whom President William R. Harper called to the University of Chicago in 1893. In 1895 he established *The American Journal of Sociology*, which quickly assumed leadership in its field. Small's *General Sociology* (1905) introduced leading German sociologists to a generation of Americans and familiarized the latter with the various concepts of social forces. To Small, who was influenced by the current emphasis on social Christianity, social forces had a very practical mission: "to interpret the meaning of human experience, and to find out how human experience may be directed in the future toward a larger output of life's values." He opposed Spencer's extreme individualism, but his interest in the attainment of the better life did not prevent his emphasis on scientific method as a prerequisite to advancement.

Among the first to teach formal courses in sociology was William Graham Sumner of Yale, the founder of a sociological school who entered the final decade of his active life as the new century began. Unlike Ward and Small, Sumner was an uncompromising individualist of the Spencer variety who held fast to an extreme social Darwinism which condemned even moderate social legislation. He coined the striking term "forgotten man" to designate the unfortunate taxpayer compelled to bear the burden of increased governmental social services. In 1907 appeared his *Folkways,* which became one of the most influential works in sociology. To many readers it seemed to attack objective social values in favor of a form of moral relativism—the idea that the mores, or group sanctions, make anything right or wrong and have no rational basis except in group beliefs and desires. This sociology had iconoclastic effects on ethics and politics as well as on economics, for it apparently explained orthodox ideas of right and wrong as products of an evolutionary process in which mere caprice played a large role. It implied a deep distrust of the state and of majority rule as well, and left a huge anarchic sphere for the individual.

"SOCIOLOGICAL EVANGELISM" AND THE SETTLEMENT MOVEMENT

One of the dynamic intellectual forces in the Progressive revolt was social Christianity, which, after several decades of rapid growth, reached its climax just prior to World War I and influenced many of the chief reform leaders of the era. From nineteenth-century England, Charles Kingsley and F. D. Maurice had spread the "social gospel" of reconstructing the modern social and economic order upon the doctrinal principles of Christianity. This was part of the popular rebellion against the industrial evils which were associated with the factory system and against the increasing secular indifference to traditional values which accompanied the rise of large cities.

In the United States, notably after 1880, a vast reformist literature on social Christianity—novels, short stories, essays, tracts—written by both ministers and laymen came into existence and circulated widely. Chautauqua speakers, eminent college professors and religious leaders, and journalists took a militant stand for the social teachings of Christ. In the forefront were such representative Americans as Richard T. Ely, John R. Commons, Albion W. Small, E. A. Ross, Graham Taylor, Jane Addams, Frances E. Willard, Shailer Mathews, Hamlin Garland, Walter Rauschenbusch, and Norman Thomas (who became the Socialist leader after Debs). Social Christianity frankly met the challenge offered by the current labor unrest, poverty, ruthless business practices, and other questions that absorbed the Progressives. It found a doctrinal basis in the dogma of God's presence within human society and the mission of religion to build a kingdom of righteousness on earth. Secular and sacred interests lost their distinctiveness, being fused into a common religious experience which was applied to everyday problems. A large wing of these reformers rejected the competitive economic order in favor of a cooperative system. Others contented themselves with formulations of a "Christian sociology" which would put this study in the direct service of religion.

Walter Rauschenbusch of the Rochester Theological Seminary in New York, who had been influenced by Henry George, Marx, and Tolstoy, as well as by the Scriptures, did much to popularize the Social Gospel as well as to provide a theological framework for it. His most popular book, *The Social Principles of Jesus* (1916), was written in the earnest spirit of the ancient prophets. At the University of Wisconsin, Richard T. Ely, the economist, vigorously championed these ideals in many publications and lecture halls. He regarded the emphasis on the otherworldly nature of Christianity as a gross mistake and demanded that divinity schools teach more economics and sociology to emphasize "preventive philanthropy" aimed at poverty and disease. Another influential religious teacher and author, George D. Herron of Grinnell College, fervently preached the "Christian State" and "industrial democracy" based on a socialist system administered in a spirit of "social sacrifice." As noted previously, this movement culminated in the organization in 1908 of the Federal Council of the Churches of Christ in America, a Protestant group which stressed "a living wage" for labor and "the application of Christian principles to the acquisition and use of property, and for the most equitable division of the products of industry that can ultimately be devised."

This type of "sociological evangelism," as it has been called, provided a major impulse (although not the only one) for the settlement movement, the social survey, and to some extent the professionalization of social work. The American settlement movement, led by Jane Addams of Hull House in Chicago and Lillian Wald of the Henry Street Settlement in New York City, had been inspired by Toynbee Hall, an English organization founded in 1884 to solve the problems of poverty and social adjustment by means of university-trained "residents" rather than through any "superimposed institutions." By living among the European newcomers to this country, the residents came to respect the culture of the immigrants. Americanization did not seem to require the wanton destruction of the traditions of an alien people. Lillian Wald did much on New York's East Side in originating public health nursing by combining the nurse's technique with that of the social worker, thus affording an intimacy and scientific approach previously absent. Jane Addams and her associates were able to create at Hull House a laboratory for essential social legislation on the basis of their experience with the bewildered, inarticulate masses of Chicago's poverty-stricken West Side. Out of the settlement movement—in large part at least—came valuable educational institutions which were later adopted by the public school system: playgrounds, nursery schools, adult education, home economics classes, and manual training, as well as public health nursing.

At Kingsley House in Pittsburgh, a settlement center significantly named after the British Christian Socialist, Charles Kingsley, there developed the institution of the social survey. Borrowing the technique of the Booth survey of the London slums, Paul U. Kellogg, a noted social statistician, and his associates turned their trained minds upon the economic status of the steel workers' community in Pittsburgh. Their *Findings*, published in six volumes during 1909–1914, afforded a comprehensive analysis of the economic and social structure of community life which was supplemented by various documentary photographs and exhibits. Thus a scientific basis for social action was laid; it was perpetuated after 1914 by such organizations as the Russell Sage Foundation.

Although social work in the professional sense was still in its infancy during this period, definite advances were made in the expansion of a specialized social work curriculum. Summer school courses and one-year programs in academic social work were still the rule. Ultimately, full-time professional schools were modeled on the New York School of Philanthropy and the Boston Training School for Social Workers, both of which were established in 1904. As late as 1915, however, Abraham Flexner, an authority on the subject, could still insist that social work was not a profession. A new era was heralded in 1917 by the publication of Mary E. Richmond's textbook, *Social Diagnosis*, the first authoritative presentation of social case work techniques; it was written from a sociological point of view.

SOCIOLOGICAL JURISPRUDENCE

This sociological trend in academic thinking furnished one of pragmatism's most distinctive triumphs—sociological judisprudence. Certain European legal theorists had already prepared the way for the idea that law must concern itself less with the traditional emphasis on abstract principles and laws divorced from a social context and more with the actual working of judicial processes in their application to present-day situations. Legal institutions, the sociological school believed, must primarily fulfill social ends; lawyers should not retire behind the walls of a self-sufficient jurisprudence but should study the sociological bearings of the application of law in a changing world. This position, which greatly strengthened the state's role in serving social interests above individual property rights—the enhancement of the police power—received its early formulation in the United States from Oliver Wendell Holmes before 1900. Somewhat later Roscoe Pound of Harvard, teaching the continuous adaptation of law to changing human needs, still further elaborated the philosophy of legal pragmatism.

Perhaps the flowering of sociological jurisprudence appeared in the creation of the "Brandeis brief"; for in Muller *v.* Oregon (1908), Louis Brandeis argued successfully in behalf of an Oregon ten-hour law for women by introducing considerable sociological data to support his contentions. This case did much to destroy the baleful effect of the over-legalistic opinion in Ritchie *v.* Illinois (1895), which invalidated Governor Altgeld's humane program to reduce the working hours of women. Among the influential sociological jurists was a professorial friend of William James, Associate Justice Oliver Wendell Holmes of the Supreme Court, who preferred to rely on the practical experience of legislators regarding property rights rather than trust too much in the a priori abstractions of the traditional courtroom. Finally, sociological jurisprudence thrived in the law school atmosphere fostered by the relatively new casebook method of legal education which discarded traditional textbook maxims in favor of concrete applications drawn from the world of experience as well as historic precedent.

REALISM IN POLITICS AND HISTORY

Spurred on by the practical aspects of the new economics and sociology, political scientists rejected the older absolutist doctrines regarding sovereignty and the state in favor of a pragmatic view of the workings of politics and actual government and the evolution of political institutions. The most striking work among that of the younger professors was *An Economic Interpretation of the Constitution* (1913) by Charles A. Beard, who explained the movement for the Constitution as being prompted by economic pressure groups rather than by the common desire of the people as a whole. Beard's emphasis upon economic interests as the motivating force behind a hallowed national document shocked his colleagues at Columbia University.

Prewar political science profited by the scientific methods taught in German seminars. John W. Burgess of Columbia, who in 1906 was honored by being made the first exchange professor to Germany, had studied with von Ranke, Gneist, and Waitz, and as a result taught the practical importance of critical scientific methods and stressed the evolutionary approach. Politically individualistic, he feared the encroachment of government upon individual rights; he expressed this fear in *The Reconciliation of Government with Liberty* (1915), which intimates that any government is best served by an aristocracy of "the wise and the good." However, he was ready to preach the imperialist mission of all the Teutonic nations to civilize backward peoples by strong methods. One of Burgess's colleagues, William A. Dunning, attracted many brilliant students to his seminars in political theory and the history of Reconstruction. Dunning taught, even if he did not always practice it, that political theories must be studied not as logical formulas within a social vacuum but as an integral expression of their times. Among other of the more realistic works in political science were Albert B. Hart's *Actual Government* (1903) and A. Laurence Lowell's studies of the British government.

Early twentieth-century history, too, reflected the new realistic trend, particularly in the vogue for regional history in its economic and social setting. While the authors of the various encyclopedic histories of the United States no longer sought, like George Bancroft, to find a mystical message regarding the will of Providence in history, most of the later encyclopedists continued to give a heavily political interpretation of the nation's past. But even here a note of greater realism was present. In 1906 James Ford Rhodes, a retired Cleveland businessman and amateur historian, completed the sixth and seventh volumes of his *History of the United States from the Compromise of 1850.* Although Rhodes showed little interest in the West and in economic history, he now devoted more space than previously to social history; and in his interpretation of the Civil War and Reconstruction, even if biased in favor of New England—in the opinion of his successors—he made a far greater attempt to achieve objectivity than earlier historians had.

John Bach McMaster of the University of Pennsylvania produced during 1900–1913 the final four volumes of his *History of the People of the United States from the Revolution to the Civil War,* which gave serious attention to social history and recognized the importance of the West. His realism, however, was marred by a nationalist tone and a predominantly descriptive treatment based heavily on the newspapers; but his revealing footnotes became the starting point for many a lesser scholar. Far more aware of the social forces in history was Edward Channing of Harvard, who completed the first four volumes of his *History of the United States* between 1905 and 1917. But by this time the younger sectional historians were finding even this work inadequate in its discussion of western and southern history.

THE TURNER FRONTIER SCHOOL OF HISTORIANS

The most original contribution to history was made by a professor who rebelled against the overemphasis given at Johns Hopkins to the Teutonic origins of American institutions. This was Frederick Jackson Turner of the University of Wisconsin, a social evolutionist who had opened new vistas of research and speculation for historians in 1893 by his paper, "The Significance of the Frontier in American History," which he read before the American Historical Association at Chicago. The frontier process, he insisted, conditioned the growth of American nationality by encouraging individualism, democracy, inventiveness, and a grasp of material things. "The true point of view in the history of this nation," he said, "is not the Atlantic Coast, it is the Great West." Whatever was unique in American historical experience was due to the influence of the various "wests" on our development. But the frontier process had now ended, he warned, and with it began a new stage of history. Turner usually preferred to state his thoughts in numerous scattered essays, but he made a noteworthy exception in 1906 by publishing *The Rise of the New West* in the "American Nation Series" edited by Albert B. Hart; it is one of the best volumes in the series. His method was sociological, and it excelled in clarity and illuminating generalizations.

A Turner school of historians arose so quickly and in so authoritative a form that it was not altogether certain that the unorthodox Turner himself could always be persuaded to remain within its limits. In *The Mississippi Valley in British Politics* (1917) Clarence W. Alvord proved that western fur interests and land speculation explained much of the content of British imperial diplomacy. Working along these lines, the younger historians, particularly in the Old Northwest, discovered a new factor in the frontier influence upon diplomatic and social questions once deemed restricted to the Atlantic seaboard. The fresh concern with social and economic history was exemplified in Beard's *Economic Origins of Jeffersonian Democracy* (1915), in Gustavus Myer's critical *History of the Great American Fortunes* (1911), and in the socio-economic histories of Virginia written by Philip A. Bruce. Southern historical research, particularly, was spurred on by these dynamic influences; it found its chief Jeffersonian apostle in William E. Dodd, whose *Expansion and Conflict* appeared in 1915. Thus the historian, too, felt the impulse to rewrite the record of the nation in realistic terms of the everyday social and economic forces pressing about him.

Through the work of Ellen C. Semple another link was forged between history and geography. Miss Semple was influenced by Friedrich Ratzel of Leipzig, whose *Anthropogeographie* was a pioneer factor in adding the science of human geography to the usual physiographic studies. In 1903 she broke new ground in two fields simultaneously by publishing *American History and Its Geographic Conditions;* this became the model for many successors in historical geography. Her chief theme was that historical events are to be understood in terms of the conditioning influence of the physical environment. A later volume, *The Influences of Geographic Environment* (1911), gave Americans a thorough introduction to Ratzel's geographic theories but suggested that Miss Semple clung to an extreme form of geographical determinism and ignored the influence of independent cultural factors upon human development.

BIOLOGY AND SCIENTIFIC MATERIALISM

The continued vogue for Darwinism, despite the rise of formidable rival theories, brought biology into a position of eminence among the sciences. To many individuals, often without their quite realizing it, natural science became a philosophy in the form of scientific materialism. Mind itself seemed the mechanical product of an evolutionary process, and in this new world of scientific determinism the human will seemed an illusion—except among those who raised will to an instinct. The pragmatism of William James waived aside the absolutes of truth, offering instead "the will to believe." The new literary naturalism often pictured man as a helpless pawn of circumstance. In general, however, American psychology was too optimistic to accept the full implications of blind determinism.

Among those who wished to solve philosophical questions in the scientist's laboratory was the brilliant German, Jacques Loeb, a physiologist who came to the United States in 1891. He taught at various universities and after 1910 became a member of the Rockefeller Institute for Medical Research. He aroused international attention by his discovery of tropisms, which explained animal behavior as mechanically motivated by inherent chemical substances. In 1900, his experiments at the University of Chicago in developing the egg of certain marine animals by artificial fertilization led the newspapers to draw the most extravagant inferences as to the possibilities for controlling human life. Loeb himself, for all his indubitable genius, was not far behind in creating a complete mechanistic philosophy from his laboratory researches. In 1912 he stated in his book, *The Mechanistic Conception of Life*: "If our existence is based on the play of blind forces and only a matter of chance; if we ourselves are only chemical mechanisms—how can there be an ethics for us? The answer is, that our instincts are the root of our ethics and that the instincts are just as hereditary as is the form of our body. . . . We struggle for justice and truth since we are instinctively compelled to see our fellow beings happy. Economic, social and political conditions, or ignorance and superstition may warp and inhibit the inherited instincts and thus create a civilization with a faulty or low development of ethics."[1] In this way Loeb's own temperamental idealism converted his mechanistic philosophy into an optimistic theory of human progress looking toward the abolition of hatred and superstition.

Before coming to Chicago, Loeb lectured at Bryn Mawr where he met the distinguished biologist, Thomas Hunt Morgan, who did much to give the United States a position of leadership in the field of genetics and evolutionary theory. Later, when he joined the Columbia faculty, Morgan drew to himself many students of future note—the so-called Morgan School—and successfully applied to animal forms (in this case the prolific fruit fly *Drosophila melanogaster*) the laws of heredity which the Austrian priest, Gregor Mendel, had developed from plant life. Going beyond Darwin and his successors, Morgan expanded evolutionary theory by demonstrating how one species can actually give rise to another through the occasional birth of a new type (or mutant) which breeds true. The Columbia group taught that the genes (this is Morgan's own term) constituted primary units of inheritance and that hereditary characteristics are often linked to a single sex. Unlike Loeb, Morgan did not try to build a mechanistic philosophy upon his researches, and he ignored the vitalists on the other side who gave a supernatural explanation for the processes of life.

MEDICINE AND MENTAL HYGIENE

In this atmosphere of achievement, natural science was frequently the pacemaker for other learned disciplines. A study of the periodical literature of 1905–1918 indicates that the commercial applications of science came to occupy a leading place in American journals. While periodical discussions of pure science declined by a third, the number of articles devoted to applied science increased sixfold.

In medicine, Americans were most aware of the great discoveries that were made in connection with our advance into the Caribbean.

[1] Jacques Loeb, *The Mechanistic Conception of Life,* University of Chicago. Reprinted by permission.

Particularly dramatic was the eradication of yellow fever in Havana after 1900 by a sanitary commission headed by Dr. Walter Reed. In an effort to discover the cause of this disease through self-experiment, one member of the commission, Dr. Jesse W. Lazear, lost his life and another suffered a physical breakdown. Volunteers came forward; nurses, soldiers, and Cuban natives risked their lives to help the commission. Only by deliberately exposing these heroes to the disease was it possible to demonstrate that the *Stegomyia* mosquito (subsequently referred to as *Aëdes aegypti*) was exclusively responsible for its transmission. Armed with this information, Major William C. Gorgas not only cleared Havana of the disease effectively but in 1904 began similarly successful work in the Canal Zone and ultimately attacked it in South America itself.

Another by-product of Caribbean penetration was Colonel Bailey K. Ashford's important discovery that the anemia prevalent in Puerto Rico was due to hookworm. A zoologist, Dr. Charles W. Stiles, identified the parasite as the major cause of the apparent backwardness of many poor whites in the southern United States. The results of treatment in both Puerto Rico and the South were gratifying. For example, physical examinations in 1911–1914 revealed that almost 60 per cent of southern school children had hookworm infestation. By 1918 this figure had been reduced by one-third and the downward trend continued subsequently.

A new spirit of cooperation between research and philanthropy ushered in preventive medicine, a major gain in this era. Persistent attempts to reduce infant mortality led to the official recording of birth rate statistics in 1915 and soon made child hygiene a recognized professional study. The establishment of the Rockefeller Institute for Medical Research in 1901 meant a frontal attack on many problems of preventive medicine and supplemented the work of the inadequately equipped university laboratories. To combat the rising menace of tuberculosis by preventive methods, the Henry Phipps Institute was opened during 1903 in Philadelphia—the first institute for research in this disease. A year later the National Tuberculosis Association was launched for preventive as well as curative purposes, and thereafter a widespread sanitorium movement began.

Rejecting the prevalent attitude of hopelessness toward insanity,

American physicians and intelligent laymen pioneered in the field of mental hygiene in an effort to prevent mental illness by clinical methods. Foremost among these was the eminent psychiatrist, Dr. Adolf Meyer, who stressed detailed case histories and personality studies as a method of discovering the causes of psychoneuroses. The greatest impetus for the mental hygiene movement came from the publication in 1908 of Clifford W. Beers' sensational autobiography, *A Mind That Found Itself*. In it he described vividly the brutalities which he and the other inmates in an institution suffered at the hands of ignorant attendants. He recovered in spite of the harsh treatment and on his release devoted himself to the mental hygiene movement. The ensuing reaction to his exposé helped him in establishing the National Committee for Mental Hygiene to provide scientific care for mental cases and to eliminate the stigma attached to the mentally ill. Partly as the result of this movement, trained psychiatrists enjoyed an accepted role in the new child guidance clinics and juvenile courts as well as in the older courts and prisons.

THE TRIUMPH OF CHEMISTRY

Of the various natural sciences, chemistry was most at home in the increasingly complex world of commerce and industry. Commercial laboratories, in fact, drained college faculties of many able chemists. At the General Electric Laboratories a former college instructor, Irving Langmuir of New York, invented a gas-filled tungsten lamp while making a theoretical study of atomic hydrogen. "Langmuir, the theorist," asserts Bernard Jaffe in his book *Crucibles,* "saved America a million dollars a night on its light bill of over a billion dollars a year." Aided by the General Electric Company's sympathetic policy toward pure research, Langmuir made a significant theoretical contribution in his concentric shell idea of the atom, in which he explained chemical reactions in terms of electronic groupings within a single atom.

The du Ponts, long famous as manufacturers of explosives, began to experiment with rayon, artificial leather, and various lacquers, and became noteworthy pioneers in these fields. Experiments in extracting aluminum from the ore had been in progress for many decades, but not until 1886 was a satisfactory process found. Its discovery by Charles M. Hall made possible a decrease in the price of this vital metal from five dollars a pound in 1888 to 18 cents in 1914, thus opening an era which was to be prolific in its use of aluminum. Chemists of this period succeeded in reclaiming used rubber economically and in processing synthetic rubber, but manufacture of the latter was discouraged by the fact that large supplies of natural rubber were available. Another branch of chemistry saw the discovery of novocain in 1905. This was epochal in importance for dental surgery and helped to make more credible the reassuring slogan of "painless dentistry."

In nutrition a revolution was in the making. Scientists were absorbed in measuring the caloric (or energy-producing) value of various foods to man and beast, but several noted chemists both here and abroad came to regard this dietary approach as inadequate. During 1912–1916 Professor Elmer V. McCollum of Yale, while studying various ailments caused by dietary deficiency, discovered that retarded growth could be remedied in many instances by a chemical designated as vitamin A, which is found in butter fat, and that certain enervating nerve diseases were eliminated by vitamin B, which is present in yeast, rice, and certain other foods. Other vitamin discoveries continued into the succeeding decades. The new theories of diet awakened extraordinary popular interest but frequently opened the door to the most exaggerated claims by producers of packaged foods.

Unfortunately the achievements of chemistry were partly obscured by the sensational publicity given to the manufacturing chemist's role in the unscrupulous adulteration of foods. An entire division of the army of muckrakers was concerned with persistent attacks on food adulterants and patent medicine frauds; they found sympathetic audiences among the readers of the *Ladies' Home Journal* and *Collier's Weekly*. Nevertheless, by 1917 the prestige of the American chemist came close to overtaking the world preeminence of German chemistry.

LITERARY REALISM: FALL OF THE "GENTEEL TRADITION"

The literary aspect of pragmatism sought expression in an intensive realism based on the varying models of Tolstoy, George Eliot, and Zola, which broke sharply with the evasions and conventionalities of the Puritan "genteel tradition." William Dean Howells, whose novels had opened new vistas of realism to Americans during the later nineteenth century, continued to influence the novelists of the early twentieth, stressing everyday situations, minimizing the importance of plots, and even descending to the monotony of the strictly commonplace in order to achieve reality. More devastating to the Victorian mind was the gradual emergence of naturalism. This school sometimes buried the traditions of literary esthetics in its endeavor to portray life with the fullest scientific detachment. To the naturalists who followed Zola, man was a helpless pawn controlled by the determinist forces of his environment and heredity. Free will, in the sense of genuine choice, was an illusion. Morality was replaced by amorality in which ethical judgments were totally irrelevant. Descriptions of sex life, mental perversions, and human irrationality flowed easily from the pen of the fatalistic and pessimistic naturalists and shocked the older realists by their utter frankness.

Although men like Mark Twain, Bret Harte, George W. Cable, and Joel Chandler Harris, who represented the older realism of an optimistic epoch, lived into the new century, their work was done. Far less confident were the younger realists who dealt with the declining frontier, such writers as Hamlin Garland, Jack London, and Willa Cather. Garland wrote grim tales of the Middle Border, not overlooking the sordidness of rural life intensified by the exploitative forces of the new economics. His autobiography, *A Son of the Middle Border* (1917), united the scattered threads of his short stories and novels into a candid picture of the harsh realities of life on the late-nineteenth-century frontier of the Dakotas, where his family struggled vainly for a stable existence.

Just as Garland expressed the thwarted psychology of the rural Middle West which had gone down to defeat in the nineties with Bryan, so Jack London, at various times a rancher and a vagabond on the Pacific coast, carried his revolt against the entire *bourgeoisie*. Although his numerous socialistic works such as *The War of the Classes* (1905) and *The Iron Heel* (1907) were limited in influence, the American public knew him well for his extraordinary storytelling ability, particularly in tales of the Alaskan frontier. For all his collectivist philosophy, London was fascinated by the sheer will-to-power of the rising industrial leaders. Even his *Call of the Wild* (1903), an animal story, is an allegory of the resurgence of a long-lost predatory instinct in Buck, a domesticated dog that returns to the forests and wins leadership of the pack after a primitive struggle for survival in which cunning as well as strength plays a part. *The Sea Wolf* (1904) utilizes this theme of domination through the crude will-to-power on the part of a sea captain, Wolf Larsen. But in his journalism London stressed the world mission of the Anglo-Saxon to win political supremacy and warned against the "yellow peril."

Willa Cather's realistic treatment of the late frontier was tempered by her own sympathies for the Nebraskan prairies where she was reared and for the Bohemian, Russian, and Scandinavian people whom she knew. Miss Cather could depict the tragedies and insecurity of the immigrants' lot in the Northwest, but she preferred the heroic and colorful in their daily life. Her novel of a struggling immigrant artist, *The Song of the Lark* (1915), was praised by Professor Vernon Parrington as "the most convincing story of artist life written by an American." To the critics Willa Cather defied easy classification; belonging to no school, she was primarily a craftsman.

Naturalism, according to some critics, made its debut among American readers before 1900 in the work of the New York reporter, Stephen Crane, whose psychological Civil War novel, *The Red Badge of Courage* (1895), left little room for heroics or the human will. A member of Crane's school but even more directly affected by Zola, Frank Norris displayed a modified determinist philosophy in his novels. He was too much a rebel at heart, however, to preserve the detachment of the consistent mechanistic philosopher. In *The Octopus* (1901) and *The Pit* (1903), Norris dealt with a social epic of wheat and the abuses arising in its production and distribution. The story of irresponsible speculation, corruption, exploitation, parasitism, and the passing struggle for power fills these novels. To Norris, railroad monopolies were "the octopus," and the Chicago grain exchange was symbolized as "the pit," the term used colloquially for the traders' room.

Chief proponent of the naturalistic school, which was to win its greatest victories during the twenties, was Theodore Dreiser. His *Sister Carrie* (1900), dealing with the mistress of several sordid figures, won early recognition from Frank Norris but shocked most of the reviewers and frightened publishers away. In Dreiser's mechanistic philosophy there seemed little room for human sympathies and his skepticism barred any real hope for a better world. In *Jennie Gerhardt* (1911) and *The Genius* (1915), he portrays good and evil with cool detachment, creating living characters in all their selfish, brutal, decadent, or lustful reality. His interest in social history is seen in the fictional account of Charles T. Yerkes of Philadelphia and Chicago, who appears as Frank Cowperwood in *The Financier* (1912) and *The Titan* (1914). After studying newspaper accounts of Yerkes and then interviewing numerous businessmen who knew the man, Dreiser embarked on these thinly fictionized two volumes that depict an utterly unscrupulous, lustful, and predatory financier, as he saw him. Substituting the effect of careful, overwhelming detail for any personal note of protest, Dreiser attempted to show how Cowperwood's corrupt individualism disintegrated the social life of a community, down to the most trivial occupation. Readers gasped at the offhand frankness with which he portrayed the illicit sex life of his characters and at the starkness of his realism.

Literary men who clung to the older estheticism of the eighties fared harshly at the hands of critics in this atmosphere of naturalism. If the genteel tradition meant "the divorce between our educated minds and experience," there was now little room in the pragmatic gospel of action for the older esthetic ideal of "art for art's sake." Ironically it was Henry James, the brother of the high priest of pragmatism, who suffered most among the novelists of his day from the literary canons of naturalist critics. He professed a realism of the inner life and drew exquisite pictures and subtle characterizations of people who existed only in his own delicate imagination. Rejecting the American emphasis on the deed, James fled to England, where he found a congenial home in which the esthetic traditions of Walter Pater and Oscar Wilde survived. In *The Ambassadors* (1902), the novel that James considered his best, he characterizes a New Englander, not unlike the author himself, who despises the materialism of his factory community and is fascinated by the charm of the historic cities and traditional countrysides of Europe. Only in 1904, after an absence of twenty-one years, did Henry James return home.

THE NEW ROMANTICISM

But the "gentle reader" to whom popular novelists had addressed themselves for the past century was far from extinct. Publishers still derived their chief income from those who insisted that literature remain an escape from life rather than a dissection of it. At the turn of the century the best seller was apt to be a highly fanciful historical romance like Charles Major's *When Knighthood Was in Flower* (1898) or George B. McCutcheon's *Graustark* (1901), a love story laid in a mythical Balkan country, or the entertaining historical novels of the prolific F. Marion Crawford. Mary Johnston's *To Have and to Hold* (1899), a graceful adventure story about Indians and pioneer scouts, sold 285,000 copies. In 1901 alone, the historical romances by Sir Walter Scott found more than 100,000 American customers, besides those who read the well-thumbed copies in the libraries.

The new romanticism reflected the popular optimism and expansiveness in an era of triumphant capitalist enterprise, even if current fiction harked back to an idealized Middle Ages of brave knights and fair ladies. Adventure stories were in great demand. Rudyard Kipling's engrossing tales and stirring ballads of India popularized imperialist adventures as "the white man's burden" for civilization and attracted many American readers. Although Robert Louis Stevenson died in 1894, his stories of adventure had an extraordinary American following. Escape from the prosaic world of business and the machine could be guaranteed for the reader of Jack London's stories of the Yukon. Outstanding among the writers of ephemeral literature was Richard Harding Davis, the famous war correspondent whose plots seldom lacked action. He showed amazing versatility in adapting his numerous novels and short stories to the changing styles in popular reading, and he won a host of admirers for his resourceful soldiers of fortune and the Van Bibber tales of Manhattan's upper society. Trite copybook formulas in the sentimental vein of the Sunday school brought wealth to the retired minister, Harold Bell Wright, whose books, *The Shepherd of the Hills* (1907) and *The Winning of Barbara Worth* (1911), each sold one and a half million copies.

In 1899 a literary meteor shot up in the field of the short story and blazed brightly for at least a decade before it began to fade. William Sydney Porter, better known by his pen name O. Henry, came originally from North Carolina. Unknown to his readers, he served four years in prison for embezzling funds from a Texas bank in which he was a teller. His rich fund of experience was gained in South America while he was evading officers of the law. Hailed for a time as the "American Maupassant," he turned out hundreds of stories marked by frontier humor, a whimsical form of sentiment, and a fascinating trick of surprise endings. The literary critic, Fred L. Pattee, has pointed out O. Henry's peculiar sympathy for the philosophy of his lawbreaker characters and his inability to draw individuals who were not caricatures, but notes his influence on the technical style of the American short story. Over four million copies of O. Henry's books, especially his *Cabbages and Kings* (1904), had been sold by 1919.

In the field of autobiography, fame eventually overtook Henry Adams' book of self-analysis, *The Education of Henry Adams.* Written in the detached third person, it was completed in 1906 but was cautiously withheld from publication until 1918. Adams, at one time private secretary to his father, Charles Francis Adams, the ambassador to England, became a professor of history at Harvard during the seventies and wrote an outstanding nine-volume *History of the United States During the Administration of Jefferson and Madison* (1889–1891). His family's comfortable income did not prevent his inner rebellion against the commercialism and scientific materialism of the age. He tended to idealize the precapitalist period and expressed detestation of the new national leadership won by the men of finance. Fleeing to a psychological sanctuary in the Middle Ages, a period in which he was a specialist, he wrote *Mont-Saint-Michel and Chartres* (1913); he found a mystical warmth in romanticizing feudalism, with its courtly literature, its soaring cathedrals, the scholastic wisdom of Saint Thomas Aquinas, and the cult of the Virgin. Adams followed the path taken by English romanticists like William Morris and John Ruskin, who rediscovered the Middle Ages in their revolt against the pecuniary values of the modern commercial spirit.

IMAGISM: THE RENAISSANCE OF POETRY

In American poetry, particularly after 1912, a period of relative sterility came to an end. Spurred on by the imagist school that originated in London under the gifted American expatriate Ezra Pound, poets avowed their allegiance to greater realism in theme and expression. Amy Lowell pioneered after the ideal of the imagists, discarding conventional rhythms and strained effect by using free verse and "the language of common speech." She despised the "cosmic poet" who dealt in generalities, insisting that poetry must present an image —hence the name of the movement—and "render particulars exactly." This ideal came close to realization in her exquisite poem of love and war, "Patterns" (1915).

Literary critics often credited Chicago rather than Boston with beginning the renaissance in poetry. Harriet Monroe discovered significant talent among the "prairie poets" of the Middle West through her magazine, *Poetry*. From Carl Sandburg, the son of a Swedish immigrant, came the *Chicago Poems,* inspired by the democratic and prophetic qualities of Walt Whitman's verse, and dramatizing the will-to-power, immorality, confusion, and braggadocio of the "Hog Butcher for the World." Untrammeled by orthodox meters, Sandburg tried to express the moral strength and dignity of the common man. Much more disconcerting was the psychological realism of Edgar Lee Masters in his caustic *Spoon River Anthology,* which reviewed the true lives of men and women buried with the usual flattering epitaphs near an Illinois town. Although Masters' poetry was praised to the skies, it revolted Amy Lowell; she condemned *Spoon River Anthology* as "one long chronicle of rapes, seductions, liaisons, and perversions." Somewhat apart from this group was the romantic lyrical poet, Vachel Lindsay of Illinois, who liked to sing his "ragtime rhythms" of the Congo aloud, or dramatize the beating drums and banjo music of the Salvation Army, as in "General William Booth Enters into Heaven." A preacher in love with the "gospel of beauty" after the fashion of John Ruskin and William Morris, Lindsay added to this esthetic impulse the emotional idealism of social Christianity. To Altgeld the humanitarian he paid the magnificent compliment of "The Eagle That Is Forgotten"; in "Abraham Lincoln Walks at Midnight," written at the outbreak of the First World War, he expressed the hope of "A league of sober folk, the Workers' Earth, bringing long peace to Cornland, Alp and sea." The poetic renaissance had begun.

More directly in the English tradition of nineteenth-century poetry was William Vaughn Moody, a professor of literature at the University of Chicago. Until his death in 1910, he was hailed as the greatest living American poet. Some of the rebellious social tendencies of the new poetry had begun to appear in his work, as in his "The Brute," in which he criticized the new slavery to materialism and the machine. In "An Ode in Time of Hesitation" Moody assailed the rising imperialist spirit that followed the Spanish-American War and called for the earlier unselfish attitude with which we had gone to Cuba's rescue. Edwin Arlington Robinson of New England had already begun to win distinction as the interpreter of that aging section's somber mood. Popularity made Edwin Markham of the Pacific coast a man of one poem, "The Man with the Hoe" (1899). This was a challenge to exploited labor everywhere.

NATIVE TRENDS IN PAINTING AND SCULPTURE

American painting at the opening of the century continued to cling to colonial dependence upon Europe. Many native artists like John Sloan were stimulated by the luminous and realistic French impressionism which was soon followed by the more analytical post-impressionism of Paul Cézanne. Americans were dazzled—and bewildered—at the famous New York Armory Show in 1913 by the suggestive cubism of Pablo Picasso, leader of the Paris school, who sought deeper reality through the symbolism of abstract and geometric forms. Imitators were legion in the United States in the ensuing decades.

High among the great native artists were Winslow Homer and Albert P. Ryder. Homer was praised for his "pragmatic directness," his refusal to be confined by historic traditions or current patriotic exaggerations, and his preference for experiment in landscape art within the everyday realm of visual experience. In Albert P. Ryder critics found the coming of age of native genius. His imaginative "Toilers of the Sea" revealed the profound insight and otherworldliness typical of his marines and landscapes which set him apart from Homer and most of his contemporaries. Both men, unlike their Europeanized fellow artists, drew many of their subjects from the American scene. Perhaps America's declaration of independence in art came in 1908 with the revolt of "The Eight" against the domination of European authority. This group, which stressed visual honesty, included such important native painters as Robert Henri, George W. Bellows, John Sloan, and George Luks.

Sculpture submitted to a long apprenticeship under the French genius of Auguste Rodin, one of the greatest sculptors in the history of art and best known in the United States for his bronze figure, "The Thinker." He gave his subjects deeper realism and profound psychological expression through an ingenious play of light and shadow achieved by a lifelike succession of skillful hollows and projections. Among his chief American disciples were George Gray Barnard and, to some extent, the gifted Augustus Saint-Gaudens; the latter expressed American pioneer idealism, as was apparent in the inspiring statue of Lincoln which he did for the city of Chicago. Historical themes were immensely popular at the time. New York invited Saint-Gaudens to do a statue of Sherman. John Quincy Adams Ward, who unlike Saint-Gaudens was American-trained, produced impressive statues of Sheridan and Hancock.

CHICAGO AND THE BIRTH OF MODERN ARCHITECTURE

In the nineties Chicago had come to occupy a commanding position as the cultural center of the nation, just as New York City was to dominate intellectual life in the twenties. Chicago was the city of Theodore Thomas and his orchestral music, the home of Jane Addams and the settlement movement, and the adopted center of the significant Middle West novelists and poets for whom there was now a growing list of publishers. The wealthy merchant and industrial class, from the Marshall Fields to the McCormicks, Armours, Swifts, and Palmers, had shown extraordinary enterprise in building up a sturdy metropolis to serve the Mississippi Valley. The merchants had initiated the nation-wide vogue for city planning through Daniel Burnham and Charles Wacker and had thrilled the world with their spectacular exhibits and architectural taste in the Columbian Exposition of 1893.

Following its devastation by fire in 1871, the rebuilding of Chicago proceeded rapidly under the direction of such leading architects as Daniel Burnham and John Root. The Columbian Exposition in 1893 served to advertise that city's growth as no other event did, and it brought admiring visitors from all over the world. The beautiful landscape work was planned by Frederick Law Olmsted, a prominent architect who had done much to raise his specialty from its humble beginnings in landscape gardening to his imaginative conception of Central Park in New York, Prospect Park in Brooklyn, and Franklin Park in Boston. The older generation still remembered him as the famous author of *The Cotton Kingdom* (1861), which attempted to explain the ante-bellum South to northern readers. Despite his advanced age, Olmsted gave the Exposition in Jackson Park its graceful network of lagoons, wooded islands, and shrubbery. In erecting the main buildings of the Fair, the architects combined plaster of Paris and jute fiber to produce an illusion of white marble, thus giving Chicago its flattering name, "The White City." Burnham, who was in charge of the general architectural plans, deferred to eastern architects who insisted upon classical and Renaissance building models. So sensational was the popularity of the Fair, despite its curtailment by the depression of 1893, that the nation was soon swept by a vigorous demand for the historical styles in architecture which had been revived at the lake front.

A young Irish-American architect of Chicago, Louis H. Sullivan, viewed this imitative trend with severe condemnation and later denounced the "virus of the World's Fair" for spreading an epidemic of "bogus antique" and delaying the progress of truly modern architecture by half a century—an exaggerated estimate. He derided the "classic and Renaissance merchants" for creating a "culture lost in ghostly *mésalliance* with abstractions." After Greek and Roman temples ceased to attract enthusiasts, the country was swept by a vogue for eclecticism in art, with free American adaptations of almost every conceivable European style. Abroad, especially in Austria, some experiments had already been made with modernism, but they had little influence in this country.

Sullivan had been trained in France and had studied the historical styles of architecture, but, an enthusiastic reader of Darwin and Spencer, he was influenced by the skepticism of the modern scientific spirit. Rebelling against the conventional historical patterns, he insisted on experimenting with a plastic art that would meet all the practical demands of modern living and industry without suppressing the function of the structure beneath an alien design appropriate to a bygone age. He emphasized that "form follows function" and that this function created and organized the architectural form to be taken. He introduced modernism in architecture in the Transportation Building at the Columbian Exposition, and perhaps even before this. To Sullivan, Burnham's successes seemed merely triumphs of "colossal merchandising," a mania for what was the tallest and the biggest, and the product of work delegated to and done by good subordinates rather than by himself.

The rapid crowding and the rising land values in the cities during the nineties made the skyscraper a necessity, especially in Chicago and New York. Manhattan had begun to build these giants, regardless of the congested narrow streets inherited from a simpler era. A light factory building became a Roman temple if the architect willed it. The increasing use of thick concrete walls reduced the size of the windows and darkened the rooms. Struck by the incongruity of these buildings sheathed in a classical exterior amid modern surroundings, Sullivan taught his disciples to adapt the structure to its environment.

Meanwhile, to achieve efficient lighting, Chicago architects, less wedded to custom than their New York rivals, were experimenting with a new all-steel framework, the result of recent technological advances in treating steel. Sullivan profited from these experiments and launched his idea of emphasizing the tallness of the skyscraper by continuous vertical lines. This theory was to be expressed in a graceful, slender building that would fulfill its purpose efficiently and look "like a proud and soaring thing." Although as a good ornamentalist Sullivan liked to add decorations at variance with his strictly functional theory, he taught the early modernists that architecture must represent the social expression of an age. This gave immense vitality to American design. From Sullivan developed the Chicago school of architects. His famous pupil and assistant, Frank Lloyd Wright, elaborated the ideas of his master and with superb artistry (especially in private dwellings) applied the theory of adapting a building to its natural setting. Although eclecticism continued well into the twenties, functionalism had definitely arrived and the art of the skyscraper became a leading American contribution in the field of esthetics.

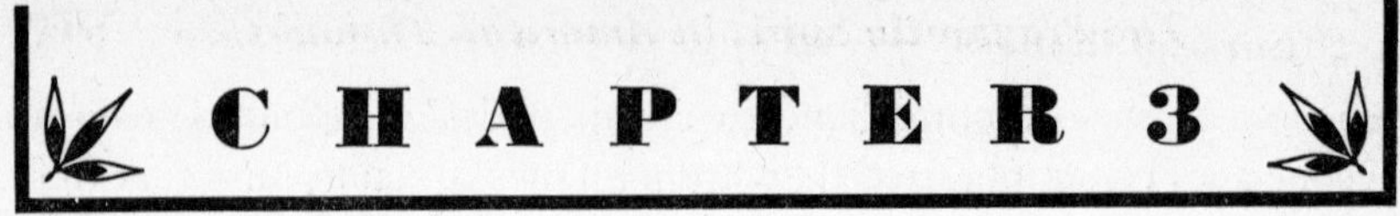

"The Curse of Bigness"—Challenge to Business Leadership: 1900-1913

SOCIAL DARWINISM AND THE DECLINE OF COMPETITION

The success of American business enterprise in achieving a higher standard of living for the nation as a whole was obscured during the prewar era by the widespread resentment against the "trusts," as the new industrial and financial combinations were popularly called. As industry came increasingly under the domination of bankers and the ownership of big business assumed a more impersonal form in the corporation, the small businessman, the farm owner, and various middle-class reform elements rebelled against the allegedly sinister—and often exaggerated—influence of the "money power," "Wall Street," and the "international banker." After the Civil War, falling prices and a narrow margin of profit made competition frequently destructive and led to price wars and peace through consolidation. This result was facilitated by irrational overproduction in the belief that bigness made for profits. Moreover, integration, the spirit of the age, attracted industrialists who enjoyed the struggle for power and the opportunity for spoils which monopoly afforded.

The first revolutionary cycle of consolidation occurred between the two depression years of 1886 and 1893. By the end of the century, adventurous promoters had created trusts in tobacco, oil, sugar, whisky, cash registers, and meat packing, among a host of lesser combines. During the recovery years 1897–1903, the combination process, having exhausted the pioneer forms of profitable expansion, entered a period of super-trusts that united the existing combinations in a "pyramid of pyramids." John Pierpont Morgan, the leading financier of the period, intervened repeatedly in behalf of his stockholder-clients to end the conflict of industrial giants by promoting such huge combines as the United States Steel Corporation, the International Harvester Company, and the American Telephone and Telegraph Company. However, his indifference to public relations permitted the press to distort his motives as being calculated malevolence. To those who criticized the United States Steel Corporation, which was formed in 1901, as being overcapitalized at one and a third billion dollars, he maintained that this figure was not excessive in view of the raised earning potential. In Europe too, it must be noted, the advance of finance capitalism awakened deep popular distrust that sometimes, as in Germany, was channelized into anti-Semitism.

Bigness arose only in part from purely economic causes such as the compelling motive to increase size as a method of reducing costs, for in many instances this alleged benefit was illusory. In fact, the conviction that mere bigness did not pay was brought home to the stockholder during the panic of 1903, for it revealed that too many combines had paid deceptively handsome dividends out of working capital, thus impairing efficiency. Thereafter, for a few years, new combinations declined in number. The super-entrepreneur in some instances sought bigness for the sake of power rather than riches alone. A crude pragmatism—the worship of success—was evident in the evasion of law characteristic of the Age of Trusts. This was the era of social Darwinism as expressed in Herbert Spencer's extremely individualist philosophy of the survival of the fittest and in the amoral ideal of Nietzsche's superman. The old traditions of moderate growth and stability that had been sanctioned by local community loyalties broke down before the impersonal force of the rootless urban-commercial spirit. This same impersonality governed the dominant unit of business—the corporation—which now relegated the field of production management to the expert; this permitted the entrepreneur to specialize in the purchase and sale of securities and thus combined banking and industrial power. An outmoded legal system inherited from the Jeffersonian era of unregulated individual freedom afforded little protection to the laborer, the small competitor, and the consumer. "Let the buyer beware!" too often remained the individualist legal formula in practice.

Louis D. Brandeis, who had built up a highly successful law practice in Boston since the eighties, became the spokesman of the competitive philosophy of the small businessman. As already noted, he did much to popularize the efficiency ideal of Frederick W. Taylor, but his intimate knowledge of huge corporations had convinced him that mere bigness did not guarantee lower prices and a better product to the consumer. More than that, he assailed the incompetence of the banker-entrepreneur in industry, pointing out the evil implications of the "money power" for democratic control of government. His challenging books, *Other People's Money* and *Business a Profession,* which appeared in 1914, were an assault on the abuses of investment trusts; and his essay, "The Curse of Bigness," published in *Harper's Weekly,* became famous for its arraignment of monopoly and its justification of a regulated competitive ideal. He had closely observed the revelations made by Charles Evans Hughes in 1905 regarding the gross inefficiency, high costs, and corrupt political activities of some of New York's largest insurance firms, a field in which competition was at a minimum. Two years later he campaigned successfully for a system of cheap insurance for the workmen of Massachusetts. His ideas of business reform subsequently enriched Wilson's program of the New Freedom.

History favored the nineteenth-century rise of social Darwinism in business. The almost universal victory of *laissez-faire* liberalism had destroyed slavery in the New World and the remnants of serfdom in the Old. But "freedom of contract"—including the right of the workman to bargain freely for his services—while replacing chattel slavery and paternalism, served as a legal doctrine to declare trade unions and strikes conspiracies, and it encouraged long hours and low wages in many fields. Frequently this doctrine prevented the reforms sought in popular legislation.

When the Civil War destroyed the might of the agrarian South, the proponents of untrammeled corporate enterprise inscribed their terms into the Constitution itself. The Fourteenth Amendment, which northern voters in 1866 had intended to protect Negro civil rights in the South, actually came to offer the rising corporation a large measure of immunity from hostile state legislation. "No State," reads the crucial section, "shall make or enforce any law which shall abridge the privileges or immunities of citizens of the United States; nor shall any

State deprive any person of life, liberty, or property, without due process of law; nor deny to any person within its jurisdiction the equal protection of the laws." Within a few years the federal courts came forward as the guardian of the "person"—a corporation was also a "person" in law—against the regulatory acts of a local legislature which, in the light of an intricate legalism, violated "due process of law." As a result, the popular control of monopolies remained impotent and numerous state reforms involving shorter hours, factory inspection, and child labor failed to meet the test of constitutionality. The lawyers and the Supreme Court itself became converted to the unrestrained individualism of social Darwinism. Justice Oliver Wendell Holmes sharply reproved his colleagues in Lochner *v.* New York (1905), which invalidated a New York law limiting the weekly hours of bakery workers to sixty. "The Fourteenth Amendment," he observed caustically, "does not enact Mr. Herbert Spencer's Social Statics." In this statement Holmes denied that extreme individualism had become part of the Constitution.

Northern and western farmers who had joined eastern manufacturers in 1860 to bring victory to the new Republican party never quite realized that they had struck down their historic ally, the agrarian South. Ante-bellum America had been largely ruled by the Democratic alliance between the South and the expanding West. Although declining crop prices and stationary debts afflicted the farmer after 1865, he won only specious local successes against the high rates charged by the railroads and grain-elevator owners during the revolt of the Grangers and the era of Farmers' Alliances that followed. Ever attracted by inflationary panaceas to offset the hard-money policies of eastern creditors, he turned successively to demands for unsecured paper currency—the Greenback movement—and for the free coinage of silver at the ratio of sixteen of silver to one of gold.

The farm insurgents, organized as Populists, were joined by labor, which had grown restless during the severe depression of the early nineties. Popular resentment flared when the Income Tax Law was declared unconstitutional by the Supreme Court in 1895 (Pollock *v.* Farmers Loan and Trust Co.) and when President Cleveland hastily moved troops into Chicago during the Pullman strike of 1894 prior to any rioting. Governor John P. Altgeld of Illinois and William Jennings

Bryan, the Democratic presidential candidate, sought unsuccessfully to revive the historic agrarian-labor coalition of ante-bellum days. *Laissez-faire* liberalism, represented by William McKinley's party, thrust back this effort to invoke a popular crusade against corporate enterprise. The election of 1900, in which the same presidential candidates faced each other, merely confirmed the decision of 1896, which was enhanced by the Republican promise of the "full dinner pail."

THEODORE ROOSEVELT, TRUST BUSTER

On September 6, 1901, an assassin's bullet ended President McKinley's career on the eve, apparently, of certain concessions to reform. His successor, Vice-President Theodore Roosevelt, eagerly reassured the worried business and financial community that he was retaining both McKinley's Cabinet and his policies. There was much, however, in Roosevelt's mercurial temperament to give concern to those who loved the more predictable ways of the late President, even if "Teddy's" social philosophy was fairly conservative.

Born in 1858 of a mercantile middle-class family in New York City and educated at Harvard, the comparatively youthful President—the youngest in our history—had a long record of political experience. Beginning as a regular party man in the New York Assembly, he served successively on the federal Civil Service Commission, as head of the New York City police board, as Assistant Secretary of the Navy under McKinley, and in 1898 as governor of New York. His selection as running mate for McKinley in 1900 was aided by the desire of Thomas E. ("Boss") Platt to eliminate him from New York politics. Roosevelt had shown vigorous executive ability and moral fervor, particularly on behalf of civil service reform. In foreign affairs he was an enthusiastic admirer of the expansionist philosophy of Admiral Alfred T. Mahan. During the campaigns of 1896 and 1900 he did yeoman service against the alleged menace of Altgeld and Bryanism. Altogether, the new President should have been a reassuring influence for the friends of the existing order.

As he prepared his first annual message to Congress, Roosevelt thought it expedient to consult the party oracle, Mark Hanna—"Dollar Mark," as the cartoonists loved to label him because of his intimate relations with big business. Hanna came close to earning the distinction of being the first national boss of a major political party. Both as a political realist and from sincere conviction, he believed that certain concessions to labor and public opinion were essential. Nevertheless, he found himself not ready fully to endorse Roosevelt's program of using federal supervision to save corporate business from the consequences of its own sins, and he succeeded in having the President delete from his message certain phrases likely to antagonize businessmen; besides, Hanna felt, it was politically dangerous to make an issue of corporation control. Both men realized that inactivity might also be dangerous. No one could ignore the resounding blows against railroad abuses struck by Governor Robert M. La Follette of Wisconsin, or wholly overlook congressional revelations regarding monopolies, facts which were publicized by the Industrial Commission in 1899–1902 and inspired a flood of petitions to the Department of Justice for relief. Equally disturbing was the journalistic literature of dissent written by Henry Demarest Lloyd, Ida M. Tarbell, Ray Stannard Baker, and a host of other critics of bigness. The Middle West, particularly, was sensitive to the rising cost of living that was popularly if erroneously attributed to the machinations of the trusts. Professional economists and businessmen might minimize the influence or extent of the trust movement, but they won few conversions among the laity.

Written in cautious language, the President's message set the tone of his first term in office. He pictured the large corporate fortunes as being due to increased productivity and natural economic factors operative in Europe as well as America, rather than as arising from tariffs and other governmental factors. It was desirable, he thought, to leave as unhampered as the public interest permitted "the strong and forceful men upon whom the success of business operations inevitably rests." He deplored the class hatred aroused in the popular campaign against big business, but pointed out gently that certain features of corporate practice were harmful to the general welfare. Overcapitalization he specified as the chief evil and he proposed a program of limited federal supervision of corporations to cope with it. The main weapon of the government would be to publicize the workings of the great corporations engaged in interstate commerce. Public opinion, apparently, could be relied on to do the rest. Not without justification was this message mildly satirized by Finley Peter Dunne's "Mr. Dooley," when he summarized it aptly to Mr. Hennessey: "Th' trusts, says he, are heejoous monsthers built up be th' enlightened intherprize iv th' men that have done so much to advance progress in our beloved country, he says. On wan hand I wud stamp thim undher fut; on th' other hand not so fast."

While Roosevelt's moral earnestness cannot be gainsaid, his proposal to publicize corporate operations, even when supplemented by his badly misnamed "trust-busting" laws, was already antedated by events. Such alleviative measures had long since failed. When the courts and the legislatures of the 1880's had partly succeeded in thwarting the attempts of the railroads and of industry to fix prices through pooling agreements, a new evil genie had arisen in the trust, which achieved monopoly by the device of centralizing control through the group ownership of trust certificates. Then came the illusory Sherman Anti-Trust Act of 1890 which solemnly warned, "Every contract, combination in the form of trust or otherwise, or conspiracy, in restraint of trade or commerce among the several states, or with foreign nations, is hereby declared to be illegal." Penalties for officials were to be not less than $5000 fine or a year's imprisonment. This legislation, badly written from a legal standpoint and vitiated by judicial interpretation, accomplished little more than to drive trusts into the underground channel of informal understandings known euphoniously as "community of interest." In the Debs injunction case arising out of the Pullman strike of 1894, the Sherman Act came dangerously close to becoming a club against labor unions, which were classified by Attorney General Richard Olney as combinations coming under this law.

Worse still, in 1895 the Supreme Court indirectly gave its blessing to industrial monopoly in United States *v.* E. C. Knight Co., a suit involving the powerful sugar combine which then controlled no less than 98 per cent of the domestic refining industry. The Court, influenced by the inept presentation of the Attorney General, argued that control of the manufacturing process affected commerce only incidentally and indirectly, hence industrial monopoly was a fit subject for state rather than federal regulation. Fortunately, subsequent decisions, such as the Trans-Missouri Freight case (1897), prevented the influence of the Knight precedent from strengthening railroad combinations, but industrial monopoly remained under the spell of the Sugar Trust case and enjoyed relative immunity.

A wave of state anti-trust legislation that began in the seventies had proved futile in dealing with a problem which was clearly national in scope. By President Roosevelt's time, in fact, certain revenue-seeking states such as New Jersey, "mother of trusts," had opened a new door to monopoly through charters granted to holding companies. The financier was now able to exercise control over a far-flung empire by indirection; he was at the apex of a pyramid of stockholding corporations cemented together by means of interlocking directorates and informal agreements. Thus the final result of the anti-trust movement was to change the form of the combine without altering its essence. The Standard Oil Company, for example, during its troubled career since 1870, had turned successively, in response to legal pressure, from the pool to the trust, from the trust to community of interest, and from the latter to the holding company, New Jersey style. Nor had this process of transformation ended in 1901. "The more it changes, the more it is the same thing," runs a witty French saying that is singularly appropriate to the history of American industrial combinations.

Against this record of futility, Roosevelt's policy of publicizing monopolistic evils and occasionally dissolving combines, although salutary, was clearly inadequate in the face of an ambiguous Sherman Act and the individualist bias of the courts. His approach was moral rather than scientific; it embodied the crusading spirit and disregarded any philosophical understanding of the theory of free competition held by men like Brandeis. But in many respects Roosevelt knew how to promote reform, believing as he did in vigorous presidential leadership and a strong federal government capable of removing the worst excesses of bigness. Nevertheless, he continued to defer to the wisdom of Senator Nelson W. Aldrich, unyielding leader of the standpat element in his party, and the masters of finance and industry continued to enjoy the intimate contacts with the Chief Executive that they had had under McKinley. After three years of Roosevelt's well-publicized victories against monopoly, it must have been a chastening experience for his admirers to learn, from a subsequent congressional investigation, that the interests against which he fulminated, from the Standard Oil

Company down, had contributed to his campaign fund of 1904 with almost unprecedented generosity.

One of the President's first major victories was gained in connection with the projected combination of the leading transcontinental railroads. The ambitious Edward H. Harriman, whose dreams of railroad conquest not only spanned the continent but took in the Orient as well, had succeeded, with the financial backing of Kuhn, Loeb, and Company, in merging the already extensive Union Pacific and Southern Pacific railroads. His rival, the mighty James J. Hill, with J. P. Morgan's support, had combined the Northern Pacific with his Great Northern lines. The plan was for Hill and Morgan to purchase the Chicago, Burlington, and Quincy Railroad jointly; this would give Hill his own connection with Chicago. When the Harriman forces staged a stock market raid in May, 1901, to get control of the Northern Pacific and indirectly of the Burlington system, the battle precipitated a Wall Street panic. Peace was reached when the contending parties agreed to organize, under New Jersey law, the Northern Securities Company, a holding company capitalized at 400 million dollars; it would combine the railroad stock ownership of both parties. Their lawyers advised them that they had nothing to fear from the Sherman Act.

This situation gave Roosevelt an opportunity for a dramatic coup whose preliminaries had been secretly arranged. On February 19, 1902, his Attorney General, Philander C. Knox, former counsel for Andrew Carnegie in the steel merger of 1901, announced publicly that the Administration intended to file suit at St. Paul to dissolve the Northern Securities Company as a violator of the Sherman Act. Simultaneously, however, Roosevelt reassured big business in a speech at Charleston, South Carolina; in it he said that this was an era of combinations in labor as well as capital and that both types of combinations were frequently for the public good. He assailed the demagogue "who raves against the wealth which is simply the form of embodied thrift, foresight, and intelligence."

The defeat of the Northern Securities in 1904 by the Supreme Court, although by a narrow margin, gave new life to the Sherman Act and a temporary setback to the holding company device, if not to the combination movement itself, for the latter was driven to new underground channels. James J. Hill, who sincerely believed that his plans for combination would stabilize the erratic railroad business in the public interest, saw only a selfish political adventure in the anti-trust assault. "What has been the result?" he asked caustically. "To the owners of the properties, merely the inconvenience of holding two certificates of stock [of the Northern Pacific and the Great Northern] of different colours instead of one, and of keeping track of two different sets of securities. To the public, no difference at all except that it has missed the advantages which the simpler and more businesslike plan would have secured. . . ." Nevertheless, Roosevelt took pride in overthrowing the dead weight of the sugar case precedent which, because of the Supreme Court's refusal to recognize the implicit intent of the sugar combine to restrain interstate commerce, had discouraged indictments under the Sherman Act. Justice Harlan's opinion in the Northern Securities case was so sweeping in its denunciation of trade conspiracies in both manufacturing and transportation as to offer some support for Roosevelt's contention that the E. C. Knight decision had been reversed. The Sherman Anti-Trust Act had been reinvigorated.

The Northern Securities case brought Roosevelt popularity, especially in the Northwest, where the Hill railroad combine was cordially disliked. Even professional economists added their praise, although subsequent years of monopolist advances were to disillusion them. If railroad monopolists were at all displeased with this alleged defeat, they were given more than a crumb of comfort in the Elkins Act of 1903, which, written at their behest, compelled the roads to observe published rates usually prepared by the dominant railroad interests. Only a largely ineffective provision forbidding rebates to shippers removed the law from the category of pure class legislation.

Spectacular prosecutions were instituted in 1902 at Roosevelt's request against the Beef Trust of Chicago, beginning with Swift and Company and extending in 1905 to Armour and Company and other large packers, for various monopolist practices including price-fixing, the blacklisting of rebellious independents, and railroad rebates. Once more a specious victory was won when the Supreme Court enjoined these methods; but later the various packers achieved the control they desired through informal marketing agreements.

Within the Department of Commerce and Labor, newly established in 1903, Roosevelt compelled a reluctant Congress to create the Bureau of Corporations to investigate "the organization, conduct, and management of the business of any corporation, joint-stock company, or corporate combination." Witnesses might be subpoenaed and special studies of industrial operations made, thereby furnishing a basis for legislative recommendations. The Bureau's fact-finding services invigorated the Department of Justice and assisted W. H. Moody, Roosevelt's conscientious Attorney General from 1904 to 1906, in establishing an excellent record of prosecutions. But even this active Bureau, the predecessor of Wilson's Federal Trade Commission, suffered a setback in the Beef Trust cases, when the defendants successfully claimed immunity from criminal action on the ground that their testimony had originally been given before the Bureau of Corporations and hence enjoyed an "immunity bath."

In taking issue with the powerful anthracite coal combine during a major strike in 1902, Roosevelt could claim a tangible achievement. He felt little sympathy for the coal operators, whom he held responsible for the impoverishment of the miner, and he would have prosecuted them under the Sherman Act had he not been advised that this would be futile. Irregular and exceptionally hazardous employment, squalid company towns, long hours, and extremely low wages marked the lot of the anthracite miner in eastern Pennsylvania. In 1900, John Mitchell and his United Mine Workers had taken advantage of Roosevelt's fear of losing the presidential election by demanding and securing through party pressure a 10 per cent increase in pay—the first since 1880. In 1902, 140,000 miners struck again, after asking another wage increase, a shorter working day, the removal of current abuses in weighing coal, and union recognition. This time the coal operators refused to yield to political or union pressure; they displayed such arrogance in contrast to the modest behavior of John Mitchell that Roosevelt was antagonized. Five months of this deadlock saw coal prices soar, schools close, and imminent disaster face the Administration. "The Socialistic feeling is growing apace," warned Henry Cabot Lodge in a letter to the President.

With a keen sense of economic realities, Roosevelt invoked the aid of the financier John Pierpont Morgan, whose interests interlocked with those of the operators. At the same time he summoned both sides to a private conference in Washington, but found the employers unwilling to accept arbitration. Then came his dramatic threat to use the Army to run the mines as receivers, thus dispossessing the operators; this proved unnecessary, however, for Morgan's continued pressure on the coal barons now brought results. An arbitral commission on March 22, 1903, awarded a 10 per cent wage increase with a three-year contract and eliminated certain abuses. But the United Mine Workers had to wait until 1916 before the operators granted the crucial demand for union recognition. Thus the election of 1904, like its predecessor of 1900, was safeguarded for the G.O.P.

THE ELECTION OF 1904

If Roosevelt's trust-busting reputation had earned him a host of enemies among those in high places, the presidential election of 1904 failed most embarrassingly to disclose the fact. With a commendable Christian sense of turning the other cheek for further chastisement, big business contributed almost three-fourths of the $2,195,000 collected by the Republican national chairman, George B. Cortelyou, Roosevelt's Secretary of Commerce and Labor. E. H. Harriman, his monopolist leadership in the Northern Securities railway combine evidently forgotten, was high in the private counsels of the President; he contributed $50,000 personally and collected $200,000 more from other sources for a Roosevelt victory. Far from feeling any malice over this affair, Morgan gave $150,000 cash and an associate added over $165,000. Representatives of Standard Oil, the President's favorite whipping boy, were compelled to conceal their $125,000 gift behind anonymity in fear of White House displeasure. Railway, steel, insurance, the Beef Trust, and other corporations added their mite to defeat the financially orthodox Democratic candidate, Alton B. Parker, chief justice of the New York State Court of Appeals. Despite Parker's rejection of inflationism, he was known to favor certain heretical Populist ideas and had been long associated with Bryanism.

Although the Republicans rested on the laurels of their hero, who was given the colorless Charles W. Fairbanks of Indiana as a running mate, their platform stressed the party's record on trust control, advocated a sound currency and a glorious foreign policy, and denounced the low-tariff ideals of their chief opponents. The Democrats, temporarily repudiating the twice-defeated Bryan and avoiding the insistent claims of the sensation-loving newspaper publisher William Randolph Hearst, chose Parker and the wealthy octogenarian, Henry G. Davis of West Virginia. Their platform cautiously dropped the usual demand for an income tax law as well as the inflationist free-silver proposal of 1896, but retained an anti-trust plank which could scarcely outshine the glory of the arch trust buster on the Republican side; their plea for tariff revision was insufficient in itself to turn popular sentiment into victory. Joseph Pulitzer's New York *World* raised the single significant issue of the campaign when it denounced the heavy corporate contributions to Roosevelt—which could then only be surmised—and pointed out that Cortelyou, the Republican national chairman, as Secretary of Commerce and Labor was actually head of the Bureau of Corporations, an organization which so far had done nothing—so it was alleged—to lay the trusts low. Was business buying protection from Cortelyou? Judge Parker chose this as his cue and in a speech on "Cortelyouism" delivered shortly before election day charged that these corporate donations were a species of blackmail. Such charges Roosevelt hotly labeled as a "wicked falsehood."

The electorate apparently was convinced, for the President won overwhelmingly by a popular majority of over 2,500,000 votes; Parker carried scarcely any section beyond the Solid South. The electoral vote, 336 to 140, also reflected a far worse defeat for the Democrats than any Bryan had suffered. A protest vote against both parties was partially absorbed by the Socialist candidate, Eugene V. Debs, leader of the Pullman strike, who polled over 400,000 ballots, four times as many as in 1900. With a substantial Republican majority in both Houses of Congress, Roosevelt's elation was expressed in an election night declaration that under no circumstances would he be a "candidate for or accept another nomination." He was to regret this statement deeply in 1912.

MUCKRAKING AND REFORM

During his second administration Roosevelt returned to his campaign against monopolies, insisting unsuccessfully in 1907 that Congress provide a national corporation license law for the adequate control of large concerns. Temperamentally anything but thorough, the Presi-

1900 - 1910

Theodore Roosevelt as President. (Brown Brothers.)

Theodore Roosevelt, Rough Rider, During the Spanish-American War. (The National Archives.)

The Three Philosophers, by Winifred Rieber. Josiah Royce (left, seated), George H. Palmer (standing), and William James—all of Harvard.

avorable Interpretation of the Campaign Con-
ution of Big Business to Roosevelt in 1904. (From
k, November 2, 1904.)

A Critical View of Roosevelt's Trust Busting in *Puck* (September 20, 1905).

Wilbur Wright, with King Alfonso of Spain, in his latest model in 1908. (Brown Brothers.)

Italian Family—Ellis Island, 1905. (Lewis Hine Memorial Collection Committee.)

Lower East Side New York at the Turn of the Century. (Brown Brothers.)

John Barrymore in *Uncle Sam*
Farce That Ran in 1911. (Harv
Theatre Collection.)

William Gillette as Sherl
Holmes in 1899. (Harvard The
Collection.)

Sterling, Al St. John, Hank
n, and Fatty Arbuckle in a
stone Film, *In the Clutches of*
Law. (The Museum of Modern
Film Library.)

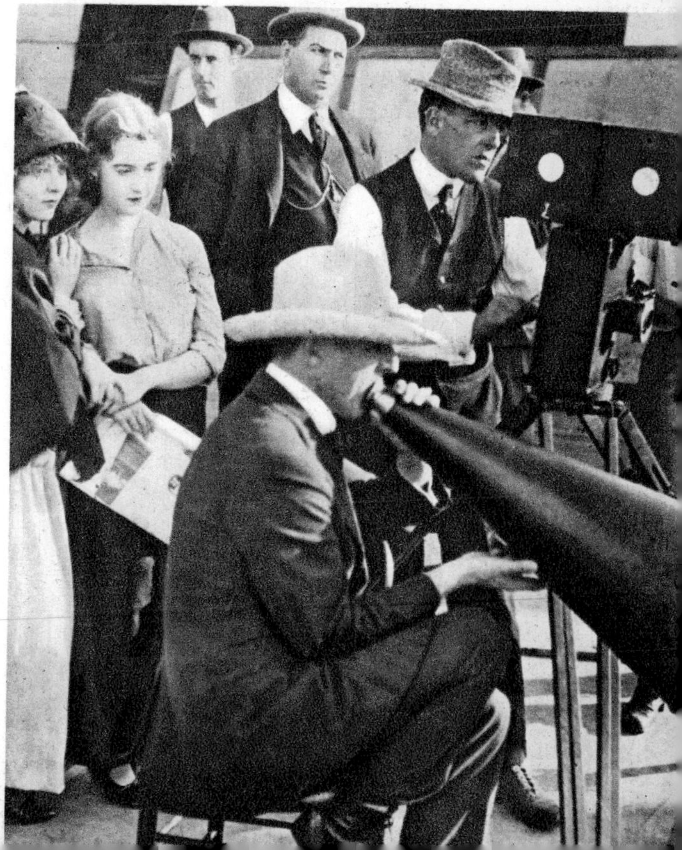

. Griffith Directing; Blanche
et and Dorothy Gish in Back-
nd. (The Museum of Modern
ilm Library.)

Eugene V. Debs Campaigning in New York During 1912 (?) as Presidential Candidate of the Socialist Party. (The National Archives.)

William Howard Taft, Retiring President, Riding with Woodrow Wilson to the Latter's Inauguration. (Brown Brothers.)

dent carried only a few major cases to completion; the bulk of the Department of Justice prosecutions were against minor pools. In twenty-five criminal cases involving monopolies, eleven convictions were obtained, a record inferior to Taft's. Two major suits against the Standard Oil Company and the American Tobacco Company were begun but were left for the succeeding administration to complete—with the usual specious victory. However, vindication was definitely won with the decision against the monopolistic American Sugar Refining Company, victor in the famous E. C. Knight case, when certain of its officials were convicted of tampering with the customhouse scales and the company had to pay over $4,000,000 for using these crude methods of self-enrichment.

The Administration could also take comfort for the ineffectual decision over the Beef Trust in 1905, for the Meat Inspection Act was passed the following year. Ground had been laid by the Socialist, Upton Sinclair, whose novel *The Jungle,* as already noted, had revealed the loathsome conditions prevailing among the great packing houses of Chicago where competition had declined substantially. Despite departmental skepticism regarding Sinclair's revelations, Roosevelt chose to begin an inquiry at once. This resulted in the Neill-Reynolds report, which substantially upheld Sinclair's case. The packers fought back stubbornly through their Washington lobby, denying official charges that their food products were prepared in a filthy and disease-ridden environment. House indifference almost defeated the inspection bill, which was introduced by the progressive Senator, Albert J. Beveridge; but news that unfavorable foreign reaction to the Neill-Reynolds report might curtail American meat exports, together with Administration pressure, compelled passage on July 1, 1906, of an Act requiring federal inspection of domestic meats.

Even while utilizing Sinclair's exposé of packing-house conditions Roosevelt could not refrain from offering some crumbs of consolation to the packers themselves. In March, 1906, at a dinner given by the ultra-conservative Speaker of the House, "Uncle Joe" Cannon, the President compared popular writers who assailed business with the "muckraker" in *Pilgrim's Progress,* the man whose eyes were ever fixed on the vile and debasing. Although Roosevelt later qualified his remarks to exclude useful exposures, he had again removed much of the stigma of wrongdoing as well as the sting of defeat from his late opponents. The name muckraker clung to the popular literature of dissent, but the relatively high plane of these writings deprived the term of opprobrium in the public mind.

The general outcry over *The Jungle* hastened the passage of another pioneer Act calling for government intervention in behalf of the consumer. This was the Pure Food and Drug Act of 1906, prepared by Dr. Harvey W. Wiley, chief chemist of the Department of Agriculture. Roosevelt had recommended legislation of this type in his message in December, 1905, but it required Upton Sinclair's book and the Neill-Reynolds report to obtain congressional action. The Act emphasized proper branding, insisted that certain harmful ingredients be listed on the label, and provided additional penalties for adulteration of contents, especially the use of decomposed ingredients. Unfortunately, enforcement of this legislation was hampered by inadequate funds, and the unscrupulous manufacturer could evade the label provision by using technical language and small print. Not until 1938 did the original hopes of its sponsors come close to realization.

THE PANIC OF 1907

The biographer, Henry F. Pringle, found Roosevelt's ignorance of economics naïvely displayed during the panic of 1907. At Harvard Roosevelt had been trained under the gold-standard enthusiast, J. Laurence Laughlin, and he admittedly retained only the stock arguments with which to combat free-silver heretics. Although publicly he expressed his belief that eastern financiers were responsible for the panics of 1903 and 1907, he turned to them instinctively whenever business squalls threatened. When the stock crash in October, 1907, began to imperil the huge Knickerbocker Trust Company of New York, Morgan was hastily called upon to stop the impending ruin of many financial institutions and Secretary of the Treasury Cortelyou quickly agreed to deposit $25,000,000 of government funds in the national banks. Roosevelt returned from a bear-hunting trip in Louisiana during a temporary market respite and he publicly thanked "those influential and splendid business men . . . who have acted with such wisdom and public spirit." But the Knickerbocker went down, accompanied by several large trust companies and banks. There was a strong suspicion that the government funds had been used to save several stockbrokers rather than the banks themselves. Bank runs, currency shortages, sharp business retrenchments, and unemployment all blended into a disturbing situation which Roosevelt stubbornly attributed to international causes.

Certain financiers associated with Morgan now approached the President with a patriotic offer. Elbert H. Gary and Henry C. Frick of the United States Steel Corporation sought his sanction for the outright purchase of the extensive properties of the Tennessee Coal and Iron Co., whose stock was held by many New York brokerage firms, some of which faced extinction. Explaining that their sole motive was to save from bankruptcy a certain large brokerage house that held these securities, Gary and Frick asked immunity from prosecution under the Sherman Act. Roosevelt yielded, apparently badly frightened by the sweep of events and the dark picture presented by these men. Soon after, Gary admitted to congressional investigators that the purchase of the Tennessee properties, which included units in Alabama and Georgia, had been an extraordinarily good stroke of business for the United States Steel Corporation. Congressmen learned from representatives of Moore and Schley, the brokerage firm concerned, that a loan of perhaps five or six million would have been sufficient without the sale of the securities to Gary. Thus President Roosevelt unwittingly assisted big business to evade the Sherman Anti-Trust Act in an instance where the public interest scarcely justified his intervention.

CURBING THE RAILROADS

On the advice of party stalwarts in Congress, Roosevelt avoided a fight over tariff revision, although he endorsed the reciprocal trade agreement ideal as expressed by McKinley on the eve of his assassination. Instead of the tariff, railroad rate legislation became the heart of Roosevelt's program for his second term. After the turn of the century, railroad abuses were revived on a large scale as new consolidations took place. The muckraker Ray Stannard Baker wrote a lengthy exposé of railroad monopolies, revealing their favoritism to certain shippers and their extortionate rates in areas where competition had disappeared. Rate discriminations sometimes took the indirect form of "smokeless rebates" whereby the railroad refunded a portion of the freight charges to a favored shipper, the transaction being concealed behind various ingenious bookkeeping and other devices. As governor of Wisconsin, La Follette had led a spectacular war against railroad monopolies. When he took his seat in the Senate, he contended that government regulation required rate determining on the basis of a physical valuation of the railroads. It was clear that the Interstate Commerce Commission, which had been established in 1887 to cope with the railroads, was seriously in need of implementation.

Although Roosevelt's demand for railroad regulation was ultimately embodied in the Hepburn Bill, it was blocked for a time by a strong lobby in the Senate led by Nelson Aldrich, son-in-law of John D. Rockefeller, whose Standard Oil Company, the President learned, profited from rebates to the extent of at least $750,000 annually. The Bureau of Corporations revealed similar profits for the Sugar Trust. A series of federal prosecutions against railroads violating the Interstate Commerce Act and the Elkins Act was announced by Attorney General William H. Moody on December 11, 1905. Many a Roosevelt campaign contributor had to face the unfavorable publicity created by Moody's suits.

Despite certain weaknesses, the Hepburn Act of 1906 did much to curb railroad abuses. An enlarged Interstate Commerce Commission, serving a longer term at increased remuneration, was empowered to regulate Pullmans, express and pipe-line companies, and terminal facilities, thus closing the chief gaps in federal transportation control. More important, the Commission was given partial rate-fixing power; should its investigation of a formal complaint determine that prevailing rates were unreasonable, maximum rates could be imposed. Objections to its rates could be filed by the carrier and a temporary injunction holding the new rates in abeyance could be obtained. While this meant that the burden of bringing suit now fell upon the railroads instead of the Commission, prolonged litigation that would defeat the ends of justice could be profitable for the carriers. A commodity clause provided for the separation of transportation activities from actual business or manufacture, thus aiming to remove a fruitful source of concealed discriminatory provisions. Published rates could not be changed without thirty days' notice, and penalties for rebates were strengthened. The Commission could require a standardized accounting system and itself supervise accounting practices. Future railroad legislation was to be built on the foundations of the Hepburn Act, but the door to prolonged litigation was left open too wide for completely effective regulation of rates.

CONSERVING THE NATION'S RESOURCES

Not content with striking at monopoly in manufacturing, finance, and transportation, Roosevelt maintained an active second front—his most successful—against private monopoly of the nation's resources in power sites, mineral deposits, and lumber. His love of the outdoors, continuing since his youthful search for health in the West, fanned his interest in the subject of conservation. Immediate inspiration came from the enthusiastic conservationist, Gifford Pinchot, chief of the Forestry Bureau since 1898. Furthermore, the passing of the frontier with its cheap lands made conservation a live public issue, particularly in the eastern states where the unfortunate results of unregulated exploitation of natural resources could be visualized. Various Presidents from Benjamin Harrison to McKinley had followed the policy of setting aside huge forest reserves in the public interest. With Roosevelt, however, these sporadic acts of conservation became a crusade and in his first message to Congress he urged the primary importance of forest and irrigation problems for the country. The powerful position of large mining and lumbering interests challenged his combativeness.

Much of the initiative for the first conservation Acts passed during Roosevelt's term of office came from Senator Francis G. Newlands of Nevada, a Democrat. His Reclamation Bill, encouraged by the President and enacted in 1902, provided for extensive government development of irrigation projects covering some 3,000,000 acres in the West. Roosevelt was convinced that the benefits of water power belonged to the public. His gospel of conservation, urged repeatedly on the public platform and before Congress, emphasized systematic surveying and planning for the future use of the nation's natural resources as well as the setting aside of large areas of the public domain for federal preservation.

An Inland Waterways Commission which was appointed in 1907 to elaborate a modern water conservation policy made certain recommendations which led Roosevelt to call a National Conservation Conference at the White House on May 15, 1908; this was composed of governors, Congressmen, justices of the Supreme Court, and other men high in public office. At this conference was born the National Conservation Commission, headed by Gifford Pinchot, created to prepare an inventory of the nation's resources as a basis for future legislation. This was supplemented by many new active conservation commissions in the states and by numerous private conservation committees. At the end of Roosevelt's administration almost 150,000,000 acres of timberland had been set aside, together with over 85,000,000 acres of Alaskan mineral lands and other large tracts rich in untapped mineral wealth. Roosevelt's repeated use of implied executive authority in administering the national domain made his legalist Secretary of War, William Howard Taft, wince more than once. Many Westerners, eager to explore the possibilities of undeveloped resources, grew hostile to the conservationist crusade of Roosevelt and the East.

THE PRESIDENTIAL MESSAGE OF 1908

Aside from these victories for conservation, the President became increasingly dubious toward the end of his term as to the effectiveness of his campaign against bigness. He was disagreeably surprised in 1908 when the federal Circuit Court of Appeals in Illinois set aside the sensational fine of $29,000,000 imposed by Judge Kenesaw M. Landis against the Standard Oil Company of Indiana for extorting rebates from the railroads. In his congressional message of 1908 Roosevelt struck a new crusading note which suggested his later career as standard-bearer of the Progressive party. He asked federal leadership in the extension of workmen's compensation and assailed the abuse of court injunctions in labor disputes as unjust to the striker. He even took up La Follette's demand for the physical valuation of railroads as a basis for rate-fixing, which he had hitherto rejected. Pleading for the "moral regeneration" of business, he attacked stock market abuses, the sins of corporation lawyers in shielding the injustice of their clients, and the prevalence of scandals throughout the business community. In spite of a host of conservative critics who expressed shock at this message, Roosevelt publicly branded the power wielded by the judiciary as excessive.

Most of these sweeping recommendations were ignored by Congress, for the end of a presidential term hardly offered an opportunity to enact such a powerful program. Roosevelt's new militancy reflected both his own sense of futility in attempting to curb business and the rising tide of insurgency during 1908 as shown by the increasing strength of the Republican insurgents in Congress. He feared the growing Socialist vote and the return of Bryanism as a political factor. Ever a crusader by temperament, he found his middle-of-the-road policies too conservative for the changing times.

MAKING TAFT PRESIDENT

Casting about for a successor to take up the task of disciplining business, Roosevelt at various times considered the brilliant Elihu Root, who had served successively as Secretary of War and Secretary of State in his Cabinet, and, more briefly, the exceptionally deserving Governor Charles Evans Hughes of New York, the able prosecutor of insurance abuses and monopoly and a practical reform type of executive, but a man whom Roosevelt regarded suspiciously. The President's choice fell upon William Howard Taft of Ohio, his genial Secretary of War who had acted in an official and a confidential capacity that was of importance for Roosevelt both at home and abroad. Since Taft's ambition was to crown his judicial career in the federal courts with the chief justiceship of the Supreme Court, he accepted the higher honor largely as a duty thrust upon him.

In pre-convention maneuvers Roosevelt cleverly outdid the academic Hughes in reformist pronouncements, and he marshaled in advance the formidable delegation of federal officeholders, especially in the South, thus insuring the nomination of his protégé. Big business quickly added its blessings and financial contributions. As Roosevelt put it, Taft was "oversensitive" regarding the sources of campaign gifts, but fortunately well-organized propaganda of the National Association of Manufacturers brought in from small businessmen alone, $1,600,000 of a total of $2,200,000. To Taft's disappointment, the party platform vacillated on the issue of labor injunctions, thus driving Samuel Gompers and the American Federation of Labor to Denver, where the Democratic convention met. Roosevelt's enforcement of the Sherman Anti-Trust Act received the anticipated party endorsement, as did his railroad legislation, and further extension of these policies was promised. A tariff revision plank, which Taft took very seriously, was given routine approval by the party regulars.

After their severe defeat with Parker in 1904, the Democrats turned once more to the idealistic, if twice-defeated, Bryan and his program of curbing monopoly by specific penalties, the enactment of an income tax law, and the forthright prohibition of court injunctions in labor disputes. Bryan, however, aroused fears of socialism when he declared publicly that the railroads tended so much to monopoly by nature that they must ultimately become public property. Taft, profiting by the nation's recovery from the panic of 1907, maintained a cautious position, pointing out the dangers to private property implicit in Bryanism. Hearst's newspapers enlivened the campaign by revealing the intimate transactions between Rockefeller's oil monopoly and Senator Foraker of Ohio, a Republican party leader; thus was destroyed the political career of a man who had been seriously considered for the Republican presidential nomination that year. Later, the jubilance of the Democrats was stilled by Hearst's revelations of similar intimate ties between the Standard Oil Company and the treasurer of the Democratic National Committee.

Once more the Nebraskan failed to secure the coveted prize, for Taft won 321 electoral votes to Bryan's 162, a large popular vote for the Republican candidate coming especially from the northeastern states. The Democrats could claim gains in recovering the Far West and reducing Taft's popular margin to one-half of the lead held by Roosevelt over Parker in 1904. Besides, Democratic governors captured at least five more middlewestern states, including Taft's own Ohio. There was indeed a promise of a transfer of power in 1912.

THE FAILURE OF TARIFF REFORM

Taft's single term was in large part an extension of Roosevelt's policies on almost every front. If his Cabinet differed considerably from that of his predecessor, particularly in the inclusion of five corporation lawyers, he could defend this deviation by urging the necessity of strengthening Roosevelt's reforms through sound judicial interpretation. Ever legalistic in his thinking, he believed that the courts were the chief highway of progress. His selection of the able

George W. Wickersham as Attorney General proved exceedingly fortunate and enabled him to establish a record for trust busting that ultimately surpassed Roosevelt's for both his terms. But Taft's ignorance of the ways of favorable publicity, so well understood by his predecessor, and the inevitable unfortunate comparison in the press of his own and Roosevelt's more vigorous and colorful personality gave an exaggerated impression of the differences in policy and execution between the two men.

Like Roosevelt, Taft repeatedly urged upon Congress the federal incorporation of interstate businesses for the purpose of supervising stock issues and detecting monopolist practices. He invited defeat by failing to use his patronage powers and party leadership sufficiently to exercise pressure upon the Republican conservative wing. Speaker "Uncle Joe" Cannon in the House and suave Senator Nelson W. Aldrich remained the bulwark of obstruction without any real challenge from the White House. Cannon was to be dethroned in 1910, but without Taft's assistance. Ultimately Congress accepted a watered-down measure of business control in the Payne-Aldrich tariff provision for an excise tax of one per cent on the earnings of interstate corporations, which indirectly afforded some publicity regarding monopolist practices. This proved important from the standpoint of revenue but was far too mild as a curb on bigness.

Taft's major fight against the existing high tariff, the alleged "mother of trusts," revealed true courage as compared with Roosevelt's evasion of the issue. The general (and erroneous) belief that the existing Dingley Tariff Act of 1897 was solely responsible for the high cost of living might have brought the President genuine popularity had his course not been marked by ineptitude both in dealing with obstructionists in his party and in his relations with the press. Standpatters insisted that the tariff revision called for in the party platform did not mean tariff reduction, and further complexity arose from the Republican formula that tariff duties should "equal the difference between the cost of production at home and abroad, together with a reasonable profit to American industries." The difficulty of determining the cost of production seemed to sanction the simpler method of writing schedules according to the political strength of each economic interest that desired protection.

Although Sereno E. Payne of New York, who had collaborated with Nelson Dingley of Maine in writing the high protective tariff bill of 1897, was the author of the bill introduced in the House in 1909, important reductions were made which even the Cannon-appointed Ways and Means Committee permitted to stand. But in the Senate, where the arch-protectionist Aldrich was in command, the Payne reductions began to be whittled away. Resistance came not only from the Democratic minority but from the Republican insurgents as well, particularly La Follette of Wisconsin, Albert J. Beveridge of Indiana, and Albert B. Cummins and J. P. Dolliver of Iowa. Unfortunately Taft had too deep a personal dislike for the insurgents and too great a respect for "regularity" to combat the extreme protectionists. He did, however, succeed in securing several important reductions, notably on hides, but only after some last-minute threats to withhold patronage from certain protectionist Congressmen.

Altogether, the Payne-Aldrich Act of 1909 brought little essential change in the system of protection. Besides hides, some reductions were made on lumber, iron ore, coal, and leather goods. As Henry F. Pringle has shown, the famous—or infamous—Schedule K, which the newspaper cartoonists portrayed as a sinister conspiracy of wool growers and wool manufacturers, actually contained few changes in comparison with the Dingley tariff. Enterprising clothing merchants who announced that their increased prices were caused by the tariff were merely capitalizing on newspaper misconstruction of Schedule K. Certain advantages were won by the Havemeyer sugar refining interests—the Sugar Trust—for, having recently acquired control of the domestic beet sugar industry, they now obtained decisive tariff protection for it. The protectionists had inserted a flexible clause that permitted the President, upon evidence of European discrimination against American products, to raise duties through an increased valuation of goods up to 25 per cent, but Taft nullified these hopes by denying that any European discrimination existed. Scientific tariff-making received a short-lived concession in the creation of a tariff board, but the later victorious Democrats abolished it.

In a speech-making tour intended to silence his critics, Taft argued that the Payne-Aldrich Act had effected decreases on goods valued at $5,000,000,000, and increases that affected only 600,000,000 dollars' worth of goods, half of them luxury products. This argument unfortunately ignored the fact that many of these alleged decreases affected products in which there was little European competition. Warming up to his subject, the President then made his greatest blunder of all, at Winona, Minnesota, in August, 1909. After admitting certain defects in the tariff but insisting that the high cost of living was the result of world factors, he concluded: "On the whole, however, I am bound to say that I think the Payne bill is the best bill that the Republican party ever passed." This statement aroused newspaper publishers, already smarting under the new tariff's protective duties on newsprint, and left Taft startled by the popular storm he had aroused. The subsequent congressional campaign proved how seriously the President had miscalculated in publicly endorsing the Payne-Aldrich Act.

RAILROAD AND BANKING REFORMS

One of Taft's most solid achievements in anti-monopoly legislation was the Mann-Elkins Act of 1910 strengthening federal supervision of the railroads. Roosevelt's Hepburn Act of 1906 had encouraged protracted litigation and even rate increases by permitting the railroads to apply for a court injunction suspending new maximum rates imposed by the Interstate Commerce Commission. The carriers could retain the former rates until the question of reasonableness had been determined, thus enriching themselves during the period of court action. This benefit was sharply curtailed under the Mann-Elkins Act, for it empowered the Commission to suspend any carrier-imposed new rate or regulation for a maximum of ten months without waiting for formal complaints from shippers, and to investigate the reasonableness of the changes demanded. Irresponsible railroads were at least partly deterred from imposing unreasonable rates by the fear that the Commission might suspend the schedules and leave them the expensive alternative of court appeal without the former advantage of operating temporarily under the old rates.

Another benefit of the new law was the removal of a dangerous ambiguity in the Interstate Commerce Act of 1887, which provided that no greater charge should be made for the transportation of passengers or goods for a shorter distance over the same line than for a longer one "under substantially similar circumstances and conditions."

This latter phrase, as interpreted by a lenient court, often nullified the entire provision against discrimination in favor of powerful shippers. It was dropped in the new Act. Railroads desiring to charge more for a short haul than a long one were required to obtain the consent of the Commission. To expedite cases on the crowded dockets and to avoid the unspecialized purview of the regular courts, a Commerce Court was created; its decisions could be appealed only to the Supreme Court. Unfortunately the Commerce Court, after a period of conflict with the Commission and a scandal involving one of its justices, had to be abandoned several years later. Finally, the Act of 1910 extended the Commission's authority to cover the new fields of telephone, telegraph, and wireless regulation. Thereafter the Interstate Commerce Commission became one of the most powerful administrative agencies, an indication of the path of future developments in the evolution of government control over business.

In 1910 Taft sought to obtain certain salutary changes in the banking system that had been suggested by the experiences of the panic of 1907. The inflexible nature of American currency had long been evident in the conflict between western debtors, who demanded inflation, and eastern creditors, who insisted on sound money as the only alternative to dishonor. Not only did the monetary system fail to correspond with the requirements of business expansion and contraction, but the panic of 1907 led to an absolute breakdown in the supply of currency. The Roosevelt administration had secured the passage of the Aldrich-Vreeland Act of 1908, which created additional currency that was to be retired ultimately by taxation, but this was intended as a palliative for the emergency. The same Act established a monetary commission to study the subject. By Taft's administration, the leadership of the commission had been given to Aldrich, who favored centralized banking after the English model, with moderate government control.

Opposition came from the American Bankers' Association, which insisted on the Jacksonian idea of preserving the individuality of the nation's banks. Although the quarrel between government control and banker control prevented immediate legislation, the commission's recommendations in 1912 furnished the nucleus of Wilson's Federal Reserve System. One of its chief suggestions was the establishment of a

Reserve Association of America which would have the function of creating a flexible currency based on rediscounted commercial paper of the member banks.

Both Roosevelt and Taft endorsed the establishment of a postal savings system to encourage thrift and prevent currency hoarding on the part of small investors. Many European immigrants, accustomed to the security of such systems already functioning in their native countries, had no high opinion of the soundness of American banks. Taft estimated that in 1908 these newcomers sent $90,000,000 to postal banks in their homeland. Moreover, he feared that the western states would themselves experiment in guaranteeing bank deposits, with dangerous possibilities of chaos; and there was Bryan's radical proposal for a federal guarantee of small savings accounts. Taft's plan offered a postal savings system which would both give the small depositor security and, by limiting the interest rate, avoid competition with private banking; furthermore, the funds would be available to bankers for local investment. Nevertheless, the bankers denounced the plan as socialistic, warned that the average post office was easy prey for bank thieves, and said that the system might encourage the wholesale withdrawal of bank deposits during critical periods of financial stringency. But Taft obtained the passage of the bill. Three Cabinet members formed a board of trustees to administer the system, and deposits up to $500 were accepted; the interest rate was 2 per cent. The postal savings system enjoyed moderate growth until 1931, but the bank crash of 1933 brought such a sharp increase in postal deposits at the expense of the private banks as to justify some of the fears expressed by bankers in 1910.

THE ELUSIVE "RULE OF REASON"

In Roosevelt's favorite field of trust busting, Taft and Attorney General Wickersham achieved a vigorous record. From 1890, the year the Sherman Act was passed, up to 1909, sixty-two anti-trust suits had been introduced, but Taft's one term accounted for seventy-eight court actions. Most sensational were the government victories of 1911 in the Standard Oil and American Tobacco cases, originally instituted by the Roosevelt administration. By that time Standard Oil had secured control of over 90 per cent of the refining industry through its New Jersey holding company. Special Prosecutor Frank B. Kellogg, later Coolidge's Secretary of State, pushed the government's demand for dissolution to a successful close in the federal courts. The Standard Oil Company of New Jersey was ordered to divest itself of all its subsidiaries within thirty days. This decision, originally handed down by a circuit court in 1909, was upheld two years later in the Supreme Court, but no one, critics noted, went to jail. Thereafter the oil combine turned to more subtle methods of achieving control through Rockefeller's personal ownership of stock and a community of interest understanding among the various Standard units.

A similar resounding but hollow victory was won over the American Tobacco Company of New Jersey. This combination owed its inception in 1890 to the efforts of the famous manufacturer, James B. Duke of North Carolina. Its methods of eliminating competition were regarded as being in many respects more reprehensible than those of Standard Oil. From the beginning it had been an extraordinarily successful combine, paying huge dividends and capitalizing on the fact that it controlled the best patents for the machinery needed by the industry. Ruinous price wars disposed of recalcitrant competitors, who were compelled to promise never to reenter the field. To cope with the rising resistance of the independent retail distributors the combine sponsored the United Cigar Stores, a chain of retail stores in the leading cities. So ambitious were the promoters that in 1901 they entered the British tobacco field in the same monopolist spirit. Next they went into Germany. Finally, in agreement with the English-owned Imperial Tobacco Company, they divided the entire world into three parts for exploitation: Britain for the English company, the United States for the American Tobacco Company, and the remainder of the globe for a company owned jointly by the two groups.

The Supreme Court formally dissolved the American Tobacco Company after severely denouncing its ruthless methods. But no fines were imposed, and the "dissolved" company was allowed to follow the plan of reorganization which it had presented to the courts. Louis Brandeis, counsel in one of the dissolution proceedings, observed caustically at the time: "A combination heretofore illegal has been legalized. The value of that legalization is shown by the high market value of the common stock of the American Tobacco Company." To him the moral was: "What man has illegally joined together, let no court put asunder."

Admittedly the two decisions, highly praised by Taft as a government victory, strengthened the application of the Sherman Act to consolidations in manufacturing, but the legal doctrine of the "rule of reason," which accompanied it did infinite damage by introducing new uncertainty into anti-trust cases. Chief Justice Edward D. White, who had recently been elevated to the position by Taft, delivered the majority opinion in both cases in language that revealed the most naïve assumptions as to the automatic self-correcting character of pure *laissez-faire* economics. Although he condemned the two holding companies as violators of the Sherman Act, he based his argument on the defendants' intent to achieve monopoly rather than on their obvious practices to destroy competition. The "standard of reason," he said, would determine for the Court whether a businessman intended primarily to injure the public by restraint of trade, or if such restraint was merely incidental to the perfectly legal objective of gain, and hence permissible. Regarding unintentional restraint of trade, White was confident that "the operation of the centrifugal and centripetal forces resulting from the right to freely contract was the means by which monopoly would be inevitably prevented if no extraneous or sovereign power imposed it and no rights to make unlawful contracts having a monopolistic tendency were permitted."

A vigorous dissenting opinion castigating the "rule of reason" came from Justice Harlan, who asserted that the Supreme Court had, "by mere interpretation, modified the act of congress, and deprived it of practical value as a defensive measure against the evils to be remedied." Liberals joined him in denouncing the doctrine of reason which left the courts to decide which were the "good trusts." The President, however, strongly defended the doctrine and in a special message to Congress in December, 1911, argued that White's common-law distinctions, had they been observed prior to this time, would not have affected the outcome of any cases which had come under the Sherman Act.

Subsequent federal suits soon demonstrated the increasing individualist trend of the courts in favor of monopolies whenever, in the judgment of the high court, the company had certain commendatory aspects such as the offering of economies in production or the creating of useful patents. This was the case with the United Shoe Machinery Company, for example, which used its control of patents on essential shoe machinery leased to manufacturers to compel them to accept its complete line of products. Its predominant position in the manufacture of the nation's shoe machinery and its avowed purpose of controlling this field did not make for a violation of the Sherman Act in the mind of the Supreme Court; instead, the Court extolled the excellence of the machines made by the company. The "reformed" trusts, especially the United States Steel Company which had also been prosecuted by Taft, basked in the new immunity conferred by the justices, despite evidence of collusion to prevent competition. Much of the popular discontent with the courts was channelized into the Progressive revolt of 1912.

THE BALLINGER CONTROVERSY

In conservation, as in almost everything else, Taft shared his predecessor's enthusiasm, tempered by a more profound respect for the niceties of constitutional law; but he succeeded only in arousing the most erroneous suspicions of his intentions regarding fraudulent corporate claims to the public domain. The western states, alarmed by Roosevelt's withdrawal of large areas there from private exploitation and the consequent loss of revenue, had by 1907 secured the enactment of a law forbidding the President to set aside additional public lands in the Northwest. Before signing the measure, Roosevelt had nullified its effect by ordering the immediate withdrawal of forest areas in the Northwest comprising 16,000,000 acres.

President Taft, pledged to conservatism but outraged by what he considered illegal executive action, replaced Roosevelt's Secretary of the Interior, James R. Garfield, with the more cautious Richard A. Ballinger of Seattle, who opened large tracts of previously withdrawn lands to private settlement but reserved federal control over waterpower sites. Chief Forester Pinchot was instructed to abandon his supposedly implied power to regulate the rates of power-transmission lines through the national forests. Pursuing Roosevelt's policies if not his methods, Taft obtained from Congress additional conservation powers that protected valuable mineral lands by separating titles to the land surface from subsoil ownership. The Weeks Law of 1911 authorized the President to acquire additional forest reserves by purchase; hence vast mineral lands were withdrawn from settlement.

During 1909–1910 the Taft administration was rudely shaken by the Glavis-Pinchot-Ballinger controversy, whose reverberations helped to estrange Roosevelt and Taft. A youthful government field agent, Louis R. Glavis, published in *Collier's Weekly* a series of articles charging Ballinger with conspiracy to aid the wealthy Guggenheim interests in acquiring control of Alaska's coal deposits. The prevalent fear that the nation's coal resources were being exhausted or given away fraudulently to the "interests" made Glavis's charges sensational indeed, despite the fact that little coal had ever come from Alaska. The immediate issue concerned Ballinger's personal relations with Clarence Cunningham of Idaho, whose controversial claims to over 5000 acres of Alaskan land were supported by the Department of the Interior. Ballinger admitted performing a routine legal service for Cunningham for a fee of $250 prior to taking office as Secretary of the Interior, but suspicious Progressives leaned toward Glavis's belief that a much more intimate relation existed between the two men. Gifford Pinchot, conservationist leader, immediately plunged into the controversy despite the President's appeal for neutrality. An open letter supporting Glavis which Pinchot addressed to Senator Dolliver of Iowa compelled Taft to dismiss Pinchot in January, 1910. Glavis had already been discharged. Ballinger demanded a congressional investigation and was officially exonerated.

Most embarrassing for Taft's own reputation was the sensational discovery by Louis Brandeis, acting for Glavis and Pinchot, that the President and Wickersham had antedated by two months the latter's report dated September 11, 1909, on which Taft had justified his dismissal of Glavis. The President publicly explained that he had acted on the oral testimony available on that date; the later Wickersham report, containing the same material, was therefore antedated. It was difficult, however, to destroy the popular impression that Taft had first decided to drop Glavis and had found his reasons afterward. In the ensuing controversy, Pinchot appealed his case to Roosevelt, who was returning from an African hunting trip, and sought to convince the touchy ex-President that Taft had repudiated his predecessor as well as the conservation cause itself. Taft's tragedy in 1912 was now imminent.

Despite the picturesque crusades of Roosevelt and Taft against bigness, the end of their administrations left the rising Progressive movement with a sense of non-fulfillment, even betrayal. More huge combinations existed in 1912 than in 1900. Pioneer advances in federal authority had been made experimentally, but they seemed fragmentary rather than thoroughgoing, if one assumes that the intended objective was popular control over economic life. However, the rudimentary forms of scientific rate-making for the railroads and the increasing number of investigatory commissions on currency, tariffs, labor conditions, industrial control, and other vital problems suggest that the atmosphere of political crusading was gradually yielding to the scientific detachment of the expert in government.

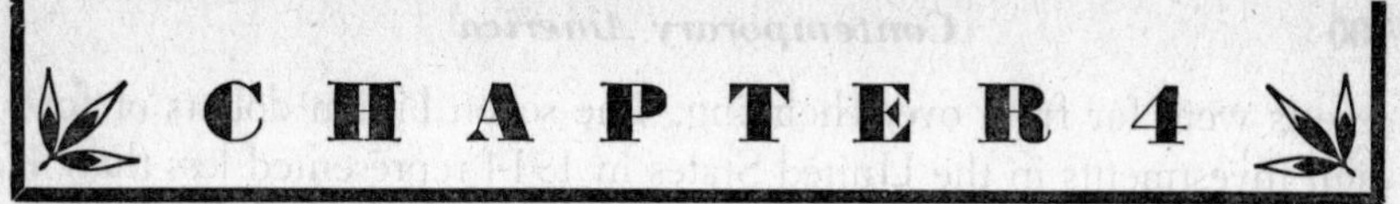

CHAPTER 4

Echoes of Imperialism: 1900-1913

INVESTMENTS AND A MATURING INDUSTRIAL SOCIETY

For centuries the western hemisphere had been the chief frontier of expanding Europe. By 1900 it seemed that the United States had already reached her continental limits and was herself a contestant in the race to acquire unexploited frontiers, especially in Latin America and the Far East. American business, too, wanted its place in the sun as the nation moved belatedly to a commanding status in the markets of the world. As the century opened, Americans held half a billion dollars in foreign investments; by 1914 this figure had soared to over 3.5 billions. The industrial economy had come of age, for by 1914 the value of exported manufactured goods had finally caught up with that of the traditionally dominant agricultural surplus which was sent abroad. After 1900 American heavy industry hastened to open hundreds of factory branches all over the world; their value more than quadrupled before the First World War. The United States Steel Corporation established 268 agencies in some sixty nations. Another giant, the International Harvester Company, opened 53 branches by 1912; within the preceding decade, the proportion of its foreign business had risen from 18 to 44.3 per cent.

Fundamentally, America was shifting from her colonial status as a debtor nation, as far as international economic relations were concerned, to that of a creditor nation. Although investment obligations to foreigners doubled during 1897–1914, American investments abroad multiplied five times. The World War merely accentuated this trend toward a creditor's status as hard-pressed Europeans frantically sought to liquidate their American investments. Furthermore, European interests were far from overwhelming. The seven billion dollars of foreign investments in the United States in 1914 represented less than 4 per cent of our total national wealth, which was then 212 billions; and this proportion was steadily declining. Although investments abroad increased, the vast potentialities of the domestic market made imperialist adventures an expensive luxury and weakened the economic pressures for colonial empire that seemed irresistible to less-favored countries. In a nation with continental dimensions, blessed in this Age of Steel with the vital resources of coal, iron, copper, and oil, as well as various agricultural products, American business and finance continued as in the preceding century to find rich opportunities largely in the United States herself.

American investments of all types in Europe amounted to almost 692 million dollars by 1914, a fivefold increase since 1897. Our Canadian holdings, especially in the pulp and paper industries, had risen at a similar ratio and aggregated 867 millions. Mexico's extraordinary diplomatic importance was forecast by a fourfold gain in this period which brought the total to 853 millions in 1914; these investments were largely in oil, minerals, and factories. Among the men encouraged by the favorable concessions given by President Porfirio Diaz was Edward L. Doheny, who later figured in the Teapot Dome scandal. In 1900 he bought 280,000 acres of oil lands at slightly above a dollar an acre; his holdings, which constituted the largest oil wells in Mexico, were valued at 58 million dollars in 1914. His friend, Senator Albert B. Fall, led a movement for military intervention in behalf of Mexican investments like Doheny's, as well as the safety of American lives. In the vital Caribbean zone of Central America, Cuba, and the West Indies, which had both strategic and economic importance, investments grew six and a half times over their total in 1897 and involved almost 460 millions. In a sensational advance, the South American interests of American investors increased ninefold during 1897–1914 to a total of 365.7 millions. Most of the 246 million dollars invested in Asia in 1914 represented loans made to Japan, then favorably regarded in this country, for her war with Russia in 1904–1905.

From 1874 on, the repayment of past loans and the substantial interest charges paid made it possible for Europeans to finance more purchases of American goods, thus stimulating our export industries and creating a so-called favorable balance of trade. In the opening years of the century, exports averaged 1.33 billion dollars annually and exceeded the two-billion mark by 1914. Although much of this trade and investment involved well-developed countries and was not calculated to stimulate political expansionism, there was sufficient penetration into so-called backward countries to encourage diplomatic intervention.

THE EXPANSIONIST SPIRIT

Aggressive nationalism and armament races in Europe, fostered particularly by the "Big Navy" men, swept aside the liberal ideals of free markets, equal access to raw materials, and the sovereignty of weaker states. Fierce rivalries among the great powers for political or economic domination, reminiscent of the bitter price wars in the formative period of industrial monopolies, too often ended in utter repudiation of the liberal spirit of fair competition. Just as domestic legislation proved unable to take the bold steps necessary to maintain the delicate balance of free competition, so international law, enjoying far less effective sanctions, failed to curb the giant national rivals.

Echoes of European and Japanese imperialism reached the expansionists in the United States who won ascendancy during the Spanish-American War. This group, as suggested elsewhere, had its Kipling-inspired literature of "the white man's burden" and its ideology which held that the Anglo-Saxon peoples (including Germany, England, and the United States) were destined to inherit the earth. Some of its members, like the Reverend Josiah Strong, sought an Anglo-Saxon alliance with the missionary element. Social Darwinists, following the philosopher and historian John Fiske, tended to make imperialism a fierce jungle doctrine of the survival of the fittest. A few Progressives like Senator Albert J. Beveridge, Jack London, and the Kansas editor, William Allen White, echoed the mysticism of empire-building and revived the nineteenth-century slogan of Manifest Destiny.

Most significant of the ardent expansionists was Captain Alfred Thayer Mahan, renowned strategist and strong advocate of a large Navy equipped with numerous naval bases. The dual motive of security in a war-prone world and national ambition dominated his writings. His favorite theme was expressed in the title of his most popular work, *The Influence of Sea Power upon History* (2 vols., 1892). Professing himself a "realist" who believed that self-interest was the sole basis for statecraft, he fought both disarmament and the compulsory arbitration of vital questions. This was clear at the Hague Conference of 1899, called by the Czar in a movement for peace which Mahan appraised (probably accurately) as insincere. "When he [Mahan] speaks," observed a fellow American delegate, Andrew D. White, "the millennium fades and this stern, severe, actual world appears." During the Spanish-American War, Mahan helped to convert Congress to his belief that Hawaii must be annexed as "the first line of American defense" in the vital Pacific. In 1900 he wrote *The Problem of Asia,* which called for the annexation of the Philippines and territorial integrity for China as part of a grand strategy designed to offset the penetration of Germany and Russia—and Japan—into dominating Pacific positions. Theodore Roosevelt and Henry Cabot Lodge deferred continually to Mahan's views, which they seemed to have substantially adopted. The revised perspective on Pacific affairs after Japan's attack on Pearl Harbor in 1941 revived Mahan's prestige as the great apostle of sea power.

On the other hand, the drift to empire aroused the deep anger of the powerful movement for social democracy (except in a small imperialist wing) which attributed expansionism to the influence of large capitalist enterprises. Much of this resentment was channelized at the opening of the century by Bryan and Altgeld in the Democratic party, and in the anti-imperialism of the minor Social Democratic party led by the Socialist, Eugene V. Debs. President Grover Cleveland had publicly rebuked American sugar expansionists in 1893 by withdrawing the treaty pending in the Senate for annexing Hawaii. The Spanish-American War began, in large part, as a middle-western crusade against Spanish atrocities in Cuba. Although the jingoist Hearst newspaper, the New York *Journal,* by its provocative tone and gross sensationalism sharply increased its circulation in leading the nation to war, Altgeld of Illinois in all sincerity wrote editorials for Hearst, also demanding military intervention in Cuba. Many who had followed Bryan in 1896 as the knight of the disinherited clamored for justice for the suffering Cubans. American business interests in Cuba, whose holdings amounted to some $50,000,000, preferred the strong arm of

Spain to the unpredictable and possibly confiscatory tendencies of a native Cuban regime. McKinley, Mark Hanna, Wall Street—all had opposed war until overwhelmed by popular sentiment. The altruistic impulse of the true crusader was injected into the anti-imperialist Teller Amendment providing for an independent Cuba, which was passed with the war resolution on April 19, 1898.

Victory brought us the Philippines, Puerto Rico, and Guam, together with the temporary military administration of Cuba, and crystallized national attitudes on imperialism. Although the older crusading sentiment, especially among the adherents of social democracy, demanded withdrawal from the Philippines and sought to make the issue of imperialism paramount in Bryan's Democratic platform of 1900, McKinley, spurred on by the expansionists, regarded the retention of these islands as a divine trust for civilization. American business leaders echoed Mark Hanna's hope that the Philippines would serve as a geographic approach to increased trade in the Orient; and Havemeyer's Sugar Trust, previously indifferent or hostile to the war, argued for the annexation of Cuba as a secure foundation for American economic penetration. Mahan saw his wish realized in the annexation of Hawaii on July 7, 1898, by a joint resolution of Congress. At the same time fresh sentiment for an Isthmian canal arose following the dramatic voyage of the battleship *Oregon* from the northern Pacific coast all the way around South America in order to reach the combat zone near Cuba. Japan, observing these developments, was frankly worried and stiffened her attitude accordingly.

THE PHILIPPINE EXPERIMENT

Such an incipient growth of imperialism invited complications. Filipino soldiers led by the professional revolutionary, Aguinaldo, raised the banner of revolt once more during 1899–1902, convinced that they had been betrayed by promises of independence into merely exchanging an old master for a new one. McKinley's avowed policy of beneficent assimilation antagonized the revolutionists, as did the condescending attitude of certain American officers who regarded the natives as children and commended the uncompromising tactics of the British in subjugating Burma. "There is no Philippine people," asserted McKinley's Secretary of War, Elihu Root, in pointing out the numerous tribes, languages, and religions among the 9,000,000 inhabitants; Christians, Mohammedan Moros, and Igorot head-hunters were scattered over the thousand islands. The first Philippine Commission, originally an investigatory body, concluded that a free commonwealth was conceivable only with American occupation.

Meanwhile the Philippine insurrection degenerated into savage guerrilla warfare in which 130,000 American troops had to fight on unfamiliar terrain. Increasing reports of anti-native atrocities, some of them well authenticated, reached the United States. There seemed to be an embarrassing parallel to Spain's unfortunate record in Cuba, even to the use of concentration camps. From Bryan and the forces of social democracy came bitter attacks upon the Administration. Secretary Root, somewhat belatedly, took strong measures to stamp out the use of torture by Americans regardless of the provocation. Finally on July 4, 1902, a presidential proclamation announced the restoration of peace, except among the wild Moro tribes, and offered a general pardon to the revolutionists.

Equally complex were the problems of colonial administration. The recognizable features of an American colonial office in the British tradition appeared in McKinley's Bureau of Insular Affairs. A framework of imperial theory was laid with the Supreme Court's decisions in the famous insular cases of 1900–1904 which displaced the historical tradition, established by the Northwest Ordinance of 1787, of an equal democratic partnership between new territories and the states of the Union. In one of these cases, Downes *v.* Bidwell (1901), the court warned, "A false step at this time might be fatal to the development of what Chief Justice John Marshall called the American empire." The judge asserted that Congress had the power to decide upon the status of inhabitants of newly acquired territory because the civil rights guaranteed by the Constitution did not automatically go into force. Among the "artificial rights" which Congress might withhold were citizenship, suffrage, and the judicial procedure prescribed in the Constitution. Commenting on this decision, Secretary of War Root remarked with his customary humor, "The Constitution follows the flag but doesn't quite catch up with it."

McKinley's first civil governor for the Philippines was William Howard Taft, former judge of the Circuit Court of Appeals. Root's instructions to him practically conceded the guarantees of the federal Bill of Rights to the islands, except trial by jury and the right to bear arms. Strong local governments that would allow the maximum native control compatible with the cultural level of the people were to be established. Filipinos were to be given preference in government posts and the utmost respect was to be shown for local customs and prejudices. Root sincerely believed with McKinley that America held the Philippines only in trust for the future.

In this enlightened spirit, Taft wrestled with serious Philippine problems of agriculture, health, unemployment, and administration. He intervened effectively in Aguinaldo's long-smoldering war on the local clergy, which had culminated in bloody attacks on the Spanish priests and in the confiscation of 420,000 acres of the so-called Friar Lands. To appease the landless Filipino insurgents as well as Catholic sentiment, Taft even visited the Vatican. As a result, these land claims were settled for $7,543,000, a sum which was ultimately met by selling the church lands to the natives. Philippine criticism of the monastic orders and their alleged political domination over the islands was eventually quieted after Rome introduced American priests to replace the traditional Spanish clergy. In 1907 the Philippine Islands, given the limited status of an "unincorporated territory," held their first national election for the Assembly. The Philippine Commission, however, offset increased popular control to some extent by itself assuming the legislative function of a senate body, although by the time of Wilson's inauguration four of its nine members were Filipinos.

CUBA UNDER THE PLATT AMENDMENT

The administrative record of American military occupation in Cuba during 1899–1901 was far better than that of the Army in the Philippines before Taft became governor. This was due largely to the effective cooperation of General Leonard Wood and the Secretary of War. Although Wood preferred outright annexation of Cuba, he accepted the contrary opinion of his superior with soldierly loyalty.

Cuba in 1899 was poverty-stricken, overwhelmingly illiterate, disease-ridden, and in the throes of postwar reconstruction. The Foraker Act, which attempted to eliminate corrupt economic concessions to businessmen, forbade the granting of public franchises during the period of Cuban occupation and thus unfortunately hampered the island's economic development. However, an exception was made in the case of certain American and Canadian railroad men led by Sir William Van Horne, noted as the builder of the Canadian Pacific Railroad; this group opened the hitherto impassable route from Havana to the easternmost province of Oriente. A gigantic task was achieved in the creation of a modern school system for Cuba; the generosity of Harvard University, in particular, made it possible during the summers of 1900 and 1901 for almost 1500 Cuban teachers to enjoy a free program of travel and recreation, as well as classroom study.

Most famous in the annals of colonial administration was the stamping out of the island's scourge—yellow fever—through the cooperation of American and Cuban doctors. Havana was transformed into a healthful modern city. Important advances were made in the administration of Cuban hospitals, charitable institutions, and prisons, and local laws were honestly enforced.

The Cubans were not altogether satisfied with American prescriptions as to what was good for them and local politicians awaited their rise to power with ill-concealed impatience. Most serious in Secretary Root's estimation was the fear of Spanish businessmen that American withdrawal would mean bloody reprisals against them on the part of the natives. Other causes for hesitation in granting complete freedom to Cuba were the exaggerated fears of our War and State Departments that Germany was planning to dominate the Caribbean. Nevertheless, preparations were completed in December, 1901, for the first Cuban election; it was expected that this would terminate American occupation.

To strengthen the Monroe Doctrine, formulated in 1823 to prevent further European penetration into the Americas, Root decided that some diplomatic safeguard was necessary in Cuba. Accordingly he wrote the famous Platt Amendment, which was passed in 1901. This provided that Cuba could not make any treaties which might impair her independence or assume any public debts which could not be met by ordinary revenues. All the official acts of the American military administration in Cuba were held binding upon the incoming native government. The amendment also included provisions regarding the future lease or sale of Cuban coaling and naval stations. Most important of all was the provision that the United States was to retain "the right to intervene for the preservation of Cuban independence, the maintenance of a government adequate for the protection of life, property, and individual liberty," and in certain other contingencies. With great reluctance and only because of American pressure, the Cubans incorporated into their fundamental law the Platt Amendment which gave them the position of a protectorate of their powerful northern neighbor.

Root, who continued to serve as Secretary of War under Roosevelt, proved indeed to be a friend of Cuba and Latin America, despite his authorship of the much-criticized Platt Amendment. He defended the creation of the protectorate on the ground that it conferred no powers of intervention not already exercised by the United States in 1898 or required for our safety in keeping with the Monroe Doctrine. Moreover, he admitted privately that the famous document had no standing in international law; therefore it was decidedly preferable to base any action on behalf of Cuban independence on the generally recognized Platt Amendment. As Philip C. Jessup, his biographer, has shown, Root opposed the annexationists, helped to make General Wood's military government—intended as a transition to civil control—exemplary in most respects, and fought for a generous reciprocal trade agreement which would enable Cuba to live. As far as the American naval bases in Cuba were concerned, Root agreed to accept the lesser ports of Guantánamo and Bahía Honda rather than embarrass the succeeding native administration by insisting on a base at Havana. Despite adverse pressure at home, he was convinced that the contested title to the Isle of Pines belonged to Cuba and he vigorously repelled the efforts of American land speculators to seize the island.

The merits of our occupation of Cuba were obscured by the severe depression suffered by the sugar planters, a depression aggravated by the beet sugar interests in Europe and the United States who used high tariffs and export bounties to protect their increasing output from Cuban competition. Independence for Cuba meant the island's commercial ruin unless the American market could be reached. The beet sugar interests in the Northwest and the cane sugar growers of Louisiana, Hawaii, and Puerto Rico organized a powerful lobby against any Cuban-American reciprocal trade agreement. Only when Europe abolished export bounties on sugar and thereby assured Cuba of new markets did President Roosevelt act, and then without the authorization of Congress. Fear of losing the island as a market for American exports and the threatened weakening of Cuban-American ties, together with Secretary Root's solicitude for Cuba's prosperity, led to a reciprocity treaty which was finally ratified in 1903. The tariff on Cuban imports to the United States was put at 20 per cent below our regular schedule, and that on our exports to Cuba was reduced 20 to 40 per cent. American consumers enjoyed cheaper sugar and Cuban planters benefited by the agreement to the extent of $20,000,000 up to 1910. By 1914 the United States was importing almost all her sugar from Cuba, and American-owned mills on the island were processing over one-third of the cane.

Yankee capital, closely followed by British, poured into Cuba in a swelling stream. In 1906, the year of our second military intervention, it amounted to the significant total of $159,500,000, which was largely invested in sugar, tobacco, cattle, and railroads. Despite our investments, the Roosevelt administration showed the utmost disinclination to intervene when official reports reached Washington that the first president of Cuba, Dr. Tomás Estrada Palma, was unable to maintain order. In 1905 Palma's followers, the Moderates, were attempting to insure their lease on power by evicting their opponents, the Liberals, from municipal offices and encouraging fraud at the national elections held that year. When the Liberals struck back the following year with the time-honored weapon of revolution, thus alarming both native and foreign property holders, Palma immediately appealed for American military intervention. Roosevelt hesitated to act in the absence of Elihu Root, who had been transferred to the State Department in 1905 and was making a crucial—and successful—good-will tour of South America, whereupon the Cuban President forced the issue by threatening to resign. He remarked privately to a friend, "I have never feared to admit nor am I afraid to say aloud that a political dependence which assures us fecund boons of liberty is a hundred times preferable for our beloved Cuba to a sovereign and independent republic discredited and made miserable by the baneful action of periodic civil wars." Despite the embarrassment it caused Root, Roosevelt was compelled to send armed forces to Cuba; and Taft, the new Secretary of War, was instructed to proclaim himself provisional governor after attempts to persuade Palma to continue as President had proved fruitless.

Although American business, reinforced by the northern press, clamored for annexation, Roosevelt ignored the outcry and proceeded to appoint a new provisional governor to succeed Taft. Judge Charles E. Magoon, the new incumbent, a man thoroughly experienced in colonial affairs, was instructed to prepare the way for a revival of Cuban self-government. Energetic and personally honest, he was seriously handicapped by political pressure in Washington and Havana. In his desire to soothe American as well as Cuban public opinion, especially in view of Roosevelt's desire to elect Taft as his successor, Magoon proceeded to placate insistent Cuban office seekers by a systematic use of patronage, thus creating a general if erroneous impression of personal corruption. Although our second intervention resulted in useful public works, favorable labor legislation, and a democratic apparatus for elections, the Cubans were unenthusiastic, partly because of the severe economic depression which occurred during this period as a result of climatic and marketing conditions. Cuban critics denounced the Magoon administration for favoritism in awarding public contracts and blamed the governor for the scandalous traffic in pardons and other official favors which in reality had been freely granted but had been corruptly sold by private individuals. Roosevelt withdrew our troops on January 28, 1909; only this administrative act was held worthy of commendation by the Cubans.

PUERTO RICO, STRATEGIC OUTPOST

Much more intimate were our relations with Puerto Rico, which, it was assumed from the beginning, would be permanently included in the United States for strategic reasons. This beggared Spanish colony became part of the new American empire under tragic circumstances, for on August 8, 1899, a terrific hurricane killed 3000 of its people; the survivors, reduced to destitution, required extensive aid from their wealthy neighbor. Like the Philippines, Puerto Rico was given the status of an "unincorporated territory" under the Foraker Act of 1900, which denied American citizenship to the inhabitants but allowed considerable freedom to local institutions and customs in the hope of ultimate home rule. The partially elective government which was set up was similar to that in the Philippines, especially in the popularly chosen Assembly which was balanced by an American-dominated upper council and an American governor. In spite of pressure from tariff lobbies in the United States, Secretary Root succeeded by 1901 in achieving virtual free trade between this country and Puerto Rico, thus saving the island's economy from disaster. Within a few years large American-owned sugar, coffee, and tobacco plantations had begun to replace the traditional subsistence farms of the Puerto Ricans. New industries arose, exports climbed sharply, and an elaborate system of public works modernized the island. Illiteracy, the heritage of 85 per cent of the population, declined steadily. Especially noteworthy was the work of American medical research in curbing hookworm, yellow fever, smallpox, and tuberculosis. Although the rise of absentee ownership under American occupation created serious social and economic problems, there is little question that the transfer from Spanish to American rule brought a better day to Puerto Rico.

"I TOOK THE CANAL ZONE"

Overshadowing in importance almost every other phase of Caribbean diplomacy during this period was our acquisition of the Panama Zone, so vital to American strategy. Interest in an interoceanic canal had been shown long before by Cortés, Simon Bolívar, and Henry Clay among many others. The new spirit of expansion which arose after the Spanish-American War in 1898 demanded the immediate removal of all technical obstacles to an Isthmian canal under exclusively American control. Newspapers drove home the lesson of the *Oregon's* voyage around Cape Horn during the recent war, and by 1900 both political parties were pledged to a program calling for the early construction of a canal. Our special interests in the Isthmus had been implied in the treaty of 1846 with Colombia (then New Granada), which permitted the United States to guarantee the neutrality of the Panama area. Britain, whose interests in Central America antedated the Monroe Doctrine, had fought the extension of American influence after the discovery of gold in California. A collision was avoided by the Clayton-Bulwer Treaty of 1850, which provided that neither country would fortify, colonize, or dominate the Isthmus or obtain exclusive control over any canal in that region. At the time only Britain was in a financial position to build a canal, but a half century of inactivity made it clear that she had no intention of undertaking such a project.

Jingoist newspapers like the New York *Journal* whipped up nationalist sentiment in 1900 for the abrogation of the Clayton-Bulwer Treaty. Fortunately for peace, the British were in desperate need of friends to offset the rising might of Bismarck's Triple Alliance and hence were receptive to the "hands across the sea" gesture made by John Hay, the Anglophile Secretary of State in the Cabinets of McKinley and Roosevelt. In a public address at Birmingham, the British Colonial Secretary, Joseph Chamberlain, expressed his hope of a future alliance with the United States which would balance the growing bloc of military powers on the Continent. "I go even so far as to say that, terrible as a war may be, even war itself would be cheaply purchased if, in a great and noble cause, the Stars and Stripes and the Union Jack should wave together over an Anglo-Saxon Alliance." Democrats, particularly Irish- and German-American, charged that Hay had actually engineered an alliance with England.

Preliminary negotiations for an exclusively American canal seemed on the point of success in 1900, but anti-British sentiment as well as reasons of security compelled the Senate to demand American fortification of the canal and the complete abrogation of the Clayton-Bulwer Treaty. Her isolation endangered by the Boer War, Britain yielded to necessity and, despite criticism at home, accepted the amended Hay-Pauncefote Treaty on November 18, 1901. This treaty, which embodied the Senate's demands, removed an important obstacle to the construction of the canal by the United States.

Both Roosevelt and Congress had almost been persuaded by the engineers of the Walker Commission that the Nicaraguan route was preferable to the Panama Zone for the proposed canal. At this juncture, however, a powerful lobby intervened on behalf of the New Panama Canal Company which had succeeded the bankrupt French Construction Company of Ferdinand de Lesseps, builder of the Suez Canal. The new company, represented by Philippe Bunau-Varilla, the French engineer, and William N. Cromwell, a New York lawyer, offered to sell its properties for $40,000,000. This won Roosevelt and the Congressmen over to the Panama route as being considerably cheaper than that across Nicaragua. Cromwell, who eventually received an $800,000 fee for his services in connection with the canal, had already contributed $60,000 to McKinley's campaign chest in 1900 in order to prevent unqualified Republican endorsement of the Nicaragua route. Bunau-Varilla, proud of his role as promoter, boasted later that he had influenced the Senate vote by publicizing a recent volcanic eruption in Nicaragua. He managed to find, at various stamp dealers in Washington, ninety stamps imprinted with a picture of the volcano "belching forth in magnificent eruption"; each Senator received one of these stamps labeled "An official witness of the volcanic activity of Nicaragua." Subsequently the Senate voted the Spooner Amendment of June 28, 1902, which empowered the President to negotiate with Colombia for the Panama route; if he failed to secure this "within a reasonable time and upon reasonable terms," he was to initiate plans for the Nicaraguan canal.

Hay quickly proceeded to negotiate the Hay-Herran Treaty with Colombia; this established a canal zone six miles wide for the sum of $10,000,000 in cash and an annual rental of $250,000. For once the Senate offered no opposition to the Secretary of State and approved the treaty on March 17, 1903. Much to the indignation of Roosevelt and Congress, however, the Colombian Senate refused to accept it. The chronic threat of revolution there made it unwise for the government to barter the country's resources too cheaply. American threats to use force merely stiffened Colombia's attitude. Roosevelt, anxious to begin construction of the canal in time to aid his reelection in 1904, contemplated a legalist formula evolved by the State Department which justified seizure of the proposed canal zone, but this step was superseded by events.

Meanwhile Bunau-Varilla and Cromwell had decided to take no chances on a possible decision in favor of the Nicaraguan route. Apparently without formal authorization from any responsible American authority, the Frenchman convinced a small band of professional revolutionists in Panama that the United States would actively assist that country to regain her long-lost independence. Conversations with the President and members of the State Department made him feel certain that in the event of a revolution the United States would exercise the right given her by the treaty of 1846 with Colombia, and land troops on the Isthmus for the purpose of protecting "free transit"; in fact, exactly this had been done on several similar occasions. If there was no actual collusion between Bunau-Varilla and Roosevelt, it is at least clear that the latter had advance knowledge of the plot and intended to profit from it. Furthermore, the French engineer knew that the U.S.S. *Nashville* would arrive at Colón, Panama, on November 2, 1903, but he claimed later that he had deduced this from the newspapers.

On November 3 the "revolutionists," consisting largely of employees of the New Panama Canal Company and its affiliate, the Panama Railroad Company, and of bribed Colombian troops and local soldiers of fortune, staged their carefully rehearsed uprising. Madame Bunau-Varilla acted as the Betsy Ross of Panama by making a flag for the nation. As anticipated, loyal Colombian troops were unable to land because of American naval forces. With more than undignified haste, Roosevelt immediately extended recognition to the Republic of Panama. (In 1911 he boasted to an audience at the University of California, "If I had followed traditional, conservative methods I would have submitted a dignified State paper of probably 200 pages to Congress and the debates on it would have been going on yet; but I took the Canal Zone and let Congress debate; and while the debate goes on the Canal does also." This boast proved costly to Latin American friendship, for it apparently confirmed the worst suspicions of our neighbors to the south.) Liberal newspapers in the United States criticized the Administration and charged that powerful American financiers actually owned much of the New Panama Canal Company in 1903 and had exercised pressure to precipitate the revolution in their own interest.

THE VENEZUELA BLOCKADE

During 1902 Colombia's neighbor, Venezuela, was the cause of another troublesome episode in Rooseveltian diplomacy. In 1895, through the belligerent insistence of President Cleveland that England accept arbitration, this republic settled a long-standing boundary dispute with Britain over British Guiana. This gave Venezuelan politicians a feeling of security in challenging the major European powers, for they were confident that the United States would intervene in accordance with the idea of hemisphere exclusiveness fostered by the Monroe Doctrine.

In 1899 Cipriano Castro, an "unspeakably villainous little monkey," —the words are Roosevelt's—became dictator through a revolution and soon contracted huge foreign debts for an elaborate program of public works. After futile attempts at collection, his creditors appealed to their home governments for assistance and in 1902 England proposed to Germany that they act jointly to compel Castro to accept arbitration. Both powers were reassured by the attitude of our State Department and by Roosevelt's dictum that in case of wrongdoing by any Latin American state, the offended European country might "spank it." Since there was no question of a permanent occupation of Venezuela, the Roosevelt administration remained quiescent while the two chief creditors, later joined by Italy, blockaded Venezuelan ports, bombarded Puerto Cabello, and sank three gunboats. Castro, realizing that American diplomats had deserted him, yielded quickly to this determined onslaught and offered to accept the original demand that the Hague Tribunal arbitrate the issues. Nevertheless, the blockade continued until February, 1903, the blockading powers demanding preferential treatment among Venezuela's numerous creditors.

One of the chief factors which finally brought the blockade to an end was the widespread indignation expressed by American newspapers in January, 1903, when Germany, acting independently, bombarded Fort San Carlos in Venezuela and destroyed an entire village. The Pan-German press, which preached aggressive expansionism and German racial superiority, added fuel to the flames by bitterly assailing the American right to intervene under the Monroe Doctrine. The State Department had long been disturbed over German penetration into Latin America, particularly Brazil, where 300,000 Germans stubbornly preserved their cultural identity through German-language schools, churches, and recreation, and maintained intimate ties with their homeland. Pan-German propagandists said frankly that Germany needed a huge fleet to protect her advance into South America, the only unexploited portion of the earth left for belated German imperialism. American diplomats erroneously suspected that Germany was responsible for Denmark's refusal to sell us the Virgin Islands in 1902.

It now seems fairly clear that the German Foreign Office, in contrast with the Pan-German extremists, followed a circumspect diplomatic policy toward the United States at the turn of the century.

That Latin America was not altogether unconcerned over the Venezuela dispute was apparent in the now famous memorandum of Luis M. Drago, Argentine Minister of Foreign Affairs, to the State Department on December 29, 1902. In this he stated a principle that has become known as the Drago doctrine: "The public debt can not occasion armed intervention nor even the actual occupation of the territory of American nations by a European power." Much to Drago's disappointment, Secretary of State Root in submitting this to the Hague Conference in 1907 added several major exceptions when he held that the Drago doctrine was "not applicable when the debtor State refuses or neglects to reply to an offer of arbitration, or, after accepting the offer, prevents any *compromis* [the preliminary agreement regarding the subject of the dispute and the powers of the arbitrators] from being agreed on, or, after the arbitration, fails to submit to the award." In this form, despite Latin American dissatisfaction with the loopholes, the Drago doctrine became an important auxiliary to international law.

As long as Castro remained in power, Venezuela continued to embarrass American foreign policy. In 1904 his soldiers seized an asphalt lake that was being exploited by a New York firm and he himself began to ship asphalt to the company's competitor in the United States. The American minister at Caracas demanded that warships be sent to Venezuela, but Root, who had just become Secretary of State, refused to go beyond diplomatic methods of solution. Castro's interference in the affairs of a large French company brought irate protests from France, the breaking off of diplomatic relations with Venezuela, and the threat of war. Castro, apparently impressed, appealed to the United States for assistance under the Monroe Doctrine, but Root replied that the circumstances did not warrant intervention and instead offered his favorite remedy, arbitration. Despite other repeated provocations from Castro, Root refused to use force, for he believed that this would only strengthen the nationalist sentiment behind the dictator. Fortunately the latter's overthrow in 1908 made it possible for Venezuela to return to normal diplomatic methods.

THE ROOSEVELT COROLLARY TO THE MONROE DOCTRINE

England's decision to withdraw from the Venezuela blockade had been prompted largely by criticism at home over the Navy's prolonged association with Germany and by the desire to strengthen Anglo-American friendship. Yet British ties with Latin America—economic, cultural, and historical—were in many respects even firmer than ours. British statesmen, perhaps echoing the sentiments of the Council of Foreign Bondholders, argued that any assertion by the United States of the right to protect Latin American countries from the consequences of their misdeeds carried with it the duty of controlling these nations. Roosevelt was thus offered the role of international policeman, a congenial part to a man of his active temperament. There was not a little of Kaiser Wilhelm's self-conscious strut in the President. In 1900, while inveighing against the New York Republican machine, he declared that he had always liked a certain West African proverb, "Speak softly and carry a big stick, you will go far." Fortunately for Roosevelt's administration, the moderating influence of Root, Hay, and Taft kept the Big Stick policy subordinate in foreign affairs.

The international policeman had his first chance to act when financial difficulties beset the turbulent Dominican Republic, a vital area of the strategic waters of the Caribbean. An American firm, the Santo Domingo Improvement Company, had controlled the country's customs collections since 1893. Eight years later, its contract was arbitrarily revoked by the local government, whereupon the State Department successfully reinstated the company. Reports of negotiations between the Dominican Republic and Germany regarding naval bases and coaling stations alarmed the United States, despite Chancellor von Bülow's rejection of them. The little republic was financially hard-pressed and its European creditors were gathering about ominously, encouraged by the Hague Tribunal's unanimous decision in 1904 that the powers who had used coercion against Castro were entitled to preferential treatment over all other creditors.

Fearing that the Hague decision had put a premium on foreign intervention and violence, the State Department moved to avert a second Venezuela affair by arranging a treaty with the Dominican Republic that gave the United States official control of the customs revenue, in line with the precedent set in the case of the Santo Domingo Improvement Company. In his annual message of December, 1904, the President formulated the famous "Roosevelt Corollary to the Monroe Doctrine," which accepted the British-inspired suggestion that we make European coercion of any American nation unnecessary by ourselves assuming the task of preserving order and protecting lives and property. He denied any territorial designs and assured Latin America that our interest was concerned solely with her prosperity. "If a nation shows that it knows how to act with reasonable efficiency and decency in social and political matters, if it keeps order and pays its obligations, it need fear no interference from the United States. Chronic wrongdoing, or an impotence which results in a general loosening of the ties of civilized society, may in America, as elsewhere, ultimately require intervention by some civilized nation. The adherence of the United States to the Monroe Doctrine may force the United States, however reluctantly, in flagrant cases of such wrongdoing or impotence, to the exercise of an international police power."

This extension of the Monroe Doctrine was elaborated the following year in Roosevelt's message explaining that the Corollary did not mean American intervention when normal redress was sought by a foreign country in behalf of injured citizens. We would intervene only when there was danger that such a nation might take even temporary possession of a Latin American customhouse to compel payment of an obligation and thus open the door to permanent occupation.

Senate Democrats, distrusting the Corollary as rank imperialism, blocked the Dominican agreement. But Roosevelt, with his customary strong belief in the prerogatives of the Chief Executive, proceeded to act without the Senate and issued an Executive Letter that established an American customs receivership for the Dominican Republic and refunded its foreign debt among New York bankers. Haste was made vital by the arrival of an Italian cruiser in Caribbean waters. Since this move was suspected of embodying a plan to obtain a harbor in Samaná Bay, American warships moved in to emphasize the special position of their government in Dominican affairs. The Executive Letter proved so successful financially as well as diplomatically that the British Council of Foreign Bondholders endorsed similar American action in

Costa Rica, Honduras, Guatemala, and elsewhere. Roosevelt and Root, however, now showing marked deference to Latin American opinion, were reluctant to extend the Corollary. Customs duties were collected honestly and efficiently, bringing in much-needed revenue for internal construction as well as for foreign obligations. Order was restored, at least for several years, without seriously infringing upon native civil liberties. Even our suspicious Senate finally consented in February, 1907, to incorporate most of these arrangements in treaty form.

The necessities of Caribbean strategy, rather than pressure from private investors, dictated our course in Cuba, Puerto Rico, Venezuela, and even Panama. Inevitably these motives, justified by the State Department in the name of national defense, brought all of Central America within the zone of American interests. But during Roosevelt's administration, thanks to the cautious Root, American intervention was sporadic and circumspect. Zelaya of Nicaragua, chief intriguer in Central America, attempted to revive the one-time political unity of this area but found the cooperation between President Porfirio Diaz of Mexico and President Roosevelt during 1906–1907 an effective check. Joint Mexican-American mediation temporarily halted the revolutionary disturbances fomented by Zelaya, and a Central American Bureau was created in the hope of restoring regional unity under democratic auspices. United States Marines were instructed by Root not to land in Central America during revolutions unless American lives were in actual jeopardy.

ROOT'S "GOOD NEIGHBOR" POLICY

Root's consistent efforts to build a lasting foundation for Latin American friendship toward the United States reached its dramatic climax, as Philip C. Jessup, his biographer, has shown, in the summer of 1906 when he embarked upon a good-will tour of South America, thus setting an important precedent for similar visits by other American statesmen. His trip was timed to coincide with the Pan-American Conference at Rio de Janeiro; even the Hague Conference had been deferred until 1907 in order to provide the most favorable setting for the Rio conference. Root's simple, dignified bearing and his sincerity in speaking impressed many Latin Americans. Although the conference itself proved relatively unimportant in achievement, our Secretary of War allayed suspicions of Yankee imperialism by assuring the independence and equal rights of the smallest as well as the largest states: "We neither claim nor desire any rights, or privileges, or powers that we do not freely concede to every American republic." Americans, he went on, desired Latin American cooperation in order to achieve prosperity through trade and were not interested in acquiring territory.

After extravagant receptions in the South American capitals and enthusiastic demonstrations in the streets, Root returned home eager to make Americans aware of the potentialities for economic and cultural cooperation with their neighbors to the south. He told business groups that American foreign trade was steadily shifting from one based on loans and imports to one based on investments and exports. The program he proposed was still widely endorsed a generation later. It called for businessmen who operated in Latin America to have agents familiar with Spanish or Portuguese; for manufacturers to adjust their exports to Latin American tastes and their credit practices to Latin American standards; for tact and respect to replace condescension; and for new systems of communication, especially steamship facilities, to be initiated immediately. In the cultural sphere, Root declared that the "strenuous utilitarianism" of Americans could profitably be blended with the social charm of their southern neighbors. Roosevelt paid his Secretary of State the compliment of recommending to Congress legislation favorable to this program, but no immediate action was taken. A later generation was to rediscover the principles formulated by Elihu Root as its "Good Neighbor" policy.

THE OPEN-DOOR POLICY

The mounting importance of the Far East was clearly reflected in the diplomacy of John Hay. At the end of the Sino-Japanese War of 1895, when the despised "dwarfs" had humiliated the giant Chinese empire, the aggressive western powers descended eagerly upon the prostrate nation to secure spheres of influence, the cession of coastal lands, and exclusively controlled trade centers, factories, and leased properties. The practice of extraterritoriality permitted the Occident to apply its own judicial standards in the case of European residents, and the foreign control of the Chinese tariff system reduced the authority of Peking still more drastically. While Russia and Japan quarreled over the spoils in Manchuria, England expanded into the Yangtze valley and across the bay at Hong Kong to Kowloon, at the same time keeping a vigilant eye on a southward Russian drive across Afghanistan to India itself. France continued to expand in the south around Indo-China. Germany, late in the race for empire, demanded certain portions of the Chinese coast which Japan had allocated to herself after the war. American interests in this potentially rich oriental market seemed well on the way to extinction when we decided to retain the Philippines as a foothold in the Far East.

Britain, finding her "splendid isolation" a handicap in the Orient as well as in Europe, sought American assistance in preserving her extensive trade interests, especially against Russian absorption. During 1898, British statesmen and business leaders urged the United States to join Great Britain in maintaining the territorial integrity of China and an open door for trade. Lord Charles Beresford of the Associated Chambers of Commerce in particular advocated British-American collaboration in his much-discussed volume, *The Break-Up of China.* A former English customs inspector in China, Alfred E. Hippisley, was the immediate inspiration for Hay's famous open-door notes. Hippisley privately warned the State Department that Russia's rapid penetration into North China meant another Manchuria ruled by the Czar. It was likewise evident that England wanted to avoid arousing American Anglophobes by following the United States, rather than leading, in proclaiming the principle of equal trade opportunities in China.

On September 6, 1899, Hay addressed identical notes to the five chief contending powers in China—Great Britain, Russia, Japan, France, and Germany—in which he asked that they formally adhere to certain principles governing commercial practices in the various spheres of interest. These principles included the following: that no power would interfere with any treaty port or vested interest within another nation's sphere of interest; that the Chinese tariff would be applied impartially within these spheres, the duties to be collected by the Chinese government; and that in the same areas there would be no discrimination in levying harbor duties and railroad charges against foreign nationals. Britain, as expected, adopted these principles but reserved Hong Kong and Kowloon; Germany, Japan, France, and Italy (who had no "sphere") agreed on condition that all the other interested powers accept them. Russia, however, unwilling to yield her dominating position around Port Arthur in Manchuria, was evasive. Professing to believe that all the powers had adopted his proposals, Hay then announced that the United States would consider the open-door doctrine of commercial equality as final. The American press, though critical of Hay's Anglophile tendencies, praised the Secretary extravagantly for saving China from partition at no cost to the United States.

THE BOXER REBELLION: WIDENING THE OPEN DOOR

The occasion for an extension of the open-door policy came several months later with the Boxer Rebellion in 1900. Crop failures and mounting taxes, as well as the rapacity of the foreigners, inspired a group of Chinese extremists known as Boxers to lead an uprising in North China which would drive the "foreign devils" into the sea. Missionaries and foreign legations were the primary objects of attack. Over three hundred Europeans were brutally massacred. To save the 920 foreigners who sought refuge in their legations, an international army was organized; the United States sent 5000 troops, largely from the Philippines.

Embarrassed by McKinley's campaign for reelection in which imperialism was a major issue, Hay informed the American Minister at Peking that, as far as limited cooperation with the other powers was concerned, "There must be no alliances." He worked steadily to protect China from disintegration and insisted that our intervention was merely a relief expedition to protect our nationals, and not a war effort against the Chinese government. Although fully aware that the Empress Dowager was secretly encouraging the Boxers, Hay professed to see only isolated bandit groups involved. Other nations followed his lead. In an important circular dated July 3, 1900, and addressed to the major powers, he expanded the open-door idea: American policy stressed not only the "principle of equal and impartial trade," as stated a year earlier, but also the preservation of "Chinese territorial and administrative entity" and the protection of all the rights guaranteed to the various powers by treaty and international law. Once again, comment from the other interested states was favorable on the whole.

This open-door note, which was issued the day preceding the Democratic convention at Kansas City, was praised by Republicans as a refutation of Bryan's charges of imperialism. Hay even pointed out that the "principle of equal and impartial trade" had been proclaimed by Buchanan's Democratic administration in 1858 when the British and French were fighting China. Other nations were not averse to accepting a temporary solution that called for equality of treatment in rich anarchic countries like the Ottoman Empire and China until a permanent division of spoils could be effected. Possibly the Hay notes did a great deal to retard the partition of China by other greedy nations. McKinley, however, in his desire to withdraw American troops from China and prevent any complications in the Far East, made it difficult for Hay to assist England further in blocking Russia's advance into North China and Manchuria. Britain, left without American aid, drifted into an alliance with Japan which was formally announced in 1902, whereupon our policy, favoring England and hostile to Russia, became increasingly complacent toward Japanese imperialist expansion.

Hay's influence probably modified the terms of the Boxer Protocol of September 7, 1901, which demanded from China an indemnity of $333,000,000 and the punishment of guilty Chinese officials. The United States asked only to be reimbursed for the cost of her expedition, not for punitive damages; when this amount, $25,000,000, proved to be far above the claims of her nationals, she returned $10,785,286 to China in 1907. Following the suggestion of an American missionary, the Roosevelt administration and the Chinese government cooperated in using the money as an educational trust fund for Chinese youths in their own country and in the United States. A final payment of over $6,000,000 made in 1924 was also returned to China. Generous action like this was needed to calm Chinese indignation over the increasingly severe immigration rules which began to exclude even businessmen and students from the United States early in the present century. American goods were boycotted semi-officially in China during the spring of 1905; this was followed by riots, the assassination of five American missionaries, and considerable destruction of property. In the face of conditions like these, the remission of the indemnity in 1907 was plain common sense.

MEDIATING THE RUSSO-JAPANESE WAR

Most serious from the standpoint of war and peace were our relations with the ambitious Japanese empire. Recognized as a powerful nation after the war with China in 1895, Japan once more became involved in a major war during February, 1904, while attempting to halt Russia's absorption of Manchuria and Korea. Both Britain and the United States, hostile to Czarist Russia, maintained a friendly neutrality to Japan and helped to preclude outside intervention in the conflict. Roosevelt evinced great respect for the Japanese soldier's fighting qualities which were demonstrated in an amazing series of victories over the supposedly more powerful Russians. The victors, however, found the effort exhausting; they were saved from collapse only by revolutionary dissensions in Russia and their own willingness to request mediation (secretly) of Roosevelt.

Japan promised to restore Manchuria to China and accept the open-door policy in that province; more than this she refused to promise. Roosevelt met both belligerents in Portsmouth, New Hampshire, in August, 1905, and removed the chief obstacle to mediation by convincing Japan that she must give up all ideas of a huge indemnity from Russia. He effected a compromise by which the southern half of the island of Sakhalin was awarded to Japan. In addition, the Russians yielded to Japan both the valuable Liaotung leasehold in Manchuria and control of the politically and economically significant South Manchurian Railway, and acknowledged Japan's special position in Korea; the latter proved to be a prelude to outright annexation. Roosevelt was rewarded by receiving the Nobel Peace Prize. But the Japanese populace, ignorant of their own leaders' responsibility in initiating the peace overtures, rioted in demonstrations against the United States, who had robbed them of a huge indemnity and other fruits of their glorious victory. Just before the Portsmouth conference Roosevelt made a major concession to Japan in the informal Taft-Katsura agreement of July, 1905, which recognized Japan's "paramount interests" in Korea in return for her assurance that she had no aggressive intentions against the Philippines. For our partial retreat from the open-door policy in this instance, Roosevelt and Root felt there was no alternative but war with the Japanese, who were determined to take Korea.

THE GENTLEMEN'S AGREEMENT

A dangerous rift in Japanese-American relations was caused when, on October 11, 1906, the San Francisco Board of Education ordered Japanese school children to be segregated in special schools. The proud Japanese, refusing to be considered on the same level with the Chinese, formally protested this "stigma and odium." Moreover, it was recalled that the Japanese government had headed the list of contributors of funds for the victims of the devastating San Francisco earthquake a few months earlier. Several factors motivated this action by the Board of Education. Organized labor, including the national convention of the American Federation of Labor as well as the corrupt Ruef labor machine which dominated politics in San Francisco, demanded the elimination of Japanese competition just as a generation earlier it had successfully insisted on the elimination of Chinese labor. Racial hatred was augmented by the powerful but chauvinistic Hearst press of San Francisco, which emphasized the racial factor when it branded the Japanese as the "yellow peril." Finally, anti-Japanese legislation of dubious constitutionality was impending in the state capital, for, like the planters of the Old South, Californians resisted federal pressure by proclaiming the ideal of states' rights.

Fearing the loss of trade with Japan and aware that war would find the nation unprepared, President Roosevelt took vigorous steps to compel California to accept a compromise. A basis for the famous Gentlemen's Agreement of February 18, 1907, was discovered in McKinley's agreement with Japan which was still in force and by which Japan promised to refuse passports to laborers bound for the United States mainland. Hawaiian sugar interests, eager for cheap and efficient labor, had encouraged Japanese immigration to Hawaii, and many of these Japanese eventually immigrated to the Pacific coast, where they were welcomed by wealthy California fruit growers and the transcontinental railroads. The Act of 1907 empowered the President to exclude from the United States all aliens who had passports only for our island possessions or for Canada or Mexico. Thus this Act spared Japan's feelings by omitting any mention of exclusion, offering merely to enforce a policy which she had already undertaken voluntarily.

PLACATING TOKYO

Although California legislators, both state and municipal, had agreed to suspend legislation against the Japanese, a mob, unrestrained by the police, attacked several Japanese buildings in San Francisco on May 20, 1907. This effectively reopened the controversy. Government opposition leaders in Japan threatened war against the United States, and some European diplomats even speculated on a possible Nipponese victory. Relations between Canada and Japan were strained because of similar racial animosities at Vancouver. Since this involved Japan's ally England, through the Dominion of Canada, British diplomats joined the Americans in settling the dispute by paying Japan for relatively small damages caused by rioters. Taft was sent to placate Tokyo.

Roosevelt, however, characteristically chose to impress the Japanese with our naval strength by sending the fleet to the Pacific, ostensibly the first part of a spectacular good-will cruise around the world. It is possible that the President, who feared a surprise attack on Hawaii and the Panama Canal, believed that in this way he could insure the fleet's being completely prepared to fight without having to risk the threat of war inherent in his ordering it to mobilize. A former Navy Department official, Franklin D. Roosevelt, recalled later in 1923, "Outside the executive departments at Washington it has never been known in this country that, during the nervous days in the early summer of 1908, the United States hovered on the edge of an ultimatum from Japan." Fortunately the fleet was received everywhere with cordiality, even in Japan, where 10,000 school children greeted the American sailors with "Hail Columbia, Happy Land." Australia, ever fearful of Japanese designs on her thinly populated farms and cities, gave the fleet a heartfelt ovation.

Peace came closer with the Root-Takahira Agreement of November 30, 1908, by which both countries agreed to respect each other's territories in the Pacific, to uphold the open door in China, and through diplomatic means to preserve the "independence and integrity of

China." Taft had already informed the President that Japan had every intention of dominating China; furthermore, the Chinese themselves looked upon this agreement as a prelude to further Japanese encroachment. Nevertheless, Roosevelt hoped that this understanding, which implied the recognition of Japan's economic position in Manchuria, would postpone war until America was better prepared.

ARBITRATION VERSUS NATIONAL HONOR

After 1899, when the first Hague Conference met, arbitration enjoyed extraordinary international prestige among enlightened statesmen and jurists as a peaceful means of outlawing war. High among the ideals of both Hay and Root was the hope that disputes between nations could be settled in accordance with the decision of an impartial body. Whereas Hay was unable to progress far along this path because of the Senate's fear of surrendering its authority in foreign affairs, Root secured general treaties of arbitration with twenty-five nations by agreeing to accept certain vitiating Senate amendments. Not only was the Senate's approval necessary on the *compromis* formula, but these treaties exempted from consideration any disputes involving "vital interests," "independence," or "national honor." This, Root hoped, was at least a beginning.

He enjoyed a signal triumph in the arbitration of the long-standing fisheries dispute with Newfoundland. Less fortunate, however, was the arbitration of the Alaskan boundary conflict between the United States and Canada. This conflict was aggravated by the discovery of gold in the Klondike, which raised the question of access through the disputed coastal strip. Ill feeling on both sides increased as the result of exaggerated reports of strife and insurrection between American and Canadian miners. Although a tentative agreement was reached in 1899, Roosevelt in 1903 demanded a final settlement which would recognize that our position regarding the Alaskan boundary line was unassailable. The arbitral board supposedly consisted of six "impartial jurists of repute," but the President insisted on selecting three members who were already pledged to his own views. One was the Anglophobe Senator Henry Cabot Lodge; another was Senator Turner of Washington, who echoed his state's belligerent insistence on the fullest extent of our claim; the third was Secretary Root, whom the British considered unqualified because of his connection with the Administration.

While the arbitrators were at work, Roosevelt warned indirectly through Root that he would tolerate only a favorable decision; should the judges decide otherwise, he would appeal to Congress for action. "I do wish," he wrote to Root, "that they [the British arbitrators] could understand that this is the last chance and that though it will be unpleasant for us, if they force me to do what I must do in case they fail to take advantage of this chance, it will be a thousandfold more unpleasant for them." Luckily the British, unwilling to take any chance of forfeiting American friendship, had chosen the truly impartial Lord Alverstone, Lord Chief Justice of England. He recognized the strength of the American case and voted with Lodge, Turner, and Root, much to the wrath of the two Canadian jurists. The conflict was decided almost entirely in favor of the United States, but Roosevelt's attitude reflected the obstacle that nationalism presents to the achievement of genuine arbitration.

ROOSEVELT AND EUROPE

Roosevelt showed publicly a greater interest in European affairs than any of his predecessors. He denounced the massacres of Russian Jews in 1903, although he followed conventional diplomacy on domestic questions by refraining from sending a formal protest directly to Russia. When the German Foreign Office asked the Kaiser in 1905 to protest personally at Tangiers against France's growing domination in Morocco, an international crisis broke out that arrested Roosevelt's attention. At the Kaiser's request he agreed to exert diplomatic pressure on the Entente powers in favor of an international conference. Although isolationists opposed this intervention in European affairs as contrary to our historic policy, American representatives were sent to the Algeciras Conference in 1906. As one scholar has suggested, Roosevelt may have taken this step on the theory that the preservation of peace in Europe was essential to American security.

DOLLAR DIPLOMACY: INSTRUMENT OF STATECRAFT

Taft on becoming President sought to continue his predecessor's policies but was less fortunate in the men and the measures he employed. After the depression of 1907, American capital sharply increased; it was now seeking more foreign investment outlets and new markets for goods. Taft believed that the major aspect of our foreign policy should include "active intervention to secure for our merchandise and our capitalists opportunity for profitable investment which shall insure to the benefit of both countries concerned." To further this end, he chose as his Secretary of State Philander C. Knox, who had served as Attorney General in the Cabinets of McKinley and Roosevelt and was intimately connected with big business. Progressives quickly labeled the Taft-Knox program "dollar diplomacy"; some even hinted that sinister commercial interests had enslaved the State Department. Actually Knox's background was similar to Root's and his larger policies received the latter's endorsement. Root himself had sought actively to promote American business abroad, especially in Latin America, and Hay's open-door policy was frankly based on the idea of equal commercial opportunities in China. With apparent sincerity, Knox, like Hay and Root, claimed an altruistic purpose in his activities. Unfortunately, however, he proved far less adept in his diplomacy than his predecessors; as a result, he found himself committed to an unpopular course of intervention in the Caribbean and a quasi-alliance with big business that was offensive to liberal opinion.

Taft's ministers and ambassadors, as his biographer, Henry F. Pringle, points out, labored successfully abroad to secure Greek naval contracts for the Bethlehem Steel Company, orders from Peru for American submarines, and Argentine contracts for two major battleships. Secretary of War Henry L. Stimson, destined to serve again in this office a generation later under more momentous circumstances, urged that American officers replace the Europeans in the armies of Latin American countries, especially since this would mean the purchase of American materials. American businessmen were directly encouraged to invest in Latin America and China.

A significant application of dollar diplomacy occurred in China, inspired by Willard D. Straight, a former American consul general at Mukden, whose motives were indubitably sincere. Straight argued that China's territorial integrity could best be maintained by means of American investments in Manchuria, where Japanese penetration was most menacing. A strong economic interest in that area, he felt, would greatly strengthen our diplomatic efforts in behalf of the open-door policy, already compromised by Roosevelt's concessions to Japan. "Dollar diplomacy," wrote Straight, "is a logical manifestation of our national growth, and of the rightful assumption by the United States of a more important place at the council table of nations." In 1905 Straight had been associated with E. H. Harriman's original project to build a Manchurian railroad as a link in a privately owned American transportation system which was to circle the globe. This scheme had failed because of Japanese opposition. When Taft took office, Straight was acting as agent for the New York banks that were interested in underwriting any Far Eastern loan. The new Administration, influenced by Straight's ideas, supported this group by strong diplomatic measures.

In an ambitious endeavor to eject Japan and Russia from Manchuria through dollar diplomacy, Knox proposed to these powers as well as France, Great Britain, and Germany that an international syndicate purchase and operate the railway holdings of Russia and Japan in Manchuria on behalf of the Chinese government, which would appear as the nominal purchaser. Thus the political role of the railroads, the chief instrument of Japanese and Russian domination, would be neutralized and the open-door policy reasserted. Knox apparently counted on the serious financial plight of these two countries to compel acquiescence, but his bungling attempts at diplomatic pressure had the effect only of drawing the two imperialist rivals together in joint resistance. The other powers were too far committed to a partisan position to follow Knox's proposal. France supported her ally, Russia; England sided with Japan, with whom she was still allied; only Germany, isolated diplomatically, supported the Secretary. The treaty of friendship signed by Japan and Russia on July 4, 1910, administered the final resounding rebuke to Knox and the open-door policy in Manchuria. The New York bankers were disgruntled by the State Department's failure. Worse still, the jingoist press revived an anti-Japanese campaign which required the best efforts of moderate statesmen to subdue. While the Japanese press treated the Knox proposals as "nothing but selfish ambition and unreasonable jealousy," the Tokyo government left no doubt that it intended to dominate the railroads of South Manchuria.

THE LODGE COROLLARY

Suspicions of Japanese designs on the New World furnished the occasion for another extension of the Monroe Doctrine, this time by Senator Henry Cabot Lodge. During 1911 the Hearst newspapers created a sensation by claiming that a Japanese company was negotiating with an American group for the purchase of a huge tract of land on Magdalena Bay in Lower California; such a move would constitute a threat to the Panama Canal. Although the State Department put a speedy end to this proposal, the agitation it aroused led to the passage of a Senate resolution known as the Lodge Corollary to the Monroe Doctrine. This resolution declared that the United States would oppose possession of any place of strategic importance in the western hemisphere by a private concern whose relation to a non-American nation was such as to give that nation practical control. Although Taft considered this resolution provocative, he was unable to prevent its adoption.

DOLLAR DIPLOMACY IN THE CARIBBEAN

Critics of dollar diplomacy usually singled out Taft's Latin American policies for censure. Recurrent civil wars in the turbulent republics made even the good-natured Taft confess privately to Knox that he would like to "knock their heads together until they should maintain peace between them." The period of peace which had been painfully maintained in the Dominican Republic since 1905 by the customs control established by Roosevelt ended suddenly in November, 1911, with the assassination of President Cáceres and the subsequent struggle for power. The situation was further complicated by a boundary dispute between the Dominicans and Haiti. Meanwhile the customs control had been undermined by the extravagance and incompetence of Dominican officials. Fearing that European nations would intervene, in spite of the Roosevelt Corollary to the Monroe Doctrine, Taft rushed 750 Marines to the little republic in October, 1912; naval reinforcements were required before peace was finally restored.

Conditions were far more serious in Central America, for the ambitious dictator José Zelaya continued to play a leading role in disturbing the peace in Nicaragua. However, his doom came with the revolution of October, 1909, in which American mining companies were interested. When Zelaya executed two American soldiers of fortune, Secretary Knox broke off relations with Nicaragua and denounced the dictator as a "blot on the history" of his country. Zelaya yielded to this pressure and resigned; his followers were defeated with the help of American naval forces which indirectly kept open certain strategic points to save his opponents from entrapment.

The vice-president chosen by the incoming Conservative government was Adolfo Díaz, who had been secretary of the American Mining Company at Bluefields, Nicaragua; this firm had once employed Knox as its legal representative. In 1910 Díaz became president. His appeal to the United States for financial aid in meeting the burdensome debts of Nicaragua was answered by the Knox-Castrillo treaty of June 6, 1911. Although this agreement followed the Dominican pattern, suspicious Senate Democrats rejected Taft's request for ratification, despite his statement that the New York bankers were only waiting for Senate approval to extend a loan of $15,000,000 to Nicaragua. In 1912 civil war again broke out in the republic and American Marines were landed. This time they openly defended the Conservative government and left a "legation guard" of one hundred soldiers to stabilize the regime.

Elsewhere in Central America Knox failed miserably. In Honduras he attempted to block British financial and political domination by persuading American bankers to acquire control of British-held loans. He arranged a treaty based on the Dominican model and providing for American control of Honduras customs, but the Senate's refusal to ratify it made the bankers lose interest in his proposal. A similar attempt to acquire control of the Guatemalan debt held in Great Britain was unsuccessful because of energetic British action. Thus dollar diplomacy in Central America failed its sponsors, partly as the result of Knox's inept methods which made the press, already dissatisfied with Taft's domestic policies, even more suspicious.

In Cuba, this policy, reinforced by the interventionist Platt Amendment, took on a crude imperialist flavor because of the large American investments there; the holdings of non-resident Americans alone reached the huge total of $205,000,000. Adopting a policy intended to forestall European intervention, Knox tried to increase the American economic stake in Cuba by securing contracts for our businessmen there; he defended their interests by military means under the Platt Amendment. When American firms insisted on protection during a Negro insurrection in 1912, the Secretary of State, ignoring claims by Cuban officials that the situation was under control, landed Marines at several points. Roosevelt and Root, as Leland Jenks observes, would have deferred military action until the actual collapse of native authority was clear. Taft and Knox, however, took precipitate measures which had a deleterious effect on Latin American relations.

THE MADERO REVOLUTION

During 1910–1911, Mexico was shaken by a social and political revolution whose far-reaching consequences intimately affected the lives and property of both natives and foreigners. Porfirio Diaz, the dictator-president since 1876, had long before restored peace and order to his revolution-ridden land but had ruthlessly destroyed his critics. At the same time he rewarded his supporters by wholesale grants of land taken from the helpless Indians, in accordance with his law of 1886, which required all landholders to prove their titles. Both Roosevelt and Taft were oblivious to the high price in civil liberties that the Mexican masses paid for their nation's well-publicized prosperity (which failed to trickle down to the lower classes) and hence remained great admirers of the dictator. American capitalists, impressed by the extremely generous concessions offered them by Diaz, were also inclined to think well of him. Henry Lane Wilson, whom Taft appointed as Ambassador to Mexico, became an influential spokesman for Yankee business, then valued at two billion dollars; he also faced the problem of providing safety for 70,000 Americans living in that southern republic.

Long resentful over their grievances, Mexican farmers and laborers in 1910 joined a revolutionary plot against Diaz, led by the idealistic Francisco Madero. Madero, who came from a wealthy family in Coahuila, demanded the restoration of the democratic but anti-clerical Constitution of 1857, a system of public education, and various agrarian and industrial reforms. His armies drove back the dictator's demoralized troops in a march on Mexico City from the north, and on May 25, 1911, compelled Diaz to flee. Unfortunately for Mexico,

Madero failed to maintain order. A rival revolutionary movement led by Emiliano Zapata demanded that the large estates be divided among the landless, and several former associates of Madero intrigued against the new President. Ambassador Wilson, who admired Diaz, was openly hostile to Madero. Our Congress, however, supported the revolutionary government and attempted to weaken its opponents by forbidding, on March 14, 1912, the shipment of arms to any nation in the western hemisphere which was in the throes of domestic violence. Knox threatened to have this embargo repealed unless Madero could give American lives and properties more effective protection. When Madero, in reply, reminded him of the Mexican citizens in Texas and California who had been lynched or beaten while the Americans responsible for these outrages had escaped unpunished, the Secretary ignored him.

American troops, considerably reinforced, were stationed along the border, but Taft firmly resisted the attempts of the jingoists, especially the Hearst press and the representatives of American oil interests in Mexico, to precipitate war. The most tragic blow to Taft's Mexican policy was struck by Ambassador Henry Wilson, who apparently encouraged, even if he did not actually connive with, Madero's former adherent, General Victoriano Huerta, to seize the power and overthrow Madero. When Madero was assassinated, apparently at Huerta's instigation, Wilson denied the latter's responsibility and urged prompt recognition of the Huerta government. But Knox joined with the American press in holding Huerta guilty and instructed the Ambassador to avoid any action that would imply our formal recognition of the Huerta regime. At this stage of the crisis the new Democratic administration in the United States took office.

DEFEAT OF CANADIAN RECIPROCITY

Although Canadian-American relations brought some minor triumphs to Taft, particularly in the international agreement of 1911 calling for the preservation of seals in the North Pacific and the final settlement of the Newfoundland fisheries dispute, the major issue—Canadian reciprocity—brought a stunning defeat. As an economic liberal and internationalist, Taft believed with McKinley in reciprocity because it would compel the wholesale reduction of world tariffs through negotiation. Here was an opportunity to offset the general dissatisfaction with the Payne-Aldrich tariff and the high cost of living. Although many earlier attempts at reciprocity with Canada had failed because of private interests, at least one—the Elgin-Marcy Treaty of 1854—had operated to Canada's benefit until its abrogation twelve years later by the United States. Canadian Liberals under Prime Minister Sir Wilfrid Laurier and low-tariff Democrats in the United States joined with administration Republicans in supporting a new reciprocity agreement.

The President's plan, embodied in a bill submitted in 1911, called for concurrent legislation in both countries which would admit without duty a long list of agricultural products, farm machinery, meats, automobiles, and certain other items. A favorable American press was assured by the free entry of Canadian paper and wood pulp to the United States, and Congress was favorably inclined toward the bill. Canadian nationalists, however, encouraged by the British press, looked upon reciprocity as a prelude to annexation and therefore fought the agreement. These fears rose to a high point when Champ Clark, the Democratic leader, told the House on February 11, 1911, that he desired passage of the bill because he hoped to see the day "when the American flag will float on every square foot of the British North American possessions clear to the North Pole." In addition to the nationalist sentiment in Canada against reciprocity, numerous economic interests there strongly opposed it. Some of these companies, artificially created by tariff favors, were threatened with extinction. The Canadian transcontinental railroads, which had been heavily subsidized by the government to link the Far West and the East, seemed to be endangered by the competitive north-south movement of traffic. Prime Minister Laurier dissolved parliament and appealed to the country on the reciprocity issue; in spite of a gallant fight, he was defeated in the ensuing elections. Thus Taft suffered another, and undeserved, defeat to his foreign policy.

THE TAFT ARBITRATION PROPOSALS

Like Root, Taft believed firmly in the power of judicial processes to bring about international peace. During 1911, Secretary of State Knox drew up arbitration treaties with Great Britain and France which in scope went far beyond any of the treaties formulated by Root. Instead of excluding as usual those questions affecting "national honor" or "vital interests," Taft held that all "justiciable" disputes should be submitted to arbitration. Here again, despite the President's vigorous defense of his position, the Senate refused to yield any of the prerogatives which enabled it to share in the direction of our foreign policy. Led by the nationalist Henry Cabot Lodge, the Senate amended the treaties so drastically by exempting practically every important question from arbitration that Taft refused to accept his mutilated handiwork.

Despite the varied character of the McKinley, Roosevelt, and Taft administrations, it is clear that the period from 1900 to 1913 saw a steady transition of American diplomacy from the traditional hemisphere defense policies to a broader "preventive" policy which involved the State Department in repeated intervention in the Caribbean and meant the formulation of an active policy with respect to Japan and China. Although commerce and industry exercised increasing influence on diplomacy, they were not the mainspring of our major policies. The open-door policy, for example, was adopted not because of the immediate pressure of big business but because of our belief in the huge potentialities of the Chinese market for future generations. Even dollar diplomacy in Latin America, so profitable to American investors and industrialists, was devised primarily to preserve the new strategic defense policy in the Panama Canal area by establishing an economic stake.

Roosevelt's conduct in the acquisition of the Canal Zone and Taft's hasty intervention in Cuba were undoubtedly serious blunders imperialistically, but they were a departure from the usual circumspect means used in creating formidable defenses for 100,000,000 people in a world which was coming to rely increasingly on war as an instrument of national policy. Nevertheless, the very exigencies of defense and the rising nationalist spirit after 1898 led us to make certain experiments in imperialism which permitted critics to point out obvious parallels in the expansionist adventures of Russia, Great Britain, Japan, Germany, and Italy. To a later generation it seems clear that some Americans of that period, like William Randolph Hearst, thought in imperialist terms but that they never dominated our foreign policy. Even Roosevelt, the theatrical apostle of nationalism, usually bowed to the moderate views of the internationally-minded Elihu Root and of the other experts among the State Department officials. In the end, the Progressive movement—with certain exceptions—was suspicious of an aggressive foreign policy which might be inspired by big business, and thus held aspiring imperialists in check.

The Progressive Revolt: Political Phase

THE TEMPER OF PROGRESSIVISM

"Roosevelt was the Bull Moose movement," asserted Elihu Root to Philip C. Jessup, revealing an exaggerated estimate typical of those who came under the spell of the former President's vigorous personality. Actually this American movement of social protest was only one phase of a pragmatic process that was then affecting most of western civilization. In England, the New Liberalism led by David Lloyd George was fighting to overthrow Tory landlordism which was monopolizing the best lands of an increasingly congested country. In an effort to shatter the complacent *laissez-faire* spirit of Victorian England, labor unions in 1906 founded the militant Labor party, which included many Socialists. Simultaneously with the United States, Great Britain embarked on a pioneer program of welfare legislation that provided compensation laws for injured workmen and assistance to children through such means as factory laws, scientific procedures in juvenile courts, educational aid, and wholesome recreational facilities. England, however, surpassed the American effort by establishing old-age pensions, sickness insurance, unemployment compensation, and model housing.

Just as the leading issue in the election of 1912 in the United States was direct popular control of government, so the parliamentary elections in Great Britain in 1910 marked a sensational struggle to overthrow the power of entrenched minority interests in the House of Lords in an effort to achieve a more democratic constitution. Even a casual glance at prewar Germany, France, and Italy reveals similar popular movements imbued with the ideal of social democracy expressed in the Progressive or Bull Moose platform.

Strikingly enough, the intellectual mentor of Lloyd George was a New York reformer of the same name, Henry George, whose *Progress and Poverty* (1879) deeply influenced the British statesman as it did many American Progressives. Henry George, observing the fast-disappearing public domain and the speculators' increasing tendency toward land monopoly, concluded that as the population increased, this monopoly would dominate society, sharpen class lines, and entail widespread misery. The single tax, his proposed solution, would practically eliminate all other forms of taxation in favor of a tax on land values exclusive of improvements. He contended that since all land values were enhanced by the growth of a community rather than by an individual's effort, the community was justified in confiscating this "unearned increment" through taxation. Innumerable Americans, like the millionaire traction owner Tom L. Johnson of Cleveland, who became a model mayor, dated their conversion to social democracy from their first reading of Henry George. As early as 1905, more than two million copies of *Progress and Poverty* had been printed and an estimated three million copies of George's other reformist books had been sold both here and abroad. Despite the scoffing of professional economists, his doctrines made steady advances especially among middle-class reformers.

A common trait of the various movements of social protest in the United States and western Europe was an increasing urban and agrarian distrust of capitalism's amazing growth and of the often ruthless methods of big business in achieving power. This found expression in various Socialist parties and factions, in anti-monopoly movements, municipal ownership of public utilities, and reform of electoral laws in the interest of curbing bigness. Sometimes, as in central and eastern Europe, this anti-capitalistic sentiment took the form of anti-Semitism when it created the myth of a Jewish financial hegemony. In the United States, agrarian reformers adopted Bryan's slogans of 1896 regarding the "international banker" and the supposedly sinister "money power." The world-wide depressions of the 1870's and 1890's imposed new forms of insecurity on the average man, and the recurrent financial and industrial scandals seemed to confirm his naïve impression that some personalized evil force was corrupting a world naturally prone to goodness. Congressional investigations of business, sometimes conducted by incompetent committees, led to sensational revelations which seemed to condemn the entire industrial order. The Roosevelt and Taft administrations sought to channelize this sentiment by effecting pioneer measures of government control over business, but this taste of popular influence and the failure of the trust-busting movement served only to increase the demand for more far-reaching reforms.

The breakdown of traditional ethical standards in business was hastened by the march of unrestrained individualism and the corroding influence of rapid urbanization. If success and wealth alone were the pragmatic test, the question of how to obtain them honorably was irrelevant. Many small businessmen emulated the ruthlessness of the Tobacco Trust and, failing to achieve success, denounced the corruptness of their more favored competitors. Although muckrakers assailed the low ethics of business and politics, Lincoln Steffens, the prince of them all, observed that the respectable leaders of the community actually preferred to have a boss in power, for this gave unique opportunities for self-enrichment through public contracts and utility franchises. Besides, they felt, reformers and the exposures they made hurt business. Too many reform mayors and governors had been voted out of office as soon as the original mood of popular indignation subsided. In some cities a single economic interest, such as the largest railroad or an important utility company, found it expedient to bribe the voters, directly or indirectly, in order to maintain its favored position against outside competition or prevent the passage of nuisance bills intended as political blackmail.

A decided handicap in the Progressive effort to introduce responsible government was the individualist tradition of the frontier, which opposed managerial experts in local government and confused voters by overburdening the ballot with scores of unnecessary elective offices. The same individualism led the middle-western and western states to solve corrupt politics by adopting the various pioneer devices of direct election, including direct primaries and the recall of public officials. With incredible faith in the average citizen's ability to decide extremely complex governmental problems, these two sections enthusiastically presented the electorate with new tasks. Among them were the initiative, which permitted voters to compel popular consideration of a measure by a certain percentage of them petitioning for a public vote to be held on it; the referendum, which allowed a specified percentage of the voters, acting by petition, to remove a bill from the legislative body and submit it to popular vote; and the recall, exercised similarly by petition, which permitted the electorate to vote on the dismissal of an elected official. This system of direct election, popularly known as the Oregon system, awakened premature hopes that the day of crooked elections was over.

EARLY PROGRESSIVISM

From the literature and politics of social protest during the late 1880's and 1890's came the germinal ideas of Progressivism. Edward Bellamy of Massachusetts revived the Utopian socialism of a half century before in his influential novel, *Looking Backward, 2000–1887* (1888), which painted an idealistic picture of an efficient state socialism that gave the individual considerable scope. Over a million copies were sold quickly—it was still in demand during the Bull Moose era—and scores of Bellamy clubs spread the "nationalist movement," as it was called, throughout the country. The nationalists were swallowed during the early nineties in the tidal wave of agrarian protest known as Populism, the inflationist and anti-monopoly platform of the People's party.

The falling farm prices, stationary debts, and high railroad and warehouse rates that followed the Civil War inspired widespread unrest that was manifested in such movements as the inflationist Greenback party of the 1870's and the Farmers' Alliances. Workingmen's anti-monopoly movements antedated the Civil War; their dissatisfaction was reflected in the program of the idealistic but inchoate Knights of Labor, which with the Farmers' Alliances formed the new People's or Populist party in 1891. Except for the emphasis on inflation, its platform in 1892 anticipated in large part the major demands made by the Roosevelt and Wilson Progressives. Although they called for the free and unlimited coinage of silver in an effort to raise farm prices and ease the debt burden, the Populists also agitated for a flexible currency that would be under government control; this issue was to be dealt with by Wilson in his Federal Reserve Act. They demanded a graduated income tax; public ownership and operation of railroads, telegraphs, and telephones; an eight-hour day for labor and the abolition of industrial spies like the Pinkertons; the direct election of Senators, a single term for the President, the initiative and referendum, and the Australian ballot; a subtreasury system that would permit generous federal loans to be extended on farm products in storage; the abolition of land monopolies; and a postal savings system. After polling over a million votes in the presidential election of 1892, the Populists decided four years later to join with the Democrats after the inflationist wing under Bryan and Altgeld had expelled the followers of the conservative Cleveland. Bryan remained faithful to the Populist heritage which later became the basis of Woodrow Wilson's New Freedom. The Republican Progressives under Robert La Follette and Roosevelt likewise emphasized federal responsibility for social welfare.

In 1881, Henry Demarest Lloyd, the financial editor of the Chicago *Tribune* assailed Rockefeller's Standard Oil Company in "The Story of a Great Monopoly," which aroused national attention when it appeared in the *Atlantic Monthly*. Lloyd's criticisms of monopoly and corruption were amplified in his challenging book, *Wealth Against Commonwealth* (1894), which became the literary prototype for Ida Tarbell's muckraking exposé of the following decade, *The History of the Standard Oil Company*. In other books and articles Lloyd sought to awaken the public conscience against mining and factory abuses, and he advocated compulsory arbitration of labor disputes after the New Zealand pattern. He worked with the leaders of Hull House and his friend Governor Altgeld in promoting social legislation in Illinois and the municipal ownership of Chicago's traction system, then dominated by Charles T. Yerkes. Disappointed at the failure of these reform measures, he joined the Socialist party in 1903, the year of his death.

Among the most influential of the reform governors who upheld early Progressivism was John Peter Altgeld of Illinois, a wealthy lawyer and real estate promoter—he lost this fortune while governor —whose administration (1893–1897) was devoted to pioneer labor legislation, anti-trust activity, civil service and tax reform, and the introduction of scientific procedures into penal institutions and mental hospitals. His battle against the traction and gas monopolies was largely responsible for his defeat as governor in 1896, but despite ill health and poverty he continued until his death in 1902 to demand municipal ownership as the solution to the corrupt alliance between politicians and utilities in Chicago. On the national scene, as noted elsewhere, he did much to promote the Populist-Democratic fusion of 1896 which liberalized his party. He denounced the conservative Cleveland wing for repealing the inflationary Sherman Silver Act of 1890 and claimed that the move had been instigated by creditor interests. During the Pullman strike of 1894, he strongly protested Cleveland's sending federal troops to Chicago before rioting actually broke out. Despite Altgeld's feud with the Chicago *Tribune,* which lampooned his motives, and his much-criticized pardon of the Haymarket "anarchists," his idealism crystallized into a vigorous Progressive tradition after his death.

MUCKRAKING AT ITS ZENITH

Lincoln Steffens, staff writer for *McClure's Magazine,* shocked thousands of readers during 1902–1903 by his revelations of civic corruption and initiated a vogue of exposé journalism which Roosevelt labeled "muckraking." *The Shame of the Cities* (1904) and *The Struggle for Self-Government* (1906) included certain of his McClure articles and won national attention. In refuting those who blamed civic corruption on illiterate immigrants, Steffens chose the predominantly native American city of "Philadelphia: Corrupt and Contented"—as he branded it—as the worst-governed municipality in the nation. The city's Republican machine, which was dominated by the state boss, Senator Matthew S. Quay, gave away city franchises with a facility comparable to that of New York's Tammany Hall.

Delighting in assailing popular idols, Steffens publicized the degradation of San Francisco, where the Schmitz administration, claiming to be a labor government because it was elected by trade-union votes, held sway. Actually, however, it was ruled by a boss, Abe Ruef, in the interest of large corporations, especially the railroads and some lesser political grafters. It was this demagogic ring that created international complications in 1906 by its order segregating the relatively few Japanese children in special schools. A small band of reformers led by Fremont Older, editor of the San Francisco *Bulletin,* revealed startling cases of bribery that involved the entire Board of

Supervisors, as the city's legislative council was known, and certain large utility companies in the state. As a result, Ruef and Schmitz were sent to jail. But they were soon freed by the higher courts, although Ruef was returned to prison after a bitter legal battle.

The reformers encountered the most stubborn resistance from various substantial citizens and were lampooned in Hearst's *Examiner*. When the belligerent prosecutor, Francis J. Heney, challenged an ex-convict who had been called for jury duty, he was so seriously wounded that he had to withdraw from the case. Another attorney, Hiram Johnson, continued the prosecution and on the whole was successful, although he failed to convict the bribe-givers. In 1910 Johnson was elected as reform governor of California with the slogan, "The Southern Pacific Railroad must be kicked out of state politics," and a few years later began his long career as United States Senator. The citizenry of San Francisco grew tired of the reformers and reinstated the old political machine.

Steffens observed that a similar series of prosecutions and confessions in St. Louis had uncovered an elaborate network of graft centering about Boss Edward R. Butler, who acted as intermediary between the city council and certain corrupt businessmen who wanted bargains in profitable franchises. The trail of corruption eventually led the tireless prosecutor, Joseph W. Folk, to the state legislature and to various powerful lobbyists working on behalf of utility companies, railroads, and schoolbook publishers. To Folk, this systematic bribery was a social revolution in the interests of plutocracy. Hampered in his reform efforts by the machine-controlled local courts, he turned to politics and became the outstanding reform governor in Missouri's history.

Among the most colorful opponents of civic corruption was Mayor Samuel M. Jones of Toledo, a wealthy oil owner and manufacturer of Welsh descent, whose idealism in managing his factory won him the title of "Golden Rule" Jones. A philosophic anarchist, Jones looked upon mankind as inherently good, attributing man's acquisitive and predatory characteristics to the evils inherent in our social structure. The newspapers were startled when he ordered the police to dispense with their nightsticks, and fears of Socialism were awakened by his advocacy of public ownership of local utilities. To the children of

Toledo he made public playgrounds and free kindergartens available; to labor he offered factory reforms and free recreational opportunities. Despite his repudiation by the Republican regulars, Jones remained in office as an independent until his death in 1904, when his former secretary, Brand Whitlock, became mayor. Whitlock, who had served his political apprenticeship in Illinois under Governor Altgeld, was a worthy successor of Jones. In his efforts to strengthen popular government he secured from the Ohio legislature a new charter for Toledo which contained provisions for the primary system and for the adoption of the initiative, referendum, and recall.

From 1901 to 1909 Cleveland had its own idealistic equivalent of both "Golden Rule" Jones and Brand Whitlock in Mayor Thomas L. Johnson, a wealthy steel manufacturer and street car magnate who had, confessedly, once bribed the city councilmen and other politicians to secure special concessions. Johnson, the son of a former Confederate officer, had risen from poverty during Reconstruction days and, aided by an inventive turn of mind, had learned early in life the possibilities of self-enrichment through monopolist methods. One day, on the chance recommendation of a train conductor, he purchased Henry George's *Social Problems* and was so impressed by the single-tax idea that he experienced an intellectual and moral conversion. Convinced that the monopoly of land and natural resources was unjustified, he sold his railway properties and in 1901 ran successfully as a reform candidate for mayor on a platform demanding municipal ownership of public utilities and a three-cent fare.

Aided by a remarkable personal following which included Newton D. Baker, later Wilson's Secretary of War, Edward W. Bemis the economist, and Dr. Frederick C. Howe, lifelong champion of reform, Johnson soon established a nation-wide reputation as an efficient executive and a dauntless fighter for the more abundant life. Among the benefits brought to Cleveland were a system of city planning, tax reforms, and reduced fares; extensive parks, playgrounds, and other recreational facilities; effective sanitation; and new, scientifically managed institutions for delinquents and the mentally handicapped. Under his administration Cleveland was in many respects the best-governed city in the nation. In 1909, however, the entrenched political and economic cliques defeated Johnson at the polls by a narrow margin, but the civic spirit he had invoked was revived two years later by the new mayor, Newton D. Baker.

"FIGHTING BOB" LA FOLLETTE

The man whose name was most intimately associated with the Progressive movement was Robert M. La Follette of Wisconsin, the dynamic spokesman of agrarian discontent and a bitter foe of corporate privilege. Although formally a Republican, he showed a heretical disposition to disregard party lines in favor of definite principles. As governor during 1900–1906 he challenged the political power of the railroads and utilities by creating forceful regulative commissions that had authority to determine rates on a basis of the valuation of physical assets. He was a pioneer in demanding a state income tax graduated on the principle of ability to pay; he secured passage of an inheritance tax, and he sought to eliminate industrial monopolies through legislative restraints. Workmen's compensation laws were passed and hours of work for women and children were shortened. State forest reserves were set aside for the people's benefit.

A strong believer in popular government, La Follette introduced a sweeping program of electoral reforms, including the direct primary and the initiative, referendum, and recall. He chose to enhance popular control by frequently submitting his policies to the voters. After his election to the United States Senate in 1906, he became the leader of the Republican insurgents and the prime spirit behind the National Progressive Republican League, founded in January, 1911. Theodore Roosevelt's stupendous personal following deprived him of the well-earned presidential nomination by the Progressive party in 1912. Thereafter, until his death in 1925, Senator La Follette remained the leader of the Progressive movement, especially in Wisconsin.

POLITICAL REFORM IN NEW YORK AND ILLINOIS

Few Progressives had any illusions about accomplishing lasting improvements in New York City politics, despite the salutary but extremely brief terms of reform mayors like Seth Low and William L. Strong. Roosevelt's term of office as police commissioner failed to change the "system," with its protected vice, its perennially fraudulent public contracts, and the unsavory political adventures of Tammany Hall.

New York State, however, enjoyed a short period of effective government under Governor Charles Evans Hughes, who defeated William Randolph Hearst in 1906 and was reelected for a second term. Hughes' victory at the polls was made possible by his energetic prosecution of three of the nation's leading insurance companies that were incorporated under New York State laws; gross bribery, irresponsible control, and inflated salaries, he revealed, were reflected in the correspondingly heavy premiums paid by the policyholders. As governor, Hughes sought far-reaching changes in the insurance laws that would remove the worst of the abuses he had uncovered. He set up a state commission to regulate public utility companies and tried to effect a change in the voting laws that would make elections more direct. The party regulars, including Roosevelt, were antagonized by Hughes' refusal to cooperate with them; other men resented his "goody-goody" legislation that prohibited race-track gambling which constituted a valuable source of revenue for politicians. "The fact is that Hughes is a thoroly unhealthy element in public life," wrote Roosevelt to a friend in 1908, "for just the same reason that the professional prohibitionist is an unhealthy element in public life."

Chicago and Illinois, like New York City and New York State, fluctuated between reform administrations and the old bipartisan machine. A reform "boss," George E. Cole (popularly called "Old King Cole"), who was backed by leading citizens, began a well-planned movement to clean up Chicago politics. His Municipal Voters' League, a pressure group, ultimately showed the progressive potentialities inherent in a non-partisan government. One of his successors, Walter L. Fisher, did much to elect honest aldermanic candidates. Fisher eventually succeeded Ballinger as Secretary of the Interior under Taft. But there were too few Coles and Fishers, and Chicago reverted to its routinized pattern of corruption.

"THE TREASON OF THE SENATE"

In 1911 the Chicago *Tribune* published sensational details regarding the wholesale bribery which attended the Illinois state legislature's election of William Lorimer to the United States Senate. As a member of the state legislature and a political boss, Lorimer had long been an opponent of reform. Before the Senate had time to exercise its privilege of passing on the qualifications of its new member, Theodore Roosevelt, the most active American ex-President in history, drew nation-wide attention to the case when, in a widely publicized letter to the Chicago Republicans who were sponsoring a dinner to be given in his honor, he stated that he would not attend if Senator-elect Lorimer were present. Accordingly Lorimer's invitation was withdrawn. Newspapers quickly played up the incident, and official Washington from President Taft on down was eventually involved in the controversy. Although the Senate Committee on Privileges and Elections, aware that the Illinois legislature was not unique in its method of electing Senators, attempted to validate Lorimer's title, the pressure of Taft and Root—the latter was then serving as Senator from New York—united enough regular Republicans to unseat the newcomer.

The Lorimer case gave final impetus to the growing movement for the direct election of Senators which had begun during the nineties. In a series of articles called "The Treason of the Senate," David Graham Phillips excoriated that body as a rich man's club that was representative only of corporate privilege. By 1912, when the Seventeenth Amendment was passed in both houses of Congress, Senators in twenty-nine states were being directly elected by the people rather than the state legislature. These states achieved this result by indirection; that is, they provided for the popular nomination of Senators, with the understanding that the legislature would automatically accept the nominees. New York's resolution of 1911 calling for congressional action on the prospective Seventeenth Amendment was offered by a rising young state senator, Franklin Delano Roosevelt. Although legalists like Root distrusted the increasing demand for constitutional reform on the ground that it constituted an expression of distrust in representative government, thirty-six states quickly endorsed the New York resolution and the amendment became law on May 31, 1913. Later critics lamented the fact that the new amendment seemed to produce mediocrities rather than senatorial giants like Webster, Clay, and Calhoun.

DIRECT DEMOCRACY

Popular impatience with the state legislatures, the lobbyists, and the boss-controlled party conventions hastened the adoption, in the West and Middle West, of the various devices for direct election, especially direct primaries and the initiative, referendum, and recall. South Dakota under Democratic and Populist leaders introduced the initiative and referendum in 1898, but Oregon's thoroughgoing espousal of these and other similar devices in 1902, under the leadership of William S. U'ren, furnished the model for the other states. U'ren, "the lawgiver, father of the initiative and referendum," was the leading crusader for the Oregon system. Born in Wisconsin, the son of a Welsh blacksmith, he knew poverty as a youth; like many other progressives, he had been started on his career of systematic political activity by Henry George's doctrines. During the nineties he introduced in Oregon the Australian, or secret, ballot and a voter's registration law, both aimed at fraudulent voting; in 1902 the Populists and independent voters under his leadership forced the adoption of the initiative and referendum; two years later a direct primary law was passed, followed closely by a corrupt practices act and the adoption of the recall. U'ren's reform lobby, like Chicago's Municipal Voters' League, demonstrated the effectiveness of a well-organized minority in reducing if not eliminating civic corruption.

The movement for direct primaries on a state-wide scale began in Wisconsin with the law of 1903 which enabled Governor La Follette to break the Republican machine's control of nominations in his state. This example proved so contagious that by 1915 at least two-thirds of the states had adopted direct primaries. La Follette also set the precedent in 1905 of allowing the voters at the primaries to instruct their party's delegates to the national convention regarding their choice for President. Although the preferential primary, as this system was called, was not mandatory as a rule, fifteen states had provided for it by 1912. This fact encouraged Roosevelt in believing that he might thus win over many of Taft's delegates in the Republican convention.

THE EXPERT IN GOVERNMENT

The Progressive movement, by its strong interest in novel electoral devices, undoubtedly contributed to the science of politics; conversely, the latter aided the attempt to replace the alleged efficiency of the boss system by administrative experts and simplified governmental machinery. In 1900 the National Municipal League campaigned for city home rule and government by experts; subsequently bureaus of municipal research were organized to provide a scientific basis for remedial legislation, and a host of courses in city administration were offered by various universities. An attempt to overcome public apathy and blind voting was made by the National Short Ballot Organization, founded in 1909. This group sought to reduce the long list of offices that usually appeared on a ballot to a few important policy-making positions and to make the elected officers responsible for the appointment of lesser officials. It was expected that eventually government would thus attain the centralized responsibility and simplicity requisite for intelligent voting at the polls. Woodrow Wilson, when president of the association, declared that the short ballot movement was the key to the entire problem of the "restoration of popular government."

An important step toward responsible leadership came with the commission system initiated in Galveston, Texas. In September, 1900, a gigantic tidal wave overwhelmed the Gulf city; one-sixth of the inhabitants were killed and considerable property was destroyed. Galveston's inefficient mayor and council system had shown little but an ability to accumulate huge annual deficits during normal times; in abnormal times such as followed the catastrophe, the Texas legislature had to intervene in order to save the city from bankruptcy. As an emergency measure the state replaced the mayor and councilmen with a combined executive and legislative board of five commissioners, one member of which acted as mayor-president. So well did this centralized board operate that the commission system, as it became known, was soon made permanent in an elective form. By 1912, two hundred municipalities had adopted the commission system with minor variations, and two years later it was in force in more than four hundred cities in the United States and Canada.

It became apparent, however, that the commission idea itself embodied certain of the cumbersome features of the old mayor and council system with its checks and balances and divided authority; for one thing, the five-headed executive too frequently lacked administrative unity. A wholesale reversion to the earlier form of government was partially checked by the rise of the council-manager plan, popularly known as the city-manager system, which Staunton, Virginia, adopted in 1908. This system supplemented the mayor and council system with an appointed professional manager who was held responsible for the administrative and business aspects of government; legislative action was left to the elected officials. The city-manager's powers were carefully defined in the city charter, which usually emphasized the nonpartisan and completely objective role that he was expected to fill. Dayton, Ohio, installed this system in 1914, and thereafter a host of other adoptions followed, beginning with the smaller cities. Political scientists praised the city-manager movement as a promising blend of government by the expert and the political will of the majority.

HOME RULE AND THE RECALL

Popular distrust of the state legislature often inspired the wholesale rewriting of constitutions during this period. Hence tinkering with the constitution became a favorite diversion of the Progressive mind. The home rule movement that sprang up among the cities expressed the desire of an increasingly urbanized people to legislate for themselves with a minimum of state and rural interference; consequently many cities won "charters," sometimes at the expense of the general welfare of the state as a whole. After 1903, when the Los Angeles city charter was amended to provide for the recall of undesirable political officials, other western cities fought for this device in their state legislatures, but after 1912 the recall declined in importance. The succeeding generation had less confidence than its parents in direct government and the frontier ideal of primitive democracy.

SOCIAL LEGISLATION

Aside from the controversial value of its political nostrums, the Progressive movement experimented with basic social reforms for the underprivileged. Somewhat belatedly, following the leadership of Germany and Great Britain, one state after another enacted effective workmen's compensation laws. It had long been apparent that damage suits brought by injured workmen were usually ineffectual, largely because of the numerous legal loopholes which barred compensation.

Legislators now insisted on automatic and adequate payment for injuries, regardless of cause or responsibility. Despite a false start resulting from judicial vetoes of the early state laws, persistent efforts brought victory. Nine states enacted compensation laws in 1911 alone, and most of the other states as well as the federal government itself had fallen in line by the time America entered the First World War. In other respects, however, the bold advances of northern Europe toward social security were far less successful here. Only Wisconsin adopted a system of sickness insurance, and no state went beyond creating public employment agencies in aiding its unemployed.

The social conscience of this generation was stirred by the plight of hundreds of thousands of children, some no more than seven or eight years old, who, unprotected by adequate legislation, worked long hours in field and factory. An important step forward in this sphere was taken in 1904 when the National Child Labor Committee was formed as an agency of public enlightenment. Aided by organized labor, the reformers secured the passage in most states of laws which prohibited child labor in industry, but this achievement was counteracted by the lack of enforcement. On another front President Roosevelt endorsed the movement to aid dependent children by removing such children from institutionalized orphanages and placing them in foster homes which would provide them with a normal environment. He called a White House Conference on the Care of Dependent Children in 1909 to draft the necessary program. Following this trend, President Taft in 1912 created the Children's Bureau, the first federal bureau concerned solely with child welfare. Julia Lathrop, whom he appointed as its head, thus became the first woman to head a government agency. Miss Lathrop, a former resident of Hull House, was well prepared for this work, for she had been appointed by Governor Altgeld to do similar work in Illinois.

The increased popular interest in child welfare was attested by the public playground movement which spread quickly from the East to other areas. Baden-Powell's Boy Scout movement was introduced to the United States in 1910 and followed two years later by the founding of the Camp Fire Girls. Youthful mortality declined with the scientific application of methods of child hygiene. A juvenile court system which would rehabilitate delinquent children attracted nation-wide attention when Judge Ben B. Lindsey of Denver secured in 1901 the passage of a law establishing special court procedures for minors in Colorado. Lindsey, an idealistic but unconventional magistrate, looked upon the delinquent child as the product of an unwholesome environment for whose existence society was responsible. His efforts along these lines led him to enter politics; his fight against child labor and civic corruption in every form finally antagonized politicians in both parties. Fortunately for Denver, Lindsey managed to retain his influence for several decades.

Women, too, benefited from the aroused social conscience. Florence Kelley of Hull House, whom Altgeld appointed the first chief factory inspector in Illinois, had succeeded in 1893 in securing a factory inspection act which restricted women's hours in industry to forty-eight per week. Although this law was less far-reaching than similar ones in Massachusetts and New York, and Inspector Kelley's first report revealed gross abuses of woman and child labor, the law was assailed by the Illinois Manufacturers Association, which tested its constitutionality in Ritchie *v.* Illinois (1895). The Illinois supreme court, at that time dominated by an ultra-conservative judiciary, decided that the act was an unconstitutional deprivation of the individual's freedom of contract guaranteed by the Fourteenth Amendment's "due process" clause. "What a mockery it is," commented the Chicago *Times-Herald*, "to read that the supreme court has demolished this humane, this civilizing law, on the plea that it robs the poor of their right to sell their labor as they will." Similar legislation in other states was jeopardized.

In 1903 Oregon enacted a ten-hour law for women in industry which was contested in the United States Supreme Court in Muller *v.* Oregon (1908) and aroused wide interest. Fortunately, Oregon's chief counsel was Louis Brandeis, whose sociological rather than legalist approach established the reasonableness of legislation that restricted hours of work for women. Although the Supreme Court had decided in Lochner *v.* New York (1905) that a state law which limited working hours in bakeries was unconstitutional because it violated the rights of property and freedom of contract guaranteed in the Fourteenth Amendment, it now followed Brandeis and held that women's maternal and familial functions brought laws calling for shorter hours legitimately within the police power of the state.

This decision opened the road to other industrial legislation for women. In 1913, nine states, nearly all of them west of the Mississippi, initiated minimum wage laws for women; this move received moral rather than economic justification, for it was hoped that higher wages would help to eliminate prostitution. Further legislative assistance came during 1908–1913, when twenty states established mothers' pensions in the case of destitute or disrupted families. As administered, however, the pension system resembled institutionalized charity to such an extent that many women refused to apply for aid. A far-sighted critic, Dr. Edward T. Devine, observed at the time that only compulsory social insurance, in which pension benefits automatically accrued to every contributor, would be satisfactory.

REDISTRIBUTING THE TAX BURDEN

Tax reform was another inevitable result of the democratic progressive spirit that seriously alarmed the propertied classes. Senator Elihu Root suspected that Progressivism actually meant the confiscation and redistribution of private wealth along Communist lines. Although the liberal press labeled Taft a reactionary because of his legalist outlook, in reality he was imbued with many progressive ideas. In 1909 he proposed and eventually carried through a 2 per cent excise tax on corporate incomes which brought publicity to the affairs of big business.

When Taft took office, at least thirty-six states had passed a graduated inheritance tax. The President favored a federal law to this effect, but the Senate rejected the proposal. The dispute over the income tax brought Taft considerable adverse criticism. This form of taxation, based on ability to pay, had been used during the Civil War, but President Cleveland's attempt to revive it in 1894 had been blocked by an adverse decision of the Supreme Court in Pollock *v.* Farmers' Loan and Trust Company. The majority opinion held that the income tax measure involved a direct tax and hence was unconstitutional since such taxes should be apportioned among the states in accordance with the Constitution. Backed by the liberal elements of both parties and confident that the high court would reverse its decision, Senator Joseph Bailey, a Democrat of Texas, attempted in 1909 to revive the movement for an income tax law. But President Taft, to whom the Supreme Court was sacred, was able to block Bailey by forcing standpat Republicans to accept his own proposal for a constitutional amendment that would permit Congress to enact an income tax law. This would at least delay action and enable him to avoid a contest with the Court. Thus, on February 25, 1913, after the requisite number of states had ratified it, the Sixteenth Amendment empowering Congress to impose income taxes without apportionment among the states became law.

SOCIALIST MOVEMENTS

Many moderates as well as extremists of the period before World War I were dissatisfied with piecemeal reform—the pragmatic method of Progressivism—and demanded that society be remolded along Socialist lines. The thriving European Socialist movement and the philosophical absolutes of Marxism made both native and foreign converts in most American industrial centers. Daniel De Leon, a former Columbia University lecturer whom Lenin praised later as "the greatest of modern socialists," joined the Socialist-Labor party in 1890, became its leader, and sought to wean the labor movement away from its philosophy of compromise as expressed in Gomper's "pure and simple" craft objectives of better wages, hours, and working conditions. Attacking the leaders of the American Federation of Labor as "labor fakers," he proposed the overthrow of capitalism in favor of a Socialist state in which trade-union syndicates would be the primary political and social units. With this purpose in mind, he aided the organization of the Industrial Workers of the World (I.W.W.), whose major goal was "one big union." Intellectually, however, he was too doctrinaire to be able to win any considerable following. In the presidential elections from 1900 to 1912 the Socialist-Labor party maintained a uniform average of little more than thirty thousand votes.

Far more effective in gathering protest votes than De Leon's followers was the Socialist party of America, organized by Eugene V. Debs of Indiana. Formerly secretary of the Brotherhood of Locomotive Firemen, a conservative craft union, Debs by the late nineties had become convinced that labor was facing a reactionary alliance between employers, politicians, and the press, and hence his philosophy became more militant. During the nation-wide Pullman strike of 1894 he headed the American Railway Union, a powerful industrial organization, but was sent to jail for ignoring Attorney General Olney's anti-strike injunction. His admiration for Altgeld, who protested publicly against federal intervention in the Pullman strike, led Debs to aid the Democrats in the critical election of 1896. This experience, which confirmed his belief that liberal reform was not enough, converted him to Socialism.

Even in his Socialism, however, Debs retained many of his reformist ideas. The Socialist party, which he founded in 1897 as the Social Democratic party, supported a Populist platform whose planks, it was said, were shamelessly stolen by Roosevelt and the Progressives. Perennial standard-bearer of his party, Debs polled 94,768 votes for President in 1900, and in each of the next two elections he received over 400,000. In the exciting election of 1912 he won 897,011 votes, despite the progressive appeal of both Roosevelt and Wilson. Debs helped De Leon in organizing the I.W.W., but his desire to achieve Socialism gradually through democratic processes soon estranged him from his fiery co-worker and the sabotage tactics employed by the I.W.W. According to his leftist critics, Debs had made Socialism respectable. Although the Socialists never won a single vote in the electoral college and left the rural South and the craft-conscious American Federation of Labor practically untouched, by 1912 there were Socialist office-holders in more than 300 urban communities.

PROGRESSIVISM IN THE SOUTH

In the states of the old Confederacy the Progressive movement, as Daniel M. Robison has suggested, displayed a curious blend of agrarian reform idealism after the Populist pattern, and a crude demagogic emphasis on white supremacy. The disfranchisement of the Negro, especially after 1890, tended to weaken the political power of the mercantile- and industrial-minded Bourbons. Not only did these post-bellum aristocrats maintain a paternalistic policy toward the Negroes which contrasted sharply with the competitive attitude of the poorer white classes, but they also found a valuable political instrument of control in the black vote. Senator Benjamin R. Tillman of South Carolina, who in the early nineties led the rural "masses against the classes" to dethrone the Charleston conservative leaders, proved to be a strong ally not only of Bryan and Altgeld but even—despite party differences—of the Republican trust buster, President Roosevelt. This revolt of small farmers resulted in Jeff Davis's election as governor of Arkansas. Davis, another advocate of white supremacy, prosecuted and legislated against the monopolies, restricted child labor, demanded pure food laws, and extended public education. Regardless of their Democratic affiliation, he and his followers ardently supported Roosevelt's attack on bigness. This group of "demagogues"—nearly all of them were college men—included Governor James K. Vardaman of Mississippi, who successfully fought against state corruption and corporate privilege on behalf of the poorer classes of whites.

This type of Progressivism lowered the status of the Negro. The "demagogues" in some states tried to limit education for Negroes on the basis of the actual taxes contributed by them and to make the informal practice of racial segregation mandatory by law. In 1915 the Supreme Court voided the notorious Grandfather Clause as constituting an attempt to disfranchise the Negro by reestablishing conditions that existed prior to the adoption of the Fifteenth Amendment, but the same end was accomplished by the white primaries that were soon thereafter instituted in the South. Reflecting more truly the liberal spirit of the time was Charles B. Aycock of North Carolina, who actually was elected governor at the opening of the century on a platform that demanded education for the Negro as well as the white; but he too wanted Negroes to be disfranchised.

As the colored folk moved into the cities and thus increased the threat of racial disturbances, southern legislatures turned belatedly to the national prohibition movement in an effort to remove alcohol as a potential cause of race riots. In 1907 Georgia, Alabama, and the new state of Oklahoma passed bone-dry constitutional amendments—mere temperance was not enough—a move which most of the South followed within a decade. In alliance with the rural dry sentiment throughout the country, southern Congressmen played a decisive role in the enactment of the Eighteenth Amendment, which became effective on January 17, 1920. The Anti-Saloon League, which led the Dry Crusade, had a powerful constituency in the South.

More enlightened southern liberals like Walter Hines Page of North Carolina, later Wilson's Ambassador to England, lashed out at the "professional Southerners" who made political capital of sectional prejudices. In his blunt address at Greensboro in 1897 on "The Forgotten Man" he demanded the elimination of mass illiteracy and rural poverty in the South. In the decade following Rockefeller's establishment of the General Education Board in 1903, Page directed its extensive work. In addition to its interest in the nation as a whole, the Board sought to raise the level of rural life and education in the South through scentific demonstrations to stimulate farm productivity, educational surveys of rural areas, contributions to medical schools, and endowment funds for white and Negro colleges; its aid to Negro education totaled almost $700,000 by 1914. North Carolina under Governor Aycock experienced a genuine educational renaissance which spread at a somewhat slower pace to the other southern states.

BACKGROUND OF THE PROGRESSIVE PARTY

On the national scene, a new political party was taking shape as a group of progressive-minded Republican Senators and Congressmen, under the leadership of Senator La Follette, fought to promote popular control of our economic and political life. More than any other issue, the Payne-Aldrich tariff of 1909 revealed the ideological cleavage between men like La Follette and Albert B. Cummins on the one hand and old-line leaders like Nelson W. Aldrich and Speaker Joseph Cannon on the other. The Insurgents, as the La Follette men were called, were determined to prevent excessive protection to favored interests. Senator Beveridge of Indiana, a moderate protectionist, grew increasingly impatient at the Old Guard's power to block vital social legislation. For example, Beveridge's defense of a child labor law was outflanked by the substitute proposal made by Lodge, the Senator from industrial Massachusetts, to outlaw child labor in the District of Columbia—where there were practically no factories!

A major Insurgent victory over the Old Guard came with the "Revolution of 1910" which deprived the Speaker of the House of his dictatorial powers. The Speaker's position had developed into one of centralized control, since he held the right to appoint the members of the all-powerful congressional committees. As Congress became more and more concerned with the technical problems inherent in the new spheres of federal activity, these committees became correspondingly important and the House itself was relegated to a minor role. The Speaker could control the order of business in the House because he was an ex-officio member of the vital Committee on Rules, whose members he appointed; moreover, he could almost arbitrarily deny any Congressman the floor. Such broad disciplinary powers brought him party leadership. In the hands of strong men like Thomas (Czar) Reed and Joseph Cannon, the Speakership meant power second only to that of the Presidency itself.

Profiting by the Democrats' congressional victories at the polls, the Insurgents in the House combined with them to overthrow "Uncle Joe" Cannon. A young Progressive, George W. Norris of Nebraska, opened the attack by proposing that the Speaker cease to sit on the Rules Committee; the debate that followed lasted three days. Seasoned politicians wept at the thought of Cannon divested of his committee powers and of his power to recognize members. When Cannon himself realized that he had lost, he offered a proposal to declare the Speaker's chair vacant. This proved too much for certain sentimental Congressmen and they insisted that he retain the Speakership. Actually the office retained many significant parliamentary controls, especially through its informal leadership of the party, but the days of unchecked Cannonism had ended.

ROOSEVELT AND THE PROGRESSIVE PARTY

Meanwhile Theodore Roosevelt had returned from his adventures in the African jungle, having been honored by ovations and by elaborate receptions tendered him by the rulers of the Old World. With unerring political instinct he saw the seriousness of the breach which the Taft administration had permitted to develop between itself and the rising Progressive forces. At first Roosevelt formally cooperated with his protégé, for in 1910 he professed to believe that Taft was well meaning but had "no instinct of leadership." Roosevelt had been deeply impressed with the reformist philosophy presented in Herbert Croly's *The Promise of American Life,* which was published at the end of 1909. Croly's belief in a national government that could rise above existing constitutional checks and achieve a more socially-minded leadership became Roosevelt's "New Nationalism."

While touring the West in behalf of Republican congressional candidates, Roosevelt chose to elaborate upon his Croly-inspired principles. On August 29, 1910, at Osawatomie, Kansas, where John Brown's attack on the proslavery men had once electrified the nation, Roosevelt spoke on the New Nationalism. "I stand for the square deal," he declared, going on to say that this meant more than fair play under the prevailing rules. "I stand for having those rules changed so as to work for a more substantial equality of opportunity and reward." The government must be freed from the "sinister influence" of special interests. In specific details his program did not differ essentially from the reforms advocated by Taft, but it was phrased in far more challenging language than the perplexed man in the White House customarily used.

"The New Nationalism," explained Roosevelt, "regards the executive power as the steward of the public welfare. It demands of the judiciary that it shall be interested primarily in human welfare rather than in property." He gave an ancient ethical ideal an alarming Socialistic ring when he said: "The man who wrongly holds that every human right is secondary to his profit must now give way to the advocate of human welfare, who rightly maintains that every man holds his property subject to the general right of the community to regulate its use to whatever degree the public welfare may require it." Thinking about this speech shortly afterward, Roosevelt feared he had expressed himself in too unqualified terms.

Such advanced sentiments should have made him a sponsor of the National Progressive Republican League which was organized by La Follette's followers on January 21, 1911. This organization advocated direct popular election of United States Senators, a system of direct primaries, the adoption of the initiative, referendum, and recall by all the states, and a "thoroughgoing corrupt practices act." Roosevelt, however, gave this program only qualified endorsement; privately he referred to certain League members who contemplated forming a third party as "ultra-extremists." Actually—perhaps unwittingly—he was undermining La Follette's leadership of the Progressive wing of the Republican party by his ambiguous position regarding the presidential nomination in 1912 and his persistent attempts to keep himself in the public eye.

During January, 1912, Roosevelt was active behind the scenes in crystallizing the growing sentiment that he make a pre-convention race for the Presidency as candidate of the progressive Republican forces. His friends agreed with him that his nomination should be urged in a petition signed by seven or eight governors. Roosevelt displayed such alacrity that his reply, in which he offered to accept the nomination if the citizens demanded it, was made public before the petition itself. This maneuver so distressed Taft that he lashed out three days later at the "political emotionalists or neurotics"—this obviously included Roosevelt—who had so far lost their sense of proportion as to want to make government depend on the "momentary passion of a people necessarily indifferently informed"; Taft here referred to the initiative, referendum, and recall. "My hat is in the ring" was Roosevelt's reply two days later in Cleveland.

The final break with his former friends, especially Root, Stimson, Taft, Lodge, and Knox, came with his speech, "A Charter of Democracy," before the Ohio Constitutional Convention at Columbus on February 21, 1912. Advising this body that it must create sufficient instruments of popular control to enable the people to enact all the social legislation necessary, Roosevelt went so far as to recommend the popular recall of judicial decisions as preferable to the popular recall of judges—although the latter was also desirable—since good judges sometimes made bad decisions. Taft and his circle were aghast at this assault on the judiciary. The Administration's position on the recall of judges and judicial decisions had been clarified as recently as 1911, when the Arizona constitution-makers had inserted such a provision into their organic law. Congress, at Taft's behest, compelled the state to strike out this article as a preliminary to admission to the Union. Arizona yielded and was admitted in February, 1912. (By November, it was to assert the privilege of a sovereign state to retain the offending clause.) "A popular government," Taft declared in his veto of the Arizona Enabling Act in 1911, "is not a government of a majority, by a majority, for a majority of the people. It is a government of the whole people under such rules and checks as will secure a wise, just, and beneficent government for all the people." An essential ingredient of such government, he felt, was "an independent and untrammeled judiciary."

The Republican convention which met at the Chicago Coliseum on June 18, 1912, was dominated by Taft's delegates despite popular preference for Roosevelt. Taking advantage of the presidential preferential primaries, Roosevelt swept every state but the two which La Follette received; of the total of 388 delegates on the primary ballots, Roosevelt won 281 to Taft's 71. Since the Republican rank and file obviously preferred Roosevelt to Taft, it was clear that the ex-President's nomination was prevented only by the Administration steam roller, in whose effective operation Roosevelt himself had played no small part in 1904 and 1908. Regular Republicans refused to alter the existing rules in favor of an anti-Administration man and adhered to the historic procedure used in convention nominations. Consequently, the all-powerful Republican National Committee, which Roosevelt had appointed in 1908, remained loyal to Taft as titular head of the party and adopted a routine procedure which unseated many of the Roosevelt delegates. It is doubtful whether the ex-President could have won the nomination even if he had retained all the contested seats. Taft's victory was a foregone conclusion in the first trial of voting strength, when Root, who was now supporting the President, was voted temporary chairman. Taft, nominated at his request by the urbane Warren G. Harding of Ohio, received 561 votes, while Roosevelt obtained 107 and La Follette 41. The protégé had defeated his patron.

"I'm feeling like a bull moose!" Roosevelt told an admiring crowd in Chicago during his struggle with Taft. From this picturesque phrase was derived the emblem of the newly formed Progressive party which met in convention at Orchestra Hall, Chicago, on August 5. The keynote address delivered by Albert J. Beveridge, chairman of the convention, before ten thousand enthusiastic listeners assailed the ineffectiveness of the existing parties and the domination of an "invisible government." The Progressive party, he asserted, represented a liberal movement "to make little business big, and all business honest, instead of striving to make Big Business little, and yet letting it remain dishonest." The next day Roosevelt himself addressed the convention, which seemed to be animated by the spirit of a religious revival. His speech, "A Confession of Faith," elaborated on the ideals of direct democracy held by the Progressive movement and attacked the major parties as "boss-ridden and privilege-controlled. Summarizing the record of his presidential war against monopoly, he called for the creation of a special administrative commission to enforce the Sherman Anti-Trust Act. In an emotional atmosphere of hymns and waving banners the Progressives nominated Roosevelt for President and Hiram Johnson of California as Vice-President.

The Progressive platform, like that of its Socialist rival, epitomized the prewar spirit of social revolt and in the most sweeping terms reaffirmed practically every reform in the field of labor, government, conservation, and currency which had absorbed the attention of that generation. Although George Perkins, one of the directors of the monopolist International Harvester Company and financial "angel" of the Progressives, managed to have the anti-trust plank withdrawn, enough remained of the party's objectives to offer such forward-looking proposals as a thoroughly modern system of social insurance, minimum wage standards for women, and the protection of labor against the injunction. "Unhampered by tradition," read the platform, "uncorrupted by power, undismayed by the magnitude of the task, the new party offers itself as the instrument of the people to sweep away old abuses, to build a new and nobler commonwealth." Nevertheless, the Progressive party's Republican origin revealed itself in the support given to the protective tariff.

THE NOMINATION OF WILSON

Hopelessly divided between Roosevelt and Taft, the Republican schism of 1912 insured the victory of the Democratic nominee. The beneficiary was the Democratic standard-bearer, Woodrow Wilson of New Jersey, marked by fate for the most crucial tasks in American history since the Civil War. An adherent of the liberal Jeffersonian school, Wilson was endowed with a seriousness of purpose and a moral fervor that suggested his Calvinist Presbyterianism and his Scotch-Irish ancestry. He was born in 1856 in Staunton, Virginia, the son of a scholarly minister. His early life was spent in Columbia, South Carolina, and in nearby Augusta, Georgia, communities which had ardently supported slavery and secession before the Civil War and fiercely resented the abuses of Reconstruction. Wilson graduated from Princeton University, then a Presbyterian citadel, in 1879, and took a degree in law at the University of Virginia Law School. Finding the law both unremunerative and distasteful, he enrolled for graduate work in political science at Johns Hopkins University. His political ideals during this period were crystallized in his doctoral dissertation, *Congressional Government* (1886), which revealed his admiration for Great Britain's parliamentary system, especially the political leadership by which cabinet government controlled the diverse impulses of the legislators. He condemned the system of divided responsibility inherent in the American theory of separation of powers and upheld the idea that the President, not a leaderless Congress, should formulate and guide legislation. As a state and national executive, Wilson later attempted to realize the major thesis of *Congressional Government.*

After an academic career of teaching, research, and the writing of books on American history, Wilson first attracted political attention in 1902 when he became president of Princeton University. His insistence on higher intellectual standards for the college and his demand that student life be democratized won favorable publicity outside the university, if not altogether within it. His vigorous personality attracted the attention of George Harvey, wealthy publisher of the conservative *Harper's Weekly,* who hoped that the moderate reform spirit of this college president might be an antidote to Bryan's radical leadership of the Democratic party. At the behest of Harvey and other powerful conservatives, the New Jersey machine secured Wilson's election to the governorship as a necessary political apprenticeship for the Presidency.

During the 1910 campaign in New Jersey it was clear that Wilson had moved intellectually to the left and that his hitherto critical attitude toward Bryanism and social reform was being replaced by a more sympathetic outlook. To the consternation of his backers, he showed such independence in his new zeal for effective reform that he quickly antagonized his former supporters, attracting instead the younger, more liberal members of his party. During his first year as governor he dethroned the state boss and proceeded to bring backward New Jersey abreast of the progressive states; this program, however, was blocked by a hostile Republican majority the following year. The Employers' Liability Act which was passed during his term of office strengthened the provision of compensation to injured workmen and their families by the state. The Corrupt Practices Act was designed to remove the worst electoral abuses, and the Direct Primaries Act brought New Jersey into the nation-wide movement for the popular control of nominations. A public utilities law providing for state regulation was also passed; its purpose was to weaken one of the most flagrant sources of political corruption in New Jersey. Wilson's insistence on maintaining leadership of the legislature as long as his party held control showed tangible results in spite of his brief term in office. By 1912 he had become a national figure. Socially-minded citizens were greatly pleased by his speeches, which exalted the role of the states as the "political laboratories of a free people"—the pragmatic ideal of Progressivism.

At the Democratic national convention which met on June 25 in Baltimore, Bryan fought to nominate a progressive candidate in spite of the upsurge of conservative sentiment which confidently expected victory in any event because of the Republican split. Speaker of the House Champ Clark of Missouri had apparently won Bryan's support, but this was withdrawn when it became known that the eastern conservatives who had backed Alton B. Parker in 1904 were sponsoring Clark; Bryan regarded this earlier contest as a war between the Bourbon-Tammany machine and the western liberal forces. Wilson was no "dark horse" candidate; on the contrary, he was supported with every expectation of success by such sophisticates as Roger Sullivan, the Democratic boss of Illinois, as well as by the idealists. When the nomination struggle narrowed down to Clark and Wilson, the Tammany delegation's switch from Harmon to Clark made Wilson's chance of success look black indeed. A stampede to Clark was prevented when "Alfalfa Bill" Murray, the colorful Oklahoma delegate who later became governor of the state, demanded rhetorically: "Is this convention going to surrender its leadership to the Tammany Tiger?"

By the next session the picture had changed. Bryan prepared a bombshell of his own in a resolution which declared the convention to be opposed to any candidate "under obligation to J. Pierpont Morgan, Thomas F. Ryan, August Belmont, or any other member of the privilege-hunting and favor-seeking class." Fearful of the effect of an adverse vote on public opinion, the delegates accepted the resolution 883 to 201 and thus by clear implication weakened the Clark forces. Sullivan's success in shifting the Illinois vote from Clark to Wilson insured victory for the governor of New Jersey. The Democratic party's requirement of a two-thirds majority for a presidential candidate was a major factor in defeating Clark's nomination. In the balloting for Vice-President, the convention chose Thomas R. Marshall, governor of Indiana.

The progressive wing's victory was reflected in the Bryanesque quality of the party's platform, which denounced various monopolist practices in business and finance and provided for the adoption of La Follette's plan of basing rate-fixing on the valuation of a railroad's physical assets. It condemned the use of the labor injunction and promised currency reform and federal assistance in extending farm credit. Most important from the Democratic point of view was the tariff plank, which called for low duties and assailed the high rates under the Payne-Aldrich Act. As far as foreign policy was concerned, the Democrats reechoed the anti-imperialist sentiment current in 1900 and pledged Philippine independence as soon as it was practicable.

THE BULL MOOSE CAMPAIGN

In the ensuing campaign, liberals were at a loss to distinguish between Roosevelt's "New Nationalism" and Wilson's "New Freedom"; both candidates advocated strengthening competitive capitalism by extensive federal regulation of business. Roosevelt's reformist ideas apparently partook of the paternalistic socialism of Bismarck, who made an enlightened system of social insurance serve the nationalist and militaristic ideals of the Prussian aristocracy. Wilson, reared in the tradition of international liberalism, had become converted to the "New Liberalism" of David Lloyd George; he recognized the social dangers implicit in the older *laissez-faire* philosophy. It was the context of their thinking rather than the specific remedies they proposed that differentiated Roosevelt and Wilson.

In view of his almost certain defeat, Taft was unwilling to make a strenuous fight and conceded the field to his opponents early in the campaign. Although he considered Wilson cold and dictatorial, even superficial, he preferred him to Roosevelt. The latter found his oratorical shafts blunted by the undeniable progressivism of the Democratic candidate. Wilson attacked Roosevelt as an extreme egoist whose actual accomplishments fell far short of the expected. "He promised too often the millennium," observed Wilson of Roosevelt.

Election day brought victory to Wilson, but as a minority President, for he won approximately 6,286,000 votes of the over fourteen million cast. Roosevelt's vote, 4,126,000, was a tribute to his personal popularity, for no professional party machine had aided his campaign. Taft trailed behind with 3,484,000 votes. Wilson, however, made a far better showing in electoral votes, for he had 435 against Roosevelt's 88 and Taft's forlorn 8, the latter representing only Vermont and Utah. Equally pleasing to the President-elect was the fact that his party won control of both houses of Congress, thus assuring him favorable legislative support.

The hungry Democrats, who so long had constituted the opposition —the party's last victory had occurred in 1892 with Cleveland's election—were now enjoying the fruits of power. But analysis of the election returns made the Republicans feel confident that the Wilson administration would be only a brief interim in the normally Republican control of the federal government. As far as the Progressive movement was concerned, the election of Wilson meant the perpetuation of the reform spirit rather than the beginning of an uncharted social revolution. The future hopes of the Progressive party itself were doomed when Roosevelt observed privately, "There is only one thing to do and that is to go back to the Republican party."

CHAPTER 6

Toward the New Freedom

THE WILSON-HOUSE REGIME

Admirers of the American educational system could take heart as Woodrow Wilson became President, for no man with better academic qualifications had ever attained this high office. Enjoying a national reputation in his own right as a creative historian and political scientist, Wilson had indeed forged the intellectual tools most serviceable to a President; but for a man who believed in ruling rather than in merely reigning, these gifts were none too much. His limited political experience compelled him to rely heavily on the advice of his shrewd private secretary, Joseph Tumulty, and even more on the extraordinary Colonel Edward M. House, a former banker and cotton planter of Texas, and long a staunch supporter of Bryan. Critics were wont to compare Wilson's Colonel House with Richelieu's unobtrusive Father Joseph who played so large a part behind the scenes in French statecraft. Even Roosevelt's dependence on Root offered only a faint parallel to the Wilson-House friendship. "Mr. House is my second personality," Wilson was reported to have said. "He is my independent self. His thoughts and mine are one."

Wilson's democratic ideals as president of Princeton and governor of New Jersey had attracted House's own idealistic nature and awakened his desire to attach himself to this rising star. In 1911 House wrote anonymously a political novel, *Philip Dru: Administrator,* which furnished a model of statesmanship for Wilson. Dru, a West Point graduate who was unable to enter active military service because of ill health, led to victory an armed revolt against entrenched privileged groups. As a beneficent dictator during the revolutionary transition period, he destroyed the "credit trust" by enacting a flexible currency law and curbed the trust movement by imposing a corporate income tax and abolishing the protective tariff. In language strangely anticipatory of Wilson's Clayton Act, Dru said, "Labor is no longer to be classed as an inert commodity to be bought and sold by the law of supply and demand." Hence labor was benefited by far-reaching social legislation. To crown these accomplishments, Dru founded a league of nations based primarily on Anglo-Saxon solidarity. As Wilson's Secretary of the Interior, Franklin K. Lane, later observed; "The President comes to 'Philip Dru' in the end."

House inevitably played a major role in selecting the new Cabinet members. Bryan was chosen as Secretary of State because of his party influence and his political services to Wilson in 1912, rather than because of his knowledge of diplomacy. William G. McAdoo of New York, a liberal financial leader who as an "original" Wilson man had helped to promote the President's victory, became Secretary of the Treasury. After an unsuccessful attempt to secure Louis D. Brandeis as Attorney General, the President and Colonel House turned to James C. McReynolds of Tennessee, at that time regarded as progressive because of his energetic prosecution of the tobacco and coal trusts. McReynolds' militant reformism evidently evaporated after 1914 when Wilson appointed him to the Supreme Court, for Brandeis, whom the President also elevated to the high court in 1916, frequently found himself in opposition to Justice McReynolds in defending ideals once championed by the New Freedom. Wilsonian disciples in 1933 regarded McReynolds as an ultra-conservative, the chief foe of the New Deal in the judiciary.

Josephus Daniels, a North Carolina editor and a staunch Bryanite, was made Secretary of the Navy. Although this appointment was said to involve payment of a political debt incurred when Wilson accepted his help before the convention, the wisdom of this choice was shown in his ability in connection with naval policies during World War I. Later, however, Daniels was overshadowed by the rise of Assistant Secretary of the Navy Franklin D. Roosevelt of New York. Equally fortunate was the selection of two of Colonel House's intimate friends, Albert S. Burleson and David F. Houston, both from Texas. Burleson seemed highly eligible for Postmaster General because of his long experience in Congress which would be of value in dispensing patronage, a task usually associated with this post. He proved an able and farsighted administrator. David F. Houston, chancellor of Washington

University in St. Louis, whom House regarded as an expert in agricultural economics, became Secretary of Agriculture.

The choice of Lindley M. Garrison as Secretary of War was casual in the extreme, for Tumulty, to whom Wilson had appealed for advice on this question, discovered Garrison's name in a law register and recalled that he was "a high type of equity judge." Both Garrison and the public were equally surprised by this unexpected honor. Franklin K. Lane, vigorous chairman of the Interstate Commerce Commission, became Secretary of the Interior. Since the formerly dual role of the Secretary of Commerce and Labor had been separated by Taft, the new President had two offices instead of one to fill. The Commerce post went to William C. Redfield, an experienced manufacturer, and the Labor appointment to William B. Wilson of Pennsylvania, a conservative union leader recommended by the American Federation of Labor. The Cabinet as a whole was moderately strong; an interesting addition was made in 1916 when the pacifist-minded Newton D. Baker became Secretary of War.

From the beginning Woodrow Wilson, following his cherished British parliamentary ideals, acted on the assumption that the election of 1912 was a popular mandate to promote social reform. With this solemn purpose in mind, he delivered an inspiring inaugural address, couched in the unusually felicitous language that distinguished his speeches and impressed many people with his Calvinist belief in a divine "calling" for a high task. "There can be no equality of opportunity, the first essential of justice in the body politic," he said, "if men and women and children be not shielded in their lives, their very vitality, from the consequences of great industrial and social processes which they cannot alter, control, or singly cope with." He asked for a reduced tariff to free the channels of world commerce, a stable banking system, protective labor laws, and an active conservation program. "This is not a day of triumph," he concluded, "it is a day of dedication. Here muster, not the forces of party, but the forces of humanity. . . ."

REVERSING THE PROTECTIONIST TREND

Anxious to fulfill his ambitious program, Wilson attempted to arouse public interest by personally addressing Congress, thus reviving a custom dormant since the Presidency of John Adams. He called for a special session to meet in April, 1913, and in a brief but eloquent message appealed for the abolition of a tariff structure that was based on pressure exerted by various private interests. Only with difficulty was he dissuaded from "purging" the obstructionist members of vital committees; nevertheless, administrative patronage, now dispensed by Colonel House and Postmaster General Burleson, was held as a threat against Democratic opponents of his legislative program. To forestall the influence of industrial lobbies on wavering Congressmen the President denounced such groups in a press release: "Washington has seldom seen so numerous, so industrious or so insidious a lobby." In decided contrast to Taft's inept conduct during the sessions of Congress that produced the futile Payne-Aldrich Tariff Act, there was no mistaking Wilson's determination to exert the full strength of his leadership at the outset.

Although Oscar Underwood of Alabama, chairman of the pivotal Ways and Means Committee that was entrusted with the House tariff bill, had been a presidential aspirant at the Baltimore convention, he cooperated warmly with Wilson in securing a genuine low-tariff law, for he had long supported downward tariff revision. Bryan's political experience also proved a distinct asset for the Administration. The resulting Underwood-Simmons Tariff Act of 1913 drastically reduced existing tariffs; if the World War had not intervened, this law might have become the keystone of a scientific tariff policy by reducing the pressure of private interests for protectionist favors. The average rates were reduced by a third, but many of the reductions applied to foodstuffs on which foreign competition was negligible. The free list now covered such important commodities as wool and sugar, besides various everyday necessities. Free trade with the Philippines was granted and the Cuban reciprocity agreement, so vital to that island—and profitable to American-owned business there—was renewed. Wilson also created a Tariff Commission in 1916 to undertake a fact-finding study of tariff problems.

To Cordell Hull, a young Democrat of Carthage, Tennessee, and a member of the Ways and Means Committee, was delegated the task of preparing an income tax clause for the Underwood Tariff Bill. The Sixteenth Amendment had become law shortly before Wilson's inauguration and the Democrats chose to offset the probable loss in revenue due to the lowered tariff by enacting an income tax measure. Hull insisted on the taxation ideal of the Progressive movement, namely, a tax based on ability to pay rather than on the older basis of special benefits derived. His graduated income tax called for a one per cent levy on incomes of $3000 or more in the case of single individuals, and $4000 and over for married men; incomes of $20,000 and over were subject to graduated surtaxes. Hull had worked out these provisions after studying European experience with income taxes; despite his critics' charges to the contrary, he maintained that he was interested in formulating a revenue measure, not a "share the wealth" program. Americans, he felt, could easily adjust themselves to these moderate taxes; furthermore, in the event of a national emergency the transition to the necessarily higher rates could be made more smoothly than would otherwise be the case. Thus he hoped to end the makeshift financial expedients that had been resorted to in times of national crisis.

BIRTH OF THE FEDERAL RESERVE SYSTEM

Scarcely had Congress passed the tariff measure before Wilson once more resorted to the audacious techniques of leadership he had used previously and began to urge the necessity for major banking reforms. Colonel House worked assiduously behind the scenes on the numerous details of the proposed banking legislation, collecting an enormous array of technical data, interviewing every important banker and academic economist he could find, and personally directing Wilson's fight for the sweeping reconstruction of the American financial system. Recognized by the initiate as the "guardian angel" of the Federal Reserve Act, House smoothed the way for the experts. At this time Wilson was not a little embarrassed at having in his Cabinet William J. Bryan, the ardent apostle of free silver, whose dreams of inflation had not been wholly dissipated by his successive defeats at the polls. Both Bryan and Robert L. Owen, Senate sponsor of the bill, were successful in overcoming the opposition of Wilson and the bankers to a proposal that the federal reserve notes become obligations of the United States, instead of the note-issuing power being left to private banks.

No Democrat could afford to overlook his party's traditional hostility to centralized banking, which had been firmly established by Jefferson and Jackson. The party's agrarian background involved an inveterate hatred, on the part of western and southern farmers of the debtor class, toward the eastern creditor groups and their alleged diabolic machinations. President Jackson, prodded into action by his political opponents, had found it simple in 1832 to launch a popular crusade against the "Monster," as he called the eastern-dominated United States Bank and its branches, and the fall of this centralized banking system meant a major Democratic victory. But subsequent expedients, from the Independent Treasury System to the National Banking Act of 1863, had likewise failed to solve the hard-pressed debtor's dilemma. The revivalist fervor which attended various inflationist panaceas from Greenbackism to "16 to 1" free silver merely sidetracked the more scientific proposals made by impartial experts.

Although many creditors found the post-Civil War rise in the value of the dollar far from intolerable, to farsighted businessmen at the turn of the century the absurd gyrations of an inelastic currency appeared an increasing handicap. Under the Banking Law of 1863 which was then in force, currency was issued by national banks in proportion to their purchase of government bonds at relatively high prices. So seriously did this system of note issue fail to keep pace with the needs of business that during the panics of 1893 and 1907 it was necessary for the bankers to obtain clearinghouse currency certificates to settle interbank accounts temporarily; actual cash was doled out only in accordance with stringent regulations. Monetary experts of the Wilsonian period believed that many bankruptcies might have been prevented in 1907 if it had been possible to convert acceptable but "frozen" commercial assets into currency at the critical time. Another perennial complaint of the debtor farming classes was the fact that credit sources seemed to dry up long before the Mississippi was reached, thus leaving needy agriculturalists without requisite funds. For this reason there was a strong demand for a decentralized banking system, particularly throughout the West.

Carter Glass of Virginia, chairman of the House Banking and Currency Committee, had begun working with the President-elect in 1912 on a federal reserve bill. While neither Glass nor Wilson was an expert in finance, both men fully realized the popular demands for revision; fortunately they had the exceptionally able assistance of Secretary McAdoo and of Professor H. Parker Willis, a national authority in this field. Furthermore, the Taft administration had left an extraordinary legacy of monetary studies in the work of the National Monetary Commission, headed by Senator Nelson W. Aldrich. This largely Republican group issued a comprehensive report in 1912, embodied in the Aldrich bill, which urged the establishment of a central bank with fifteen branches empowered to issue bank notes for member banks against rediscounted commercial paper. But the Democrats shelved the Aldrich bill before it even reached the committee stage and in its place eventually substituted the Glass-Owen bill. The latter created considerable opposition on the part of bankers. When Congress prepared to adjourn for the summer recess of 1913 without passing the bill, Wilson forced its immediate consideration by threatening to call a special session despite the oppressive heat of a Washington midsummer.

The new Federal Reserve Act, which became law on December 23, 1913, was Wilson's second major triumph in domestic affairs within a few months. In keeping with the Democratic tradition, this Act created a decentralized banking system which consisted of twelve regional banks administered by a Federal Reserve Board, whose members originally included the Secretary of the Treasury, the Comptroller of the Currency, and five members appointed by the President with senatorial confirmation. The capital of each of the twelve reserve banks was subscribed by the private banks that were members of the Federal Reserve System; administrative control rested in regional boards chosen for the most part by private bankers. Thus the latter retained considerable local autonomy while the federal government undertook to harmonize regional banking practices. One of the chief methods used to attain a flexible currency was to permit each member bank to present its eligible commercial paper to the reserve bank for rediscounting; the Federal Reserve currency notes issued to the member banks were partially secured by this commercial paper. Currency expansion was controlled primarily by the district reserve bank, which was authorized to adjust the rediscount rate and could thus accelerate or retard the issuance of Federal Reserve notes by making it profitable or unprofitable for member banks to rediscount their commercial paper.

On November 16, 1914, the "bankers' banks," as the reserve institutions were in fact, opened their doors for business. Even the staunch Republican newspaper, the New York *Tribune,* praised the new system when it said: "President Wilson has brought his party out of the wilderness of Bryanism." During the First World War the Federal Reserve System enhanced its prestige by successfully preventing the general suspension of payments characteristic of earlier crises and by effectively channelizing government efforts to finance the war. Serious defects in the banking legislation of 1913 had become apparent by the time Franklin D. Roosevelt became President, but amendment rather than repeal provided the remedy.

PENALIZING MONOPOLY

Shortly after the tariff and banking reforms had been consummated Wilson again came before Congress on January 20, 1914, to demand special anti-monopoly laws. Public opinion was prepared for sweeping changes in trust control, the need for which had been emphasized in the campaign of 1912. Sensational disclosures regarding the "money power" exercised by a few eastern bankers had been made by the Pujo Committee shortly before Wilson's inauguration. The keen cross-examination of this House committee's attorney, Samuel Untermeyer of New York, brought out startling inferences that suggested the concentration of an unprecedented degree of economic control in relatively few hands, especially in the case of industry, credit, and transportation.

Although the extremely sinister implications which this committee left in the public mind were far worse than the facts actually warranted, fair-minded critics felt that the future of democracy was imperiled by this trend toward centralized ownership and control of the nation's wealth. For example, the Pujo Committee showed that three New York financial institutions—Morgan and Company, the First National Bank, and the National City Bank—together held 341 directorships in 112 corporations of various types whose resources totaled $22,245,000,000. This financial pyramid had been made possible largely by interlocking directorates, especially in potentially competitive firms, and by outright consolidation of competitors. Thus Morgan directors sat on the boards of leading financial, industrial, and commercial companies and presumably shaped their policies—at least so the committee inferred—in the interests of the House of Morgan.

In a conciliatory gesture to industry Wilson declared, "The antagonism between business and Government is over." Both groups, he insisted, believed in the philosophy of competition. To safeguard this ideal he proposed to prohibit interlocking directorates among large corporations. Instead of dismembering bigness itself—which now appeared to be futile—he would outlaw certain well-defined monopolist practices "item by item." To help the businessman who was discouraged by the ambiguities in the Sherman Anti-Trust Act, he would clarify this legislation, and he would make the penalties imposed on the unscrupulous equally clear. In line with Brandeis' oft-repeated complaint, Wilson pointed out that the prevailing judicial practice prevented an injured firm from obtaining damages in an anti-trust suit because it was required to establish the facts anew despite the proofs already presented by the Attorney General. Moreover, the statute of limitations, which determined the time limit for prosecution, was frequently invoked after the government completed its litigation. Wilson asked for the elimination of all obstacles to recovery on the part of injured parties. Most important in the interest of effective anti-trust legislation, he believed, was the creation of a federal trade commission with powers analogous to those of the powerful Interstate Commerce Commission.

Brandeis' ideal of competition expressed in Wilson's program had already taken tangible form in the bills prepared by Senators La Follette and Newlands, among other progressive-minded legislators. Although Brandeis was unable to participate as actively in the committee hearings on the President's legislative proposals as he had planned, his numerous articles in *Harper's Weekly* had accurately forecast the essential features of the Clayton Anti-Trust Act and the Federal Trade Commission Act which resulted. In fact, in "The Solution of the Trust Problem," which appeared in this periodical on November 8, 1913, Brandeis anticipated practically every leading idea of the President's special message on monopolies. Little wonder, therefore, that Brandeis could publicly praise Wilson's program for regulating competition as inherently superior to the trust-busting ideas of Roosevelt and Taft.

Wilson's plan of assailing bigness by penalizing specific monopolist practices rather than dissolving huge enterprises was already widely supported. Many Supreme Court decisions had called attention to certain "unfair competitive methods" apart from actual monopoly. Brandeis had long maintained that natural economic forces favored an efficient moderate-sized business unit and that the abnormally swollen units characteristic of the period were made possible by artificial advantages that violated competitive ethics. If the government outlawed the unfair practices upon which monopoly rested, he believed that the inherent inefficiency of bigness would prove its undoing and there would be no need to resort to wholesale dissolutions. Small businessmen, especially middlemen, wanted a halt put to the tyrannical domination of certain manufacturers who were enabled by "tying clauses" to compel a retailer to accept an entire line of goods in order to purchase the particular item he ordered. Retail price-cutting aroused the ire of many manufacturers and some retailers, but opinion on this practice was sharply divided. Another interested group was the American Federation of Labor, which had assisted the Democrats in 1908 and 1912; it demanded the exclusion of labor and farmer organizations from the operation of the anti-trust laws.

Curiously enough, the monopoly-minded also expected to derive benefits from Wilson's program. Judge Gary of the United States Steel Corporation hoped that a federal trade commission would assist in stabilizing production and fixing prices. Well-established monopolies virtuously objected to cutthroat competition, and even prospective monopolists thought that such a commission would confer legal immunity in advance upon their projects. Business also objected to the uncertainties inherent in the Supreme Court's rule of reason which made the definition of "good" and "bad" trusts in specific cases wholly unpredictable.

Out of a welter of diverse and conflicting anti-trust bills emerged the Act creating the Federal Trade Commission in September, 1914, and its companion, the Clayton Anti-Trust Act, which became law in October of that year. Henry D. Clayton, chairman of the House Judiciary Committee, became the foremost Administration spokesman for this legislation, even declining a nomination to the Senate in deference to the President's desire that he remain in the House to lead the battle there. The new Federal Trade Commission, which absorbed Roosevelt's Bureau of Corporations, was empowered not only to investigate any business corporation engaged in interstate commerce, but also to take an active part in prosecuting those guilty of unfair methods of competition. This five-man administrative board was chosen by the President but remained independent of the ordinary Executive departments.

Wilson hoped that the growth of administrative precedent within the Federal Trade Commission would afford it sufficient flexibility, experience, and power to cope with whatever weaknesses the Clayton Act might reveal in the future, for this Act provided the Commission with its major tasks of enforcement. It forbade price discrimination among purchasers where the effect was to lessen competition; it outlawed "tying contracts"; and it forbade both intercorporate stock ownership if the result was lessened competition, and interlocking directorates among banks with more than a $5,000,000 capitalization and industrial corporations in the million-dollar class. Labor was given its "Magna Carta," as Samuel Gompers called it, in Section VI, which exempted trade unions and their members from prosecution as illegal combinations. In language suggestive of the famous papal encyclical *Rerum Novarum*, this clause proclaimed that "the labor of a human being is not a commodity or article of commerce."

The nationalizing influence of the First World War, with its huge enterprises and integrated economic life, was to weaken the competitive ideal of small business and destroy the effectiveness of antimonopolist legislation. Business-minded Presidents and conservative courts during the 1920's sabotaged the Clayton Act, and the altered membership of the Federal Trade Commission showed an increasing indifference to the purposes envisaged by Wilson. Not until another Democratic administration took office in 1933 was there a revival of the prewar belief in competition as the life of trade. By that time, the almost complete emasculation of the Clayton Act made necessary a fresh onslaught on the same monopolist evils that Wilson had fought in 1914.

RURAL CREDIT AND SCIENTIFIC FARMING

With the Democrats in the saddle and a Southerner as President, it was inevitable that the agrarian South would secure sweeping farm legislation. The Federal Reserve Act offered only a partial answer to the farmer's need for credit. Encouraged by the proponents of rural credit, Wilson urged repeatedly upon Congress, beginning in 1913, the establishment of a national system of farm loan banks which would provide long-term loans at moderate rates. A congressional commission, on the basis of its study of mortgage credit institutions in Europe, recommended non-profit land mortgage banks that would be owned and controlled by the borrowers. This idea was denounced as socialistic by private bankers.

The Federal Farm Loan Act of July 17, 1916, represented a compromise between these two positions. Although the federal loan banks were non-profit and coöperative in character, as "bankers' banks" they permitted private bankers to share in the benefits bestowed on cooperative farm associations; that is, they could borrow at moderate rates on land mortgages as security. Decentralization of credit, as in the Federal Reserve System, was provided by setting up twelve regional farm loan banks supervised by a Farm Loan Board. The capital came largely from the federal Treasury, although the framers of the Act contemplated ultimate ownership by national farm loan associations.

Scientific farming was spurred on not only by the excellent administration of Secretary of Agriculture David F. Houston but by the passage of the Smith-Lever Act in 1914, which provided for federal grants-in-aid to promote agricultural extension programs. As a result of this legislation, county agents bring directly to the farm community the most up-to-date scientific findings of agricultural colleges and of various local and national farm bureaus. This Act also fostered a greater cooperative spirit among the farmers, thus eliminating to a great extent the isolation characteristic of rural areas.

EXPERIMENTS IN PUBLIC OWNERSHIP

Wilson's Postmaster General, A. S. Burleson, aroused a widespread fear of Socialism because of his repeated attempts to extend government ownership into new fields. The parcel post system, established toward the end of Taft's administration, received Burleson's emphatic support, particularly the shipment of small packages at low cost by mail. The express companies bitterly assailed government competition and in 1914 one large concern, the United States Express Company, decided to cease operation. A few weeks later, with the blessing of the Wilson administration, the various companies were consolidated into the American Railway Express Company. In the communications field likewise, Burleson, influenced by the European example of government-owned systems which offered cheap and efficient service to the consumer, recommended a federal telegraph, telephone, and radio monopoly. But Congress, after prolonged debate, empowered the President to take over these systems only in case of war.

In the interests of competition—paradoxical as it seemed—Wilson instituted new government controls over economic life and made certain experiments in socializing business that his opponents considered were tinged with Marxist red. The World War demonstrated how far and how fast he was willing to go toward public ownership in order to preserve the New Freedom. Wilson cherished Jefferson's ideals of popular government but sought to realize them by an expansion of federal activity that would have made the Sage of Monticello gasp. Had Wilson completely brought about the New Freedom in foreign affairs, he would have implemented the freedom of small nations by an effective international super-government whose extensive powers would have been generously construed to enable it to cope with the enormous problems before it. Wilson was no passive liberal of the nineteenth century.

GOLDEN RULE DIPLOMACY: THE PANAMA TOLLS CONTROVERSY

Both the President and Bryan in 1913 appeared to be amateurs in the diplomatic field, eager to substitute the ethics of the Golden Rule for the historic policies and subtle methods of professional diplomacy. Both of them publicly repudiated Taft's dollar diplomacy as another phase of monopoly, this time on an international scale, although later events tended to shake this judgment. Wilson held the expert in diplomacy in high regard and wanted an end put to the spoils system as the basis of appointments to diplomatic posts. Bryan on the other hand represented the older Jacksonians who believed that public administration both at home and abroad was sufficiently simple so that "deserving Democrats" could easily satisfy requirements. Colonel House, more familiar with foreign affairs, sided with Wilson and became his alter ego in promoting our leadership of the movement for international peace. Later historians have tended to challenge the assertion that Wilson, Bryan, and House were hopelessly naïve in diplomacy, although admitting that the three displayed serious shortcomings in putting certain major policies into effect.

One of the earliest tests of Wilson's diplomacy in Congress occurred in 1914, when he tried to have repealed the clause in the Panama Canal Act of 1912 exempting American coast-wise vessels from paying tolls. According to the President, this clause violated the Hay-Pauncefote Treaty made in 1901 with Great Britain, which provided that the Canal should be open to ships of all nations on "terms of entire equality." Britain and the other nations regarded tolls exemption for American vessels as a flagrant violation of this treaty. Nationalist sentiment in the United States insisted that since the canal had been built and financed by this country, it should be operated primarily for our benefit. Republicans, Democrats, and Progressives—all except a few independents—were largely agreed on this point. Even Taft's legalist mind, after initially objecting to the exemption proposal, yielded to this sentiment. Senator Elihu Root, who had participated in the treaty negotiations in 1901, disagreed with Taft and gave his powerful support to the Wilsonians who sought repeal of the toll exemption clause.

Despite the warning of political experts that this issue would split the party, Wilson and House kept to their course, firmly convinced that the principle of the sanctity of treaties was at stake. Professor Charles Seymour, a careful student of this period, has stated that Wilson was eager to secure British assistance in ousting Huerta from Mexico. According to Seymour, the President may have believed that England was backing Huerta in the interests of Lord Cowdray's extensive oil holdings in Mexico; hence concession to Britain would mean success for us in our Mexican policy. Moreover, despite the outcries of such Anglophobes as the belligerent Hearst press, Wilson was always eager to cultivate England's friendship.

In a brief but urgent message concerning the repeal of the tolls clause which he delivered personally to Congress on March 5, 1914, the President stated that "we are too big, too powerful, too self-respecting a nation to interpret with a too strained or refined reading the words of our own promises just because we have power enough to give us leave to read them as we please." In spite of a mass desertion of the Democratic leaders, the clause was repealed in June, 1914, on the eve of a war in which Wilson found it necessary to urge the sanctity of treaties as the foundation of international order.

DISCOURAGING IMPERIALISM IN THE FAR EAST

Wilson's far-eastern policy struck the same note of idealism. In line with his public condemnation of dollar diplomacy, the President refused to support Taft's plan for American bankers to participate in a six-power loan of $125,000,000 to China. The terms of the loan, said Wilson, compromised the sovereignty of China and might necessitate American intervention abroad. The next day the various bankers, who from the beginning had been cool to Taft's project, withdrew from the proposed loan pool. Thereupon American diplomacy in China returned to the traditional non-interventionist policies. American loans and industrial assistance to China continued without the solicitation of the State Department, but our investments had to compete with European and Japanese enterprises which were strongly supported by their governments. Belatedly, Wilson came to appreciate Taft's dollar diplomacy as a potential check on Japan's relentless advance into China.

The Philippines had been promised their independence by the Democratic party, and Wilson and Bryan were therefore pledged to introduce immediate measures to this end. Under the Taft administration the number of American officials in the islands had remained stationary at 2600; but Wilson's new governor general, Francis B. Harrison of New York, in line with our new policy of "Filipinization," replaced 2000 of these officials by Filipinos. Naturally this move was bitterly criticized by the American colony. In 1913 the Filipinos were also given control of the Philippine Commission, which constituted the upper house of the legislature. A major step toward self-government was made possible by the Jones Law of 1916, which converted the appointive Commission into an elective senate and promised independence as soon as a stable government existed. Harrison upheld the Jones Law and used his discretionary powers with wise restraint. During these years important experiments in public ownership, such as the Manila Railroad and the Philippine National Bank, were successfully completed. But in 1920, when Wilson asked Congress for Philippine independence, claiming that the conditions imposed by the Jones Law had been satisfied, he could make no headway against a hostile legislature.

A TRUCE WITH JAPAN

Once more in 1913, as during the preceding administrations, the Japanese problem in California approached a crisis. Although the state had been dissuaded from enacting hostile legislation by compromises offered by McKinley, Roosevelt, and Taft, the Republican legislature in 1913 saw no reason for forbearance with a Democrat in the White House and hence proceeded to bar Japanese landownership in California. Japan protested in vain. Bryan intervened personally with Governor Hiram Johnson and the legislature, but this had little result except to indicate the federal government's sympathetic attitude toward the Japanese. A concession that "saved face" for Japan was finally obtained in a diplomatic phrase that forbade landownership by "persons ineligible to citizenship." When the Japanese ambassador inquired whether this decision was final, Bryan replied in his conciliatory manner, "There is nothing final between friends, Mr. Ambassador."

Within a few years, Japanese nationalists viewed American diplomacy in a darker perspective. Taking advantage of the preoccupation of the European powers with the war, Japan in 1915 presented the sweeping "Twenty-One Demands" upon China which would have reduced that country to complete economic and political vassalage. Thereupon Bryan intervened to assert the territorial integrity of China which had been formally guaranteed by Japan and other powers on repeated occasions; he warned that the United States "could not regard with indifference the assumption of political, military, or economic domination over China by a foreign power." Nevertheless, he left the door open for further negotiations by admitting that as far as certain portions of northeastern China were concerned, "territorial contiguity creates special relations between Japan and those districts." This nebulous concession encouraged the Japanese to demand our specific recognition of their "paramount interests" in China.

Confusion mounted with the Lansing-Ishii Agreement, signed on November 2, 1917, after America and Japan had become co-belligerents. Secretary of State Robert Lansing, Bryan's successor, broad-ened the latter's concession in regard to China when he stated in the agreement that "territorial propinquity creates special relations between countries," but he failed to specify what those relations might be. Evidently he had in mind the privileged position of the United States in the Caribbean. As usual, the Japanese promised to respect the open door and China's territorial integrity. When Viscount Ishii later chose to interpret the agreement as an outright admission of his country's "paramount interests" politically in China, Lansing denied that anything more was involved than certain economic interests arising from geographic propinquity. In concluding such an agreement, he apparently was motivated by the hope of preventing Japanese aggression in China while the western powers were at war.

STRATEGY AND RELUCTANT INTERVENTION IN THE CARIBBEAN

In October, 1913, Wilson symbolically united the waters of the Atlantic and the Pacific in the Panama Canal by pressing a button at the White House which set off a charge of dynamite that blasted away the final obstacles of soil and rock in the Canal. Shortly afterward, at Mobile, Alabama, he said that this was the beginning of a new day in hemisphere relations, that it marked the "spiritual union" of the United States with the Latin American nations. "We must show ourselves friends," he declared, "by comprehending their interest whether it squares with our own interest or not. It is a very perilous thing to determine the foreign policy of a nation in the terms of material interest." To promote the spread of constitutional liberty in the world, "human rights" must take precedence over material interests. "I want to take this occasion to say," he observed significantly, "that the United States will never again seek one additional foot of territory by conquest."

Latin American friendship was indeed close to Wilson's heart, but, tragically enough, his Administration surpassed all others in bloody interventions among the Caribbean nations. The countries of South America itself could be wooed in the gallant spirit of Elihu Root, but the problems raised by the Canal invoked a totally different attitude toward the nations along its route. Naval administrators and State Department officials felt justified in putting aside Wilson's policy of forbearance in the case of Santo Domingo, Haiti, and Cuba when the

United States was on the brink of entering the World War. Roosevelt and Taft had thought it necessary to intervene in the Caribbean in behalf of a prospective canal route; Wilson, with the Canal completed, still found intervention necessary in the face of unsettled world conditions. Even so, he had difficulty in convincing his critics that his motives were entirely free from the commercialism of dollar diplomacy.

When a revolution broke out in Santo Domingo in 1913, Bryan, for all his anti-imperialist beliefs, insisted on direct methods to restore order and prosperity to the republic. Even the customs receivership set up by the Roosevelt treaty of 1907 appeared inadequate to the Secretary of State, for he imposed new economic and political restraints in order to insure a fair election and prevent foreign intervention. When these failed, Marines were landed in the spring of 1915 to protect American and other foreign property, a step which aroused popular clamor at home. In November of the following year, Wilson authorized the complete military occupation of Santo Domingo. "It is with the deepest reluctance that I approve the course here proposed," he wrote to the State Department, "but I am convinced that it is the least of the evils in sight in this very perplexing situation." Although our occupation greatly promoted the material progress of the Dominican Republic, our entrance into the World War encouraged numerous abuses—even brutalities—against the natives on the part of Naval officials stationed there. Republicans were quick to capitalize on this during the campaign of 1920; nevertheless, American troops were not evacuated until 1924.

Wilson became even more inextricably involved in the Negro republic of Haiti, Santo Domingo's turbulent neighbor. The heritage of slavery under French rule and the destructive wars for independence had intensified gross illiteracy, extreme poverty, and chronic civil war. A small and well-educated governing class that relied on dictators supported by professional revolutionaries to maintain them in power exploited the Haitian masses and fought popular education. Border disputes with Santo Domingo, controversies with European powers over the destruction of foreign property by revolutionists, and the scandalous condition of the country's public finances marked Haiti as a likely place for European intervention. During the disorders of 1913–1914, American Marines, together with similar forces from England, France, and Germany, were sent to Haiti to protect foreign lives and property. Wilson and Bryan attempted to persuade the republic to accept American supervision of customs and internal finance in order to assure the payment of creditors. Germany on this occasion insisted on participating in any plan for customs control and therefore sent a landing party of well-armed marines to Haiti in July, 1914, but she recalled them after her declaration of war against Russia.

Another revolution which broke out in 1915 and attained new extremes of meaningless brutalities compelled Wilson to act vigorously. When the dominant faction led by General Guillaume Sam, president of Haiti, ordered the mass execution of 167 prisoners, the revolutionists retaliated by breaking into the French and Dominican legations where the government leaders had sought refuge, and dismembering the bodies of the President and his top-ranking general; later they paraded through the streets with these gruesome fragments. On July 28, 1915, an American warship carrying Marines arrived to impose a treaty which established a political and financial protectorate over Haiti. Assistant Secretary of the Navy Franklin D. Roosevelt drew up a constitution for the republic which became law despite the opposition of the local politicians, who objected to a clause intended to attract outside capital by permitting whites as well as Negroes to own land. Increasing friction between the Marines and the Haitians led to the outbreak of a formidable war in 1918; its leader, Charlemagne, was variously described as a patriot and a bandit chieftain, and his followers were inspired by the fear that the whites intended to revive slavery. The war was brought to an end with heavy loss of life, especially among the natives, and our intervention was severely criticized by Americans as well as Haitians. During the unwonted period of internal peace in the twenty years that our protectorate was in force, much was accomplished in modernizing Haiti and raising her standards of well-being.

Wilson's anxiety to insure supplies for the Allied armies led to armed intervention also in Cuba during a political revolt early in 1917. Marines patrolled the areas where important American enterprises were located. "As the Allied Powers and the United States must depend to a large extent upon the sugar production of Cuba," read Wilson's proclamation of May 15, 1917, "all disturbances which interfere with this production must be considered as hostile acts." Bound to the United States by geographic, economic, and political ties, Cuba entered the World War immediately after we did, but our troops were not withdrawn until 1922.

In Nicaragua, Wilson learned that Taft's dollar diplomacy harmonized too well with the need of defending the Canal to be lightly discarded. Because that country's San Juan River offered a route for a rival canal, he sought to embody Taft's policies in the Bryan-Chamorro Treaty of 1916, by which the United States paid Nicaragua $3,000,000 for an option in perpetuity to this route. The fact that the American bankers who were that nation's creditors would be the primary beneficiaries of this payment proved embarrassing to the President. However, he unobtrusively sent a financial adviser to Nicaragua and by 1918 the financial system had been stabilized.

Strategy dictated Wilson's purchase of the Danish West Indies (thereafter known as the Virgin Islands) in 1916 for $25,000,000, thus closing half a century of intermittent negotiations. Although it was realized that these tiny islands, predominantly Negro, would prove an economic liability because of their limited resources, the Navy Department, which exercised authority over them, justified the purchase as furnishing "the key to the defense of the Panama Canal." Feeling that the sum was not excessive for the purpose, Wilson therefore refused to haggle over "a question of money."

THE COLOMBIA "APOLOGY" ISSUE

Colombians anticipated that Wilson's accession to the Presidency meant complete financial and moral compensation for the injuries they had suffered as a result of the Panama revolution of 1903, whose success had been largely due to American aid. They were not disappointed. Wilson arranged the treaty of April 6, 1914, which expressed "sincere regret" for the interruption of Colombian-American friendship and offered Colombia $25,000,000 in gold, together with special privileges in using the Canal. Roosevelt, still active in spite of his nominal retirement, sounded the battle cry of his friends in the Senate when he said: "The payment can only be justified on the ground that this nation has played the part of a thief, or of a receiver of stolen goods." The World War temporarily suspended Senate action on the treaty.

When the treaty finally came before the Senate in 1919, the "apology clause" was withdrawn, but Roosevelt's friend Senator Lodge raised another obstacle when he pointed out that Colombia's new oil laws threatened to confiscate American property. Not until 1922, during the Harding administration, did the treaty pass the Senate; its ratification was apparently due in no small extent to the part played by the leading American oil interests who feared that Colombia's rich oil concessions might go to European competitors. What Wilson could not accomplish in the name of Pan-American friendship commercial groups succeeded in achieving through the naked appeal of self-interest.

WILSON RESCUES THE MADERO REVOLUTION

Nothing set off the idealism of Wilson and Bryan from the "realism" of professional diplomats so much as the new administration's Mexican policy. Critics who could understand intervention when life and property were scarcely endangered failed to comprehend Wilson's crusade in behalf of the Mexican revolution of 1910 which offered sweeping agrarian and labor reforms at the expense, in large part, of established American interests there. Nor did the Mexicans themselves, observing his intervention in Santo Domingo, Haiti, and Cuba, readily believe that the President was motivated solely by the desire to see their country freed from the economic and political domination of a selfish ruling class.

Henry Lane Wilson, our Ambassador to Mexico, had made the special privileges of American businessmen almost the sole basis of his diplomatic policy and had labored unconvincingly to establish the innocence of the new dictator, General Victoriano Huerta, in the murder of President Madero and Vice-President Suarez. Huerta seemed "safe" for foreign concessionaires, whereas Madero brought with him the menace of a national upheaval that would endanger the economic privileges accumulated during the regime of the complacent and generous dictator, Porfirio Diaz. Despite the countless precedents for automatically recognizing any revolutionary *de facto* government, President Wilson refused to recognize the bloody Huerta regime; to him it was the complete negation of any hope for the spiritual and social regeneration of Mexico. "The people of Mexico," he stated on one occasion, "are striving for the rights that are fundamental to life and happiness—fifteen million oppressed men, overburdened women, and pitiful children in virtual bondage in their own home of fertile lands and inexhaustible treasure!" Ambassador Wilson was recalled in the interests of Mexico.

While General Huerta was autocratically dissolving the Mexican Congress and arresting, and in some cases murdering, deputies who dared criticize him, Wilson steadily increased the pressure upon him. John Lind, former governor of Minnesota who during 1913 acted as the President's confidential agent in Mexico, urged Huerta to permit a fair election to be held in which he would not be a candidate, but this proposal was flatly rejected. Thereupon Wilson announced: "The present policy . . . is to isolate General Huerta entirely; to cut him off from foreign sympathy and aid and from domestic credit, whether moral or material, and to force him out. . . . If General Huerta does not retire by force of circumstances it will become the duty of the United States to use less peaceful means to put him out." Early in 1914 the President lifted an existing embargo on arms to Mexico in order to aid the rebel, Venustiano Carranza of the Constitutionalist party, in offering armed resistance to Huerta. Carranza was popularly identified with the democratic followers of the murdered President Madero.

An apparently trivial incident encouraged Wilson to strengthen his pressure. On April 9, 1914, several American sailors from the U.S.S. *Dolphin,* while loading supplies at Tampico, were arrested on the charge that they had entered a forbidden zone. Although they were released an hour and a half later with an apology from Huerta himself, Admiral Mayo demanded further redress and insisted on severe punishment for the Mexican officer responsible for the arrest, and a twenty-one-gun salute to our flag. The admiral conveyed this to Huerta in the emphatic form of a twenty-four-hour ultimatum. The dictator agreed to punish the officer but refused to humiliate himself by saluting the flag; however, he offered to arbitrate the dispute. Wilson not only supported Mayo but in a personal appeal to Congress requested permission to use arms in enforcing the admiral's demands. The affair, he declared, was no isolated instance of Huerta's hostility to the United States.

The night that the President appeared before Congress, news came that a German vessel was due at Vera Cruz with munitions for Huerta. Wilson, Bryan, and Secretary of the Navy Daniels quickly agreed that the vessel must not be permitted to land her cargo, and the President had Daniels order Mayo to take Vera Cruz at once. This order was fulfilled all too well, at a cost of nearly two hundred Mexicans—mostly young naval cadets—and twenty-one Americans. Every Mexican faction froze into common hostility in the face of this tragic invasion of their soil, however well intended; Mexican mobs stormed American buildings, and even Carranza, who benefited from this action, denounced the attack on Vera Cruz.

Wilson belatedly took the wise step of inviting Argentina, Brazil, and Chile to mediate regarding the relative claims of Huerta and Carranza; but, despite Wilson's efforts to make him Huerta's successor, Carranza refused to accept foreign mediation in a domestic matter. The Constitutionalist leader found it politically wise to characterize our intervention as "mistaken kindness"; furthermore, his army, strengthened by American supplies, was gradually driving Huerta from power. At the end of August, 1914, Carranza became President and his request that we end our military occupation of Vera Cruz was granted.

A quarrel between Carranza and his ambitious but irresponsible associate, General Francisco (Pancho) Villa, plunged Mexico into worse anarchy than ever. Wilson offered to recognize Carranza if he would confer with the opposing faction to achieve order, but the headstrong Mexican leader refused. Notwithstanding this refusal, the State Department on October 19, 1915, extended *de facto* recognition to Carranza. "We will aid and befriend Mexico," said the President in a message to Congress, "but we will not coerce her." During 1913–1915 at least 76 Americans were killed on Mexican soil, and in retaliation a similar or even larger number of Mexicans were murdered on American territory. Property losses increased, and the Hearst press, whose proprietor owned extensive mineral properties in Mexico, led the American interventionist sentiment for war. Once more Wilson invited the A.B.C. countries to mediate—this time Guatemala, Bolivia, and Uruguay were included—but again Carranza refused.

During 1915, armed bands of Mexicans, some of them Carranza's soldiers, crossed the Rio Grande on raiding expeditions. Native leaders whipped up Mexican nationalist feeling indiscriminately against "gringos" and political opponents. General Villa, embittered by Wilson's preference for Carranza, sought revenge by murderous attacks on Americans. On January 10, 1916, the Villistas halted a train near Santa Ysabel, Chihuahua, and removed seventeen American mining engineers whom Carranza had invited to Mexico. One of them escaped; the rest were shot down. Although Congress was now ready for military intervention, Wilson chose to rely on Carranza's promise to punish the Villistas; the promise was not fulfilled. On March 9, Villa himself led a raid on the small town of Columbus, New Mexico, killing sixteen Americans and burning considerable property.

"Get Villa alive or dead!" was the popular version of Wilson's emphatic order to General John J. Pershing on sending him at the head of a punitive expedition into Mexico. After expressing his regret at the Villa outrages in qualified terms, Carranza refused to cooperate with Pershing's efforts to capture the bandits and finally threatened outright opposition to the American advance. Despite clashes between our own and Carranza's troops, Wilson refused to yield to the mounting clamor at home, led by Theodore Roosevelt, for war with Mexico. The imminence of war with Germany ultimately led to the withdrawal of Pershing, although Villa was still at large. Thereafter Carranza showed more energy in dissolving the various bands of guerillas; as the World War progressed, his attitude toward the United States was so hostile that Germany was encouraged to believe him to be a potential ally.

Nevertheless, Wilson's role of knight-errant in upholding Madero's principles against the revival of Mexican "personalism" with its endless internal warfare was not without its results. Carranza's victory made possible the liberal Constitution of 1917, which furnished the younger disciples of Madero with a blueprint of basic reforms and heralded a new era for the exploited peon and laborer of Porfirio Diaz' day. American businessmen, it is true, mourned the economic advantages they had previously enjoyed, and Catholic churchmen protested the anticlerical spirit of the revolution. But Wilson's supporters saw with satisfaction the beginnings of democracy south of the border.

Carranza himself did not always remain faithful to the principles of the revolution. He was overthrown in the spring of 1920 by one of his generals, Alvaro Obregón, who denounced his former commander for playing on anti-American prejudice. The Obregón government succeeded in restoring order in time to forestall the efforts of Senator Albert B. Fall of New Mexico to precipitate a declaration of war on Mexico because of long-standing American property claims. Fall, who later was involved in the notorious Teapot Dome oil scandal, was the influential chairman of the Senate Foreign Relations Subcommittee on Mexican affairs; he also represented the Doheny oil interests. When the Harding administration took office, the United States still had not recognized the Obregón government because of President Wilson's insistence that a specific understanding on all of our claims was a necessary preliminary to normal diplomatic relations.

DREAM OF A PAN-AMERICAN LEAGUE

When the First World War broke out, Wilson and Colonel House were at work on an elaborate plan for a Pan-American league of nations which would be the nucleus of a future world organization for international peace. The mediation in Mexico attempted by the A.B.C. countries, abortive though it was, suggested a framework for systematic cooperation. Colonel House, who originally conceived the idea, wanted to transform the Monroe Doctrine from a one-nation guarantee of Latin American freedom from European intervention into a multilateral hemisphere agreement by which every nation in South America would guarantee the independence and territorial integrity of every other nation—a striking forerunner of Article X of the League of Nations Covenant. The manufacture and sale of munitions, always a source of disturbance, were to be controlled by each government, and diplomatic machinery was to be set up for the investigation and arbitration of certain classes of disputes. "This is a matter of such far-reaching consequence," wrote House to Wilson in December, 1914, "that I feel we should pay more attention to it just now than even the European affair, for the reason that, if brought to a successful conclusion, the one must have a decided influence upon the other."

Although Bryan showed little interest in the Pan-American pact idea, Wilson pressed it in Congress, particularly in the Senate Foreign Relations Committee. House approached the ambassadors of the A.B.C. nations and found both Argentina and Brazil receptive, but Chile, fearful of losing her long-standing boundary dispute with Peru, proved a stumbling block; furthermore, the increasing friction between the United States and Mexico created an unfavorable atmosphere for hemisphere unity. The idea received its *coup de grâce* when we entered the World War.

In the perspective possible to a later generation, it is clear that in both domestic and foreign policy the New Freedom represented the final flowering of the progressive spirit, the welfare state ideal that was awakened during the nineties by the Populists and the rebels in the two major parties. The World War and its aftermath terminated this era of social consciousness by introducing unbridled individualism. Not until the economic depression of the 1930's did the prewar search for social democracy revive. During that decade the intellectual affinity between the prewar progressives and many of those who supported the far-reaching social legislation of the New Deal became apparent.

CHAPTER 7

The Peace Crusade: World War Neutrality

PACIFISM ON THE EVE OF WAR

Never perhaps in all history did world peace sentiment attain loftier heights than during the period that preceded World War I. Although selfish nationalist rivalries laid the foundation of the holocaust, internationalists of every description vowed undying devotion to peace. Even though powerful groups of European Socialists—those in Germany and France, for example—had been denouncing war for almost half a century as a capitalistic and feudal adventure in imperialism, the Socialist comrades who had managed to achieve political power by 1914 patriotically voted war appropriations in the name of democracy. The Autocrat of All the Russias, Czar Nicholas II, had occupied the center of the world stage in 1899 and 1907 when he inaugurated the Hague Conference whose goal was ultimate disarmament and an international system of arbitration and conciliation; nevertheless, this same Czar, albeit with tears, signed the fateful mobilization order of July 31, 1914, which helped to set off the European powder keg. The benefits of war are illusory, cried the pacifists; its profits accrue solely to munitions profiteers. But the total number of conscientious objectors proved to be astonishingly small.

Peacemakers sought inspiration in widely diverse sources. William Jennings Bryan, who had long preached the ideals of the Prince of Peace before Chautauquas, prepared to practice them as Wilson's Secretary of State. Believers in the Enlightenment of the eighteenth century and the liberalism of the nineteenth rejected war as an irrational intrusion upon an otherwise orderly universe. American progressives, fresh from their combat with the money power and the great industrial conspiracies to stifle competition, regarded war as the handiwork of sinister plotters against the innocence of the masses. In the historic isolationist tradition of early America, as expressed in the writings of Washington and Jefferson, there persisted the assumption that war reflected Europe's decadence and loss of ideals. But this isolationist spirit did not deny, it actually encouraged, the belief in many quarters that America's ultimate mission was to propagate her youthful democratic ideals as leader of a world peace crusade. From John Quincy Adams' conception of the Monroe Doctrine through Wilson's Pan-American Pact to the League of Nations ran a stream of thought expressive of America's growing sense of being entrusted with a democratic mission to achieve universal peace.

Among the foremost apostles of peace in this country was the idealistic schoolbook publisher, Edward Ginn, who enlisted in the cause in 1901 at the age of sixty-three, after a successful business career marked by sympathetic labor relations. With continuing generosity he financed various educational societies and publications whose aim was to promote world peace; he climaxed this work in 1910 with the endowment of the World Peace Foundation for the diffusion of an informed peace sentiment. He was particularly interested in projects for disarmament, arbitration, and a league of nations that would have a permanent armed force. In 1910 also, another philanthropist, Andrew Carnegie, the steel magnate, established a similar propagandist and scientific organization, the Carnegie Endowment for International Peace; this represented a gift of $10,000,000 to the cause of peace. The same year he contributed most of the funds for the beautiful Pan-American Union building in Washington and three years later presented the peacemakers with an imposing headquarters, the Palace of Peace at The Hague. Although Carnegie's record on arbitration was poor where labor was concerned, he nevertheless aspired to promote diplomatic arbitration on a world scale in order to abolish war. From all these groups, together with numerous religious organizations, women's clubs, and experts on international law, flowed millions of pamphlets and books at various popular and scientific levels, all urging the construction of a harmonious world order.

Arbitration treaties in particular seemed to offer a royal road to peace, but nationalist suspicions in the Senate, as we have seen, blocked the submission of really vital questions to arbitration. Elihu Root, who in 1911 became a trustee of the Carnegie Endowment for International Peace, had been a pioneer in the movement for compulsory arbitration of international disputes; but his twenty-five pacts concluded in 1908–1909 while he was Secretary of State did not cover disputes that affected the "vital interests, the independence, or the honor, of the two contracting states." President Taft evoked sympathetic response from Britain as well as the United States in 1911, when he proposed that questions of national honor also be referred to arbitration, but again the Senate refused to accept the proposal.

With exaggerated trust in the efficacy of simple conciliation pacts, Secretary of State Bryan negotiated thirty of them during 1913–1914; both parties to a dispute were bound to submit it to an international commission but its decision was scarcely more than advisory in force. The commission's investigation usually involved considerable time, and since neither side could resort to war during this period it was hoped that the countries concerned would "cool off" in the meantime. Subsequent decades found the Bryan "cooling-off" pacts of questionable utility. Germany, evidently fearful of the advantage that the slow-moving but overwhelming Russian forces would gain from the period of investigation, frankly rejected this type of treaty. "Our strength," the Kaiser explained to Colonel House, "lies in being always prepared for war at a second's notice." To House, this remark was a confession of militaristic aims.

While Bryan pursued his scheme for peace independently, Colonel House, with Wilson's support, was busily engaged in constructing the society of nations described in *Philip Dru*. During the spring of 1914 he visited the capitals of western Europe in the interest of achieving a framework for diplomatic cooperation, including a system of international trustees for backward areas to replace the colonial regimes with their potentialities for war; this last anticipated the mandate system set up under the League of Nations. House was greatly disturbed by the tense diplomatic atmosphere, its tenseness accentuated by armament rivalries. "The situation is extraordinary," he wrote from Berlin on May 29, 1914. "It is militarism run stark mad." He shared the view, generally held by prewar American statesmen, that the Pan-German extremists led by Admiral von Tirpitz' big navy clique were courting a major war.

"IMPARTIAL" NEUTRAL THOUGHT

August, 1914, saw the unbelievable happen as a titanic war engulfed most of Europe. Nationalist anarchy had proved more decisive than cosmopolitan ties, even those welded by the international force of the modern scientific spirit. American peace advocates, particularly among the progressives, nevertheless accepted the challenge and worked for the resuscitation of their battered ideal. For them—Wilson belonged to this group—neutrality never meant simply isolation; it was a program that called for American leadership in mediating between warring nations and in establishing the foundation of a permanent peace. When official neutrality failed, the lovers of peace justified our entrance into the struggle with the phrase that has since fallen into derision, "a war to end war."

Much to the disappointment of House, Wilson in 1914 was too interested in completing his domestic program to take a vigorous stand on the war. Although the President privately condemned Germany for her responsibility, he refused to take any steps which might arouse a war spirit in this country. For this reason he opposed the preparedness program recommended by Colonel House; furthermore he believed that Germany, if victorious, would be too exhausted to attack the United States. Colonel House admitted that an Allied victory would mean Russia's domination on the Continent, but he tried to convince Wilson that a German victory constituted a far greater menace to the United States. "We will in that event have to abandon the path which you are blazing as a standard for future generations, with permanent peace as its goal and a new international ethical code as its guiding star, and build up a military machine of vast proportions."

Wilson agreed in January, 1915, to send House to Europe once more, this time to explore the possibilities of American mediation and to suggest the principles of a just and lasting peace that might possibly guarantee the territory of each belligerent and clear the way for disarmament. The conflicting war aims of both the Allies and the Central Powers, however, proved a stumbling block and the belligerents' expectations of victory prohibited any concessions that even suggested defeat. For reasons of self-interest England did not wish to see her trade with Germany destroyed by the latter's annihilation, whereas her allies, France and Russia, insisted on annexation of territory. Moreover, wrote House, Germany was unwilling to indemnify Belgium for the destruction caused by invasion. Popular distrust ended another of Colonel House's promising plans, this one to guarantee the freedom of the seas to enemy as well as neutral merchant vessels which carried non-contraband goods. Such a proposal implied the restriction of submarine attacks to actual vessels of war.

American public opinion, while firmly opposed to war, did not take Wilson too seriously when at the outbreak of hostilities he begged the people to remain "impartial in thought as well as in action." Even before the paid propagandists on both sides went to work, various factors which determined predominant Allied sentiment were active. Our Anglo-Saxon cultural heritage and our love for French liberal ideas created strong sympathy for Great Britain and France. On the other hand, considerable feeling for the Central Powers existed in this country among the eleven million people of central European parentage and the more than four million Irish-Americans, many of whom recalled Britain's oppression of Ireland all too well.

Although England's stern measures against the instigators of the Easter Rebellion of 1916 in Ireland awakened a storm of anti-British sentiment among the Irish, this was outweighed by the widespread hatred of Germany that followed the invasion and occupation of Belgium and the frequent sinkings of merchant vessels by German submarines. Even the British Admiralty's high-handed interference with the traditional rights of neutrals on the high seas could not of itself make American public opinion demand war against England. The average man saw clearly that at the worst Great Britain's illegal actions affected only property rights, whereas Germany's ruthless depredations involved the loss of human life.

For this reason organized propaganda, while impressive in extent, was not the determining factor in our entering the war. Pro-German sentiment was nourished by the hotbeds of propaganda in the embassies and consulates of the Central Powers, with their abnormally large staffs. Young George Sylvester Viereck, an amateur poet from Munich, edited the German-subsidized *The Fatherland,* a periodical which stressed the "hate England" theme as the most effective bond between

German-Americans and Irish-Americans. However, the German ambassador, Count von Bernstorff, complained bitterly that German propagandists failed to comprehend the American mind.

The British, who found the environment more congenial, employed such influential figures as Lord Northcliffe, the publisher, and two well-known novelists, H. G. Wells and Sir Gilbert Parker. The famous report on German atrocities signed by Viscount James Bryce, the noted scholar and observer of the American scene, carried more conviction than the complete facts warranted. By culling from the writings of the most ardent German foes of democracy, the Allies convinced many Americans that Germany had deliberately instigated the war in the interest of Prussian autocracy and was conducting it with calculated brutality. They cited Treitschke, the German professor of history, who glorified the militarist mission of Prussia, and Bernhardi, one of his followers, who preached a war conducted by frightfulness (*Schrecklichkeit*) in his *Germany in the Next War* (1911); from the Kaiser's own bombastic speeches came the justification for the term "Huns," the damning epithet applied to the Germans. The Allies made certain that Americans realized that Germany regarded treaties as mere "scraps of paper"—at least that was the conclusion to be drawn from Chancellor Bethmann-Hollweg's remark to the British Ambassador on England's declaration of war in 1914, when he is reported to have expressed surprise at England's willingness to go to war for a "scrap of paper" like Prussia's neutrality guarantee to Belgium in 1839.

THE FREEDOM OF THE SEAS

At the outset of the war, Wilson attempted to prevent any quarrel with England from arising over his efforts in behalf of the rights of neutrals on the seas. He invited her to sign the long-pending Declaration of London, formulated in 1909, which codified blockade and contraband rules and stipulated the procedure pertaining to other aspects of sea warfare. Great Britain, however, unwilling to yield her tactical advantages as the foremost sea power in the world, refused to accept the Declaration unless certain vitiating amendments were included. Contending that she was fighting for her life and that modern warfare had necessarily altered certain rules of international law, England began to "waive the rules," as the Germans put it. When submarines made impractical an effective blockade of German ports, the British nevertheless declared a blockade in defiance of accepted practice; neutral ships bound for Germany were intercepted on the ocean and shipments made by neighboring neutral nations which might indirectly reach the Central Powers were seized. To tighten the blockade, the British on November 3, 1914, declared the North Sea a military zone and began to mine it; this compelled neutral merchant vessels to stop for instructions as to safe channels, and incidentally for search.

Pointing out that new uses for commodities hitherto considered non-contraband had altered the exemption traditionally accorded these products, England gradually enlarged the list of goods liable to seizure as contraband. An additional reason for her arbitrary course was the sensational effectiveness of the German U-boats against enemy vessels in utter disregard of the safety of the passengers. To forestall being attacked while searching neutral ships at sea, British cruisers compelled neutral vessels to accept the expense and delay involved in being examined in an Allied port. There were other causes of irritation against Great Britain, as when American mails were opened by the British or imports of essential drugs from Germany were restricted or cargoes bound for "blacklisted" firms in neutral countries were seized. The revered doctrine that "free ships make free goods" seemed to have been discarded.

Encouraged by the success of her U-boats and alleging England's gross violations of international law as an excuse, Germany resorted to a new device when she declared a submarine blockade of the British Isles, to become effective on February 18, 1915. Since submarines were too fragile to be exposed to possible attack on the surface, the conventional rules of visit and search would be dispensed with and any enemy merchant ship would be sunk on sight. Neutrals were warned that the British misuse of neutral flags made the blockade zone perilous for non-belligerents.

The State Department protested these flagrant departures from international law on the part of both Britain and Germany in several sharp notes. On December 26, 1914, Wilson reviewed Great Britain's violations of international law and denounced her North Sea blockade as "ineffective, illegal, and indefensible." He concluded: "This task of championing the integrity of neutral rights which have received the sanction of the civilized world against the lawless conduct of belligerents . . . the United States unhesitatingly assumes, and to the accomplishment of that task it will devote its energies. . . ." Since the German blockade of the British Isles endangered American lives on enemy and even neutral merchant vessels, Wilson on February 10, 1915, sent Germany an even stronger note in which he warned that the United States would hold her "to a strict accountability" for the acts of her naval authorities.

Although the Germans appeared willing to modify their stand, the British, encouraged by Walter Hines Page, our Anglophile Ambassador, were not convinced that Wilson would resort to strong action; therefore the diplomatic discussions were extended. Page believed that the Allied cause was that of civilization itself, and he made every effort to soften the impact of Wilson's protests upon England. "It's no time," he complained to Colonel House, "to quarrel or to be bumptious about a cargo of oil or of copper, or to deal with these Governments as if things were normal." Furthermore, the fact that Great Britain gave financial compensation for much of the loss she caused prevented too great a general outcry. Nevertheless, Wilson's protests were made in all sincerity. On September 30, 1914, he commented to Colonel House on the coincidence that James Madison and himself had been the only Princeton men to become President and that both had faced a similar situation. "The circumstances of the War of 1812 and now run parallel," he observed grimly; "I sincerely hope they will not go further." House informed Sir Edward Grey, the British Foreign Secretary, of Wilson's remark.

THE FINANCIAL STAKE IN ALLIED VICTORY

While the diplomats were exchanging notes, an economic link with the Allies was being forged. American bankers like Morgan who had sentimental as well as financial ties with England and France wanted to make loans to these countries and asked the State Department what its attitude would be. Since both Bryan and Wilson opposed any transactions which might create a material interest in an Allied victory, the State Department announced on August 15, 1914, that loans to belligerent nations were "inconsistent with the true spirit of neutrality."

For the time being, this policy did not embarrass the Allies, for they could sell their large American holdings and realize funds from other sources as well.

Meanwhile the serious depression in the United States in 1914 had turned into prosperity as the Allies placed with us huge orders for munitions; the total actually exported by December, 1915, amounted to over $500,000,000. Germany, of course, was theoretically free to place similar orders but was restrained by the British blockade. Since this resulted in a virtual embargo on shipments to Germany, our new mushroom prosperity was precariously based on Allied ability to pay cash. Responding to the suggestions of bankers who desired to facilitate Allied purchases in the United States, Robert Lansing, then counselor to the State Department, convinced Wilson in October, 1914, that extending short-term credit to the Allies was not an unneutral act. This concession was followed in September, 1915, by approval of a long-term Anglo-French loan of $500,000,000 promoted by Morgan and Company. So high had the value of our exports risen by then that Wilson feared that Europe would be unable to make payment unless credit was extended to her, and a major depression would therefore develop. "The result," Lansing warned in urging the President to support a loan policy, "would be restriction of output, industrial depression, idle capital and idle labor, numerous failures, financial demoralization, and general unrest and suffering among the laboring classes." National interest, he reiterated, required a reversal of our former anti-credit policy.

Only irresponsible sensationalists could argue that the several hundred Americans who had financial stakes in the Anglo-French loan were deliberately bringing the United States into war. That retaliatory economic measures against British violations of neutral rights were not instituted was due to other factors, particularly the popular resentment aroused by German submarine depredations. Furthermore, the people themselves were benefiting from the only important source of foreign trade that remained after 1914 and hence were opposed to an embargo which would have brought on a major depression. Although Wilson believed that the cause of the war was commercial and industrial rivalry, he felt confident that under his leadership this country would never be brought into it because of economic factors.

THE *LUSITANIA* AWAKENS A WAR PARTY

The failure of American diplomacy in 1915 to compel either side to accept the traditional practices of international law in regard to blockade spelled tragedy. It was inevitable that a German submarine would attack a British merchantman carrying American passengers and precipitate a crisis that would imperil German-American relations. This occurred on March 28, 1915, when the British steamer *Falaba* was sunk in the Irish sea; one of the 104 people who went down with her was an American citizen. In an attempt to avoid a clash with Germany, Bryan told Wilson that Americans who chose to travel on the ships of belligerents should not expect protection from the government. The President, however, regarded the case as setting a dangerous precedent which would sanction illegal attacks on unarmed vessels at sea. On April 28, before any decision regarding our action had been made, an American steamer, the *Cushing,* was attacked by a German seaplane, and on May 1 an American tanker, the *Gulflight,* was torpedoed. Although there were no fatalities on the *Cushing,* two of the *Gulflight's* sailors were drowned and her captain died of heart failure the next day. Germany promptly disavowed these attacks as mistakes and offered "full recompense." Nevertheless, Lansing and House urged that a sharp note of protest implying a possible break in diplomatic relations be sent to Germany. German-paid notices warning Americans not to travel on British vessels in the war zone appeared in numerous American newspapers on May 1.

While Wilson was studying the various courses of action, the most sensational attack of all occurred. On the afternoon of May 7, a German submarine torpedoed and sank a huge Cunard liner, the *Lusitania,* just off the Irish coast; 1198 persons, including 270 women and 94 children, perished. Of these, 128 were Americans, some of them—like Charles Frohman, the theatrical producer, and Elbert Hubbard, the middlewestern poet—nationally prominent men. This attack threw a sinister light on the *Falaba, Cushing,* and *Gulflight* incidents. Newspapers poured out bitter denunciations of Germany; comparatively few, however, demanded an immediate declaration of war. The German contention that the *Lusitania* was carrying arms and possibly heavy explosives had little weight. Most opportunely, a few days after the sinking of the *Lusitania,* the British released the Bryce report on alleged

German atrocities in Belgium. This strengthened anti-German sentiment to such an extent that Colonel House predicted war within a month.

Newspapers, closely watching the President's public utterances for some indication as to the action he would take on the *Lusitania* affair, singled out a statement made on May 10 in a speech to several thousand newly naturalized citizens in Philadelphia: "There is such a thing as a nation being so right that it does not need to convince others by force that it is right." Although Wilson had expressed similar sentiments on several earlier occasions, the *Lusitania* crisis led to this statement being unfavorably interpreted as calling for peace at any price. The President, who had intended merely to emphasize America's general policy of peace, quickly disavowed the "too proud to fight" phrase he had used in this speech, but not before his critics had roundly denounced his pacifism and a new faction, ready to lead the nation in war against Germany, had come into being. Theodore Roosevelt, a convert to the new party, hurled his choice invectives against Wilson as he had once hurled them against the peace-minded McKinley; one of his epithets for Wilson was a "Byzantine logothete."

Colonel House, then in England as Wilson's confidential agent, sought to solve the *Lusitania* crisis by a compromise restricting submarine warfare. The Germans justified this form of war on the ground that Britain's food blockade was starving millions of German women and children and other noncombatants. Sir Edward Grey, the British Foreign Minister, declared that Great Britain was willing to let food shipments go through the blockade if German submarines ceased their attacks on merchant vessels. That Germany's claim of the inhumane food blockade justifying her unrestricted submarine warfare was largely propaganda was made clear when she demanded, in addition to the cessation of food restrictions, that raw materials as well be permitted to pass through. Germany, it was apparent, was facing a shortage of materials needed for warfare rather than an imminent food crisis. This put an end to House's attempts at mediation. for England naturally refused to give up the chief advantage still to be derived from the blockade.

Wilson was convinced that, Bryan's ideas to the contrary, any warning to Americans regarding travel on belligerent ships was unnecessary and even harmful because it would be understood as yielding on the issue of neutral rights. Americans could not be restrained from traveling on Allied vessels; moreover, no presidential proclamation to this effect could be any more effective than the tragic warning offered by the *Lusitania.* Consequently the note on the *Lusitania* crisis, handed to Germany on May 13, 1915, and signed by Bryan, reviewed the record of German violations of American rights and pointed out that since the nature of the submarine prevented it from offering merchantmen the customary measures of safety, it could not be used against merchant vessels "without an inevitable violation of many sacred principles of justice and humanity." The note insisted that American rights on the high seas could not be abolished by Germany's warning that our citizens travel at their own risk. After a tactful reference to the "high principles of equity" that heretofore had guided the German government, the note closed with a request that an official disavowal of the illegal attacks be made, that reparation be offered, and that similar incidents be effectively prevented.

Germany's reply on May 28, while conciliatory, was unsatisfactory to Wilson, for it gave a special explanation for each attack in which Americans were involved but did not disavow the *Lusitania* sinking or concede the rights of Americans on enemy merchantmen. The *Lusitania,* it said, was an armed auxiliary cruiser of the British Navy that was carrying munitions of war; her rapid sinking was due to an internal explosion after the torpedoing. Furthermore, the Germans insisted, British merchant vessels were instructed to ram submarines; this made it impossible for the latter to comply with the rules of international law and give warning in advance of an attack. Germany's reply seemed as offensive to the press as it did to the Administration.

While Wilson contemplated a second and more forceful note, Bryan signified his intention to resign. He was convinced that diplomatic pressure meant war; the German reply, he felt, offered sufficient basis for satisfactory negotations without recourse to an ultimatum. Since the President seemed to consider him only as a figurehead, Bryan would carry on his work for peace as a private citizen. His resignation was greeted with relief by the press, which had long questioned his qualifications as a diplomat. Actually, the second *Lusitania* note of June 9, 1915, signed by Bryan's successor Robert Lansing, whose sympathies were strongly pro-Ally, was far from an ultimatum. It maintained that "the sinking of passenger ships involves principles of humanity which throw into the background any special circumstances of detail. . . ." In firm but conciliatory language it signified our expectation that Germany would seek to safeguard American lives and American ships. Altogether, it impressed Americans as an anticlimax to a tense situation.

To mitigate the crisis, Germany ordered her submarine commanders to avoid torpedoing large passenger vessels but she still refused to disavow the *Lusitania* sinking. Such half-measures did not prevent the sinking on August 19 of the *Arabic*, a large British liner bound for New York; two American lives were lost. Colonel House and Secretary of State Lansing favored breaking relations with Germany immediately unless a complete disavowal was forthcoming. Fortunately, Ambassador von Bernstorff quickly intervened with a promise to secure a definite guarantee of American rights; he transmitted this assurance from Berlin on September 1: "Liners will not be sunk by our submarines without warning and without safety of the lives of noncombatants, provided that the liners do not try to escape or offer resistance." (The *Arabic*, according to the captain of the submarine, had attempted to ram his U-boat.) This statement was followed by official German offers of indemnity and by promises to avoid similar incidents in the future. This gratifying victory justified Wilson's faith in the peaceful processes of diplomacy.

SABOTAGE

During these months of repeated submarine incidents, American public opinion was shocked by newspaper revelations of German and Austrian sabotage in munitions and shipping centers in the United States. The swelling stream of American munitions destined for the Allies was imperiling the war efforts of the Central Powers and consequently was the chief concern of enemy agents. On Memorial Day, 1915, only a few weeks after the *Lusitania* went down, a barge loaded with munitions for the Russians at Vladivostok blew up at a dock in Seattle Harbor. This was one of a series of plots, some extending as far as India, which involved Franz Bopp, the German consul general of San Francisco, and scores of his associates, many of whom were even tually indicted by the federal authorities. Similar plots in the East were engineered by Captain Karl Boy-Ed, naval attaché at the German Embassy, and Captain Franz von Papen, the dapper military attaché who was involved in many Nazi intrigues a generation later. Our seizure of his papers revealed a huge spy ring that was engaged in the systematic sabotage of munitions factories, railroad bridges, and other points of military importance. On the basis of this damning evidence Lansing demanded the recall of both von Papen and Boy-Ed.

At this same time the State Department also requested the recall of the Austro-Hungarian Ambassador, Count Constantin Dumba, for participation in sabotage and strike activities on the part of Hungarian workers—charges which he freely admitted in later years. Particularly colorful were the newspaper accounts regarding Dr. Heinrich F. Albert, a spy for the German Embassy, whose brief case was picked up by an American Secret Service man on an elevated train in New York City while Dr. Albert was dozing in the next seat. Although the evidence was too incomplete for court action, the New York *World*, which had secured some of the documents from Secretary of the Treasury McAdoo, revealed that attempts had been made to purchase munitions factories to prevent them from producing for the Allies, and that negotiations had been begun to foment strikes among munitions workers and to buy the press for the dissemination of anti-British propaganda. The *World* asserted that Germany was sending about $2,000,000 each week to the United States to be used in such conspiracies. A year later, on the night of July 29, 1916, occurred the Black Tom explosion near Jersey City which caused a heavy loss of life and property and involved some $40,000,000 in damages; even the ponderous Statue of Liberty was shaken. Over twenty years of litigation before a Mixed Claims Commission were required to adjust the claims arising from this disastrous explosion.

THE PREPAREDNESS MOVEMENT AND PACIFISM

In a speech at Milwaukee on January 31, 1916, Wilson expressed his foreboding that the nation might be forced into the war in spite of every effort to remain at peace: "I know that you are depending upon me to keep this nation out of the war. So far I have done so and I will pledge you my word that, God helping me, I will—if it is possible.

But you have laid another duty upon me. You have bidden me to see to it that nothing stains or impairs the honor of the United States, and that is a matter not within my control; that depends upon what others do, not upon what the Government of the United States does. Therefore there may at any moment come a time when I cannot preserve both the honor and the peace of the United States. Do not exact of me an impossible and contradictory thing."

This speech, which was one of the earliest expressions of the President's conversion to preparedness, marked the keynote of his tour of the North and Middle West. At the time, war with Mexico seemed a greater possibility than involvement in the European war, but both had a part in convincing Wilson that an adequate nation-wide defense could not be achieved overnight. There was danger also from the political standpoint, for 1916 was an election year and this might mean that, because of the President's pacifist ideas, the leadership of the nation might pass to the war-minded Theodore Roosevelt and his followers who were now demanding the unprecedented peacetime introduction of compulsory military service.

Preparedness advocates—among them General Leonard Wood, Wilson's Chief of Staff, Secretary of War Garrison, and Admiral Peary—severely criticized the pacifist ideas held by Bryan, now a leader of the organized peace movement, and pointed out the extent to which pro-German agents had infiltrated the movement. Jane Addams and Carrie Chapman Catt, the feminist leader, conducted a vigorous campaign to keep the nation out of war and in January, 1915, organized the Women's Peace Party. With bewildering profusion there appeared the National Peace Council, the American Truth Society, the Friends of Peace, and many other anti-war organizations. So rapid was their growth that an Emergency Peace Federation was formed a month later to unite the various groups into a common front. Bryan, anxious to spread his gospel, unwittingly played into pro-German hands by lending his name and prestige to groups affiliated with German and Austrian activities in behalf of the Fatherland.

Among the chief advocates of pacifism was Senator La Follette, whose *La Follette's Magazine* assailed the war as a munition-maker's plot. "What do Morgan and Schwab care for world peace," he demanded, "when there are big profits in war?" Far more naïve was

Henry Ford, who felt certain that international finance had caused the war. Inspired by the counsels of Madame Rosika Schwimmer, the idealistic Hungarian suffragette leader, and Jane Addams, Ford urged Wilson to organize an international peace commission and chartered the steamer *Oscar II* of the Scandinavian-American line to carry a huge delegation of pacifists to Europe. According to the newspapers, Ford promised to "get the boys out of the trenches by Christmas"; but Colonel House, who heard him expound his views in December, 1915, found them "crude and unimportant."

Close to Wilson's heart were the advocates of plans for a lasting peace. Mayor Newton D. Baker of Cleveland, a progressive Democratic leader who later became Wilson's Secretary of War, and Bainbridge Colby, later his Secretary of State, were actively behind a plan for a world court. Particularly vigorous in the effort to promote a league of nations during 1915–1916 were ex-President William Howard Taft, who had become an ardent supporter of the League to Enforce Peace, and President Nicholas Murray Butler of Columbia and President A. Lawrence Lowell of Harvard, both of whom were sponsors of this organization. In a speech before the League on May 27, 1916, Wilson painted a glowing picture of a cooperative world system that would offer "self-determination"—and preserve the rights of small as well as large nations and of a "universal association of nations" that would maintain peace. He vigorously denounced isolationism in these words: "We are participants, whether we would or not, in the life of the world. The interests of all nations are our own also."

Convinced that large-scale defense measures were "absolutely imperative," Wilson declared in a speech at St. Louis that the United States Navy must be second to none. On his return to Washington he was drawn into the controversy between Congress and the Army as to methods of enlarging the armed forces. Congress, swayed by the democratic tradition of a volunteer citizens' army such as was represented in the state National Guards, opposed the professional Army men, whose spokesman was Secretary of War Garrison and who wanted an expanded regular army with centralized control. Anxious for immediate action, Wilson supported the Hay bill advocated by Congress and thereby lost his Secretary of War, who promptly resigned in protest. Newton D. Baker, who was generally regarded as a pacifist and a de-

1910 - 1920

President Woodrow Wilson. (The National Archives.)

Henry Ford, Thomas A. Edison, and Warren G. Harding. (Brown Brothers.)

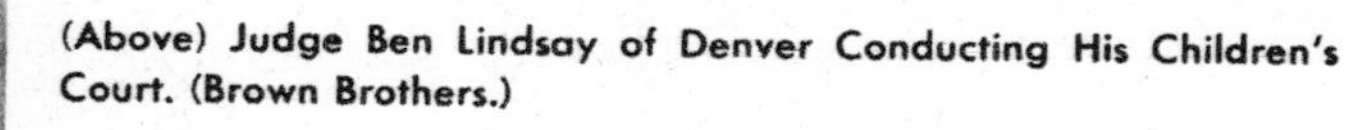

(Above) Judge Ben Lindsay of Denver Conducting His Children's Court. (Brown Brothers.)

(Left) Senator Robert M. (Fighting Bob) La Follette in Front of the Capitol, 1917. (The National Archives.)

(Right) Walter Wellman's Dirigible, *America*, in the First Attempt to Cross the Atlantic by Air in 1912. (Brown Brothers.)

Preparedness Parade Marching Along Fifth Avenue in New York City in 1916. (Brown Brothers.)

The 1915 Suffragette Parade in Washington, D. C. (Brown Brothers.)

General John J. (Black Jack) Pershing During the Mexican Border Campaign. (Brown Brothers.)

Henry Ford Aboard the Ford Peace Ship. (Brown Brothers.)

Sabotage in World War I—The Black Tom Explosion, New Jersey. (Brown Brothers.)

The Boston Police Strike in 1919. (Courtesy of the Boston *Globe*.)

Frank Lloyd Wright. (Hedrick-Blessing Studio.)

A Suburban Development Where Homes Stressed Standardized Comfort over Architectural Significance. (Brown Brothers.)

... Premier Orlando of Italy, Prime Minister Lloyd George of

votee of the New Freedom, was appointed head of the War Department.

The National Defense Act passed in June, 1916, represented a compromise. Generous provisions were made for the enlargement and training of National Guard units, and the Regular Army was increased from its existing strength of 106,000 men to 175,000; this insured a nucleus of trained men for the Army's rapid expansion in case of war. Federal funds were allocated for General Wood's training camps for civilians which had practically initiated the preparedness movement with the camp at Plattsburg, New York. Congress began a three-year naval expansion program in October, 1915, with an appropriation of half a billion dollars. By August, 1916, the Navy Department asked for another billion and a half. That same month the Council of National Defense was established for the purpose of coordinating all national resources for the common security; six Cabinet members served on it. In September, Congress created the United States Shipping Board to build and otherwise acquire the fleet of merchant vessels necessary to relieve the extraordinary shipping shortage caused by the war. Both Wilson and McAdoo had urged such a measure since 1914, but its passage had been blocked by a filibuster by Congressmen who regarded it as socialistic.

At the same time colleges increased their courses in military training. Propagandist agencies like the National Security League advocated compulsory military service, a proposal that won support particularly in Republican ranks. The League sponsored preparedness parades and created a formidable public sentiment which might have destroyed presidential leadership. But Wilson's decision to lead one of these parades in the District of Columbia on Flag Day symbolized his complete command of the preparedness movement. In San Francisco, however, a preparedness parade ended in tragedy on July 22 when a bomb thrown by an unknown hand killed many spectators. Two labor leaders, Thomas J. Mooney and Warren K. Billings, who were seized as suspects were saved from execution only when the governor commuted their sentence to life imprisonment. Subsequent investigations indicated that perjured evidence and mass hysteria had played a major role in convicting the two men. Their case became a rallying point of leftist organizations until both were released in 1940.

THE SUSSEX PLEDGE

At the beginning of 1916 Colonel House was again in Europe, this time with a startling proposal for American intervention in the war. Wilson apparently had decided to use every possible means to end the war. Sir Edward Grey's memorandum of February 22 read: "Colonel House told me that President Wilson was ready, on hearing from France and England that the moment was opportune, to propose that a Conference should be summoned to put an end to the war. Should the Allies accept this proposal, and should Germany refuse it, the United States would probably enter the war against Germany." Wilson cautiously insisted on the insertion of the word "probably" in deference to Congress; not even the enthusiastic Colonel House could ignore this body. The Allies found this statement far from a satisfactory pledge of military assistance and consequently rejected the proposal. Meanwhile Britain continued her aggressive policy toward neutrals on the high seas and in addition blacklisted American firms suspected of giving aid to Germany.

Congressional fears that Wilson had joined the advocates of war mounted after the so-called Sunrise Conference on February 21, 1916, at which the President was reported to have asked the Democratic leaders to cooperate with him in bringing us into the war against Germany in order to shorten the conflict. According to one account, Wilson proposed to sever diplomatic relations if American lives were lost on another vessel sunk by a submarine; Ambassador Bernstorff had assured the State Department that this would be followed automatically by a declaration of war by Germany. The reaction to this plan was quickly apparent in the McLemore-Gore resolution, which warned American citizens against traveling on armed ships of belligerent nations. Wilson met this challenge by an open letter to Senator William J. Stone of Missouri, chairman of the Senate Committee on Foreign Relations, in which he said: "For my own part, I cannot consent to any abridgment of the rights of American citizens in any respect. . . . To forbid our people to exercise their rights for fear we might be called upon to vindicate them would be a deep humiliation, indeed. . . . Once accept a single abatement of right, and many other humiliations would follow, and the whole fine fabric of international law might crumble under our own hands piece by piece. What we are contending for in this matter is of the very essence of the things that have made America a sovereign nation." This letter swung public opinion back to the President and the resolution was defeated in Congress.

The most serious crisis since the *Lusitania* occurred a few weeks later when an unarmed French passenger steamer, the *Sussex,* was torpedoed on March 24. Although she did not go to the bottom, some eighty of her passengers—some of them Americans—were killed or injured. Nevertheless, the attack on the *Sussex* was a violation of Germany's pledge not to sink an unarmed vessel without warning. Wilson was then involved with Mexico over Villa; furthermore, the congressional action on the McLemore-Gore resolution had convinced him that the peace sentiment in Congress as well as in the country at large was still powerful. Accordingly, instead of breaking off diplomatic relations with Germany, he instructed the State Department to send the following stern warning to her on April 18: "Unless the Imperial Government should now immediately declare and effect an abandonment of its present methods of submarine warfare against passenger and freight-carrying vessels, the Government of the United States can have no choice but to sever diplomatic relations with the German Empire altogether."

Because Germany considered her submarine fleet too inadequate to offset our entrance into the war, the German Foreign Office promised that merchant vessels would not be sunk without warning and without saving passengers unless resistance or escape were attempted. However, Germany reserved to herself "complete liberty of decision" if the United States could not persuade the Allies to relax the food blockade. Thus Wilson again staved off war, to the great disappointment of his pro-Allied friends and associates. Bernstorff later remarked that, after the *Sussex* note, there was no longer any doubt in Berlin that persistence in unrestricted submarine warfare meant war with the United States.

"HE KEPT US OUT OF WAR"

The presidential election of 1916 was one crisis that Wilson could not avert and he prepared himself for battle in spite of his increasing responsibilities elsewhere. The foreign situation inevitably colored the campaign, despite the fact that neither party favored an outright declaration of war. Republicans hailed their September victory in Maine as portending a national victory in November, in line with the tradition, "As Maine goes, so goes the nation." To reunite their party they had only to heal the breach that appeared in 1912 between the regulars and the Progressives. This hope seemed realized when the congressional elections of 1914 reduced the number of Progressives by one-half and Roosevelt began to move back into regular Republican ranks, possibly aspiring to win the party nomination for President in 1916.

The Republican convention in Chicago was presided over by Senator Warren G. Harding of Ohio as both temporary and permanent chairman; he was useful to party unity because he had avoided becoming entangled with the interparty animosities of 1912. In the same interest of conciliation Associate Justice Charles Evans Hughes of New York, a regular with progressive tendencies, was nominated for the Presidency. Partisan newspapers made capital of the fact that Hughes was reported to have written privately in 1912: "A man on the Supreme Bench who would run for political office is neither fit for the office he holds nor for the one to which he aspires." Roosevelt himself gave the *coup de grâce* to the Progressive party by belatedly rejecting its nomination and publicly advising its members to return to the Republican fold.

The Democrats, as expected, nominated Wilson by acclamation. The party had great hopes of winning the independent and Progressive votes on the basis of the President's domestic legislation and his appointment of liberals to the Supreme Court. In the summer of 1916 Wilson signed the Keating-Owen bill to bar from interstate commerce any goods produced by child labor, a measure long desired by Beveridge and other liberals. The President's campaign managers attempted to popularize his foreign policy with the slogan, "He kept us out of war!" and at the same time suggested that Hughes was secretly allied with the disloyal "hyphen" element—a reference to German- and Irish-American supporters of the Central Powers. But the Democrats were worried about New York State, whose Tammany-led machine was in revolt against Wilson; only two Democrats, Madison and Buchanan, had won a presidential election without New York votes.

Hughes conducted a lawyer-like campaign in which he was careful not to jeopardize what seemed to be certain victory, although his criticism of Wilson's reforms antagonized many liberals. Friends who knew how brilliant he was intellectually were astonished at the endless platitudes in the name of "America First" which filled his speeches. Moreover, his chances were seriously weakened in the important state of California, the happy hunting grounds of Hiram Johnson's Progressives, when a feud broke out between the party's central committee and Johnson. Hughes himself did little to heal this breach and inadvertently weakened his chances further by attending a political luncheon at the Commercial Club in San Francisco where scabs were employed in open defiance of the city's powerful unions.

Wilson scored a major triumph on the "hyphenate" issue which came to the forefront of the campaign. Jeremiah O'Leary, the truculent head of the anti-British American Truth Society, sought to organize the Irish- and German-American vote against Wilson and wrote the President an offensive letter questioning his sincerity and expressing the hope of his defeat in November. Wilson shrewdly chose to give this nation-wide publicity by releasing to the newspapers his reply to O'Leary in which he said: "I would feel deeply mortified to have you or anybody like you vote for me. Since you have access to many disloyal Americans and I have not, I will ask you to convey this message to them." Skilled politicians like Joseph Tumulty and Colonel House considered this the best move of the campaign in discrediting the anti-British societies.

Early in September, 1916, a nation-wide railroad strike was called; in addition to interrupting the campaign, it threatened to cut off vital supplies for the Allies and to paralyze our own preparedness activities. In 1915 the four great Railroad Brotherhoods had demanded an eight-hour day instead of the existing ten-hour day, but with no decrease in pay scales and time and a half for overtime. These demands were stubbornly resisted by the operators, who claimed that their profits were limited by the low rates fixed by the Interstate Commerce Commission, by the higher costs resulting from the newly required safety devices and workmen's compensation acts, and by the general rise in the price level. In a personal appeal to the patriotism of both sides Wilson on August 12, 1916, proposed arbitration, but failed to win over either side. Thereupon the Brotherhoods voted to strike at midnight on September 4, the day before Labor Day; the strike order affected nearly 400,000 men.

Wilson's next step set a record for speedy congressional action. Appearing before a joint session on August 29, he asked for legislation that would halt the strike. He warned that the nation's economic life faced a complete breakdown and he called for an eight-hour day and a factual study of possible rate increases by the I.C.C. He also sought (but failed to secure) greater power for the Commission, provision for effective mediation, conciliation, and arbitration, and emergency powers that would enable the government to take over the railroads and if necessary draft all their employees into military service. On September 3, a few hours before the strike was to begin, the Adamson Eight Hour Law, which embodied his chief recommendations, was sent to Wilson for his signature. Although the strike was immediately called off by the unions, the operators refused to put in the new wage scale until after the Supreme Court had upheld its constitutionality. Hughes' denunciation of the bill swung Progressives to Wilson; conservative members of the press branded the Act as cheap politics to win the labor vote.

Election day brought some of the uncertainties of the famous disputed election of 1876, for the results indicated victory at first for Wilson, then for Hughes, and then for Wilson again. By evening it was clear that Hughes had carried New York State and the industrial Northeast and was winning most of the Middle West as well; the next morning even staunch Democratic newspapers conceded a Republican victory. However, later that day Colonel House's prediction of a clean Democratic sweep in the "Bryan country" and the Far West as well as the South began to be realized. California's electoral votes ultimately became the margin of success; Wilson won 277 to Hughes' 254. The popular vote gave Wilson 9,129,600; Hughes, 8,538,200; and Allan Benson, the Socialist candidate, 585,100. Altogether, the President's total well exceeded that of 1912, even though his electoral votes fell off. The Democrats also triumphed in the congressional elections, retaining control of both houses. This close battle forecast the Republican return to power in 1920.

THE FAILURE OF "PEACE WITHOUT VICTORY"

With the election over, Wilson hoped to resume his role of peacemaker. The European struggle seemed to be degenerating into a war of attrition in which both sides were stalemated in strongly fortified trenches facing each other. On December 12, 1916, Germany suggested that both sides discuss peace, and six days later Wilson, acting independently, addressed similar notes to each belligerent, asking for a statement of its war aims and suggesting the creation of a League of Nations. Germany's reply recommended only a conference of the belligerents. The Allies, on the other hand, although insisting that Wilson's step was premature, expressed their war aims as the reorganization of Europe on the basis of nationalities (this meant the dismembering of Austria-Hungary), the political restoration of Belgium, Serbia, and Montenegro, and the payment of various indemnities. Thereupon Wilson addressed the Senate on January 22, 1917, in behalf of "peace without victory" as the foundation of a League for Peace in which the peoples of the New World also would cooperate. Its principles would include equality of all nations, democratic government, freedom of the seas, and partial disarmament. He proposed that the Monroe Doctrine be made universal by extending it to protect every nation, small as well as large, from domination by other nations.

The Allies' unsatisfactory reply to Wilson's note of December 18 strengthened the determination of the German military leaders to press the war to a conclusion regardless of cost, and correspondingly weakened the political leaders who, struggling desperately to keep the United States out of the war, had up to now managed to restrain the militarists. On January 9, Hindenburg and Admiral Holtzendorf informed the German government that no chance for a negotiated peace remained and that resumption of the intensive submarine warfare would starve Britain into submission before American armed forces could become effective. This policy was motivated not by fear of our munitions exports but by the belief that the unusually poor harvests of 1916–1917 in Great Britain and North America might make it possible to isolate England by means of unrestricted U-boat warfare within four to six months and thus end the war. This was made clear later, when Bethmann-Hollweg, the former Chancellor, testified before the Reichstag in 1919 as follows: "The U-boat war meant a break and later war with America. It was on this point that for years the argument between the military and the political branch had turned. The decisive point was that the Supreme High Command of the Army from now on was absolutely determined to assume the responsibility of the risk which an American war meant."

WAR

On January 31, 1917, the German government announced that on and after February 1 submarines would sink all ships, including neutral vessels, that entered the waters around the British Isles, France, and Italy, or the eastern Mediterranean. Germany magnanimously made a concession in allowing one American vessel to pass each week through a designated shipping lane in the war zone, provided it carried no contraband and was painted with broad red and white stripes. This move stunned Wilson, for in view of his earlier statements it left him no alternative but war. On January 4 he had said to Colonel House: "There will be no war. This country does not intend to become involved in this war." To enter the conflict at this time, he went on, would be a "crime against civilization." Moreover, he had begun to be skeptical regarding the Allied motives, and our relations with Great Britain as a result of the blockade had seldom been worse. The German Ambassador later commented: "After January 31, 1917, Wilson himself was a different man. Our rejection of his proposal to mediate, by our announcement of the unrestricted U-boat war, which was to him utterly incomprehensible, turned him into an embittered enemy of the Imperial Government."

After consulting his Cabinet, Wilson asked Congress on February 3 to sever diplomatic relations with Germany. In view of the long-standing friendship between the German people and ourselves, he said, only overt acts of hostility would convince him that Germany intended to carry out her new policy. His own opinion was made clear in his comment to Tumulty regarding the German announcement: "This means war. The break that we have tried so hard to prevent now seems inevitable."

Overt acts were not long in coming. On February 26 Wilson informed Congress of the sinking of two American ships and requested authority to arm merchant vessels. The House acted promptly, but the measure was shelved in the Senate when twelve Senators led by La Follette filibustered until the end of the session. These insurgents were convinced that such a bill meant the end of neutrality and the advent of actual war. Wilson publicly asserted that "a little group of willful men have rendered the great government of the United States helpless and contemptible." On being advised of his inherent emergency powers as President, Wilson acted independently of Congress on March 12 and ordered merchant vessels to be armed.

Among the factors that strengthened the President's position was the nation-wide outcry early in March over the Zimmermann conspiracy. On January 19, 1917, the German Secretary of State, Alfred Zimmermann, sent a telegram to the German Minister at Mexico City, outlining a military alliance with Mexico in the event that Germany became involved in war with the United States. "We shall give generous financial support [to Mexico]," the telegram read, "and it is understood that Mexico is to recover the lost territory in New Mexico, Texas, and Arizona." The President of Mexico was to offer to mediate between Germany and Japan; if this was successful it might bring the Japanese into a hostile alliance against the United States. The telegram, which had been intercepted and decoded by the British intelligence service, served to awaken Americans to the immediacy of war as few other things could.

Additional overt acts occurred in March. On March 12 a submarine sank the *Algonquin*, an unarmed American merchantmen. A week later the public learned of the sinking of three more such vessels, with heavy casualties among the crews. This news solidified the Cabinet's pro-war sentiment, and by the end of March Wilson himself was convinced that the time had come for a declaration of war. A new note was added when the autocratic regime of Czar Nicholas II was overthrown by a revolution, then in its democratic phase. Free of the liability of a despotic government as an ally, Wilson and House could envisage a "war for democracy."

On the evening of April 2, 1917, the President addressed a joint session of the new Congress. "The present German submarine warfare against commerce," he declared, "is a warfare against mankind. . . . Neutrality is no longer feasible or desirable where the peace of the world is involved and the freedom of its peoples, and the menace to that peace and freedom lies in the existence of autocratic governments backed by organized force which is controlled wholly by their will, not by the will of the people. We have seen the last of neutrality in such circumstances." His remark, "We have no quarrel with the German people," made it clear that he held the German government solely responsible for the war. Aggressive designs, he contended, could not thrive when popular opinion ruled and no privileged class existed.

He saw the beginning of a new era of world cooperation after the war. The "wonderful and heartening things" that were taking place in Russia he hailed as marking the accession of fresh democratic forces in the fight for freedom and justice. The overthrow of autocracy heralded the recovery of the "great generous Russian people . . . in all their naïve majesty and might. . . ." The Prussian autocracy, he said, had long demonstrated its untrustworthiness, its tendency to spy and intrigue abroad—even, as witness the Zimmermann plot, at the threshold of the United States herself. Our fight, then, would be "for the ultimate peace of the world and for the liberation of its peoples, the German peoples included; for the rights of nations great and small and the privilege of men everywhere to choose their way of life and of obedience."

Then in powerful and inspiring language which aroused hopes whose later blighting by circumstances caused the cynical to laugh, Wilson said: "The world must be made safe for democracy. Its peace must be planted upon the tested foundations of political liberty. We have no selfish ends to serve. We desire no conquest, no dominion. We seek no indemnities for ourselves, no material compensation for the sacrifices we shall freely make. We are but one of the champions of the rights of mankind. We shall be satisfied when those rights have been made as secure as the faith and the freedom of nations can make them."

Wilson's innate pacifism became evident toward the end of his message when he observed sadly: "It is a fearful thing to lead this great peaceful people into war, into the most terrible and disastrous of all wars, civilization itself seeming to be in the balance. But the right is more precious than peace, and we shall fight for the things which we have always carried nearest our hearts, for democracy, for the right of those who submit to authority to have a voice in their own governments, for the rights and liberties of small nations, for a universal dominion of right by such a concert of free peoples as shall bring peace and safety to all nations and make the world itself at last free."

An enthusiastic Congress cheered Wilson when he ended his speech. Two days later the Senate voted for war 82 to 6 and early on April 6 the House supported the war resolution 373 to 50. That same day President Wilson affixed his signature to the resolution. Thus in the eyes of Wilsonian idealists, the European war, whose cause the President believed lay in selfish commercial rivalry, was transformed into a world peace crusade by the altruistic mission undertaken by the United States. After the smoke of battle had cleared, it was hoped that a democratic social order would emerge that would achieve on the world stage what the Progressives had dreamed of accomplishing on a smaller scale at home.

Latin America, on the whole, heartily endorsed Wilson's war message. Ties of interest if not sentiment were responsible for a wave of diplomatic pressure to break off relations with the Central Powers. Declarations of war were made automatically by Cuba and Panama, bound as they were by treaties with the United States. The danger of German espionage plots in the Caribbean was checked by similar declarations by Honduras, Nicaragua, Haiti, and Guatemala. Brazil's declaration in October, 1917, was precipitated by the submarine sinking of two of her vessels. Diplomatic relations with Germany were quickly severed by Peru, Ecuador, Bolivia, Uruguay, and Costa Rica, thus removing a possible source of embarrassment to our own war effort.

Popular sentiment in Argentina favored war with Germany, particularly after the infamous Luxburg dispatches. On May 19, 1917, Count Luxburg, the German Minister to Argentina, wrote Berlin regarding his country's submarine policy: "I beg that the small steamers *Oran* and *Guazo* [Argentine vessels] . . . may be spared if possible, or else sunk without a trace being left [*spurlos versenkt*]." Anglo-American cooperation made possible the interception of this message, and its publication in Argentina led to serious riots against the Germans. But President Hipólito Irigoyen, intent on domestic reforms, refused to do more than ask for Luxburg's dismissal. Mexico's neutrality seemed cold to

Wilson, but the Mexican-German collaboration suggested in the Zimmermann telegram was never realized. Chile, torn by internal crises and far from the fighting scene, also elected to remain neutral. Colombia's aloof attitude reflected her continued grievance at losing Panama because of Roosevelt. Nevertheless, a large measure of hemisphere solidarity had been achieved against the Central Powers.

"A People's War"

DRAFTING A NATION

"The great fact that stands out above all the rest," observed Wilson in his Flag Day speech in 1917, "is that this is a People's War. . . ." With the crusading zeal of Peter the Hermit, the one-time college professor prepared to lead the masses—including the German people—against the autocracy he believed inherent in the Prussian militaristic spirit. These idealistic pronouncements ultimately penetrated into Germany; their effectiveness, comparable to that of Marshal Foch's artillery, seriously alarmed Hindenburg and Ludendorff. America's entry into the war seemed to transform the struggle overnight into a crusade for social democracy whose revolutionary implications might well give pause to the Allies themselves. Failure to satisfy Wilson's liberal ideals could lead to a mass disillusionment whose consequences no one could foresee. Even though Wilson may have known that the Allied leaders had already concluded secret treaties which dismembered the enemy in traditional fashion, he relied on the power of a democratic public opinion to achieve a cooperative world order in spite of selfish leadership.

Conscious of the magnitude of modern war, the President warned the nation on May 18, 1917, that few could expect to remain untouched by the existing conflict. "In the sense in which we have been wont to think of armies there are no armies in this struggle," he said; "there are entire nations armed. . . . The whole Nation must be a team in which each man shall play the part for which he is best fitted." The eighteenth-century ideal of a professional army which left the bourgeois citizen free to pursue his daily life quietly above the din of battle was shattered by the French Revolution with its emphasis on a "nation in arms." Just as that struggle had improved on Bourbon experiments with mass troop levies, so the rising German state had perfected the organization of an entire nation geared to war. Nothing less than a similar nation-wide effort in the United States would suffice for victory.

When the movement for preparedness was first organized, Wilson fought military conscription, for it was his belief that a call for volunteers would result in an overwhelming response. For example, England, always averse to the continental practice of compulsory military service, had relied on volunteers during the first eighteen months of the war. Before April 6, 1917, however, the President had been entirely converted to the idea of a draft and was working closely with Secretary of War Baker and Major Enoch H. Crowder to assemble the conscription machinery. Although it was believed that America would make her major contribution to the war effort by furnishing supplies rather than an expeditionary force, the latter, too, was essential and the desire to have "every man in the right place" made conscription the most effective method of recruiting. Many Congressmen, recalling the bloody riots of the Civil War and fearful of their constituents' reaction, bitterly assailed the Selective Service Bill. Speaker Champ Clark went so far as to say that "there is precious little difference between a conscript and a convict." In spite of further controversy over age limits, the Administration forces won and the bill became law on May 18; it gave the President broad powers in enforcing it.

All men between 21 and 30 inclusive were ordered to register for war service on June 5 at their regular voting places, it being Baker's idea that civilian draft boards rather than military recruiting officers would soften the transition to Army life. Volunteer medical, legal, and other specialized staffs, cooperating with state and local officials, supplied the conscription machinery. Over 9.5 million men registered. Generous exemptions were made in the first draft in the case of men with dependents, men skilled in war industries, certain high elective officials, ministers and theological students, pacifists and other "conscientious objectors" to war, and certain classes of aliens. Captain Hugh S. Johnson, a colorful and vigorous administrator who as Major Johnson became famous two decades later in connection with the NRA and the Blue Eagle emblem signifying industrial cooperation, originated the basic provisions of the Selective Service Act and assisted Major Crowder in preparations for the actual draft. The first drawing was made in the Senate Office Building on July 20, 1917, by Secretary of War Baker, who, blindfolded, drew the capsules containing the draft numbers from a large glass bowl.

Anti-draft and anti-war demonstrations promptly broke out in the large cities. In Boston, Socialists carried placards reading, "If this is a popular war, why conscription?" Thousands of anti-war pamphlets were circulated by pacifist, radical, and pro-German elements. The pacifist Farmers' Non-Partisan League in the Dakotas brought public condemnation upon itself for its stand. The governor of Minnesota had to intervene to stop the People's Council of America for Democracy and Peace, an anti-war organization, from holding a meeting in Minneapolis. All these pacifist demonstrations were systematically stamped out by federal and local authorities aided by zealous citizens. Neither anti-union elements nor patriotic groups were displeased when I.W.W. headquarters were closed by federal agents on the charge of "obstructing the recruitment and enlistment service of the United States."

Some 338,000 draft evaders—almost half remained at large—constituted the major problem of enforcing the draft. Police covered pool rooms, ball parks, and other recreation centers in an effort to trap "slackers" who were unable to produce a draft registration card. There was a boom in marriages, but it collapsed quickly when it was announced that these belated unions carried no exemption. Men who fled to Mexico found themselves isolated by the contempt of the native population.

The most sensational case of draft dodging involved Grover Cleveland Bergdoll, member of a wealthy brewing family. Bergdoll, who had been a favorite pupil of the Wright brothers, became one of the foremost sportsman flyers in the country. Apparently resentful at his failure to secure an Army commission as an aviator, he ignored his draft summons and disappeared. He was captured in 1920 and sentenced to five years at hard labor, but he escaped his guards on the pretext of recovering a chest of gold that he had hidden in a mountain retreat. He promptly made his way to Germany where he was given an enthusiastic welcome. Almost two decades later he returned to the United States and was rearrested by Army officials who wished to punish draft evasion, especially since a new war loomed.

A NATION IN ARMS

As soon as the United States entered the war, Wilson and an Anglo-French mission agreed that a token force of 2000 men would be sent overseas under General John J. Pershing, to be followed in the summer of 1917 by enough additional men to make up a full division. Hence, in accordance with the War Department's original plan calling for a large defensive army at home, by the end of 1917 over half a million men were undergoing rigorous training in huge, hastily constructed Army camps resembling miniature cities. But the collapse of Russia that summer, together with further reverses in France and Italy, led the Allies to adopt a policy of attrition in France until large-scale aid from us could restore the balance in our favor. Accordingly, the Army was expanded to over 1.25 million men by the spring of 1918. At the same time, more than 100,000 officers were rapidly recruited from special training camps, college military units, and men on the inactive list. This sudden increase bred considerable confusion within the War Department in readjusting supply services, especially clothing, and pneumonia took a heavy toll in northern camps that winter.

As the war progressed, new sources of manpower were tapped. A special registration was ordered on June 5, 1918, for men who had reached their twenty-first birthday during the preceding year; the draft lists were swelled by almost a million new names. On August 31, 1918, another draft registration was held for men between 18 and 45; almost 13.5 million men and boys registered. Many of these men, it was believed, would be needed for the victory drive in 1919. Furthermore, this census was valuable as a basis for the new "work or fight" program in which able-bodied men would be allocated to industry or the fighting front as required.

Despite initial problems, the morale of the soldiers was high. Considerable success followed the introduction, on a gigantic scale, of psychological testing as a means of selecting the right man for each post. Postwar progress in intelligence and achievement testing was heavily indebted to these experiments. Morale was further raised by the clubhouses, Christmas parties, vaudeville performances, movies, and concerts provided by such organizations as the Red Cross, the Y.M.C.A., the Knights of Columbus, the Salvation Army, and the

Jewish Welfare Board. The Army learned to sing, and "Tipperary," "Keep the Home Fires Burning," "Good-Bye Broadway, Hello France," and "Over There" quickly became favorites. Irving Berlin, then a sergeant in a New York camp, struck a popular note of "doughboy" humor in his ditty, "Oh! How I Hate to Get Up in the Morning!"

In choosing Army leaders Wilson was indebted to the pioneer work done by his Republican predecessors. Elihu Root as Secretary of War under McKinley and Roosevelt had created the General Staff in 1903 as a planning group to study the technical needs of possible future theaters of operations and to plan for the mobilization and strategic use of all the forces required by the nation. He was also instrumental in replacing seniority, the conventional basis for promotion in the Army, with merit. John J. Pershing, whom Wilson chose as commander of the American Expeditionary Force, had already been recognized as a skillful organizer by President Roosevelt, who promoted him from captain to brigadier-general—a long step forward.

Pershing, who was fifty-seven years old in 1917, had had experience in Cuba, the Philippines, and Mexico; a visit to Europe had given him a speaking knowledge of French. His appearance was impressive and his personal qualities were solid if not brilliant. A firm believer in offensive warfare in the open field, he tended to minimize the importance of defensive trench tactics. He found his task as commander of the A.E.F. a heavy one and felt that the assistance he might have received from the General Staff had been reduced by congressional economies and the Chief of Staff's failure to anticipate a possible increase in the A.E.F. Wilson realized the political danger in appointing a lifelong Republican like Pershing as commander, for presidential aspirants always emerged from among the victorious generals after every war. Nevertheless, the nation's interests made the selection of Pershing imperative. When Pershing refused to appoint General Leonard Wood to an overseas post under circumstances that publicly humiliated the latter, Wilson loyally bore the severe newspaper criticism that followed.

Theodore Roosevelt's attempts to organize and head an overseas group of volunteers similar to his Rough Riders of 1898 provoked a minor war in itself, for his admirers were insistent in his behalf. Congress had provided for such a contingency by authorizing the establishment of an independent command for volunteer divisions. Even Clemenceau, the French Premier, said that all his poilus were asking, "Where is Roosevelt?" However, the War Department and the Chief of Staff refused to handicap Pershing's expedition by diverting to Roosevelt the officers and highly trained men he required. Wilson's support of his military experts once again brought him harsh rebukes in the press and Roosevelt's bitter hatred.

"OVER THERE"

In the spring of 1918 arrangements were made with the British government to assist in the mass transportation of our troops to France. The steady stream of heavily loaded American troopships that were sent to France suffered few losses because of the huge Anglo-American convoys that protected them from submarines. At the end of 1917 there were only 195,000 American soldiers in France, but when the armistice was signed in November, 1918, almost two million men out of a total of 3.5 million had already arrived in France, and three-fourths of these newcomers had been in actual battle on the western front.

Wilson and Pershing agreed that our men should constitute a separate American army instead of being scattered among the depleted Anglo-French forces as the Allied High Command advised. This goal of an independent force could not be achieved before August, 1918, because the restricted shipping facilities limited us to transporting infantry and machine-gun units without any artillery. Another important factor was the pressing need for infantry reinforcements for the battered British and French units thrown against Hindenburg's spring offensive in 1918. When the armistice was signed, American soldiers were still using our Allies' artillery and airplanes.

Despite their inexperience in actual large-scale warfare, the A.E.F. showed a buoyant offensive spirit that gave their war-weary Allies new encouragement; their superb skill with the rifle won the admiration of French and British alike. Official German reports revealed later that the enemy too was impressed by the effectiveness of our men, particularly their steadfastness in the face of withering gunfire. A London *Times* war correspondent, after observing our machine gunners in the bitterly contested battle of Château-Thierry in May, 1918, sent this enthusiastic wire to his paper: "These are allies worth having. That is what the French feel and say, and every Englishman will agree with him."

After occupying the extreme southern end of the western front in October, 1917, our men held but one per cent of the long Allied lines by the opening of the new year. So rapidly did we move after this, however, that at the armistice our forces were holding almost one-quarter of the entire front. Engaging at first in raids along the quiet Lorraine sector, they carried on full-scale offensives during the spring of 1918. At Château-Thierry American soldiers aided by French colonials helped to block the German advance to Paris early in June, and soon afterward they opened a vigorous counteroffensive at Belleau Wood, clearing a critical point of machine-gun nests and recapturing several villages.

When the final German offensive of July 15 began to slow up, Marshal Foch gave the signal for a mighty counterdrive in which Americans fought at various points, especially between Soissons and Château-Thierry. Led by the experienced First and Second Divisions, our men acted as a spearhead and forced the Marne salient; the attack compelled the Germans to retreat. The final phase of the campaign was begun on August 30, 1918, when Pershing prepared to throw more than a million men into a major independent drive against the St. Mihiel salient at the southern tip of the Hindenburg Line in order to free the Paris-Nancy railroad from a paralyzing German fire and open the road to the strategic iron basin at Briey. This army went into action on September 12, pinched off the salient, and captured 16,000 prisoners and 450 guns at the relatively moderate cost of 7000 casualties. As the British and French drives to the north developed, a huge American force of 1,200,000 troops began to pour through the Meuse-Argonne sector toward Sedan on September 26. Although the French leaders criticized the faulty staff work to which they attributed our heavy losses—120,000 men—in the Argonne Forest, all our objectives were taken, including thousands of German prisoners and considerable equipment. The British break-through of the Hindenburg Line on the north in a converging attack which complemented the Franco-American thrusts to the south made the enemy realize his defeat. Accordingly the Germans requested an armistice, which they formally accepted at 11 A.M. on November 11, 1918.

When the reckoning was made, some 50,000 Americans had been killed in action and another quarter of a million had been wounded. The French lost over 1.33 million killed; the British, over 900,000 killed. Russia and Germany both suffered staggering losses.

While the American Army performed a brilliant role in the war, our Navy also lived up to its historic traditions, despite the altered conditions of sea warfare. Under Josephus Daniels, the Navy Department reached a high level of efficiency; its personnel expanded from an initial 65,000 men to almost half a million in November, 1918. Assistant Secretary Franklin D. Roosevelt, like Theodore Roosevelt in 1898, showed considerable foresight in the strategic allocation of the fleet on the eve of our entrance into the war. Rear Admiral William S. Sims, who was in command of naval operations, had long since demonstrated his originality as tactical expert and had instituted significant changes, especially in raising the standards of marksmanship and inventing an excellent system of controlling fires. Although the vociferous Hearst press and its satellites timorously insisted that most of our Navy be kept at home for coastal defense, Sims came out in favor of offensive operations abroad. Since the major portion of the German fleet was immobilized by the British blockade, our Navy's task was to strengthen convoys, hunt down submarines, engage in extensive mine-laying operations in the North Sea, and clear away the enemy's mines elsewhere.

Beginning in the spring of 1918, a wave of submarine attacks on American shipping brought the war to our Atlantic coast, especially off Virginia. Germany boasted of her new submarines which could cross the ocean, and panic-filled Americans saw the shadow of a periscope everywhere along the Atlantic. To the sharp criticism which began to be leveled against the Navy Department, Secretary Daniels replied firmly: "The activities of the German submarines off the American coast have not in any way changed the policy of the Government. . . . There will be no weakening of our naval forces in European waters as a result of the new activity on our coast." The convoy system and our efficient anti-submarine devices eventually prevented the U-boats from paralyzing Allied shipping, and the newly awakened energies of American shipbuilders rapidly replaced the ships that were lost.

Despite his pacifist background, Wilson could be as realistic as professional Army and Navy men in devising offensive strategy, and he sharply criticized what he called the "prudence" of the British fleet. He was a party to our Navy's ambitious plan of laying over two hundred miles of mines in the North Sea area and he advised that the submarine menace be combated at its source. Marshal Joffre of France, who visited Wilson during the spring of 1917, praised his "perfect mastery of the military situation." When Allied fortunes were threatened by the unchecked German drive early in 1918, it was Wilson who urged a unified command under General Foch.

A WAR ECONOMY

The World War, because of its extensive operations and its new mechanized aspects, raised the importance of the home front to unprecedented heights. To equip, feed, and transport millions of soldiers required another army of civilian workers trained to meet the unique production demands of large-scale warfare. These efforts involved the raising of the President's authority to extraordinary heights and a degree of governmental centralization whose influence would inevitably remain even after the conflict ended. The fact that Wilson's New Freedom involved far-reaching federal control over business in peacetime made conservatives fear that "war socialism" might become permanent. Liberals were apprehensive lest the civil liberties so painfully acquired through the ages be destroyed as the result of the enormous powers conferred on the President as commander-in-chief of the nation's armed forces.

Republicans, suspicious that the fortunes of the Democrats might be enhanced by the powers granted the Administration, pressed for a voice in the government. When the War Department seemed bogged down by the sudden change in Allied plans at the end of 1917, Theodore Roosevelt thought the moment opportune to demand a bipartisan Cabinet. But Wilson refused to yield to this proposal on the ground that it would end unified direction of the war, although he showed every willingness to give able Republicans key positions in the government. He propitiated the leaders of business by giving them important posts on the home front, and a stream of "dollar-a-year men" began to flow into Washington.

The Council of National Defense, hitherto a purely advisory group, emerged in part as the powerful War Industries Board headed by Bernard Baruch. The Board was given sweeping powers to centralize and control industry in the interests of war and civilian needs. Although Baruch found that its powers were far from adequate, especially where price-fixing was concerned, he could exert pressure on any recalcitrant industry by threatening to curtail its priority rating on materials; if necessary, he could nationalize any factory. President Wilson was sufficiently realistic to see that persuasion alone was not enough. "Let the manufacturer see the club behind your door," he advised Robert S. Brookings, chairman of the price-fixing commission of which Baruch was a member.

The War Industries Board, among its manifold activities, sought to cooperate with employers in standardizing and using materials. Generous price concessions for essential commodities and the assistance of experts such as comprised its Chemical Division stimulated the production of much-needed materials. One of Baruch's associates, A. W. Shaw, who published business books and magazines in Chicago, claimed that the elimination of so-called non-essential businesses was fallacious; instead he advocated the removal of "non-essential uses of labor, capital, and equipment from all business." In this way he hoped to preserve the skeleton of the normal business structure necessary for the transition to postwar industrial expansion. The Board apparently agreed with Mr. Shaw; for example, it planned to convert the nation's automobile industry to war work late in 1918, and the first step was a drastic reduction in tire and passenger car production during the summer of that year.

LABOR'S STATUS DURING THE WAR

An inflationary rise in prices that began in 1914 canceled only part of the wage gains made by labor, for there were many offsetting factors. Felix Frankfurter, head of the War Labor Policies Board, accepted local union standards for wages and conditions in plants engaged in war production. The cost-plus basis on which government contracts were figured acted as a stimulant to high wages because wages were reckoned as part of the producer's cost. When a mounting wave of strikes and lockouts induced by the rising cost of living swept the country during the fall of 1917, President Wilson intervened and by presidential proclamation established the National War Labor Board. Ex-President Taft and Frank P. Walsh were selected as co-chairmen, and the remaining members were drawn equally from the American Federation of Labor and the National Industrial Conference Board, an employer's organization.

The new Board, which was empowered to act in disputes between labor and management, embodied a pioneer step in democratizing labor relations. Its expressed ideal was a living wage, and to this end the President guaranteed labor the right to organize unions and to bargain collectively; even the closed shop was sanctioned under certain circumstances. Co-Chairman Taft, to the surprise of his colleagues, proved aggressively pro-labor, in contrast to his former legalist conservatism. Munitions plants, such as the Smith & Wesson Arms Company of Springfield, Massachusetts, which resisted unionization by forbidding prospective employees to join a labor organization, were commandeered by the War Department. A clash with the Western Union Telegraph Company, which steadfastly refused to reinstate 450 men who had been discharged for union activities, led ultimately to the wartime nationalization of the telegraph and telephone industries. Recalcitrant workers also had to face a determined Board. For example, when the munitions workers in Bridgeport, Connecticut, struck for additional concessions which the Board considered unjustifiable, President Wilson warned them that they were liable to exclusion from employment in any war industry and that they would lose the military exemption allowed war workers by the draft boards. This quickly ended the strike.

The steady march of unskilled workers into industry brought with it a strong advance of industrial unionism against the well-entrenched lines of craft unionism. This held true even within the American Federation of Labor, whose dues-paying membership increased by 2,000,000 between 1917 and 1920. This gain was made largely in mining, shipbuilding, railway shops, packing houses, and federal agencies. Union membership as a whole increased over 70 per cent during the period 1914–1920. Most of the new members were men, for although women invaded the ranks of elevator operators, munitions workers, streetcar conductors, and messengers, few of them joined a union.

With the outspoken assistance of a sympathetic national Administration, women made measurable gains in industry, despite the fears of feminist leaders. When the United States entered the war in 1917, Jane Addams predicted to Ida Tarbell: "Everything that we have gained in the way of social legislation will be destroyed. It will throw us back where we were twenty-five years ago." This pessimism proved unjustified, for Wilson, in creating the National War Labor Board, called for equal pay for men and women doing the same work. Although this turned out to be the exception in practice, appreciable advances were made along other lines. For example, women were given unprecedented representation on key industrial boards such as the Board of Control of Labor Standards for Army clothing, of which Florence Kelley was a member. The leading defense organizations had their women's committees. The effect of this advance was evident when Julia Lathrop reported that the Children's Bureau had never before been engaged in such far-reaching activities. However, in too many cases, as Mary Van Kleeck, head of the Women's Branch of the Ordnance Department, later pointed out, the persistence of traditional prejudice toward women in industry meant flagrant violations of the labor laws pertaining to long hours and night work.

The wartime need for labor, intensified by the sudden curtailment of immigration, sharply accentuated the prewar migration of Negroes to northern cities. This new labor supply was rapidly absorbed by steel mills, packing houses, and automobile plants in Chicago, Detroit, and Pittsburgh. The newcomers overflowed the segregated areas into restricted white residential districts despite exorbitant rents, intimidation, and occasional riots. One such riot in East St. Louis, Illinois, in 1917 caused the death of thirty-nine Negroes and eight whites. Local union branches were dismayed by this new competition but took no effective steps to organize the Negroes, despite the potential threat to working standards. The Negroes' bitter race consciousness, already aggravated by the knowledge that colored soldiers were fighting abroad for democracy, deepened in such hostile environments.

One of the greatest tasks of government and labor was to replace the tremendous shipping losses resulting from U-boat attacks and to build additional ships to transport men and supplies to Europe. Since the great days of the speedy clipper ships before the Civil War, American shippers had depended increasingly on foreign vessels. Although the rates were cheaper, the drawbacks to such a policy were revealed at the beginning of the World War when the Allies had to divert their ships to other uses. Acting on repeated recommendations, Wilson in September, 1916, brought about the creation of the United States Shipping Board, which operated the Emergency Fleet Corporation. Shipbuilding was retarded during the early months of our war effort by disputes as to whether the new ships should be made of steel or of wood; wood construction made possible greater speed in production. The fabulous wages paid shipyard workers and the extravagance and waste practiced in construction caused widespread criticism and further retarded production.

However, the appointment of Charles M. Schwab of the Bethlehem Steel Company as director general of shipbuilding resulted in a sharp rise in efficiency. Marshy wastes were transformed into shipbuilding centers, and a system of pre-fabricated standardized parts made rapid construction possible. When the armistice was signed, over 350,000 men, instead of the 50,000 employed in 1917, were engaged in shipbuilding. The Allies were greatly encouraged by the spectacular launching of 95 ships on July 4, 1918. During that one year 533 American vessels, aggregating over three million tons, were completed. These ships, together with the interned German vessels and various private craft which had been commandeered, meant that the "bridge to France," so ardently desired by the Shipping Board, had been built.

NATIONALIZING THE RAILROADS

The movement of troops and war materials put an unprecedented burden on the railroads. Early in the war, Wilson relied on the voluntary cooperation of the railroad operators, but conditions at the end of 1917 made it clear that individual patriotism and the profit motive were insufficient to give the war effort complete priority over purely civilian needs. For one thing, the railroad industry's strong individualist spirit, so characteristic throughout its history, prevented effective joint action by competing roads. Consequently, on December 26, 1917, Wilson proclaimed the complete unification of the railroads under a federal Railway Administration for the duration of the emergency; all private property rights were fully guaranteed. "Only under Government administration," the President told Congress, "can an absolutely unrestricted and unembarrassed common use be made of all tracks, terminals, terminal facilities and equipment of every kind."

Secretary William G. McAdoo, as the new director general of the railroads, became the "dictator of traffic." Passenger service and civilian freight were cut to a minimum, and trains, tracks, stations, and other facilities were operated as a unit regardless of ownership; both schedules and rates were made uniform. Because federal rates did not cover the higher costs resulting from the government's uneconomic use of the railroads, additional subsidies from the federal Treasury had to be drawn to meet the payments guaranteed the stockholders. Since its primary concern was to win the war, the Railway Administration gave precedence to financially unprofitable traffic at the expense of more lucrative civilian traffic. Before the war ended, the telephone and telegraph systems were nationalized by the Railway Administration and the leading express companies were consolidated under government management as the American Railway Express Company.

Many railroad officials, lamenting the government's tendency to "pamper" railroad employees, feared that federal policies would revolutionize labor relations completely. Long-standing restrictions to unionization were removed, and the privileged status of the powerful railway Brotherhoods, whose membership was composed of the most skilled employees, was reduced by a new policy of equal treatment for all. Wage increases were granted frequently because of the high cost of living. The Adamson Eight Hour Law, which offered time and a half for overtime, became firmly entrenched in the industry. Little wonder, therefore, that the employees vigorously resisted the postwar effort to turn the clock back to 1916. Management continued to hold the unionized shop committees responsible for a serious drop in efficiency, and opponents of government ownership cited this venture as proof of their contention.

THE FUEL CRISIS

Intimately related to the railroad problem was the serious fuel crisis caused by the shortage of coal and labor. One reason for the nationalization of the railroads was the fact that most of the nation's coal cars were being used during the fall and winter of 1917 for the shipment of last-minute orders placed by consumers who had waited in vain for the federal coal authorities to lower the prices. That winter several strategic harbors froze over and immobilized coal barges; overloaded trains were stalled by labor shortages and increased traffic. Particularly serious was the fact that thirty-seven munitions-laden ships were tied up in New York Harbor by the fuel shortage. The extremely cold weather that brought mining operations to a stop aggravated the situation even further. Thousands of cars had to be diverted to regions in urgent need of coal. Coal yards were repeatedly raided by crowds of shivering people; and churches, schools, factories, offices, homes, and theaters were poorly heated. So dangerously irregular was the gas service in some cities that gas burners were apt to go on or off without warning.

In desperation, Fuel Administrator Harry A. Garfield ordered all manufacturing plants east of the Mississippi River to close down for five days; heatless Mondays were to be observed until spring by all business and factory buildings not absolutely essential to the war effort. Miners responded generously to Garfield's appeal for their cooperation by working on holidays. State fuel boards imposed further restrictions on the use of coal and oil, and the following spring daylight-saving time was adopted to conserve fuel. From Marshal Foch came the grim warning, "If you don't keep up your oil supply, we shall lose the war." Sunday motoring was discontinued as the result of Garfield's appeal to an aroused public opinion. Meanwhile our output of oil steadily increased. It was inevitable that Garfield's program, particularly the curtailment of essential factory production at a time when the war demanded every ounce of industrial effort, should arouse considerable criticism. Ultimately, however, the public accepted its seeming inconsistencies and cooperated to the fullest extent.

HOOVER AND THE BATTLE OF FOOD

While the fuel crisis was at its height, Wilson was also struggling with the equally vital problem of food, so badly needed by the fighting forces abroad. Herbert Hoover of California, whom Wilson appointed Food Administrator, had already demonstrated his ability along these lines as head of the Commission for Relief in Belgium. At the outbreak of the war in Europe, Hoover, a graduate of Stanford University and a wealthy mining engineer, decided to devote himself henceforth to public service. He went to London, where Ambassador Page asked him to assist American refugees from the war zones. Page reported to Wilson that Hoover was a man of extraordinary energy and generosity.

After Belgium was reduced to destitution by the German invasion and the curtailment of vital food imports, Page asked Hoover to set up an emergency organization. The new Commission for Relief in Belgium was soon distributing $5,000,000 a month in foodstuffs alone; the thirty-five ships that sailed under its flag brought clothes donated by sympathetic Americans and wheat from the bountiful Argentine harvest, for American and Canadian crops were poor that year. "But for Hoover, Belgium would have starved," Page wrote Wilson. Hoover's work in Belgium was harassed by British charges—they were far from unjustified—that the supplies of food often went to the Germans or encouraged them further to deplete Belgium's own supplies on the theory that the Americans would make good the loss. The German occupation authorities sometimes doubted the military expediency of feeding the rebellious Belgians.

Although, as Baruch later observed, the Food Control Act of August 10, 1917, "fairly bristled with penal provisions" for its enforcement and gave the President and the Food Administrator the authority of food dictators, Hoover chose to rely on voluntary cooperation. He told Wilson that he would ask the women of the country to help, and that his staff, except for the clerks, would be composed of volunteers; he himself would serve without payment. Pleased at this repudiation of bureaucracy, Wilson praised the "justified reliance upon the freedom of individual initiative."

Hoover's task proved to be crucial in winning the war. Early in 1918 Lord Rhondda, British Food Controller, cabled him: "Unless you are able to send the Allies at least 75,000,000 bushels of wheat over and above what you have exported up to January 1, and in addition to the exportable surplus from Canada, I cannot take the responsibility of assuring our people that there will be food enough to win the war." When this message arrived, our own wheat stocks were low—only 30,000,000 bushels had been stored from our last harvest—Belgium needed 15,000,000 bushels if she was to avert starvation, and Cuba, on whom the Allies relied increasingly for sugar, required 10,000,000 bushels. Nevertheless, Hoover replied to Lord Rhondda: "We will export every grain that the American people save from their normal consumption."

Wilson's influence over Congress enabled Hoover to prevent farmers from hoarding their crops in the expectation of higher prices; however, a Senate farm bloc put up a strong fight against this program. Speculation on the grain exchange was curbed. To encourage greater wheat production, the price of wheat for the farmer was fixed at $2.20 per bushel; this was twenty cents above the minimum guaranteed by Congress. Women and children were urged to join a land army to combat the farm labor shortage. Wheat areas were expanded by forty million acres. Despite a severe drought during the summer of 1918, all types of farm production soared to record-breaking heights.

Hoover avoided using food cards and compulsory rationing for consumers. Instead, hoarders and profiteers were watched carefully; some dealers lost their licenses or were cut off from their source of supply. All wholesale food dealers, such as the great packing houses, were subject to a licensing system, and prices for basic foodstuffs like wheat, sugar, and meat were fixed after consultations with the major distributors. To provide shipping space for Cuba's exports of sugar to the Allies, the people accepted a voluntary form of rationing which limited each individual to three pounds of sugar per month; in July, 1918, this was cut to two pounds.

Most spectacular of Hoover's activities were those in behalf of food saving, a program popularized by George Creel's Committee of Public Information and its propaganda, such as the "Food Will Win the War!" posters. To "Hooverize" meant to live according to the "gospel of the clean plate"; so well was this lesson driven home to the American housewife that the decrease in garbage put some large collection agencies out of business. The wheatless and meatless days which helped to conserve essential foods for the Allies required no great sacrifice from the average citizen because ample supplies of other foods, particularly fruits and vegetables, were available. Hotels and restaurants were asked to cut down or eliminate the wheat products on their menus, and bakeries were expected to use substitutes for at least 20 per cent of this grain in their bread. Even small home owners became farmers on a modest scale through war gardens. To a nation where natural abundance encouraged wastefulness, the war food program had an intriguing element of novelty.

One significant provision of the Food Control Act authorized the President to forbid the manufacture of distilled spirits from foodstuffs. This was the first step toward prohibition. The sale and consumption of intoxicating liquors were temporarily prohibited in September, 1918, by the Agricultural Appropriation Act. Neither Wilson nor Hoover actually wanted prohibition as a wartime food control measure, for they believed that as a result beer drinkers would turn to whisky, which was more harmful and of which huge quantities of old stock were then available. Wilson advocated temperance or local option on prohibition but insisted that public opinion was the best regulator of the individual consumer. An important motive that gave prohibition a patriotic basis in some quarters was the bitter anti-German feeling created by the fact that many of the prominent brewers were German and hence were suspected of giving active aid to the enemy.

Screened behind a food economy measure, the dry forces, under the banner of the Anti-Saloon League, culminated a temperance crusade that had begun over a century before. Rural America, particularly the South, had already achieved prohibition by local action, for half of the states had voted to become dry. Nation-wide prohibition was to take permanent form with the passage of the Eighteenth Amendment in 1920. Grudgingly, the cities yielded to the will of the rural communities and undertook a half-hearted campaign against the saloon.

Another result of food control was our increasing economic hegemony over Cuba as we spurred the island on to produce one-fourth of the world's sugar. Using her dependence on American foodstuffs as a lever, the Food Administration exercised absolute control over the price of her sugar. A new federal corporation, the Sugar Equalization Board headed by Hoover, contracted for Cuba's entire crop at a price substantially below the world price. At the same time Hoover conceded the political wisdom of encouraging the organized American beet- and cane-sugar planters by granting them special price advantages. Despite this restriction on her profits, Cuba began to expand her sugar industry and attracted American capital in ever-increasing amounts.

All this activity culminated in the fantastic but short-lived prosperity of the immediate post-war era—the so-called Dance of the Millions.

LIBERTY BOND DRIVES

Financing the World War was a problem significant not only for its unprecedented magnitude but also for the social philosophy underlying the methods that were finally chosen to cope with it. The direct cost of the war, including loans of $9,500,000,000 to the Allies, totaled over $36,583,000,000. By 1918 the United States was spending one-fourth of her national income for war purposes. As the proponent of a people's war, Wilson inevitably aroused bitter criticism from business by the sweeping excess profits taxes imposed on corporate earnings, in addition to the heavy progressive income tax also paid by corporations. Certain classes of war profits were taxed a minimum of 80 per cent, and even the capital stock of corporations was subject to a steadily increasing levy. Small taxpayers likewise had to pay numerous excise taxes and higher income taxes.

Despite these pioneer and democratic steps in war taxation, the Wilson administration found it expedient, as the war effort expanded, to secure the bulk of its revenue from public borrowing, notably by the mass sale of Liberty and Victory bonds. An elaborate propaganda organization, the Committee on Public Information, vigorously pressed home the necessity of buying war bonds. Motion picture stars like Douglas Fairbanks, Sr., were among the "four-minute" men who spoke in theaters, churches, and community centers; artists, cartoonists, and publications of all types urged citizens to invest their savings in bonds. The first Liberty Loan drive for two billion dollars in June, 1917, was oversubscribed; almost twenty million Americans responded to the second drive in October, 1917; its goal was $3,800,000,000. This trend continued unabated in successive loan drives which were accompanied by the most extensive use of publicity in our history.

CREEL'S WAR

The Creel Committee, as the Committee on Public Information was often called, proved remarkable in many other ways besides selling war bonds on a mammoth scale. It represented a novel experiment in organized propaganda calculated to aid the war effort both at home and abroad. George Creel himself, a Denver journalist and an "original" Wilson man, had a crusader's temperament mellowed by a sense of humor. His journalistic gifts of persuasion had been signally demonstrated during the campaign of 1916 when he showed himself an effective champion of the New Freedom.

Wilson, who disliked censorship of the press even in wartime, was consequently impressed by Creel's argument that "expression, not repression" provided the remedy for disloyalty and war weariness. The program Creel outlined called for carrying our war aims to the man in the street, to Allies and neutrals, and, above all, to the enemy. Censorship should be voluntary and achieved by indirection, he maintained. An aroused public opinion would be more effective against disloyalty than any censor's arbitrary pencil. Newspapers, thirsty for real news under war restrictions, welcomed the exciting releases his committee offered them. Ultimately some 150,000 men and women from every walk of life participated in its far-flung activities. Creel's tactics were assailed by fastidious critics as pugnacious and intrusive, but his surprising success marked him as a master of mass psychology.

Creel's unyielding refusal to permit the publication of news that would aid the enemy was tempered by the interesting news stories prepared and released by his staff. Although his stories were frequently colored in the Allies' behalf, few of them were actually challenged because of untruth. Creel's ubiquitous connections with the Censorship Board, the Post Office Department, and the Department of Justice were sufficiently well known to suggest the power he might exercise in the case of a refractory newsman. Fortunately he used his authority with considerable restraint, although some of his decisions, particularly in connection with books, were questionable. For example, Thorstein Veblen's thoughtful analysis, *Imperial Germany and the Industrial Revolution* (1915), was regarded as damaging to the war effort and Postmaster General Burleson was asked to exclude it from the mails. In some cases radical labor propaganda was also conveniently disposed of as "pro-German."

Creel enlisted a host of scholars in several of the numerous divisions of his organization. Eminent historians in the Division of Civic and Educational Cooperation under Professor Guy Stanton Ford of the University of Minnesota published scores of pamphlets, articles, and encyclopedias to present the Allied case against Germany. Five and a half million copies of one pamphlet, *The Kaiserite in America,* were distributed. Some of the publications, especially those dealing with atrocities, were rather lurid for sober historians. There was a temptation to represent the extreme reactionary element in Germany as typical of the entire people. German *Kultur* became a sinister term for Teutonic brutality.

The Committee's divisions of labor publications and of industrial relations attempted to present the war as a conflict in behalf of better working conditions and greater regulation of capitalism by the government. Community singing was fostered to keep home morale high; the popular war song, "Keep the Home Fires Burning," was typical. A film division, in line with a taste already discovered by Hollywood, offered "wholesome" pictures to the exhibitors, and crowds gathered to see the *Wolves of Kultur, The Prussian Cur,* and most popular of all, *The Beast of Berlin.* The prewar Mexican screen villains yielded to monocled German plotters, often impersonated by Eric von Stroheim. Loyalty was encouraged among alien groups by various bureaus which prepared translations of pertinent material for immigrants in the interest of Americanization. The sale of war bonds and the popularizing of the draft drew upon the artistic talents of the Division of Pictorial Publicity headed by Charles Dana Gibson, originator of the attractive Gibson Girl and Miss Columbia. James Montgomery Flagg's poster showing an American citizen's reaction to a newspaper report of German brutality—"Tell That to the Marines"—had a sensational effect, as did also the recruiting poster on which Uncle Sam had his finger pointed at the spectator—"I want YOU for the United States Army."

Extremely significant among Creel's diverse activities were his efforts to foster a revolution in Germany; in this he used Wilson's idealistic speeches as his major weapon. The name of one of his organizations, Friends of German Democracy, implied the coming of a new social order in that country. Creel made certain that Wilson's program for the postwar world reached almost every part of the earth through newspapers, pamphlets, books, and posters. Germany, he proudly observed, was deluged with this type of propaganda; nor did the Germans on the battle line escape it. Perhaps Creel did his task too well, for his work contributed to the postwar disillusionment and hampered the defense effort of whole peoples two decades later when a worse danger than the Germany of 1914–1918 confronted the world.

THE DECLINE OF CIVIL LIBERTIES

Although during 1917–1918 Wilson devoted his energies to the restoration of freedom everywhere in the world, he seemed tragically unaware of the full extent to which federal and local agencies were repressing freedom at home. The responsibility rested in large part on the intolerant mob spirit that the war aroused and that condemned judicial restraint as unpatriotic and dangerous. Exaggerated reports of sabotage, spies, and systematic draft evasion fostered this popular intolerance. Professor Zechariah Chafee suggests that the old Civil War fear of mass disloyalty, such as that displayed by the Copperheads of the Old Northwest, was still alive. Nearly two thousand federal and local court actions were taken during the war against the perpetrators of allegedly seditious acts, many of which were merely the expression of radical economic and social doctrines.

Acting at first in a more moderate spirit, Congress passed the Espionage Act in June, 1917; this forbade any false statement which might injure the prosecution of the war and penalized any incitement to disloyalty or obstruction to recruiting. Much more restrictive was the Sedition Act passed on May 16, 1918; in effect it made punishable all statements calculated to bring into "contempt, scorn, contumely, or disrepute" our form of government, the Constitution, the armed forces, the flag, or the military uniform. Severe penalties up to twenty years' imprisonment were attached.

The effect of this legislation is made clear in Chafee's *Freedom of Speech* in which he says: "It became criminal to advocate heavier taxation instead of bond issues, to state that conscription was unconstitutional though the Supreme Court had not yet held it valid, to say that the sinking of merchant vessels was legal, to urge that a referendum should have preceded our declaration of war, to say that war was contrary to the teachings of Christ." A boardinghouse or smoking-car dispute over one of these points might bring the participant to court. Under a Minnesota espionage law an individual was imprisoned for saying to a group of women who were knitting for the Army, "No soldier ever sees these socks."

The movies occasionally felt the strong hand of censorship. One film, *The Spirit of '76,* which was produced before the United States entered the war, was seized by federal agents acting under the Espionage Act, on the ground that the Wyoming Massacre, which was shown in it, was offensive to our British allies because it depicted them killing women and children. The prosecution claimed that this episode had been deleted in the version that was submitted to the censor. The producer, after being sentenced to ten years in a federal penitentiary, was paroled at the end of three years and emerged from prison a bankrupt.

Under the legal doctrine of "remote bad tendency," critical and especially radical journals lost their vital mailing privilege. This was the case with the New York magazine, *The Masses,* and Victor Berger's socialistic *Milwaukee Leader,* both of which were suppressed by Burleson. The mild protest made by *The Nation* against the conduct of a slacker roundup by New York police brought its temporary suspension. Periodicals that criticized the British Empire or showed pro-Soviet leanings likewise faced suppression.

Radical leaders and organizations were given short shrift. The Socialist leader Eugene V. Debs was convicted of an alleged attempt to cause insubordination in the Army and to obstruct recruiting. In reality his offense lay in the fact that in a speech at a Socialist party convention he had declared parenthetically that war was the supreme curse of capitalism. State criminal syndicalist laws frequently made radicalism a form of sedition—the I.W.W. was pursued by both federal and state authorities on grounds of sedition.

Popular intolerance proved an active enforcement agency against suspects. Citizens of German extraction were always subject to attack in certain rural communities. The German language was barred in the schools, and even German music, German food, and German names suffered at the hands of self-appointed patriots.

Wartime restrictive legislation on freedom of speech and the press survived the war itself and proved a source of danger in the postwar reconstruction period. The statutes that attacked civil liberties during the war and that were originally intended solely to defend the nation from enemies within its borders were often made the means of insuring economic and social orthodoxy. This menace to freedom forecast the coming twilight of pre-1917 progressivism and of the New Freedom in particular.

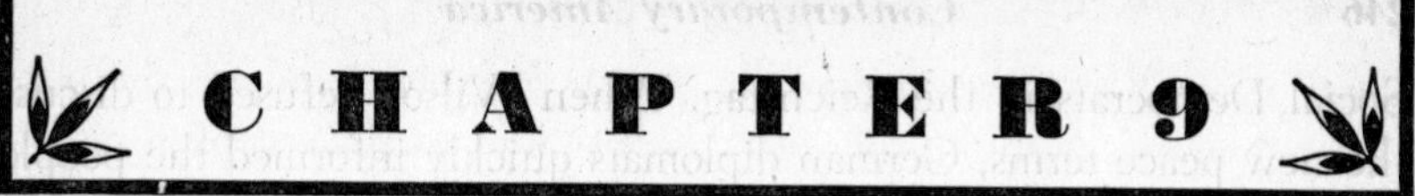

The Lost Peace

THE FOURTEEN POINTS AND LIBERAL NATIONALISM

"This agony must not be gone through with again," declared Wilson in rejecting Pope Benedict's appeal for a negotiated peace on August 15, 1917, while mighty armies were locked in bloody but seemingly indecisive combat on the vast European front. "We seek no material advantage of any kind, . . ." he asserted. "Punitive damages, the dismemberment of empires, the establishment of selfish and exclusive economic leagues we deem inexpedient and in the end worse than futile, no proper basis for a peace of any kind, least of all for an enduring peace." Apparently, now that the nation was a full-fledged belligerent, the President was convinced that peace without victory could not last. Certainly it would have been denounced by Americans and the other Allies.

"Let there be no next war!" reiterated the leading newspapers in New York, Baltimore, and Philadelphia in demanding unconditional surrender of the enemy. But the Central Powers, who had inflicted a crushing defeat on Italy at Caporetto shortly after annihilating the Russians in 1917, considered that anything less than a negotiated peace was fantastic. After still more spectacular victories on the western front during the spring of 1918, the German government, spurred on by the Social Democrats, addressed a new peace offensive to Wilson as the Allied spokesman. The German people were informed of the Bolshevik revelations regarding the secret treaties between the Czarist regime and the British and French, calling for the dismemberment of the Central Powers in the traditional imperialist style. This propaganda advantage was offset, however, by the harsh Treaty of Brest-Litovsk which Germany and Austria-Hungary imposed upon revolution-torn Russia in March, 1918, despite the outcry of "No annexations!" by the

Social Democrats in the Reichstag. When Wilson refused to discuss the new peace terms, German diplomats quickly informed the people that even Wilson demanded their country's total destruction as a requisite for peace.

On January 8, 1918, Wilson gave Congress a statement of our war aims formulated in the famous Fourteen Points. The idealism embodied therein shook the enemy people's will to resist and compelled their diplomats to exert themselves to the fullest in order to discredit the American President. The Fourteen Points may be summarized as follows:

1. Open covenants; openly arrived at. . . .

2. Absolute freedom of navigation upon the seas . . . alike in peace and in war. . . .

3. The removal, so far as possible, of all economic barriers. . . .

4. Adequate guarantees given and taken that national armaments will be reduced to the lowest point consistent with domestic safety.

5. A free, open-minded, and absolutely impartial adjustment of all colonial claims. . . . [The] interests of the populations concerned must have equal weight with the equitable claims of the government whose title is to be determined.

6. The evacuation of all Russian territory and such a settlement of all questions affecting Russia as will secure the best and freest cooperation of the other nations of the world in obtaining for her an unhampered and unembarrassed opportunity for the independent determination of her own political development and national policy. . . .

7. Belgium . . . must be evacuated and restored. . . .

8. All French territory should be freed and the invaded portions restored, and the wrong done to France by Prussia in 1871 in the matter of Alsace-Lorraine . . . should be righted. . . .

9. A readjustment of the frontiers of Italy should be effected along clearly recognizable lines of nationality.

10. The peoples of Austria-Hungary . . . should be accorded the freest opportunity of autonomous development.

11. Rumania, Serbia, and Montenegro should be evacuated; occupied territories restored; Serbia accorded free and secure access to the sea . . . and international guarantees of the political and economic independence and territorial integrity of the several Balkan states should be entered into.

12. The Turkish portions of the present Ottoman Empire should be assured a secure sovereignty, but the other nationalities which are now under Turkish rule should be assured an undoubted security of life and an absolutely unmolested opportunity to autonomous development, and

the Dardanelles should be permanently opened as a free passage to the ships and commerce of all nations under international guarantees.

13. An independent Polish state should be erected . . . which should be assured a free and secure access to the sea, and whose political and economic independence and territorial integrity should be guaranteed by international covenant.

14. A general association of nations must be formed under specific covenants for the purpose of affording mutual guarantees of political independence and territorial integrity to great and small states alike.

Although the Fourteen Points were ultimately discredited by the Allies themselves, in 1918 they seemed to herald the belated victory of liberal nationalism which had been arrested at the Congress of Vienna in 1815 by Metternich's feudally inspired paternalistic traditionalism. After one hundred years of nationalist struggles, the seal of legality was now to be given to the "self-determination" of peoples, and nations were expected to evolve peacefully under a powerful league of nations. The freeing of world channels of travel and trade would permit the smaller nations to live. That these war aims were conceived in no spirit of vindictiveness toward the enemy was made clear in Wilson's statement to Congress: "We have no jealousy of German greatness, and there is nothing in this program that impairs it."

WILSON'S APPEAL FOR A DEMOCRATIC CONGRESS

The failure of Germany's great offensive on the western front in July, 1918, followed by the Allies' sustained counterdrive, hastened the Central Powers' realization that they could not win the war. Accordingly Austria asked for peace terms on September 16 and on Wilson's insistence accepted an armistice based on the Fourteen Points and specifically recognizing the national aspirations of the Czechs, Slovaks, Serbs, Croats, and Slovenes. This demand for Austria-Hungary's virtual dissolution into component states indicated that the terms of Germany's surrender would also be rigorous. On October 6 Prince Max von Baden, the new German Chancellor, proposed a general armistice, but Wilson refused to accept the limited nature of the new constitutional reforms offered the German people. If the United States must deal with the "military masters and the monarchical autocrats of Germany," he insisted, we must demand surrender and not enter into peace negotiations. Thus in effect a republican revolution was forced upon Germany. On November 9 the Kaiser fled to Holland and two days later the armistice was signed.

The stage seemed set for the achievement of Wilson's fondest dream, a cooperative world order. Although our European allies were committed to secret treaties and objectives wholly at variance with the Fourteen Points, the President knew that Europe's dependence on us for financial and material aid in reconstruction would influence her to make concessions. Herbert Hoover was already feeding the people whom Germany and Austria-Hungary had conquered, and Creel had inspired Europeans with a fervent admiration of Wilson's ideals and with trust in America's leadership in creating a world society based on justice.

The President, however, committed a serious political blunder when on October 25, against Colonel House's advice, he appealed to the nation to elect a Democratic Congress. Numerous Democratic Congressmen who feared a Republican landslide had already asked his help privately in the coming election, but Wilson chose to follow the British custom of seeking the electorate's mandate for the government's policies. There was some precedent for such an appeal, for during the Spanish-American War President McKinley, supported by Roosevelt and Lodge, had tried to convince the voters that they must not repudiate the Administration in the critical months preceding peace. "If you have approved of my leadership," pleaded Wilson, "and wish me to continue to be your unembarrassed spokesman in affairs at home and abroad, I earnestly beg that you will express yourself unmistakably to that effect by returning a Democratic majority to both the Senate and the House of Representatives. . . ."

The Republicans indignantly charged that the President had violated the wartime truce on partisan politics; their attack was led by Theodore Roosevelt, despite his own repeated appeals to the electorate for support in the past. The G.O.P. won control of Congress by a narrow margin. Although the elections involved a host of personal and general issues unconnected with peace, disgruntled Democrats feared that Europe would regard the Republican success as a repudiation of Wilson's leadership. Wilson, however, interpreted it as the natural reaction to so long-lived an Administration and a rebuke to certain Congressmen but he could not disguise the fact that he was now a minority leader.

PARIS

In a dramatic move Wilson announced that he intended personally to head our peace delegation in Paris—an unprecedented step on the part of an American President. In accordance with a gentleman's agreement with Congress, important bills would be deferred until his return and certain minor bills would become law without his signature—a novel constitutional procedure. Secretary of State Lansing regarded Wilson's decision to take part in the peace negotiations abroad as a serious mistake, but his influence over the President had begun to wane. Nor was Wilson's poor health enough to thwart his desire to be present at the birth of a new world order.

His selection of members of the peace delegation aroused bitter criticism from the Republicans. Rather than include Henry Cabot Lodge, the obstructionist who later became chairman of the powerful Senate Foreign Relations Committee, Wilson chose the dangerous alternative of ignoring the Senate altogether. The delegates included only one Republican—Henry White, whose long record as a capable diplomat indicated no tendency toward party leadership. The other members were Colonel House, Secretary of State Lansing, and General Tasker H. Bliss. Some 300 experts of mixed political affiliations also accompanied the President. It was to be regretted that Taft and Root, both of them pioneer leaders of pro-league sentiment, were not among the delegates, but their exclusion was perhaps attributable to Wilson's distrust of lawyers. Nevertheless, the suggestions which the delegation received from Taft later in Paris were of great assistance.

On December 4, 1918, after solemn warnings from Senator William E. Borah of Idaho against any departure from our traditional isolationist policy, the President and the peace delegation sailed on the *George Washington*, formerly a German transport. During the voyage Wilson made it clear that he would defer to expert opinion on international problems and would accept the judgment of specialists in their own sphere. "Tell me what is right," he said, "and I will fight for it." The staff of experts which Colonel House had been collecting since

September, 1917, included numerous college professors and was armed with detailed investigations and reports.

Before the Peace Conference assembled, Wilson visited France, England, and Italy; the popular demonstrations he received everywhere were on a scale rarely accorded a visiting statesman. Pictures of him were displayed in windows in Italy, and some peasants were reported to be burning candles before his portrait. Premier Orlando, who headed the Italian delegation to the Peace Conference, told an Italian editor that his main policy was Wilsonism. Enthusiastic students at Polish universities greeted each other with the magic name of the "liberator of Poland." Persecuted Armenians and Jews, and suppressed Albanian, Ukrainian, Rumanian, and Jugoslav minorities made fervent appeals to Wilson in the confident expectation that all the wrongs of centuries would be righted. Almost every one of Wilson's speeches struck a note of idealism and emphasized a permanent organization for the maintenance of peace and justice rather than the everlasting punishment of Germany advocated by President Poincaré of France.

When the Conference convened on January 12, 1919, Wilson faced the most astute diplomats of Europe and Asia. Prime Minister Lloyd George brought with him the electorate's mandate, "Make Germany pay" (popularly construed as "Hang the Kaiser"). A decade earlier young Lloyd George had electrified reformers by his courageous attack on the evils of aristocratic land tenure in Britain, but the responsibilities of power thereafter led him to adopt a more temporizing attitude toward social panaceas. Nevertheless, despite the demand for vengeance, British opinion, from the conservative London *Times* and the House of Lords to the radical Labour and Socialist conferences, emphatically endorsed a league of nations. As a matter of fact, a detailed plan for such a league had been formulated in Britain years before the idea had crystallized in Wilson's mind.

Far less ebullient than Wilson and Lloyd George was Clemenceau of France, the elderly Premier who sustained his country's morale during the darkest hours of the war. Two decades earlier he had led the endangered democracy of France against the insidious attacks of reactionary monarchists when, with Émile Zola, he stubbornly defended the innocence of Alfred Dreyfus, the Alsatian Jew accused of selling military secrets to Germany; now the aged Premier seemed only to realize that he had seen two German invasions of his beloved country. Therefore he believed that salvation was to be found in the alliances of traditional diplomacy and the crushing of the enemy across the Rhine. Moreover, Clemenceau, who had little organized political strength in the National Assembly, was convinced that his countrymen would not support any treaty that made possible a future revival of German strength. Marshal Foch, the Allies' outspoken commander in chief, showed an even greater impatience with Wilsonian ideals; he advocated at least military control on the Continent as a prelude to the partitioning of Germany and the overthrow of the Bolsheviks in Russia.

Orlando of Italy admired Wilson, but he was committed to the realist policy of his nationalist-minded Foreign Minister, Sonnino, who demanded the complete fulfillment of the secret treaties of 1915 which had brought Italy into the war. Interventionists in Italy like the rising editor Mussolini and the poet d'Annunzio insisted that the Allies must give their country control of the Adriatic and the Brenner Pass, a slice of Asia Minor, and "compensation" in Africa. The Italian crowds which had cheered Wilson could not understand that these territorial demands were incompatible with the principles of a just and lasting peace.

THE LEAGUE COVENANT AND THE TREATY

Although Wilson lost an initial skirmish in behalf of wider publicity for Conference proceedings, he won the much more important battle to make the League project an integral part of the peace treaty. With the reluctant consent of the major powers, he sidetracked the controversial territorial questions in order to complete the Covenant of the League. To him the term "Covenant" suggested the organization established by his rebellious Presbyterian ancestors, the Covenanters. By becoming chairman of the League of Nations Commission the President made it impossible for the other Allies to ignore the Covenant. He also understood the task involved in reconciling the numerous conflicting League projects suggested by Europeans as well as Americans. While the language was unmistakably Wilsonian, the architects of the League's structure included not only the American President and his legal expert but also the idealistic Lord Robert

Cecil, Vice-Chairman of the Commission, General Jan Smuts, and a British law expert.

The League itself consisted of an executive Council of the five permanent members, Great Britain, France, Italy, Japan, and the United States; and four temporary members chosen by a second and larger body, the Assembly. Although the Council studied any threat to the peace of member states, it could render a decision in a dispute only by a unanimous vote. In the Assembly each League member received a single vote, but this body was primarily a deliberative rather than an executive group. The controversial Article X, which Wilson considered "the heart of the Convenant," required each nation "to respect and preserve against external aggression the territorial integrity and existing political independence of all members of the League." This broad commitment had a precedent in our own Articles of Confederation and Wilson's abortive Pan-American Pact of 1916. Scarcely less controversial was Article XVI, which imposed an economic boycott against League members who went to war in violation of their promise to submit the issue to arbitration or to the Council's decision. If necessary, the Council might even recommend specific military action by the League nations against an aggressor.

In the writings of Jan Smuts, a brilliant young South African general who had fought against the British in the Boer War and was now on the League of Nations Commission, Wilson found the mandate or trusteeship idea for the administration of the colonies formerly held by the defeated powers. Instead of being annexed outright in defiance of the wishes of its people, each colony would be administered by some nation in trust for the League until it showed itself to be ready for independence. Strangely enough, Smuts himself and the representatives of Australia and New Zealand insisted that defensive strategy required outright annexation of former German possessions in their own immediate vicinity. In fighting for the mandate system, Wilson was influenced by the precedents established by McKinley and Root in providing for the ultimate independence of the Philippines by gradual stages.

Deeply moved by the plight of the various racial minorities in Europe, Wilson insisted that such nations as Poland and Rumania, both of which received extensive benefits from the peace treaty, sign special treaties guaranteeing the political and cultural rights of the numerous minority groups within their borders. Article XI of the Covenant gave any nation the right, hitherto undetermined under international law, to call attention to "any circumstance whatever affecting international relations which threatens to disturb international peace or the good understanding between nations upon which peace depends." Such a provision in international law in 1903 would have enabled the United States to protest the Czarist pogrom against the Kishenev Jews through regular diplomatic channels. That minority rights continued to suffer in spite of Article XI is a commentary on the weakness of the League rather than the result of any real shortcomings in the written document.

After ten days of continuous work, Wilson appeared before a plenary session of the Conference on February 14 and read the completed Covenant. The fact that it was the unanimous report of fourteen nations seemed to assure its acceptance in Europe, but the attitude of the United States was uncertain. Accordingly he prepared to return to Washington for a short stay during which he would insure our acceptance of the Covenant and also attend to various official matters. During his absence from Paris, the nationalist forces strove to remake Europe in accordance with the secret treaties.

THE LODGE "ROUND ROBIN"

Isolationist Senators, chafing under the President's request to delay debate on the League until he could confer with the Senate leaders, were overtly impatient to assail the League Covenant. Senator Borah in a public controversy with Taft claimed that Article X nullified the traditional policy of the Monroe Doctrine and in support quoted a Brazilian diplomat who said: "The Monroe Doctrine, as I see it, is destroyed by the new League. There is no longer any reason why the United States should attempt to protect the Republics of the new world." Senator James Reed of Missouri, another isolationist, denounced the League as a British tool to insure world domination and a weapon to destroy our sovereignty.

Wilson chose to arrive in Boston rather than in New York, for he hoped by his public appearance in Massachusetts to undermine the strength of Senator Lodge in his home constituency. With prophetic vision the President warned in a speech made just after his arrival: "The peace of the world could not endure for a generation unless guaranteed by the united forces of the civilized world." Old powerful enemies, he said, were ready to pounce on each of the new nations of Europe at the first favorable moment. Much more difficult was Wilson's task of persuading his opponents in the Senate to accept the League without reservations. He held that the Monroe Doctrine had not been abandoned and that Congress still had the power to decide whether to send troops to Europe when in its opinion a League obligation was involved.

The President's Republican opponents chose the eve of his return to Paris to filibuster against a bill appropriating $750,000,000 for the railroads and they prevented action from being taken on other essential bills before adjournment. On March 4, the final day of the session, Henry Cabot Lodge hurled a parting shot at Wilson in his famous "Round Robin," a resolution signed by thirty-nine Senators and Senators-elect: "Resolved . . . That it is the sense of the Senate that while it is their sincere desire that the nations of the world should unite to promote peace and general disarmament, the constitution of the League of Nations in the form now proposed to the peace conference should not be accepted by the United States. . . ." Furthermore, the resolution demanded that the League should not be considered until a peace treaty had been signed. Wilson's defiant answer to this was given a few days later before a New York crowd as he was embarking for Europe: "When that treaty comes back, gentlemen on this side will find the covenant not only in it, but so many threads of the treaty tied to the covenant that you cannot dissect the covenant from the treaty without destroying the whole vital structure."

THE CONFERENCE: SECOND PHASE

On his return to Paris Wilson faced new difficulties which he suspected—perhaps unjustly—arose from concessions made by House and Lansing to the European nationalists. He yielded to Taft's insistence that an amendment regarding the Monroe Doctrine be offered to satisfy Lodge's supporters, and this was embodied in Article XXI: "Nothing in this Covenant shall be deemed to affect the validity of international engagements, such as treaties of arbitration or regional understandings like the Monroe Doctrine, for securing the maintenance of peace."

Wilson was indeed averse to "watering" any part of the Covenant, but he finally agreed to accept three other amendments (largely Taft's) as the price of support by moderate Republicans. In essence these amendments provided that (1) any member might withdraw from the League after two years' notice; (2) armament standards, the basis for future disarmament control, must be revised every two years; and (3) domestic questions should be withdrawn from the jurisdiction of the League. When these concessions ultimately failed to satisfy his opponents, Wilson was forced to doubt the sincerity of the Republican Senators. One concession led directly to another; moreover, each amendment that Wilson forced through usually compelled him to make some concession to the demands of Clemenceau and Lloyd George.

The inevitable conflict with Clemenceau was brought to a head by France's demands for the utmost protection against Germany. Despite the recommendation of American experts that the amount of reparations be definitely stated, the French and British, fearing political repercussions at home if the figure was too low, were successful in obtaining a blank check against Germany. While Wilson was pleading for rapid disarmament on the basis of League guarantees, France demanded an international army and navy and compulsory military service. In addition, the French economic experts sought Germany's economic disarmament through international control of her munitions factories; as an alternative they wanted military control of the Rhineland. Both Lloyd George and Wilson opposed compulsory military service in peacetime as alien to their country's traditions. Wilson further antagonized the French by refusing to permit Pershing's forces to cooperate in a French plan to form an independent Rhineland Republic from western Germany. For this he was sharply criticized by the extreme nationalist wing of the Paris press.

Even though he was stricken by influenza on April 3, Wilson's iron determination to hold French demands in check kept him busy, and eventually he was able to secure a compromise. The French were given the rich Saar coal basin for fifteen years, after which the status of the Saar would be determined by plebiscite. In return, Wilson promised to sign a treaty of alliance with Great Britain which provided that the armed forces of the two nations would assist France if Germany attacked her without provocation. The President regarded this as a temporary arrangement which would soon be supplanted by the cooperative machinery of the League of Nations; this treaty project was quietly forgotten in the struggle over the final ratification of the peace treaty.

The bitter controversy with France left its mark, for Wilson found himself almost isolated when the expansive demands of Italy and Japan were under consideration. Great Britain likewise resented our desire to reduce the size of her Navy. In November, 1918, Winston Churchill, then a member of the Cabinet, had said: "A league of nations is no substitute for the supremacy of the British fleet." Germany ended a dispute at the Peace Conference over the disposition of her fleet by scuttling it. Another undercurrent at the Conference was the fear that Communism might overwhelm Europe, particularly Hungary, which had been made a Soviet state temporarily, and Germany. French Army men supported the Jugoslavs against the Austrians, the Rumanians against the Hungarians, and the Poles against the Russians, in order to create a line of strong buffer states between Germany and Russia. Small nations looked to France rather than the League for protection in the future. Even American troops stationed in northern Russia and Siberia were drawn into the Franco-British intervention against Russia.

FIUME AND SHANTUNG

Italian claims for territory promised under the secret Treaty of London signed on April 26, 1915, found Wilson adamant, except for his earlier and much-regretted commitment by which, for strategic reasons, Italy was given the Brenner Pass and some 250,000 Germans in Tyrol. Orlando continued to insist that the important Dalmatian port of Fiume be ceded to Italy, a demand which Italian nationalists regarded as the core of their plan for Italy's complete domination of the Adriatic. In the secret Treaty of London Fiume had been promised to Croatia by the English and French, the Italians having originally given up their claim to it on the basis of a territorial "deal" with Bulgaria and Serbia that was never consummated. Sonnino said frankly that Italy had been offered territorial inducements by both the Central Powers and the Allies but had chosen to fight on the Allied side after a definite promise of large grants of territory. Lloyd George and Clemenceau, embarrassed by Italy's exaggerated claims which exceeded the concessions made in the Treaty of London, privately supported Wilson's position.

Wilson, following the recommendations of his advisers on Adriatic problems, refused to be bound by the secret treaties or to yield on the question of Fiume. His guiding principle of self-determination forbade such an injustice to the Jugoslavs. Much to the wrath of the Italian delegation but with the consent of Lloyd George and Clemenceau, Wilson attempted to bring this dispute to the attention of the world by issuing on April 23 a press statement which he specified was to be given wide publicity. When the Italian diplomats denounced this act as a subversive effort to create a breach between the Italians and their government, Wilson replied that he was interested only in having the problem receive consideration in the Italian Parliament. Unfortunately for Wilson, however, the nationalists had done their work too thoroughly for any democratic reaction to be possible on the part of the people. The Italian delegation applied additional pressure to Wilson by encouraging the circulation of a rumor that they intended to desert the Conference—as they did temporarily—if Fiume were awarded to the Jugoslavs. Eventually Italian nationalists, led by d'Annunzio, seized Fiume. The complete breakdown of the Conference seemed imminent when the Belgian delegation, dissatisfied with the reparations settlement, threatened to withdraw. At this point the hitherto quiet Japanese delegates broke their silence by emphatically demanding Germany's economic privileges in the Shantung peninsula which Japan had seized during the war. This made Wilson's position even more delicate. He had already expressed opposition to Japan's earlier proposal for an amendment to the Covenant that would provide for racial equality. Fully cognizant of California's position on Japanese immigration and landownership, Wilson had argued that the League guaranteed the equality of nations but could not be expected to deal with such purely domestic questions as immigration.

Here too Wilson learned that a secret treaty had been concluded between Japan and the Allies in 1917 which promised Japan both Germany's rights in the Shantung peninsula and her island possessions north of the equator; the islands she owned to the south were to be annexed by Australia and New Zealand. Lloyd George, whose nation had been allied with Japan since 1902, explained that the British and French had made these commitments in return for valuable assistance received from her in the submarine warfare. Wilson in turn informed Lloyd George of the infamous Twenty-One Demands which Japan had secretly imposed upon China in January, 1915, in an attempt to establish a protectorate and economic control over eastern Asia. Wilson had learned of these demands despite Japan's threats to China if they were divulged and had exerted as much diplomatic pressure against them as was possible.

Britain had been unenthusiastic regarding Japan's entrance into the World War. The Nipponese quickly ejected the Germans from Shantung and demanded, as a price for its ultimate return to China, more economic concessions than Germany had ever enjoyed. China's eloquent delegate to the Peace Conference, Wellington Koo, protested Japan's retention of Shantung because this peninsula with its 36,000,000 people was strategically important to China in safeguarding against domination by a foreign power; furthermore, as the birthplace of Confucius it was sacred to the Chinese. The Japanese ignored China's appeal and threatened to bolt the Conference if the Shantung question was not settled immediately.

Wilson finally yielded to a compromise which gave Shantung to Japan if she would formally declare her intention ultimately to restore it to China. This was the price he paid to save the League in the face of a possible Japanese-German-Russian alliance against the Allies. Japan refused to give anything but an oral promise or to agree to seek peaceful redress through the League of Nations if China failed to live up to her promise that Shantung would be policed by both Japanese and Chinese. Wilson in turn insisted that nothing he said should be construed as recognition of the Sino-Japanese "agreements" of 1915 and thereafter. The Chinese, bitterly disappointed at this "betrayal," refused to sign the Treaty of Versailles.

END OF THE CONFERENCE

Misunderstandings and disappointments surrounded Wilson. For example, Irish-Americans, unaware of his informal efforts in behalf of Irish independence, denounced him as a British puppet because he failed to demand self-determination for Ireland at the peace table. It was difficult to convince these partisans that the Peace Conference had dealt only with the disposition of territory held by the Central Powers; moreover, the prospect that the new League of Nations would solve the Irish problem seemed remote in view of the six votes exercised by Great Britain and her dominions in the Assembly, where each nation had one vote. Similarly, American Zionists were disappointed by the report of the American Commission to Syria and Palestine which was unfavorable to the establishment of the Jewish homeland in Palestine that the famous Balfour Declaration had promised. To Clemenceau, Wilson seemed pro-German at times, whereas the Italians assailed him as pro-Jugoslav. Since signing the Treaty of Versailles was a prerequisite to sharing in the reparations paid by Germany, Italy finally affixed her signature, but she did so in the conviction that Wilson had robbed her of a well-earned reward.

Although politically Wilson's peace program was well integrated, economically it was uncoordinated. For one thing, he could scarcely attempt the removal of tariff barriers called for in his Fourteen Points because Congress, in which the protectionist Republicans were in the majority, would almost certainly repudiate such a move. The economic experts Wilson chose were all able men—Herbert Hoover, Bernard Baruch, Thomas Lamont, Norman H. Davis, and Vance McCormick, for example—but their strong individualist bias opposed any effective economic cooperation among nations. Apparently all of them favored a strict policy of private initiative, tempered, however, by generous relief to the distressed areas. Thus when Wilson argued that Germany must not only be fed but have access to raw materials if she were to make any reparations payments, Clemenceau retorted: "To do this would be to turn the world upside down. It would not be the conquerors but the conquered who came out best."

The peace treaty was finally signed on June 28, 1919, at Versailles, where the previous generation of victorious Germans had celebrated their country's unification symbolically over the body of a prostrate France. Now vanquished, Germany was curtly asked to sign a document which imposed a heavy burden on her people and included the humiliating "war guilt clause" (Article 231) in which she accepted the responsibility for all Allied loss and damage caused by "the war imposed upon them [the Allies] by the aggression of Germany and her allies." Wilson, although aware of the shortcomings of the treaty, did not consider it basically unjust. "I believe, even, that a hard peace is a good thing for Germany herself, in order that she may know what an unjust war means," he observed. "We must not forget what our soldiers fought for, even if it means that we may have to fight again." However, both Wilson and Colonel House believed that the League of Nations, if universally accepted, would eliminate the injustices of the treaty.

To Professor Charles Seymour of Yale, who had intimate knowledge of the Conference, Wilson's Fourteen Points seemed far from being hopelessly lost in the final treaty, despite such charges by many liberal critics; actually, these principles were realized to a surprising extent. The broad concept of the self-determination of peoples had to be whittled down in practice in a number of instances because of economic, geographic, strategic, and conflicting nationalist factors. Nevertheless, Czechs and Slovaks, Serbs, Croats, and Slovenes, Russian and Austrian Poles, and other nationalities had been freed to begin an independent if troubled national existence. France yielded several vital guarantees she had originally demanded for her defense, only to realize scarcely a generation later how well founded were her fears of future German aggression.

The peacemakers, however, could not foresee the full evil consequences of the unworkable economic settlement, nor did they allay the rising nationalist fever and the fear of Communism that lingered among Europe's medley of peoples. The Fascist spirit, far from affecting only the vanquished at the Versailles Conference, quickly infiltrated a victorious Allied power like Italy as well as a defeated Germany brooding over her lost cause. German critics of the Versailles Treaty were to forget that the war rather than the peace bankrupted the world of 1914; and the extreme German nationalists of the 1930's, convinced by the Hitler myth that an unconquered German Army had been "stabbed in the back" in the "final quarter of the hour" before victory, avidly believed that all the evils of postwar Germany grew out of the Versailles Treaty.

"MR. WILSON'S LEAGUE"

In spite of persistent objections to the treaty on the part of the Senate, Wilson was optimistic regarding its final acceptance by the United States. Public opinion polls indicated that the majority of the people supported the League, and at least thirty-two state legislatures had already passed resolutions endorsing it. Only a handful of Senators—the thirteen irreconcilables led by Borah, Hiram Johnson, and La Follette—actually opposed the treaty *in toto* and denounced the sinister international interests allegedly behind it. Even Lodge was known to have favored some form of league, but his strong nationalism and his dislike of Wilson compelled him to insist on sweeping reservations and amendments. From the outset Wilson indicated his intention of forcing the treaty through in its present form; for he had no desire to reopen negotiations which might conceivably break down and leave the world ripe for revolution and new wars. On June 25, shortly before his departure from Europe, Wilson cabled Tumulty as follows: "My clear conviction is that the adoption of the treaty by the Senate with reservations will put the United States as clearly out of the concert of nations as a rejection."

On July 10 Wilson presented his case to the Senate in person. The United States, he said, was "no longer isolated and devoted to a policy which has only our own interests and advantage for its object. It is our duty to go in, if we are indeed the champions of liberty and right." At first the debate was encouraging. Senator Knox's resolution to the effect that the Senate would reject the treaty if it included the League Covenant failed to receive sufficient votes for its passage. Forty Senators, most of them Democrats, favored the treaty without reservations, and forty-three others were prepared to accept it with reservations; only eight opposed the League in any form, and five were still undecided. The overwhelming majority of Senators favored some plan for a league of nations—if not "Mr. Wilson's League."

In an attempt to win support, the President conferred privately with certain Senators on August 19. After the conference, however. Borah and Johnson released a statement declaring that their worst fears had been justified: The President wished the United States to guarantee unjust territorial settlements made on the basis of secret treaties. Wilson had been the only disinterested person at the peace table, they claimed, and now he was unwilling to give full details regarding certain negotiations. Article X, which provided for a League guarantee of the territory and independence of each member, implied no ordinary moral obligation but "compelling force," as the President himself admitted.

To men like Lodge and Fall of New Mexico who were actively marshaling the extreme reservationists behind the Senators who wanted to dilute the League just as they had done earlier in connection with arbitration, the major source of inspiration at first was, strangely enough, the Republican "elder statesman," Elihu Root. The one-time Cabinet member under McKinley and Roosevelt had been a lifelong advocate of the rule of international law, and he was one of the original proponents of the World Court suggested in the League of Nations Covenant. But in conservative legalist fashion he had frequently shown an inclination to defer to Senate nationalists like Lodge who demanded that all vital national questions be exempt from the procedures embodied in the arbitration treaties made by Root as Secretary of State under Roosevelt. Root opposed Article X in its entirety because the treaty provided for territorial boundaries which violated the principle of nationality. Nothing in the treaty, he felt, must be construed as giving up our "traditional attitude toward purely American questions" (the Monroe Doctrine) or submitting such questions to other powers. Theoretically Root recognized that a bona fide international agreement meant the limitation of national sovereignty, but he seemed unwilling to fight for this principle as vigorously as did Wilson or Taft. Not until it was too late did Root attempt to restrain Lodge in opposing the President's program. He had already provided a much-needed justification for Lodge's reservations.

WILSON'S COLLAPSE

Democratic Senators, fearful of defeat, encouraged Wilson to undertake a three-week trip, a "swing around the circle," through the Middle West and Far West in September to give the electorate firsthand information regarding his program. Wilson's physician, convinced that this might cost him his life in view of his poor physical condition, tried to dissuade him, but the President persisted in regarding himself as a soldier on the field of battle and refused to be deterred by daily headaches and accumulated fatigue. At Columbus, Ohio, he gave the first of some thirty-seven speeches that comprised his heavy program. In vigorous and persuasive language he urged the ratification of the treaty as marking the beginning of a new era of world cooperation. The League Covenant, and particularly Article X, received most of his attention. Even Henry Cabot Lodge, he pointed out in one speech, had once concurred in the principle embodied in this article, for in an address at Union College in June, 1915, he had said: "Nations must unite as men unite in order to preserve peace and order. . . . In differences between nations which go beyond the limited range of arbitral questions, peace can only be maintained by putting behind it the force of united nations determined to uphold it and prevent war." Lodge had reaffirmed this a year later in a speech before the League to Enforce Peace, when he decried isolationism in no uncertain terms.

So successful was Wilson in his appeal to the people that the isolationists arranged for Borah and Johnson to follow him in an effort to refute his arguments. Shortly afterward, however, the President was stricken by partial paralysis at Pueblo, Colorado, and was brought back to Washington. An invalid thereafter, he was carefully shielded—perhaps too carefully—from political affairs by his wife and Tumulty. Meanwhile, the Senate was growing in stature politically and the reservationists were steadily winning ground.

DEFEAT OF THE TREATY

The first tactics resorted to by the Lodge forces were to prolong the debate over the treaty in order to dampen the popular enthusiasm for it. To this end the Lodge-dominated Senate Committee on Foreign Relations showed extraordinary interest and patience in according public hearings to numerous private individuals and representatives of organizations who professed an opinion on the treaty. Not until September 4 did the Committee make its report, and then it decried the impatience of the Administration press and the alleged sinister force exerted by "certain great banking firms."

The treaty as reported contained forty-five amendments and four reservations, which if adopted would probably compel renegotiation in Europe. Betraying a strong nationalist bias, the majority report assailed Articles X and XVI, providing respectively for economic sanctions against aggressors and that the United States agree to administer at least one of the territorial mandates offered by the League. It denounced the League as a system of alliances that would breed war rather than insure peace. After consulting various Republican leaders, Lodge succeeded in having his fourteen reservations substituted for the original four. In line with a suggestion made by Root, Lodge demanded that ratification of the treaty by the United States be withheld until the reservations had been accepted by three of the four principal powers.

Lodge's reservations showed clearly his deep-seated suspicion of international engagements on really vital issues which might be binding in effect and possibly diminish the power of Congress in foreign affairs. They completely rejected Article X, left the use of military force entirely up to Congress, and insisted that the United States was to be the sole judge regarding her obligations should she decide to withdraw from the League. The question whether the nation was to accept or reject a territorial mandate under the League was likewise to be decided only by Congress. As for the Monroe Doctrine, this was placed emphatically outside the League's jurisdiction. In regard to the unpopular Shantung settlement at Versailles, we reserved complete freedom of action. Finally, the reservations provided that this country be protected against any inequality in voting such as that resulting from the combined votes of Great Britain and her Dominions.

The Lodge resolutions, wrote Wilson to Hitchcock, Democratic leader in the Senate, would nullify the treaty, not ratify it; whereupon Hitchcock warned his opponents: "President Wilson will pocket the treaty if the Lodge program of reservations is carried out in the ratifying resolution." Wilson asked his supporters to vote against the amended treaty in order to open the door to a "genuine resolution of ratification"—a move already decided upon by the majority of Democratic Senators. The result of this maneuver, when the vote was taken on November 19, was to unite Borah's thirteen irreconcilables with Wilson's forty-two Democratic supporters, which meant the defeat of the treaty; thirty-nine reservationists, including four Democrats, voted for it. At no time was either side able to muster the two-thirds vote needed for ratification.

Some true friends of the League, like Taft, feared that Wilson himself might kill it unless he made additional concessions. Lodge, casting the responsibility for the defeat of ratification wholly on the President, refused to heed the pleas of Root and Taft for compromise. Herbert Hoover, who soon became a mild reservationist, had supported Wilson unreservedly in a speech a few weeks earlier. "I am confident," he stated, "that if we attempt now to revise the treaty we shall tread on a road through European chaos. Even if we managed to keep our soldiers out of it we shall not escape fearful economic losses. If the League is to break down we must at once prepare to fight. Few people seem to realize the desperation to which Europe has been reduced."

Reconsideration of the treaty was inevitable and the forces which insisted on compromise were already in motion. Wilson refused to yield —as did Lodge—insisting that the Senate reservations must not go beyond an interpretation of the treaty. He evidently distrusted the motives of his opponents and regarded the struggle as a selfish partisan attack on the treaty and himself. In a message to fellow Democrats at the Jackson Day dinner on January 8, 1920, Wilson called his party to battle. Assailing halfway measures toward world cooperation, he said: "The maintenance of the peace of the world and the effective execution of the treaty depend upon the whole-hearted participation of the United States." Refusing to accept the decision of the Senate as that of the nation, Wilson demanded "a solemn referendum" on the treaty in the forthcoming presidential election. Lodge had previously indicated his desire to make the treaty an election issue. Bryan disagreed with the President and pointed out that while he had supported Wilson on the treaty up to that time, the situation now called either for compromise or for an admission of defeat. Other Democrats realized that to make the treaty an issue in a heated presidential election might destroy the League completely and end any possibility of a compromise between the Senate factions. Nevertheless, the party stood by the President and partly as a result met crushing disaster.

A few weeks later the British tried tactfully to bridge the gap between Lodge and Wilson. Viscount Grey, who had been Foreign Secretary and was now a special ambassador to the United States, wrote an open letter to the London *Times* ostensibly to present our position on the treaty to Englishmen. After pointing out that the League would be severely limited if the United States failed to join it, he intimated that the Allies would welcome us even with such resolutions as those suggested by Lodge, except for the one dealing with the British Empire's plural votes. This opinion, it was surmised, had been approved by Prime Minister Lloyd George.

Wilson, however, had already indicated his willingness to compromise along the lines suggested in Grey's letter by accepting certain reservations proposed by Senator Hitchcock which went far toward meeting the chief objections of the Republican reservationists to the treaty. Especially encouraging was the fact that most of the Senate Democrats signed a round robin definitely agreeing to Taft's proposed reservation to Article X. This reservation denied any "binding obligations" by the United States to preserve the territory or independence of any nation except when Congress decided that a moral obligation exists. Compromise between parties seemed close. At this juncture all hopes of agreement were dashed by the emphatic threat of Senator Borah and his intransigent group to depose Lodge as Senate leader and disrupt the party if the Republicans voted for the treaty. To preserve party unity, Lodge submitted the Democratic compromise offer to his Foreign Relations Committee without any recommendation, thus terminating the episode. On March 19, 1920, the Senate voted on the original fourteen reservations, which had been increased to fifteen by the addition of one dealing with Irish independence that was almost certain to irritate England and perhaps prevent us from joining the League. Even though Wilson's supporters had dwindled, only 49 Senators could be mustered for Lodge's version of the treaty. Since this was insufficient to meet the two-thirds requirement, the treaty became an issue in the presidential election that year.

THE SENATE CLIQUE AND THE VICTORY OF NORMALCY

The Democrats gathered at San Francisco on June 28 to nominate their presidential candidate. The platform they drew up indicated their firm intention to endorse Wilson's handling of the League controversy, and demanded immediate ratification of the treaty with no vitiating reservations. It also promised independence to the Filipinos and expressed sympathy with Ireland's struggle for freedom. Foreign affairs rather than domestic issues were emphasized.

Wilson, unable to leave the White House, maintained only indirect contact with the convention and refused to exert any pressure even when leaderless Democrats became deadlocked while voting on the nomination of a candidate for the Presidency. When Attorney General A. Mitchell Palmer of Pennsylvania announced his candidacy and offered to resign from the Cabinet if his presence embarrassed his chief, Wilson refused to accept the offer. Even more embarrassing was the fact that his son-in-law William G. McAdoo was a candidate; but here too the President remained strictly neutral, refusing to discuss McAdoo's candidacy with even such an intimate adviser as Tumulty.

After the convention had reached its forty-fourth ballot, Governor James M. Cox of Ohio, a former newspaper publisher, was chosen, the vice-presidential nomination going to the Assistant Secretary of the Navy, Franklin D. Roosevelt of New York. Both men were strong advocates of the League as formulated by Wilson. In fact, despite the warnings of his political advisers, Cox paid Wilson a visit at the White House in order to identify his course of action publicly as the President's. In the campaign, Cox emphasized the League issue but failed to arouse any great degree of public interest.

The Republicans, confident that the congressional elections of 1918 portended victory in 1920, convened on June 8 in Chicago. There were several strong contenders for the presidential nomination. The party was particularly interested in the hard-fought pre-convention campaign from which General Leonard Wood, Governor Frank O. Lowden of Illinois, and Senator Hiram Johnson of California emerged as the three most likely possibilities. Further down the list were Herbert Hoover, Senator Warren G. Harding, Charles Evans Hughes, and Calvin Coolidge, governor of Massachusetts. Pre-nomination contributions by oil, steel, and utility corporations reached unprecedented figures; a Senate investigation prompted by the charges made by Borah and Johnson revealed that Wood and Lowden, the leading candidates, were heavily indebted to big business. Leadership at the convention was assumed by the party Senators—Lodge, Fall, Smoot, Brandegee, and their colleagues—several of whom were themselves candidates. In the now-famous "smoke-filled rooms," the Senate clique decided to support Warren G. Harding of Ohio. Harding was nominated on the tenth ballot, with Calvin Coolidge as his running mate.

Harding owed his victory both to the brilliant leadership of his manager, Harry M. Daugherty, and to the exhausting battle waged by the candidates whose chances had been considered far stronger than his. As the owner of a small newspaper in Marion, Ohio, and as Senator, his record had been undistinguished. In the treaty fight he was close to Lodge, but his background in foreign and domestic affairs alike was extremely weak. Personally honest, always amiable, and with few enemies among Republicans, he had an accepted place among the party's standpatters. His chief weaknesses, as later events revealed, were his overdeveloped sense of loyalty to his political associates regardless of their misdeeds, and his naïve trust in political adventurers who sought favors from him. Regardless of his modest record of achievement, Harding seemed attractive to an electorate that was experiencing a general slump in idealism.

The Senate clique faced a difficult task in formulating a platform that would deal adequately with the League. On one side there were the rabid irreconcilables like Borah and Johnson who wanted no league whatsoever; in the center were the extreme reservationists like Lodge; and on the other side were the mild reservationists like Root, Taft, Hoover, and Hughes. Root cut the Gordian knot by pledging the party in vague terms to "agreement among the nations to preserve the peace of the world." The rest of the platform, which was devoted to foreign policy, criticized Wilson to such an extent, especially his treatment of Mexico, that the party's future trend toward strict isolationism was clear. Lodge's speech at the convention made it evident that the chief issue was Wilson and his associates and that they must be divested of all control and influence in the government. The New Freedom in business and industry and Wilson's strong League of Nations were to be destroyed—at least many campaign contributors believed this.

While Cox was actively canvassing the nation in a vain effort to win votes, Harding shrewdly engaged in a front-porch campaign in the McKinley tradition and read carefully prepared speeches to various visiting delegations. Following a lifelong habit, he so obscured his position on the League as to satisfy each audience he addressed. Party members who favored the League were alternately encouraged and disappointed as Harding spoke enthusiastically about an "association of nations" one day and the next day denounced the League as a "fraud." Cox's support of the Covenant forced Harding to assume an increasingly hostile attitude toward ratification, even with reservations.

Characteristically, the Republican advocates of a strong league of nations once more deceived themselves into thinking that they could accomplish their object by defeating Cox. Accordingly, in October, 1920, they formed the Committee of Thirty-One, whose function was to convince the voters that Cox's election would mean another stalemate between the Executive and the Senate because he was pledged to Wilson's uncompromising methods; therefore only a Harding victory could save the League. This Committee included some of the most distinguished members of the Republican party—Hoover, Hughes, Root, A. Lawrence Lowell, president of Harvard, Nicholas Murray Butler, president of Columbia, and William Allen White, the journalist, among others. At the same time Borah and Johnson were urging the election of Harding as a guarantee of our not joining the League. Such confusion prevented the appearance of any clear-cut issue in the election that year.

Harding's platitudes were pleasing to many people who were anxious to forget the war and return to their everyday tasks. His emphasis on the homely virtues, the glory of womanhood, and the rural tradition was evidently more effective than Cox's well-reasoned and forthright appeals. One statement in particular appealed to a large portion of the press: Harding's declaration in May that the nation needed "not heroism but healing, not nostrums but normalcy, not revolution but restoration, not agitation but adjustment, not surgery but serenity, not the dramatic but the dispassionate, not experiment but equipoise, not submergence in internationality but sustainment in triumphant nationality." In this were implied all of Wilson's failings—heroics, nostrums, revolution, agitation, drastic action, dramatization, experimentation, and internationalism. No more professorial supermen! was the note struck by Republican campaigners.

Coolidge, although friendly to the idea of a League, felt compelled to follow the line adopted by Harding in regard to Wilson. Referring to the proposed Covenant without reservations, he remarked: "To a league in that form, subversive of the traditions and the independence of America, the Republican party is opposed." But other issues influenced the campaign—the high cost of living, complaints of gross profiteering, and the increasing unemployment. The postwar discontent tended to endow Harding with fanciful virtues, for the country was preparing to return to its traditional allegiance to the Republican party, from which it had departed only occasionally since the Civil War.

Election day brought victory to Harding in genuine landslide fashion, as witness his 404 electoral votes to Cox's 127. In the popular vote he received over 16,100,000 ballots, while Cox polled slightly less than 9,150,000. The Democratic candidate failed to carry any state outside the Solid South and even there Tennessee swung to Harding. Eugene V. Debs, whom Wilson denounced as a traitor when he refused him a pardon, campaigned for President on the Socialist ticket from the penitentiary (his campaign pictures showed him behind bars in the regulation prison stripes) and won almost 920,000 votes. The election seemed a tragic repudiation of the sick man in the White House who had dreamed of world-wide victory for his New Freedom.

In his victory speech Harding announced that the League was dead, that it had been killed by the election which he now interpreted as being a popular referendum on the question. The fight over whether the League was to be adopted with or without reservations had in his mind become a question of having any league at all. After his inauguration, Harding declared that his administration had "definitely and decisively" put the League aside. "It doesn't propose to enter now by the side door, back door, or cellar door." The Committee of Thirty-One was rewarded when two of its members, Hughes and Hoover, were given posts in the new Cabinet. Subsequently Harding made an attempt to bring the United States into the World Court, but he retreated gracefully at the first sign of Senate disapproval. Technically the United States remained at war with Germany until July 21, 1921, when Congress passed a joint resolution simply declaring the war at an end.

Wilson was thoroughly embittered by his resounding defeat. Of those who spurned the League he observed privately: "They have disgraced us in the eyes of the world. The people of America have repudiated a fruitful leadership for a barren independence. . . . The enemies of this enterprise cleverly aroused every racial passion and prejudice, and by poisonous propaganda made it appear that the League of Nations was a great Juggernaut which was intended to crush and destroy instead of saving and bringing peace to the world." Because we had lost world leadership, he grimly predicted, "soon we will be witnessing the tragedy of it all."

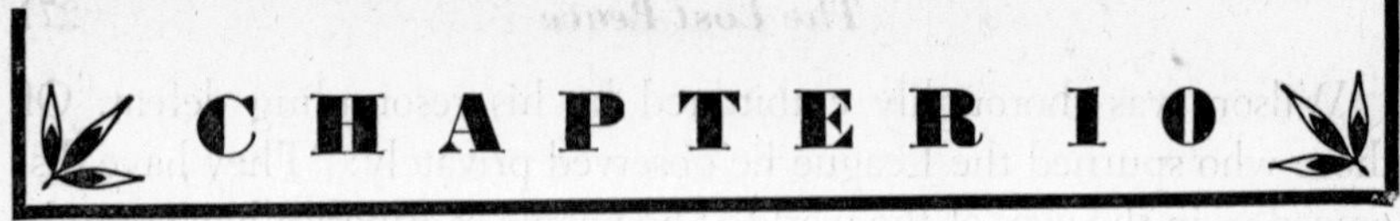

Demobilization and the Red Hunt

THE CHAOS OF RECONSTRUCTION

Germany's surrender caught the United States woefully unprepared for any concerted plan of domestic reconstruction. Wilson's defeat in the congressional elections of 1918, as we have seen, destroyed his effectiveness as the nation's leader during the postwar reconstruction period. Throughout the critical year of 1919, all his energies were concentrated on the single object of winning the peace; but thereafter, because he was an invalid as well as a minority President, he was unable to serve his country as its active leader. Anarchic forces of capital and labor, of nationalism and revolution, and of mass intolerance shook the nation. Business sought to undo the progress of unionism which Wilson and the necessities of war had promoted. Labor, conscious of new power and solidarity, struck back fiercely in its determination to retain all it had gained since 1914.

Congress and the President were soon deeply absorbed in the League issue and partisan conflicts, leaving the process of demobilization to the individual military and civilian agencies. As James R. Mock and Evangeline Thurber point out in *Report on Demobilization,* Congress, suspicious of the President's wartime powers, passed no important measure of reconstruction during the critical months before and after the Armistice.

Pressure from the veterans and their families compelled the speedy demobilization of most of the 4.5 million servicemen, regardless of employment opportunities—a process largely finished within a year. In their search for jobs these men were aided only by scattered efforts of governmental and private agencies. To make matters worse, Congress practically abolished the experienced United States Employment Service in response to conservative charges that this agency was manned by sentimental and radical social workers who coddled labor. Hundreds of thousands of war workers were suddenly discharged during the winter of 1918–1919 as the War Industries Board (minus the steadying hand of Bernard Baruch, who resigned in protest) and other agencies ruthlessly canceled war contracts, thus eliminating industrial "war babies" and in many cases shifting the burden of plant conversion to businessmen who were frequently handicapped by obsolete machinery and the loss of prewar customers. Thousands of federal employees were stranded in Washington because no provision had been made for the contingency of peace. Plans were nebulous for the disposition of the huge surplus of war materials which acted as a depressing influence on industry and employment.

"It is surprising," observed Wilson optimistically in his annual message on December 2, 1918, "how fast the process of return to a peace footing has moved in the three weeks since the fighting stopped." The American businessman, according to the President, was showing a "quick initiative" in shaping the course of reconstruction. All the government could do was to "mediate the process of change"; no quarter had advocated forcing any scheme upon "our spirited businessmen and self-reliant laborers." For these reasons Wilson wished to relax the wartime restraints on business as rapidly as possible, especially by a prompt reduction of taxes and by economy in government. Although he was ready to scrap wartime controls over business, he had no desire to return to the prewar anarchy of unregulated competition. He asked that the railroads retain some form of public regulation which would eliminate wasteful competition by promoting a unified transportation system. Believing that *laissez faire* would not provide immediate jobs for discharged veterans, he asked Congress to authorize large-scale public works which would hasten the development of hitherto unused lands and natural resources. A reclamation program which would use submarginal lands for the resettlement of veterans, he believed, would aid the nation as a whole as well as the returning servicemen.

Despite certain progressive ideas, the President's message dismayed many liberals, for they interpreted it as bringing to an end the prewar crusade against capitalist monopoly. Congressional conservatives, distrustful of Wilson, defeated his demobilization program. Farmers, organized in the National Grange, feared the competition of servicemen in newly reclaimed lands. Businessmen in the name of economy objected to an expensive public works program and chafed at the continuation of bureaucratic controls over economic life. As unemployment rose, Wilson called a conference of governors and mayors at Washington in March, 1919, but the atmosphere was distinctly unfriendly to any extension of leadership by the White House. At this meeting Governor Calvin Coolidge reported that "90 per cent of the boys were able to take care of themselves." Current riots and unrest were popularly attributed to the machinations of radicals. It was indeed fortunate that some measure of recovery, spurred on by the expanding automobile industry, took place by the summer of 1919, but the severe recession of 1920–1921 and the Red hunt hysteria demonstrated the weakness of a peace that no one planned.

THE SHADOW OF MOSCOW

The domestic scene was further hopelessly confused by the reverberations of Russia's Communist Revolution, for its social and economic implications quickly overshadowed the political idealism that had been aroused by the war. Fears of a world revolution, however exaggerated, had their foundation in the intermittent success of Socialism and Communism in the new republic of Austria, in Bela Kun's short-lived Hungarian Soviet Republic, in Kurt Eisner's Bavarian People's Republic, and in the Communist danger presented by the Spartacist followers of Karl Liebknecht and Rosa Luxemburg in northern Germany. Reaction soon set in. The clerical party in Austria repressed democratic reform as well as "Red" Vienna. Admiral Horthy's blood-stained Whites destroyed democrats as well as Bela Kun's Bolsheviks; and Ludendorff, Kapp, and young Adolf Hitler awakened violent nationalist hatreds in their attempts to destroy both democracy and Communism. Mussolini's war veterans posed as Italy's protectors against Communism while they robbed shopkeepers and beat duly elected government officials. Fascism, feeding on the employer's fear of labor, the widespread apprehension of Communism, and the postwar disillusionment of youthful nationalists, offered what appeared to be a transitional if harsh dictatorship in place of the permanent domination of Moscow.

Closely related to the common fear of impending world-wide Communism were the mixed humanitarian and political motives behind

American and Allied postwar relief efforts for the famine-stricken masses of Europe. Herbert Hoover, appointed by Wilson to administer the relief program abroad, urged ever larger federal loans for the destitute peoples. "I need not repeat," he cabled from Paris on January 5, 1919, "that strong liberal relief is today the only hope of stemming the tide of Bolshevism, without the expenditure of lives and vast sums on military action." A week later, Wilson successfully persuaded congressional leaders to enact a relief appropriation involving $100,000,000; ultimately over one billion dollars was required for relief loans to Europe. In this appeal to Congress, Wilson stated emphatically, "Food relief is now the key to the whole European situation and to the solution of peace. Bolshevism is steadily advancing westward, has overwhelmed Poland, and is poisoning Germany. It cannot be stopped by force, but it can be stopped by food. . . ." Hungry men and economic chaos, it seemed obvious, furnished a simple lever for Communist penetration.

Although during the Peace Conference Wilson had frowned on our active military participation in any campaign to overthrow the government of Lenin and Trotsky, he obviously shared the general fear that Communism was spreading. "If you had been across the sea with me," he told an audience in Montana on September 11, 1919, "you would know that the dread in the mind of every thoughtful man in Europe is that that distemper [Communism] will spread to their countries"; this was the poison "running through the veins of the world." "There are apostles of Lenin in our own midst," he warned his listeners. Guided by the advice of his overzealous Attorney General, A. Mitchell Palmer, Wilson persuaded Congress to extend the life of certain wartime controls in the Lever Act (the Food Control law) in order to combat subversive movements. "With the free expression of opinion," he told Congress in his annual message in 1919, "and with the advocacy of orderly political change, however fundamental, there must be no interference, but towards passion and malevolence tending to incite crime and insurrection under guise of political revolution there should be no leniency." Unfortunately, Palmer proved a poor judge of "passion and malevolence" and shortly afterward inspired one of the severest peacetime onslaughts on civil liberties in American history.

CURBING LABOR MILITANCY

In a modified form, the social ingredients of the turbulent European cauldron appeared here after the war. Here as elsewhere, labor fought both a rising cost of living and employers' attempts to reduce working standards; occasionally it flirted with radical measures of social reconstruction. Capital professed to see a plan for world revolution behind labor's demands for union recognition, wage increases, and greater participation in personnel policies. Against the menace of Moscow there rallied the new American Legion formed by our veterans in the name of "God and country" to foster "one hundred per cent Americanism"; violent clashes occurred frequently between its members and parading Socialists, striking I.W.W. workers, and editors of radical and labor publications. A revived Ku Klux Klan fostered an aggressive nationalist spirit not only against radicals but against Negroes, Catholics, Jews, and their liberal allies. Class war, intolerance, blatant nationalism, extreme economic individualism, radicalism—all of them helped to fill the void left by the absence of effective leadership at Washington. To put down a strike might establish the reputation of a local politician and lead to high office—to even the highest in the land.

Postwar labor militants came from the rank and file, rather than from the recognized leaders of national trade unions. During 1920, Samuel Gompers' American Federation of Labor doubled its 1916 membership figures when it passed the four-million mark, but it cautiously followed a policy of piecemeal advance. The most radical demands in its reconstruction program of February, 1919, were the right of public employees to organize, the municipal ownership of utilities, and a graduated tax on undeveloped land. Hailing a new era in labor history, the A. F. of L. went on record for an "American standard of living" with reasonable hours, equal pay for men and women for equal work, and the abolition of child labor. But Gompers vigorously resisted labor's radical doctrinaires, hazardous strike adventures, and the formation of independent labor parties. "There is nothing to be gained," he said, "in taking an immovable stand for an impossible cause."

Despite the rising cost of living, wage increases continued to outstrip inflated prices until 1920, although this did not hold true in every part of the country. Having experienced the wartime increase in purchasing power, organized labor insisted that adequate wages, satisfactory hours, and union recognition must be maintained. Had not the Creel Committee promised American labor a better postwar world? President Wilson himself repeatedly endorsed the expansive ideal of a "living wage," and his Administration had given practical aid to collective bargaining, especially under the National War Labor Board. Hence labor assumed that this favorable trend would continue. The new feeling of labor solidarity that emerged was expressed in sympathy strikes and in financial aid to less fortunate unskilled workers in the steel and textile mills and the coal fields, and to the various classes of municipal, state, and federal employees. For such unorganized groups, inflation was stark tragedy. During 1919 this ferment resulted in no less than four million men and women being either on strike or locked out by their employers. Most alarming to the average citizen was the occasional threat of a general strike, with all its revolutionary implications.

Early in 1919 nation-wide attention was focused on a general strike in Seattle, Washington, which paralyzed all but the most essential activities. Organized labor turned out en masse on February 6 in support of the demand made by over 30,000 shipyard workers for a revised wage scale and a forty-four-hour week. Strict discipline among the strikers made the walkout an orderly one, but Mayor Ole Hanson persisted in denouncing the shutdown as an effort to overthrow organized society. Pressure from high labor officials, who opposed the wholesale breaking of existing union contracts with the wartime Shipbuilding Adjustment Board, ended the strike a few days later. Nevertheless, Mayor Hanson won national acclaim because he had presumedly halted the progress of Bolshevism. Another general strike that was called shortly afterward across the border in Winnipeg, Canada, confirmed the panic-inspired belief that revolution threatened on all sides. The Canadian authorities promptly took stern repressive measures against the strikers, and several of their leaders were deported or imprisoned.

The major battle of 1919 involved the great steel strike, especially in the Chicago-Gary area dominated by the United States Steel Corporation. Ten years previously, a flourishing union in the steel mills had been crushed. As a result, almost half of the men worked twelve hours a day, seven days a week; the average working week for all employees was slightly under sixty-nine hours. Anti-union spies and *agents provocateurs* strove to destroy any incipient unionism. Under such conditions even the preponderantly Italian, Serbian, and Polish workers, who had been chosen for their docility, grew restive.

During 1918, the Chicago branch of the American Federation of Labor had begun an active campaign to organize the steel workers in behalf of an eight-hour day and had chosen William Z. Foster to head the organization drive. Foster had once been a follower of Bryan; then he became a radical syndicalist, and now he claimed to be an orthodox trade unionist. During the war he sold war bonds as one of the Creel Committee's "four-minute men." Only after the steel strike did he publicly emerge as a Communist; in 1924, he became this party's presidential candidate. He proved highly successful as an organizer, for by the beginning of 1919 every steel district had its own local. The United States Steel Corporation promptly discharged all the union men, and Judge Gary, the chairman of the board, refused to discuss the situation with Gompers, Foster, or any other union official.

After prolonged efforts to confer with Gary had failed, the union voted to strike on September 22, 1919, unless the corporation would agree to a conference. President Wilson pleaded with the A. F. of L. that it was in the public interest that no strike be called, at least not until the National Industrial Conference could meet to discuss the situation. Gompers was ready to comply with the President's request, but by this time many of the men, under Foster's militant leadership, were impatient of further delay. Consequently the strike began as planned, and over 343,000 men walked out. The strike spread to western Pennsylvania, where union meetings were suppressed by local officials amid bloody clashes.

While the press, reflecting the company point of view, portrayed the strike leaders as Communists, aid came to the strikers from another quarter, the church. During October the Industrial Relations Department of the Interchurch World Movement undertook a sweeping investigation of the steel strike; their report completely supported the workers. Among the evidence they uncovered was a letter of instructions to a company agent that revealed the tactics employed by the big steel operators: "We want you to stir up as much bad feeling as you possibly can between the Serbians and Italians. . . . Call up every question you can in reference to racial hatred between these two nationalities. . . . Urge them [The Serbians] to go back to work or the Italians will get their jobs." But this report likewise failed to influence the operators.

When Negroes, long the object of union discrimination, were brought in as strikebreakers, rioting broke out in Gary. Governor Goodrich of Indiana ordered the state militia to the scene and in the face of continued defiance from the strikers appealed for federal assistance. General Leonard Wood arrived at the head of United States Army troops and, after proclaiming martial law, restored order. Eighteen of the twenty men killed during the disturbance were strikers. As their savings disappeared and the public was still gripped by the Red scare, many of the discouraged steel workers deserted the strike even before union leaders officially announced that the strikers would return to work on January 8, 1920. The unionization of steel workers suffered a setback that lasted a decade and a half.

PURITAN REACTION: THE BOSTON POLICE STRIKE

New England watched with alarm as unionism became entrenched among poorly paid natives and aliens alike. The numerous foreign-language groups became articulate when the United Textile Workers demanded a basic eight-hour day early in 1919. Local unions, impatient for action, called out over 120,000 workers on strike. Radical organizers who frankly acknowledged that their aim was a revolution led the strike to victory, but it soon became apparent that their talk of revolution only masked the usual demand for wage and hour adjustments. New England telephone operators, emulating the militancy of the workmen in overalls, likewise demanded that their salaries be brought within closer range of the high cost of living. Postmaster General Albert S. Burleson, who still retained wartime control over the nation's telephone systems, stubbornly refused even to recognize the operators' union. Only after service had been halted in twenty-six cities and towns and the governors of the New England states had appealed to President Wilson to avert an even wider strike did Burleson agree to accept union demands.

Most dramatic and significant of all was the Boston police strike in 1919. Police salaries in that city began at $1100 per year, an amount that in no wise corresponded with the increased living costs; long hours and poor conditions in the police stations were causes of further dissatisfaction. In London and Liverpool, policemen's unions were winning hard-fought battles for better conditions; and in the United States also, despite severe criticism from their local unions, policemen in thirty-seven cities had affiliated themselves with the A. F. of L. Furthermore, labor's recent victories in New England encouraged Boston's policemen to organize. However, the police commissioner, Edwin U. Curtis, following a well-established precedent in Boston, was emphatically opposed to a policemen's union, although he was responsible for a $200 annual raise in wages. "I desire to say to the members of the force," he told his men, "that I am firmly of the opinion that a police officer cannot consistently belong to a union and perform his sworn duty."

Nevertheless, the Boston Social Club, as the policemen's organization was called, applied to the A. F. of L. for a charter on August 10, 1919. In spite of the threat of a police strike, Curtis promptly ordered that eight officials of the club be disciplined for insubordination. Mayor Peters of Boston sought a compromise by organizing a Citizens' Committee of Thirty-Four, who, although far from being prejudiced in the policemen's favor, were conciliatory to their demands. The Committee's report recommended that the club be granted the status of an independent union not affiliated with the A. F. of L., that all grievances be submitted to arbitration, and that the eight officers be reinstated. The policemen apparently were ready to accept these recommendations, according to the leaders of the Committee, but Curtis refused to consider any compromise; on the contrary, he suspended nineteen additional club members. Accordingly, on September 9, 1117 out of the 1544 members of the force went out on strike. Their sympathizers cheered them, but every newspaper in Boston condemned them for leaving the city without protection.

That evening, mischief-makers enjoyed an advance Hallowe'en celebration. Tires were removed from autos, streetcars were stopped or stones were hurled at them, and hats were knocked off of people's heads. The more venturesome began to smash store windows and carry off the merchandise. Curtis, apparently stunned by the strike, hesitated to take action, but Mayor Peters superseded Curtis the next morning—the police commissioner considered himself responsible only to the governor—and ordered out the Boston companies of state troops. President Lowell of Harvard appealed for student volunteers to assist in policing Boston. Mayor Peters, a Democrat, chose this moment for a newspaper interview in which he criticized the inactivity of Calvin Coolidge, the Republican governor of Massachusetts, who had decided to support Curtis. Stung into action on the third day of the strike, Coolidge sent troops from outside Boston to patrol the city, even though order had been largely restored the day previously. When reports reached him that the Central Labor Union with which the police were affiliated was considering a general strike, the governor appealed to the Secretary of War for aid in the event that it became necessary. Curtis announced that no striking policeman would ever be reinstated, a decision which the governor immediately supported.

By this time the entire nation was closely watching the police strike. President Wilson, speaking at Helena, Montana, in behalf of the League of Nations, denounced the strike as "a crime against civilization" and declared that the obligation of a policeman was as sacred as the duty of a soldier. On the fourth day, the police themselves, completely discouraged by the way things were going, were ready to return to work but were halted by Curtis' lockout order. Gompers' decision to appeal directly to Coolidge for their reinstatement unwittingly made political capital for the governor. With his eye on his political future—so his autobiography implies—Coolidge wired Gompers his refusal; his statement included this epigrammatic sentence which captured the public imagination: "There is no right to strike against the public safety by anybody, anywhere, anytime."

The common hysteria, fed by a press which constantly warned of the imminent organization of Soviets on our soil, took comfort in this statement. Although the total damages in the Boston strike did not exceed $34,000, the grateful city collected over $500,000 for the members of the force who had remained at their posts. Scarcely heard above the din of acclamation was the criticism of the *New Republic*, the *Nation*, and men like Harold J. Laski of Harvard, who publicly denounced Commissioner Curtis as the real deserter. But few, even among the liberals, could justify the policemen's decision to use the strike as a weapon, despite the provocation.

As the result of his policy during the strike, Coolidge, a competent if unspectacular state executive who felt that the limits of his political career had been reached, now saw new vistas unfold that might lead to the White House. Not only was Coolidge reelected for governor—with Wilson's congratulations—but his candidacy for the Republican presidential nomination in 1920 presented a formidable threat to his opponents. It was only the fact that Harding's campaign, directed by Harry M. Daugherty, was better planned that finally deprived the Coolidge forces of victory after Lowden, Wood, and Johnson had withdrawn from the race. Even so, Coolidge's consolation prize of the Vice Presidency opened the door to the presidential office itself.

INSURGENCY AMONG THE MINERS

In spite of declining health, President Wilson struggled against the rising tide of labor discontent in 1919 to reach a solution that would be fair to both sides. The National Industrial Conference, which he had confidently expected would be an instrument of peace between labor and capital, failed to reach any agreement when it met at Washington on October 6, 1919. Gompers' insistence on a resolution advocating collective bargaining and a closed shop met immediate resistance from the employers. Wilson vainly appealed for the Conference to set up the necessary machinery for cooperation. "At a time when the nations of the world are endeavoring to find a way to avoid international wars," he wrote in his message to the Conference, "are we to confess that there is no method to be found for carrying on industry except in the spirit and with the very method of war?"

No industry required as much mediation from the President as coal mining. Although American coal fields were far better off than the long-exploited British mines, competitive factors within the industry resulted in considerable inequality among our miners. The miners' unions were striving to organize the entire industry in order to remove these inequalities. Furthermore, the high cost of living bore heavily on the bituminous coal miners, for their wages had not been increased since the agreement with the Fuel Administration in September, 1917. Insurgency among district unions, and the wild-cat strikes called by independent unions like those in Illinois, made it difficult for the central organization of the United Mine Workers to maintain a unified policy.

New unity, comparatively speaking, was achieved when the United Mine Workers held an "international" convention in September, 1919, under the aggressive leadership of young John L. Lewis, the new president. Except for an unfortunate tendency to carry on protracted personal feuds with union rivals, Lewis showed himself a master of strategy. Although cool to a union proposal to nationalize the coal industry, he supported such novel policies as the thirty-hour week to spread employment and a national contract for miners. He advocated the termination of the 1917 agreement and was ready to call a nationwide strike, if necessary, to secure a new wage contract. Specifically, the convention demanded a six-hour day, a five-day week, and a 60 per cent wage increase. When the operators resisted these demands, a strike was ordered for November 1. President Wilson's appeal to the convention, in which he denounced the strike as "morally and legally wrong" in view of the danger to the public safety, failed to move the miners. Accordingly, on November 1, some 450,000 miners left their pits.

At Wilson's request, Attorney General Palmer, acting under the wartime Food and Fuel Control Act, secured a sweeping injunction on November 8 restraining all officers of the United Mine Workers from carrying on strike activities. Liberals denounced this move as a violation of the Administration's pledge not to use this Act to prohibit strikes. Lewis agreed to cancel the strike order; as he told the press, "We cannot fight the government." But the miners refused to return to work. Finally, a month later, Palmer and Tumulty, as representatives of the President, conferred with the union leaders and secured their acceptance of Wilson's compromise offer of an immediate token wage increase, this and other disputed points to be arbitrated in the near future. Ultimately the miners received a 27 per cent wage increase instead of the 60 per cent requested, but no reduction in hours of work. The operators in turn yielded to Wilson's insistence that they absorb the wage increase instead of passing it on to the consumer in higher prices. Despite general disappointment with the agreement, Lewis' leadership was now well established, and Wilson found it advantageous to work closely with him during subsequent labor conflicts in the industry.

One of the by-products of the perennial mining disputes, some of which involved considerable violence, was the well-publicized Court of Industrial Relations established by the Kansas legislature early in 1920. This provided an elaborate system of compulsory arbitration for labor disputes in industries affecting the public interest; severe penalties were imposed on those who failed to abide by the arbitrator's decision. Thirty years earlier, when labor organizations were still weak, such a plan would have found appreciable support among the unions, but now it was violently denounced and many miners were fined or arrested for flatly defying it. Ultimately the Supreme Court nullified the substance of this law.

SACCO AND VANZETTI, SYMBOLS

Even more than the Boston police strike, the Sacco-Vanzetti case revealed the dangerous social cleavage in New England and the nation. In April, 1920, the paymaster and a guard of a Massachusetts shoe factory were killed on a street in South Braintree and their payroll was seized by five men who drove away swiftly in an automobile. Three weeks later, Nicola Sacco, a shoemaker, and Bartolomeo Vanzetti, a fish peddler in the Italian colony near Boston, were arrested for the crime. Both men were admittedly radicals in their philosophy; they had organized protest meetings against Attorney General Palmer's raids of 1919–1920 and were active in encouraging strikes. In their trial, over which Judge Webster Thayer presided, witnesses whose reliability was questionable convinced the jury that Sacco and Vanzetti were indeed the guilty men. Accordingly on July 14, 1921, they were sentenced to death.

Execution was deferred until August 23, 1927, as a result of the active intervention of the supporters of labor and liberal sympathizers. "Save Sacco and Vanzetti!" became an international slogan, and demonstrations in their behalf took place outside our embassies and consulates in Latin America and Europe. Prominent New Englanders who investigated the case took opposing sides. Thus President Lowell of Harvard upheld the processes of the court, whereas Felix Frankfurter, the legal expert, condemned the evidence as flimsy.

Critics of the verdict, like the journalist Eugene Lyons, portrayed the trial as evidence of the deep racial, religious, and economic prejudice in New England. Conservatives, Lyons implied, shaken by repeated strikes, the militancy of labor, the gradual loss of the textile industry to the South, and the westward shift of the shoe industry, had sacrificed Sacco and Vanzetti to expiate the economic and social ills of postwar New England.

THE I.W.W. AND CRIMINAL SYNDICALISM

During this era when the strike fever was at its height, the casual newspaper reader found it simpler to attribute the basic unrest to the machinations of the Reds than to more complex economic maladjustments. As a result criminal syndicalism appeared, reaching its peak a few years after the war. By 1920, at least one-third of our state legislatures had fashioned their statutes pertaining to criminal syndicalism after the New York model, which defined it as "advocating, teaching, or aiding and abetting the commission of crime, sabotage, or unlawful acts of force and violence or unlawful methods of terrorism as a means of accomplishing a change in industrial ownership or control, or effecting any political change." The mere possession of radical literature might suffice to determine the culprit, and those found guilty of criminal syndicalism were liable to imprisonment for ten years or longer.

Ostensibly the new statutes were aimed in particular at the semi-revolutionary I.W.W., whose success in organizing unskilled workers constituted a threat to the prevailing low wage standards. In spite of the raids on their headquarters during the war, the I.W.W. were still active among the miners, longshoremen, lumbermen, and agricultural workers of the Pacific coast. Migratory laborers, going from one poorly paid seasonal job to another, their pace hastened by hostile local deputies, found it difficult to develop the patriotism felt by the citizen with a stake in America and were an easy prey for the bitter rebelliousness preached by the I.W.W. Their songs of social hate heard in the wheat lands and across the timber belt were not the optimistic notes that our early pioneers had sung. Studying their behavior, Professor D. D. Lescohier of the University of Wisconsin concluded, "They are a social tragedy rather than a social menace." Nevertheless, these men did burn the crops of hostile employers and sabotage farm machinery.

Simultaneously with the repressive campaign undertaken by the states, Palmer's Department of Justice speeded up its activities under the Espionage and Selective Service Acts that had been so effective during the war. Wholesale convictions and deportations picked off the leaders of the I.W.W., leaving only inexperienced organizers who frittered away their energies in private feuds. Fifteen of the leaders received sentences of twenty years, and in Chicago alone the I.W.W. members who were tried before Judge Kenesaw M. Landis were fined an aggregate of $2,300,000. By 1919, the organization's prewar membership of 100,000 had dropped to 35,000 and it continued to decline, many of the radicals now joining the newly organized American Communist party.

State prosecutions of the I.W.W. revealed much less regard for civil liberties than was shown by Palmer's federal agents. Even organized labor, which was hostile to the radicals, charged that California used professional witnesses in prosecuting criminal syndicalists. Organized attempts by lumber operators and World War veterans to combat radicalism and unionism in the State of Washington resulted in bloodshed. On Armistice Day, 1919, an American Legion parade in Centralia attacked an I.W.W. hall; the members had been warned beforehand and hence were prepared for the assault. The death of four Legionnaires in the encounter inflamed public opinion and led to arbitrary mass arrests of I.W.W. adherents. Seven of them were found guilty of second-degree murder and sentenced to the penitentiary for from twenty-five to forty years. The combined blows of federal and state authorities forced the dwindling members of the I.W.W. to exhaust their remaining resources in expensive legal battles.

THE PALMER RAIDS

Most sensational of the repressive measures of the postwar years was Palmer's Red hunt of 1919–1920. Late in April, 1919, the country was electrified by reports of a nation-wide Communist plot to celebrate May day by murdering every outstanding public official who was involved in any labor case. Packages containing bombs had been found addressed to such prominent figures as Secretary of Labor Wilson, Postmaster General Burleson, Judge Kenesaw M. Landis, Supreme Court Justice Oliver W. Holmes, and the Attorney General himself.

On June 2 Palmer's home was bombed, but he himself escaped injury. Impatient at the time required for legal action against the radicals, Palmer determined to ferret out the unknown criminals, even at the risk of subjecting innocent suspects to arrest. At first his authority was almost unchallenged because of the simultaneous illness of the President and the Secretary of Labor.

Palmer's preliminary blow fell on December 21, 1919, with the mass deportation of 249 Russians on the transport *Buford.* In January over 4000 aliens were rounded up in a sudden concerted attempt to wipe out the Communist and the Communist Labor parties. Without the formality of a warrant, agents of the Bureau of Investigation, acting on Palmer's instructions, staged night raids on club rooms, homes, and other meeting places of workingmen and seized everyone suspected of revolutionary affiliations. Families were separated, some being left without support; prisoners were held incommunicado and deprived of their right to legal counsel. The mayor of Detroit assailed the authorities for holding one hundred men for a week in a room 24 by 30 feet. The radicals who were American citizens were turned over to state authorities for prosecution under the criminal syndicalist laws. Legal formalities were dispensed with in the case of aliens—many of whom could not speak English—save for a hasty trial before an immigration inspector in the presence of a Bureau of Investigation agent. The bail demanded was frequently excessive. The American Civil Liberties Union vainly strove to offset this roughshod procedure by providing financial and legal assistance wherever possible. Nevertheless, Palmer eventually deported 550 radicals.

By the end of January, 1920, Secretary of Labor Wilson and his liberal assistant, Louis F. Post, both of whom had been ill, were able to intervene to stem the tide of arrests and deportations. Members of the Communist Labor party, as distinguished from the rival Communist party, were released. Prisoners had access to counsel and the rules of evidence were more strictly adhered to; as a result, over one-third of those who had been arrested were released. President Wilson's own attitude toward repression had been expressed a few weeks earlier in his congressional message on December 2, 1919, when he pleaded for a comprehensive program of labor reform: "The real antidote for the unrest which manifests itself is not suppression, but a deep consideration of the wrongs that beset our national life and the application of a remedy."

Palmer, besieged by critical Congressmen, insisted that the traditional procedure of making an arrest had proved ineffective in suppressing radicalism. He defended his arrests of people who visited convicted radicals in jail on the ground that their friendship for the convicted men indicated a dangerous political affiliation. Radical violence was not extirpated, however, for on September 16, 1920, a mighty blast of dynamite in front of the Wall Street offices of J. P. Morgan and Company killed thirty-eight people and injured hundreds more. Morgan himself was abroad. Property damage was estimated at over $2,000,000. This crime was never solved, but the public assumed that it was instigated by radicals.

Competent observers claimed that the actual membership of revolutionary parties was very small. The new Communist party of America, which had seceded from the "gradualist"-minded Socialist party in September, 1919, had a total membership of well under 60,000. The Communist Labor party, which was ultimately absorbed by the Communist party, had perhaps between ten and thirty thousand members. These parties drew most of their adherents from various foreign-language associations, the Russian in particular. The Socialist party, on the other hand, lost its most militant element when the Communists seceded, and like the British Labour Party it became increasingly parliamentary and reformist in its platforms and methods. Ironically enough, the Socialist convention called on the police on August 30, 1919, to oust Communists and other extremist delegates from the hall. Despite a small dues-paying membership of 39,000, Debs, the Socialist candidate for President, received 920,000 votes in 1920.

"UNDIVIDED AMERICANISM": THE ANTI-SOCIALIST CAMPAIGN

The wave of hysterical nationalism, encouraged by anti-labor forces, resulted in a series of cases in 1919–1920 which brought our traditional observance of civil liberties to an unprecedented low point. The Socialist party itself was put on trial in the person of one of its founders, Victor L. Berger of Milwaukee, who came to the United States from Austria in 1878. As editor of the Socialist *Leader,* a Milwaukee paper which criticized our entrance into the war, he was indicted under the Espionage Act in February, 1918, and sentenced the following December by Federal Judge Landis to twenty years' imprisonment. The situation was complicated by the fact that in November he was elected to Congress, defeating both his Republican and Democratic opponents. Berger appealed his case, and the Supreme Court set aside the Landis sentence on the ground of judicial prejudice; thereafter, the federal charges against Berger were dropped.

When the Milwaukee Socialist presented himself to be sworn in as a member of the House of Representatives, he was denied his seat because as a Socialist he professed doctrines inconsistent with the oath of office. Ignoring the Democratic candidate's claim to Berger's seat, the impartial governor of Wisconsin ordered a special election. Despite a Republican-Democratic fusion movement, Berger won again, this time by an even larger majority vote. Again the House of Representatives refused to admit him. Eventually, however, when the Red scare had abated, Berger was admitted.

In January, 1920, while Palmer was hunting Reds and Berger was fighting for his seat in Congress, the New York State assembly burst into an orgy of patriotism induced by the Lusk Committee, which was investigating allegedly subversive activies. When the legislative session opened on January 7, Speaker Sweet called upon the five Socialist members to rise, denounced their membership in an unpatriotic organization like the Socialist party, and referred to a forthcoming resolution of the assembly to declare their seats vacant. Theodore Roosevelt, Jr., a member of the assembly, condemned the proposed resolution as contrary to American traditions. Speaker Sweet, in refutation, read excerpts from the writings of the elder Roosevelt on one hundred per cent Americanism, and the Socialists were expelled by an overwhelming vote on a variety of personal, political, and religious grounds.

Incisive criticism of the assembly came from Charles Evans Hughes, a former governor of New York and now a liberal member of the Supreme Court. Revolutionists, he said, should be punished, but it was an extremely serious mistake to deprive entire groups of citizens, who had combined for political action, of the only means of peaceful government, the ballot. Hughes was backed by the New York Bar

Association, which had asked him to serve as chairman of a special committee to investigate the expulsion. When the assembly's own investigating committee refused to admit the Hughes committee to its hearings, Hughes left, delivering a parting shot in his statement that the entire proceedings were legally indefensible.

Further attempts of the Lusk Committee to Americanize New York State failed. The Committee organized raids on the Rand School in New York, a famous labor institution with Socialist affiliations, and it secured the passage of bills barring all subversive organizations from the ballot. When the progressive-minded governor, Alfred E. Smith, vetoed these bills, the assembly retaliated by adjourning without action on the governor's welfare measures, a victory, as Speaker Sweet put it, for "undivided Americanism." Several years later, with another governor at Albany, the Lusk bills, amended to include sweeping penalties for teaching or otherwise advocating subversive ideas, became law. They remained in effect until Smith's second term as governor, when they were repealed.

VICTORY OF THE OPEN SHOP

By 1920, employers had begun to cooperate in order to capitalize on the strong anti-radical feeling and the nationalist spirit. To this end they proposed a program, under the attractive name of "the American Plan," which called for the non-union open shop and wage deflation, and constituted a concerted flank attack on labor's gains under the New Freedom. Farmers as well as industrialists were invited to subscribe to the "hallowed American principle" whereby every individual has the inalienable right to enter any trade or business without interference—union interference being understood. These open-shop associations, sponsored by Chambers of Commerce, Boards of Trade, and manufacturing associations, appeared in every state in the Union. Southern industry, profiting by the low wages prevalent in that section, supported the movement vigorously, and Los Angeles became its headquarters in the West.

A spectacular victory was won in Chicago when the "Big Five" meat packers, by abrogating their agreement with the unions, provoked a strike and then broke union control of the industry. The building-trade unions throughout the nation, many of them wealthy and corrupt, were an especially vulnerable target for an open-shop drive. The Chamber of Commerce in San Francisco, labor's citadel, led the assault on the corrupt dictatorship exercised by the building-trade leaders; the weapon was a threat to boycott non-cooperative contractors. Chicago was more difficult, for there the building trades had the united support of liberal sympathizers as well as labor. Even the Amalgamated Clothing Workers of New York, one of the most powerful unions in the country, was able to retain the closed shop only after a lockout which resulted in lowered wage scales. The war-bred unions which had been stimulated by the Administration's policies were the real casualties of this drive. After initial victories in the various fields, the open-shop advocates were compelled to yield some ground.

LABOR AND THE CRISES OF 1920–1922

At the end of 1920 occurred the worst economic depression since the nineties; it lasted less than a year, but it was so severe that it threatened to wipe out all the gains made by labor. Agriculture, unable to adapt its overexpanded acreage to the reduced peacetime needs, felt the depression first. The high cost of living reached its peak in November, 1920, and a buyer's strike, encouraged by the Administration itself, made rapid headway in many sections of the country. It is true that prices fell as the depression developed, but five or six million wage earners were soon unemployed, and employers insisted that wages must come down to offset the decline in prices. In 1919 the Department of Labor had asked for federal and state cooperation in formulating public works projects to prevent unemployment during the period of demobilization, and blueprints for almost two billion dollars' worth of such projects had been prepared before Harding took office.

President Harding, whose sympathy for labor had been actively manifested in his newspaper office in Marion, Ohio, stated publicly, as Wilson had done, that he would fight for the ideal of a living wage. To this end he called for a national conference to be held on unemployment. His Secretary of Commerce, Herbert Hoover, took a leading role in this pioneer meeting, and outlined a policy of reserving all but the most essential public works and private construction for periods of depression. This had the further advantage of economy because building projects would be undertaken when costs were low. The conference's recommendations for an immediate expansion of local and federal construction projects brought considerable response and an unprecedented volume of building. After the emergency was over, however, protests came in from various industries which claimed that they would suffer hardships if their normal operations had to be curtailed; and when Hoover himself, as President, confronted an even worse depression than that of 1920–1921, he found his plan as far from realization as it had been a decade earlier.

The depression made a violent impact on the railroads, which had just been restored to their owners by the Transportation Act of 1920. One of the provisions of this Act created a Railroad Labor Board to regulate labor conditions and called for the Board to intervene whenever negotiations between operator and employee failed. Actually the Board had no effective means of securing compliance with its decisions. Worse yet, its impartiality was open to question; thus labor complained that the Board had ordered wage cuts before other industries thought this step essential. Railroad shopmen, in particular, suffered severely from the Board's policies, but they refrained from striking until their union organization was perfected.

In May, 1922, the Board won temporary popularity by a decision that outlawed one of labor's worst grievances. The railroads had been evading union regulations and wage scales by farming out much of their work to outside shops, a practice which the shopmen said accounted for the abnormally high unemployment in their ranks; some 40 per cent of the shopmen had been discharged. The carriers, who refused to acknowledge that this practice ran counter to the Transportation Act as the Board contended, evaded compliance with the Board's decision by engaging in prolonged court action and discharging employees who agitated for the new ruling. The Board, apparently without power to enforce its decision on the carriers, agreed to the latter's proposals for new wage cuts averaging 12.5 per cent, to go into effect July 1, 1922.

Thereupon the shopmen voted overwhelmingly to go on strike and 400,000 walked out on July 1. The Board denounced the strike as a wildcat action and encouraged the carriers to form company unions, as the Pennsylvania Railroad had done, and to deprive the strikers of their seniority rights. President Harding intervened in an effort to end the strike by arbitration but was unsuccessful because the carriers refused to restore the men's seniority rights. Thereupon Attorney General Harry M. Daugherty obtained an injunction from Federal Judge James Wilkerson of Chicago against all strike activities as a violation of the conspiracy clause in the Sherman Anti-Trust Act. The cautious influence of the American Federation of Labor prevented the strike from becoming general, even though the resentment of labor as a whole flared to new heights. Finally, the moderate group of carriers, led by Daniel Willard of the Baltimore and Ohio Railroad, arranged a separate agreement with their employees by which the situation was restored as of July 1, 1922. The Pennsylvania group, however, exacted a far more rigorous peace, for the seniority rights of 175,000 strikers were canceled. The only crumb of comfort left for the badly defeated workmen was the fact that the Railway Labor Board was thoroughly discredited and soon ceased to function.

The years 1921–1922 were a period of recurrent labor violence, especially in the coal industry, which experienced more strikes than ever before in its history. Efforts of the United Mine Workers to organize the West Virginia bituminous fields, where labor standards were exceptionally low, resulted in armed clashes with private detectives, local police, and the militia. In August, 1921, President Harding had to send an Army detachment there to halt a miniature civil war between union miners and armed deputies.

This fight for union practices brought on another small-scale civil war in Herrin, Illinois. Herrin, a prosperous and progressive town, was the center of a mining community that included forty-four mines. Its predominantly native American population showed an aggressive sympathy for the Illinois coal workers who were out on strike in 1922, despite the prevailing newspaper belief that violence was an alien importation. The crisis was reached when the Illinois Coal Company violated an "armistice" understanding that no coal would be shipped during the strike and proceeded to import strikebreakers and detectives. On June 21, the strikers besieged the company's barricade and met the opening gunfire of the guards with overwhelming force. When the strikebreakers surrendered, nineteen of them were massacred by an angry mob of strikers. So strong was the feeling against the operators that the local jury acquitted the strikers.

AGRARIAN RADICALISM

The farmer, too, proved to be a persistent rebel in the postwar period as his plight grew worse after the depression of 1920–1921. The exceptionally heavy demand for farm products during the war not only had encouraged overexpansion but had fastened the evil one-crop system on the Middle West. By 1921 the price of corn and wheat had fallen by half and cotton prices dropped even more.

Agrarian radicalism was not new in the North Central states, for the farmers in that section had fought vigorously for agrarian reforms under Granger and Populist leadership during the post-Civil War era, under Bryan in the nineties, and since 1915 under Arthur C. Townley and his Farmers' Non-partisan League. In 1920, the scattered agrarian rebels organized the Farmer-Labor party, which was especially strong in Minnesota, the independent votes of the Scandinavian-American farmers accounting for much of its strength. The party's vote for President in 1920 was trivial, but shortly afterward it sent two Senators to Congress when it elected Henrik Shipstead and Magnus Johnson of Minnesota; thereafter it dominated politics in that state. Regional discontent was eventually channelized in the famous farm bloc, formed in Congress under the leadership of the Senators from Iowa and Kansas and destined to complicate domestic politics for over a decade.

ERA OF THE KU KLUX KLAN

Postwar intolerance compounded of economic discontent and blatant nationalism fell with crushing force on the Negro. His war record failed to impress the southern advocates of white supremacy and his invasion of northern urban centers and factories alarmed people in that section. Negroes were charged fantastic rents for crowded unsanitary quarters in segregated areas of northern cities; and the whites who owned homes on the fringe of Negro neighborhoods used every means, from economic pressure to physical violence, to halt their further encroachment.

The Ku Klux Klan had been revived in 1915 by "Colonel" William J. Simmons, and in 1920 it was given a new lease on life by leaders (like the Imperial Wizard Hiram S. Evans) who made the fostering of intolerance financially attractive by means of an elaborate fee system. Although the Klan relied on its diverse anti-Semitic, anti-Catholic, anti-alien, and anti-Red activities for northern support, the hoary banner of white supremacy was sufficient in the South. A new bigotry had apparently healed the wounds left by the Civil War and united Northerners and Southerners alike against a common object of hatred. This army of intolerance had an estimated four to six million members throughout the nation by 1924. The New York *World*, tabulating the Klan's activities in the South during 1920–1921, included four murders, two mutilations, forty-one floggings, twenty-seven tar and feather parties, and five kidnapings. Forty-three citizens were warned to leave their towns and fourteen communities were threatened; on numerous occasions masked men in Klan regalia paraded through the streets with warning placards. An investigation of Klan violence in Oklahoma revealed over 2000 outrages of various kinds during a two-year period. In Texas, which became a center of the movement, the Klan secured the passage of a law excluding Negroes from Democratic primaries, thus virtually disfranchising this race since primaries were usually equivalent to elections in the South. But in Nixon *v.* Herndon (1927) the Supreme Court ruled this law unconstitutional as a violation of the "equal protection" clause of the Fourteenth Amendment. By the late 1920's the Klan, especially in Indiana, so overreached itself in immorality and corrupt state and national politics that it hastend its own end.

During 1919, anti-Negro groups in the South could point complacently to the race riots in the North, some of them far bloodier than any of their southern counterparts. In Chicago an argument between whites and Negroes on a bathing beach developed into an alarming race war that lasted four days. Gangs raided the Negro district, beating many of its inhabitants and destroying considerable property, and mobs of Negroes clashed with whites in hysterical fury. Twenty-three Negroes and fifteen whites were killed and over five hundred of both races were injured; around one thousand people, largely Negroes, were left homeless. Underlying the race war was the newly aroused fear among the whites that the Negro migration from the South, which had doubled in a decade, threatened their security, both personal and economic. A similar large-scale race riot broke out in Washington, D. C., whose white residents were aroused by the specter of the rapidly mounting Negro population. The year ended with a total of twenty-six such riots, including those that occurred in the South and other scattered riots in factory towns.

Negro resentment, conforming to the nationalist pattern of the time, took the form of a strong race consciousness that was evident in the challenging pages of postwar Negro writers. The most pathetic manifestation of this race consciousness was the "Back to Africa" movement headed by Marcus Garvey, a Jamaican Negro who dreamed of converting Africa into a huge Black Republic. The movement reached large proportions in 1921, especially among the Negroes who had moved to the North, like those in New York's Harlem, for it offered emotional satisfaction to uprooted Negroes, most of whom enjoyed their leader's extraordinary showmanship and the titles and colorful uniforms displayed by his followers.

An International Negro Convention was held by Garvey's followers in New York in August, 1920, to draw up a Negro Declaration of Independence; it proclaimed that the Negro would never enjoy the "full rights of manhood and liberty" except under a Negro government in Africa. To Garvey, the white worker was an inherent enemy of the Negro worker and hence the latter must ally himself with his employer and eventually launch his own enterprises. As president of the Universal Negro Improvement Association which he founded, Garvey collected no less than a million dollars among as many Negro members—at least so his adherents claimed. He also promoted several promising cooperative grocery stores, but he dissipated his funds on worthless vessels for the Black Star Steamship Line which he formed to transport Negro emigrants to Africa and to carry on trade between Negroes on the two continents. Finally, like other false messiahs of history, Garvey fell from grace; he was imprisoned for swindling and deported to Jamaica in 1927.

NORDICS AND THE IMMIGRATION POLICY

The immigration laws of the postwar period likewise reflected the intolerant spirit of nationalism. Organized labor as usual urged restriction of immigration and won unexpected support from the American Legion and the Ku Klux Klan. The economists' fear of a flood of starving European immigrants was augmented by the propagandists of "Nordic superiority" who were anxious to protect the nation from the allegedly inferior southern and eastern Europeans. Fears were also expressed that the crushing poverty of this section of Europe would endanger our own economic standards; furthermore, by its diligent exploitation the press had made Russia's alleged Red peril a cause for worry. Still popular at the time was Madison Grant's *The Passing of the Great Race,* a pseudo-scientific discussion of the Nordic that was published originally in 1916.

Close on the heels of the literacy law, which favored northwestern Europe and had been passed over Wilson's veto in 1917, came the demand for a quota system in immigration, coupled with a selective test that also favored Nordic peoples, in spite of the fact that our late enemy, Germany, was thus included. Although the House of Representatives was in favor of suspending all immigration for the time being, the Senate forced a compromise in the Emergency Law of 1921. This Act established a quota system which limited the number of immigrants from each country per year to 3 per cent of the number of its nationals shown by the Census to be residing in the United States in 1910. This meant that the British, German, and Scandinavian countries had the largest quotas, for their nationals were numerically preponderant in 1910. Only certain non-quota nations, primarily in this hemisphere, were unaffected. The new bill was temporarily held up by Wilson's pocket veto but was reenacted at once by the incoming Harding administration; thereafter it was extended in an even more restrictive form. The liberal immigration policy of the nineteenth century was dead.

TOWARD ECONOMIC NATIONALISM

The outgoing Congress, animated by nationalist fears and partisan pressure, passed the Emergency Tariff Act of 1921 over Wilson's veto. The President pointed out that practically all the proposed rates equaled or exceeded those of the iniquitous Payne-Aldrich Act. Furthermore, the relief offered American farmers by the bill was an illusion in view of the fact that our agricultural production and efficiency made foreign competition of little moment; besides, our farmers depended on the foreign markets now threatened by this bill. Even more important, Wilson emphasized that this nation's newly acquired position as a creditor in the world market demanded a liberal tariff policy that would enable debtor countries to use their exports to us in payment of their debts. He declared that the bill, far from being an emergency measure, was intended as the foundation of a permanent tariff policy, and, pointing out the grave problems of reconstruction, he concluded: "Clearly this is no time for the erection of high trade barriers." But the President appealed in vain. The passage of the Emergency Tariff Act inaugurated an era of high tariffs that accentuated our growing nationalism and invited retaliation from abroad.

Despite the prosperity of the next decade, the turbulent spirit of the postwar years had a deep influence on the American people. The anarchic individualism of the twenties owed much to the breakdown, during 1919–1921, of the cooperative ideal characteristic of the Progressive era. The World War unleashed the destructive forces of chauvinism and class war, and after the war this heritage of hate imbued the problems of reconstruction with hysteria. Misdirected mass emotion replaced the wartime spirit of sacrifice, provoked resentment on the part of labor and capital, arbitrarily infringed on the traditional civil liberties of American citizens, and threatened the security of the Negro, the Jew, the Catholic, and the alien. The peace had been lost, and the stage was set for the rampant individualism of the twenties.

CHAPTER 11

The Twenties: Triumph of Mature Capitalism

STABILIZATION OF BUSINESS

Despite the turmoil of the postwar period, such consistent levels of prosperity were attained during the 1920's as to inspire sober economists as well as ecstatic Rotarians with the belief that economic life had been stabilized and that violent fluctuations of the business cycle were a thing of the past. The high priests of efficiency and service had apparently triumphed—in America at least—and Europe came hat in hand to her former pupil to learn the secrets of rationalization, standardization, and other mysteries of mass production. Man stood on the threshold of the abolition of poverty—or so it seemed.

To Werner Sombart, a brilliant if erratic German economist, the postwar decade represented an extraordinary change in the nature of capitalism itself. The bright summer of ripening prewar capitalism had yielded to the golden autumn of mature capitalism, he believed; the businessman's former daring decision and intuitive judgment were replaced by the impersonal and objective operations of management, the systematic planning of production, and the self-imposed regulations along bureaucratic lines. Spontaneity gave way to systematized knowledge. "'Stabilization of business,'" wrote Sombart, "seems to be both the slogan and the accomplishment of this period." It was indeed fitting that the twenties were to close with Herbert Hoover, the chief evangelist of stabilization, in the White House.

The domination of the engineering ideal had been foreshadowed by prewar trends, and the blueprints of economic planning in industry, or rationalization, had been prepared two decades before by Frederick W. Taylor and his disciples. The fragments of handicraft techniques that still survived, as in shoemaking, quickly succumbed to the machine. Engineering experts who standardized the size and shape of various manufactured products claimed that the automobile industry alone was saving $750,000,000 annually through the processes of standardization. Himself an engineer, Hoover served as Secretary of Commerce under both Harding and Coolidge and preached the gospel of simplification to businessmen. For example, the Bureau of Standards in the Department of Commerce fostered new economies by reducing the prevailing 66 varieties of paving brick to 4, and the approximately 44 types of hospital beds to one or two. These, together with scores of other similar simplifications, were estimated to have saved the nation almost five billion dollars by 1929.

That rational planning in the form of systematized invention had come fully into its own seemed evident from the numerous million-dollar expenditures made annually for research work in the chemical, electrical, petroleum, and machine industries. New efficiency was made possible by cost accounting, many types of statistical services, and job analysis in the personnel field. Marketing devices ranging from sales promotion to elaborate style-making bureaus grew increasingly sensitive in anticipating and even creating demands. Business forecasting, still in the rudimentary stages, became popular in many quarters as a valuable planning tool. Inventory control methods and improved transportation facilities made possible a drastic reduction in goods that were hitherto stored in company warehouses far in excess of any immediate demand—merchants recalled all too well the serious difficulties created by huge inventories during the depression of 1920–1921. Secretary Hoover, in an address in April, 1927, attributed the nation's current abundance of capital to the sharply decreased inventories of almost every commodity. Thus capital became more mobile, and mobility itself was a dominant characteristic of life in the 1920's.

These engineering techniques insured the most effective use of the extraordinary mechanization that took place during this decade. So rapidly did the productivity of the average worker increase, especially in the automobile industry, mining, and agriculture, that the American Federation of Labor was deeply concerned over the potential menace of technological unemployment. The imaginative dramatist Karl

Čapek crystallized the popular fear of human mechanization in the docile mechanical slaves, the robots, that toiled efficiently and impersonally in his play, *R.U.R.* Electricity dwarfed steam as the traditional source of industrial power and gave the factory greater mobility, much to the dismay of the older industrial regions.

BUSINESS FRONTIERS AND MERGERS

New England's textile mills moved closer to the cotton fields of the South, where they enjoyed a new freedom from labor unions and effective social legislation, and her historic boot and shoe industry found more favorable manufacturing and distributing conditions in the Middle West. Philadelphia's leadership in rug making was challenged, and despite increases in the total output she lost almost half her share of the nation's production. Chicago continued to expand as the leading butcher of the nation but surrendered much of her one-time major part of the packing industry to other cities. The water power of Alabama, Tennessee, and North Carolina provided the basis for an industrial revolution in the South. North Carolina enjoyed spectacular prosperity, the value of her manufactures alone rising during 1910–1927 from $216,000,000 to more than one billion dollars. Many people visualized the prospect of a future tariff-minded South. Along the Pacific coast, too, new frontiers of industry arose.

Prewar trends toward centralization of business control continued in the tolerant atmosphere of the Harding-Coolidge-Hoover era. Despite the appearance of various new enterprises, the twenties saw the disappearance of over 6000 independent manufacturing and mining companies and over 4000 public utility firms; there were nearly 1800 bank mergers. The holding company was especially popular in the utility field since it offered an inexpensive and effective method of consolidation to well-entrenched groups that aspired to control huge aggregations of capital. So rapid was the growth of chain stores that by 1929 they had captured one-fifth of the nation's retail trade. Sensational advances by chain enterprises were made in the drug field by Walgreen, and in food distribution by the Great Atlantic and Pacific Tea Company, and by Kroger, Safeway, and National Tea. Almost all the variety goods, nearly one-third of all the tobacco products, and a large proportion of general merchandise and wearing apparel were sold by chain stores; and Woolworth, Sears Roebuck, and Childs became household words throughout the nation.

THE GREAT BULL MARKET

Business apologists were convinced that a democratic revolution had taken place in stock ownership. By the end of the twenties, the former two million shareholders in American enterprises had become seventeen million, and the large proportion of employee-shareholders suggested that the ownership of business had become socialized. But this inference was grossly exaggerated, for the diffusion of stock ownership increased rather than decreased the centralized control of corporations by "insiders." Highly negotiable stock certificates offered a type of mobile ownership that was advantageous to small cliques of managers and directors; moreover, the latter were also aided in maintaining control by the device of non-voting stock and the small shareholders' indifference to questions of policy. As for the employee-shareholders, the amount of stock they could purchase was usually limited.

Capital poured into industry from widespread sources as stenographers and office clerks, encouraged by the new investment departments created in the large banks, stormed the stock market. Speculation has always characterized American economic life, but seldom has it been so well channeled by new credit institutions and a trained army of promoters. To many the mercurial stock market offered an attraction for idle capital that even the boom in urban real estate could not match. Moreover, it was part of the current patriotic faith in Coolidge prosperity to believe what Secretary Hoover said in 1928: "We seem only to have touched the fringe of our potentialities." No stock price seemed fantastic to one imbued with this faith, and the climactic bull market of 1927–1929—while it lasted—strengthened this illusion.

Organized business, no longer shamefaced as in trust-busting days, eagerly sang its own praises. Boosters' clubs, trade associations, Chambers of Commerce, and service clubs emphasized the sanctity of private enterprise, the "American way." The Rotary International, a social organization devoted to the interests of business promotion, claimed that it had 3000 clubs in some forty-four countries; and the Kiwanis International (a name taken, interestingly enough, from an Indian word meaning "to make oneself known") and the Lions made similar claims. Few considered Bruce Barton, a New York advertising executive, irreverent when he wrote *The Man Nobody Knows*, in which Christ was pictured as a great business executive who used parables as advertisements in behalf of the ideal of service. The association between business and religion was further stimulated by the Calvinist virtues of sobriety, perseverance, and labor preached by President Coolidge.

Innumerable books on business ethics were published during this decade, as industry, led by advertising, assumed the role of crusader for a prosperous society. In 1927 over 1.5 billion dollars was spent on publicizing the products and services of business—a function that became big business in itself. Even college professors and ministers spoke of "selling" their messages to their audience.

The striking prosperity which made Europe gasp was in reality unevenly distributed, for large groups of farmers, miners, textile workers, and many others failed to share the good fortune of their commercial brothers in the cities. Nevertheless, the material gains for the nation as a whole were unmistakable. According to Slosson, real income rose from 40.25 billion dollars in 1917 to over 54 billion in 1928. Savings accounts increased from 8 to 23 billion dollars during 1914–1925; the major part of this was due to the fact that the number of predominantly small depositors increased from 11 million to 43 million. Between 1921 and 1929, wages on the whole made the most substantial advance over prices in more than three decades.

Even the brief economic recessions of 1924 and 1927 did not alter this favorable picture. Although there was little evidence of any radical tendency toward greater equality in the distribution of wealth, the greater amount of goods and services available meant a higher standard of living for most groups. By 1929, the infant automobile industry was providing a motor car for one out of every five people; in Muncie, Indiana—the Lynds' Middletown—sixty out of 123 working-class families owned cars. Unprecedented expenditures for education, health, recreation, and furniture bore out the general feeling of a steadily rising level of well-being.

Producers and distributors showed marked impatience at the consumer who failed to replace his old possessions with new products and models. The advertisers' appeal to "keep up with the Joneses" was made easy for the consumer by the appearance of an aggressive breed of personal finance companies that promoted new expenditures on a large scale. Installment selling, which before the war had been largely confined to furniture, sewing machines, and books and had totaled less than a billion dollars in 1910, reached new peaks in spite of its high costs. The volume of retail installment selling reached five billion dollars in 1925 and seven billion in 1929, with automobiles and radios leading the procession.

THE AUTOMOBILE AND THE REAL ESTATE BOOM

Much of the flavor and speed of life during the twenties was due to the popularity of the automobile. Almost four million people, from assembly-line mechanics to private chauffeurs, secured their livelihood from this, the largest of all our industries. German technicians who came here to study our methods of production returning home to spread the gospel of *Fordismus,* which ultimately aided Germany to rearm.

Henry Ford retained his undisputed leadership throughout the twenties, although in 1927 he had to replace his standardized ugly duckling, the Model T, with a more ornate car in order to meet increasing competition from Chevrolet in the lower price field. Millions came to see his Model A on display, their interest aroused by the widespread publicity the new model received in the press. Ford's nearest rival was the General Motors Company, which was established by William C. Durant but was now owned largely by the du Pont and Morgan interests. This company made not only the economical Chevrolet automobile but also various high-priced cars, as well as trucks. Completing the "big three" was the Chrysler Corporation, founded by Walter P. Chrysler, who through his bold financial and engineering policies secured a dominant position for his company in the automobile field. These three concerns, together with their powerful satellites—petroleum, rubber, plate glass, and leather upholstery plants in and around Detroit and other automobile centers—handled four-fifths of the industry's total volume of business.

As 23,000,000 cars appeared throughout the country, startling alterations in the national way of life took place. Highway construction on a lavish scale became a requisite for men who aspired to be elected to office. The highways brought urban patterns of living to hitherto isolated communities, and regional cultural differences declined. Recreation became a major industry as millions poured each year into the national parks and forests and the numerous resorts, camps, and other vacation spots. The picturesque but inefficient little red schoolhouse yielded to the new order as the automobile made possible the consolidated school with its modern equipment and its better-trained and better-paid teachers.

The automobile was likewise primarily responsible for the extraordinary nation-wide real estate boom, especially in Florida. The advance in real estate values during this decade accounted for much of the general increase in the nation's wealth. New suburbs were developed partly as the result of the increased mobility of the population made possible by the automobile, and this in turn led to the appearance of "realtors," whose importance in the business structure of the twenties was depicted in Sinclair Lewis's *Babbitt*.

Promoters made the hitherto inaccessible beaches of southern Florida a tourists' paradise. New highways were built to supplement the limited facilities offered by the railroads, and solicitous legislators called attention to the absence of inheritance and income tax laws in Florida and added special inducements to corporations. Miami, Palm Beach, and Tampa grew almost overnight from sleepy villages to bustling and attractive cities. Even William Jennings Bryan, who was in the midst of his battle for Fundamentalism, found time to praise "Magic Miami" to tourists and incidentally to earn almost half a million dollars by selling Florida real estate. During the 1926 season alone, it was estimated that visitors spent a billion dollars in Florida's vacation resorts. By the end of the decade the population of the state had been increased 50 per cent by the influx of Northerners. (This trend jeopardized the orthodox southern politics of Florida, once a member of the Confederacy.)

New suburban subdivisions sprang up near New York, Chicago, Detroit, and other large cities as the result of the mass migration of the middle classes made possible by the automobile. Realtors, succumbing perhaps to their own eloquence, promoted future suburbs that were not even at the blueprint stage. California's boom owed much to the railroad as well as to the automobile, for the average Easterner found a trip of over two thousand miles in a car that could make only twenty-five or thirty miles an hour too strenuous and time-consuming. Tourists echoed the indefatigable Los Angeles Chamber of Commerce in singing the superior virtues of California's year-round climate in comparison to Florida's. People from less-favored sections swelled the population by 2.25 millions during the 1920's; many of them settled permanently in the southern part of the state, especially in Los Angeles.

On the other hand, the automobile introduced certain problems that were profoundly disturbing. For one thing, deaths from automobile accidents between 1919 and 1929 increased from slightly over 11,000 a year to well over 31,000. Furthermore, the automobile proved an exceptional convenience to criminals in evading police and for kidnaping and bank robberies. Finally, the motor car was regarded by sociologists as a major contributing cause of juvenile delinquency.

THE RAILROAD AND THE AIRPLANE

That the railroads managed to retain most of their long-distance traffic despite the gradual inroads made by the new local and regional motor buses was due in part to their purchase of these competitors. A far more serious threat was the reduction in interurban passenger revenues which accompanied the enhanced popularity of the automobile; freight revenues also dropped as farmers began to make general use of motor trucks for marketing their produce. Attempts to alleviate the competition from this source by putting motor transport under the control of the Interstate Commerce Commission failed in these years as a result of the determined resistance of automobile and truck manufacturers. In view of their stationary or even declining revenue, and other difficulties which they attributed to restrictive government regulation, the railroads introduced rigid economies and abandoned thousands of miles of track.

Over the protests of the big railway operators, the framers of the Transportation Act of 1920, which returned the railroads to private control, included a "recapture clause," whereby half of a road's earnings in excess of 6 per cent was deposited in a general fund to aid the weaker rail systems. Recognizing the inherent weaknesses of the railroads' economic structure, Congress also empowered a revitalized Interstate Commerce Commission to offer plans for outright consolidations and to authorize traffic pools, unrestricted by the anti-trust laws, thus relegating competition to fewer and economically sounder railway systems. The Commission, newly entrusted with the power to fix minimum rates, was instructed to maintain rates that would yield a fair return on the aggregate value of all railroad property in the nation. These sections of the Transportation Act not only reflected the railroads' plight, but also revealed the willingness of Wilsonian liberals to modify their distrust of bigness. Although the rail executives were critical of certain features of the Act, they too bowed to the necessity of seeking government assistance.

The technical advances made in airplane construction during the First World War removed the airplane from its earlier association with sport and made it an important part of our transportation system. But while such nations as Germany heavily subsidized commercial aviation, the United States, feeling secure from air attack because of her geographic isolation, did little during the early twenties beyond providing air-mail service. A new day came with the Kelley Act of 1925, which authorized postal officials to contract with private operators to carry air mail and allowed a generous profit at the Treasury's expense.

Popular attention was focused on aviation for the first time by the spectacular transatlantic flights of Lindbergh, Byrd, and Chamberlin during 1927–1928. Most important for the immediate future of the industry was the bull market of 1928–1929, for millions of dollars poured into aviation. As a result, approximately 7400 planes were in operation in 1929, the passenger traffic almost reached the three-million mark, and the annual output of the aircraft industry was valued at around 100 million dollars. This record was indeed unique considering that commercial aviation dated back no further than 1926.

THE RADIO AND URBANIZATION

Even more intrusive than the automobile and airplane as the missionary of urban sophistication was the radio, which first became popular in the winter of 1921–1922. Although the basic inventions had been made before the war, they had scarcely been applied commercially when the Westinghouse Electric Company set up Station KDKA in East Pittsburgh in 1920 and broadcast the Harding-Cox election results. Within a brief period, radio receiving sets and incidentally the programs had so improved that the sales of radios and radio accessories soared from $60,000,000 in 1922 to over $842,000,000 in 1929, and practically one family out of every three owned a radio. Newspaper owners were apprehensive at first over having to compete with the radio in the dissemination of news but soon discovered that their circulation figures continued to rise.

Although the earlier programs were sponsored by the radio manufacturers themselves, the burden of financing them was soon assumed by individual companies who spent from seven to twenty million dollars annually to bring their products before the millions of radio listeners. This vast audience was apparently more than willing to hear about the merits of Campbell's Soup or Ipana Tooth Paste if in addition it was provided with entertainment by highly paid stars. Although the din of jazz monopolized the programs, radio stations also offered concerts, operas, plays, and lectures—undoubtedly a higher level of entertainment than that provided by the average motion picture of the twenties.

Sociologists were quick to point out the rich social implications of the radio. Like the automobile, the radio broke down regional and national cultural barriers; it standardized speech and brought an urban outlook to the village. It provided greater safety for airplanes and ships. It was a means of popularization, for it could rapidly exploit various pieces of music, in some cases to the saturation point; it stimulated interest in sports and gave travel added pleasure. The radio aided adult education, although early hopes for a "university of the air" failed to materialize as fully as expected; it popularized domestic science, health information, and scientific farming, and quickened the general interest in current events. The Republican and Democratic parties spent $1,250,000 for radio time during the 1928 campaign.

Radio fostered centralization of every type and made the nation a more cohesive community because the traditional states' rights variety of federalism declined. Governor Franklin D. Roosevelt of New York found the radio an ideal instrument in defending his policies before the people of that state. Had radio been available on a popular scale in 1919, Wilson might have been spared to the nation, for he broke down in the attempt to bring his appeal for the League personally to the voters. On the other hand, there were complaints that radio advertisers and other interested groups kept important issues off the air. Thus the radio commentator, H. V. Kaltenborn, who then favored our diplomatic recognition of Russia, was temporarily deprived of his time on the radio.

The formative period in the history of radio culminated in 1929, when 606 broadcasting stations were in existence in the United States; some of them had joined one of the two major networks, the National Broadcasting Company and the Columbia Broadcasting System. Two years before this, in an effort to bring order out of the welter of overlapping wave lengths and avoid the resultant conflict in radio programs, Congress had created the Federal Radio Commission.

"WELFARE CAPITALISM" AND THE UNIONS

The position of labor in the wake of expanding industry was far more favorable than it had ever been. Wages rose, the eight-hour day became almost universal, even in the steel industry, and the five-day week made considerable progress in the building and painting trades, the New York clothing industry, and various seasonal occupations. Industrial prosperity and the "welfare capitalism" preached in the Chambers of Commerce as well as in the White House emphasized the high cost of a heavy labor turnover and the advantage to be derived from friendly labor relations.

Daniel Willard's Baltimore and Ohio Railroad led the way, after the shopmen's strike of 1922, in introducing democratic shop representation within a union framework and assuring steady employment by eliminating outside contracts. "Business scientists" were quick to see the advantage gained by industry from high wages, shorter hours, profit-sharing plans, facilities for employee recreation, and pleasant working conditions. Many corporations instituted group insurance plans covering death, disability, and retirement. Here indeed was the enlightened self-interest that the philosophers of the eighteenth century had dreamed of.

But technological unemployment gave the picture a less favorable aspect. For example, in 1929 the Railway Brotherhoods demanded a six-hour day in order to employ the "victims of the machine." As the result of the progress in efficiency, they claimed, one train crew and one engine crew could now do the work for which five had formerly been needed, and some 350,000 men had accordingly been laid off since 1920. Mechanized industry undeniably demanded speed and agility rather than experience and mature judgment; this meant a reduction in the number of older men employed. However, part of this reduction may have been due to discrimination against older men because of group insurance and pension plans.

Contrary to precedent in the history of American labor, the ranks of organized labor experienced no expansion, for the craft-conscious leaders of the American Federation of Labor had no strong desire to organize the unskilled workers on whom mechanized industry depended. Consequently trade-union membership declined to its prewar figure of slightly over three million. Part of this decline was undoubtedly due to the increasingly poor conditions in the coal mines and to the open-shop movement in 1920–1921, as well as to the elimination of the highly paid skilled workers in the new machine shops.

Critics charged that William Green, and particularly Matthew Woll, president and vice president respectively of the A. F. of L., were too much interested in "patrioteering nationalism"—that is, in lobbying for high tariff rates and immigration restriction—to be concerned with the advance of genuine labor aims. As a result, the pioneer impulse for the social security movement came from outside the ranks of the A. F. of L. Political corruption and union racketeering went unchecked. Some of the A. F. of L. locals in the South, not satisfied with the long-standing rules which excluded Negroes from certain trades, introduced bills in several state legislatures to exclude Negro barbers from serving whites, despite the fact that this was a well-established custom.

Certain of the larger independent unions accepted the popular philosophy of "welfare capitalism" but sought to maintain their own initiative and control in promoting better labor conditions. The powerful clothing unions, led by the Amalgamated Clothing Workers and the International Ladies Garment Workers, had won outstanding victories in the past in the battle for collective bargaining. They entered the field of unemployment insurance in 1923; in 1929, when the crash came, they continued this experiment and had an excellent record of solvency. Frankly accepting the ideal of efficiency, the Amalgamated sought to cooperate with employers in eliminating waste in production and even financed certain manufacturers. Piece rates were cut in order to stimulate business and bring about greater annual earnings. This union was also a pioneer in experimenting with low-cost housing, for it sponsored a huge cooperative project for its members in the crowded sections of New York City. The Congressmen who were then assailing the dangers to be expected from eastern European immigration might better have paid tribute to the members of this union who, predominantly of Russian and Polish descent, apparently had mastered the most difficult techniques of industrial democracy.

Less fortunate were the experiments in labor banking initiated by the Brotherhood of Locomotive Engineers. This movement was designed, among other things, to create from the workers' savings a fund, earmarked for investment, that would be large enough to influence an employer's labor policy. By 1926 thirty-five banks with total resources of over $126,500,000 had been established, but thereafter a steady decline set in, the result of inefficient management as well as adverse financial conditions. Like the short-lived cooperative labor and Granger enterprises of the 1870's, this attempt of labor to turn capitalist failed.

"BORING FROM WITHIN"

In the face of the generally optimistic labor picture, the plight of the mine worker was deplorable. Bituminous coal operators, faced by destructive competition, began to turn to the cheaper non-union mines of West Virginia, Kentucky, and Alabama. As a result, 3300 mines were closed during 1923–1929, a quarter of a million men were deprived of work, and the wages of those who were kept on were cut drastically. John L. Lewis, acting for the United Mine Workers, stubbornly insisted on the existing wage contracts, a policy which critics within the union ranks claimed had in the first place forced the operators to abandon the union mines and work non-union pits. As an alternative these insurgents demanded an aggressive campaign to unionize the southern mine workers. When union miners in western Pennsylvania were evicted from their homes by company police and denied the right of assemblage, sympathy was expressed openly by a Senate investigating committee and the A. F. of L. The situation was further complicated when Communists rallied to the support of the anti-Lewis faction; this enabled Lewis to stigmatize union factionalism as a Communist product and to expel his enemies from the U.M.W. Although Lewis scored a personal triumph, the tragedy of the coal miner remained unsolved except among the more fortunate anthracite workers.

After the labor upsurge of 1919–1922, strikes declined steadily, but one major conflict aroused the nation. This occurred in January, 1925, at Passaic, New Jersey, a leading woolen center, when over 20,000 textile workers struck in protest against a wage cut and long hours. When Polish priests encouraged their poverty-stricken parishioners to hold street demonstrations, the sheriff invoked a Civil War statute outlawing union meetings as well as picketing. Norman Thomas, the Socialist, went to Passaic to test the statute and was promptly jailed, whereupon the American Civil Liberties Union secured an injunction which restrained the sheriff from interfering with the strikers' meetings. After a year marked by considerable violence and by futile efforts at mediation by the governor and Senators La Follette and Borah and by still more futile appeals to Coolidge, the strike came to a successful end. Suspicion in the ranks of organized labor that this strike was called primarily to serve the political aims of Communism created serious confusion in the policy adopted by the A. F. of L. toward this and similar disputes. A fear that the Communists were using their well-known tactics of "boring from within" strengthened the conservatives' control of the Federation throughout the twenties.

THE NATIONAL ORIGINS ACT

American labor, eager to win access to trades dominated by immigrants, joined with other restrictionist groups in urging Congress to curb immigration, but the Act that was finally passed in 1924 was more nationalist than economic in nature. The existing law allotted to each country (except for certain non-quota nations, largely in this hemisphere) a quota of 3 per cent of its nationals who had been residents of the United States in 1910. Although this new Act was intended to favor northwestern Europe, immigrants from that section had been so few as to constitute only half of the quota, whereas those from the impoverished southeastern section represented practically the entire quota; furthermore, there was no drop in immigration totals. Accordingly, the nationalists insisted that 1890, the census year before immigration from southern and eastern Europe became heavy, be used as the quota basis in order to reduce the Slav, Italian, Greek, and Russian Jewish figures. As a concession particularly to the economic argument for restriction, the quota for each country was cut from 3 per cent to 2. Racialist sentiment apparently was so strong that a complicated "national origins" clause, to become effective on July 1, 1927, had to be included in the 1924 Act. This clause (delayed in execution until 1929) provided that the total number of immigrants should be fixed at 150,000 per year, and that national quotas should be determined on the basis of the proportion of the number of American descendants of each nationality in 1920 to the total population of that year—a fine puzzle for genealogists!

If labor expected to benefit from this law, its hopes were quickly dissipated, for hundreds of thousands of Mexicans, Canadians, and French-Canadians, all non-quota peoples, crossed the border into this country, and a large but undetermined number of European immigrants entered illegally. Puerto Ricans swarmed into New York City, and Filipinos came in sufficient numbers—to California in particular—to be the cause of an occasional race riot. The results were tragic for the immigrants from southern and eastern Europe; families were separated, and desperate attempts to enter the United States, illegally if need be, brought the total number of deportations to a new high. Jane Addams at Hull House noted the pathetic feeling of rejection suffered by the children of alien parents in school. When Chicago's Mayor William Hale Thompson opened a well-publicized campaign against pro-English textbooks in history and offered to "punch King George on the snoot," he not only garnered the Irish and German vote, as he had anticipated, but also became the champion of the Slovaks, Greeks, Italians, Negroes, and other minority groups against the Anglo-Saxons' flamboyant theories of superiority.

"RACIAL INTEGRITY" LAWS

Well within the immigration walls but facing similar restrictions of racialism was the Negro. A wave of "racial integrity" laws, perhaps resulting from the new interest in heredity and eugenics, swept twenty-nine states, largely in the South. These laws forbade marriage between Negroes and whites and essayed a definition of the word "Negro"—a task that was apparently elusive. Eleven states considered an eighth of Negro blood damning; others, like Alabama, Georgia, and Virginia, applied the new intermarriage ban to whites who had even a suspicion of Negro blood. Whereas old-line Southerners ignored the discussion over the long-established custom of "passing" because it would embarrass many a famous name, aggressive politicians raised the threadbare banner of white supremacy and launched a program calling for increased segregation of the races. The Richmond *News Leader* aroused a furore in the South by pointing out that if the racial integrity laws had been in effect early enough, two Presidents, two Senators, an ambassador to France, three governors, five generals, and various other members of the "first families of Virginia" would have been branded as "Negroes."

There was, however, a marked decline in lynchings. According to a study made by the Tuskegee Institute, there were 76 in 1919; this had dropped to 16 in 1924, and to the exceptionally low number, 7, in 1929. Furthermore, more southern police officials showed a determination to punish lynchers and to protect prisoners from mob attacks. But, on the other hand, a federal anti-lynching bill was killed by a Senate filibuster.

The prevalent prosperity inevitably improved the economic status of the Negro. Despite the concerted effort of the unions and of unemployed white people in rural sections to oust Negroes from the building trades and from barber shops that catered to white people, Negroes found a multitude of new jobs in the lumbering and tobacco industries, in garages and filling stations, and in the large factories of the North, especially in automobile construction, metal work, and meat packing. Open-shop employers welcomed them. The number of Negroes employed by the federal government practically doubled during the decade and increasing numbers found civil service positions in New York, Chicago, and other northern cities.

The Negro vote in Chicago proved strong enough to elect a colored Congressman, Oscar de Priest, who could now champion his people's cause in Washington. Negro businessmen, frankly accepting segregation, strove to establish their own banking, insurance, personal service, and retail store enterprises. The musical genius of Roland Hayes and Paul Robeson won the enthusiastic patronage of their fellow men, regardless of color. Negro education made spectacular advances, especially in high school and college enrollment. The South built more high schools for Negroes during this decade than during her entire past. By the end of the twenties there were an estimated 15,000 Negro college graduates, of whom forty were doctors of philosophy, sixty-five were members of Phi Beta Kappa, and at least one was a Rhodes scholar. The avalanche of books sympathetic to the Negro testified to a marked improvement in race relations.

FORD'S EXPERIMENT IN ANTI-SEMITISM

Before the full effects of prosperity were felt during the late twenties, America's minority peoples were harassed by racialism and nationalism, fed by similar trends in Europe. Even before the war, many Jews had been discriminated against in employment and in summer resorts. Now, however, the racialists assailed this people, regardless of place of birth or achievement, as insufferable aliens and tried to restrict the proportionate number of Jewish college students and teachers by the medieval *numerus clausus*. Klan propaganda and debates on immigration made it clear that tired Israel must gird itself once more for a struggle for survival.

Strongly suggestive of czarist and medieval German anti-Semitism were the many corrosive attacks on the "international Jew" in Henry Ford's magazine, *The Dearborn Independent;* its anti-Semitic arguments were later of great value to Hitler's National Socialists. But after 1925 a racialism founded on social insecurity ceased—for the time being at least—to be popular. As the hunt for dollars became more exciting than the pursuit of Jews, Henry Ford publicly, if belatedly, completely disavowed the magazine articles. The Jews, like the Negroes, were more optimistic at the end of the decade than they had been at the beginning.

POPULATION TRENDS AND THE FARMER

Whatever population problems there were during the twenties, the specters of "standing room only" conjured up by certain journalists was not among them. Although the 1930 census showed a gain of over seventeen million since 1920, the rate of increase was downward as compared with the trend during the nineteenth century. It was easy to envisage the future with a stationary and ultimately declining population. During 1920–1930, the 45–64 age group grew in number by one-fourth, and the 65–74 age group increased by a third. This trend reflected an increased life expectancy from an average slightly above 51 years in 1919 to a new high of 59.09 in 1930, and was accompanied by a greater public interest in old age pensions, adult education, and security. On the other hand, the number of children under 5 decreased sharply, for the World War, as anticipated, resulted in an immediate drop in the birth rate; and despite prosperity, or perhaps because of it, the rate never fully recovered. Urban migration, especially to New York City, continued as before the war; it resulted in a net change of six million persons and involved entire families rather than individuals.

The decline of at least 1,200,000 in the farm population, especially in New England, and the population gain in non-farm areas reflected the farmer's failure to share fully in the general prosperity after 1922. But there were other factors—for example, the increasing mechanization of the farm and the inevitable contraction of overexpanded acreages. Moreover, as farm productivity more than kept pace with consumption, overproduction became a chronic complaint. Changes in the American diet also affected certain farmers adversely, for many people turned from the traditional cereal diet to meals balanced with dairy products, vegetables, fruits, and sugar. Thus milk consumption increased by one-half during the decade.

For farmers who could adjust themselves to the changing demand by diversifying their crops, and for the average large-scale farmer as well, the twenties meant increased incomes. Considerable agricultural advance was made in Virginia with the aid of northern capital, and North Carolina's tobacco planters prospered as their output soared ninefold in value. But the innumerable small farmers who raised staple crops welcomed farm tenancy as a release from pressing obligations. These farmers could not understand why the city distributor of farm products was so prosperous while they themselves received so little for their produce; they showed little patience with the explanations of economists. Farm real estate values, measured in terms of purchasing power, averaged 20 per cent less at the beginning of 1929 than in 1914. Hence, as we shall see later, the farmers' rebellion assumed formidable proportions in the politics of the twenties.

FAMILY TRENDS: "ACCENT ON YOUTH"

Just as the new technology broke down the traditional patterns of economic organization and behavior, so the individualism of the postwar decade, encouraged by the apparent victory over the material universe, upset conventional patterns of family, church, school, and press. But much of this individualism, as Sinclair Lewis suggested in *Babbitt* and *Main Street,* involved the uncritical acceptance of machine-inspired values and of stereotyped prejudices clad in modern dress. The commercialization of social life brought with it a new orthodoxy, but social conformity, as ever, remained an indispensable virtue. Although the rapid social changes during the twenties indicated that the younger generation would at first be a problem to the older, the new orthodoxy won out so quickly that matrons were soon pathetically imitating the ways of the "flapper"—cocktails, cigarettes, bobbed hair, short skirts, and all. Expenditures for cosmetics and perfumes increased eightfold during 1914–1925. "Accent on youth" became the theme of this pleasure-loving decade.

Emancipated women, so bravely portrayed in Ibsen's *A Doll's House* during the nineties, were now part of the new orthodoxy. Increasing numbers of women sought "careers" as stenographers, teachers, nurses, and clerks. The reduction in housework and home interests was reflected in the small apartment with its kitchenette, its delicatessen meals, and its numerous electrical appliances to economize time and labor. Families had fewer children, and pre-kindergarten "nursery schools" were available for infants of middle-class parents. In 1914 one couple out of every ten was divorced, but by 1929 the rate had risen to one out of six. The brief residence that Reno, Nevada, required for a divorce enabled that "wide-open" western town to offer a cheap and convivial substitute for the speedier but more expensive Paris decree.

To the emancipated woman of the twenties, the grant of suffrage by the Nineteenth Amendment seemed a matter of course. The agitation for woman suffrage, which dated back to the days of Frances Wright and Lucretia Mott, had achieved partial success after 1868, when Wyoming Territory led a group of western states in enfranchising women. Nation-wide woman suffrage lagged, however, until August 18, 1920, when Tennessee, at Wilson's instigation, became the thirty-sixth state to ratify the so-called Susan B. Anthony Amendment, thus assuring its passage. Even so, almost two years had elapsed since September, 1918, when he had urged Congress to pass the amendment as "vital to the winning of the war."

Although the enfranchisement of women did not double the electorate because of the indifference of many of the new voters, the amendment was valuable in that it enabled several powerful women's lobbies to promote essential social legislation. In 1921 they secured the passage of the Shepard-Towner Act, which created cooperative state and federal bureaus of child hygiene and also prenatal centers that offered free instruction to mothers. The following year they achieved another victory in the Cable Act, which made the citizenship of a married woman independent of her husband's status. In 1924 they started the ill-fated child labor amendment on its way through the state legislatures. By the end of the decade, organized lobbies like the Women's Joint Congressional Committee had put through 436 state and local laws in behalf of child welfare, education, social hygiene, and honest government, and women were holding prominent offices on the national, state, and local scene. Politicians came to fear the intelligent scrutiny of leagues of women voters. If woman suffrage did not bring the millennium, neither, it must be admitted, did the votes of the men.

The World War hastened the trend, which had been apparent earlier, toward new sex standards. Adolescent precocity as regards sex marked the 1920's. The automobile and bootleg liquor made many a "petting party" far from innocuous. Pointing out the increasing number of illicit unions, Judge Ben B. Lindsey of Denver caused a nationwide controversy by proposing "companionate marriage," a plan that called for a preliminary trial period. The semi-literate imbibed the new standards through such channels as Bernarr McFadden's *True Story Magazine,* which had a circulation of almost two million in 1926; but the sophisticated preferred the sex theories propounded by Sigmund Freud, a Viennese doctor who became high priest of the easy elimination of inhibitions and repressions in sexual behavior.

Vainly—and unintelligently—the Customs Office, the Post Office Department, the police, and Will Hays' office in Hollywood strove to curb the new trend by means of censorship. Even as sophisticated a critic as George Jean Nathan bluntly labeled the plays then running in New York, Boston, and Chicago as "open-and-shut sex exhibits" and "anatomical clinics." In summing up the season of 1929 he observed, "Not a single clean play has enjoyed a really profitable engagement." The authors of popular books on sexual perversion received a "safe and certain revenue." But the untrained censors frequently blacklisted worth-while books and plays in their fumbling and overzealous attempts to eradicate "smut."

THE SCHOOL IN AN ERA OF ECONOMIC EXPANSION

Prosperity made possible a sensational increase in education, particularly in the secondary schools. Three per cent of the nation's income, or almost three billion dollars, was expended for this purpose in 1928, making education the most expensive single activity of the American community, outside of waging war. A high school education became almost universal during the decade, partly as a result of the new labor laws which strained existing school facilities. The number of junior colleges at least tripled, and colleges and professional schools numbered over a thousand. The 532 doctor of philosophy degrees granted by graduate schools in 1920 had quadrupled by the end of the decade. This mushroom growth of Ph.D.'s brought a sharp criticism of graduate schools from the American Association of Colleges in 1929; it charged that college teachers were superficially trained in institutions which stressed formal and barren research. Adult education, especially Americanization courses, showed remarkable growth, as did also pre-school or nursery school education. Schools for the blind, the deaf, and the mentally defective increased greatly in number. Significantly, the crowded classroom of the 1920's reflected the declining influence on the individual of the traditional home and church environment; the weight of personality adjustment and vocational training was thrown upon the school.

Vocational training in the spirit of John Dewey's "learning by doing" gained momentum, spurred on by industry and government. The increase in high school subjects from twenty-three in 1910 to forty-seven in 1928 occurred largely in home economics, manual training, machine shop, music, typewriting, and bookkeeping. Partly as the result of Dewey's influence in the elementary school field, foreign languages in the grade schools were replaced by applied civics, industrial arts, and supervised play. Practical courses in commerce, applied arts and sciences, and law usurped the long-established place in the college curricula held by classical studies. The federal government itself expanded the high school and college curriculum by introducing Reserve Officers Training Corps courses and generously subsidizing vocational education under the provisions of the Smith-Hughes Act of 1917.

Despite vociferous protests, sex education was included in high schools and college curricula, a move which was strongly supported by the American Social Hygiene Association and such religious groups as the Y.M.C.A. and the Federal Council of Churches. The World War helped to dissipate the traditional silence concerning venereal diseases and stimulated medical research in this field. Moreover, the writings of G. Stanley Hall and Havelock Ellis advocated frank scientific instruction in sex for adolescents.

The press of the 1920's waged bitter warfare on the evils in American schools and colleges. For example, in his book *The Goose Step* (1923), Upton Sinclair called attention—albeit with considerable exaggeration—to the close connection between education and capitalism as evidenced by heavy college endowments and the dismissal of liberal professors. But no one could dismiss as exaggerated the revelations of the Federal Trade Commission regarding the presence of propaganda in certain textbooks that assailed government ownership and defended private utilities. Certain commerce professors at well-known colleges were shown to have been paid fees by the public utility lobby.

The current emphasis on commercial ideals relegated the teacher to a minor social status in the community. Few states protected instructors as far as academic tenure was concerned. Hysterically patriotic agencies, like New York's Lusk Committee, frequently deprived teachers of their civic right to criticize the social order or to express opinions on controversial subjects; thus, New York teachers were required to take a sweeping "loyalty" test which could be used as a legal weapon against unorthodox ideas. During the war the Chicago *Tribune,* under the slogan, "My Country, Right or Wrong," demanded the dismissal of every pacifist teacher. The prevalent theory that taxpayers had the right to decide what should be taught in schools supported by public funds made it possible to ban the teaching of evolution in several states and to prescribe the inculcation of approved nationalist principles in many more. There was little dignity in a profession whose members were usually paid less than semi-skilled workers and were all too often subjected to the bullying of unsympathetic school boards and deans.

RELIGION: THE FUNDAMENTALIST CRUSADE

The iconoclastic spirit of the twenties forced organized religion to the defensive, although church membership, it was claimed, continued to increase proportionately with the population. While Catholic and Fundamentalist leaders stoutly condemned birth control, other churches split on the issue. The large convention representing Lutheran youth that the International Walther League held in San Francisco in 1928 unanimously passed a resolution condemning "modernism, liberalism, evolution, and radicalism." The number of Catholics was adversely affected, for immigration restrictions cut down the number of Italian and Slav newcomers. Foreign missionary activities suffered from the rise of nationalism in Japan, China, and Turkey. The Japanese, in particular, replaced occidental clergymen by natives and nationalized the church.

Churches met the increasingly secular interests of their members by providing gymnasiums, game rooms, and athletic fields both to attract young people and—in keeping with Dewey's progressive ideas—to aid religious education through a beneficial environment. Religious funds poured into hospitals, colleges, orphanages, and charities in ever larger amounts. The sharp increase in the number of parochial schools inspired Klansmen and Fundamentalists in Oregon to combine in initiating a measure designed to outlaw all such schools, but court action brought by Catholics and Lutherans nullified the law as interfering with parental control over a child's education. The Federal Council of the Churches of Christ in America, which embraced over twenty Protestant sects, displayed considerable militancy in campaigning against poor industrial conditions, race prejudice, and war; its role in the steel strike of 1919 has already been mentioned. Peter Odegard, a social scientist, considers it significant that in forty-one sermons delivered in New York City on September 22, 1929, the word "sin" was used only once.

One feature of the history of the church during this decade was the upsurge of conservative Fundamentalism in the South and Middle West. This anti-liberal wing of Protestantism emphasized "revealed fundamental religion" and the literal interpretation of the Bible, particularly in relation to the creation of man; it was vehement in its denunciation of the Darwinian theory of evolution. Neither instruction in the sciences nor secular interests were encouraged, as a rule, in educational institutions dominated by Fundamentalists. Teachers not only were required to accept the "five points" of Fundamentalism but were severely restricted as to dancing, "going out," wearing short dresses, and pursuing any other activity which the church school board regarded as unorthodox. To rid the public schools of the taint of evolution, the Fundamentalists had by 1925 secured the passage of laws prohibiting the teaching of this subject in Arkansas, Florida, Oklahoma, Kentucky, and Tennessee, among others. William Jennings Bryan, now a resident of Florida and the outstanding lobbyist for all these activities, appeared before joint legislative sessions in various southern states to plead that the teaching of evolution be banned. In Miami he conducted the "largest Bible class in the world," and he entreated its two or three thousand students to manifest the faith traditionally shown by rural America against the inroads of modernism. So successful was he that Fundamentalists came to regard him as their particular champion.

Both Fundamentalists and their opponents seized eagerly upon a chance to test the constitutionality of Tennessee's law against the teaching of evolution. This chance was offered when John Thomas Scopes, a young biology instructor at Central High School in Dayton, Tennessee, deliberately gave himself up as a violator of the statute. Fundamentalists, eager to win a public victory for the "old-time religion," immediately retained Bryan to represent them. The liberals turned to Clarence Darrow, a frankly agnostic criminal lawyer of Chicago who had recently won nation-wide fame by his successful defense of young Nathan Leopold, Jr., and Richard Loeb against charges of murdering Robert Franks. Dudley Field Malone and Arthur Garfield Hays, two distinguished lawyers employed by the Civil Liberties Union, also appeared for Scopes.

In a celebrated trial before a jury composed almost exclusively of Baptist and Methodist farmers, Bryan and Darrow fought each other on the stand, practically ignoring Scopes. The press sent its best reporters to Dayton, inspiring the greatest fanfare of publicity in its history; as a result, the trial benefited newspaper revenue more than religion or science. Darrow, who considered Bryan a "jackass," asked him to name the date of the creation of the earth and to give a logical explanation for the story of Jonah and the whale and of Joshua and the sun; but Bryan, confident that religion itself was on trial, seldom lost his composure. "The purpose of this examination," he charged, "is to cast ridicule on everybody who believes in the Bible," whereupon Darrow shouted, "We think the purpose is preventing bigots and ignoramuses from controlling the education of the United States." Scopes, as expected, was convicted but was soon released at the instance of the prosecutor. The trial, however, ended tragically for Bryan, for, worn out by his strenuous efforts during the heat of a Tennessee July, the Great Commoner died a few days after adjournment, his lifetime of service stained by the buffoonish proceedings at the Dayton "monkey trial."

THE NEWSPAPERS AND THE TABLOID ERA

The press thrived on the sensationalism of the Leopold-Loeb murder case, the Dayton trial, and the Hall-Mills murder, giving these and other similar events an exaggerated emphasis for its readers.

Hearst instructed his editors to "disregard, or cover perfunctorily, subjects which are merely important, but not interesting." Most papers gave feature articles, sports, crime, advertising, and business news the space once reserved for editorial opinion, local news, and politics; as the result, there were few papers like Adolph Ochs' New York *Times* which still presented "all the news that's fit to print."

Various reasons account for the heightened commercialization of the press. The newspaper business in the twenties was a battle between giants, even more than it had been before the war. Smaller papers were gobbled up by the great chains; thus there were 2000 fewer papers in 1929 than in 1914, and some large cities were left without any morning newspapers. But million-dollar journalistic enterprises required greater caution and conservatism on the part of the publisher; he had to guard against any taint of radicalism and be more attentive to his advertisers' sensibilities. A Federal Trade Commission investigation of public utility propaganda revealed gross venality on the part of numerous newspapers in accepting what amounted to bribes in the form of advertising intended to convert critics to supporters. Although one editor, Ernest Gruening, pointed out that the majority of the papers in Klan territory were discreetly silent regarding the depredations of Klan members, there were exceptions; for example, the Indianapolis *Times* lost fifteen or twenty thousand readers by assailing the Klan, but it continued the campaign, regardless of cost, until the grip of the Klan was broken.

The Scripps-Howard chain of newspapers was undoubtedly a force for good, but like its contemporaries, even it had to make its editorial policies increasingly impersonal. A survival of a better day in intelligent personal journalism was William Allen White's Emporia (Kansas) *Gazette*. Some progress in covering foreign news was made, especially with the development of foreign correspondents during the war; but as a rule the proportion of foreign to domestic news scarcely exceeded 5 per cent. The *Christian Science Monitor* of Boston was an important exception, for its foreign news dispatches were extensive and they proved invaluable to intelligent observers of world affairs. Perhaps our diplomacy during the twenties would not have been so bleakly isolationist if our press had given us adequate foreign news reports.

Millions of converts were won over to newspaper reading during this decade by the rise of tabloids, most of which purveyed unadulterated yellow journalism in compact form. When the McCormick-Patterson group discovered that the press had ignored one potential group of readers in New York City—the semi-literate who could easily be persuaded to read simple accounts about crime, sex, and publicity-seekers presented mostly by means of pictures—they promptly founded the New York *Daily News,* a tabloid which attained great success. Not to be outdone, Hearst followed with the New York *Mirror,* and Bernarr McFadden with the *Graphic;* the latter outdid both the others in salacious journalism.

BOOTLEGGING AS A VOCATION

The hedonist tendencies of the twenties ran sharply counter to the Eighteenth Amendment, ratified in January, 1920, which forbade the manufacture, transportation, or sale of intoxicating liquors. Still worse was the Volstead Act which was passed immediately afterward to enforce the prohibition amendment, for it defined an intoxicating beverage as one that contained one-half of one per cent alcohol and in addition it imposed severe penalties for violation. Thereafter, as evasion of the new law grew widespread, the sentiment for prohibition declined rapidly. Thus a poll of nearly two million people conducted in 1926 by the Newspaper Enterprise Association showed that only 19 per cent favored the Volstead Act, 50 per cent wanted it modified to permit the sale of light wines and beer, and 31 per cent were for repeal. Although he favored temperance by independent state and local action, Wilson vetoed the Volstead Act as too restrictive, but Congress passed it over his veto.

The social results of prohibition are obscured by controversy and by the dearth of trustworthy statistics. Rural America, on the whole, remained dry, but urban areas evaded the law, as witness the popularity of cocktail and beer parties and the countless "speakeasies" that sprang up almost overnight. Prohibition was particularly resented by beer-drinking Germans and wine-drinking Italians. The wealthy probably consumed as much liquor as ever, even if it was worse, but the poorer classes necessarily became comparatively dry. Bootlegging grew into a major enterprise which was closely integrated with smuggling and the illicit brewing business. Enforcement officials were able to halt rumrunning by larger vessels, but after 1925 it was taken up by small motor boats, especially in the Great Lakes. The officials seized hundreds of millions of dollars' worth of property, ranging from home-brew outfits to the rumrunners' launches and automobiles. Between 1920 and 1928, 135 persons were killed by federal officers and 55 of the latter lost their lives. A congressional committee reported in 1929 that 3000 bootleggers were active in the one city of Washington, D. C.

Gangsters in Chicago aspired to national leadership in the bootlegging business because of the city's strategic location near Canada and its undisputed control over the liquor supplies of the West and North West. The enormous potential profits led to gang wars and to desperate attempts at the wholesale bribery of local government officials for "protection." The obvious necessity of decentralizing the liquor business and the reversion to home methods of production made ambitious men compete bitterly in their effort to control as many stills as possible. "Hijackers" seized the liquor trucks of bootleggers who could rely only on their own high-priced bodyguards or gangs for protection. Although consolidation methods, as Jane Addams observed, were ruthless and terroristic, they were not unlike the desperate methods adopted earlier in the Pennsylvania oil fields.

Legendary exploits were attributed to such bootleg kings as Al Capone, Dean O'Bannion, and the O'Donnells. Such events as the Valentine Day Massacre of 1929, in which seven men were lined up against the wall of a garage in Chicago and then shot down by machine-gun fire, were usually clear proof that rival gangs had been at work. The infamous six Genna brothers, originally from Sicily, eventually dominated much of the city's traffic in domestic alcohol by underselling all their competitors; they became millionaires, but three of them were slain in a gang war. Syndicates were formed by bootleggers to dictate prices within a specified territory; uncooperative dealers were threatened with being "taken for a ride." A mushroom growth of roadhouses in "safe" outlying areas forced the older cabarets in the city to close, and the "alky cookers" on Chicago's West Side, especially along the dilapidated river front, experienced new prosperity.

Prohibition furnished one of many opportunities for criminals, but here again the statistics are incomplete. Newspapers repeatedly asserted that a "crime wave" was in progress, but the accuracy of this description was effectively disputed by Professor George W. Kirchwey of Columbia University, a noted criminologist. Prohibition and traffic violations, many of them for drunken driving, did swell the totals for minor offenses, but the available evidence did not indicate any sharply accelerated increase in the activities of professional criminals. Nor did many criminologists accept the popular theory which attributed the so-called "crime wave" to the confusion resulting from the prevalent multiplicity of laws. But new types of crime did arise—for example, the "rackets" that permeated numerous service trades in Chicago, especially during the "open-town" era while Thompson was mayor. Cleaners and dyers, teamsters and painters were bombed for failing to pay tribute—or protection, as it was more politely called—to racketeers.

The bandits of the twenties drove high-powered motor cars and fought with automatic guns, sometimes with machine guns. To fight them, the police were organized into well-armed squads which used armored cars equipped with radio communication devices and provided with tear-gas bombs. Federal officials were increasingly drawn into the fight as the automobile made crimes like kidnaping interstate offenses. Cooperation between local and federal officials increased, especially as regards fingerprinting. But too little was done in the way of prison reform. The unscientific methods and overcrowded conditions characteristic of our prisons led to the great prison riots of 1929, in which a score of men were killed and prison property suffered heavy damage. This was, at least in part, a protest against the dark, ill-ventilated cells, the practice of handcuffing prisoners to walls and floors, the brutal lashing of inmates, and the "sweat boxes" for trouble-makers.

THE MOVIES: ERA OF CECIL B. DE MILLE

By 1930, movies had become so deeply imbedded in American life that between eighty-five and one hundred million people were attending local theaters weekly and paying over $1,500,000,000 annually in admissions. The period of World War I marked the transformation of the motion picture from a spectacle intended for the poorer classes into a leading form of middle-class entertainment. Although Hollywood could on occasion produce great films that surpassed the best stage plays, it was involved too deeply in mammoth investments—almost two billion dollars' worth—to be able to disregard the cultural tastes of the least critical groups among its world-wide audiences. Since nine-tenths of all the movies originated in Hollywood, this caution led to so many cocktail and gangster movies that foreigners were given a grossly distorted idea of life in the United States. Of necessity, whatever incipient progressivism the prewar film had shown was discarded in favor of escapist themes and the individualist attitudes so popular in the 1920's.

Mergers snuffed out independents and led to such powerful combinations of producers, distributors, and exhibitors as Paramount, Metro-Goldwyn-Mayer, and First National, that controlled some 20,000 theaters in 1927. Warner Brothers surmounted its financial crisis that same year by introducing the first feature-length "talkie" in *The Jazz Singer*. Elaborate theaters sprang up everywhere. Producers spent an average of well over $100,000 on a picture; *Ben Hur,* the most expensive of all, cost $6,000,000, according to *Variety*. Movie salaries reached fabulous proportions; in two years William S. Hart earned $900,000 as the star in cowboy films. However, thousands of musicians in small theaters were driven from their jobs by the advent of sound motion pictures, and many stars of the "silent" screen were unable to meet the voice requirements of sound films. To formulate a common business code and to counter a rising demand for federal censorship, the movie magnates introduced self-regulation in 1922 through the Motion Picture Producer's and Distributor's Association and chose Harding's Postmaster General, Will H. Hays, to head it. Hays, who had had considerable political experience as chairman of the Republican National Committee, turned these talents effectively to his exacting task in public relations.

The sophistication of the 1920's was faithfully mirrored in the films. Lewis Jacobs' excellent analysis, *The Rise of the American Film,* reveals the determining influence exercised by the director, Cecil B. De Mille, over postwar motion pictures. De Mille capitalized on the fact that even the poor reveled in seeing films showing luxurious boudoirs, upper-class manners and fine clothes, and "super-colossal" spectacles. The average audience, he knew, was attracted by sex motifs and sensationalism, and he furnished these qualities in generous measure. The vogue spread, bringing the sophistication of Greenwich Village to the entire country. Clara Bow, famed as the "it" girl of the film versions of Elinor Glyn's novels, became the symbol of "flaming youth" and "sex appeal" (conveniently abbreviated as S.A.). Rudolph Valentino's torrid love scenes, especially in *The Sheik,* made him the idol of countless women; his sudden death brought mobs of these admirers to the undertaking parlor where his body lay in state.

In *The Freshman,* Harold Lloyd amused his audiences with the "collegiate" idea in which hectic extracurricular activities summed up the modern university. Among those who preferred the Pollyanna variety of prewar innocence, Mary Pickford earned the title of "America's Sweetheart." Douglas Fairbanks, Sr., led all his rivals as the exponent of the strenuous life, jumping and swinging from the housetops, notably in the spectacular film, *The Thief of Bagdad.* In comedy, the gifted Charlie Chaplin held leadership, especially in serio-comic melodrama of prewar vintage. That Hollywood would eventually escape futility and become a vital agency of art was foreshadowed toward the end of the decade when a reaction set in, inspired by German experimental photography and direction and the forceful realism of the Russian, Sergei Eisenstein.

THE NEW EMPHASIS ON SPORT

Recreation was too integral a part of the twenties to be considered as incidental: Stuart Chase has estimated that perhaps one-fourth of our national income was spent for this purpose. College football receipts (as reported by sixty-five institutions) gained eightfold and the attendance at games more than doubled. In 1927 alone, some thirty million people paid $50,000,000 for admission; this bore out the statement that we had become a "nation of spectators." The publicity technique of the twenties quickly made national heroes of such players as Red Grange of the University of Illinois. Colleges gladly went into debt, even to the point of starving the regular academic departments, in order to build magnificent stadia. So successful was the commercialization of college football that it retarded the development of professional football despite the latter's advantage of long-tested gridiron stars.

Professional baseball continued to enjoy a huge following that was attracted by such players as George Herman (Babe) Ruth of the New York Yankees, who hit sixty home runs in 1927. The World Series continued as always to fill the ball parks to capacity, but attendance at the regular season's games was only moderate, except in the case of games which promised to be unusually close and thus brought out otherwise indifferent spectators. Moreover, other sports and amusements competed strongly with professional baseball for public attention. Thus the total attendance at the major league games in 1920 was 9,134,000, but in 1929 it showed an increase of less than half a million.

Prize fighting enjoyed tremendous popularity under the arch-promoter George (Tex) Rickard, who thoroughly understood the art of publicity. Boxing fans readily believed that the fight at Jersey City on July 2, 1921, between the "world's heavy-weight champion" Jack Dempsey and the French challenger, Georges Carpentier, was indeed the "Battle of the Century." That one spectacle brought gate receipts of $1,118,603. But the all-time peak of general interest was reached in the Dempsey-Tunney match on September 22, 1927, in Chicago, in which Dempsey, the ex-champion and challenger, strove desperately but unsuccessfully to recover his crown. The crowd paid $2,658,660 to see the ten rounds that this fight lasted. However, Gene Tunney as champion was unable to gain the popularity accorded to Dempsey—for one thing, he was reputed to be a highbrow and to admire Shakespeare—and his voluntary retirement was unlamented.

The extraordinary popularity of golf during the decade, despite its "dude" background and the expensive equipment required, testified to the patronage of innumerable business and professional men. The twenties were a period of the rapid construction, in almost every corner of the nation, of municipal and private golf courses whose value amounted to approximately $850,000,000. The golf equipment manufactured in 1929 alone was valued at more than $21,000,000, representing well over a third of the value of all sporting goods. Private clubs dominated the golf courses; clubhouses were elaborate and membership fees high.

Tennis, like golf, was extraordinarily popular, with an estimated 1,200,000 players using courts in the public parks alone. Winter sports, stimulated by the spectacular rise in the tourist traffic, likewise flourished, especially in New England and the great national parks along the Pacific coast. The older types of commercial amusements—cabarets, small dance halls, amusement parks, and pool rooms—declined in importance in favor of roadhouses, elaborate public ballrooms, and bowling alleys, the latter patronized by women as well as men.

ELEVATING RAGTIME TO JAZZ

Popular dancing was vulgarized by the vogue for syncopated acrobatics like the Charleston and the Black Bottom, and was dominated by jazz, the sophisticated successor of ragtime, which Paul Whiteman, the popular band leader, defended as the "folk music of the machine age." The new dances, with their eccentric syncopation and their intimate embrace, quickly gained popularity; "dance marathons," some of which lasted for days, were held in the larger dance halls. Urban night clubs offered sophisticated entertainment and liquor—the latter in defiance of the Volstead Act—at fabulous prices. Youth idolized Rudy Vallee, the sentimental crooner from Maine. No song was too extravagant to attain nation-wide popularity, as witness "Show Me the Way to Go Home" and "Makin' Whoopee," greatly enjoyed by imbibers during this decade, and "Yes! We Have No Bananas," "Crazy Over Horses," and "Collegiate!" The saxophone's grotesque improvisations of a jazz version of Schumann's "Träumerei" probably captured the youthful mood of this period better than did the more restrained art.

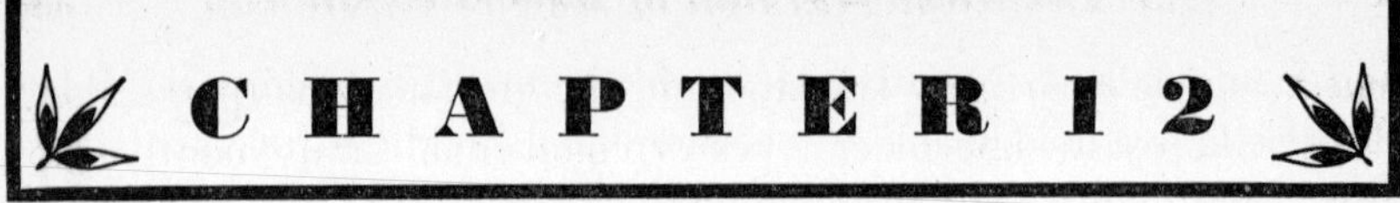

The Twenties: Cult of Individualism

THE LOST GENERATION

"Whirl is King, having driven out Zeus," wrote the brilliant journalist Walter Lippmann in his *A Preface to Morals* (1929), quoting the arch-conservative Aristophanes. The satirical playwright of ancient Greece might easily have accepted as true of his own time Lippmann's characterization of the twenties as "the dissolution of the ancestral order." Nevertheless, just as the bustling commercial civilization of Greece could produce an Aristophanes, an Aeschylus, a Plato, and an Aristotle, so the capitalist culture of America could present, on a lesser scale, a Lippmann, a Dewey, a Eugene O'Neill, and a Frank Lloyd Wright.

Although frequently sterile and blatantly critical of traditions, the individualism enshrined in the spirit of the twenties was more often creative of sound techniques and fertile interpretations of humanity. The new prosperity brought forth wealthy patrons and comfortable taxpayers to enhance the arts and the citadels of learning, but the cultural distinctiveness of the period was imparted by that Bohemian band of literary rebels, from H. L. Mencken to James Branch Cabell, who made a cult of "decadent" individualism, flouted the traditional Puritanical reticence in regard to sex, considered the "herd" and democracy with contempt, and was cynically dubious of the accepted ideals and meaning of existence.

Postwar disillusionment and the collapse of Wilsonian idealism undoubtedly contributed to the rise of this youthful intelligentsia who preferred to worship Nietzsche's superman rather than Wilson's New Freedom—except as the latter came to mean licentiousness. This type of individualism had a strong introspective side that was often morbid and neurotic and was steeped in the animalistic inferences of behavioristic psychology and an oversimplified Freudian psychoanalysis. Just as the dominant prewar tone was sociological, that is, committed to the ideal of social reform by means of cooperative action, so the new era of individualism ushered in a preoccupation with self that was psychological in emphasis. A renewed interest in eugenics encouraged the "smart set" to believe that they were indeed of nature's aristocracy. The social mobility of the decade was reflected in their restlessness, "debunking," experimentalism, and indifference to group values. "Naturalism," which they intended to be understood as the scientific realism of Zola and Maupassant, pervaded their novels and critical essays.

Many of the young intellectuals like the poet Ezra Pound and the novelist Ernest Hemingway sought refuge from the "Philistines" in America by living abroad. "You are all a lost generation," Gertrude Stein once told Hemingway in Paris, and this phrase, "the lost generation," was quickly taken up to characterize the plight of those between two worlds—one dead and the other yet unborn. Hemingway, a native of Oak Park, Illinois, was severely wounded in World War I while fighting with the Italian shock troops, the *Arditi,* and was decorated for valor. His novel, *A Farewell to Arms* (1929), in which he related his experiences in the war, enjoyed an immense vogue, in spite of its realistic indifference to the glamour of war, but the critics preferred *The Sun Also Rises* (1926), which revealed his deep disillusionment and his loss of traditional values.

Another idealist who turned cynic after that war was John Dos Passos of Chicago; he was then in his esthetic individualist period, and on the basis of his own experiences wrote naturalistic accounts of the war and its aftermath. Later he achieved a particularly depressing —yet successful—effect in *Manhattan Transfer* (1925), an impressionist novel of modern New York in which the individual characters are made to appear helplessly and almost meaninglessly dwarfed in the face of the all-encompassing power of the great metropolis. Here was the pessimistic implication of the complete dominance of urbanism and of machine civilization.

For a brief time in this atmosphere of sophistication James Branch Cabell of Richmond, Virginia, held a commanding position as the darling of the intelligentsia for his clever combination of romanticism, disillusionment, eroticism, and an exotic style. When his novel *Jurgen* (1919) was barred from the mails by the Post Office Department, he was made, according to the canons of the day; he was taken to the bosom of the smart set and vociferously championed by the oracular Mencken. Even the literary historian Vernon L. Parrington regarded the "incomparable Mr. Cabell" as a great philosopher-poet who was endowed with a broad Chaucerian humor and was basically an idealist in flight from the ugliness of modern life to a charming medieval never-never land, "all shimmer and sheen." Few reputations of the twenties suffered such deflation as Cabell's at the hands of later critics and readers, for the adolescent sophistication of *Jurgen* ceased to attract readers after the crash of 1929.

THE PSYCHOANALYTIC NOVEL AND ITS RIVALS

Much more lasting but scarcely less controversial was the reputation made by Theodore Dreiser, whom Parrington hailed as the chief of American naturalists and a worthy exponent of the modern Russian and French literary tradition of disillusionment. Using a psychoanalytic technique suggestive of Dostoevski, Dreiser in his two-volume work, *The American Tragedy* (1925), advanced beyond the economic realism of his earlier novels and embraced the new vogue for the psychological novel. Conservative critics like Professor Arthur Hobson Quinn thought that this story of a young man who murders his mistress was painfully labored as to style, unbearably long, and spiritually morbid, especially on the theme of sex expression. But the *Nation,* the *New Republic,* and Mencken's *American Mercury* loudly proclaimed the worth of Dreiser's novel.

Among the social chroniclers of the time were the two Minnesota-born novelists, F. Scott Fitzgerald and Sinclair Lewis. Fitzgerald's highly popular *This Side of Paradise* (1921) and *The Great Gatsby* (1926) pictured the sophisticated "flaming youth," "flappers," and cocktail parties of the period and aroused some apprehension over the postwar generation; most of his work, however, rarely rose above mediocrity. Much more disquieting was Sinclair Lewis, a rebellious satirist who carried the struggle waged by urban individualism against social conformity and smug "philistinism" to a new battlefield in *Main Street* (1920), a cruel portrait of the small town and its revered native traditions. This story of Gopher Prairie, Minnesota, a town with 3000 people, was a severe indictment of its hypocrisy, cultural intolerance, and parasitic relation to the nearby farmers. These Gopher Prairies, Lewis feared, would establish the cultural tone of the nation.

Not content with this attack, Lewis next turned to the Kiwanis type of small-town "booster" whom he satirized in *Babbitt* (1922), a portrayal of the complacency and intellectual poverty of the commercial classes who reveled in their materialism. Thereafter the term "Babbittry" was widely used to denote the smugness of middle-class respectability. In *Elmer Gantry* (1927), Lewis offended more than the usual number of people by bitterly satirizing the "booster spirit" in evangelical religion in the person of a sensual and ignorant minister. Critics considered that this picture of religion as a business was more than a little overdone and, moreover, that it was weak from the literary point of view. *Arrowsmith* (1925) was obviously written with greater care and was much more popular. This novel portrayed only incidentally the commercialism that invaded medicine; it was primarily concerned with the lifelong pursuit of truth on the part of Martin Arrowsmith, an idealistic medical student.

Although tainted somewhat in the minds of the intelligentsia with the much-loathed "genteel tradition," Willa Cather, Edith Wharton, and Ellen Glasgow continued to have a large following among discriminating readers. In *Death Comes for the Archbishop* (1927), a story of the tolerant French missionaries of New Mexico in the mid-nineteenth century, Miss Cather combined realism and a persistent love of diverse frontier and alien cultures. Ellen Glasgow, faithful to her prewar southern realism, wrote *Barren Ground* (1925), an account of the struggle of small independent farmers in southern Virginia against a difficult natural environment. Most grimly realistic, perhaps, of the agrarian novelists of the twenties was the Norwegian-born Ole Edvart Rölvaag of Minnesota, whose *Giants in the Earth* (1929) Parrington considered to be of epic proportions and to suggest the frontier realism of Hamlin Garland. Rölvaag reflected the intense psychological interest of the twenties in this description of the disintegration of a pioneer woman's mind as the result of the overwhelming loneliness and power of a harsh, unconquered frontier.

For those who indiscriminately put aside all the new realistic novels as "morbid," there was always escape in Booth Tarkington's novels of comfortable middle-class life in Indiana; his *The Magnificent Ambersons* (1918) was awarded the Pulitzer Prize as the novel representing "the highest standard of American manners and manhood." A mystery thriller like Mary Roberts Rinehart's *The Red Lamp* (1925) sold over a million copies the first year; Mrs. E. M. Hull's *The Sheik,* which was particularly attractive to romantic adolescents, did almost as well, especially after Rudolph Valentino, the handsome movie idol, appeared in a motion picture version. Extremely popular on a much higher level was the work of Edna Ferber, whose stirring novels *So Big* (1925), *Show Boat* (1926), and *Cimarron* (1929), suggesting Bret Harte and O'Henry, were made into stage plays and motion pictures.

Although few of these novelists failed to experiment with the short story, which was enjoying an ever-increasing vogue, one writer, Sherwood Anderson of Ohio, became outstanding in this field. His *Winesburg, Ohio* (1919), a story of small-town life in Ohio, was a series of sketches which departed from the sex conventions of the American short story. Borrowing heavily from the new psychoanalytic literature, Anderson dismayed academic critics by portraying the town's warped personalities in all their naked abnormalities, ranging from a peeping-Tom minister to a homosexual villager.

DRAMA AND POETRY

Contemporary drama likewise reflected the psychological emphasis of the novelists and short-story writers. Furthermore, the stage provided an admirable vehicle for a serious treatment of the Negro in line with the spirit of greater tolerance. Thus Eugene O'Neill, the most creative playwright in American drama, achieved notable success in his interpretation of primitive Negro psychology in *Emperor Jones* (1920), a play that depicted the mental collapse of a Negro dictator fleeing as much from his own fears as from actual pursuit by his subjects. Most ambitious of O'Neill's attempts at psychoanalysis in drama

1920 - 1930

President Harding at a Baseball Game at Fort Benning, Georgia, in 1922. Near him are Secretary of War Weeks (wearing a top hat) and Secretary of the Interior Albert B. Fall. (The National Archives.)

President Coolidge, Senator Smoot of Uta
Secretary Mellon. (Courtesy of the Boston

The Election of 1928. (McCutcheon in the C
Tribune.)

Sacco and Vanzetti. (Courtesy of the Boston *Globe*.)

A Ku Klux Klan Ceremony. (Brown Brothers.)

Renée Adorée and John Gilbert in the Anti-War Motion Picture, *The Big Parade*, Which Was Released in 1932. (Harvard Theatre Collection.)

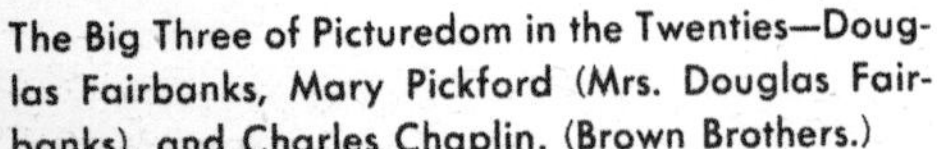

The Big Three of Picturedom in the Twenties—Douglas Fairbanks, Mary Pickford (Mrs. Douglas Fairbanks), and Charles Chaplin. (Brown Brothers.)

Walter Hampden as Cyrano de Bergerac in (Courtesy of Mary Dale Clarke.)

The Circus, Part of the Life of Each Generat Americans. (Brown Brothers.)

Douglas Fairbanks in a Scene from *The Black Pirate* in 1926. (The Museum of Modern Art Film Library.)

Mary Pickford, Spec O'Donnell, Monty O'Grady, and Mary Louise Miller in *Sparrows*, Released in 1926. (Brown Brothers.)

(Upper left) *Baptism in Kansas* by John Steuart Curry. (Whitney Museum of American Art.) (Lower left) *Tornado* by John Steuart Curry. (Brown Brothers.) (Upper right) *Arts of the South*, a Mural Panel by Thomas Benton. (Library of Whitney Museum of Modern Art.) (Lower right) *6th Ave. Elevated at 3rd Street* by John Sloan. (Whitney Museum of American Art.)

The Country Club, the Eighteenth Green, and Plus-Fours—Characteristics of the Twenties. (Brown Brothers.)

Fishing, America's Most Popular Sport of the Decade. (Brown Brothers.)

was *Strange Interlude* (1928), a nine-act play which resorted freely to the "aside" so that the four leading characters could express their inner thoughts. Especially sympathetic to the Negro was Paul Green, whose play *In Abraham's Bosom* (1926) gave an honest and frank picture of Negro life in the South. In striking contrast with these plays, the motion pictures continued to use Al Jolson's well-worn stereotype of the Negro minstrel.

Naturalism in all its unadorned starkness of theme and language appeared on the stage in *What Price Glory?* (1924), written by Maxwell Anderson and Lawrence Stallings. The postwar disillusionment, especially with life at the front, that was clearly mirrored in the play represented the American equivalent of the popular German pacifist novel, *All Quiet on the Western Front*. Some of the outstanding playwrights like Eugene O'Neill were given an opportunity to experiment with new themes by the Little Theatre movement. Although George Jean Nathan grumbled that its numerous profitable ventures had commercialized this movement, it was the solvency of such groups as the New York Theatre Guild that made it possible to bring the best of European plays to America and to raise the level of popular taste. Colleges also became increasingly important as sponsors of amateur dramatics of a high order.

High in the rostrum of the smart set was the individualist George Jean Nathan, the "great dissenter" who bluntly spoke his mind on the personalities of the stage. Contemptuous of academic theories of criticism, this Indiana-born theatrical critic insisted that the main duty of the theater was to please intelligent audiences. His comments showed an unabashed confidence in the ability of his own taste to provide a dependable standard for measuring dramatic excellence. He was able to appreciate the Broadway showmanship of Florenz Ziegfeld in "glorifying the American girl" as well as the finesse of the Moscow Art Theatre and the Provincetown Players. In his favor was the fact that he had "discovered" Eugene O'Neill.

Seldom was the stage so captivating as during the 1920's. Walter Hampden, a scholarly actor and producer of New York who had achieved great success on the London stage, drew warm praise for his original and profound interpretation of Hamlet. In the complex title role of Edmond Rostand's *Cyrano de Bergerac,* Hampden caught the bluster and romanticism of the sentimental Gascon soldier-poet. Katharine Cornell, whose superb poise and distinctive manner attracted a large following, scored one of her greatest successes in *A Bill of Divorcement* (1923), a psychological play that suggested the fatalism of Ibsen's *Ghosts*. In the unique couple, Alfred Lunt and Lynn Fontanne, the Theatre Guild possessed an effective combination of actors who seemed to live the roles they assumed. Another outstanding stage figure was the energetic Eva Le Gallienne, born in London of a famous theatrical family. Rebelling against the monotony of playing the same part over and over for months or even years, she took the bold course in 1926 of organizing the Civic Repertory Theatre in New York which changed bills every night. This theater reflected the owner's fondness for the plays of Ibsen and Chekhov.

As one might expect, the introspective twenties fulfilled the promise of the prewar revival in American poetry. The expression of Walt Whitman's challenging sensualistic spirit, if not his robust democratic faith, could be appreciated anew. From T. S. Eliot, who had been influenced by the aristocratic estheticism of Ezra Pound, came the overpowering *The Waste Land* (1922) which depicted the spiritual drought of his day and won extraordinary acclaim as the greatest poem of the century. The sardonic humor of Edwin Arlington Robinson of Maine expressed the strong fatalistic strain of his literary confreres and, according to the critic, Fred B. Millett, revealed "the fading glories and backwater neuroses of New England in decline." From Maine also came Edna St. Vincent Millay, whose love sonnets appeared in a Bohemian setting of frank feminine sensuality; her poem *The Harp Weaver* (1923) won the Pulitzer Prize. More definitely in the new psychoanalytic mold was Robinson Jeffers, whose *Tamar and Other Poems* (1924) is exotic, violent, and colorful. In its expression of spiritual decay, sex frustration, and introspection, his poetry impressed his followers as powerful in content and interpretative in quality.

Poetry, too, proved to be an ideal vehicle for the emotional expression of the rising Negro intelligentsia, especially in cosmopolitan New York; their poems filled a significant anthology compiled by James Weldon Johnson, *The Book of American Negro Poetry* (1922). Johnson, an able scholar and a cultural pioneer who contended that the Negro's artistic expression represented the true indigenous American spirit, felt intimately the religious psychology of his people. Certain poets, like New York's Countee Cullen, wrote in the style of Tennyson and Keats, but Cullen, like others of his race, found the tragedy of the Negro in a white man's world his most compelling theme. Claude McKay, best known for his sophisticated *Harlem Shadows* (1922), tended more to the leftist tradition of proletarian literature. These writers reflected a growing race consciousness that was sometimes expressed in ill-concealed bitterness. Many Negro poets adopted the free verse and the sensual interpretation of life characteristic of the 1920's.

CRITICISM: THE AGE OF H. L. MENCKEN

The *Zeitgeist* was particularly favorable to literary criticism because self-consciousness marked this period. Young novelists, poets, and dramatists, for all their assumed indifference, hoped for a friendly nod from the inner sanctum of the *American Mercury,* dominated by the turbulent Henry L. Mencken of Baltimore. Confident that he and his fellow intellectuals were among the elect chosen to create all art and civilization, Mencken popularized the aristocratic game of ridiculing the "mob," the "Boobus Americanus," and the "Bible-belt Fundamentalists." Absolute truth and progress were illusions; hence there remained only the superior man's privilege of laughing at the antics of the herd. Mencken's works, *A Book of Prefaces* (1917) and several volumes of *Prejudices* (1919–1927), expressed this comfortable fatalistic philosophy. Doctrinaire novels were abhorrent to him, for his radicalism was confined only to the extremes to which his Nietzschean ideas of aristocracy led him. To the sophisticated intelligentsia of the twenties, Mencken was an admirable arbiter of the taste and literary achievement of America. More important, however, was the fact that his preoccupation with the American scene led him to produce a scholarly work of philology in *The American Language* (1919).

Far more solid was the literary criticism of Vernon L. Parrington, a professor of English at the University of Washington who achieved his reputation suddenly toward the end of the decade. In 1927 appeared his two-volume work, *Main Currents in American Thought,* which reinterpreted American letters in realistic socio-economic terms and from a liberal agrarian point of view. Few if any of his predecessors possessed such a gift of integrating every phase of American life and placing our literary heritage in a context of contemporary social forces. Frankly more Marxist in thought were the critical essays by V. F. Calverton, who abhorred the "sophisticated futility" of his literary generation. Another extremely important liberal force in criticism was the *Nation,* the *New Republic,* and the *New Freeman.*

At the exotic level of literary criticism and philosophy was a small determined group of college professors, among them Irving Babbitt of Harvard and Paul Elmer More of Princeton, who called themselves "neo-humanists." Neo-humanism, they claimed, was the authentic successor of classical and Renaissance humanism; it decried the naturalism and utilitarian ideals of their own age in favor of the aristocratic ideal of a gentleman—"squirearchy" their opponents called it. Impatient with the intellectual anarchy, sensualism, and skepticism of the day, they advocated traditional moral values, lofty estheticism, and an educational system founded on the idea of leisure rather than the current gospel of service. In his *Preface to Morals* (1929), Walter Lippmann professed himself a humanist in terms that sharply differentiated humanism from the liberalism of his former radical associate, Lincoln Steffens. But Lippmann's humanism had too basic a strain of liberal utilitarianism to please Irving Babbitt and his circle.

THE VOGUE FOR FICTIONIZED BIOGRAPHY

Quite properly, this age of psychology produced an unprecedented vogue for biography and autobiography. Here was an admirable vehicle for literary psychoanalysis, with opportunities for the naturalist, the entertaining "debunker," and the simple realist. Influenced largely by the work of the English biographer Lytton Strachey, who in his biographies of eminent Victorians attempted to depict the play of psychological motives, fictionized biography became fashionable in America after the war. Even Amy Lowell, the Imagist poet, turned much of her prodigious energies to an intensive two-volume study, *John Keats* (1925), a labor which hastened her untimely death that year. Few popular biographers made such extensive use of the psychoanalytic method as Katharine Anthony, whose interpretation of

Catherine the Great, published in 1925, shocked readers not accustomed to a dissection of the sexual life of famous men and women. Volumes on Roosevelt, Lincoln, and Wilson, written in the older tradition of idealized biography, bulked particularly large. In this group was Albert J. Beveridge's *Life of John Marshall* (1916–1919), which was awarded the Pulitzer Prize in 1920. It was especially fitting for an era of biography that the decade should close with the appearance of the first volume in the monumental *Dictionary of American Biography* (1928–1944), published by the American Council of Learned Societies and the New York *Times.*

PSYCHOLOGY, QUEEN OF THE SOCIAL SCIENCES

Contemporary literature was not alone in establishing the preeminence of psychology among the social sciences during the twenties, for few fields were untouched by its influence. Students eagerly enrolled in college courses on psychology in the hope of solving the ever-pressing problem of the Ego and the Unconscious. Even people who had never been to college talked knowingly about inhibitions, repressions, inferiority complexes, and fixations, and were familiar with all the jargon of psychoanalysis. There were few academic disciplines that did not boast of offering a "psychological approach." Case workers, personnel managers, teachers, advertisers—all steeped themselves directly or indirectly in the new psychology, often with most profitable results.

The World War afforded a proving ground for experimental psychology in this country, a branch which at the time had scarcely progressed beyond its apprenticeship to Wundt's laboratory techniques and the French and German mental test procedures. Armies of recruits appeared before trained psychologists who hoped by means of tests to put "the right man in the right place." In addition to enabling research on routine mental and personnel tests, the war afforded opportunities to study shell shock, rehabilitation, emotional stability, propaganda, military intelligence, acoustics, and a variety of other important subjects.

The intelligentsia were vastly amused by the early, and frequently exaggerated, implications of the Army mental tests as to the low mentality of the average man. (Mencken and his followers wore it threadbare as an argument against democracy.) Champions of Nordic supremacy, some of them psychologists, claimed, quite erroneously, that these tests proved the native inferiority of Negroes and southern Europeans. Despite this intellectual fog, psychology emerged triumphantly during the twenties with practical tests of all kinds, ranging from those for college freshmen to those for commercial telegraphers and industrial workers. Although some enthusiastic psychologists made exaggerated claims for their tests, the fact remains that the line between mental tests and achievement tests was much more vague at the end of the decade than at the beginning.

Far more gratifying to believers in the influence of the environment upon the individual was the temporary flutter over behaviorism. The chief impetus came from the animal experiments of I. P. Pavlov, the Russian physiological psychologist whose famous experiments with a dog inspired the term "conditioned reflex" or, in its closely related form, "conditioned response." In these experiments a dog which had at first secreted saliva at the sight of food accompanied by a certain sound, eventually reacted the same way to the sound alone. This type of association became the basis of behaviorism, a school of psychology headed by Dr. John B. Watson. His *Psychology from the Standpoint of a Behaviorist,* which appeared in 1919, stirred psychologists and the lay public alike. Never, perhaps, did a scientist state the theory of environmental determinism in such positive terms as Watson, when he said: "Give me a dozen healthy infants, well-formed, and my own specified world to bring them up in and I'll guarantee to take any one at random and train him to become any type of specialist I might select—doctor, lawyer, artist, merchant, chief and, yes, even beggarman and thief, regardless of his habits, penchants, tendencies, abilities, vocations, and race of his ancestors." Not even Jefferson would have dared to state human equality so conclusively. Discarding formal psychological terms, Watson taught that personality was merely the product of conditioning our "habit systems" along certain lines. "Instinctive behavior" was a fraud; in reality it was learned and therefore was capable of being unlearned. Here indeed was a cheerful view for the exponents of social control. (Incidentally, it was not inappropriate that in 1924 Dr. Watson became vice president of one of the nation's leading advertising firms. The prospective consumer, presumably, could be "conditioned" to respond favorably to the products advertised by the firm.)

Another school of psychology appeared during the decade in the form of psychoanalysis; where behaviorism made one disciple, psychoanalysts won three or four. As a young neurologist in Vienna in the 1880's, Dr. Sigmund Freud began an intensive study of hysteria and came to conclusions which turned him toward psychology. Discarding medicine and hypnosis, the conventional treatment for neuroses at that time, Freud experimented with psychoanalysis, a method which emphasized the unconscious but important influence of sex motivations—the libido—on behavior from infancy through adulthood. Dreams provide release for repressed desires and therefore, when interpreted as symbols, serve as a clinical instrument for the psychoanalyst. Finally, in cooperation with the patient, the psychoanalyst uses mental associations to recall the event responsible for the abnormal behavior. By thus enabling the patient frankly to face the initial fact which he has unconsciously repressed, the psychoanalyst endeavors to restore mental equilibrium.

The possibilities of psychoanalysis were promoted by Freud's American disciple, Dr. A. A. Brill, and by the great psychiatrist, Dr. Adolph Meyer, who did much to transform our "insane asylums" into scientific "mental hospitals." Inevitably, charlatans who set themselves up as psychoanalysts preyed on susceptible wealthy women, a fact which led skeptics to jeer at Freud's revolutionary technique. Nevertheless, the potentialities in psychoanalysis have stimulated the mental hygiene movement as a whole. Rapid progress was made in modernizing mental hospitals, especially in New York, Massachusetts, and Illinois. More and more physicians were trained in the psychoanalytic technique, and social workers learned it in order to understand childhood abnormalities. This new interest in psychiatry after 1920 gave rise to the child guidance clinics which by 1928 were serving 40,000 children all over the nation.

DEWEY AND PROGRESSIVE EDUCATION

Educational theory, dominated by John Dewey and his associates at Columbia University, inclined heavily toward social psychology. Dewey, whose fame as a philosopher, psychologist, and educator had been established before the war, became the undisputed leader of the progressive teaching world during the twenties. In reality unsympathetic to crude vocationalism, he stressed the socializing benefits to the pupil of active participation in the learning process. The subject matter must be subordinated to the needs of the child's personality, and facts must be identified with his experience and psychological growth. Above all, Dewey taught that school is not merely a preparation for life but a part of life itself; the school community is a society in miniature. His disciples discarded the formal recitation in favor of socialized recitations, field trips, library research, and creative individual projects.

Influenced by these concepts of a school society, progressive communities when building new schools provided rooms for all types of activity—assembly rooms, gymnasiums, dining rooms, and rooms for shopwork and art; movable furniture gave the classrooms an atmosphere of informality. Although taxpayers sometimes grumbled at the "fads and frills" of progressive education, the necessary money was forthcoming. Dewey's influence swept the Soviet Union, China, Turkey, and, to a lesser extent, Germany. Latin Americans sought to introduce his ideas into their schools. The celebration of Dewey's seventieth birthday in 1930 brought testimonials from world-famous educators that here indeed was a giant among us.

THE STUDY OF SOCIETY

American sociology, as the editors of the *Encyclopedia of the Social Sciences* observed, was dominated by psychological interests during the twenties, in keeping with the current trend both here and abroad. The concern with the process of social interaction and the new techniques of psychology, psychoanalysis, and education gave rise to the disciplines of educational sociology, rural sociology, and urban sociology. Pioneer studies in group behavior in a specific geographic setting were made by the ecological school at the University of Chicago led by Robert Park and Ernest W. Burgess, among other brilliant sociologists. This group applied quantitative and descriptive methods to various social units in Chicago, and produced numerous studies on such topics as the West Madison Street hobo, the North Side "gold coast" and the slums, the West Side Ghetto, and the gang. Ignoring the formal limits of the academic disciplines, this school of sociologists cooperated freely with historians, geographers, anthropologists, economists, and others who were interested in a regional approach to various problems.

The vogue of the case study, the sociologist's version of biography, was strikingly emphasized in the work of W. I. Thomas and F. Znaniecki. Their book, *The Polish Peasant in Europe and America* (1918–1920), based on correspondence between Poles both here and in Poland, is a concrete study of social interaction that suggests certain Freudian principles as motivating conduct. Another sociological classic, this one a modification of the social survey method, was *Middletown* (1929), a cross-sectional description of Muncie, Indiana, by R. S. and H. M. Lynd. These two sociologists drew so incisive and analytical a picture of an entire community in terms of its social, political, and economic behavior that social historians consider this book a guide to American society of the 1920's. Other noted sociologists, like William F. Ogburn of the University of Chicago, made increasing use of statistical methods in social analysis and interpretation.

Influenced by both psychiatry and the psychoanalytic method, social work moved ever further away from the parent field of sociology and became increasingly independent during this decade. Professional status for the social worker seemed clearly established when the American Association of Social Workers was organized in 1921. By the end of the decade scientific social work included within its rapidly expanding sphere not only mental hygiene, poverty, and delinquency, but also problems of family disorganization, vocational guidance, and medical assistance, in its effort to substitute technical investigation and diagnosis for indiscriminate and patronizing charity. This trend was partly reflected in the expansion of scientific social agencies for child protection, such as the new child guidance clinics, juvenile courts, and policewomen, as well as the promotion of wholesome recreational opportunities. With these developments came a host of books on numerous aspects of social work, especially on child delinquency, written from the new point of view; of these, *The Child, The Clinic, and the Court* by Jane Addams and her associates was representative.

Anthropology likewise attained swift popularity as it shook off its alliance with sociology, despite the parallel nature of their investigations. There were many reasons for this upsurge of interest. For one thing the current controversy over Darwinism raised new questions regarding alleged racial differences and the cultural traits of primitive societies. Closely related to this was the controversy over our immigration policy in which those who favored the restriction of southern and eastern Europeans frequently resorted to the racialist theories of Madison Grant's *The Passing of the Great Race* (1916) to prove the superiority of the Nordic (or Aryan) race. Another influence was Freudian psychology, which stimulated a renewed interest in primitive behavior, thus suggesting further problems for the anthropologist. Finally, there was the natural curiosity of an iconoclastic generation which sought to justify its distaste for traditional values by exploring the psychological norms of the family, the church, sex relations, and other aspects of community life to be found in the cultures of primitive peoples.

The ordinary citizen was only too likely to be impressed by Madison Grant's assumption that America's greatness rested upon the inherited traits of the fair, tall, longheaded Nordic race, whose numbers were declining in favor of the "insidious" southern European races. This myth of racial superiority was devastatingly examined by scientific anthropologists, notably Aleš Hrdlička of the National Museum at Washington and Professor Franz Boas of Columbia University. Hrdlička's study, *The Old Americans* (1925), revealed that the original colonists were mostly roundheaded, medium in stature, and almost dark in complexion—scarcely the longheaded blond giant of the Nordic myth. Even more emphatic were Boas' conclusions in his *Anthropology and Modern Life* (1928): "Up to this time none of the mental tests gives us any insight into significant racial differences that might not be adequately explained by the effect of social experience." Race and culture, he demonstrated, were separate entities. Thus, while German nationalists were eagerly imbibing the racial superiority theories of Houston S. Chamberlain and Count Arthur de Gobineau, American anthropologists fought the invasion of such corrosive ideas introduced by the disciples of the racialists.

What Dewey was to education, his colleague, Boas, was to anthropology. Boas wrote for the layman as well as the specialist; he stressed the practical importance of his subject for social workers, teachers, public health officials, physicians, legislators, and, above all, for the average citizen seeking enlightenment on race, nationalism, immigration, and other civic problems. His early training in the natural sciences impressed him with the value of actual field studies as against secondhand library research. In line with this belief, Boas conducted many anthropological expeditions; those to Alaska and elsewhere in North America, where he studied Indian cultures, resulted in impressive findings regarding the languages, traits, and tribal organizations of these people. The historical school which Boas headed remained the orthodox wing; it emphasized rigidly scientific methods in uncovering the historical diffusion of primitive cultures. To have been a student of Boas at Columbia became almost a necessary distinction for an aspiring young anthropologist. Among the students thus distinguished was Professor Edward Sapir of the University of Chicago, who announced in 1925 that his Indian linguistic researches led him to believe that a cultural affiliation existed between the Indians and certain primitive Chinese groups, thus supporting the theory that America was peopled from Asia by way of the Bering Strait. However, the increasing insistence of professional anthropologists on a sane, balanced picture of primitive psychology failed to restrain the science popularizers of the decade, entranced as they were by the bizarre and exotic, from describing primitive peoples in terms of pathological tabus and ubiquitous sex symbolism.

TRENDS IN POLITICS AND LAW

Political science was immeasurably enriched by contemporary developments. The current interest in psychology stimulated countless studies on public opinion, propaganda, pressure groups, and civic training. The World War gave rise to a profound curiosity regarding the nature of propaganda and censorship. Harold D. Lasswell of the University of Chicago, a student of propaganda processes, frankly accepted a Freudian interpretation in his *Propaganda Technique in the World War* (1927) and especially in his *Psychopathology and Politics* (1930). Lobbyist propaganda was investigated by Peter H. Odegard in *Pressure Politics: The Story of the Anti-Saloon League*

(1928). Other political scientists, like Charles Merriam and Herbert W. Schneider, studied propaganda in relation to civic loyalty both here, in the Soviet Union, and in Mussolini's Italy. Related to these inquiries into the nature of propaganda was Walter Lippmann's widely discussed *Public Opinion* (1922) which offered a psychological explanation of mental "stereotypes," irrational responses which act as a substitute for genuine thinking by distorting human behavior in such forms as group bigotry, uncritical party loyalties, and even revolutionary movements.

Woodrow Wilson, himself a political scientist and historian by training, inspired many of his former colleagues with renewed interest in international organization and law, the democratization of diplomatic methods, political geography, and public administration. The latter, the culmination of the prewar agitation for more experts in government, was encouraged by the scientific budget system advocated by Wilson and adopted by Harding. Observing the rise of dictatorships, one group of political scientists, the younger "pluralists" led by Harold J. Laski (then at Harvard), attacked the all-powerful modern state. This group held that an individual owed allegiance to many other associations besides the state—his family and his church, for example—and that this challenged the pretensions of any political state to absolute domination over its citizens.

Law continued its earlier swing from analytical to sociological jurisprudence as broader interpretations were given to legal concepts by anthropologists, psychologists, political scientists, and historians. Thus its unity with the other social sciences became more apparent and the psychological elements in the judicial process were increasingly realized. Along these sociological lines, the Supreme Court decisions of Justices Louis D. Brandeis and Oliver Wendell Holmes and the teachings of Roscoe Pound of Harvard strengthened the police power of the states and enabled them to legislate more broadly in behalf of the social welfare of their citizens. On the whole, however, the courts reflected the postwar emphasis on individual and particularly business rights rather than community rights; and lawyers were preoccupied with the new complexities inherent in the corporate form of business and the elaborate credit system. Dean Roscoe Pound complained in 1922 that prominent legal firms had become huge business organizations, that "the leaders of the bar in the cities are coming to be divorced not only from the administration of criminal justice, but from the whole work of the courts, and the most effective check upon judicial administration of justice is ceasing to be operative."

Justice Benjamin N. Cardozo of New York, whom Hoover later appointed to the Supreme Court, awakened considerable criticism among those who believed in the certainties of law by his book, *The Nature of the Judicial Process* (1922), which pointed out the broad discretion that a judge actually possesses. Conservative lawyers were even more shocked by Jerome Frank's *Law and the Modern Mind* (1929), which employed Freud's psychoanalytic method to explode the myth of the certainty of the law. Frank traced this myth back to the mental security a child enjoys before birth, and to his subsequent fear of confusion and change. Although this explanation was open to considerable question, it indicated a trend toward greater realism in analyzing a judge's mentality, background, preconceptions, and social environment.

TRENDS IN ECONOMICS AND HISTORY

Economists moved into closer intimacy with business during the twenties, as was evident from the numerous statistical studies that were immediately related to current business problems. This trend had been noted as early as 1919 by Wesley C. Mitchell, the famous student of the business cycle, who observed at that time: "The economists seem more concerned than formerly with the practical bearings of their work." J. M. Clark, an outstanding theorist, joined Mitchell in insisting that economic theory must be "actively relevant to the issues of its time." Noteworthy among the numerous statistical studies was the work of Irving Fisher of Yale, whose *Stabilizing the Dollar* (1919) offered a plan which would lessen the violence of price fluctuations. As before the war, studies in economic history increased; in this field appeared the monumental three-volume *History of Manufactures in the United States* (1929) by V. S. Clark. Lulled into optimism by the current prosperity that preceded the crash late in 1929, more and more economists asserted their belief in the power of such modern safeguards as the Federal Reserve System to make the violent changes of the business cycle from prosperity to depression a thing of the past.

Contemporary advances in the other social sciences compelled the professional historian to bring his specialty abreast of the times or be threatened with the eclipse that overtook philosophy during the decade. In 1911 James Harvey Robinson had published several papers on "the new history," which suggested a cross-sectional approach to the entire scope of man's activities patterned on the German *Kulturgeschichte*. These ideas took definite root among historians during the 1920's, especially through Robinson and his students. He predicted that the historian would ally himself increasingly with anthropology, economics, psychology, and sociology; thus equipped, he could write a penetrating history of thought capable of "dissolving the bonds of prejudice." Spurred on by men like Robinson and Harry Elmer Barnes of Smith College, the vogue for intellectual history attained its maturity.

Carleton J. H. Hayes, a professorial colleague of Robinson's, achieved notable sucess in the methods of the new history when he applied them to studies of European nationalism. He showed a mastery of cultural integration that few scholars of American history possessed. Arthur M. Schlesinger of Iowa and Harvard pioneered in the application of such integrative patterns as urbanization in American history; this spirit of synthesis marks *A History of American Life* (1927–), a series of which he and Dixon R. Fox were co-editors. Charles A. Beard, once a member of the brilliant group of cultural historians at Columbia, interpreted American life in the economic terms of James Madison, thus achieving a cultural synthesis which stressed self-interest as a mainspring of history. *The Rise of American Civilization* (2 vols., 1927), on which he and his wife Mary collaborated, is a significant social interpretation that has attained nation-wide popularity.

Following the older and simpler style but nevertheless containing much that is relevant to the modern spirit is the extensive *Chronicles of America* (1918–1921), a series of some fifty pocket-size volumes edited by Allen Johnson. One of the volumes, William E. Dodd's *Cotton Kingdom,* is a masterpiece of synthesis and condensation applied to the culture and politics of the Old South. As a matter of fact, the interpretation of the Old South, the Civil War, and Reconstruction became increasingly pro-southern as the decade wore on, until the "Lost Cause" seemed on the point of recovering the ground lost at Appomattox.

The World War stimulated considerable interest in diplomatic history and archival studies. From a Europe engaged in bitter controversy over war guilt came new revisionist interpretations. The revisionists in this country were led by Bernadotte E. Schmitt of the University of Chicago, who held a modified pro-Entente position, and Harry Elmer Barnes, who made Czarist Russia primarily responsible for the war. Midway between the two was Sidney B. Fay of Smith College, whose two-volume *Origins of the World War* (1926) became almost the standard American interpretation.

THE ADVANCE OF SCIENCE

The applied sciences, particularly, flourished during the twenties as the result of the mushroom growth of commercial and university laboratories financed by heavy endowments and appropriations. If chemistry made little progress in laying bare the ultimate mystery of matter, it created unheard-of new conveniences for housewives, automobile owners, and physicians, partly because the huge laboratories built for war purposes were available thereafter to private research.

During the war, a semi-governmental agency, the Chemical Foundation, had been organized to acquire all the patent rights held by enemy aliens, especially the vital coal-tar dyes and drugs, a field hitherto dominated by Germany and the astute monopolist methods of her chemists. After 1918, however, this field was open to American chemists, and valuable bacteriological and medical products, such as rare sugars, chemical stains, and new drugs, were manufactured here for the first time. Chemistry made possible the production of inexpensive artificial silk, or "rayon," from cellulose; enthusiasts claimed that its use in hose and other articles of clothing leveled the difference between shop girls and ladies of leisure. From the gas mask used in the war were developed devices that protected workmen against fumes and poisonous dusts. Another advance was our production of helium from Texas natural gas, which gave us a major supply of this indispensable and non-inflammable gas for dirigibles. More economical fuel mixtures and "anti-freeze" preparations were available for automobile owners.

Physics moved closer to chemistry and the market place, especially in depth photography, aviation instruments, engineering, and the use of X-rays in medicine. Nevertheless, the decade witnessed several outstanding developments in the purely theoretical field, the most important of which resulted from the work of A. A. Michelson on the velocity of light, and of Arthur H. Compton on X-ray diffraction. Michelson, who had already received the Nobel Prize in 1907 (Compton received it later), won further recognition as a critic of the sensational theory of relativity, formulated by Albert Einstein of Germany, which apparently nullified the older idea of a static universe when it claimed that motion and velocity are relative qualities, and threatened an imminent revolution in physical science. California's huge observatories served as a testing ground for Einstein's calculations. The press, undeterred by the complex mathematics of relativity, watched these experiments with absorption, and curious laymen wondered if relativity in physics, like the evolutionary hypothesis in biology, would apply to the social sciences as well and overturn the traditional certainties regarding man's place in society as well as in the physical world.

Biology remained an intellectual storm center of controversies ranging from eugenics to evolution. Scores of popular writers, convinced that the laws of heredity had been too long ignored in this country, urged the passage of laws that would compel sterilization for the feeble-minded and insane. As a result, over twenty states had passed such laws by the end of the decade. Working along more cautious experimental lines, T. H. Morgan and his associates at Columbia continued their prewar discoveries regarding the genes that control inheritance and thus advanced our understanding of the mechanism of heredity.

Wartime science and prosperous research foundations helped to make the decade memorable in American medicine. Part of this advance was due to the fact that the selective draft gave the medical profession wider representation than it had had in any other war. From the grim experience of the battlefield came important advances in chest surgery made possible by new antiseptic methods. Malaria, typhoid, and dysentery, which had been responsible for a large proportion of the lives lost during the Civil and Spanish-American Wars, became almost negligible as a cause of death during the World War. Pneumonia, however, took their place, accounting for almost nine-tenths of all disease fatalities in the Army. The influenza epidemic of 1918–1919 led to important advances in techniques of isolating the disease and thus preventing its spread. The study and experiments by G. F. and G. H. Dick of Chicago on scarlet fever led to the preparation of a concentrated antitoxin in 1925. The Mayo Clinic at Rochester, Minnesota, became world-famous for its outstanding medical research in such vital fields as the functions of the liver.

A host of scientific workers, whose experiments antedated the war, contributed to the most significant development in public health during the decade—the application of the recently discovered vitamins to revolutionize dietary theories and food habits. The proper vitamin was found to aid the normal growth of children, to cure certain diseases that are due to diet deficiencies, and to strengthen adult body structure. The irradiation of foods by ultraviolet rays was devised as a means of correcting calcium deficiency in teeth and bones. This discovery, however, opened a new field not only for scientists but for charlatans as well because irresponsible distributors could charge the consumer high prices for products that supposedly contained additional vitamins or were irradiated.

ART: THE EPOCH OF FRANK LLOYD WRIGHT

Architectural art was greatly affected by the current trend toward naturalistic expression. Louis Sullivan of Chicago had appreciated the esthetic possibilities of the skyscraper as a "proud and soaring thing" and had taught that "form follows function," that the design must be inherent in the structure rather than merely superimposed. His outstanding pupil, Frank Lloyd Wright of Wisconsin, who had come to Chicago during the stimulating days of the Columbian Exposition, elaborated Sullivan's ideas of architecture as a plastic and organic art which reflected the continued evolution of things as well as the purpose of the inner structure. He rejected the "borrowed fineries" of eclectic styles and historic decorations. "Let no one . . . be the cause of a style," advised Wright, "or ever increase the number of the peddlers of a style." He used materials that would lend themselves most effectively to both the purpose of the building and the nature of its environment, and made ample provision for sunlight, fresh air, and comfort. Architecture was to him a form of sculpture. His "prairie houses," for example, emphasized horizontal lines close to the earth but had magnificent open interiors; these won him an enviable reputation in Europe and even in faraway Japan as well as in the United States. Foreign critics often referred to his work as "the American expression in architecture." To the contemporary historian his theories seem to partake of the restless experimental spirit of the era and its craving for the utmost in individual expression.

Numerous architects followed this modernist trend, although conservatism was still evident in the frequent resort to traditional Greek and Roman decorative elements. Impressive perpendicular lines, sometimes blended with the popular Gothic motif, accentuated the "soaring" idea, as in the Chicago Tribune Tower, whose designers, John Mead Howells and Raymond Hood, won a world-wide architectural contest with their plans for this building. Some who criticized the judges' decision preferred the designs submitted by Eliel Saarinen, a Finn; his design, which won second prize, emphasized the beauty of the steel structure in its functional setting and was devoid of classical columns and cornices. Building codes frequently limited the unbroken height of a building on the basis of the width of the street, but architects solved this problem by using a succession of structures that were set back from the street front and often were topped by a narrow tower. Domestic architects found their greatest field in homes for wealthy suburban sections. An attractive adaptation of the Spanish style of architecture was widely used in California and Florida. However, most small home owners were unable to afford the services of an architect and hence followed standardized models.

Closely related to architecture was the art of city planning, which made unprecedented progress during the twenties, particularly in zoning. In 1916, only eight cities had zoning ordinances which restricted the type of building that could be erected in certain districts, but by 1929 there were 821 cities with such ordinances, and three-fifths of the entire urban population was thereby affected. Community planning ranged from the "garden city" model suburb or town to regional plans intended to integrate sprawling metropolitan areas. Large appropriations for recreation produced beautiful park systems and playgrounds. San Francisco's ambitious plans provided for air, rail, and highway transportation, for flood control, sewerage, and water supply protection, and for zoning. Thus an important step forward was taken in combining beauty and utility.

Although purchasers paid dealers a quarter of a billion dollars in 1929 for all types of imported works of art, many American painters complained of a lack of both appreciation and financial support. Nevertheless, important work, less bound to the European tradition than ever before, was produced, especially in the thriving field of cubism. Small paintings were in demand, now that limited wall space made the hanging of large canvases impossible. Georgia O'Keeffe's delicate patterns of flowers and leaves led Thomas Craven, the critic, to characterize this artist from Virginia as "the foremost woman painter of the world." Also outstanding were the abstract landscapes of John Marin. The vogue for huge ornate buildings made the painting of murals popular once again; the distinguished Jules Guerin completed seven allegorical murals for the Cleveland terminal by 1929.

Better fed than the struggling painters in oil and more in the dominant spirit of the decade were the commercial artists whose work was done largely for advertisers. Commercial art became important as businessmen who had hitherto been preoccupied with utility considerations began to demand that their products be more esthetic in appearance and attractively presented in catalogues and magazine advertisements.

MUSIC: *RHAPSODY IN BLUE*

The new technology of the twenties profoundly altered the field of music. Thousands of professional musicians were deprived of work by the sound movies, the radio, and the continued popularity of the phonograph; only the better artists survived. A sharp drop in piano sales suggested a decline in at least one form of active musical participation in the home. This was partially offset by a vigorous movement for music education in the schools and colleges, beginning with vocal and choral instruction and finally including extensive orchestral training that sometimes was symphonic in scope.

Lovers of "classical" music were greatly disturbed by the "jazz invasion" of the twenties. Thus, Daniel Gregory Mason of Columbia, himself a distinguished composer whose work was achieving increasing recognition in this country, denounced jazz as the attempt of "a joyless industrial civilization to arouse its fatigue-poisoned mind and its drudgery-jaded bodies." Far from being vital or spontaneous, he asserted, jazz was actually "a trick rubber stamp, a mechanical formula by which a slight rhythmical kink or twist is put into utterly commonplace musical progressions."

Paul Whiteman, who left his native Denver to try his luck leading a jazz band in San Francisco, antagonized British sensibilities by presenting jazz versions of several English musical classics. Older musicians considered it the height of arrogance when, in 1924, he sought to give jazz the respectable setting of traditional music by hiring a large concert hall for one of his programs, "An Experiment in Modern Music." This program included George Gershwin's *A Rhapsody in Blue,* whose enthusiastic reception helped immeasurably in winning over numerous critics to the belief that jazz had enormous potentialities as an indigenous form of American art. Gershwin, a Brooklyn composer who won heartfelt applause for his serious music as well as his musical comedy tunes, was highly regarded even outside jazz circles. American composers of traditional music, whose work was frequently viewed by Europeans as imitative, were annoyed to note the generous praise given by certain renowned French and other continental critics to the work of Gershwin and his colleagues.

Although Professor Mason deplored our lack of musical background and taste, he noted optimistically that at least twenty-six compositions by Americans had won a steady place on hitherto thoroughly Europeanized orchestral programs. Deems Taylor's opera, *The King's Henchman* received an ovation from the critics when it was produced in 1927. Among a host of talented musicians from other countries, the modernist composer, Ernest Bloch, won an established place on symphony programs with *America,* a magnificent compliment to his adopted land. Negro themes became increasingly popular among composers, and Negro composers, like William Grant Still who expressed the exoticism, emotional depth, and rhythm of his people, were acclaimed by the critics.

Popular musical tastes, as before the war, clung to the romantic waltz mood of the operetta exemplified in Victor Herbert's work. This beloved Irish-American composer who died in 1924 had many successors, of whom the best known are Jerome Kern and Sigmund Romberg. Kern, who had produced at least twenty-six operettas by 1929, rose to leadership in this field once preempted by the Viennese. His adaptation of Edna Ferber's *Show Boat* in 1929, with its stirring "Old Man River," won enormous popularity. No less popular among waltz-lovers was the Hungarian-American composer, Sigmund Romberg, who had been trained in Vienna and who charmed millions with the sentimental tunes and romantic atmosphere of *Maytime, The Student Prince, Blossom Time,* and the *Desert Song.*

The 1920's marked a turning point in the cultural history of America. The prewar promise of emancipation from the intellectual tutelage of Europe was partly fulfilled during the decade, for all its materialism and manifestations of egoism. European science, art, and literature enjoyed high esteem among Americans, but in turn the fruits of our intellectual creativeness reached Old World shores. Fittingly, however, for a period which emphasized technology, the average European knew us best through our motion pictures, most of them produced in Hollywood, our assembly-line methods of production, and our syncopated music. Nevertheless, Dewey's educational theories received homage abroad; American writers like Theodore Dreiser, Sinclair Lewis, Eugene O'Neill, and Upton Sinclair had a large following in Britain and on the Continent; and American science as well as American philanthropy likewise crossed the Atlantic.

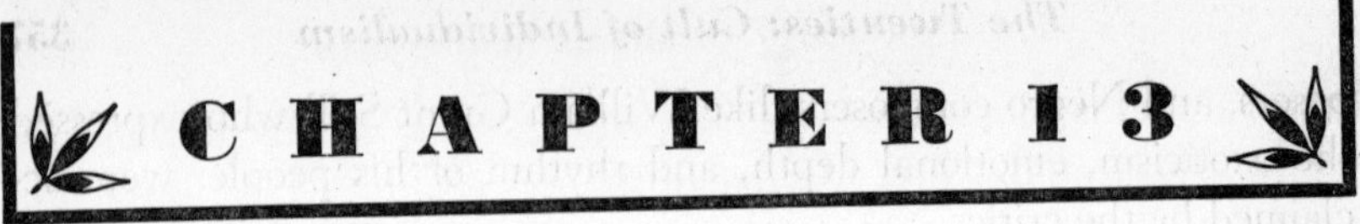

CHAPTER 13

The Politics of Business Leadership: 1921-1929

THE VOTER ABDICATES

"Less government in business, more business in government!" This slogan, used in Harding's campaign in 1920, thus frankly accepted the avowed ideal of the United States Chamber of Commerce which became the dominant political faith of the decade. Government enterprise, trust busting, and Wilsonian restraints on business were discarded in favor of free play for industrial and financial giants and strict government economies—except for the traditional subsidies afforded manufacturers through the protective tariff and for favors to various business interests. Jefferson had proclaimed a philosophy calling for "less government," but that was during an almost self-sufficient age when farmers suspected Hamilton's political and economic schemes that advanced the interest of business. In the twenties, however, the prestige of the businessman soared to new heights and government was fashioned in his image.

The decline of popular interest in both national and local government, marked by the "vanishing voter," reflected the subordination of politics to business and the professional politician's subservience to the business man to a greater degree than ever before. The similarities in party platforms, each of them intent on courting business, suggested a sham battle and helped to keep half of the electorate away from the polls.

Utility magnates frequently made and unmade the men who had been elected to public office. Although easygoing President Harding may himself have been unaware of the political scandals that marked his Administration, the fact remains that he brought to Washington the "Ohio gang" which later became notorious as having flourished on bribes from oil companies, graft in private supply contracts, traffic in public offices, and a host of other dishonest dealings. Like President Grant during the Reconstruction period, Harding admired the rising postwar industrialists, merchants, and financiers who were the embodiment of power; and he, like Grant, was betrayed by friends whom he had placed in high office and who had succumbed to the prevailing acquisitive spirit.

LIGHTENING THE TAX BURDEN

Perhaps no greater hostage to business leadership in politics could have been found than Andrew W. Mellon of Pennsylvania, Secretary of the Treasury under Harding, Coolidge, and Hoover. Estimated to be one of the wealthiest men in the country, Mellon had amassed a huge fortune in banking, aluminum, and steel; his bank in Philadelphia was extremely powerful, and progressives claimed that the family's aluminum investments approximated a national monopoly in that vital product. Although Mellon formally resigned from his own business enterprises on being appointed to the Cabinet, he still retained his distaste for government enterprise and his conviction that any program of economy in government must be particularly generous to businessmen and that this generosity must take the form of drastic reductions in tax rates and large tax refunds. Senator James Couzens of Michigan promptly pointed out the slightly embarrassing fact that such a policy would result in direct, and probably exceptional, benefits to the various enterprises controlled by the Mellon family. Conservative Republicans basked in the reflected glory of the "greatest Secretary of the Treasury since Alexander Hamilton."

It is true that President Wilson anticipated both Harding and Coolidge in demanding rigid economies and businesslike budget procedures, but his tax program favored the common man. Prosperity, especially after 1922, had created mounting surpluses which necessitated wholesale tax revision and encouraged the reduction of the national debt. Mellon claimed that business was handicapped by the present high taxes and that wealth was escaping to tax-exempt government securities. Accordingly, his first steps were to reduce the income tax rates in the higher brackets and to recommend a constitutional amendment which would prohibit the issuance of tax-exempt bonds

(Coolidge considered the latter proposal impractical from a political standpoint). The Secretary battled in congressional committees for the abolition of federal inheritance and gift taxes, which he branded as socialistic, for the reduction of excess profits taxes, and for the repeal of the section of the existing revenue law that provided for publicity regarding tax returns.

Mellon was obliged to beat a temporary retreat when the rebels in his party joined John Nance Garner of the House Ways and Means Committee. Among other things, these critics wanted to know why incomes below $5000 should not be exempted from all income taxes. Mellon's reply was somewhat reminiscent of Hamilton's defense of the excise tax which resulted in the famous Whisky Rebellion. "As a matter of policy," the Secretary said, "nothing so brings home to a man the feeling that he personally has an interest in seeing that Government revenues are not squandered, but intelligently expended, as the fact that he contributes individually a direct tax, no matter how small, to his Government." With the strong support of Harding, Coolidge, and Hoover in succession, Mellon succeeded in slashing by one-third the huge war-swollen national debt; in 1920, some $24,061,000,000 was outstanding, but a decade later this had fallen to $16,185,000,000. Wartime taxes almost disappeared. With a jealous eye on the nation's revenues, Mellon fought legislation that would extend federal aid to the states and stiffened the three Presidents' resistance to veterans' bonus laws despite the political repercussions. "Economy," President Coolidge once said, "is idealism in its most practical form."

SCANDAL IN THE VETERANS' BUREAU

Hoping to avert the extraordinary pension burden that followed the Civil War, Congress had passed a War Risk Insurance Act in October, 1917, that provided both life insurance and generous hospitalization for war veterans, and support for their orphaned dependents. This legislation proved anything but final, for by 1924 almost one hundred changes had been incorporated in it. The newly organized American Legion, which in 1922 had an estimated 850,000 members, exerted powerful pressure for legislation which would provide permanent pensions for all who wore a uniform during 1917–1918, regardless of actual combat service. It also attempted to supplement the discharge bonus, which by 1922 had cost the nation a quarter of a billion dollars, by paid-up insurance. Although the bill which would have made this possible was passed in both the House and the Senate, it was vetoed by President Harding on Mellon's insistence, and the veto was sustained in the Senate, with Borah of Idaho firmly holding the line for economy.

In response to group pressure from veterans, Harding in 1921 had combined the various federal offices dealing with ex-soldiers into a single semi-independent body, the United States Veterans' Bureau, for which some half billion dollars was to be appropriated each year. Unfortunately, however, he chose as its director Charles R. Forbes, whose dishonesty cost the Bureau at least $200,000,000. At a time when veterans' hospitals were suffering from desperate shortages in supplies, Forbes enriched himself and his friends by labeling as "worthless" valuable materials, including Red Cross donations, and selling them to certain men who, acting in collusion, resold the identical items to the Bureau at exorbitant prices. Fraud likewise was rife in the awarding of contracts and the purchase of hospital sites. The American Legion vigorously criticized Forbes' apparent lack of interest in administering to the needs of disabled veterans, but Harding loyally accepted the explanations made by his appointee. The scandal was eventually brought into the open by disgruntled contractors who resented the favors shown to Forbes' own men; the ensuing Senate investigation, although long delayed, confirmed the worst fears. Forbes resigned his office in 1923 but was convicted two years later by a federal court; one of his chief associates committed suicide. This was one of the first of the major scandals of the Harding administration; the others came to light only after the President's death.

BUDGET REFORM

Far more in keeping with Harding's campaign slogan, "More business in government," was the passage in 1921 of the Budget and Accounting Act which had been sponsored by both Taft and Wilson when President. Instead of each executive department submitting inflated and conflicting estimates of expenditures and revenues to Congress, there to be considered by nine different legislative committees, the new Act created a Bureau of the Budget which afforded complete centralization of control directly under the President. The Bureau was not only to examine and revise estimates but also to simplify the numerous administrative bodies and departmental processes. A vigilant "watchdog of the Treasury"—sometimes too vigilant—was provided in the person of the semi-independent Comptroller General who headed the new General Accounting Office; he was empowered both to audit accounts and to set aside expenditures he judged illegal. Finally, the House of Representatives decided that a single enlarged Committee on Appropriations should examine budget expenditures. This was a long forward step in curbing logrolling, a practice which had drained the Treasury in behalf of politically useful local projects.

As his first Director of the Budget President Harding chose the exceptionally able Chicago banker, Charles G. Dawes, whose name later won respect in the chancelleries of Europe in connection with reparation payments. Availing himself of his new prestige as the President's direct financial representative, Dawes set valuable precedents for future budget directors by his coordinated policies that broke down the separation between departments. High officials met occasionally to hear his vigorous lectures on economy and efficiency, and refractory Congressmen soon learned to respect his opinions on government finance.

THE REVIVAL OF ECONOMIC NATIONALISM

Wilson's low-tariff policies were hastily scrapped by the incoming Republican administration. "I believe in the protection of American industry," Harding declared in his special message on April 12, 1921, "and it is our purpose to prosper America first." The Emergency Act of 1921 gave illusory protection to middle-western farmers and more substantial aid to the sugar, wool, and chemical interests. The Fordney-McCumber Tariff Act of 1922 went far toward restoring—in some cases it even surpassed—the sharply criticized prohibitive schedules of the Payne-Aldrich tariff of 1909, especially in textiles. Because protectionists inserted the dubious "flexible" clause which equalized costs here and abroad, a new tariff commission was entrusted with the task of determining duties that would offset the lower costs of labor and materials in other countries. Acting on the commission's report, the President could increase or decrease the prevailing duties by as much as 50 per cent, if necessary.

Objective economists in this country severely criticized this "flexible" clause as unworkable. To make matters worse, both Harding and Coolidge appointed frankly partisan protectionists to the tariff commission, thus ending the hope that the tariff could be kept out of politics. The commission, torn as it was by internal dissensions, contrasted sharply with Wilson's advisory group of six distinguished economists, under Professor Taussig of Harvard, who made scientific data available for tariff-framers. European debtor nations found our tariff an obstacle to payment of debts as well as an excuse for retaliatory measures. Republican defenders of the Fordney-McCumber Act could, however, point to the fact that many protectionist votes came from Democratic ranks.

CALVIN COOLIDGE AS PRESIDENT

President Harding's death in San Francisco on August 2, 1923, mercifully spared him from knowledge of the scandals that resulted from his lax administration and his indifference to his responsibilities as a public servant. For the time being, the nation mourned him as a martyred President whose death was caused by the burdens of his office; according to some newspapers, he was comparable to Lincoln. Conscientious Republicans who had shown misgivings over his fitness for high office seemed convinced of their error, in view of the economic recovery which imbued the few achievements of his Administration with a golden aura.

Vice President Calvin Coolidge, who took the oath as President at his father's home in Plymouth, Vermont, reassured his countrymen that he would follow in the footsteps of his illustrious predecessor and would retain the same Cabinet. Journalists who had loved the jovial, handsome Harding eyed critically the solemn, puritanical New Englander who was by contrast so physically unimpressive, sparing of words, and socially aloof. But those who knew Coolidge well appreciated his excellent training and abilities, his innate shrewdness, and his high-minded sincerity. Conservatives were reassured by his handling of the Boston police strike in 1919 and by his oft-quoted statement that "the business of America is business." The perpetuation of business leadership in politics was certain.

THE TEAPOT DOME SCANDAL

Within a few months of Coolidge's accession to the Presidency, there were heard the first ugly rumors of scandal involving Harding's Secretary of the Interior, Albert B. Fall of New Mexico, whose appointment had been regarded as an affront to Mexico because of his belligerent advocacy of intervention while a Senator. Now, after a decade of financial difficulties, Fall was suddenly showing evidences of considerable prosperity, especially in expanding his ranch in New Mexico. On October 25, 1923, Senator Thomas J. Walsh of Montana, a Democrat, called for a public hearing on the peculiar circumstances surrounding the leasing of two naval oil reserves to private corporations. One of these reserves, the Teapot Dome oil field, was located in Wyoming and had been set aside for the Navy's use by Wilson; the other, at Elk Hills, California, had likewise been withdrawn from private use by Taft.

The mystery of how Fall could accumulate almost $125,000 on an annual salary of $12,000 was slowly dispelled by the Senate committee. Secretary Fall had convinced both Harding and Secretary of the Navy Edwin Denby that the two reserves should be transferred to the Department of the Interior. Thereupon he leased Elk Hills to Edward L. Doheny, multimillionaire president of the Pan-American Petroleum Company; this transaction, Doheny told the Senate, should net the company at least $100,000,000 profit. At practically the same time, Doheny's son turned over to Fall a satchel containing $100,000, covered only by an unsecured note for whose origin the Secretary could give no convincing explanation. The other beneficiary of federal largess was Harry F. Sinclair, another oil magnate who was interested in Teapot Dome. The lease for this field, which was believed to be worth at least as much as the Elk Hills unit, was awarded to Sinclair in 1922 without the inconvenience of competitive bids. Once more a Senate investigating committee found evidence that Fall had been bribed when it disclosed the transfer of $223,000 in Liberty Bonds from a Sinclair corporation to the Secretary's son-in-law, supplemented by a gift of $85,000 in cash and some choice cattle for Fall's ranch.

President Coolidge promised that the guilty would be punished. He followed the excellent advice of Harlan F. Stone, a prominent lawyer, in selecting Owen J. Roberts and Atlee W. Pomerene as special counsel to prosecute the oil cases. The lethargic Department of Justice headed by Harry M. Daugherty, Harding's intimate friend, was ignored. When Fall, Doheny, Sinclair, and their associates took the stand, their memories grew poor and their testimony was conflicting. Sinclair's refusal to answer many of Senator Walsh's questions brought him a contempt citation from the Senate and three months in jail, in addition to a fine of $1000. During the court trial of Fall and Sinclair, the latter employed detectives to shadow the jury; this brought him a second contempt citation and six months more in jail. Ultimately, after protracted court proceedings, both he and Doheny managed to be acquitted. Curiously enough, only Fall the bribe-taker was convicted; he was sentenced to a year in jail and a fine of $100,000. The federal prosecutors eventually obtained the cancellation of the oil leases. The publicity given the trial cast a shadow on various political notables—even, by implication, on Harding himself—but their names were cleared after the excitement died down.

THE DOWNFALL OF DAUGHERTY

Although the oil cases led Denby to resign as Secretary of the Navy, Daugherty clung obstinately to his post as Attorney General in spite of suspicions against him. These charges became concrete during the middle twenties when another Harding scandal was unearthed; this one involved Daugherty and the Alien Property Custodian, Thomas W. Miller, a Harding appointee. Among the enemy alien property seized by the federal government during the World War was the American Metal Company, supposedly German owned, whose assets were put at $6,500,000, including interest, in 1921. To secure possession of this property, a German representative paid John T. King, a "go-between" politician, some $441,000. Of this sum, $50,000 found its way to the Alien Property Custodian; another $50,000, in easily identified Liberty Bonds, was deposited to the account of Jesse Smith, a close friend and business associate of

Daugherty. Before the case was brought to trial, however, King died and Smith committed suicide; some of the latter's personal records were reported destroyed by Daugherty or his agents.

This chain of circumstantial evidence called for a formal investigation of the Attorney General. To everyone's surprise—and Coolidge's disgust—Daugherty refused to testify on the technical ground that his testimony might incriminate him. Instead he issued a remarkable statement to the effect that his relations with Harding, as his personal attorney and Cabinet officer in particular, and with other high officials were most confidential, the obvious inference being that his refusal to testify was based solely on a praiseworthy desire to protect the late President. Miller alone was convicted and jailed.

This proved the last straw even for Coolidge, who was notoriously slow in taking action, and Daugherty was forced to resign from the Cabinet. More evidence was accumulated against the unofficial "attorney general," Jesse Smith, who had maintained an office in the Department of Justice and seemed to have acted as an intermediary for Daugherty. Also disclosed was the unsuccessful attempt of the Department of Justice to prosecute Senator Burton K. Wheeler of Montana, the leader of the Senators who had challenged Daugherty's probity. Special agents of the Attorney General, charged members of the Senate, were creating a "government by blackmail." The resulting lack of confidence in government officials was so widespread that even the Democrats, who naturally were glorying in their assault on Republican virtue, failed to gain an unprecedented number of the nation's votes in either 1924 or 1928.

BUSINESS AND THE ELECTION OF 1924

In his campaign for the Presidency in 1924, Coolidge carefully dissociated himself from the Senate clique, led by Lodge, which had promoted Harding's election in 1920. The professional politicians were replaced by a group of New England businessmen which included Frank W. Stearns, the Boston cotton mill owner, and Senator William M. Butler. The latter, a traction magnate and textile manufacturer of Massachusetts, managed Coolidge's campaign.

The Republican state primaries indicated an overwhelming preference for Coolidge's renomination, a preference borne out at the convention in Cleveland when he won an easy victory on the first ballot; La Follette and Hiram Johnson, who also sought the nomination, received only a few scattered votes. Charles G. Dawes, whose record as Budget Director and reparations expert had been outstanding, was nominated for the Vice Presidency. The party platform embodied Mellon's ideas on economy and tax reduction.

The Democratic convention, which was held in New York's Madison Square Garden, was far less harmonious. A fierce battle raged between the delegates pledged to support Tammany's Alfred E. Smith, and those from the rural South and West who supported William G. McAdoo of California, Wilson's son-in-law and political heir apparent. Smith, though a conservative from an economic point of view, had advocated progressive measures as governor of New York, but had antagonized William Jennings Bryan and the dry forces by his activities in securing the repeal of the state prohibition law. Smith's boast that he came from the sidewalks of New York and that the Fulton Street fish market was the only university he had ever attended failed to endear him to the delegates from the rural sections. Nevertheless, an enthusiastic roar went up when his name was placed before the convention by Franklin D. Roosevelt.

A Pandora's box of trouble was opened when Smith's managers, who represented the urban, Catholic, Jewish, and liberal elements, demanded that the party platform condemn the rampant Ku Klux Klan by name. McAdoo and Bryan, assuredly no friends of intolerance, sought to avoid the political trap laid for them on account of their southern following, by substituting a general plank that assailed "any effort to arouse religious or racial dissension." The McAdoo forces won this costly skirmish by a narrow margin, but dangerous feelings had been aroused between the forces of rural, Protestant, dry America and the motley urban, wet elements.

The balloting continued for well over a week, with McAdoo leading but unable to win the two-thirds vote needed for nomination. Many of the delegates, worried by the specter of mounting hotel bills, began a frantic search for a compromise candidate. Their choice, John W. Davis of New York, received the nomination on the hundred and third ballot.

Davis, once a vigorous Wilsonian liberal, was a supporter of the

League of Nations and a moderate on the prohibition issue, but, as Republican and Progressive critics soon pointed out, he had served as counsel for the Morgan interests. This was a serious drawback, in view of the tradition that however generously corporations might contribute to campaign funds, the President himself must not be too ostensibly associated with big business. Davis and his supporters at once made a bid for Bryan's cooperation by securing the vice-presidential nomination for his brother, Governor Charles W. Bryan of Nebraska. The party platform assailed the Teapot Dome scandal, emphasized honesty in government, and advocated a scientific revision of the tariff, farm relief, and a cautious modification of Wilson's policies in foreign affairs.

THE DEFEAT OF PROGRESSIVISM

Even before it became clear that Davis would be nominated, various dissident Progressives sponsored by the Conference for Progressive Political Action, a farmer-labor organization, offered the presidential nomination to Senator Robert M. La Follette on a platform of his own making. Senator Burton K. Wheeler of Montana, nominally a Democrat, was their vice-presidential candidate. The two men were heartily endorsed by the great Railroad Brotherhoods, the Socialist party, and the American Federation of Labor, which thus temporarily shelved Gompers' policy of avoiding party politics.

As before the war, La Follette's platform declared: "The great issue before the American people today is the control of government and industry by private monopoly." The veteran Senator asserted that more than 600,000 farmers in the fifteen leading wheat-growing states had been virtually bankrupt since 1920, in the face of continuing prosperity for industry. He attributed this to the exorbitant tariff, the favoritism shown powerful corporations, the excessive freight rates paid by farmers, and speculation in farm products. He promised a thorough cleanup of the Departments of Justice and the Interior. The platform also included protection of labor against the injunction, a promise of judicial reform, and a popular referendum on war and peace. Finally, the Senator outlined a program for government ownership of water and power resources which would lower the rates paid by the consumer.

During the campaign La Follette effectively neutralized the magic of the Bryan name in the Middle West as the famous Democrat took the stump with his brother in behalf of Davis. That the people were apathetic to crusading issues and to Davis's charges of corruption among Republicans was manifest on election day, when Coolidge won 382 electoral votes and Davis 136; La Follette had only the 13 cast by Wisconsin. Davis was supported exclusively by the Solid South and Oklahoma. Coolidge's popular vote was 15,725,000; Davis's, 8,386,000; and La Follette's, 4,826,000. The latter was stronger than Davis in twelve midwestern and western states. The Republicans increased their slight margin in the House and Senate—it had been dangerously cut in 1922—but farm bloc Republicans constituted a hazard to the Administration program. Shortly after the strenuous campaign of 1924, La Follette and William J. Bryan both died, having witnessed the crushing defeat of the prewar Progressive leaders.

THE ATROPHY OF GOVERNMENT REGULATION

Coolidge's inaugural address struck the usual note of economy and dwelt upon the current prosperity of the land. Much more unexpected was the sharp harangue which Vice President Dawes gave the Senate on the subject of the waste involved in prolonged debate. "Who would dare maintain," he asked, "that the right of the Senate itself to act should ever be subordinate to the right of one Senator to make a speech?" However, this assault on the time-honored filibuster and kindred dilatory tactics brought no response from his increasingly cool audience. Progressive Senators more than once had found the filibuster a valuable weapon in protecting minority groups such as the farm bloc against the conservatism of the majority, and southern Senators regarded it as infallible when anti-lynching legislation was being considered.

Like Harding, Coolidge did not advocate strong executive control over Congress, nor did he favor any far-reaching program of social reform. Although sympathetic toward those whom the new prosperity had passed by, he nevertheless firmly rejected every suggestion that involved "federal paternalism"; the states, he insisted, were responsible for providing relief for their underprivileged groups. In his message to Congress in 1925, he said: "It does not at all follow that because abuses exist, it is the concern of the federal government to attempt their reform." Critics noted that his public utterances emphasized the Calvinist virtues of thrift, sobriety, honesty, self-denial, and the glory of labor in the attainment of individual wealth.

Seldom had commerce and industry enjoyed such favor at the White House. The Federal Trade Commission, Wilson's chief instrument of business regulation, declined in both importance and prestige after the new Coolidge-appointed members introduced their policy of "self-government for industry." For a time it seemed that the F.T.C. was concerned solely in aiding businessmen to circumvent the anti-trust laws. This added function became apparent when William E. Humphrey of Washington, a former Republican Congressman and one of Coolidge's campaign managers, was appointed to the Commission. Immediately its investigative and judicial activities were reduced and Wilson's policy of "pitiless publicity" was largely discarded. Business and trade associations, always an object of suspicion to reformers before the war, were given open encouragement in the new Trade Practice Conference system, which promoted price uniformity rather than competition.

Writing in *The Magazine of Wall Street* on April 5, 1927, Humphrey boasted of the revolutionary "wholesale fusion of political and economic life." This he attributed to the increasing ownership of stocks and bonds by every class of people. The three or four hundred trade associations that were represented at Washington, he said, constituted "a sort of parliament of the people as business units"; as a result, "The ballot follows the bond; the vote is the voice of business." Economic life was regulated more and more by the decisions of these associations. "Instead of passing obstructive laws for political purposes," Humphrey said caustically, "Congress now satisfies its demagogic tendencies by ordering all sorts of investigations—which come to nothing." These opinions brought Humphrey under the fire of Senate liberals who demanded the abolition of the F.T.C. as the pawn of big business.

A similar tendency to atrophy was apparent in the declining activities of other regulatory agencies, for example the Interstate Commerce Commission, which had come into being in 1887 as the result of the farmers' revolt against railroad monopoly. Coolidge urged Congress to authorize railroad consolidations under the supervision of the Commission; actually, however, this body had a minor part in the subsequent plans for combination, for the large railroad operators called the tune. The Railroad Labor Board was replaced by informal boards of adjustment which reduced the government's role in labor relations. Hard-pressed farmers demanded that the I.C.C. reduce railroad rates, but no action was taken. Another declining regulatory agency, the Federal Power Commission, created by the Federal Water Power Act of 1920 to supervise power activities primarily through a licensing and rate-fixing system, suffered from inadequate personnel (it consisted of three Cabinet members) and frequently succumbed to the pressure of the power interests. Not until June, 1930, did Congress set up a power commission of five full-time members with functions analogous to those of the Interstate Commerce Commission, and even then serious loopholes in power regulation still existed. Moreover, the Tariff Commission, according to Democrats as well as Republican insurgents, seemed ineffective and biased in favor of special interests that demanded protection.

This trend toward greater self-regulation on the part of business was paralleled by similar developments elsewhere, as in various state governments. The New Jersey legislature, which had enacted the sweeping program advanced by Governor Woodrow Wilson for business control, repealed all such restrictions on big business. Even the Supreme Court moved gradually to Brandeis' belief that it was better to permit the restraints on competition advocated by trade associations in their efforts to "rationalize competition" than to force industry to enter "the inviting field of consolidation."

THE POWER INDUSTRY VERSUS PROGRESSIVISM

Senate Progressives like Norris and Walsh joined the Democratic regulars in selecting publicity as a weapon against the steady encroachment of business on government. During 1927–1928 these dissidents, with great reluctance, entrusted the Federal Trade Commission with the task of investigating the power industry. Gifford Pinchot, former governor of Pennsylvania and a lifelong crusader for conservation, had aroused congressional interest by his open letter to Senator Thomas J. Walsh of Montana, in which he asserted that four-fifths of all the electrical energy produced in the United States was controlled by forty-one corporations. These corporations, which represented a total capitalization of well over ten billion dollars, were controlled by relatively few men.

The Commission's subsequent investigation substantiated many of Pinchot's fears regarding the concentration of power in the electrical industry through fantastically pyramided holding companies. In one instance cited by the F.T.C., a single million-dollar investment resulted in control of companies worth several hundred million dollars. Prominent among those at the top in the industry were the Anglo-American Company, Samuel Insull of Chicago, the General Electric Company, and the North American group. The penetration of public utility propaganda against government ownership in the schools and press has already been mentioned in another connection. Even the infant radio industry, firmly based on patent monopoly, seemed to have reached the consolidation stage by 1927, when the General Electric Company organized the Radio Corporation of America.

One of the most sustained efforts against the power trust was the battle waged by Senator Norris of Nebraska for permanent federal operation of Muscle Shoals, the forerunner of the Tennessee Valley Authority. Muscle Shoals, located on the Tennessee River falls in northern Alabama, was built in 1918 by the federal government to supply power for the manufacture of nitrate explosives needed in our war effort. The total cost of developing the project, including a series of dams, was $145,000,000. Both Harding and Coolidge favored disposing of the property as quickly as possible to private corporations; accordingly, work on the Wilson Dam unit was stopped. On July 8, 1921, Henry Ford submitted a bid for a hundred-year lease; the amount he quoted would apparently enable farmers to buy nitrate fertilizers at a low price. The question of the large-scale development of electric power seemed forgotten in Congress, which was in favor of accepting Ford's offer.

Senator Norris, convinced that the future of America was closely connected with electric power, argued that an independent government corporation must enter the field in order to safeguard later generations against private monopoly; moreover, he contended that federal operation of Muscle Shoals as a power source would provide a yardstick for determining the fairness of the rates paid by consumers. As southern and western Congressmen slowly became converted to Norris's views, Ford withdrew his bid. In 1925 Coolidge put his support behind the Underwood Bill, which would have leased the waterpower rights of Muscle Shoals to a private corporation, but the measure failed to pass Congress. Coolidge had his revenge three years later when he pocket-vetoed the Norris-Morin resolution, which represented a partial acceptance of Norris's ideas on public power. Convinced that the war on the power trust was of paramount importance to the nation, Norris deserted the Republican party in 1928 to support Alfred E. Smith, who was sympathetic to federal power projects, but not until the middle 1930's did his project become a reality.

Power lobbies were busily engaged between 1921 and 1928 in a fight against the huge dam to be constructed and operated by the government at Boulder Dam on the Colorado River. Taking advantage of the clause in the Constitution that provides for interstate compacts under congressional authorization, seven southwest states signed an agreement in 1922 that disposed of the ownership of the waters of the Colorado River. However, various business and sectional controversies delayed congressional approval until December 21, 1928, when Coolidge signed the Johnson-Swing Bill. This Act provided the reclamation and flood control features of Boulder Dam. The framers of the law envisaged the private sale of power while permitting government construction of the dam. This was also the view held by Coolidge and Secretary of Commerce Hoover, who opposed government competition with private power companies.

The influence of the utility companies upon politicians was clearly illustrated in the Senate disputes over seating William S. Vare, boss of the Philadelphia Republican machine, and Frank L. Smith of Illinois; both cases involved the excessive expenditure of money in the primaries. Once before, in 1918, the Senate had yielded to the Harding administration, which wanted to retain a Republican majority in the upper chamber, and seated Senator-elect Truman H. Newberry of Michigan. Although he had defeated Henry Ford, Newberry was barred because of the huge amount—$195,000—he spent in the primaries. The fact that many Senators who supported Newberry had lost their seats in the election of 1922 caused the Senate in 1926 to view with considerable disfavor the admission of Vare and Smith.

Vare's campaign fund amounted to the modest sum of $800,000, and it was claimed that, despite the fact that this was a Pennsylvania contest, out-of-state public utility corporations had contributed to it substantially. Frank L. Smith, chairman of the Illinois Commerce Commission which supervised utility practices, received $158,735, directly and indirectly, from Samuel Insull of the Commonwealth Edison Company; other utility officers also gave large sums to his campaign fund, which totaled over $285,000. Collusion in the Smith case was hotly denied by the utility magnates. First Vare and then Smith were denied their seats by the Senate, which relied on a generous interpretation of its constitutional power to pass on the election and qualifications of its members. Editorial comment likened Insull's bipartisan attitude on contributions (he had aided both parties) to the position taken by Jay Gould, who in an earlier era had boasted, "In a Democratic district, I am for the Democratic candidate; in a Republican district, I am for the Republican candidate; but always I am for the Erie Railroad."

DEFEAT OF FARM SUBSIDY

Coolidge's unrelenting opposition to government in business was forcefully presented in his war on the farm bloc's McNary-Haugen Bill. As early as 1923, Senator Charles L. McNary of Oregon and Congressman Gilbert N. Haugen of Iowa had introduced a controversial measure (it was later amended) that called for federal aid in raising farm prices, especially for wheat, corn, and hogs, the leading farm products of the Middle West. Under this bill, a federal board would be created to purchase the surplus remaining after domestic needs were satisfied, the surplus to be either held or disposed of abroad at the current world market price. The artificial scarcity thus induced at home by eliminating current surpluses would raise domestic prices. To help finance this scheme, an "equalization fee" clause in the bill provided that farmers who raised the commodities covered in the plan should pay the difference between the new domestic price and the world price. Clearly, the tariff, the traditional cure for depressed farm prices, had been discarded by the farm bloc in favor of more direct price control.

Coolidge was advised by the Department of Agriculture that, as in earlier decades, the present farm problem was primarily one of credit and that a solution might be found in scientific farming and cooperative farmers' associations. Furthermore, Secretary Jardine reported, farm income had increased greatly since 1921. An attack on the credit aspect of the problem had been made by Harding in 1923, when, spurred by the farm bloc, he had signed the Intermediate Credits Act which made economical short-term credit available to farmers through special federally owned banks. Attempts had also been made to curb market manipulations of farm prices. Coolidge's position was made clear in an address to the American Farm Bureau Corporation on December 7, 1925, in which he said that the federal government should not fix prices for farm products either directly or indirectly, nor should it engage in the purchase or sale of these products.

The McNary-Haugen Bill passed both houses of Congress in February, 1927, but was vetoed by Coolidge in terms that vigorously denounced it as socialistic in principle. He held that it would "put a premium on one-crop farming" because it gave special encouragement to the great staple crops and discouraged diversified agriculture; moreover, the farmer's hope of higher prices would lead to ever-increasing surpluses. Meanwhile, the consumer would bear the brunt of the higher prices. "Government price fixing, once started, has alike no justice and no end," Coolidge warned. "It is an economic folly from which this country has every right to be spared." Finally, he said that in the opinion of the Attorney General the bill was unconstitutional.

In view of the forthcoming election in 1928, the political implications of the McNary-Haugen Bill seemed menacing. Some critics of the President's veto failed to see any difference between the subsidy principle inherent in a tariff like the Fordney-McCumber Act and that in the rejected bill. A second bill, a modification of the first, was passed by Congress in 1928 but was vetoed by Coolidge. This veto had the support of cotton and tobacco planters who were interested in a profitable foreign market, for this version of the bill offered them only limited protection. Not only did Coolidge win his battle, but the farm problem presented no serious obstacle to party unity in the election of 1928.

SUBSIDIES FOR THE MERCHANT MARINE

Shipping owners were far more fortunate than farmers in securing financial aid from the government. Toward the end of Wilson's administration, the adherents of less government in business compelled the wholesale transfer of the huge wartime merchant marine to private groups. Therefore, with this purpose in mind, Congress passed the Merchant Marine Act in 1920, which extended the life of the United States Shipping Board, the agency that acted as government salesman, and the Emergency Fleet Corporation, which would operate the ships as yet unsold and would encourage the development of new shipping routes by making loans. As a result—this created a minor public scandal—the Board between 1921 and 1928 sold 1164 comparatively new ships for $41,500,000, a fractional part of their original cost, $516,000,000. Most of the unsold ships were operated by private agents under federal contracts that guaranteed them against loss.

Coolidge opposed direct money subsidies for the merchant marine, but advocated temporary and direct federal aid to private shipping. Although he urged American businessmen to use American-owned ships, he was against granting preferential rates to American shippers as a dangerous form of discrimination that was likely to invite retaliation from other nations. The Act of 1920 had excluded foreign ships from our coastal trade and from trade with the Philippines and various other American possessions. The President's annual message on December 5, 1927, aroused considerable comment because of the blunt statement, "The Shipping Board is constantly under pressure, to which it too often yields, to protect private interests rather than serve the public welfare." A few days later he removed an official from the Board for accepting a large loan from Pacific coast shipping interests under suspicious circumstances.

Since the private shipping industry continued to lag, despite earlier measures in its behalf, Congress passed the Jones-White Mail Subsidy Act in 1928. This important bill not only granted generous long-term contracts for carrying mail across the oceans but offered liberal loans for the construction of new vessels and reduced even further the price of the ships still unsold. Despite these measures, the merchant marine could not meet European competition and hence continued to decline. This was due in part to the fact that our operating expenses were relatively high as a result of the La Follette Seamen's Act of 1915, which established wage and living standards considerably higher than those of other nations, although lower than the standards of American semiskilled factory workers.

OTHER PROBLEMS OF THE COOLIDGE ERA

One setback to Coolidge's program of economy during 1923–1929 was the passage, on May 19, 1924, of the veterans' bonus bill over his veto. A week earlier he had vetoed the Bursum Pension Bill appropriating $58,000,000 for the veterans of earlier wars and their widows, and that veto had stood; but this time Congress yielded to the pressure exerted by the powerful veterans' lobby. The American Legion had campaigned for preference for veterans in civil service appointments, had introduced universal military training in the schools, and had strengthened the federal Veterans' Bureau. It reached the peak of success in the new bonus law, which granted twenty-year endowment policies to veterans in the form of adjusted service certificates based on length of service; these notes could be used by veterans as collateral for loans.

A major irritant for Coolidge during these years was prohibition enforcement. Although more conscientious than Harding, who occasionally had aroused the wrath of Wayne Wheeler's all-powerful Anti-Saloon League, Coolidge also faced much criticism. One federal enforcement administrator in New York, who resigned his position in 1927, charged publicly that the spoils system had demoralized every effort to enforce the Volstead Act and that "three-quarters of the 2500 dry agents are ward heelers and sycophants, named by the politicians." Coolidge responded promptly by placing the Prohibition Service under civil service rules, a step greatly commended by impartial observers. Smuggling was reduced considerably, but the problem of enforcement in the face of increasing urban hostility to prohibition remained serious and constituted a delicate political issue in 1928.

Coolidge looked on the roseate bull market of 1927–1929 with the optimism of Secretary Mellon and the Federal Reserve Board and upheld the then popular policy of rapid credit expansion. No more at fault than certain professional economists of high repute, the President and the Secretary repeatedly issued statements during 1928 to the effect that the existing high market levels were far from unjustified by the nation's economic progress. Government economy, tax refunds, and the Federal Reserve bank rediscounting policies that had favored the speculative trend prior to 1928 contributed to the overabundant funds that poured into the stock market. The New York Stock Exchange, which had disposed of 223,000,000 shares in 1920, an active year, handled the unprecedented volume of 1,124,000,000 shares in 1929.

THE HOOVER SUCCESSION

On August 2, 1927, Coolidge electrified the country by his statement, "I do not choose to run for President in nineteen twenty-eight." Although political experts considered his reelection a reasonable certainty, the President refused to be swayed from his decision by those who favored drafting him for a second term. The press was unconvinced by his avowed desire to leave public life. Possibly, as Claude M. Fuess, his biographer, has suggested, his failing health, which caused his death in 1933, was a factor. At any rate, the stock market dropped decidedly, reflecting the loss of a benevolent influence in business life.

The Republican heir-apparent was obviously Herbert Hoover, who symbolized this period in a profound sense. His choice foreshadowed by success in the state primaries, he was nominated by the Republican convention in Kansas City on the first ballot. An independent and energetic Secretary of Commerce, he had escaped in large part the stigma attached to the members of Harding's scandal-ridden Cabinet. Although some eastern financiers would have preferred Charles G. Dawes or Frank O. Lowden, Hoover won the confidence of the people who advocated less government in business by his encouragement of trade association leadership in business and other measures calling for voluntary collective action. His record as an administrative expert forecast his future policy of "government by commission." In 1929 he stated his laissez-faire ideal, "Progress is born of cooperation in the community, not from governmental restraints. The government should assist and encourage these movements of collective self-help by itself cooperating with them." Like Coolidge, Hoover had an undramatic, even colorless, personality, despite his vivid record as a humanitarian in war-torn Europe and as head of the relief agencies who worked during the catastrophic Mississippi floods in 1927.

Hoover had contributed a great deal to the positive achievements of the Harding and Coolidge administrations, as he had to those of the Wilson era. As Secretary of Commerce, he had waged a long and difficult but successful struggle with Congress on the question of federal regulation of radio communication in 1927, the outcome of which was the beginning of the scientific allocation of wave lengths and the strengthening of the principles of free speech on the air and of local control of broadcasting stations. He had encouraged the infant aircraft industry and promoted interstate compacts for reclamation and flood control. He had warned European countries against instituting production restrictions and price controls on raw materials essential to the United States, and had even threatened trade reprisals. But he was cool to all proposals, such as Senator Norris's plan embodying large-scale competition between the government and private electrical companies, which would put the government in business. On prohibition he stood for vigorous enforcement regardless of the unpopularity of the law, but his support was not as wholehearted as the Anti-Saloon League wished.

As Hoover's running mate the Republicans chose the relatively weak Senator Charles Curtis of Kansas. The platform spelled the doom of the McNary-Haugen Bill, despite a vigorous fight for it at the convention in behalf of middlewestern farmers. Instead, a Hoover-sponsored plank was adopted which would create a Federal Farm Board to encourage cooperative marketing. In his acceptance speech Hoover declared optimistically, "We in America are nearer to the final triumph over poverty than ever before in the history of any land. . . . We shall soon, with the help of God, be in sight of the day when poverty will be banished from this nation." Once again, prosperity was the overwhelming factor presented to the electorate.

At the Democratic convention in Houston, Texas, Alfred E. Smith received his hard-earned reward of the party's presidential nomination, without serious competition, on the first ballot. The vice-presidential nominee was the liberal Senator, Joseph T. Robinson of Arkansas. Discussing the prohibition plank of the platform, Smith said frankly that while he would enforce the law as long as it remained in effect and would oppose the return of the saloon, he favored modification of the law. The farmers who had deserted the Republican party in an "On to Houston!" movement were promised an agricultural bill which would cope with the problem of surpluses along the lines of equalization fees. One Republican malcontent, Senator George Norris, was won over to the opposing party's cause by Smith's avowed friendliness to federal development of Muscle Shoals.

Hoover struck back at Smith's concessions to government in business by insisting, in his important address at New York on October 22, 1928, that the true issue was between "the American system of rugged individualism" and European doctrines of paternalism and state socialism. Economic freedom, he maintained, could not be sacrificed if political freedom was to be preserved. He said that while he did not advocate laissez faire to a "devil take the hindmost" extreme and would uphold economic justice, he subscribed to "decentralized self-government, ordered liberty, equal opportunity, and freedom to the individual." These principles, in contrast with those in effect in Soviet Russia, had achieved unparalleled success in bettering the welfare of the American people.

Smith proved pitifully vulnerable to religious bigots and attacks by the drys, particularly in the Solid South and the rural areas of the North. The Anti-Saloon League, newly financed by a recent campaign for funds, joined rural Fundamentalists and other organized dry groups in assailing him. Proponents of white supremacy in the South argued that Smith favored giving liquor to the Negroes. Worst of all were the vituperative attacks of anti-Catholic forces which represented him as a pawn of the Pope, intent on abolishing immigration restrictions. So low did the tone of the campaign sink that Democratic regulars in the South publicized the fact that Hoover swore occasionally and frequently went fishing on Sunday.

The Solid South broke ranks on election day, for Virginia, North Carolina, Florida, Tennessee, Texas, and the southern "border states" gave Hoover their electoral votes. Altogether he received 444 electoral votes to Smith's 87, the latter's coming from the other southern states plus Massachusetts and Rhode Island, where the recent immigration of Catholics had affected New England's traditional support of the Republican party. On the basis of popular votes—Hoover, 21,943,000; Smith, 15,430,000—Hoover's victory was less impressive because of the urban vote and that of the southern states that remained Democratic. The Republicans swept both houses of Congress. The Socialist party won only 267,800 votes for its candidate, Norman Thomas.

When the reports on campaign expenditures reached Congress, it became evident that the 1928 campaigns were unique in the huge amount of money spent. Hoover's campaign cost $9,433,604 and Smith's $7,152,511, whereas the highest totals heretofore spent amounted to less than half the Republican expenditure. The single item of radio time, which both parties used daily, cost at least $1,250,000.

THE BUSINESS EXPERT IN GOVERNMENT

The "Hoover bull market," as the newspapers called the post-election boom, cast a beneficent light over the new Administration. The Cabinet, which someone has described as "neither stars nor third-raters," once again included Mellon, the acknowledged financial wizard who had originally been Harding's Secretary of the Treasury. In the Agricultural Marketing Act of 1929, President Hoover secured the enactment of the farm program he had promised during his campaign. This Act created the Federal Farm Board, gave it a revolving fund of half a billion dollars, and empowered it to make loans through farm cooperatives and stabilization corporations; the latter were to help farmers keep their surplus crops off depressed markets until prices rose. Although these hopes of price stabilization at high levels were shattered by the depressing influence of mounting world surpluses as the great depression began, at the time Hoover seemed justified in his boast that the Agricultural Marketing Act was the "most important measure ever passed by Congress in aid of a single industry." Apparently it made unnecessary government price fixing and outright purchase of agricultural products.

In an attempt to solve the prohibition problem, Hoover called for "a searching investigation of the whole structure of our Federal system of jurisprudence, to include the methods of enforcement of the Eighteenth Amendment and the causes of abuse under it." This resulted in the creation of the National Commission on Law Observance and Enforcement, popularly known as the Wickersham Commission, whose members included Dean Roscoe Pound of Harvard, Newton D. Baker, a member of Wilson's Cabinet, George W. Wickersham, who had been Taft's Attorney General, and other acknowledged experts. The drys complained that the Commission's primary interest was general judicial problems and that it was therefore unable to deal with prohibition adequately. Wickersham appealed for greater cooperation with federal prohibition agents on the part of the states, and for the adoption of a uniform system of crime statistics. That prohibition was doomed became clear when Wisconsin in April, 1929, joined New York and Maryland in repealing their own enforcement laws and abolishing their prohibition enforcement agencies. Other states were soon swept by agitation for similar action.

As the summer of 1929 progressed, it seemed as if the decade might end in complete vindication of the ideal of business leadership. There were some who felt that, under Hoover, even government might be transformed and rationalized just as the assembly line and standardization had altered the industrial scene. Rarely had economic radicalism been at so heavy a discount. The substantial unemployment in the factories and fields as early as the middle twenties, and the rampant stock market speculation that sometimes suggested a harsh future reckoning could be waved aside as transient problems ultimately to be solved by the engineer in politics. The rational universe of the eighteenth-century philosophers, with its neatly formulated "laws of nature," had never been so close to realization.

CHAPTER 14

Retreat Toward Isolationism: 1921-1929

IGNORING THE LEAGUE OF NATIONS

Although Harding and Coolidge chose Secretaries of State who spoke the language of internationalism, powerful isolationist sentiment opposed any effective plan for world peace as a British snare to bring the United States into the League of Nations through a back door. American investors poured billions of dollars into foreign enterprises, but even here the fiction of isolationism was maintained. Nationalists, seeking to aid the hard-pressed staple farmer, could boast of such triumphs as the reversion to high-tariff protection under the Fordney-McCumber Act, but it largely failed of its purpose as far as farmers were concerned, invited retaliation, and made repayment of both government and private loans abroad extremely difficult. The anomaly of such a tariff for a nation which, as a creditor, required increased imports as a method of payment did not trouble the protectionists. However, the isolationist trend was modified by our continued adherence to certain historic foreign policies that were based on our conception of defensive strategy and by the permanent tenure of many State Department experts.

Harding preferred Albert B. Fall as his Secretary of State, despite the imperialist oil program that the Senator had advocated for Mexico and Colombia, but he was prevailed upon to accept Charles E. Hughes, of the pro-League Republican faction. Similarly, the choice of Herbert Hoover, a man who had been close to Wilson, as Secretary of Commerce seemed to place certain economic aspects of foreign affairs in the hands of one opposed to isolationism. Actually, both men tacitly accepted President Harding's dictum that the League was dead; Hughes, in particular, set himself to build a new framework of cooperation wholly outside the League of Nations. For months, at least until adverse publicity compelled a change, he refused to acknowledge letters from Geneva and discouraged American citizens from accepting important positions with the League. Inasmuch as Congress had rejected the Treaty of Versailles, which included the League Covenant, a separate peace treaty was signed with Germany on August 25, 1921; it ended the "state of war" but reserved all treaty rights acquired by Wilson.

Embarrassing to the League were Hughes' attempts to prevent diplomatic questions from reaching its jurisdiction and to keep alive the older international organizations which it wanted to absorb. When the fact that the League could survive without the United States finally became apparent, Harding and Hughes began the practice of permitting "unofficial observers" to attend certain League committee meetings that dealt with non-political questions. Miss Grace Abbott, appointed in October, 1922, to head the Children's Bureau, was the first of an increasing number of such observers who were chosen to cooperate actively on such problems as white slavery, the opium traffic, poison gas, anthrax control, and the international regulation of the private munitions traffic. This limited collaboration, which avoided all political responsibility, was not always effective, especially as regards major issues.

ISOLATIONISTS AND THE WORLD COURT

As a substitute for the League, President Harding, in a message which he sent to Congress (he dispensed with Wilson's practice of reading his messages in person), urged our membership in the Permanent Court of International Justice, popularly called the World Court. Unlike Wilson, Harding brought forth his own reservations before the Senate could think of any. These had been drawn up by Hughes in order to avoid any legal relationship between the Court and the League under which it had been created. Although the United States refused to assume any obligations under the League Covenant, she desired equal participation in the election of judges and consequently agreed to bear a fair share of the Court's expenses.

Americans had long been vigorous champions of arbitration, and during the Hague Conference of 1899 Republican statesmen had played a major role in setting up the Permanent Court of Arbitration, a tribunal intended to be a panel of judges rather than a court. Elihu Root, who had been Secretary of State under Roosevelt and had for a long time urged the creation of a court with permanent judges, became one of the jurists who drew up the World Court plan in 1920. It provided that judges were to be elected by the Council and the Assembly of the League of Nations, thus assuring representation to large and small nations alike. Although the League was not ready to make the Court's jurisdiction over disputes compulsory, it granted the judges regular judicial power in cases of an international character and the right to offer advisory opinions on questions submitted to the Court.

Harding, a Republican President with considerable Democratic support on the Court issue, faced an isolationist onslaught within his own party. Once again stubborn resistance was marshaled by Senator Lodge as chairman of the Committee on Foreign Relations, aided by Senator Borah, who was vigorously opposed to the "League Court." The resulting struggle bore an ominous similarity to the fight over the League in 1919–1920. Opponents insisted that the British Empire would dominate the election of judges because of the six votes to which she was entitled through the inclusion of the Dominions in the Assembly. Secretary Hughes replied that in the League Council, whose power in judicial elections was certainly not inferior to that of the Assembly, both the United States and Great Britain would be equally represented. President Harding, however, immediately retreated and was apparently on the point of utter capitulation at the time of his death.

Calvin Coolidge, who had been sympathetic to Wilson's League in 1919, showed greater vigor as President than his predecessor had displayed in attempting to bring the nation into the World Court. Both parties endorsed the Court in the campaign of 1924. The death of Lodge at this time caused only a temporary flurry in the isolationist ranks, for Borah filled the breach completely. Filibustering tactics delayed a vote on the Court until finally the Administration resorted to the cloture rule, thus shutting off further debate. The Senate yielded only after five reservations, all of them involving far-reaching changes in the structure of the Court, had been voted. Most significant was the fifth, which was intended to remove such policies as the Monroe Doctrine or immigration exclusion from the purview of the Court. It provided that the Court should render no advisory opinion without the consent of all interested parties, nor should it, without our consent, offer such an opinion on any question in which we claimed to have an interest. Thereupon, on January 27, 1926, the Senate voted to adhere by a vote of 76 to 16.

Recognizing that these reservations meant a drastic revision of the Court protocol, the League members met in conference at Geneva, accepted all the reservations except the last part of the fifth, and invited the United States to confer with the League Council in order to define the scope and operation of that clause. Since this clause was the most essential of all, Coolidge and the Senate regarded this reply as a rejection, and the President accordingly announced that the issue was closed.

In December, 1928, Elihu Root offered a compromise which, in case of a specific disagreement with the League as to what constituted our "interest," would have allowed us to withdraw from the Court without ill feeling, but the Senate proved cool. Although unsuccessful in achieving the requisite two-thirds majority, both Hoover and Franklin D. Roosevelt favored the Court, and Secretaries of State Hughes and Kellogg later served as judges. But the isolationist minority, suspicious of alleged international conspiracies to involve the United States in purely European wars, continued to hold firm; nor were they daunted by the pro-Court agitation of the American Federation of Labor, the Federal Council of Churches, the United States Chamber of Commerce, the American Bar Association, and numerous women's groups.

WAR BECOMES ILLEGAL

Typical of the lawyer's approach—which Wilson had always distrusted—was the postwar campaign among various nations to attain peace by outlawing war. This scheme was originally intended to be based upon the authority of the World Court, but the Republican sponsors of the plan were willing, if necessary, to proceed without the Court. On April 6, 1927, the tenth anniversary of our entrance into the World War, Foreign Minister Aristide Briand of France announced that his country would sign any treaty with the United States "tending to outlaw war, to use an American expression." This brought to public attention the agitation of Salmon O. Levinson, a prominent Chicago lawyer, and his American Committee for the Outlawry of War which had been founded in 1918. Levinson claimed that there were rules for war but no rules against war, and that if war were outlawed, all international conflicts would immediately assume a judicial character. While Wilson was President, Levinson advocated the use of organized international force to curb lawbreaking nations, but after the defeat of the League he put his chief reliance on the efficacy of public opinion.

One of Levinson's converts was Senator Borah, who had fought bitterly against a strong League Court but was eager for the creation of an independent court of nations modeled on our own Supreme Court, except that he would have enforcement rest only on enlightened public opinion. On February 14, 1923, he offered a Senate resolution which proposed that war be outlawed as an institution and that all international disputes be referred to the new independent court. Despite the fact that this proposal excluded military sanctions as a basis of enforcement, progressives like John Dewey, Senator Thomas Walsh of Montana, Dr. James T. Shotwell, and John Haynes Holmes gave it their enthusiastic support in the hope that thus outlawing war would arouse public opinion to demand the removal of the fundamental causes of international conflicts.

Borah's proposal, unlike Briand's, recommended that, instead of a Franco-American pact renouncing war, such an agreement be signed by all the principal nations of the world. Secretary of State Kellogg likewise advocated a multilateral pact. Briand agreed enthusiastically that the moral force of public opinion would afford valuable sanctions and would lead the way to the next step, organizing peace. Thus the Pact of Paris, or the Kellogg Pact, as the treaty came to be called, was officially proclaimed on July 24, 1929, after thirty-one nations had signed it. They agreed to "condemn recourse to war for the solution of international controversies, and [to] renounce it as an instrument of national policy in their relations with one another." None would resort to any but "pacific means" in settling disputes of any type.

That the millennium had not arrived was evident from the various reservations and interpretations. Senate isolationists, apprehensive of any infringement of the Monroe Doctrine, were reassured by Kellogg that it was protected by the fact that nothing in the treaty affected the sovereign right of self-defense. Britain likewise insisted on a "Monroe Doctrine" of her own for certain designated areas. Kellogg agreed to the demands of France and certain other powers that each nation remain the sole judge of what constituted self-defense. Only aggressive wars—whatever this might mean—were to be considered illegal. By 1935 the Pact of Paris had become almost universal; it even included the nations that precipitated a second world war shortly thereafter.

Levinson's Committee for the Outlawry of War maintained that the distinction between aggressive and non-aggressive wars vitiated the Pact, and he expressed disappointment at the failure to link it with an international supreme court. One concrete result of the Pact of Paris was the fact that territorial gains made in violation of it were not recognized; however, this failed to deter Japan from her decision to seize Manchuria and North China. Secretary of State Stimson invoked the Pact in December, 1929, during the Sino-Russian clash in Manchuria over China's seizure of the Soviet-owned Chinese Eastern Railway. His intervention was belated, for the two powers were on the point of concluding an agreement. The Soviet Union replied angrily that Stimson was interfering with her right of self-defense; furthermore, she pointed out, the United States had not recognized the Russian government. Stimson was also embarrassed by the indifference of the great powers, especially Germany, Japan, and France; apparently the Pact of Paris offered nothing corresponding to the economic and military sanctions provided by the League of Nations.

ISOLATING RUSSIA

Among Borah's more realistic plans to promote world peace was the recognition of the Soviet Union, but his efforts were unavailing. One reason was the fact that on January 21, 1918, the Soviet government repudiated its financial obligations abroad. "Absolutely and without exception," read the decree of the Council of People's Commissars, "all foreign loans are annulled." Later, however, Russia modified her position when she offered to meet certain obligations if we granted her generous credits.

The original debt principal of $192,601,297 owed the United States government consisted of a State Department loan of $187,729,750 extended to Kerensky's anti-Communist government in 1917; $4,465,-465 was due for American relief supplies; and $406,082 covered surplus war materials. Far greater in magnitude were the estimated claims, amounting to 400 million dollars, of American private investors, businessmen, and former residents whose property had been confiscated by the Soviets or destroyed during the revolution; among the heaviest single losers were the International Harvester Company and the Singer Sewing Machine Company. Most disconcerting to the United States were Russia's huge counterclaims for compensation for the villages in northern Russia and Siberia destroyed by our troops during the period of foreign intervention following the collapse of her resistance to Germany. The Soviet government maintained that it was difficult to understand why it must clear up debts, some of which had been incurred to put down the Bolshevik Revolution.

Although Wilson permitted American troops to play a minor part alongside the Allies in the military intervention against Soviet Russia, he refused to follow England and France in their active and large-scale support of counterrevolution. Nevertheless, the cost of the Archangel expedition in northern Russia was 244 Americans killed and 305 wounded; the direct financial cost reached three million dollars. The firm attitude of General William S. Graves prevented our occupation troops in Siberia from becoming militarily involved in anti-Soviet hostilities. Liberals assailed Wilson's Archangel adventure as imperialistic and criticized his keeping of American soldiers in Russia long after the 1918 Armistice. The President cautiously maintained unofficial contact with the Soviet government, notably through William C. Bullitt, a State Department official. Although Bullitt reported growing stability of the new regime, he failed to convince Wilson that diplomatic recognition should be extended. Private American loans of some $50,000,000 were made to Poland in her war against the Soviet Union in 1920, and that same year Bainbridge Colby, Wilson's last Secretary of State, reaffirmed our policy of not recognizing Soviet Russia. He expressed doubt as to the permanence of the new regime, denounced its unrepresentative character, and insisted that it violated "every principle of honor and good faith"; furthermore, he said, the

Russians were heavily subsidizing world-wide revolution by means of the Third (Communist) International. Thus Wilson's policy of not recognizing usurper governments, which had been followed with Mexico, was applied to Russia.

Soviet hopes that Harding would reverse this policy were quickly dashed, despite large economic concessions in Siberia granted the Sinclair interests and other business groups close to the Administration. Secretary of Commerce Hoover rebuffed the plea made by the Soviet diplomat, Maxim Litvinov, for the resumption of normal business relations. Believing that Communist Russia was an "economic vacuum," the Secretary maintained that it was impossible for such a system either to produce a surplus for export or to purchase large quantities of imports. Secretary Hughes, concurring, went so far as to suggest that Russia alter her fundamental policies as a prelude to recognition by the United States. However, when severe famine descended on the Soviet Union in 1921–1922, Secretary Hoover, supported by a generous federal appropriation for relief, came to the rescue of the starving millions in the Volga region.

Although Harding had denounced the Soviet government as one based on "confiscation and repudiation," President Coolidge seemed to be more conciliatory. This was evident in his first message to Congress on December 6, 1923, when he said that "whenever there appear works meet for repentance, our country ought to be the first to go to the economic and moral rescue of Russia." This hope of reopening negotiations was killed by Hughes. Kellogg, his successor, refused to use any but the most indirect methods of communicating with the Soviet Union, and he worked actively to prevent her from being one of the original signatories to his prized Pact of Paris. Borah alone argued that the isolation of Russia was a hazard to world peace and that recognition did not imply approval of a nation's political and economic doctrines. But more than a decade went by before the United States recognized the Soviet Union.

THE WASHINGTON CONFERENCE: JAPAN'S VICTORY?

Most ambitious of all the nation's peace enterprises during the twenties was the Washington Conference of 1921–1922, called to deal with disarmament and far-eastern questions. The peace treaty with Germany in 1921 had incorporated the section of the Treaty of Versailles which called for Germany to disarm as a step toward general disarmament for all nations. But instead of arms limitation, a huge naval race began, aggravated by increasing Japanese-American tension in the Pacific. Warnings about the yellow peril appeared regularly in the Hearst newspapers and other bellicose sheets, and the fatalistic cry, "The next war will be in the Pacific!" was commonly heard. The near-completion of Japan's "monster" battleship, the *Mutsu,* was given tremendous publicity; popular belief held that it was the most formidable warship afloat. On the other hand, the American Navy was racing to fulfill its huge program, originally laid down in 1916 by which it threatened to eclipse even the British Navy in new, heavily armed vessels.

The Philippine Islands, it was repeatedly observed, would be defenseless against any Japanese thrust. There was fear that Japan would strike before 1923, for then her naval strength would begin to be offset by our new vessels. Japan herself, worried by our fleet's shift to the Pacific, was anxious to prevent us from fortifying our insular possessions. Since their victorious war with China in 1895, the Nipponese had been steadily cutting off our Pacific approaches to Asia and had acquired a chain of islands stretching from southern Sakhalin on the north to Formosa on the south, in addition to the strategic areas once held by Germany in the Pacific. Japan's conquest of Korea and her penetration into Manchuria and the Shantung peninsula opened new paths into the interior of China and threatened the open-door policy because of her exclusionist economic and political policies.

At the Peace Conference in 1919, Japan doggedly refused to yield economic control over Shantung, which she acquired from Germany in spite of Wilson's objections, but she agreed informally to restore this to China in the future. One of the chief concerns of the subsequent Washington Conference was to persuade Japan to fulfill her pledge regarding Shantung and to guarantee the territorial integrity of China, for the great industrial nations of the West still clung to the yet unrealized dream of "four hundred million customers" absorbing their products. Another major problem was the Anglo-Japanese alliance, which was increasingly resented by the Dominions of Australia, New Zealand, and Canada, inasmuch as their immigration policies favored Japanese exclusion. Premier Hughes of Australia voiced the insecurity felt by a thinly populated white nation in an oriental world dominated by the belligerent Japanese when he declared that his people welcomed news of every battleship laid down in American shipyards and regarded our naval might as a bulwark against the "oriental menace."

Borah introduced a Senate resolution in December, 1920, calling for an international conference to halt the naval arms race. Here again it was necessary to proceed outside the framework of the League because the United States was not a member. The incoming Harding administration, at first cool to Borah's proposal, acted after it learned that Great Britain would take the initiative in this if we failed to do so. British taxpayers were demanding relief from the expensive program of naval expansion in which the greater financial resources of the United States were pitted against those of Great Britain. American taxpayers likewise were anxious to lighten the heavy tax burdens of the war years. Economy in government was so important an issue in foreign as well as domestic politics that eventually the Administration pressed for land as well as naval disarmament.

The Washington Conference, which opened on November 12, 1921, was attended by the ranking diplomats of the five leading naval powers—the United States, Great Britain, Japan, France, and Italy—and of Holland, Belgium, Portugal, and China, all of which had important far-eastern interests. The Senate was represented by Lodge, Oscar Underwood, a ranking Democrat, and ex-Senator Elihu Root. Secretary of State Hughes, coming bluntly to the point, demanded that the construction of capital ships be abandoned and that the existing ratios of such ships among the naval powers become the permanent basis of naval strength. Avoiding generalities, he mentioned the specific vessels that he maintained should be scrapped.

The admirals fumed, but public opinion applauded this bold move. In fact, William Jennings Bryan, who was attending the Conference as a reporter, was so vociferous in his approval that there was general fear that he might make a speech. The Japanese were glum indeed at the naval—and psychological—inferiority forced upon them by the ratios—5:5:3:1.75:1.75—finally adopted for the United States, Great Britain, Japan, France, and Italy respectively. However, they managed to save their precious *Mutsu* by demanding an upward revision of the tonnage estimates of the other naval powers. The Five-Power Naval Treaty which resulted from the Conference provided for a ten-year naval "holiday," after which replacements would be permitted at these ratios. Under this treaty the United States, Britain, and Japan were to scrap seventy vessels built and building, or 40 per cent of their capital ships. The United States had to scrap thirty vessels.

When it came to applying this principle to other types of naval vessels, France refused to cooperate. There were several reasons for her refusal. During the war she had put her once-powerful fleet on short rations in order to build up her Army; now she refused to be designated as a minor naval power. Furthermore, the French people were generally disappointed by the continued failure of the United States and Great Britain to ratify Wilson's treaty of alliance with France in the face of possible attack by a resurrected Germany. Perhaps most important of all was the fact that French diplomats were convinced that security must precede disarmament. At first the French amazed the Conference—and aroused ugly suspicions of militarism—by demanding twice the tonnage of capital ships assigned her, but she finally yielded on this point.

More serious was her adamant demand for a minimum submarine tonnage of 90,000 tons—more than the combined total for Great Britain and the United States. Thereupon the British refused to accept any reduction in destroyers and other auxiliary ships, which they insisted were the answer to the submarine menace. Thus the extremely important cruisers, at times prized even above battleships, escaped being scrapped. A futile declaration which the French refused to sign denounced the use of submarines to destroy vessels of the merchant marine because they could not be used without violating international law protecting neutrals. It condemned as piracy the sinking of ships without regard for the safety of their passengers and crews.

Another agreement made during the Conference was the Nine-Power Treaty dealing with the Far East and signed February 6, 1922. This treaty, much of which was the work of Elihu Root, reaffirmed the principle of the open door for China in concrete pledges to respect the sovereignty, independence, and administrative integrity of that country. Although the Chinese desired the abolition of the unequal treaties with Japan and the western powers which restricted their freedom, they were granted only limited concessions. The treaty called for the elimination of imperialist spheres of interest in China and for Chinese control of the tariff system. The Four-Power Treaty advocated by Lodge abrogated the Anglo-Japanese alliance and pledged that Great Britain, the United States, Japan, and France would respect one another's rights in the Pacific and would hold four-power conferences in case disputes arose. Underestimated in importance at the time was our own pledge not to fortify our Pacific possessions; this exposed the Philippines to Japan and made Hawaii the limit of our strength to the west. A separate agreement between Japan and China provided for the restoration of economic privileges in the Shantung peninsula and modified certain of the infamous twenty-one demands made earlier on China.

All in all, Japan was not as heavy a loser at the Washington Conference as at first appeared. She could not afford a naval race against the powerful United States in which Great Britain and her Dominions might join. As for the Anglo-Japanese alliance, it was moribund before 1921 and was therefore no longer an asset to Japan. That her withdrawal from Shantung was never carried through completely was clear during 1927–1928 when Baron Tanaka moved troops into the peninsula at the first threat of Chinese violation of Japanese interests. Our own pledge—Japan and Britain made similar promises—not to fortify our far-eastern possessions, including the Aleutian Islands, meant that Japan was secure from our Navy and allowed her to concentrate on advancing in the Asiatic mainland. At that time the liberal members of the Tokyo Cabinet were able to formulate a foreign policy that called for new markets, especially in Manchuria and Korea, and equal access to raw materials rather than continued territorial expansion. For these reasons Japan withdrew from Siberia soon after the Conference, and restored the northern half of Sakhalin to Russia, except for certain valuable mineral and fishery concessions which she retained. In reality, it was the United States rather than Japan which retreated in the Far East to a position of increased isolation and peril.

THE FAILURE OF DISARMAMENT

As anticipated, the inability of the Conference to restrict the construction of cruisers led to a naval race after 1922 in this and other auxiliary craft. The new 10,000-ton cruisers armed with heavy guns made the reduction in capital ships a hollow victory. Between 1922 and 1927 Japan laid down fourteen cruisers, largely of the heavy type, Britain thirteen, and the United States two; we had six more in the blueprint stage. Since we did not fully adhere to the League's disarmament program, President Coolidge on February 10, 1927, invited the five leading naval powers to another conference to be held at Geneva in June. France, disappointed by the earlier conferences and still firmly convinced that security must precede disarmament, refused to attend, as did Italy, then wholly enthralled by Mussolini's imperialism. Since Japan at this time was primarily interested in land armaments in view of her plans for Asia, the three-power conference which met on June 20 developed largely into a contest between Great Britain and the United States over the type of naval disarmament to be adopted.

Our disagreement with Britain at the Geneva Conference sprang from the diverse defense needs of the two nations. Britain, who had many naval bases scattered over the globe, wanted at least seventy light cruisers, whereas the United States, with extremely few bases, needed a smaller number of heavy cruisers that would be able to make long voyages without refueling. Coolidge charged publicly that the British made "a tentative offer which would limit the kinds of cruisers and submarines adapted to the use of the United States but left without limit the kind adapted to their own use." The Conference ended in a stalemate on August 4, whereupon Congress proceeded at once to pass record-breaking appropriations for naval expansion.

Two years later there was a repercussion of the Geneva Conference when a Senate investigation proved that certain leading steel and shipbuilding firms had been actively engaged in efforts to defeat disarmament during the twenties. The chief lobbyist was William B. Shearer, a former night-club owner who had been charged with income tax fraud. As an "observer" at Geneva, he engaged in vicious anti-British propaganda and issued a steady stream of biased news releases to American newspapers, especially the Hearst papers which had subsidized him generously. He was provided with large sums of money with which to entertain key figures in our naval circles and in superpatriotic societies. In numerous pamphlets and articles written by him but signed by influential men he assailed Hughes and Kellogg as traitors and claimed that the most grotesquely sinister conspiracies were being plotted against the defense of our land by "internationalists," radicals, college professors, movie magnates, labor leaders, and other "paid agents of Moscow." The shipbuilding interests spent no less than $150,000 on lobbyists like Shearer who worked for the successful passage of the Jones-White Merchant Marine Act of 1928 that increased the federal subsidy for private shipping, particularly in the form of lucrative government mail contracts.

The munitions industry, like the steel and shipbuilding interests, was also vitally interested in disarmament. Increasingly since the World War the armament business had assumed the aspect of a monopoly with significant international ramifications. In view of the enlarged plants and heavy inventories when the armistice was signed, lobbyists were active in their attempts to thwart disarmament, particularly on land. Wilson wanted to abolish the private manufacture of arms, but the Allies refused. Although the Harding and Coolidge administrations rejected Wilson's proposal as unconstitutional, they advocated control of the international traffic in munitions, as opposed to control of manufacture. Despite successive conferences on the arms problem, no agreement was reached; the failure was attributed to the Republicans' unwillingness to have an international office for arms control established within the structure of the League.

THE JAPANESE EXCLUSION ACT

Relations with Japan grew worse during the twenties, in spite of our relief efforts in the earthquake disaster of 1923 and our heavy investments in the rebuilding and industrialization of Japan. One factor was the popular Japanese belief that the 5–5–3 naval ratio established by the Washington Conference was degrading. Another and more serious cause was the Japanese Exclusion Act of 1924 and the numerous earlier anti-alien land laws, all aimed primarily at the Japanese and based on the California model, which had been passed in the western and southern states. Segregation laws increased, particularly on the Pacific coast. During Wilson's administration exclusionists assailed the Japanese custom of proxy marriage by means of "picture brides," large numbers of whom were coming to the United States. They charged that Japan had connived in this way to evade the Gentlemen's Agreement restricting immigration and had violated the anti-alien land laws. Nor did Japan's agreement in 1920 to ban the issuance of passports to picture brides satisfy the exclusionists.

Congressmen from the Pacific coast introduced a bill excluding "aliens ineligible to citizenship." Although this did not bar aliens hitherto exempt under the Gentlemen's Agreement, in essence it transferred enforcement from the Japanese government to our own, and put Japan on the same basis as other oriental nations. Secretary Hughes, anxious to avoid antagonizing Japan, especially since her officials were willing to make the required concessions as long as no formal exclusion policy was adopted, advocated the quota system, and pointed out that this would limit Japanese immigrants to only 146 each year.

An unfortunate statement by Ambassador Hanihara regarding the "grave consequences" which would follow any exclusion act was quickly interpreted in Congress as a "veiled threat," despite emphatic denials by both Hanihara and Hughes. The exclusion bill was thereupon passed promptly on July 1, 1924, although Coolidge signed it under protest as "unnecessary and deplorable at this time." Japan immediately issued a formal protest in which she assailed the Act as constituting racial discrimination and violating the Treaty of 1911. The Japanese people reacted violently, and everything American was boycotted. One student who committed hara-kiri in protest against exclusion became a national hero. Anti-American demonstrations raged, and the atmosphere was surcharged with suspicion. Liberalism in Japan was increasingly discredited as the chauvinists triumphed.

CHINA AND THE PHILIPPINES

The resurgence of Chinese nationalism during the twenties, both under Chiang Kai-Shek and under Communist influence, was aimed at the unification of China and the expulsion of foreign imperialism, and ultimately led to attacks on foreigners. A miniature Boxer Rebellion occurred on March 24, 1927, when a Chinese force attacked

Nanking, killed half a dozen foreigners of various nationalities, and invaded several consulates before it was halted by the British and American gunboats that were protecting the evacuation of foreigners. An international force was organized to remove endangered foreigners in the Yangtse valley. Chiang eventually agreed to a settlement that called for reparations, but he made it clear that the day of the unequal treaties was over.

The Chinese Nationalists frequently employed the boycott as a weapon against Japan and the western nations; however, they excepted the United States because of her conciliatory attitude. Secretary of State Kellogg declared in 1927 that we were ready to negotiate in order to abolish extraterritorial privileges and establish China's control over her tariff, but that we were uncertain with whom to negotiate. For this reason we would maintain a strictly neutral attitude toward the rival Chinese factions, and our naval forces would remain in Chinese waters solely to protect our nationals. The Nanking incident was entirely settled by the spring of 1928.

Wilson's policy of early independence for the Philippines was reversed by the Harding administration and the return of the civil service to Filipinos was slowed up. In 1921 President Harding sent General Leonard Wood and W. Cameron Forbes (the latter had served as Governor General of the islands) to investigate the readiness of the Filipinos for independence. Their report was far from favorable, for it condemned the rapid influx of natives into important government positions under Wilson as harmful to efficiency, criticized the increasing number of government-owned businesses, and urged that the Governor General's powers be strengthened so that Washington's decisions would be backed by the necessary authority. Unfortunately, General Wood's own administration as Governor General from 1921 to 1927 was largely paralyzed by his feud with the native leaders.

President Coolidge, also interested in the problem of independence for the Filipinos, was advised by his investigator that few of the Wood-Forbes suggestions had borne fruit, and that economic reforms were needed to revive business in the islands. Upon Wood's death in 1927, the President appointed Henry L. Stimson, Taft's Secretary of War, as Governor General. Stimson, an able administrator, conciliated the Filipino leaders—at least in part—by making his cabinet responsible to the legislature and reestablishing a greater measure of home rule, such as had been enjoyed under Wilson. Independence, however, was still in the distant future, for the problem was complicated by our need for defense against possible Japanese aggression as well as by the economic instability of the islands.

MEXICAN NATIONALISM AND AMERICAN BUSINESSMEN

Mexico presented as perplexing a problem to Harding and Coolidge as she had to Wilson. Americans who had business interests there feared that the nationalist articles of the Constitution of 1917 would be enforced. For example, Article XXVII, which vested ownership of the subsoil in the national government, was retroactive and hence threatened mineral properties acquired by foreigners before 1917. The State Department refused to acknowledge the clause requiring Americans to be treated as Mexican citizens in respect to their property, for this waived their right to diplomatic intervention. The United States resented Mexico's harsh anticlerical legislation. On the other hand, suspicious anti-imperialists like Bryan and Borah insisted that Americans who did business abroad should not ask their government for special protection but should act at their own risk. Harding and Coolidge employed Wilson's policy of non-recognition to demand from Mexico written guarantees against property confiscation.

But Mexico could point out during 1922–1923 that our treatment of her nationals who lived north of the Rio Grande, especially in Texas—the lynchings, mob attacks, and social discrimination—by no means indicated any fundamental respect for law and order. She refused to attend the Fifth Pan American Conference at Santiago, Chile, in March, 1923, giving as her reason the fact that she was not represented on the governing board of the Pan American Union. However, Mexican-American conferences were finally successful, in 1923, in effecting a truce which included a general claims convention covering the damages suffered by our nationals during the revolutionary decade of 1910–1920. Not only was recognition extended to the Obregon government, but President Coolidge saved it from being overthrown during the de la Huerta rebellion in December, 1923, by selling arms exclusively to Obregon.

The long-deferred legislation to carry out the intent of the revolutionary fathers of the Mexican Constitution was introduced by President Plutarco Elías Calles after lengthy correspondence with the United States. Kellogg, however, created an unnecessary crisis at this tense moment by the statement he made to the press on June 12, 1925: "The Government of Mexico is now on trial before the world." He also warned Mexico that the United States expected to be paid for any property taken illegally. The State Department stirred up another crisis in 1926 when it declared that "a steady stream of Bolshevist propaganda" was filtering into Central America from Mexico. When Calles' efforts to enforce the anticlerical sections of the Constitution brought about violent resistance by the church party during 1926–1927, American Catholics were quick to denounce the government for its persecution of religion. The crucial oil laws went into effect on January 1, 1927; they compelled owners of oil lands who had acquired title before 1917 to exchange the titles for fifty-year leases. Practically all the oil companies complied except the Doheny-Sinclair-Mellon group. The crisis became even more serious when President Coolidge ten days later made the accusation before Congress that Mexico was shipping munitions to rebel troops in Nicaragua; this, he said, justified our intervening in Central America to protect the Canal.

Coolidge as well as the nation as a whole had no real desire for war with Mexico; hence our policy at this stage was definitely conciliatory. Dwight W. Morrow, whom Coolidge appointed as Ambassador to Mexico, proved liberal in his sympathies, despite his affiliation with the Morgan banking interests. Without abrogating Calles' legislation, Morrow was able to secure a compromise that protected American titles to oil lands acquired before 1917. He also was instrumental in effecting a temporary truce in the bloody dispute between church and state in which many priests had been executed as rebels, church schools and convents closed, and religious services suspended. Mexican public opinion was gratified by our Ambassador's tact in arranging for Lindbergh to make a special flight to Mexico City in December, 1927, and Calles himself came to look upon the new Ambassador as a close confidant. Largely through Morrow's efforts, a needless war was averted and the popular charge of economic imperialism was stilled

CHASTISING SANDINO

The Nicaraguan imbroglio, in which Mexico had offended Coolidge by showing overt partisanship, touched an established policy of our State Department. This largely Indian nation had the best alternative canal route in Central America and hence it was to our advantage to discourage revolutions in that section. Because of the recurrent disturbances, American Marines had been stationed in Nicaragua since 1912; they were withdrawn by Coolidge in 1925. Later that year a revolutionary chieftain sought to overthrow the Conservative President, Adolfo Diaz, and make himself dictator; but our State Department refused to recognize him and instead supported Diaz in his struggle to remain President. Thereupon Sacasa, a Liberal who had formerly served as Vice President, claimed the Presidency on technical grounds. When we refused to recognize or otherwise support him, Sacasa accepted arms from Mexico, which recognized his government. During the civil war that followed, Diaz appealed to us for aid, and accordingly in December, 1926, we sent warships and Marines to Nicaragua; we also supplied him with machine guns, rifles, and ammunition. "Towards the governments of the countries which we have recognized this side of the Panama Canal," declared President Coolidge in April, 1927, "we feel a moral responsibility that does not attach to other nations." In accordance with this sentiment, he sent Henry L. Stimson to Nicaragua later that month to try to induce the Liberals to end the war. As a result of Stimson's efforts and his promise that United States Marines would supervise the election in 1928, both sides surrendered their arms.

In spite of the fact that the Liberals had agreed to the armistice and that a Liberal was elected to the Presidency the next year, Sandino, another Liberal who headed a popular faction, raised the standard of revolt anew. Our Marines, after being considerably reinforced, were ordered to destroy his army. When it proved more costly than had been expected, American anti-imperialists, suspecting that business groups were behind "Mr. Coolidge's private war," bitterly attacked the Administration. They pointed out that $12,000,000 had been invested by Americans in Nicaragua alone, of which the powerful United Fruit Company, a leading interventionist, held $200,000, in addition to many millions invested in nearby countries. The total of American investments in Central America amounted to almost $125,000,000. But Coolidge replied: "We are not making war on Nicaragua any more than a policeman on the street is making war on passers-by." Although our Marines remained there until 1933, they prepared the groundwork for a stable regime by organizing a non-partisan native constabulary.

STABILIZING THE CARIBBEAN

Elsewhere in Central America and the Caribbean, maintenance of the Monroe Doctrine required no such military intervention as Nicaragua did. A working arrangement between the State Department and New York bankers which provided for financial advisers in the various countries helped to maintain stability. Although we held Panama as a protectorate, this made no difference when she refused to accept our arbitral decision in a boundary dispute with Costa Rica. She yielded only before our threat to enforce the decision with arms if necessary.

Cuba suffered severely from the depression of 1921 that followed the orgy of wild spending. Her sugar industry, in which American interests were paramount, was already in a precarious position and was further injured by the discriminatory tariffs imposed by the Fordney-McCumber Act. The island's own tariff, corruptly administered and regulated in accordance with the calculating nationalism of certain native politicians, imposed so heavy a burden on the poorer classes that it was characterized as "extortion for revenue only." Puerto Rico had no tariff problems because she was within the tariff wall of the United States, but a small but vigorous movement for independence sprang up; this, however, was ignored by our State Department.

For Haiti, in spite of being occupied by American Marines, the twenties represented a period of prosperity and stability that was unique in her history. Senate investigations and criticisms of offenses against the natives on the part of our Marines led to more circumspect race relations. Modern hospitals, free clinics, and trained native doctors transformed the Negro republic as far as health was concerned. Education, hitherto the prerogative of the elite leisure class which revered the classics, became increasingly vocational and reached peasant and craftsman alike. The tax burden, which was lightened for the poorer classes, was further eased by the honest administration of the customs. Nevertheless, we failed to encourage sufficiently the native capacity for self-rule; hence dictatorship under American auspices remained. It was difficult for some Americans to believe Hughes when he insisted in 1928 that we would withdraw from Haiti as soon as her stability and prosperity were assured.

Marine-occupied Santo Domingo, adjacent to Haiti, fared better, for the last of our Marines left in September, 1924. Especially valuable in the organization of the new government were the services of Sumner Welles, the skillful diplomat who formerly had headed the Latin American Division of the State Department, and of Charles G. Dawes, who helped to formulate plans for a scientific budget and a civil service system.

ARGENTINE CATTLEMEN AND RECIPROCITY

South America continued to eye our Caribbean policy with distrust. The rapid infiltration of American investments since the World War—by 1928 they totaled around $2,250,000,000—and the corresponding advance in our foreign trade offered us an economic role which threatened to eclipse Great Britain's historic importance in the continent. The Standard Oil Company of New Jersey and its affiliates and the great Chicago meat-packing firms of Swift and Armour were thoroughly familiar to the residents of Argentina, Uruguay, and their neighbors.

Argentina, aspiring to leadership on the southern continent, showed an increasing truculence toward American policies that was inspired by both real and fancied grievances. Her powerful cattlemen were smarting under the restrictive quarantine regulations imposed on Argentine cattle by our Department of Agriculture because of disease. The discriminatory duties of the Fordney-McCumber tariff aroused such resentment that in 1928, when the American tariff commission planned to send members to Argentina to study her costs of production as a basis for tariff rates, Señor Pueyrredón, the Argentine ambassador, declared that they would not be welcome.

Repercussions of this quarrel were felt at the Havana Pan American Conference that year, when Pueyrredón pointed out that cost of production as a tariff basis would wipe out the comparative economic advantages of every nation that was engaged in international trade. He called for the reduction of inter-American trade barriers and the enforcement of the cattle quarantine in a non-arbitrary fashion. When Hughes replied that for the Pan American Conference to advocate such a tariff policy would create opposition in the legislatures of each country concerned, Pueyrredón, who had the support of Mexico, Colombia, Bolivia, and Paraguay, immediately resigned, and the whole question of tariff reciprocity remained unsolved.

THE INVESTOR'S STAKE ABROAD

Prosperous American manufacturers and investors of the twenties came to look upon the world as their oyster, with a complaisant State Department ready to do their bidding. On one occasion Assistant Secretary of State William R. Castle, Jr., reassured his audience of exporters in these words: "Mr. Hoover is your advance agent and Mr. Kellogg is your attorney." The modest 3.5 billion dollars in foreign securities held by American investors in 1914 was offset at that time by the approximately seven billions owed to European holders of American securities. However, Europe's need for funds to finance the war had liquidated her holdings here, and with them our prewar position as a debtor nation. Moreover, the flotation of Liberty and Victory Loans created a habit of investment among the lower middle class which helped to account for the huge volume of our foreign investments; in 1927 they totaled $25,000,000,000 (including some $11,000,000,000 in war debts to us). An estimated fifteen million Americans—roughly one in every eight—were actively concerned with foreign securities.

So eager were we to find an outlet for our savings that these funds sometimes failed to raise the standard of living abroad. They enabled dictators like Machado in Cuba and Mussolini in Italy to strengthen their position, and many extensive but wasteful public works were undertaken; such steps could only portend the eventual repudiation to which so many of these loans were subject. In May, 1927, Thomas W. Lamont, a member of J. P. Morgan and Company, warned against this indiscriminate lending in these words: "Naturally, it is a tempting thing for certain of the European governments to find a horde of American bankers sitting on their doorsteps offering them money. It is rather demoralizing for municipalities and corporations in the same countries to have money pressed upon them. That sort of competition tends to insecurity and unsound practice."

American industrialists, in their search for additional markets to absorb an increasing volume of production, frequently established branches in such countries as Canada; this enabled them to avoid paying duties and to take advantage of various local inducements. The value of these branch plants in foreign countries quadrupled between 1914 and 1929, reaching a total of 1.8 billion dollars at the end of the decade. Our motion picture industry owned a forty-million-dollar chain of theaters which distributed American films throughout the world.

The volume of foreign trade, which had averaged two or three billions per year before the World War, rose to an annual average of well over $8,000,000,000 during the twenties. Agricultural and other raw materials, which had topped the export list before the war, tended to give way to finished products; cotton and petroleum, however, still remained at the head of the list and were closely followed by machinery and automobiles. Our leading imports—crude rubber, raw silk, coffee, and sugar—reflected the needs of a maturing industrial economy. But the free flow of goods was obstructed by the world-wide protectionism which was then on the rise. Thus our nationalist Fordney-McCumber tariff of 1922 was matched by "Buy British" campaigns and protective measures by the Italians. The United States was faced with the dilemma of slavishly adhering to the "favorable balance of trade" ideal—the excess of exports over imports that the mercantilists had deified—and at the same time becoming a creditor nation and acquiring an increasing proportion of the world's gold supply, a situation which threatened the stability of foreign currency systems. The various measures adopted by protectionists in the United States (including federal subsidies to the merchant marine) practically blocked normal methods of repaying foreign debts.

When Hoover headed the Department of Commerce, it was active not only as a fact-collecting agency but also, through its agencies in forty-six foreign countries, as a promoter of American enterprise abroad. Secretary Hoover was influential in curbing American loans which would further foreign monopolies or would be used for "nonproductive" purposes like militarism. Of the thirteen or fourteen billion dollars of American investments abroad in 1928 (exclusive of the war debt), Europe held about 4⅓ billions; Canada, intimately bound to us by economic ties after the war, held almost four billions; Central America and the Caribbean (including Mexico) held almost three billions; and South America, 2.25 billions. Our holdings in China and Japan, which had amounted to $200,000,000 in 1913, swelled to $726,500,000 after the war. Hordes of American tourists spent $770,-000,000 in Europe and Canada in 1927 alone.

In the light of such economic stakes abroad, even the traditional protection of lives and property took on a new meaning which liberal critics somewhat hastily dubbed "economic imperialism." During 1921–1922, President Harding took official cognizance of the investment situation by establishing a special policy in regard to foreign loans. Pointing out the increasing interdependence of international and national interests, he asked our bankers to give the State Department an opportunity to examine such loans informally before they were actually extended so that it could determine whether there were any political objections. This meant a form of supervision which would discourage loans for revolutions, for monopolies in raw materials, and for aid to nations like Russia and possibly others that had defaulted on their war debts. President Coolidge continued this policy, for he feared that otherwise a suspicious Congress would take the regulation of foreign loans into its own hands and perhaps discourage such investments altogether.

BUSINESS EXPERTS AND REPARATIONS

Our economic expansion abroad during the 1920's made our traditional isolationism seem antiquated. The bitter political controversy over German reparations and inter-Allied debts was too obvious an obstacle to the free flow of American investments and credit for bankers to be content with a hands-off policy. American financiers and industrialists like Charles G. Dawes, J. Pierpont Morgan, and Owen D. Young played a dominant role in solving the reparations tangle; and it was American investors who indirectly made possible not only Germany's partial reparations payment but also Allied payments on war debts owed our government.

At the Paris Conference of 1919, Wilson had fought unavailingly against imposing heavy "punitive damages" upon Germany, whereas France and Great Britain wanted all direct war costs included, particularly pension costs. Although Allied estimates of reparations ranged from eight to 120 billion dollars, American experts believed that about fifteen billion dollars would constitute a just figure. France wanted not only to restore her devastated country but also to destroy Germany's economic power. As Tardieu, her nationalist leader, observed, "We cannot accept the risk of German industrial revival, therefore we must compel her to pay mountainous indemnities." In Britain, where unemployment had become increasingly severe immediately after the war, official opinion veered to the policy advocated by the noted economist J. M. Keynes, that the best road to recovery lay in lightening the burden of Germany, who before the war had been Britain's second-best customer. German reparations payments in goods and services threatened to injure the peacetime markets of France and Great Britain while stimulating her own productive capacity.

Meanwhile, Germany's currency system, weakened first by the war and then by reparations, collapsed during 1921–1923, and her stock of gold fled to safety abroad. The French broke with their British allies and exerted economic and military pressure upon Germany; this culminated in the French occupation of the Ruhr, which exhausted both nations. Germany had appealed to us to mediate the reparations dispute in 1921, but, after consulting France and Britain, we rejected the request. In December, 1922, Secretary Hughes suggested that reparations be taken out of politics and turned over to economic experts, but nothing was done until October, 1923, when President Coolidge made the same suggestion. Thereupon the Reparations Commission asked well-known economists to serve on it, one of the most important committees of experts being headed by Charles G. Dawes.

The famous Dawes Plan won laurels for its author, although Dawes gave Owen D. Young credit for its chief features. Dawes wisely avoided a clash with France by completely evading the problem of determining the grand total of reparations payments; instead, he worked in terms of annuities, which he maintained must not strain Germany's economic structure. To guard against defaulting, he set up in Germany machinery for the supervision and control of payments, with Owen D. Young as Agent General for Reparations Payments. The Dawes Plan eased the burden of the German government and of various state enterprises by bearing down on large industries which had wiped out their private debts through inflation; it also recommended a more democratic tax system. American investors subscribed to more than half of the loan of 800,000,000 gold marks which Dawes obtained to protect Germany's gold reserve and to revive her credit abroad.

Inasmuch as the Dawes Plan had operated successfully, Allied creditors of Germany looked to the experts for the final liquidation of reparations. Accordingly, the Young Plan, named after Dawes' brilliant associate, Owen D. Young, was formulated in 1929. Under this plan, German reparations annuities were to run for fifty-nine years (until 1988) and to aggregate $28,800,000,000 (including interest)—a relatively moderate sum in contrast to earlier figures. Financial supervision was exercised by the new Bank for International Settlements at Basel, which was to collect and disburse reparations payments. Because the Allies by now were apparently satisfied with any arrangement that covered their own indebtedness to the United States, the Young Plan provided that if we reduced our claims on them, the annuities would be correspondingly scaled down. However, this plan had to be discarded within two years because the depression which shook the financial foundations of almost all Europe made it unworkable.

THE REPARATIONS-WAR DEBT LINK

A more stubborn problem for the financiers was the repayment of the war debt owed by the Allies to the United States; in 1920 it amounted to $10,000,000,000 and interest payments were increasing steadily. Most of this debt represented credit extended by us during the war; the balance constituted credits we extended after the armistice for European relief and for the sale of surplus war materials there. Congress had made it clear at the time these debts were incurred that we expected them to be paid, and French statesmen had agreed. Subsequently, however, France pointed out that the various loans had been spent in the United States, whereas the heaviest sacrifices in men and materials had been sustained by herself, Russia, Great Britain, and Italy.

By 1920, France and England were claiming that all the Allied war financing had been interdependent because all the Allies' gold, much of it earmarked for purchases in the United States, had been pooled in Britain's vaults. Not only were both countries heavily in debt to us, but France was simultaneously in debt to England and a creditor of the rest of the Allies. Since German reparations were expected to offset these inter-Allied debts, the money owed us was firmly linked, in the minds of the Allies, with reparations. All-round cancellation, Britain maintained, was the only measure that would restore normal world trade.

Wilson, disavowing this attempt to link war debts and reparations, had pointed out that Congress had given him no power to revise or cancel any part of these debts. However, in his message on December 1, 1919, he had observed realistically that since Americans had purchased most of the American securities that formerly had been held abroad and, moreover, were building a merchant marine, Europe was being deprived of the usual means of meeting international obligations. "Europe is in no position at the present time to ship gold," he said, "nor could we contemplate larger further imports of gold into this country without concern." Secretary of the Treasury Carter Glass, with Wilson's support, laid down the official policy of regarding the war debt settlement entirely apart from reparations, in spite of the obvious relation between them.

The Republican platform in 1920 assailed Wilson for his laxity regarding war debts and pledged Harding to regularize debt payments. Both Harding and Coolidge accepted the Wilson-Glass policy but in addition advocated a high tariff which made it difficult for Europe to sell sufficient goods and services to make any debt payments. President Harding looked upon the debts as upon any ordinary domestic debt; all that was necessary was honesty on the part of the debtor. "The call of the world today," he said, "is for the integrity of agreements, the sanctity of covenants, the validity of contracts." President Coolidge disposed of the problem with his usual terseness when he said, "They hired the money, didn't they?"

Congress kept a vigilant eye on Secretary of the Treasury Mellon, for it feared that he would cancel a portion of the debts in order to free American investment channels abroad. Harding and the State Department used their self-assumed veto power on foreign loan issues to put pressure on the Allied nations that refused to make "reasonable efforts" to pay their debts to us. On February 9, 1922, Congress created the World War Foreign Debt Commission, whose members included Hughes, Mellon, Hoover, Senator Reed Smoot, and Congressman Theodore E. Burton. The Commission invited the debtor nations to present their proposals for funding their debts, and promised that interest rates would be scaled down on the basis of "capacity to pay," a standard that the major powers resented.

Great Britain, whose $4,600,000,000 debt made her the heaviest debtor, led the procession to Washington. However, the determination of the French, who likewise owed us over four billions, to collect substantial reparations from Germany before they paid us anything, led to bitter recriminations in French and American newspapers. Some continental newspapers wounded our sentiments by caricaturing Uncle Sam as "Uncle Shylock," and others asked, "Who won the World War?" The French finally agreed in 1925 to negotiate directly with us regarding principal and annuity payments, but negotiations dragged along until the end of the decade before any settlement was made. Actually the Allies continued to follow the policy of making payments to the United States only with funds received from German reparations payments. Consequently, when the depression dried up the stream of American investments that was pouring into Germany, inter-Allied debt payments dwindled to mere "token" payments.

In the literal sense, the foreign policy of the United States after the war was not isolationist. But our rejection of the moral leadership of the world assumed by Wilson meant reversion to our traditional hemispheric policies at a time when our economic and political power might have turned the scales in favor of organized peace. Instead, the fictions and antiquated techniques of isolationism were maintained in spite of the earnest but tentative efforts of Hughes, Coolidge, Hoover, Borah, and Kellogg to collaborate with Europe. "Unofficial observers" at nonpolitical meetings of the League of Nations, the adoption of watered-down substitutes for the League, and generous financial aid to Europe and Asia were used to achieve peace without incurring the risks of membership in a League that bristled with economic and military "sanctions" against aggressors. Whereas Wilson had largely convinced the democratic elements in Europe, particularly in Germany, of America's sincere desire to lead them through the dark paths of renascent nationalism, his successors failed to attain his vision, a failure which carried a severe penalty.

CHAPTER 15

Hoover and the Great Depression

COLLAPSE

President-elect Herbert Hoover assumed office amid the warm plaudits of his countrymen who hailed him as a brilliant liberal who had earned his position by his distinguished humanitarian and administrative services for over fifteen years. Yet, long before his term ended, he had endured greater ridicule and more bitter attacks than most of his predecessors. The less-talented Calvin Coolidge staved off a second term with difficulty; and even Warren G. Harding, who died before the Teapot Dome scandal broke in force, was eulogized in terms which compared him with the martyred Lincoln. Not a little of whatever substantial achievement had been made during the two preceding Administrations was due to the ingenuity and foresight of the Secretary of Commerce under Harding and Coolidge, for it was he who was responsible for major aspects of farm relief, labor reforms, increased business efficiency, and the economic aspects of our foreign policy. Hoover's personal tragedy was in large part a reflection of the millions of individual tragedies which struck American homes during the worst depression in the history of capitalism. Never a member of the reactionary wing of the Republican party, Hoover nevertheless came to be identified by the liberal press with the selfish and unintelligent Bourbonism of a dying social order. The world-wide trend toward state intervention in economic life and the various socialistic expedients that were advocated left his ideal of "collective self-help" far behind. The shibboleths of rugged individualism failed to impress those who were stranded in the morass of insecurity and suffering.

American economists like Wesley C. Mitchell had long called attention to the alternations of prosperity and depression in the business cycle. Hoover, as we have seen, had for many years been deeply interested in methods of economic stabilization. As Secretary of Commerce during the depression of 1921, he proposed to President Harding that the severe fluctuations of economic activity be modified by deferring public construction projects until a period of depression, but businessmen resisted this because they would have to forgo immediate profits; furthermore, federal tax policies encouraged spending on the part of city and state governments. By 1929, the intricate world-wide interdependence of capitalist enterprise had reached such a degree that many orthodox economists believed with Hoover that no nation, acting alone, could achieve real recovery from a period of depression.

World War tax burdens, unprecedented armament costs, insurmountable tariff barriers, and a persistent decline of agricultural prices were among the international factors leading to the crash of 1929. In the United States, where the economic decline was more precipitate than in Europe, additional elements of weakness appeared not only in the low purchasing power of our farmers, but especially in the inadequate banking control exercised by local governments and the extraordinary increase of funds which poured into the stock market and raised the price of stocks far beyond any sober expectation of increased earnings. The bull market of 1927–1929 was satiated with the funds of millions of people who enthusiastically bid up the price of stocks without examining them as investment possibilities and reaped huge paper profits on small margin payments. Brokers' loans had passed the 8.5-billion mark by October, 1929. The myth of eternal prosperity was in the air and skepticism was considered unpatriotic.

Hoover, who did not share Coolidge's equanimity regarding the stock market, took steps two days after his inauguration to reduce stock market credits. At his instigation, the Federal Reserve Board put pressure on banks to curtail loans for speculative purposes. Resistance to this policy sprang up at once from Charles E. Mitchell, the head of the powerful National City Bank of New York, who indignantly assailed the "weasel" spirit shown by political leaders in Washington. He defiantly offered large credits to the stock market, an act of confidence that gratified Wall Street. Mitchell's action followed Secretary of the Treasury Mellon's thinly disguised warning: "Bonds are low in price compared to stocks." Believing that effective stock market regulation could be carried out constitutionally only by the State of New York, Hoover decided on a limited drive against market tipsters who used the mails to stimulate speculation. This was undertaken by the Department of Justice after the President had publicly appealed to the press for support.

Meanwhile the behavior of the stock market grew increasingly erratic. News of the failure of investment houses in European, Latin American, and Australian cities augmented the general uneasiness in financial circles. Nevertheless, even as late as September, 1929, the monetary authority, Professor Irving Fisher, declared reassuringly, "There may be a recession but not anything in the nature of a crash." At the same time, however, Roger Babson, the business forecaster, warned the people that a major break was due; still another warning was given in a speech on October 1 by the president of the American Bankers' Association, who called for a check on credit expansion.

The market collapse which began two days later struck the great electrical equipment companies like Westinghouse with heavy force. On October 15, after a temporary rally, Charles E. Mitchell (then in London) assured the world that American markets were in a healthy condition. Thereafter the market declined in earnest. On October 24 the Morgan interests attempted to stem the tide by buying stocks, but this produced only a temporary respite, and a similar effort by John D. Rockefeller six days later was hardly more successful. The decline reached panic proportions on October 29, when 16,410,030 shares were dumped by frightened investors, an all-time record for market transactions. Only after weeks of wild trading did the rout assume the more orderly phases of liquidation. Some large firms who failed were found later by the Senate to have saved their heaviest investors by carefully staged rallies which were aided by obliging financial writers who drew roseate pictures of conditions and encouraged gullible investors to take over the worthless securities. Weaker companies put pressure on their employees to buy their company's stock.

Hoover recognized the gravity of the crisis, although, in common with most men, he underestimated the length of the depression. He considered that his chief task was to prevent panic and to insure the orderly liquidation of weak firms. He avoided any statement on the future stability of the stock market, although he said confidently, "The fundamental business of the country, that is, production and distribution, is on a sound and prosperous basis." Relying on his oft-tried technique of conference and persuasion, he held successive meetings during the latter part of November, 1929, with leaders of industry, transportation, and organized labor. He said frankly that heavy liquidation and severe unemployment were inevitable; he pleaded against regarding labor as a commodity subject merely to supply and demand and urged that each industry make long-range plans for construction work to protect labor from distress.

BUSINESS LEADERSHIP AND RECOVERY

Industrialists responded by pledging to increase their plant expenditures, which were estimated at $2,000,000,000 for 1930; in return they asked that labor promise to suspend strikes and that current demands for wage increases be withdrawn. The American Railway Association later reported an increase of $300,000,000 in plant expenditures over the previous high in 1929. Although some public utility leaders—among them Samuel Insull of Chicago, whose gigantic empire was soon to crumble into ruin—claimed that the situation was not as serious as it was pictured, others agreed to maintain existing wage and employment levels as far as possible. Hoover's conference with labor leaders, who included William Green, John L. Lewis, and Matthew Woll, pledged the American Federation of Labor and various independent unions to withdraw new wage demands and to cooperate on the President's program. Henry Ford offered a solution by increasing wages and cutting prices in his plants, a policy which he urged his fellow industrialists to follow; but even his vast resources proved unequal to maintaining it for long.

Hoover insisted that forces outside the United States were largely responsible for the depression, for otherwise recovery would have taken place long before. His message to Congress on December 2, 1930, made it clear that he opposed any drastic program which would put the government in business. "Economic depression," he declared, "cannot be cured by legislative action or executive pronouncement. . . ." Nevertheless, he raised government expenditures for public works to the highest level in peacetime history by more than doubling the 1929–1930 total of $253,000,000, and he drew up plans for public works that exceeded $650,000,000 for the fiscal year 1931–1932.

EXPERIMENTS IN EMERGENCY LEGISLATION

At least during the early phase of the depression, organized labor seemed to approve of the President's policies and to appreciate his efforts to maintain existing wage levels. Hoover was known to have been responsible for President Harding's intercession on behalf of an eight-hour day for the steel workers, and his extraordinary administration of mass relief in Belgium, Russia, and central Europe, as well as in our own Mississippi flood in 1927, was also well known. As Food Administrator during the war he had worked closely with farmer, laborer, and housewife. Now, as President, he ordered continuous publicity for unemployment figures so that false optimism as well as panic would be avoided. That 1930 was far from the worst year of the depression was attributed by several able critics to the stabilizing measures taken by Hoover to avert new catastrophes.

Unemployment was steadily mounting. The Department of Labor estimated that some 4,500,000 people were idle at the beginning of 1931, a figure close to the unemployment peak in the depression of 1921. This estimate was low in comparison to unofficial figures; the Cleveland Trust Company, for example, reported 6,000,000 unemployed early in 1931. Bread-lines lengthened in the cities and police commissioners grew apprehensive. In October, 1930, Hoover organized the President's Committee for Unemployment Relief, composed of distinguished non-partisans from the ranks of labor and business who sought to coordinate the work of national and local welfare agencies. He opposed direct federal relief to individuals, for he held that relief was a responsibility of state and local governments which must not be shifted to Washington. The various state governors, at Hoover's appeal, pledged their enthusiastic support to his program for large-scale state relief and public works projects. However, it soon became apparent that only the larger and wealthier states could meet their relief burdens adequately, for as private philanthropy exhausted its sources of income, welfare agencies became increasingly helpless before the swelling demands of the needy.

Democratic leaders in the congressional campaigns of 1930 placed the responsibility for the depression on Hoover and his Republican predecessors in the twenties. As a result, the Democrats not only captured the House but dominated the Senate through their alliance with several progressive Republicans. John Nance Garner of Texas, who was chosen Speaker of the House, led the congressional assault on Hoover, and the Democratic national chairman, Charles Michelson, planned an adroit campaign of nation-wide propaganda against Republican leadership as a prelude to a Democratic victory in 1932.

Differences between the Democratic Congress and Hoover quickly multiplied. When the President sought to consolidate and reorganize the railroads as a means of forestalling bankruptcy, a suspicious Senate blocked this as a move toward monopoly. Later, the federal government had to lend hundreds of millions to the weakened railroads in order to save them. Far more bitter was the question of direct federal relief. Hoover insisted that such relief should be provided only when state and local resources were exhausted, for he claimed that to do otherwise would destroy local responsibility and lead to a vast, corrupt, and inefficient bureaucracy. He rejected congressional suggestions that billions be appropriated for "made" work in order to stimulate business, because he feared that this would unbalance the budget. Instead, he suggested that self-liquidating income-producing projects, such as toll bridges and toll tunnels, be undertaken; loans for such projects could be obtained from the new federal lending agency, the Reconstruction Finance Corporation.

His opponents regarded these counterproposals as too limited for so great an emergency, nor were they convinced that an unbalanced budget was the dread calamity pictured by Hoover. By the spring of 1932, various European nations had already resorted to a separate "extraordinary budget" for the unusual expenses involved in combating a major depression. The President was also accused of permitting his concern for constitutional abstractions to overshadow any sympathy for human suffering. To this he replied in a press statement on February 3, 1931, in which he maintained that the emergency was not one that required revolutionary legislative action, and he went on to say: "I am willing to pledge myself that if the time should ever come that the voluntary agencies of the country together with the local and State governments are unable to find resources with which to prevent hunger and suffering in my country, I will ask the aid of every resource of the Federal Government because I would no more see starvation amongst our countrymen than would any senator or congressman. I have faith in the American people that such a day will not come." In his mind, the danger of emergency measures that tended toward greater centralization was the creation of a "superstate" and the destruction of local civil liberties characteristic of state socialism and the new Fascism. The Democrats, he charged repeatedly, were "playing politics at the expense of human misery."

When in February, 1931, Senator Robert Wagner of New York, a liberal Democrat, introduced a bill providing for a federally aided system of state employment agencies to replace the existing inefficient federal agencies, Hoover vetoed the measure. He based his veto on his belief that such a system would require too long a time before it could function effectively, especially since he considered that the existing system was satisfactory; furthermore, federal subsidies to state employment agencies and their possible administration by federal authorities would merely relieve local government units of their responsibilities. Here again was the familiar pattern of divergence between Congress and the President. But this time labor leaders, social service workers, and economists criticized Hoover severely, and the House rejected a substitute Administration bill which would have curbed federal aid to state agencies.

Wagner's other proposal for the advance planning and regulated construction of public works, a step long favored by the President, was heartily endorsed by Congress. Nor could reactionaries take comfort in Hoover's signing of the liberal Norris-La Guardia Anti-Injunction Act in March, 1932. This measure reduced the scope of federal injunctions in labor disputes, especially those used to punish labor unions under the anti-trust laws, and it made yellow-dog contracts, which some employers used to compel workers to forswear future union membership, unenforceable in federal courts. Early in 1932, when Congress advocated cutting the wages of federal employees and the possible discharge of 50,000 post-office workers as an economy measure, Hoover averted this by ordering a five-day week, with payment at the same hourly rate as hitherto.

Responding to pressure from organized labor, the President was instrumental in reducing immigration to a mere trickle. The law already provided that persons likely to become public charges should be excluded, and the unemployment crisis was considered sufficient grounds for declaring most immigrants to be potential public charges. In 1929, 279,678 individuals entered the United States; by 1933, because of the depression and the new immigration policies, this had dropped to an unprecedented low of 23,068. At the same time, Hoover enforced the deportation laws against illegal entrants to such an extent that between sixteen and nineteen thousand people were deported annually.

THE BONUS EXPEDITIONARY FORCE

During 1930–1932, innumerable proposals were made in Congress for additional compensation to war veterans, many of whom were reduced to selling apples on street corners in order to earn a living. Democratic leaders, anxious to combat the depression by means of huge governmental expenditures, wanted to double the loan value of the adjusted service certificates and to reduce the interest charged. Hoover estimated that this might cost the Treasury $1,700,000,000; furthermore, he was unwilling to support any veterans' subsidy plan which disregarded the fact that a vast proportion of these men did not need relief. Consequently he vetoed the bonus loan bill, but it was passed over his veto by record majorities.

Hoover showed that he could outdo other Administrations in providing for needy and disabled veterans when he advocated bills which provided increased disability allowances, virtually unlimited hospitalization, and vocational training and placement. But even these measures, involving an annual expenditure of hundreds of millions of dollars, became ineffectual by the fall of 1931 when the depression reached new depths. When Congress showed itself ready to vote payment of the entire bonus, amounting to $3,400,000,000, the President appealed to the patriotism of the American Legion, then in convention at Detroit; he warned of the imminent danger faced by the nation because of mounting deficits and the drop in the national revenue at the rate of a billion a year. Thereupon the Legionnaires voted to support Hoover, thus checking the bonus movement in Congress.

Most humiliating to Hoover was the "bonus march" to Washington during the late spring and summer of 1932. Approximately 11,000 men—some brought their families—milled around the Capitol and settled down in an improvised shantytown just outside Washington;

others occupied decrepit buildings on historic Pennsylvania Avenue. When Congress defeated the bonus bill and prepared to adjourn on July 16, thus leaving the veterans stranded, Hoover quickly obtained $100,000 from Congress to enable the men to return to their homes. Six thousand thereupon left Washington. The agents who were sent to investigate the veterans reported that a check of 2000 cases showed that less than one-third were actual veterans, and that the self-styled "Bonus Expeditionary Force" included a small but active group of Communists.

On July 28, police of the District of Columbia undertook the delicate task of removing fifty veterans from some condemned buildings along Pennsylvania Avenue which were to be demolished. The police met opposition, and during a tense moment one of them drew his pistol, killed two veterans, and wounded two more. President Hoover then ordered General Douglas MacArthur to complete the evacuation of the capital. Cavalrymen, at first greeted by cheers from the veterans, suddenly wheeled into large crowds of men, women, and children; infantrymen threw tear-gas bombs into the lines of curious spectators. No one was killed, but many were injured in the stampede that followed. Finally the leader of the veterans' colony waved a white flag.

This was scarcely good publicity for the Republican presidential campaign of 1932. Journalists were cold to the President's public statement: "A challenge to the authority of the United States Government has been met, swiftly and firmly. . . . It is my sincere hope that those agitators who inspired yesterday's attack upon federal authority may be speedily brought to trial." Veterans' organizations bitterly assailed the treatment given the B.E.F. Even the American Legion, which had previously supported Hoover, reversed its stand. Nearly all of the B.E.F., claimed the Veterans' Bureau, were bona fide servicemen, not Communists or vicious hoodlums. The entire incident was humiliating to the nation's dignity.

SUPER-PROTECTIONISM

One of the earliest congressional conflicts during the Hoover administration appeared when the Republicans attempted to revise the tariff of 1922 upward, especially in the interests of farmers. As a lifelong internationalist, the President was opposed to extending protection except for certain farm products; in this he was supported by Borah. When a special session of Congress was called in 1929 to deal with the tariff and with farm legislation, the extreme protectionists, under the leadership of J. R. Grundy, president of the Pennsylvania Manufacturers' Association, immediately began a fight to convert moderate revision into "prohibitive superprotection," as Congressman Cordell Hull of Tennessee put it. Borah's Republican insurgents in the Senate, including young La Follette, Norris, Brookhart, and Nye, cooperated with the Democrats in trying to prevent the industrial states from winning new tariff concessions, but were unsuccessful. The Democratic assault on protectionism in the House was led by Cordell Hull, who denounced the "continuous and corrupt political partnership between tariff beneficiaries and dominant Republican leadership." He pointed out that, except for Spain's tariff rates, the existing Fordney-McCumber tariff imposed the highest general rates in the world, and he predicted economic retaliation from abroad.

Both Hoover's moderates and the Democratic minority met defeat on the tariff issue. The Republican Old Guard won a sweeping victory in the Hawley-Smoot Act of June, 1930, which gave generous protection not only to farmers but to many industrialists as well. Although more than one thousand economists in the country petitioned to veto the bill, the President decided to sign it. Like Taft during the Payne-Aldrich tariff controversy, Hoover made a virtue of necessity and praised the new Act as completely fulfilling his party's pledges. Since our imports were curtailed by the new increased rates, foreign debtors, both public and private, were severely restricted in financing their payments on the billions they owed to our government and to private creditors. Not only did taxpayers and investors suffer, but consumers were on the whole forced to pay higher prices for protected goods because the tariff encouraged wasteful and inefficient concerns to remain in business.

Retaliation from abroad came quickly, especially as the depression deepened. British Tories like Lord Beaverbrook, who had long advocated "imperial preference," eventually overthrew Great Britain's historic free-trade policy in favor of protectionism; their opponents could be silenced by a reference to the Hawley-Smoot Act. Scores of other nations revived economic nationalism in a move to bar American goods. Critics of the tariff law charged that the drastic decline in our exports—from $5,200,000,000 in 1929 to $1,647,000,000 in 1933—had far more obvious causes than the depression. These consequences both at home and abroad had been predicted by economists when the new tariff was under consideration.

THE FARM EMERGENCY

The farm legislation enacted by the special session in 1929 included the Agricultural Marketing Act, which provided for a Federal Farm Board with a revolving fund of half a billion dollars with which to finance loans to agricultural cooperatives; this would permit farmers to withhold their surpluses from the market until prices rose. But the farmers, whose property values had already declined twenty billion dollars during the decade, were dealt a blow by the depression that even the Farm Board's heroic efforts could scarcely soften. The crash of 1929 caught farmers with much of their harvest unsold, still heavily in debt, and in danger of having to accept lower prices than ever. Only the Farm Board's prompt advance of large loans on wheat and cotton prevented a sharp price break in these and other basic commodities.

The world-wide bumper harvest in 1930 constituted a new peril for American farm prices, and again the Farm Board promptly extended additional loans. Ugly rumors, which the Administration accepted, had it that Russia was deliberately dumping her huge crops on the American market as a means of fomenting revolution. As prices continued to fall, farmers increased their production in order to secure a livelihood. Open resentment flared when it became apparent that the price levels of 1928 could not be restored. The Farm Board pleaded for farmers voluntarily to cut their crop acreage by 30 per cent, but this individualist group responded by putting additional acres into cultivation. The Administration refused to resort to compulsory crop restriction, which it denounced as unconstitutional. By 1932 it became evident that the government's own stocks of wheat and cotton were acting as a price depressant.

The desperate plight of farmers, reminiscent of the days of Shays' Rebellion, made rural leaders resort to wild schemes of repudiation and, in some cases, even violence. Farmers faced with the loss of their property through foreclosure defied court orders and mobbed the lawyers who sought to serve foreclosure notices. Crude attempts to withhold crops from the market led farmers to barricade roads and to dump milk. Some farm leaders in the Dakotas, taking their cue from the moratorium that was being sought on international debts, also demanded a moratorium on farm loans. As in Bryan's campaign of 1896, demands for inflation through free silver and fiat money were already being made.

Nature added a new load to the farmers' already heavy burden in the drought which in 1930 affected at least a million families and threatened some 20,000,000 animals in the lower Mississippi valley, especially Arkansas, and in scattered areas along the Ohio and Potomac Rivers. The Red Cross declared itself ready to meet the drought emergency, but told questioning Senators that any congressional attempt to apply direct federal relief through it might alienate its heaviest contributors. The governors in the affected areas pledged their cooperation to the President in alleviating drought distress, and Hoover secured from all the railroads a 50 per cent reduction in feed freight rates. Contrary to precedent, farm prices continued to decline in spite of the destruction of crops. Nevertheless, Hoover was convinced that a direct federal dole to farmers in the drought area patterned after the British model was unnecessary.

Insurgent Republicans and liberal Democrats in Congress were openly caustic of the Administration's attempt to avoid a dole by relying on the American Red Cross, contributions to which were slow in coming in, despite a well-publicized national campaign. The Senate's attempt to donate $25,000,000 to the Red Cross for the relief of human starvation was blocked by Administration pressure. The Red Cross found too many instances in which it was difficult to determine whether the depression or the drought was primarily responsible for the farmer's plight. Critics complained that the Department of Agriculture had funds to feed farm animals but none for humans. Finally, on December 20, 1930, Republican leaders in Congress agreed to a drought relief bill which set up a $20,000,000 fund for "agricultural rehabilitation" by means of loans to farmers. Loans of $47,000,000 for seed, fertilizer, and feed had already been extended. A total of some 350,000 or 400,000 farm families in thirty-one states availed themselves of this assistance. For farm tenants and others who owned no property and were consequently ineligible for these loans, there remained only the increasingly threadbare resources of private charity and the pitifully small contributions of impoverished local governments.

NORRIS AND THE POWER ISSUE

Rugged individualism in the White House meant strong hostility toward government competition with private enterprise. This was particularly evident in Hoover's veto of the Norris bill on March 3, 1931. The Nebraskan insurgent, despite the rebuffs of Harding and Coolidge, once more sought federal operation of the power plants at Muscle Shoals; his bill gave private interests a year in which to decide between leasing the plants from the government or yielding them to a federal agency. The Democrats had pledged themselves in 1928 to convert the federal government's costly "white elephant" in the Southeast into a popular asset, and Norris himself had switched to Smith because of the latter's stand on the power issue. But all these hopes were struck down by Hoover's veto, which denounced the plan advocated by the Norris bill as a dangerous assault on private initiative and free enterprise. A countersuggestion was made that the Muscle Shoals units be turned over to a joint commission composed of farmers' cooperatives, which would naturally be interested in cheap nitrates, and of local government agencies. Instead, a stalemate ensued.

At this stage the issue of government operation of power plants rested until the Roosevelt regime. In 1930 Norris was made the victim of a petty partisan plot, attributed to the executive director of the Republican National Committee, to prevent his reelection to the Senate. In order to defeat the "renegade" Republican, Nebraska politicians arranged for an obscure grocer with the same name as the Senator's to run in the primaries. Before he finally succeeded in being reelected, Norris was the target of a well-financed campaign employing deliberate falsifications and defamatory leaflets.

But those among the Senator's enemies who had solemnly warned the nation of the corrupt political consequences of government competition with private utility interests were deeply disturbed by the sensational collapse of Samuel Insull's Middle West Utilities in 1931.

The Chicago millionaire, who had dominated both the politics and the social circles of that city for years, eventually revealed some of the financial subterfuges and highly speculative methods by which he had built up a gigantic national holding company whose value was estimated at around three billion dollars. One of the greatest bankruptcies in American economic life, the Insull failure impoverished innumerable investors, including company employees who had firmly believed in the myth of their chief's financial invulnerability.

THE SMALL DEPOSITORS' PANIC

Paralyzing in their effect on our morale during the depression were the recurrent cycles of bank panics, depositors' runs, and the closing of thousands of banks. Forty-eight states, many of them dominated by the debtor psychology that favored easy credit, offered as many varieties of banking regulations. Every bank suffered from the wholesale decline in the pre-depression value of bank assets, particularly real estate, investment securities, and unpaid notes, all of them aptly called "frozen" assets because they could be thawed out only at a heavy loss. Panic-stricken, many erstwhile depositors resorted to hoarding their cash, thus increasing the weakness of the nation's economy.

The 659 banks closed in 1929, tying up about $230,000,000 in deposits, represented a normal annual average for the decade. A year later there were 1352 suspensions involving $853,000,000; 1931, however, set a new record, with 2294 banks, representing $1,690,669,000 in deposits, closing their doors. One of the most startling failures was that of the huge New York state bank, The Bank of the United States, whose name suggested to its 400,000 depositors—many of them immigrants—that the federal government stood solidly behind it. This bank, which held $180,000,000 in deposits, closed its doors on December 12, 1930, a failure which subsequent investigation revealed had been hastened by fraudulent banking practices and the negligence of the state banking authorities.

In an effort to meet the recurrent crises that were aggravated by the failure of European banks, Hoover conferred with leading bankers and with the powerful American Bankers' Association. One plan that was put into effect in October, 1931, established a National Credit Association, capitalized at half a billion dollars, the capital being subscribed by the banks themselves. The new agency was to convert quickly into cash all frozen but sound assets not eligible for rediscounting at Federal Reserve banks; in many instances this would avoid sacrificing assets in order to meet immediate demands. The Association was also permitted to make loans against the assets of closed banks so that depositors could be paid without delay. Another step in the same direction was taken when the Federal Reserve banks extended their rediscount operations as a means of thawing out frozen assets. The National Credit Association averted crises in the South and West by lending $400,000,000 to over 750 banks. But this and similar measures were recognized as palliatives which failed to penetrate to the basic reasons for insolvency.

In a vain attempt to halt the flood of mortgage foreclosures on homes and to stimulate construction, Congress in July, 1932, belatedly established a federal home loan bank system. It was set up along the lines of the Federal Reserve System, but its loans to mortgagors were cautiously limited to 50 per cent of the value of the property. Few took advantage of it, but the President nevertheless declared emphatically that the new law was "the greatest act yet undertaken by any government at any time on behalf of the thousands of owners of small homes."

With some reluctance, Hoover decided at the end of 1931 that the government must halt deflation and prevent further bankruptcies by extending huge loans to the hard-pressed banks, business enterprises, railroads, and insurance companies. Consequently, on January 22, 1932, the Reconstruction Finance Corporation, a federal agency modeled on the earlier War Finance Corporation, was created; it was backed by government funds amounting to $500,000,000 and had additional borrowing power. Dissatisfied with the limited scope of the R.F.C., Hoover urged Congress to enlarge its emergency powers, although he refused to go as far as his opponents wished in lending money for local relief. Accordingly, the Relief Bill of July, 1932, permitted the R.F.C. to make temporary loans of $300,000,000 to states which, as he put it, were "absolutely unable to finance the relief of distress." In addition, it could lend up to $1,500,000,000 for public construction projects of a self-liquidating character, i.e., those whose revenues assured repayment, and it would offer generous loans to farmers. This far-reaching legislation made it clear that the proponent of "rugged individualism" in the White House had come a long way since 1928, for the new agency bordered perilously near the brink of state enterprise.

Although Hoover chose most of the R.F.C. directors from Democratic ranks, his opponents failed to be appeased. Speaker Garner charged that the agency was lending its funds primarily to big business, and to Republicans at that. An emphatic denial came from the President. Democrats raised a clamor when, shortly after resigning as president of the R.F.C. on June 6, 1932, former Vice President Dawes borrowed $80,000,000 for his Central Republic Bank and Trust Company in Chicago, which was then in difficulties. This aid proved timely indeed, for a series of runs which began on June 18 wiped out thirty-nine of that city's other banks. Although Dawes himself neither solicited nor voted for the loan, he severed his connection with the R.F.C. so abruptly that many Democrats charged him with using his influence with it on his own behalf. Garner thereupon secured an amendment to the Relief Bill which required the R.F.C. to publish the names of all borrowers. Later, this amendment was severely condemned by business leaders, for they regarded it as directly responsible for the further loss of the people's confidence in business and for new runs on otherwise sound banks.

By the beginning of March, 1933, the R.F.C. had actually disbursed $1,842,151,761 and additional amounts were authorized; the lion's share of this sum, $732,279,141, went to banks and insurance companies. Largely as a result of the R.F.C.'s policy in thawing out frozen assets, bank suspensions in 1932 dropped sharply, as is evident from the fact that 1456 banks with deposits of $715,626,000 were closed that year, as against the 1931 figures—2294 banks and $1,690,-669,000 in deposits. By the end of 1932, the precipitate liquidation characteristic of 1930 and 1931 seemed to have been halted, and a leveling-out process apparently had set in.

THE HOOVER MORATORIUM

Financial conditions in this country became increasingly intertwined with the depression in Europe until the thin partition between foreign and domestic affairs was finally broken down. During the twenties, American investors had loaned one country alone—Germany—the huge sum of $2,475,000,000. The inter-Allied war debts to us soared above the original $10,000,000,000, and several debtors found themselves unable to meet even their interest payments. A threat to the stability of American banks was the fact that at least $1,000,000,000 in short-term bills issued by Germany and held by our own banks was in danger of being repudiated if the bank crisis spread.

Germany, bereft of her former outside sources of investment, was desperate by 1931. Her attempt in March of that year to form a customs union with Austria was blocked by France, who regarded it as a clever attempt at *Anschluss* and hence withdrew her powerful financial support from Austrian banks. In May came the startling news that the *Kreditanstalt* of Vienna, one of the largest banks in Europe, had appealed to the Austrian government and the Rothschilds for help. Repercussions were felt at once in the stock markets in Berlin, London, Paris, and New York. Depositors in Germany crowded the streets outside the banks, and capital fled from Germany to other countries. Britain, who had many interests in Central Europe, was hard-pressed for gold during this crisis, and eventually, in September, 1931, she was compelled to go off the gold standard. Bankers both here and in Europe pleaded for the cancellation of reparations and war debts as the only possible preliminary to world recovery. Many people feared that a Communist revolution would break out in Germany and spread elsewhere.

In June, 1931, President Paul von Hindenburg appealed directly to Hoover to avert the impending catastrophe. England thus far had been unwilling to underwrite Germany's financial solvency, and the French apparently believed that the Weimar Republic was in better shape than it professed to be. These were the crucial weeks of the banking crisis in Chicago, when the huge Foreman banks had to be taken over by other banks, and innumerable smaller ones, weakened by highly speculative practices, were closing their doors. Since Congress was not in session, Hoover secured support for his intended action from leaders of both parties, including Borah, Glass, Cordell Hull, and Arthur Vandenberg; and on June 20, after being advised by American financial experts, he announced his proposal for a one-year moratorium on all intergovernmental debts. Fully aware that this meant a budget deficit of some $250,000,000 for the United States, he said, "I am suggesting to the American people that they be wise creditors in their own interest and be good neighbors." Supplementing the breathing spell afforded Germany by the moratorium, American banks, including the Federal Reserve Bank of New York, joined European banks in extending short-term loans to stabilize Germany's financial institutions. As a result, trade activity revived, prices rose, and some measure of stability had been attained by the end of the year.

Once the moratorium came into effect, the question of war debt cancellation was raised immediately. Certain administration opponents charged, with considerable exaggeration, that the advocates of cancellation were primarily international bankers who were anxious to clear the path for the resumption of large-scale private loans to Europe, and that this amounted to pouring good money after bad. When Hoover in his December message to Congress suggested the creation of a World War Foreign Debt Commission, patterned after the Harding-Coolidge board, to reconsider the war debt question, isolationists like Hearst branded it as inviting wholesale cancellation and they succeeded in getting Congress to pass a resolution declaring that the inter-Allied debts to the United States should not be "in any manner cancelled or reduced." Hoover predicted that this refusal to make concessions would encourage our debtors to repudiate their obligations.

This resolution against cancellation blocked any plan for reparations revision discussed in Hoover's private conference with the French premier, Pierre Laval, during the fall of 1931. Nevertheless, our European Allies met at Lausanne the following summer and virtually cancelled German reparations, except for a modest sum of $750,000,000. Evidently expecting that public opinion in the United States would react by advocating the partial cancellation of inter-Allied debts, the Lausanne conference made the whole agreement contingent on a proportionate reduction in the debts owed our government. Hoover's last hope for the elimination of intergovernmental debts as barriers to world recovery vanished with President-elect Roosevelt's refusal to commit himself to any immediate international settlement before his domestic program was under way. Consequently, for this and other reasons, the London Economic Conference, which met in the spring of 1933 to consider problems of international finance, was doomed to failure.

THE END OF DISARMAMENT

Disarmament appealed to Hoover both as a Quaker who detested war and as an ardent advocate of economy; he even hoped, after the failure of the Geneva Conference of 1927, that the war debts might be used to bring it about, but this remained unrealized. After informal discussions during the fall of 1929 with British Prime Minister Ramsay MacDonald, the President sent an impressive delegation, headed by Secretary of State Stimson, to London to attend a five-power naval conference which began on January 21, 1930. As in previous conferences, France demanded definite assurance of military aid in case of a German invasion, and when this was not forthcoming she joined Mussolini's Italy in refusing to consider any of the major proposals for disarmament. The treaty signed in April, 1930, gave the United States complete naval parity with Great Britain; but bringing our Navy up to the British level actually meant an increase in our naval expenditures. The new 10–10–6 ratio for heavy cruisers put Japan in third place, but the 10–10–7 basis for light cruisers was a significant gain for her, and she achieved equality in submarines; in other words, she now was strong enough to dominate the South Pacific. We reaffirmed our 1922 agreement with Japan not to increase the fortifications of our eastern Pacific bases. Hence, from the perspective of the Second World War, it is clear that Japan was the real beneficiary of the London Conference, for Britain and the United States limited their naval strength but gained neither security nor real economy. The Senate, unimpressed by the results and fearing some secret entanglement, grudgingly approved the treaty.

Going far beyond his predecessors in cooperating with the League, Hoover sought a leading part in the World Disarmament Conference which met in Geneva on February 2, 1932. He first urged that all offensive weapons be abolished, but later proposed that all existing armaments be reduced by a third. France now had an even better reason than ever for non-cooperation, for Hitler's National Socialist party was leading a movement for nationalism in Germany and was advocating rearmament in disregard of the Treaty of Versailles. While the Conference was in session, Japan made disarmament a dead issue by suddenly attacking Shanghai.

JAPAN VERSUS THE STIMSON DOCTRINE

The revival of Japan's dormant imperialism was spurred on by the loss of her vital foreign markets, increasing unemployment, and a lower salary scale for civil servants—all of these factors products of the world-wide depression. Seeking to strengthen her economic penetration of Manchuria through her South Manchurian railroad, Japan came in conflict with Chinese Nationalists determined to halt her advance. After a series of incidents in Manchuria which culminated in an alleged bomb attack on the railroad by Chinese soldiers, the Japanese struck out suddenly on the night of September 18, 1931, and occupied many cities and towns in southern Manchuria, a move which must have been planned long before the alleged bombing of the railroad. China appealed to the League of Nations and to the signatories of the Kellogg Pact.

Secretary Stimson, anxious to strengthen the Pact in a concrete case which involved our interests, promptly warned Japan of her obligations and on October 10 declared that "the American Government, acting independently through its diplomatic representatives, will endeavor to reinforce what the League does." When the League proceeded to order an investigation, Japan insisted that there was no actual war and completed her occupation of Manchuria in defiance of the League. The Secretary of State then issued on January 7, 1932, what has become known as the Stimson Doctrine; this stated that the United States would not "recognize any situation, treaty, or agreement which may be brought about by means contrary to the covenants and obligations of the Pact of Paris. . . ." Japan replied by converting Manchuria into the puppet state of Manchukuo.

The Chinese Nationalists retaliated with a boycott on Japanese goods that cut trade with the island empire by 60 per cent. Thereupon Japanese marines, later reinforced by army units, invaded Shanghai on some slight pretext, killing thousands of civilians and finally colliding with the well-trained Chinese Nineteenth Route Army, which offered fierce resistance. At this point, the Japanese were willing to be persuaded to accept an armistice. In a public letter of February 24 to Senator Borah, Secretary Stimson restated his policy of not recognizing territorial changes made in violation of international law. He pointed out that America's agreement in 1922 to surrender her lead in battleship construction and to leave Guam and the Philippines unfortified had been based on Japan's acceptance of the open-door policy as embodied in the Nine-Power Treaty.

This should have been clear warning to Japan. China was encouraged by the favorable report of the Lytton Commission of the League: "The military operations of the Japanese troops . . . cannot be regarded as measures of self-defense." Japan immediately gave notice of her intention to withdraw from the League, thereby further weakening its authority in the face of the later aggressions of Italy and Germany. No sanctions of any type were invoked against her, for Hoover, and probably Congress as well, were opposed to such a step for fear of bringing on war with the island empire. In view of her important economic interests in the Far East and the vulnerability of India, Australia, New Zealand, and other British areas, Great Britain decided upon appeasement. American critics of Britain overlooked the fact that Stimson's policy of threatening without imposing penalties was scarcely effective in restraining aggressors and not at all reassuring to the British. As it was, the isolationists and isolationist newspapers like the Chicago *Tribune* and the Hearst chain were thoroughly convinced that we had already gone too far toward cooperating with the League.

THE GOOD NEIGHBOR IDEAL

Hoover's Latin American policy constituted one of the great successes of his Administration. As President-elect, he made a good-will tour of Latin America late in 1928, in which he said that the United States was eager to maintain "the relations of good neighbors" with the southern republics. As a step in this direction, he insisted that the diplomatic and consular services be staffed by men acquainted with the language and people of the countries to which they were assigned. Those who feared that he was advocating dollar diplomacy were answered in his public statement on April 13, 1929: "I can say at once it never has been and ought not to be the policy of the United States to intervene by force to secure or maintain contracts between our citizens and foreign States and their citizens."

Latin Americans were reassured when they learned that Hoover and Stimson opposed the so-called Roosevelt Corollary to the Monroe Doctrine, which empowered the United States, as a hemisphere policeman, to intervene in the domestic affairs of the southern republics in order to prevent foreign penetration. The Clark Memorandum on the Monroe Doctrine, which was prepared toward the end of Coolidge's term but was not issued until 1930, clarified the State Department's position and was the basis of Hoover's policy of non-intervention.

To reduce the possible need for intervention, the Administration discarded Woodrow Wilson's policy of not recognizing *de facto* governments established by revolution or violence. Stimson announced that the United States would return to Jefferson's theory of basing recognition "not upon the question of the constitutional legitimacy of the new government but upon its *de facto* capacity to fulfill its obligations as a member of the family of nations." He pointed out that Wilson's refusal to recognize the Huerta government had led to armed conflict with Mexico. However, he said that one exception to this policy of recognition was revolution-ridden Central America. Since these republics had themselves agreed in 1907 and 1923 not to recognize governments based on revolution or violence, the United States, apparently for reasons of strategic necessity, would therefore do likewise. Stimson repeatedly invoked this special Central American agreement to compel revolution-bred administrations to retire, as in the Guatemala revolution. Our war against the Sandistas was continued in Nicaragua but was more and more turned over to the newly trained native gendarmes. By January, 1933, all our Marines had been withdrawn.

Hoover also had the satisfaction of bringing about the solution of the "Question of the Pacific" which had been a bone of contention between Peru and Chile since 1883. This involved the disposition of the frontier provinces of Tacna and Arica after the bloody war of the Pacific (1879–1883), in which Chile had been victorious. Chile, desirous of retaining the provinces as buffer states against Peru, proceeded to Chileanize them and to intimidate Peruvian voters who sought to participate in the plebiscites arranged through the earlier mediation of the United States. President Coolidge had sent Generals John J. Pershing and William Lassiter to supervise a plebiscite, but none could be held. Finally, Peru and Chile agreed to ask President Hoover to mediate. Chile was given Arica, and Peru received not only Tacna but also an indemnity and certain other compensations.

THE NOMINATION OF FRANKLIN DELANO ROOSEVELT

Hoover's renomination by the Republicans in 1932 was virtually uncontested, although there were reports of a lack of any genuine enthusiasm at the convention. The Administration was endorsed, the Democrats being blamed for the long deadlock between Congress and the President. The contest for the Democratic nomination was much more spirited, particularly in view of the two-thirds requirement for nomination. Governor Franklin D. Roosevelt of New York had a majority on the first ballot but lacked the necessary two-thirds. Speaker John N. Garner of Texas, who was strongly supported by the Hearst newspapers, held second place. In the background, ever hopeful that a deadlock might end in his favor, was former Governor Alfred E. Smith, the unsuccessful candidate in 1928. This hope proved vain, however, for the Garner forces finally compromised by accepting the vice-presidential nomination for their leader, thus enabling Roosevelt to be nominated on the fourth ballot. He broke tradition by flying to Chicago to make his acceptance speech, in which he promised "a new deal for the American people."

While the Republican campaign stressed the international causes of the depression, the Democrats attributed it to their opponents' post-war policies which they claimed fostered economic nationalism and private monopoly. They emphasized federal aid to the poorer states for unemployment relief, and promised regulation of security-issuing holding companies engaged in interstate commerce. Old age and unemployment insurance under state laws offered another popular attraction, responsibilities which the Republicans held should be assumed by private industry. The Democratic platform called for the repeal of the Eighteenth Amendment as a step toward recovery; that of their opponents advocated an amendment which would permit local option and thus protect the dry states. With studied evasion, the Democrats supported "sound" currency and a "competitive" tariff for revenue.

Roosevelt at the age of fifty was far more vigorous-looking than he was when he nominated Alfred E. Smith for President in 1924. His opponents might refer to him deprecatingly as a "country squire" who had been born in a well-to-do home at Hyde Park, New York, but his actions showed a sympathy for the "forgotten man"—a phrase he popularized—that his rivals could scarcely surpass, regardless of whether they had risen from a humble farm or city streets. He was trained at Harvard University and the Columbia University Law School. When he entered politics in New York, he fought the Tammany wing of his party and supported its liberal candidates. As a delegate to the Baltimore convention in 1912 he worked for Wilson's nomination and afterward received the important position of Assistant Secretary of the Navy; here he distinguished himself in preparing our Navy for action in World War I as the first Roosevelt, a distant relative, had done under McKinley. When, a year after his defeat in 1920 as Cox's running mate, he was stricken by infantile paralysis, it seemed that his political career must be over. Nevertheless, after partial recovery, he agreed, in answer to Smith's appeal in 1928, to run for governor of New York in order to strengthen the Democratic national ticket; Smith was defeated, but Roosevelt won by a small margin. Two years later he was reelected by an overwhelming vote.

As governor, Roosevelt learned many lessons he used later as President. He became an enthusiastic advocate of public ownership of water-power sources and strove to lower the cost of electric power to the people. Among the reforms he supported were workmen's compensation laws, effective factory inspection, unemployment insurance, and an eight-hour day for government workers. He initiated an old-age pension system in New York State and met many able social workers whom he later appointed to federal government posts. Already familiar with the problems of agriculture, he had become interested in reciprocal trade agreements as a substitute for the traditional tariff bargaining. Significantly, he fought the depression in his state by promptly appropriating state funds for relief.

The impact of the depression led him, when he became President, to experiment with unorthodox ideas that he considered were adapted to the changing national scene. To aid him in this, he surrounded himself with a group of eager men, many of them college professors, whom John Kieran of the New York *Times* dubbed the "brains' trust" (later the "brain trust"). Raymond Moley, a professor at Columbia who brought some of these experts together, had considered Hoover too inflexible in his ideas, however good; but subsequently he himself dropped behind Roosevelt as the latter's experimental spirit led him down new paths. Close to Roosevelt, but apart from his academic experts, were his devoted political mentors, Louis McHenry Howe and Judge Samuel Rosenman of New York, who had steered their protégé through the pitfalls that beset a candidate for office. Finally, there was James Farley of New York, whose acute political genius had planned Roosevelt's campaign with a thoroughness that helped to insure both nomination and election.

NEW DEAL VICTORY

Roosevelt's insistence during the campaign that the federal government extend its authority by regulating and protecting economic life met emphatic opposition from Hoover. Assailing the "well-meaning reformer" who was discouraged by the failure of local communities to rise to their responsibilities, Hoover declared that such failures were better "than that we should drive this Republic to a centralization which will mean the deadening of its great mainspring of progress, which is the discovery and experimentation and advancement by the local community." He also denounced the reciprocal trade agreements advocated by Roosevelt as injurious to one industry at the expense of another. The President was nettled by his opponent's characterization of the Hawley-Smoot tariff as a "ghastly jest," for to him this tariff was the bulwark of the country's high wages. Roosevelt's "new deal," said Hoover, meant a revolutionary change in the foundations of national life that would lead to regimentation and socialism.

But both the depression and Hoover's cautious methods of meeting it worked against him. According to the Cleveland Trust Company's estimates, unemployment had risen from around six million in November, 1930, to more than ten million a year later and to over fourteen million two years later. Banks, utility companies, and other businesses of all types were still closing. Although there had been some recovery, it was apparent only in the realm of cold statistics; the modest upturn was entirely lost in the overwhelming human tragedy of personal insecurity.

In the election, Roosevelt received 472 electoral votes to Hoover's 59. Only New England, protectionist Pennsylvania, and Delaware remained loyal to the President. The popular vote, however, was far less impressive, for Roosevelt polled 22,821,513 votes—only 57.4 per cent of the total vote—to his opponent's 15,761,787. Nevertheless, this wiped out the Democrats' humiliation in 1928. Both parties cut their election expenditures drastically, but Hoover's managers reported expenses of $2,670,000 to Roosevelt's $1,700,000.

Symptomatic of the depression was the sharp increase in the leftist vote, some of which was a protest against the major parties rather than a sign of Marxist penetration. Norman Thomas, who received 267,627 votes in 1928, won 884,274 in 1932. William Z. Foster, the Communist candidate, polled 102,991 votes to more than double his 1928 total. Temporarily committed to Roosevelt's program were Senator Huey Long of Louisiana, who offered a "Share the Wealth" plan, and Father Charles Coughlin, radio priest of the Shrine of the Little Flower in Michigan, whose "Roosevelt or Ruin!" revived an extreme form of the inflation called for in Bryan's 1896 campaign.

THE DEEPENING CRISIS

The final months of Hoover's administration were a nightmare for the tired and repudiated President. He clashed with Congress over the Philippine Independence Act, which was passed over his veto early in 1933. In his mind, Philippine independence was motivated primarily by American sugar interests in their desire to escape competition and it could result only in social and economic chaos. He recommended that the bill include guarantees which would preclude any future intervention on our part to restore order and would also insure against attack on the islands from another quarter—obviously Japan. Our motives, he declared, must remain altruistic.

Hoover considered it futile to embark on other new policies because the next Administration might discard them, a fact of which European diplomats were well aware. When he sought a commitment from

Roosevelt on December 19 regarding plans for the World Economic Conference, the President-elect answered, "I think you will realize that it would be unwise for me to accept an apparent joint responsibility with you when, as a matter of constitutional fact, I would be wholly lacking in any attendant authority." The press quoted Roosevelt as remarking informally that the war debt problem was "not my baby."

In Michigan, the once-prosperous automobile industry and the real estate boom had sunk deep under the depression, and the weakened banks, especially in Detroit, were faced with repeated runs by depositors. Consequently, on February 14, 1933, Governor Comstock ordered an eight-day "banking holiday" which would tie up perhaps $1,500,000,000. An epidemic of such holidays soon swept the nation. Hoover attributed this resurgence of the panic to the fears aroused by Roosevelt's unorthodox monetary policies, and on February 17 he sent a Secret Service messenger to the President-elect to warn him of the impending national panic; his message stressed the psychological causes of the crisis which, he said, could be eliminated by Roosevelt's prompt assurance that he would not tamper with the currency. The President-elect replied that the fire was bound to spread in spite of any statement he might make. "The real trouble," he said, "is that on present values very few financial institutions anywhere in the country are actually able to pay off their deposits in full, and the knowledge of this fact is widely held." That this was overly pessimistic was shown by the subsequent reopening of the banks.

Hoover anxiously watched Roosevelt's attempts to persuade the conservative Carter Glass to serve as Secretary of the Treasury, a choice which might be regarded as reassuring to the bankers; but Glass refused, in view of the inflationary experiments likely under the new Administration. Meanwhile, weakened banks in the interior began to draw heavily on New York and Chicago banks. Since this was endangering the nation's entire financial structure, Hoover a few days before the inauguration considered proclaiming a nation-wide bank holiday to halt the panic, but many financiers feared that such a move would have catastrophic results; he also sent to the Federal Reserve Board a suggested plan for the federal guarantee of bank deposits. Once more he appealed to Roosevelt for collaboration; the latter, however, regarded any temporary closing of the nation's banks as unnecessary, and suggested instead that Hoover use certain war emergency powers to regulate foreign exchange and withdrawals of deposits. Hoover considered this suggestion as not only unconstitutional but as liable to rejection by the Democratic Congress. Consequently the crisis was left in the hands of state governors.

By March 4, 1933, when President Hoover, wearied by forty-eight hours of continuous labor with no sleep, rode solemnly down Pennsylvania Avenue beside Franklin D. Roosevelt, practically every governor in the nation, including Lehman of New York and Horner of Illinois, had either declared a bank holiday or imposed severe restrictions on withdrawals. For the first time in its history, our country's economic life faced complete paralysis. Trade was reduced in many instances to barter, and fears of worse things haunted the man in the street. Revolutions had flamed in other countries with far less provocation. This was the grim setting for the New Deal.

CHAPTER 16

The New Deal Revolution; Collapse of Business Leadership: 1933-1936

THE NEW DEALERS TAKE OVER

In this inaugural crisis, the gravest since Lincoln's inauguration in 1861, the bold unruffled confidence manifest in Roosevelt's inaugural address that March afternoon in 1933 was an inspiriting tonic to a worried nation. Two weeks earlier, on February 15, the President-elect had narrowly escaped death in Miami, Florida, when an assassin's bullet aimed at him hit Mayor Anton Cermak of Chicago, who later died from the wound. Three days afterward, Roosevelt received Hoover's message on the peril facing the nation in the banking crisis. Refusing to be daunted, the new President spoke reassuringly: "This great Nation will endure as it has endured, will revive and will prosper. So, first of all, let me assert my firm belief that the only thing we have to fear is fear itself—nameless, unreasoning, unjustified terror which paralyzes needed efforts to convert retreat into advance."

The crisis was far from insoluble, in his opinion. "We are stricken by no plague of locusts. . . . Plenty is at our doorstep, but a generous use of it languishes in the very sight of the supply." This failure he attributed to the stubbornness and incompetence of "the rulers of the exchange of mankind's goods" who had relinquished their power after resorting to exhortations and "pleading tearfully for restored confidence." Herbert Hoover, as he listened to the address, could scarcely have missed this thrust at himself. Roosevelt went on to outline the problems involved in farm and urban relief and unemployment, and advocated national planning in the fields of transportation, communications, and public utilities. "We must act," he insisted; "we must act quickly."

International trade relations he placed second to the establishment of a "sound national economy"; nevertheless, these relations need not be "narrowly nationalistic." In foreign affairs he sounded the tocsin of the "good neighbor" policy—"the neighbor who resolutely respects himself and, because he does so, respects the rights of others. . . ." He promised vigorous leadership, but said frankly that if the emergency required it, he would ask for broad executive power comparable to "the power that would be given to me if we were in fact invaded by a foreign foe." He expressed his goal in the following terms: "We aim at the assurance of a rounded and permanent national life."

Although there was little indication in Roosevelt's Cabinet appointments that revolutionary changes were in prospect, the strongly progressive elements became increasingly apparent as the New Deal was translated into action. Senator Cordell Hull of Tennessee, who became Secretary of State, was commonly considered a nineteenth-century apostle of free trade and moderate competition. The Treasury post went to William H. Woodin, president of the American Car and Foundry Company and a Republican until 1928; his appointment was expected to reassure business. Not until his resignation in 1934 because of illness did an ardent New Dealer succeed to this key post. Henry Morgenthau, Jr., of New York, the next Secretary of the Treasury, was the son of Wilson's Ambassador to Turkey and had been Governor Roosevelt's chief adviser on farm problems; thereafter he had served successively as governor of the Federal Farm Board, governor of the Farm Credit Administration, and Under Secretary of the Treasury.

The post of Secretary of Agriculture, for which Morgenthau was apparently well fitted, went instead to Henry A. Wallace, an Iowa dirt farmer of strong progressive tendencies, whose father, Henry C. Wallace, had held the same post under Harding and Coolidge. Another consistent liberal, then comparatively unknown to the country, was the new Secretary of the Interior, Harold L. Ickes of Chicago. Frances Perkins, who had been New York State Commissioner of Labor under Roosevelt, became the Secretary of Labor, the first woman to be appointed to any Cabinet. The President had planned to give the attorney-generalship to Thomas J. Walsh, the militant Montana reformer who was primarily responsible for unearthing the Teapot Dome scandal, but Walsh's death two days before the inauguration resulted in the selection of Homer S. Cummings of Connecticut for the post.

Vital for the success of the New Deal was the patronage power which was entrusted in large part to the astute new Postmaster General, James A. Farley of New York. "Deserving Democrats"—their ranks had swollen during the twelve-year political drought—were persistent applicants for the many thousands of new posts not yet brought under civil service rules. The mushroom growth of new government agencies meant, at least for several years, a parallel increase in patronage. Not only was the President's power in Congress enhanced in this way, but men sympathetic to the Administration's novel program could be given key positions in important agencies which were still in the experimental stage. The New Deal subsidies and reforms on behalf of farmers, laborers, the unemployed, and Negroes, among others, swung millions of traditionally Republican votes to the Democratic column.

REOPENING THE BANKS

During the exciting "hundred days" after his inauguration, the President, hoping to achieve recovery and reform simultaneously, kept a weary Congress in session so that his numerous emergency measures could be enacted with the utmost rapidity. To meet the paralyzing banking crisis, the Administration hit on the expedient of invoking an unrepealed war emergency act dating from Wilson's time, the Trading with the Enemy Act of 1917. This permitted Roosevelt to issue an executive proclamation on March 6 declaring a four-day nation-wide banking holiday—subsequently extended to March 13—suspending gold and silver exports, and delegating to the Secretary of the Treasury certain broad powers in the emergency. When Congress convened on March 9, Roosevelt was ready with a draft of the Emergency Banking Bill which gave him authority to reopen the banks and asked for the issuance of Federal Reserve banknotes to help meet depositors' runs when the bank holiday ended. So rapidly did Congress act that the President signed the bill the same day it was presented.

While Treasury officials were struggling with the herculean task of deciding which banks should be permitted to reopen, Roosevelt on March 10 sent Congress another bill calculated to reassure businessmen regarding the orthodoxy of his proposed financial measures. This was a sweeping economy bill which the proponents of inflationary spending deeply resented. "For three long years," declared Roosevelt, "the Federal Government has been on the road toward bankruptcy." He estimated that the accumulated deficit left by the preceding Administration would total $5,000,000,000 by 1934, and he considered this a direct threat to the credit of the United States. The bill specified a cut of possibly half a billion dollars in government employees' salaries and in veterans' compensation; the latter was aimed in particular at pension abuses on the part of ex-soldiers who had suffered no disabilities in actual battle. Although scores of Democratic Congressmen deserted their leader on the economy issue, enough conservative Republicans supported the bill to save Roosevelt from humiliating defeat at the outset of his term of office.

On Sunday evening, March 12, the President delivered the first of his simple but psychologically effective "fireside chats" over the radio. In it he reassured the people as to the measures taken to strengthen the banks and he urged depositors to redeposit their money. Shortly afterward the banks were allowed to reopen and the immediate crisis ended. Roosevelt had convinced depositors that the remaining banks were solvent, although no actual federal guarantee was given. Not until June, 1933, did Congress create the Federal Deposit Insurance Corporation to guarantee the funds of small depositors in full and of larger depositors in part.

PROHIBITION REPEAL AND INFLATION

Even while the banks were reopening, the President acted to fulfill a party pledge which it was believed would stimulate recovery, provide substantial taxes for the government, and curb certain abuses of law enforcement. This was the immediate modification of the Volstead Act to permit the sale of beer and light wine. In fact, the entire prohibition experiment that had lasted over a decade came to a largely unlamented end on December 5, 1933, when Utah became the thirty-sixth state to ratify the Twenty-First Amendment repealing the controversial Eighteenth. Only in the Old South and in Oklahoma, Kansas, and North Dakota did the drys retain their control. The "tavern" and the well-upholstered cocktail lounge replaced the prewar saloon.

Roosevelt bowed to the powerful wave of inflationist sentiment from the western and southern farm states led by Senators Burton K. Wheeler of Montana and Elmer Thomas of Oklahoma, as distressed farmers once again sought to achieve higher prices and mortgage debt reductions through tinkering with the currency. The President, who thought it expedient to depart from the gold standard in order to save our gold reserve, issued a proclamation on April 20 forbidding gold exports except under Treasury license. The ghost of Bryan's free-silver ideas of 1896 appeared in Wheeler's narrowly defeated proposal for the free coinage of silver at the ratio of sixteen to one.

The President accepted a modified inflation bill, sponsored by Senator Thomas as an amendment to the Farm Relief Bill, which empowered him to reduce the gold content of the dollar up to 50 per cent. Among other inflationary powers, he could compel the Federal Reserve System to undertake open market operations in government bonds and to buy Treasury certificates up to three billion dollars, and he could issue up to three billion dollars in greenbacks to retire federal bonds. He could also coin silver at a ratio to gold fixed by himself and accept silver from foreign debtors up to $100,000,000 (this was later increased to $200,000,000).

Although Roosevelt acted slowly in using his new powers, both the Thomas amendment and the gold embargo were strongly criticized abroad, especially in England, as a breach of international faith. Other nations, said the British press, had been forced off the gold standard by the pressure of external events, but the United States was pursuing purely inflationary aims. Lewis W. Douglas, Roosevelt's orthodox-minded Director of the Budget, commented discouragedly, "Well, this is the end of Western civilization"; and Raymond Moley feared that the "wild men" from the farm states would open the road to ruinous inflation. Popular anticipation of inflation was followed by depreciation of the dollar, a three-month rise in prices, and a feeling of optimism that became general despite the fact that Roosevelt still refrained from actually using his new inflationary powers.

SAFEGUARDING INVESTORS

Seldom was the prestige of bankers so low as during the spring of 1933, a fact due in large part to the Senate investigation of the investment field, as well as the current bank crash. Most sensational were the disclosures which not only brought up to date the Pujo Committee's revelations in 1912 regarding the Morgan interests' concentrated financial organization and industrial credit control but also proved that the Morgan partners, by taking advantage of loopholes in the federal tax law, had paid little or no income taxes during 1930, 1931, and 1932. Ernest K. Lindley, the journalist, compared the immoral practices that numerous bankers admitted were being followed in floating and managing investments, with the worst that Tammany Hall had ever offered. As a result of the Senate investigation, the reformist Glass-Steagall Act was passed in June, 1933. To curb the speculative mania characteristic of the late twenties, it separated investment banking from commercial banking, thus ending the existence of the latter's profitable investment affiliates which had access to the funds of commercial bank depositors. To prevent another speculative spree, the Act empowered the Federal Reserve Board to refuse banks an excessive use of credit for speculation in securities, real estate, or commodities. Provision for the Federal Deposit Insurance Corporation was also made, despite Administration criticism of it as both unnecessary and burdensome to sound banks.

The Securities Act of 1933 came more specifically to the defense of investors. Britain's experience in this field, particularly Gladstone's British Companies Act of 1844, proved invaluable to the New Deal. Louis D. Brandeis' challenging book, *Other People's Money* (1913), had called attention to the British practice of requiring investment houses to furnish prospective investors with accurate information on the financial status of various issues. Many of our own states had blue-sky laws to protect investors, but this legislation proved ineffectual because the states lacked power under the Constitution to enforce these laws adequately. In a message to Congress on March 29, the President proposed a federal law that would require full information on investment issues. "It puts the burden of telling the whole truth on the seller," he said; and then, consciously borrowing a phrase from Brandeis, he maintained that people who handled "other people's money" were trustees for the investors.

The drafting of the Securities Act was left to three lawyers, all Harvard men—Professor Felix Frankfurter, a disciple of Brandeis and

Wilson, Professor James M. Landis, and Benjamin V. Cohen. One factor that contributed directly to the severity of the depression was brought out by the Senate's revelations concerning the frauds and misrepresentations involved in the sale of billions of dollars' worth of worthless securities during the twenties. Consequently, the Securities Act was stringent and detailed; it insured the provision of full and accurate information by the seller through the heavy penalties it imposed for violations. Enforcement was entrusted to the renovated Federal Trade Commission. Opponents of the measure immediately charged that it discouraged new flotations of securities, but the more serious aspects of these charges were eventually removed by amendments and wise enforcement.

RAISING FARM PRICES AND INCOME

High on the agenda of the crowded "hundred days" was the Agricultural Adjustment Act. The desperate position of the farmers, revealed by their receptivity to any and all inflationist panaceas, made drastic action imperative. No political leader could afford to adopt a *laissez-faire* attitude and wait for farm bankruptcies to establish an equilibrium between supply and demand. Hoover's policy in purchasing surpluses had actually encouraged overproduction; for this reason some form of crop restriction like acreage reduction appeared necessary.

On the assumption that the depression was largely due to domestic causes, Roosevelt's brain-trusters emphasized internal remedies rather than international price-raising programs. The crystallizing philosophy of the New Deal embodied the ideal of the government as an agency that would equalize agriculture with industry, labor with capital, and consumption with production. Hence the President's inner circle welcomed with open arms the "equality for agriculture" program—later known as parity—proposed by Professor M. L. Wilson of the Montana State College for Agricultural and Mechanic Arts at Bozeman. As editor of *Iowa Homestead and Wallace's Farmer,* Secretary Wallace had been keenly interested in Wilson's idea of raising prices by crop allotment. Temporarily eclipsed was Cordell Hull, who stressed international agreements and drastic tariff cuts, especially through reciprocal treaties, as the chief approach to recovery.

On March 16 Roosevelt sent to Congress his farm relief message asking for reduction of acreage in certain basic crops and for credit relief to farmers who were in immediate danger of losing their homes, and calling for immediate action so that crop restriction could go into effect before the spring planting. "I tell you frankly," he said, "that it is a new and untrod path, but I tell you with equal frankness that an unprecedented condition calls for the trial of new means to rescue agriculture." The resulting Agricultural Adjustment Act, passed in May, 1933, declared as its objective the reestablishment of farm prices at a level "that will give agricultural commodities a purchasing power with respect to articles farmers buy, equivalent to the purchasing power of agricultural commodities in the base period—August, 1909–July, 1914." During these years agriculture had approached the equality to industry envisaged by Professor Wilson.

The A.A.A., as it quickly became known, sought crop and acreage restriction primarily by means of government contracts that provided attractive benefit payments or commodity loans to cooperating farmers. Beginning with the basic staples—wheat, cotton, corn, hogs, rice, milk, and tobacco—the list of restricted crops was steadily expanded. To finance the program, a processing tax was levied at intermediate points such as cotton mills, and from there was passed on to the ultimate consumer. George N. Peek, a manufacturer of farm implements who had been active in the McNary-Haugen agitation of the twenties, was appointed to enforce the Act. An army of A.A.A. agents drove through farm counties to persuade farmers to plow under or otherwise reduce their crop production. According to Ernest K. Lindley, who was sympathetic to the New Deal, even the southern mules that drew the plows were outraged at having to tread down young cotton plants which they had painstakingly learned to avoid. Cotton immediately rose from the ruinous price of five cents per pound in 1932 to nine cents, and soon afterward to twelve cents, which was considered a fair price. Cotton growers plowed under, or otherwise eliminated, some 10.5 million acres out of a total of forty million.

The farmers' cash income rose from $4,500,000,000 in 1932 to $6,900,000,000 in 1935. Nevertheless, it was difficult to make the average man see that the wholesale slaughtering of pigs was equivalent to similar restrictive policies in agriculture and industry, and to convince Father Coughlin's radio converts that restriction was not a criminal extension of "want in the midst of plenty." Hoover characterized this program as being "an economy of scarcity" rather than abundance. Other opponents emphasized the new burdens put on urban workers by the processing taxes, to which they attributed an exaggerated influence on the urban cost of living. Still others pointed out that while the New Deal was seeking to restrict world grain exports by agreements with Canada, Argentina, and Australia, wheat production was being subsidized by Mussolini, Hitler, and even democratic France. The A.A.A. program was commonly charged with sacrificing our own foreign markets in favor of our overseas competitors. But it was supported by the farmers, who had been severely derogatory of the program advocated by Coolidge and Hoover; and Roosevelt hailed it as the "expression of an enduring principle carved in stone by a nation come to maturity."

AIDING THE MORTGAGE-HOLDER

The New Deal struck out boldly at the critical problem presented by the twelve billion dollars of farm indebtedness, three-fourths of which consisted of mortgages. Because the orthodox methods undertaken during Hoover's administration had failed to stem the flood of foreclosures, the new Administration saw clearly that many bad risks would have to be assumed by the government and that this would mean numerous defaults. The Emergency Farm Mortgage Act made it possible to refinance farm loans over generously extended periods at reduced interest, and the Farm Credit Act gave some relief to farmers with short-term obligations. To simplify and coordinate the government's credit agencies, both new and old, the President consolidated all of them in a centralized Farm Credit Administration. By 1936, the federal government had assumed or underwritten some 40 per cent of the total farm mortgage debt.

Small home owners who faced eviction were saved by the Home Owners' Loan Corporation, capitalized at $200,000,000 from the funds of the Reconstruction Finance Corporation and authorized to issue interest-guaranteed bonds up to two billion dollars. These bonds were exchanged for mortgages, thus bringing in the federal government as a lenient creditor who was willing to wait fifteen years for repayment. Credit was also available for those who wanted to redeem property already foreclosed or to reduce other claims on their homes. When the H.O.L.C. ceased its lending operations in 1936, it had made over one million loans involving well over three billion dollars. It seems unquestionable that this agency played a major role in halting the wholesale collapse of real estate values, with the attending tragic mass evictions.

THE N.R.A. AND PLANNED ECONOMY

The crowning glory of the "hundred days" was the ambitious National Industrial Recovery Act, which was conceived by the Administration as "a great co-operative movement directed by the Government." It sought to eliminate overproduction, destructive competition, and industrial planlessness, and at the same time it encouraged labor unions, imposed minimum wage and maximum hour limits, abolished child labor, and increased employment. The labor provisions were intended as a moderate substitute for Senator Black's impending thirty-hour-week bill—popularly dubbed the "share-the-work bill"—which would require a drastic, perhaps dangerous, reorganization of the nation's economy. Finally, the N.I.R.A. called for a huge public works program.

One aspect of this program, self-rule in business, originated among the large industries who were suffering from the price-cutting tactics employed by the more fiercely competitive small business units. In September, 1931, Gerard Swope, president of the General Electric Company, had proposed that industry consolidate itself into huge trade associations which would be authorized by the government to enter price-fixing agreements in order to stabilize prices. A similar plan had been offered a few months later by the United States Chamber of Commerce as the result of a vote among its members. These plans not only implied the suspension of anti-trust laws against trade associations but also meant government enforcement of price and production agreements. Hoover had rejected these suggestions, convinced that such plans would lead to Mussolini's corporate state or to some form of socialism; furthermore, he pointed out, obsolete plants and inferior management would be perpetuated by legalized price-fixing. In his mind, such proposals constituted "the most gigantic proposal of monopoly ever made in history."

Roosevelt looked upon the N.I.R.A. as a vital step in the direction of national planning. "History," he declared optimistically, "probably will record the National Industrial Recovery Act as the most important and far-reaching legislation ever enacted by the American Congress. It represents a supreme effort to stabilize for all time the many factors which make for the prosperity of the Nation, and the preservation of American standards." Opponents were not slow in comparing this attempt at a planned economy with Soviet Russia's Five-Year Plan, which was then enjoying considerable prestige abroad, especially in leftist circles. Members of the brain trust talked about the need for "a balanced and dynamic economic system" to replace the existing chaos of undisciplined competition. Cooperation among capital, labor, and government, the President believed, would achieve what state and federal legislation had ever failed to accomplish. Members of the United States Chamber of Commerce who assembled in Washington early in May, 1933, went so far in reaffirming their demand for government aid in regulating competition as to recommend that the government adopt compulsory methods. Labor leaders likewise seemed willing to strike a bargain in order to guarantee collective bargaining and large-scale public employment.

The National Industrial Recovery Act, which became law on June 16, 1933, permitted trade and industrial associations to draw up codes of fair competition subject to the President's approval. Considerable authority was delegated to Roosevelt to impose codes in industries where none existed and to enforce them through his licensing power. Anti-trust laws were relaxed to permit the codes to operate. Most famous of the provisions was Section 7(a), which guaranteed labor's right "to organize and bargain collectively through representatives of their own choosing, . . ." free from interference by employers. Company unions were discouraged, although not banned. Under Administration pressure, the code provisions set the minimum wage usually at fifteen dollars a week, reduced working hours in most instances to forty hours per week or less, and forbade child labor. Regarding the wage provisions of the Act, the President said that "no business which depends for existence on paying less than living wages to its workers has any right to continue in this country."

The second section of the N.I.R.A. outlined a huge public works program, such as Senator Wagner of New York had persistently advocated for several years. A total of $3,300,000,000 was allocated for highway projects, flood control, inland navigation, and naval construction; in addition, a series of large loans or outright grants was made to needy local governments. Such a plan, it was hoped, would "prime the pump" of dormant private enterprise. To administer this part of the Act, the Public Works Administration, headed by Secretary of the Interior Ickes, was created.

The man chosen as administrator for the N.I.R.A. was the belligerent General Hugh S. Johnson, who had helped to write the draft regulations in force during World War I and had served on Bernard Baruch's War Industries Board. Convinced that the high-pressure application of World War psychology was needed to defeat the depression, and wishing to avoid expensive and unpredictable court contests, he turned to public opinion as a weapon to keep "chiselers" (a term he popularized) in line. His rugged personality and the choice epithets he reserved for unfriendly critics were enlisted in an effort to make the Blue Eagle emblem a respected symbol of compliance with the N.I.R.A. Jeering newspapermen, no less fertile as far as epithets were concerned, promptly lampooned this campaign "ballyhoo" and did much to reduce the potency of the Blue Eagle.

"NOBODY IS GOING TO STARVE"

After the N.I.R.A. was set up to stimulate the economic machine, there still remained the pressing problem of relief; to meet this, the Administration resorted to bold measures. It adopted the idea of work camps, still in a tentative stage in Europe, in the form of the Civilian Conservation Corps, which employed some 300,000 young men from relief-supported families for work on soil conservation and forest protection projects. This had a twofold result: it saved idle youths from the hazards of delinquency and it removed their impoverished families from relief rolls since a C.C.C. youth had to contribute a substantial portion of his salary to his family. In addition, the nation's natural resources were benefited by reforestation, by the prevention of costly soil erosion, and by flood control; and its human resources—eventually over two million young men—were benefited by living in well-equipped, healthful camps.

Direct relief, up to $500,000,000, was provided for in the Federal Emergency Relief Act of May, 1933. Half of this amount was granted to states at a ratio of one dollar of government funds to every three dollars expended locally; the other half was available to those states which were in such poor financial condition that they lacked funds for relief. In effect, by means of the Federal Emergency Relief Administration created by this Act, the burden of relief was shifted to the federal government. Whereas Hoover had not gone beyond making a $300,000,000 loan to needy states, Roosevelt eventually canceled state liability for even this circumspect loan. "Nobody is going to starve in this country" was Roosevelt's constant reassurance to the nation.

SAVING THE RAILROADS

The recovery program gave considerable attention to the railroads, whose operating revenues had been cut in half since 1929 in spite of the emergency rate increases belatedly permitted by the Interstate Commerce Commission during Hoover's term of office. The Reconstruction Finance Corporation gave some financial assistance in 1932, and the railroads cut salaries and took other steps toward economy. Nevertheless, motor vehicle and waterway competition continued to weaken them.

Roosevelt, himself the son of a vice president of the Delaware and Hudson Railroad, was keenly interested in the whole problem of transportation. This interest resulted in the Emergency Railroad Transportation Act, passed by Congress in 1933, which sought to integrate our transportation system by means of a Federal Coordinator who was to promote economies, largely on a voluntary basis. New authority granted the I.C.C. would enable it to eliminate railroad holding-company abuses and prevent fraudulent receiverships, and railroad employees were to be protected as far as salary and job tenure were concerned. The regulatory powers of the federal government were strengthened by the fact that the R.F.C. was one of the largest creditors of the railroads.

T.V.A. BLUEPRINT OF THE FUTURE

Roosevelt and his supporters found time during the first few months for a gigantic planning experiment that, in his own words, had "no parallel in our history." The recently completed Five-Year Plan of the Soviet Union had stimulated the proponents of economic planning everywhere; but Roosevelt's interest antedated this, for as governor of New York he had been active in the planning movement which sought to determine the best use of the state's thirty million acres by classifying each ten-acre square. Now, after conferring with Senator Norris, the President decided to convert the long-controversial Muscle Shoals property into a land-use project covering the entire Tennessee valley. "By controlling every river and creek and rivulet in this vast watershed," he wrote some time later, "and by planning for a highly civilized use of the land by the population of the whole area, we believed that we could make a lasting contribution to American life." He asked Congress to create the Tennessee Valley Authority, which would be empowered to develop the section's power resources and to deal with flood control, soil erosion, afforestation, the elimination of marginal land, and the industrialization of the region. A new Nile River was envisioned which would fructify the decaying Southeast, and it was hoped that other regions would eventually be benefited by similar projects.

The Tennessee Valley Authority which was created on May 18, 1933, consisted of a three-member board entrusted with the economic development of a region comprising 640,000 square miles. A moribund government investment of nearly $165,000,000 was to be revitalized. The Authority could sell any surplus power produced, but governmental and cooperative organizations were to be given preference as purchasers. As Norris put it, the T.V.A. would serve as a regulatory standard—a "yardstick"—for measuring the unit cost of electrical power and determining fair rates to be charged consumers by private companies. The New Deal's invasion of the Tennessee valley was deeply resented by the Commonwealth and Southern system, which had hitherto served this area. Its president, Wendell L. Willkie, challenged the fairness and validity of the T.V.A.'s yardstick as applied to private utilities and sought to protect his company's property interests by blocking the power-distributing activities of the T.V.A. Although the ensuing litigation to clarify and define the functions of the new agency hampered its progress for several years, government engineers continued to work toward their goal of cheap power, particularly for backward rural areas which had never before had electricity.

A MANAGED CURRENCY

The historic special session of Congress which ended on June 16, 1933, saw the rapid enactment of the most far-reaching domestic legislation ever sought in American history. An economic upturn was already in evidence. According to the estimates of the Cleveland Trust Company, unemployment had declined from the all-time high of over 16,000,000 in March, 1933, to 14,500,000 by the following July; this downward trend continued, for by October the number of unemployed had dropped below 12,000,000. Taking heart from this measure of recovery, the conservative press had already begun to indicate the lines which partisan resistance to the New Deal would take.

Public attention veered that summer to the World Economic Conference which had recently convened in London. Unfortunately the press, encouraged not a little by Roosevelt, gave an exaggerated idea of the results that were expected, among them being the stabilization of currencies, the leveling of tariff walls, and the raising of price levels by international action. At this time the New Deal was too deeply committed to its adventurous domestic program to accept any international agreement which threatened to tie its hands in currency experiments aimed at raising prices. In a public statement on July 3, Roosevelt himself hurled the bombshell that ended the possibility of constructive action by the Conference. "Let me be frank in saying that the United States seeks the kind of dollar which a generation hence will have the same purchasing and debt-paying power as the dollar value we hope to attain in the near future. That objective means more to the good of other nations than a fixed ratio for a month or two in terms of the pound or franc." He assailed the "old fetishes of so-called international bankers," referring apparently to the traditional gold standard, and came out in favor of a managed currency, evidently along the lines then being popularized by the distinguished British economist, John M. Keynes.

Then began a brief period of currency manipulation in the hope of raising prices and achieving the "commodity dollar" which Professor George F. Warren and Frank A. Pearson advocated on the theory that changes in the price of gold will cause a corresponding change in commodity prices. Invoking his power under the Thomas amendment to the Farm Relief Act of 1933, Roosevelt on January 31, 1934, fixed the weight of the gold dollar at approximately 59.06 per cent of its former weight. From the profit thus derived, a fund of $2,000,000,000 would be set up to stabilize our currency in terms of that of other nations. The President's action followed by a day the Gold Reserve Act which gave the federal government title to all the stock of monetary gold in the country and authorized the President to make further devaluations of the dollar in terms of gold. Other provisions were included to prevent the hoarding of gold and its shipment abroad.

Prices rose, but for reasons attributable to other factors than currency devaluation. Since the over-all result was far less satisfactory than the Administration had anticipated, Roosevelt refrained from further steps toward devaluing the dollar. A halfhearted concession to the inflationists was made in May, 1934, by the controversial Silver Purchase Act, which empowered the Treasury to buy silver. The purchases, however, were scarcely adequate to have any marked inflationary effects, for by this time the Administration was seeking other methods of bringing about recovery.

REFORMS IN HOUSING

In order to revive the dormant capital goods industries, especially through building construction, Congress passed the National Housing Act on June 27, 1934. This measure, in the drafting of which leading bankers and real estate men as well as housing authorities were consulted, encouraged small home owners to borrow money for repairing and improving their property. These loans, which were limited to $2000, were handled through the usual private channels, but a substantial part of each loan was protected against default by a federal guarantee. New construction was stimulated by a system of government-insured mortgages with low interest rates and a long period for amortization.

The financial phases of the National Housing Act were largely entrusted to the Federal Housing Administration, which soon became interested in the highly important related problem of community and national planning. At the same time, the Administration entered the field directly with the slum clearance and low-cost housing projects undertaken by the Housing Division of the P.W.A.; in addition, the government extended loans for these purposes to local governments. In spite of this progress, housing enthusiasts regarded these measures as scarcely more than the initial step, and there was considerable disagreement as to the importance of the role played by the F.H.A. in the subsequent building activity.

STOCK EXCHANGE REFORMS

While Congress was in session in 1934, Roosevelt insisted that legislation "with teeth in it" be enacted to control the nation's stock exchanges. The Securities Act of 1933 had offered investors considerable protection against fraud in purchasing securities, but the Administration now wanted to halt the worst of the manipulative practices which had characterized the stock market during the twenties. This led to a clash between the New Deal and the Senate conservatives led by Carter Glass, for Roosevelt advocated placing stock market regulation under vigorous control by the Federal Trade Commission and demanded fixed margin requirements, whereas Senator Glass believed that a special and more moderate regulatory body was necessary. The Securities and Exchange Act, which was finally passed on June 6, 1934, created a Securities and Exchange Commission of five members who not only were charged with stock market control but assumed other regulatory functions hitherto vested in the F.T.C. by the Securities Act of 1933.

A long list of sharp practices, from "wash sales" to "straddles," was outlawed by the new Act. A new method of registration required all security companies affiliated with stock exchanges to furnish detailed and confidential information regarding their financial status, the salaries received by their officers, and the speculative activities of the latter. Wall Street naturally was openly resentful at this curb to the glorious freedom it had enjoyed during the 1920's, and there was sharp criticism in the press; but public opinion as a whole supported Roosevelt.

THE W.P.A.

A temporary increase in unemployment during the winter of 1933–1934 compelled the New Deal to speed up the relief measures already put in effect under the P.W.A. To meet the emergency, the Civil Works Administration was hastily set up in November, 1933, as a branch of the Federal Emergency Relief Administration to provide immediate work at prevailing wage rates for some four million persons, half of whom were to be drawn from relief rolls. Projects were selected practically overnight and too many of them were in the "leaf-raking" class in order that there should be no ground for claims that the government was competing with private industry. Consequently the entire program aroused such ridicule in the press that the C.W.A. was hastily abolished in March, 1934.

In January, 1935, Roosevelt asked Congress to enact new relief legislation which would benefit some five million families. He suggested that the "unemployables" who had weighted down the C.W.A. rolls be referred to their local relief agencies, and that the latter be assisted by grants of federal funds. In this way an estimated 3,500,000 able-bodied but unemployed individuals, primarily people on relief, would be given work on useful federal projects and would be paid a "security wage," i.e., an amount below prevailing wage rates but substantially above relief allowances. This became the core of the Works Progress Administration created by the Emergency Relief Act of April, 1935, and headed by Harry L. Hopkins of the F.E.R.A. Of the huge sum of $4,800,000,000 appropriated under the new Act, $1,400,000,000 was allotted to the W.P.A.

The new agency quickly set up numerous projects of extremely diverse types. Manual laborers built long networks of roads across the country. Skilled women were employed on practical sewing projects. Long-idle professional and white-collar workers received up to $94 a month for musical, theatrical, art, educational, and literary projects. Although critics deplored the high cost of this type of relief, New Dealers stressed the social value of conserving the skills which the depression had left unutilized. On June 26 a special relief agency, the National Youth Administration, was established within the W.P.A. The N.Y.A. provided vocational training and employment especially for needy high school and college youths.

Employment on the whole increased steadily. In December, 1935, direct relief was turned over to state and local authorities, which made every effort to reduce the number of people on relief. Nevertheless, those who considered work relief a federal extravagance demanded its abolition and the shifting of this relief load to local government units. "Boondoggling," the newly coined term for these so-called useless work relief projects, must go.

THE PROGRAM OF SOCIAL SECURITY

By the beginning of 1935, the President was convinced that something more than emergency relief was needed, for the depression-nourished feeling of insecurity was leading to increased demands that the government itself underwrite economic security. For example, a coast-to-coast radio network regularly carried Father Coughlin's emotional medley of inflationary and reform proposals for "a living annual wage" which, it was implied, embodied the "social justice" program advocated by the papal encyclicals.

More threatening at the moment, however, was the "Share the Wealth" movement led by Senator Huey P. Long, the self-styled "Louisiana Kingfish" who had gained complete control of his state by methods somewhat similar to those used by European dictators. Castigating big business and oversize private fortunes, he threatened to tax these two groups so heavily that every family would be provided with a homestead and with the "reasonable comforts of life" to a value of $6000. His buffoon-like coarseness concealed an iron will to power which aimed at nothing less than the Presidency itself, but he won popularity by his magnificent program of public works which culminated in the elaborate buildings constructed for Louisiana State University. Huey Long used the filibuster effectively in the Senate to block New Deal measures until his own more radical bills were accepted. In this way he secured the passage of the Frazier-Lemke Farm Mortgage Bill which was subsequently nullified by the Supreme Court as confiscatory in tendency. On September 10, 1935, an assassin's bullet terminated the Senator's meteoric career.

Further pressure on the Administration for fundamental social reforms came from the Far West. The former Socialist writer, Upton Sinclair, won the Democratic nomination for governor of California on his "Epic" platform—"End poverty in California." He proposed to set up a state emergency economy, reminiscent of early communistic experiments in this country, which would operate factories to employ the jobless and would provide subsistence homesteads in suburban areas. Raymond Moley derided the plan in the magazine *Today* as a "blessed retreat—back beyond industrial civilization . . . back to barter, back to nature." Other Administration spokesmen, however, were frankly worried; at first they temporized with Sinclair but were reassured by the subsequent Republican victory.

Even more persistent than these populistic programs was the Townsend old-age pension movement, which was particularly strong in California. Dr. Francis Townsend, its leader, promised everyone over sixty years of age $200 a month on condition that it be spent within thirty days. In addition, this princely pension system, which was to be financed by a sales tax, would banish the depression by the large-scale spending that was an inherent part of the Townsend program. Townsend clubs spread all over the West and even crossed the Mississippi River; in 1935 their membership was estimated at from three to ten million people. Behind the Townsend movement was the undeniable political and sociological fact that because of our declining birth rate and our increased life expectancy, persons over sixty years of age would constitute an ever-increasing proportion of the population. Here was a permanent problem, not merely one engendered by the depression. In addition to Townsend and Coughlin and the other radical reform leaders, there were the persistent Farmer-Laborites, the Communists and Socialists, and the liberals who subscribed to the tenets of *The Nation* and *The New Republic*.

In this portentous atmosphere the Social Security Act of 1935 took form; it stemmed from a social movement which had taken root in Europe at least as early as Bismarck's social insurance program of the eighties. The Act was comprehensive in scope, if far more moderate than the programs outlined by Long, Townsend, and the leftist press. The question of constitutionality, which had begun to worry the architects of the New Deal, was met by basing the Act on the powers reserved to the states under the Tenth Amendment and on the acknowledged taxing and spending powers of the federal government. Some of the states, especially since 1923, had pioneered in the field of old-age assistance, but the benefits were often pathetically small. To assist the aged who required immediate financial aid, the Social Security Act provided federal grants to states on a dollar-for-dollar matching basis up to a maximum contribution of $15 per person per month. This was expected to stimulate backward states to set up old-age assistance plans as well as to make benefit payments more substantial.

Distinct from this feature of the Act was a more elaborate provision for old-age insurance covering future dependency. This was a pension system, directly administered by the federal government, to which employers and employees contributed. Benefits were payable after the age of sixty-five on a scale corresponding only in part to previous payments made by and on behalf of the individual; in this way some adjustment was allowed for members of the low-income groups. About two-thirds of the employed were covered, but for various practical reasons agricultural and casual labor, domestic servants, people employed in non-profit institutions, and the self-employed were excluded.

The provisions for unemployment compensation were extremely significant in view of the fact that the Farmer-Laborites and some of their radical allies were then demanding passage of the Lundeen bill, which offered a minimum payment of $10 a week to all unemployed persons over eighteen years of age. The Social Security Act sought to protect workers against the hazards of unemployment as well as to stabilize the business cycle. To this end, state unemployment systems were aided by federal grants that covered administrative costs. Payrolls were taxed to provide unemployment benefits which were paid to the recipients by public employment agencies ready to examine unemployment claims and to prod those who found labor distasteful. Here again, as in old-age insurance, large groups—almost the same ones in both cases—were excluded; nevertheless, by 1940 over 28,000,000 individuals had been aided by the unemployment provision.

Nor was this all. The Act provided for federal aid in child welfare work, vocational rehabilitation, especially for the handicapped, pensions for the blind, and public health services. To administer the Act, a Social Security Board with regional branches was created. Although several serious technical defects appeared, there were few people who could disagree with the President's statement that the Social Security

Act is the most fundamental law ever passed in behalf of American wage earners.

Equally calculated to take the wind out of the sails of Huey Long's Share-the-Wealth plan were the President's tax proposals to Congress on June 18, 1935. Arguing that wealth was the result of community as well as individual effort, Roosevelt called for "a wider distribution of wealth" to be effected through federal taxes on inheritances and gifts, and through higher corporation taxes. "The transmission from generation to generation of vast fortunes by will, inheritance, or gift," he said, "is not consistent with the ideals and sentiments of the American people." Opponents at once labeled this the "soak-the-rich" bill and charged that it was dictated by political expediency rather than considerations of revenue. In the Revenue Act of 1935, Congress struck out the federal inheritance tax but imposed substantial estate and gift taxes and a higher graduated income tax on corporations and individuals.

CURBING THE POWER COMPANIES

During 1935, Roosevelt concentrated on more extensive control of the electric power industry, especially the elimination of the fantastic pyramids, the so-called "utility empires," that resulted from the holding companies. Many investors had suffered losses through manipulations by "insiders" entrenched behind the complicated structure of the holding company. State utility commissions, as the Frank L. Smith and the Vare cases had shown, were too amenable to political influence. Congressional investigations of the power industry during the Coolidge and Hoover administrations had provided a massive indictment of monopolist practices. Roosevelt was also influenced by Brandeis, who favored well-integrated moderate-sized units as against irrational "bigness." During the congressional debate on the legislation, certain utility propagandists, although skilled from past experience in combating public regulation, damaged their cause when they deluged Congress with a stream of telegrams and letters, purportedly from individuals all over the country but which were quickly traced to a few people who had combed city directories for the necessary names and addresses.

The subsequent Public Utility Holding Company Act set up a

strict regulatory system under the Securities and Exchange Commission. Most famous was the "death sentence clause" (Section 11), which called for the simplification or elimination of all types of holding companies after January 1, 1938, except those forming a "geographically and economically integrated system"—a clause inserted by Frankfurter as a compromise. The Federal Power Commission, which had been revitalized by new personnel, was given control of the interstate transmission of electric power, as well as authority to investigate rate schedules. The utilities, smarting under the competition of the T.V.A. and the financing of numerous municipal power plants by the P.W.A., were dealt another blow by this new legislation. After challenging it unsuccessfully in the courts, they sought to defeat the New Deal at the polls.

FALL OF THE N.R.A.

On May 27, 1935, by a unanimous decision in Schechter Poultry Corporation *v.* United States, the Supreme Court struck down the important National Industrial Recovery Act. The Court held that the N.R.A. infringed state control over purely intrastate commerce, the business done by the Schechter Poultry Corporation being confined primarily to New York. Arguments pleading the existence of a national emergency were dismissed. "Extraordinary conditions," wrote Chief Justice Charles E. Hughes, "do not create or enlarge constitutional power." The code-making authority conferred on Roosevelt by Congress was denounced by the Court as an unconstitutional delegation of legislative power. This decision placed the rest of the New Deal program in jeopardy. Roosevelt, deeply disappointed, declared that this case was the most important since the Dred Scott decision and that the major issue was whether the federal government could control any national economic or social problem. The Supreme Court, he was reported to have said, had relegated the powers of the federal government to the "horse and buggy age." Social workers reported a sudden spurt in child labor in factories.

The blow to the New Deal proved far less severe than was anticipated. An economic revival had already begun, and the ground lost here was recovered subsequently by other labor legislation. Small businessmen had long complained that the codes were written by the large corporations which dominated each industry and that they inserted provisions that harmed the smaller producers. In his earlier report as chairman of the National Recovery Board of Review, Clarence Darrow supported these contentions in the following words: "Monopolists [are] expected to execute a law against the law by which they operate, with the result that the biggest producers will survive and the smallest merchants be driven out of business." That manufacturers were irritated by the generous concessions to labor was evident in a poll conducted at the end of 1935 by the National Manufacturers' Association, which revealed that its members were overwhelmingly opposed to the revival of the N.R.A. in any form.

Labor had enjoyed too direct gains from the N. R. A., however, for defeat to be accepted without a struggle. Not only had this legislation stimulated more than twenty states to enact child labor laws, but the guarantee of collective bargaining had inspired a wave of unionizing unknown during previous depressions. Working conditions had improved demonstrably in such bitterly competitive industries as cotton textile manufacturing and bituminous coal mining. In fact, pressure exerted by John L. Lewis of the United Mine Workers following the Schechter decision forced the enactment in August, 1935, of the "little N.R.A." for soft-coal mines—the Bituminous Coal Conservation Act, commonly known as the Guffey Coal Act. Roosevelt urged Congress not to permit constitutional doubts, "however reasonable, to block the suggested legislation." This Act contained the usual provisions for price agreements among operators and for guarantees as to hours, wages, and collective bargaining. It imposed a federal tax of 15 per cent on the value or price of coal at the mines, 90 per cent of which would be refunded to operators who accepted this new bituminous "code."

Shortly after the Schechter decision, Senator Wagner of New York secured the passage of the National Labor Relations Act, which reestablished the National Labor Relations Board charged with the enforcement of collective bargaining under the N.R.A. Company unions were banned, as was all other employer interference with unionizing activities. The new Board was stronger than its predecessor and had full authority to supervise elections in order to assure the free selection of employee representatives. Similar in organization to the

Federal Trade Commission, which was concerned with fair trade practices, the N.L.R.B. could investigate an employee's charge of unfair labor practices (such as intimidation, espionage, discrimination, etc.) and summon the employer for a trial hearing. If the charges were upheld, the Board could issue a cease and desist order, enforceable in a federal Circuit Court of Appeals, to halt the abuse. Dissatisfied parties had the privilege of appealing through the regular courts on points of law.

Conservatives denounced the Act as class legislation; they pointed out that the power held by the N.L.R.B. as final judge of the facts—subject only to review on purely legal points—made that body "judge, jury, and prosecutor." Liberals, however, regarded it as a counterbalancing force necessary to protect employees against the natural economic strength of employers.

A SHORT "BREATHING SPELL"

By late August, 1935, the New Deal was facing renewed attacks, even on the part of its supporters. On August 26, the day Congress adjourned, Roy Howard, head of the liberal Scripps-Howard newspaper chain and hitherto a New Dealer, wrote a widely publicized open letter to the President in which he warned that "there can be no real recovery until the fears of business have been allayed through the granting of a breathing spell to industry and a recess from further experimentation until the country can recover its losses." Roosevelt's answer showed complete agreement with this point of view. "Duty and necessity required us to move on a broad front for more than two years. . . . This basic program, however, has now reached substantial completion and the 'breathing spell' of which you speak is here—very decidedly so." With this assurance, both the press and the stock market reflected greater optimism than they had since 1931.

But the promised breathing space was brought suddenly to an end in January, 1936, when the Supreme Court refused to uphold the Agricultural Adjustment Act and, later, the Bituminous Coal Conservation Act. In United States *v.* Butler, the Court decided by a six-to-three vote—Brandeis, Stone, and Cardozo dissenting—that the processing tax was intended primarily to control agricultural production and was therefore an encroachment on the powers reserved to the states to regulate agriculture; hence it was not a true tax but constituted an exaction from one group to benefit another. The later Carter *v.* Carter Coal Company decision brought victory to small operators who resented the price control advantages enjoyed by large operators under the Guffey Act. Here again a divided Court, with the liberals in the minority, rejected a major New Deal measure. The Court held that mining was production, not commerce, and was therefore outside of the federal government's power to regulate as interstate commerce. Similarly divided decisions also nullified the Municipal Bankruptcy Act, which eased the financial position of hard-pressed local governments. Liberals were particularly incensed when the Supreme Court—again divided—declared New York's minimum wage law for women unconstitutional. An election year was not the most favorable time for Roosevelt to express his full resentment at what he regarded as the reactionary trend of the Supreme Court. Nevertheless, he issued a brief criticism of these decisions in which he said, "The ultimate results of the language of these opinions will profoundly affect the lives of Americans for years to come."

Congress acted quickly to provide a constitutional successor to the production control provisions of the A.A.A. Since once again the principal objective was to maintain farm income at the satisfactory levels of 1909–1914, the legislators fell back on the conservation power of Congress as a means of insuring crop control. A Soil Erosion Act to relieve farm distress had been passed in 1935; hence the new Act of February, 1936, took the form of a Soil Conservation and Domestic Allotment Act which stressed the necessity of conserving natural resources by means of an incidental control of production. Payments were to be made to farmers who were willing to shift from soil-depleting crops to soil-building crops—the indirect equivalent of plowing under surplus acreage.

Some of the ground lost in the Schechter decision was regained in 1936 with the passage, after considerable delay, of the Walsh-Healey Act. This legislation compelled employers who received substantial government contracts to abide by minimum wage and hour standards determined, within limits, by the Secretary of Labor, and to abolish child labor. By 1937, Congress had also found a constitutional substitute for the Guffey Coal Act.

SUBSIDIES AND AN UNBALANCED BUDGET

The shadow of imminent war in Europe compelled the President to go beyond preceding Republican administrations in subsidizing the merchant marine, for despite earlier reforms American ships were carrying an ever-dwindling tonnage. Postmaster General Farley insisted that the burdensome mail subsidies awarded to shipping be replaced by direct federal grants. The resulting Merchant Marine Act of 1936 not only effected this change but also created a new United States Maritime Commission which was empowered to grant subsidies for construction and operation. In the event that these subsidies proved ineffective, the Commission could enter the shipbuilding business itself. Although this legislation was criticized by economists, its justification was more than apparent with the outbreak of World War II in 1939.

Election year was ideal for the veterans' lobby to push through its long-deferred cash bonus bill. The Patman bill, passed in May, 1935, and promptly vetoed by Roosevelt as dangerously inflationary, had combined inflationary and pension objectives by providing that the veterans' adjusted compensation certificates be paid off by a special issue of $2,200,000,000 in treasury notes. Consequently the veterans prepared for a new battle early in 1936. The resulting bill, which provided immediate cash payment for certificates and dropped Patman's inflationary proposal, was also vetoed, but Congress overrode the veto. Since Roosevelt did not want to make the veterans' bonus a campaign issue, the Administration had to find new sources of income. It did this in the Revenue Act of 1936, which included a controversial provision for a graduated surtax on the undistributed net income of corporations, a feature which was condemned by businessmen as penalizing every weak or young corporation in the country.

Business spokesmen feared that the cost of the New Deal would mean the heaviest peacetime tax burden in the nation's history. Hoover's administration, spurred on by an impatient Congress, had shown a total deficit of over $5,000,000,000 during its last two years in office. This failure to balance the nation's budget drew Roosevelt's fire in 1932, but by the end of 1936 the Administration had raised the total deficit to $11,787,000,000. However, the veterans' bonus bill, which had been passed over Roosevelt's veto, accounted for no less than $1,773,493,000 of this total. Another unforeseen item was the burden incurred by the Treasury when the Supreme Court invalidated the processing taxes of the A.A.A., thus throwing the cost of the program directly upon the government. The national debt set a new record at the end of 1936 when it totaled more than $32,500,000,000. But English economists pointed out that our total debt, including that of local and state governments, constituted only a quarter or a fifth of the burden carried by the average Briton.

In his campaign, President Roosevelt stressed the social benefits that were being derived from the New Deal reforms and promised new economies in government. He estimated that at the present rate of business improvement recovery and relief expenditures could be reduced by one-third and over $7,000,000,000 in revenue could be collected during the coming fiscal year, thus balancing the budget. He pointed out that many of the projects were self-liquidating, and called attention to the heavy repayments already being made to the Reconstruction Finance Corporation and other lending agencies.

There was indeed cause for optimism on the part of the Democrats in the economic situation on election day in 1936. Factory employment, according to the Bureau of Labor Statistics, had risen to 96.4 per cent of the average for the middle 1920's, and payrolls had shown a similar trend. The Federal Reserve Board's index of industrial production, which had dropped from 125 in 1929 to 58 in 1932, stood at 114 on November 1, 1936. Estimates made by *The Annalist* placed the index of business activity at 107.5 per cent of normal. Roosevelt's political opponents now found sinister implications in the fact that relief and recovery expenditures continued unchecked, in spite of the improvement in business conditions. The millions who were dependent on federal largess in 1936 undoubtedly constituted a mighty political asset for the Administration, but these votes could easily be garnered without resort to the direct bribery or intimidation charged by anti-New Dealers. Few conservatives of either party were willing to admit publicly that the New Deal had saved competitive capitalism from overthrow by making timely concessions to the rising demand for social security. The lessons to be learned from Fascist Italy and Nazi Germany were lost on too many of the President's critics.

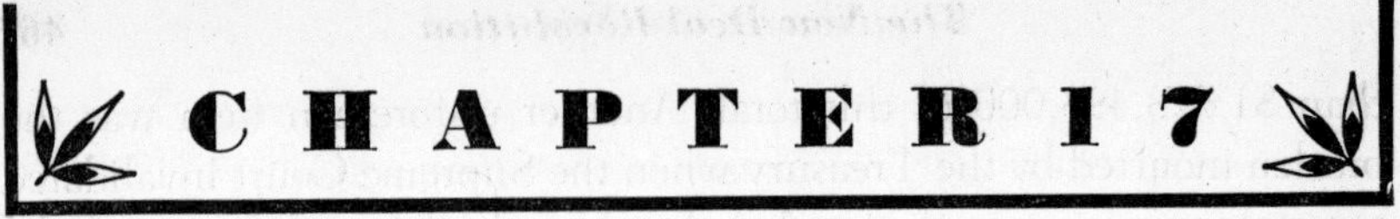

Broadening the New Deal: 1936-1941

PARTY REALIGNMENTS OF 1936

On June 9, 1936, the Republican national convention met in Cleveland, hoping to reverse the overwhelming Democratic victories of 1932 and 1934 which had swept the G.O.P. strongholds of the Middle West and the Pacific coast. Their strategy was suggested by former President Hoover when he compared the New Deal with the Communist and Fascist dictatorships in Europe and proclaimed a "holy crusade for liberty" to combat the regimentation and collectivism now held in check only by the Supreme Court. So enthusiastic was the forty-minute demonstration which followed his speech that certain observers were of the opinion that Hoover had renominated himself. Party leaders, however, had decided to bid for middle-western support by nominating Alf M. Landon of Kansas, who had been reelected governor in spite of a sectional tidal wave for the Democrats. Landon's record as a budget-balancer endeared him to those who assailed New Deal extravagance, and his support of the Bull Moose ticket in 1912 could be expected to attract progressives. His nomination on the first ballot was virtually unopposed. The vice-presidential nominee, Colonel Frank Knox, was also a former Bull Moose enthusiast and the publisher of the independent Chicago *Daily News.*

"America is in peril," warned the Republican platform as it berated the Roosevelt administration for its "frightful waste and extravagance" and its bureaucratic organization in the interest of partisan politics. The Administration was accused of prolonging the depression by frightening business and by flooding our markets with foreign goods as a result of Hull's reciprocal trade agreements. The Republican platform-writers, however, were careful to avoid giving the impression that they advocated the abolition of Roosevelt's major policies such as social security, relief, and soil-conservation subsidies to farmers; but they maintained that these aims would be best fulfilled through the honest and efficient administration of the G.O.P. Relief problems must be turned over to "non-political local agencies familiar with community problems." Further devaluation of the dollar was denounced, and Landon declared publicly that he favored a return to the gold standard—but only when this could be done without injuring the farmers. He also promised to extend the scope of the merit system and to recommend a constitutional amendment, if necessary, to abolish child labor and to protect the hours and working conditions of women in industry.

Even before the Democrats met in Philadelphia a significant bolt of northern and southern conservatives under the leadership of Alfred E. Smith had occurred. The 1928 Democratic nominee had publicly criticized the Administration's devaluation program and denounced the "boloney dollar." On January 25 he told the ultra-conservative Liberty League that, in the event the New Deal was endorsed, true Jacksonian and Cleveland Democrats could "either take on the mantle of hypocrisy or we can take a walk, and we will probably do the latter." Smith eventually threw his support to Landon. Southern Liberty Leaguers attempted vainly to break up the New Deal's hold on the Deep South by supporting the tempestuous Governor Eugene Talmadge of Georgia for President on an antiquated "white-man supremacy" and states' rights platform. In August, a short-lived conservative group, the "Jeffersonian Party," won the support of such prominent rebels as Senator James A. Reed of Missouri; former Governor Joseph B. Ely of Massachusetts; Bainbridge Colby, Wilson's Secretary of State; John W. Davis, Democratic presidential nominee in 1924; Lewis Douglas, Roosevelt's erstwhile Director of the Budget, and Alfred E. Smith himself. Here indeed was a sharp social and economic break among the Democratic leaders of the 1920's. The spirit of the conservative "gold Democrats" of 1896 had been revived after forty years. This party schism, arising from the unusual urgency of economic issues, was more than offset by a similar but less publicized Republican split caused by the desertion of low-income groups to the New Deal standard.

The Democratic convention proudly pointed to the party's record of social reform and made the New Deal philosophy the chief campaign issue. Cautiously avoiding a direct attack on the Supreme Court's power to veto unconstitutional legislation, the platform nevertheless asserted the right of Congress to legislate nationally on relief, labor conditions, and soil conservation. Roosevelt supporters secured the abolition of the historic two-thirds rule which had hitherto enabled a minority section—usually the South—to block a candidate's nomination. Southern opposition to this move was particularly strong. As anticipated, the convention renominated Roosevelt and Garner by acclamation.

The new emphasis on liberal American principles, vigorously supported by the sons of "Fighting Bob" La Follette, resulted in a national Progressive conference being held at Chicago on September 11. Among those attending were Mayor La Guardia of New York, Senator George W. Norris, Nebraska's independent Republican, and over a score of powerful labor leaders, including John L. Lewis of the United Mine Workers and Sidney Hillman of the Amalgamated Clothing Workers. The convention endorsed New Deal objectives and branded Landon as the tool of wealthy reactionaries.

Ominous charges that Fascism had become naturalized in America were heard during the summer of 1936 when a new Union party was formed. It nominated for the Presidency its founder, Representative William Lemke of North Dakota, an advocate of radical agricultural reforms, inflation, and extreme isolation in foreign affairs. His program, which included limitations on income and inheritance and restraints on finance and monopoly, was reminiscent of old-fashioned Bryanism. Lemke formed an alliance with the blatant but influential Father Charles Coughlin of Royal Oak, Michigan, and his National Union for Social Justice, an organization which claimed 8,000,000 members and supported radical monetary policies and a nebulous "living annual wage." The radio priest, who had backed Roosevelt in 1932, now publicly denounced him as a "betrayer and liar," "a scab president," and a "double-crosser." Both he and Lemke were apparently convinced that the "international bankers" had won control of the Administration in an effort to prevent the masses from wielding financial control. Townsendites, now organized as Old Age Revolving

Pensions, Ltd., were sympathetic to the Union party, for it promised more than the modest pension payments under the Social Security Act. Also pledged to Lemke was the waning Share-the-Wealth movement, now led by Huey Long's successor, the rabble-rousing Gerald L. K. Smith of Louisiana, who poured out his fiery oratory in the populist crusade of 1936. Even old General Jacob S. Coxey, famous as the leader of Coxey's Army in its march on Washington in 1894 and himself a presidential aspirant on a very minor level, joined the Lemke-Coughlin-Townsend-Smith coalition.

A NEW DEAL LANDSLIDE

To political scientists, the 1936 campaign marked a unique economic division between parties comparable only to that during the battle of 1896. Perhaps three-fourths of the metropolitan press, itself a distinct group of large business enterprises, fought the President's reelection. The small sector of big business which had supported Roosevelt in 1932 had largely deserted him for Landon; the huge steel and chemical interests in particular, and William Randolph Hearst, joined Wall Street in financing him. The Republicans' campaign expenditures totaled almost $9,000,000, as against $5,194,741 for their opponents. Most significant for the Democrats was organized labor's contribution of $770,218. Grateful liquor and tobacco interests and the sympathetic motion picture and theater industry also backed Roosevelt. In addition, Democratic officeholders were an important source of campaign revenue.

Democrats pictured Landon as a wealthy oil promoter and claimed that his budget-balancing record as governor was made possible only by federal funds and a disregard for human suffering. Father Coughlin's radio thrusts against the President were parried by the strong defense of the New Deal made by Monsignor John A. Ryan of Catholic University, who had long been considered a genuinely progressive exponent of the papal encyclicals on labor. The "old guard" Socialists broke with Norman Thomas' leftist followers and joined the American Labor party (primarily a New York State faction) in its support of the New Deal. To Landon, who sought to stress liberal aims, the backing of the ultraconservative Liberty League was a distinct liability. In campaigning, he found it difficult to convince disaffected Republicans that his election did not mean the cancellation of recent social gains. Organized labor was apathetic to his appeals.

Election day, as James Farley had predicted, brought a Democratic landslide which gave the President the electoral vote of every state except conservative Vermont and Maine, or a total of 523 to Landon's 8. His popular vote increased from 57.3 per cent of the total in 1932, to 60.7 per cent. The already large Democratic majorities in both Houses were increased by four Senators and fourteen Representatives. State and local results brought corresponding victories to the jubilant Democrats. Lemke's ambitious dream for himself and his Union party vanished when he polled only 891,858 votes. Even Norman Thomas, who had won almost 900,000 Socialist votes in 1932, lost heavily to the New Deal, receiving only 187,342 in 1936. The Communist candidates, Earl Browder and James W. Ford, the latter a Negro, polled slightly over 80,000, a decline of 22,000 since the preceding election; this, however, was probably due to the exclusion of Communist party candidates from the ballots of various states.

"NINE OLD MEN"

To Roosevelt, the election results constituted a mandate for the continuation and extension of his policies. In his second inaugural address on January 20—a new inauguration date established by the Twentieth Amendment—the President stressed the government's responsibility for the economic and social well-being of its citizens and hinted at sweeping future reforms. "The Constitution of 1787," he observed, with an eye to the conservatives on the Supreme Court bench, "did not make our democracy impotent." Turning to the pressing economic needs of the day, he said in challenging words which were swiftly broadcast throughout the country, "I see one-third of a nation ill-housed, ill-clad, ill-nourished." The past year had not brought "the promised land."

With half a dozen vital New Deal measures awaiting court tests of their constitutionality, Roosevelt determined on an immediate "frontal assault" against the Supreme Court's conservatism. His advisers, among them Thomas Corcoran, were resentful of the "nine old men" who constituted the highest federal court. Six of them had ignored the retirement age, and four of the six—McReynolds, Van Devanter, Butler, and Sutherland—were firmly opposed to the New Deal. The same criticism held true of the lower federal courts, for one out of every ten judges was over the retirement age; moreover, court opposition to the New Deal was also visible in the sweeping use of federal injunctions against Administration measures. In spite of the careful polls made by Dr. George Gallup's American Institute of Public Opinion, which showed 59 per cent of the people opposed to any effective curb on the power of the Supreme Court, the President embarked on what opponents called his "court-packing" plan.

In a message on the judiciary issued on February 5, Roosevelt proposed that for each judge in any federal court who failed to retire at the age of seventy, the President be entitled to name an additional member; the suggested maximum number of judges for the Supreme Court was put at fifteen, and that for all other federal courts at fifty. Federal judges were to be required to advise the Attorney General in advance regarding all decisions involving constitutionality and to expedite appeals to the Supreme Court. Pointing out that court dockets were overcrowded and that delay constituted a denial of justice, Roosevelt recommended that the Supreme Court appoint a proctor to facilitate its calendar and that judges of lower federal courts be transferred as needed to meet any regional pressure. This was the plan which Roosevelt believed would lead to the infusion of "new blood" into the Court. Thinking perhaps of Justice McReynolds' evolution from a Wilsonian liberal to an economic Bourbon, the President observed, "Little by little, new facts become blurred through old glasses fitted, as it were, for the needs of another generation. . . ."

When this "court-packing" plan was introduced in Congress it provoked an immediate split among the Democratic ranks that left the Republicans content to follow Senator Burton K. Wheeler of Montana and his anti-Administration Democratic wing in their fight against the bill. Roosevelt answered the charges of dictatorship in a radio address in which he asserted, "You who know me will accept my solemn assurance that in a world in which democracy is under attack, I seek to make American democracy succeed."

The battle of the judiciary lasted six months and resulted in a political defeat for the President, for the Senate Judiciary Committee reported that the judiciary bill was a "needless, futile, and utterly dangerous abandonment of constitutional principle." In effect, however, the struggle led to ultimate victory, for the Supreme Court itself took steps which made drastic court reform by Roosevelt unnecessary. One after another, basic New Deal laws were upheld during these months as Justice Roberts joined the liberal Brandeis, Stone, Cardozo, and Hughes in upholding the constitutionality of highly controversial measures. "We are now in 'Roberts' Land,'" observed Roosevelt jocosely at his press conference on April 13. In spite of early forebodings, the Wagner Labor Relations Act met the Court's approval; so did the essential features of the Social Security Act and the gold abrogation law. Then came Justice Van Devanter's announcement of his imminent retirement, thus permitting Roosevelt to make his first appointment to the Supreme Court bench. Other retirements soon followed. Although the Administration felt itself compelled to withdraw the badly battered judiciary bill and accept a watered-down substitute, its final aim had been achieved—the Court would no longer obstruct the centralizing philosophy of the New Deal's economic legislation.

An immediate outcry was raised against Roosevelt's first appointee to the Supreme Court, Senator Hugo L. Black of Alabama, long a friend of labor and civil liberties, when a Pittsburgh newspaper suddenly revealed that he had been a member of the Ku Klux Klan for a short period in 1923—a time when many a southern and middle-western politician had found it expedient to carry a Klan membership card. Black admitted this in a dramatic radio address, but repudiated the connection and pointed to the various liberal measures he had supported as evidence of his genuine opposition to intolerance. Conservatives in both Congress and the press made this a major issue, in view of Black's congressional record of New Deal loyalty. However, the Supreme Court itself interposed no objections; hence Black assumed his new position, where he soon won a reputation as a belligerent liberal and a foe of intolerance.

THE RECESSION AND THE HOUSING DRIVE

In April, 1937, Administration economists had become concerned over the sharp price rise in producers' goods. At his press conference on April 2, Roosevelt warned that certain basic materials such as copper and steel were experiencing an unjustified price rise "in an upward spiral which is at least a danger flag, judging by the past"; and he advocated a reduction in the construction of steel bridges and other permanent structures in which these high-priced materials were used. At the same time he observed that consumers' purchasing power was not keeping pace with price rises. These opinions were quickly ridiculed by business leaders and political opponents, who maintained that this was the time to curtail New Deal expenditures and to balance the budget. But by September, 1937, it was evident that the President's warning had not been unduly pessimistic, for the serious recession that began then wiped out most of the economic gains made since 1933. Not until the summer of 1938 did a decided upturn take place.

The recession afforded an ideal opportunity for attacks on the New Deal by an increasingly hostile press led by the Chicago *Tribune*. Even one-time supporters of the Administration like Raymond Moley, General Hugh Johnson, and Walter Lippmann joined conservative columnists like Mark Sullivan and Westbrook Pegler in denouncing Roosevelt's advisers—particularly Thomas Corcoran, Benjamin Cohen, and Adolph Berle—and their proposals. Conservative Democrats led by Senator Pat Harrison of Mississippi, who was chairman of the Senate Finance Committee, were convinced that business must be reassured by substantial reductions in the taxes on undistributed corporate profits and capital gains. Secretary of the Treasury Morgenthau promised to initiate an economy policy that would balance the budget.

In this crisis the President called an extraordinary session of Congress for November 15, 1937, and in successive messages outlined a broad program of domestic legislation. Housing construction, he declared, had not kept pace with the need or with population growth; at least 600,000 to 800,000 new dwelling units, costing some twelve to sixteen billion dollars, would be needed annually during the next five years. To revive the dormant construction industry would stimulate other industries; this would mean that the national income would rise and unemployment would be reduced.

Encouraged by the Supreme Court's new outlook, Roosevelt asked at the same time for another A.A.A. to curb the unprecedented crop surpluses of 1937—especially in cotton, corn, and potatoes—which threatened to cut prices to unprofitable levels. He pointed out that the year's cotton crop was the largest in history, fully five million bales more than domestic and world markets usually absorbed. Greatly extended crop restriction, he said, was imperative. For labor, he demanded effective legislation that would protect it against excessively low wages and long hours, and the abolition of child labor. He wanted to prevent local governments from using cheap labor as bait to attract industries away from other sections. Presumably, the Supreme Court in this instance would interpret the federal power to control interstate commerce generously in the interest of social reform. Finally, Roosevelt requested the reorganization of the Executive Departments in the interests of greater cohesion and efficiency, and advocated the following civil service program: "To extend the merit system upward, outward and downward to cover practically all non-policy-determining posts."

The slum-clearance plan was more than a "pump-priming" expedient to defeat the recession. As already noted, the P.W.A. had been active in this field since 1933. It had built or financed huge modern housing units for the low-income groups, such as the ambitious Jane Addams project in Chicago's "Bloody Eighteenth" ward. Enthusiasts had already announced the extinction of Memphis' "Greasy Plank" district, Atlanta's "Beaver Slide," and Cleveland's "Whiskey Island." Private initiative, aided by P.W.A. funds, undertook a slum-clearance drive in crowded New York City; the noteworthy Hillside units in the Bronx housed over 1400 families. Some fifty-one low-cost housing projects were being operated by the P.W.A. in October, 1937, when they were transferred to the newly established United States Housing Authority.

Far more intensive than the P.W.A. experiments in low-cost housing was the Wagner-Steagall Act of September, 1937, which set up the United States Housing Authority to act as banker to local public agencies in promoting low-rent apartments. The plan, which was patterned after European experience, provided for joint federal and local subsidies for every low-rent project; another section provided that as each new unit was completed, a slum area of corresponding size was to be demolished. Playgrounds might be required by the U.S.H.A. in any contract. Nathan Straus of New York, who had won a reputation as a slum-clearance expert and believed that decent housing could be provided in the larger cities at no more than five dollars per room, was chosen to head the new agency. By the beginning of 1941, the U.S.H.A. program had completed or had under construction 118,000 family dwelling units. By that time too, it was also attempting to solve the vital problem of housing accommodations for defense workers.

Roosevelt's message to the special session also stressed the need of encouraging the construction of homes apart from the government's low-rent program. To this end, the National Housing Act of 1934 was amended in February, 1938, to liberalize the loan policies of the Federal Housing Administration and to raise the total limit on insured home mortgages—if the President authorized it—from $2,000,000,000 to $3,000,000,000; by 1940 Roosevelt had used his authority to increase the limit to $4,000,000,000. In addition, the F.H.A. was authorized to insure loans made to small home owners up to 90 per cent of the appraised value of the property, instead of the former 80 per cent. Over 1,500,000 small property owners had taken advantage of these loans by 1940 and 383,000 new homes had been built. At the end of 1940, Roosevelt was able to report the heaviest amount of private construction since 1928 and to announce that the F.H.A., which had insured loans amounting to over $4,000,000,000 since 1934, was in a sound and self-sustaining position.

AIDING FARM TENANTS AND FARM OWNERS

During Roosevelt's second term, the Administration's farm program was put in motion by an assault on the evils of farm tenancy, after careful studies made by the Special Committee on Farm Tenancy. "The American dream of the family-size farm, owned by the family which operates it, has become more and more remote," the President warned Congress on February 16, 1937. "The agricultural ladder, on which an energetic young man might ascend from hired man to tenant to independent owner, is no longer serving its purpose." According to the Committee's report, one out of every four farmers was a tenant fifty years ago; now, two out of every five were in this class, and the land and buildings they occupied were valued at $11,000,000,000. Genuine security, he concluded, did not exist for half the farming population.

Congress responded by passing the Bankhead-Jones Farm Tenant Act in July, 1937; this granted federal loans to farm tenants, sharecroppers, and farm laborers who wanted to purchase farms for themselves. The program was placed under the new Farm Security Administration. Because the original appropriation of $10,000,000 was inadequate, thousands of qualified applicants were turned away. By 1940 the F.S.A. appropriation amounted to $40,000,000, and in 1941 the agency was granted $50,000,000 for its operations. The number of loans extended showed a similar rise—from 1800 the first year to 6100 three years later. Expert advice as well as loans was available to farm families on or near the relief level so that they might become self-supporting through purchasing or improving their farms. The expanding Farm Security Administration also immediately took over the homestead projects for low-income farm and city families, formerly under the Resettlement Administration.

The crop restriction plan urged by the President in his November, 1937, message to Congress became the nucleus of the Agricultural Adjustment Act of 1938, which Secretary of Agriculture Wallace called "the ever-normal granary" idea and compared with the food supply control exercised by Joseph in the land of Egypt. Glut and scarcity were to be prevented through a series of complementary programs. Marketing control of surpluses was to be imposed only after formal agreement by two-thirds of the farmers who raised the particular crops. Farmers who cooperated were to be assigned reduced acreage allotments for which they would be compensated by "conservation payments." Additional "parity payments" were to be made to cooperating farmers so that their income might be raised to its prewar relation to the income of industrial workers; but this provision was largely nullified by the failure of Congress to appropriate sufficient funds to cover its cost. Prices were to be maintained by means of government loans on surplus farm commodities which could be stored against periods of scarcity. As the result of these measures, it was expected that between fifteen and thirty million acres would be withdrawn from production in 1938. At the same time, conservation measures were to be extended to include all types of erosion control.

Congress included in the new A.A.A. an "all-risk" crop insurance plan requested by the President in February, 1937, when he called attention to the widespread demand for the equalizing of any economic burden due to such "acts of God" as droughts and floods. The

Federal Crop Insurance Corporation was accordingly set up within the Department of Agriculture to provide insurance and research that would protect wheat farmers against such losses. From 50 to 75 per cent of the crop, based on the past average yield, was insured against drought, flood, hail, tornadoes, insects, and blights. Premiums in the form of crops were gathered into storaged reserves which could be applied to lean years, thus stabilizing farm income and consumers' stocks. By 1940, 378,000 wheat growers had purchased crop insurance.

Roosevelt defended this new invasion of the insurance field by pointing out that private insurance had hitherto been handicapped by the overwhelming nature of the risk, which was necessarily confined to limited areas, and by the lack of actuarial data. However, crop insurance was not extended to cotton and other crops because of the early losses suffered by the Federal Crop Insurance Corporation in wheat insurance. The entire crop insurance idea was still in an experimental stage. The Administration expected that this program could ultimately be made an integral part of a national resources planning system that would promote soil and water conservation and better land utilization.

WAGE "FLOORS" AND HOUR "CEILINGS"

Roosevelt's message of November, 1937, spurred Congress to take long-deferred action on significant labor legislation which resulted in the Fair Labor Standards Act, passed in June, 1938. This bill had been almost buried by John J. O'Connor, chairman of the House Rules Committee, whom the Administration regarded as a reactionary obstructionist. In one of his radio "fireside chats," Roosevelt praised the new law as ranking next to the Social Security Act in being "the most far-reaching, farsighted program for the benefit of workers ever adopted here or in any other country." The law was intended, as the President put it, to place "a floor below which wages shall not fall, and a ceiling beyond which the hours of industrial labor shall not rise."

Fears regarding the constitutionality of minimum wage laws had been largely dissipated, for the Supreme Court decision in West Coast Hotel Co. *v.* Parrish in the spring of 1937 reopened the door to this type of legislation and reversed the decision in Adkins *v.* Children's Hospital (1923) which had looked upon such laws as an infringement of the freedom of contract guaranteed by the Fifth Amendment. As anticipated, the Supreme Court, now including largely New Dealers, upheld the Fair Labor Standards Act in February, 1941. This also overcame the last legal obstacle resulting from Hammer *v.* Dagenhart (1918), which had nullified a federal law forbidding the interstate shipment of goods produced with child labor. The Supreme Court seemed to have broken with its traditional economic individualism.

The Fair Labor Standards Act was expected to reduce unemployment, estimated by the Commissioner of Labor Statistics in 1938 as affecting between eight and ten million workers. A maximum basic work week of forty-eight hours was established—this was subsequently reduced to forty—and payment for overtime was fixed at one and a half times the regular rate. To increase mass purchasing power, a wage floor of twenty-five cents an hour was set; this was to be raised at stated intervals until the minimum hourly rate was forty cents. The employment of children under sixteen years of age was prohibited in industries engaged in interstate commerce. The child labor provisions were applied by the Children's Bureau of the Department of Labor, and the rest of the Act was administered by a new Wage and Hour Division established within that Department.

Here was no mere paper legislation. The new Act made unnecessary the long-debated child labor amendment, which still required action by eight states for ratification. Similarly it aided in removing the drastic regional wage and hour differences which had previously weakened state social legislation. Sweated industries, such as textile manufacturing, benefited immediately from the Act, for many employees were paid a basic rate above the thirty-cent minimum. By 1941, the minimum hourly rate had risen to thirty cents and over 13,000,000 persons were protected by the new law.

THE FIGHT FOR EXECUTIVE REORGANIZATION

Roosevelt's efforts to secure the passage of a reorganization bill met far greater resistance. The bill, as introduced, provided for six executive assistants to aid the President in departmental problems, and for two new departments—Public Works, and Social Welfare. It empowered the President to link various independent agencies with the executive departments. The bill also provided for a revision of the powers of the Comptroller General, whose extensive control over the nation's spending programs had long been a thorn in the side of the New Deal; and it called for the creation of a Civil Service Administrator and the extension of the civil service along the lines suggested in the President's November message.

However, the "dictator bill," as Colonel Robert McCormick's Chicago *Tribune* promptly labeled it, fell before the opposition of the House of Representatives, spurred on by savage newspaper attacks. To the New Dealers, the chief antagonistic propaganda seemed to come from the ubiquitous Father Coughlin, who saw in the bill a hidden scheme of the President to dominate the nation's educational system. Such fears were expressed in the flood of Coughlin-inspired telegrams and letters which swept Congress. Once more, as with the Fair Labor Standards Act, Roosevelt's chief foe, Representative O'Connor, led the House attack on the bill.

Wearily, Roosevelt reiterated that he had no inclination to be a dictator. He pointed out that the bill resulted from recommendations made by his non-partisan Committee on Administrative Management—headed by three well-known political scientists, Louis Brownlow, Dr. Charles E. Merriam, and Dr. Luther Gulick—which had been asked to provide "twentieth-century machinery with which to carry out a twentieth-century program." Most of the proposals that were now subjects of controversy had already been recommended by Republican administrations. Roosevelt was particularly criticized because of his request for authority to reorganize the various administrative departments, especially the civil service, in spite of the fact that his actions would be subject to congressional approval. Many new bureaus had been created during his Administration, and he was loath to entrust the process of their coordination directly to Congress, for individual Congressmen might insert regulations calculated to obstruct the New Deal program. Even Hoover, who as President had insisted on the need for thorough executive reorganization under his direction, saw a potential threat to civil liberties in the bill and charged that Roosevelt sought to dominate the civil service and the semi-judicial bodies within the governmental agencies.

Although the Senate passed the bill in March, 1938, by a vote of 49 to 42, the House rejected it by a similarly close vote—204 to

196. Interestingly enough, when the election of 1938 was over and the partisan clamor had died down, another reorganization bill, similar to the first in many controversial aspects, became law in 1939 without undue opposition. Roosevelt followed this victory with the successful presentation of five more plans for executive reorganization during 1939 and 1940.

In the face of resistance from certain patronage-hungry Congressmen of both parties, the President and his supporters on February 1, 1939, put in force an essential part of his civil service program. A division of Personnel Supervision and Management was set up under the Civil Service Commission to supervise the appointment and training of employees in each federal agency. Important also in this respect was the Ramspeck-O'Mahoney Postmaster Act of June, 1938, which brought all postmasterships of the first, second, and third classes under the merit system; 14,798 employees were affected. Roosevelt sought to bring 81,000 positions under the civil service by Executive order, but Congress whittled this down to 24,000. By February, 1939, three-fourths of all government employees had come under the merit system, as compared with two-thirds in June, 1938.

RECOVERY AND TAX REFORM

When the recession reached new depths during the spring of 1938, Roosevelt on April 14 made additional recommendations to Congress designed to stimulate recovery. He was convinced that the public works program of 1937 had tapered off too quickly and that the new Social Security taxes were drawing on much-needed purchasing power. His proposal for a huge public works program was favored by the fact that a congressional election campaign was not far off. The current session of Congress voted a total of $3,750,000,000 for work relief, public works, housing, rural electrification, the National Youth Administration, and other similar programs. The largest appropriation, $1,425,000,000, was for the W.P.A., which was expected to employ three million men between then and March 1, 1939; another $965,000,000 was allocated to give the P.W.A. a million workers; $300,000,000 went to slum clearance and low-cost housing; the N.Y.A. appropriation enabled it to aid an estimated 600,000 youths. Apart from this huge program, a five-year flood control system at a cost of

$375,000,000 was approved. The Reconstruction Finance Corporation was authorized to expend $1,500,000,000 in loans to business. But long before the full effect of these programs was apparent, a definite trend toward recovery became evident.

During that same congressional session the Administration fought a losing battle to retain several of the major tax reforms achieved in 1934 and 1936, notably those affecting undistributed corporate profits and capital gains. The New Dealers resented the practice of large corporations whereby, in order to escape heavy progressive income taxes, they passed their dividends and consequently left their undistributed profits subject only to a corporation tax which was relatively modest. This gave corporations a decided advantage over partnerships and individually owned firms. When the earlier tax measures were under consideration, Roosevelt had agreed to congressional demand that small corporations be exempted. But the session of 1938 reduced the tax rate on undistributed profits to a point so low as to make it ineffective in compelling corporations with surplus profits to declare dividends. The capital gains tax, which largely affected income derived from the stock market and from real estate, was reduced from the existing progressive rate to the same flat rate that applied to "productive types of income." Roosevelt considered vetoing the Revenue Act of 1938, which was supported by conservative Democrats in an attempt to mollify business, but since it contained various partly compensating features, he permitted it to become law without his signature, a novel procedure for him. He also continued his efforts, eventually with some success, to remove undesirable tax immunities and legal loopholes used by the "upper bracketeers."

THE TEMPORARY NATIONAL ECONOMIC COMMITTEE

The Administration also opened a drive against monopoly during the spring of 1938. Critics inside and out of Congress had criticized the New Deal's compromises with big business under the N.R.A., and Roosevelt himself, in discussing the unjustifiably high prices for copper and steel early in 1937, had implied that monopolist forces were responsible for the recession. Furthermore, his sustained assault on holding companies indicated that, like Brandeis, he believed in restoring a genuine competitive system. Consequently, in his message to

Congress on April 29, 1938, he denounced the increasing concentration of economic power. Less than 5 per cent of all the corporations reporting to the Bureau of Internal Revenue in 1935, he said, owned 87 per cent of the total assets; one tenth of one per cent received 50 per cent of the net income. This was reflected, he went on, in a maldistribution of income; according to the estimates of the National Resources Committee for 1935–1936, 47 per cent of the nation's families and single individuals living alone had an income of less than $1000 a year; and the upper 1.5 per cent of American households received a share of the national income equal to that of the 47 per cent at the bottom.

This concentrated private economic power, warned the President, was endangering democratic government. "No people," he declared, "least of all a people with our traditions of personal liberty, will endure the slow erosion of opportunity for the common man, the oppressive sense of helplessness under the domination of a few, which are overshadowing our whole economic life." Government leadership was needed to cope with this concentration of private power. "We must find practical controls over blind economic forces as well as over blindly selfish men." The earlier anti-trust laws, he felt, had been too limited in scope to be effective. For all these reasons he asked Congress to initiate a thorough study of economic concentration in the country, to improve anti-trust procedure by strengthening the power of the government, to extend federal control over mergers and interlocking business relationships, especially bank holding companies, and to amend the patent laws so that inventions would not be suppressed or industrial monopolies encouraged.

Congress responded by setting up the Temporary National Economic Committee, composed of Senators and Congressmen, three Cabinet members, and representatives of the Federal Trade Commission and the Securities and Exchange Commission. Senator Joseph O'Mahoney was appointed chairman. Public hearings, which began December 1, 1938, and continued until April 26, 1940, investigated almost every phase of economic life and resulted in thirty-nine volumes of reports. By the end of 1941, forty-three scientific monographs and various reports based on the findings of the T.N.E.C. had been issued.

On the whole, the Committee's conclusions supported Roosevelt's contention that the American system of private enterprise had been profoundly altered by the process of rapid economic concentration characteristic of the preceding four decades. Most of his specific recommendations, including the repeal of the controversial Miller-Tydings Act of 1937 which legalized retail price-fixing for branded or trade-marked articles, were adopted in the Committee's early reports. Although critics maintained that the Committee was biased from the outset in favor of the President's views on monopoly, its reports regarding centralized management and price and credit control—especially in insurance and in the steel, petroleum, and building industries—were nevertheless conclusive. Its final report of March 31, 1941, endorsed the competitive principle but at the same time supported such economic experiments of the government as low-cost housing. It recommended geographic decentralization of industry and the removal of interstate barriers to trade, and condemned such monopolist controls as retail price-fixing laws and monopolies in basic materials. However, it remained to be seen how far the influence of the T.N.E.C. would redirect the nation's future economic life into competitive channels.

THE CAMPAIGN TO LIBERALIZE THE DEMOCRATIC PARTY

The events that had occurred since the election of 1936 gave new importance to congressional and local elections in 1938. Bourbon Democrats and Tory Republicans joined hands to defeat the Supreme Court reform and the reorganization bill; they likewise blamed the recession on the Administration's policy of "strangling business" and they endeavored to water down its tax reforms. Public opinion, according to the press, was alarmed by the sudden upsurge of militant labor unions like John L. Lewis' Committee for Industrial Organization, encouraged as they were by the New Deal's guarantee of collective bargaining. The unprecedented wave of sit-down strikes, especially in the steel industry, suggested to the timid and conservative alike that a red revolution was at hand. Roosevelt, who with his close advisers was apparently sensitive to the charges brought by the liberals that the New Deal was still far short of its objectives, wished to prevent a return to the personal politics of the 1920's which had made Republican and Democratic philosophies almost identical. His conviction that the Democratic party must be made the genuinely liberal party of the nation was the key to his decision to intervene actively in the 1938 primaries in behalf of the nomination and election of liberal Democrats.

In the Georgia primaries, President Roosevelt opposed the renomination of Senator Walter George; as he put it, on some questions the Senator and he did not "speak the same language." But the conservative Senator undertook a strenuous campaign and won. Also unsuccessful were the President's campaigns against the renomination of Senator Millard Tydings of Maryland and of "Cotton Ed" Smith of South Carolina. However, he was successful in his efforts toward the renomination of Alben Barkley of Kentucky, the New Deal majority leader, and the elimination of Representative John J. O'Connor of New York, a bitter foe of the Administration.

The hostile press immediately labeled Roosevelt's intervention as a "purge" à la Moscow which sought to destroy everyone who disagreed with him and to dictate how the American people should vote. Despite their Democratic affiliation, conservative southern newspapers denounced the President as a new Napoleon and a "power-drunk" dictator, and the nominally Democratic New York *Times* observed, "How great an intellectual servitude the President now requires from his followers." Charges were made that Administrator Harry Hopkins was using W.P.A. funds to coerce relief workers to support Administration candidates, but investigation disproved them. There were also reports of a break between the Chief Executive and Postmaster General Farley, who held that the Democratic National Committee should support the party's nominees regardless of their views on the New Deal.

Both the primaries and the elections themselves failed to fulfill the President's desire of converting the Democratic party into a thoroughly liberal organization. The party lost 67 seats in the House of Representatives and 6 in the Senate; and even though it still retained a comfortable majority in Congress, a large number of Democratic Congressmen were hardly sympathetic to the New Deal. New York's Governor Lehman narrowly escaped defeat at the hands of Thomas E.

Dewey, New York County's vigorous district attorney. A severe disappointment to the Administration was Frank Murphy's failure to be reelected governor of Michigan, largely because his sympathy to labor during the Detroit strikes had made powerful enemies for him. The outlook for 1940 seemed uncertain for the New Deal, but the nation's increasing prosperity and the danger of war with the Axis bolstered the President's leadership.

JOHN MARSHALL'S SHADOW

As 1939 began, the country's attention was increasingly focused on foreign affairs and the menace of Fascist aggression; consolidation of past gains was the keynote in domestic affairs. Roosevelt optimistically observed in his annual message to Congress on January 4, that with a few exceptions, "the past three Congresses have met in part or in whole the pressing needs of the new order of things. . . . We have now passed the period of internal conflict in the launching of our program of social reform. Our full energies may now be released to invigorate the processes of recovery in order to preserve our reforms, and to give every man and woman who wants to work a real job at a living wage." He reassured those who were worried by the mounting national debt of $40,000,000,000—almost one-third of which was attributable to New Deal policies—by pointing out that our national income was also rising and might soon reach $80,000,000,000 annually.

Tax legislation of a novel type was repeatedly presented to Congress by the President. In two significant cases the Supreme Court had opened the way to the abolition of reciprocal federal-state tax immunities that had been firmly established by John Marshall's famous decision, "The power to tax is the power to destroy," handed down in McCulloch *v.* Maryland, a case involving Maryland's right to tax a branch of the United States Bank at Baltimore. In Helvering *v.* Gerhardt, decided May 16, 1938, the Court held that the salary received by an employee of the Port of New York Authority was subject to a federal income tax, thus depriving state employees of their traditional immunity to federal taxation. The converse of this was established on March 27, 1939, in Graves *v.* O'Keefe, which held that an employee of the federal Home Owners' Loan Corporation was subject to a state income tax.

Even before the Helvering decision in 1938, Roosevelt had proposed the abolition of these reciprocal tax immunities as they affected government employees and both federal and state bonds. Consequently, on the basis of these two significant decisions, Congress passed the Public Salary Tax Act of 1939, which allowed the taxing of federal employees by state and local governments and made employees of the latter subject to the federal income tax. Not until the Public Debt Act was enacted in 1941 did Congress remove a popular means of tax evasion when it provided that holders of U. S. government bonds must pay a federal income tax; the Senate, however, defeated an Administration attempt to extend federal income taxes to state and local bondholders and to allow local governments to tax the income derived from U. S. government obligations. "It is difficult for almost all citizens to understand why a constitutional provision permitting taxes on 'income from whatever source derived' does not mean 'from whatever source derived,'" said Roosevelt in 1939. Nevertheless, he considered these two tax bills a victory for the democratic principle of taxation on the basis of ability to pay.

LIBERALIZING THE SOCIAL SECURITY ACT

As a result of recommendations made in January, 1939, by the Social Security Board, Congress expanded the existing pension provisions that year. This legislation provided that old age insurance was hereafter to be known as Old Age and Survivors' Insurance, and created a special trust fund under that title. Maritime workers and employees of agencies affiliated with the federal government were included in the insured classes, and survivors of an insured employee—particularly dependent children, widows over 65 years of age or younger widows with dependent children, and dependent parents—were made eligible to receive his old age benefits. The tax on employers and employees was frozen at the existing rate of one per cent until 1942, instead of being sharply increased as originally planned; this meant a substantial saving to those affected.

The ideal of a "welfare state" that would actively raise the economic and social level of the people was rapidly advanced during 1939–1941. By June, 1941, over 2,170,000 aged persons who were not covered by Old Age and Survivors' Insurance were receiving from combined federal and local sources assistance averaging $21.08 a month for the nation as a whole. At the same time federal grants-in-aid stimulated extensive state welfare programs that cared for 917,000 dependent children and provided pensions for 50,000 blind persons; millions were spent annually for maternal and child welfare, for vocational retraining of the physically handicapped, and for new health services for the low-income groups. Conservatives led by the American Medical Association stubbornly resisted the wholesale extension of federal aid to the field of medicine as "socialized medicine"; they maintained that no one in this country was being denied medical care because of poverty. Congress remained cool to the Administration's National Health Bill, sponsored by Senator Robert F. Wagner of New York in 1939, which would have extended the principle of social insurance to industrially disabled workers.

THE LIQUIDATION OF RELIEF

Although relief expenditures dropped, certain agencies were continued on a declining but still appreciable scale because of their importance to the nation's welfare and defense. As conditions improved, the W.P.A. came under the fire of Senator Byrd of Virginia, who combined his drive for economy with the demand by Congress that radicals be removed from these projects. Eligibility rules for W.P.A. applicants became more stringent, appropriations were slashed repeatedly —in 1941 they dropped to less than $60,000,000—and finally, in 1942, the agency was voted out of existence. The W.P.A. administrators claimed an impressive record. Their expenditures of $10,468,-000,000 (plus an additional $2,723,000,000 contributed by those who sponsored the various projects) for 1935–1942 directly benefited some 8,500,000 people. To aid our defense effort, the W.P.A. workers built 285 airports and enlarged or improved 500 more, together with 700 miles of runways; they also constructed 77,000 bridges and viaducts, and numerous barracks, mess halls, storehouses, military and naval reservations, and other war facilities; in addition, workers were trained for vital industries. Market-bound farmers and pleasure-bound motorists could enjoy 644,000 additional miles of good roads and streets.

W.P.A. workers served school children free lunches on a large scale in working-class districts, conducted them safely across busy thoroughfares, and constructed innumerable playground and other recreational facilities for children. Among the 122,000 public buildings built by this agency were many schools, hospitals, and libraries. Women workers made millions of garments and pieces of furniture for the needy. The diversity of cultural, professional, and technical projects conserved the talents of men and women, many of whom possessed creative ability of a high order. Perhaps most important of all was the fact that the W.P.A. preserved such human intangibles as morale and dignity.

By 1941 the P.W.A. like the W.P.A. was engaged in liquidating its extensive activities, after spending over six billions of the public funds for 34,465 projects that affected practically every county in the nation. This involved substantial construction work of all types for federal agencies, local and state governments, and the railroads. Somewhat more fortunate than these two agencies was the Civilian Conservation Corps, which managed to weather Senator Byrd's campaign to abolish it until 1942, when nearly all its activities ceased. Its total expenditures of $2,900,000,000 over a nine-year period were offset by many assets. Three million men were given jobs and useful training and were enabled to send $7,000,000 home to needy dependents. They planted entire forests, built over 125,000 miles of truck trails, 89,000 miles of telephone lines, and 4000 fire and observation towers; their success in combating forest fires meant a substantial reduction in timber losses. Although the N.Y.A. survived these years, most of its activities shifted from subsidizing needy youths, especially students, to the problem of meeting labor shortages by training young men and women for defense and, finally, war jobs. All in all, the results achieved by the agencies for the nation were far more than incidental "pump priming."

By successive reorganization acts, the first of which was enacted in 1939, the President was able to consolidate the heterogeneous mass of relief agencies into an efficient cohesive form. All public construction agencies were placed under the Federal Works Agency, and an Executive Office of the President was organized to absorb such planning agencies as the National Resources Board and the Bureau of the Budget. Lending agencies, including the R.F.C., the F.H.A., and the Export-Import Bank, were brought under the Federal Loan Agency; farm lending agencies, however, were transferred to the Department of Agriculture. The Federal Security Agency absorbed most of the nation's health and welfare bureaus, among them the Public Health Service, the Social Security Board, the United States Employment Service, the Office of Education, the N.Y.A., and the C.C.C. Thus a new sense of permanence was given the revolutionary legislation of 1933–1939.

T.V.A.: POLITICAL STORM CENTER

During the later 1930's, a titanic struggle raged between the Tennessee Valley Authority and the Commonwealth and Southern Corporation, which had plants in eleven states, including six southern states. This conflict dramatized the increasing rivalry between public and private operation of electric power sources and, for many, the struggle of private enterprise for survival against the planned economy of the New Deal. On January 4, 1934, the T.V.A. had concluded contracts with several of the Corporation's subsidiaries. These contracts, which expired during the summer of 1936, provided for an interchange of power and the T.V.A.'s use of private transmission lines.

Roosevelt wanted to reduce rates by creating a southeastern power pool under the T.V.A., but he suspended negotiations abruptly when nineteen utility companies obtained an injunction restraining the agency's activities. This action he branded as "judicial sabotage." Thereafter, in drawing up new power contracts, the T.V.A. dealt directly with municipalities and cooperatives as well as private companies. Finally, on December 29, 1939, a contract was made with the Commonwealth and Southern Corporation involving limited cooperation in the exchange and sale of surplus power, both steam-generated and hydroelectric.

On January 30, 1939, in Tennessee Electric Power Company *v.* Tennessee Valley Authority, the liberalized Supreme Court again came to the rescue of the New Deal by upholding the T.V.A. and its electric power activities against the Tennessee company, a Commonwealth and Southern subsidiary. The Court also upheld the government's policy of making loans and grants to municipalities for the construction of power distribution systems. When he was unable to persuade the T.V.A. to sell its power business to the Tennessee Electric Power Company, Wendell Willkie, president of Commonwealth and

Southern, sold the thirty-five-year-old subsidiary to the T.V.A., which now dominated the valley's electrical enterprises. Willkie, however, won the applause of many businessmen for his long and skillful battle against government enterprise, and for selling the subsidiary for some $30,000,000 more than T.V.A. officials offered at first. As a result, he became the champion of those who feared that the New Deal was heading toward socialism. After the sale of the Commonwealth and Southern subsidiary, other private utilities in Tennessee, northern Alabama, and northeastern Mississippi followed its example and sold out to the T.V.A.

The T.V.A. apparently had come to stay. By January, 1941, it was supplying electric power to 425,000 consumers, many of whom were enjoying the benefits of electricity for the first time. As the war spread in Europe, the T.V.A. modernized the ammonium nitrate plant at Muscle Shoals and turned to the manufacture of munitions. Huge government-built dams, like Norris Dam, rose as symbols of a future planned economy as well as a yardstick by which to measure the cost of electricity, and served directly to stem periodic floods. In 1937 the War Department completed its ambitious Bonneville project on the Columbia River some sixty miles from Portland, Oregon, a project whose primary purpose was to improve navigation and operate the fishways; the sale of surplus power to municipalities and cooperatives was incidental. The Grand Coulee Dam, another Columbia River project, was undertaken by the Bureau of Reclamation primarily for irrigation, but also for the production and sale of electric power.

The government's activities in the power field won another victory with the Flood Control Act of 1938, which not only gave the federal government title to all flood control dams, reservoir projects, and other related properties, but empowered it to exercise authority over potential electric power sources. The dream of cheap power, serving areas never touched before and stimulating economic and social life in backward regions, seemed on the road to realization.

THE ELECTION OF 1940

By 1940, the leading political issue, according to the Gallup Poll, was keeping out of the war. But both parties and their standard-bearers held such similar positions on this issue that attention was arbitrarily focused on the domestic issues of recovery and reform. The Republican national convention which met in Philadelphia on June 24 at first seemed pledged to either Thomas E. Dewey of New York or Robert A. Taft of Ohio. However, Wendell Willkie's struggle with the T.V.A. had brought him to the fore as a potential political leader. He waged a sensational pre-convention campaign unusual in Republican annals, and received 105 votes on the first ballot and 659 votes on the sixth, whereupon he was nominated unanimously. The nomination for Vice President went to Charles L. McNary of Oregon, who had been associated with the McNary-Haugen bill in the twenties and who enjoyed considerable popularity among farmers.

This time the Republicans named a man who not only regarded himself as a La Follette liberal but had supported Roosevelt and voted the Democratic ticket as recently as 1932. As a delegate to the Democratic convention in 1924, he had backed Smith against McAdoo on the Ku Klux Klan issue. A leading utility executive who as a foe of the T.V.A. had been front-page copy for several years, he now symbolized the bipartisan conservative reaction to the New Deal. Actually, like Landon, Willkie professed himself in sympathy with many Administration objectives, but differed as to the manner of their execution. "Party lines are down," he said in his acceptance speech. "Nothing could make that clearer than the nomination by the Republicans of a liberal Democrat who changed his party affiliation because he found democracy in the Republican party and not in the New Deal party." He charged that the Administration had restricted the opportunities of businessmen and put farmers on the dole. "I say that this course will lead us to economic disintegration and dictatorship." He favored substituting "unlimited productivity" for "distributed scarcity." As far as foreign affairs were concerned, he held that Roosevelt had endangered the nation by making rash threats against Germany and Italy and had failed in our national defense program.

Before their convention met in Chicago on July 15, the Democrats made certain basic decisions as to their future course. France had already fallen before Hitler's mechanized might and events had proved that the military strength and diplomatic unscrupulousness of the Nazis had been underestimated. Despite the protests of a small minority within the party, the Democrats disregarded the anti-third term tradition and "drafted" Roosevelt on the first ballot. For full measure, they followed his recommendation and nominated Secretary of Agriculture Henry A. Wallace for Vice President. "The world is undergoing violent changes," their platform declared. "Humanity, uneasy in this machine age, is demanding a sense of security and dignity based on human values." It went on to make the following specific pledge regarding foreign affairs: "We will not participate in foreign wars, and we will not send our Army, naval or air forces to fight in foreign lands outside of the Americas, except in case of attack." The rest of the platform elaborated on the benefits of the New Deal to all Americans, Negro as well as white.

As in previous campaigns, Roosevelt made the New Deal the main issue and stressed his record of social and economic reconstruction. He made one sensational charge: "There are some banks now using money to advertise, or to send letters to their depositors, hinting that unless this administration is defeated, the deposits of their banks will be in danger." Willkie, in return, charged that the third term endangered individual liberty and warned that 1940 might be our last free election. He declared that whereas, before 1914, liberals (like himself) had fought the domination of the people by big business, "We now face the domination of the people by Big Government."

Various Gallup Polls during 1938–1940 had discovered certain interesting currents of opinion behind the election of 1940. Slightly less than half the people polled in 1938 objected to a third term for any President—but this was before Hitler had overrun Europe. Although 66 per cent favored the Administration's becoming more conservative, over 90 per cent endorsed old age pensions and 78 per cent advocated making the C.C.C. permanent. In a poll of farmers in March, 1940, 73 per cent thought that Secretary Wallace had "done a good job." Legislation in behalf of farm tenants, federal maternity care, and minimum wages and maximum hours was heavily endorsed. In March, 1940, the poll indicated victory for the Democrats by 55 per cent—an accurate estimate of the final results.

Once more Roosevelt gained a substantial victory, although by margins considerably reduced since 1936. However, an important wedge was driven in the Middle West by the Republicans, for in addition to Landon's faithful Maine and Vermont, Willkie carried Colorado, Indiana (his home state), Iowa, Kansas, Michigan, Nebraska, and North and South Dakota; this gave him a total of 82 electoral votes to the President's 449. The popular vote, following the Gallup forecast, gave Roosevelt 27,243,466 to Willkie's impressive 22,304,755. The Socialist candidate, Norman Thomas, dropped to a new low of approximately 100,000 votes, and Earl Browder, the Communist candidate, received less than 50,000. The Democrats retained their control of Congress practically unchanged. Nevertheless, there were unmistakable signs of reviving Republican strength. In New York's gubernatorial race, for example, Thomas E. Dewey would undoubtedly have beaten Governor Lehman had not the American Labor party decided the latter's election by casting its 420,000 votes in his favor. Lehman was a candidate, much against his inclination, Roosevelt having persuaded him that he was needed to keep pivotal New York in the Democratic column.

As war drew closer in 1941, liberals wondered whether our hard-won domestic gains of eight years could survive a new world catastrophe. The prestige of popular democracy in Europe was at low ebb, and Fascist paternalism was advancing to new positions along both the ideological and the military fronts. Ambitious leaders were anxious to naturalize Fascism on our soil. Would Roosevelt's New Deal reenact the tragedy ascribed to Léon Blum's Popular Front in France? This was the fear expressed by Wendell Willkie and his associates in utter disregard of the fact that the nation's leadership in Washington had seldom ever been so vigorous and determined. Would a war in the name of democracy destroy civil liberties at home and revive the Red Hunt and class hatreds of 1919–1921? Some progressives like John T. Flynn, formerly on the staff of the *New Republic,* and the young La Follettes were ready to answer in the affirmative.

CHAPTER 18

The Thirties: An Era of Social Planning

THE PSYCHOLOGY OF RESTRICTED OPPORTUNITY

The shattering impact of the great depression on the 1930's seemed to accelerate the basic trends that had characterized American life for several generations. The birth rate declined sharply; the size of families decreased; and political and economic life assumed an ever more highly centralized form at the expense of local and regional initiative. The process of secularization in religion and popular philosophy was only momentarily interrupted. Recreation became even more a business enterprise, and increased communication and transportation facilities gave greater mobility to the population.

But the social pendulum swung back from the extreme individualism of the 1920's as the economic breakdown of the early thirties revealed the tragic inadequacy of the isolated individual in the face of widespread unemployment and general insecurity. The small family unit, broken up by the increasing divorce rate and shorn of many of its traditional functions, offered only limited aid to its stranded members. Equally helpless were the church and the local community, financially unable to meet their new burdens. Any neighborhood spirit in the great urban centers had long ago declined; in fact, the depression reversed the movement from farm to city.

Our historic faith in unlimited individual opportunity gave way to a pessimistic belief that the limits of economic expansion had been reached. Competition for jobs followed the jungle spirit of survival and pitted youths against their elders, strained race relations, and gave plausibility to the Marxian concept of an eternal class war. When local and private institutions faltered, the federal government assumed the leadership and offered a new social cohesion. The active "welfare state," stressing collectivism in various degrees, had already become a reality in other parts of the world.

Those who were convinced that we had entered a period of restricted opportunity cited our current population statistics as their authority. In the decade of the thirties the population increase—from 122,775,000 to 131,669,000—showed a decline to the unprecedentedly low rate of 7.2 per cent, less than half that in any previous decade, according to Professor Philip M. Hauser, the sociologist. Marriages during the depression were relatively few and long deferred. In 1916, births had occurred at the rate of 25 per 1000 of the population, but by 1929 this had fallen to 18.9; in 1933 it declined still further, to 16.6, and rose only slightly thereafter during the decade. However, this over-all decline in the birth rate was partly offset by the decrease in the death rate resulting from gains made by medical science.

A related population phenomenon of the period was the excess of emigration over immigration, which amounted to some 47,000—a sharp contrast with the immigration excess of millions before the mid-1920's. For example, Mexicans who had come here during the 1920's returned to their homeland in overwhelming numbers. The prolific immigrant peoples, experts pointed out, would soon die out, and the nation would be left with an ever-larger old age population, with all its social and economic implications. The psychology of limited opportunity became even more manifest after 1937 when German-Jewish refugees, many of them exceptional in training and achievement, sought refuge from terrorism. Only a few were permitted to enter this country except during 1939, when 43,274—scarcely the flood envisaged by restrictionists and anti-Semites—were admitted.

The depression generated a new westward movement, especially from the stricken dust bowl of the Great Plains. The population of Los Angeles showed a spectacular increase during the decade, from 1,238,048 to 1,504,277. San Diego and other urban areas in Southern California also grew, but San Francisco and the coastal cities farther north remained almost stationary. Among the larger cities whose population decreased were Philadelphia, Cleveland, St. Louis, Boston, and Newark. The South, benefiting from its new industrialization as well as its traditionally high birth rate, lost far fewer people than did the northern and central states. Notwithstanding the general decline in urban growth, the rate of growth of southern cities was higher than ever before in their history.

FAMILY LIFE DURING THE DEPRESSION

Family life reflected the depression in a variety of ways. The marriage rate during 1932 was the lowest in history but had markedly recovered by 1934. The divorce rate also declined in 1932 but rose so rapidly thereafter that it exceeded the high record set during the 1920's. The divorce mill in Reno, Nevada, turned even more rapidly in 1934 when the residence requirement was cut from three months to a brief six weeks. The American home had an average of three children at the opening of the century, but by 1940 there were one or two. Competition for jobs forced many school boards and civil service commissions to bar married women.

At the onset of the depression, according to the Lynds, "Middletown" experienced a temporary breakdown in middle-class morals marked by sexual license and a vogue for "bathtub gin" parties. As the depression wore on, its inhabitants "ate out" less and bought fewer cars and less jewelry, candy, clothes, and furniture; filling stations, however, enjoyed relative prosperity because automobiles, even antiquated ones, were considered a necessity. During the crisis years, middle-class families feared the possibility of a radical uprising, and some even stored food in their cellars against the coming revolution. According to Dr. Elsie Clews Parsons, the noted sociologist, the average family reverted to extremely conservative habits in this decade, in contrast to the adventurousness of the 1920's.

The collapse of private and local resources compelled the federal government to assume an increasing share of the relief burden in 1932. Local charity with its bread lines and soup kitchens had failed to cope with the emergency. Professional hobos were soon joined by an army of amateurs, many of them women, who overflowed from the park benches to the cots made available by missions and churches, and even slept in city halls and public libraries. The New Deal provided temporary homes through the Farm Security Administration, and work in the Civilian Conservation Corps for some of these transients.

Early in the depression, the press regarded unemployment as a local problem and cheered such modest attempts at aid as cookies baked by high school girls for Red Cross relief. But within a few years an increasing tax burden for relief became a matter of course. Federal legislation, supported by state and local governments, did much to offset the downward trend of family life through old age pensions, maternity and dependency assistance, low-cost housing, loans to home owners, subsidized school and health programs, and other direct benefits derived from the entire recovery program. Our government went so far in providing relief that, before the decade ended, private social service agencies were disavowing any responsibility for the basic economic needs of the family and were concentrating instead on personal maladjustment.

MECHANIZED FARMING AND THE GRAPES OF WRATH

Rural life shared the vicissitudes of the urban community. The so-called "back to the farm" movement was actually directed toward the villages and small towns rather than farms, for the disturbing increase in technological unemployment and absentee ownership made life on small farms anything but secure. In common with the depression-induced tendency toward rigid economy in industry, agriculture reduced its costs by the wholesale application of large-scale methods and mechanization. Farmers who could afford it bought trucks and tractors. The number of tractors rose by 70 per cent and farm trucks increased by 16 per cent during the decade, raising productivity and thus partly offsetting the elimination of 20,000,000 acres of cotton, wheat, and tobacco by the A.A.A. Bankrupt farms were frequently taken over by corporations or banks which stressed more efficient production; a similar economy was emphasized in Kansas, where there appeared "suitcase farmers" who went from farm to farm with their tractor and tilled the soil.

Sensational gains were made in productivity. One of them, to which Carl C. Taylor, the sociologist, has called attention, was the use of hybrid corn seed, which in 1938 resulted in an increase estimated at nearly 10,000,000 bushels over the usual yield from open-pollinated seed. The production of the versatile soybean increased 238 per cent during the decade. Scientific improvements in stock farming made the lot of farm animals enviable in contrast to that of the people worst hit by the depression. Farm life in certain sections became more comfortable as well as more productive economically under the New Deal's program of rural electrification. Less than 11 per cent of all our farms had electricity in 1934, but this had risen to 27.1 per cent by 1940. In addition, various federal agencies were engaged in raising the income and living standards of farmers.

But the farm picture had a darker side, especially before 1934. Agricultural income, which had lagged behind the income from industry and commerce during the twenties, in 1922 dropped to a low of 55.6 (index=100 for the base period 1910–1914) and then rose steadily until it reached 119.3 in 1940. The plight of sharecroppers in the South was reflected in the militancy of the Southern Tenant Farmers' Union, which united white and Negro sharecroppers, their racial animosities temporarily forgotten, against the planter-merchant class in a struggle for better living standards and the halting of mass evictions. Roosevelt declared that the South was the nation's "economic problem number one." The steady increase in tenant farming that had been apparent before the depression was arrested to some extent, as Professor Taylor has pointed out, by mortgage foreclosures and increased corporate ownership.

Most destructive of all the catastrophes to which farmers are subject were the great dust storms, droughts, and floods of the thirties. Decades of soil depletion in the semi-arid Great Plains that stretch from the Texas Panhandle to Canada exhausted large areas of farm land and culminated in the "Black Blizzard," a dust storm that began on November 11, 1933. Much of the topsoil in the Dakotas, Kansas, Oklahoma, and nearby states was blown away, and houses, trees, and machinery were completely buried in the dust. Bankruptcy and wholesale evictions were the inevitable result. The tragedy of it all is laid bare in John Steinbeck's *The Grapes of Wrath,* a description of the trek of an entire farm people from their lost homes in the Great Plains to the promised land of California, where they were treated as undesirables or as dangerous radicals. Aid was given such unfortunates by the Federal Farm Security Administration and by the various credit agencies which enabled farm tenants or dispossessed farmers to become farm owners.

COMBINATIONS IN INDUSTRY AND LABOR

Although agriculture's share of the national income steadily declined from 16.7 per cent in 1918 to 5.3 in 1932, no large group wholly escaped the depression. The total value of our production dropped by 38 per cent between 1929 and 1932, and full employment was not reached until 1941. Business mortality was high. Mergers accelerated the pre-depression trend toward concentration; according to Gardiner C. Means, the social economist, by 1933 one-fifth of the nation's total wealth and one-half of its industrial wealth were controlled by 200 corporations—a substantial increase over 1929.

Competition declined correspondingly. In the automobile industry for example, the demand for low-priced cars favored mass-production methods and forced out many independents. General Motors, which had made 33 per cent of the cars produced in this country in 1929, was manufacturing more than 40 per cent by 1939; similarly, Chrysler's 9 per cent before the depression had grown to 25 per cent a decade later. These two companies—and Ford—produced 87 per cent of American-made cars during the thirties; the low-priced Chevrolet, Plymouth, and Ford had the greatest demand. According to E. D. Kennedy, a financial writer, the earnings of General Motors alone during the depression years exceeded $1,000,000,000. The decline in competition in this and other industries encouraged a popular demand for increased economic planning by the government.

The combinations in industry, together with the initial impetus given by the N.R.A., the N.L.R.B., and other New Deal labor agencies, inspired union leaders to seek similar combinations in the labor field. During the depression, organized labor dissipated its energy on "spread the work" movements, immigration restriction, jurisdictional disputes, and even occasional racketeering. Critics berated the American Federation of Labor for its neutral attitude toward "labor czars" who exacted tribute from employers in the building trades, the restaurant business, and various other fields. During 1929–1932, wages dropped 60 per cent; meanwhile the growing army of the unemployed constituted a threat to the security of those who still had jobs. Oblivious of the economic emergency, some Congressmen like Representative Hamilton Fish of New York were preoccupied solely with alleged Communist inroads into organized labor.

COLLECTIVE BARGAINING AND THE GOVERNMENT

Meanwhile, the increase in technological improvements, which was accelerated by the depression, not only reduced employment (in the short run) but transformed many complex skills into simple mechanical operations which could be learned quickly. Plant superintendents, especially in mass-production industries, used various "speed-up" devices and at the same time took advantage of the huge labor supply to eliminate men in their late forties and the less efficient youngsters. Effective unionization was hampered by court injunctions, company spies, and company unions.

The magic in the phrase "collective bargaining" had already been anticipated by the Norris-La Guardia anti-injunction law of 1932, which Hoover supported. This Act provided that workers should be free to organize for the purpose of collective bargaining or for other forms of mutual aid. It outlawed yellow-dog contracts compelling employees to agree not to join labor unions, and restricted the use of federal court injunctions in labor disputes. Far more influential in reviving moribund unionism was Section 7(a) of the National Industrial Recovery Act, which promised workers freedom from coercion in organizing and bargaining collectively "through representatives of their own choosing. . . ." This was no empty offer; on the contrary, it was an integral part of the entire code-making authority conferred by the N.I.R.A. and it was strengthened still further by the Labor Advisory Committee established under that Act.

Unionism boomed with the passage of the N.I.R.A. "The President Wants You to Join," read United Mine Workers posters. Even the timid interpreted this as meaning that belonging to a union had become respectable, patriotic in fact. The American Federation of Labor, which early in the depression had lost some 800,000 of the 2,933,500 members it had in 1929, was overwhelmed by the hundreds of thousands of prospective members in the mass-production industries. Following the invalidation of the N.I.R.A. by the Supreme Court, collective bargaining was reaffirmed and given new guarantees in the Wagner Act, which established the powerful National Labor Relations Board. This Act provided that union representatives were to be chosen under the supervision of the Board, that all complaints regarding anti-union discrimination would receive thorough investigation, and that remedial measures would be taken where necessary. Judicial "red tape" could be eliminated by the Board, which thus became the final authority on the facts of a case; an appeal was permitted only on the strictly legal aspects of a decision. Labor could afford to be jubilant.

THE RESURRECTION OF INDUSTRIAL UNIONISM

In 1935 a gigantic schism split the labor movement. Industrial unionists, who held that the only effective form of organization for mass-production industries was one based on an entire industry and not on crafts, claimed that they had been betrayed by the A. F. of L., which they said had repeatedly raided the newly formed industrial unions and drawn off skilled workmen into the numerous craft unions, thus dissipating the organizing strength of workers in the mass-production industries. Although the A. F. of L. provided for some industrial unionism, its "realistic" policies clung to the strength inherent in an aristocracy of skill. Craftsmen in the old established unions feared that they would be crowded out by the solid blocs of industrial unionists, with their adventurous policies. Dissidents like David Dubinsky, who headed the powerful International Ladies Garment Workers Union, criticized the A. F. of L. for failing, in its fifty-five years of existence, to organize any more than 3,500,000 workers out of a total of 39,000,000.

The doughty John L. Lewis, a member of the A. F. of L. Executive Council, led the industrial unionists within the Federation in demanding that it grant unrestricted charters, free from the jurisdictional claims of the craft unions, to the new locals who desired them. Industrial unions, these men argued, would eliminate the plague of jurisdictional disputes. At the A. F. of L. convention in San Francisco in 1934 the Executive Council had promised to grant such charters and to organize the crucial steel industry, which had decisively defeated unionism in the great strike of 1919. But this promise went unfulfilled, thus jeopardizing the progress already made in organizing that industry. The battle that was long brewing was joined in 1935 at the A. F. of L. convention in Atlantic City, with Lewis' challenge (in his best Elizabethan manner) to the craft unionists: "I am enraged and I am ready to rend my seducers limb from limb, including Delegate [Matthew] Woll." Old-line craft leaders were deeply perturbed when a roll call on the issue disclosed the astonishing fact that almost 40 per cent of the delegates supported Lewis.

Shortly afterward, on November 9, 1935, Lewis and his industrial bloc took the momentous step of forming the Committee for Industrial Organization in Washington, D. C., without withdrawing from the A. F. of L.; craft leaders denounced this as "dual unionism." The most progressive representatives of the labor movement went with Lewis—Sidney Hillman and his Amalgamated Clothing Workers; David Dubinsky and the I.L.G.W.U.; Philip Murray, a United Mine Workers official; Charles P. Howard of the International Typographical Union, who shared the leadership of the new C.I.O. with Lewis; and Thomas F. McMahon, president of the United Textile Workers. Behind them was the historic tradition of solidarity preached by the Knights of Labor: "An injury to one is an injury to all." A few members, it is now apparent, adhered to the more radical and class-conscious traditions of the I.W.W., now largely absorbed by the Communist party, and its militant code of One Big Union. By resurrecting industrial unionism, the C.I.O. fell heir to the radical reputation that the I.W.W. had given the movement. Lewis himself was no doctrinaire, although he advocated a powerful labor movement to combat the menace of Fascism in this country and thus prevent the unions from suffering the fate of the German and Italian unions. On January 22, the Executive Council of the A. F. of L. refused an industrial charter to radio workers, at the same time condemning the C.I.O. as the outgrowth of a radical minority scheme for dual unionism. The C.I.O. retaliated with a huge drive, headed by Philip Murray as director of the Steel Workers Organizing Committee (the S.W.O.C.), to organize the steel industry. Secession became a fact when the craft leaders refused to admit the steel workers as an industrial union.

UNIONIZING THE MASS-PRODUCTION INDUSTRIES

The C.I.O. won a sensational victory in organizing the steel industry, considering the crushing defeats suffered by the steel unions in the Homestead strike of 1892 and in the nation-wide strike of 1919 led by William Z. Foster. Hoping to repeat earlier victories, "Big Steel," led by the two-billion-dollar United States Steel Corporation, put up a stubborn fight before it yielded; union meetings were broken up by company police, plant-inspired "citizen movements" created an atmosphere of unreason and fear, and the local press beat the drums for an anti-Communist crusade. Paternalism and hand-picked company unions failed to appease the workers—many of them immigrants who lived in filthy, unpainted shacks around the steel mills and in 1932 averaged $13.20 a week—if employed. To avert an impending strike which, as Professor J. Raymond Walsh of Harvard believes, might have cost the companies lucrative armament contracts from Great Britain, Myron Taylor, chairman of the U. S. Steel Corporation, negotiated a written labor contract with John L. Lewis in March, 1937.

Four other important steel producers regarded Taylor's act as a gross betrayal and proceeded to resist the S.W.O.C. Tom Girdler of the Republic Steel Company refused to sign any labor contract on the ground that it was not required by law. Strikes broke out in the Middle West and spread eastward to the plants owned by Girdler and the three other "Little Steel" companies. In defending their position these firms could not claim serious losses during the depression, for the Securities and Exchange Commission had revealed the huge salaries and bonuses paid to executives during those years—Girdler's salary was $129,372 a year, and certain of his colleagues in other companies had received salaries that ranged from $173,750 to $250,000, in addition to bonuses.

The continued success of the S.W.O.C. in organizing the steel, automobile, and other major industries awakened fears among white-collar elements of a labor dictatorship. Consequently "Little Steel" found ready allies among small businessmen, journalists, local government officials, and farm owners. Roosevelt and the new federal Steel Mediation Board, faced by the division in the ranks of labor, leaned backward in their effort to maintain strict neutrality during the Little Steel strikes of 1937. The friendliness shown to labor by Governor Frank Murphy of Michigan, who refused to permit state troopers to be used in ending strikes, proved insufficient to turn the rising anti-union tide. Violence hastily attributed to the C.I.O. broke out. Most tragic was the Memorial Day "massacre" of 1937 near the South Chicago shops of the Republic Steel Company. When strikers attempted to form a picket line outside the company's gates, Chicago police who had been called in lost their heads and fired into the crowd of fleeing men, women, and children; ten people were killed and forty were wounded, one an eight-year-old child. Senator La Follette's investigating committee denounced this "callous indifference to human life" and proved that the strikers and their families had given no provocation for the shooting. Eventually the S.W.O.C. won a major if belated victory over the Republic Steel Company when the N.L.R.B. compelled the company to adopt collective bargaining and to reinstate several thousand discharged employees.

Meanwhile the C.I.O. had scored a resounding success in organizing the automobile industry through the United Automobile Workers of America, led by Homer S. Martin, a former Baptist minister. Despite relatively high hourly rates, 45 per cent of the automobile workers were earning $1000 or less a year. As in the steel campaign, every device for repression, espionage, and intimidation was used against the union organizers. General Motors promptly referred all labor grievances to its local plant superintendents. Since this was interpreted by the men as an evasion, they began an impromptu "sit-down" strike, without U.A.W. authorization, in the Fisher Body plant at Cleveland, the strikers refusing to leave the premises. Production was paralyzed, for not even a court injunction could dislodge the defiant men. The sit-down strike idea spread quickly, despite the fact that the legality of this form of strike was widely challenged. When the automobile workers in Michigan staged sit-down strikes, Governor Murphy again refused to send state troopers but worked earnestly for a settlement by negotiation. The strike ended after six weeks and culminated in a labor contract, signed in February, 1936, in which William S. Knudsen, vice president of General Motors, agreed to recognize the U.A.W. as the sole bargaining agency for its members.

But the Girdler of the automobile industry was the equally individualistic Henry Ford, who was still flatly opposed to unionization and who denied the constitutionality of the National Labor Relations Board. Strikes broke out in which there were ugly scenes of violence; the Ford Service Organization, led by a former prize fighter, won considerable notoriety for its crude methods of repressing the strikers. Eventually, however, Ford also recognized the signs of the times and accepted collective bargaining.

C.I.O. organizers under Sidney Hillman made rapid headway in the poorly paid textile industry except in the South, for factory owners in this section were unwilling to surrender the advantage they enjoyed over their northern rivals because of cheap wages. The Ku Klux Klan was renovated to keep out union organizers and to intimidate the Negroes, who were attracted by the unrestricted unionization offered members of their race. The C.I.O. had been critical of Jim Crowism in the A. F. of L., for it recognized the structural weakness of any labor movement which excluded Negroes. Lewis' followers also penetrated the important fields of transportation and rubber, and even the white-collar industries. The American Newspaper Guild, organized under the N.I.R.A. in 1933 by the leftist writer, Heywood Broun, was at first affiliated with the A. F. of L., but in 1936 it joined the C.I.O. and expanded its organizing program to include individualistic-minded newsmen. Newspaper publishers contended that a closed shop meant biased editorial writers, but Guild members denied these charges and pointed to the control over editorial policies exercised by the publishers themselves. Longshoremen, plagued by economic insecurity and discriminatory hiring policies, hastened to join C.I.O. unions established by Joseph Curran on the Atlantic and Gulf coasts and by Harry Bridges, a Lewis protégé, on the Pacific. Bridges' radical views led to a newspaper demand for his deportation to Australia and constituted a *cause célèbre* which many regarded as a flank attack on the C.I.O. itself.

Senate revelations during the rise of the C.I.O. indicated the partial abolition of civil liberties in many industrial communities in the effort to halt wholesale unionization. But resentment against labor flared up over the innumerable strikes that occurred between 1935 and 1940. Over 688,000 men went out on strike in 1937, and in 1939 this figure soared to over 1,170,900.

The C.I.O. was reorganized in 1938 as the Congress of Industrial Organizations. At that time it claimed four million members, a figure which approached the total membership of the A. F. of L. It entered the political field with the organization of the powerful Labor's Non-Partisan League to back progressive candidates. Friends of the C.I.O. believed that its growing pains had ended and that its leaders could curb the "outlaw strikes" and thus enhance the trustworthiness of its labor contracts.

Meanwhile, despite the C.I.O.-A. F. of L. schism, labor prospered as the recovery trend was accelerated by defense and ultimately war needs. Real wages increased by 19 per cent between 1935 and 1941 in spite of the tendency to pass wage increases on to the consumer in the form of higher prices, thus creating the danger of an inflation spiral that might eventually cancel labor's hard-won gains. A five-day forty-hour week was becoming universal and was raising the welcome problem of adequate leisure-time activities. Comforting, too, was the fact that the Supreme Court upheld practically every major labor law which came within its purview.

THE NEGRO FORSAKES LINCOLN FOR ROOSEVELT

In 1933, according to Professor Charles S. Johnson, the Negro sociologist, 2,117,044 colored people were on relief, or, in proportion to the population of the two races, twice as many Negroes as whites. "Nearly half of the Negro working population in New York was on relief," wrote Professor Johnson, "and there were food riots in Harlem." Economic competition increased interracial strife in Detroit, Pittsburgh, St. Louis, Birmingham, and other cities, north and south. The plight of underpaid Negro sharecroppers, many of whom were evicted, attracted national attention. Under such circumstances, probably no sector of the population received relatively more benefits from the New Deal than did Negroes at the marginal subsistence level.

Relief, social security, the work and subsistence projects, and the various credit agencies brought a new day to Negroes. In the face of local prejudices the Roosevelt administration insisted—not always effectively, however—on the uniform disbursement of relief regardless of color. Professor Johnson has pointed out that in one month in 1939, the W.P.A. employed 300,000 Negroes at a cost of $15,000,000. Especially significant to colored marginal workers was the Fair Labor Standards Act of 1938, with its provisions guaranteeing a wage "floor" and an hours "ceiling." Here was a clue to the Negroes' wholesale transfer of political allegiance from the party of the Great Emancipator to one which included the bulk of the Ku Klux Klan as well as the New Deal.

Population figures suggest an improvement in the status of this people, for in the decade of the thirties the Negro population increased from 11,891,000 to 12,866,000 a rate somewhat above the average for the nation as a whole. The number of lynchings had decreased markedly since the 1920's; the worst year of the new decade was 1933, with 24 lynchings. Advances in education continued and there was some improvement in the salaries of Negro teachers; the doubling of the number of Negro college graduates led to a sizable Negro intelligentsia. Victories won by Negro candidates for state and federal office in the North and Middle West gave the race an important channel of expression. Several significant court victories were won during the thirties on behalf of civil liberties for Negroes. Sympathetic white people contributed generously to the defense fund for the colored boys in Scottsboro, Alabama, whose trial for rape was based on alleged flimsy evidence. The national defense program reawakened racial discrimination, but Negroes in increasing numbers managed to enter occupations from which they had previously been excluded.

THE REVIVAL OF ANTI-SEMITISM

Seldom in our history have Jews been so conscious of their minority status as during the 1930's. Although both they and the Negroes shared in varying degree the onus of racial discrimination as well as the economic benefits of the New Deal, the Jews became increasingly conscious of powerful forces aimed at their extinction. Hitler proclaimed a world crusade against 16,000,000 Jews, 4,770,660 of whom lived in the United States. Nazi and Fascist sympathizers in this country brushed off the portrait of the "International Jew" which Henry Ford had discarded in the 1920's, and the time-honored charges of Jewish capitalism and Communism and of domination by Jews were revived. The Dies and other congressional committees discovered that ample funds from various suspect sources were available to make anti-Semitism a remunerative "racket." The Nazis sought to identify Roosevelt as a Jew and to label his Administration as an instrument of world domination wielded by the Elders of Zion.

The Jews were confronted by a bewildering array of Fascist-minded organizations, both indigenous and foreign. Fritz Kuhn, the Fuehrer of the Bund in this country, who as a Storm Trooper had goose-stepped in a parade reviewed by Hitler in 1936, continued to assail the Jews as the spearhead of Bolshevism until he was sent to Sing Sing for larceny of Bund funds and for forgery. Before the Bund was finally abolished, it staged an open rally at Madison Square Garden in New York City, attracting a crowd, estimated at 20,000, that carried placards bearing anti-Semitic slogans.

In the spirit of the moribund Ku Klux Klan, William Dudley Pelley organized the Silver Shirts the day after (as he boasted) Hitler became Chancellor of Germany. Numerous imitators of Pelley sprang up, among them the Reverend Gerald B. Winrod of Kansas, who added anti-Catholicism to his witches' brew of mass prejudices. When Winrod sought the Republican nomination for the Senate, party leaders campaigned successfully to defeat his attempt to inject religious bigotry into their ranks.

The case of the Reverend Charles Coughlin of Royal Oak, Michigan, was unique because of his extraordinarily large radio and personal following. To the embarrassment of his superiors in the Church, who hesitated to curb opinions on non-religious matters, Father Coughlin embarked on an anti-Semitic campaign in 1938 which revived the Protocols of the Elders of Zion, held Jewish bankers responsible for the Bolshevik Revolution, and in some cases used verbatim the propaganda put out by Goebbels. Claiming him as their inspiration and authority, certain rowdy elements in New York City united in the "Christian Front," and others, led by Joseph E. McWilliams, formed the "Christian Mobilizers." Thereupon assaults were made on residents of Jewish extraction in that city. When Father Coughlin, combining his vilification of President Roosevelt with that of the Jews, offered his political support to Willkie in 1940, the Republican candidate replied witheringly: "If I understand what his beliefs are, I am not only not interested in his support—I don't want it. . . . I have no place in my philosophy for such beliefs. . . . I don't have to be President of the United States but I do have to make my beliefs clear, that is, in order to live with myself."

Just as the anti-Semites identified the depression with Jewish-made capitalism, so they adopted the strategy of branding resistance to Fascism as a Jewish trick. As late as Japan's attack on Pearl Harbor, certain leading isolationists were seeking to convince the people that no war actually threatened the United States but that she was intervening in a foreign struggle at the behest of the Jews. Even Lindbergh, characteristically naïve in political matters, claimed at an America

First rally at Des Moines on September 11, 1941, that Roosevelt, abetted by Jewish and British elements, was seeking to drive the country into war. William Allen White, the famous independent journalist of Kansas, sent Lindbergh the following telegram: "Shame on you, Charles Lindbergh, for injecting the Nazi race issue into American politics. Why was it necessary to defame an honest, patriotic cause by the indefensible injection of Hitler's anti-Semitism into the issue?" Lindbergh remained silent.

RACKETEERING AND THE "GANGBUSTERS"

During the thirties the crime of kidnaping, which robbed the Lindberghs of their oldest son in 1932, replaced the liquor racket of the preceding decade as a profitable field for gangsters. Public opinion, although it enjoyed the harrowing details of the crimes reported in the daily papers, was less complacent toward the failure of our law enforcement officers. Accordingly it favored the broad expansion of federal authority in the so-called Lindbergh law of June, 1932, which made kidnaping a federal offense if the victim was taken across a state line. When kidnaping showed no signs of slackening, Congress in January, 1936, strengthened this law by making the minimum penalty ten years' imprisonment and imposing a fine of $10,000 on anyone passing, receiving, or otherwise handling ransom money. California, the scene of several kidnapings involving wealthy residents, imposed the death penalty on kidnapers who harmed their victims; Maine and Oklahoma also provided additional severe penalties for this crime.

Deprived of their customary revenues by the repeal of prohibition, racketeers turned to other sources of funds in addition to kidnaping. Various crime "syndicates" were formed; some of them extorted tribute from businessmen by means of "protective associations" and others profited handsomely from their "takes" in the notorious "numbers" racket. The low point of the depression coincided with a sharp rise in robberies, automobile thefts, and murder, but thereafter these crimes declined to their more "normal" levels. Child delinquency increased to such an extent that several conferences of social workers were held in Washington to discuss it. Pressure from labor unions compelled the elimination of prison labor, resulting in general discontent and riots on the part of idle prisoners.

Despite this formidable array of crimes and criminals, the decade became known for its vigorous prosecutors and the vigilant—and highly romanticized—Federal Bureau of Investigation headed by J. Edgar Hoover. It is suggestive of the new public conscience that Thomas E. Dewey, the outstanding district attorney of New York who successfully prosecuted important and powerful political grafters and racketeers, should not only be elected governor of the Empire State but be nominated by the Republican party for the Presidency itself. After decades of indifference, the forces of good government rid Kansas City of the notorious Tom Pendergast machine. Despite his erratic judgments, Westbrook Pegler, the syndicated columnist, won commendation for his attacks on racketeering, especially as it existed in Chicago and Kansas City. Important scientific advances were made in crime detection in Chicago, where gang feuds and organized graft, like Jack Zuta's alliance between politicos and crime, were rife. In 1933 New York City expelled the well-entrenched Tammany forces when it elected a liberal reformer, Fiorello H. La Guardia, mayor on a Republican-Fusion ticket. La Guardia not only restored the city's shaken credit but established a miniature New Deal.

"COOPERATIVE FEDERALISM"

The secretary of the National Municipal League characterized the late thirties as a "modern municipal renaissance." Although he referred largely to the success of civic reform, the record is remarkable in view of the condition of municipal and state finance. States like Florida, North Carolina, and Texas, which had expanded feverishly during the twenties, defaulted on bond issues. Huge tax delinquencies in cities during the early thirties left thousands of teachers and other employees unpaid. The New Deal came to the rescue of local governments by its policy of making grants-in-aid and relief subsidies to local units and through the second A.A.A. program reviving the long-dormant county governments, a process referred to as "cooperative federalism." To relieve debt-ridden communities, Congress passed the Municipal Bankruptcy Act in 1934 and, when this was nullified by the Supreme Court, enacted a second such law in 1937. In their frantic search for revenues to meet the cost of government and to make payments on old debts, many city officials preferred to avoid a local income tax; instead they favored the revenue-making sales tax, despite the burden which this entailed for the poorer people. In other cities, income, cigarette, and occupancy taxes were imposed; and at least seven municipalities, under the pressure of independent retailers, enacted a chain-store tax.

VOCATIONALISM INTENSIFIED

Education suffered from the depression in crowded classrooms, shortened school terms, declining endowments, slashes in teachers' salaries, generally reduced budgets, and the closing of many private schools, but much of the lost ground had been recovered by the end of the decade. During the depression young people attended school more regularly and, if they could afford it, continued their education to advanced levels of study that led to high academic degrees, rather than face enforced idleness. College enrollment increased far more rapidly than the population. In 1925, 800,000 were attending college, but ten years later this had risen to 1,200,000. Federal grants-in-aid, especially subsidies for the National Youth Administration, enabled thousands to go to high school and college.

Most spectacular were the gains in vocational education and the corresponding decline in liberal arts courses. In 1930, students in federally aided vocational schools totaled considerably less than a million; a decade later, 2,290,741 were enrolled. California, New York, Texas, and Georgia had the heaviest enrollment in vocational studies such as home economics, trades, and agriculture. A vital adjunct to this advance was the Emergency Education Program under the Federal Emergency Relief Administration, which absorbed 50,000 unemployed teachers for work in vocational rehabilitation as well as in more general school subjects. Over 1,500,000 children and adults attended classes, ranging from the nursery school level through elementary English and recreational classes to relatively advanced adult courses in current social issues, fine arts, and occupational adjustment problems. The E.E.P. also took pioneer steps in the vital field of education in labor problems, although not without persistent charges of radicalism by the anti-New Deal press.

Business courses, spurred on by the current preoccupation with job hunting, boomed to such an extent that many of the relatively new colleges of commerce dwarfed the older departments in the universities. The growing interest in economics was reflected in the increased number of such courses offered in high schools and colleges. The influence of events in Europe led to the expansion of the social science field. Leading educators preferred courses which emphasized the responsibility of the community for the welfare of its members, especially studies in labor, social economics, and international relations.

REVITALIZING THE SOCIAL GOSPEL

Church attendance, with minor exceptions, at first declined during the depression, reflecting at an accelerated pace the long-term trend toward secular interests. Interdenominationalism scored a major victory in 1939, when the four leading Methodist sects united in a single church of 8,000,000 members, and incidentally healed a schism between North and South dating from the eve of the Civil War. Sharply reduced revenues during the economic crisis compelled the churches to turn over most of their charitable activities to the government.

According to Hornell N. Hart, the sociologist, the clergy showed a marked sympathy for radical economic programs as the depression deepened. A questionnaire sent to some 100,000 Protestant clergymen in 1934 revealed an overwhelming sentiment for a "cooperative commonwealth" as against capitalism; 31 per cent wanted a socialist order, and Communism and Fascism each received one per cent of the vote. According to another poll, Congregationalists favored consumers' cooperatives by a three-to-one vote. Other sects showed similar leftist trends. A strong pacifist feeling was revealed by the fact that 75 per cent of all the Protestants included in one questionnaire wanted the church to oppose war. Alf M. Landon, the Republican standard-bearer of 1936, openly fought the tendency of his fellow Methodists to uphold the rights of conscientious objectors. On the whole, churchmen were ready to concede that waging a "just war" was a Christian duty.

Catholics in this country were placed in an awkward position by the activities of Father Coughlin, who, although he claimed to be the authentic interpreter of the famous papal encyclicals on labor, was denounced by two cardinals, an archbishop, and numerous priests, as well as by various groups which restated the Catholic principles of tolerance. The state execution of churchmen in Spain and the burning of Catholic churches led most of the Catholic press in the United States to favor Franco.

Jewish religious leaders bore the heavy burden of providing for the victims of anti-Semitic persecutions, first in Poland and then, with the rise of Hitler, throughout Europe. An important weapon against religious intolerance was created in the National Conference of Christians and Jews, which embraced all faiths and actively employed the radio, education, the church, and the lecture forum to achieve better understanding.

JOURNALISM AND THE POPULAR MAGAZINES

Newspaper circulation fell off by four million during the crisis years but a decade later had more than recovered the 39,500,000 readers it had in 1930. Nevertheless, largely as a result of mergers, there were 64 fewer newspapers in 1940 than there were ten years earlier. A serious blow to newspaper revenue was the increasing shift to the radio as an advertising medium. Pro-New Deal papers, assailing the inactive role of the press during the depression, attributed it to the fact that journalism had become a business enterprise of great financial proportions and consequently had a corresponding stake in the upper middle-class stratum of society.

Administration supporters pointed out the wide disparity in the fact that, although two-thirds of the daily papers fought Roosevelt's reelection in 1936 (this was true of three-fourths of the papers in 1940), he received an overwhelming popular vote at the polls. New Dealers labeled as camouflage the publishers' campaign for "freedom of the press," led by the arch-enemy of the Administration, Colonel Robert R. McCormick of the influential Chicago *Tribune*. McCormick's paper, an anti-union, isolationist, and thoroughly conservative (critics said reactionary) publication, had a million readers in 1940 and thus ranked second among the dailies. Furthermore, it was closely connected with the powerful anti-New Deal tabloid, the New York *Daily News,* whose circulation of 3,400,000—a tribute to the power of gross sensationalism—put it in first place. Liberals therefore found little satisfaction in the gradual dissolution of Hearst's once-vast newspaper empire. Newspaper publishers gave labor and the New Deal scant favor, but instead channelized their reform energies into campaigns against political machines and racketeering.

Reflecting the trend toward realism both here and abroad, the metropolitan press increased its pictorial contents by two-thirds during the decade. This same trend, especially when it took the form of "candid camera" pictures, accounted for the tremendous popularity of *Life* and *Look,* two new picture magazines whose subscribers quickly passed the million mark. In line with the greater interest in European affairs, the major newspapers secured a staff of able foreign correspondents and devoted considerable space to foreign news. As in the past, however, journalistic enterprise too frequently invaded the privacy of personal sorrows, a notorious example being the handling of the Lindbergh kidnaping and the Hauptmann trial.

In social trends, magazines paralleled the newspapers. Robert Cantwell, the liberal magazine editor and novelist, based the popularity of *True Story* magazine during the depression on the fact that its stories tended to quiet unrest among the unemployed. Whatever the reason, by 1937 its circulation had more than recovered its pre-depression total of 2,167,000. Commenting on the prevailing vogue for escapist literature, Cantwell estimated that the 400,000 circulation of the four "spicy stories" magazines, which featured sex themes, was equal to that of the nation's five leading intellectual and cultural magazines combined—*Harper's, Scribner's,* the *Atlantic Monthly,* the *Nation,* and the *New Republic.* The twelve leading movie magazines had a combined public of 3,500,000, and the millions who avidly read Wild West exploits turned eagerly to stories about "gang-busting" detectives and the romanticized G-men.

An arresting phenomenon in magazine history was the growth of *Reader's Digest,* a twenty-five-cent pocket-size periodical which began with a small Greenwich Village clientele in 1922 and attained a national—and international—circulation of 1,801,400 copies by 1936, despite the depression. Its editors, De Witt Wallace and his wife, tapped a new reading public eager for the condensed non-fiction articles of current interest which *Reader's Digest* provided from some thirty-five magazines. The Wallaces demonstrated that non-fiction magazines could be highly profitable even without advertising. A legion of digest imitators sprang up, capitalizing on the desire of millions for "streamlined" reading which made no great demand on concentrated attention. Popular interest in weekly news summaries was reflected in the rapid rise of two chatty and unconventional magazines, *Time* and *Newsweek*. In spite of the depression, the leftist literature of social protest, typified by the *Nation*, the *New Republic*, *Commonsense*, and the *New Masses*, appealed to an inconsiderable proportion of the population, for most magazine readers preferred politically neutral or escapist themes.

RADIO: FIRESIDE CHATS AND QUIZ PROGRAMS

Spurred on by a demand for cheaper portable or "midget" sets, radio prospered during the decade. Whereas only 9,000,000 homes possessed radios in 1929, by 1940 a radio was an integral part of 29,200,000 homes—practically universal, in fact. The total number of radios in use increased more than fivefold in the ten-year period—from 10,500,000 in 1930 to 54,000,000 in 1940. By the latter year radio sets had become self-contained units except for the electrical connection, and the cumbersome outside aerials had been eliminated; the highly popular automobile radios were equipped with short rod antennas. Tuning became automatic, a push button being provided for each station. Combination phonograph-radio sets were produced in large numbers to satisfy the demand of people with discriminating taste in music. Experiments were made with television programs, but full commercial exploitation of this field was yet to come.

A wide variety of radio programs, ranging from "crooning" and "hot jazz" to outstanding features like Toscanini's superb orchestral music, the University of Chicago Round Table, and the vital Town Hall of the Air, were available. The European crisis awakened a strong demand for foreign news and news analyses and brought into prominence a small army of news commentators, among them H. V. Kaltenborn, Lowell Thomas, Gabriel Heatter, and Boake Carter. For the most part, the newscasters avoided the biased presentation characteristic of the daily press.

Extremely important from the standpoint of a functioning democracy were President Roosevelt's "fireside chats" in which he gave the people a periodic accounting of his political stewardship. Radio stations solved the problem of political bias during campaigns by allocating time to each leading candidate for office, including Earl Browder, the Communists' perennial candidate for President. Ultimately it was thought not inconsistent with the ideal of free speech to bar Father Coughlin's incendiary speeches from the air waves. Its own system of self-regulation enabled the radio industry to avoid any real efforts at censorship on the part of the Federal Communications Commission.

The sponsors of radio programs were assured of nation-wide attention for their products when they put Hollywood stars or popular variety shows on the air, or broadcast sports events or presented dramatic or orchestral programs. There were relatively few who would not endure the repetitious "commercials" for the sake of listening to Edgar Bergen and Charlie McCarthy, Bing Crosby, Rudy Vallee, and Hollywood guest stars. Often flattering to the ego of listeners who compared themselves in factual background with the performers were the numerous question and answer programs like "Information Please," "Professor Quiz," and the precocious "Quiz Kids." Radio offered countless opportunities for talented stars who lacked the photogenic qualities necessary for Hollywood. In a decade characterized by the reformist spirit, the radio had a large part in breaking down provincial narrowness and in promoting a greater feeling of social solidarity.

MOVIES: DOUBLE FEATURES AND CENSORSHIP

The movies, perhaps more than all other forms of entertainment combined, consumed an increasing share of the average American's leisure time. This was true especially with the advent of the double feature. Although attendance in 1933 fell off by one-third from the pre-depression total, the lost ground was largely recovered within a few years; by 1940, an estimated 80,000,000 persons were attending the nation's 19,645 motion picture theaters each week. Theater managers tried to offset the decline in box office receipts during the depression by giving away premiums like dishes or washing machines or providing cash prizes to be won in "bank night" drawings or in "bingo."

Hollywood's domination of the world film market was curbed toward the end of the decade first by extreme nationalism and then by the war. Sound movies were firmly established during the depression, technicolor was introduced, and numerous other improvements in photographic and sound techniques were made. According to Louis R. Reid, the dramatic editor, more than forty pictures in the million-dollar class were produced in the boom year of 1936. Pictures were classified A, B, or C, not according to artistry but on the basis of cost.

Perhaps, as Charles and Mary Beard suggest in *America in Mid-passage,* the huge financial stakes involved in Hollywood productions and the increasing control of the industry by bankers explain the fact that motion pictures for the most part avoided the basic social and economic issues of the 1930's. But this tendency was common to journalism and radio broadcasting as well. Catering to a huge world market, Hollywood producers carefully avoided offending democratic peoples as well as Fascists, until war made this policy unnecessary. Thus, fears of Fascist displeasure seemed to explain the refusal to film Sinclair Lewis' *It Can't Happen Here.* Only a discriminating minority asked for greater realism than was implied in Walt Disney's ingenious cartoon feature, "Three Little Pigs," or the spectacular but often grossly inaccurate historical films or the gang-busting pictures.

A succession of rather sordid sex pictures during the early 1930's was arrested suddenly in 1934 by the rise of the Catholic Legion of Decency, led by the Reverend Daniel A. Lord of St. Louis, a Jesuit priest and the editor of *The Queen's Work.* Fears of an expensive boycott led Hollywood to make an about-face and establish an internal censorship office under Joseph I. Breen, an Irish-American Catholic. With exaggerated caution producers shifted from the heavily sophisticated Mae West and George White pictures to such juvenile classics as *Mrs. Wiggs of the Cabbage Patch* and *Anne of Green Gables.*

Among Hollywood's undeniable merits was the fact that from time to time classics in the artistic and intellectual sense were produced. One star, Paul Muni, always discriminating in the choice of his story, won popular acclaim in *The Good Earth, The Life of Louis Pasteur, Emile Zola,* and *Juarez.* Although child stars like Shirley Temple and Mickey Rooney led in box office popularity for years, large audiences admired the superb performances of such adult stars as Bette Davis in *Dark Victory,* Elisabeth Bergner in *Catherine the Great,* and Greta Garbo in *Ninotchka,* a gentle satire on the Soviet system.

Like the magazines, the movies of the depression era (and of course before this) were largely neutral or escapist. Not infrequently, however, a picture appeared which stressed bad housing conditions, as in *Dead End*, or the sufferings of migratory farm workers, as in *The Grapes of Wrath*, or the evils of modern industrialism, as in Charlie Chaplin's *Modern Times*. Stark realism of a high order was achieved in "documentary films," especially those sponsored by government agencies, that depicted man's reckless abuse of nature or the havoc wrought by floods and erosion; Pare Lorentz' *The Plough That Broke the Plains* and his *The River* are outstanding in this class. Will H. Hays, president of the Motion Picture Producers and Distributors of America, was probably justified when he said in 1939 that, despite all their shortcomings, motion pictures helped to remove misunderstandings by portraying the history, ideals, and culture patterns of various groups.

RECREATION AND THE DEPRESSION

The world of sport suffered severe financial setbacks during the early part of the decade but eventually recovered in large measure. Although the amateur Golden Gloves bouts sponsored by the Chicago *Tribune* became generally popular, professional boxing declined considerably from the spectacular championship bouts of the twenties. The amazing prowess of Joe Louis, the Negro world champion, never attracted the princely gate receipts that Jack Dempsey usually drew.

Baseball receipts for the 1933 World Series dropped to slightly more than half of the 1926 figure, which was $1,207,864, but this previous record was exceeded in 1936, when admissions amounted to $1,304,399. An estimated 200,000 to 300,000 fans attended the world series each year. The decade had its heroes—Lou Gehrig, the "pride of the Yankees" who in sixteen years as captain and first baseman earned $400,000 and whose life story was made into a motion picture. The New York Yankees had the mighty Joe DiMaggio, who at the end of the decade was rated as the "most valuable player."

All the other sports continued their pre-depression trends, except for inevitable losses in the early 1930's. Winter sports like skiing grew in vogue. Municipal golf courses increased at the expense of private country clubs. An extraordinary revival of bicycling, especially among women, raised the production of bicycles in 1935 to 639,435—over half the total for the peak year of 1899.

In the home, contract bridge, the recognized authority on which was Ely Culbertson, attained great popularity among all classes; as the Lynds have suggested, bridge games averted many potentially dangerous political discussions and in many cases brought prestige to people who could not hope to shine in the art of conversation. Tournaments were held for the regional, national, and world championship.

During the decade public dancing shifted from large ornate ballrooms to the more informal small dance halls. By the late 1930's jazz had been transformed into the more eccentric "swing music," with corresponding improvisations in dance steps by the youthful "jitterbugs." In *Since Yesterday,* Frederick L. Allen traces the progress of swing, from the honky-tonks in New Orleans where Negro musicians improvised as they played, to France and Britain. "During the early years of the depression," he writes; "there was little popular interest in this 'hot jazz' in the United States; what a worried public wanted was 'sweet' music, slow in rhythm, and soothingly melodious. . . ." After the depression lifted, however, New York City turned to swing music, with Benny Goodman, "King of Swing," and his numerous rivals presenting its frenzied rhythms for huge crowds.

Musical taste showed a remarkable improvement, doubtless due in some degree to the music projects of the federal government. W.P.A. orchestras were established to give employment to the thousands of musicians reduced to the relief level by the depression. Under the baton of such conductors as Toscanini and Stokowski, symphonic music enjoyed new popularity and even influenced the music used in motion pictures. The decline in the number of concert and operatic performances during the depression was offset to some extent by the revival in popularity of the phonograph. As Deems Taylor, the noted music critic and composer, observed in 1938, "The staple moneymakers of the record dealer today, outside of his dance records, are albums—recordings of entire symphonies, suites, string quartets, even entire operas—a condition that was unthinkable fifteen years ago." The economic status of composers improved with the organization of the American Society of Authors, Composers, and Publishers, which, despite criticism of monopoly, protected their patent rights and assured their royalties. The romantic ideal of the individualist artist was giving way to a more cooperative theory patterned on trade unions.

CHAPTER 19

The Security Ideal of the Thirties

NEW CERTAINTIES FOR OLD

The world-shaking decade of the 1930's, ushered in by the great depression and culminating in World War II, made a forceful impression on the thinking and beliefs of the period. Wholesale insecurity shattered the Narcissus mood of the preceding decade, preoccupied as it was with psychological interests of an egoistic nature. Individualist beliefs in the inevitability of progress and the adequacy of self-reliance yielded to an instinctive mass reaction toward the shelter of state interventionism. The old intelligentsia, with its hyper-aestheticism, its affectation of sophisticated but decadent principles, and its hedonism, surrendered to a new elite of "class-conscious" intellectuals whose god was far more likely to be Marx than Freud. Economic determinism, enhanced by the well-publicized exploits of the Soviet Union in social engineering which offered a sense of direction to a bewildered generation, ranked high among the newer values that triumphed. Nazi Germany and Fascist Italy propagandized for a militaristic brand of extreme collectivism which competed with the Marxian variety. As we have seen, the New Deal sought to avoid these extremes by experiments with a planned economy—in a limited sense—within a democratic framework.

The search for new certainties offered a variety of approaches, aside from that preempted by a relatively small band of Marxians. The great popularity of historical themes, especially in literature, reflected not only nostalgia for the past but the hope of achieving a needed perspective for the distressing immediacy of present problems. The urgent need to comprehend the current scene led not only to a sharp emphasis on economics but also to an attempt to discover some new intellectual unity in the social sciences through an "interdisciplinary" approach or perhaps a philosophic synthesis. Relatively few people followed Heywood Broun, the liberal journalist, whose quest for certainty led him to the Catholic Church. Despite its economic and social chaos, the period was too secular in spirit for a fervent revival of religious authority. Consequently, as in the years before 1917, the cultural emphasis was predominantly on sociological interests.

The intellectual relationship of Europe and America, hitherto one of patron and client, practically reversed itself by the end of the decade as Hitler and Mussolini expelled from the Continent its most creative minds, Christian rebels as well as "non-Aryans." Many of them, including Thomas Mann and Albert Einstein, came to the United States. Harvard opened its doors to the former Chanceller of democratic Germany, Dr. Heinrich Bruening, who became a member of its Government Department, and to several other distinguished German and Italian refugees. Yale welcomed Paul Hindemith, the great German musician; and the vast numbers of intellectual celebrities who flocked to the New School for Social Research in New York City transformed its Graduate School into the renowned "University-in-Exile." Here indeed was a favorable setting for something more than individual precocity or mere intellectual competence.

THE LITERARY REALISM OF THE CANDID CAMERA

To the leading American novelists of the 1930's few literary crimes eclipsed "escapism" or a bourgeois indifference to "social consciousness." In notable instances early in the depression, craftsmanship was sacrificed in the interests of the "proletarian renaissance" encouraged by the leftist *New Masses*. The new realism engendered by bread lines, labor conflicts, and slums was definitely "hard-boiled"; it reveled in an unadorned naturalism far cruder and more unrestrained in violence than the early followers of Zola ever envisaged. To the novelist society itself was desperately ill and its illness was reflected in the degradation of the people. Even the prewar socialist writings of Jack London and Upton Sinclair seemed innocuous compared to the violently predatory tone of John Dos Passos, James T. Farrell, Richard Wright, and Meyer Levin. Endless detail, often of the nauseating variety, marked the new cult of the "candid camera" and the "documentary" school.

The literary career of John Dos Passos, which bridged two decades, reflected the abrupt change in social values. In his youth Dos Passos went through the disillusionment of the famous "lost generation" and was largely concerned with the personal problems of an artist confused by the stupid scheme of the world around him. Then, as Max Lerner put it, he became a "historian of the collective mentality," influenced by Thorstein Veblen's incisive attack on the ideals and behavior of the "leisure class." In line with the prevailing tendency toward retrospection, he portrayed his generation in a trilogy, *U. S. A.* (1937), which stressed labor's struggles for status and security. In these three volumes —*The Forty-Second Parallel* (1937), *1919* (1932), and *The Big Money* (1936)—Dos Passos caught the mood of the changing scene by a kaleidoscopic use of news headlines and satirized the complacency of business leadership in American life.

Naturalistic writers like James T. Farrell, Richard Wright, and Meyer Levin portrayed the theme of social degeneration against the slums of Chicago. In *Studs Lonigan* (1935), a semi-autobiographical trilogy, Farrell told the story of a vicious South Side gang of young Irish-Americans, their predatory habits and the social excrescences surrounding their home and sex life. The inferential indictment of a society which could produce such unhealthy growths was damning. The incredible filth and poverty of Chicago's blighted Negro section provided the background chosen by the young Negro writer, Richard Wright, for his *Native Son* (1940), which pictured a warped human product of this squalor and lack of economic opportunity in Bigger Thomas, whose revolting crimes were committed in a grim sociological setting. Meyer Levin's *The Old Bunch* (1937) was, like Farrell's novels, a frank account of a gang of Jewish youths in Chicago's decaying West Side.

The rural slums of the South were no less challenging to the naturalistic school than was urban squalor. Native Southerners like William Faulkner of Mississippi and Erskine Caldwell of Georgia mercilessly flayed the degeneration of various backward rural regions and startled many a gentle reader with plots involving incest, gross carnality, and idiocy. Faulkner's *Sanctuary* (1931), perhaps the best known of his many novels, scored the stubborn backwardness and reactionary mentality of certain southern types. One of Caldwell's novels, *Tobacco Road* (1932), which enjoyed great popularity in dramatized form, presented an appalling picture of rural poverty and shiftless degeneracy in Jeeter Lester and his family. In an age when southern demagogues like Huey Long of Louisiana and Governor Talmadge of Georgia made the illiteracy, prejudices, and economic helplessness of a vast segment of the rural population the foundation stone of their power, the sweeping indictment of "poor whites" by southern liberals was comprehensible.

When Caldwell turned from fiction to write *You Have Seen Their Faces* (1927), he found a highly sympathetic audience for this candidly illustrated attack on the inertia and conservatism of journalism and politics in the South and for his plea that sharecroppers organize. Much of the tragedy of depleted soil and wasted human resources in the rural South was implied in John Steinbeck's picture of evicted Oklahoma farmers adrift on the nation's highways in jalopies, presented in the best-seller *Grapes of Wrath* (1939). More than any other novel since *Uncle Tom's Cabin,* this book awakened the people to the human cost of an exploitative agricultural system and, more important, it led to legislative action in behalf of dispossessed farmers.

Many literary expatriates of the 1920's hurried home from Europe when the depression began. Among that "lost generation" was Ernest Hemingway, who aptly expressed the changed atmosphere of his native land and now preached the new social consciousness, notably in *To Have and Have Not* (1937). His most successful theme was the Fascist threat to democracy as symbolized in the Spanish Civil War—a miniature world war between Fascist and anti-Fascist armies. In *For Whom the Bell Tolls* (1940), Hemingway depicted the martyrdom of an American college instructor who fought for Loyalist Spain and the ideal of industrial democracy. Sinclair Lewis, another outstanding individualist writer of the 1920's, also made the necessary ideological adjustment to the new social and economic emphasis. *It Can't Happen Here* (1935), his imaginative picture of the advent of Fascism in America on the heels of a prolonged economic depression, became a best-seller, although critics were not agreed on its purely literary merits.

More concerned with painstaking self-analysis and the breakdown of social values than with social panaceas was the meteoric Thomas Wolfe of North Carolina, whose death in 1938 cut short a brilliant literary career. His *Look Homeward, Angel* (1929), an autobiographical family chronicle, brought him into the front rank of novelists; subsequently the theme was continued successfully in *Of Time and the River* (1935) and in several later novels. Readers admired his personal idealism, magnificent rhetoric, and deep-seated sentiment. Certain novelists avoided harsh realism by rediscovering the comforting traditional virtues of home and fireside. This was the case with Thornton Wilder's popular *Our Town* (1938), although one of his earlier volumes, *Heaven Is My Destination* (1935), was more critical in tone. On a lower literary plane was *Gone with the Wind* (1936), an extraordinarily popular historical novel by Margaret Mitchell which blended the traditional romantic qualities of southern plantation life with a certain amount of economic realism. A flood of other historical novels, from Stark Young's *So Red the Rose* (1934) to much slighter books, constituted much of the fiction read during the 1930's. Not only was there comfort for a distressed generation in stories that told of the treasured past, but there was often a tendency to find meaningful and helpful analogies between the present and the past.

DRAMA AND THE STAGE

Dramatic literature reflected similar trends. The proletarian theme was most effectively sounded by Clifford Odets, who in *Waiting for Lefty* used an impressionist technique to dramatize labor exploitation and emphasized mass unity as against the isolated action of the individual. His *Awake and Sing,* a portrayal of the economic struggles of a Jewish family in the Bronx, struck a note of hopeful idealism. In the thirties as in the twenties, Paul Green continued to depict southern realism on the stage, but in a far less exaggerated form than *Tobacco Road.* He dealt sympathetically as well as understandingly with the relations of black and white (*The House of Connelly*), the decay of the southern aristocratic tradition, and the suffering of prisoners in chain gangs under their bosses (*Hymn to the Rising Sun*).

As in the preceding decade, Eugene O'Neill maintained his rank as an outstanding craftsman among his fellow dramatists, although his persistent interest in psychological subjects sometimes spurred the socially-minded critics to frank disparagement. In his long drama, *Mourning Becomes Electra,* he attempted to discover abiding human values in the Greek tragedy by Aeschylus. The historical theme enjoyed a major triumph in Robert E. Sherwood's *Abe Lincoln in Illinois,* which gave a timely emphasis to democratic idealism; his other success, *Idiot's Delight,* dramatized the economic mainspring of war. Among the other important dramatists of the period who were concerned with the immediate problems of a disjointed social order were Maxwell Anderson, whose *Winterset* was based on the Sacco-Vanzetti case, and Elmer Rice, who excoriated Fascism in *Judgment Day,* which dealt with the burning of the Reichstag by the Nazis.

The depression years blotted out the legitimate theater in many cities and left thousands of actors stranded. In New York, the last refuge of the drama, two-thirds of the theaters were dark in 1931. The long-established Shuberts went into receivership and A. H. Woods, the famous producer, also became bankrupt. Hollywood enticed many stage celebrities to the west coast; this resulted indirectly in raising production costs for the legitimate stage because the remaining stars had to be paid more to offset Hollywood's heavily competitive bids.

To employ the thousands of actors, musicians, and other entertainers left idle by the decline in the legitimate theater, the Federal Theatre Project was organized in 1935 with Hallie Flanagan of Vassar College as national director and Elmer Rice, the New York playwright, as regional director for the East. Under its auspices plays were performed in twenty-eight states; many of the audiences, especially in the rural sections, had never before seen a stage play. Despite broad streaks of amateurishness, the Federal Theatre gained steadily in artistic stature; at times it undertook significant dramatic experiments which the commercial stage usually avoided. Among its more striking presentations were a dramatization of Sinclair Lewis' *It Can't Happen Here,* a convincing interpretation of Sherwood's *Abe Lincoln in Illinois,* and a jazz version of Gilbert and Sullivan's *Mikado* with an all-Negro cast. The distinguished personalities connected with the Federal Theatre Project included the versatile Orson Welles, who later founded the experimental Mercury Theatre. By June, 1939, when Congress terminated it because certain critics of the Administration believed it extravagant and Communist in tendency, the Federal Theatre Project had become a seven-million-dollar enterprise employing more than 12,000 persons and had hopes of developing into a permanent national theater for the United States.

As economic conditions improved during the middle thirties, the legitimate theater recovered some of its former luster. While the depression was at its depth the most popular plays, according to the Beards, dealt with crime and mystery as a supplement to the eternal triangle. But a number of important and successful plays, such as those of Sherwood, Rice, Odets, O'Neill, and Anderson, had more serious plots that concerned contemporary problems. Caldwell's *Tobacco Road* enjoyed an astonishing five-year run in New York that eclipsed the phenomenal record set by *Abie's Irish Rose* a decade earlier. Its success was due to its appeal to an audience that ranged from socially-conscious intellectuals to those who frankly enjoyed the undisguised bawdiness of the play. As always, stage comedies usually monopolized the long runs—like *You Can't Take It With You,* a good-humored satire on current politics by George S. Kaufman and Moss Hart.

As the decade wore on, Hollywood stars in increasing numbers alternated in stage and screen roles. Theatre Guild audiences warmly applauded Helen Hayes, especially for her convincing and sympathetic interpretation of the tragic Mary Stuart in Maxwell Anderson's *Mary of Scotland.* Katharine Hepburn added to her Hollywood laurels by her buoyant performance in *The Philadelphia Story.* Paul Muni, Tallulah Bankhead, and Dorothy Gish (of the "silent" film days) were major attractions to theatrical audiences. As in previous years, the stage favorites included the Lunts, Walter Hampden, Eva Le Gallienne, and Katharine Cornell.

POETRY: ERA OF T. S. ELIOT

Poetry lost the atmosphere of unintelligibility and personal nostalgia so fashionable during the 1920's among many followers of Ezra Pound and Gertrude Stein. That Pound himself, basking on the shores of Italy, would later openly embrace Mussolini's Fascism became clear when his "Jefferson and/or Mussolini" appeared. On the whole, American poets forsook the hyper-aestheticism of "pure art" in favor of expressing the new social issues. Typical of this shift was Archibald MacLeish, who revealed the current feeling of social bewilderment in "Land of the Free," an ironic poem that described the now tragic westward movement of evicted farmers and the plight of jobless coal miners and factory workers. Likewise, although Edna St. Vincent Millay frequently reverted to her earlier emotional yearnings, she protested against economic injustice in *Wine from these Grapes* and bitterly lamented the fall of democratic Spain in "Say That We Saw Spain Die." A new rebellious spirit filled Carl Sandburg, particularly in the defiant *The People, Yes,* with its reformist theme of social democracy. But few followed Robinson Jeffers in defining anew the agony of a soul battered down by spiritual frustration.

T. S. Eliot, who had despaired over the spiritual drought and sterile skepticism of the twenties in *The Waste Land* (1922), discovered a refuge in the Church and its dogmas, for his poem "Ash Wednesday" (1930) was a public confession of his conversion to Anglo-Catholicism. This exaltation of faith and the certainties of the past as the savior of the turbulent modern world underlay his religious poem, "The Rock" (1933), and the poetical play, *Murder in the Cathedral* (1935), which was based on the martyrdom of Thomas à Becket. But Eliot's indisputable reputation as a "poet's poet" was won not primarily because of his religious message or even his metaphysical subtleties, but rather for his superb poetical technique, his invigorating imagery, and —to a considerable extent—his intellectuality. As a result the Eliot School, despite accusations of rank Toryism and cloistered detachment, proved extremely influential in both creative poetry and aesthetics.

More than ever, novelists, dramatists, and poets turned to regionalism as the key to the integrated folk life of a cultural area. Among the most self-conscious regionalists were the southern agrarians, including the so-called fugitive group of Nashville poets led by Allen Tate, a devotee of T. S. Eliot, and John Crowe Ransom. In *I'll Take My Stand* (1930) this group, joined by other southern writers and teachers, stated its belief in a rural southern traditionalism cast in a precapitalist, Jeffersonian, aesthetic mold. This series of essays was promptly labeled aristocratic romanticism in the liberal press, and its rejection of machine culture and the modern scientific temper was called reactionary. But, as already noted, few of the leading southern novelists who wrote about the Deep South continued to err on the side of romanticism.

DECLINE OF THE PSYCHOLOGICAL BIOGRAPHY

Biography, which in the 1920's had been the hunting ground of writers who used Freudian techniques to probe the inmost recesses of the soul, took a more scientific turn and reached ever-closer affinity with the professional historian's work. The biographies of the thirties tended to be heavy tomes, sometimes three or four volumes in length, and to rely more heavily on original sources. The changing emphasis in biographical writing was clearly exemplified by the abrupt transition in Carl Sandburg's six-volume life of Lincoln. The first two volumes, which appeared during the twenties, were a poetical but scarcely historical portrait of Lincoln, whereas the other four, which were published in 1939 under the title of *The War Years,* were so thoroughly steeped in source materials that historians hailed them enthusiastically. In this same realistic and factual pattern was the four-volume "definitive" life of Robert E. Lee by Douglas S. Freeman, a southern journalist. Professional historians themselves achieved new standards of unadorned realism in biography, notably in the *American Political Leaders Series* (1930–) edited by Allan Nevins. The scholarly *Dictionary of American Biography* was also completed during this decade.

Although "debunking" for its own sake ceased to be popular, the current vogue for social criticism subjected famous business leaders to unflattering portraits. In *The Robber Barons* (1934), Matthew Josephson described the financial buccaneers of the post-Civil War generation; his *The Politicos* (1938) portrayed their corrupt alliance with politicians. A mild sensation was created by Ferdinand Lundberg's *America's Sixty Families* (1937), a challenging biographical treatment of financial concentration which had sinister implications for the survival of democracy. The same writer also scored with his *Imperial Hearst* (1936), which described the enormous power of an erratic publisher who had long since forgotten his early liberalism. John D. Rockefeller, Sr., attracted several biographers, among them John T. Flynn, the liberal financial writer, and Allan Nevins, whose painstaking two-volume work was hailed as "definitive."

The decade was so rich in this type of realistic biography that adequate enumeration is impossible. Critics singled out, as particularly worth while, Carl Van Doren's life of Franklin, Marquis James' Sam Houston and Andrew Jackson, Henry S. Commager's Theodore

Parker, Lloyd Lewis' William T. Sherman, Philip C. Jessup's Elihu Root, and Harry Barnard's Altgeld. In a related field, *The Autobiography of Lincoln Steffens* (1931) revealed the evolution of an early muckraker who came to espouse Communism.

SOCIAL CONSCIOUSNESS IN HISTORY

The flood of sound historical biographies and the widespread popularity of historical novels led professional historians to capitalize on the current vogue for retrospection. Responding to the pressure for academic guidance in a topsy-turvy world, they presented social, economic, and intellectual history from a more socially conscious point of view. The progress of specialization during the past few decades had deprived historians of their earlier academic affiliations with political science, sociology, and literature, but now they hastily embarked on a search for an "interdisciplinary" unity which would give both the world and historians themselves a coherent idea of social causation.

Together with their fellow social scientists, scores of historians contributed to the *Encyclopædia of the Social Sciences,* a comprehensive fifteen-volume work edited by Edwin R. A. Seligman and Alvin Johnson in cooperation with the ten leading social science societies, ranging from history to statistics. This was no ordinary encyclopedia but a highly authoritative work which provided a sound basis for fruitful cooperation among social scientists. The same trend was reflected in the extensive activities of the Social Science Research Council of New York, which stressed the interdisciplinary approach and by subsidies enabled young scholars to escape the narrowness involved in extreme specialization in one of the social studies.

Few men were so well equipped to present the multifold phases of modern life from politics to the arts as Charles A. Beard, at one time a professor at Columbia. In 1939 he and his wife Mary reviewed the decade in *America in Midpassage,* the third volume in their brilliant survey of American civilization. They gave considerable attention to aesthetic and ideological aspects, the role of organized labor in our economy, and the economic sources of our foreign and domestic policies. Many critics, however, were antagonized by Charles Beard's isolationism, for, despite an overtone of social democracy, its dominant note was economic nationalism. In earlier books he had advocated ultimate economic self-sufficiency (*The Open Door at Home,* 1934) and justified its historical soundness (*The Idea of National Interest,* 1934). To him, the redirection of investments into home channels seemed the only alternative to exploitative imperialism and war. He derided internationalists as unrealistic and antiquated in their outlook.

Of the host of significant studies in American history written with an intimate knowledge of the social and economic environment, few ranked higher than Charles M. Andrews' four-volume *Colonial Period of American History* (1934–1938), which weighed carefully the influence of capitalistic expansion in Europe on the New World. In the field of cultural history, the path-breaking *History of American Life Series,* edited by A. M. Schlesinger and D. R. Fox, neared completion. Thomas J. Wertenbaker's *The Founding of American Civilization: The Middle Colonies* (1938) was the first volume of a promising series of regional cultural histories. Noteworthy among the several frank discussions of slave insurrections in the South was Bell I. Wiley's *Southern Negroes, 1861–1865* (1938), which swept away the myth of the docile, carefree black and revealed the Negro's fierce struggle for freedom. Interestingly enough, this book was originally subsidized by the Daughters of the Confederacy.

Among the vast numbers of regional and state histories, many of them of high quality, were the guidebooks prepared by the Federal Writers Project of the W.P.A. The W.P.A. mapped the entire nation by regions and prepared a guidebook for each of these units; the history and present-day social life of the larger cities were covered in separate guidebooks. The W.P.A. put historians under permanent obligation by assembling such comprehensive inventories of documentary materials as the Survey of Federal Archives and the Historical Records Survey, in the preparation of which local depositories were combed for letters and files of historic interest. Long-forgotten letters of Daniel Boone turned up in an old North Carolina courthouse and thousands of Lincoln war dispatches and Civil War documents were discovered in the dome of Chicago's old post office building.

American historians of the European scene joined the trend toward cultural history, rewriting the past in terms of contemporary issues. William L. Langer of Harvard edited a series, *The Rise of Modern Europe,* in which the emphasis was shifted from the purely political to social, cultural, and intellectual history. This series made possible a high degree of synthesis in historical interpretation from the point of view of the present generation. More exclusively "cultural" was Preserved Smith's erudite *History of Modern Culture,* a series which dealt with modern Europe and stressed the rise of science, in addition to treating other phases of intellectual history. The American Historical Association itself set an example to its members, especially in the European field, by arranging convention programs that high-lighted problems of direct contemporary significance.

PUBLIC ADMINISTRATION AND POLITICAL PHILOSOPHY

The fluctuating interests of political scientists constituted a sensitive barometer of the history of the 1930's. The sharply increased role of government in business—what unfriendly critics called bureaucracy—resulted in such a rapid growth in the science of public administration that few universities of any size dared not offer at least one course on the subject. Intimately bound up with this development were the widespread popularity of democratic planning and the keen interest in the efficiency of public service. As the basis for a long series of monographs to be prepared by experts, the Social Science Research Council in 1933 established the important Commission of Inquiry on Public Service Personnel to conduct extensive hearings in eleven cities. The Commission's report stressed the ideal of a non-political "career service" along the lines of Great Britain's famous administrative branch. About two years later, the Council organized the Committee on Public Administration to cooperate with public and private agencies in formulating scientific principles of administration and securing recent data on current problems and practices. Extremely important in coordinating the numerous planning bureaus and gathering basic facts concerning our national resources was the National Resources Board, which later became one of the New Deal's chief planning agencies.

Few major issues at Washington left political scientists untouched. Roosevelt's Supreme Court reform proposal brought forth a surprising number of books and articles, some of them favoring such changes and others opposing any further extension of executive control over the judiciary. Sympathy for the New Deal was so well entrenched that many academicians rebuked the increasingly conservative Walter Lippmann for the nineteenth-century individualism he advocated in *The Good Society* (1937). In view of the victories of totalitarianism abroad, Lippmann feared that New Deal "collectivism," spurred on by pressure groups, was endangering individual rights. The growth of totalitarianism and the decline of *laissez-faire* ideas helped to create a renewed interest in political philosophy which reexamined, often with devastating results, the fundamental assumptions underlying our political institutions. In this realistic departure from the conventional static analyses of the structure of political institutions Harvard and the University of Chicago furnished much of the leadership, and political theory became a major part of their courses on government. In foreign affairs, to judge from random polls, most political scientists were liberal Wilsonians in supporting some form of international association.

ECONOMISTS AND THE ASSAULT ON *LAISSEZ FAIRE*

In this period of economic dislocation, the science of political economy made vast inroads on the school curriculum; relatively few high-ranking academic economists, however, were included in the Administration's most intimate councils. President Hoover at first listened to certain orthodox economists who advised waiting for the natural market forces to reassert themselves, but soon afterward he waived them aside as "reactionary." Similarly, congressional committees found too many economic experts wedded to the conservative businessman's view of the world. Early in the New Deal, Roosevelt relied to a considerable extent on Professor James H. Rogers of Yale for advice on both domestic and foreign policy. Although Rogers favored the use of temporary budget deficits to curb depressions and restraints on spending to deflate dangerous booms, like many other economists he opposed the purchasing of silver and the philosophy of artificial scarcity implied in the N.R.A. and the A.A.A.; eventually he became openly critical of the long-deferred balancing of the budget. Thereupon Roosevelt for a time turned to unorthodox monetary theorists and other experimentally-minded economists for advice.

In speaking of this peculiar situation in his presidential address to the American Economic Association on December 27, 1935, Professor

J. M. Clark inferentially defended Roosevelt's attitude when he mentioned the failure of the existing economic system and the necessity of immediate action: "It [the future] points to the likelihood of a world full of trial-and-error experimentation, in which the more deliberate studies may seem fated to reach their goal, if at all, too late to render service. That chance some of us may take, while others grapple with the more immediate issues." Seven pro-New Deal economists at Harvard and Tufts advanced arguments for government spending in a cooperative work, *An Economic Program for American Democracy* (1939); but other economists, like N. S. B. Gras in *Business and Capitalism* (1939), upheld the orthodox economic order on the authority of history.

Critics of capitalism—and of economists as well—were legion. Representative of the extreme left was the shrewd Marxian assault on the foundations of individual enterprise and the flagrant injustice of wealth distribution embodied in Lewis Corey's *The Decline of American Capitalism* (1933). In the name of "democratic collectivism," Professor John R. Commons of the University of Wisconsin, himself a lifelong rebel against economic injustice, characterized Corey's book as totalitarianism. Middle-of-the-road critics of *laissez faire,* including some prominent New Dealers and institutional economists, discovered a fount of inspiration in Thorstein Veblen's writings, which distinguished between the creative role of the craftsman-engineer and the predatory role of business and finance. Joseph Dorfman's biography, *Thorstein Veblen and His America* (1935), provided a factual and analytical basis that was especially valuable to those who were seeking a theoretical foundation for the social control of business. Wesley Mitchell, the famous institutionalist of the business cycle, collected Veblen's writings in *What Veblen Taught* (1936). Veblen's book, *The Engineers and the Price System* (1919), was claimed by Howard Scott's industrial engineers to have inspired them in their meteoric crusade for "technocracy," which they hoped would replace the limited productivity of an economy motivated solely by price with an engineer-dominated system that permitted the maximum employment of technology. The war between capitalism and "technics" and the bankruptcy of leisure-class values, as Lewis Mumford saw the problem, would be resolved in favor of a collectivist solution.

The reiterated challenge, "Want in the midst of plenty," came under the microscope of experts with the publication of *America's Capacity to Produce* (1934), prepared by several economists of the Brookings Institution. This book maintained that even during the idyllic years of the late twenties the nation's productive capacity had been far above actual production, perhaps by as much as $15,000,000,000. The Institution also sponsored a companion volume, *America's Capacity to Consume* (1934), which revealed the almost infinite market that was still untapped in a society where, even in the peak year of prosperity, one-fifth of the families earned less than $1000 and 71 per cent received less than $2500. The goal of a more abundant life, it seemed to follow, still lay somewhere in a socially planned future rather than in the mythical golden age of the 1920's.

Economists trained in the classical tradition were reminded by M. S. Eccles, the New Deal chairman of the Federal Reserve Board, that "the economics of the system as a whole differs profoundly from the economics of the individual; that that which is economically wise behavior on the part of a single individual may on occasion be suicidal if engaged in by all individuals collectively; that the income of the nation is but the counterpart of the expenditures of the nation." Professor Richard A. Lester of Princeton argued against the older individualist economics in an article in the *American Economic Review*: "Broad social and national questions of an economic nature are not only complicated by numerous variable factors, and therefore not subject to the 'other things remaining the same' type of reasoning, but these 'other things' are often determined, not by precise calculations and mathematical equations, but by factors of social psychology." The repeated assaults on neo-classical theory were followed by the significant theories of "imperfect competition" and "monopolistic competition," whose leading exponents were Professor Edward H. Chamberlain of Harvard, author of *The Theory of Monopolistic Competition* (1933), and Joan Robinson, an Englishwoman who wrote *The Economics of Imperfect Competition* (1933). These theories held that, for the purpose of analysis, monopolist conditions rather than purely competitive factors were to be taken as "ubiquitous and determining, rather than exceptional and inconsequential, features of modern economic life."

SOCIOLOGY AND ANTHROPOLOGY

While social workers were becoming increasingly involved in the administrative aspects of poverty and personal maladjustment, they were also confronted by theoretical problems allied to sociology, psychology, economics, political science, and medicine. Sociologists turned to descriptive studies of the regional ecological type (a concept borrowed from biology) which stressed the environmental influence on social behavior. Many of these regional studies proved invaluable as the basis for social planning. An examination of over three hundred research projects under way in 1934 placed human ecology next to poverty and dependency as the field of greatest interest to sociologists. This emphasis on regionalism was most pronounced in the country's three leading sociology departments—those at the University of Chicago, Columbia University, and the University of North Carolina. Professor Howard Odum of the latter institution directed the Southern Regional Survey, which involved innumerable studies and charts of that area.

The federal government itself turned sociologist in promoting ecological research and investigating housing conditions, Negro problems, rural migration, and the history of American folk lore. One result of this ecological emphasis was the abundance of books on the city; at least half a dozen volumes on this subject appeared in 1939 alone. Among such books was George R. Leighton's case history, *Five Cities* (1939). *Middletown in Transition* (1937), the Lynds' second book about Muncie, Indiana, discussed the impact of the depression on the city's attitudes and institutions. Especially stimulating from a different point of view was Lewis Mumford's *The Culture of Cities* (1938), an interpretation of the role of cities in civilization.

A notable contribution to sociological analysis was the two-volume *Recent Social Trends in the United States* (1933) with a preface by President Herbert Hoover. This book summarized the studies made under the direction of the President's Research Committee on Social Trends, and was accompanied by a series of monographs on the chief phases of American life, from population trends to recreation and the arts. Its conclusions, well buttressed by statistical evidence, proved invaluable to teachers and students in the social sciences. Sociologists and their interests were given a commanding position in the *Encyclo-*

pædia of the Social Sciences, which has already been mentioned. Despite their leanings toward theory, sociologists were also prominent in public affairs. Practically every experienced sociologist in the country, according to Professor L. L. Bernard of Washington University, was a member of one or more of the committees formed for research work or for the active promotion of the public welfare.

In analyzing the group traits of a selected community, especially in urban areas, sociologists like the Lynds, and many of the ecological school as well, frequently turned to the descriptive methods used by cultural anthropologists. The latter, in turn, often employed a sociological and psychological approach in examining the interrelations of culture and personality. In other words, anthropology had become a science of contemporary social analysis as well as a science of primitive society. Just as Veblen had turned anthropologist in his classic *Theory of the Leisure Class* (1899) when he described the cultural traits and attitudes of society that are based on pecuniary values, Thurman Arnold, a professor of law at Yale and a high-ranking New Dealer, used cultural anthropology as an approach in his devastating critique of *laissez-faire* society, *The Folklore of Capitalism* (1937). This convergence of the social sciences was hailed in Melville Herskovits' essay in the *American Anthropologist* which bore the suggestive title, "The Significance of Thorstein Veblen for Anthropology."

Nazi theories of racial superiority were emphatically denounced by the American Anthropological Association at its annual meeting in December, 1938. Numerous books condemning "Aryanism" appeared. In *Race Differences* (1935), Otto Klineberg examined the existing knowledge regarding racial traits and variations but found no scientific proof of differences between races in psychology or mentality. Race itself, he concluded, could not be regarded as the *cause* of any cultural trait. Books and articles by Franz Boas, Max Radin, and numerous other prominent anthropologists were likewise aimed at destroying the myth of race. An influential work dealing with the controversy that attained wide popularity was J. Barzun's *Race: A Study of Modern Superstition* (1937). On the whole, Americans during the 1930's did not uphold extreme doctrines of heredity—a reversal of the emphasis on the superior individual, family, or class that was common in the preceding decade. People in this decade of social planning in the United States tended to believe optimistically in the all-powerful influence exerted by a beneficial environment on individual and group problems. Although this was not as pronounced here as it was in the Soviet Union, it was nevertheless unmistakable.

ENVIRONMENTALISM IN PSYCHOLOGY AND EDUCATION

The current interest in mass behavior, especially in the propaganda technique used by the totalitarian governments, was evidenced in the increased popularity of social psychology. This emphasis on mass psychology was shown clearly by the publication in one year—1936—of L. Doob's *Propaganda,* H. Cantril and G. W. Allport's *The Psychology of Radio,* and E. Dale's *The Control of Moving Pictures.* Psychology itself, as one psychologist put it, was "concerned increasingly with the real problems of real human beings." This was reflected in practical experiments to determine traffic judgments of automobile drivers, in vocational and industrial analysis, in adult learning programs, and in personnel tests. The many books on child psychology which appeared treated the subject not solely in relation to education but from practically every environmental aspect.

Psychiatry likewise yielded to the current emphasis on environmental causation, and neuroses tended to be attributed to environmental stresses rather than to heredity. This was notably true in K. Horney's *The Neurotic Personality of Our Time* (1937), which suggested that it was both more reasonable and more effective to alter an individual's cultural environment than to try to rehabilitate him directly. Robert L. Faris and H. W. Dunham, the sociologists, studied 34,864 patients in psychopathic institutions in preparing to write their book, *Mental Disorders in Urban Areas* (1939). These studies led them to refine the environmental theory by relating certain types of insanity to specific segments of urban environments, such as rooming-house areas and slums. Popular interest centered around the fact that increasing numbers of new patients were being admitted to mental institutions. The depression was held directly responsible by many, but others denied this, pointing out that the only relation between the two was the fact that the depression made it economically impossible for many families to care for mentally defective members at home.

Nowhere, perhaps, was environmentalism so influential as in educational theory. In the past Americans had alternately emphasized the school as an agency of beneficent change and the conservator of the existing order. The declining influence of the home and church during the depression period brought with it extravagant demands upon the school system to lead the forces of social reconstruction. Educators pointed out that more laws affecting the curriculum had been passed in the thirties than had existed in 1928. School administrators were urged to introduce courses on good citizenship, vocational subjects, and "socialized" studies. Discontent with the influence of business on education that characterized the past was openly expressed at professional meetings.

At Columbia University, where in a twofold sense progressive education had long been dominant under the continued inspiration of John Dewey, the challenge to education was undisguised. One of Dewey's leftist colleagues, George S. Counts, had insisted for over a decade that the nation was moving toward collectivism and had defied the orthodox by praising the educational experiments of the Soviet Union. He expressed his ideal of a democratic collectivism in a provocative pamphlet, "Dare the School Build a New Social Order?" Another outstanding colleague was William H. Kilpatrick, author of *Education and the Social Crisis* (1932) and frank advocate of indoctrination along socially cooperative lines. Dewey himself, believing as he did in intelligent planning along experimental lines, a "socialized" personality, and democracy, was in his element during the early years of the New Deal.

Educators of the traditional type were dismayed by the belligerent report made in 1934 by the Commission on Social Studies, which had been appointed by the American Historical Association five years earlier. The Commission announced:

"Cumulative evidence supports the conclusion that in the United States, as in other countries, the age of individualism and *laissez-faire* in economy and government is closing and that a new age of collectivism is emerging.

"The emerging age is particularly an age of transition. It is marked by numerous and severe tensions arising out of conflict between actual trends toward integrated economy and society, on the one side, and traditional practices, dispositions, ideas, and institutional arrangements inherited from the passing age of individualism on the other. . . ."

The Commission demanded that students be given a deeper knowledge of society and its problems and that teachers be better informed on contemporary events. Among the desirable goals it stressed were democratic freedom, untrammeled scholarship, economic security, intercultural tolerance, the combination of utility with aesthetics, the substitution of cooperative and moral values for acquisitive individualism, and enlightened nationalism.

Educators in progressive school systems tended to reduce individual competition among children and to hold that when a child failed it was the school that was at fault. School systems in the larger cities consciously emphasized racial tolerance and devoted considerable attention to the dangers of foreign propaganda. The nation-wide trend toward permanent tenure for competent teachers who satisfactorily completed a brief trial period made it safe for the more liberal teachers to discuss current problems freely. However, the smaller communities resisted this trend.

THE HUTCHINS-ADLER REVOLT AGAINST RELATIVISM

President Robert Maynard Hutchins of the University of Chicago attacked the college curriculum for its exaggerated vocationalism at the expense of humanist courses. In *The Higher Learning in America* (1936)—the title was borrowed from Thorstein Veblen, who had assailed the colleges for their pecuniary interests—President Hutchins created a furor among professors and college administrators by recommending a return to the medieval curriculum embodied in the *trivium* and *quadrivium,* which included grammar, rhetoric, logic, arithmetic, geometry, astronomy, and music. He advocated the establishment of junior colleges which would include the last two years of high school and the first two years of college and would deal with these subjects; the last two years of college would be devoted to the natural and social sciences and metaphysics. Mere factualism, he maintained, should be replaced by a unified conception of the universe which, he believed, would afford an unshakeable basis for democracy and social justice. Especially interesting was Hutchins' plan to recover the certainties and wisdom of the past by including in the curriculum the study of a hundred great books. This idea was successfully introduced at St. John's College, Maryland.

Hutchins and certain of his associates, notably Mortimer J. Adler of the Philosophy Department, were roundly criticized. Adler, who had come to the University of Chicago with Hutchins, was an outspoken disciple of St. Thomas Aquinas. He denounced the relativist and pragmatic philosophies of his colleagues and shared with Hutchins the medieval dream of intellectual unity as a means of meeting the challenge of modern totalitarianism and anarchic skepticism. The attack on the Hutchins-Adler group was led by John Dewey of Columbia, who labeled such ideas as dangerously reactionary. On the other hand, the Catholics, who were experiencing a notable revival of Thomistic philosophy which had begun more than a generation earlier and was currently fostered by such brilliant men as Jacques Maritain, heartily endorsed the transformation taking place at the University of Chicago.

This revival of interest in the teachings of St. Thomas gave added vitality to contemporary Catholic thought. In April, 1939, appeared a new journal, *The Thomist: A Speculative Quarterly Review,* which was edited by the Dominicans and printed by the well-known Catholic publishers, Sheed and Ward. Also serving the Thomist cause were numerous English translations of the leading French philosophers, Jacques Maritain and Étienne Gilson, which stimulated neo-scholasticism in America. Adler himself performed yeoman service in relating Thomism to current problems in *St. Thomas and the Gentiles* (1938). The trend toward neo-scholasticism was also evident in the influential *Religion and Culture Series* (1937—), edited by Dr. Joseph Husslein.

SOCIAL PHILOSOPHY

Among the newer trends in secular philosophy was an increased emphasis on social philosophy and the philosophy of science. Problems of democracy, freedom, and ethics were reexamined in their contemporary as well as their historic setting. An organized effort to attain "a philosophic synthesis of the social sciences" resulted in the appearance during 1935 of the *Journal of Social Philosophy,* edited by the social theorist, R. M. MacIver of Columbia University. Many philosophers were perturbed by the skeptical inferences of the new physics, especially the relativist idea implied in the principle of indeterminacy. In 1937 Einstein himself joined in a symposium on "The Nature of Causal Relation in the Light of Recent Physics"; the controversy led one participant, Professor Morris R. Cohen, to remark, "Without determination there is no basis for scientific search or any other planned activity."

The decade was marked by the publication of a large number of biographies and anthologies dealing with American philosophies of the past and present. Ralph Barton Perry of Harvard, a student of William James though not himself a pragmatist, won the Pulitzer Prize for his scholarly two-volume work, *The Thought and Character of William James* (1936). Paul A. Schilpp of Northwestern University edited *The Library of Living Philosophers,* the first volume of which was devoted to John Dewey's writings. Dewey himself in 1938 published *Logic: The Theory of Inquiry,* which was widely discussed because of its unconventional departure from the formal aspects of logic in favor of a broad sociological emphasis on scientific inquiry. Still a pragmatist, Dewey saw truth as something approximated rather than attained by the scientist. Indicative of the increasing interest in the history and evolution of ideas was the illuminating book, *The Great Chain of Being: A Study in the History of an Idea* (1936), by Arthur O. Lovejoy, a professor at Johns Hopkins, and his editorial efforts in behalf of the *Journal of the History of Ideas: A Quarterly Devoted to Intellectual History,* the first number of which appeared in January, 1940.

PHYSICS AND ASTRONOMY

Philosophers could indeed claim a unique intimacy with physicists and physical chemists, whose investigations of the mystery of an atom-built universe showed that reality was as elusive to scientists as to metaphysicists. So widespread was the interest in the nucleus of the atom both here and abroad that nuclear physics seemed to dominate the field. In 1931 Professor Harold C. Urey of Columbia announced his discovery of an isotype of hydrogen with an atomic weight of two instead of one; he called it deuterium. The discovery of this "heavy hydrogen," as it became known, was followed immediately by experiments to determine the physiological effects of heavy water, which contains deuterium, on plants and animals, and finally on the aging of the human body itself. Urey's research, which won him the Nobel Prize, introduced undreamed-of possibilities of new compounds of hydrogen and led Ernest E. Rutherford, a leading British scientist, to hail this development as "one of the most important discoveries of the century." It also opened a new path for the "atom-smashers," for these physicists (some of them were practically electrical engineers) now sought to discover the properties of the nucleus by bombarding atoms with deuterium particles and with the newly discovered neutrons, the non-electrically charged particles in the atom. The ancient dream of transmuting baser elements into gold would soon be realized —at least so popular science magazines implied.

Physicists—in particular Robert A. Millikan of the California Institute of Technology and Arthur H. Compton of the University of Chicago, both of whom won Nobel Prizes—made the front pages by their measurements of the cosmic rays, whose all-pervading energy was already known to both European and American scientists. Although Millikan and Compton disagreed as to whether these rays were a form of radiation or consisted of charged particles, both agreed that they originated in interstellar space beyond the Milky Way. Even sober scientists speculated on the possibility that atomic energy, perhaps from these cosmic rays, would revolutionize civilization by providing an unlimited source of motive power. A possibly important step toward this goal occurred in 1939 when German scientists split the uranium nucleus by means of neutron bombardment and released some 175,000,000 electron-volts of energy per atom. In spite of the strained relations between the two countries, American scientists were able to obtain sufficient data to confirm the experiment and to make important supplementary observations and measurements.

Despite drastic cuts in research budgets resulting from the depression, research men, especially in the larger, better-equipped laboratories, were able to make spectacular progress through the cooperation of individuals and institutions. This was particularly true in astronomy, for observatories and the other expensive equipment required could be used jointly. Ingenious applications of modern photography followed the pioneer lines laid down by George E. Hale of the University of Chicago whose spectroheliograph, invented in 1891, enabled him to photograph the sun and thus study the prominences at its edges. In 1936 Robert R. McMath and his associates at the University of Michigan took motion pictures of the sun.

During the latter part of the decade certain astronomers challenged the popular theories of the "expanding universe"; one of them maintained that, on the contrary, the universe is tending toward disintegration. To clarify this and many related problems, plans were made for the construction of a 200-inch telescope at Mount Palomar, to be completed in the 1940's, which would penetrate more than a billion light-years.

Pluto, a long-awaited planet, was finally identified from a photograph taken in 1930, which showed it beyond Neptune. The orbit of the new planet had been estimated by means of intricate calculations, and predictions as to its location had been made in 1914 by Percival Lowell of Harvard; hence its discovery was hailed as a triumph of mathematical astronomy.

APPLIED CHEMISTRY AND MEDICINE

Among the natural sciences, applied chemistry alone had little to fear from the depression. On the contrary, the demands of businessmen and manufacturers for lower costs and rigid economies created employment for industrial chemists. Cellulose wrappings, synthetic resins, and attractively colored plastics were developed and gained immediate popularity. The use of Cellophane as a sanitary, non-porous wrapper for foodstuffs and other perishable goods became universal. The astonishing advances in the field of plastics gave resilience, economy, durability, and beauty to a host of products, including radio cabinets, fountain pens, electrical appliances, and automobile parts. One movement in the field of industrial chemistry which attracted Henry Ford's keen interest was known as chemurgy; it offered a possible alternative to crop restriction by demonstrating the use of certain farm products as sources of alcohol, oil, and other needed industrial materials. In 1939, Congress subsidized huge regional laboratories employing several hundred scientists and industrial engineers for research work in chemurgy. Experiments in raising chemically fed crops suggested the enormous possibilities of "tray agriculture." These vast triumphs in the field of chemistry, according to Charles and Mary Beard, gave definite shape to our future national self-sufficiency.

Chemistry and medicine enjoyed a fruitful alliance during the thirties that resulted in the miracle-working sulfa drugs to combat certain infections and in the synthesis of vitamin K concentrate used to prevent hemorrhage, especially in surgery. The epidemic of infantile paralysis in 1935 centered public interest on the battle against it. President Roosevelt's own experience with the disease some years earlier led him to sponsor an annual drive for funds for the Warm Springs, Georgia, Foundation, devoted to treating its victims. Strong hopes that a means of controlling epidemics had been discovered arose when two New York physicians, Maurice Brodie and William H. Park, reported favorable results in preventing infantile paralysis in children by means of special vaccines. Scientific skepticism, however, tended to discount these claims.

THE ERA OF STREAMLINED INVENTIONS

Engineers and inventors also made notable progress in making people both more comfortable and more productive. The air-conditioning of factories, offices, homes, sickrooms, and department stores had interesting implications for the South, with its proverbial 90 degrees in the shade, as well as for increased comfort and efficiency elsewhere in the hot summer months. The economy, comfort, and attractiveness of prefabricated houses awakened enthusiasm as a means of eradicating slums and raising the aesthetic level of middle-class homes. Streamlining was applied lavishly to trains, automobiles, and airplanes, imparting a popular impression of beauty and speed; it soon became a vogue in itself.

Trailer cars enjoyed great popularity, for they made possible an interesting form of community life on wheels and served as an inexpensive substitute for privately owned homes. Fluorescent lighting, which made for efficiency without overheating, was used ever more widely in home and display lighting. Extremely popular toward the end of the decade was the candid camera, whose ability to catch fleeting but informal poses amused countless fans. A sad commentary on the ever-present fear of technological unemployment under an unregulated competitive system was the widespread controversy that greeted the Rust brothers' invention of a huge mechanical cotton picker; this immediately raised the nightmare of unemployment for the farm workers of the South, especially Negroes.

MODERNISM VERSUS CLASSICISM IN ARCHITECTURE

Architects suffered severely during the depression because of the halt in construction. Skyscrapers were widely resented more than ever by owners of nearby property and by real estate interests because of their harmful effect in absorbing potential tenants from the surrounding area, thus adding to the congestion and lowering values. Hence Radio City, the gigantic project which John D. Rockefeller, Jr., undertook early in the decade and which covered several blocks in crowded mid-Manhattan and cost over $250,000,000, drew considerable criticism as well as praise. The architects were Raymond Hood, famous for his design of the Chicago *Tribune* building, Harvey Corbett, and Hartley B. Alexander. Nevertheless, to many people the decorative scheme seemed garish and startling. Professor Harry F. Cunningham of the University of Nebraska deplored the "current craze for rampant geometry"—the current manifestation of "modernism"—that was being taught to students of architecture. The architectural plan of the Chicago Century of Progress in 1933 and the New York World's Fair in 1939, both of which stressed the domination of machine civilization, was criticized for similar reasons. The San Francisco Fair in 1939 was received more favorably, for despite certain Hollywood effects its central artistic theme was based on the pre-machine civilizations of Spanish and Indian America.

The creative impulse of American architecture was stimulated by President Roosevelt's statement that "one-third of a nation [is] ill-fed, ill-clad, and ill-housed." In 1939 the architectural press, hitherto somewhat critical of the New Deal's emphasis on quantity, hailed the projects undertaken by the T.V.A., especially the extensive recreational and educational facilities made available to the humblest citizen, as democracy's great achievement. The stream of orders for new government buildings, of which the more noteworthy were the National

Archives, the Supreme Court, and the New York and Chicago post office buildings, meant substantial employment for architects. Housing projects, in spite of their Spartan simplicity in the name of economy, attracted the more idealistic architects, who quickly recognized their social implications.

Modernism as visualized by Frank Lloyd Wright—the direct adaptation of a building to its purpose and environment—crowded out the classical tradition. Suggestive of the new trends were the bold effects in design, the simplicity of surface, and the stark absence of ornamentation. The individual was dwarfed by one of the huge single-story buildings, occupying a vast expanse of land, that Albert Kahn designed for automobile production. Soviet Russia, entranced with this new style, eagerly invited American architects like Kahn to come there. Streamlining effects and the preponderance of vertical and horizontal lines, with a liberal use of corner windows, became common in plans for apartment buildings and private homes.

THE NEW DEAL, PATRON OF THE ARTS

The depression struck artists with exceptional violence, leaving them with little chance of making a living but giving them ample firsthand experiences for the "socially conscious" painting that became the vogue. As the manifesto of a Communist-led Artist Congress put it, art must not be isolated as "a decorative or aristocratic phenomenon or as a precious cultural indulgence." A new day for artists began in December, 1933, with the organization of the Public Works of Art Project, financed by the C.W.A. and directed by Edward Bruce, a versatile and ardent New Dealer who had won almost equal success in finance and in painting. Bruce gained public attention in 1931 for his imaginative interpretation of the San Francisco business district, with the Bay in the foreground and the city itself in the background. Two years later, in his role as economist, he was sent to London as a delegate to the World Economic Conference.

Under Bruce's direction, art projects in all the states aroused such interest among the people as to encourage a vogue for painting among amateurs. In 1936 over 5000 artists—some of outstanding merit—were employed on these projects. At the government's insistence, the American scene was used as the leading theme, thus encouraging a departure from imitative works with an unfamiliar foreign background. Most significant was the fact that this experiment made the federal government the world's leading patron of the arts—a situation which was reflected in the creation of a Painting and Sculpture Section within the Treasury Department. Despite the grumbling of the conservative press, the traditional version of the struggling artist at work in a cold garret no longer held.

Government buildings in particular provided a huge sphere of activity and expression for mural painters. Great popularity among muralists was attained by Diego Rivera, the Mexican disciple of Trotsky, who combined colorful interpretations of the indigenous Indian culture with a leftist challenge to the economic order. Rivera, who had been "discovered" by Ambassador Dwight Morrow, visited the United States early in the decade and helped to stimulate a keen interest here in primitive art, especially that of aboriginal Mexico. A national organization for the advancement of American Indian art was formed in 1931 by John Sloan, the famous painter of the Southwest.

In the Middle West a notable revolt broke out among regionalist painters against the "international" French style of modernism typified by Picasso. An ardent champion of the regionalists, Thomas Craven asserted that the cult of Picasso had reached "the uttermost limits of infantilism and absurdity . . . geometrical litter and phony symbols." Craven believed that the middlewestern regionalists were reviving the true Renaissance emphasis on local schools. Charles E. Burchfield, a pioneer artist in rural Ohio, had turned away from the cosmopolitanism and faddism of Paris and New York to search for local color in his rustic countryside; this often led him to portray prosaic themes, bleak backgrounds, and ramshackle houses.

Under Burchfield's influence, Thomas Hart Benton of Missouri, a collateral descendant of his famous senatorial namesake, eschewed the French tradition and won repeated awards from art juries for his murals delineating sharecroppers, rural Negroes, urban sophisticates, political bosses, and the everyday realities of the Middle West and South. His sardonic humor and unflattering angular style were appropriate for that critical decade but utterly disconcerting to many fellow Missourians who regarded this artist's history of Missouri series as a caricature of their past. Another important regionalist was the Iowa-born Grant Wood, a real craftsman in technique who found his inspiration in the German and Flemish primitives. He faithfully expressed rural life through the simplicity and realism of the farmhouse scenes he knew so well at firsthand. Scarcely less significant among this group was John S. Curry of Kansas, who lent poetic depth to characteristic scenes of American life and won substantial recognition for his "Baptism in Kansas" and his circus scenes. Socially-minded landscape painters tended to forget the prettified countryside in favor of such blighted scenes as eroded lands and farmhouses buried beneath dust storms. The middlewestern origin of so many of the leading regionalists suggested a historic shift in American art during the decade from the Atlantic seaboard to the indigenous culture of the prairies.

This movement did not go unchallenged. Lewis Mumford, a keen student of cultural processes who preached the social and cosmopolitan ideals of art, derided the "patriotic school" and even charged that some of the regionalists were motivated by semi-Fascist ideals—an accusation then being made by leftists against the Nashville group of southern literary regionalists. Admitting certain exceptions like Benton, Mumford maintained nevertheless that American regionalist painters had only limited possibilities and produced merely "stale replicas" of the inferior European genre painters. To him, Craven's judgments were reactionary because they apparently ignored the role of art as an instrument of social action and turned away from the well-earned leadership held by European art. "Art is by its very nature propaganda," wrote Mumford, "that is, it seeks to share and widen a particular kind of experience." He drew a sharp distinction between art as a form of social expression and "propagandist art" in the usual narrow sense of covering only a small segment of life.

Art museums expanded considerably toward the end of the decade, a number of new ones being opened in New York and Washington. After a close study of art trends, Frederick P. Keppel noted a "shift in emphasis from custodial functions of the American Museum to its opportunities for education and other services." Also suggestive of the spirit of the thirties was the increased public support of museums; this replaced much of the support formerly received from private sources which were depleted by heavy taxes as well as by the depression. Culminating this renaissance of interest in art was the publication during 1939 of many popular books on the subject.

Sculpture followed the same general pattern, but on a smaller scale. Government aid was extended in this field also; according to Sheldon Cheney, the art historian, "Probably two-thirds of the really important sculptors are on the government rolls." Younger sculptors in particular tended to seek a theme in the bitterness and despair of contemporary life and to defy the graceful classical tradition in favor of massive pieces, suggestive of strength and power, that were often distorted or expressed in angular lines. Primitive art of the Congo or Mayan cultures rather than the traditional Greek sculpture served frequently as a source of inspiration.

Malvina Hoffman was commissioned by the Field Museum of Chicago to execute in bronze altogether one hundred works showing various racial types in their native setting. Her resulting trip around the world did much to familiarize her fellow craftsmen with authentic primitive types. Her craftsmanship and careful attention to authenticity were instrumental in uniting anthropology and art, and the pieces she did for the museum won praise as the finest racial portraiture ever executed. Gutzon Borglum's statue of Woodrow Wilson as a great humanitarian was erected in Poznan, Poland, but was destroyed by the Nazis in 1939. Jo Davidson exhibited a series of sculptures of the Loyalist leaders in the Spanish Civil War and donated the proceeds to the Spanish Children's Milk Fund. His impressive statues of Walt Whitman and of Will Rogers won favorable attention. On the whole, however, critics agreed that the European influence was still predominant in American sculpture.

THE COMING OF AGE OF NATIVE MUSIC

In music, the prestige of native composers and artists continued to rise. No longer was it necessary to conceal a homely American surname behind a pretentious Italian or Russian name. This was noteworthy on the operatic stage, where the time-honored names of Galli-Curci, Caruso, Amato, and others of their generation gave way to such American names as Grace Moore, Lawrence Tibbett, Richard Crooks, John Charles Thomas, and Helen Jepson. David Ewen, a historian of music, observed that now most Metropolitan Opera artists were Americans and that this apparently made no difference in their popularity with the public. Native writers, more frequently than ever before, composed operas that were of a quality to satisfy the fastidious tastes of the Metropolitan opera-goers. Deems Taylor—artist, composer, journalist, and music commentator—whose opera, *The King's Henchman,* had been produced at the Metropolitan during the preceding decade, scored another success in 1931 with *Peter Ibbetson,* which was based on Du Maurier's sentimental novel. Richard Hageman, who came to the United States from Holland as a youth, won praise for his colorful opera, *Caponsacchi,* drawn from Robert Browning's romantic work, *The Ring and the Book.* Another Metropolitan success was *Merrymount,* composed by Howard Hanson, director of the Eastman School of Music in Rochester; the music historian, John T. Howard, considered this composer extremely influential in the shaping of American music. American orchestral compositions in increasing numbers were performed by the leading symphony orchestras. According to Ewen, during the season of 1939–1940 no less than 121 native works were included in the repertoires of the sixteen outstanding orchestras in this country.

As in the other arts, federal relief funds played a major role in the development of native music during the decade. W.P.A. grants made possible the creation of thirty symphonic orchestras and numerous other smaller units. Government subsidies came in time to save from destitution thousands of trained musicians who had been displaced by sound films or released by deficit-ridden orchestras. Huge audiences attended the concerts given by W.P.A. orchestras. Finally, there was the artistically stimulating influence of such great European musicians as Bruno Walter and Paul Hindemith, who came to the United States after being deprived of their posts by Hitler and Mussolini.

CHAPTER 20

The Good Neighbor, Collective Security, and World Anarchy

VOGUE FOR ECONOMIC NATIONALISM

Among the medley of diverse interests supporting the New Deal in its early days were free traders like Cordell Hull and protectionists like Raymond Moley; Wilsonian internationalists and anti-British isolationists marched side by side. Even Roosevelt, who with Wilson's blessing had campaigned with Cox for the League of Nations in 1920, appeared at first to have swung over to a nationalist program in combating the depression, for the New Deal legislation that affected currency, prices, production, and labor suggested the end of the liberal competitive world of Adam Smith and paralleled uncomfortably the experiments in economic nationalism abroad.

The depression fastened a popular stigma on financiers—all too frequently well deserved—and revived the old Progressive bogy of the "international banker" who stirred up war in behalf of Wall Street or the Bank of England and bound the common folk tight in the toils of debt. The League and the World Court were portrayed in Congress and on the radio as tools of British finance, and investigators like Senator Gerald P. Nye stressed the responsibility of powerful bankers and munitions makers in 1914–1917 for our entrance into the World War. The sinister picture of predatory international capitalism drawn by many congressional isolationists had long been popularized by Marxians at home and abroad. The victory of Hitler's National Socialists in 1933 gave new energy to the world crusade against economic individualism by embellishing the myth of a conspiracy among the financiers.

The imminence of domestic catastrophe left little scope for a vigorous foreign policy during the early months of the New Deal. Moreover, our novel currency experiments helped to make impossible any genuine agreement at the World Economic Conference in 1933. The consequent failure of the Conference meant an immediate reversion to economic nationalism as practically every leading nation made a desperate attempt to retain its share of a world trade that had fallen off by 65 per cent since 1929. In an effort to win new markets, Britain extended her mercantilist system of imperial preference which gave tariff advantages to members of the Empire, and in Argentina she popularized the slogan, "Buy from those who buy from us," at the expense of the United States, which enjoyed a heavily favorable balance of trade with that Latin American country. Other European nations raised their tariffs, diverted foreign exchange from its natural channels, or set up quotas to promote exports and curtail imports. Our own prohibitive Hawley-Smoot tariff of 1930 was still securely on the statute books, unchallenged even by the New Deal, and Congress was apparently responsive to the "Buy American" campaign that the Hearst papers were waging vigorously.

A world-wide trend toward bilateral barter agreements appeared as nations sought to balance imports with declining exports or to conserve their precarious supply of foreign exchange, credits, and gold. Particularly ominous were the ruthless barter methods of Nazi Germany, which was aiming more and more at political as well as economic hegemony. Even before Roosevelt's first term ended, it was clear that the Nazis, although short on foreign exchange, were securing new markets in the Balkans and South America by means of a barter system so contrived as to make these nations buy surplus German products of any type in order to thaw out their frozen credit balances. Jugoslavia, which had gladly disposed of her wheat surpluses in a barter deal with Germany, was eventually compelled to take large quantities of aspirin in payment—an appropriate product under the circumstances. South American countries were forced to divert their precious foreign exchange to Germany; payment often took the form of a deluge of unwanted harmonicas or any other goods of which the Nazis had a surplus. The regimentation of Germany's economy to include subsidized exports gave her a distinct advantage over her democratic competitors for world trade. By the later thirties this advantage was heightened by the ideological war waged by the Nazis and Fascists against Great Britain and the United States in particular.

RECIPROCITY AND PROTECTIONISM

By the spring of 1934, Roosevelt and Hull were ready to carry out their promise, made the preceding year, to negotiate tariff agreements which would "break through trade barriers and establish foreign markets for farm and industrial products." A controversy began over the Trade Agreements Act, which empowered the President to conclude commercial agreements with foreign nations without the consent of the Senate and to reduce existing duties up to 50 per cent in return for corresponding concessions. Republican protectionists, supported by leaders of the American Federation of Labor and the National Grange, sprang to arms at once, for they suspected that Roosevelt was working toward a wholesale leveling of the tariff system. The Administration, on the other hand, was convinced that the Senate's unfavorable record on reciprocity treaties made executive control essential, and it hoped that the new bill would eliminate from tariff-making the traditionally undemocratic and sectional approach used by pressure groups. The chairman of the United States Tariff Commission testified before a Senate committee that the so-called "flexible clause" in the Hawley-Smoot tariff law was anything but flexible and that the "cost of production" theory as a basis for tariff rates was useless in practice.

Congress passed the Trade Agreements Act in June, 1934, by a largely Democratic vote, whereupon State Department experts began working on a preferential reciprocity agreement with revolution-torn Cuba. The high duty of two cents per pound imposed by the Hawley-Smoot tariff on the island's vital sugar exports to the United States was cut to 0.9 cent, and additional concessions were given to other of its leading crops. In turn, Cuba made tariff concessions in our favor on a wide range of American-made goods, from automobiles to lard. Only with difficulty, however, was the Administration able to modify the drastic sugar quota limits which the domestic beet and cane sugar interests in Congress insisted be included in the agreement.

Later reciprocity agreements extended the most-favored-nation principle in the interests of a general downward revision of the tariff. In practice, this meant that any concession in duties which we made to one country would be applied to every other country which did not discriminate against us or resort to unfair trade practices. Germany was automatically ineligible for any benefits from this policy. By the fall of 1939 Hull could report that nineteen countries, representing three-fifths of the world's trade, had entered reciprocal trade agreements with us, and that 3000 concessions affecting one-third of our exports had been made in our favor. At the same time Americans were able to buy foreign goods more cheaply which did not compete seriously with our own commodities.

Despite the critics, the reciprocal trade agreements were far from meaning absolute free trade. If anything, they erred on the side of conservatism, for they failed to make a major breach in the high tariff wall although they definitely reversed the continued upward trend. Nationalist forces at home as well as abroad hampered the drive for genuine free trade. However, Hull's program won an important political victory when Great Britain, which had adopted a mercantilist tariff system for the Empire in 1932, consented in 1938 to join Canada in entering a reciprocal trade agreement with the United States. After Britain's humiliating diplomatic defeat at Munich in her efforts to attain "peace in our time," as Prime Minister Chamberlain put it, the Anglo-Saxon countries were now moving closer together in a solidarity symbolized by a broad trade agreement which reversed the protectionist trend of the Chamberlain government.

The United Kingdom made concessions on American wheat, electrical equipment, women's shoes and hosiery, and other important products, and we in turn reduced the import duties on high-grade English textiles and other manufactured goods. Canada made concessions on American machinery, fruits, and vegetables among other imports, and in turn obtained lower duties on her grain products, maple sugar, and paper output. Agreements such as these were a political liability for the Administration because there were invariably a number of small groups that were alarmed by some particular concession. New England textile interests, for example, claimed that the agreement with Britain tended to put them out of business. In 1943, after a decade of experiment, Under Secretary of State Sumner Welles assessed reciprocity in the following terms: "Our trade agreement program represented one spark of sanity in a world outlook that seemed wholly and hopelessly dark."

THE GOOD NEIGHBOR POLICY AND COLLECTIVE SECURITY

In his inaugural address in 1933, Roosevelt gave a brief summary of foreign affairs in which he said, "In the field of world policy I would dedicate this nation to the policy of the good neighbor . . . the neighbor who respects his obligations and respects the sanctity of his agreements in and with a world of neighbors." This rather general statement took on special significance in light of the marked improvement in our relations with Latin America. President Hoover and Secretary of State Stimson had already given substance to the "good neighbor" ideal of collective security by retreating from this country's early policy of military intervention in Central America and the Caribbean under the Platt Amendment of 1901. But the incoming Roosevelt administration was faced with the problem of anarchy in Cuba, blood-drenched under the terrorism of President Gerardo Machado.

The collapse of the one-crop system in Cuba, brought on by her loss of much of the American sugar market to Puerto Rico, Hawaii, and the Philippines, led to a great and ruthlessly suppressed uprising in 1931 against the dictatorship of Machado. In the next two years both the government and its opponents resorted to terroristic methods; university professors were forcibly silenced, schools closed, and the jails filled with political prisoners, many of whom were shot while allegedly trying to escape. Machado, who apparently hoped that American businessmen interested in salvaging their Cuban loans would force our intervention in his behalf, labeled the opposition indiscriminately as "communist," although in reality his chief enemies were nationalists like the secret A.B.C. who, suspicious of our influence, were anxious to replace the huge sugar estates by a system of small independent land holdings.

Determined to forestall any military intervention in Cuba, the Administration dispatched Sumner Welles, an expert on Latin America, to Havana. Welles found that the factional issues quickly simmered down to the demand that Machado resign. New bloodshed occurred when political strikes were ruthlessly put down by the dictator. Finding mediation impossible, Welles worked for the resignation of Machado. Finally, on August 11, 1933, a revolt among Cuban army officers forced the dictator to flee and installed Dr. de Céspedes as provisional President.

Although American warships moved near Cuba's coastal cities as rioting continued against Machado's associates, there was no actual intervention. President Roosevelt summoned the various Latin American diplomats in Washington to a conference at which he assured them, as he later recalled, that the United States was not going to intervene in Cuba, that we all wanted to help Cuba, and that therefore any action that was to be taken in helping Cuba ought to be the action of all the Americas. Subsequent revolutions eventually brought Colonel Fulgencio Batista to the helm; he combined his influence over the army with a popular appeal based partly on his sweeping social legislation which was modeled after that of the New Deal. Roosevelt offered recognition to "any provisional government in Cuba in which the Cuban people demonstrate their confidence," an indication that his Administration intended to follow the Jeffersonian policy, revived by Hoover's Secretary of State Stimson, of recognizing revolutionary governments and thus reducing the need for military intervention. As already noted, valuable economic concessions were extended to Cuba in a preferential trade agreement.

Cuba thus became the proving ground of the good neighbor policy and the results gave new vigor to the hitherto ineffectual pan-American movement. At the Montevideo Conference in December, 1933, which attracted international interest because it was attended by President Roosevelt, the American delegation accepted the anti-intervention formula, "No state has the right to intervene in the internal or external affairs of another." This was translated into fact on May 29, 1934, when the generation-old Platt Amendment was abrogated by the Senate, except for the provision regarding our naval base at Guantánamo. Cubans celebrated this by declaring a holiday, and the Latin American nations were visibly impressed by our government's sincerity. The maintenance of constitutional government in other nations, declared Roosevelt shortly after this Conference, was not a sacred obligation of the United States alone; it was primarily the duty of every nation to maintain it within its borders; only when orderly processes failed did it become "the joint concern of a whole continent in which we are neighbors." Here again was the ideal of collective security.

ARGENTINE VERSUS AMERICAN CATTLEMEN

The various Pan-American Conferences revealed Argentina's persistent truculence toward the United States and indicated that she coveted leadership of the countries of South America. Hull was most tactful in allowing her delegates at the Conferences the initiative on many major questions. Argentina's proposal for an anti-war pact among the nations in this hemisphere, which Stimson had rejected as cumbersome and unnecessary, was accepted by Hull and the Senate.

But Argentina still had many grievances. Her cattlemen, the barons of the pampas who dominated the domestic political scene, had a longstanding grievance in our embargo of their famous beef for sanitary reasons. The high duties of the Hawley-Smoot tariff were another cause for complaint. Finally, it was undeniable that Argentina's principal exports—corn, wheat, beef, and hides—were strongly competitive with our own exports. Ignoring Hull's proffered reciprocity agreement, the republic adopted a policy whereby preferential treatment in allocating foreign exchange was given to those nations who bought heavily from her; this favored Great Britain.

One of the high hopes held by the Inter-American Conference for the Maintenance of Peace, which met at Buenos Aires in December, 1936, and which Roosevelt promoted and attended, was the cancellation of our quarantine on Argentine beef. But our cattlemen, who like their South American rivals were also powerful in the councils of their government, opposed all concessions. Administration supporters vainly pointed out that the dread hoof-and-mouth disease affected only a remote portion of Argentina. When our Navy Department in January, 1939, called for bids on canned corned beef, Argentina offered her acknowledgedly superior product for nine cents per pound as against the lowest American bid of twenty-three cents. When the Administration, acting on the fact that this disease cannot be carried in cooked meats, favored accepting her offer, stout resistance came immediately from our large packers and the American National Live Stock Association. As Roosevelt observed indignantly, "There then broke out a torrent of protest which was in large part based on an outrageous attempt to deceive the public, especially in the cattle-producing states." Congress rebuked the Chief Executive by ordering that only domestic foodstuffs should be purchased for the Navy. Not until early in 1941, when there was an unlimited market for American beef because of the European war, did Congress permit Argentina's canned beef to enter the United States freely.

THE PAN-AMERICAN CRUSADE

Whatever Argentine officials might think of their northern neighbor, the people of Argentina gave Roosevelt an unprecedented ovation on his arrival at Buenos Aires for the Pan-American Conference. His address to the Conference stressed "the principle of interdependence" for all the countries of this hemisphere. He pointed out how the Colombia-Peru boundary dispute in the early thirties had revealed the lack of effective peace machinery among the Latin American nations and how the League of Nations had been able to restore peace, wherefore he hoped that the League would be strengthened rather than replaced by the Pan American Union. Although our delegates were unsuccessful in effecting a united front against Fascist aggression, the member nations unanimously accepted a diluted agreement providing for consultation in the event of any threat to peace. The necessity of a common policy of neutrality was accepted on principle, but the use of the embargo was made optional for each nation. The resolutions desired by Hull for the removal of trade barriers were adopted, but their enforcement was left to each country's discretion. Far more concrete was the series of projects undertaken in the interest of all types of cultural cooperation. The interchange of educational films, scholarships, professors, art exhibits, publications, and other inter-American programs of all types helped to arouse an extraordinary interest in pan-Americanism and to spread the gospel of understanding and solidarity among the nations of the western hemisphere.

The steady stream of American investment funds which had dried up during the depression was replaced by economic assistance to Latin America which flowed with such ever-increasing force that the good neighbor policy impressed some Americans as meaning the under-

1930 - 1944

THE LABOR FRONT: *The more abundant strife.*—Phoenix Arizona Republic.

One View of the Domestic Situation in August, 1937. (Manning in the Phoenix, Arizona, *Republic*.)

(Upper left) The State or County Fair—A Recreational High Light in the Life of Rural and Suburban America. (Brown Brothers.)

(Upper right) The Small Traveling Carnival with Its Games and Prizes, a Typical Summer Amusement. (Brown Brothers.)

ored Sharecroppers of theast Missouri Camping ng the Roads in January, 9, in Protest at Being Evict- Farm mechanization and p restriction aided the nters, and federal relief ks and absentee corporate ership ended the historic ernalism of slavery days. rothea Lange photo.)

Joads on the Highway in Summer of 1938. A family nigratory farm workers, in- ling seven children, from is, Arkansas. (Dorothea ge photo.)

Brian Aherne and Katharine Cornell in *The Barretts of Wimpole Street*, a Play by Rudolf Besier Produced in 1931. (Harvard Theatre Collection.)

Helen Hayes as Mary and Philip Leigh as Rizzio, in Maxwell Anderson's *Mary of Scotland*, Which Appeared in 1933. (Harvard Theatre Collection.)

Luise Rainer and Paul Muni in *The Good Earth*, Which Was Released in 1937. (Harvard Theatre Collection.)

Midday Dinner, High Point of the Day for Harvest Hands. (Brown Brothers.)

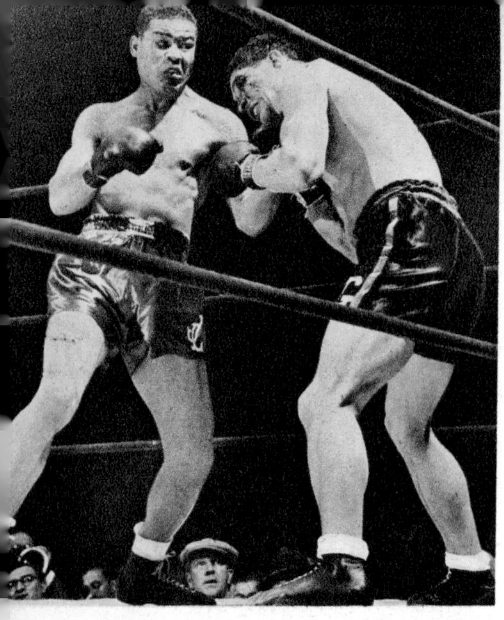

Joe Louis vs. Arturo Godoy, First Round of the Prize Fight on June 20, 1940. (N. Y. *Daily News* Photo.)

Jitterbug. (Photo by Murray Lewis; from the Dan Archives of the Museum of Modern Art.)

Snow White and the Seven Dwarfs, Walt Disney's First Full-Length Feature Produced in Technicolor. (Copyright, Walt Disney Productions.)

A Newsstand in a Village Drugstore. (Photo Lee; Farm Security Administration.)

Pearl Harbor, December 7, 1941. (Official U. S. Navy Photograph.)

Roosevelt, Stalin, and Churchill at the Teheran Conference, November

writing of hemisphere prosperity as well as security. Although more than 80 per cent of the Latin American securities held in the United States were in default, the Roosevelt administration refused to exert strong pressure for the collection of private debts. An Export-Import Bank was created by Congress in 1934 to promote trade, especially with South America. It bolstered Brazil's financial system, for example, in order to eliminate discriminatory control of the exchange rate and to expand her industry and her transportation system, especially after 1938 when the menace of Fascism made it imperative to strengthen economic bonds throughout the hemisphere. The reciprocal trade agreements themselves proved extremely important in removing the sources of trade friction and promoting collective security.

Roosevelt sought to alleviate Latin America's historic suspicions of the "Colossus of the North" by liberalizing the Monroe Doctrine in line with what he called the "Pan-American doctrine of continental self-defense," or "continentalizing" the Monroe Doctrine, as it was popularly referred to. The persistent efforts to unify the diplomatic and defense machinery of the hemisphere against Fascist aggression reflected the new belief that a threat to a single Latin American country was the concern of all the nations, not of the United States alone. Secretary Hull and Alf M. Landon, Republican presidential candidate in 1936, both attended the important Inter-American Conference at Lima in December, 1938, to make it clear that the United States would remain cordial to pan-Americanism regardless of the party in power.

The Lima Conference was overshadowed by the strained relations between Mexico and the United States. President Lázaro Cárdenas, who represented the revolutionary forces behind the socialist, nationalist, and anti-clerical Constitution of 1917, had broken with Calles, who was becoming increasingly conservative, and in 1934 embarked on a radical program of expropriating large landed properties, especially foreign oil lands. Cárdenas was determined to solve Mexico's long-standing land problem in favor of small farmers and landless Mexicans. Since the treasury would undoubtedly be unable to make proper compensation, virtual confiscation seemed likely. Cárdenas' efforts to Mexicanize his country's industry in March, 1937, were followed by a series of strikes which culminated in the nationalization of the oil industry. This affected seventeen British and American companies, representing investments which they estimated at $450,-000,000 and of which approximately $200,000,000 was American.

The British government insisted on proper compensation under international law, and a controversy followed which ended in the mutual recall of ministers. Much to the relief of the hard-pressed Cárdenas, the United States made no formal protest. Nazi Germany's imports to Mexico were steadily increasing, and Roosevelt recognized full well the danger of a Fascist state being established in Mexico if the Cárdenas regime was overthrown. However, Secretary Hull reminded the Mexican government on July 23, 1938, that expropriation was the same as confiscation even though "there may be an expressed intent to pay at some time in the future." Although there was serious danger that this application of socialization might prove contagious in other impoverished Latin American nations such as Bolivia, the Administration did not use its most effective weapon against the Cárdenas regime—halting our government's large-scale purchases of silver from Mexico at artificially high prices. In the ensuing negotiations the United States showed herself willing to make major financial concessions to retain that nation's friendship. Consequently, when we entered World War II, Mexico proclaimed that the enemies of her northern neighbor were her enemies and, following her subsequent declaration of war against the Axis, she gave valuable aid to us in men and materials. This situation was in sharp contrast to the tension between Wilson and Carranza in 1917–1918.

Latin America was also impressed by the complete evacuation of American Marines from Haiti on August 15, 1934, in accordance with the promise made by the Hoover administration and accelerated by Roosevelt. At the request of President Sténio Vincent, the United States agreed to return to Haiti the control of her financial system, hitherto administered by the National City Bank of New York. Roosevelt gave emphasis to his policy toward her by visiting the republic in July, 1934. Another opportunity to put the good neighbor policy into effect came in October, 1937, when many hundreds of impoverished Haitian squatters in the Dominican Republic were killed by the Dominicans. The liberal press in the United States held Trujillo, the dictator of the republic, responsible for the massacre. The ensuing dispute between Haiti and the Dominican Republic was finally terminated after both sides agreed to the mediation of the United States, Mexico, and Cuba.

Disturbed conditions in Puerto Rico called for considerable good neighborliness on our part. The depression had been unusually severe on the overcrowded little island. Nationalists drilled in Fascist-style black shirts; they sabotaged elections and, during 1935–1937, resorted to outright terrorism. An American police chief was assassinated, and a clash between native police and Nationalists at Ponce on March 21, 1937, ended with nineteen dead and 100 wounded. The Roosevelt administration ordered that the Nationalists be punished, and Senators introduced an independence bill to remind the Puerto Ricans that separation was economic suicide.

More important were the investigations undertaken by the Puerto Rican Policy Commission and the efforts of the new Reconstruction Administration to promote cooperative experiments in small modern farms and subsistence homesteads, rural electrification, and the development of local industries. However, jealous protectionists in Congress opposed any far-reaching program of industrialization for Puerto Rico; churchmen fought against the dissemination of information on birth control, although the island's population of 1,800,000 had doubled since 1898; and our large sugar interests continued to hold huge tracts of the best farm lands.

CANADA AND THE MONROE DOCTRINE

Canada, despite her imperial connections, was expected to play a large part in hemisphere affairs, although not actually a member of the Pan American Union. She had close trade ties with the United States, and it was hoped that she would eventually agree to the establishment of an air mail route and the construction of a coastal highway between the United States and Alaska. Most important in the late thirties were the long-pending negotiations over the proposed deepening of the St. Lawrence–Great Lakes waterway which would make such inland cities as Chicago important seaports. Railroad and power companies and the Atlantic coastal cities on both sides of the border feared this threatened competition; hence the sustained efforts of both Hoover and Roosevelt to secure adherence to the waterway pact were frustrated by the Senate. The Roosevelt administration drafted a new treaty in May, 1938, which provided for an elaborate power and navigation program to be undertaken largely at our expense. Despite the importance of defense at that time, the power interests were determined to resist any encroachment of public ownership, and local politicians across the border were also unfavorable to the suggested program.

The increasing probability that Great Britain would fight Hitler put Canada in a pivotal position as far as hemisphere defense was concerned. French-Canadian isolationists had succeeded in keeping the Ottawa government from making actual commitments regarding military aid to the mother country in case of war, but historic ties reasserted themselves during England's effort to rearm in the emergency. As a result, British student pilots were soon being sent to Canada for training and by 1938 Canadian factories were geared to manufacture armament for overseas. On August 18, 1938, President Roosevelt called the attention of the world to the military relations between his country and Canada when he went to Ontario to receive an honorary degree of doctor of laws from Queens University. "I give to you assurance," he said with deliberation, "that the people of the United States will not stand idly by if domination of Canadian soil is threatened by any other empire." He told his press conference the next day that the Monroe Doctrine had never excluded Canada. These statements were received enthusiastically by the Canadian press, for the danger of invasion from across the Atlantic had ceased to be fantastic.

ISOLATIONISM AND NEUTRALITY

However acquiescent Congress might be in supporting hemisphere solidarity, both House and Senate viewed intimacy with any European country with suspicion. Roosevelt found it politic to consider our membership in the League of Nations a closed issue, although he followed Hoover's policy of informal cooperation. His plea to the Senate in 1935 in favor of membership in the World Court was rebuffed, largely because of the radio campaign waged by Father Coughlin, the Anglophobic isolationist. Whatever leniency the Administration might have shown the hard-pressed European nations in regard to war debt revision was blocked by Senator Hiram Johnson of California and his congressional supporters. The Johnson Act, passed in 1934 after wholesale defaults on war debts, outlawed all securities issued by governments in default to the United States. Public opinion in the United States warmed toward "little Finland," the only debtor still in good standing. However, few realized that her ability to pay in gold was due to her favorable balance of trade.

Congress elbowed the President aside in the vital field of neutrality legislation. Japan's invasion of Manchuria and northern China and the bellicose threats of Hitler and Mussolini during the early years of the New Deal brought closer the possibility of our involvement in a second world war. Popular interest was aroused by "Arms and the Men," published in *Fortune* in March, 1934; this exposé stressed the profits and international ramifications of the munitions industry as factors in the creation of a war spirit. In April a Senate committee headed by Senator Gerald P. Nye of North Dakota began an investigation of the industry. Like the shipping investigation during Hoover's administration, the munitions investigation revealed the various devices employed by arms manufacturers—the high-pressure sales methods, the international lobbying against disarmament conferences, the outright bribery, and the synthetic patriotism. These disclosures were brought to the attention of the public by such sensational books as George Seldes' *Iron, Blood, and Profits* and H. C. Engelbrecht and F. C. Hanighen's *Merchants of Death.*

Senator Nye, untrained in the use of historical documents, drew extremely sinister inferences regarding our country's economic stake in an Allied victory during 1914–1917. International bankers like Morgan, as well as the munitions makers, were given a villain's role, and President Wilson was pictured as a man whom the economic pressure around him had made thoroughly unneutral. The inference was obvious to both Congress and the people—President Roosevelt, too, would have to be restrained when the question of future neutrality legislation arose. The efficacy of the Nye revelations was made clear by the Gallup Poll question in April, 1937: "Do you think it was a mistake for the United States to have entered the World War?" which 70 per cent of those questioned answered affirmatively. In a subsequent poll on the causes of our entering that war, 34 per cent believed that we were "the victim of propaganda and selfish interests" and only 26 per cent were satisfied that "America had a just and unselfish cause."

Congressional war remedies inspired scores of bills. The State Department was particularly concerned when Representative Louis Ludlow of Indiana proposed that, except in case of actual invasion, a constitutional amendment prohibit Congress from declaring war until a national referendum had been held. Among Ludlow's supporters were the isolationist Senators Nye, La Follette, Bennett Clark, and Burton K. Wheeler, as well as Representative Hamilton Fish, who was then the ranking Republican member of the House Committee on Foreign Affairs. His proposal was also favorably received by the people; according to a Gallup Poll in October, 1937, public opinion was divided 73 to 27 in favor of it. Former Secretary of State Stimson came to the rescue of the Administration by pointing out the danger of holding a referendum on war in the midst of an international crisis; he pointed out that in effect, such an amendment would abrogate the Monroe Doctrine and immobilize our Navy should danger threaten. Aided by such internationally-minded Republicans, the Administration succeeded in mustering sufficient strength to shelve the proposal. As far as munitions were concerned, Roosevelt, who favored international control over the industry, secured the Senate's belated approval of the Geneva Convention of 1925 for the suppression of international trade in arms and ammunition.

Action on neutrality legislation was finally taken in August, 1935, after Mussolini's invasion of Ethiopia threatened to bring on a world war. A joint resolution introduced by Administration leaders gave the President discretionary power, in the event of war outside the United States, to impose an embargo on the goods of one or all of the belligerents. But Nye and his followers threatened a Senate filibuster to compel the passage of a neutrality bill that would automatically prohibit the shipment of arms to any belligerent. The ensuing Neutrality Act was a compromise measure that made the embargo mandatory only when the President recognized that a state of war existed. He had no power to discriminate between aggressors or victims, a limitation which Roosevelt feared would encourage aggression and hence endanger peace. He could, however, prohibit Americans from traveling on belligerent vessels except at their own risk. Hoping that a better measure might be enacted later, the Administration gave way but succeeded in limiting the life of the Act to February 29, 1936. Roosevelt and Hull extended the scope of this law when they urgently requested American oil companies to discontinue shipments to belligerents, a move calculated to restrain Italy in Ethiopia.

In view of Nye's charge that unneutrality was responsible for our entering the First World War and in the desperate hope of averting war, Congress scrapped the traditional right, long protected by international law, of neutral vessels to freedom on the high seas, subject only to such accepted restraints as "visit and search" by belligerents. In 1936 it also forbade loans to belligerents.

Civil war suddenly broke out in Spain in the summer of 1936, when the Fascist-supported Franco attacked the leftist government at Madrid. Italy and Germany sent considerable "volunteer" aid to Franco, but Great Britain and France, unprepared for a major war, worked desperately to formulate a common non-intervention policy; thus Russia was left to assist the Loyalists alone. Since Congress was not in session and the Neutrality Act was silent on civil wars, Roosevelt adopted the Anglo-French policy and effectively discouraged the sale of arms to either side, despite the rights of the Madrid government under international law and our commercial treaty with Spain.

Congress endorsed the President's action when it convened in January, 1937, and extended the arms embargo to Spain. The liberal press agitated for the raising of the embargo, which they maintained was one-sided because Franco could still rely on Fascist aid. The Catholic press, on the other hand, fearing that the Loyalists, who were supported by Soviet Russia as well as by volunteers from the democratic nations, would establish Communism and destroy the church, pleaded for complete neutrality. Roosevelt later defended his decision on the ground that the rebels controlled more shipping than the Loyalists did and hence would have profited more from the lifting of the embargo.

On May 1, 1937, Congress passed a "permanent" Neutrality Act to replace the 1935 law. The new legislation embargoed the export of arms to belligerents when the President proclaimed that a state of civil or international war existed. It prohibited all loans and credits to either side and banned all ordinary travel by American citizens on the ships of warring countries. If the President judged it necessary, he could bar certain raw materials destined for a belligerent from being carried in American ships. However, belligerents could obtain them from us on a "cash and carry" basis, the American shipper surrendering title to the cargo before it left our shores; this would eliminate "incidents" on the high seas that might lead to war. But the President was still denied the crucial power of distinguishing between aggressor and victim in applying these measures. Isolationists were dissatisfied with the "cash and carry" clause because it would benefit the warring nation capable of controlling the seas—in all probability, Great Britain.

JAPAN CLOSES THE OPEN DOOR

The value of the automatic arms embargo to an aggressor was only too patent in the Far East, where the Japanese drive on northern China and Manchuria had continued intermittently since the Mukden incident in 1931. Hull followed the Stimson Doctrine of not recognizing territorial changes made in violation of international law and cooperated with the League regarding the Far East. While the Japanese carved out an exclusive continental market for their goods, largely at American, British, and Chinese expense, the Reconstruction Finance Corporation made loans to China, and American aviation firms helped to build the nucleus of her air strength. Our long-deferred recognition of the Soviet Union on November 16, 1933, was widely interpreted as an astute move to embarrass the Japanese in northern China, to whom the Russians were a dangerous rival. Certainly this action did not lead to any major debt or trade concessions in our favor, although these would naturally be expected, nor did the Soviet Union effectively eliminate Communist propaganda in the United States, as Ambassador Maxim Litvinov had promised.

Tokyo's diplomats struck back at us on April 17, 1934, by proclaiming Japan's right to act alone for "peace and order in Eastern Asia" and denouncing the foreign powers who were building up the military strength of China "even in the name of technical and financial assistance." This repudiation of the open door in favor of Japanese hegemony in the Far East brought a blunt reminder from Hull: "Treaties can lawfully be modified or terminated only by processes prescribed or recognized or agreed upon by the parties to them." Disregarding American, British, and Dutch interests, Japan enacted a sweeping law on oil monopoly in 1934 which compelled the oil companies of these three nations to relinquish a profitable field.

The disarmament settlement of the Washington Conference of 1922 assumed new importance after 1931 as the Japanese conquests imperiled American interests in the Far East. P.W.A. funds had been voted to replace obsolete naval ships in 1933, and the Vinson Act, passed in March, 1934, authorized the expansion of the Navy up to treaty strength by 1942. Since no funds for immediate construction were actually appropriated by Congress, this law was undoubtedly intended as a warning to Japan.

The Nipponese, however, were undeterred in their campaign to achieve parity in capital ships instead of the ignominious 5–5–3 of the Washington Treaty. As Hiroshi Saito, Japan's witty Ambassador, observed, this ratio sounded like "Rolls-Royce—Rolls-Royce—Ford" to his countrymen. Britain and the United States refused to yield, for parity in effect would give Japan unchallenged supremacy in the Pacific. Therefore, on December 29, 1934, Japan, invoking the privilege of cancellation by advance notice, repudiated the naval treaty, which would thus lapse two years later. That same day the Navy Department announced large-scale maneuvers from the Aleutians to the Midway Islands, a coincidence which Tokyo found disturbing and to which she replied with similar maneuvers close to American possessions. These developments insured the utter failure of the London Naval Conference in 1935. The disarmament era was over.

By the spring of 1935 the Japanese were busily detaching China's five northern provinces in the so-called "autonomy movement," and on December 5 our State Department and the British Foreign Office simultaneously warned Japan that they were "closely observing" the political changes in North China and were reserving all treaty rights. After a brief period for consolidating her gains, Japan embarked on a major war against China in July, 1937, while Europe was preoccupied by the civil war in Spain. Nipponese armies, the air force in particular, shocked the world by inflicting heavy losses on the civilian populations of Shanghai, Nanking, Canton, and Hankow. Several Americans were killed and others injured. Secretary Hull and most European nations protested the indiscriminate air bombardment.

Convinced that we were courting war for the sake of profit-seeking interests, many isolationists and a large section of the people demanded the immediate withdrawal of our soldiers and civilians from China. According to them, the only lesson to be learned from World War I was that peace can be maintained during a war crisis by the correctly timed surrender of rights established under international law. Administration supporters followed Senator Key Pittman, chairman of the Foreign Relations Committee, in characterizing this demand as "cowardly and unpatriotic"; they implied that it was ineffective as well. Secretary Hull denied that our policy was based solely on economic motives. Our Chinese investments and properties were substantial—they represented approximately a quarter of a billion dollars—but they were far less than our holdings in any of several regions of Latin America and Europe. "There is a broader and much more fundamental interest," Hull said, "which is that orderly processes in international relationships be maintained." Inasmuch as Japan had not declared war on China, Roosevelt avoided imposing a general arms embargo, which would have hurt China, by not formally recognizing a state of war, but he barred American merchant ships from Chinese waters. However, our industrialists continued to supply Japan outside the war area.

Simultaneously with the League's renewed efforts to halt the Japanese warlords, Roosevelt delivered one of the most significant speeches of his career in Chicago on October 5, 1937. Referring to the spread of international lawlessness in the Far East and Spain, he called for "positive endeavors" by peace-loving nations to oppose those who violated treaties and the instincts of humanity. "When an epidemic of physical disease starts to spread," he observed, " the community approves and joins in a quarantine of the patients in order to protect the health of the community against the spread of the disease." This idea of quarantining aggressors in a program of collective security was emphasized by the press. "If those things [aggressions] come to pass in other parts of the world," he went on, "let no one imagine that America will escape, that America may expect mercy, that this

Western Hemisphere will not be attacked and that it will continue tranquilly and peacefully to carry on the ethics and the arts of civilization."

But, as an informal newspaper poll revealed, Congress was overwhelmingly opposed to League sanctions against the aggressor. Dr. Gallup's survey in October showed public opinion to be divided 63 to 37 per cent against boycotting Japan. Nevertheless, private boycotts were imposed and anti-Japanese sentiment increased. Furthermore, trade friction between the two countries had become serious by this time. Successful Japanese competition with the United States for new markets, especially during 1933–1936, frightened many industrialists, who attributed it to that nation's unfair trade practices. The island empire, actually, had rationalized its industrial system and its trade was profiting from its extremely low wage scale. T. A. Bisson, an authority on the Far East, characterized our fear of Japanese competition as exaggerated.

On December 12, 1937, Americans were shocked by the bombing and sinking of the Navy gunboat *Panay* near Nanking on the Yangtze River by Japanese planes; two crew members were killed and thirty others wounded. Another bombing attack in the afternoon on three Standard Oil tankers resulted in the death of one of the captains. Several British ships were also attacked. Hull issued a severe protest in which he said that he had received reliable information from State Department sources that the attack on the *Panay* was deliberate. Tokyo, evidently anxious to avoid a clash with the United States at this time, quickly apologized, promised to discipline the air force commander responsible, and arranged for full indemnities covering property and personal damages. Even so, Japanese-American relations became definitely worse as the result of the *Panay* incident.

During 1938, when Hitler was absorbing Austria and the Sudetenland and was defying the once-victorious Allies with impunity, Japan took less pains to prevent incidents involving both Britons and Americans. United States Ambassador Grew made repeated representations at Tokyo—as when Japanese soldiers illegally entered American buildings in China to remove Chinese employees and goods, when Embassy officials were slapped by a Japanese soldier during an investigation, and when property belonging to American missions was looted. Japan made it clear that she regarded the open door as an antiquated policy which had been supplanted by the birth of her New Order in East Asia.

As a result, 1938 was a year of unprecedented expansion for the United States Navy. "A Navy second to none!" became the popular watchword. Japan's deliberate wall of secrecy around her naval program inspired wild speculations as to her actual strength and encouraged generous armament appropriations by Congress; these began in May, 1938, with a billion-dollar Navy bill to build a two-ocean Navy. But Congress, fearing to antagonize Japan, rejected even a minor appropriation for the defense of the strategic but distant island of Guam, and refused to be moved by the Navy experts who maintained that an advance fleet base would make us virtually immune to any Japanese attack upon the Philippines.

The desire to avoid war with Japan as well as the pressure exerted by domestic sugar interests hastened the movement to free the Philippines. However, the legislature of the islands rejected the Hare-Hawes-Cutting Act of January, 1933, which Congress had passed over Hoover's veto. This Act terminated the favored position of the islands in our tariff system, restricted Philippine immigration, and demanded extensive military and naval reservations for the United States. The slightly more liberal Tydings-McDuffie Act, passed on March 24, 1934, was made acceptable to the Filipinos only by Roosevelt's personal assurance: "Where imperfections or inequalities exist, I am confident that both can be corrected after proper hearing and in fairness to both peoples." A transitional government for the new Commonwealth of the Philippines was organized by the Filipinos, but certain powers over external affairs were to be exercised by the United States until 1946, when complete independence would be realized. Unfortunately, agricultural lobbies frustrated the efforts of Administration leaders to liberalize the economic provisions of the Act so that the islands would have a generous period in which to find new markets after 1946.

THE MARCH OF EUROPEAN FASCISM

While Japanese aggression was triumphing in eastern Asia, Fascist aggression was thriving in Germany and Italy. The dynamic ideologies of Hitler and Mussolini threatened to engulf the western world in revolutionary nihilism beyond the fondest dream of the Communists in 1918–1919. Far surpassing Mussolini and his pioneer Fascism which had netted an African empire for King Victor Emmanuel II, Adolf Hitler brought his National Socialists to power in 1933 and quickly transformed the democratic Weimar Republic into a totalitarian instrument for world conquest. Labor unions throughout the world looked on with indignation as the proudest trade-union movement in Europe received its death blow. Liberals saw the collapse of all the liberties that had been so painfully won in the course of centuries, and humanitarians were appalled by the most brutal persecution of Jews since the czarist pogroms. The fear of Nazi Germany helped to transform the disarmament movement into a desperate race to rearm.

One of the first problems which Hitler thrust upon the world was that of providing for the hundreds of thousands of Jewish, "non-Aryan" Christian, and purely political refugees who had been driven from their homeland after their property had been confiscated. Over 660,000 persons in Germany were seeking resettlement abroad; but the depression-ridden countries, especially those in which native Fascists had sedulously fostered anti-Semitism, were not always hospitable to the harried refugees. To facilitate their orderly migration, President Roosevelt took the initiative on March 23, 1938, in organizing an international committee for refugees, headed by Myron C. Taylor, the steel manufacturer, who was given an Ambassador's rank. The committee hoped to persuade the Nazis not to strip prospective emigrants completely of their worldly goods. A characteristic Nazi solution to the problem of these refugees was suggested by Dr. Hjalmar Schacht, who proposed that a mass exodus of Jews from Germany be financed by a trust fund derived from their property and from funds designated by other nations to be used to buy German goods on behalf of the émigrés. But the State Department indignantly rejected the idea of "asking the world to pay a ransom for the release of hostages in Germany and [to] barter human misery for increased exports." Consequently, little beyond halfway relief measures was possible.

Hitler's intention of going far beyond scrapping the Treaty of Versailles and of achieving arms equality was revealed by his intrigues in Austria, which included the murder of Chancellor Dollfuss and ended in her complete absorption in March, 1938. By September of that year, Hitler was invoking the Wilsonian right of self-determination on behalf of the German population in the Sudetenland, a section of democratic Czechoslovakia. Britain and France at first seemed ready to help Czechoslovakia resist these demands, even at the cost of war.

On September 26 President Roosevelt sent each nation involved a plea for peace. "I earnestly repeat," he said, "that so long as negotiations continue, differences may be reconciled." Hitler's reply placed the full responsibility for peace on Czechoslovakia, derided her as an abnormality created by the "dictates of 1919," and reiterated his determination to protect the "oppressed" Sudetenland Germans. Roosevelt answered Hitler on September 27, pointing out that war would mean "the mutilation and death of millions of citizens" and that the World War had shown that force had failed for victors and vanquished alike. But Prime Minister Neville Chamberlain, faced with England's unpreparedness, flew to Munich on September 29 for conferences which resulted in the surrender of the Sudetenland to Hitler in return for his supposed guarantee of the integrity of the remainder of Czechoslovakia. On his return Chamberlain naïvely told his relieved countrymen that he brought "peace in our time," but in March, 1939, Hitler absorbed the balance of Czechoslovakia.

Once again flouting public opinion, the Brown Shirts carried out a brutal pogrom against the Jews on November 9, 1938, in retaliation for the shooting of a German official in Paris by a grief-stricken Jewish boy who sought thus to avenge the sufferings of his parents at the hands of the Nazis. Innumerable Jews in Germany were arrested and tortured by Storm Troopers, their shops looted, and their synagogues burned, and all the German Jews were saddled with a fine of one billion marks.

Public opinion throughout the world was outraged as it had not been since the Kishinev pogrom of czarist times. Americans from the President down publicly expressed their revulsion. President Green of the American Federation of Labor urged a boycott of German goods. Roosevelt recalled Ambassador Hugh Wilson, ostensibly for a report on the recent anti-Semitic campaign, whereupon Hitler promptly ordered his Ambassador to return to Germany. Secretary of the Interior Ickes, who had recently prohibited the sale to Germany of any of our helium, a requisite for her dirigibles, openly denounced Hitler as a "brutal dictator." Earlier, in a speech in Cleveland, Ickes had criticized Henry Ford and Charles A. Lindbergh for accepting the German eagle which Hitler had awarded them. "How can any American," he asked, "accept a decoration at the hand of a brutal dictator who, with that same hand, is robbing and torturing thousands of fellow human beings?" The Nazis, utterly unable to comprehend outside interference in "purely domestic questions," sought a retraction of Ickes' remark but were rebuffed by the State Department.

HITLER'S WAR

By January, 1939, according to the Gallup Poll, only 43 per cent of the people questioned believed that the United States could stay out of another world war, as compared to 62 per cent who had thought so two years previously. Munich had dispelled every illusion of security. Although the extent of Germany's rearmament was not known, popular estimates claimed that the Nazis had 10,000 first-line planes and were building heavy warships. In his annual message in January, 1939, the President hinted at effective cooperation between the United States and the nations that resisted aggression when he said, "There are many methods short of war, but stronger and more effective than mere words, of bringing home to aggressor governments the aggregate sentiments of our own people." He was successful in securing a 200 per cent increase in our air force, and in March, 1939, the Navy approved the construction of two 45,000-ton battleships. Britain had signed her first contract for American-built planes in 1938, and a French air mission had obtained the President's approval for the purchase of new models of our military planes. From this it became clear that we would help these two nations strengthen themselves against the Nazis.

Hitler completed another spectacular coup on March 15, 1939, when he absorbed Czechoslovakia by occupying Bohemia and Moravia, at the same time encouraging Hungary to seize the Carpatho-Ukraine. Once again the State Department issued a futile protest against "wanton lawlessness" and "arbitrary force." Nazi troops marched into Lithuania on March 22 and took possession of Memel, a section largely settled by Germans. Mussolini followed this example by ordering the invasion of Albania on April 7, thus adding another country to Victor Emmanuel's growing empire. On April 14, in a forceful message to the Fascist dictators, President Roosevelt asked for a non-aggression guarantee covering the territory and possessions of the remaining free countries of Europe and the Near East. This message was never answered. Two weeks later Britain broke all national precedents by ordering conscription, even though she was still at peace; and on May 7 Germany and Italy announced a formal military alliance. The war clouds were gathering.

In the face of an imminent world war, the Administration forces in Congress attempted to put through a new neutrality law which would extend the "cash-and-carry" principle to all commodities and thus remove the arms embargo which was detrimental to the partly armed British and French. This meant a partial reversion to the more traditional practices of international law. But the bill failed to secure passage by a close margin, largely because of the isolationists, led by Borah and Johnson, who distrusted Roosevelt's interventionism. Consequently, when the 1937 Neutrality Act expired on May 1, it was renewed without any "cash-and-carry" provision. In commenting on this defeat the President remarked that Europe's danger from war had been increased.

By August, Hitler had turned from the now-defunct Czechoslovakia to Poland, from whom he demanded Danzig and the Corridor which Germany had lost by the Treaty of Versailles. This time the Anglo-French diplomats, having lost confidence in the Fuehrer's promises, were prepared to support Poland even to the extent of declaring war. Meanwhile the British were negotiating a military alliance with Russia, who was already allied with France and seemed a vigorous supporter of the League of Nations. On August 22, in the midst of these negotiations, the Soviet government suddenly announced the conclusion of a non-aggression pact with Germany, a development which suggested that a second Munich was in the making.

Roosevelt again appealed to Germany and Poland for peace, urging direct negotiations, mediation, or arbitration as alternate means of agreement, and offering our cooperation in solving the problems that now threatened a world catastrophe. As expected, the German reply placed complete responsibility on Poland and Britain. Not accustomed to prolonged diplomatic procedures, Hitler on September 1, 1939, launched a lightning attack on Poland without the formality of declaring war. Great Britain and France fulfilled their pledge of assistance by declaring war on Germany two days later. That evening, September 3, Roosevelt in a radio address announced his forthcoming neutrality proclamation but warned that events abroad might not leave the United States untouched. "This nation," he said, with an eye on Wilson's experience, "will remain a neutral nation, but I cannot ask that every American remain neutral in thought as well. . . . Even a neutral cannot be asked to close his mind or his conscience. . . . As long as it remains within my power to prevent, there will be no black-out of peace in the United States."

AIDING THE ALLIES "SHORT OF WAR"

During the next few weeks the Gallup Poll asked: "Do you think the United States should do everything possible to help England and France win the war—short of going to war ourselves?" Sixty-two per cent responded affirmatively. Eighty-four per cent wanted the Allies to win and 2 per cent desired a German victory, but only 5 per cent responded in favor of an immediate declaration of war which would require sending our soldiers and sailors abroad. Should Germany appear to be winning, 29 per cent indicated that the United States should declare war. Interestingly enough in view of the isolationist trend, 53 per cent favored our participation in a movement to establish an international police force to maintain world peace. On the whole, the poll corresponded with the policies advocated by the Administration. Few Americans were neutral in thought.

Congress was called in extraordinary session on September 21, 1939, to hear the President ask for the repeal of the embargo features of the Neutrality Act and a return to neutral rights under international law. Without mentioning the belligerents by name, he pointed out that the embargo "had the effect of putting land powers on the same footing as naval powers, so far as sea-borne commerce was concerned." Accordingly, despite opposition arguments that such action was unneutral in time of war, Congress repealed the embargo features on November 4 in favor of a modified "cash-and-carry" arrangement which barred American vessels from combat zones. As a result, between the outbreak of war and August, 1940, the British Empire absorbed 44.3 per cent of our exports, or a total of $1,739,-733,000. During the critical summer of 1940 which saw the fall of France, two-thirds of the total value of American exports—primarily war materials—went to Great Britain.

On September 23, a pan-American conference of foreign ministers met at Panama and issued the Declaration of Panama, which established a 300-mile "safety belt" along the coasts of this hemisphere—a radical innovation in international law—but made no provision for enforcement. The ineffectiveness of this measure became apparent when the *Graf Spee* was sunk in an Anglo-German naval battle near the port of Montevideo. More effective was the Inter-American Financial and Economic Advisory Committee which was created to help adjust the nations on this hemisphere to a war economy.

As in the First World War, neither belligerent was overmeticulous in observing the rights of neutrals. The British set up a rigorous blockade of Germany and compelled neutrals to stop at specified control bases to be inspected for contraband. Britain's practice of blacklisting business firms that dealt with the enemy was revived from World War I. Far more revolting to public opinion were the tactics of German submarines which utterly disregarded the provisions of the London Naval Treaty of 1930 forbidding the sinking of merchant ships unless they resisted their captors. At the outbreak of war the British steamship *Athenia,* half of whose 1400 passengers were Americans, was sunk with a loss of thirty Americans. Nazi propagandists claimed that this attack was ordered by the British Admiralty under Winston Churchill to involve us in the war. Two more American lives were lost shortly afterward, when a Norwegian ship, the *Rondo,* struck a mine. During November the Nazis counterblockaded Britain by means of magnetic mines which were extremely effective—for a short time. The British retaliated by seizing all German exports.

Although the war on the western front remained quiescent until the spring of 1940, Russia opened a new front by invading Finland on November 30, 1939. Various alleged frontier incidents were given as the cause of this move, but Russia was apparently motivated primarily by the need of strategic defenses for Leningrad, which would be exposed in the event of a Nazi attack. American opinion was deeply sympathetic to Finland. At the recommendation of the President, Congress empowered the Export-Import Bank to lend Finland $20,-000,000 and permitted her to defer her next war debt payment to us. The Navy released to the Finns 44 planes that were nearing completion, and many of our engineers were withdrawn from Russia. The Soviet-Finnish war ended on March 12, 1940, with Finland's cession of the Karelian Isthmus, Viborg, and the Mannerheim Line to the Soviet Union.

During April and May the Nazis suddenly revived their dormant campaign in the west by invading Denmark, Norway, Belgium, the Netherlands, and Luxembourg. Roosevelt immediately ordered that the financial assets of these nations in the United States be frozen in order to prevent their funds from getting into German hands. The Nazis were thus deprived of access to $1,619,000,000 belonging to Holland, Belgium's $760,000,000, Norwegian and Danish credits of $267,000,000, and, when France fell in June, 1940, her $1,593,000,-000 held here. By October, 1940, over $4,200,000,000, which could have served the Nazis handsomely, had been impounded in the United States.

PREPARATIONS FOR THE INEVITABLE

Following the startling German successes on the western front, the President asked Congress on May 16 for legislation that would provide for a huge preparedness program to cope with the extraordinary progress in air power. "So-called impregnable fortifications no longer exist," he said. An effective defense required equipment which could attack the aggressor before he could establish strong bases "within the territory of American vital interests." Accordingly, Roosevelt stressed the need of increasing our plane production capacity to at least 50,000 a year. Congress appropriated the unprecedented sum of $13,000,000,-000 for peacetime defense for the fiscal year 1940–1941.

To help readjust the nation's economy to the ambitious goals of defense, an Advisory Commission to the Council of National Defense, similar to Wilson's defense agency early in World War I, was set up on May 28; its members included leading industrialists and representatives of labor and consumers. Army and Navy contracts involving $825,000,000 were awarded after the fall of France in June; a month later, similar contracts amounting to $1,137,000,000 were signed. Automobile plants like Ford, Studebaker, Packard, and General Motors began the large-scale production of airplane engines; Chrysler began to turn out tanks; and other industries undertook the difficult process of partial conversion to war production. At the same time, the desperate needs of the surviving Allies were kept uppermost. We succeeded in sending large surplus stocks of war goods after the British had evacuated Dunkirk, where they had been forced to abandon huge quantities of equipment. During the final months of 1940, Britain needed aid desperately to stave off annihilation by Goering's *Luftwaffe.*

Hitler's conquest of Europe immediately made apparent the possibility that the territories of some of the conquered nations in this hemisphere might be used as centers of Nazi penetration. When Denmark fell in April, Roosevelt entered into an agreement with the Danish minister to provision Greenland; later he established close military and political ties with this strategic island, which lies in the path of any potential air invasion of the United States. Allied troop landings in the Netherland West Indies were permitted when the Nazis conquered Holland, despite this apparent violation of the "no transfer" principle of the Monroe Doctrine. However, the State Department warned the belligerents on June 18, when the French colonies were cast adrift by Weygand's defeat, that it would not allow "any attempt to transfer any geographic region of the Western Hemisphere from one non-American power to another non-American power." Discussion of this problem at the Havana Conference of foreign ministers in July led to an agreement to set up provisional administrations for the colonies of defeated European nations in this hemisphere. Here was a practical "continentalization of the Monroe Doctrine," as A. R. Elliott, the Foreign Policy Association's expert, observed.

While France was making her last stand, Italy declared war on her on June 10, 1940, for frankly avowed territorial gains. "The hand that held the dagger has struck it into the back of its neighbor," Roosevelt charged in an address at the University of Virginia. Premier Reynaud's tragic appeal to him for "clouds of war planes" to save France and the democracies from extinction brought his emphatic assurance of redoubled efforts to supply the Allies. But other French leaders like the aged Marshal Pétain, skeptical of receiving effective resistance from us, surrendered to Hitler rather than continue the devastating war from North Africa. France's salvation was left in the hands of the stubborn followers of de Gaulle, who fought on from British and French colonial bases.

At this critical moment, with Britain under a crushing aerial siege and her fleet battling singlehandedly to prevent being defeated by a concentrated submarine attack, timely assistance came from us in the form of fifty over-age destroyers that were reconditioned and turned over to England in September. In return, we gained a vital adjunct to hemisphere defense by receiving ninety-nine-year leases on valuable air and naval bases in eight British colonies ranging from Newfoundland to British Guiana. Roosevelt described this to Congress as "the most important action in the reinforcement of our national defense that has been taken since the Louisiana Purchase." In accordance with the liberalized conception of the Monroe Doctrine, the facilities of these bases were made available to all of Latin America.

Simultaneously, Congress took the unprecedented step of ordering peacetime conscription when it passed the Selective Training and Service Act on September 16, 1940. The Selective Service system, as envisioned by the General Staff, would provide an army of several millions and thus assure the defense of the entire western hemisphere. In accordance with this Act, 16,000,000 men between twenty-one and thirty-five registered for one year of service on October 16, and within a year the Army increased in size from 265,000 to 1,400,000 men.

Since Japan's intimacy with the Axis was already a recognized fact, the pact she signed with Germany and Italy on September 27 came as no surprise; this provided that aid would be forthcoming if any member was attacked by a power not yet engaged in the European or Asiatic war. The following month Greece was invaded by Italy and was promised aid from the United States. Embattled China was negotiating for a credit of $100,000,000 from us.

In a radio address on December 29, the President warned that if Great Britain went down, the Axis would rule supreme on all the other continents and that life in the United States would be lived at the point of a gun. "We must be the great arsenal of democracy," he declared. "For us this is an emergency as serious as war itself." This proposal was implemented by the far-reaching Lease-Lend Bill (H.R.-1776), which became law on March 11, 1941, after three weeks of bitter debate in the Senate. In sweeping language it authorized the President to "sell, transfer title to, exchange, lease, lend, or otherwise dispose of . . . any defense article" to any nation whose defense he "deems vital to the defense of the United States." The term "defense article" included not only all types of weapons but also transport equipment and services, factory machines, raw materials, food, and repair services of all kinds; under it Allied pilots, mechanics, and gunners could be trained in this country and the Allied nations could receive defense information from our military and civilian leaders. In return for lease-lend aid, the United States was eventually to collect "payment or repayment in kind or property, or any other direct or indirect benefit which the President deems satisfactory." This sweeping grant of aid to the Allies brought criticism outside of Congress from Hoover, Landon, and Norman Thomas, in addition to that from the extreme nationalists; on the other hand, Wendell Willkie and Thomas E. Dewey—the latter somewhat belatedly—supported it.

Two weeks later Congress appropriated $7,000,000,000 for lease-lend. "Within a few minutes," Roosevelt said later, "army and navy war materials were speeding on their way to Great Britain and Greece." New ships were built for the Allies, old ones were repaired, and British pilots were trained in the United States. The tempo of production and delivery was accelerated beyond belief. Lease-lend eliminated the thorny problem of collecting loans after the war, but far more important at the moment was the fact that we could immediately release supplies to the Allies at a time when they were desperately needed.

Meanwhile the German war machine overran Greece and Jugoslavia and forced the British to retire to Crete and finally to Egypt. In spite of the non-aggression pact, Hitler invaded Russia without warning on June 22, 1941. Once more, in keeping with our policy of assisting all those who resisted Nazi domination, the Administration arranged for the extension of lease-lend to Russia. To insure the safety of the North Atlantic sea lanes and of Greenland, American soldiers were landed in Iceland on July 1. Since April, lease-lend shipments had been sent on American vessels to the Allies via the Red Sea, which the President had declared to be outside the combat zone. The spread of the war to Russia and our deteriorating relations with Japan led the Administration to demand on July 21, 1941, in line with a recommendation by Chief of Staff General George Marshall, that Selective Service men be retained in the Army beyond the original one-year period.

In his annual message in January, 1941, Roosevelt proclaimed that a moral world order must be based on "four freedoms": freedom of speech and expression, freedom of religion, freedom from want, and freedom from fear. These aims were significantly amplified in the Atlantic Charter, drawn up in August at a secret conference on the Atlantic attended by Prime Minister Winston Churchill and President Roosevelt. The Charter renounced territorial aggrandizement and territorial changes which did not accord with the "freely expressed wishes of the people concerned." It pledged the right of all peoples to choose their own form of government, and restoration of the sovereignty of the conquered nations. Both countries agreed that raw materials should be accessible to all nations without discrimination. The Charter recommended economic collaboration to improve labor standards and create social security. The peace which would follow this war would, it was hoped, bring freedom from fear and from want. A permanent system of collective security was suggested, to be based at first on the complete disarmament of the aggressor nations. Although the Atlantic Charter was heralded as both wise and liberal, realists who remembered the fate of Wilson's Fourteen Points preferred to reserve judgment until it had been translated into concrete proposals.

Our relations with the Axis continued to deteriorate rapidly. In June we froze the assets of Germany and Italy and a few days later closed the Nazi consulates because of their propagandist activities. In July the President blacklisted some 1800 firms in Latin America which were suspected of being agents for the Fascist powers. On July 25, Japanese assets in the United States were frozen, and the day afterward General Douglas A. MacArthur, former Chief of Staff, was recalled to active service and put in command of American and native forces in the Philippines. On August 26, an American military mission was sent to aid China in her defense against Japan. Meanwhile, after German submarines had begun openly to attack American ships and had sunk a few, our Navy was instructed to take action against any Nazi submarine operating in American defensive waters. By October 9, the President was urging that our merchant ships be armed against the U-boats. That same month he stated that he had in his possession a Nazi map on which South America was divided into five puppet states, and a German document calling for the abolition of all churches and the establishment of an international Nazi "church." In November, Congress, reverting to the theory that the United States should refuse to give up her legal rights as a neutral on the seas, revised the Neutrality Law as recommended by the Administration.

"AMERICA FIRST" AND THE "CHRISTIAN FRONT"

Meanwhile, the President's foreign policy was being challenged, despite the fact that Wendell Willkie, the 1940 Republican presidential candidate, supported its main features. Senator Robert A. Taft of Ohio, who had come close to winning the presidential nomination that year, favored lease-lend aid to Britain but not to Russia because of his deep-rooted fear of Communism; furthermore, he criticized the convoying of our merchant ships in the combat zone by Navy vessels. Former President Hoover assailed our assistance to the Allies as an alliance with Communism and maintained that the United States could best serve democracy by keeping the "lamp of liberty alight in this world"; according to him, mobilization would lead to Fascism in this country.

Particularly active in the isolationist America First movement was Senator Burton K. Wheeler of Montana, who strongly opposed taking any risk of entering the war in order to defeat the Fascists. Another isolationist leader was John L. Lewis of the United Mine Workers, but his influence was offset by that of other labor groups, like Labor's Non-Partisan League. Father Coughlin and the irresponsible Christian Front fanned the flames of extreme nationalism and anti-Semitism in an effort to defeat Roosevelt's foreign policy. Avowed adherents of the Nazis joined him and others of his ilk in applauding the naïve isolationism of Charles A. Lindbergh when he accused the British, the Jews, and the Roosevelt administration of propagandizing for war. Many of the more intelligent isolationists in the America First ranks were embarrassed by their bigoted associates and consequently withdrew their support.

PEARL HARBOR

Japanese-American relations paralleled the European situation. Japan had cleverly utilized the European war for continued expansion in the southeast, timing each major step on the basis of the relative impotence of Hitler's enemies. Thus the fall of France led to Japanese penetration into Indo-China. Our policy was to keep the orphaned Dutch East Indies from being absorbed by Japan. Consequently, hoping to stay Tokyo's aggressive designs, the Administration resisted the heavy pressure to embargo the export of oil products and scrap iron to Japan. Our collaboration with Great Britain and China in resisting Japan's attempt to dominate eastern Asia during 1939–1941 led to numerous incidents involving the three nations; and our material assistance, especially in protecting China's vital Burma road, marked us as an ally of Japan's enemies.

During the late summer and fall Japan kept up a smoke screen of peace negotiations with the United States to mask the elaborate war preparations that had been going on for many busy months. Ambassador Nomura blandly informed our government that any idea of war was "unthinkable." Allied aid led the Dutch East Indies to stiffen their resistance to Japan's demands for sweeping economic concessions, and it seemed as if the Japanese had been checkmated in the southeast. Churchill publicly promised aid to us should we become involved in the Far East. But the Japanese had no intention of yielding to the pressure of the United States, Britain, China, and the Netherlands—the A.B.C.D. powers. A special envoy, Saburu Kurusu, arrived in Washington on November 14 with scarcely new proposals which involved our recognition of his country's advances in southeast Asia, the resumption of normal commercial relations, and the sale of our oil to Japan. In return, Japan would make no further advances into that section of Asia. Secretary Hull, in line with the established liberal policy of the open door, offered a counterproposal promising economic and commercial concessions to Japan in return for her withdrawal from China. Thereafter the Japanese delegation was ominously silent, and Japanese warships and troops assembled around Indo-China. On November 21, Premier Tojo informed the Japanese Diet that hostilities were impending. Roosevelt finally appealed directly to the Emperor on December 6, asking for a peaceful settlement of the issues.

Japan's real reply, which preceded the formal note, took the form of a mass air raid on December 7, 1941, which completely surprised our forces at Pearl Harbor, Hawaii, where 86 vessels of the Pacific Fleet were stationed. Although the State Department had warned of possible attack and had called for the utmost vigilance, the Army and Navy officers in command failed to prevent the sinking of the battleship *Arizona* the capsizing of another, and severe damage to four more battleships and three destroyers. First reports magnified these losses into the annihilation of our entire Pacific Fleet. Of the Navy and Marine forces, 2117 were killed, 876 wounded, and 960 missing; the Army lost 226 men killed and 396 wounded.

Japan's treacherous attack on American territory finally convinced those who had refused to believe that any nation could be so mad as to attack this country. With public opinion thus united in support of the President, Congress declared war on December 8 by a vote that was unanimous except for the single dissenting voice of Representative Jeannette Rankin of Montana, who had voted against the declaration of war in 1917. In accordance with their alliance with Japan, Germany and Italy at once made a formal declaration of war—a novel procedure for any Axis nation—against the United States, whereupon Congress voted war against Germany and Italy, this time unanimously. In his radio broadcast on December 9, Roosevelt asserted that to his knowledge Germany for weeks had been urging Japan to make war on us or forgo any share in the spoils of victory. "When we resort to force, as now we must," he said with an eye to the postwar world, "we are determined that this force shall be directed toward ultimate good as well as against immediate evil. We Americans are not destroyers—we are builders."

War of the United Nations

THE WAR OF ATTRITION AGAINST JAPAN

The United States entered World War II in a grim mood that resulted from the need of fighting two world wars within a quarter of a century. Yet it was generally realized that the Germany of Hitler posed a far greater menace to western concepts of civilization than had the Hohenzollern state of Wilhelm II. Japan's aggression also displayed an ideological aspect of domination in eastern Asia that went far beyond her limited imperialist war aims of 1895, 1905, and 1914. Stressing this fascist threat to the security of the common man, Vice President Henry Wallace revived Wilson's slogan for World War I, "a people's war," a phrase which gained poignancy as desperate, poorly armed underground resistance groups within the occupied countries struck repeatedly against the invader. For the United States, with her highly developed industries, the enhanced role of civilians as well as the military in winning a mechanized war lent conviction to those who spoke of a people's war.

Five months of incredibly rapid advances by the Japanese in the Pacific, made possible by the treacherous blow at Pearl Harbor, left unchanged the Anglo-American decision to defeat Hitler first. China, Australia, New Zealand, and our own west coast criticized this decision, for they feared the strength of a consolidated Greater Japan, revitalized by her recent conquests. However, Allied strategists considered Germany's industrial capacity and military power a far more imminent danger in view of the proximity of the British Isles. Therefore, until Hitler was defeated, Japan was to be kept in check by a policy of attrition and her ships and planes were to be destroyed at a rate beyond her ability to replace them.

The attack on Pearl Harbor temporarily disabled every American battleship and most of our planes in that area—not without serious losses to Japan—and thus secured the enemy's flank for the invasion of the Philippines and Malaya. Japan immediately launched an attack against the Philippines and isolated General Douglas MacArthur on Luzon, with a force composed of only 15,000 American Marines and Army troops, 40,000 Filipino soldiers, and a few hundred planes, in addition to our small Asiatic fleet. Japanese planes attacked our air bases and soon destroyed our air force. Within several weeks after Pearl Harbor the Japanese landed an estimated 200,000 well-equipped men on Luzon, but they paid heavily for their subsequent advance into the Bataan peninsula, for MacArthur's forces held them at bay until April, 1942. The Filipino troops fought with the fierce loyalty of men defending their homes; few of them followed Emilio Aguinaldo, the revolutionary leader of 1899 who, won over by Japanese blandishments, now counseled his countrymen in a radio broadcast to cooperate with the invaders.

The fact that American supply ships were unable to penetrate the Japanese blockade except in small numbers sealed the doom of Bataan, despite the bravery of its defenders. Australia, which provided a natural base for eventual countermeasures against Japan, received the bulk of the assistance sent to the Far East. MacArthur himself was ordered to Australia by President Roosevelt, being replaced in the Philippines by Major General Jonathan M. Wainwright. After battling the Japanese for "ninety-eight tortured days," Wainwright and his army—now reduced to some 35,000 men—yielded Bataan in April. He carried on the final struggle for the 12,000 remaining troops from the adjacent island fortress of Corregidor, whose guns exacted a heavy toll from the enemy before the starving, disease-wracked Americans and Filipinos surrendered on May 6. Thereafter little news of the Philippine Islands reached the outside world. MacArthur vowed to liberate them and the United States government pledged them political independence at the end of the war.

The British and Dutch fared no better in Malaya, where the Japanese penetrated the jungle hinterland and seized the prized bastion of Singapore; by March they had overrun the Dutch East Indies. Aided by a Burmese fifth column, Japanese troops advancing in the west toward India had driven the British out of Burma by May 10, 1942, thus cutting the vital Burma Road over which desperately needed supplies were transported from the Allies to China and imperiling India. Australia to the south, aided by steady American reinforcements, worked feverishly to avert invasion as the triumphant Japanese poured into New Guinea, New Britain, and other adjacent islands. At this juncture Gandhi and Nehru, although sympathetic to the Allied cause, demanded India's immediate independence as the condition for her cooperation against Japan. A few other Indian leaders apparently favored a policy of benevolent neutrality toward the Japanese. Doubting the efficacy of India's war effort under Nationalist leadership, the British refused to offer anything more than dominion status after the war. President Roosevelt vainly sought to arbitrate the dispute, but England regarded additional concessions as suicidal in the face of the Japanese menace.

Rounding out her advances in the Pacific, possibly in preparation either for the invasion of Hawaii or, as west coast Congressmen feared, for an attack on our Pacific states, Japan occupied Kiska, Attu, and Agattu in the bleak Aleutian Islands that project from the fringes of Alaska. Her Navy moved into the South Pacific in May, 1942, apparently ready for a crushing blow northeast of Australia. But our carrier-based planes struck back in the Battle of the Coral Sea, inflicting heavy losses—seventeen enemy warships probably sunk or damaged—at the cost of one American aircraft carrier, the *Lexington*. Early in June our land-based planes intercepted a Japanese flotilla off Midway Island and sank at least four enemy carriers in addition to inflicting heavy damage on other Japanese warships. Our crushing victory at Midway marked a definite turn in our favor, for thereafter the Japanese Navy began to shift from offensive to defensive tactics. Our submarines played havoc with enemy shipping and in January, 1943, our aviators, piloting the efficient new machines being turned out in ever-increasing numbers in the United States, were shooting down the Japanese Zeros and other enemy planes at a ratio of four to one, according to President Roosevelt.

Meanwhile General MacArthur and Admiral Chester Nimitz had been working on a coordinated campaign up the "ladder of the Solomons." This got under way at dawn on August 7, when our Marines landed at Tulagi Harbor on Florida Island; this was followed by successive landings on Guadalcanal and neighboring islands. Concurrently our naval forces defeated units of the Japanese fleet in the Solomons area and the Bismarck Sea, thus cutting off much-needed supplies and reinforcements for the Japanese garrisons then in combat with Allied troops. Thereafter Australian and American troops opened a long but successful campaign in New Guinea which drove the Japanese back into the jungle after their advance on Fort Moresby. By January, 1944, MacArthur's men were threatening the strong enemy base at Rabaul, New Britain, in their effort to execute a pincers movement in cooperation with troops at Bougainville. These campaigns, claimed Roosevelt, involved more than "island-hopping" strategy; they were a necessary preliminary to direct attacks on Japan herself. Between May and August, 1943, the enemy was driven out of the Aleutians and American fliers from these bases began to bomb the outer fringes of the Japanese homeland. This was followed by landings on the Japanese-held Gilbert Islands and the intensive air bombing of the Marshalls, a prelude to their capture in February, 1944.

The smashing invasion of the Marshalls which wiped out enemy resistance in that area signified the precipitate decline of Japan's air power as well as her sea power. This exploit was followed by an unbroken series of sea victories and the capture of various strategic western Pacific island bases essential to the final assault on Japan herself. During October 20–21, 1944, after many months of painful advance through the jungles of New Guinea, General MacArthur unloosed the heaviest blow of the war—the mass invasion of the Philippine Islands. Some 600 ships landed American troops and supplies upon Leyte in the central Philippines, an army comparable in size to the one that invaded Normandy on the first day; our forces quickly overran most of the island and extended their operations into the neighboring islands. In a desperate gamble calculated to cut off and destroy MacArthur's expedition, the Japanese fleet emerged into the Philippine Sea in a three-pronged pincers movement, only to be severely beaten in an engagement that lasted days and was comparable to the famous battle of Jutland in World War I. Admiral Chester W. Nimitz estimated that our combined Navy, air force, and submarines had definitely sunk at least 24 Japanese warships, including four carriers and two battleships, and damaged at least 36 more (some of these may have been sunk); few escaped unscathed. Our principal losses—

the light carrier *Princeton*, two escort carriers, two destroyers, one destroyer escort, and a few lesser craft—were not excessive in view of the total gains, which included domination of the invaded land area. American strategists jubilantly calculated the strength of the remaining Japanese fleet. As a result of this victory, MacArthur's men, accompanied by the long-exiled Philippine government (President Quezon, however, had died a short time previously), moved forward rapidly on their mission of liberating the Filipino people from nearly three years of harsh subjection to Japan. Something more ambitious than a war of attrition and "island hopping" had begun.

Although a frontal attack on Japan from Asiatic bases was apparently envisaged, China received relatively limited supplies from the Allied powers, primarily because of transportation difficulties. The sensational bombing of Tokyo in April, 1942, by American carrier-based fliers under James Doolittle offered a heartening if isolated promise of things to come. A small but remarkably effective United States air force, originally a volunteer group known as the "Flying Tigers" and commanded by Brigadier General Claire L. Chennault, helped the poorly equipped Chinese soldiers to check Japanese advances inland. As 1944 began, China looked to Lord Mountbatten's new Allied armies—including Americans—in India to take the initiative in driving the enemy out of continental Asia. However, the preoccupation of Allied forces elsewhere, together with jungle barriers and the paralyzing monsoons, made Japanese resistance in Burma formidable and reduced this campaign almost to a stalemate until late in 1944.

THE EUROPEAN THEATER

On January 26, 1942, the first American troops to be sent to the European theater reached North Ireland. Soon thereafter the Rangers, the counterpart of the British Commandos, were organized with specially selected men from our fighting forces, and units of our Navy joined the British home fleet. Roosevelt and Churchill met at Teheran in June to plan a large-scale Anglo-American attack in the Mediterranean, and named Major General Dwight D. Eisenhower as head of Allied military and air forces in the European sphere. The Soviet Union, which up to now had borne the brunt of the Nazi strength, was incessant in her demand for the opening of a second front by her allies. Millions of her soldiers had perished in the herculean effort to prevent the Nazis from capturing Stalingrad and reaching the precious oil of the Caucasus.

During the spring and summer of 1942, American equipment and supplies arrived in the Middle East in sufficient quantities to turn the tide against General Erwin Rommel, the "desert fox" whose clever strategy had driven the British from Bengasi back to Egypt and was now threatening Alexandria. By that fall, General Sir Bernard L. Montgomery, having taken the measure of his opponent, forced the Germans and Italians to withdraw to Tripoli and Tunisia.

On November 7, 1942, the "largest amphibious expedition in history" began when 500 troop transports escorted by 350 warships landed British and American soldiers on the coasts of French Morocco and Algeria. These French possessions were under the Vichy government headed by Marshal Henri Pétain, who advocated a policy of abject collaboration with Nazi Germany. General Eisenhower and our State Department avoided prolonged bloodshed by successful negotiations with Admiral Jean François Darlan, a hitherto anti-British member of the Vichy regime who was able to bring about the surrender of the French garrisons at Algiers on the first day and at Casablanca on the third; Allied losses were thus comparatively light. With the first stage of the campaign ended, Allied troops, soon augmented by French contingents, marched on the Axis-held French protectorate of Tunisia. Darlan brought French West Africa over to the Allied side and then turned his efforts to winning over the important French fleet at Toulon. But as soon as the Allies invaded North Africa the Nazis overran the hitherto unoccupied southern portion of France and marched quickly into Toulon. Thereupon, except for a few units which escaped from the harbor, the French fleet was scuttled by its crews.

The liberal press condemned our recognition of Darlan, the ex-collaborationist, as political head of North Africa and charged him with Fascist leanings; but Roosevelt, pointing out that the arrangement was only temporary, supported Eisenhower and the State Department. Darlan was assassinated on December 24 and was succeeded by the popular but politically neutral General Henri Giraud, who had escaped from the Nazis with Allied aid. This was a source of dissatisfaction to General de Gaulle and his Fighting French, who had never collaborated with Hitler. Although de Gaulle eventually was recognized as political leader of the liberated French people, Roosevelt made it clear that only the French people themselves, after all of France had been liberated, could decide on their country's permanent government. American pressure on Giraud's new North African regime hastened the nullification of laws, especially those against the Jews, which had been enacted by the Vichy government after the fall of France in 1940. Giraud, promised ample lease-lend supplies by the United States, planned to organize a new French army of perhaps 500,000 men to fight against the Nazis.

Meanwhile the Allies had moved into Tunisia but were hampered for months by a reinforced German-Italian army and a combination of poor weather and difficult terrain; nevertheless, they conquered all Tunisia by early summer. General Eisenhower thereupon ordered the invasion of Sicily, an amphibious operation on a far larger scale than any preceding one; 3266 transports and other vessels took part. While General Montgomery led his Eighth Army into eastern Sicily and Canadian troops advanced into the center, American forces under Lieutenant General George S. Patton, Jr., invaded western Sicily. The morale of the Italian soldiers—it had been declining steadily for some time—collapsed, leaving the bulk of the fighting to small numbers of picked German troops. As a result, the battle of Sicily, which began on the night of July 9, ended abruptly.

Mussolini was overthrown in a palace revolution on July 25 but was subsequently rescued by the Nazis. The new government set up by Marshal Badoglio signed an armistice on September 3 which gave Italy the status of co-belligerent on the Allied side. By this time the first stage of the invasion of the Italian mainland, with Rome as the objective, was being completed. Montgomery's troops were advancing up the heel of the Italian boot and along the western slope of the Apennines, and Lieutenant General Mark W. Clark was leading an Anglo-American amphibious expedition which captured "bloody Salerno" and eventually drove on to Naples.

The Nazis, profiting from the uneven miry terrain, the snow-covered mountains, and the miserable weather which aided defensive operations, fought a fierce delaying action that held the British and Americans in 1943 to small gains beyond Naples. Although the Allies failed to cut off the German forces retreating from southern Italy, they succeeded in establishing the Mediterranean air bases that were vital for bombing Germany from the south and in assisting Jugoslav guerrillas against Nazi occupation troops.

If this campaign was not the second front envisaged by the hard-pressed Russians, it at least diverted several Nazi divisions from the east. The opening of the Mediterranean sea lanes eased the transportation problem for the Allies, strengthened the supply lines to the Far East, and made available warships hitherto kept in Atlantic waters to reduce the Nazi submarine menace. Rome itself was taken by units of General Clark's Fifth Army on June 4, 1944—an event which heralded the prompt abdication of Victor Emmanuel III in favor of his son Prince Humbert (in accordance with his promise), the resignation of Premier Badoglio, and the formation of a government untainted by Fascism.

Russia's rapid advance during 1943–1944 across her pre-1939 borders as well as the Italian campaign gave Britain and the United States much-needed time in which to prepare the long-heralded invasion of France. In the meantime American and British airmen were accelerating the "softening up" of the industrial cities of the Reich and were methodically wiping out entire factory sections; large sections of Berlin, Hamburg, and other cities were reported to be in ruins early in 1944. American bombers of the Eighth Air Force dealt Germany's aircraft industry a severe blow and forced the Luftwaffe to go on the defensive. From across the Atlantic came huge convoys of American fighting men and supplies that were landed in Great Britain.

On June 6, 1944—D Day—3200 transports and landing craft, supported by some 8000 Allied planes of all types, opened the initial phase of the battle for France. The Allies poured nearly 2,500,000 troops, 500,000 vehicles, and 17,000,000 ship tons of munitions and supplies into this campaign during the first 109 days. General Eisenhower was made supreme commander of the operation. Lessons learned in the Pacific proved invaluable for the large-scale amphibious operations in Normandy. Novel prefabricated ports solved the problem of landing supplies on the coast. American land forces under General

Omar N. Bradley in conjunction with the British overwhelmed Germany's vaunted Atlantic Wall. Paris fell during the last week of August. By August 25, the retreating Germans had lost an estimated 400,000 men in northern France. Meanwhile, new British, American, and French armies landed on a hundred-mile coastal strip of southern France around Toulon and Nice on August 15 and helped to bring about the total collapse of the German defense of France. While the British moved into Belgium and Holland and Canadian divisions captured Antwerp, American armies to the south probed sections of the formidable Siegfried Line. The American First Army under Lieutenant General Courtney H. Hodges fought a fierce prolonged battle for Aachen, the medieval seat of Charlemagne's empire. Virtually demolished by artillery and air attacks, this vital bastion of the Siegfried Line was in our hands on October 20. This news, which coincided with despatches reporting Russia's capture of Belgrade and our invasion of the Philippines, was an excellent augury for the United Nations.

INTER-ALLIED UNITY

Inter-Allied cooperation became increasingly integrated. Joint war staffs and various international boards concerned with munitions, raw materials, shipping, food supplies, rehabilitation, and production increased in number, suggesting possible machinery for postwar collaboration. American lease-lend shipments to the Soviet Union alone were valued at over $3,287,000,000 on October 1, 1943; most of the goods had been shipped during the preceding nine months, Russia's darkest hour. Britain likewise contributed heavily to the mechanization and supplying of the Red Army. All the Allies, with a few exceptions, interchanged some goods on a lease-lend basis, so that the United States, as Roosevelt pointed out, shared in a "two-way" system.

Outstanding among various Allied meetings was the Moscow Conference in October, 1943, in which Secretary of State Hull participated, together with British Foreign Minister Anthony Eden, Soviet Foreign Commissar Molotov, and, later, the Chinese Ambassador to Moscow. The four-power Moscow Declaration which they formulated emphasized unconditional surrender, pledged the destruction of the remnants of Italian Fascism, promised Austria independence, and agreed upon postwar cooperation and the need for a "general international organization" to maintain peace and security. The four countries pledged that they would not use military force against other nations after the war except for purposes commonly agreed upon and that they would cooperate in efforts to regulate postwar armament. European Advisory Commissions were set up in Britain and Italy to make recommendations on non-military problems relating to enemy territory.

On November 5, by a vote of 85 to 5 on the Connally resolution, the Senate implemented the Moscow Declaration by a cautiously worded statement on the need for an international peace organization "at the earliest practicable date" after the war, to be "based on the principle of the sovereign equality of all peace-loving States." The resolution provided that any treaty covering our participation in such an association must be made with the advice and consent of two-thirds of the Senate as provided by the Constitution. Even strong reservationists like Lodge, who had emasculated the League of Nations, could have agreed to such a proposal in 1919 with equanimity. Popular hopes for an early victory and a postwar order in which Russia would collaborate were raised by the second conference at Teheran in November, 1943, which was attended by Churchill, Stalin, and Roosevelt.

Roosevelt, Churchill, and Chiang Kai-Shek met in Cairo later that month to discuss the final disposition of Japan after her unconditional surrender. She was to be deprived of every Pacific island she had taken (or been granted) since World War I, together with the hitherto Chinese territories of Manchuria, Formosa, and the Pescadores. Even Korea, which Japan had formally annexed back in 1910, was promised freedom and independence. Thus the predatory Land of the Rising Sun would be reduced to the status of a third-rate power and China's power would be correspondingly increased—a development already foreshadowed in the treaties China signed with Britain and the United States in January, 1943. In them the two western powers surrendered their long-standing extraterritorial rights, which ignored China's sovereignty, and also their unique policing powers and economic privileges which were so detrimental to China's independence and development. It was hoped that other western powers would follow this example of democratic good will and banish foreign imperialism.

Significant both as a "world community chest" and as a potential world peace organization was the creation, on November 9, 1943, of the United Nations Relief and Rehabilitation Administration, which included forty-four nations. This agency, intended primarily as an emergency council, was concerned with the relocation and feeding of the 20 or 30 million people uprooted by the war. Each member nation contributed on the basis of its national income to a pool which it was estimated would amount to 2.5 billion dollars. The Big Four—the United States, Great Britain, China, and the Soviet Union—constituted an executive Central Committee, and the forty-four nations were represented in a policy-making council. Herbert H. Lehman, former governor of New York, was named Director General, a position which required close liaison with the various Anglo-American strategic boards in Washington as well as with numerous private humanitarian agencies. Special overseas personnel were trained for relief administration and regional committees were set up for Europe and the Far East.

On June 15, 1944, Roosevelt announced plans for a new league and world court formulated after consultations with State Department officials and other experts. "We are not thinking of a superstate with its own police forces and other paraphernalia of coercive power," he asserted. "We are seeking effective agreements and arrangements through which the nations would maintain, according to their capacities, adequate forces to meet the needs of preventing war and of making impossible deliberate preparation for war, and to have such forces available for joint action when necessary."

The translation of these hopes into deeds was attempted at the much-heralded Dumbarton Oaks Conference which opened August 21, 1944, in Georgetown, just outside of Washington, D. C. This Conference followed other international discussions on such questions as monetary stability. Cordell Hull and the other American delegates met with British, Russian, and Chinese representatives at the beautiful Dumbarton Oaks manor house to explore the organizational forms that a postwar security league might take. It was readily apparent that the peace of the world rested primarily on the decisions made by the Big Four and that therefore these nations (with the expected addition of France) must occupy a special position in the projected league.

On October 9 the Conference revealed its recommendations: An international security organization, obviously intended to absorb the existing League of Nations, was to be known as "The United Nations" and would be empowered "to take such action by air, naval, or land forces as may be necessary to maintain or restore international peace and security." An eleven-nation Security Council with five permanent members—the Big Four and France—was to be empowered to keep the peace. Second, a General Assembly of all nations was to be created, but its activities would be largely advisory in nature. Third, an international Court of Justice was to be established along the lines of the existing World Court. Finally, an Economic and Social Council of eighteen members was to be created; it would be under the control of the General Assembly and would make recommendations on international economic and humanitarian problems. This project was favorably received in the press—except for such isolationist newspapers as the Chicago *Tribune*—and Dewey's support as a presidential candidate assured it of bipartisan backing.

HEMISPHERE SOLIDARITY

War brought the western hemisphere into ever greater economic and political intimacy. Military and economic cooperation with Canada advanced far beyond the joint defensive plans of pre-Pearl Harbor days. Japan's early successes and the threat to our own west coast clearly indicated the need for us to guard our communications with Alaska. Accordingly construction on the Alcan Highway was begun in March, 1942. The road was cut through the wilderness from Dawson Creek on the eastern border of British Columbia to Fairbanks, Alaska—a distance of 1670 miles—and was completed by November, 1942. Canada not only consented to this project but supplied some of the materials, the agreement being that the portion of the road within her borders would revert to her after the war.

Latin America's solidarity with the United States was apparently in proportion to the geographic proximity of the various nations. Thus Mexico declared war on the Axis in May, 1942, after several of her oil tankers had been torpedoed by German submarines. She cooperated with us in home defense measures and entered an agreement with us for the reciprocal use of air bases. Our lease-lend supplies enabled her to expand and modernize her army and to produce essential war materials for the Allies. Under the stimulus of the war and of subsidies from us, Mexico turned more than ever from agriculture to industry and mining and enjoyed a major economic boom. Cut off from her European markets, she depended heavily on closer economic relations with us. Our acute shortage of agricultural labor, especially in the Southwest, was relieved by a carefully planned program which brought Mexican workers to this country, assured them the prevailing wage rates and adequate housing, and guaranteed them against racial discrimination.

The basic blueprints for inter-American cooperation as a whole were drawn at Rio de Janeiro in January, 1942, when the third Conference of Foreign Ministers met to adopt common measures against the Axis and to adjust the hemisphere economy to the loss of normal trade channels abroad. The United States was interested in stamping out fifth-column activities in Latin America and in developing nearby resources which could supply strategic materials—especially rubber, cordage, and various agricultural and forest products—that had been lost to the Japanese. The leading hemisphere powers, including recalcitrant Argentina, had agreed a month before the Conference to consider the United States a non-belligerent; this allowed us to use harbors and airports that were closed to the warring nations. Although Argentina's isolationist Castillo government had an important part in preventing the Conference from taking a vigorous anti-Axis stand, it was recommended that diplomatic relations be broken with Rome, Berlin, and Tokyo. The Conference laid plans for economic and financial cooperation, gave tacit support to our blacklisting of Axis-dominated firms, and agreed to cooperate in developing sources of strategic materials.

At the same time our government completed agreements with fifteen Latin American countries designed to stimulate a long-range rubber program and the introduction of sanitation measures; the plans called for the opening of the malaria-infested Amazon basin. Countries in the accessible Caribbean area were encouraged to raise the fiber plants and mahogany which we formerly obtained from the Philippines, and American experts—men from the new Inter-American Institute of Agricultural Sciences at Washington, for example—attempted to conquer other material shortages. Tiny Costa Rica helped to lighten our shipping problem by furnishing supplies for American soldiers in the Canal Zone. Thus loans, technical aid, and lease-lend supplies welded the western hemisphere into an economic unit—except for Argentina, which was left to enjoy a costly isolationism.

MOBILIZATION

Total war meant a degree of mobilization which far surpassed that in World War I; however, the experience gained from the earlier conflict proved invaluable. Early in 1943 Congress reluctantly extended the draft limits to include men between eighteen and thirty-eight in an effort to defer as long as possible the drafting of fathers; but by the beginning of 1944 "pre-Pearl Harbor fathers" were being called up. Only a few classifications were exempt from service; however, deferments were granted to farm workers in order to keep up food production and similar exceptions were made in the case of men in certain essential industries. To carry on war in perhaps sixteen theaters, the Army alone required no less than 10,800,000 men, according to Selective Service officials. The problems involved in such a sudden expansion of our armed forces—selecting, training, equipping, and housing the draftees—were handled far more efficiently than in World War I, and detailed plans for the soldiers' return to civilian life after the war were formulated. To release men for combat duty wherever possible, the various branches of the armed forces were augmented by the Wacs (Army), the Waves (Navy); the Spars (Coast Guard), and the Women's Auxiliary of the Marines. A War Manpower Commission, headed by Paul V. McNutt of Indiana, was created in April, 1942, and later that year its powers were extended to include jurisdiction over Selective Service, the U. S. Employment Service, and other recruiting and training agencies related to the war. Home defense was strengthened by the Office of Civilian Defense, which in 1942 included more than 5,000,000 volunteer air raid wardens, persons trained to give first aid, nurses' aides, and other workers.

By the time the War Manpower Commission was set up, Donald Nelson's War Production Board had completed the gigantic task of converting most of our 184,000 factories into war plants. The next problem was to find the millions of additional workers, especially women, required in war production. Not only did unemployment disappear, but many of the hitherto "unemployables" found jobs. McNutt's demand for a bill to draft labor met stubborn resistance in Congress. Because of the labor shortage, Roosevelt was compelled early in 1943 to decree a forty-eight-hour week for most war industries, but he succeeded in saving the hard-won basic forty-hour week by stipulating overtime rates for the additional eight hours. To combat the unusual labor turnover caused by employees "shopping around" for higher-paying jobs, workers in war plants were "frozen" to their jobs; however, exceptions were permitted in certain cases.

The W.P.B.'s control of critical materials gave it a dominating position on the industrial scene. Since these materials were allocated on the basis of military and essential civilian demands, many factories not engaged in what was regarded as necessary production were compelled to close for lack of materials, even though they had survived the labor shortage. Periodic statistics released by the W.P.B. indicated that in most instances American industry, especially steel and aviation, was bettering the peak production records set in World War I. To meet the potentially disastrous shortage of rubber, a special division headed by William M. Jeffers was set up in the W.P.B. Its work in reclaiming old rubber and in producing synthetic rubber averted our military collapse for want of mechanized equipment (even though there were fewer cars on the highways to use up rubber).

INFLATION AND LABOR PROBLEMS

The conversion of factories to war production and the competition of the high-income groups for the dwindling amount of civilian goods and services raised the menace of inflation, which would crush the people with fixed or low incomes and eventually would raise the cost of war supplies to the government. By December, 1941, food had risen 61 per cent above the pre-1939 level and the prices of other civilian goods were correspondingly higher. Wage agreements rapidly became obsolete. The Office of Price Administration, created in the spring of 1941, had been able to keep the prices of basic defense materials down by means of voluntary agreements but was helpless to take any further steps. Congress was torn between the farm bloc's demand for higher prices and Administration pressure to stabilize the cost of living.

The Price Control Act of January, 1942, which authorized the O.P.A. to set ceilings on prices and rents, yielded—at least in part—to the farm bloc by providing a new parity formula intended to protect the farmers' share of the national income. Farm bloc leaders stubbornly resisted the attempt of the Southern Tenant Farmers Union to increase farm labor rates to thirty cents an hour. The importation of Mexican workers and the draft deferment eventually granted men engaged in farming kept labor costs down, but the Secretary of Agriculture had no power to regulate wages and conditions of farm labor, except in the case of the Mexicans. According to Professor Paul S. Taylor, the economist, a Kansas Congressman who feared the impact of New Deal wage standards on farm labor said, "You can leave out the wage scales and standards of living and all of that. We do not need any of them." In other words, farmers remembered the long lean years of the twenties and thirties too well to be willing to surrender any economic advantages deriving from the war. Taylor also pointed out that local statutes in various farming sections permitted the hoarding of farm labor.

Organized labor was likewise unwilling to lose either the favorable position it had won under the New Deal or the general rise in real wages. This resulted in widespread newspaper attacks on the unions for lack of patriotism; editorials frequently contrasted the pittance received by the soldier who faced death on the battlefield, with the high wages paid organized labor in the United States. Shortly after Pearl Harbor the President called representatives of the C.I.O. and of the A.F. of L. and various industrial leaders to Washington for a conference. The outcome was that labor signed a "no strike" pledge for the duration and industry agreed not to use lockouts. More important, however, were recommendations made by the conference leading to the establishment of the National War Labor Board, whose members were to be drawn equally from labor, industry, and the public. Its authority to stabilize wages during this period of sharply rising prices was put to a significant test when the United Steel Workers of America, a C.I.O. affiliate, demanded a raise of one dollar per day in the smaller steel plants. In its award of July 16, 1942, the War Labor Board allowed a 15 per cent wage increase—in this case forty-four cents a day—to cover a proportionate rise in the cost of living between January 1, 1941, and May, 1942. This award, which became known as the Little Steel formula, was later extended by Roosevelt to other industries. Inevitably this formula was outstripped by the continued rise in prices. The W.L.B. was flooded by petitions for wage increases as labor discontent mounted. "Wildcat" strikes accounted for most of the 3000 work stoppages in 1942 that involved approximately 840,000 employees.

In a statement on April 27, 1942, Roosevelt advocated curbing excess purchasing power and profiteering through heavier taxes, wholesale purchases of war bonds by the public, and restrictions on installment buying. He also suggested that consumers and laborers be protected by price ceilings and by the rationing of scarce commodities, and that the basic forty-hour week, with additional payment for overtime, remain unchanged. Farm bloc Congressmen joined anti-Administration men during 1942 in fighting this program. When the cost of living continued to rise in 1943, despite this largely successful program for "holding the line" against inflation, the A. F. of L. and the C.I.O. sought to have the Little Steel formula set aside. On the grounds of the extreme hardships resulting from the rising living costs under the existing system of company stores, John L. Lewis and his United Mine Workers rebelled against the Little Steel Formula and the War Labor Board itself. When the miners threatened a nationwide strike in November, 1943, President Roosevelt ordered Secretary of the Interior Ickes to take over the mines. Anti-union forces in Congress, profiting by the widespread condemnation of strikes and threats of strikes, passed the Smith-Connally Act over the President's objections. This Act subjected strike votes and union finances to federal scrutiny and imposed penalties on leaders of strikes in plants engaged on government contracts. The year 1943 ended with the President compelled to intervene again, this time to place the railroads of the nation under Army control in order to avert a wholesale walkout on the eve of the contemplated invasion of northwestern Europe.

In one of the most publicized labor cases of the war, Roosevelt ordered United States Army troops to Chicago on April 25, 1944, to take over the huge mail-order house of Montgomery Ward and Company after its chairman, Sewell Avery, defied an order of the National Labor Relations Board to continue its contract with the local union. Alleging a federal violation of the Bill of Rights, Avery refused to leave his office; he was finally carried out bodily. The N.L.R.B. held an election to determine the union preferences of the employees; the C.I.O. won, and the soldiers were withdrawn.

One step to halt inflation was the creation, in October, 1942, of the Office of Economic Stabilization, headed by the former Supreme Court Justice, James Byrnes, and empowered to formulate an economic policy which would stabilize the various factors in the rising cost of living such as excessively high salaries. Meanwhile the O.P.A. had rapidly expanded its rationing program until by 1943 most essential foods were included. Its effort to enforce price ceilings on more than 400 items created a host of enemies among producers and retailers. "Price control may influence people," wrote Professor Clair Wilcox of Swarthmore, a former O.P.A. official, "but it does not win friends." As with the tariff problem, Congressmen tended to reflect the pressure of their constituents. Thus congressional displeasure was responsible for the resignation, on December 17, 1942, of Leon Henderson, a noted economist who had served as Director of the O.P.A. Many "long-haired professors," too mindful perhaps of consumer interests, were ousted in 1943 when Congress refused to pass the War Agencies Act unless "theorists" were replaced by men "qualified by experience in business, industry, or commerce." Once more the prestige of businessmen and business leadership was rising to the eminent position it held before the depression. Anti-New Dealers suspected that the Administration was using the war emergency as a "front" behind which to socialize the nation's economy. In defense of the O.P.A., Professor Wilcox declared that it would save the government and the people no less than $90,000,000,000 by the end of 1943.

During 1943–1944 the Department of Agriculture became involved in a controversy with the farm bloc over food subsidies. In an effort to block or to "roll back" rising food prices and relieve farmers and processors from the pressure of higher costs, the Department began to extend subsidies for some twenty-five food crops and to make incentive payments to farmers. Although its official charts for October, 1943, indicated that the farmer was already receiving fifty-eight cents of the consumer's dollar—a record that had not been reached since 1917—the food subsidy program antagonized the farm bloc, for they preferred to have higher prices for agricultural products take the natural wartime course to ever-higher levels. The controversy continued to simmer through 1944, with no decisive gains for consumer groups.

The problem of paying for the most expensive war in history raised many related issues in addition to inflation curbs. One of them involved taxation. Budget estimates—$56,000,000,000 for the fiscal year 1943—were continually revised upward to meet the expanding needs of global warfare. Going far beyond the tax rates enacted in World War I, Congress imposed a 5 per cent Victory Tax on gross annual incomes over $624 and in addition sharply increased the normal and surtax rates; exemptions were slashed repeatedly. The 1943 corporate taxes, which included a 90 per cent excess profits tax, cut profits drastically. Tax exemptions for inheritances declined; excise taxes were not only increased but widely extended. The prospect for 1944 was even worse, according to Secretary Morgenthau. Encouraged by the testimony of several large business associations, many conservative Congressmen agitated for a federal sales tax on the ground that this would reach the most dangerous sources of inflation, but liberal publications denounced it as class legislation because of its disproportionately heavy burden on poor people. To serve the dual purpose of supplementing taxation and reducing inflation, a series of highly successful war bond drives, publicized by every means of appeal from radio programs to caravans of Hollywood stars, was undertaken.

ELIMINATING INTERNAL ENEMIES

Recalling the Red Hunt during the last war, liberals were keenly interested in how the Administration planned to reconcile the needs of internal security with civil liberty. Although the Alien Registration Act of 1940 exposed a possible source of danger when it revealed that almost 5,000,000 residents were not American citizens, the Federal Bureau of Investigation under J. Edgar Hoover found the problem far less serious than was anticipated. Relatively few Italian-Americans were implicated in plots against this country, but thousands of suspect German-Americans were interned. To prevent race riots on the Pacific coast, especially in Los Angeles County with its numerous Japanese colonies, and to guard against possible disloyalty, the government decided to evacuate some 110,000 individuals of Japanese ancestry, despite the fact that nearly two-thirds of them were born in the United States. The evacuees were taken to carefully planned inland relocation centers, at which a large measure of self-government was encouraged; and their property interests were protected. Certain groups of disloyal Japanese made it a point of honor to create periodic disturbances, but most of the internees were cooperative. A few Americans who were serving as propaganda agents for the Japanese government were arrested, and scores of fanatic Negro cultists were jailed in Chicago and elsewhere for spreading Japanese-inspired doctrines of racial affinity with the Nipponese and race hatred against whites. Their leaders, who claimed to have a nation-wide organization, also sought to discourage Negroes from entering military service.

The mushroom prewar growth of Nazi "front" organizations and their sympathizers was stopped swiftly. Not only was the German-American Bund dissolved, but its leaders were jailed and many of its naturalized members lost their American citizenship. Agents of the F.B.I. moved against William Dudley Pelley's Silver Shirts, the pro-Coughlin Christian Front, the "Crusaders," and other subversive groups. Father Coughlin's *Social Justice* continued to attack the British, the Jews, and President Roosevelt until Postmaster General Frank C. Walker, himself a Catholic, took steps to revoke its vital second-class mailing privileges, whereupon Coughlin withdrew it from general circulation. George Sylvester Viereck, avowed propagandist for the Kaiser in World War I, was imprisoned once more for similar activity in behalf of Hitler. Over 500 Axis-controlled businesses were impounded by federal officers during 1941–1942. The most sensational roundup of all was the F.B.I.'s arrest of eight Germans, completely equipped for two years of sabotage, who were landed on the Atlantic coast by two submarines. Convicted before a secret military tribunal of seven generals appointed by Roosevelt, six of them were electrocuted and the other two were given long prison terms. In the light of these developments in our battle against internal enemies, the American Civil Liberties Union in its report, *Freedom in Wartime* (1943), praised the "commendable restraint" of the Department of

Justice and compared present conditions with the hysteria, anti-German mob violence, and suppression of free discussion characteristic of World War I.

RACE HATRED AND THE WAR

Axis propagandists delighted in thrusts at the weakest link in our democratic armor—the status of the Negro. As in World War I, Negroes moved from rural sections to the industrial cities, especially in the North. During 1940–1943 the "black belt" in Norfolk, Virginia, grew by over 200 per cent; in Charleston, South Carolina, by 39 per cent; in Los Angeles, by 30 per cent; in Chicago, by 20 per cent; and in Detroit, by 19 per cent. Citing the slogans of a democracy at war, Negroes demanded the end of racial discrimination both in factories engaged in war work and in the armed forces. Roosevelt, whose policies had won strong Negro support, averted a march on Washington by some 50,000 colored citizens in 1941 by issuing an Executive Order forbidding discrimination in war plants. A Fair Employment Practice Committee, headed by sympathetic leaders, was set up to cope with Jim Crowism. At the same time the Army extended new opportunities for officer training to Negroes and the Navy lowered certain of its barriers. But patriotic Negroes were given a gratuitous insult in 1941 when it was learned that the Red Cross segregated the blood of Negro donors, despite the criticism of medical men.

Race tension, North and South, nevertheless increased. The situation was especially acute in crowded Detroit, where the hard-pressed whites resented the federal housing projects for the even worse-pressed Negroes. Attracted by the paternalistic hiring policies of Henry Ford, who was still resisting unionism, the heavy influx of Negro workers to the hovels of Paradise Valley in Detroit overflowed into hitherto restricted areas and enraged white property owners. Furthermore, the "upgrading" of Negro workers in the automobile plants led to "wildcat" strikes in protest. While the Negro press added its provocative weight of racial chauvinism, traditional group antipathies were fanned by certain obscurantist elements among an estimated half million southern whites, some of whom were Klansmen and over-emotional backwoods evangelists, who had migrated to Detroit in recent years. Southern and central Michigan, for all its enlightened communities, could now boast of such popular orators as the Reverend Gerald L. K. Smith, Huey Long's successor, who stressed Fascist ideas, ran unsuccessfully for the Republican senatorial nomination on a platform of "Tires for Everybody," and endeavored to fill the gap left by Father Coughlin's abrupt silence.

The riot that had been freely predicted in the Detroit press for over a year began suddenly on June 20, 1943, with isolated fist fights, but spread quickly when exaggerated rumors arose regarding atrocities on both sides. According to Earl Brown, writing in *Harper's Magazine,* the riot was preceded by "hate strikes" against Negro workers in Detroit factories. At its height, hundreds of sailors and hoodlums clashed with infuriated Negroes; the police were powerless. The governor of Michigan finally appealed to President Roosevelt for federal troops, which promptly put an end to the rioting. At least twenty-five Negroes and nineteen whites were killed and hundreds seriously injured in the worst race riot since 1919. Local officials criticized Negro leaders and the Negro press, but some objective reporters maintained that the race tension was rooted in the glaring economic and social inequalities as well as in traditional race prejudices. Turner Catledge has pointed out that most of the rioters who were arrested were newcomers with foreign names, which suggests that one factor may have been competition between eastern Europeans and Negroes for employment.

An exceptionally tense racial situation existed in crowded Philadelphia. Thus when Negro employees of the Philadelphia Transportation Company were upgraded, a city-wide strike that paralyzed public transportation in this vital defense area broke out on August 1, 1944. In response to the appeal of the War Labor Board, President Roosevelt ordered Secretary of War Stimson to take over the entire transit system. The Army quickly restored order and normal transportation facilities, and the strike ended without undue concessions to the anti-Negro leaders who had instigated it.

Race violence occurred in other cities as well, among them southern cities in which most of the white population, according to a Gallup Poll, were dissatisfied with the New Deal's concessions to Negroes. In Harlem, New York's squalid "black belt," mobs of Negroes plundered neighborhood stores, particularly those owned by Jews; however, Mayor La Guardia held the police in partial check to avert a worse riot. Five people were killed and around 500 wounded; property losses were estimated at $5,000,000. New York papers reported a serious "crime wave" among Negro youth and tried to find some connection between the eccentric "zoot suit," with its extremely long coat and very tight trouser cuffs, and lawbreaking.

Early in June, 1943, over a thousand servicemen and other young men attacked "zoot-suited" Mexican boys in Los Angeles' decayed Main Street district. These clashes followed exaggerated local press reports of assaults on young couples by gangs of Mexican-Americans. Although the police stated that the delinquency rate was somewhat higher among Mexicans than other groups, the most vicious gangs were found to stem from other nationalities. Here again a background of extreme poverty, race discrimination, and the absence of normal recreation helped to explain much of the restlessness and delinquency among Mexican-Americans.

During the fall of 1943, *PM,* a New York liberal paper, revealed that gangs of boys were beating and terrorizing Jewish children in the shabby Dorchester area of Greater Boston, a situation which finally compelled Governor Saltonstall to remove the city's police commissioner. Shortly afterward Jews were beaten and youthful vandals appeared in the poorer sections of New York. Suspicious that this was Nazi-inspired, clergymen immediately opened a campaign against anti-Semitism as a menace to democracy and progressive communities hastened to indoctrinate school children in race tolerance.

FAMILY DISORGANIZATION AND THE SCHOOL

The social dislocations wrought by the war stimulated restlessness among adolescents to a new and alarming degree. A report of the Federal Children's Bureau disclosed a 31 per cent increase in juvenile delinquency in 1943 over the high figures for the previous year. Traditional restraints were necessarily weakened in a floating population that moved from one industrial center to another. War marriages, the disruption of normal relations between the sexes, the instability of a home in which the mother was working, and the intensely crowded housing conditions contributed to abnormal behavior patterns. At least 4,000,000 women were employed in war plants by the beginning of 1944. Many young wives followed their soldier husbands to camp, despite the absence of normal living facilities. Prostitution and sexual promiscuity flourished as they usually do in time of war. Government housing projects were inadequate to meet the demand for living quarters, and the building of private homes was impossible because of the diversion of materials to war uses. Tire and gasoline rationing restricted wholesome recreation and left many rural communities isolated.

The war had a strong impact on the schools. For one thing, the number of employed children tripled in 1940–1941 and many of them put in long hours at adult jobs in restaurants and stores; some even drove trucks. In spite of teacher shortages, especially in technical subjects, the curriculum stressed vocational courses more than ever before. High schools organized Victory Corps to guide boys into occupations that would be useful for the war effort. Colleges and universities suffered major enrollment losses during 1941–1942, but many were saved by the sudden influx of men from the armed forces who came for officers' training courses and other technical work. The quality of class work necessarily decreased for civilians also in many quarters as courses were streamlined in the interest of speed.

Despite four decades of wholesale emphasis on vocational subjects in the schools, the military services were severely handicapped by the lack of technically skilled men—only 15 per cent of the inductees had this type of training. Hence they were compelled to train men for modern mechanized warfare, which requires that over 50 per cent of the armed forces be skilled in mechanics, radio, aviation, the natural sciences, and other technical fields. However, the educational average of the draftees was high, compared with that in other armies and in our own forces in 1917–1918. At least 41 per cent had graduated from high school as against the 9 per cent in World War I. More chastening to educators was the common observation that these young men were woefully deficient in geography, especially that of the Far East, a part of the world which had been largely ignored by colleges in the past. The New York *Times* created a nation-wide controversy on June 21, 1942, when it published an article intended to prove that most of our colleges had shirked a major responsibility toward citizenship in time of crisis by neglecting American history. This newspaper demanded that courses on this subject be made compulsory, but historians and educators were not entirely convinced of the desirability of this step for they felt that poor quality rather than scarcity of courses had characterized the teaching of history.

THE REPUBLICANS GAIN: 1942–1943

Meanwhile there was no truce on partisanship, particularly on domestic issues, in the great game of politics. The prewar trend toward the Republican party gained momentum. In the November, 1942, elections the Democrats lost 34 seats in the House, which reduced their majority to 5; they also lost 8 seats in the Senate, but this left 57 Democrats to 38 Republicans and 1 Progressive. The defeat of the ardent New Dealer, Senator George Norris of Nebraska, was lamented by liberals, who attributed it to the fact that he was 81 years old. This trend continued in the elections of 1943, when a Republican candidate for governor captured the normally Democratic state of Kentucky and almost every state in the North came under G.O.P. control. Confident of victory in 1944, the Republicans began to evaluate the claims of their various presidential aspirants, particularly Wendell Willkie, their 1940 candidate, whose extremely popular book, *One World,* had made him the outstanding representative of postwar internationalism within the party. Even more formidable as a contender for the nomination was Governor Thomas E. Dewey of New York, who had moved steadily away from his earlier semi-isolationism in the direction of world cooperation. Various polls indicated that, against Roosevelt, Dewey would be somewhat stronger than Willkie. Senator Vandenberg sought to convince the nation that General MacArthur was the logical man to defeat Roosevelt in 1944.

Democratic party leaders, in spite of dissent from the conservative South, were increasingly convinced that only a "draft Roosevelt" movement could prevent a debacle in 1944. That the anti-fourth-term obstacle would not be insurmountable if the war continued was indicated by a Gallup Poll in June, 1943, which reported that 56 per cent of the voters wanted Roosevelt reelected in 1944 if the war continued; if it were over, 69 per cent would vote against him. The preceding April the Gallup Poll had asked bluntly: "Do you approve or disapprove of the way Roosevelt is handling his job as President today?" Eighty per cent expressed approval, as against 69 per cent in September, 1941. Most of the President's strength came from the lower-income groups, and from labor and the Negroes. On the other hand, farmers who expressed an opinion on the Administration's domestic policies in 1943 were undecided—49 per cent were favorable, 42 per cent opposed; western farmers were especially cool. Dissident Southerners who were polled regarding their grounds for criticism underlined the "poor handling" of the labor situation, bureaucracy, too much equality for Negroes, and injustice to southern farmers.

These polls revealed the difficulty in interpreting the Republican victories of 1942 and 1943 as clear-cut mandates against Administration policies. If anything, the President's popularity was even greater, but the Democratic party failed to keep pace with it. In a poll that asked people whether they voted Republican or Democratic in 1942 and whether Roosevelt was "doing a good job in running the country," 35 per cent of the Republican voters, but only 67 per cent of the Democratic voters, thought he was. As far as foreign affairs and the war were concerned, according to analysts, the press favored the Administration overwhelmingly early in 1944 but parted with it on most domestic issues. Even the potential difficulties in fostering good relations with Soviet Russia did not trouble the average citizen, said the Gallup statisticians, for at the end of 1943 at least 80 per cent favored collaboration with her both during and after the war.

A SECOND BILL OF RIGHTS

The future of the New Deal was shrouded by the war, but Vice President Wallace made no secret of his conviction that victory and the New Deal were interdependent. In his famous "Free World" speech delivered in 1942, he expressed belief in the coming industrial democracy: "The new democracy, the democracy of the common man, includes not only the Bill of Rights but also economic democracy. . . ." While the Administration was preoccupied with war problems, Wallace assailed the menace of monopoly to American institutions inherent in transportation and in other fields, and reiterated the government's responsibility to continue its huge expenditures after the war if necessary to aid returning soldiers to resume civilian life. His cordial interest in and visits to Latin America, where his forthright manner and facility in Spanish endeared him to his hosts, and his emphatic championship of the Good Neighbor policy, even under the trying conditions of war, made him, next to the President, the nation's foremost spokesman for the progressive tradition.

President Roosevelt's annual message to Congress on January 11, 1944, dissipated liberal fears that winning the war had killed the New Deal. Flatly rejecting the pending tax bill which Congress had drawn up in defiance of the much heavier rates proposed by Secretary Morgenthau, he demanded "a realistic tax law—which would tax all unreasonable profits, both individual and corporate, and reduce the ultimate cost of the war to our sons and daughters." He called for the renegotiation of war contracts to prevent exorbitant profits. To secure fair prices to consumers and an adequate return to farmers, he advocated a federal subsidy program and the removal of the price stabilization law of 1942. Finally, defying organized labor, he recommended a national service law to outlaw strikes for the duration and to make available for essential war purposes the services of every adult male in the nation. "We are united in determination that this war shall not be followed by another interim which leads to new disaster—that we shall not repeat the tragic errors of ostrich isolationism—that we shall not repeat the excesses of the wild twenties when this nation went for a joy ride on a roller coaster which ended in a tragic crash." Commenting on the possibility of a postwar rightist reaction, he said bluntly, "Indeed, . . . if history were to repeat itself and we were to return to the so-called 'normalcy' of the 1920's—then it is certain that even though we shall have conquered our enemies on the battlefields abroad, we shall have yielded to the spirit of Fascism here at home."

He concluded with a striking plea for a "second Bill of Rights," already popularized by Vice President Wallace, which would include economic security. Political rights were no longer enough—"Necessitous men are not free men." This new Bill of Rights would offer everyone "a useful and remunerative job" which would enable him to secure adequate food, clothing, "a decent home," and recreation. It would also provide for social insurance, including sickness and accident protection, and for adequate medical care. Farmers were rightfully entitled to a fair return for their services; similarly, businessmen were entitled to competitive conditions as against monopoly. Finally, this program of a New Liberalism would include "the right to a good education." These were the factors which Roosevelt believed not only meant economic security but were preliminary to any lasting peace in the world. Congress, he maintained, must explore the means for implementing this economic bill of rights. To his followers at least, it seemed clear that the President had defined the issues of 1944 in their broad world setting.

THE ELECTION OF 1944

The month of April, 1944, witnessed the elimination of two Republican presidential candidates, Wendell Willkie and General Douglas MacArthur. Disregarding all dictates of political expediency, Willkie staked his hopes on open war against the isolationists of his party, who were championed by the Chicago *Tribune*. Making the Wisconsin primary campaign the focus of his pre-convention battle, he stumped the state exhaustively, delivering some twenty-five speeches in thirteen days. However, his Republican rivals defeated him so overwhelmingly that he felt compelled to withdraw his name from the race. His sudden death the following October ended the meteoric career of a man whose magnificent courage and idealism had come to be increasingly appreciated. The second Republican hope to retire from the race was General MacArthur. The fact that he was engaged in fighting the Pacific war and that he lacked adequate political support led him to withdraw his name on April 19.

The somewhat listless Republican Convention that met in Chicago during an unbearably hot week in June nominated Dewey for President on the first ballot and his zealous but unsuccessful rival, Governor John Bricker of Ohio, as Vice President. Bricker had attracted Republican advocates of economy in government by his refusal to call a special session of the Ohio legislature to aid Cleveland during that city's relief crisis; this problem, he maintained, should be handled by the cities, not the state. He cited his record in balancing Ohio's budget (critics questioned his methods) as an example of what could be done on a national scope. The Republican platform did not differ fundamentally from those upon which Landon and Willkie had run, although its advocacy of "organized international cooperation" proved too nebulous for Willkie and eventually drove Republican Senator Joseph Ball of Minnesota to vote for Roosevelt. "Four years more of

New Deal policy," read the platform, "would centralize all power in the President and would daily subject every act of every citizen to regulation by his henchmen." As in preceding presidential campaigns, the Republican platform accepted the major social reforms of the New Deal but criticized their administration as partisan, bureaucratic, and wasteful. It proposed a constitutional amendment limiting the President to two terms of four years each, demanded the abolition of the poll tax, and called for federal anti-lynching legislation. In his acceptance speech, Dewey lashed out at the "tired and quarrelsome" administration and promised to drive it out of power.

The Democrats also met at Chicago, but their convention was marked by more internecine feuds which crystallized about the vice-presidential contest. Many southern delegates, dissatisfied with the New Deal's C.I.O. affiliation and its anti-segregation policies for Negroes, were outraged by Vice President Wallace's emphatic liberalism, especially his dictum, "The poll tax must go!" Conservatives in Texas, Mississippi, and South Carolina had even threatened, if Roosevelt was nominated, to name Democratic electors not pledged to cast their electoral college votes for him. Roosevelt himself had had to beat a hasty retreat a few months earlier when his Senate floor leader, Alben Barkley of Kentucky, usually considered a staunch Administration man, resigned his post (he was immediately chosen again) rather than carry out the President's sweeping war tax policies—an incident which reflected the anti-New Deal tide in Kentucky and other southern states.

Roosevelt secured the anticipated endorsement on the first ballot, but the struggle for the vice-presidential nomination was not settled so quickly. In one letter to the Democratic national chairman, the President endorsed Wallace and said that he did not "wish to appear in any way as dictating to the convention"; but in another—and fatal—note, he declared himself also ready to accept Senator Harry S. Truman or Associate Justice William O. Douglas. It may be that Roosevelt was forced to drop Wallace as a concession to the South and to the urban machine "bosses" who regarded the uncompromising Iowan as a political liability. Nevertheless Wallace, convinced that this was a struggle for the survival of the New Deal against the Bourbonism within his party, persisted in battling for the nomination with the support of Sidney Hillman's new C.I.O.-sponsored Political Action Committee.

After showing unexpected strength on the early ballots, he lost to the compromise candidate, Senator Truman of Missouri. Truman, although at one time intimately associated with the Pendergast machine in Kansas City, was no reactionary and was undoubtedly a New Dealer of considerable experience and ability. He had won high praise for the war economies effected by the Senate's Special Committee investigating the national defense program, of which he was chairman.

In an unusually strenuous campaign—the first wartime presidential election since 1864—Dewey scored the "fourth-term candidate" and the bankruptcy of the former idealism of the New Deal, charged that Roosevelt had failed to prepare the nation adequately for a war he had forecast, and characterized the President's foreign policy as personal, secret, and unpredictable. He repudiated the extreme isolationism and intolerance of such men as Hamilton Fish and Gerald L. K. Smith. His adherents branded the New Deal red because the Communists and the leftist Political Action Committee of the C.I.O. were backing Roosevelt and Truman. In conservative Evanston, Illinois, Republican leaflets read: "Sidney Hillman and Earl Browder's Communists Are Registered. Are You?"

Roosevelt sought to offset Dewey's appeal of youth by stressing the need for experience in winning the peace as well as the war; he also elaborated on his "economic bill of rights." He won some Willkie Republicans like Senator Ball by advocating that the American delegation in the United Nations Council should be empowered in advance by Congress "with authority to act" in time of crisis. He and his supporters warned internationally-minded citizens of both parties that, in accordance with congressional rules of seniority, a Republican victory would automatically elevate Hiram Johnson, veteran isolationist, to the chairmanship of the Senate Foreign Relations Committee—a reminder of Henry Cabot Lodge's successful obstructionism in that key position; that another isolationist, Gerald P. Nye, would become chairman of the Senate Appropriations Committee; and that Hamilton Fish would succeed to the chairmanship of the House Rules Committee. The P.A.C., convinced that Roosevelt's victory hinged upon a large registration in the urban areas, concentrated on registering working-class voters in Chicago, Detroit, and Cleveland in order to carry the doubtful states of Illinois, Michigan, and Ohio, where rural voters tended to go Republican. Both sides anxiously eyed the soldier vote, which Democrats assumed would favor them. During 1943–1944, Roosevelt had appealed to Congress for a simplified federal ballot for the armed forces, subject to each state's approval, but southern Democrats and conservative Republicans insisted on a complicated "states' rights" soldier vote law that defeated the plan to get out the maximum servicemen's vote.

Despite some delay occasioned by the record-breaking vote and absentee soldier ballots, it soon became clear that the President had won the election by the overwhelming electoral vote of 432 to 99 (Willkie won 82 in 1940); his popular vote, however—25,610,946 to 22,018,-177—was much closer than in 1940. The urban-rural cleavage was apparently sharper than ever, for the states carried by Dewey—Wyoming, Colorado, North Dakota, South Dakota, Nebraska, Kansas, Iowa, Wisconsin, Indiana, Ohio, Maine, and Vermont—were largely in the western farm and cattle areas. The Democratic vote in the cities, especially New York, Chicago, and Detroit, offset Dewey's strength in the rural counties. A relatively strong Republican vote came from the Democratic states of the Deep South, where political disaffection sought unsuccessfully to break the traditional party allegiance of that section. Reassuring to the President was his party's gain of 21 seats in the House and its unbroken control of the Senate, 57 Democrats to 38 Republicans and one Progressive. The Republicans managed to retain 23 governorships instead of their former 26.

Those who feared that American voters might turn the clock back to the isolationism of the 1920's were relieved to see the wholesale defeat of extreme isolationists like Representatives Stephen A. Day of Illinois and Hamilton Fish of New York and Gerald P. Nye, the veteran Senator from North Dakota. The Political Action Committee of the C.I.O., which had concentrated its attack on these isolationists, claimed credit for the result and announced that this political organization would become permanent. Isolationists actively backed by the Chicago *Tribune* were likewise beaten. The primaries and local pressure had already eliminated Senators Bennett Clark of Missouri and Robert R. Reynolds of North Carolina and Representative Martin Dies of Texas. Massachusetts, which went strongly Democratic, nevertheless gave a huge majority to Leverett Saltonstall, the internationally-minded Republican candidate for the Senate. Jubilantly the New York *Times* observed, "With considerable discernment the voters winnowed out isolationists, both Democratic and Republican, and sent men to Congress who are committed to American membership in an international organization." Here was the popular mandate which James Cox and young Franklin D. Roosevelt had sought so vainly in 1920. It remained to be seen whether Woodrow Wilson's idealistic aspirations for world peace could be resurrected on an international scale after a quarter of a century in which nationalism and totalitarianism had run rampant.

CHAPTER 22

Reconstruction: "One World—or None" (1944-1948)

V-E DAY

The *grande finale* of the worst war in history, culminating in the atomic bomb, began in the spring of 1945. In mid-April, the Anglo-American Fifteenth Army Group under Lieutenant General Mark W. Clark opened its decisive advance upon Bologna, driving the Germans through the Po Valley. On the twenty-ninth, the German commander hastily surrendered without consulting the higher command. The day previously, Italian partisans executed their prisoner, Benito Mussolini, chief architect of Fascism, and hanged his body by the heels. All hostilities on the Italian front ceased on May 2.

In central Europe, eight powerful Soviet armies sped across a huge battlefront from the Baltic to the Danubian Valley, sweeping 2,000,000 Nazi troops before them, taking Warsaw in January, Budapest in February, Danzig in March, and finally capturing Berlin itself the day Italian hostilities ceased. Scarcely less spectacular were the advancing Allied armies in France and western Germany under Dwight D. Eisenhower and his associates, Omar N. Bradley to the south and Field Marshal Sir Bernard L. Montgomery to the north. Before the Russian offensive had been fully mounted in December, 1944, Nazi General von Rundstedt had gambled on a last desperate offensive in the Ardennes which threw the American soldiers back about fifty miles in the first onslaught. However, this forlorn hope crumbled before Eisenhower's methodical land and air blows in the Battle of the Bulge. By February the Allies had launched a giant counteroffensive along the Roer River and had advanced to the Elbe. On March 7 an armored division of the First Army reached the Rhine, luckily found the Remagen Bridge intact, and won a major bridgehead which proved decisive for the Rhine crossing. By the end of the month a skillful "double development" maneuver had encircled the Ruhr basin. Three weeks later, Russian and American troops made contact and halted to prevent any accidental clashes. German resistance had vanished. On April 30 a Hamburg radio announced that Hitler had been killed.

General Bradley jubilantly declared to his soldiers on April 25, "the [Soviet] armies have come to you from the ruins of Stalingrad and Sevastopol—across the scorched cities of the Ukraine. In two years, they have smashed 1400 miles through German armies to drive the enemy from Russia and pursue him to the Elbe." Turning to the armies of the West, he added proudly, "Across 3500 miles of an ocean supply line, you forced a coast the enemy has been years in preparing against you. Within four months after landing, you destroyed whole armies—to take Paris, free France, and give the world a symbol of freedom."

In a French schoolhouse at Reims on May 7, 1945, Eisenhower and the Allied commanders, including Soviet officers, accepted the unconditional surrender of Germany's armed forces from Colonel General Alfred Jodl, chief of the Wehrmacht and chief of staff to Grand Admiral Karl Doenitz, Hitler's successor. To the silent Allied victors Jodl spoke briefly, pleading for generosity to his beaten country—an odd predicament for a Nazi. Fighting in Europe ended May 8, 1945, officially designated as V-E Day. With Germany and her European satellites eliminated, there remained only Japan.

Mixed with the rejoicing over the armistice was a deep note of sorrow. On April 12, the day American Ninth Army troops reached the Elbe, sixty miles from Berlin, and our Third Army took Weimar, President Franklin D. Roosevelt, who had come to symbolize the resistance of the United Nations to Fascism, died of a cerebral hemorrhage at his home in Warm Springs, Georgia. Although his work as a war leader had been almost completed, the world looked to his leadership in the difficult task of reconstruction and the achievement of a lasting peace. At home, it is true, the congressional coalition of Southern Democrats and Republicans had blocked his cherished "Economic Bill of Rights," and the end of war would unleash powerful pressures for *laissez-faire* long repressed by the New Deal and the war. Possibly Roosevelt had thus escaped the living martyrdom awaiting the leader who tries to harness the anarchic forces of national rivalries and domestic reaction. In these trying circumstances, Vice President Harry S. Truman of Missouri, then 61 years of age, was sworn in as thirty-second President. Before Congress, he promised that there would be "no relaxation in our efforts to improve the lot of the common people" and that he would carry out the bipartisan foreign policy of Roosevelt as well as bring the war to an early successful conclusion. He retained Roosevelt's Cabinet, but all the members had been replaced by 1947.

THE ATOM BOMB AND JAPAN'S DEFEAT

In the Pacific War, American, British, Dutch, and Chinese forces were blockading Japan by land and sea. On the Burmese front the Japanese fled northward before the Allied troops of Admiral Lord Louis Mountbatten. American soldiers and engineers moved their supply lines for China toward the southeastern Chinese coast and prepared the way for important victories in that area. In February, 1945, General Douglas MacArthur let the enemy know that he had returned to the Philippines, as promised, by consolidating his control over the islands and expelling the Japanese from Manila in bloody house-to-house fighting. On the sea the American fleet and air forces "softened" the approaches to Tokyo for the growing invasion armies.

One of the most spectacular engagements was the marine assault of February 19 on the island of Iwo Jima, 750 miles south of Tokyo, which was needed to neutralize other Japanese bases and to serve as a springboard for major blows by B-29 bombers upon the heart of Japan. Here fanatical Japanese soldiers behind a string of inland defenses held up the Americans for twenty-seven days, killing 4189 and wounding 15,749 men; but they paid with 21,000 lives and 1259 taken as prisoners. Scarcely had this costly battle ended than a new island battle absorbed the world's attention. On April 1, the Tenth United States Army of Lieutenant General Simon Bolivar Buckner advanced in a huge amphibious attack—some 200,000 men were thrown into battle—on Okinawa, an island in the Ryukyus 825 miles west of Iwo Jima and of great strategic importance as Japan's sea lane to the East Indies. Once more the task proved painfully dear, for the enemy was entrenched in intercommunicating caves and behind well-prepared gun emplacements which could be taken only with flame-throwing tanks and dynamite squads. Far more costly than Iwo Jima, the battle cost the Americans 11,260 men killed and 33,308 wounded; the Japanese were almost wiped out, with 90,401 dead and 4000 captured. General Buckner, commander of the ground forces, was himself killed by Japanese shell fire. The supporting American fleet was badly damaged by the sensational Japanese Kamikaze planes; these were dynamite-filled bombers, guided by suicide pilots, which exploded by direct contact with the large vessels into which they were driven, often sinking the warships. This expensive victory convinced Allied leaders that the final invasion of the Japanese mainland might cost them more than a million lives.

Nevertheless, on July 26, 1945, both President Truman and Prime Minister Churchill knew when, with Chiang Kai-shek, they issued the Potsdam Declaration calling for Japan's unconditional surrender on pain of "annihilation" that the war could not be long protracted. For they were armed with a "secret weapon" which verged on the fantastic in its devastating power—the atomic bomb. Without hinting at this secret, the Proclamation warned Japan of the fate of Germany and offered the terms already formulated at the Cairo Conference. Japan was to be stripped of all her annexations since 1894, to give up her war industries, and to accept the work of a military occupation force to guarantee disarmament and democratic methods. She was assured of help in securing access to raw materials and of future participation in world trade on a basis of equality. No Japanese would be enslaved, but all war criminals would be punished. Japan chose to disregard this ultimatum as mere propaganda and the Allies prepared for the final blow.

On August 5, 1945, an atomic bomb was dropped with devastating results on a major Japanese ordnance-making center, Hiroshima. Fully 60 per cent of the city was wiped out, with over 78,000 of its 343,000 inhabitants killed and relatively few escaping without some injury. Nearly all green vegetation was obliterated. This grim event did not immediately convince the Japanese government of its doom. Therefore on August 8 a second bomb, more deadly than the first, was dropped on Nagasaki, a leading shipping and industrial center; it obliterated one-third of this city of 253,000, and left almost 40,000 dead or missing. That same day the Soviet Union, in keeping with its previous commitment, declared war on Japan and launched a lightning drive into Manchuria, Korea, and the southern part of Sakhalin island. Truman declared emphatically, "We are now prepared to obliterate more rapidly and completely every productive enterprise the Japanese have left above the ground in any city. . . . Let there be no mistake: We shall completely destroy Japan's power to make war." On August 10, Japan offered to surrender on the basis of the Potsdam Declaration, and hostilities ended four days later; the signing of the articles of surrender took place on September 1, 1945—proclaimed as V-J Day.

Behind the story of the atom bomb was the revelation of the race that we had been running against Germany for the discovery of the weapon. Spurred on since 1942 by news of sensational German advances in experiments with atomic power, Roosevelt and Churchill, aided by Canada, had decided to pool their previously independent efforts in this field into a mammoth cooperative scientific venture, "the Manhattan Project," under Brigadier General Leslie R. Groves; nearly $2,000,000,000 was spent and 125,000 scientists and workers were employed in laboratories and factories. While German atomic plants were being bombed incessantly by British and American planes, Allied scientists, including key German *emigrés* whom Hitler had expelled as non-Aryan, worked in the security of American soil. Thus, Professor Albert Einstein, refugee from Hitlerism, who in 1905 had written the basic mathematical equation for the conversion of matter into energy, had advised the Administration in 1939 of the likely possibilities of harnessing atomic energy released through the "fission" of Uranium 235. The pioneer test of the atom bomb took place secretly on July 16, 1945, at the Alamogordo Air Base in the New Mexico desert; the reverberations of the terrific blast shattered plate-glass windows in Silver City a hundred miles away. Nature had yielded one of its most incredible sources of energy and the atomic age was born.

Despite the shortening of the war and the hope that atomic power might usher in an age of plenty, the Allied peoples were shocked and saddened by the horrible potentialities of the bomb. It required little imagination to recognize the possibilities for international blackmail and intimidation that could be exercised by those ready and willing to use the bomb to the fullest extent. General Henry H. Arnold, Commander of the Army Air Forces, visualized a cheaper and improved atomic bomb in the near future, carried in pilotless aircraft over the oceans at supersonic speed. Here was the greatest test facing the collective intelligence of the world—to escape annihilation.

It is still too early to assess the full human and material costs of World War II. Vatican estimates placed the total dead, both military and civilian, at 22,060,000. Almost 300,000 American soldiers and sailors lost their lives, nearly three times our losses in the First World War; the British Empire reported 353,000 killed. Among all the belligerents, the Soviet Union paid most heavily, with combined military and civilian dead estimated at twelve to fifteen million people. Nazi Germany lost 2,100,000 servicemen, with 4,000,000 wounded; 468,000 Japanese were killed and 4, 616,000 wounded. The most shocking civilian tragedy occurred in Nazi-occupied countries where some 6,000,000 men, women, and children, largely Jews, were put to death, starved, or tortured in German concentration camps like those at Buchenwald, Maidenek, Belsen, and Dachau. Semi-official estimates for the military cost of the war for both sides (excluding China) aggregated $1,116,000,000,000, of which the United States paid $330,030,000,000. There still remained the incalculable burden of feeding the starving peoples of the world, reconstructing their homes, factories, and railroads, and stabilizing bankrupt economies.

SHAPING A NEW FOREIGN POLICY

The peacemakers, even more than in 1919, moved in an emotional atmosphere of keen national rivalries and conflicting ideologies. Once more the fear of a missionary Communism enveloping the western world became a prime factor in the diplomacy of the United States, Britain, and the smaller powers. The desperate mood of the starving and homeless central European peoples fostered substantial Communist groups, often organized by Moscow-trained leaders, in almost every nation on the continent. In Yugoslavia, where guerrilla and regular resistance against the Axis had killed or wounded 1,685,000 patriots, the Partisan leader and dictator Tito proved a loyal ally of the Kremlin and a thorn in the side of the western powers. Even in western Europe, where less damage had been done, millions of frustrated Frenchmen (and many newly enfranchised women) voted for the Communist party candidates.

Strategic factors, almost a constant quantity under czar and commissar, led to sustained Soviet pressure in eastern Europe, the Balkans, the Far East, and the Middle East. Huge landlocked Russia, weak in internal transportation, still sought ice-free port outlets to the Pacific and the Mediterranean; again she hoped to control the Turkish Straits and the Black Sea; the oil of Iran was even more important in this mechanized age than in czarist days when it had been appropriated by an Anglo-Russian diplomatic deal; and Communism had merely supplemented Pan-Slavism as a tool of Russian penetration in the Balkans and eastern Europe. The most basic factor, perhaps, was the ability of the Red armies to fill the military vacuum left by the collapse of Germany, recently the successor to France's military hegemony on the continent. With the Red armies in actual control of all liberated eastern areas up to the Elbe River, Russian diplomats had an obvious tactical and propagandistic advantage in a pivotal region. In a shrinking postwar world, only three first-rate military powers remained: the United States, Great Britain, and the Soviet Union; and the first two were already gravitating toward a western diplomatic bloc of nations against the growing Soviet coalition in the East. Europe was urged by the Russians not to stake her future upon the United States, whose economy was subject to major depressions and whose diplomacy had only recently emerged from isolationism.

Roosevelt had been sanguine in his belief that a broad basis for agreement with Russia existed, despite doctrinal differences. But, although ready to concede that the Soviet Union had special interests in eastern Europe necessitated by defensive needs, he had insisted at Yalta on free elections in Poland and the broadening of the political control (by democratic parties) of Rumania and Bulgaria, then heavily pro-Soviet. Although the Soviet Union's absorption of Latvia, Lithuania, and Estonia (onetime czarist states) had not been recognized by the Roosevelt administration, no challenge had been raised. Henry Wallace, who claimed to represent the Roosevelt policies, insisted that the Truman administration had substituted a "get-tough-with-Russia" policy, flanked by generals in the State Department, for the conciliatory policy of the late President. This was vehemently denied by other Roosevelt adherents, who pointed out the violations of the free election pledge taken by Russia at Yalta.

Truman's decision in 1945 to withhold essential atomic information from the world until a system of adequate international controls could be devised angered Soviet diplomats, who made violent charges against the United States of aggressive intent and high-pressure "atomic diplomacy." Vishinsky, for example, compared American control of the atomic bomb to the sword of Damocles suspended over the heads of the world. A fatalistic "house-divided" antithesis between East and West crept into popular discussions. Anglo-American press opinion tended to believe that Soviet Russia's previously arrested trend toward achieving world Communism had been resumed, and a Canadian spy case involving Russian-directed espionage into atomic secrets inspired official probes in the United States against "Red" suspects and "fellow travelers" in key posts. The combustibles for a new "Red scare" on the 1919 model were at hand. Soviet diplomats and newspapers did not improve matters by their soapbox flourishes and charges of sinister Anglo-American conspiracies.

Especially resented by the Soviets as "clearly offensive in character" was the new American emphasis on winning naval and military bases as part of a revised postwar concept of national security. This policy, the Russians assumed, could be directed only against them. President Truman, upon the advice of strategists, insisted that the United States be given a U.N. strategic trusteeship under the Security Council for the former Japanese-mandated islands, the Marshalls, the Carolines, and the Marianas. Although the Philippines were granted complete independence on July 4, 1946, as promised, no strategic military bases were surrendered. Spurred on by nationalist sentiment, Congress gave liberal grants for the Pacific bases and for the improvement of the eight Atlantic bases leased from England.

However, the Russians were scarcely the forgotten men in this picture, for they had inherited through a "top secret" protocol of the Yalta Agreement in February, 1945, a string of valuable strategic bases in the Kuriles uncomfortably close to the American Aleutians off Alaska; besides, they received the vital areas of southern Sakhalin flanking the Asiatic continent and the lease of the old czarist-held naval base of Port Arthur, shared in the internationalization of the key

Manchurian port of Dairen, and held a partnership with China in the dominating Chinese eastern and south Manchurian railroads. In addition to regaining practically all the ground lost in the Russo-Japanese War of 1905, Soviet interests were safeguarded by troops in northern Korea offsetting American soldiers in southern Korea; Red troops were of course stationed in nearby Siberia. Russia held the active sympathies of the powerful Chinese Communists, who were driving the Nationalists from one province after another. Indicative of the revised security concepts of both sides were the ambitious Soviet and American expeditions in the Arctic, the logical crossroads for any future air war between the two nations. To block an oft-used road for invaders from the west, the Russians used direct military, political, and economic pressure to bring Poland, Rumania, Bulgaria, and Hungary within their orbit.

To compensate for her geographic remoteness in this new security plan, the United States sent large and efficient army and navy missions abroad, thus developing close ties in these countries. Military personnel took an unprecedented position in the shaping of foreign policy. Lieutenant General Walter B. Smith became ambassador to Russia; and our former chief of staff, General George C. Marshall, after serving as special envoy and ambassador to China until January, 1947, became the very active successor of James F. Byrnes as Secretary of State. To raise the efficiency of our defenses through better coordination, the army, navy, and air forces were unified under a single Secretary of National Defense. This meant the end of costly duplication of certain administrative activities without an actual merging of the personnel of the older branches.

Truman, in his Army Day speech in 1946, also urged universal military training. "Only so long as we remain strong," he observed, "can we insure the peace of the world." We had undertaken foreign commitments in almost every part of the globe and adopted the immediate goal of supporting the United Nations to the utmost. He added this pointed argument for preparedness: "We know, too, that we are not likely again to be given two years or more by heroic allies to get ready. Next time—if there must be a next time—we are likely to be the first target." Unofficial estimates of the cost of military training were as high as two or three billions annually; only this would provide for a trained reserve of millions of men. Critics as diverse as Henry Wallace, Albert Einstein, and Senator Robert Taft of Ohio condemned the plan as militaristic; however, the Gallup Poll showed 65 per cent favoring the idea. As the election of 1948 approached, politicians tended to defer a decision on this momentous and explosive issue until spurred by the Czech crisis.

In keeping with our new global policy, Congress passed the Foreign Service Act of 1946, the most important legislation of the kind since the original Rogers Act of 1924 which set up the merit system in the diplomatic and consular services. The 1946 Act extended the merit system, under a new Director General, to an expanded personnel. Salaries were raised to attract first-class men and a more flexible promotion system was created to eliminate incompetents. As a result of this law, the staff of 4000 employed in 1939 grew to 11,000 by 1947. Hoping to influence world opinion along democratic and pro-American lines, the Foreign Service began an ambitious cultural program under an Assistant Secretary of State, utilizing the radio, motion pictures, library services, press releases, student exchange plans, and other activities formerly carried on by the Office of War Information and the Office of Inter-American Affairs. Foreign Service officers together with high-ranking military and naval officers were sent for expert training to the new National War College opened in July, 1946, as part of a major move toward the coordination of the joint chiefs of staff with the State Department.

THE OCCUPATION OF GERMANY

Two months after Germany's surrender, President Truman met with Stalin and Churchill (and his Laborite successor, Clement R. Attlee) during July 17–25, 1945, at Potsdam, near Berlin. This Tripartite Conference not only sought to settle the fate of Germany—the Declaration on Japan *followed* the Conference—but also entrusted a Council of Foreign Ministers representing the five principal powers to draft peace treaties for Italy, Rumania, Bulgaria, Hungary, and Finland. By this time, both Americans and British had withdrawn the Roosevelt-Churchill endorsement, given at the Quebec Conference in September, 1944, of Secretary Morgenthau's plan for converting Germany to an agrarian state by removing her heavy industries and thus her war-making potential. The Potsdam Declaration took middle ground by demanding the "elimination or control of all German industry that could be used for military production." Agriculture and "peaceful domestic industries" were stressed. An Allied Control Commission charged with the occupation was expected to break up "the present excessive concentration of economic power as exemplified in particular by cartels, syndicates, trusts and other monopolistic arrangements." This was aimed at the great German industrialists who had backed Nazi rearmament and aggression. Germany was to be treated as an economic unit during the occupation—a promise never kept because of Russian suspicions of the western Allies.

Russia, permitted by Yalta to compensate Poland for loss of eastern territory to the Soviets by a cession of western German lands, had agreed to a controversial clause which left the western boundary of Poland to be finally settled by the future peace treaty; but she came with a *fait accompli* which gave the Poles immediate control of that area. This opened a prolonged quarrel between East and West among the Allies. Again, the Russians wanted ten billion dollars in German reparations to offset their enormous losses from the Nazi invasion; this sum Roosevelt had been willing to consider "as a basis for discussion" at Yalta, according to Byrnes, but the Russians asserted that such reparations had been promised them. The Conference formula was that these payments were "to leave enough resources to enable the German people to subsist without external assistance"—another source of later controversy.

The Big Three at Potsdam declared as their policy:

> German militarism and Nazism will be extirpated and the Allies will take in agreement together, now and in the future, the other measures necessary to assure that Germany never again will threaten her neighbors or the peace of the world.
>
> It is not the intention of the Allies to destroy or enslave the German people. It is the intention of the Allies that the German people be given the opportunity to prepare for the eventual construction of their life on a democratic and peaceful basis.

Although Germany was not partitioned as her uneasy neighbor France would have liked, she was stripped of all Nazi-annexed territories and lost part of East Prussia to Russia and another part—her "breadbasket"—to Poland. Within her present restricted boundaries she was compelled to receive millions of Germans from abroad, many of whom had agitated for Nazi aims in Poland, Czechoslovakia, and Hungary. This was to be done "in an orderly and humane manner"—a forlorn hope. Details and final approval were left for the future peace treaty.

Eventually Germany was divided among the four occupying powers. United States forces, first under Eisenhower then under General Joseph T. McNarney, occupied the southwest, which included Frankfort, Munich, and Nuremberg. The northwest, including Cologne, Aachen, and Dusseldorf, went to Britain. The fertile east—particularly Saxony, Thuringia, Anhalt, and Mecklenberg—was left to Soviet policing. The French, who had been neglected at Potsdam, were stationed on either side of the Rhine and controlled the rich Saar basin, which they hoped to keep. All four powers shared in governing Berlin. This zonal division of Germany, contrary to the Anglo-American plans of economic cooperation for the country, remained a series of economic barriers as well as political-military lines, largely because of the Russians, and tended to cripple further the ruined country and to worsen existing shortages of food and materials. In 1946 the British and Americans combined their zones into "Bizonia" for economic cooperation, but the Russians refused to join and the French delayed entering negotiations for another year.

Soviet authorities, disappointed in the poor returns obtained from dismantling German factories as reparations, chose to take further compensation out of current German production—a step strongly protested by Americans and Britons as certain to prevent German recovery and likely to put increased relief burdens on the western powers. On May 25, 1946, the American authorities halted further reparations shipments to Russia from the American zone, which led to an acrimonious exchange. Byrnes complained that the Russian insistence on isolated zones was largely responsible for the American taxpayer spending $200,000,000 annually to support our zone in Germany, which had never been self-sufficient.

Another basic divergence of views appeared in the controversy regarding the allowable steel production for Germany. Russia and

France were anxious to keep German industrialization at as low a level as possible; but the Americans and British, undoubtedly influenced by fear of future Russian expansion, had no intention now of reducing Germany to an economic cipher and argued for a relatively high steel production quota to aid Germany's early recovery and thus promote western Europe's economic stability and halt Communist inroads. So far did Secretary Byrnes go in urging Germany's recovery as an economic and political factor in European affairs that in his Stuttgart speech in September, 1946, he called for the early creation of a provisional government.

Reporters investigating the temper of the defeated people found little by which to justify such optimism as shown by Byrnes. If a sense of guilt and atonement was essential for Germany's rehabilitation, this was notably lacking. The sensational Nuremberg trials of Hermann Goering and twenty other Nazi leaders, intended as a grim day of judgment, produced little mass reaction. Revelations of inhuman scientific experiments, the callous enslavement of foreign workers, and the calculated wholesale murder of at least six million people did not arouse the expected revulsion. Some observers attributed this to the average German's absorption in the harsh task of survival. Justice Robert Jackson, American chief prosecutor, did effective work in presenting the Allied sense of outrage at the proved atrocities to those who listened. He expected that the Nuremberg trials would strengthen international law and set precedents against clear-cut military aggression, useful for the control of the atomic bomb. The Kellogg-Briand Treaty (the Pact of Paris), which renounced war as an instrument of national policy, was cited by Jackson as a legal basis for these unprecedented trials.

Whatever the real psychological results, "denazification" by the occupying powers produced major changes in the cultural institutions of Germany. Despite a shortage of non-Nazi teachers, objective textbooks, and politically reliable civil servants, the American authorities worked vigorously to oust Nazi officials on Eisenhower's original directive of "no indispensable Nazi." The ideal of sportsmanship rather than competitive rivalry was fostered. Overhastily perhaps, the American zone allowed German local self-government to proceed quickly, and by 1947 state governments were in process of formation. The voting pattern approximated that of the democratic Weimar period, but with far weaker Communist representation.

Secretary of State Marshall, who had recently succeeded Byrnes, declared in April, 1947, at the Moscow Conference of Foreign Ministers that his country, Britain, and France wished to see a unified but federal Germany with strong state governments possessing reserved powers and capable of checking any centralized dictatorial group at the helm. But the Russians argued for a strong centralized government—a plan suspected in the west as offering a Trojan horse for a Communist Germany. To meet Russian fears of a future German attack upon them, Marshall offered the Soviets a security plan, originated by Byrnes and favored by Britain and France since 1945, for a four-power alliance guaranteeing the disarmament and demilitarization of Germany for forty years. This resembled the ill-fated Franco-American alliance project of Woodrow Wilson in 1919 which was not even considered by the United States Senate. Although Stalin had once agreed to the security plan in principle, Molotov showed increasing coolness to any proposal which kept American forces in Europe and insisted on preliminary agreements that included more reparations to Russia.

The Soviets were apparently not so much afraid of a revived Germany acting independently as of a German state used as a spearhead of Anglo-French and American aggression toward Russia. In February, 1948, their newspapers charged that captured German documents revealed an Anglo-French plot at Munich in 1938 to divert Hitler's wrath to the east. These harsh charges followed publication by our State Department of German documents revealing close collaboration between Russia and Germany from the signing of the Non-Aggression Pact in 1939 to Germany's attack on Russia in 1941. Hopes for early German and Austrian peace treaties languished as 1948 began.

RELIEF, DIPLOMACY, AND THE MARSHALL PLAN

Once more, as after World War I, the task of caring for the distressed of Europe and Asia assumed political as well as humanitarian significance. Wilson and Hoover had stressed large relief appropriations by Congress as a major weapon to combat renascent Communism among Europe's uprooted peoples; then too, relief loans were also influenced by the desire to maintain the momentum of huge war-time exports and thus avoid a depression. These props of self-interest supplemented genuine humanitarianism. Now, the United States, which had escaped actual want and physical destruction at home, was again expected to share her vastly increased food output and to bear most of the burden for the nations capable of acting as donors.

The Nazis had stripped Europe of surpluses; the fighting men had destroyed railroads, bridges, homes, and factories; and nature itself had provided unusual droughts and crop failures through 1945–1947, especially in northern Europe and the Mediterranean. In China, India, and Japan, mass starvation and disease reaped a grim harvest. Hoover, this time a food adviser to Truman, found that even the victorious nations were subsisting on starvation diets, but he tended seriously to overestimate the ability of Europe to feed herself in the near future and counseled voluntary cuts in American food consumption rather than continued food rationing and price controls.

American relief poured into Europe, first through the military commanders in liberated and occupied areas, and then through lend-lease shipments and U.N.R.R.A. which soon took over the major share of this task. Food exports from this country reached $1,678,000,000 in 1945 and rose to $2,172,000,000 the following year. Voluntary agencies like the American Red Cross and church groups provided clothes for 25,000,000 persons in 1945 and exceeded this total in 1946. The Gallup Poll indicated that fully 85 per cent of all Americans were ready to suffer shortages to supply Europe and Asia, but the political decision to drop rationing quickly handicapped adequate relief in this large-scale emergency.

The United Nations Relief and Rehabilitation Administration (U.N.R.R.A.), which had been established in November, 1943, eventually spent four billions (of which this country contributed 72 per cent) on food, supplies, epidemic control, and other forms of aid. U.N.R.R.A. camps in western Germany, Austria, and Italy cared for 6,770,000 "displaced persons"—stateless and homeless refugees—in 1945 alone, finding new homes for many of them. The Soviet Union, which had won victories by the costly policy of scorching its own towns and villages in the face of the Nazi advance, was given a half billion dollars in American relief. However, Congressmen, suspicious that Soviet agents were using U.N.R.R.A. to build up Communist factions in eastern Europe, failed to appropriate sufficient funds to meet our full pledge to that agency; other member nations scarcely went beyond the first of the required payments. During Europe's critical months of 1946, American food deliveries dropped.

Toward the end of 1946, the State Department decided to scrap U.N.R.R.A. altogether, despite the reasoned protests of former Director General Herbert Lehmann and his successor, Fiorello La Guardia. The State Department publicly charged U.N.R.R.A. with political favoritism and gross inefficiency. "Those in power," declared one spokesman of the pro-Communist European politicians in November, 1946, "will not be allowed to feed their political supporters and starve their political opponents." Relief must not be used for militarism or radical social experiments. Besides, it was claimed that the food crisis was over in most nations and that rehabilitation would be taken over by the new International Bank and the International Monetary Fund. However, the scuttling of U.N.R.R.A. did not mean the end of humanitarian relief; rather, a new plan guaranteeing exclusive control by the United States over her relief expenditures was proposed. Critics deplored the destruction of an international agency like U.N.R.R.A. in favor of unilateral action; but the State Department, like Congress, felt convinced that to continue U.N.R.R.A. was to subsidize Communistic factions in eastern Europe.

On June 5, 1947, Secretary of State Marshall announced a new plan of large-scale economic aid abroad as a bulwark against the collapse of western Europe (an event which would endanger our own economy); moreover, stability would halt the advance of Communism. Europe was in progressively worse straits as her war-time shortages in food and goods were aggravated by poor crops and disorganized economies. The newly signed peace treaties with Soviet-dominated Hungary, Bulgaria, and Rumania involved recognition of these semi-Communist regimes by the United States and implied defeat for our policy of confining Communism to its older boundaries. In effect, Marshall called upon all friendly-minded European nations to decide independently and as a group upon their financial needs and to present these estimates for the consideration of the United States. However, Europe was expected to show how far she was ready to help herself before she would receive assistance.

In September, 1947, sixteen European nations, including representatives of the Anglo-American combined zone in Germany, met in Paris to discuss the Marshall Plan. The western powers were anxious to benefit from American aid, but the Russians seemed convinced that Marshall intended to build a western military coalition against them and therefore kept the Slavic bloc of nations and Finland out of the Conference. Besides, it was obvious to Moscow that a major purpose of the plan was to halt the spread of Communism. The Conference on European Economic Cooperation reported, "Industrial production in Belgium, France and the Netherlands was [now] reduced to 30 to 40 per cent of pre-war and in Italy to only 20 per cent; production of bread grains fell to only two-thirds of pre-war." Finally, it recommended credits and loans of $21,780,000,000 over the period 1948–1951; of this total, the United States was expected to contribute $15,810,000,000 and Latin America and Canada were to offer the remainder. The International Bank, to which the United States was the chief contributor, and private investors were asked for additional credits of $3,130,000,000 for machinery and other equipment. Haste was urged upon the United States as the only alternative to calamity.

Secretary Marshall, strongly supported by the President, advised Congress that prompt action on his European Recovery Plan was vital to save sixteen southern and western European states from Communist domination as well as economic chaos. He frankly conceded the risk involved in pushing this program against the resistance of Russia, but saw no alternative. This meant a 51-month program of foreign aid, for which $6,800,000,000 would be needed in the first fifteen months. State Department officials also pointed out that E.R.P. would serve as a prop for our economy as deferred war demands tapered off, for continued heavy exports would be needed to perpetuate full employment and prosperity here. Congress, spurred on by current fears of Russia's designs as well as by humanitarianism, seemed generally favorable but was embarrassed by a partisan mood of economy during an election year. Some, like Taft, questioned the wisdom of a long-term commitment as well as the size of the sums requested; many were concerned by the impact of the anticipated exports on the grave inflationary situation. As a stopgap measure, Congress in December, 1947, voted winter relief of $597,000,000 for France, Italy, Austria, and China.

Public opinion polls showed overwhelming support for E.R.P. and discussion ended abruptly after the Red coup in Czechoslovakia. In April, 1948, Congress provided an Economic Cooperation Administration to supervise a four-year program, beginning with a twelve-month appropriation of $5.3 billion, of which $463 million went to China and $275 million to Greece and Turkey for military aid; the remainder went to the original sixteen European nations and western Germany. Exports to pro-Soviet countries behind the Iron Curtain, especially of strategic goods, were to be curbed—a hazardous step economically in view of current trade necessities of eastern and western European nations; and American deliveries were to be partly balanced by the imports here of strategic European materials. Among those to assist the Administrator were a five-member National Advisory Council on Fiscal Problems, including three Cabinet members, and a twelve-man Public Advisory Board appointed by the President. E.R.P. was expected to be the most effective American move in the "cold war" waged against the Soviet Union since 1945. Critics disagreed as to the extent of the risk involved, but President Truman himself admitted that this risk existed.

THE "COLD WAR" IN EASTERN EUROPE: THE TRUMAN DOCTRINE

The most sensitive points of contact between Russian and American spheres of control lay in eastern Europe and the Balkans. At the Yalta Conference on February 4–12, 1945, Roosevelt, Stalin, and Churchill had agreed upon a new Polish government "on a broader democratic basis with the inclusion of democratic leaders from Poland itself and from Poles abroad," this government to hold "free and unfettered elections as soon as possible," with all democratic parties being allowed to campaign freely. Russia was promised the eastern section of Poland, largely non-Polish in population, along the old Curzon line; in return, despite the principle of self-determination, Poland was to be compensated in eastern Germany. Most significantly, the Yalta Declaration on Liberated Europe provided that the Big Three would "jointly assist" the liberated peoples "to form interim governmental authorities broadly representative of all democratic elements in the population and pledged to the earliest possible establishment, through free elections, of governments responsive to the will of the people."

Hopefully President Roosevelt told Congress on March 1, 1945, that the Yalta Conference, in spite of painful compromises, meant "the end of the system of unilateral action, exclusive alliances, and spheres of influence, and balances of power, and all the other expedients which have been tried for centuries and have always failed." But the next day news arrived that Russia was repudiating the Polish Government-in-Exile of London to sponsor a pro-Soviet coalition at Warsaw. The Soviets made it clear that they had no intention of permitting Poland, as in Pilsudski's day, to become the springboard for western military intervention against Russia. Considerably disturbed, Roosevelt supported by Churchill protested directly to Stalin, only to learn that the Russian interpretation of Yalta differed fundamentally from the Anglo-American. This was all the more disquieting, coming as it did shortly after Rumania's postwar government had been replaced by Russia with a Communist-led coalition. Apparently Soviet concepts of security differed but little from those of the czarist regime.

Poland had been a spearhead of French-sponsored military intervention under Pilsudski after World War I and thereafter it had been a hotbed of extreme nationalism and feudal reaction; meanwhile the condition of the peasants remained poor and attempts at land reform were blocked by the aristocracy. Still, the Polish armies had fought valiantly, if futilely, against Hitler until their government officials fled to London. The Russians originally set up a regime at Lublin which was non-Communist though pro-Soviet, broke with the Polish Government-in-Exile as "reactionary," and gradually picked off all critics of the new Warsaw coalition after irregular elections which were scarcely those envisaged by Roosevelt and Churchill at Yalta. After the January, 1947, elections, which were condemned as fraudulent by Mikolajczyk, the liberal Peasant party leader, Truman recalled our ambassador. Subsequently Mikolajczyk himself fled to the

United States, where he joined other eastern European leaders like Ferenc Nagy, former premier of Hungary. Extreme Polish nationalists hoped to profit from this Soviet-American rift; on one occasion they launched the worst anti-Jewish pogrom in Poland's history—except for those during the German occupation. The new Warsaw regime weakened the extreme nationalists by undertaking the long-overdue land reforms and redistributing the huge estates of the former aristocratic ruling class among the landless. As expected Poland's delegate to the U.N. usually argued on the Soviet side.

Byrnes has recently revealed this episode in Polish affairs: On the day that Roosevelt died, April 12, 1945, the President sent a message of advice to Churchill on the Polish issue and related Russian problems in which he said, "I would minimize the general Soviet problem as much as possible because these problems, in one form or another, seem to arise every day and most of them straighten out. . . . We must be firm, however, and our course thus far is correct." Whether this tolerant view would have continued after 1945 had Roosevelt lived is not easily determined. His strong protests in regard to Poland suggest that Truman's policy was not necessarily an abrupt departure from that of his predecessor.

From the very beginning of the postwar era it was clear that Tito's Yugoslavia had come within the Soviet orbit and was actively engaged in collectivist plans along the lines of the Soviet experiment during the 1920's when a nation of small farmers seemed the ideal. Although he extinguished political democracy (the limited aspect of it known previously), Tito expelled the Karageorge dynasty and its followers who had ruled during the Serb domination over the Croats and Slovenes and had been noted for military intrigues. Among the international irritants was Tito's refusal to permit former American officers in wartime Yugoslavia to testify in behalf of the Chetnik (guerrilla) leader, Draja Mikhailovitch, who was condemned and executed for alleged collaboration with the Nazis. Much more serious was the crisis in August, 1946, when Yugoslav soldiers shot down two United States transport planes flying without permission over a narrow corner of the country—apparently an innocent "short-cut" of the pilots—killing five American soldiers in one and arresting the occupants of the other. Secretary Byrnes, threatening to bring this issue before the Security

Council, forced Tito to release the survivors and to pay indemnities for those killed.

Also disquieting was the surprising revival of Pan-Slavism, reminiscent of czarist days, as a movement under Yugoslav and Russian auspices uniting eastern Europe against the West. Peace negotiations over Italy were violently disturbed by Yugoslav mobs which supported Tito's demand for all of Trieste and seemed determined to seize disputed territory in the high-handed manner of the Italian extremist d'Annunzio at Fiume after World War I. Communist propaganda and organizations originating in Yugoslavia and Albania inevitably affected Italian and Greek politics. Guerrillas from these countries as well as Bulgaria helped keep alive the civil war in Greece.

Czechoslovakia, once more under President Beneš and Foreign Minister Jan Masaryk, desperately tried to maintain a neutral role as a "bridge between East and West," but a substantial Communist movement led to the choice of a Communist premier and a strong pro-Soviet policy. When the Czech government and press spoke accusingly of the United States enslaving weaker nations by her economic power, our State Department suspended credits to that country. The western nations were startled to read, in late February and early March, 1948, that Premier Gottwald's Communists, who already dominated the unions and the army policy, had taken over complete control of the police and expelled all effective opposition from the ministry. Communist "action committees" purged "disloyal" elements in the state; newspapers, radio, police, and factories came under the revolutionary dictatorship, and Beneš yielded to the inevitable. Shortly afterward appeared the shocking news that Jan Masaryk, son of the revered first president of Czechoslovakia, had committed suicide for reasons of alleged ill health. In the west, where Masaryk was well known and respected, his death was interpreted as a final despairing protest against the Communist overthrow of the "bridge" between Russia and the western nations. Coupled with news that Finland was being compelled to sign a military alliance with Russia and that the Italian elections seemed in danger of going Communist, the Czech crisis created new tension and brought the United States into closer cooperation with Britain, France, Belgium, and the Scandinavian countries.

After many months of futile protest, the United States in 1947 virtually conceded the loss of Bulgaria, Rumania, and Hungary to Soviet influence. But in September of that year, our State Department intervened vigorously at Moscow and Sofia in a vain effort to save the life of Nikola Petkov, the leader of Bulgaria's Agrarian party, who was charged with plotting to overthrow the government. His hanging was regarded as a violation of the Yalta promise of a broadly representative democratic government for Bulgaria, and little credence was given to the treason charge. The Soviet-influenced regimes in the Balkans won some leftist support for the land distribution program which in Hungary, for example, dealt a staggering blow to the hereditary landowning Magyar aristocracy and to the Catholic Church whose endowments were primarily in land. Defenders of Soviet policy argued that Russia's method of Balkan infiltration was basically similar to American strategic moves in the Caribbean decades before. They explained Russian foreign policy as a defensive reaction to the moves of the United States and England in the eastern Mediterranean. But, as the Gallup Polls indicated, this failed to convince American public opinion. Bilateral Soviet treaties involving the partial integration of her neighbors' economies with Russian economic organizations antagonized the State Department, which, despite congressional high-tariff policies, had hoped for freer international trade. But among the economic weapons of persuasion the Soviets had little to offer aside from temporary relief through limited grain exports, and they therefore turned to other tools of penetration.

Although Stalin was determined to prevent in eastern Europe any *cordon sanitaire* of the 1919 type which might serve as a springboard for anti-Russian intervention, the expansion of Soviet influence stirred public opinion in the United States and Britain. On March 5, 1946, former Prime Minister Churchill, considered by Russia to be the arch-plotter of the old *cordon sanitaire*, opened a frank anti-Soviet campaign at Fulton, Missouri. "From Stettin in the Baltic to Trieste in the Adriatic," he asserted, "an iron curtain has descended across the Continent." In later speeches he called for a United States of Europe which evidently excluded the Soviet Union. William C. Bullitt, former champion of Soviet-American collaboration, suggested in a book, *The Great Globe Itself* (1946), that our high international moral standards did not mean "that we should hesitate to use the atomic bomb to stop new crimes of Soviet Imperialism." No less extreme was former Governor George H. Earle of Pennsylvania, who demanded an ultimatum to halt Russian expansion; "if they refuse I would use the atomic bomb on them while we have it and before they get it."

By the beginning of 1947 it was clear that the State Department had determined on an active policy of "firm containment" of the Soviet Union, the line being drawn in Greece and Turkey. On March 12, 1947, the President asked Congress for $400,000,000 for these two countries, of which $100,000,000 was intended to strengthen Turkey militarily. The Truman Doctrine, as it came to be called, was "to assist free peoples to work out their own destinies in their own way." Like the Monroe Doctrine of 1823 which was intended in part to halt Russia's advance along the Pacific coast, the Truman manifesto—if consistently applied—marked a radically expanded concept of strategic frontiers in regard to Russia. Apart from the Communist issue, Greece's need for food and supplies was desperately urgent, despite a half billion already received up to that time from England and the United States. However, as Greece's Premier announced, most of her $300,000,000 was to be spent for military purposes. Her treasury was bankrupt, her economy more hopelessly impoverished than ever, and a runaway inflation was embittering class feelings. A civil war between right and left forces flared in the Greek mountains in the north, in which leftist guerrillas were aided from pro-Soviet sources in Bulgaria, Yugoslavia, and Albania. British troops of occupation intervened to halt the civil war but found the task beyond their financial resources. The Greek election and plebiscite, judged to be fairly honest by an army of American observers, had resulted in bringing back an unpopular monarchy, apparently as an alternative to Communism, and an irresponsible ruling class. Bled white by the successive Italian Fascist and Nazi invasions and then by an exhausting guerrilla war, Greece could not easily recover. Supporters of the Truman Doctrine insisted that only American aid could save her from falling a prey to Communism and Soviet control. As for aid to Turkey, untouched by war or economic breakdown, this rested on the belief that Russia was exercising pressure on her neighbor by demanding joint control—regarded as in fact sole Russian domination—over the strategic Straits, gateway to the Mediterranean and key to the Middle East.

Once more, as in the case of U.N.R.R.A., the Truman administration had found it expedient to bypass an international agency—the United Nations this time—in order to deal with Soviet power in eastern Europe. In the U.N., where Russia's veto could block the Greek-Turkish program, Americans believed that they had little chance. Chief foe of the Truman Doctrine was former Secretary of Commerce Henry Wallace. In his Madison Square Garden speech on September 12, 1946, which led to his dismissal at the insistence of Byrnes, he had said bluntly, "On our part we should recognize that we have no more business in the political affairs of Eastern Europe than Russia has in the political affairs of Latin America, Western Europe and the United States." He rallied the opposition through speeches all over the country and as editor of the *New Republic*. Finally, in January, 1948, his dissent from the policy of "propping up Greek reaction" and using relief as a weapon to halt Russia and Communism led him to announce that he would run for President at the head of a third party in 1948.

Popular sentiment, as measured by George Gallup's American Institute of Public Opinion, seemed to favor Truman's Russian policy. A poll of September 24, 1947, showed that 40 per cent even wished "to tell Russia any further move into Greece will be considered a declaration of war against the rest of the world"; another 28 per cent voted: "In cooperation with the United Nations organization, send United States troops to patrol the Greek border to stop armed men from coming into the country to make trouble." Only 4 per cent wanted a strictly "hands off" policy; 6 per cent thought that the Greek issue should be allowed to die but that Russia should be halted upon her next move of expansion. A month later Gallup Poll interviewers asked, "Do you think the United States is being too soft or too tough in its policy toward Russia?" The response was 62 per cent "too soft," 6 per cent "too tough," and 24 per cent "about right." It is a fair assumption that Truman's Russian policies were far milder than those that the excited public of 1946–1948 were willing to support. So far had isolationism waned—and again the Russian issue had much to do with this—that according to a poll in November, 1947, by the National Opinion Research Center, 75 per cent wanted the United States to join in a movement for an international police force to maintain world peace.

Despite periodic crises, exaggerated in the Hearst and McCormick press as well as in the no less blatant Soviet newspapers, the Council of Foreign Ministers managed by December 12, 1946, to complete the five treaties with Hitler's former satellites, Bulgaria, Italy, Rumania, Hungary, and Finland. Molotov withdrew his support of Yugoslavia's demand for Trieste, allowing that key area to become a free territory under the Security Council's control. He agreed to free navigation on the Danube, although Russia, who was directly concerned, had previously expressed misgivings. Finally, he gave up his demand for a Soviet trusteeship of Italian Tripolitania which had embarrassed the western powers. In return, Russia received $100,000,000 and Yugoslavia $125,000,000 in reparations from Italy, leaving $105,000,000 to Greece, $25,000,000 to Ethiopia, and $5,000,000 to Albania.

Despite her change of side in the war, Italy lost the Dodecanese Islands to Greece, eastern Venezia Giulia and 25 per cent of her limited and precious coal fields to Yugoslavia, and certain Alpine areas to France; she expected to lose her African empire at a future conference. However, after the Czech crisis, the United States urged that Trieste be given to Italy, much to the embarrassment of Russia which sided with Tito's Yugoslavia but also hoped, apparently, for a Communist Italy. Reluctantly, the western powers recognized the Soviet-dominated regimes of Bulgaria and Rumania. Hungary lost her gains won under Hitler—although she could assert an older historic title to them—of the partly Magyar area taken from Czechoslovakia and the eastern half of Transylvania which was returned to Rumania. In keeping with previous arrangements, Russia received the Karelian Isthmus sector and Petsamo Province from Finland, and Bessarabia and northern Bukovina from Rumania; and Bulgaria was awarded Rumania's southern Dobruja. Despite the expanded boundaries of the Soviet Union, previously enlarged by Latvia, Lithuania, and Esthonia—a situation which invited bitter journalistic attacks in the West—she could still claim to be short of the czarist boundaries of 1914 if one did not reckon Communist satellite states abroad.

NEW TIES WITH BRITAIN

The postwar years brought British and American foreign policies, welded together by a common front against Soviet expansion, into ever-increasing harmony. Even England's shift to partial socialism under Prime Minister Clement Attlee and the Labor party scarcely affected the continuity of their war-time collaboration. But the wide disparity in resources between the two countries left England a junior partner. The burden of six exhausting years of war, the havoc wrought by Nazi bombs, and the breakdown of her best European customers forced her tired people to endure a new "austerity" program in view of the shortages in food, clothing, and housing. England's shortage of manpower and finances, as well as the anti-imperialistic views of the Labor party, led her to free India and to withdraw her troops from Greece, where they had been fighting the leftist guerrillas.

The intensive industrial specialization of Britain, with its emphasis on heavy exports, required imports of foods and raw materials; but her dwindling foreign trade, declining investments abroad, and the war-time loss of shipping tonnage reduced her supply of foreign exchange to the danger point. To correct this situation, the Labor government campaigned for more "austerities" to reduce imports and increase exports, hoping thus to regain a favorable balance of international payments. Failure might force the adoption of a nationalist self-sufficient economy with its inevitably low standard of living. The Labor program was hampered by Europe's prolonged economic crisis and the amazingly bad spring and winter weather in 1945–1946 which destroyed roads and crops and reduced the fuel supply.

England's grave situation was of direct political and economic concern to the United States. Her situation had been worsened by President Truman's abrupt termination of the lend-lease program after V-J Day. The Administration, however, had no intention of bankrupting England and in December, 1945, after three months of delay by Congress, it extended a large credit of $3,750,000,000 to that country at the relatively low interest rate of 2 per cent, which was to be waived whenever the foreign exchange position of Britain required it. In addition, the British received $650,000,000 as credit on the much-reduced money repayment for Lend-lease and surplus property shipments. The English had hoped for an interest-free $5,000,000,000 loan but managed to make up the difference by means of a Canadian loan.

The State Department's purpose in pushing this loan was not only to stabilize Britain's economy as essential for Europe and therefore the United States, but to use this opportunity to free international trade and promote world recovery by eliminating artificial barriers such as currency controls. Hence the British were required to give up their exchange controls through which they had obtained much-needed American dollars. More serious for Britain's shaky position was the requirement that the existing blocked sterling balances of $14,000,000,000 held by foreigners in London banks were to be freely convertible into dollars. These blocked funds limited their owners to British goods in large part; but the new conversion rule meant a heavy raid on Britain's limited dollar supply and by mid-1947 threatened to nullify the benefits of the loan. Moreover, since the borrowed money was to be spent in the United States, the loan benefits were further dissipated by inflated American prices. Therefore, to conserve dollars, the British were compelled to cut down on American tobacco and Hollywood movies, among other imports. By the beginning of 1948, hopes for solution rested heavily upon the Marshall Plan.

Anglo-American relations were somewhat disturbed by the Palestine problem, in which the United States took a keen interest. The British held a League of Nations mandate which guaranteed England's Balfour Declaration of 1917 promising a Jewish home in the Bible land though protecting Arab civil and religious rights. But England's position in the Middle East after 1918 led her to show an increasing sensitivity to Mohammedan opinion which made fulfillment of the mandate difficult if not impossible. Thus it happened that while British-sponsored Arab states in the defunct Ottoman Empire won independence, the Jewish state of Palestine remained a mere blueprint; furthermore, England met Arab demands in 1921 by creating independent Transjordania out of the larger part of the original Palestine area. After World War II, Jewish "displaced persons," frustrated by violent anti-semitism in their former European homes and barred by immigration rules elsewhere, looked intently upon the ancient Hebrew Holy Land as the last hope for survival. They were blocked by the British, who were already seriously weakened in nationalist Egypt and elsewhere in the Middle East and who depended upon the precious oil reserves of that area dominated by the Moslems. To placate the Arabs the British reduced Jewish immigration to a trickle—a policy which had already prevented many European Jews from escaping Hitler's gas chambers. In desperation a group of Jewish extremists sought to force world action in their behalf by acts of terrorism against the British.

In the United States, where some 5,000,000 Jews resided, Truman had emphatically supported the Zionist request for the entrance of 100,000 Jews into Palestine and had sought unsuccessfully to secure congressional action to liberalize our immigration laws. Our policy, like that of Britain, had to reckon with strategic factors in the Middle East and the military importance of the oil reserves, especially in Saudi Arabia; this meant strong reluctance by our State Department to antagonizing the powerful Arab League of seven states. Britain, smarting under American criticism, insisted that such attacks were meaningless unless we would share the military risk of a possible Arab uprising in the event of large-scale Jewish immigration. Foreign Minister Bevin declared in 1947 that the mandate was "unworkable in practice" and that his country's obligations to Arabs and Jews were irreconcilable; therefore he was appealing to the U.N. for a solution.

A U.N. committee acted promptly in investigating the Palestine situation and reported a plan for partitioning the country but allowing for economic cooperation between the Arab and Jewish states. Zionists quickly accepted the plan, but the Arab League spurned any form of partition. Nevertheless, a Jewish state was voted by the U.N. in November, 1947, with the strong support of Russia and this country. However, rejoicings in Israel were suddenly stilled by sporadic Arab attacks which were closely followed by Jewish reprisals, leaving 2000 dead on both sides by April, 1948. Meanwhile, Britain prepared to end her mandate on May 15 regardless of what the U.N. might do to implement the partition resolution. Both England and the United States placed an arms embargo on Palestine, much to the distress of the Jews, whose defense depended heavily on imports of guns from the West. In March, after the Czech revolution had dismayed the West, the State Department suddenly reversed its policy on partition in favor of a U.N. trusteeship for Palestine. The Arab world, whose oil and neutrality were useful in the anti-communist front, was apparently not to be antagonized. After the trusteeship plan was defeated by the U.N., Truman closely followed by Russia, reverted to the partition idea and recognized the newly-proclaimed state of Israel.

THE CHINESE PUZZLE

American leadership took a sharp setback in China, despite heavy expenditures and well-intended efforts. During the war, Americans had been at least partly successful in bringing Chiang Kai-shek's conservative Central Government and the forces of Communist China together in military cooperation. The defeat of Japan led to a race between Nationalists and Communists for the key cities of north China and Manchuria. American troops, instructed to protect Chiang's communications while his men disarmed the Japanese, occupied vital transfer centers and gave the Nationalists their surplus weapons, thereby losing their previous status as impartial peacemaker between the two factions. They found themselves involved indirectly in the revived civil war between Chiang and the Communists.

While the right-wing Kuomintang faction of Chiang's party had neglected badly needed economic reforms for China's impoverished people, the native Communists, of whom few were actually Marxists, pushed forward sweeping revolutionary changes in their territories, redistributing land among the peasantry, lowering rents and taxes, and breaking the grip of the feudal landowning class. Although the civil war doubtless offset many of these economic gains and burdened the suffering Chinese with endless battles, the Communists by 1947 could claim more than a dozen provinces in China and Manchuria and a combined population of 131,000,000. How much they owed to the Soviet Union was disputed by observers, although it was clear that Russian occupation troops gave considerable indirect aid to the native Communists in the form of Japanese war booty.

In December, 1945, General Marshall arrived as special envoy and ambassador to China, with instructions to unify China by combining Nationalist and Communist factions, thus ending the civil war. President Truman knew the one-party nature of Chiang's dictatorship and its regressive tendency; therefore he wanted a broader popular basis for the Central Government. Marshall, benefiting by his military prestige as chief of staff as well as by the fact that the United States was expected to aid heavily in China's economic rehabilitation, did secure a truce on January 10, 1946, and made a short-lived agreement for the merger of Communist forces with the Nationalist Army and for Communist political representation in the government. However, neither faction was anxious to surrender its existing military gains; the Communists were dissatisfied with the representation accorded them, and war broke out again. The Soviet-American rift undoubtedly contributed to the difficulties of reaching a compromise. In the end, Marshall had to admit failure, which he attributed to extremists on both sides. Thereafter he worked to liberalize the Chiang regime and to spur it on to undertake economic reforms. Postwar lend-lease, terminated for other nations, continued for Chiang's China; it exceeded a billion dollars by October 1, 1946, and more was demanded for 1948 when the Nationalists appeared to be losing north and south.

Floundering in the mesh of Soviet-American conflict, Korea, "the Hermit Kingdom" absorbed by Japan in 1910, impatiently awaited the independence promised by the Cairo Conference. Besides Korea's own sixty quarreling parties, there was the occupational split between Russians in the north and Americans in the south. Each power set up provisional regimes, the Russians introducing a revolutionary land distribution program among the peasants. After negotiations for unity broke down in 1947, Soviet-occupied Korea announced on February 16, 1948, that a radical "Democratic People's Republic" guaranteeing the expropriated lands for the peasants had been formed and expected ultimately to embrace the American zone. Protests came from the American military authorities, who denounced this step as a Russian violation of the Allied agreement to work together for an independent Korea. The strategic location of Korea relative to Manchuria, Japan, and China proper gave that area major importance.

MacARTHUR, JAPAN, AND THE PHILIPPINES

With American troops controlling Japan, MacArthur enjoyed a relatively free hand, though the Soviets protested occasionally in the Allied Councils. As Supreme Commander for the Allied Powers

(S.C.A.P.), he demobilized 4,000,000 Japanese, purged the civil service of known militarists, tried and punished "war criminals," abolished the incendiary patriotic societies, and put Japan—so it was hoped—back on the road to democracy. Very helpfully, Emperor Hirohito himself told his people that he was not divine and that Shintoism, which MacArthur had disestablished, had taught a false doctrine that the Japanese were "superior to other races and fated to rule the world."

A new constitution along American lines, with a Bill of Rights and a genuine party system, replaced the rule of the military and big-business groups in May, 1947. Women were enfranchised and their legal status was raised. Labor was encouraged to form free unions and to agitate for better conditions; however, political strikes and those against the public interest were repressed. Education was revolutionized through a program of democratic and anti-militarist indoctrination in the schools and via the radio. The feudal and inefficient landowning system was broken up, thus enabling 2,000,000 Japanese tenant farmers to become farm owners. On the commercial-industrial front, the monopoly of the *Zaibatsu* (Japan's dozen leading families) was dissolved and competitive enterprise fostered. Most of these changes by S.C.A.P. were brought about through the agency of the Japanese Diet. But the Russians seemed suspicious that MacArthur was grooming Japan as a potential enemy on the flank of the Soviet Union.

Although MacArthur was working for the revival of Japan's economy, he bowed to the pressure of other Pacific powers, including Russia, and earmarked one-third of Japan's industries for reparation seizures. Famine conditions around Greater Tokyo, aggravated by food hoarding in rural areas, compelled S.C.A.P. to import foodstuffs from the United States. Conservative Japanese politicians hesitated to apply MacArthur's suggestions for rigid price and rationing controls, but allowed inflation and the black market to have full sway. American policy assumed that world stability rested upon the economic recovery of the vanquished as well as the victors. This meant heavy financial obligations by this country, at least until the German and Japanese peace treaties decided the future.

On July 4, 1946, the Philippine Islands became an independent republic and thus the American pledge was honorably fulfilled. The long period of tutelage had not been used to enrich Americans, for our total investments of $250,000,000 fell far short of our interests in other parts of the globe. In the Philippine Rehabilitation Act, Congress gave $400,000,000 to war damage claimants and turned over $100,-000,000 of surplus property to the islands and another $120,000,000 for Filipino technical education. The islands had suffered losses close to $800,000,000, half of Manila was in ruins, and land reform was long overdue. Americans had not interfered in the basic economic structure, leaving sharp class divisions antedating their era of occupation for the natives to deal with.

Very unfortunate for an independent nation was the colonial nature of the Philippine economy, which stressed exports of sugar, hemp, coconuts, and tobacco, largely destined for the United States. President Roosevelt had favored diversification, but little had been accomplished. Congress, deciding to break off economic ties with the islands, passed the Philippine Trade Act of 1946 (the Bell Act), which continued free trade for eight years and then eliminated the prevailing system of tariff preference at an annually accelerated rate until 1974, when the process of separation would be completed. Prewar producers, many of them American, were granted exclusive export quotas of the chief crops—a provision resented by many Filipinos.

In return for accepting this law, which ran counter to the State Department's multilateral trading policy, the natives were given the benefits of the Philippine Rehabilitation Act. The native Democratic Alliance and the semi-Communist Hukbalahap group assailed the Trade Act as imperialistic. Nationalists attacked a stipulation that United States citizens must receive equal economic treatment with natives in developing Philippine resources. This, too, was suspected as concealing imperialistic aims. However, President Roxas managed to put the Trade Act through his legislature and also guaranteed to the United States the continued ownership of military bases on the islands and the cooperation of his government on all defense measures.

BUILDING AN INTERNATIONAL ORDER

At the San Francisco Conference in June, 1945, the Charter of the United Nations, modeled after the draft of the Dumbarton Oaks agreement, was signed by some fifty nations. One of the stumbling blocks then and thereafter was the veto power given each of the permanent members of the all-powerful Security Council—namely, China, France, the Soviet Union, the United Kingdom, and the United States—on all but procedural matters; that is, unanimity among these big powers was required on all non-procedural decisions. However, a party to a dispute was expected to abstain from voting on decisions involving a pacific settlement of the dispute and small powers were reassured that the veto would be used sparingly. Both the United States and the Soviet Union wished to retain the veto power, especially on military sanctions, but disagreed as to the extent that the veto be used. By the fall of 1947 it was estimated that the Soviet delegate had invoked the veto power over twenty times, mostly on quite minor issues, thus blocking action by the Security Council. By that time Secretary Marshall was striving to solve the stalemate by proposing a permanent Assembly Committee—the Little Assembly—to handle certain peace and security cases. Despite violent Soviet criticism, an Interim Committee of the General Assembly was approved on November 13, 1947, and given investigatory and advisory power on questions affecting the peace, save for those issues already being considered by the Security Council.

Among the numerous vexations facing the youthful U.N. was the serious issue of Iran, from which Soviet, American, and British troops were pledged to withdraw six months after the war, but where the Russians, entrenched in the rebel area of Azerbaijan in the north, were suspected of fomenting civil war. Iran, formerly Persia, had been a focal point of Anglo-Russian oil rivalry for over a generation; this time the Soviets were asserting the old Russian demand for oil concessions. The United States, suffering from depleted oil reserves at home and holding huge concessions in neighboring Saudi Arabia, was interested in preventing any Soviet monopoly of Iran oil and any extension of Russian influence in that country. Encouraged by Anglo-American support, Iran arraigned the Soviet Union before U.N. for military interference in her affairs. The Russians denied these charges and called attention to British military intervention in Greece and Indonesia; nevertheless, they agreed to settle these matters by direct negotiations. By April 15, 1946, Iran seemed satisfied that the Russians were out and withdrew her complaint, but she refused to consider any further Soviet negotiations for oil concessions.

No less serious was the U.N. rift over the international control of atomic power. In December, 1945, the Moscow Conference of Britain, the United States, and the U.S.S.R. had agreed to sponsor a U.N. Atomic Energy Commission. Thereupon the United States, as sole custodian of the atom bomb, took the initiative in preparing the Acheson-Lilienthal Report on the international control of this deadly weapon. Bernard M. Baruch, American representative on the U.N. Atomic Energy Commission, presented on June 14, 1946, a modified version of the Lilienthal Report to the Commission. "We are here to make a choice between the quick and the dead," he observed solemnly. He proposed an International Atomic Development Authority—without the veto power being allowed to any nation—to deal with every phase of atomic energy—a kind of world T.V.A. (Lilienthal had been chairman of the T.V.A. board). The agency would have:

1. Managerial control or ownership of all atomic energy activities potentially dangerous to world security.
2. Power to control, inspect, and license all other atomic activities.
3. The duty of fostering the beneficial uses of atomic energy.
4. Research and development responsibilities of an affirmative character intended to put the Authority in the forefront of atomic knowledge. . . .

Once the agency established conditions of security, he added, the United States would then propose that all atom bomb–making cease, that existing bomb stocks be disposed of, and that penalties be fixed for the illegal possession or use of atomic bombs or materials or for willful interference with the Authority.

This proposal, at least in principle, seemed satisfactory to all but Russia and Poland. The Soviet representative, Gromyko, made it clear that his country would not tolerate international inspection by a committee roaming at will through the Soviet Union or relinquish the veto power in the proposed Authority. These concessions were incompatible with national sovereignty. Instead he proposed the immediate outlawry of the bomb, the destruction of all such stocks, and a system of committees for the exchange of scientific information, each nation being left to execute any agreements for the punishment of atomic bomb criminals. Gromyko's newly found nationalism seemed to have cast him for the role of a resurrected Henry Cabot Lodge.

Disagreement over atomic control opened the door to a vicious armament race in the deadliest weapon known to man. After such a setback, other agreements to surrender conventional weapons seemed futile. The Bikini tests undertaken in July, 1946, in the Marshall Islands by the United States Joint Chiefs of Staff revealed more of the atomic bomb's capacity and proved that it could damage every ship within a mile of the blast. While Russia was apprehensive of our atomic strength, the United States also feared Soviet progress toward manufacturing the bomb—a feat already accomplished, according to Molotov. Optimistically, the U.N. General Assembly resolved on December 14, 1946, on ultimate disarmament and the abolition of the atomic bomb and other new destructive weapons.

Another snag in the efforts toward Soviet-American understanding was struck in the formation of the United Nations Educational, Scientific, and Cultural Organization (U.N.E.S.C.O.) on November 16, 1945. President Truman, announcing our adherence on July 30, 1946, remarked, "I attach the greatest importance to this agency. U.N.E.S.C.O. will summon to service in the cause of peace the forces of education, science, learning, and the creative arts and the agencies of the film, the radio and the printed word through which knowledge and ideas are diffused among mankind." The constitution of U.N.E.S.C.O. asserted that "since wars begin in the minds of men, it is in the minds of men that the defenses of peace must be constructed." It sought agreements between nations to promote the free flow of ideas, advised upon educational rehabilitation in war-torn areas, and encouraged democratic educational methods although respecting "the fruitful diversity of cultures."

The Soviets abstained from joining, their point of view best expressed by a Yugoslav spokesman who criticized the "cultural centralization" fostered by U.N.E.S.C.O., assailed its missionary "humanistic" ideas as contrary to Marxist thought, and took issue with the assumption that wars are caused by ignorance of each other's ways and lives. Observers wondered whether U.N.E.S.C.O. would in effect deepen the ideological rift between Marxist and non-Marxist nations.

Among the new agencies of peace, much was hoped from the International Bank for Reconstruction and Development and from the International Monetary Fund, both of which had been born in the significant Bretton Woods Agreements of 1944, which the United States had ratified in July, 1945. The International Bank, popularly called the World Bank, was, like the Federal Housing Administration, a mutual loan insurance and guaranty institution. It did not supplant international lending, but guaranteed loans for productive development projects to countries which could not borrow the money otherwise. The United States controlled 40 per cent of the votes and could veto unfavorable decisions. Many had counted upon the Bank to take over all reconstruction loans at once, but for various reasons the first loan was not issued until May, 1947. The Bank's companion, the International Monetary Fund, in which the United States director cast 31.68 per cent of the vote, was intended to stabilize the exchange of currencies through short-term credits and expert advice; nations would be helped to achieve a balanced trade without resorting to harmful deflationary policies and exchange restrictions. Thus, it was hoped, the free flow of international trade would be unimpeded and the dangerous and unjust consequences of bilateral deals would be avoided. By 1948, the U.S.S.R. was still the chief U.N. member to abstain from joining the World Bank or the Fund.

These agencies, which sought to liberalize trade and aid fuller world employment, were invaluable to the American goal of stabilizing Europe and Asia. Toward the same end, the U.N. members—except those like the U.S.S.R. which had a state trading monopoly—set up the International Trade Organization (I.T.O.) to encourage fair trading practices among nations; it would discourage the "dumping" of surpluses on the world market when this tended to have a depressing effect on price stability; the chief instrument for enforcement of its recommendations was world opinion. The urgent problem of postwar malnutrition and agricultural production was turned over to the Food and Agricultural Organization (F.A.O.). Such international measures were powerfully strengthened by the direct aid given by the United States. Congress extended this direct financial help to

Europe through the Export-Import Bank Act of 1945 which increased the Bank's lending authority from $700,000,000 to $3,500,000,000. The former emphasis on Latin American loans was replaced by the new stress upon European reconstruction. A large loan to France was timed strategically to help the French moderates defeat the rising Communists. Loans were sometimes withheld from nations which seemed ready to follow on the Soviet path.

HEMISPHERE COLLABORATION

Pan-American solidarity, strengthened by common efforts in World War II, advanced during the postwar era, marred only by Argentine nationalist acts of defiance and the resurgence of Communist anti-Yankee propaganda. A significant step toward hemisphere peace was taken in the war-time Act of Chapultepec of March 6, 1945, which pledged the Pan American states: "That every attack of a State against the integrity or the inviolability of territory, or against the sovereignty or political independence of an American State shall . . . be considered as an act of aggression against the other States which sign this declaration."

In such a case the members would decide as to the necessary collective measures. Specific procedures for sanctions were to be set up in a future treaty. By seeking to guarantee the peace regionally, the members went beyond the Monroe Doctrine concept of an external aggressor. The hemisphere system, far from being obsolete in the new age of the United Nations, was expected by the U.N. Charter to play a vital part in giving regional support to the edicts of U.N. However, the scheduled Inter-American Conference on the Maintenance of Continental Peace and Security at Rio de Janeiro, envisaged in the Act of Chapultepec, was delayed by the refusal of the United States to sign with Peron's Argentina. Only in September, 1947, did the United States reluctantly decide upon cooperation with the Peron regime and Truman and Marshall journeyed to Brazil to sign the Inter-American Defense Treaty binding the hemisphere to military action against both internal and external aggressors.

In Argentina, an ultra-Nationalist revolution in 1943, led by Colonel Juan Domingo Peron, forced that country to maintain a war-time policy of "strict neutrality" until the final months of World

War II, intrigue with Nazi leaders, emulate certain of their Fascist ideas, and conspire against the safety of her neighbors. Spruille Braden, an outspoken American hostile to Peron's system, was sent as our ambassador to Argentina as an expression of official condemnation. When Peron decided to run for president in the election of 1946, rather than remain an untitled power behind the throne, the State Department suddenly issued the startling *Blue Book,* which proved in documentary fashion that Argentina's regime had aided the Nazis after Pearl Harbor and even now continued to shelter dangerous Nazi interests. Former President Castillo as well as Peron had plotted to form an anti-Yankee Nazi coalition in South America. Peron denied all allegations, attacked Braden as a foreign meddler, and appealed emotionally to Argentine national pride. Despite the *Blue Book,* Peron won the presidency, a fact which compelled Secretary Byrnes to reconsider his policy and to accept Argentina as a co-signatory to the long-delayed Inter-American Defense Treaty. Undoubtedly, Argentine wheat, which was a vital factor in the world relief problem, as well as the disturbed European situation, influenced this retreat.

A new factor to be reckoned with in Latin American affairs was the rising influence of Soviet ideology, strengthened by the recent renewal of diplomatic ties with most hemisphere nations during the war years and thereafter. Brazil's temporary venture into a free election system revealed a Communist vote of a half million in the election of December, 1946. Her dynamic Communist leader, Luis Carlos Prestes, sounded the new anti-Yankee line which had succeeded the friendly war-time slogans. Latin American poverty and illiteracy offered a fertile breeding ground for Communist growth. In Chile, the anti-Yankee outbursts of the Communists included a note of generous tolerance for Peron. In most cases, however, the friends of the United States held the political reins in Latin America.

DEMOBILIZATION AND RECONVERSION

Despite postwar commitments in foreign policy, public opinion forced a large-scale demobilization of our armed forces ahead of schedule, beginning with those longest in the services and family men. To offset this sudden depletion of soldiers, President Truman and General Eisenhower persuaded Congress to extend the Selective

Training and Service Act until March, 1947, a program which in practice stressed voluntary enlistment and a prolonged "draft holiday." As 1947 began, scarcely a half million soldiers remained abroad, largely as occupation troops. A record number of 13,909,000 veterans of World War II eventually resumed civilian life, aided by government grants. A "G.I. Bill of Rights," largely in the Servicemen's Readjustment Act, offered education and maintenance to the veterans, depending on length of service. Enrollments soared in high schools, colleges, and vocational schools of all types. Veterans' loans on easy terms for homes, farms, and business property were guaranteed by federal agencies, and encouraged many to assume debts beyond discretionary bounds at a time when values were badly inflated. A vast program for veterans' life insurance, medical aid, vocational rehabilitation, disability pensions, hospitalization, and other services was set up under the Veterans Administration headed by General Omar N. Bradley.

War industries, which had produced $186,000,000,000 of military weapons and supplies, were rapidly converted to peacetime uses, aided by generous federal provisions during the process of canceling war contracts. Motivated by *laissez-faire* ideas, Congress forced the hands of the Administration in quickly abolishing war-time agencies like the War Production Board and the War Labor Board. Spurred on by a tremendous backlog of consumer demand, accumulated savings, and the need for machinery for reconversion, American industry achieved record employment—the realization of Henry Wallace's goal of "sixty million jobs"—by 1947. Individual incomes totaled $164,000,000,000 in 1946 and consumer expenditures reached $127,-000,000,000 that same year. Despite record-making strikes and shortages, industrial production in 1946 was 50 per cent above 1939 levels.

This challenging picture was severely marred by the worst housing crisis in our history—unique for a nation which had escaped air bombardment. Truman's Housing Expediter, Wilson W. Wyatt, undertook to solve this problem, which was aggravated by the fact that too little residential building had been done in the depression and war years and that increased consumer income absorbed housing facilities as it did other types of commodities and services. The veterans came home to a situation already at a critical stage and these millions of young men and women were forced to double up, often under the most pathetic circumstances. The government program of low-cost housing, control over scarce building materials, and price ceilings for veterans' housing met severe criticism from real estate lobbies and conservative groups that eventually forced the Administration to abandon Wyatt and most of the program to private initiative. The Taft-Ellender-Wagner Bill, which might have offered some relief in the form of subsidized and low-cost housing, passed in the Senate, but was buried in the House.

LABOR UNDER INFLATION

As overtime pay fell off in the postwar years and prices rose steadily, labor became increasingly restive. Strikes reached the emergency stage by late 1945 and an all-time record in 1946, when 4,750,000 workers left their jobs at a loss of 110,700,000 man-days. A 27-day power strike by city employees in Pittsburgh cost $300,000,000 and created considerable hardship before it was settled by arbitration. Oakland experienced a general strike when the American Federation of Labor called out 100,000 members to protect their picket lines in a department store strike. New York City suffered severely from a tugboat strike which tied up food and other supplies. The worst tie-ups occurred in the General Motors strike, the railroads, the soft coal pits, the maritime industry, and steel. Bitter public reaction was reflected in anti-union bills before Congress and many state legislatures.

In May, 1946, a 48-hour strike of 250,000 railroad unionists paralyzed the nation and led to the federal seizure of the railroads. President Truman made a dramatic appeal before Congress for emergency authority to draft the strikers into the army and to impose other drastic punishments on those who struck against the government. But even as he spoke, a note was handed him which he read aloud: Just a few minutes before, the rail strike had been settled by a wage compromise. When Congress followed up Truman's proposal for anti-strike legislation with the Case Bill, the President vetoed it as dangerous for permanent legislation. "Men cannot be forced in a peacetime democracy to work for a private employer under compulsion," he declared.

A particularly crippling strike began on April 1, 1946, when John

L. Lewis' 400,000 United Mine Workers went out on a 45-day strike to demand higher wages and a health and welfare program. By May 4, the Office of War Mobilization and Reconversion reported to the President that the soft coal strike was already a "national disaster" whose inevitable effects would endanger reconversion. Truman thereupon seized the mines and negotiated a settlement directly with the miners. However, the operators refused to accept the government-sponsored contract and Lewis ordered another strike on November 20, this time for seventeen days, despite the fact that his employer was now the federal government. His strike was met by a federal injunction which he defied as a violation of the Norris-La Guardia Anti-Injunction Act. Thereupon Justice T. Alan Goldsborough of the federal district court for the District of Columbia declared Lewis and his U.M.W. in contempt of court and fined the leader $10,000 and his men $3,500,000. In reviewing the case on March 6, 1947, the Supreme Court upheld the Goldsborough decision, ruling that the Norris-La Guardia Act did not prevent the federal government, as acting coal operator, from issuing labor injunctions. But the U.M.W. fine was ordered reduced to $700,000 if Lewis canceled his notice terminating the current contract—as he did. Subsequently, Lewis won a highly favorable contract for his loyal miners.

Sympathy veered back to the miners, who had included safety measures among their demands, after the Centralia, Illinois, disaster on March 25 when a gas-filled mine exploded, killing 111 trapped miners. This was the worst mine disaster since 1928. Although Secretary of the Interior Julius A. Krug closed 518 pits for safety reasons and investigated the accident, Lewis fiercely charged Krug with responsibility for conditions in the government-run mines and proclaimed a six-day memorial shutdown of the soft coal mines. Local and company negligence was found as a contributing cause of the accident, though Krug blamed Lewis for non-cooperation in previous attempts to install safety devices.

Employers were deeply disturbed in 1947 by labor's concerted drive behind a new federal decision of January 23 in the Mount Clemens Pottery Company case involving an interpretation of the Fair Labor Standards Act (the Wage and Hour Law) which was held to mean "portal-to-portal" pay for employees, that is, payment for all necessary time consumed preparatory to and following the actual factory work performed. The unions, who were eager to offset the losses due to inflated prices, encouraged an avalanche of retroactive pay-suits that totaled $5,000,000,000 by May. That month, Congress acted to outlaw before May 14, 1947, all such claims not specifically provided for in labor contracts and also placed a two-year time limit on future claims. Truman signed this bill, but attempted to placate labor by urging Congress to raise minimum wage rates under the Fair Labor Standards Act and to extend its benefits to workers not yet covered. By this time, however, Congress was too deeply absorbed in anti-union legislation to respond.

LABOR ON THE DEFENSIVE: THE TAFT-HARTLEY ACT

Like the tense labor-employer clashes after World War I, the conflicts following the Second World War were due to inflationary pressures, fears of Communism, and determination of the unions to defend their war-time gains. Instead of three or four million organized workers as in 1919, there were now almost 14,000,000 actually working under written collective bargaining agreements, and union agents were organizing occupations affecting 29,000,000 men and women. The Wagner Act of 1935, successful in its objective of protecting collective bargaining, had been based on the belief that the employer's strength was so immense as to discourage really effective labor bargaining and that the forces of government had to be thrown in on the side of labor to correct the balance; hence the National Labor Relations Board had come into being.

By mid-1947 a conservative Congress, acting on the conviction that labor no longer needed extra advantages over capital, insisted that not only must unfair employer practices against labor be penalized, but that abusive actions by unions too must be given strong penalties beyond those currently provided by the statute books and in the courts. Large sections of public opinion had been antagonized by the wholesale work stoppages of 1946, by the defiant attitude of John L. Lewis, and by the backward methods of the building trades in handling the housing crisis. State laws against labor were beginning to sweep the country. In this emotional setting the Taft-Hartley Act was passed and later repassed over the President's stinging veto in June, 1947. In the House a bipartisan group of 225 Republicans and 106 Democrats supported the bill, leaving only 71 Democrats and 11 Republicans standing by Truman. A pro-labor filibuster in the Senate collapsed when 20 Democrats joined 48 Republicans to override the veto.

To meet the long-standing charge that the National Labor Relations Board was "judge, jury, and prosecutor" to the injury of management, the Act transferred considerable administrative power from the Board to a President-appointed general counsel. He dealt with employers' complaints regarding unfair practices by labor. The N.L.R.B. had now the unpopular task of acting as umpire in jurisdictional disputes—some of them bloody civil wars between unions for the exclusive right to perform certain types of work—and strikes on such jurisdictional grounds were outlawed. To offset newspaper charges that unions were secretive, demanded extortionate fees, and paid exorbitant salaries, union officers were expected to file with the Department of Labor all relevant facts regarding finances, the size of initiation fees, and the dues collected. Above all, they were to file affidavits with the N.L.R.B. stating that they were not Communists. The officers of federated bodies like the C.I.O. and the A. F. of L. who neglected to make an anti-Communist affidavit, according to General Counsel Robert Denham, forfeited the rights of the constituent national unions to the services of the N.L.R.B. This was later reversed by the N.L.R.B., which held that only officers of independent or national unions rather than the officers of the C.I.O. or the A. F. of L. need file anti-Communist affidavits.

To reduce work stoppages by strikes, a 60-day cooling-off period was required for changes in labor contracts. Secondary boycotts by labor, which forced a business not directly involved in a dispute to cease dealing with another company or to cease using or handling its products, were banned. Also forbidden were strikes by one group intended to force the employer of another group to recognize a union. In cases where strikes violated labor contracts, such as a strike in defiance of a no-strike pledge, the unions might be sued in the federal courts, and damage claims against them were permissible. More definitely than ever before, unions were made suable and bound by the acts of their agents. Furthermore, the Norris-La Guardia Act was amended by the Taft-Hartley Law to allow the government to obtain injunctions in the federal courts against certain illegal strikes, thus resurrecting the injunction as a weapon against unions. Should a strike create a national emergency, such as the recent railroad strike, the federal Attorney General could seek an 80-day injunction during which a solution might be obtained through investigation, mediation, or, in the last resort, action by Congress. An independent mediation board under a director appointed by the President was established to speed up conciliation work. No compulsory arbitration was attempted.

Among the new rules for collective bargaining were those outlawing closed-shop agreements which required that all employees hired be union members. However, a contract might require union membership of employees 30 days after hiring. Thus a *union shop,* but not a *closed shop,* was permitted. Employers were cheered by the elimination of "featherbedding" by which unions demanded payment for standby workers who might do nothing whatever. More difficult from the union point of view was the rule that a majority of all the employees in a plant, not merely of those voting, was required to approve a negotiated union-shop contract. After a year the contract might be challenged by 30 per cent or more of the employees, or the employees might "decertify" or reject their bargaining agents and new elections would be ordered. Employers, too, could petition for new elections. A serious political blow was the ban on union contributions or expenditures for national primaries or elections. The New Deal had drawn heavily from union contributions.

Altogether, the Taft-Hartley Law, though not as strong as anti-union forces would have liked, angered many union leaders, who promptly dubbed it the "slave labor act" and campaigned for the President's veto. Defiant "wildcat" strikes broke out in ten states as a protest against the law. There were potentialities in the Act for costly, destructive litigation, crippling injunctions, and frequent unsettling elections which might wear down union resources and discourage effective organizing. The attempt to eliminate Communists and "fellow-travelers" among union leaders might become a boomerang against non-doctrinaire but militant labor leaders. William

Green of the A. F. of L. denounced the law as "reprehensible and vicious and destructive to the legal and civil rights of workers." The C.I.O. under Philip Murray moved to make a test case of the ban on political contributions. John L. Lewis was even more open in his boycott of the law. He refused to sign the affidavit on Communism as "insulting" and withdrew his United Mine Workers from the less-obdurate A. F. of L. which had only recently welcomed him back to the fold.

President Truman, issuing the most belligerent veto message in recent history, argued that the law was unworkable, would force the government to intervene to a novel and injurious extent in labor bargaining, and would shift settlements from the informal bargaining tables to the more inflexible courts of law. He held that the law constituted class legislation in its unequal penalties, and that the ban on political activity was "a dangerous intrusion on free speech." To this Senator Taft replied at length over the radio, denying practically every assertion of the President as erroneous. On the subject of prolonged litigation he retorted, "Everyone else in the United States is subject to harassment by lawsuits. Why not unions? . . . We have simply provided that unions are subject to the same general laws as any other corporation or agency or citizen." The Wagner Act, he contended, had been one-sided in its administration; the new law made it operate both ways. He insisted that the ordinary worker, if not the union leader, was pleased with the law.

THE INFLATIONARY SPIRAL

Scarcely had the war ended before the Administration was beset by increasing pressure for the elimination of all wage and price controls and compelled to make concessions. By 1945 the average consumers' price index, according to the Department of Labor, had risen to 128.4 from 125.5 the previous year (1935–1939 = 100), but this was mild compared to what was to follow when controls disappeared. Labor spokesmen denied that moderate wage raises need cause higher prices. The C.I.O. economist, Robert Nathan, for example, contended that industry could raise wages 25 per cent out of high current profits without raising prices. Henry Wallace popularized this view in his speeches and interviews, but employers and most newspapers tended to treat it as fantastic.

Soon the battle line on prices formed before the pivotal Office of Price Administration under Chester Bowles, entrusted with the war against inflation. Consumers armed with unprecedented incomes bought eagerly almost beyond the current rate of production in certain lines. Strikes maimed the general output. Scarcities plagued the housewife and homebuilder, encouraging a "black market" over which public opinion seemed only mildly exercised. Business protested the narrowing margin of profit under O.P.A. controls because of uncontrolled factors of cost; uneven controls led some to abandon production in basic fields in favor of more attractive and often less essential consumer goods. Newspapers campaigned for the end of controls as a panacea for current ills.

By mid-1946, Truman had already made wage and price concessions which inevitably forced the cost of living further upward. It remained for a bipartisan Congress, under Taft's leadership, to destroy price control on the theory that higher prices would stimulate production and eventually the increased supply would itself force prices down. On June 28, 1946, Congress sent the President a "compromise" bill extending the O.P.A. for a year but removing government controls over numerous items. Truman, disregarding his party leaders, vetoed it as a deceptive choice between "inflation with a statute and inflation without one." He broadcast an appeal to the people to send their protests to their Congressmen, and an avalanche of critical letters and telegrams descended on Congress. The veto was upheld, but the Administration failed to get another bill at once, and O.P.A. controls expired. The country was left exposed for a month to gouging and profiteering as prices soared for scarce commodities and rents rose to fantastic heights in numerous instances. By the time Congress acted on July 25 to restore an emasculated O.P.A. on somewhat better terms than those in the vetoed measure, irreparable damage had been done to the cause of effective controls.

Livestock owners particularly, suffering from high food prices, rebelled at the revived low price ceilings and meat almost disappeared from legitimate sales channels. On October 14, Truman yielded to the angry clamor of housewives and newspapers by removing meat ceilings. Thereafter ceilings were rapidly eliminated except on rents, sugar, and rice. Real estate lobbies, protesting that the landlord alone was being neglected in the upward trend of prices and costs, secured partial relief in the Hawkes Rent Control Act of 1947 thrust upon an unwilling President. While extending rent control for a year, the law provided "voluntary" increases in rentals up to 15 per cent if both parties signed eighteen-month leases; enforcement was left to the local courts rather than the O.P.A. rent boards and evictions were made considerably easier.

Food prices rose 34 per cent in 1946 alone. John R. Steelman, Director of War Mobilization and Reconversion, reported that prices had risen higher in the three months since the original price control act had expired than they had in the previous thirty-eight months. Heavy foreign exports to needy Europe strengthened the inflationary trend, leading the Administration in October, 1947, to organize a Citizen's Food Committee in order to reduce consumption of bread and meat through voluntary "meatless" Tuesdays and "poultry-less" and "egg-less" Thursdays and other conservation rules. Thus it was hoped to save 100,000,000 bushels of grain for export to Europe during the next nine months without unduly affecting prices. But grain and other prices continued to go skyward, encouraged by the prospects of further exports under the European Recovery Program.

By the end of 1947, the President's Council of Economic Advisers reported ominously a steady decline in both real wages and the rate of savings, despite the fact that dividends and profits continued to increase at an accelerated rate and achieved the highest totals in history. Corporate profits during 1947 as compared with the previous year rose from $21.1 billion to $28 billion before taxes, and from $12.5 billion to $17 billion after taxes; the latter total was actually 73 per cent higher than the average for war-time profits. From the time price controls ended in mid-June of 1946 to the end of 1947, the cost of living rose 23 per cent compared with an increase of 18 per cent in weekly earnings. Although the dollar volume of production in 1947 increased 15 per cent over totals for the previous year, physical production actually rose less than 5 per cent. Demand in certain lines was tapering off. Food prices were almost double the 1935–1939 average, although rents, it is true, had risen only mildly. Public opinion polls agreed that high prices were the chief problem of the day. Buyer strikes in New York and other large cities broke out in 1947 but made little impression on inflation. Senator Taft won some notoriety for advising his countrymen to eat less extravagantly and thus curb inflation. The President embarked on a campaign to halt food prices by punishing grain speculators.

To combat this dangerous as well as painful inflation which far exceeded the 1919–1920 price rise in scope, President Truman in December, 1947, offered Congress a sweeping anti-inflation program. He requested authority to impose controls as needed (including rationing) on wages, prices, rents, consumers' credit, exports, transportation, and certain other phases of the national economy. However, the coalition of conservative Democrats and Republicans was not yet convinced that such drastic steps were necessary; some of the Congressmen expressed a fear of reversing the inflationary trend into a dangerous deflationary tailspin and depression. The resulting Anti-Inflation Law of January, 1948, which the President characterized as better than nothing at all, was therefore a partial series of concessions. It gave the Administration certain controls over exports, transportation, consumers' credit, rent facilities, and industrial materials—the latter to be controlled through voluntary agreements. The requested pivotal powers of direct price and wage controls were rejected.

Beginning on Wednesday, February 4, 1948, wheat prices, already at famine levels, felt the severe impact of the worst break in commodity prices in history, falling sixty cents per bushel in eight days and carrying stock market values back to the levels of the previous summer. Most observers agreed that some downward price adjustment was inevitable, but the current skyrocketing of prices left fears that the process of adjustment might be drastic and extremely painful. While many favorable factors in the economy seemed to militate against the possibility of a severe depression at this time, a strong note of uncertainty existed and led to cautious plans by investors, consumers, and others.

THE RED SCARE AND CIVIL LIBERTIES

Meanwhile the nation, which had shown an exemplary war-time record for civil liberties, reverted to the familiar "Red scare" psychology of 1919. The worsening international situation, the Canadian spy case (involving atomic bomb secrets betrayed to the Soviets) which had ramifications in this country, and the anti-union feeling stimulated congressional investigations of an alleged Red network here and led to the strong possibility that legislation would be passed which might endanger civil liberties. The Communists themselves did little to improve the situation. By expelling their leader, Earl Browder, in 1945 they had thereby rejected his currently moderate policy of "bourgeois collaboration" as mere opportunism, and had turned to the latest international line proclaimed by the French Communist leader, Jacques Duclos, which called for an attack on "American imperialism" and the allegedly sinister conspiracies of "monopoly capitalism."

The most spectacular hunt for Communists was led by the House Committee on Un-American Activities headed by J. Parnell Thomas of New Jersey, the zealous successor of Martin Dies. Progressives were disturbed by the Committee's methods of conducting hearings into supposed Communist infiltration in Hollywood. The publicity frightened the motion-picture industry into discharging ten screen writers who had incurred contempt charges for refusing to answer questions about their political affiliations. Those involved regarded this as an invasion of their privacy, since they were not themselves on trial.

A *Fortune* poll of October, 1947, showed 64 per cent in favor of barring Communists from public positions or high labor posts. Possibly, as his friends suggested, to head off even worse congressional legislation, Truman issued an Executive Order on March 21, 1947, eliminating disloyal federal employees by a legal procedure intended to observe basic civil rights. However, as George Britt, managing editor of *Survey Graphic,* put it ten months afterwards, the program "loosed such a swarm of unrestricted intimidation, snooping, and tattling upon government employees as Washington perhaps never in all its days had seen before." Even such an event as the confirmation of David Lilienthal, head of T.V.A., as chairman of the United States Atomic Energy Commission afforded the Senate an exciting opportunity for Communist-hunting.

President Truman's chief contribution to civil liberties was his Committee on Civil Rights, which in October, 1947, issued sweeping recommendations that the Chief Executive embodied in large part in a message to Congress. The Truman Committee declared that "public excitement about 'Communists' has gone far beyond the dictates of the 'good judgment' and 'calmness' of which Holmes and Brandeis spoke. A state of near hysteria now threatens to inhibit the freedom of genuine democrats." The report assailed the prevailing discrimination against Negroes and Jews and called for a "new charter of human freedom." Pointing to the recurrent lynching cases, the Committee observed, "While a society permits private and arbitrary violence done to its members, its own integrity is inevitably corrupted." It called for a fair employment practices act to end discrimination in hiring by private concerns, federal anti-lynching laws, abolition of poll taxes and white primaries, exposure of "native Fascists" as well as Communists, removal of residential restrictions on grounds of race, and equal opportunities for education and health.

The President's recommendations to Congress stressed the political and economic disfranchisement of the Negro and employment discrimination between groups, rather than educational and residential restrictions. Poll taxes, white primaries, and lynching among other abuses were condemned and legislation was asked for. "We know the way," declared the President. "We need only the will." His surprisingly far-reaching program, which the *New Republic* asserted "would change the face of our democracy," unleashed a storm of protests in the South, where a number of organized groups threatened to block the nomination or election of the Democratic leader.

In civil liberties, the Supreme Court majority in 1945–1948 stood in large measure where the "great dissenters" like Holmes had been in 1919–1920. A series of cases in 1946 are particularly noteworthy. In Morgan *v.* Virginia, involving a Negro woman ejected from a Virginia-Maryland bus for not complying with the Jim Crow seating rules, the Court denied the state's police power over segregation in interstate commerce, criticizing this as a violation of the need for national uniformity. In Hannegan *v.* Esquire, which tested the power of the Postmaster General to revoke second-class mailing privileges for *Esquire* magazine on grounds of morals, the judges decided that the Postmaster had no power to prescribe standards for literature or art. Again, in Marsh *v.* Alabama, the arrest of allegedly fanatical members of the cult of Jehovah's Witnesses for distributing religious tracts was denounced as an abridgment of the freedom of religion and of the press. Other rulings on southern white primaries encouraged many hitherto-disfranchised Negroes to vote, even under unfavorable circumstances.

While these gains could not altogether refute charges of racialism from United Nations members, they represented considerable advance. On the debit side were the perennial southern filibusters in the Senate blocking anti-lynching and anti–poll tax laws—new bills were scheduled for 1948—and the defeat of the Fair Employment Practices Bill in 1945. In 1946, after a campaign based on white supremacy slogans, Mississippi reelected the reactionary Senator Theodore Bilbo and Georgia chose his counterpart for governor, Eugene Talmadge; but death eliminated both men and more tolerant officials succeeded them. A Georgia mob lynched four Negroes that year; most discouraging was the verdict of a South Carolina jury which acquitted 28 self-confessed lynchers in an exceptionally brutal affair. Once more newspapers carried accounts of the reviving Ku Klux Klan in their self-delegated campaign of intimidation for the protection of "white womanhood."

POLITICS IN AN ERA OF CONSERVATIVE REACTION

Truman's conflict with a conservative Congress during 1945–1948 had already been forecast in 1944 when Roosevelt sought vainly to introduce major New Deal legislation and found the Democrats divided. He failed to secure a "full employment" bill intended to prevent future depressions if possible, obtaining instead the limited bill for research granted in the Maximum Employment Act of 1946. Nor was he able to liberalize unemployment insurance benefits, except for minor changes. The Administration-sponsored Murray-Wagner-Dingell Bill which proposed to add health insurance to the social security system was rejected. Moving on a less ambitious scale, Congress passed the National Mental Health Act in 1946, which reflected the strong current interest in psychiatry and set up a National Institute for Mental Health to investigate and develop methods of preventing insanity. For this purpose, federal grants were made to the states. A National School Lunch Act removed some of the regional inequities as far as diet for school children is concerned, by extending federal grants-in-aid to help the states operate a non-profit school lunch program.

Very important from the standpoint of parliamentary efficiency was the Reorganization Act of 1946 which modernized Congress by reducing the numerous House standing committees from 48 to 19 and the Senate committees from 33 to 15. Registration of lobbyists, a step long regarded as desirable, became mandatory. Congressmen recognized the high cost of living by raising their salaries from $10,000 to $12,500, establishing a tax-free expense account of $2500, and providing themselves civil service retirement benefits. On the other hand, this Congress passed major European relief legislation and provisions for veterans' benefits.

In a brilliantly conducted campaign during 1946, the Republicans capitalized on the popular disgust with shortages and controls that marked mid-1946 before the full effects of price decontrol had been felt. Anti-strike feeling and fears of Communist leadership in the trade unions affected the vote. "Had enough? Vote Republican!" proved an effective slogan in winning a huge vote for Republican candidates. The G.O.P. won both houses for the first time in sixteen years, gaining 12 seats in the Senate and 56 in the House. Besides, it now held 25 governorships and control over 28 state legislatures. Rock-ribbed conservatives like Bricker of Ohio, candidate for the Senate, won impressive victories. Thomas Dewey in New York and Earl Warren in California were overwhelmingly reelected to the governorship, thus increasing their chances for the Presidency. New England, the Middle West, and the Northwest, particularly the rural areas, proved strongholds of Republican strength. Negroes, embittered by several flagrant cases of lynchings and brutalities in the Southeast, drifted away in substantial numbers from their alliance with the Democrats. Prosperous farm owners, now indifferent to New Deal farm programs, returned to their distrust of radical labor organizations. Alleged Communist penetration drove some religious groups out of the Democratic fold.

The Eightieth Congress, a Republican body, differed little from its Democratic predecessor and merely intensified the deadlock between the executive and legislative branches. On foreign affairs there appeared greater reluctance to follow Truman's leadership, but internationalists like Senator Arthur Vandenberg of Michigan and fears of Communism prevented any serious break in policy. The shade of Roosevelt affected Congressmen sufficiently so that they passed a constitutional amendment, for consideration by the states, limiting Presidents to two terms of office. Another constitutional change, inspired by the current situation, took the form of a statute rather than an amendment. This was the Presidential Succession Act of 1947, replacing the law of 1886. President Truman, who had risen from the Vice Presidency, felt that it was undemocratic for him to be succeeded under the prevailing law by his own appointees in the Cabinet beginning with the Secretary of State. He proposed that the elected Speaker of the House and after him the Senate President pro tempore succeed as acting President until a special presidential election could be arranged. Congress, apparently pleased by the proposal—though it ignored the separation of powers principle—adopted the suggestion but dropped the special election idea. The law called for the Speaker, the Senate President pro tempore, and after them the Cabinet members, in the usual order, to succeed to the Presidency whenever the President and Vice President both died or failed to qualify for office.

One major defeat for the Republican majority came in their 1947 program of tax reduction to which they had pledged themselves in the election. Some tax relief had already been afforded in the Revenue Act of 1945 which sought to aid reconversion by repealing excess corporate profits taxes and offering other retroactive concessions that reduced the tax liabilities of corporations by two billions. By restoring the $500 income tax exemption for each spouse and dependent, some twelve million persons had been relieved from paying taxes. Now in the 1946–1947 revenue bill, the Republicans attempted an "across the board" reduction in income tax of 10 to 30 per cent, an estimated four billions in tax relief. Truman rejected this bill as offering too little to the small taxpayer and too much to the large one. Besides, he argued that periods of high employment and national income should be used to help retire the huge national debt of $269,422,009,173. To do otherwise was to add to inflationary pressures. In April, 1948, Congress finally defeated the Administration overwhelmingly, raised exemptions and deductions generously, and offered a community property law which enabled wealthy couples among others to escape higher surtaxes.

The coming presidential election of 1948 colored much of the legislation and programs of this session. A *Fortune* poll of September, 1947, showed that only Thomas Dewey among the Republican candidates was managing to keep ahead of Truman but was losing ground, retaining 45 per cent to the President's 43 per cent. Most confusing for the political picture was Henry Wallace's announcement in January, 1948, that he would head a third party to protest the drift to war against Russia and to fight the bipartisan reaction that infected Congress. A Gallup Poll and a New York by-election revealed that he would draw heavily from Truman's strength, thus endangering the President's chances for reelection. However, both C.I.O. and A. F. of L. leaders repudiated the third-party movement; rather than tolerate a conservative Republican in the White House, even the Railroad Brotherhoods forgave the President for breaking their strike. Taft made no secret of his desire for the Republican nomination in 1948; nor did Harold Stassen, former governor of Minnesota, a moderate on labor issues and a decided internationalist. The most threatening contender for the Republican nomination, according to the Gallup Poll, was General Dwight Eisenhower, but he chose to make a forthright refusal to run and accepted the presidency of Columbia University. The Republicans were encouraged by another Gallup Poll in April, 1948, which indicated that Truman was slipping so rapidly that not only Dewey but Stassen, Vandenberg, and Douglas MacArthur were running ahead of the President. By this time, the southern revolt against the President's Civil Liberties program, the Wallace defection, and the Zionist resentment over the reversal of the Palestine partition plan made Truman's renomination seem far from an attractive prospect to many Democratic party leaders. But with so many variables in the political picture, the battle of 1948 seemed capable of many surprises, even some unforeseen by Dr. Gallup.

Epilogue

Despite two world wars and an extremely painful depression, the United States approached the mid-century mark stronger and richer than ever. Even the staggering national debt of some $258 billion in 1947 raised no serious doubts regarding stability. The citizen in McKinley's day patiently carried a per capita debt, newly enlarged by the Spanish-American War, of $16.60; but almost a half century later this had been multiplied a hundredfold. However, the federal income, which was then less than a half billion dollars, was now over $43¼ billion and the debt was being paid by a prosperous people with a national income of $178 billion and a per capita consumption of food, goods, and services that reached unprecedented heights. Frederick W. Taylor's dream of industrial and managerial efficiency was an amazing reality, as whole industries like the telephone business became nearly automatic in operation; even the individualistic farmer of tradition was witnessing the transformation of his farm into a factory where valuable industrial by-products as well as foods were produced; 3,000,000 tractors were in active use across the land. The specter of recurrent depressions might linger, but the means to combat them multiplied.

Without any notable accession of territory, 144 millions lived far more comfortably than did the 76 millions of Theodore Roosevelt's time. Even the long-term downward birth rate seemed at least temporarily to have reversed itself and the population growth curve was now expected to advance beyond the year 2000. Still, despite a current trend to somewhat larger families, the divorce rate shot upward from 0.7 per 1000 population in 1900 to 4.4 in 1946. Here was a disturbing factor in the picture of national stability. On the other hand, minority groups like the Negro shared in the general upward population increase and the decline of the mortality rate. If there was an Achilles heel in this situation, it lay in the second-class citizenship and limited economic opportunities for so many of the 12,865,518 Negroes, especially in the South, and the millions of white sharecroppers and tenant farmers whose income lagged sadly behind that of their fellow citizens in more favored sections. But more than ever there appeared a greater will to use the collective wisdom and resources of the nation to rectify such inequities.

Illiteracy, which averaged 10.7 per cent in 1900, had fallen to 4.3 in 1930 and continued downward thereafter. Over two million were attending college in 1946, and much larger enrollments were predicted within the next few years. However, World War II revealed grave weaknesses in social education among our veterans, despite their schooling, particularly on questions relating to democratic ideas, reflecting the void left in the classroom by educators' fears of indoctrination. Progress in science and literature was attested in the growing monopoly of Nobel prizes held by Americans. During 1901–1918, Michelson had won the prize in physics, the French-born scientist Carrel held it for medicine and physiology, and Theodore Roosevelt and Elihu Root received awards for contributions to peace. Since then, thirty-three have been honored with the Nobel Prize and distinguished foreign recipients like Einstein, Thomas Mann, and Enrico Fermi have made their homes here.

Pragmatism, secularism, and an optimistic faith in progress, though in a far less naïve form than in 1900, still seemed to dominate the American mind. However, disturbing doubts were raised by the dawning atomic age with its suicidal as well as beneficent potentialities. Catholic and Protestant churchmen decried the secular faith which had enshrined science as a philosophy as well as an instrument for the better life. Some, like the brilliant Reinhold Niebuhr, reverted to long-dormant theological doctrines of original sin and divine wrath. Hundreds of thousands of converts joined evangelical cults, particularly the new "holy" cults such as the Assemblies of God and Jehovah's Witnesses. The social gospel of a kingdom of righteousness on earth had spent some of its youthful enthusiasm, but its objectives seemed more fully accepted than in 1900; critics remained who feared its challenge to the purely spiritual mission of the church.

The historic and adventurous belief in inevitable progress had been whittled down since 1900 by a realistic drive for genuine social security forecast, it is true, by the Progressive movement of Theodore Roosevelt and Woodrow Wilson. Federal and state laws, catching up finally with the best practices of progressive European countries, had built around the citizen a protective rampart of old age and unemployment insurance, minimum wage and maximum hour guarantees, effective workmen's compensation laws, and industrial safety measures. These were not likely to be surrendered even under partisan attacks. Unions, which had grown from the three million members of Gompers' day to more than fourteen million, brought the security of written labor contracts and better conditions to millions under federally protected processes of collective bargaining. Security was underwritten in scores of ways by an increasingly powerful central government—state and local governments also grew in economic functions—capable not only of waging total war but of protecting citizens in their daily life. Regulatory agencies scarcely dreamed of in 1900 protected the consumer from impure foods and drugs, fraudulent investments, and unfair trade practices. Small bank depositors were insured, homebuilders were secured against certain unnecessary losses, farmers enjoyed a long list of benefits—from higher "parity" prices to generous credit terms—and low-income groups received subsidies in the form of school lunches at cost or cheaper electric power as in the area of the Tennessee Valley Authority. In addition, the New Deal had set an undeniable precedent for the future, that in any major depression the forces of government would be thrown in heavily to reduce the impact of suffering, rather than awaiting the uncertain results of private charities. Yet the search for security, which some believed would lead to stagnation, did not seem to reveal any real decline in self-reliance or dynamic leadership.

While the old Progressive war against economic monopoly continued to win only specious victories against the steadily mounting force of industrial and financial concentration, none could prove that the nation was bound helplessly in the meshes of "monopoly capitalism." The majority, informed or uninformed, continued to rule through the ballot box. If Congress seemed at times distressingly conservative or "reactionary," its decisions bore too frequently an undeniable likeness to those of the voice of the people as revealed in the carefully prepared public opinion polls as well as in the ballots. If the results were not always commendable, what was at fault was not popular consultation but the failure of conflicting interest groups, restless in any free society, to achieve a just equilibrium. Only the confused and the cynical would seek alternatives in the examples of totalitarianism so recently exposed at Nuremberg or in the czarist-bred Soviet absolutism that ruled 200,000,000 people. Political democracy since 1900 had probably gained only a minor skirmish in the progressive victory for such direct democracy devices as the initiative, the referendum, the recall, and the primary. More undoubtedly had been won through the ideal of the expert in government as embodied in an expanding merit system, the city-manager plan, and the specialized knowledge of governmental commissions of inquiry and research. Still more had been achieved in the broadening of political democracy into a more responsive social democracy, leaving behind the old nineteenth-century liberal concept of the weak state capable indeed of dealing with aggression but limited to the task of observing that the rules needed to maintain an allegedly self-correcting economic system were obeyed.

As the mid-century year moved closer, regional wars and rumors of war filled the air, as after World War I, while some Americans congratulated themselves that none outside of this country seemed capable of embarking upon a global war. Both parties seemed far more aware of the leadership this nation must exercise in foreign affairs than did the Lodges and the Coolidges in their day. America had moved from the fringes of the world stage to its very center within a half century. Americans, like other peoples, dreamed of making the U.N. the instrument of world fellowship; they had long learned the vanity of conquest by arms alone and of endless empire where the sun never set. Since 1900, a far wealthier, a more powerful, and a spiritually more chastened nation had emerged. Despite certain surviving injustices and narrow concepts of interest, no nation had ever been so well equipped in so many ways to face problems even of the magnitude of those confronting the mid-twentieth century.

Bibliography

1. THE PROMISE OF AMERICAN LIFE: 1900–1917

Invaluable for twentieth-century social and economic developments is the Report of the President's Research Committee on Social Trends, *Recent Social Trends in the United States* (one vol. ed., McGraw-Hill, 1933); especially noteworthy are the various sociological monographs growing out of these studies and referred to in the volume. In the newer historical mode, which stresses social and cultural history, Harold U. Faulkner interprets an era in *The Quest for Social Justice, 1898–1914* (A History of American Life Series, A. M. Schlesinger and D. R. Fox [eds.], Vol. XI, Macmillan, 1931). Along similar lines, with additional chapters on political events, is the noteworthy though briefer synthesis in the second volume of Charles and Mary Beard, *The Rise of American Civilization* (2 vols., Macmillan, 1927). Most fascinating in visualizing a changing America is the popular historical series by Mark Sullivan, *Our Times: The United States, 1900–1925* (Scribner, 1926–35), especially the first three volumes.

Among the excellent general economic histories are Harold U. Faulkner, *American Economic History* (Harper, 5th ed., 1943); Edward E. Kirkland, *History of American Economic Life* (Crofts, 1932); and Fred A. Shannon, *America's Economic Growth* (Macmillan, 1940). Particularly useful for the special topics discussed in this chapter are Ellwood P. Cubberley, *Public Education in the United States* (Houghton Mifflin, 1934); Arthur W. Calhoun, *A Social History of the American Family from Colonial Times to the Present* (3 vols., Clark, Cleveland, 1917–19); and G. M. Stephenson, *A History of American Immigration, 1820–1924* (Ginn, 1926). The "classics" of the settlement movement are Jane Addams, *Twenty Years at Hull House* (Macmillan, 1923), and Lillian D. Wald, *The House on Henry Street* (Holt, 1925). Other special topics in social history are discussed in Selig Perlman and Philip Taft, *Labor Movements* (Vol. IV of the series *History of Labor in the United States, 1896–1932*, Macmillan, 1935), an outstanding book; Don D. Lescohier and Elizabeth Brandeis, *Working Conditions, Labor Legislation* (*ibid.*, Vol. III), an extremely valuable analysis; Charles H. Wesley, *Negro Labor in the United States, 1850–1925* (Vanguard, 1927); Paul H. Douglas, *Real Wages in the United States, 1890–1926* (Houghton Mifflin, 1930), the standard work on the subject; W. G. Bleyer, *Main Currents in the History of American Journalism* (Houghton Mifflin, 1927); R. B. Weaver, *Amusements and Sports in American Life* (University of Chicago Press, 1939); Arthur Hornblow, *A History of the Theatre in America from Its Begin-*

nings to the Present Time (2 vols., Lippincott, 1919); Lewis Jacobs, *The Rise of the American Film* (Harcourt, Brace, 1939); William W. Sweet, *The Story of Religions in America* (Harper, 1931); and Charles H. Hopkins, *The Rise of the Social Gospel in American Protestantism, 1865–1915* (Yale University Press, 1940).

2. THE PRAGMATIC SPIRIT IN AMERICAN THOUGHT: 1900–1917

Representative works of exceptional merit in each field are frequently indicated in the chapter itself. The pragmatic theme is best understood through Ralph Barton Perry's Pulitzer Prize winner, *The Thought and Character of William James* (2 vols., Little, Brown, 1935). For short but scholarly biographic sketches of most of the individuals discussed, see the appropriate articles in Allen Johnson and Dumas Malone (eds.), *Dictionary of American Biography* (20 vols. and index, Scribner, 1928–37). Similarly, brief but sound treatments of intellectual themes can usually be found in the *Encyclopædia of the Social Sciences* (15 vols., Macmillan, 1930–35). Fundamental for the pragmatic idea in philosophy and education are Paul A. Schillp (ed.), *The Philosophy of John Dewey* (Vol. I of *The Library of Living Philosophers,* Northwestern University Press, 1939), and the excellent final chapters in Merle Curti's *The Social Ideas of American Educators* (Scribner, 1935). Curti's more recent *The Growth of American Thought* (Harper, 1943) is a valuable handbook on the entire intellectual history of the United States. This may be supplemented by Charles and Mary Beard, *The American Spirit* (Macmillan, 1942).

The ideas of many of the social scientists mentioned in this chapter are carefully presented in Ralph H. Gabriel, *The Course of American Democratic Thought* (Ronald, 1940). Albion W. Small summarizes the genesis of American sociology in "Fifty Years of Sociology in the United States," *American Journal of Sociology,* XXI (1915–1916), 721–864. A hitherto overlooked source of sociology in the United States is discussed for the pre-1900 period in Harvey Wish, "George Frederick Holmes and the Genesis of American Sociology," *ibid.,* XLVI (1941), 698–707. Very informative for the various social sciences are Howard Odum (ed.), *American Masters of Social Science* (Holt, 1927); Michael Kraus, *A History of American History* (Farrar & Rinehart, 1937); Lewis H. Haney, *History of Economic Thought* (Macmillan, 1936); and Joseph Dorfman, *Thorstein Veblen and His America* (Viking, 1934), a brilliant interpretive and factual account of Veblen and of the social-economic conditions which explain his economics. The influential legal philosophy of Louis D. Brandeis can be studied in his important *Other People's Money* (National Home Library Foundation, Washington, D. C.,1933), and in *The Curse of Bigness* (O. K. Fraenkel (ed.), Viking, 1934), a series of essays and court decisions. A good case study of Brandeis' democratic methods—in this instance his application of the Massachusetts mutual insurance idea—appears in Alpheus T. Mason's *The Brandeis Way* (Princeton University Press, 1938).

Literary trends for the prewar period are evaluated in Alfred Kazin, *On Native Grounds* (Reynal & Hitchcock, 1942), an exceptionally keen survey; Oscar Cargill, *Intellectual America: The March of Ideas* (Macmillan, 1941), which presents the schools and strands of literary traditions in a penetrating study; F. L. Pattee's suggestive *The New American Literature, 1890–1930* (Appleton-Century, 1930; Van Wyck Brooks, *New England: Indian Summer, 1865–1915* (Dutton, 1940), an important work; and A. H. Quinn, *A History of American Drama from the Civil War to the Present Day* (2 vols., Harper, 1927). Every reader should acquaint himself with the pioneer literary-intellectual history by Vernon L. Parrington, *Main Currents in American Thought: An Interpretation of American Literature from the Beginnings to 1920* (3 vols. in one, Harcourt, Brace, 1930).

The trends of American art are discussed in S. Isham (and Royal Corlissoz), *History of American Painting* (Macmillan, 1936); Lorado Taft, *The History of American Sculpture* (Macmillan, 1931); and T. E. Tallmadge, *The Story of Architecture in America* (Norton, 1929). In architecture there is Frank Lloyd Wright's significant *Autobiography* (Longmans, Green, 1932). Excellent background materials are given in David M. Robb and J. J. Garrison, *Art in the Western World* (Harper, rev. ed., 1942). John T. Howard is extremely informative in *Our American Music* (Crowell, 1939); and David Ewen's *Music Comes to America* (Crowell, 1942) is a good brief popular account.

The social aspects of science and invention are dealt with in *Recent Social Trends,* cited; Waldemar Kaempffert (ed.), *A Popular History of American Invention* (2 vols., Scribner, 1924); and Roger Burlingame, *Engines of Democracy: Inventions and Society in Mature America* (Scribner, 1940). Recent scientific advances are interestingly explained to laymen in Bernard Jaffe, *Outposts of Science* (Simon & Schuster, 1935); and in George W. Gray, *The Advancing Front of Science* (McGraw-Hill, 1937). Paul de Kruif has written several good biographic sketches of scientists of this period, especially of Walter Reed and Theobald Smith, in his popular *Hunger Fighters* (Harcourt, Brace, 1926).

3. "THE CURSE OF BIGNESS"—CHALLENGE TO BUSINESS LEADERSHIP: 1900–1913

For Brandeis, see the references on him in the Bibliography for Chapter 2. The best biography of Theodore Roosevelt is Henry F. Pringle, *Theodore Roosevelt* (Harcourt, Brace, 1931); also useful is the authorized work by Joseph B. Bishop, *Theodore Roosevelt and His Time* (Scribner, 1920); Harold Howland gives a good general account in *Theodore Roosevelt and His Times* (Yale University Press, 1921). Robert M. La Follette's *Autobiography* (*La Follette's Magazine*, Madison, 1913) is a prime source for early Progressivism. The biographic approach to big business and politics is well executed in Allan Nevins' excellent *John D. Rockefeller* (2 vols., Scribner, 1940); John T. Flynn, *God's Gold: The Story of Rockefeller and His Times* (Harcourt, Brace, 1932); F. L. Allen, *The Lords of Creation* (Harper, 1935); Matthew Josephson, *The Robber Barons: The Great American Capitalists, 1861–1901* (Harcourt, Brace, 1934) and his *The President Makers* (Harcourt, Brace, 1940); John Moody, *Masters of Capital* (Yale University Press, 1919); and N. W. Stephenson, *Nelson W. Aldrich* (Scribner, 1930).

Among the more important books on government and business during this era, especially in relation to trust busting and economic concentration, are W. Z. Ripley, *Trusts, Pools, and Corporations* (Ginn, 1916); C. R. Van Hise, *Concentration and Control* (Macmillan, 1914); A. A. Berle, Jr., and G. C. Means, *The Modern Corporation and Private Property* (Commerce Clearing House, Chicago, 1932), a classic on the process of economic concentration; Merle Fainsod and Lincoln Gordon, *Government and the American Economy* (Norton, 1941); and Slason Thompson, *Short History of American Railroads* (Appleton-Century, 1925). Mark Sullivan's *Our Times, III, Prewar America* (Scribner, 1930) gives a good popular account of the trust movement. The literature on the Standard Oil Company is critically appraised in Chester McA. Destler, "Wealth Against Commonwealth, 1894 and 1944," *The American Historical Review,* L (1944), 49–72.

4. ECHOES OF IMPERIALISM: 1900–1913

The creative role played by Elihu Root in our foreign policy before 1914 is thoroughly discussed in Philip C. Jessup's magnificent study, *Elihu Root* (2 vols., Dodd, Mead, 1938). New light on the foreign policy of McKinley and Roosevelt—the Far East in particular—is thrown by Tyler Dennett's interesting *John Hay* (Dodd, Mead, 1933). Henry F. Pringle has illuminated certain aspects of our foreign affairs during this period in his *Theodore Roosevelt,* already cited, and in *The Life and Times of William Howard Taft* (2 vols., Farrar & Rinehart, 1939). General works of value include Samuel F. Bemis's scholarly *A Diplomatic History of the United States* (Holt, 1936), and T. A. Bailey's fascinating textbook, *A Diplomatic History of the American People* (Crofts, 1942). Informative essays on foreign policies, written by specialists, appear in S. F. Bemis (ed.), *The American Secretaries of State and Their Diplomacy* (10 vols., Knopf, 1927–), of which Vol. IX covers this chapter.

The genesis of "dollar diplomacy" can be studied in Herbert D. Croly's *Willard Straight* (Macmillan, 1924), and in Pringle's book on Taft, cited above. T. A. Bailey challenges a popular notion regarding the election of 1900 in "Was the Presidential Election of 1900 a Mandate on Imperialism?" *Mississippi Valley Historical Review,* XXIV (1937–1938), 43–52. Another interesting side of this picture is dealt with in F. H. Harrington, "Literary Aspects of American Anti-Imperialism, 1898–1902," *New England Quarterly,* X (1937), 650–667. Imperialism, "dollar diplomacy," and, in particular, the strategic factors underlying the Monroe Doctrine are weighed by Dexter Perkins in *The Monroe Doctrine, 1867–1907* (Johns Hopkins Press, 1937). General readers, however, usually prefer his interesting synthesis of the subject in *Hands Off; A History of the Monroe Doctrine* (Little, Brown, 1941). Latin-American diplomatic problems are well discussed in Howard C. Hill, *Roosevelt and the Caribbean* (University of Chicago Press, 1927); Ernest H. Gruening's challenging study of Mexico's social and economic difficulties, *Mexico and Its Heritage* (Appleton-Century, 1928); and J. Fred Rippy, *The United States and Mexico* (Knopf, 1926). A severe but enlightening criticism of our older Caribbean policy is given in Leland H. Jenks, *Our Cuban Colony* (Vanguard, 1928).

An extremely useful single volume on the Far East is A. W. Griswold, *The Far Eastern Policy of the United States* (Harcourt, Brace, 1938). T. A. Bailey deals with an important and hitherto shrouded question in *Theodore Roosevelt and the Japanese-American Crises* (Stanford University Press, 1934). Tyler Dennett has found significant material in Roosevelt's private papers for his *Roosevelt and the Russo-Japanese War* (Doubleday, Doran, 1925). An optimistic view of Japanese-American relations is given by Payson J. Treat in *Japan and the United States, 1853–1921* (Houghton Mifflin, 1921). For the contemporary European scene, the general and biographic works already cited are useful; they should be supplemented by Allan Nevins, *Henry White, Thirty Years of American Diplomacy* (Harper, 1930); and W. D. Puleston, *Mahan* (Yale University Press, 1939). An important work is Cleona Lewis, *America's Stake in International Investments* (Brookings Institution, 1938).

5. THE PROGRESSIVE REVOLT: POLITICAL PHASE

In addition to the books already cited—notably those by Jessup, Pringle, Faulkner, the Beards, Brandeis, and La Follette—the most relevant for political Progressivism include Lincoln Steffens' *Autobiography* (Harcourt, Brace, 1931); *The Shame of the Cities* (McClure, Phillips, 1904); and *The Struggle for Self-Government* (McClure, Phillips, 1904), all written by the same author largely in a pessimistic vein. The interesting account by Louis Filler, *Crusaders for American Liberalism* (Harcourt,

Brace, 1939) supplements the earlier standard books such as C. E. Regier, *The Era of the Muckrakers* (University of North Carolina Press, 1932); B. P. De Witt, *The Progressive Movement* (Macmillan, 1915); and F. E. Haynes, *Social Politics in the United States* (Houghton Mifflin, 1924). An informative autobiographic account of middlewestern Progressivism is given in Brand Whitlock, *Forty Years of It* (Appleton-Century, 1930), and in his more recent *Letters and Journals* (Allan Nevins [ed.], 2 vols., Appleton-Century, 1936). Other important firsthand accounts are Tom L. Johnson, *My Story* (Huebsch, 1911); John Chamberlain's disillusioned *Farewell to Reform* (Liveright, 1932); and Herbert Croly's *The Promise of American Life* (Macmillan, 1909), which influenced Theodore Roosevelt during the Bull Moose era.

Among recent studies of personalities of this period are Claude G. Bowers, *Beveridge and the Progressive Era* (Houghton Mifflin, 1932), an intimate picture; K. W. Hechler, *Insurgency: Personalities and Policies of the Taft Era* (Columbia University Press, 1940); and, somewhat earlier, H. F. Gosnell, *Boss Platt and His New York Machine* (University of Chicago Press, 1924). Harold L. Ickes criticizes George W. Perkins of the International Harvester Company in "Who Killed the Progressive Party?" *American Historical Review,* XLVI (1940–1941), 306–337. The origins of Progressivism as revealed in the career of an outstanding liberal are discussed by Harvey Wish in "Altgeld and the Progressive Tradition," *ibid.,* XLVI (1940–1941), 813–831. Histories of left-wing parties include *A History of Socialist Thought* (Crowell, 1927), by Harry W. Laidler, a Socialist leader in this country; and Nathan Fine's informative *Labor and Farmer Parties in the United States, 1828–1928* (Rand School, 1928). See also the Roosevelt biographies cited in the Bibliography for Chapter 3.

6. TOWARD THE NEW FREEDOM

The most definitive study on the life and times of Wilson is the yet incomplete work by Ray Stannard Baker, *Woodrow Wilson, Life and Letters* (6 vols., Doubleday, Doran, 1927–), the last two volumes of which deal with this period. J. P. Tumulty's *Woodrow Wilson as I Knew Him* (Garden City, 1925) is an intimate account by his private secretary. William E. Dodd offers a useful if laudatory biography in *Woodrow Wilson and His Work* (Peter Smith, New York, 1932). Extremely revealing and sometimes critical is *The Intimate Papers of Colonel House* (Charles Seymour [ed.], 4 vols., Houghton Mifflin, 1926–28). R. S. Baker and W. E. Dodd have edited *The Public Papers of Woodrow Wilson* (3 vols., Harper, 1927). Important domestic information on the early Wilsonian period as well as diplomatic observations appears in Burton J. Hendrick (ed.), *The Life and Letters of Walter H. Page* (3 vols., Houghton Mifflin, 1924–25). An excellent history of this period is F. L. Paxson, *Pre-War Years, 1913–1917* (Houghton Mifflin, 1936).

An interesting analysis of Wilson's personal and public motives in foreign affairs is given in Harley Notter, *The Origins of the Foreign Policy of Woodrow Wilson* (Johns Hopkins Press, 1937). Bryan's prewar role is carefully studied in Merle E. Curti, *Bryan and World Peace* (Smith College, 1931), and more briefly in Paxton Hibben, *The Peerless Leader* (Farrar & Rinehart, 1929). For other books on foreign affairs see the Bibliography for Chapter 4. References to World War I are cited in the Bibliography for Chapter 7.

7. THE PEACE CRUSADE: WORLD WAR NEUTRALITY

C. C. Tansill, *America Goes to War* (Little, Brown, 1938), is a highly detailed analysis of the period of neutrality which gives considerable weight to the economic and propagandist factors. It should be read in conjunction with Charles Seymour's *American Neutrality, 1914–1917* (Yale University Press, 1935), which defends Wilson's position against the extreme charges made by the Nye Committee, and with Alice M. Morrissey, *The American Defense of Neutral Rights, 1914–1917* (Harvard University Press, 1939). Indispensable background material is given in Sidney B. Fay, *Origins of the World War* (rev. ed., 2 vols., Macmillan, 1930), and B. E. Schmitt, *Coming of the War* (2 vols., Scribner, 1930). Recent additions to autobiographic information are J. von Bernstorff's *Memoirs* (Random House, 1936), the recollections of Germany's prewar Ambassador to the United States who was critical of his country's policy; and the defensive *War Memoirs* (Bobbs-Merrill, 1935) by Robert Lansing, Wilson's Secretary of State.

An interpretive picture of one of America's belligerent interventionists is presented by Russell Buchanan in "Theodore Roosevelt and American Neutrality," *American Historical Review,* XLIII (1938), 775–790. Horace C. Peterson stresses the role of British propaganda in *Propaganda for War, the Campaign Against American Neutrality, 1914–1917* (University of Oklahoma Press, 1937). Universally popular is Mark Sullivan's fourth volume of *Our Times, The War Begins* (Scribner, 1932). Other authors who deal with neutrality are Curti, Paxson, Dodd, Baker, House, Page, Notter, Tumulty, and Hibben, already cited in the preceding Bibliography.

8. "A PEOPLE'S WAR"

The war mobilization problem is dealt with in detail by B. Crowell and R. F. Wilson (eds.), *How America Went to War* (6 vols., Yale University Press, 1921); in Frederick Palmer's *Newton D. Baker: America at War* (2 vols., Dodd, Mead, 1931); and in Bernard M. Baruch, *American Industry in the War* (Prentice-Hall, 1941). F. L. Paxson's informative book, *America at War, 1917–1918* (Houghton Mifflin, 1939), supplements John B. McMaster, *The United States in the World War, 1918–1920* (2 vols., Appleton-Century, 1927). Mark Sullivan gives his usually vivid picture of the average citizen's role, this time during World War I, in the fifth volume of *Our Times, Over Here* (Scribner, 1933). A good reference volume for the military aspects is C. J. H. Hayes, *Brief History of the Great War* (Macmillan, 1920). Very useful for the diplomatic scene is Charles Seymour, *American Diplomacy During the World War* (Johns Hopkins Press, 1934).

Propaganda in wartime has been analyzed from rich archival materials in *Words That Won the War: Story of the Committee on Public Information* (Princeton University Press, 1940), a fascinating book on George Creel's Bureau by James R. Mock and Cedric Larson. The best study on the breakdown of civil liberties at home is Zechariah Chafee, Jr., *Free Speech in the United States* (Harvard University Press, 1941). An interesting introductory volume is Charles Seymour's *Woodrow Wilson and the World War* (Allen Johnson [ed.],*The Chronicles of America Series,* vol. XLVIII, Yale University Press, 1918–21).

9. THE LOST PEACE

Among the documentary accounts of Wilson at the Peace Conference are David H. Miller, *The Drafting of the Covenant* (2 vols., Putnam, 1928); Ray S. Baker, *Woodrow Wilson and the World Settlement* (3 vols., Doubleday, Doran, 1922); and the papers of Colonel House previously cited. Excellent firsthand interpretations include James T. Shotwell, *At the Paris Peace Conference* (Macmillan, 1937), a diary; Harold Nicholson, *Peacemaking: 1919* (Harcourt, Brace, 1939); Oswald G. Villard, *Fighting Years, Memoirs of a Liberal Editor* (Harcourt, Brace, 1939); and Tumulty's work already cited. Relevant chapters appear in Arthur D. W. Smith, *Mr. House of Texas* (Funk & Wagnalls, 1940); in George C. Osborn, *John Sharp Williams, Planter-Statesman of the Deep South* (Louisiana State University Press, 1943); and, among the books already cited, in Philip Jessup's *Elihu Root,* Henry Pringle's *The Life and Times of William Howard Taft* (Vol. II), Charles Seymour's *Woodrow Wilson and the World War,* and the diplomatic histories by S. F. Bemis and Thomas A. Bailey. A recent analysis, friendly to Wilson's adherents, is Clarence A. Berdahl, "Myths About the Peace Treaties of 1919–1920," *The American Scholar,* XI (1942), 261–274. Critical of Wilson's "blunders" as a statesman and parliamentarian is Thomas Bailey's *Woodrow Wilson and the Lost Peace* (Macmillan, 1944).

10. DEMOBILIZATION AND THE RED HUNT

The transition from war to peace is discussed in J. R. Mock and E. Thurber, *Report on Demobilization* (University of Oklahoma Press,

1944), and F. L. Paxson, "The Great Demobilization," *American Historical Review,* XLIV (1938), 237–251. Postwar trends are thoughtfully analyzed in J. C. Malin, *The United States After the World War* (Ginn, 1930); this is based on original sources. F. L. Allen's best-seller, *Only Yesterday* (Harper, 1931), is a highly useful as well as entertaining picture of the 1920's; the same is true of Mark Sullivan's *Our Times, VI, The Twenties* (Scribner, 1935).

Among the most informative accounts of postwar labor and radicalism are Selig Perlman and Philip Taft, *History of Labor in the United States, 1896–1932: Labor Movements,* already cited; W. Z. Foster, *The Great Steel Strike and Its Lessons* (Viking, 1920); J. S. Gambs, *The Decline of the I.W.W.* (Columbia University Press, 1932); and Felix Frankfurter, *The Case of Sacco and Vanzetti* (Little, Brown, 1927). Covering the same topic of labor radicalism and social reaction are the firsthand account in the early chapters of Eugene Lyons, *Assignment in Utopia* (Harcourt, Brace, 1937), and J. M. Mecklin, *The Ku Klux Klan: A Study of the American Mind* (Harcourt, Brace, 1924). For another aspect of popular psychology, see Bessie L. Pierce, *Public Opinion and the Teaching of History in the United States* (Knopf, 1926). One of the most important books on the postwar as well as the wartime decline of civil liberties is Zechariah Chafee, Jr., *Free Speech in the United States* (Harvard University Press, 1941).

11. THE TWENTIES: TRIUMPH OF MATURE CAPITALISM

Perhaps the most informative social history of the 1920's is Preston W. Slosson, *The Great Crusade and After: 1914–1928* (in A. M. Schlesinger and D. R. Fox [eds.], A History of American Life Series, Macmillan, 1931). Louis M. Hacker gives an excellent historical survey in *American Problems of Today: A History of the United States Since the World War* (Crofts, 1938). Indispensable is the sociological analysis of the decade in *Recent Social Trends,* already cited. R. S. and Helen M. Lynd describe an average American city of the 1920's in the sociological classic, *Middletown: A Study in Contemporary American Culture* (Harcourt, Brace, 1929). Among the books previously cited, relevant social and economic material appears in J. C. Malin, *The United States After the World War;* the sixth volume of Mark Sullivan's *Our Times;* F. L. Allen's *Only Yesterday;* F. A. Shannon's *America's Economic Growth;* and the Beards' *Rise of American Civilization,* Vol. II.

Some contemporary evaluations of the social and economic scene during the 1920's are given in Kirby Page (ed.), *Recent Gains in American Civilization* (Harcourt, Brace, 1928); André Siegfried, *America Comes of Age* (Harcourt, Brace, 1927); and Harold E. Stearns (ed.), *Civilization in the*

United States: An Inquiry by Thirty Americans (Harcourt, Brace, 1922). For labor, consult the valuable work by Selig Perlman and Philip Taft, *Labor Movements* and Don D. Lescohier and Elizabeth Brandeis, *Working Conditions, Labor Legislation,* both already cited; and L. L. Lorwin and J. A. Flexner, *The American Federation of Labor* (Brookings Institution, 1933). The political structure of the time, with considerable attention to corruption, is analyzed in Peter Odegard, *Pressure Politics: The Story of the Anti-Saloon League* (Columbia University Press, 1928); Frank R. Kent, *The Great Game of Politics* (Doubleday, Doran, 1928); Lloyd Lewis and H. J. Smith, *Chicago: The History of Its Reputation* (Harcourt, Brace, 1929); Carroll H. Wooddy, *The Case of Frank L. Smith* (University of Chicago Press, 1931); and M. R. Werner, *Tammany Hall* (Doubleday, Doran, 1928). Among the newer books, special attention is due Thomas C. Cochran and William Miller, *The Age of Enterprise: A Social History of Industrial America* (Macmillan, 1942); and Allan Nevins and Louis M. Hacker (eds.), *The United States and Its Place in World Affairs, 1918–1943* (Heath, 1943).

12. THE TWENTIES: CULT OF INDIVIDUALISM

This chapter itself is in part a bibliographic guide, to which should be added the relevant books listed for Chapters 2 and 11. Excellent summaries of current intellectual trends appear in the *American Year Book* (Doubleday, Doran, 1910–) and *The New International Year Book* (Dodd, Mead; especially 1920–30). Among the useful symposiums not cited previously which deal with cultural developments are Charles A. Beard (ed.), *Whither Mankind?* (Longmans, Green, 1928), and S. S. Schmalhausen (ed.), *Behold America!* (Farrar & Rinehart, 1931). For special topics in the history of the various social studies, see the *Encyclopædia of the Social Sciences* (E. R. A. Seligman and A. Johnson [eds.], Macmillan, 1930–35). The literary trends are discussed in Malcolm Cowley (ed.), *After the Genteel Tradition* (Norton, 1936), which contains some excellent critical essays; Bernard Smith, *Forces in American Criticism* (Harcourt, Brace, 1939); Arthur H. Quinn, *American Fiction* (Appleton-Century, 1936), very informative as to specific books and authors; V. F. Calverton, *Liberation of American Literature* (Scribner, 1932), a semi-Marxian interpretation stressing a sociological approach; Fred L. Pattee, *The New American Literature* (Appleton-Century, 1930). Merle Curti's comprehensive *The Growth of American Thought,* cited, is useful throughout this chapter.

For science and other aspects of learning and the arts, see the Bibliography for Chapter 2, especially the works of Burlingame, Jaffe, Gray, and *Recent Social Trends* in science; to this should be added Richard Goldschmidt, *Ascaris: The Biologist's Story of Life* (Prentice-Hall, 1937). In music, see John T. Howard; in the arts, Isham, Taft, Tallmadge, and

Keppel; and in the social studies, Barnes, Haney, Curti, Odum, Schilpp, and the *Encyclopædia of the Social Sciences.* See also Caroline Ware's sociological interpretation of an important urban phenomenon, *Greenwich Village, 1920–1930* (Houghton Mifflin, 1935); Joseph W. Krutch, *The Modern Temper* (Harcourt, Brace, 1929), a literary critic's analysis of the period; Ralph Borsodi, *This Ugly Civilization* (Harper, 1929), an attack on this mechanistic age; and Lewis Mumford's important *Technics and Civilization* (Harcourt, Brace, 1934).

13. THE POLITICS OF BUSINESS LEADERSHIP: 1921–1929

Of the leading personalities of this decade, a critical biography of Harding appears in Samuel Hopkins Adams' popular book, *The Incredible Era* (Houghton Mifflin, 1939). Coolidge is thoughtfully examined in William Allen White, *A Puritan in Babylon* (Macmillan, 1938); more authorized in flavor but nevertheless useful is Claude M. Fuess, *Calvin Coolidge* (Little, Brown, 1940). Two good biographies of George W. Norris are available: Richard L. Neuberger and Stephen B. Kahn, *Integrity, the Life Story of George W. Norris* (Vanguard, 1937); and Alfred Lief, *Democracy's Norris* (Stackpole Sons, 1939). Pertinent studies of contemporary politics appear in Carroll H. Wooddy, *The Case of Frank L. Smith* (University of Chicago Press, 1931), a scientific political analysis of the corrupt alliance between business and politics during the 1920's; Wayne Williams, *William Jennings Bryan* (Putnam, 1936); Henry F. Pringle, *Alfred E. Smith, A Critical Study* (Macy-Masius, 1937); M. R. Werner, *Tammany Hall,* cited. The most useful account of the Teapot Dome scandals and the "Ohio Gang" is given in Mark Sullivan, *Our Times, VI, The Twenties.*

Good general discussions of this period appear in the political works already cited, especially James C. Malin, *The United States After the World War;* Charles and Mary Beard, *The Rise of American Civilization,* Vol. II; Preston Slosson, *The Great Crusade and After;* and Louis Hacker, *American Problems of Today.*

14. RETREAT TOWARD ISOLATIONISM: 1921–1929

Valuable among contemporary discussions of diplomatic history are Charles P. Howland (ed.), *Survey of American Foreign Relations* (Council on Foreign Relations, Yale University Press, 1928–); Foreign Policy Association, *Pamphlet Series* (New York, 1928); *International Conciliation* (Carnegie Endowment for International Peace, New York; particularly 1920–29), a monthly series of pamphlets largely on problems of international organizations; and the World Peace Foundation studies.

Among the leading volumes on American diplomacy during the 1920's are D. F. Fleming, *The United States and World Organization, 1920–1933*

(Columbia University Press, 1938); M. E. Curti, *Peace or War* (Norton, 1936), a history of the American peace movement; B. H. Williams, *Economic Foreign Policy of the United States* (McGraw-Hill, 1929), and his textbook, *American Diplomacy* (McGraw-Hill, 1936); Louis Fischer, *Why Recognize Russia?* (Ballou, 1931), an argument for recognition. A particularly comprehensive and scholarly work on Russo-American relations is Frederick L. Schuman, *American Policy Toward Russia Since 1917* (International Publishers, 1928). Polish-American relations during the twenties are discussed in H. H. Fisher, *America and the New Poland* (Macmillan, 1928). Isaac J. Cox, *Nicaragua and the United States* (World Peace Foundation, 1927, is a splendid synthesis by an expert who has considerable firsthand experience. Extremely interesting, informative, and up-to-date is Edgar W. McInnis, *The Unguarded Frontier: A History of American-Canadian Relations* (Doubleday, Doran, 1942).

A biographic approach to postwar diplomacy is provided in such books as Harold Nicolson, *Dwight Morrow* (Harcourt, Brace, 1935), the story of the influential financier and diplomat who was praised for his conciliatory diplomacy in Mexico. David Bryn-Jones, *Frank B. Kellogg* (Putnam, 1937), is a sympathetic study of Coolidge's Secretary of State by a professor of international relations. For further references, see the Bibliography for Chapters 4, 6, and 9; the titles cited for Bemis, Bailey, Jessup, Gruening, Jenks, Perkins, and Mark Sullivan are especially pertinent.

15. HOOVER AND THE GREAT DEPRESSION

Hoover's course during the depression is shrewdly defended in William S. Myers and Walter H. Newton, *The Hoover Administration: A Documented Narrative* (Scribner, 1936), and in Ray L. Wilbur and Arthur M. Hyde, *The Hoover Policies* (Scribner, 1937). W. S. Myers has also written *The Foreign Policies of Herbert Hoover, 1929–1933* (Scribner, 1940), and has edited *The State Papers and Other Public Writings of Herbert Hoover* (2 vols., Scribner, 1934). These books offer an interesting contrast to most contemporary accounts, especially those written during 1931–1933, which criticize Hoover's administration.

Much historical and analytical material on the relation between government and business is well integrated in Merle Fainsod and Lincoln Gordon, *Government and the American Economy* (Norton, 1941). A Socialist's view of labor conditions during the early 1930's is given by Norman Thomas, *Human Exploitation in the United States* (Stokes, 1934). Annual events are summarized in the *American Year Book,* cited, and the *World Almanac* (New York *World Telegram,* 1929–32). The domestic and diplomatic aspects of the depression are viewed critically in Charles and Mary Beard, *America in Midpassage* (Macmillan, 1939). Hoover's final year is briefly discussed in the early chapters of Raymond Moley, *After*

Seven Years (Harper, 1939). Vividly written and informative is Frederick Allen, *Since Yesterday: The Nineteen-Thirties in America* (Harper, 1940). Domestic and foreign problems of the period, as discussed in the influential editorials of the New York *Herald Tribune*, are presented in Walter Lippmann, *Interpretations, 1931–1932* (Allan Nevins [ed.], Macmillan, 1932). An intimate picture of Anglo-American relations and of certain aspects of our European policy during the Hoover administration is given in Charles G. Dawes, *Journal as Ambassador to Great Britain* (Macmillan, 1939).

16. THE NEW DEAL REVOLUTION: COLLAPSE OF BUSINESS LEADERSHIP: 1933–1936

A source of exceptional value for the New Deal is Samuel I. Rosenman (ed.), *The Public Papers and Addresses of Franklin D. Roosevelt* (9 vols., Random House, 1938–), which contains revealing notes and comments by the President, in addition to the documents themselves. Raymond Moley, *After Seven Years,* cited, covers the early New Deal from a critical and sometimes unfriendly point of view but contains valuable firsthand information. Among the best general analyses of Roosevelt's first term are Ernest K. Lindley, *The Roosevelt Revolution* (Viking, 1933), and his *Halfway with Roosevelt* (Viking, 1937); Frederick Allen, *Since Yesterday,* cited; Editors of the *Economist, The New Deal: An Analysis and Appraisal* (Knopf, 1937), an excellent brief synthesis; L. S. Lyon, *et al., The National Recovery Administration* (Brookings Institution, 1935); and Arthur M. Schlesinger, *The New Deal in Action, 1933–1939* (Macmillan, 1940).

In addition to Moley's book, there are innumerable firsthand accounts by members of the inner group of the New Deal, such as Henry A. Wallace, *New Frontiers* (Reynal & Hitchcock, 1934; Harold L. Ickes, *Back to Work: The Story of PWA* (Macmillan, 1935); Hugh S. Johnson, *The Blue Eagle from Egg to Earth* (Doubleday, Doran, 1935); Franklin D. Roosevelt, *On Our Way* (Day, 1934); and James A. Farley, *Behind the Ballots, the Personal History of a Politician* (Harcourt, Brace, 1938). An excellent series of biographic essays of early New Dealers written by political experts appears in J. T. Salter (ed.), *The American Politician* (University of North Carolina Press, 1938); it includes Fiorello La Guardia, Paul V. McNutt, George Norris, Robert Wagner, Robert La Follette, Jr., Maury Maverick, John L. Lewis, James Farley, and critics of the New Deal like Arthur Vandenberg, Millard Tydings, and Norman Thomas. A left-wing criticism of liberal reform is given in Lewis Corey, *The Decline of American Capitalism* (Covici, Friede, 1934). A leading journalist assails the New Deal in Frank R. Kent, *Without Grease* (Morrow, 1936). Especially worth while are the selected New York *Herald*

Tribune editorials in Walter Lippmann, *Interpretations, 1933–1935,* cited. Sympathetic to New Deal objectives is the informative journalistic account of Marquis W. Childs, *I Write from Washington* (Harper, 1942).

17. BROADENING THE NEW DEAL: 1936–1941

The best source is Judge Rosenman's *The Public Papers and Addresses of Franklin Delano Roosevelt,* cited. The Supreme Court struggle in 1937 gave rise to a voluminous literature of which the more useful books are R. H. Jackson, *The Struggle for Judicial Supremacy* (Knopf, 1941); Henry A. Wallace, *Whose Constitution?* (Reynal & Hitchcock, 1936); Edward S. Corwin, *Court over Constitution* (Princeton University Press, 1938); Erik M. Eriksson, *The Supreme Court and the New Deal* (Lymanhouse, Los Angeles, 1941); and F. L. Allen, *Since Yesterday,* cited. Public opinion on leading questions of the day is gauged in George H. Gallup and Saul F. Rae, *The Pulse of Democracy: The Public Opinion Poll and How it Works* (Simon & Schuster, 1940). A good review of recent New Deal legislation is included in Merle Fainsod and Lincoln Gordon, *Government and the American Economy,* cited.

Among the leading criticisms of the New Deal are Wendell Willkie, *This is Wendell Willkie* (Dodd, Mead, 1940); and Herbert Hoover, *Addresses upon the American Road, 1933–1938* (Scribner, 1938), and *Further Addresses upon the American Road* (Scribner, 1940).

18. THE THIRTIES: AN ERA OF SOCIAL PLANNING

The special issue of the *American Journal of Sociology* for May, 1942, "Recent Social Trends," has been invaluable in the preparation of this chapter. It does for the 1930's what the famous two-volume work of the same title does for 1900–1930, and contains noteworthy articles by W. F. Ogburn, C. S. Johnson, P. M. Hauser, Louis Wirth, H. Hart, C. H. Judd, G. C. Means, and other recognized specialists in the various fields. A case study of an American city is given in Robert and Helen Lynd, *Middletown in Transition* (Harcourt, Brace, 1937); this should be compared with their earlier book, *Middletown* (Harcourt, Brace, 1929). Excellent essays on the social and cultural scene appear in Harold E. Stearns (ed.), *America Now* (Scribner, 1938). Appropriate articles are available in the American *Year Book,* the *New International Year Book,* the various *Fortune* surveys, the *Survey Graphic,* the *New Republic,* and *The Nation.*

In *America in Midpassage,* cited, Charles and Mary Beard present pertinent articles on labor, business, the movies, and other social and economic institutions; F. L. Allen, *Since Yesterday,* cited, is also valuable. Among the books dealing with labor are R. R. Brooks, *When Labor Organizes* (Yale University Press, 1938), and his *Unions of Their Own Choosing* (Yale University Press, 1939), the latter a discussion of labor under the Wagner Act. The extremely informative *C.I.O., Industrial Unionism in Action* (Norton, 1937) is written by J. R. Walsh, a former Harvard professor who is sympathetic to labor. Louis Adamic, *My America, 1928–1938* (Harper, 1938), is militantly pro-labor. On the Negro worker, see Horace R. Cayton and G. S. Mitchell, *Black Workers and the New Unions* (University of North Carolina Press, 1939). Important reactionary currents in the American scene are presented in Alfred M. and Elizabeth B. Lee, *The Fine Art of Propaganda: A Study of Father Coughlin's Speeches* (Harcourt, Brace, 1939).

19. THE SECURITY IDEAL OF THE THIRTIES

This chapter is in itself an annotated bibliography and can be supplemented by the relevant books cited in the Bibliography for Chapter 2. Especially useful are the Beards' *America in Midpassage;* Curti's *The Growth of American Thought* and *The Social Ideas of American Educators;* H. E. Barnes, H. Becker, and F. B. Becker, *Contemporary Social Theory* (Appleton-Century, 1940); Harold Stearns, *America Now;* Oscar Cargill, *Intellectual America;* Alfred Kazin, *On Native Grounds,* which deals with the literature of the decade; Halford E. Luccock, *American Mirror* (Macmillan, 1940), a penetrating sociological interpretation of the literature of the 1930's. *The New International Year Book* series and the *American Year Book* series are also valuable.

Other writings of value on the social sciences are Max Lerner, *Ideas Are Weapons* (Viking, 1939), a collection of his excellent essays on political theory, literature, economics, constitutional history, etc.; Simeon Strunsky, *The Living Tradition: Change and America* (Doubleday, Doran, 1939), a thoughtful cultural interpretation of the 1930's; and J. M. Clark, "Past Accomplishments and Present Prospects of American Economics," *American Economic Review,* XXXVI (1936), 1–11, a significant presidential address; Horace G. White, Jr., "A Review of Monopolistic and Imperfect Competition Theories," *ibid.,* 637–649. The humanist revolt in education, especially at the University of Chicago, is made clear in Robert M. Hutchins, *The Higher Learning in America* (Yale University Press, 1936), and in John U. Nef, *The United States and Civilization* (University of Chicago Press, 1942).

The reader will find interesting surveys on music of the period in John T. Howard, *Our American Music,* cited; in David Ewen's briefer popular account, *Music Comes to America,* also cited; and in the Stearns symposium, cited. The relevant books on science for the layman include Bernard Jaffe, *Outposts of Science,* cited; George W. Gray, *The Advancing Front of Science* (McGraw-Hill, 1937); Richard Goldschmidt, *Ascaris: The Biologist's Story of Life* (Prentice-Hall, 1937); and Arthur K. Solomon, *Why Smash Atoms?* (Harvard University Press, 1940).

20. THE GOOD NEIGHBOR, COLLECTIVE SECURITY, AND WORLD ANARCHY

In addition to the Roosevelt papers, documentary materials are presented in S. S. Jones and D. P. Meyers (eds.), *Documents on American Foreign Relations, 1938–1940* (2 vols., World Peace Foundation, 1939–), and the United States Department of State, *Press Releases* (20 vols., 1929–). A useful one-volume collection is Wilfred Funk (ed.) *Roosevelt's Foreign Policy, 1933–1941* (Wilfred Funk, Inc., 1942). The *Foreign Policy Reports,* issued by the Foreign Policy Association and usually prepared by experts, offer indispensable material for contemporary diplomacy. Equally important is the series, *The United States in World Affairs* (Harper, 1932–), originally edited by Walter Lippmann for the Council on Foreign Relations. Important summaries of foreign affairs appear in the current volumes of the *American Year Book,* cited.

T. A. Bisson's brief *American Policy in the Far East, 1931–1940* (Institute of Pacific Relations, 1940) is extremely valuable. Among the leading criticisms of isolationism are Raymond L. Buell, *Isolated America* (Knopf, 1940), and Charles G. Fenwick, *American Neutrality, Trial and Failure* (New York University Press, 1940). Non-interventionism is strongly defended in Charles A. Beard, *A Foreign Policy for America* (Knopf, 1940). Two non-interventionists look at neutrality from the standpoint of international law in Edwin Borchard and William P. Lage's *Neutrality for the United States* (Yale University Press, 1937). Excellent articles, although selected primarily for debaters, are available in J. V. Garland (ed.), *War and the Americas* (H. W. Wilson, 1941). David Lawrence, the anti-New Deal journalist, gives contemporary notes on the coming of war in *Diary of a Washington Correspondent* (Kinsey, 1942). The role of William Allen White in influencing opinion is carefully assessed in Walter Johnson, *The Battle Against Isolation* (University of Chicago Press, 1944).

21. WAR OF THE UNITED NATIONS

Periodical materials most useful for this chapter include Sidney B. Fay, "The Meaning of the Moscow Conference," *Current History,* December, 1943; Hadley Cantril and John Harding, "The 1942 Elections: A Case Study in Political Psychology," *Public Opinion Quarterly,* Summer, 1943; George Soule, "Roosevelt in 1943," *New Republic,* September 6, 1943; Ruth D. Tuck, "Behind the Zoot Suit Riots," *Survey Graphic,* August, 1943; William C. Headrick, "Race Riots—Segregated Slums," *Current History,* September, 1943; Turner Catledge, "Our Greatest Social Problem," *New York Times Magazine,* December 19, 1943; Earl Brown, "The Truth About the Detroit Riot," *Harper's Magazine,* November, 1943; Robert A. Polson, "The Impact of the War on Rural Community Life: State and Local Viewpoint," *Rural Sociology,* June, 1943; Paul S.

Taylor, "Effects of the War on the Social and Economic Status of Farm Laborers," *ibid.*; Alfred G. Buehler, "How the United States Is Financing the War," *Foreign Policy Reports,* November 1, 1942; "Minority Peoples in a Nation at War" (entire issue), *The Annals of the American Academy of Political and Social Science,* September, 1942; "The American Family in World War II" (entire issue), *ibid.,* September, 1943; Clair Wilcox, "In Defense of Price Control," *New York Times Magazine,* October 10, 1943; Louis Stark, "What's the Matter With Labor?" *Survey Graphic,* July, 1943; David H. Popper, "The Rio de Janeiro Conference of 1942," *Foreign Policy Reports,* April 15, 1942; Ernest S. Hediger, "Agricultural Cooperation in the Americas," *ibid.,* September 15, 1943; Payson S. Wild, Jr., "Machinery of Collaboration Between the United Nations," *ibid.,* July 1, 1942; Hanson W. Baldwin, "The First Year," *Foreign Affairs,* January, 1943, and his "America at War—The End of the Second Year," *ibid.,* January, 1944; Lawrence K. Rosinger, "Strategy of the War in Asia," *Foreign Policy Reports,* April 15, 1943; Allan Spalding, "Food Subsidies v. Inflation," *New Republic,* November 15, 1943.

Indispensable for current history are the various yearbooks such as the *American Year Book* and the *New International Year Book.* The 1943 edition of the latter includes two informative articles, "Mobilization for Total War," by Allan Nevins, and "Education," by Charles H. Judd, in addition to excellent summaries of war trends by Kenneth Colegrove. This chapter has leaned heavily on the polls summarized in each issue of *The Public Opinion Quarterly.* The New York *Times,* the Chicago *Sun, Current History,* and the *Christian Science Monitor* are particularly useful. Allan Nevins and Louis M. Hacker (eds.), *The United States and Its Place in World Affairs, 1918–1943* (Heath, 1943), is extremely valuable for the period. A careful sociological analysis of the factors behind the Detroit riot of 1943 is A. M. Lee and N. D. Humphrey, *Race Riot* (Dryden Press, 1943). An important phase of the war and the home front is discussed in E. R. Stettinius, Jr., *Lend-Lease, Weapon for Victory* (Macmillan, 1944).

22. RECONSTRUCTION: "ONE WORLD—OR NONE" (1945–1948)

The most comprehensive surveys of American diplomacy for these years are in John C. Campbell, *The United States in World Affairs, 1945–1947* (Council on Foreign Relations: Harper, 1947) and Wilbur W. White's critical appraisal, "The United States and World Peace," *Rice Institute Pamphlet,* Vol. XXXIV (April, 1947), No. 2. Of first-hand value are *Documents on American Foreign Relations,* Vol. VII, June, 1944–July, 1945, and Vol. VIII, July, 1945–December, 1946 (World Peace Foundation, Princeton University Press, 1947) and former Secretary of State

James F. Byrnes' *Speaking Frankly* (Harper, 1947). Some attempt to understand the Soviet point of view is made in Frederick L. Schuman's *Soviet Politics at Home and Abroad* (Knopf, 1946) and Vera M. Dean's *The United States and Russia* (Harvard University Press, 1947). Experts analyze the Far East in Harley F. MacNair (ed.), *China* (University of California Press, 1946, Berkeley); the most convenient introduction to the Near East is E. A. Speiser, *The United States and the Near East* (Harvard University Press, 1947). Alvin H. Hansen's *America's Role in the World Economy* (Penguin, 1946) covers authoritatively and clearly the World Bank, the International Monetary Fund, and other leading international economic problems. Invaluable articles appear in *Foreign Affairs, Foreign Policy Reports, Current History, International Conciliation* (especially for documents), and the New York *Times* (see *Index* to *Times*).

Literature on World War II in practically every aspect has already assumed mammoth dimensions; some of it is of high quality, such as Samuel E. Morison's series, *History of United States Naval Operations in World War II* (Little, Brown, 1947) and C. Vann Woodward, *The Battle for Leyte Gulf* (Macmillan, 1947). Henry S. Commager has skillfully edited a fascinating narrative woven from first-hand reports in *The Pocket History of the Second World War* (Pocket Books, 1945); a detailed account prepared by the Military Intelligence Division of the War Department is *The World at War, 1939–1944* (Infantry Journal, 1945). See also Walter P. Hall, *Iron Out of Calvary: An Interpretive History of the Second World War* (Appleton-Century, 1946) and Roger W. Shugg and H. A. De Weerd, *World War II: A Concise History* (Infantry Journal, 1946). Science in World War II is explained for the layman in James P. Baxter III, *Scientists Against Time* (Little, Brown, 1946) and David Dietz, *Atomic Energy in the Coming Era* (Dodd, Mead, 1945).

On the domestic scene there is considerable information in the journalistic Tris Coffin's *Missouri Compromise* (Little, Brown, 1947); Henry Wallace, *Sixty Million Jobs* (Simon and Schuster, 1945); and Chester Bowles, *Tomorrow Without Fear* (Simon and Schuster, 1946). Some contemporary southern problems are examined by a liberal in Ellis G. Arnall, *The Shore Dimly Seen* (Lippincott, 1946) and A. D. Mezerik, *The Revolt of the South and West* (Duell, Sloan, and Pearce, 1946). For public opinion polls such as the Gallup Poll, see *Public Opinion Quarterly* and *Fortune*. Very serviceable are the current numbers of *New International Yearbook, American Year Book, Annals of the American Academy of Political and Social Science,* Henry Wallace's critical *New Republic,* and the New York *Times* Magazine.

Index